masculine or feminine	*mf*	maschile o femm
military	*Mil*	militare
music	*Mus*	musica
noun	*n*	sostantivo
nautical	*Naut*	nautica
pejorative	*pej*	peggiorativo
personal	*pers*	personale
photography	*Phot*	fotografia
physics	*Phys*	fisica
plural	*pl*	plurale
politics	*Pol*	politica
possessive	*poss*	possessivo
past participle	*pp*	participio pass
prefix	*pref*	prefisso
preposition	*prep*	preposizione
present tense	*pres*	presente
pronoun	*pron*	pronome
psychology	*Psych*	psicologia
past tense	*pt*	tempo passat
someone	*qcno*	qualcuno
something	*qcsa*	qualcosa
rail	*Rail*	ferrovia
reflexive	*refl*	riflessivo
religion	*Relig*	religione
relative pronoun	*rel pron*	pronome relativo
somebody	*sb*	qualcuno
school	*Sch*	scuola
singular	*sg*	singolare
something	*sth*	qualcosa
technical	*Techn*	tecnico
telephone	*Teleph*	telefono
theatrical	*Theat*	teatrale
television	*TV*	televisione
typography	*Typ*	tipografia
university	*Univ*	università
auxiliary verb	*v aux*	verbo ausiliare
intransitive verb	*vi*	verbo intransitivo
reflexive verb	*vr*	verbo riflessivo
transitive verb	*vt*	verbo transitivo
transitive and intransitivo intransitive verb	*vt/i*	verbo transitivo e
vulgar	*vulg*	volgare
familiar	!	familiare
slang	✖	gergo
cultural equivalent	≈	equivalenza culturale

Oxford
Italian
Mini Dictionary

FOURTH EDITION

Italian–English
English–Italian

Italiano–Inglese
Inglese–Italiano

OXFORD
UNIVERSITY PRESS

OXFORD

UNIVERSITY PRESS

Great Clarendon Street, Oxford OX2 6DP

Oxford University Press is a department of the University of Oxford.
It furthers the University's objective of excellence in research, scholarship,
and education by publishing worldwide in

Oxford New York

Auckland Cape Town Dar es Salaam Hong Kong Karachi Kuala Lumpur
Madrid Melbourne Mexico City Nairobi New Delhi Shanghai Taipei
Toronto

With offices in
Argentina Austria Brazil Chile Czech Republic France Greece
Guatemala Hungary Italy Japan Poland Portugal
Singapore South Korea Switzerland Thailand Turkey Ukraine Vietnam

Oxford is a registered trade mark of Oxford University Press
in the UK and in certain other countries

First published 1986
Second edition published 1997
Third edition published 2005
This edition published 2009

British Library Cataloguing in Publication Data
Data available

Library of Congress Cataloging in Publication Data
Data available

ISBN 978-0-19-956682-2 (special edition)
ISBN 978-0-19-953434-0

10 9 8 7 6 5 4 3 2

Typeset by Interactive Sciences Ltd, Gloucester
Printed and bound in Italy
by L.E.G.O.S.p.A, Lavis (TN)

Contents/Indice

Fourth edition/Quarta edizione
Editors/Redazione
Joanna Rubery, Loredana Riu, Pat
Bulhosen

Third Edition/Terza edizione
Editors/Redazione
Nicholas Rollin, Francesca Logi

Second Edition/Seconda edizione
Editors/Redazione
Debora Mazza, Donatella Boi, Sonia
Tinagli-Baxter, Peter Terrell, Jane
Goldie, Francesca Logi, Carla Zipoli

First Edition/Prima edizione
Editor/Redazione
Joyce Andrews

Phrasefinder/Trovafrasi
Colin McIntosh, Francesca Logi
Loredana Riu, Neil and Roswitha
Morris

Proprietary terms

This dictionary includes some words which are or are asserted to be, proprietary names or trademarks. Their inclusion does not imply that they have acquired for legal purposes a non-proprietary or general significance, nor is any other judgement implied concerning their legal status. In cases where the editor has some evidence that a word is used as proprietary name or trade mark this is indicated by the symbol (®), but no judgement concerning the legal status of such words is made or implied thereby.

Marchi registrati

Questo dizionario include alcune parole che sono o vengono considerate marchi registrati. La loro presenza non implica che abbiano acquisito legalmente un significato generale, né si suggerisce alcun altro giudizio riguardo il loro stato giuridico. Qualora il redattore abbia trovato testimonianza dell'uso di una parola come marchio registrato, quest'ultima è stata contrassegnata dal simbolo ®, ma nessun giudizio riguardo lo stato giuridico di tale parola viene espresso o suggerito in tal modo.

Preface/Prefazione

This new edition of the *Oxford Italian Mini Dictionary* has been updated to reflect the changes in English and Italian since the last edition in 2005. Notable additions include terms from the spheres of computing, business and communications, that have become common in modern life. The *Phrasefinder* section has been expanded to provide more useful expressions needed for everyday communication. The section is arranged thematically and covers nine key topics: *going places, keeping in touch, food and drink, places to stay, shopping and money, sport and leisure, good timing, health and beauty* and *weights and measures*.

Questa nuova edizione del *Mini Dizionario Oxford* è stata aggiornata per riflettere i cambiamenti avvenuti nell'inglese e nell'italiano dopo la scorsa edizione del 2005. Tra le voci aggiunte si segnalano in particolare termini del settore informatico, commerciale e delle comunicazioni divenuti ricorrenti nella lingua di tutti i giorni. La sezione *Trovafrasi* è stata infine ampliata per dare maggior spazio alle espressioni necessarie alla comunicazione quotidiana. Tale sezione è presentata per tema e copre nove aree chiave: *in viaggio, comunicazioni, mangiare e bere, dove alloggiare, spese e soldi, sport e tempo libero, l'ora giusta, salute e bellezza,* e *pesi e misure.*

Introduzione

Allo scopo di fornire il maggior numero possibile di informazioni riguardo all'inglese e all'italiano, questo dizionario ricorre ad alcune convenzioni per sfruttare al meglio lo spazio disponibile.

All'interno della voce un trattino ondulato ∿ è utilizzato al posto del lemma.

Qualora il lemma contenga una barra verticale |, il trattino ondulato sostituisce solo la parte del lemma che precede la barra. Ad es.: **dark|en** *vt* oscurare. **∿ness** *n* buio *m* (la seconda parola in neretto va letta **darkness**).

Vengono forniti indicatori per indirizzare l'utente verso la traduzione del senso voluto di una parola. I tipi di indicatori sono:

- etichette semantiche, indicanti lo specifico settore d'uso di una parola o di un senso (commercio, informatica, fotografia ecc.);

- indicatori di significato, ad es.: **redazione** *f* (ufficio) editorial office; (di testi) editing;

- soggetti tipici di verbi, ad es.: **trovarsi** *vr* (luogo:) be;

- complementi oggetti tipici di verbi, collocati dopo la traduzione del verbo stesso, ad es.: **superare** *vt* overtake (veicolo); pass (esame);

- sostantivi che ricorrono tipicamete con certi aggettivi, ad es.: **solare** *adj* (energia, raggi) solar; (crema) sun.

Il pallino nero indica che la stessa parola viene tradotta come una diversa parte del discorso, ad es.: **calcolatore** *adj* ... ● *m* ...

La pronuncia inglese è trascritta usando l'Alfabetico Fonetico Internazionale (vedi pag. viii).

L'accento tonico nelle parole italiane è indicato dal segno ' collocato davanti alla sillaba accentata.

Le parentesi quadre racchiudono parti di espressioni che possono essere omesse senza alterazioni di significato.

Introduction

In order to give the maximum information about English and Italian in the space available, this new dictionary uses certain space-saving conventions.

A swung dash ~ is used to replace the headword within the entry.

Where the headword contains a vertical bar | the swung dash replaces only the part of the headword that comes before the |. For example:

efficien|te *adj* efficient. **~za** *f* efficiency (the second bold word reads efficienza).

Indicators are provided to guide the user to the best translation for a specific sense of a word. Types of indicator are:

- field labels, which indicate a general area of usage (commercial, computing, photography etc);

- sense indicators, eg: **bore** *n* (of gun) calibro *m*; (person) seccatore, -trice *mf*;

- typical subjects of verbs, eg: **bond** *vt* (glue:) attaccare;

- typical objects of verbs, placed after the translation of the verb, eg: **boost** *vt* stimolare (sales); sollevare (morale);

- nouns that typically go together with certain adjectives, eg: **rich** *adj* ricco; (food) pesante;

A bullet point means that a headword has changed its part of speech within an entry, eg: **partition** *n* ... ● *vt* ...

English pronunciation is given for the Italian user in the International Phonetic Alphabet (see p viii).

Italian stress is shown by a ' placed in front of the stressed syllable in a word.

Square brackets are used around parts of an expression which can be omitted without altering its sense.

Pronuncia inglese

Simboli fonetici

Vocali e dittonghi

iː	see	ɔː	saw	eɪ	page	ɔɪ	join
ɪ	sit	ʊ	put	əʊ	home	ɪə	near
e	ten	uː	too	aɪ	five	eə	hair
æ	hat	ʌ	cup	aɪə	fire	ʊə	poor
ɑː	arm	ɜː	fur	aʊ	now		
ɒ	got	ə	ago	aʊə	flour		

Consonanti-

p	pen	tʃ	chin	s	so	n	no
b	bad	dʒ	June	z	zoo	ŋ	sing
t	tea	f	fall	ʃ	she	l	leg
d	dip	v	voice	ʒ	measure	r	red
k	cat	θ	thin	h	how	j	yes
g	got	ð	then	m	man	w	wet

Note: ' precede la sillaba accentata.

Pronunciation of Italian

Vowels

a is broad like *a* in *father*: **casa**

e has two sounds: closed like *ey* in *they*: **sera**; open like *e* in *egg*: **sette**

i is like *ee* in *feet*: **venire**.

o 1. closed like *o* in *show*: **croma**. 2. open like *o* in *dog*: **bocca**.

u is like *oo* in *moon*: **luna**

When two or more vowels come together each vowel is pronounced separately: **buono; baia**.

Consonants

b, d, f, l, m, n, p, t, v are pronounced as in English. When these are double, they are pronounced as separate sounds: **bello**.

c before **a, o** or **u** and before consonants is like *k* in *king*: **cane**.
Before **e** or **i** it is like *ch* in *church*: **cena**.

ch is also like *k* in *king*: **chiesa**

g before **a, o** or **u** is hard like *g* in *got*: **gufo**.
Before **e** or **i** it is like *j* in *jelly*: **gentile**.

gh is like *g* in *gun*: **ghiaccio**.

gl when followed by **a, e, o** and **u** is like *gl* in *glass*: **gloria**.

gli is like *lli* in *million*: **figlio**.

gn is like *ni* in *onion*: **bagno**.

h is silent.

ng is like *ng* in *finger*: **ringraziare**.

r is pronounced distinctly.

s between two vowels is like *s* in *rose*: **riso**. at the beginning of a word it is like *s* in *soap*: **sapone**.

sc before **e** or **i** is like *sh* in *shell*: **scienza**.

z sounds like *ts* within a word: **fazione**; like *dz* at the beginning: **zoo**.

Stress is shown by the sign ' printed before the stressed syllable.

Aa

a (*ad before vowel*) *prep* to; (*stato in luogo, tempo, età*) at; (*con mese, città*) in; (*mezzo, modo*) by; **dire qcsa a qcno** tell sb sth; **alle tre** at three o'clock; **a vent'anni** at the age of twenty; **a Natale** at Christmas; **a dicembre** in December; **ero al cinema** I was at the cinema; **vivo a Londra** I live in London; **a due a due** two by two; **a piedi** on o by foot; **maglia a maniche lunghe** long-sleeved sweater; **casa a tre piani** house with three floors; **giocare a tennis** play tennis; **50 km all'ora** 50 km an hour; **4 euro al chilo** 4 euros a kilo; **al mattino/alla sera** in the morning/evening; **a venti chilometri/due ore da qui** twenty kilometres/two hours away

a'bate *m* abbot

abbacchi'ato *adj* downhearted

ab'bacchio *m* [young] lamb

abbagli'ante *adj* dazzling ●*m* headlight, high beam

abbagli'are *vt* dazzle. **ab'baglio** *m* blunder; **prendere un ~** make a blunder

abbai'are *vi* bark

abba'ino *m* dormer window

abbando'na|re *vt* abandon; leave (*luogo*); give up (*piani ecc*). **~rsi** *vr* let oneself go; **~rsi a** give oneself up to (*ricordi ecc*). **~to** *adj* abandoned. **abban'dono** *m* abandoning; *fig* abandon; (*stato*) neglect

abbassa'mento *m* (*di temperatura, prezzi ecc*) drop

abbas'sar|e *vt* lower; turn down (radio, tv); **~e i fari** dip the headlights. **~si** *vr* stoop; (*sole ecc*) sink; *fig* demean oneself

ab'basso *adv* below ●*int* down with

abba'stanza *adv* enough; (*alquanto*) quite

ab'batter|e *vt* demolish; shoot down (aereo); put down (animale); topple (regime); (*fig: demoralizzare*) dishearten. **~si** *vr* (*cadere*) fall; *fig* be discouraged

abbatti'mento *m* (*morale*) despondency

abbat'tuto *adj* despondent

abba'zia *f* abbey

abbel'lir|e *vt* embellish. **~si** *vr* adorn oneself

abbeve'ra|re *vt* water. **~'toio** *m* drinking trough

abbi'ente *adj* well-to-do

abbiglia'mento *m* clothes *pl*; (*industria*) clothing industry

abbigli'ar|e *vt* dress. **~si** *vr* dress up

abbina'mento *m* combining

abbi'nare *vt* combine; match (colori)

abbindo'lare *vt* cheat

abbocca'mento *m* interview; (*conversazione*) talk

abboc'care *vi* bite; (tubi:) join; *fig* swallow the bait

abboc'cato *adj* (vino) fairly sweet

abbof'farsi *vr* stuff oneself

abbona'mento *m* subscription; (*ferroviario ecc*) season-ticket; **fare l'~** take out a subscription

abbo'na|rsi *vr* subscribe (a to); take out a season-ticket (a for) (teatro, stadio).

∼to, -a *mf* subscriber

abbon'dan|te *adj* abundant; (quantità) copious; (nevicata) heavy; (vestiario) roomy. ∼te di abounding in. ∼te'mente *adv* (mangiare) copiously. ∼za *f* abundance

abbon'dare *vi* abound

abbor'da|bile *adj* (persona) approachable; (prezzo) reasonable. ∼ggio *m* (Mil) boarding. ∼re *vt* board (nave); approach (persona); (🌐: attaccar bottone a) chat up; tackle (compito ecc)

abbotto'na|re *vt* button up. ∼'tura *f* [row of] buttons. ∼to *adj fig* tight-lipped

abboz'zare *vt* sketch [out]; ∼ un sorriso give a hint of a smile. ab'bozzo *m* sketch

abbracci'are *vt* embrace; take up (professione); *fig* include. ab'braccio *m* hug

abbrevi'a|re *vt* shorten; (ridurre) curtail; abbreviate (parola). ∼zi'one *f* abbreviation

abbron'zante *m* sun-tan lotion

abbron'za|re *vt* bronze; tan (pelle). ∼rsi *vr* get a tan. ∼to *adj* tanned. ∼'tura *f* [sun-]tan

abbrusto'lire *vt* toast; roast (caffè ecc)

abbruti'mento *m* brutalization. abbru'tire *vt* brutalize. **abbru'tirsi** *vr* become brutalized

abbuf'fa|rsi *vr* 🌐 stuff oneself. ∼ta *f* blowout

abbuo'nare *vt* reduce

abbu'ono *m* allowance; *Sport* handicap

abdi'ca|re *vi* abdicate. ∼zi'one *f* abdication

aber'rante *adj* aberrant

a'bete *m* fir

abi'etto *adj* despicable

'abil|e *adj* able; (idoneo) fit; (astuto) clever. ∼ità *f inv* ability; (idoneità) fit-

ness; (astuzia) cleverness. ∼'mente *adv* ably; (con astuzia) cleverly

abili'ta|re *vt* qualify. ∼to *adj* qualified. ∼zi'one *f* qualification; (titolo) diploma

abis'sale *adj* abysmal. a'bisso *m* abyss

abi'tabile *adj* inhabitable

abi'tacolo *m* (Auto) passenger compartment

abi'tante *mf* inhabitant

abi'ta|re *vi* live. ∼to *adj* inhabited ● *m* built-up area. ∼zi'one *f* house

'abito *m* (da donna) dress; (da uomo) suit. ∼ da cerimonia/da sera formal/evening dress

abitu'al|e *adj* usual. ∼'mente *adv* usually

abitu'ar|e *vt* accustom. ∼si a *vr* get used to

abitudi'nario, -a *adj* of fixed habits ● *mf* person of fixed habits

abi'tudine *f* habit; d'∼ usually; per ∼ out of habit; avere l'∼ di fare qcsa be in the habit of doing sth

abnegazi'one *f* self-sacrifice

ab'norme *adj* abnormal

abo'li|re *vt* abolish; repeal (legge). ∼zi'one *f* abolition; repeal

abomi'nevole *adj* abominable

abor'rire *vt* abhor

abor'ti|re *vi* miscarry; (volontariamente) have an abortion; *fig* fail. ∼vo *adj* abortive. a'borto *m* miscarriage; (volontario) abortion. ∼sta *adj* pro-choice

abrasi'one *f* abrasion. abra'sivo *adj* & *n* abrasive

abro'ga|re *vt* repeal. ∼zi'one *f* repeal

'abside *f* apse

abu'lia *f* apathy. a'bulico *adj* apathetic

abu'sare *vi* ∼ di abuse; overindulge in (alcol); (approfittare di) take advantage of; (*violentare*) rape. ∼**ivo** *adj* illegal

a'**buso** *m* abuse. ∼ **di confidenza** breach of confidence

a.C. *abbr* (avanti Cristo) BC

'**acca** *f* 🄸 **non ho capito un'**∼ I understood damn all

acca'**demi|a** *f* academy. A∼**a di Belle Arti** Academy of Fine Arts. ∼**co, -a** *adj* academic ●*mf* academician

acca'**d|ere** *vi* happen; accada quel che accada come what may. ∼**uto** *m* event

accalappia're *vt* catch; *fig* allure

accal'**carsi** *vr* crowd

accal'**da|rsi** *vr* get overheated; *fig* get excited. ∼**to** *adj* overheated

accalo'**rarsi** *vr* get excited

accampa'**mento** *m* camp. accam'**pare** *vt* fig put forth. accam'**parsi** *vr* camp

accani'**mento** *m* tenacity; (*odio*) rage

acca'**ni|rsi** *vr* persist; (*infierire*) rage. ∼**to** *adj* persistent; (*odio*) fierce; *fig* inveterate

ac'**canto** *adv* near; ∼ *prep* next to

accanto'**nare** *vt* set aside; (*Mil*) billet

accaparra'**mento** *m* hoarding; (*Comm*) cornering

accapar'**ra|re** *vt* hoard. ∼**rsi** *vr* grab; corner (mercato). ∼'**tore, ∼'trice** *mf* hoarder

accapigli'**arsi** *vr* scuffle; (*litigare*) squabble

accappa'**toio** *m* bathrobe; (*per spiaggia*) beachrobe

accappo'**nare** *vt* fare ∼ **la pelle a** qcno make sb's flesh creep

accarez'**zare** *vt* caress; *fig* cherish

accartocci'**ar|e** *vt* scrunch up. ∼**si** *vr* curl up

acca'**sarsi** *vr* get married

accasci'**arsi** *vr* flop down; *fig*

lose heart

accata'**stare** *vt* pile up

accatti'**vante** *adj* beguiling

accatti'**varsi** *vr* ∼ **le simpatie/la stima/l'affetto di** qcno gain sb's sympathy/respect/affection

accatto'**naggio** *m* begging. ac-cat'**tone, -a** *mf* beggar

accaval'**lar|e** *vt* cross (gambe). ∼**si** *vr* pile up; *fig* overlap

acce'**cante** *adj* (luce) blinding

acce'**care** *vt* blind ●*vi* go blind

ac'**cedere** *vi* ∼ **a** enter; (*acconsentire*) comply with

accele'**ra|re** *vi* accelerate ●*vt* accelerate. ∼**to** *adj* rapid. ∼'**tore** *m* accelerator. ∼**zi'one** *f* acceleration

ac'**cender|e** *vt* light; turn on (luce, TV ecc); *fig* inflame; **ha da** ∼**e?** have you got a light? ∼**si** *vr* catch fire; (*illuminarsi*) light up; (TV ecc.) turn on; *fig* become inflamed

accendi'**gas** *m inv* gas lighter; (*su cucina*) automatic ignition

accen'**dino** *m* lighter

accendi'**sigari** *m* cigar-lighter

accen'**nare** *vt* indicate; hum (melodia) ●*vi* ∼ **a** beckon to; *fig* hint at; (*far l'atto di*) make as if to; accenna a piovere it looks like rain. ac'**cenno** *m* gesture; (*con il capo*) nod; *fig* hint

accensi'**one** *f* lighting; (*di motore*) ignition

accen'**ta|re** *vt* accent; (*con accento tonico*) stress. ∼**zi'one** *f* accentuation. ac'**cento** *m* accent; (*tonico*) stress

accentra'**mento** *m* centralizing

accen'**trare** *vt* centralize

accentu'**a|re** *vt* accentuate. ∼**rsi** *vr* become more noticeable. ∼**to** *adj* marked

accerchia'**mento** *m* surrounding

accerchi'**are** *vt* surround

accerta'**mento** *m* check

accer'**tare** *vt* ascertain; (*controllare*) check; assess (reddito)

ac'ceso *adj* lighted; (radio, TV ecc) on; (colore) bright

acces'sibile *adj* accessible; (persona) approachable; (spesa) reasonable

ac'cesso *m* access; (Med: di rabbia) fit; vietato l'~ no entry

acces'sorio *adj* accessory; (secondario) of secondary importance ● *m* accessory; **accessori** *pl* (rifiniture) fittings

ac'cetta *f* hatchet

accet'tabile *adj* acceptable

accet'tare *vt* accept; (aderire a) agree to

accettazi'one *f* acceptance; (luogo) reception. [bagagli] check-in. [banco] ~ check-in [desk]

ac'cetto *adj* agreeable; essere bene ~ be very welcome

accezi'one *f* meaning

acchiap'pare *vt* catch

acchito *m* di primo ~ at first

acciac'ca|re *vt* crush; *fig* prostrate. ~to, -a *adj* essere ~to ache all over. **acci'acco** *m* infirmity; **acciacchi** *pl* aches and pains

acciaie'ria *f* steelworks

acci'aio *m* steel; ~ inossidabile stainless steel

acciden'ta|le *adj* accidental. ~l'mente *adv* accidentally. ~to *adj* (terreno) uneven

acci'dente *m* accident; (Med) stroke; non capisce un ~ 𝕋 he doesn't understand a damn thing. **acci'denti!** *int* damn!

acciglia|rsi *vr* frown. ~to *adj* frowning

ac'cingersi *vr* ~ a be about to

acci'picchia *int* good Lord!

acciuf'fare *vt* catch

acci'uga *f* anchovy

accla'ma|re *vt* applaud; (eleggere) acclaim. ~zi'one *f* applause

acclima'tar|e *vt* acclimatize. ~si *vr* get acclimatized

ac'clu|dere *vt* enclose. ~so *adj* enclosed

accocco'larsi *vr* squat

accogli'en|te *adj* welcoming; (confortevole) cosy. ~za *f* welcome

ac'cogliere *vt* receive; (con piacere) welcome; (contenere) hold

accol'larsi *vr* take on (responsabilità, debiti, doveri). **accol'lato** *adj* high-necked

accoltel'lare *vt* knife

accomia'tar|e *vt* dismiss. ~si take one's leave (da of)

accomo'dante *adj* accommodating

accomo'dar|e *vt* (riparare) mend; (disporre) arrange. ~si *vr* make oneself at home; si accomodi! come in!; (si sieda) take a seat!

accompagna'mento *m* accompaniment; (seguito) retinue

accompa'gna|re *vt* accompany; ~re qcno a casa see sb home; ~re qcno alla porta show sb out. ~'tore, ~'trice *mf* companion; (di comitiva) escort; (Mus) accompanist

accomu'nare *vt* pool

acconci'a|re *vt* arrange. ~'tura *f* hair-style; (ornamento) head-dress

accondiscen'den|te *adj* too obliging. ~za *f* excessive desire to please

accondi'scendere *vi* ~ a condescend; comply with (desiderio); (acconsentire) consent to

acconsen'tire *vi* consent

acconten'tar|e *vt* satisfy. ~si *vr* be content (di with)

ac'conto *m* deposit; in ~ on account; lasciare un ~ leave a deposit

accop'pare *vt* 𝕋 bump off

accoppia'mento *m* coupling; (di animali) mating

accoppi'a|re *vt* couple; mate (animali). ~rsi *vr* pair off; mate. ~ta *f* (scommessa) bet on two horses for first *and second place*

acco'rato *adj* sorrowful

accorci'ar|e *vt* shorten. **~si** *vr* get shorter

accor'dar|e *vt* concede; match (colori ecc); (*Mus*) tune. **~si** *vr* agree

ac'cordo *m* agreement; (*Mus*) chord; (*armonia*) harmony; andare d'~ get on well; d'~! agreed!; essere d'~ agree; prendere accordi con qcno make arrangements with sb

ac'corgersi *vr* ~ di notice; (*capire*) realize

accorgi'mento *m* shrewdness; (*espediente*) device

ac'correre *vi* hasten

accor'tezza *f* (*previdenza*) forethought

ac'corto *adj* shrewd; mal ~ incautious

accosta'mento *m* combination

acco'star|e *vt* draw close to; approach (persona); set ajar (porta ecc). **~si** *vr* **~si a** come near to

accovacci'a|rsi *vr* crouch

accoz'zaglia *f* jumble, (*di persone*) mob

accoz'zare *vt* ~ colori mix colours that clash

accredita'mento *m* credit; ~ tramite bancogiro Bank Giro Credit

accredi'tare *vt* confirm (notizia); (*Comm*) credit

ac'crescere *vt* increase. **~ersi** *vr* grow larger. **~i'tivo** *adj* augmentative

accucci'arsi *vr* (cane:) lie down; (persona:) crouch

accu'dire *vi* ~ a attend to

accumu'la|re *vt* accumulate. **~rsi** *vr* accumulate. **~tore** *m* accumulator; (*Auto*) battery. **~zi'one** *f* accumulation.

accura'tezza *f* care

accu'rato *adj* careful

ac'cusa *f* accusation; (*Jur*) charge; essere in stato di ~ have been charged; la Pubblica A~ the public prosecutor

accu'sa|re *vt* accuse; (*Jur*) charge; complain of (dolore); **~re ricevuta di** acknowledge receipt of. **~to, -a** *mf* accused. **~'tore** *m* prosecutor

a'cerbo *adj* sharp; (*non maturo*) unripe

'acero *m* maple

a'cerrimo *adj* implacable

a'ceto *m* vinegar

ace'tone *m* nail-polish remover

A.C.I. *abbr* (Automobile Club d'Italia) Italian Automobile Association

acidità *f* acidity. ~ di stomaco acid stomach

'acido *adj* acid; (persona) sour
  ● *m* acid

a'cidulo *adj* slightly sour

'acino *m* berry; (*chicco*) grape

'acne *f* acne

'acqua *f* water; fare ~ leak; ~ in bocca! *fig* mum's the word!. ~ corrente running water. ~ dolce fresh water. ~ minerale mineral water. ~ minerale gassata fizzy mineral water. ~ naturale still mineral water. ~ potabile drinking water. ~ salata salt water. ~ tonica tonic water

acqua'forte *f* etching

ac'quaio *m* sink

acquama'rina *adj* aquamarine

acqua'rello *m* = ACQUERELLO

ac'quario *m* aquarium; (*Astr*) Aquarius

acqua'santa *f* holy water

acqua'scooter *m inv* water-scooter

ac'quatico *adj* aquatic

acquat'tarsi *vr* crouch

acqua'vite *f* brandy

acquaz'zone *m* downpour

acque'dotto *m* aqueduct

'acqueo *adj* vapore ~

a

water vapour

acque'rello m water-colour

acqui'rente mf purchaser

acqui'si|re vt acquire. ~to adj acquired. ~zi'one f attainment

acqui'st|are vt purchase; (ottenere) acquire. **ac'quisto** m purchase; uscire per ~i go shopping; fare ~i shop

acqui'trino m marsh

acquo'lina f far venire l'~ in bocca a qcno make sb's mouth water

ac'quoso adj watery

'acre adj acrid; (al gusto) sour; fig harsh

a'crilico m acrylic

a'croba|ta mf acrobat. ~'zia f acrobatics pl

a'cronimo m acronym

acu'ir|e vt sharpen. ~si vr become more intense

a'culeo m sting; (Bot) prickle

acumi'nato adj pointed

a'custic|a f acoustics pl. ~o adj acoustic

acu'tezza f acuteness

acutiz'zarsi vr become worse

a'cuto adj sharp; (suono) shrill; (freddo, odore) intense; (Gram, Math, Med) acute ●m (Mus) high note

ad prep = A (davanti a vocale)

adagi'ar|e vt lay down. ~si vr lie down

a'dagio adv slowly ●m (Mus) adagio; (proverbio) adage

adattabilità f adaptability

adatta'mento m adaptation; avere spirito di ~ be adaptable

adat'ta|re vt adapt; (aggiustare) fit. ~rsi vr adapt. ~'tore m adaptor. a'datto adj suitable (a for); (giusto) right

addebita'mento m debit. ~ di-retto direct debit

addebi'tare vt debit; ascribe (colpa)

ad'debito m charge

addensa'mento m thickening; (di persone) gathering

adden'sar|e vt thicken. ~si vr thicken; (affollarsi) gather

adden'tare vt bite

adden'trarsi vr penetrate

ad'dentro adv deeply; essere ~ in be in on

addestra'mento m training

adde'str|are vt train. ~si vr train

ad'detto, -a adj assigned ●mf employee; (diplomatico) attaché. ~ stampa press officer

addiaccio m dormire all'~ sleep in the open

addi'etro adv (indietro) back; (nel passato) before

ad'dio m & int goodbye. ~ al celi-bato stag party

addirit'tura adv (perfino) even; (assolutamente) absolutely; ~! really!

ad'dirsi vr ~ a suit

addit'tare vt point at; (in mezzo a un gruppo) point out; fig point to

addi'tivo adj & m additive

addizio'nal|e adj additional. ~'mente adv additionally

addizio'nare vt add [up]. ~zi'one f addition

addob'bare vt decorate. **ad'dobbo** m decoration

addol'cir|e vt sweeten; tone down (colore); fig soften. ~si vr fig mellow

addolo'ra|re vt grieve. ~rsi vr be upset (per by). ~to adj distressed

ad'dom|e m abdomen. ~i'nale adj abdominal; [muscoli] addominali pl abdominals

addomesti'ca|re vt tame. ~tore m tamer

addormen'ta|re vt put to sleep. ~rsi vr go to sleep. ~to adj asleep; fig slow

addos'sar|e vt ~e a (appoggiare) lean against; (attribuire) lay on. ~si vr (ammassarsi) crowd; shoulder (responsabilità ecc)

ad'dosso adv on; ~ a prep on; (molto vicino) right next to; mettere gli occhi ~ a qcno/qcsa hanker after sb/sth; non mettermi le mani ~! keep your hands off me!; stare ~ a qcno fig be on sb's back

ad'durre vt produce (prova, documento); give (pretesto, esempio)

adegua'mento m adjustment

adegu'a|re vt adjust. ~rsi vr conform. ~to adj adequate; (conforme) consistent

a'dempi|ere vt fulfil. ~'mento m fulfilment

ade'noidi fpl adenoids

ade'ren|te adj adhesive; (vestito) tight ● mf follower. ~za f adhesion. ~ze pl connections

ade'rire vi ~ a adhere to; support (petizione); agree to (richiesta)

adesca'mento m (Jur) soliciting

ade'scare vt bait, fig entice

adesi'one f adhesion; fig agreement

ade'sivo adj adhesive ● m sticker; (Auto) bumper sticker

a'desso adv now; (poco fa) just now; (tra poco) any moment now; da ~ in poi from now on; per ~ for the moment

adia'cente adj adjacent; ~ a next to

adi'bire vt ~ a put to use as

'adipe m adipose tissue

adi'ra|rsi vr get irate. ~to adj irate

a'dire vt resort to; ~ le vie legali take legal proceedings

'adito m dare ~ a give rise to

adocchi'are vt eye; (con desiderio) covet

adole'scen|te adj & mf adolescent. ~za f adolescence. ~zi'ale adj

adolescent

adom'brar|e vt darken; fig veil. ~si vr (offendersi) take offence

adope'rar|e vt use. ~si vr take trouble

ado'rabile adj adorable

ado'ra|re vt adore. ~zi'one f adoration

ador'nare vt adorn

adot't|are vt adopt. ~ivo adj adoptive. adozi'one f adoption

adrena'lina f adrenalin

adri'atico adj Adriatic ● m l'A~ the Adriatic

adu'la|re vt flatter. ~'tore, ~'trice mf flatterer. ~zi'one f flattery

adulte'ra|re vt adulterate. ~to adj adulterated

adul'terio m adultery. a'dultero, -a adj adulterous ● m adulterer ● f adulteress

a'dulto, -a adj & mf adult; (maturo) mature

adu'nanza f assembly

adu'na|re vt gather. ~ta f (Mil) parade

a'dunco adj hooked

ae'rare vt air (stanza)

a'ereo adj aerial; (dell'aviazione) air attrib ● m aeroplane, plane

ae'robic|a f aerobics. ~o adj aerobic

aerodi'namic|a f aerodynamics sg. ~o adj aerodynamic

aero'nautic|a f aeronautics sg; (Mil) Air Force. ~o adj aeronautical

aero'plano m aeroplane

aero'porto m airport

aero'scalo m cargo and servicing area

aero'sol m inv aerosol

'afa f sultriness

af'fabil|e adj affable. ~ità f affability

affaccen'da|rsi vr busy oneself (a

with). ~**to** *adj* busy

affacciˈarsi *vr* show oneself; ~ **alla finestra** appear at the window

affaˈmaˈre *vt* starve [out]. ~**to** *adj* starving

affanˈnaˈre *vt* leave breathless. ~**rsi** *vr* busy oneself; (*agitarsi*) get worked up. ~**to** *adj* breathless; **dal respiro** ~ wheezy. **afˈfanno** *m* breathlessness; *fig* worry

afˈfare *m* matter; (*Comm*) deal; (*occasione*) bargain; **affari** *pl* business; **non sono affari tuoi** it's none of your business. **affaˈrista** *mf* wheeler-dealer

affasciˈnante *adj* fascinating; (*persona, sorriso*) bewitching

affasciˈnare *vt* bewitch; *fig* charm

affaticaˈmento *m* fatigue

affatiˈcaˈre *vt* tire; (*sfinire*) exhaust. ~**si** *vr* tire oneself out; (*affannarsi*) strive

afˈfatto *adv* completely; **non... ~** not... at all; **niente ~!** not at all!

afferˈmaˈre *vt* affirm; (*sostenere*) assert. ~**rsi** *vr* establish oneself

affermativaˈmente *adv* in the affirmative

affermaˈtivo *adj* affirmative

affermaziˈone *f* assertion; (*successo*) achievement

afferˈraˈre *vt* seize; catch (*oggetto*); (*capire*) grasp; ~**e al volo** *fig* be quick on the uptake. ~**si** *vr* ~**si a** grasp at

affetˈtaˈre *vt* slice; (*ostentare*) affect. ~**to** *adj* sliced; (*maniere*) affected ●**m** cold meat.

affetˈtivo *adj* affective; **rapporto ~** emotional tie

afˈfetto[1] *m* affection

afˈfetto[2] *adj* ~ **da** suffering from

affettuosˈità *f inv* (*gesto*) affectionate gesture

affetuˈoso *adj* affectionate

affezioˈnaˈrsi *vr* ~**rsi a** grow fond of. ~**to** *adj* devoted (**a** to)

affianˈcaˈre *vt* put side by side; (*Mil*) flank; *fig* support. ~**si** *vr* come side by side; *fig* stand together; ~**si a qcno** *fig* help sb out

affiataˈmento *m* harmony

affiaˈtaˈrsi *vr* get on well together. ~**to** *adj* close-knit; **una coppia ~ta** a very close couple

affibˈbiˈare *vt* ~ **qcsa a qcno** saddle sb with sth; ~ **un pugno a qcno** let fly at sb

affiˈdabile *adj* dependable. ~**ità** *f* dependability

affidaˈmento *m* (*Jur: dei minori*) custody; **fare ~ su qcno** rely on sb; **non dare ~** not inspire confidence

affiˈdaˈre *vt* entrust. ~**si** *vr* ~**si a** rely on

affievoˈlirsi *vr* grow weak

afˈfiggere *vt* affix

affiˈlare *vt* sharpen

affiliˈaˈre *vt* affiliate. ~**si** *vr* become affiliated

affiˈnare *vt* sharpen; (*perfezionare*) refine

affinˈché *conj* so that, in order that

afˈfine *adj* similar. ~**ità** *f* affinity

affioraˈmento *m* emergence; (*Naut*) surfacing

affioˈrare *vi* emerge; *fig* come to light

afˈfisso *m* bill; (*Gram*) affix

affitˈtaˈcamere *m inv* landlord ●**f inv** landlady

affitˈtaˈre *vt* rent; **'afˈfittasi'** 'for rent'

afˈfitto *m* rent; **contratto d'~o** lease; **dare in ~o** let; **prendere in ~o** rent. ~**uˈario, -a** *mf* (*Jur*) lessee

afˈfliggere *vt* torment. ~**si** *vr* distress oneself

afˈflitto *adj* distressed. ~**ziˈone** *f* distress; *fig* affliction

afˈflosciˈarsi *vr* become floppy; (*accasciarsi*) flop down; (*morale:*) decline

affluˈente *adj & m* tributary. ~**za** *f*

flow; (*di gente*) crowd

afflu'ire *vi* flow; *fig* pour in

af'flusso *m* influx

affo'ga|re *vt/i* drown; (*Culin*) poach; ~**re** *in fig* be swamped with. ~**to** *adj* (*persona*) drowned; (*uova*) poached. ~**to al caffè** *m* ice cream *with hot espresso poured over it*

affol'la|re *vt*, ~**rsi** *vr* crowd. ~**to** *adj* crowded

affonda'mento *m* sinking

affon'dare *vt/i* sink

affossa'mento *m* pothole

affran'ca|re *vt* redeem (*bene*); stamp (*lettera*); free (*schiavo*). ~**rsi** *vr* free oneself. ~**trice** *f* franking machine. ~**tura** *f* stamping; (*di spedizione*) postage

af'franto *adj* prostrated; (*esausto*) worn out

af'fresco *m* fresco

affret'ta|re *vt* speed up. ~**rsi** *vr* hurry. ~**ta'mente** *adv* hastily. ~**to** *adj* hasty

affron'tar|e *vt* face; confront (*nemico*); meet (*spese*) ~**si** *vr* clash

af'fronto *m* affront, insult; **fare un** ~ **a qcno** insult sb

affumi'ca|re *vt* fill with smoke; (*Culin*) smoke. ~**to** *adj* (*prosciutto, formaggio*) smoked

affuso'la|re *vt* taper [off]. ~**to** *adj* tapering

afo'risma *m* aphorism

a'foso *adj* sultry

'Africa *f* Africa. **afri'cano, -a** *agg & mf* African

afrodi'siaco *adj & m* aphrodisiac

a'genda *f* diary

agen'dina *f* pocket-diary

a'gente *m* agent; **agenti** *pl* atmo-sferici atmospheric agents. ~ **di cambio** stockbroker. ~ **di polizia** police officer

agen'zia *f* agency; (*filiale*) branch office; (*di banca*) branch. ~ **di viaggi**

travel agency. ~ **immobiliare** estate agency

agevo'la|re *vt* facilitate. ~**zi'one** *f* facilitation

a'gevol|e *adj* easy; (*strada*) smooth. ~**mente** *adv* easily

agganci'ar|e *vt* hook up; (*Rail*) couple. ~**si** *vr* (*vestito:*) hook up

ag'geggio *m* gadget

agget'tivo *m* adjective

agghiacci'ante *adj* terrifying

agghiacci'ar|e *vt fig* ~ **qcno** make sb's blood run cold. ~**si** *vr* freeze

agghin'da|re *vt* [i] dress up. ~**rsi** *vr* [i] doll oneself up. ~**to** *adj* dressed up

aggiorna'mento *m* up-date

aggior'na|re *vt* (*rinviare*) postpone; (*mettere a giorno*) bring up to date. ~**rsi** *vr* get up to date. ~**to** *adj* up-to-date; (*versione*) updated

aggi'rar|e *vt* surround; (*fig: ingannare*) trick. ~**si** *vr* hang about; ~**si su** (*discorso ecc:*) be about; (*somma:*) be around

aggiudi'car|e *vt* award; (*all'asta*) knock down. ~**si** *vr* win

aggi'un|gere *vt* add. ~**ta** *f* addition. ~**tivo** *adj* supplementary. ~**to** *adj* added ● *adj & m* (*assistente*) assistant

aggiu'star|e *vt* mend; (*sistemare*) settle; ([i]: *mettere a posto*) fix. ~**si** *vr* adapt; (*mettersi in ordine*) tidy oneself up; (*decidere*) sort things out; (*tempo:*) clear up

agglomera'mento *m* conglomeration

agglome'rato *m* built-up area

aggrap'par|e *vt* grasp. ~**si** *vr* ~**si a** cling to

aggra'vante (*Jur*) *f* aggravation ● *adj* aggravating

aggra'var|e *vt* (*peggiorare*) make worse; increase (*pena*); (*appesantire*)

a

weigh down. ~**si** vr worsen

aggrazi'ato adj graceful

aggre'dire vt attack

aggre'ga|re vt add; (*associare a un gruppo ecc*) admit. ~**rsi** vr ~**rsi a** join. ~**to a** associated ● m aggregate; (*di case*) block

aggressi'one f aggression; (*atto*) attack

aggres's|ivo adj aggressive. ~**ività** f aggressiveness. ~**ore** m aggressor

aggrin'zare, aggrin'zire vt wrinkle

aggrot'tare vt ~ **le ciglia/la fronte** frown

aggrovigli'a|re vt tangle. ~**rsi** vr get entangled; fig get complicated. ~**to** adj entangled; fig confused

agguan'tare vt catch

aggu'ato m ambush; (*tranello*) trap; **stare in** ~ lie in wait

agguer'rito adj fierce

agia'tezza f comfort

agi'ato adj (*persona*) well off; (*vita*) comfortable

a'gibil|e adj (*palazzo*) fit for human habitation. ~**ità** f fitness for human habitation

agil|e adj agile. ~**ità** f agility

'agio m ease; **mettersi a proprio** ~ make oneself at home

a'gire vi act; (*comportarsi*) behave; (*funzionare*) work; ~ **su** affect

agi'ta|re vt shake; wave (mano); (fig: *turbare*) trouble. ~**rsi** vr toss about; (*essere inquieto*) be restless; (mare:) get rough. ~**to** adj restless; (mare) rough. ~**tore**, ~**trice** mf (*persona*) agitator. ~**zi'one** f agitation; **mettere in** ~**zione** qcno make sb worried

'agli = A + GLI

'aglio m garlic

a'gnello m lamb

agno'lotti mpl ravioli sg

a'gnostico, -a adj & mf agnostic

'ago m needle

ago'ni|a f agony. ~**z'zare** vi be on one's deathbed

ago'nistic|a f competition. ~**o** adj competitive

agopun'tura f acupuncture

a'gosto m August

a'grari|a f agriculture. ~**o** adj agricultural ● m landowner

a'gricol|o adj agricultural. ~**tore** m farmer. ~**tura** f agriculture

agri'foglio m holly

agritu'rismo m farm holidays, agro-tourism

> **Agriturismo** In the 1980s many farmers began to supplement their falling incomes by offering tourists an authentic experience of the Italian countryside. *Agriturismo* is now a very popular form of tourism in Italy. Guests can learn traditional skills and crafts, such as cooking and wine-making, all of which helps to preserve a threatened way of life. ***i***

'agro adj sour

agroalimen'tare adj food attrib

agro'dolce adj bitter-sweet; (*Culin*) sweet-and-sour; **in** ~ sweet and sour

agro'nomia f agronomy

a'grume m citrus fruit; (*pianta*) citrus tree

aguz'zare vt sharpen; ~ **le orecchie** prick up one's ears; ~ **la vista** look hard

aguz'zino m slave-driver; (*carceriere*) jailer

ahimè int alas

'ai = A + I

'aia f threshing-floor

'Aia f L'~ The Hague

Aids _mf_ Aids

ai'rone _m_ heron

ai'tante _adj_ sturdy

aiu'ola _f_ flower-bed

aiu'tante _mf_ assistant •_m_ (_Mil_) adjutant. ~ di campo aide-decamp

aiu'tare _vt_ help

ai'uto _m_ help, aid; (_assistente_) assistant

aiz'zare _vt_ incite; ~ contro set on

al = A+IL

'ala _f_ wing; fare ~ make way

ala'bastro _m_ alabaster

'alacre _adj_ brisk

a'lano _m_ Great Dane

'alba _f_ dawn

Alba'n|ia _f_ Albania. a~ese _adj & f_ Albanian

albeggi'are _vi_ dawn

albe'ra|to _adj_ wooded; (_viale_) tree-lined. ~'tura _f_ (_Naut_) masts _pl_. albe-'rello _m_ sapling

al'berg|o _m_ hotel. ~o diurno _hotel where rooms are rented during the daytime._ ~a'tore, ~a'trice _mf_ hotel-keeper. ~hi'ero _adj_ hotel _attrib_

'albero _m_ tree; (_Naut_) mast; (_Mech_) shaft. ~ genealogico family tree. ~ maestro (_Naut_) mainmast. ~ di Natale Christmas tree

albi'cocc|a _f_ apricot. ~o _m_ apricot-tree

al'bino, -a _mf_ albino

'albo _m_ register; (_libro ecc_) album; (_per avvisi_) notice board

'album _m_ album. ~ da disegno sketch-book

al'bume _m_ albumen

'alce _m_ elk

'alcol _m_ alcohol; (_Med_) spirit; (_liquori forti_) spirits _pl_; darsi all'~ take to drink. al'colici _mpl_ alcoholic drinks. al'colico _adj_ alcoholic. alco'lismo _m_ alcoholism. ~iz'zato, -a _adj & mf_ alcoholic

alco'test® _m inv_ Breathalyser®

al'cova _f_ alcove

al'cun, al'cuno _adj & pron_ any; non ha ~ amico he hasn't any/no friends. alcuni _pl_ some, a few; ~i suoi amici some of his friends

alea'torio _adj_ unpredictable

a'letta _f_ (_Mech_) fin

alfa'betico _adj_ alphabetical

alfabetizzazi'one _f_ ~ della popolazione teaching people to read and write

alfa'beto _m_ alphabet

alfi'ere _m_ (_negli scacchi_) bishop

al'fine _adv_ eventually, in the end

'alga _f_ seaweed

'algebra _f_ algebra

Alge'ri|a _f_ Algeria. a~no, -a _agg & mf_ Algerian

ali'ante _m_ glider

'alibi _m inv_ alibi

alie'na|re _vt_ alienate. ~rsi _vr_ become estranged; ~rsi le simpatie di qcno lose sb's good will. ~to, _a adj_ alienated •_mf_ lunatic

a'lieno, -a _adj_ alien •_adj_ è ~ da invidia envy is foreign to him

alimen'ta|re _vt_ feed; _fig_ foment •_adj_ food _attrib_; (_abitudine_) dietary •_m_ ~ri _pl_ food-stuffs. ~'tore _m_ power unit. ~zi'one _f_ feeding

ali'mento _m_ food; alimenti _pl_ food; (_Jur_) alimony

a'liquota _f_ share; (_di imposta_) rate

a

ali'scafo m hydrofoil

'alito m breath

'alla = A + LA

allaccia'mento m connection

allacci'ar|e vt fasten (cintura); lace up (scarpe); do up (vestito); (collegare) connect; form (amicizia). ~si vr do up, fasten

allaga'mento m flooding

alla'gar|e vt flood. ~si vr become flooded

allampa'nato adj lanky

allarga'mento m widening

allar'gar|e vt widen; open (braccia, gambe); let out (vestito ecc); fig extend. ~si vr widen

allar'mante adj alarming

allar'ma|re vt alarm. ~to adj panicky

al'larme m alarm; dare l'~ raise the alarm; falso ~ fig false alarm. ~ aereo air raid warning

allar'mis|mo m alarmism. ~ta mf alarmist

allatta'mento m (di animale) suckling; (di neonato) feeding

allat'tare vt suckle (animale); feed (neonato)

'alle = A + LE

alle'a|nza f alliance. ~to, -a adj allied ● mf ally

alle'ar|e vt unite. ~si vr form an alliance

alle'ga|re¹ vt (Jur) allege

alle'ga|re² vt (accludere) enclose; set on edge (denti). ~to adj enclosed ● m enclosure; (Comput) attachment; in ~to attached. ~zi'one f (Jur) allegation

allegge'rir|e vt lighten; fig alleviate. ~si vr become lighter; (vestirsi leggero) put on lighter clothes

allego'ria f allegory. alle'gorico adj allegorical

allegra'mente adv breezily

alle'gria f gaiety

al'legro adj cheerful; (colore) bright; (brillo) tipsy ● m (Mus) allegro

alle'luia int hallelujah!

allena'mento m training

alle'na|re vt, ~rsi vr train. ~'tore, ~'trice mf trainer, coach

allen'tar|e vt loosen; fig relax. ~si vr become loose; (Mech) work loose

aller'gia f allergy. al'lergico adj allergic

all'erta f stare ~ be alert

allesti'mento m preparation. ~ scenico (Theat) set

alle'stire vt prepare; stage (spettacolo); (Naut) fit out

allet'tante adj alluring

allet'tare vt entice

alleva'mento m breeding; (processo) bringing up; (luogo) farm; (per piante) nursery; pollo di ~ battery chicken

alle'vare vt bring up (bambini); breed (animali); grow (piante)

allevi'are vt alleviate; fig lighten

alli'bito adj astounded

allibra'tore m bookmaker

alli'e|tar|e vt gladden. ~si vr rejoice

alli'evo, -a mf pupil ● m (Mil) cadet

alliga'tore m alligator

alline'amento m alignment

alline'ar|e vt line up here; (Typ) align; Fin adjust. ~si vr fall into line

'allo = A + LO

al'locco m Zool tawny owl

al'lodola f [sky]lark

alloggi'a|re vt put up; (casa:) provide accommodation for; (Mil) billet ● vi stay; (Mil) be billeted. al'loggio m apartment; (Mil) billet

allonta'na'mento m removal

allonta'nar|e vt move away; (licenziare) dismiss; avert (pericolo). ~si vr go away

al'lora adv then; (a quel tempo) at that time; (in tal caso) in that case;

d'~ in poi from then on; **e ~?** what now?; **(e con ciò?)** so what?; **fino ~** until then

al'loro m laurel; (Culin) bay

'alluce m big toe

alluci'na|nte adj 🅱 incredible; **sostanza ~nte** hallucinogen. **~to, -a** mf 🅱 space cadet. **~zi'one** f hallucination

allucino'geno adj (sostanza) hallucinogenic

al'ludere vi **~ a** allude to

allu'minio m aluminium

allun'gar|e vt lengthen; stretch [out] (gamba); extend (tavolo); (diluire) dilute; **~ e il collo** crane one's neck. **~e le mani su qcno** touch sb up. **~e il passo** quicken one's step. **~si** vr grow longer; (crescere) grow taller; (sdraiarsi) lie down

allusi'one f allusion

allu'sivo adj allusive

alluvio'nale adj alluvial

alluvi'one f flood

al'meno adv at least; **[se] ~ venisse il sole!** if only the sun would come out!

a'logeno m halogen ● adj **lampada alogena** halogen lamp

a'lone m halo

'Alpi fpl **le ~** the Alps

alpi'nis|mo m mountaineering. **~ta** mf mountaineer

al'pino adj Alpine ● m (Mil) **gli alpini** the Alpine troops

al'quanto adj a certain amount of ● adv rather

alt int stop

alta'lena f swing; (tavola in bilico) see-saw

altale'nare vi fig vacillate

alta'mente adv highly

al'tare m altar

alta'rino m **scoprire gli altarini di qcno** reveal sb's guilty secrets

alte'ra|re vt alter; adulterate (vino);

(falsificare) falsify. **~rsi** vr be altered; (cibo:) go bad; (merci:) deteriorate; (arrabbiarsi) get angry. **~to** adj (vino) adulterated. **~zi'one** f alteration; (di vino) adulteration

al'terco m altercation

alter'nanza f alternation

alter'na|re vt, **~rsi** vr alternate. **~'tiva** f alternative. **~'tivo** adj alternate. **~to** adj alternating. **~'tore** m (Electr) alternator

al'tern|o adj alternate; **a giorni ~i** every other day

al'tero adj haughty

al'tezza f height; (profondità) depth; (suono) pitch; (di tessuto) width; (titolo) Highness; **essere all'~ di** be on a level with; fig be up to

altezzos'a'mente adv haughtily. **~ità** f haughtiness

altez'zoso adj haughty

al'ticcio adj tipsy, merry

alti'piano m plateau

alti'tudine f altitude

'alto adj high; (di statura) tall; (profondo) deep; (suono) high-pitched; (tessuto) wide; (Geog) northern; **a notte alta** in the middle of the night; **avere degli alti e bassi** have some ups and downs; **ad alta fedeltà** high-fidelity; **a voce alta, ad alta voce** in a loud voice; (leggere) aloud; **essere in ~ mare** be on the high seas. **alta finanza** f high finance. **alta moda** f high fashion. **alta tensione** f high voltage ● adv high; **in ~** at the top; (guardare:) up; **mani in ~!** hands up!

alto'forno m blast-furnace

altolà int halt there!

altolo'cato adj highly placed

altopar'lante m loudspeaker

altopi'ano m plateau

altret'tanto adj & pron as much; (pl) as many ● adv likewise; **buona fortuna! – grazie, ~** good luck! – thank you, the same to you

altri'menti adv otherwise

'altro adj other; un ~, un'altra another; l'altr'anno last year; domani l'~ the day after tomorrow; l'ho visto l'~ giorno I saw him the other day ●pron other [one]; un ~, un'altra another [one]; ne vuoi dell'~? would you like some more?; l'un l'~ one another; nessun ~ nobody else; gli altri (la gente) other people ●m something else; non fa ~ che lavorare he does nothing but work; desidera ~? (in negozio) anything else?; più che ~, sono stanco I'm tired more than anything; se non ~ at least; senz'~ certainly; tra l'~ what's more; ~ che! and how!

altro'eri m l'~ the day before yesterday

al'tronde adv d'~ on the other hand

al'trove adv elsewhere

al'trui adj other people's ●m other people's belongings pl

al'tura f high ground; (Naut) deep sea

a'lunno, -a mf pupil

alve'are m hive

al'za|re vt lift; (costruire) build; (Naut) hoist; ~re le spalle shrug one's shoulders. ~rsi vr rise; (in piedi) stand up; (da letto) get up; ~rsi in piedi get to one's feet. ~ta f lifting; (aumento) rise; (da letto) getting up; (Archit) elevation. ~to adj up

a'mabile adj lovable; (vino) sweet

a'maca f hammock

amalga'mar|e vt, ~si vr amalgamate

a'mante adj ~ di fond of ●m lover ●f mistress, lover

a'ma|re vt love; like (musica, ecc). ~to, -a adj loved ●mf beloved

ama'rena f sour black cherry

ama'retto m macaroon

ama'rezza f bitterness;

(dolore) sorrow

a'maro adj bitter ●m bitterness; (liquore) bitters pl

ama'rognolo adj rather bitter

ama'tore, -'trice mf lover

ambasci'a|ta f embassy; (messaggio) message. ~'tore, -'trice m ambassador ●f ambassadress

ambe'due adj & pron both

ambien'ta|le adj environmental. ~'lista adj & mf environmentalist

ambien'tar|e vt acclimatize; set (personaggio, film ecc). ~si vr get acclimatized

ambi'ente m environment; (stanza) room; fig milieu

ambiguità f inv ambiguity; (di persona) shadiness

am'biguo adj ambiguous; (persona) shady

am'bire vi ~ a aspire to

'ambito m sphere

ambiva'len|te adj ambivalent. ~za f ambivalence

ambizi'o|ne f ambition. ~so adj ambitious

ambu'lante adj wandering; venditore ~ hawker

ambu'lanza f ambulance

ambula'torio m (di medico) surgery; (di ospedale) out-patients'

a'meba f amoeba

a'meno adj pleasant

A'merica f America. ~ del Sud South America. ameri'cano, -a agg & mf American

ami'anto m asbestos

ami'chevole adj friendly

ami'cizia f friendship; fare ~ con qcno make friends with sb; amicizie pl (amici) friends

a'mico, -a mf friend; ~ del cuore bosom friend

'amido m starch

ammac'ca|re vt dent; bruise

(frutto). **~rsi** vr (metallo:) get dented; (frutto) bruise. **~to** adj dented; (frutto) bruised. **~'tura** f dent; (livido) bruise

ammae'stra|re vt (istruire) teach; train (animale). **~to** adj trained

ammai'nare vt lower (bandiera); furl (vele)

amma'la|rsi vr fall ill. **~to**, **-a** adj ill ● mf sick person; (paziente) patient

ammali'are vt bewitch

am'manco m deficit

ammanet'tare vt handcuff

ammani'cato adj essere ~ have connections

amma'raggio m splashdown

amma'rare vi put down on the sea; (nave spaziale:) splash down

ammas'sar|e vt amass. **~si** vr crowd together. **am'masso** m mass; (mucchio) pile

ammat'tire vi go mad

ammaz'zar|e vt kill. **~si** vr (suicidarsi) kill oneself, (rimanere ucciso) be killed

am'menda f amends pl; (multa) fine; fare ~ di qcsa make amends for sth

am'messo pp di ammettere ● conj ~ che supposing that

am'mettere vt admit; (riconoscere) acknowledge; (supporre) suppose

ammic'care vi wink

ammini'stra|re vt administer; (gestire) run. **~'tivo** adj administrative. **~'tore**, **~'trice** mf administrator; (di azienda) manager; (di società) director. **~tore delegato** managing director. **~zi'one** f administration; fatti di ordinaria **~zione** fig routine matters

ammi'ragli|o m admiral. **~'ato** m admiralty

ammi'ra|re vt admire. **~to** adj restare/essere **~to** be full of admiration. **~'tore**, **~'trice** mf admirer. **~zi'one** f admiration. **ammi'revole**

adj admirable

ammis'sibile adj admissible

ammissi'one f admission; (approvazione) acknowledgement

ammobili'a|re vt furnish. **~to** adj furnished

am'modo adj proper ● adv properly

am'mollo m in ~ soaking

ammo'niaca f ammonia

ammoni'mento m warning; (di rimprovero) admonishment

ammo'ni|re vt warn; (rimproverare) admonish. **~'tore** adj admonishing. **~zi'one** f Sport warning

ammon'tare vi ~ a amount to ● m amount

ammonticchi'are vt heap up

ammorbi'dente m (per panni) softener

ammorbi'dir|e vt, **~si** vr soften

ammorta'mento m (Comm) amortization

ammor'tare vt pay off (spesa); (Comm) amortize (debito)

ammortiz'za|re vt (Comm) = AM-MORTARE; (Mech) damp. **~'tore** m shock-absorber

ammosci'ar|e vt make flabby. **~si** vi get flabby

ammucchi'a|re vt, **~rsi** vr pile up. **~ta** f ([⊠]: orgia) orgy

ammuf'fi|re vi go mouldy. **~to** adj mouldy

ammutina'mento m mutiny

ammuti'narsi vr mutiny

ammuto'lire vi be struck dumb

amni'stia f amnesty

'amo m hook; fig bait

a'more m love; fare l'~ make love; per l'amor di Dio/del cielo! for heaven's sake!; andare d'~ e d'accordo get on like a house on fire; amor proprio self-respect; è un ~ (persona) he/she is a darling; per ~ di for the sake of; amori pl love affairs. **~ggi'are** vi flirt.

a

amo'revole adj loving

a'morfo adj shapeless; (fig) grey

amo'roso adj loving; (sguardo ecc) amorous; (lettera, relazione) love

ampi'ezza f (di esperienza) breadth; (di stanza) spaciousness; (di gonna) fullness; (importanza) scale

'ampio adj ample; (esperienza) wide; (stanza) spacious; (vestito) loose; (gonna) full; (pantaloni) baggy

am'plesso m embrace

amplia'mento m (di casa, porto) enlargement; (di strada) widening

ampli'are vt broaden (conoscenze)

amplifi'ca|re vt amplify; fig magnify. ~'tore m amplifier. ~zi'one f amplification

am'polla f cruet

ampu'ta|re vt amputate. ~zi'one f amputation

amu'leto m amulet

anabba'gliante adj (Auto) dipped ●mpl anabbaglianti dipped headlights

anacro'nis|mo m anachronism. ~tico adj anachronistic

a'nagrafe f (ufficio) register office; (registro) register of births, marriages and deaths

ana'grafico adj dati mpl ana-grafici personal data

ana'gramma m anagram

anal'colico adj non-alcoholic ●m soft drink, non-alcoholic drink

analfabe'ta adj & mf illiterate. ~'tismo m illiteracy

anal'gesico m painkiller

a'nalisi f inv analysis; (Med) test. ~ grammaticale/del periodo/logica parsing. ~ del sangue blood test

anali'sta mf analyst. ~tico adj analytical. ~z'zare vt analyse; (Med) test

anal'lergico adj hypoallergenic

analo'gia f analogy. a'nalogo adj analogous

'ananas m inv pineapple

anar'chi|a f anarchy. a'narchico, -a adj anarchic ●mf anarchist. ~smo m anarchism

A.N.A.S. f abbr (Azienda Nazionale Autonoma delle Strade) national road maintenance authority

anato'mia f anatomy. ana'tomico adj anatomical; (sedia) contoured

'anatra f duck

ana'troccolo m duckling

'anca f hip; (di animale) flank

ance'strale adj ancestral

'anche conj also, too; (persino) even; ~ se even if

anchilo'sato adj fig stiff

an'cora adv still, yet; (di nuovo) again; (di più) some more; ~ una volta once more

'anco|ra² f anchor; gettare l'~ra drop anchor. ~'raggio m anchorage. ~'rare vt anchor

anda'mento m (del mercato, degli affari) trend

an'dante adj (corrente) current; (di poco valore) cheap ●m (Mus) andante

an'da|re vi go; (funzionare) work; ~ via (partire) leave; (macchia) come out; ~ [bene] (confarsi) suit; (taglia) fit; ti va bene alle tre? does three o'clock suit you?; non mi va di mangiare I don't feel like eating; ~ di fretta be in a hurry; ~ fiero di be proud of; ~ di moda be in fashion; va per i 20 anni he's nearly 20; ma va! [là]! come on!; come va? how are things?; ~ a male go off; ~ a fuoco go up in flames; va spedito [entro] stamattina it must be sent this morning; ne va del mio lavoro my job is at stake; come è andata a finire? how did it turn out?; cosa vai dicendo? what are you talking about?; ~rsene go away; (morire) pass away ●m going; a lungo ~re eventually

'andito m passage

an'drone m entrance

a'neddoto m anecdote

ane'lare vt ~ a long for. **a'nelito** m longing

a'nello m ring; (di catena) link

ane'mia f anaemia. **a'nemico** adj anaemic

a'nemone m anemone

aneste'si|a f anaesthesia; (sostanza) anaesthetic. ~**sta** mf anaesthetist. **ane'stetico** adj & m anaesthetic

an'fibi mpl (stivali) army boots

an'fibio m (animale) amphibian ●adj amphibious

anfite'atro m amphitheatre

'anfora f amphora

an'fratto m ravine

an'gelico adj angelic

'angelo m angel. ~ **custode** guardian angel

angli'c|ano adj Anglican.

angli'smo m Anglicism

an'glofilo, -a adj & mf Anglophile

an'glofono, -a mf English-speaker

anglo'sassone adj & mf Anglo-Saxon

ango'la|re adj angular. ~**zi'one** f angle shot

'angolo m corner; (Math) angle. ~ **[di] cottura** kitchenette

ango'loso adj angular

an'gosci|a f anguish. ~**'are** vt torment. ~**'ato** adj agonized. ~**'oso** adj (disperato) anguished; (che dà angoscia) distressing

angu'illa f eel

an'guria f water-melon

an'gusti|a f (ansia) anxiety; (penuria) poverty. ~**'are** vt distress. ~**'arsi** vr be very worried (**per** about)

an'gusto adj narrow

'anice m anise; (Culin) aniseed; (liquore) anisette

ani'dride f ~ **carbonica** carbon dioxide

'anima f soul; non c'era ~ viva there was not a soul about; all'~! good grief!; un'~ in pena a soul in torment. ~ **gemella** soul mate

ani'ma|le adj & m animal; ~**li domestici** pl pets. ~**'lesco** adj animal

ani'ma|re vt give life to; (ravvivare) enliven; (incoraggiare) encourage. ~**rsi** vr come to life; (accalorarsi) become animated. ~**to** adj animate; (discussione) animated; (paese) lively. ~**tore**, ~**'trice** mf leading spirit; Cinema animator. ~**zi'one** f animation

'animo m (mente) mind; (indole) disposition; (cuore) heart; **perdersi d'**~ lose heart; **farsi** ~ take heart. ~**sità** f animosity

ani'moso adj brave; (ostile) hostile

'anitra f = ANATRA

annac'qua|re vt water down. ~**to** adj watered down

annaffi'a|re vt water. ~**'toio** m watering-can

an'nali mpl annals

anna'spare vi flounder

an'nata f year; (importo annuale) annual amount; (di vino) vintage

annebbia'mento m fog build-up; fig clouding

annebbi'ar|e vt cloud (vista, mente). ~**si** vr become foggy; (vista, mente) grow dim

annega'mento m drowning

anne'ga|re vt/i drown

anne'ri|re vt/i blacken. ~**si** vr become black

annessi'one f (di nazione) annexation

an'nesso pp di annettere ●adj attached; (stato) annexed

an'nettere vt add; (accludere) enclose; annex (stato)

annichi'lire vt annihilate

anni'darsi vr nest

annienta'mento m annihilation

a

annien'tar|e vt annihilate. ~**si** vr abase oneself

anniver'sario adj & m anniversary. ~ **di matrimonio** wedding anniversary

'anno m year; **Buon A~!** Happy New Year!; **quanti anni ha?** how old are you?; **Tommaso ha dieci anni** Thomas is ten [years old]. ~ **bisestile** leap year

anno'dar|e vt knot; do up (cintura); fig form. ~**si** vr become knotted

annoi'a|re vt bore; (recare fastidio) annoy. ~**rsi** vr get bored; (condizione) be bored. ~**to** adj bored

anno'ta|re vt note down; annotate (testo). ~**zi'one** f note

annove'rare vt number

annu'a|le adj annual, yearly. ~**rio** m year-book

annu'ire vi nod; (acconsentire) agree

annulla'mento m annulment; (di appuntamento) cancellation

annul'lar|e vt annul; cancel (appuntamento); (togliere efficacia a) undo; disallow (gol); (distruggere) destroy. ~**si** vr cancel each other out

annunci'a|re vt announce; (preannunciare) foretell. ~**tore**, ~**trice** mf announcer. A~**zi'one** f Annunciation

an'nuncio m announcement; (pubblicitario) advertisement; (notizia) news. **annunci** pl **economici** classified advertisements

'annuo adj annual, yearly

annu'sare vt sniff

annuvo'lar|e vt cloud. ~**si** vr cloud over

'ano m anus

a'nomalo adj anomalous

anoni'mato m **mantenere l'~** remain anonymous

a'nonimo, -a adj anonymous ● mf (pittore, scrittore) anonymous painter/writer

ano'ressico, -a mf anorexic

anor'mal|e adj abnormal ● mf deviant. ~**ità** f inv abnormality

'ansa f handle; (di fiume) bend

an'sare vi pant

'ansia, ansietà f anxiety; **stare in ~ per** be anxious about

ansi'oso adj anxious

antago'nis|mo m antagonism. ~**ta** mf antagonist

an'tartico adj & m Antarctic

antece'dente adj preceding ● m precedent

ante'fatto m prior event

ante'guerra adj pre-war ● m pre-war period

ante'nato, -a mf ancestor

an'tenna f (Radio, TV) aerial; (di animale) antenna; (Naut) yard. ~ **parabolica** satellite dish

ante'porre vt put before

ante'prima f preview; **vedere qcsa in ~** have a sneak preview of sth

anteri'ore adj front attrib; (nel tempo) previous

anti'aereo adj anti-aircraft attrib

antial'lergico adj hypoallergenic

antia'tomico adj **rifugio ~** fallout shelter

antibi'otico adj & m antibiotic

anti'caglia f (oggetto) piece of old junk

antica'mente adv long ago

anti'camera f ante-room; **far ~** be kept waiting

antichità f inv antiquity; (oggetto) antique

anti'clone m anticyclone

antici'pa|re vt advance; (Comm) pay in advance; (prevedere) anticipate; (prevenire) forestall ● vi be early. ~**'mente** adv in advance. ~**zi'one** f anticipation; (notizia) advance news

an'ticipo m advance; (caparra) deposit; **in** ~ early; (*nel lavoro*) ahead of schedule

an'tico *adj* ancient; (mobile ecc) antique; (*vecchio*) old; **all'antica** old-fashioned ●*mpl* **gli antichi** the ancients

anticoncezio'nale *adj & m* contraceptive

anticonfor'mis|mo *m* unconventionality. ~ta *mf* nonconformist. ~tico *adj* unconventional

anticonge'lante *adj & m* antifreeze

anticostituzio'nale *adj* unconstitutional

anti'crimine *adj inv* (squadra) crime *attrib*

antidemo'cratico *adj* undemocratic

antidolo'rifico *m* painkiller

an'tidoto *m* antidote

anti'droga *adj inv* (campagna) anti-drugs; (squadra) drug *attrib*

antie'stetico *adj* ugly

antifa'scismo *m* anti fascism

antifa'scista *adj & mf* anti-fascist

anti'furto *m* anti-theft device; (allarme) alarm ●*adj inv* (sistema) anti-theft

anti'gelo *m* antifreeze; (parabrezza) defroster

antigi'enico *adj* unhygienic

An'tille *fpl* le ~ the West Indies

an'tilope *f* antelope

antin'cendio *adj inv* allarme ~ fire alarm; porta ~ fire door

anti'nebbia *m inv* (Auto) [faro] ~ foglamp

antinfiamma'torio *adj & m* anti-inflammatory

antinucle'are *adj* anti-nuclear

antio'rario *adj* anti-clockwise

anti'pasto *m* hors d'oeuvre

an'tipodi *mpl* antipodes; **essere agli** ~ *fig* be poles apart

antiquari'ato *m* antique trade

anti'quario, -a *mf* antique dealer

anti'quato *adj* antiquated

anti'ruggine *m inv* rust-inhibitor

anti'rughe *adj inv* anti-wrinkle *attrib*

anti'scippo *adj inv* theft-proof

anti'settico *adj & m* antiseptic

antisoci'ale *adj* anti-social

anti'stante a *prep* in front of

anti'staminico *m* antihistamine

anti'stante a *prep* in front of

anti'tarlo *m inv* woodworm treatment

antiterro'ristico *adj* antiterrorist *attrib*

an'titesi *f inv* antithesis

'antivirus *m inv* virus checker

antolo'gia *f* anthology

'antro *m* cavern

antropolo'gia *f* anthropology. an-tro'pologo, -a *mf* anthropologist

anu'lare *m* ring-finger

'anzi *conj* in fact; (o meglin) or better still; (al contrario) on the contrary

anzianità *f* old age; (di servizio) seniority

anzi'ano, -a *adj* elderly; (di grado) senior ●*mf* elderly person

anziché *conj* rather than

anzi'tempo *adv* prematurely

anzi'tutto *adv* first of all

a'orta *f* aorta

apar'titico *adj* unaligned

apa'tia *f* apathy. a'patico *adj* apathetic

'ape *f* bee; **nido di api** honeycomb

aperi'tivo *m* aperitif

aperta'mente *adv* openly

a'perto *adj* open; **all'aria aperta** in the open air; **all'**~ open-air

aper'tura *f* opening; (inizio) beginning; (ampiezza) spread; (di arco) span; (Pol) overtures *pl*; (Phot) aperture; ~ **mentale** openness

'apice *m* apex

a

apicol'tura f beekeeping

ap'nea f immersione in ~ free diving

a'polide adj stateless ● mf stateless person

a'postolo m apostle

apostro'fare vt (mettere un apostrofo a) write with an apostrophe; reprimand (persona)

a'postrofo m apostrophe

appaga'mento m fulfilment

appa'ga|re vt satisfy. ~rsi vr ~rsi di be satisfied with

appai'are vt pair; mate (animali)

appallotto'lare vt roll into a ball

appal'ta'tore m contractor

ap'palto m contract; dare in ~ to contract

appan'naggio m (in denaro) annuity; fig prerogative

appan'nar|e vt mist (vetro); dim (vista). ~si vr mist over; (vista:) grow dim

appa'rato m apparatus; (pompa) display

apparecchi'a|re vt prepare ● vi lay the table. ~'tura f (impianti) equipment

appa'recchio m apparatus; (congegno) device; (radio, tv ecc) set; (aeroplano) aircraft. ~ acustico hearing aid

appa'ren|te adj apparent. ~te'mente adv apparently. ~za f appearance; in ~za apparently

appa'ri|re vi appear; (sembrare) look. ~'scente adj striking; pej gaudy. ~zi'one f apparition

apparta'mento m apartment

appar'ta|rsi vr withdraw. ~to adj secluded

apparte'nenza f membership

apparte'nere vi belong

appassio'nante adj (storia, argomento) exciting

appassio'na|re vt excite; (commuo-

vere). move. ~rsi vr ~rsi a become excited by. ~to adj passionate; ~to di (entusiastico) fond of

appas'sir|e vi wither. ~si vr fade

appel'larsi vr ~ a appeal to

ap'pello m appeal; (chiamata per nome) rollcall; (esami) exam session; fare l'~ to call the roll

ap'pena adv just; (a fatica) hardly ● conj [non] ~ as soon as

ap'pendere vt hang [up]

appen'dice f appendix. **appendi-'cite** f appendicitis

Appen'nini mpl gli ~ the Apennines

appesan'tir|e vt weigh down. ~si vr become heavy

ap'peso pp di appendere adj hanging; (impiccato) hanged

appe'ti|to m appetite; aver ~to be hungry; buon ~to! enjoy your meal!. ~'toso adj appetizing; fig tempting

appezza'mento m plot of land

appia'nar|e vt level; fig smooth over. ~si vr improve

appiat'tir|e vt flatten. ~si vr flatten oneself

appic'care vt ~ il fuoco a set fire to

appicci'car|e vt stick; ~e a (fig: appioppare) palm off on ● vi be sticky. ~si vr stick; (cose:) stick together; ~si a qcno fig stick to sb like glue

appicci'caticcio adj sticky; fig clingy

appicci'coso adj sticky; fig clingy

appie'dato adj sono ~ I don't have the car; sono rimasto ~ I was stranded

appi'eno adv fully

appigli'arsi vr ~ a get hold of; fig stick to. **ap'piglio** m fingerhold; (per piedi) foothold; fig pretext

appiop'pare vt ~ a palm off on; (🔢: dare) give

appiso'larsi vr doze off

applau'dire vt/i applaud. **ap'plauso** m applause

appli'cabile adj applicable

appli'ca|re vt apply; enforce (legge ecc). **~rsi** vr apply oneself. **~tore** m applicator. **~zi'one** f application; (di legge) enforcement

appoggi'ar|e vt lean (a against); (mettere) put; (sostenere) back. **~si** vr **~si a** lean against; fig rely on. **ap'poggio** m support

appollai'arsi vr fig perch

ap'porre vt affix

appor'tare vt bring; (causare) cause. **ap'porto** m contribution

apposita'mente adv especially

appo'sito adj proper

ap'posta adv on purpose; (espressamente) specially

apposta'mento m ambush; (caccia) lying in wait

appo'star|e vt post (soldati). **~si** vr lie in wait

ap'prend|ere vt understand; (imparare) learn. **~i'mento** m learning

appren'di|sta mf apprentice. **~'stato** m apprenticeship

apprensi'one f apprehension; **essere in ~ per** be anxious about. **appren'sivo** adj apprehensive

ap'presso adv & prep (vicino) near; (dietro) behind; **come ~** as follows

appre'star|e vt prepare. **~si** vr get ready

apprez'za|bile adj appreciable. **~'mento** m appreciation; (giudizio) opinion

apprez'za|re vt appreciate. **~to** adj appreciated

ap'proccio m approach

appro'dare vi land; **~ a** fig come to; **non ~ a nulla** come to nothing. **ap'prodo** m landing; (luogo) landing-stage

approfit'ta|re vi take advantage

(di of), profit (di by). **~'tore**, **~'trice** mf chancer

approfondi'mento m deepening; **di ~** fig: (esame) further

approfon'di|re vt deepen. **~rsi** vr (divario:) widen. **~to** adj (studio, ricerca) in-depth

appropri'a|rsi vr (essere adatto a) suit; **~rsi di** take possession of. **~to** adj appropriate. **~zi'one** f (Jur) appropriation. **~zione indebita** (Jur) embezzlement

approssi'ma|re vt **~re per eccesso/difetto** round up/down. **~rsi** vr draw near. **~tiva'mente** adv approximately. **~'tivo** adj approximate. **~zi'one** f approximation

appro'va|re vt approve of; approve (legge). **~zi'one** f approval

approvvigiona'mento m supplying; **approvvigionamenti** pl provisions

approvvigio'nar|e vt supply. **~si** vr stock up

appunta'mento m appointment; **fissare un ~** make an appointment; **darsi ~** decide to meet

appun'tar|e vt (annotare) take notes; (fissare) fix; (con spillo) pin; (appuntire) sharpen. **~si** vr **~si su** (teoria:) be based on

appun'ti|re vt sharpen. **~to** adj (mento) pointed

ap'punto¹ m note; (piccola critica) niggle

ap'punto² adv exactly; **per l'~!** exactly!; **stavo ~ dicendo...** I was just saying...

appu'rare vt verify

a'pribile adj that can be opened

apribot'tiglie m inv bottle-opener

a'prile m April; **il primo d'~** April Fools' Day

a'prir|e vt open; turn on (acqua ecc); (con chiave) unlock; open up (ferita ecc). **~si** vr open; (spaccarsi) split; (confidarsi) confide (con in)

a

apri'scatole f inv tin-opener

aqua'planing m andare in ∼ aquaplane

'aqui|la f eagle; non è un'∼a! he is no genius!. ∼'lino adj aquiline

aqui'lone m (giocattolo) kite

ara'besco m arabesque; hum scribble

A'rabia Sau'dita f l'∼ Saudi Arabia

'arabo, -a adj Arab; (lingua) Arabic ●mf Arab ●m (lingua) Arabic

a'rachide f peanut

ara'gosta f lobster

a'ranci|a f orange. ∼'ata f orangeade. ∼o m orange-tree; (colore) orange. ∼'one adj & m orange

a'ra|re vt plough. ∼tro m plough

ara'tura f ploughing

a'razzo m tapestry

arbi'trar|e vt arbitrate in; Sport referee. ∼ietà f arbitrariness. ∼io adj arbitrary

ar'bitrio m will; è un ∼ it's very high-handed

'arbitro m arbiter; Sport referee; (nel baseball) umpire

ar'busto m shrub

'arca f ark; (cassa) chest

ar'ca|ico adj archaic. ∼'ismo m archaism

ar'cangelo m archangel

ar'cata f arch; (serie di archi) arcade

arche|olo'gia f archaeology. ∼o'logico adj archaeological. ∼'ologo, -a mf archaeologist

ar'chetto m (Mus) bow

architet'tare vt fig devise; cosa state architettando? fig what are you plotting?

archi'tet|to m architect. ∼'tonico adj architectural. ∼'tura f architecture

archivi'are vt file; (Jur) close

ar'chivio m archives pl; (Comput) file

archi'vista mf filing clerk

ar'cigno adj grim

arci'pelago m archipelago

arci'vescovo m archbishop

'arco m arch; (Math) arc; (Mus, Arms) bow; nell'∼ di una giornata/due mesi in the space of a day/two months

arcoba'leno m rainbow

arcu'a|re vt bend. ∼rsi vr bend. ∼to adj bent, curved

ar'dente adj burning; fig ardent. ∼'mente adv ardently

'ardere vt/i burn

ar'desia f slate

ar'di|re vi dare. ∼to adj daring; (coraggioso) bold; (sfacciato) impudent

ar'dore m (calore) heat; fig ardour

'arduo adj arduous; (ripido) steep

'area f area. ∼ di rigore (nel calcio) penalty area. ∼ di servizio service area

a'rena f arena

are'narsi vr run aground; fig: (trattative) reach deadlock; mi sono arenato I'm stuck

'argano m winch

argen'tato adj silver-plated

argente'ria f silver[ware]

ar'gento m silver

ar'gil|la f clay. ∼'loso adj (terreno) clayey

argi'nare vt embank; fig hold in check, contain

'argine m embankment; (diga) dike

argomen'tare vi argue

argo'mento m argument; (motivo) reason; (soggetto) subject

argu'ire vt deduce

ar'gu|to adj witty. ∼zia f wit; (battuta) witticism

'aria f air; (aspetto) appearance; (Mus) tune; andare all'∼ fig come to nothing; avere l'∼... look...; corrente d'∼ draught; mandare all'∼ qcsa *fig* ruin sth

aridità *f* aridity, dryness

'arido *adj* arid

arieggi'a|re *vt* air. ~to *adj* airy

ari'ete *m* ram. A~ (*Astr*) Aries

ari'etta *f* (*brezza*) breeze

a'ringa *f* herring

ari'oso *adj* (*locale*) light and airy

aristo'cra|tico, -a *adj* aristocratic ● *mf* aristocrat. ~'zia *f* aristocracy

arit'metica *f* arithmetic

arlec'chino *m* Harlequin; *fig* buffoon

'arma *f* weapon; **armi** *pl* arms; (*forze armate*) [armed] forces; **chiamare alle armi** call up; **sotto le armi** in the army; **alle prime armi** *fig* inexperienced. ~ **da fuoco** firearm. **armi** *mpl* **di distruzione di massa** weapons of mass destruction.

armadi'etto *m* locker, cupboard

ar'madio *m* cupboard; (*guardaroba*) wardrobe

armamen'tario *m* tools *pl*; *fig* paraphernalia

arma'mento *m* armament; (*Naut*) fitting out

ar'ma|re *vt* arm; (*equipaggiare*) fit out; (*Archit*) reinforce. ~**rsi** *vr* arm oneself (di with). ~**ta** *f* army; (*flotta*) fleet. ~**tore** *m* shipowner. ~**tura** *f* framework; (*impalcatura*) scaffolding; (*di guerriero*) armour

armeggi'are *vi fig* manoeuvre

armi'stizio *m* armistice

armo'ni|a *f* harmony. **ar'monica** *f* ~ [**a bocca**] mouth organ. **ar'monico** *adj* harmonic. ~**oso** *adj* harmonious

armoniz'zar|e *vt* harmonize ● *vi* match. ~**si** *vr* (*colori*) match

ar'nese *m* tool; (*oggetto*) thing; (*congegno*) gadget; **male in** ~ in bad condition

arnia *f* beehive

a'roma *m* aroma; **aromi** *pl* herbs.

~**tera'pia** *f* aromatherapy

aro'matico *adj* aromatic

aromatiz'zare *vt* flavour

'arpa *f* harp

ar'peggio *m* arpeggio

ar'pia *f* harpy

arpi'one *m* hook; (*pesca*) harpoon

arrabat'tarsi *vr* do all one can

arrabbi'a|rsi *vr* get angry. ~**to** *adj* angry. ~**tura** *f* rage; **prendersi una** ~**tura** fly into a rage

arraf'fare *vt* grab

arrampi'ca|rsi *vr* climb [up]. ~**ta** *f* climb. ~**tore, ~'trice** *mf* climber. ~**'tore sociale** social climber

arran'care *vi* limp, hobble

arrangia'mento *m* arrangement

arrangi'ar|e *vt* arrange. ~**si** *vr* manage; ~**si alla meglio** get by; **arrangiati!** get on with it!

arra'parsi *vr* 🔲 get randy

arre'care *vt* bring; (*causare*) cause

arreda'mento *m* interior decoration; (*l'arredare*) furnishing; (*mobili ecc*) furnishings *pl*

arre'da|re *vt* furnish. ~**tore, ~'trice** *mf* interior designer. **ar'redo** *m* furnishings *pl*

ar'rendersi *vr* surrender

arren'devo|le *adj* (*persona*) yielding. ~**lezza** *f* softness

arre'star|e *vt* arrest; (*fermare*) stop. ~**si** *vr* halt. **ar'resto** *m* stop; (*Med, Jur*) arrest; **la dichiaro in [stato d']** **arresto** you are under arrest; **mandato di arresto** warrant. **arresti** *pl* **domiciliari** (*Jur*) house arrest

arre'tra|re *vt/i* withdraw; pull back (*giocatore*). ~**to** *adj* (*paese ecc*) backward; (*Mil: posizione*) rear; **numero** ~**to** (*di rivista*) back number; **del lavoro** ~**to** a backlog of work ● *m* (*di stipendio*) back pay

arre'trati *mpl* arrears

arricchi'mento *m* enrichment

arric'chi|re *vt* enrich. ~**rsi** *vr* get

rich. ~to, -a mf nouveau riche

arric'ci|are vt curl; ~ il naso turn up one's nose

ar'ringa f harangue; (Jur) closing address

arrischi'a|rsi vr dare. ~to adj risky; (imprudente) rash

arri'va|re vi arrive; ~re a (raggiungere) reach; (ridursi) be reduced to. ~to, -a adj successful; ben ~to! welcome! ●mf successful person

arrive'derci int goodbye; ~ a domani see you tomorrow

arri'vis|mo m social climbing; (nel lavoro) careerism. ~ta mf social climber; (nel lavoro) careerist

ar'rivo m arrival; Sport finish

arro'gan|te adj arrogant. ~za f arrogance

arro'garsi vr ~ il diritto di fare qcsa take it upon oneself to do sth

arrossa'mento m reddening

arros'sa|re vt make red (occhi). ~si vr go red

arros'sire vi blush, go red

arro'stire vt roast; toast (pane); (ai ferri) grill. ar'rosto adj & m roast

arroto'lare vt roll up

arroton'dar|e vt round; (Math ecc) round off. ~si vr become round; (persona): get plump

arrovel'larsi vr ~ il cervello rack one's brains

arroven'ta|re vt make red-hot. ~rsi vr become red-hot. ~to adj red-hot

arruf'fa|re vt ruffle; fig confuse. ~to adj (capelli) ruffled

arruffianarsi vr ~ qcno fig butter sb up

arruggi'ni|re vt rust. ~rsi vr go rusty; fig (physically) stiffen up; (conoscenze): go rusty. ~to adj rusty

arruola'mento m enlistment

arruo'lar|e vt/i, ~si vr enlist

arse'nale m arsenal; (cantiere)

[naval] dockyard

ar'senico m arsenic

'arso pp di ardere ●adj burnt; (arido) dry. ar'sura f burning heat; (sete) parching thirst

'arte f art; (abilità) craftsmanship; le belle arti the fine arts. arti figurative figurative arts

arte'fa|re vt adulterate (vino); disguise (voce). ~tto adj fake; (vino) adulterated

ar'tefice m craftsman; craftswoman; fig author

ar'teria f artery. ~ [stradale] arterial road

arteriosclerosi f arteriosclerosis

'artico adj & m Arctic

artico'la|re adj articular ●vt articulate; (suddividere) divide. ~rsi vr fig ~rsi in consist of. ~to adj (Auto) articulated; fig well-constructed. ~zi'one f (Anat) articulation

ar'ticolo m article. ~ di fondo leader

artifici'ale adj artificial

arti'fici|o m artifice; (affettazione) affectation. ~'oso adj artful; (affettato) affected

artigia'na|le adj made by hand; hum amateurish. ~'mente adv with craftsmanship; hum amateurishly

artigia'nato m craftsmanship; (ceto) craftsmen pl. ~'ano, -a m craftsman ●f craftswoman

artigli'ere m artilleryman. ~e'ria f artillery

ar'tiglio m claw; fig clutch

ar'tist|a mf artist. ~ica'mente adv artistically. ~ico adj artistic

'arto m limb

ar'trite f arthritis

ar'trosi f rheumatism

arzigogo'lato adj bizarre

ar'zillo adj sprightly

a'scella f armpit

ascen'den|te adj ascending ●m

(*antenato*) ancestor; (*influenza*) ascendancy; (*Astr*) ascendant

ascensi'one f ascent; **l'A∼** the Ascension

ascen'sore m lift, elevator Am

a'scesa f ascent; (*al trono*) accession; (*al potere*) rise

a'scesso m abscess

a'sceta mf ascetic

'ascia f axe

asciugabianche'ria m inv (*stenditoio*) clothes horse

asciuga'capelli m inv hair dryer

asciuga'mano m towel

asciu'gar|e vt dry. ∼**si** vr dry oneself; (*diventare asciutto*) dry up

asci'utto adj dry; (*magro*) wiry; (*risposta*) curt; **essere all'∼** fig be hard up

ascol'ta|re vt listen to ● vi listen. ∼'**tore**, ∼'**trice** mf listener

a'scolto m listening; **dare ∼ a** listen to; **mettersi in ∼** Radio tune in

asfal'tare vt asphalt

a'sfalto m asphalt

asfis'si|a f asphyxia. ∼'**ante** adj oppressive; fig: (*persona*) annoying. ∼'**are** vt asphyxiate; fig annoy

'Asia f Asia. **a si'atico, -a** agg & mf Asian

a'silo m shelter; (*d'infanzia*) nursery school. **∼ nido** day nursery. **∼ politico** political asylum

asim'metrico adj asymmetrical

'asino m donkey; (*fig: persona stupida*) ass

'asma f asthma. **a'smatico** adj asthmatic

asoci'ale adj asocial

a'sola f buttonhole

a'sparagi mpl asparagus sg

a'sparago m asparagus spear

asperità f inv harshness; (*di terreno*) roughness

aspet'ta|re vt wait for; (*prevedere*)

expect; ∼**re un bambino** be expecting [a baby]; **fare ∼re** qcno keep sb waiting ● vi wait. ∼**rsi** vr expect. ∼'**tiva** f expectation

a'spetto[1] m appearance; (*di problema*) aspect; **di bell'∼** goodlooking

a'spetto[2] m **sala f d'∼** waiting room

aspi'rante adj aspiring; (*pompa*) suction attrib ● mf (*a un posto*) applicant; (*al trono*) aspirant; **gli aspiranti al titolo** the contenders for the title

aspira'polvere m inv vacuum cleaner

aspi'ra|re vt inhale; (*Mech*) suck in ● vi **∼ re a** aspire to. ∼'**tore** m extractor fan. ∼**zi'one** f inhalation; (*Mech*) suction; (*ambizione*) ambition

aspi'rina f aspirin

aspor'tare vt take away

aspra'mente adv (*duramente*) severely

a'sprezza f (*al gusto*) sourness; (*di clima*) severity; (*di suono*) harshness; (*di odore*) pungency

'aspro adj (*al gusto*) sour; (*clima*) severe; (*suono, parole*) harsh; (*odore*) pungent; (*litigio*) bitter

assag'gi|are vt taste. ∼'**gini** mpl (*Culin*) samples. **as'saggio** m tasting; (*piccola quantità*) taste

as'sai adv very; (*moltissimo*) very much; (*abbastanza*) enough

assa'lire vt attack. ∼'**tore**, ∼'**trice** mf assailant

as'salto m attack; **prendere d'∼** storm (*città*); fig mob (*persona*); hold up (*banca*)

assapo'rare vt savour

assassi'nare vt murder, assassinate

assas'sin|io m murder, assassination. **∼o, -a** adj murderous ● m murderer ● f murderess

'asse f board ● m (*Techn*) axle; (*Math*) axis. **∼ da stiro** ironing board

a

assecon'dare vt satisfy; (*favorire*) support

assedi'are vt besiege. **as'sedio** m siege

assegna'mento m allotment; **fare ∼ su** rely on

asse'gna|re vt allot; award (premio). **∼'tario** mf recipient. **∼zi'one** f (*di alloggio, borsa di studio*) allocation; (*di premio*) award

as'segno m allowance; (*bancario*) cheque; **contro ∼** cash on delivery. **∼ circolare** bank draft. **assegni** pl **familiari** family allowance. **∼ non trasferibile** non-transferable cheque.

assem'blea f assembly; (*adunanza*) gathering

assembra'mento m gathering

assen'nato adj sensible

as'senso m assent

assen'tarsi vr go away; (*da stanza*) leave the room

as'sen|te adj absent; (*distratto*) absent-minded ● mf absentee. **∼te'ismo** m absenteeism. **∼te'ista** mf frequent absentee. **∼za** f absence; (*mancanza*) lack

asse'r|ire vt assert. **∼'tivo** adj assertive. **∼zi'one** f assertion

asses'sorato m department

asses'sore m councillor

assesta'mento m settlement

asse'star|e vt arrange; **∼e un colpo** deal a blow. **∼si** vr settle oneself

asse'tato adj parched

as'setto m order; (*Aeron, Naut*) trim

assicu'ra|re vt assure; (*Comm*) insure; register (posta); (*fissare*) secure; (*accertare*) ensure. **∼rsi** vr (*con contratto*) insure oneself; (*legarsi*) fasten oneself; **∼rsi che** make sure that. **∼'tivo** adj insurance attrib. **∼'tore,** **∼'trice** mf insurance agent ● adj insurance attrib. **∼zi'one** f assurance; (*contratto*) insurance

assidera'mento m exposure. **asside'rato** adj (*Med*) suffering from exposure; T frozen

assidu|a'mente adv assiduously. **∼ità** f assiduity

as'siduo adj assiduous; (*cliente*) regular

assil'lante adj (persona, pensiero) nagging

assil'lare vt pester

as'sillo m worry

assimi'la|re vt assimilate. **∼zi'one** f assimilation

as'sise fpl assizes; **Corte d'A∼** Court of Assize[s]

assi'sten|te mf assistant. **∼te sociale** social worker. **∼te di volo** flight attendant. **∼za** f assistance; (*presenza*) presence. **∼za sociale** social work

assistenzi'a|le adj welfare attrib. **∼'lismo** m welfare

as'sistere vt assist; (*curare*) nurse ● vi **∼ a** (*essere presente*) be present at; watch (spettacolo ecc)

'asso m ace; **piantare in ∼** leave in the lurch

associ'a|re vt join; (*collegare*) associate. **∼rsi** vr join forces; (*Comm*) enter into partnership. **∼rsi a** join. **∼zi'one** f association

assogget'tar|e vt subject. **∼si** vr submit

asso'lato adj sunny

assol'dare vt recruit

as'solo m (*Mus*) solo

as'solto pp di assolvere

assoluta'mente adv absolutely

assolu'tismo m absolutism

asso'lu|to adj absolute. **∼zi'one** f acquittal; (*Relig*) absolution

as'solvere vt perform (compito); (*Jur*) acquit; (*Relig*) absolve

assomigli'ar|e vi **∼e a** resemble. **∼si** vr resemble each other

assom'marsi vr combine; ∼ a qcsa add to sth

asso'nanza f assonance

asson'nato adj drowsy

asso'pirsi vr doze off

assor'bente adj & m absorbent. ∼ igienico sanitary towel

assor'bire vt absorb

assor'da|re vt deafen. ∼nte adj deafening

assorti'mento m assortment

assor'ti|re vt match (colori). ∼to adj assorted; (colori, persone) matched

as'sorto adj engrossed

assottigli'ar|e vt make thin; (aguzzare) sharpen; (ridurre) reduce. ∼si vr grow thin; (finanze): be whittled away

assue'fa|re vt accustom. ∼rsi vr ∼rsi a get used to. ∼tto adj (a caffè, aspirina) immune to the effects; (a droga) addicted. ∼zi'one f (a caffè, aspirina) immunity to the effects; (a droga) addiction

as'sumere vt assume; take on (impiegato); ∼ informazioni make inquiries

as'sunto pp di assumere ● m task. assunzi'one f (di impiegato) employment

assurdità f inv absurdity; ∼ pl nonsense

as'surdo adj absurd

'asta f pole; (Mech) bar; (Comm) auction; a mezz'∼ at half-mast

a'stemio adj abstemious

aste'n|ersi vr abstain (da from). ∼si'one f abstention

aste'nuto, -a mf abstainer

aste'risco m asterisk

astig'ma|tico adj astigmatic. ∼'tismo m astigmatism

'astio m rancour; avere ∼o contro qcno bear sb a grudge. ∼'oso adj resentful

a'stratto adj abstract

astrin'gente adj & m astringent

'astro m star

astrolo'gia f astrology. a'strologo, -a mf astrologer

astro'nauta mf astronaut

astro'nave f spaceship

astro|no'mia f astronomy. ∼o'no-mico adj astronomical. a'stronomo m astronomer

astrusità f abstruseness

a'stuccio m case

a'stu|to adj shrewd; (furbo) cunning. ∼zia f shrewdness; (azione) trick

ate'ismo m atheism

A'tene f Athens

a'teo, -a adj & mf atheist

a'tipico adj atypical

at'lant|e m atlas. ∼ico adj Atlantic; l' [Oceano] A∼ico the Atlantic [Ocean]

at'let|a mf athlete. ∼ica f athletics sg ∼ica leggera track and field events. ∼ica pesante weight-lifting, boxing, wrestling, etc. ∼ico adj athletic

atmo'sfer|a f atmosphere. ∼ico adj atmospheric

a'tomic|a f atom bomb. ∼o adj atomic

'atomo m atom

'atrio m entrance hall

a'troc|e adj atrocious; (terrible) dreadful. ∼ità f inv atrocity

atrofiz'zarsi vr atrophy

attaccabot'toni mf inv [crashing] bore

attacca'brighe mf inv troublemaker

attacca'mento m attachment

attacca'panni m inv [coat-]hanger; (a muro) clothes hook

attac'car|e vt attach; (legare) tie; (appendere) hang; (cucire) sew on; (contagiare) pass on; (assalire) attack; (iniziare) start ● vi stick; (diffondersi) catch

a

on. ∼si vr cling; (affezionarsi) become
attached; (litigare) quarrel

attacca'ticcio adj sticky

at'tacco m attack; (punto d'unione)
junction

attar'darsi vr stay late; (indugiare)
linger

attec'chire vi take; (moda ecc:)
catch on

atteggia'mento m attitude

atteggi'ar|e vt assume. ∼si vr ∼si
a pose as

attem'pato adj elderly

at'tender|e vt wait for •vi ∼e a
attend to. ∼si vr expect

atten'dibil|e adj reliable. ∼ità f re-
liability

atte'nersi vr ∼ a stick to

attenta'mente adv attentively

atten'ta|re vi ∼ re a make an at-
tempt on. ∼to m act of violence;
(contro politico ecc) assassination attempt. ∼tore, ∼trice mf (a scopo
politico) terrorist

at'tento adj attentive; (accurato)
careful; ∼! look out!; stare ∼ pay
attention

attenu'ante f extenuating circumstance

attenu'a|re vt attenuate; (minimiz-
zare) minimize; subdue (colori ecc);
calm (dolore); soften (colpo). ∼rsi
vr diminish. ∼zi'one f lessening

attenzi'one f attention; ∼!
watch out!

atter'ra|ggio m landing. ∼re vt
knock down •vi land

atter'rir|e vt terrorize. ∼si vr be
terrified

at'tesa f waiting; (aspettativa) expectation; in ∼a di waiting for. ∼o
pp di attendere

atte'sta|re vt state; (certificare) certi-
fy. ∼to m certificate. ∼zi'one f
certificate; (dichiarazione) declaration

'attico m attic

at'tiguo adj adjacent

attil'lato adj (vestito) close-fitting

'attimo m moment

atti'nente adj ∼ a pertaining to

at'tingere vt draw; fig obtain

atti'rare vt attract

atti'tudine f (disposizione) aptitude;
(atteggiamento) attitude

atti'v|are vt activate. ∼ismo m acti-
vism. ∼ista mf activist. attività f inv
activity; (Comm) assets pl. ∼o adj active; (Comm) productive •m assets pl

attiz'za|re vt poke; fig stir up.
∼'toio m poker

'atto m act; (azione) action; (Comm,
Jur) deed; (certificato) certificate; atti pl
(di società ecc) proceedings; mettere
in ∼ put into effect

at'tonito adj astonished

attorcigli'ar|e vt twist. ∼si vr get
twisted

at'tore m actor

attorni'ar|e vt surround. ∼si vr
∼si di surround oneself with

at'torno adv around, about •prep
∼ a around, about

attrac'care vt/i dock

attra'ente adj attractive

at'tra|rre vt attract. ∼rsi vr be at-
tracted to each other. ∼t'tiva
f charm

attraversa'mento m crossing. ∼
pedonale crossing, crosswalk Am

attraver'sare vt cross; (passare) go
through

attra'verso prep through; (obliquamente) across

attrazi'on|e f attraction. ∼i pl tu-
ristiche tourist attractions

attrez'za|re vt equip; (Naut) rig.
∼rsi vr kit oneself out; ∼'tura f
equipment; (Naut) rigging

at'trezzo m tool; attrezzi pl equipment; Sport appliances pl; (Theat)
props pl

attribu'ir|e vt attribute. ∼si vr

ascribe to oneself; ∼**si il merito di** claim credit for

attri'buto *m* attribute. ∼**zi'one** *f* attribution

at'trice *f* actress

at'trito *m* friction

attu'abile *adj* feasible

attu'al|e *adj* present; (*di attualità*) topical; (*effettivo*) actual. ∼**ità** *f* topicality; (*avvenimento*) news; **programma di** ∼**ità** current affairs programme. ∼**iz'zare** *vt* update. ∼**'mente** *adv* at present

attu'a|re *vt* carry out. ∼**rsi** *vr* be realized. ∼**zi'one** *f* carrying out

attu'tire *vt* deaden; ∼ **il colpo** soften the blow

au'dac|e *adj* audacious;. ∼**ia** *f* boldness; (*insolenza*) audacity

'audience *f inv* (*telespettatori*) audience

'audio *m* audio

audiovi'sivo *adj* audiovisual

audi'torio *m* auditorium

audizi'one *f* audition; (*Jur*) hearing

'auge *m* height; **essere in** ∼ be popular

augu'rar|e *vt* wish. ∼**si** *vr* hope. **au'gurio** *m* wish; (*presagio*) omen; **auguri** all the best!; (*a Natale*) Happy Christmas!; **tanti auguri** best wishes

'aula *f* classroom; (*università*) lecture-hall; (*sala*) hall. ∼ **magna** (*in università*) great hall. ∼ **del tribunale** courtroom

aumen'tare *vt/i* increase. **au'mento** *m* increase; (*di stipendio*) [pay] rise

au'reola *f* halo

au'rora *f* dawn

auscul'tare *vt* (*Med*) auscultate

ausili'are *adj & mf* auxiliary

auspi'cabile *adj* è ∼ **che...** it is to be hoped that...

auspi'care *vt* hope for

au'spicio *m* omen; **auspici** (*pl: protezione*) auspices

auste'rità *f* austerity

au'stero *adj* austere.

Au'strali|a *f* Australia. a∼**'ano, -a** *adj & mf* Australian

'Austria *f* Austria. **au'striaco, -a** *agg & mf* Austrian

autar'chia *f* autarchy. **au'tarchico** *adj* autarchic

autenti'c|are *vt* authenticate. ∼**ità** *f* authenticity

au'tentico *adj* authentic; (*vero*) true

au'tista *m* driver

'auto+ *pref* self +; auto-

autoabbron'zante *m* self-tan ● *adj* self-tanning

autoambu'lanza *f* ambulance

autoarticolato *m* articulated lorry

autobio'gra'fia *f* autobiography. ∼**'grafico** *adj* autobiographical

auto'botte *f* tanker

'autobus *m inv* bus

auto'carro *m* lorry

autocommiserazi'one *f* self-pity

autoconcessio'nario *m* car dealer

auto'critica *f* self-criticism

autodi'fesa *f* self-defence

auto'gol *m inv* own goal

au'tografo *adj & m* autograph

autolesio'nis|**mo** *m fig* self-destruction. ∼**tico** *adj* self-destructive

auto'linea *f* bus line

au'toma *m* robot

automatica'mente *adv* automatically

auto'matico *adj* automatic ● *m* (*bottone*) press-stud; (*fucile*) automatic

automatiz'za|re *vt* automate. ∼**zi'one** *f* automation

auto'mezzo *m* motor vehicle

auto'mobi|le f [motor] car.
~'lismo m motoring. ~'lista mf
motorist. ~'listico adj (industria)
automobile attrib

autonoma'mente adv autono-
mously

autono'mia f autonomy; (Auto)
range; (di laptop, cellulare) battery life.
au'tonomo adj autonomous

auto'psia f autopsy

auto'radio f inv car radio; (veicolo)
radio car

au'tore, -'trice mf author; (di pinti)
painter; (di furto ecc) perpetrator;
quadro d'~ genuine master

auto'revo|le adj authoritative; (che
ha influenza) influential. ~'lezza f authority

autori'carica f mobile phone tariff
where users' accounts are credited depending on usage

autori'messa f garage

autori|tà f inv authority. ~'tario adj
autocratic. ~ta'rismo m authoritar-
ianism

autori'tratto m self-portrait

autoriz'za|re vt authorize.
~zi'one f authorization

auto'scontro m inv bumper car

autoscu'ola f driving school

auto'stop m hitch-hiking; **fare l'~**
hitch-hike. ~'pista mf hitch-hiker

auto'strada f motorway

autostra'dale adj motorway attrib

autosuffici'en|te adj self-
sufficient. ~za f self-sufficiency

autotrasporta'|tore, ~'trice
mf haulier, carrier

auto'treno m articulated lorry

autove'icolo m motor vehicle

Auto've'lox® m inv speed camera

autovet'tura f motor vehicle

autun'nale adj autumn[al]

au'tunno m autumn

aval'lare vt endorse

a'vallo m endorsement

avam'braccio m forearm

avan'guardia f vanguard; fig
avant-garde; **essere all'~** be in the
forefront

a'vanti adv (in avanti) forward; (davanti) in front; (prima) before; ~! (entrate) come in!; (suvvia) come on!; (su
semaforo) cross now; **va' ~!** go
ahead!; **andare ~** (precedere) go
ahead; (orologio:) be fast; **~ e indietro** backwards and forwards ●adj
before ●prep **~ a** before; (in presenza
di) in the presence of

avanti'eri adv the day before yesterday

avanza'mento m progress; (promozione) promotion

avan'za|re vi advance; (progredire)
progress; (essere d'avanzo) be left
[over] ●vt advance; (superare) surpass; (promuovere) promote. ~rsi vr
advance; (avvicinarsi) approach. ~ta f
advance. ~to adj advanced; (nella
notte) late; **in età ~ta** elderly.
a'vanzo m remainder; (Comm) surplus; **avanzi** pl (rovine) remains; (di
cibo) left-overs

ava'ri|a f (di motore) engine failure.
~'ato adj (frutta, verdura) rotten;
(carne) tainted

ava'rizia f avarice. a'varo, -a adj
stingy ●mf miser

a'vena f oats pl

a'vere

Si può usare **have** o **have got**
per parlare di ciò che si pos-
siede. **have got** non si usa
nell'inglese americano

●vt have; (ottenere) get; (indossare)
wear; (provare) feel; **ho trent'-
anni** I'm thirty; **ha avuto il
posto** he got the job; **~ fame/
freddo** be hungry/cold; **ho mal
di denti** I've got toothache;
cos'ha a che fare con lui? what

has it got to do with him?; ~ **da fare** be busy; **che hai?** what's the matter with you?; **nei hai per molto?** will you be long?; **quanti ne abbiamo oggi?** what date is it today?; avercela con qcno have it in for sb

● v *aux* have; **non l'ho visto I** haven't seen him; **lo hai visto?** have you seen him?; **l'ho visto ieri** I saw him yesterday

● m averi *pl* wealth *sg*

avia|'tore m flyer, aviator. ~**zi'one** f aviation; (Mil) Air Force

avidità f avidness. **'avido** adj avid

avio'getto m jet

'avo, -a mf ancestor

avo'cado m *inv* avocado

a'vorio m ivory

Avv. abbr avvocato

avva'lersi vr avail oneself (**di** of)

avvalla'mento m depression

avvalo'rare vt beaɪ out (tèsi); (endorse (documento); (accrescere) enhance

avvam'pare vi flare up; (arrossire) blush

avvantaggi'ar|e vt favour. ~**si** vr ~**si di** benefit from; (approfittare) take advantage of

avve'd|ersi (accorgersi) notice; (capire) realize. ~**uto** adj shrewd

avvelena'mento m poisoning

avvele'na|re vt poison. ~**rsi** vr poison oneself. ~**to** adj poisoned

avve'nente adj attractive

avveni'mento m event

avve'nire[1] vi happen; (aver luogo) take place

avve'ni|re[2] m future. ~**'ristico** adj futuristic

avven'ta|rsi vr fling oneself. ~**to** adj (decisione) rash

av'vento m advent; (Relig) Advent

avven'tore m regular customer

avven'tu|ra f adventure; (amorosa) affair; **d'~** (film) adventure *attrib*. ~**'rarsi** vr venture. ~**ri'ero, -a** adventurer ● f adventur-ess. ~**'roso** adj adventurous

avve'ra|bile adj (previsione) that may come true. ~**rsi** vr come true

av'verbio m adverb

avver'sar|e vt oppose. ~**io, -a** adj opposing ● mf opponent

avversi|'one f aversion. ~**tà** f *inv* adversity

av'verso adj (sfavorevole) adverse; (contrario) averse

avver'tenza f (cura) care; (avvertimento) warning; (avviso) notice; (premessa) foreword; avvertenze pl (istruzioni) instructions

avverti'mento m warning

avver'tire vt warn; (informare) inform; (sentire) feel

avvez'zar|e vt accustom. ~**si** vr accustom oneself to. **av'vezzo** adj avvezzo a used to

avvia'mento m starting; (Comm) goodwill

avvi'a|re vt start. ~**rsi** vr set out. ~**to** adj under way; **bene ~to** thriving

avvi'cenda|re m (in agricoltura) rotation; (nel lavoro) replacement

avvicen'darsi vr alternate

avvicina'mento m approach

avvici'nar|e vt bring near; approach (persona). ~**si** vr approach; ~**si a** approach

avvi'lente adj demoralizing; (umiliante) humiliating

avvili'mento m despondency; (degradazione) degradation

avvi'li|re vt dishearten; (degradare) degrade. ~**rsi** vr lose heart; (degradarsi) degrade oneself. ~**to** adj disheartened; (degradato) degraded

avvilup'par|e vt envelop. ~**si** vr

wrap oneself up; (*aggrovigliarsi*) get entangled

avvinaz'zato *adj* drunk

avvin'cente *adj* (*libro ecc*) enthralling. **av'vincere** *vt* enthral

avvinghi'ar|e *vt* clutch. **~si** *vr* cling

av'vio *m* start-up; **dare l'~ a qcsa** get sth under way; **prendere l'~** get under way

avvi'sare *vt* inform; (*mettere in guardia*) warn

av'viso *m* notice; (*annuncio*) announcement; (*avvertimento*) warning; (*pubblicitario*) advertisement; **a mio ~** in my opinion. **~ di garanzia** (*Jur*) notification that one is to be the subject of a legal enquiry

avvi'stare *vt* catch sight of

avvi'tare *vt* screw in; screw down (*coperchio*)

avviz'zire *vi* wither

avvo'ca|to *m* lawyer; *fig* advocate. **~'tura** *f* legal profession

av'volger|e *vt* wrap [up]. **~si** *vr* wrap oneself up

avvol'gibile *m* roller blind

avvol'toio *m* vulture

aza'lea *f* azalea

azi'en|da *f* business. **~ agricola** farm. **~ di soggiorno** tourist bureau. **~'dale** *adj* (*politica*) corporate; (*giornale*) in-house

aziona'mento *m* operation

azio'nare *vt* operate

azio'nario *adj* share *attrib*

azi'one *f* action; *Fin* share; **d'~** (*romanzo, film*) action[-packed]. **azio'nista** *mf* shareholder

a'zoto *m* nitrogen

azzan'nare *vt* seize with its teeth; sink its teeth into (*gamba*)

azzar'd|are *vt* risk. **~arsi** *vr* dare. **~ato** *adj* risky; (*precipitoso*) rash. **az'zardo** *m* hazard; **gioco d'azzardo** game of chance

azzec'care *vt* hit; (*indovinare*) guess

azzuf'farsi *vr* come to blows

az'zur|ro *adj & m* blue; **il principe ~** Prince Charming. **~'rognolo** *adj* bluish

Bb

bab'beo *adj* foolish ● *m* idiot

'babbo *m* 🇮🇹 dad, daddy. **B~ Natale** Father Christmas

bab'buccia *f* slipper

babbu'ino *m* baboon

ba'bordo *m* (*Naut*) port side

baby'sitter *mf inv* baby-sitter; **fare la ~** babysit

ba'cato *adj* wormeaten

'bacca *f* berry

baccalà *m inv* dried salted cod

bac'cano *m* din

bac'cello *m* pod

bac'chetta *f* rod; (*magica*) wand; (*di direttore d'orchestra*) baton; (*di tamburo*) drumstick

ba'checa *f* showcase; (*in ufficio*) notice board. **~ elettronica** (*Comput*) bulletin board

bacia'mano *m* kiss on the hand; **fare il ~ a qcno** kiss sb's hand

baci'ar|e *vt* kiss. **~si** *vr* kiss [each other]

ba'cillo *m* bacillus

baci'nella *f* basin

ba'cino *m* basin; (*Anat*) pelvis; (*di porto*) dock; (*di minerali*) field

'bacio *m* kiss

'baco *m* worm. **~ da seta** silkworm

ba'cucco *adj* **un vecchio ~** senile old man

'bada *f* **tenere qcno a ~** keep sb at bay

ba'dante *mf* carer

ba'dare *vi* take care (a of); (*fare attenzione*) look out; **bada ai fatti tuoi!** mind your own business!

ba'dia *f* abbey

ba'dile *m* shovel

'badminton *m* badminton

'baffi *mpl* moustache *sg*; (*di animale*) whiskers; **mi fa un baffo** I don't give a damn; **ridere sotto i ~** laugh up one's sleeve

baf'futo *adj* moustached

ba'gagli *mpl* baggage. **~'aio** *m* (*Rail*) baggage car; (*Auto*) boot

ba'gaglio *m* baggage; **un ~** a piece of baggage. **~ a mano** hand baggage

baggia'nata *f* **non dire baggianate** don't talk nonsense

bagli'ore *m* glare; (*improvviso*) flash; (*fig: di speranza*) glimmer

ba'gnante *mf* bather

ba'gna|re *vt* wet; (*inzuppare*) soak; (*immergere*) dip; (*innaffiare*) water; (*mare:*) wash; (*fiume:*) flow through. **~rsi** *vr* get wet; (*al mare ecc*) bathe

ba'gnato *adj* wet

ba'gnino, -a *mf* life guard

'bagno *m* bath; (*stanza*) bathroom; (*gabinetto*) toilet; (*in casa*) toilet; (*al mare*) bathe; **bagni** *pl* (*stabilimento*) lido; **fare il ~** have a bath; (*nel mare ecc*) [have a] swim; **andare in ~** go to the toilet; **mettere a ~** soak. **~ turco** Turkish bath

bagnoma'ria *m* bain marie

bagnoschi'uma *m inv* bubble bath

baia *f* bay

baio'netta *f* bayonet

baita *f* mountain chalet

bala'ustra, balaus'trata *f* balustrade

balbet't|are *vt/i* stammer; (*bambino:*) babble. **~io** *m* stammering; babble

bal'buzi|e *f* stutter. **~ente** *adj* stuttering • *mf* stutterer

Bal'can|i *mpl* Balkans. **b~ico** *adj* Balkan

balco'nata *f* (*Theat*) balcony

balcon'cino *m* **reggiseno a ~** underwired bra

bal'cone *m* balcony

baldac'chino *m* canopy; **letto a ~** four-poster bed

bal'dan|za *f* boldness. **~'zoso** *adj* bold

bal'doria *f* revelry; **far ~** have a riotous time

ba'lena *f* whale

bale'nare *vi* lighten; *fig* flash; **mi è balenata un'idea** I've just had an idea

bale'niera *f* whaler

ba'leno *m* **in un ~** in a flash

ba'lera *f* dance hall

ba'lia *f* **in ~ di** at the mercy of

'balla *f* bale; ([🄵]: *frottola*) tall story

bal'labile *adj* good for dancing to

bal'la|re *vi* dance. **~ta** *f* ballad

balla'toio *m* (*nelle scale*) landing

balle'rino, -a *mf* dancer; (*classico*) ballet dancer; **ballerina** (*classica*) ballet dancer, ballerina

bal'letto *m* ballet

'ballo *m* dance; (*il ballare*) dancing; **sala da ~** ballroom; **essere in ~** (*lavoro, vita:*) be at stake; (*persona:*) be committed; **tirare qcno in ~** involve sb

ballonzo'lare *vi* skip about

ballot'taggio *m* second count (*of votes*)

balne'a|re *adj* bathing *attrib*. **sta-gione ~** swimming season. **sta-zione ~** seaside resort. **~zi'one** *f* è vietata la **~zione** no swimming

ba'lordo *adj* foolish; (*stordito*) stunned; **tempo ~** nasty weather

'balsamo *m* balsam; (*per capelli*) conditioner; (*lenimento*) remedy

'baltico adj Baltic. il [mar] B∼ the Baltic [Sea]

balu'ardo m bulwark

'balza f crag; (di abito) flounce

bal'zano adj (idea) weird

bal'zare vi bounce; (saltare) jump; ∼ in piedi leap to one's feet. **'balzo** m bounce; (salto) jump; prendere la palla al balzo seize an opportunity

bam'bagia f cotton wool

bambi'nata f childish thing to do/say

bam'bi|no, -a mf child; (appena nato) baby; avere un ∼no have a baby. ∼'none, -a mf pej big or over-grown child

bam'boccio m chubby child; (sciocco) simpleton; (fantoccio) rag doll

'bambo|la f doll. ∼'lotto m male doll

bambù m bamboo

ba'nal|e adj banal; ∼ità f inv banality; ∼iz'zare vt trivialize

ba'nan|a f banana. ∼o m banana-tree

'banca f bank. ∼ [di] dati databank

banca'rella f stall

ban'cario, -a adj banking attrib; trasferimento ∼ bank transfer ● mf bank employee

banca'rotta f bankruptcy; fare ∼ go bankrupt

banchet'tare vi banquet. ban'chetto m banquet

banchi'ere m banker

ban'china f (Naut) quay; (in stazione) platform; (di strada) path; ∼ non transitabile soft verge

ban'chisa f floe

'banco m (di scuola) desk; (di negozio) counter; (di officina) bench; (di gioco, banca) bank; (di mercato) stall; (degli imputati) dock; sotto ∼ under the counter; medicinale da ∼ over the counter medicines. ∼ informazioni information desk. ∼ di nebbia fog bank

'bancomat® m inv cashpoint, ATM; (carta) bank card

ban'cone m counter; (in bar) bar

banco'nota f banknote, bill Am; banco'note pl paper currency

'banda f band; (di delinquenti) gang. ∼ d'atterraggio landing strip. ∼ larga broad band. ∼ rumorosa rumble strip

banderu'ola f weathercock; (Naut) pennant

bandi'e|ra f flag. ∼'rina f (nel calcio) corner flag. ∼'rine pl bunting sg

ban'di|re vt banish; (pubblicare) publish; fig dispense with (formalità, complimenti). ∼to m bandit. ∼'tore m (di aste) auctioneer

'bando m proclamation; ∼ di concorso job advertisement (published in an official gazette for a job for which a competitive examination has to be taken)

bar m inv bar

'bara f coffin

ba'rac|ca f hut; (catapecchia) hovel; mandare avanti la ∼ca keep the ship afloat. ∼'cato m person living in a makeshift shelter. ∼'chino m (di gelati, giornali) kiosk; Radio CB radio. ∼'cone m (roulotte) circus caravan; (in luna park) booth. ∼'copoli f inv shanty town

bara'onda f chaos

ba'rare vi cheat

'baratro m chasm

barat'tare vt barter. **ba'ratto** m barter

ba'rattolo m jar; (di latta) tin

'barba f beard; (🔲: *noia*) bore; **farsi la ~** shave; **è una ~** (*noia*) it's boring

barbabi'etola f beetroot. **~ da zucchero** sugar-beet

bar'barico adj barbaric. **bar'barie** f barbarity. **'barbaro** adj barbarous ● m barbarian

barbecue m inv barbecue

barbi'ere m barber; (*negozio*) barber's

barbi'turico m barbiturate

bar'bone m (*vagabondo*) vagrant; (*cane*) poodle

bar'boso adj 🔲 boring

barbu'gliare vi mumble

bar'buto adj bearded

'barca f boat. **~ a motore** motorboat. **~ da pesca** fishing boat. **~ a remi** rowing boat. **~ di salvataggio** lifeboat. **~ a vela** sailing boat. **~i'olo** m boatman

barcame'narsi vr manage

barcol'lare vi stagger

bar'cone m barge; (*di ponte*) pontoon

bar'dare vt harness. **~si** vr hum dress up

ba'rel|la f stretcher. **~li'ere** m stretcher-bearer

'Barents il mare di **~** the Barents Sea

bari'centro m centre of gravity

ba'ri|le m barrel. **~'lotto** m fig tub of lard

ba'rista m barman ● f barmaid

ba'ritono m baritone

bar'lume m glimmer; **un ~ di speranza** a glimmer of hope

'barman m inv barman

'baro m cardsharper

ba'rocco adj & m baroque

ba'rometro m barometer

ba'rone m baron; **i baroni** fig the

top brass. **baro'nessa** f baroness

'barra f bar; (*lineetta*) oblique; (*Naut*) tiller. **~ spazio** (*Comput*) space bar. **~ strumenti** (*Comput*) tool bar

bar'rare vt block off (*strada*)

barri'ca|re vt barricade. **~ta** f barricade

barri'era f barrier; (*stradale*) roadblock; (*Geol*) reef. **~ razziale** colour bar

bar'ri|re vi trumpet. **~to** m trumpeting

barzel'letta f joke; **~ sporca** o **spinta** dirty joke

basa'mento m base

ba'sar|e vt base. **~si** vr **~si su** be based on; **mi baso su ciò che ho visto** I'm going on [the basis of] what I saw

'basco, -a mf & adj Basque ● m (*copricapo*) beret

'base f basis; (*fondamento*) foundation; (*Mil*) base; (*Pol*) rank and file; **a ~ di** containing; **in ~ a** on the basis of. **~ dati** database

'baseball m baseball

ba'setta f sideburn

basi'lare adj basic

ba'silica f basilica

ba'silico m basil

ba'sista m grass roots politician; (*di un crimine*) mastermind

'basket m basketball

bas'sezza f lowness; (*di statura*) shortness; (*viltà*) vileness

bas'sista mf bassist

'basso adj low; (*di statura*) short; (*acqua*) shallow; (*televisione*) quiet; (*vile*) despicable; **parlare a bassa voce** speak in a low voice; **la bassa Italia** southern Italy ● m lower part; (*Mus*) bass. **guardare in ~** look down

basso'fondo m (*pl* bassifondi) shallows pl; bassifondi pl (*quartieri* *poveri)* slums

bassorili'evo *m* bas-relief

b **bas'sotto** *m* dachshund

ba'stardo, -a *adj* bastard; *(di animale)* mongrel ●*mf* bastard; *(animale)* mongrel

ba'stare *vi* be enough; *(durare)* last; basta! that's enough!; basta che *(purché)* provided that; basta così that's enough; basta così? is that enough?; *(in negozio)* anything else?; basta andare alla posta you only have to go to the post office

Basti'an con'trario *m* contrary old so-and-so

basti'one *m* bastion

basto'nare *vt* beat

baston'cino *m* ski pole. ~ di pesce fish finger, fish stick *Am*

ba'stone *m* stick; *(da golf)* club; *(da passeggio)* walking stick

ba'tosta *f* blow

bat'tagli|a *f* battle; *(lotta)* fight. ~'are *vi* battle; *fig* fight

bat'taglio *m* *(di campana)* clapper; *(di porta)* knocker

battagli'one *m* battalion

bat'tello *m* boat; *(motonave)* steamer

bat'tente *m* *(di porta)* wing; *(di finestra)* shutter; *(battaglio)* knocker

'batter|e *vt* beat; *(percorrere)* scour; thresh *(grano)*; break *(record)* ●*vi* *(bussare, urtare)* knock; *(cuore)* beat; *(ali ecc)* flap; *Tennis* serve; ~e a macchina type; ~e le palpebre blink; ~e le mani clap [one's hands]; ~e le ore strike the hours. ~si *vr* fight

bat'teri *mpl* bacteria

batte'ria *f* battery; *(Mus)* drums *pl*

bat'terio *m* bacterium. ~'logico *adj* bacteriological

batte'rista *mf* drummer

bat'tesimo *m* baptism

battez'zare *vt* baptize

battiba'leno *m* in un ~ in a flash

batti'becco *m* squabble

batticu'ore *m* palpitation; mi venne il ~ I was scared

bat'tigia *f* water's edge

batti'mano *m* applause

batti'panni *m* *inv* carpetbeater

batti'stero *m* baptistery

batti'strada *m* *inv* outrider; *(di pneumatico)* tread; *Sport* pacesetter

battitap'peto *m* *inv* carpet sweeper

'battito *m* [heart]beat; *(alle tempie)* throbbing; *(di orologio)* ticking; *(della pioggia)* beating

bat'tuta *f* beat; *(colpo)* knock; *(spiritosaggine)* wisecrack; *(osservazione)* remark; *(Mus)* bar; *Tennis* service; *(Theat)* cue; *(dattilografia)* stroke

ba'tuffolo *m* flock

ba'ule *m* trunk

'bava *f* dribble; *(di cane ecc)* slobber; aver la ~ alla bocca foam at the mouth

bava'glino *m* bib

ba'vaglio *m* gag

'bavero *m* collar

ba'zar *m* *inv* bazaar

baz'zecola *f* trifle

bazzi'care *vt/i* haunt

be'arsi *vr* delight *(di* in*)*

beati'tudine *f* bliss. **be'ato** *adj* blissful; *(Relig)* blessed; **beato te!** lucky you!

beauty-'case *m* *inv* toilet bag

bebè *m* *inv* baby

bec'caccia *f* woodcock

bec'ca|re *vt* peck; *fig* catch. ~rsi *vr* *(litigare)* quarrel. ~ta *f* peck

beccheggi'are *vi* pitch

bec'chino *m* grave-digger

'bec|co *m* beak; *(di caffettiera ecc)* spout. ~'cuccio *m* spout

be'fana *f* Epiphany; *(donna brutta)* old witch

Befana *La Befana*, whose name is derived from *Epifania* (Epiphany), is an old woman who is said to visit children on 6 January, bringing presents and sweets. *Befana* is also the name for the Epiphany holiday and usually signals the end of the Christmas celebrations and the return to school.

'beffa *f* hoax; **farsi beffe di qcno** mock sb. **bef'fardo** *adj* derisory; (*persona*) mocking

bef'far|e *vt* mock. **~si** *vr* **~si di** make fun of

'bega *f* quarrel; **è una bella ~** it's really annoying

'beige *adj & m* beige

be'la|re *vi* bleat. **~to** *m* bleating

'belga *adj & mf* Belgian

'Belgio *m* Belgium

'bella *f* (*in carte*, *Sport*) decider

bel'lezza *f* beauty; **che ~!** how lovely!; **chiudere/finire in ~** end on a high note

'belli|co *adj* war *attrib.* **~'coso** *adj* warlike. **~ge'rante** *adj & mf* belligerent

'bello *adj* nice; (*di aspetto*) beautiful; (*uomo*) handsome; (*moralmente*) good; **cosa fai di ~ stasera?** what are you up to tonight?; **oggi fa ~** it's a nice day; **una bella cifra** a lot; **un bel piatto di pasta** a big plate of pasta; **nel bel mezzo** right in the middle; **un bel niente** absolutely nothing; **bell'e fatto** over and done with; **bell'amico!** [a] fine friend he is/you are!; **questa è bella!** that's a good one!; **scamparla bella** have a narrow escape ●*m* (*bellezza*) beauty; (*innamorato*) sweetheart; **sul più ~** at the crucial moment; **il ~ è che...** the funny thing is that...

'belva *f* wild beast

be'molle *m* (*Mus*) flat

ben ▷**BENE**

benché *conj* though, although

'benda *f* bandage; (*per occhi*) blindfold. **ben'dare** *vt* bandage; blindfold (*occhi*)

'bene *adv* well; **ben ~** thoroughly; **~!** good!; **star ~** (*di salute*) be well; (*vestito*, *stile:*) suit; (*finanziariamente*) be well off; **non sta ~** (*non è educato*) it's not nice; **sta/va ~!** all right!; **ti sta ~!** [it] serves you right!; **ti auguro ogni ~** I wish you well; **di ~ in meglio** better and better; **fare ~** (*aver ragione*) do the right thing; **fare ~ a** (*cibo:*) be good for; **una persona per ~** a good person; **per ~** (*fare*) properly; **è ben difficile** it's very difficult; **come tu ben sai** as you well know; **lo credo ~! I** can well believe it! ●*m* good; **per il tuo ~** for your own good. **beni** *mpl* (*averi*) property *sg*; **un ~ di famiglia** a family heirloom

bene'detto *adj* blessed

bene'di|re *vt* bless. **~zi'one** *f* blessing

benedu'cato *adj* well-mannered

benefat'tore, **-'trice** *m* benefactor ●*f* benefactress

benefi'care *vt* help

benefi'cenza *f* charity

benefici'ar|e *vi* **~e di** profit by. **~io**, **-a** *adj & mf* beneficiary. **bene'ficio** *m* benefit. **be'nefico** *adj* beneficial; (*di beneficenza*) charitable

bene'placito *m* approval

be'nessere *m* well-being

bene'stante *adj* well-off ●*mf* well-off person

bene'stare *m* consent

be'nevolo *adj* benevolent

ben'fatto *adj* well-made

'beni *mpl* property *sg*; *Fin* assets; **~ di consumo** consumer goods

benia'mino *m* favourite

be'nigno *adj* kindly; (*Med*) benign

beninfor'mato adj well-informed

benintenzio'nato, -a adj well-meaning ● mf well-meaning person

benin'teso adv of course

benpen'sante adj selfrighteous

benser'vito m dare il ~ a qcno fire sb

bensi conj but rather

benve'nuto adj & m welcome

ben'visto adj essere ~ go down well (da with)

benvo'lere vt farsi ~ da qcno win sb's affection; prendere qcno in ~ take a liking to sb; essere benvoluto da tutti to be well-liked by everyone

ben'zina f petrol, gas Am; far ~ get petrol. ~ **verde** unleaded petrol. benzi'naio, -a mf petrol station attendant

'bere vt drink; (assorbire) absorb; fig swallow ● m drinking; (bevande) drinks pl

berga'motto m bergamot

ber'lina f (Auto) saloon

Ber'lino m Berlin

ber'muda mpl (pantaloni) Bermuda shorts

ber'noccolo m bump; (disposizione) flair

ber'retto m beret, cap

bersagli'are vt fig bombard. ber'saglio m target

be'stemmia f swear-word; (maledizione) oath; (sproposito) blasphemy. ~'are vi swear

'besti|a f animal; (persona brutale) beast; (persona sciocca) fool; andare in ~a ⚹ blow one's top. ~'ale adj bestial; (espressione, violenza) brutal; ⚹: (freddo, fame) terrible. ~alità f inv bestiality; fig nonsense. ~'ame m livestock

'bettola f fig dive

be'tulla f birch

be'vanda f drink

bevi'tore, -'trice mf drinker

be'vut|a f drink. ~o pp di bere

bi'ada f fodder

bianche'ria f linen. ~ intima underwear

bi'anco adj white; (foglio, pagina ecc) blank ● m white; mangiare in ~ not eat rich food; in ~ e nero (film, fotografia) black and white; passare una notte in ~ have a sleepless night

bian'core m whiteness

bianco'spino m hawthorn

biasci'care vt (mangiare) eat noisily; (parlare) mumble

biasi'mare vt blame. bi'asimo m blame

'Bibbia f Bible

bibe'ron m inv [baby's] bottle

'bibita f [soft] drink

'biblico adj biblical

bibliogra'fia f bibliography

biblio'te|ca f library; (mobile) bookcase. ~'cario, -a mf librarian

bicarbo'nato m bicarbonate

bicchi'ere m glass

bicchie'rino m ⚹ tipple

bici'cletta f bicycle; andare in ~ ride a bicycle

bico'lore adj two-coloured

bidè m inv bidet

bi'dello, -a mf janitor

bido'nata f ⚹ swindle

bi'done m bin; (⚹: truffa) swindle; fare un ~ a qcno ⚹ stand sb up

bien'nale adj biennial

bi'ennio m two-year period

bi'etola f beet

bifo'cale adj bifocal

bi'folco, -a mf fig boor

bifor'c|arsi vr fork. ~azi'one f fork. ~uto adj forked

biga'mia f bigamy. 'bigamo, -a adj bigamous ● mf bigamist

bighello'nare vi loaf around. bi-

ghel'lone m loafer

bigiotte'ria f costume jewellery; (*negozio*) jeweller's

bigliet't|aio m booking clerk; (*sui treni*) ticket-collector. ~e'ria f ticket-office; (*Theat*) box-office

bigli'et|to m ticket; (*lettera breve*) note; (*cartoncino*) card; (*di banca*) bank-note. ~to da visita business card. ~'tone m (❶: *soldi*) big one

bignè m inv cream puff

bigo'dino m roller

bi'gotto m bigot

bi'kini m inv bikini

bi'lanci|a f scales pl; (*Comm*) balance; B~a (*Astr*) Libra. ~'are vt balance; fig weigh. ~o m budget; (*Comm*) balance sheet; fare il ~o balance the books; fig take stock

'bil|e f bile; fig rage

bili'ardo m billiards sg

'bilico m equilibrium; in ~ in the balance

bi'lingue adj bilingual

bili'one m billion

bilo'cale adj two-room

'bimbo, -a mf child

bimen'sile adj fortnightly

bime'strale adj bimonthly

bi'nario m track; (*piattaforma*) platform

bi'nocolo m binoculars pl

bio'chimica f biochemistry

biodegra'dabile adj biodegradable

bio'etica f bioethics

bio'fisica f biophysics

biogra'fia f biography. **bio'grafico** adj biographical. **bi'ografo, -a** mf biographer

biolo'gia f biology. **bio'logico** adj biological; (*alimento, agricoltura*) organic. **bi'ologo, -a** mf biologist

bi'ond|a f blonde. ~o adj blond ●m fair colour; (*uomo*) fair-haired man

bio'sfera f biosphere

bi'ossido m ~ di carbonio carbon dioxide

bioterro'rismo m bioterrorism

biparti'tismo m two-party system

'birba f, **bir'bante** m rascal, rogue. **bir'bone** adj wicked

biri'chino, -a adj naughty ●mf little devil

bi'rillo m skittle

'birr|a f beer; a tutta ~a fig flat out. ~a chiara lager. ~a scura brown ale. ~e'ria f beer-house; (*fabbrica*) brewery

bis m inv encore

bi'saccia f haversack

bi'sbetic|a f shrew. ~o adj bad-tempered

bisbigli'are vt/i whisper. **bi'sbiglio** m whisper

'bisca f gambling-house

'biscia f snake

bi'scotto m biscuit

bisessu'ale adj & mf bisexual

bise'stile adj anno ~ leap year

bisettima'nale adj fortnightly

bi'slacco adj peculiar

bis'nonno, -a mf great-grandfather; great-grandmother

biso'gn|are vi ~a agire subito we must act at once; ~a farlo it is necessary to do it; non ~a venire you don't have to come. ~o m need; (*povertà*) poverty; aver ~o di need. ~oso adj needy; (*povero*) poor; ~oso di in need of

bi'sonte m bison

bi'stecca f steak

bisticci'are vi quarrel. **bi'sticcio** m quarrel; (*gioco di parole*) pun

bistrat'tare vt mistreat

bi'torzolo m lump

'bitter m inv (bitter) aperitif

b

bivacco | bombardamento

bi'vacco m bivouac

'bivio m crossroads; (di strada) fork

bizan'tino adj Byzantine

'bizza f tantrum; **fare le bizze** (bambini:) play up

biz'zarro adj bizarre

biz'zeffe adv a ~ galore

blan'dire vt soothe; (allettare) flatter. **'blando** adj mild

bla'sone m coat of arms

'blatta f cockroach

blin'da|re vt armour-plate. ~**to** adj armoured

blitz m inv blitz

bloc'car|e vt block; (isolare) cut off; (Mil) blockade; (Comm) freeze. ~**si** vr (Mech) jam

blocca'sterzo m steering lock

'blocco m block; (Mil) blockade; (dei fitti) restriction; (di carta) pad; (unione) coalition; **in** ~ (Comm) in bulk. ~**stradale** road-block

bloc-'notes m inv writing pad

blog'gista mf blogger

blu adj & m blue

blue-'jeans mpl jeans

bluff m inv (carte, fig) bluff

'blusa f blouse

'boa m boa [constrictor]; (sciarpa) [feather] boa ● f (Naut) buoy

bo'ato m rumbling

bo'bina f spool; (di film) reel; (Electr) coil

'bocca f mouth; **a** ~ **aperta** fig dumbfounded; **in** ~ **al lupo!** 🔲 break a leg!; **fare la respirazione a** ~ **a qcno** give sb mouth to mouth resuscitation or the kiss of life

boc'caccia f grimace; **far boccacce** make faces

boc'caglio m nozzle

boc'cale m jug; (da birra) tankard

bocca'porto m (Naut) hatch

boc'cata f (di fumo) puff; **prendere una** ~ **d'aria** get a breath of

fresh air

boc'cetta f small bottle

bocchegg'iare vi gasp

boc'chino m cigarette holder; (Mus, di pipa) mouthpiece

'bocc|ia f (palla) bowl; ~**e** pl (gioco) bowls sg

bocci'a|re vt (agli esami) fail; (respingere) reject; (alle bocce) hit; **essere** ~**to** fail; (ripetere) repeat a year. ~**tura** f failure

bocci'olo m bud

boccon'cino m morsel

boc'cone m mouthful; (piccolo pasto) snack

boc'coni adv face downwards

'boia m executioner

boi'ata f 🔲 rubbish

boicot'tare vt boycott

bo'lero m bolero

'bolgia f (caos) bedlam

'bolide m meteor; **passare come un** ~ shoot past [like a rocket]

Bo'livi|a f Bolivia. **b~'ano, -a** agg & mf Bolivian

'bolla f bubble; (pustola) blister

bol'la|re vt stamp; fig brand. ~**to** adj fig branded; **carta** ~**ta** paper with stamp showing payment of duty

bol'lente adj boiling [hot]

bol'let|ta f bill; **essere in** ~**ta** be hard up. ~**tino** m bulletin; (Comm) list

bol'lino m coupon

bol'li|re vt/i boil. ~**to** m boiled meat. ~**tore** m boiler; (per l'acqua) kettle. ~**tura** f boiling

'bollo m stamp

bol'lore m boil; (caldo) intense heat; fig ardour

'bomba f bomb; **a prova di** ~ bomb-proof

bombarda'mento m shelling; (con aerei) bombing; fig bombardment. ~ **aereo** air raid

bombar'd|are vt shell; (con aerei) bomb; fig bombard. ~i'ere m bomber

bom'betta f bowler [hat]

'bombola f cylinder. ~ **di gas** gas cylinder

bombo'lone m doughnut

bomboni'era f wedding keep-sake

bo'naccia f (Naut) calm

bonacci'one, -a mf goodnatured person ●adj good-natured

bo'nario adj kindly

bo'nifica f land reclamation. **bonifi-'care** vt reclaim

bo'nifico m (Comm) discount; (bancario) [credit] transfer

bontà f goodness; (gentilezza) kindness

'bora f bora (cold north-east wind in the upper Adriatic)

'borchia f stud. ~'**ato** adj studded

bor'da|re vt border. ~'**tura** f border

bor'deaux adj inv maroon

bor'dello m brothel; fig bedlam; (disordine) mess

'bordo m border; (estremità) edge; **a** ~ (Aeron, Naut) on board

bor'gata f hamlet

bor'ghese adj bourgeois; (abito) civilian; **in** ~ in civilian dress; (poliziotto) in plain clothes

borghe'sia f middle classes pl

'borgo m village

bori|a f conceit. ~'**oso** adj conceited

bor'lotto m [fagiolo] ~ borlotto bean

boro'talco m talcum powder

bor'raccia f flask

bors|a f bag; (borsetta) handbag; (valori) Stock Exchange. ~ **dell'acqua calda** hot-water bottle. ~**a frigo** cool-box. ~**a della spesa** shopping bag. ~**a di studio** scholarship. ~**ai'olo** m pickpocket. ~**el'lino** m

purse. **bor'sista** mf Fin speculator; (Sch) scholarship holder

bor'se|llo m purse; (borsetto) man's handbag. ~**tta** f handbag. ~**tto** m man's handbag

bo'scaglia f woodlands pl

boscai'olo m woodman; (guardaboschi) forester

'bosco m wood. **bo'scoso** adj wooded

'Bosnia f Bosnia

'bossolo m cartridge case

bo'tanic|a f botany. ~**o** adj botanical ●m botanist

'botta f blow; (rumore) bang; **fare a botte** come to blows. ~ **e risposta** fig thrust and counter-thrust

'botte f barrel

bot'te|ga f shop; (di artigiano) workshop. ~'**gaio, -a** mf shopkeeper. ~'**ghino** m Theatr boxoffice; (del lotto) lottery-shop

bot'tiglia f bottle; **in** ~**a** bottled. ~**e'ria** f wine shop

bot'tino m loot; (Mil) booty

'botto m bang; **di** ~ all of a sudden

bot'tone m button; (Bot) bud

bo'vino adj bovine; **bovini** pl cattle

box m inv (per cavalli) loosebox; (recinto per bambini) play-pen

'boxe f boxing

'bozza f draft; (Typ) proof; (bernoccolo) bump. **boz'zetto** m sketch

'bozzolo m cocoon

brac'care vt hunt

brac'cetto m **a** ~ arm in arm

bracci'a|le m bracelet; (fascia) armband. ~'**letto** m bracelet; (di orologio) watch-strap

bracci'ante m day labourer

bracci'ata f (nel nuoto) stroke

'bracci|o m (pl f **braccia**) arm; (di fiume, di bracci) arm. ~'**olo** m (di sedia) arm[rest]; (da nuoto) armband

'bracco m hound

bracconi'ere m poacher

'brac|e f embers pl; alla ~e chargrilled. ~i'ere m brazier. ~i'ola f chop

'brado adj allo stato ~ in the wild

'brama f longing. **bra'mare** vt long for. **bramo'sia** f yearning

'branca f branch

'branchia f gill

'branco m (di cani) pack; (pej: di persone) gang

branco'lare vi grope

'branda f camp-bed

bran'dello m scrap; a brandelli in tatters

bran'dire vt brandish

'brano m piece; (di libro) passage

Bra'sil|e m Brazil. **b~i'ano, -a** agg & mf Brazilian

bra'vata f bragging

'bravo adj good; (abile) clever; (coraggioso) brave; **~!** well done!. **bra'vura** f skill

'breccia f breach; sulla ~ fig very successful, at the top

bre'saola f dried, salted beef sliced thinly and eaten cold

bre'tella f shoulder-strap; **bretelle** pl (di calzoni) braces

'breve adj brief; in ~ briefly; tra ~ shortly

brevet'tare vt patent. **bre'vetto** m patent; (attestato) licence

brevità f shortness

'brezza f breeze

'bricco m jug

bric'cone m blackguard; hum rascal

bricio|la f crumb; fig grain. **~o** m fragment

'briga f (fastidio) trouble; (lite) quarrel; **attaccar ~** pick a quarrel; **prendersi la ~ di fare qcsa** go to the trouble of doing sth

brigadi'ere m (dei carabinieri) sergeant

bri'gante m bandit; hum rogue

bri'gare vi intrigue

bri'gata f brigade; (gruppo) group

briga'tista mf (Pol) member of the Red Brigades

'briglia f rein; a ~ sciolta at breakneck speed

bril'lante adj brilliant; (scintillante) sparkling ●m diamond

bril'lare vi shine; (metallo:) glitter; (scintillare) sparkle

'brillo adj tipsy

'brina f hoar-frost

brin'dare vi toast; ~ a qcno drink a toast to sb

'brindisi m inv toast

bri'tannico adj British

'brivido m shiver; (di paura ecc) shudder; (di emozione) thrill

brizzo'lato adj greying

'brocca f jug

broc'cato m brocade

'broccoli mpl broccoli sg

'brodo m broth; (per cucinare) stock. **~ ristretto** consommé

'broglio m ~ elettorale gerrymandering

bron'chite f bronchitis

'broncio m sulk; **fare il ~** sulk

bronto'l|are vi grumble; (tuono ecc:) rumble. **~io** m grumbling; (di tuono) rumbling. **~one, -a** mf grumbler

'bronzo m bronze

bros'sura f edizione in ~ paperback

bru'care vt (pecora:) graze

bruciacchi'are vt scorch

brucia'pelo adv a ~ point-blank

bruci'a|re vt burn; (scottare) scald; (incendiare) set fire to ●vi burn; (scottare) scald. **~rsi** vr burn oneself. **~to** adj burnt; fig burnt-out. **~'tore** m burner. **~'tura** f burn. **bruci'ore** m burning sensation

'**bruco** m grub

'**brufolo** m spot

brughi'era f heath

bruli'c|are vi swarm

'**brullo** adj bare

'**bruma** f mist

'**bruno** adj brown; (occhi, capelli) dark

brusca'mente adv (di colpo) suddenly

bru'schetta f toasted bread rubbed with garlic and sprinkled with olive oil

'**brusco** adj sharp; (persona) brusque; (improvviso) sudden

bru'sio m buzzing

bru'tal|e adj brutal. ~ità f inv brutality. ~iz'zare vt brutalize. '**bruto** adj & m brute

brut'tezza f ugliness

'**brut|to** adj ugly; (tempo, tipo, situazione, affare) nasty; (cattivo) bad; ~ta copia rough copy; ~to tiro dirty trick. ~'tura f ugly thing

'**buca** f hole; (avvallamento) hollow. ~ delle lettere (a casa) letter-box

buca'neve m inv snowdrop

bu'car|e vt make a hole in; (pungere) prick; punch (biglietti) ● vi have a puncture. ~si vr prick oneself; (con droga) shoot up

bu'cato m washing

'**buccia** f peel, skin

bucherel'lare vt riddle

'**buco** m hole

bu'dello m (pl f budella) bowel

bu'dino m pudding

'**bue** m (pl buoi) ox; carne di ~ beef

'**bufalo** m buffalo

bu'fera f storm; (di neve) blizzard

buf'fetto m cuff

'**buffo** adj funny; (Theat) comic ● m funny thing. ~'nata f (scherzo) joke. buf'fone m buffoon; fare il buffone play the fool

---

bu'gi|a f lie; ~a pietosa white lie. ~'ardo, -a adj lying ● mf liar

bugi'gattolo m cubby-hole

'**buio** adj dark ● m darkness; al ~ in the dark; ~ pesto pitch dark

'**bulbo** m bulb; (dell'occhio) eyeball

Bulga'ria f Bulgaria. '**bulgaro, -a** adj & mf Bulgarian

'**bullo** m bully

bul'lone m bolt

'**bunker** m inv bunker

buona'fede f good faith

buona'notte int good night

buona'sera int good evening

buon'giorno int good morning; (di pomeriggio) good afternoon

buon'grado: di ~ adv willingly

buongu'staio, -a mf gourmet. **buon'gusto** m good taste

bu'ono adj good; (momento) right; dar ~ (convalidare) accept; alla buona easy-going; (cena) informal; buona notte/sera good night/evening; buon compleanno/Natale! happy birthday/merry Christmas!; buon senso common sense; di buon'ora early; una buona volta once and for all; buona parte di the best part of; tre ore buone three good hours ● m good; (in film) goody; (tagliando) voucher; (titolo) bond; con le buone gently; ~ sconto money-off coupon ● mf buono, -a a nulla dead loss

buontem'pone, -a mf happy-go-lucky person

buonu'more m good temper

buonu'scita f retirement bonus; (di dirigente) golden handshake

burat'tino m puppet

'**burbero** adj surly; (nei modi) rough

buro'cra|te m bureaucrat. buro-'cratico adj bureaucratic. ~'zia f bureaucracy

bur'ra|sca f storm. ~'scoso adj stormy

'**burro** m butter

bur'rone m ravine

bu'scar|e vt, **∼si** vr catch

bus'sare vt knock

'bussola f compass; **perdere la ∼** lose one's bearings

'busta f envelope; (astuccio) case. **∼ paga** pay packet. **∼'rella** f bribe. **bu'stina** f (di tè) tea bag; (per medicine) sachet

'busto m bust; (indumento) girdle

but'tar|e vt throw; **∼e giù** (demolire) knock down; (inghiottire) gulp down; scribble down (scritto); ⊤ put on (pasta); (scoraggiare) dishearten; **∼e via** throw away. **∼si** vr throw oneself; (saltare) jump

butte'rato adj pock-marked

Cc

caba'ret m inv cabaret

ca'bina f (Aeron, Naut) cabin; (balneare) beach hut. **∼ elettorale** polling booth. **∼ di pilotaggio** cockpit. **∼ telefonica** telephone box. **cabi'nato** m cabin cruiser

ca'cao m cocoa

'cacca f ⊤ pooh

'caccia f hunt; (con fucile) shooting; (inseguimento) chase; (selvaggina) game ● m inv (Aeron) fighter; (Naut) destroyer

cacciabombardi'ere m fighter-bomber

cacciagi'one f game

cacci'a|re vt hunt; (mandar via) chase away; (scacciare) drive out; (ficcare) shove ● vi go hunting. **∼rsi** vr (nascondersi) hide; (andare a finire) get to; **∼rsi nei guai** get into trouble; **alla ∼'tora** adj (Culin) chasseur. **∼'tore, ∼'trice** mf hunter. **∼tore di frodo** poacher

caccia'vite m inv screwdriver

ca'chet m inv (Med) capsule; (colorante) colour rinse; (stile) cachet

'cachi m inv (albero, frutta) persimmon

'cacio m (formaggio) cheese

'cactus m inv cactus

ca'da|vere m corpse. **∼'verico** adj fig deathly pale

ca'dente adj falling; (casa) crumbling

ca'denza f cadence; (ritmo) rhythm; (Mus) cadenza

ca'dere vi fall; (capelli ecc) fall out; (capitombolare) tumble; (vestito ecc:) hang; **far ∼** (di mano) drop; **∼ dal sonno** feel very sleepy; **lasciar ∼** drop; **∼ dalle nuvole** fig be taken aback

ca'detto m cadet

ca'duta f fall; (di capelli) loss; fig downfall

caffè m inv coffee; (locale) café. **∼ corretto** espresso coffee with a dash of liqueur. **∼ lungo** weak black coffee. **∼ macchiato** coffee with a dash of milk. **∼ ristretto** strong espresso coffee. **∼ solubile** instant coffee. **caffe'ina** f caffeine, **caffe l'latte** m inv white coffee.

> **Caffè** If you ask for a caffè *i* in an Italian bar you will be served an espresso, a small amount of very strong coffee in a small cup. A macchiato is the same, but with the addition of a little frothy milk. Cappuccino is drunk in the morning or afternoon, never at the end of a meal. A corretto has a dash of spirits in it.

caffetti'era f coffee-pot

cafo'naggine f boorishness

cafo'nata f boorishness

ca'fone, -a mf boor

ca'gare vi ⓘ crap

cagio'nare vt cause

cagio'nevole adj delicate

cagli'ar|e vi, **∼si** vr curdle

'cagna f bitch

ca'gnara f ⓘ din

ca'gnesco adj guardare qcno in ∼ scowl at sb

'cala f creek

cala'brone m hornet

cala'maio m inkpot

cala'mari mpl squid sg

cala'mita f magnet

calamità f inv calamity

ca'lar|e vi come down; (vento:) drop; (diminuire) fall; (tramontare) set ●vt (abbassare) lower; (nei lavori a maglia) decrease ●m (di luna) waning. **∼si** vr lower oneself

'calca f throng

cal'cagno m heel

cal'care[1] m limestone

cal'care[2] vt tread; (premere) press [down]; ∼ **la mano** fig exaggerate; ∼ **le orme di qcno** fig follow in sb's footsteps

'calce[1] f lime

'calce[2] m in ∼ at the foot of the page

calce'struzzo m concrete

cal'cetto m Sport five-a-side [football]

calci'a|re vt kick. **∼tore** m footballer

cal'cina f mortar

calci'naccio m (pezzo di intonaco) flake of plaster

'calcio[1] m kick; (Sport) football; (di arma da fuoco) butt; **dare un ∼ a** kick. ∼ **d'angolo** corner [kick]

'calcio[2] m (chimica) calcium

'calco m tracing; (arte) cast

calco'la|re vt calculate; (considerare) consider. **∼tore** adj calculating ●m calculator; (macchina elettronica)

computer

'calcolo m calculation; (Med) stone

cal'daia f boiler

caldar'rosta f roast chestnut

caldeggi'are vt support

'caldo adj warm; (molto caldo) hot ●m heat; **avere ∼** be warm/hot; **fa ∼** it is warm/hot

calen'dario m calendar

ca'libro m calibre; (strumento) callipers pl; **di grosso ∼** (persona) top attrib

'calice m goblet; (Relig) chalice

ca'ligine m fog; (industriale) smog

'call centre m inv call centre

calligra'fia f handwriting; (cinese) calligraphy

cal'lista mf chiropodist. **'callo** m corn; **fare il callo a** become hardened to. **cal'loso** adj callous

'calma f calm. **cal'mante** adj calming ●m sedative. **cal'mare** vt calm [down]; (lenire) soothe. **cal'marsi** vr calm down; (vento:) drop; (dolore:) die down. **'calmo** adj calm

'calo m (Comm) fall; (di volume) shrinkage; (di peso) loss

ca'lore m heat; (moderato) warmth; **in ∼** (animale) on heat. **calo'roso** adj warm

calo'ria f calorie

ca'lorico adj calorific

calo'rifero m radiator

calorosa'mente adv (cordialmente) warmly

calpe'stare vt trample [down]; fig trample on (diritti, sentimenti); **vietato ∼ l'erba** keep off the grass

calpe'stio m (passi) footsteps

ca'lunni|a f slander. **∼'are** vt slander. **∼'oso** adj slanderous

ca'lura f heat

cal'vario m Calvary; fig trial

cal'vizie f baldness. **'calvo** adj bald

'calz|a f (da donna) stocking; (da uomo)

sock. ~a'maglia f tights pl; (per danza) leotard

cal'zante adj fig fitting

cal'za|re vt (indossare) wear; (mettersi) put on ● vi fit

calza'scarpe m inv shoehorn

calza'tura f footwear

calzaturi'ficio m shoe factory

cal'zetta f è una mezza ~ fig he's no use

calzet'tone m knee-length woollen sock. cal'zino m sock

calzo'l|aio m shoemaker. ~e'ria f (negozio) shoe shop

calzon'cini mpl shorts. ~ da bagno swimming trunks

cal'zone m folded pizza with tomato and mozzarella or ricotta

cal'zoni mpl trousers, pants Am

camale'onte m chameleon

cambi'ale f bill of exchange

cambia'mento m change. ~ climatico climate change

cambi'ar|e vt/i change; move (casa); (fare cambio di) exchange. ~si vr change. 'cambio m change; (Comm, scambio) exchange; (Mech) gear; dare il ~ a qcno relieve sb; in ~ di in exchange for

'camera f room; (mobili) [bedroom] suite; (Phot) camera; C~ (Comm, Pol) Chamber. ~ ardente funeral parlour. ~ d'aria inner tube. C~ di Commercio Chamber of Commerce. C~ dei Deputati (Pol) ≈House of Commons. ~ doppia double room. ~ da letto bedroom. ~ matrimoniale double room. ~ oscura darkroom. ~ singola single room

came'rata¹ f (dormitorio) dormitory; (Mil) barrack room

came'ra|ta² f (amico) mate; (Pol) comrade. ~'tismo m comradeship

cameri'era f maid; (di ristorante) waitress; (in albergo) chamber-maid; (di bordo) stewardess

cameri'ere m manservant; (di ristorante) waiter; (di bordo) steward

came'rino m dressing-room

'camice m overall. cami'cetta f blouse. ca'micia f shirt; uovo in ~ poached egg. camicia da notte nightdress

cami'netto m fireplace

ca'mino m chimney; (focolare) fireplace

'camion m inv truck, lorry Br

camion'cino m van

camio'netta f jeep

camio'nista mf truck driver

cam'mello m camel; (tessuto) camel-hair ● adj inv (colore) camel

cam'meo m cameo

cammi'na|re vi walk; (auto, orologio:) go. ~ta f walk; fare una ~ta go for a walk. cam'mino m way; essere in ~ be on the way; mettersi in ~ set out

camo'milla f camomile; (bevanda) camomile tea

ca'morra f local mafia

ca'moscio m chamois; (pelle) suede

cam'pagna f country; (paesaggio) countryside; (Comm, Mil) campaign; in ~ in the country. ~ elettorale election campaign. ~ pubblicitaria marketing campaign. campa'gnolo, -a adj rustic ● m countryman ● f countrywoman

cam'pale adj fig attrib; giornata ~ fig strenuous day

cam'pa|na f bell; (di vetro) belljar. ~'nella f (di tenda) curtain ring. ~'nello m door-bell; (cicalino) buzzer

campa'nile m belfry

campani'lismo m parochialism

campani'lista mf person with a parochial outlook

cam'panula f (Bot) campanula

cam'pare vi live; (a stento) get by

cam'pato adj ~ in aria unfounded

campeggi'a|re vi camp; (spiccare)

stand out. ~'tore, ~'trice *mf* camper. **cam'peggio** *m* camping; (*terreno*) campsite

cam'pestre *adj* rural

'camping *m inv* campsite

campio'nari|o *m* [set of] samples ●*adj* samples; **fiera** ~**a** trade fair

campio'nato *m* championship

campiona'tura *f* (*di merce*) range of samples

campi'on|e *m* champion; (*Comm*) sample; (*esemplare*) specimen. ~**essa** *f* ladies' champion

'campo *m* field; (*accampamento*) camp. ~ **da calcio** football pitch. ~ **di concentramento** concentration camp. ~ **da golf** golf course. ~ **da tennis** tennis court. ~ **profughi** refugee camp

campo'santo *m* cemetery

camuf'far|e *vt* disguise. ~**si** *vr* disguise oneself

'Cana|da *m* Canada. ~**dese** *agg* & *mf* Canadian

ca'naglia *f* scoundrel, (*plebaglia*) rabble

ca'nal|e *m* channel; (*artificiale*) canal. ~**izzare** *vt* channel (*acque*). ~**izzazi'one** *f* channelling; (*rete*) pipes *pl*

'canapa *f* hemp

cana'rino *m* canary

cancel'la|re *vt* cross out; (*con la gomma*) rub out; (*annullare*) cancel; (*Comput*) delete. ~**tura** *f* erasure. ~**zi'one** *f* cancellation; (*Comput*) deletion

cancelle'ria *f* chancellery; (*articoli per scrivere*) stationery

cancelli'ere *m* chancellor; (*di tribunale*) clerk

can'cello *m* gate

cance'ro|geno *m* carcinogen ●*adj* carcinogenic. ~**'so** *adj* cancerous

can'crena *f* gangrene

'cancro *m* cancer. **C~** (*Astr*) Cancer

candeg'gi|na *f* bleach. ~**'are** *vt*

bleach. **can'deggio** *m* bleaching

can'de|la *f* candle; (*Auto*) spark plug. ~**li'ere** *m* candlestick

candi'da|rsi *vr* stand as a candidate. ~**to, -a** *mf* candidate. ~**'tura** *f* (*Pol*) candidacy; (*per lavoro*) application

'candido *adj* snow-white; (*sincero*) candid; (*puro*) pure

can'dito *adj* candied

can'dore *m* whiteness; *fig* innocence

'cane *m* dog; (*di arma da fuoco*) cock; **un tempo da cani** foul weather. ~ **da caccia** hunting dog

ca'nestro *m* basket

cangi'ante *adj* iridescent; **seta** ~ shot silk

can'guro *m* kangaroo

ca'nile *m* kennel; (*di allevamento*) kennels *pl*. ~ **municipale** dog pound

ca'nino *adj* & *m* canine

'canna *f* reed; (*da zucchero*) cane; (*di fucile*) barrel; (*bastone*) stick; (*di bicicletta*) crossbar; (*asta*) rod; (🅸: *hascish*) joint; **povero in** ~ destitute. ~ **da pesca** fishingrod

can'nella *f* cinnamon

can'neto *m* bed of reeds

canni'ba|le *m* cannibal. ~**'lismo** *m* cannibalism

cannocchi'ale *m* telescope

canno'nata *f* cannon shot; **è una** ~ *fig* it's brilliant

cannon'cino *m* (*dolce*) cream horn

can'none *m* cannon; *fig* ace

can'nuccia *f* [drinking] straw; (*di pipa*) stem

ca'noa *f* canoe

ca'none *m* canon; (*affitto*) rent; **equo** ~ fair rents act

ca'noni|co *m* canon. ~**z'zare** *vt* canonize. ~**zzazi'one** *f* canonization

ca'noro *adj* melodious

ca'notta *f* (*estiva*) vest top

canot'taggio m canoeing; (voga) rowing

canotti'era f singlet

canotti'ere m oarsman

ca'notto m (rubber) dinghy

cano'vaccio m (trama) plot; (straccio) duster

can'tante mf singer

can't|are vt/i sing. **~au'tore, ~au'trice** mf singer-songwriter. **~ic'chi'are** vt sing softly; (a bocca chiusa) hum

canti'ere m yard; (Naut) shipyard; (di edificio) construction site. **~ navale** naval dockyard

canti'lena f singsong; (ninna-nanna) lullaby

can'tina f cellar; (osteria) wine shop

'canto¹ m singing; (canzone) song; (Relig) chant; (poesia) poem

canto² m (angolo) corner; (lato) side; **dal ~ mio** for my part; **d'altro ~** on the other hand

canto'nata f **prendere una ~** fig be sadly mistaken

can'tone m canton; (angolo) corner

can'tuccio m nook

canzo'na|re vt tease. **~'torio** adj teasing. **~'tura** f teasing

can'zo|ne f song. **~'netta** f 🅵 pop song. **~ni'ere** m songbook

---

Canzone Italians are very proud of their tradition of popular song and it is celebrated at the Festival di Sanremo (Festival della Canzone Italiana). The festival has been held since 1951 and is watched by millions on Italian TV every year. The festival is a competition for the best new song and the winner is guaranteed chart success. *i*

'caos m chaos. **ca'otico** adj chaotic

C.A.P. m abbr (Codice di Avviamento Postale) post code, zip code Am

ca'pac|e adj able; (esperto) skilled; (stadio, contenitore) big; **~e di** (disposto a) capable of. **~ità** f inv ability; (attitudine) skill; (capienza) capacity

capaci'tarsi vr **~ di** (rendersi conto) understand; (accorgersi) realize

ca'panna f hut

capan'nello m **fare ~ intorno a** qcno/qcsa gather round sb/sth

capan'none m shed; (Aeron) hangar

ca'parbio adj obstinate

ca'parra f deposit

capa'tina f short visit; **fare una ~ in città/da qcno** pop into town/in on sb

ca'pel|lo m hair; **~li** pl (capigliatura) hair sg. **~'lone** m hippie. **~'luto** adj hairy

capez'zale m bolster; fig bedside

ca'pezzolo m nipple

capi'en|te adj capacious. **~za** f capacity

capiglia'tura f hair

ca'pire vt understand; **~ male** misunderstand; **si capisce!** naturally!; **sì, ho capito** yes, I see

capi'tale adj (Jur) capital; (principale) main ● f (città) capital ● m (Comm) capital. **~'lismo** m capitalism. **~'lista** mf capitalist. **~'listico** adj capitalist

capitane'ria f **~ di porto** port authorities pl

capi'tano m captain

capi'tare vi (giungere per caso) come; (accadere) happen

capi'tello m (Archit) capital

capito'la|re vi capitulate. **~zi'one** f capitulation

ca'pitolo m chapter

capi'tombolo m headlong fall; **fare un ~** tumble down

'capo m head; (chi comanda) boss 🅵; (di vestiario) item; (Geog) cape; (in tribù) chief; (parte estrema) top; **a ~ new** paragraph; **da ~** over again; **in ~ a**

un **mese** within a month; **gira-mento di** ~ dizziness; **mal di** ~ headache; ~ **d'abbigliamento** item of clothing. ~ **d'accusa** (*Jur*) charge. ~ **di bestiame** head of cattle

capo'banda *m* (*Mus*) bandmaster; (*di delinquenti*) ringleader

ca'poccia *m* (⊞: *testa*) nut

capocci'one, -a *mf* ⊞ brainbox

capo'danno *m* New Year's Day

capofa'miglia *m* head of the family

capo'fitto *m* **a** ~ headlong

capo'giro *m* giddiness

capola'voro *m* masterpiece

capo'linea *m* terminus

capo'lino *m* fare ~ peep in

capolu'ogo *m* main town

capo'rale *m* lance-corporal

capo'squadra *mf Sport* team captain

capo'stipite *mf* (*di famiglia*) pro-genitor

capo'tavola *mf* head of the table

capo'treno *m* guard

capouf'ficio *mf* head clerk

capo'verso *m* first line

capo'vol|gere *vt* overturn; *fig* re-verse. ~**gersi** *vr* overturn; (*barca:*) capsize; *fig* be reversed. ~**to** *pp* di ca-povolgere ● *adj* upside-down

'**cappa** *f* cloak; (*di camino*) cowl; (*di cucina*) hood

cap'pel|la *f* chapel. ~'**lano** *m* chaplain

cap'pello *m* hat. ~ **a cilindro** top hat

'**cappero** *m* caper

'**cappio** *m* noose

cap'pone *m* capon

cap'potto *m* [over]coat

cappuc'cino *m* (*frate*) Capuchin; (*bevanda*) white coffee

cap'puccio *m* hood; (*di penna stilo-grafica*) cap

'**capra** *f* goat. **ca'pretto** *m* kid

ca'pricci|o *m* whim; (*bizzarria*) freak; **fare i capricci** have tantrums. ~**oso** *adj* capricious; (*bambino*) naughty

Capri'corno *m* (*Astr*) Capricorn

capri'ola *f* somersault

capri'olo *m* roe-deer

'**capro** *m* [billy-]goat. ~ **espiatorio** scapegoat.

ca'prone *m* [billy] goat

'**capsula** *f* capsule; (*di proiettile*) cap; (*di dente*) crown

cap'tare *vt* (*Radio*, *TV*) pick up; catch (*attenzione*)

carabini'ere *m* carabiniere; **carabi-ni'eri** *pl Italian police*

Carabinieri The *Carabinieri* are a national Italian police force which is part of the army. They deal with issues of pub-lic order and serious crimes, but there is a certain amount of over-lap with the duties of the *Polizia di Stato*, which is not part of the army and is controlled by the Interior Ministry. *Carabinieri* wear a distinct-ive dark uniform with a red stripe.

ca'raffa *f* carafe

Ca'raibi *mpl* (*zona*) Caribbean *sg*; (*isole*) Caribbean Islands; **il mar dei** ~ the Caribbean [Sea]

cara'mella *f* sweet

cara'mello *m* caramel

ca'rato *m* carat

ca'ratte|re *m* character; (*caratteri-stica*) characteristic; (*Typ*) type; **di buon** ~**re** good-natured. ~'**ristico, -a** *adj* characteristic; (*pittoresco*) quaint ● *f* characteristic. ~**riz'zare** *vt* char-acterize

carbon'cino *m* charcoal

car'bone *m* coal

car'bonio *m* carbon

carbu'rante *m* fuel

carbura'tore m carburettor

car'cassa f carcass; fig old wreck

carce'ra|rio adj prison attrib. ~to, -a mf prisoner. ~zi'one f imprisonment. ~zione preventiva preventive detention

'carcer|e m prison; (punizione) imprisonment. ~i'ere, -a mf gaoler

carci'ofo m artichoke

cardi'nale adj & m cardinal

'cardine m hinge

cardio|chi'rurgo m heart surgeon. ~lo'gia f cardiology. cardi'ologo m heart specialist. ~'tonico m heart stimulant

'cardo m thistle

ca'rena f (Naut) bottom

ca'ren|te adj ~te di lacking in. ~za f lack; (scarsità) scarcity

care'stia f famine; (mancanza) dearth

ca'rezza f caress

cari'a|rsi vi decay. ~to adj decayed

'carica f office; (Electr, Mil) charge; fig drive. cari'care vt load; (Electr, Mil) charge; wind up (orologio). ~'tore m (per proiettile) magazine

carica'tu|ra f caricature. ~'rale adj grotesque. ~'rista mf caricaturist

'carico adj loaded (di with); (colore) strong; (orologio) wound [up]; (batteria) charged ● m load; (di nave) cargo; (il caricare) loading; a ~ di (Comm) to be charged to; (persona) dependent on

'carie f [tooth] decay

ca'rino adj pretty; (piacevole) agreeable

ca'risma m charisma

carit|à f charity; per ~à! (come rifiuto) God forbid!. ~a'tevole adj charitable

carnagi'one f complexion

car'naio m fig shambles

car'nale adj carnal; cugino ~ first cousin

'carne f flesh; (alimento) meat; ~ di manzo/maiale/vitello beef/pork/veal

car'nefi|ce m executioner. ~'cina f slaughter

carne'va|le m carnival. ~'lesco adj carnival

car'noso adj fleshy

'caro, -a adj dear; cari saluti kind regards ● mf ① darling, dear; i miei cari my nearest and dearest

ca'rogna f carcass; fig bastard

caro'sello m merry-go-round

ca'rota f carrot

caro'vana f caravan; (di veicoli) convoy

caro'vita m high cost of living

'carpa f carp

carpenti'ere m carpenter

car'pire vt seize; (con difficoltà) extort

car'poni adv on all fours

car'rabile adj suitable for vehicles; passo ~ ▷CARRAIO

car'raio adj passo ~ entrance to drive-way, garage etc where parking is forbidden

carreggi'ata f roadway; doppia ~ dual carriageway, divided highway Am

carrel'lata f (TV) pan

car'rello m trolley; (di macchina da scrivere) carriage; (Aeron) undercarriage; (Cinema, TV) dolly. ~ d'atterraggio (Aeron) landing gear

car'retto m cart

carri'e|ra f career; di gran ~ra at full speed; fare ~ra get on. ~'rismo m careerism

carri'ola f wheelbarrow

'carro m cart. ~ armato tank. ~ attrezzi breakdown vehicle. ~ funebre hearse. ~ merci truck

car'rozza f carriage; (Rail) car. ~ cuccette sleeping car. ~ ristorante restaurant car

carroz'zella f (per bambini) pram;

(*per disabili*) wheelchair

carrozze'ria *f* bodywork; (*officina*) bodyshop

carroz'zina *f* pram; (*pieghevole*) push-chair, stroller *Am*

carroz'zone *m* (*di circo*) caravan

'**carta** *f* paper; (*da gioco*) card; (*statuto*) charter; (*Geog*) map. ~ **d'argento** ≈ senior citizens' railcard. ~ **assorbente** blotting-paper. ~ **di credito** credit card. ~ **geografica** map. ~ **d'identità** identity card. ~ **igienica** toilet-paper. ~ **di imbarco** boarding card *or* pass. ~ **da lettere** writing-paper. ~ **da parati** wallpaper. ~ **SIM** SIM card. ~ **stagnola** silver paper; (*Culin*) aluminium foil. ~ **straccia** waste paper. ~ **stradale** road map. ~ **velina** tissue-paper. ~ **verde** (*Auto*) green card. ~ **vetrata** sandpaper

cartacar'bone *f* carbon paper

car'taccia *f* waste paper

carta'modello *m* pattern

cartamo'neta *f* paper money

carta'pesta *f* papier mâché

carta'straccia *f* waste paper

cartave'trare *vt* sand [down]

car'tel|la *f* briefcase; (*di cartone*) folder; (*di scolaro*) satchel. ~**la clinica** medical record. ~'**lina** *f* folder

cartel'lino *m* (*etichetta*) label; (*dei prezzi*) price-tag; (*di presenza*) time-card; **timbrare il ~** clock in; (*all'uscita*) clock out

car'tel|lo *m* sign; (*pubblicitario*) poster; (*stradale*) road sign; (*di protesta*) placard; (*Comm*) cartel. ~'**lone** *m* poster; (*Theat*) bill

car'tiera *f* paper-mill

car'tina *f* map

car'toccio *m* paper bag; **al ~** (*Culin*) baked in foil

carto'|laio, -a *mf* stationer. ~**le'ria** *f* stationer's. ~**libre'ria** *f* stationer's and book shop

carto'lina *f* postcard. ~ **postale** postcard

carto'mante *mf* fortune-teller

carton'cino *m* (*materiale*) card

car'tone *m* cardboard; (*arte*) cartoon. ~ **animato** [animated] cartoon

car'tuccia *f* cartridge

'**casa** *f* house; (*abitazione propria*) home; (*ditta*) firm; **amico di ~** family friend; **andare a ~** go home; **essere di ~** be like one of the family; **fatto in ~** home-made; **padrone di ~** (*di pensione ecc*) landlord; (*proprietario*) house owner. ~ **di cura** nursing home. ~ **popolare** council house. ~ **dello studente** hall of residence

ca'sacca *f* military coat; (*giacca*) jacket

ca'saccio *adv* **a ~** at random

casa'ling|a *f* housewife. ~**o** *adj* domestic; (*fatto in casa*) home-made; (*amante della casa*) home-loving; (*semplice*) homely

ca'scante *adj* falling; (*floscio*) flabby

ca'sca|re *vi* fall [down]. ~**ta** *f* (*di acqua*) waterfall

ca'schetto *m* (*capelli a*) ~ bob

ca'scina *f* farm building

'**casco** *m* crash-helmet; (*asciuga-capelli*) [hair-]drier; ~ **di banane** bunch of bananas

caseg'giato *m* apartment block

casei'ficio *m* dairy

ca'sella *f* pigeon-hole. ~ **postale** post office box; (*Comput*) mailbox

casel'lante *mf* (*per treni*) signalman

casel'lario *m* ~ **giudiziario** record of convictions; **avere il ~ giudiziario vergine** have no criminal record

ca'sello [autostra'dale] *m* [motorway] toll booth

case'reccio *adj* home-made

ca'serma *f* barracks *pl*; (*dei carabinieri*) [police] station

casi'nista *mf* 🇮🇹 muddler. **ca'sino** *m* 🇮🇹 (*bordello*) brothel; (*fig: confusione*) racket; (*disordine*) mess; **un casino di** loads of

casinò *m inv* casino

ca'sistica *f* (*classificazione*) case records *pl*

'caso *m* chance; (*Gram, Med*), (*fatto, circostanza*) case; **a ~** at random; **~ mai** if need be; **far ~ a** pay attention to; **non far ~ a** take no account of; **per ~** by chance. **~** [**giudiziario**] [**legal**] case

caso'lare *m* farmhouse

'caspita *int* good gracious!

'cassa *f* till; cash; (*luogo di pagamento*) cash desk; (*mobile*) chest; (*istituto bancario*) bank. **~ automatica prelievi** cash dispenser, ATM. **~ da morto** coffin. **~ toracica** ribcage

cassa'forte *f* safe

cassa'panca *f* linen chest

casseru'ola *f* saucepan

cas'setta *f* case; (*per registratore*) cassette. **~ delle lettere** letterbox. **~ di sicurezza** strong-box

cas'set|to *m* drawer. **~'tone** *m* chest of drawers

cassi'ere, -a *mf* cashier; (*di supermercato*) checkout assistant; (*di banca*) teller

'casta *f* caste

ca'stagn|a *f* chestnut. **casta'gneto** *m* chestnut grove. **~o** *m* chestnut[-tree]

ca'stano *adj* chestnut

ca'stello *m* castle; (*impalcatura*) scaffold

casti'gare *vt* punish

casti'gato *adj* (*casto*) chaste

ca'stigo *m* punishment

castità *f* chastity. **'casto** *adj* chaste

ca'storo *m* beaver

ca'strare *vt* castrate

casu'al|e *adj* chance *attrib*. **~'mente** *adv* by chance

ca'supola *f* little house

cata'clisma *m fig* upheaval

cata'comba *f* catacomb

cata'fascio *m* **andare a ~** go to rack and ruin

cata'litico *adj* **marmitta catalitica** (*Auto*) catalytic converter

cataliz'za|re *vt* heighten. **~'tore** *m* (*Auto*) catalytic converter

catalo'gare *vt* catalogue. **ca'talogo** *m* catalogue

catama'rano *m* (*da diporto*) catamaran

cata'pecchia *f* hovel; ⊞ dump

catapul'tar|e *vt* eject. **~si** *vr* (*precipitarsi*) dive

catarifran'gente *m* reflector

ca'tarro *m* catarrh

ca'tasta *f* pile

ca'tasto *m* land register

ca'tastrofe *f* catastrophe. **cata'strofico** *adj* catastrophic

cate'chismo *m* catechism

cate|go'ria *f* category. **~'gorico** *adj* categorical

ca'tena *f* chain. **~ montuosa** mountain range. **catene** *pl* **da neve** tyre-chains. **cate'naccio** *m* bolt

cate'|nella *f* (*collana*) chain. **~'nina** *f* chain

cate'ratta *f* cataract

ca'terva *f* **una ~ di** heaps of

cati'nell|a *f* basin; **piovere a ~e** bucket down

ca'tino *m* basin

ca'trame *m* tar

'cattedra *f* (*tavolo di insegnante*) desk; (*di università*) chair

catte'drale *f* cathedral

catti'veria *f* wickedness; (*azione*) wicked action

cattività *f* captivity

cat'tivo *adj* bad; (*bambino*)

naughty

cattoli'cesimo m Catholicism

cat'tolico, -a adj & mf [Roman] Catholic

cat'tura f capture. **∼'rare** vt capture

caucciù m rubber

'causa f cause; (Jur) lawsuit; far ∼ a qcno sue sb. **cau'sare** vt cause

'caustico adj caustic

cauta'mente adv cautiously

cau'tela f caution

caute'lar|e vt protect. **∼si** vr take precautions

cauteriz'z|are vt cauterize. **cauterizzazi'one** f cauterization

'cauto adj cautious

cauzi'one f security; (per libertà provvisoria) bail

'cava f quarry; fig mine

caval'ca|re vt ride; (stare a cavalcioni) sit astride. **∼ta** f ride; (corteo) cavalcade. **∼'via** m flyover

cavalci'oni: a ∼ adv astride

cavali'ere m rider; (titolo) knight; (accompagnatore) escort; (al ballo) partner

cavalle|'resco adj chivalrous. **∼'ria** f chivalry; (Mil) cavalry. **∼'rizzo, -a** m horseman ●f horsewoman

caval'letta f grasshopper

caval'letto m trestle; (di macchina fotografica) tripod; (di pittore) easel

caval'lina f (ginnastica) horse

ca'vallo m horse; (misura di potenza) horsepower; (scacchi) knight; (dei pantaloni) crotch; a ∼ on horseback; andare a ∼ go horse-riding. ∼ a dondolo rocking-horse

caval'lone m (ondata) roller

caval'luccio ma'rino m sea horse

ca'var|e vt take out; (di dosso) take off; **∼sela** get away with it; **se la cava bene** he's doing all right

cava'tappi m inv corkscrew

ca'ver|na f cave. **∼'noso** adj (voce) deep

'cavia f guinea-pig

cavi'ale m caviar

cavi'glia f ankle

cavil'lare vi quibble. **ca'villo** m quibble

cavità f inv cavity

'cavo adj hollow ●m cavity; (di metallo) cable; (Naut) rope

cavo'lata f 🗉 rubbish

cavo'letto m ∼ di Bruxelles Brussels sprout

cavolfi'ore m cauliflower

'cavolo m cabbage; ∼! 🗉 sugar!

caz'zo int vulg fuck!

caz'zott|o m punch; prendere qcno a ∼i beat sb up

cazzu'ola f trowel

c/c abbr (conto corrente) c/a

CD-Rom m inv CD-Rom

ce pers pron (a noi) (to) us ●adv there; ∼ ne sono molti there are many

'cece m chick-pea

cecità f blindness

'ceco, -a adj & mf Czech; la Repubblica Ceca the Czech Republic

'cedere vi (arrendersi) surrender; (concedere) yield; (sprofondare) subside ●vt give up; make over (proprietà ecc). **ce'devole** adj (terreno ecc) soft; fig yielding. **cedi'mento** m (di terreno) subsidence

cedola f coupon

'cedro m (albero) cedar; (frutto) citron

'ceffo m (muso) snout; (pej: persona) mug

cef'fone m slap

ce'lar|e vt conceal. **∼si** vr hide

cele'bra|re vt celebrate. **∼zi'one** f

celebration

'celebr|e adj famous. ∼**ità** f inv celebrity

'celere adj swift

ce'leste adj (divino) heavenly ● agg & m (colore) sky-blue

celi'bato m celibacy

'celibe adj single ● m bachelor

'cella f cell

'cellofan m inv cellophane; (Culin) cling film

'cellula f cell. ∼ **fotoelettrica** electronic eye

cellu'lare m (telefono) cellular phone ● adj [furgone] ∼ police van. [telefono] ∼ m cellular phone

cellu'lite f cellulite

cellu'loide adj celluloid

cellu'losa f cellulose

'Celt|i mpl Celts. ∼**ico** adj Celtic

cemen'tare vt cement. **ce'mento** m cement. **cemento armato** reinforced concrete

'cena f dinner; (leggera) supper

Cena Cena is the evening meal, usually a lighter meal than pranzo, although it too may start with a primo (often small pasta shapes in broth). A cena can also be a dinner party or a dinner at a restaurant, two of the principal ways in which Italians socialize.

ce'nacolo m circle

ce'nare vi have dinner

'cenci|o m rag; (per spolverare) duster. ∼**oso** adj in rags

'cenere f ash; (di carbone ecc) cinders

ce'netta f (cena semplice) informal dinner

'cenno m sign; (col capo) nod; (con la mano) wave; (allusione) hint; (breve resoconto) mention

ce'none m il ∼ **di Capodanno/ Natale** special New Year's Eve/Christmas Eve dinner

censi'mento m census

cen's|ore m censor. ∼**ura** f censorship. ∼**u'rare** vt censor

'cent m inv cent

centelli'nare vt sip

cente'n|ario, -a adj & mf centenarian ● m centenary. ∼**'nale** adj centennial

cen'tesimo adj hundredth ● m (di moneta) cent; **non avere un** ∼ **be** penniless

cen'ti|grado adj centigrade. ∼**metro** m centimetre

centi'naio m hundred

'cento adj & m one or a hundred; **per** ∼ **per cent**

centome'trista mf Sport one hundred metres runner

cento'mila m one or a hundred thousand

cen'trale adj central ● f (di società ecc) head office. ∼ **atomica** atomic power station. ∼ **elettrica** power station. ∼ **nucleare** nuclear power station. ∼ **telefonica** [telephone] exchange

centra'li|na f (Teleph) switchboard. ∼**'nista** mf operator

centra'lino m (Teleph) exchange; (di albergo ecc) switchboard

centra'li|smo m centralism. ∼**z'zare** vt centralize

cen'trare vt ∼ **qcsa** hit sth in the centre; (fissare nel centro) centre; fig hit on the head (idea)

cen'trifu|ga f spin-drier. **centrifuga** [asciugaverdure] shaker. ∼**'gare** vt centrifuge; (lavatrice:) spin

'centro m centre. ∼ **[città]** city centre. ∼ **commerciale** mall. ∼ **di accoglienza** reception centre. ∼ **sociale** community centre

'**ceppo** m (di albero) stump; (da ardere) log; (fig: gruppo) stock

'**cera** f wax; (aspetto) look. ~ **per il pavimento** floor-polish

ce'**ramica** f (arte) ceramics; (materia) pottery; (oggetto) pot

ce'**rato** adj (tela) waxed

cer'**biatto** m fawn

'**cerca** f **andare in** ~ **di** look for

cerca'per'**sone** m inv beeper

cer'**care** vt look for ●vi ~ **di** try to

'**cerchia** f circle. ~**are** vt circle (parola). ~**ato** adj (occhi) black-ringed. ~**etto** m (per capelli) hairband

'**cerchio** m circle; (giocattolo) hoop. ~**one** m alloy wheel

cere'**ale** m cereal

cere'**brale** adj cerebral

'**cereo** adj waxen

ce'**retta** f depilatory wax

ceri'**monia** f ceremony. ~**ale** m ceremonial. ~**oso** adj ceremonious

ce'**rino** m [wax] match

cerni'**era** f hinge; (di vestito) clasp. ~ **lampo** zip[-fastener], zipper Am

'**cernita** f selection

'**cero** m candle

ce'**rone** m grease-paint

ce'**rotto** m [sticking] plaster

certa'**mente** adv certainly

cer'**tezza** f certainty

certifi'**ca|re** vt certify. ~**to** m certificate

'**certo** adj certain; (notizia) definite; (indeterminativo) some; **sono** ~ **di riuscire** I am certain to succeed; **certi giorni** some days; **un** ~ **signor Giardini** a Mr Giardini; **una certa Anna** somebody called Anna; **certa gente** pej some people; **ho certi dolori!** I'm in such pain!; **certi** pron pl some; (alcune persone) some people ●adv of course; **sapere per** ~ know for certain; **di** ~ surely; ~ **che** sì of course!

cer'**vello** m brain.

'**cervo** m deer

ce'**sareo** adj (Med) Caesarean

cesel'**la|re** vt chisel. ~**to** adj chiselled. ce'**sello** m chisel

ce'**soie** fpl shears

ce'**spuglio** m bush. ~**oso** adj (terreno) bushy

ces'**sa|re** vi stop, cease ●vt stop. ~**te il fuoco** ceasefire

cessi'**one** f handover

'**cesso** m ✗ (gabinetto) bog, john Am; (fig: locale, luogo) dump

'**cesta** f [large] basket. ce'**stello** m (di lavatrice) drum

cesti'**nare** vt throw away. ce'**stino** m [small] basket; (per la carta straccia) waste-paper basket. '**cesto** m basket

'**ceto** m [social] class

'**cetra** f lyre

cetrio'**lino** m gherkin. cetri'**olo** m cucumber

cfr abbr (confronta) cf.

chat'**tare** vi (Comput) chat

che

●pron rel (persona: soggetto) who; (persona: oggetto) that, who, whom fml; (cosa, animale) that, which; **questa è la casa** ~ **ho comprato** this is the house [that] I've bought; **il** ~ **mi sorprende** which surprises me; **dal**

~ **deduco che...** from which I gather that...; **avere di ~ vivere** have enough to live on; **grazie! – non c'è di ~!** thank you! – don't mention it!; **il giorno ~ ti ho visto** 🔢 the day I saw you

● *adj inter* which, what; (*esclamativo: con aggettivo*) how; (*con nome*) what a; ~ **macchina prendiamo, la tua o la mia?** which car are we taking, yours or mine?; ~ **bello!** how nice!; ~ **idea!** what an ideal!; ~ **bella giornata!** what a lovely day!

● *pron inter* what; **a ~ pensi?** what are you thinking about?

● *conj* that; (*con comparazioni*) than; **credo ~ abbia ragione** I think [that] he is right; **era così commosso ~ non riusciva a parlare** he was so moved [that] he couldn't speak; **aspetto ~ telefoni** I'm waiting for him to phone; **è da un po' ~ non lo vedo** it's been a while since I saw him; **mi piace più Roma ~ Milano** I like Rome better than Milan; ~ **ti piaccia o no** whether you like it or not; ~ **io sappia** as far as I know

checché *indef pron* whatever
chemiotera'pia *f* chemotherapy
chero'sene *m* paraffin
cheti'chella: alla ~ *adv* silently
'cheto *adj* quiet

chi

● *rel pron* whoever; (*coloro che*) people who; **ho trovato ~ ti può aiutare** I found somebody who can help you; **c'è ~ dice che...** some people say that...; **senti ~ parla!** listen to who's talking!

● *inter pron* (*soggetto*) who; (*oggetto,*

con preposizione) who, whom *fml*; (*possessivo*) **di ~** whose; ~ **sei?** who are you?; ~ **hai incontrato?** who did you meet?; **di ~ sono questi libri?** whose books are these?; **con ~ parli?** who are you talking to?; **a ~ lo dici!** tell me about it!

chi'acchie|ra *f* chat; (*pettegolezzo*) gossip. ~**rare** *vi* chat; (*far pettegolezzi*) gossip. ~**'rato** *adj* **essere** ~**rato** (*persona*): be the subject of gossip; ~**re** *pl* chitchat; **far quattro** ~**re** have a chat. ~**'rone, -a** *adj* talkative ● *mf* chatterer
chia'ma|re *vt* call; (*far venire*) send for; **come ti chiami?** what's your name?; **mi chiamo Roberto** my name is Robert; ~**re alle armi** call up. ~**rsi** *vr* be called. ~**ta** *f* call; (*Mil*) call-up
chi'appa *f* 🔢 cheek
chiara'mente *adv* clearly
chia'rezza *f* clarity; (*limpidezza*) clearness
chiarifi'ca|re *vt* clarify. ~**'tore** *adj* clarificatory. ~**zi'one** *f* clarification
chiari'mento *m* clarification
chia'rir|e *vt* make clear; (*spiegare*) clear up. ~**si** *vr* become clear
chi'aro *adj* clear; (*luminoso*) bright; (*colore*) light. **chia'rore** *m* glimmer
chiaroveg'gente *adj* clear-sighted ● *mf* clairvoyant
chi'as|so *m* din. ~**'soso** *adj* rowdy
chi'av|e *f* key; **chiudere a ~e** lock. ~**e inglese** spanner. ~**i'stello** *m* latch
chiaz|za *f* stain. ~**'zare** *vt* stain
chic *adj inv* chic
chicches'sia *pron* anybody
'chicco *m* grain; (*di caffè*) bean; (*d'uva*) grape
chi'eder|e *vt* ask; (*per avere*) ask for; (*esigere*) demand. ~**si** *vr* wonder
chi'esa *f* church

chi'esto pp di **chiedere**

'chiglia f keel

'chilo m kilo

chilo'grammo m kilogram[me]

chilome'traggio m (Auto) mileage

chilo'metrico adj in kilometres

chi'lometro m kilometre

chi'mera f fig illusion

'chimic|a f chemistry. **~o, -a** adj chemical ● mf chemist

'china f (declivio) slope; **inchiostro di ~** Indian ink

chi'nar|e vt lower. **~si** vr stoop

chincaglie'rie fpl knick-knacks

chinesitera'pia f physiotherapy

chi'nino m quinine

'chino adj bent

chi'notto m sparkling soft drink

chi'occia f sitting hen

chi'occiola f snail; (Comput) at sign; **scala a ~** spiral staircase

chi'odo m nail; (idea fissa) obsession. **~ di garofano** clove

chi'oma f head of hair; (fogliame) foliage

chi'osco m kiosk

chi'ostro m cloister

chiro'man|te mf palmist. **~'zia** f palmistry

chirur'gia f surgery. **chi'rurgico** adj surgical. **chi'rurgo** m surgeon

chissà adv who knows; **~ quando arriverà** I wonder when he will arrive

chi'tar|ra f guitar. **~'rista** mf guitarist

chi'uder|e vt close; (con la chiave) lock; turn off (luce, acqua); (per sempre) close down (negozio ecc); (recingere) enclose ● vt shut, close. **~si** vr shut; (tempo:) cloud over; (ferita:) heal up.

chi'unque pron anyone, anybody ● rel pron whoever

chi'usa f enclosure; (di canale) lock;

(conclusione) close

chi'uso pp di **chiudere** ● adj shut; (tempo) overcast; (persona) reserved. **~'sura** f closing; (sistema) lock; (allacciatura) fastener. **~sura lampo** zip, zipper Am

ci
● pron (personale) us; (riflessivo) ourselves; (reciproco) each other; (a ciò, di ciò ecc) about it; **non ci disturbare** don't disturb us; **aspettateci** wait for us, **ci ha detto tutto** he told us everything; **ce lo manderanno** they'll send it to us; **ci consideriamo...** we consider ourselves...; **ci laviamo le mani** we wash our hands; **ci odiamo** we hate each other; **ci non ci penso mai** I never think about it; **pensaci!** think about it!
● adv (qui) here; (lì) there; (moto per luogo) through it; **ci siamo** we are here; **ci siete?** are you there?; **ci siamo passati tutti** we all went through it; **c'è** there is; **ce ne sono molti** there are many; **ci vuole pazienza** it takes patience; **non ci vedo/sento** I can't see/hear

cia'bat|ta f slipper. **~'tare** vi shuffle

ciabat'tino m cobbler

ci'alda f wafer

cial'trone m scoundrel

ciam'bella f (Culin) ring-shaped cake; (salvagente) lifebelt; (gonfiabile) rubber ring

cianci'are vi gossip

cia'notico adj (colorito) puce

ci'ao int [1] (all'arrivo) hello!, hi!; (alla partenza) bye-bye!

ciar'la|re vi chat. **~tano** m charlatan

cias'cuno adj each ● pron everyone,

everybody; (*distributivo*) each [one]; per ~ each

ci'bar|e vt feed. ~ie fpl provisions ~ si vr eat; ~si di live on

ciber'netico adj cybernetic

'cibo m food

ci'cala f cicada

cica'lino m buzzer

cica'tri|ce f scar. ~z'zante m ointment

cicatriz'zarsi vr heal [up]. cicatrizzazi'one f healing

'cicca f cigarette end; ([T]: *sigaretta*) fag; ([T]: *gomma*) [chewing] gum

cic'chetto m [T] (*bicchierino*) nip; (*rimprovero*) telling-off

'ciccia f fat, flab

cice'rone m guide

cicla'mino m cyclamen

ci'clis|mo m cycling. ~ta mf cyclist

'ciclo m cycle; (*di malattia*) course

ciclomo'tore m moped

ci'clone m cyclone

ci'cogna f stork

ci'coria f chicory

ci'eco, -a adj blind ●m blind man ●f blind woman

ci'elo m sky; (*Relig*) heaven; santo ~! good heavens!

'cifra f figure; (*somma*) sum; (*monogramma*) monogram; (*codice*) code

ci'fra|re vt embroider with a monogram; (*codificare*) code. ~to adj monogrammed; coded

'ciglio m (*bordo*) edge; (*pl f ciglia: delle palpebre*) eyelash

'cigno m swan

cigo'l|are vi squeak. ~io m squeak

'Cile m Chile

ci'lecca f far ~ miss

ci'leno, -a adj & mf Chilean

cili'egi|a f cherry. ~o m cherry [tree]

cilin'drata f cubic capacity; macchina di alta ~ highpowered car

ci'lindro m cylinder; (*cappello*) top hat

'cima f top; (*fig: persona*) genius; da ~ a fondo from top to bottom

ci'melio m relic

cimen'tar|e vt put to the test. ~si vr (*provare*) try one's hand

'cimice f bug; (*puntina*) drawing pin, thumbtack Am

cimini'era f chimney; (*Naut*) funnel

cimi'tero m cemetery

ci'murro m distemper

'Cina f China

cin cin! int cheers!

cincischi'are vi fiddle

'cine m [T] cinema

cine'asta mf film maker

'cinema m inv cinema. cine'presa f cine-camera

ci'nese adj & mf Chinese

cine'teca f film collection

'cingere vt (*circondare*) surround

'cinghia f strap; (*cintura*) belt

cinghi'ale m wild boar; pelle di ~ pigskin

cinguet't|are vi twitter. ~io m twittering

'cinico adj cynical

ci'niglia f (*tessuto*) chenille

ci'nismo m cynicism

ci'nofilo adj dog-loving

cin'quanta adj & m fifty. cinquan'tenne adj & mf fifty-year-old. cinquan'tesimo adj fiftieth. cinquan'tina f una cinquantina f about fifty

'cinque adj & m five

cinquecen'tesco adj sixteenth-century

cinque'cento adj five hundred ●m il C~ the sixteenth century

cinque'mila adj & m five thousand

'cinta f (*di pantaloni*) belt; muro di ~ [boundary] wall. cin'tare vt enclose

'cintola f (*di pantaloni*) belt

cin'tura f belt. ~ **di salvataggio** lifebelt. ~ **di sicurezza** (Aeron), (Auto) seat-belt

cintu'rino m ~ **dell'orologio** watch-strap

ciò pron this; that; ~ **che** what; ~ **nondimeno** nevertheless

ci'occa f lock

ciocco'la|ta f chocolate; (bevanda) [hot] chocolate. ~**tino** m chocolate. ~**to** m chocolate. ~**to al latte/ fondente** milk/plain chocolate

cioè adv that is

cion'dola|re vi dangle. **ci'ondolo** m pendant

cionono'stante adv nonetheless

ci'otola f bowl

ci'ottolo m pebble

ci'polla f onion; (bulbo) bulb

ci'presso m cypress

'cipria f [face] powder

'Cipro m Cyprus. **cipri'ota** adj & mf Cypriot

'circa adv & prep about

'circo m circus

circo'la|re adj circular ●f circular; (di metropolitana) circle line ●vi circulate. ~**torio** adj (Med) circulatory. ~**zi'one** f circulation; (traffico) traffic

'circolo m circle; (società) club

circon'ci|dere vt circumcise. ~**si'one** f circumcision

circon'dar|e vt surround. ~**io** m (amministrativo) administrative district. ~**si di** vr surround oneself with

circonfe'renza f circumference. ~ **dei fianchi** hip measurement

circonvallazi'one f ring road

circo'scritto adj limited

circoscrizi'one f area. ~ **elettorale** constituency

circo'spetto adj wary

circospezi'one f con ~ warily

circo'stante adj surrounding

circo'stanza f circumstance; (occa-

sione) occasion

circu'ire vt (ingannare) trick

cir'cuito m circuit

circumnavi'ga|re vt circumnavigate. ~**zi'one** f circumnavigation

ci'sterna f cistern; (serbatoio) tank

'cisti f inv cyst

ci'ta|re vt quote; (come esempio) cite; (Jur) summons. ~**zi'one** f quotation; (Jur) summons sg

citofo'nare vt buzz. **ci'tofono** m entry phone; (in ufficio, su aereo ecc) intercom

ci'trullo, -a mf 🗓 dimwit

città f inv town; (grande) city

citta'della f citadel

citta|di'nanza f citizenship; (popolazione) citizens pl. ~**'dino, -a** mf citizen; (abitante di città) city dweller

ciucci'are vt 🗓 suck. **ci'uccio** m 🗓 dummy

ci'uffo m tuft

ci'urma f (Naut) crew

ci'vet|ta f owl; (fig: donna) flirt; [auto] ~**ta** unmarked police car. ~**'tare** vi flirt. ~**te'ria** f coquettishness

'civico adj civic

ci'vil|e adj civil. ~**iz'zare** vt civilize. ~**iz'zato** adj (paese) civilized. ~**izzazi'one** f civilization. ~**'mente** adv civilly

civiltà f inv civilization; (cortesia) civility

'clacson m inv (car) horn

clacsonare vi hoot; honk

cla'mo|re m clamour; **fare** ~**re** cause a sensation. ~**rosa'mente** adv (sbagliare) sensationally. ~**'roso** adj noisy; (sbaglio) sensational

clan m inv clan; fig clique

clandestinità f secrecy

clande'stino adj secret; **movimento** ~ underground movement; **passeggero** ~ stowaway

clari'netto m clarinet

c

'**classe** f class. ~ **turistica** tourist class

classi'cis|mo m classicism. ~**ta** mf classicist

'**classico** adj classical; (tipico) classic ● m classic

clas'sifi|ca f classification; Sport results pl. ~'**care** vt classify. ~'**carsi** vr be placed. ~**ca'tore** m (cartella) folder. ~**cazi'one** f classification

clas'sista mf class-conscious person

'**clausola** f clause

claustro|fo'bia f claustrophobia. ~'**fobico** adj claustrophobic

clau'sura f (Relig) enclosed order

clavi'cembalo m harpsichord

cla'vicola f collar-bone

cle'men|te adj merciful; (tempo) mild. ~**za** f mercy

cleri'cale adj clerical. '**clero** m clergy

clic m (Comput) click; **fare** ~ **su** click on; **fare doppio** ~ **su** double-click on

clic'care vi click (**su** on)

cli'en|te mf client; (di negozio) customer. ~'**tela** f customers pl

'**clima** m climate. **cli'matico** adj climatic; **stazione climatica** health resort

'**clinica** f clinic. **clinico** adj clinical ● m clinician

clo'na|re vt clone. ~'**zione** f cloning

'**cloro** m chlorine

clou adj inv **i momenti** ~ the highlights

coabi'ta|re vi live together. ~**zi'one** f cohabitation

coagu'la|re vt, ~**rsi** vr coagulate. ~**zi'one** f coagulation

coaliz|i'one f coalition. ~'**zarsi** vr unite

co'atto adj (Jur) compulsory

'**cobra** m inv cobra

coca'ina f cocaine. **cocai'nomane** mf cocaine addict

cocci'nella f ladybird

'**coccio** m earthenware; (frammento) fragment

cocci|u'taggine f stubbornness. ~'**uto** adj stubborn

'**cocco** m coconut palm; 🔲 love; **noce di** ~ coconut

cocco'drillo m crocodile

cocco'lare vt cuddle

co'cente adj (sole) burning

'**cocktail** m inv (ricevimento) cocktail party

co'comero m watermelon

co'cuzzolo m top; (di testa, cappello) crown

'**coda** f tail; (di abito) train; (fila) queue; **fare la** ~ queue [up], stand in line Am. ~ **di cavallo** (acconciatura) ponytail.

co'dardo, -a adj cowardly ● mf coward

'**codice** m code. ~ **di avviamento postale** postal code, zip code Am. ~ **a barre** bar-code. ~ **fiscale** tax code. ~ **della strada** highway code.

codifi'care vt codify

coe'ren|te adj consistent. ~**za** f consistency

coesi'one f cohesion

coe'taneo, -a adj & mf contemporary

cofa'netto m casket. '**cofano** m chest; (Auto) bonnet, hood Am

'**cogliere** vt pick; (sorprendere) catch; (afferrare) seize; (colpire) hit

co'gnato, -a mf brother-in-law; sister-in-law

cogni'zione f knowledge

co'gnome m surname

'**coi** = **con** + **i**

coinci'denza f coincidence; (di treno ecc) connection

coin'cidere vi coincide

coinqui'lino m flatmate

coin'vol|gere vt involve. ∼**gi-
'mento** m involvement. ∼**to** adj involved

'coito m coitus

col = CON + IL

colà adv there

cola|'brodo m inv strainer; ridotto
a un ∼**brodo** 🅣 full of holes.
∼**pasta** m inv colander

colazi'one f (del mattino) breakfast;
(di mezzogiorno) lunch; **prima** ∼
breakfast; **far** ∼ have breakfast/
lunch. ∼ **al sacco** packed lunch

co'lei pron f the one

co'lera m cholera

coleste'rolo m cholesterol

colf f abbr (collaboratrice familiare)
home help

'colica f colic

co'lino m [tea] strainer

'colla f glue; (di farina) paste. ∼ **di
pesce** gelatine

collabo'ra|re vi collaborate.
∼**tore**, ∼**trice** mf collaborator.
∼**zi'one** f collaboration

col'lana f necklace; (serie) series

col'lant m inv tights pl

col'lare m collar

col'lasso m collapse

collau'dare vt test. **col'laudo**
m test

'colle m hill

col'lega mf colleague

collega'mento m connection;
(Mil) liaison; Radio link; ∼ **iperte-
stuale** hypertext link. **colle'gar|e** vt
connect. ∼**si** vr link up

collegi'ale mf boarder ●adj (responsabilità, decisione) collective

col'legio m (convitto) boarding-
school. ∼ **elettorale** constituency

'collera f anger; **andare in** ∼ get

angry. **col'lerico** adj irascible

col'letta f collection

collet|tività f inv community.
∼**'tivo** adj collective; (interesse) general; **biglietto** ∼**tivo** group ticket

col'letto m collar

collezi|o'nare vt collect. ∼**'one** f
collection. ∼**o'nista** mf collector

colli'mare vi coincide

col'li|na f hill. ∼**'noso** adj (ter-
reno) hilly

col'lirio m eyewash

collisi'one f collision

'collo m neck; (pacco) package; a ∼
alto high-necked. ∼ **del piede**
instep

colloca'mento m placing; (impiego)
employment

collo'ca|re vt place. ∼**rsi** vr take
one's place. ∼**zi'one** f placing

colloqui'ale adj (termine) colloquial. **col'loquio** m conversation;
(udienza ecc) interview; (esame) oral
[exam]

collusi'one f collusion

colluttazi'one f scuffle

col'mare vt fill [to the brim];
bridge (divario); ∼ **qcno di genti-
lezze** overwhelm sb with kindness.
'colmo adj full ●m top; fig height; **al
colmo della disperazione** in the
depths of despair; **questo è il
colmo!** (con indignazione) this is the
last straw!; (con stupore) I don't believe it!

co'lomb|a f dove. ∼**o** m pigeon

co'lonia¹ f colony; ∼**a** [estiva]
(per bambini) holiday camp. ∼**'ale** adj
colonial

co'lonia² f [acqua di] ∼ [eau de]
Cologne

co'lonico adj (terreno, casa) farm

coloniz'za|re vt colonize. ∼**'tore**,
∼**'trice** mf colonizer

co'lon|na f column. ∼ **sonora**
sound-track. ∼ **vertebrale** spine.

~'nato m colonnade

colon'nello m colonel

co'lono m tenant farmer

colo'rante m colouring

colo'rare vt colour; colour in (disegno)

co'lore m colour; a colori in colour; di ~ coloured. **colo'rito** adj coloured; (viso) rosy; (racconto) colourful ● m complexion

co'loro pron pl the ones

colos'sale adj colossal. **co'losso** m colossus

'**colpa** f fault; (biasimo) blame; (colpevolezza) guilt; (peccato) sin; dare la ~ a blame; essere in ~ be at fault; per ~ di because of. **col'pevole** adj guilty ● mf culprit

col'pire vt hit, strike

'**colpo** m blow; (di arma da fuoco) shot; (urto) knock; (emozione) shock; (Med, Sport) stroke; (furto) raid; di ~ suddenly; far ~ make a strong impression; far venire un ~ a qcno fig give sb a fright; perdere colpi (motore:) keep missing; a ~ d'occhio at a glance; a ~ sicuro for certain. ~ d'aria chill. ~ di sole sunstroke; colpi di sole (su capelli) highlights. ~ di stato coup [d'état]. ~ di telefono ring; dare un ~ di telefono a qn give sb a ring. ~ di testa [sudden] impulse. ~ di vento gust of wind

col'poso adj omicidio ~ manslaughter

coltel'lata f stab. **col'tello** m knife

colti'va|re vt cultivate. ~'tore, ~'trice mf farmer. ~zi'one f farming; (di piante) growing

'**colto** pp di cogliere ● adj cultured

'**coltre** f blanket

col'tura f cultivation

co'lui pron inv m the one

'**coma** m coma; in ~ in a coma

comanda'mento m

commandment

coman'dante m commander; (Aeron, Naut) captain

coman'dare vt command; (Mech) control ● vi be in charge. **co'mando** m command; (di macchina) control

co'mare f (madrina) godmother

combaci'are vi fit together; (testimonianze:) concur

combat'tente adj fighting ● m combattant. ex ~ ex-serviceman

com'bat|tere vt/i fight. ~ti-'mento m fight; (Mil) battle; fuori ~timento (pugilato) knocked out. ~'tuto adj (gara) hard fought

combi'na|re vt/i arrange; (mettere insieme) combine; (fam: fare) do; cosa stai ~ndo? what are you doing?. ~rsi vr combine; (mettersi d'accordo) come to an agreement. ~zi'one f combination; (caso) coincidence; per ~zione by chance

com'briccola f gang

combu'sti|bile adj combustible ● m fuel. ~one f combustion

com'butta f gang; in ~ in league

'**come**
● adv like; (in qualità di) as; (interrogativo, esclamativo) how; questo vestito è ~ il tuo this dress is like yours; ~ stai? how are you?; ~ va? how are things?; ~ mai? how come?; ~? what?; non sa ~ fare he doesn't know what to do; ~ sta bene! how well he looks!; ~ no! that will be right!; ~ tu sai as you know; fa ~ vuoi do as you like; ~ se as if

● conj (non appena) as soon as

co'meta f comet

'**comico, -a** adj comic ● m funny side ● mf (attore) comedian ● f (a torte in faccia) slapstick sketch

co'mignolo m chimney-pot

cominci'are vt/i begin, start; **a ∼ da oggi** from today.

comi'tato m committee

comi'tiva f party, group

co'mizio m meeting

com'mando m inv commando

com'medi|a f comedy; (opera teatrale) play; fig sham. **∼a musicale** musical. **∼'ante** mf comedian; fig reg phoney. **∼'ografo, -a** mf playwright

commemo'ra|re vt commemorate. **∼zi'one** f commemoration

commen'sale mf fellow diner

commen't|are vt comment on; (annotare) annotate. **∼ario** m commentary. **∼a'tore, ∼a'trice** mf commentator. **com'mento** m comment

commerci'a|le adj commercial; (relazioni, trattative) trade; (attività) business. **centro ∼le** shopping centre. **∼'lista** mf business consultant; (contabile) accountant. **∼liz'zare** vt market. **∼lizzazi'one** f marketing

commerci'ante mf trader; (negoziante) shopkeeper. **∼ all'ingrosso** wholesaler

commerci'are vi **∼ in** deal in

com'mercio m commerce; (internazionale) trade; (affari) business; **in ∼** (prodotto) on sale. **∼ equo e solidale** fair trade. **∼ all'ingrosso** wholesale trade. **∼ al minuto** retail trade

com'messo, -a pp di **committere** ●mf shop assistant. **∼ viaggiatore** commercial traveller ●f (ordine) order

comme'stibile adj edible. **commestibili** mpl groceries

com'mettere vt commit; make (sbaglio)

commi'ato m leave; **prendere ∼ da** take leave of

commise'rar|e vt commiserate with. **∼si** vr feel sorry for oneself

commissari'ato m (di polizia) police station

commis's|ario m [police] superin-

tendent; (membro di commissione) commissioner; Sport steward; (Comm) commission agent. **∼ario d'esame** examiner. **∼'one** f (incarico) errand; (comitato ecc) commission; (Comm: di merce) order; **∼ioni** pl (acquisti) **fare ∼ioni** go shopping. **∼ione d'esame** board of examiners. **C∼ione Europea** European Commission

commit'tente mf purchaser

com'mo|sso pp di **commuovere** ●adj moved. **∼'vente** adj moving

commozi'one f emotion. **∼ cerebrale** concussion

commu'over|e vt touch, move. **∼si** vr be touched

commu'tare vt change; (Jur) commute

comò m inv chest of drawers

comoda'mente adv comfortably

como'dino m bedside table

comodità f inv comfort; (convenienza) convenience

'comodo adj comfortable; (conveniente) convenient; (spazioso) roomy; (facile) easy; **stia ∼!** don't get up!; **far ∼** be useful ●m comfort; **fare il proprio ∼** do as one pleases

compae'sano, -a mf fellow countryman

com'pagine f (squadra) team

compa'gnia f company; (gruppo) party; **fare ∼ a** qcno keep sb company; **essere di ∼** be sociable. **∼ aerea** airline

com'pagno, -a mf companion; (Comm, Sport, in coppia) partner; (Pol) comrade. **∼ di scuola** schoolmate

compa'rabile adj comparable

compa'ra|re vt compare. **∼'tivo** adj & m comparative. **∼zi'one** f comparison

com'pare m (padrino) godfather; (testimone di matrimonio) witness

compa'rire vi appear; (spiccare) stand out; **∼ in giudizio** appear in court

com'parso, -a pp di comparire ● f appearance; Cinema extra

compartecipazi'one f sharing; (quota) share

comparti'mento m compartment; (amministrativo) department

compas'sato adj calm and collected

compassi'o|ne f compassion; aver ∼ne per feel pity for; far ∼ne arouse pity. ∼'nevole adj compassionate

com'passo m [pair of] compasses pl

compa'tibil|e adj (conciliabile) compatible; (scusabile) excusable. ∼ità f compatibility. ∼'mente adv ∼mente con i miei impegni if my commitments allow

compa'tire vt pity; (scusare) make allowances for

compat'tezza f (di materia) compactness. **com'patto** adj compact; (denso) dense; (solido) solid; fig united

compene'trare vt pervade

compen'sar|e vt compensate; (supplire) make up for. ∼si vr balance each other out

compen'sato m (legno) plywood

compensazi'one f compensation

com'penso m compensation; (retribuzione) remuneration; in ∼ (in cambio) in return; (d'altra parte) on the other hand; (invece) instead

'comper|a f purchase; far ∼e do some shopping

compe'rare vt buy

compe'ten|te adj competent. ∼za f competence; (responsabilità) responsibility

com'petere vi compete; ∼ a (compito:) be the responsibility of

competi'tività f competitiveness. ∼'tivo adj (prezzo, carattere) competitive. ∼'tore, ∼'trice mf competitor. ∼zi'one f competition

compia'cen|te adj obliging. ∼za f obligingness

compia'c|ere vt/i please. ∼ersi vr (congratularsi) congratulate. ∼ersi di (degnarsi) condescend. ∼i'mento m satisfaction; pej smugness. ∼i'uto adj satisfied; (aria, sorriso) smug

compi'an|gere vt pity; (per lutto ecc) sympathize with. ∼to adj lamented ● m grief

'compier|e vt (concludere) complete; commit (delitto); ∼e gli anni have one's birthday. ∼si vr end; (avverarsi) come true

compi'la|re vt compile; fill in (modulo). ∼zi'one f compilation

compi'mento m portare a ∼ qcsa conclude sth

com'pire vt = COMPIERE

compi'tare vt spell

com'pito¹ adj polite

'compito² m task; (Sch) homework

compi'ut|o adj avere 30 anni ∼i be over 30

comple'anno m birthday

comple'mentare adj complementary; (secondario) subsidiary

comple'mento m complement; (Mil) draft. ∼ oggetto direct object

comples'sità f complexity. ∼siva'mente adv on the whole. ∼sivo adj comprehensive; (totale) total. com'plesso adj complex; (difficile) complicated ● m complex; (di cantanti ecc) group; (di circostanze, fattori) combination; in ∼so on the whole

completa'mente adv completely

comple'tare vt complete

com'pleto adj complete; (pieno) full [up]; essere al ∼ (teatro:) be sold out; la famiglia al ∼ the whole family ∼ ● m (vestito) suit; (insieme di cose) set

compli'ca|re vt complicate. ∼rsi vr become complicated. ∼to complicated. ∼zi'one f complication; salvo ∼zioni all being well '**complic|e** *mf* accomplice ● *adj* (sguardo) knowing. ∼**ità** *f* complicity

complimen'tar|e *vt* compliment. ∼**si** *vr* ∼**si con** congratulate

compli'menti *mpl* (ossequi) regards; (congratulazioni) congratulations; **far** ∼ stand on ceremony

compli'mento *m* compliment

complot'tare *vi* plot

compo'nente *adj* & *m* component ● *mf* member

compo'nibile *adj* (cucina) fitted; (mobili) modular

componi'mento *m* composition; (letterario) work

com'por|re *vt* compose; (ordinare) put in order; (Typ) set. ∼**si** *vr* ∼**si di** be made up of

comporta'mento *m* behaviour

compor'tar|e *vt* involve; (consentire) allow. ∼**si** *vr* behave

composi'tore, -'trice *mf* composer; (Typ) compositor. ∼**zi'one** *f* composition

com'posta *f* stewed fruit; (concime) compost

compo'stezza *f* composure

com'posto *pp di* **comporre** ● *adj* composed; (costituito) comprising; **stai** ∼**!** sit properly! ● *m* (Chem) compound

compra're *vt* buy. ∼'**tore**, ∼'**trice** *mf* buyer

compra'vendita *f* buying and selling

com'pren|dere *vt* understand; (includere) comprise. ∼'**sibile** *adj* understandable. ∼**sibil'mente** *adv* understandably. ∼**si'one** *f* understanding. ∼'**sivo** *adj* understanding; (che include) inclusive. **com'preso** *pp di* **comprendere** ● *adj* included; **tutto compreso** (prezzo) all-in

com'pressa *f* compress; (pastiglia) tablet

compressi'one *f* compression. **com'presso** *pp di* **comprimere** ● *adj* compressed

com'primere *vt* press; (reprimere) repress

compro'me|sso *pp di* **compromettere** ● *m* compromise. ∼**t'tente** *adj* compromising. ∼**ttere** *vt* compromise

comproprietà *f* multiple ownership

compro'vare *vt* prove

compu'tare *vt* calculate

com'puter *m inv* computer. ∼**iz'zare** *vt* computerize. ∼**iz'zato** *adj* computerized

computiste'ria *f* book-keeping. '**computo** *m* calculation

comu'nale *adj* municipal

co'mune *adj* common; (condiviso) mutual; (ordinario) ordinary ● *m* borough; (amministrativo) commune; **fuori del** ∼ extraordinary. ∼'**mente** *adv* commonly

comuni'ca|re *vt* communicate; pass on (malattia); (Relig) administer Communion to. ∼**rsi** *vr* receive Communion. ∼**tiva** *f* communicativeness. ∼'**tivo** *adj* communicative. ∼**to** *m* communiqué. ∼**to stampa** press release. ∼**zi'one** *f* communication; (Teleph) [phone] call; **avere la** ∼**zione** get through; **dare la** ∼**zione a qcno** put sb through

comuni'one *f* communion; (Relig) [Holy] Communion

comu'nis|mo *m* communism. ∼**ta** *adj* & *mf* communist

comunità *f inv* community. **C**∼ **[Economica] Europea** European [Economic] Community

co'munque *conj* however ● *adv* anyhow

con *prep* with; (mezzo) by; ∼ **facilità** easily; ∼ **mia grande gioia** to my great delight; **è gentile** ∼ **tutti** he is kind to everyone; **col treno** by train; ~ **questo tempo** in this weather

co'nato m ~ **di vomito** retching

'conca f basin; (valle) dell

concate'nare vt link together. ~**zi'one** f connection

'concavo adj concave

con'ceder|e vt grant; award (premio); (ammettere) admit. ~**si** vr allow oneself (pausa)

concentra'mento m concentration

concen'tra|re vt, ~**rsi** vr concentrate. ~**to** adj concentrated ● m ~**to di pomodoro** tomato pureé. ~**zi'one** f concentration

concepi'mento m conception

conce'pire vt conceive (bambino); (capire) understand; (figurarsi) conceive ● devise (piano ecc)

con'cernere vt concern

concer'tar|e vt (Mus) harmonize; (organizzare) arrange. ~**si** vr agree

concer'tista mf concert performer. **con'certo** m concert; (composizione) concerto

concessio'nario m agent

concessi'one f concession

con'cesso pp di concedere

con'cetto m concept; (opinione) opinion

concezi'one f conception; (idea) concept

con'chiglia f [sea] shell

'concia f tanning; (di tabacco) curing

conci'a|re vt tan; cure (tabacco); ~**re** qcno per le feste give sb a good hiding. ~**rsi** vr (sporcarsi) get dirty; (vestirsi male) dress badly. ~**to** adj (pelle, cuoio) tanned

concili'abile adj compatible

concili'a|re vt reconcile; settle (contravvenzione); (favorire) induce. ~**rsi** vr go together; (mettersi d'accordo) become reconciled. ~**zi'one** f

reconciliation; (Jur) settlement

con'cilio m (Relig) council; (riunione) assembly

conci'mare vt feed (pianta). ~**'cime** m fertilizer; (chimico) fertilizer

concisi'one f conciseness. **con'ciso** adj concise

conci'tato adj excited

concitta'dino, -a mf fellow citizen

con'clu|dere vt conclude; (finire con successo) achieve. ~**dersi** vr come to an end. ~**si'one** f conclusion; in ~**sione** (insomma) in short. ~**'sivo** adj conclusive. ~**so** pp di concludere

concomi'tanza f (di circostanze, fatti) combination

concor'da|nza f agreement. ~**re** vt agree; (Gram) make agree. ~**to** m agreement; (Comm, Jur) arrangement

con'cord|e adj in agreement; (unanime) unanimous

concor'ren|te adj concurrent; (rivale) competing ● mf (Comm), Sport competitor; (candidato) candidate. ~**za** f competition. ~**zi'ale** adj competitive

con'cor|rere vi (contribuire) concur; (andare insieme) go together; (competere) compete. ~**so** pp di concorrere ● m competition; **fuori** ~**so** not in the official competition. ~**so di bellezza** beauty contest

concreta'mente adv specifically

concre|'tare vt (concludere) achieve. ~**tiz'zare** vt put into concrete form (idea, progetto)

con'creto adj concrete; **in** ~ in concrete terms

concussi'one f extortion

con'danna f sentence; pronunziare una ~ pass a sentence. con-dan'nare vt condemn; (Jur) sentence. condan'nato, -a mf convict

conden'sa|re vt, ~**rsi** vr condense. ~**zi'one** f condensation

condi'mento m seasoning; (salsa) dressing. **con'dire** vt flavour; dress (insalata)

condiscen'den|te adj indulgent; pej condescending. ∼**za** f indulgence; pej condescension

condi'videre vt share

condizio'na|le adj & m conditional ● f (Jur) suspended sentence

condizio'nare vt condition. ∼**to** adj conditional. ∼**tore** m air conditioner

condizi'one f condition; a ∼ che on condition that

condogli'anze fpl condolences; fare le ∼ a offer condolences to

condomini'ale adj (spese) common. **condo'minio** m joint ownership; (edificio) condominium

condo'nare vt remit. **con'dono** m remission

con'dotta f conduct, (circoscrizione di medico) district; (di gara ecc) management; (tubazione) piping

con'dotto pp di **condurre** ● adj **medico** ~ district doctor ● m pipe; (Anat) duct

condu'cente m driver

con'du|rre vt lead; drive (veicoli); (accompagnare) take; conduct (gas, elettricità ecc); (gestire) run. ∼**rsi** vr behave. ∼**t'tore**, ∼**t'trice** mf (TV) presenter; (di veicolo) driver ● m (Electr) conductor. ∼**t'tura** f duct

confabu'lare vi have a confab

confa'cente adj suitable. **con'farsi** vr confarsi a suit

confederazi'one f confederation

confe'renz|a f (discorso) lecture; (congresso) conference. ∼**a stampa** news conference. ∼**i'ere, -a** mf lecturer

confe'rire vt (donare) give ● vi confer

con'ferma f confirmation. **confer'mare** vt confirm

confes'|sare vt, ∼**arsi** vr confess. ∼**io'nale** adj & m confessional. ∼**i'one** f confession. ∼**ore** m confessor

con'fetto m sugared almond

confet'tura f jam

confezio'na|re vt manufacture; make (abiti); package (merci). ∼**to** adj (vestiti) off-the-peg; (gelato) wrapped

confezi'one f manufacture; (di abiti) tailoring; (di pacchi) packaging; **confezioni** pl clothes. ∼ **regalo** gift pack

confic'car|e vt thrust. ∼**si** vr run into

confi'd|are vi ∼**are** in trust ● vt confide. ∼**arsi** vr ∼**arsi con** confide in. ∼**ente** adj confident ● mf confidant

confi'denz|a f confidence; (familiarità) familiarity; prendersi delle ∼**e** take liberties. ∼**i'ale** adj confidential; (rapporto, tono) familiar

configu'ra|re vt (Comput) configure. ∼**zi'one** f configuration

confi'nante adj neighbouring

confi'na|re vi (relegare) confine ● vi ∼**re con** border on. ∼**rsi** vr withdraw. ∼**to** adj confined

con'fin|e m border; (tra terreni) boundary. ∼**o** m political exile

con'fisca f (di proprietà) forfeiture. ∼**'scare** vt confiscate

con'flitt|o m conflict. ∼**u'ale** adj adversarial

conflu'enza f confluence; (di strade) junction

conflu'ire vi (fiumi) flow together; (strade:) meet

con'fonder|e vt confuse; (turbare) confound; (imbarazzare) embarrass. ∼**si** vr (mescolarsi) mingle; (turbarsi) become confused; (sbagliarsi) be mistaken

confor'ma|re vt adapt. ∼**rsi** vr conform. ∼**zi'one** f conformity (a

with); (del terreno) composition
con'forme adj according. **~'mente**
adv accordingly

confor'mi|smo m conformity.
~sta mf conformist. **~tà** f (a norma)
conformity

confor'tante adj comforting
confor't|are vt comfort. **~evole**
adj (comodo) comfortable. **con'forto** m
comfort

confron'tare vt compare
con'fronto m comparison; **in ~** a
by comparison with; **nei tuoi con-
fronti** towards you; **senza ~** far
and away

confusi|o'nario adj (persona)
muddle-headed. **~'one** f confusion;
(baccano) (disordine) mess; (imbarazzo) embarrassment. **con'fuso** pp
di **confondere** ● adj confused; (indi-
stinto) (imbarazzo) embar-
rassed

conge'dar|e vt dismiss; (Mil) dis-
charge. **~si** vr take one's leave
con'gedo m leave; **essere in ~** be
on leave. **~ malattia** sick leave. **~
maternità** maternity leave
conge'gnare vt devise; (mettere insieme) assemble. **con'gegno** m device
congela'mento m freezing; (Med)
frost-bite
congela|re vt freeze. **~to** adj
(cibo) deep-frozen. **~'tore** m freezer
congeni'ale adj congenial
con'genito adj congenital
congestio'na|re vt congest. **~to**
adj (traffico) congested. **conge-
sti'one** f congestion
conget'tura f conjecture
congi'unger|e vt join; combine
(sforzi). **~si** vr join
congiunti'vite f conjunctivitis
congiun'tivo m subjunctive
congi'unto pp di **congiungere** ● adj
joined ● m relative
congiun'tu|ra f joint; (circostanza)

juncture; (situazione) situation. **~'rale**
adj economic
congiunzi'one f conjunction
congi'u|ra f conspiracy. **~'rare** vi
conspire
conglome'rato m conglomerate;
(fig) conglomeration; (da costruzione)
concrete
congratu'la|rsi vr **~rsi con qcno
per** congratulate sb on. **~zi'oni** fpl
congratulations
con'grega f band
congre'ga|re vt, **~rsi** vr congre-
gate. **~zi'one** f congregation
con'gresso m congress
'congruo adj proper; (giusto) fair
conguagli'are vt balance. **con-
gu'aglio** m balance
coni'are vt coin
'conico adj conical
co'nifera f conifer
co'niglio m rabbit
coniu'gale adj marital; (vita)
married
coniu'ga|re vt conjugate. **~rsi** vr
get married. **~zi'one** f conjugation
'coniuge mf spouse
connessi'one f connection. **con-
'nesso** pp di **connettere**
con'netter|e vt connect ● vi think
rationally. **~rsi** vr go online
conni'vente adj conniving
conno'ta|re vt connote. **~to** m
distinguishing feature; **~ti** pl de-
scription
con'nubio m fig union
'cono m cone
cono'scen|te mf acquaintance.
~za f knowledge; (persona) acquaint-
ance; (sensi) consciousness; **perdere
~za** lose consciousness; **riprendere
~za** regain consciousness
co'nosc|ere vt know; (essere a cono-
scenza di) be acquainted with; (fare la
conoscenza di) meet. **~i'tore**, **~i'trice**
mf connoisseur. **~i'uto** pp di **cono-**

scere ● *adj* well-known

con'quist|a *f* conquest. conqui'stare *vt* conquer; *fig* win

consa'cra|re *vt* consecrate; ordain (sacerdote); (*dedicare*) dedicate. ~rsi *vr* devote oneself

consangu'ineo, -a *mf* bloodrelation

consa'pevo|le *adj* conscious. ~'lezza *f* consciousness. ~l'mente *adv* consciously

'conscio *adj* conscious

consecu'tivo *adj* consecutive; (*seguente*) next

con'segna *f* delivery; (*merce*) consignment; (*custodia*) care; (*di prigioniero*) handover; (*Mil: ordine*) orders *pl*; (*Mil: punizione*) confinement; **pagamento alla ~** cash on delivery

conse'gnare *vt* deliver; (*affidare*) give in charge; (*Mil*) confine to barracks

consegu'en|te *adj* consequent. ~za *f* consequence; **di ~za** (*perciò*) consequently

consegui'mento *m* achievement

consegu'ire *vt* achieve ● *vi* follow

con'senso *m* consent

consensu'ale *adj* consensus-based

consen'tire *vi* consent ● *vt* allow

con'serva *f* preserve; (*di frutta*) jam; (*di agrumi*) marmalade. **~ di pomodoro** tomato sauce

conser'var|e *vt* preserve; (*mantenere*) keep. ~si *vr* keep; ~si in salute keep well

conserva|'tore, -'trice *mf* (*Pol*) conservative

conserva'torio *m* conservatory

conservazi'one *f* preservation; **a lunga ~** long-life

conside'ra|re *vt* consider; (*stimare*) regard. ~to *adj* (*stimato*) esteemed. ~zi'one *f* (*osservazione, riflessione*) remark

conside'revole *adj* considerable

consigli'abile *adj* advisable

consigli|'are *vt* advise; (*raccomandare*) recommend. ~'arsi *vr* ~arsi con qcno ask sb's advice. ~'ere, -a *mf* adviser; (*membro di consiglio*) councillor

con'siglio *m* advice; (*ente*) council. **~ d'amministrazione** board of directors. **C~ dei Ministri** Cabinet

consi'sten|te *adj* substantial; (*spesso*) thick; (*fig: argomento*) valid

con'sistere *vi* ~ **in** consist of

consoci'ata *f* associate company

conso'lar|e¹ *vt* console; (*rallegrare*) cheer. ~si *vr* console oneself

conso'la|re² *adj* consular. ~to *m* consulate

consolazi'one *f* consolation; (*gioia*) joy

'console *m* consul

consoli'dar|e *vt*, ~si *vr* consolidate

conso'nante *f* consonant

'consono *adj* consistent

con'sorte *mf* consort

con'sorzio *m* consortium

con'stare *vi* ~ **di** consist of; (*risultare*) appear; **a quanto mi consta as** far as I know; **mi consta che it** appears that

consta'ta|re *vt* ascertain. ~zi'one *f* observation

consu'e|to *adj & m* usual. ~tudi'nario *adj* (*diritto*) common; (*persona*) set in one's ways. ~'tudine *f* habit; (*usanza*) custom

consu'len|te *mf* consultant. ~za *f* consultancy

consul'ta|re *vt* consult. ~rsi *rsi* con consult with. ~zi'one *f* consultation

consul'tivo *adj* consultative. ~orio *m* clinic

consu'ma|re *vt* (*usare*) consume; wear out (abito, scarpe); consummate (matrimonio); commit (delitto). ~rsi *vr* consume; (abito, scarpe:) wear out; (*struggersi*) pine

consu'mato adj (politico) seasoned; (scarpe, tappeto) worn

consuma|'tore, -'trice mf consumer. **~zi'one** f (bibita) drink; (spuntino) snack

consu'mismo m consumerism. **~ta** mf consumerist

con'sumo m consumption; (di abito, scarpe) wear; (uso) use; **generi di ~** consumer goods or items. **~ [di carburante]** [fuel] consumption

consun'tivo m [bilancio] **~** final statement

conta'balle mf ① storyteller

con'tabil|e adj book-keeping • mf accountant. **~ità** f accounting; tenere la **~ità** keep the accounts

contachi'lometri m inv mileometer, odometer Am

conta'dino, -a mf farm-worker; (medievale) peasant

contagi|'are vt infect. **con'tagio** m infection. **~'oso** adj infectious

conta'gocce m inv dropper

contami'na|re vt contaminate. **~zi'one** f contamination

con'tante m cash; **pagare in contanti** pay cash

con'tare vt/i count; (tenere conto di) take into account; (proporsi) intend

conta'scatti m inv (Teleph) time-unit counter

conta'tore m meter

contat'tare vt contact. **con'tatto** m contact

'conte m count

conteggi|'are vt put on the bill • vi calculate. **con'teggio** m calculation. **conteggio alla rovescia** countdown

con'te|gno m behaviour; (atteggiamento) attitude. **~'gnoso** adj dignified

contem'pla|re vt contemplate; (fissare) gaze at. **~zi'one** f contemplation

con'tempo m **nel ~** in the meantime

contempo|ranea'mente adv at once. **~raneo, -a** adj & mf contemporary

conten'dente mf competitor. con'tendere vi compete; (litigare) quarrel • vt contend

conte'n|ere vt contain; (reprimere) repress. **~ersi** vr contain oneself. **~i'tore** m container

conten'tarsi vr **~ di** be content with

conten'tezza f joy

conten'tino m placebo

con'tento adj glad; (soddisfatto) contented

conte'nuto m contents pl; (soggetto) content

contenzi'oso m legal department

con'tesa f disagreement; Sport contest. **~o** pp di contendere • adj contested

con'tessa f countess

conte'sta|re vt contest; (Jur) notify. **~'tario** adj anti-establishment. **~'tore, ~'trice** mf protester. **~zi'one** f (disputa) dispute

con'testo m context

con'tiguo adj adjacent

continen'tale adj continental. **conti'nente** m continent

conti'nenza f continence

contin'gen|te m contingent; (quota) quota. **~za** f contingency

continua'mente adv (senza interruzione) continuously; (frequentemente) continually

continu|'are vt/i continue; (riprendere) resume. **~'ativo** adj permanent. **~azi'one** f continuation. **~ità** f continuity

con'tinu|o adj continuous; (molto frequente) continual. corrente **~a** direct current; **di ~o** continually

'conto m calculation; (Comm) account; (*di ristorante ecc*) bill; (*stima*) consideration; **a conti fatti** all things considered; **far ~ di** (*supporre*) suppose; (*proporsi*) intend; **far ~ su** rely on; **in fin dei conti** when all is said and done; **per ~ di** on behalf of; **per ~ mio** (*a mio parere*) in my opinion; (*da solo*) on my own; **starsene per ~ proprio** be on one's own; **rendersi ~ di** qcsa realize sth; **sul ~ di** qcno (*voci, informazioni*) about sb; **tener ~ di** qcsa take sth into account; **tenere da ~** qcsa look after sth. **~ corrente** current account, checking account *Am*. **~ alla rovescia** countdown

con'torcer|e *vt* twist. **~si** *vr* twist about

contor'nare *vt* surround

con'torno *m* contour; (*Culin*) vegetables *pl*

contorsi'one *f* contortion. **con'torto** *pp di* **contorcere** *adj* twisted

contrabban'dare *vt* smuggle. **~di'ere, -a** *mf* smuggler. **contrab'bando** *m* contraband

contrab'basso *m* double bass

contraccambi'are *vt* return. **contrac'cambio** *m* return

contracce|t'tivo *m* contraceptive. **~zi'one** *f* contraception

contrac'col|po *m* rebound; (*di arma da fuoco*) recoil; (*fig*) repercussion

con'trada *f* (*rione*) district

contrad'detto *pp di* **contraddire**

contrad'di|re *vt* contradict. **~t'torio** *adj* contradictory. **~zi'one** *f* contradiction

ontraddi'stin|guere *vt* differentiate. **~to** *adj* distinct

ontra'ente *mf* contracting party

ontra'ereo *adj* anti-aircraft

contraf'fa|re *vt* (*imitare*) imitate; (*falsificare*) forge. **~tto** *adj* forged. **~zi'one** *f* (*imitazione*) imitation; (*falsificazione*) forgery

on'tralto *m* countertenor ● *f*

contralto

contrap'peso *m* counterbalance

contrap'por|re *vt* counter; (*confrontare*) compare. **~si** *vr* contrast; **~si a** be opposed to

contraria'mente *adv* contrary (a to)

contrari'are *vt* oppose; (*infastidire*) annoy. **~'arsi** *vr* get annoyed. **~età** *f inv* adversity; (*ostacolo*) set-back

con'trario *adj* contrary; (*direzione*) opposite; (*sfavorevole*) unfavourable ● *m* contrary; **al ~** on the contrary

con'trarre *vt* contract

contras'se|gnare *vt* mark. **~'segno** *m* mark; **[in] ~segno** (*spedizione*) cash on delivery

contra'stare *vt* oppose; (*contestare*) contest ● *vi* clash. **con'trasto** *m* contrast; (*litigio*) dispute

contrattac'care *vt* counterattack. **contrat'tacco** *m* counter-attack

contrat'ta|re *vt/i* negotiate; (*mercanteggiare*) barqain. **~zi'one** *f* (*salariale*) bargaining

contrat'tempo *m* hitch

con'tratt|o *pp di* **contrarre** ● *m* contract. **~o a termine** fixed-term contract. **~u'ale** *adj* contractual

contravve'ni|re *vi* contravene. **~zi'one** *f* contravention; (*multa*) fine

contrazi'one *f* contraction; (*di prezzi*) reduction

contribu'ente *mf* contributor; (*del fisco*) taxpayer

contribu'ire *vi* contribute. **contri'buto** *m* contribution

'contro *prep* against; **~ di me** against me ● *m* **i pro e i ~** the pros and cons

contro'battere *vt* counter

controbilanci'are *vt* counterbalance

controcor'rente *adj* nonconformist ● *adv* upriver; *fig* upstream

controffen'siva *f* counteroffensive

controfi'gura f stand-in

controindicazi'one f (Med) contraindication

control'la|re vt control; (verificare) check; (collaudare) test. **~rsi** vr have self-control. **~to** adj controlled

con'trol|lo m control; (verifica) check; (Med) check-up. **~lo delle nascite** birth control. **~'lore** m controller; (sui treni ecc) [ticket] inspector. **~lore di volo** air-traffic controller

contro'mano adv in the wrong direction

contromi'sura f countermeasure

contropi'ede m **prendere in ~** catch off guard

controprodu'cente adj self-defeating

con'trordin|e m counter order; **salvo ~i** unless I/you hear to the contrary

contro'senso m contradiction in terms

controspio'naggio m counterespionage

contro'vento adv against the wind

contro'vers|ia f controversy; (Jur) dispute. **~o** adj controversial

contro'voglia adv unwillingly

contu'macia f default; **in ~** in one's absence

contun'dente adj (corpo, arma) blunt

contur'ba|nte adj perturbing

contusi'one f bruise

convale'scen|te adj convalescent

con'vali|da f validation. **~'dare** vt confirm; validate (atto, biglietto)

con'vegno m meeting; (congresso) congress

conve'nevol|e adj suitable; **~i** pl pleasantries

conveni'en|te adj convenient; (prezzo) attractive; (vantaggioso) ad-

vantageous. **~za** f convenience; (interesse) advantage; (di prezzo) attractiveness

conve'nire vi (riunirsi) gather; (concordare) agree; (ammettere) admit; (essere opportuno) be convenient ● vt agree on; **ci conviene andare** it is better to go; **non mi conviene stancarmi** I'd better not tire myself out

con'vento m (di suore) convent; (di frati) monastery

conve'nuto adj fixed

convenzi|o'nale adj conventional. **~'one** f convention

conver'gen|te adj converging. **~za** f fig confluence

con'vergere vi converge

conver'sa|re vi converse. **~zi'one** f conversation

conversi'one f conversion

con'verso pp di convergere

conver'tibile f (Auto) convertible

conver'ti|re vt convert. **~rsi** vr be converted. **~to, -a** mf convert

con'vesso adj convex

convin'cente adj convincing

con'vin|cere vt convince. **~to** adj convinced. **~zi'one** f conviction

con'vitto m boarding school

convi'ven|te m common-law husband ● f common-law wife. **~za** f cohabitation. **con'vivere** vi live together

convivi'ale adj convivial

convo'ca|re vt convene. **~zi'one** f convening

convogli'are vt convey; convoy (navi) **con'voglio** m convoy; (ferroviario) train

convulsi'one f convulsion. **con'vulso** adj convulsive; (febbrile) feverish

coope'ra|re vi co-operate. **~'tiva** f co-operative. **~zi'one** f co-operatio

coordina'mento m co-ordinatio

coordi'na|re vt co-ordinate. **~ta** f (Math) coordinate. **~te bancarie** bank (account) details. **~zi'one** f co-ordination

co'perchio m lid; (copertura) cover

co'perta f blanket; (copertura) cover; (Naut) deck

coper'tina f cover; (di libro) dust-jacket

co'perto pp di **coprire** ● adj covered; (cielo) overcast ● m (a tavola) place; (prezzo del coperto) cover charge; **al ~** under cover

coper'tone m tarpaulin; (gomma) tyre

coper'tura f covering; (Comm, Fin) cover

'copia f copy; **bella/brutta ~** fair/rough copy; **~ carbone** carbon copy. **~ su carta** hardcopy. **copi'are** vt copy

copi'one m script

copi'oso adj plentiful

'coppa f (calice) goblet; (per gelato ecc) dish, Sport cup. **~ [di] gelato** ice-cream (served in a dish)

cop'petta f bowl; (di gelato) small tub

'coppia f couple; (in carte) pair

co'prente adj (cipria, vernice) covering

copri'capo m headgear

coprifu'oco m curfew

copri'letto m bedspread

copripiu'mino m duvet cover

co'prir|e vt cover; drown (suono); hold (carica). **~si** vr (vestirsi) cover up; fig cover oneself; (cielo): become overcast

coque f **alla ~** (uovo) soft-boiled

:o'raggio m courage; (sfacciataggine) nerve; **~o!** come on. **~'oso** adj courageous

co'rale adj choral

co'rallo m coral

co'rano m Koran

co'raz|za f armour; (di animali) shell. **~zata** f battleship. **~'zato** adj (nave) armour-clad

corbelle'ria f nonsense; (sproposito) blunder

'corda f cord; (Mus, spago) string; (fune) rope; (cavo) cable; **essere giù di ~** be depressed; **dare ~ a qcno** encourage sb. **corde vocali** vocal cords

cordi'al|e adj cordial ● m (bevanda) cordial; **~i saluti** best wishes. **~ità** f cordiality

'cordless m inv cordless phone

cor'doglio m grief; (lutto) mourning

cor'done m cord; (schieramento) cordon

core|ogra'fia f choreography. **~'ografo, -a** mf choreographer

cori'andoli mpl confetti sg

cori'andolo m (spezia) coriander

cori'car|e vt put to bed. **~si** vr go to bed

co'rista mf choir member

corna ▷**CORNO**

cor'nacchia f crow

corna'musa f bagpipes pl

cor'nett|a f (Mus) cornet; (del telefono) receiver. **~o** m (brioche) croissant

cor'ni|ce f frame. **~ci'one** m cornice

'corno m (pl f **corna**) horn; **fare le corna a qcno** be unfaithful to sb; **fare le corna** (per scongiuro) touch wood. **cor'nuto** adj horned ● m (ℤ: marito tradito) cuckold; (insulto) bastard

'coro m chorus; (Relig) choir

co'rolla f corolla

co'rona f crown; (di fiori) wreath; (rosario) rosary. **~'mento** m (di impresa) crowning. **coro'nare** vt crown; (sogno) fulfil

cor'petto m bodice

'corpo m body; (Mil, diplomatico) corps inv; **~ a ~** man to man; **andare**

di ~ move one's bowels. ~ **di ballo** corps de ballet. ~ **insegnante** teaching staff. ~ **del reato** incriminating item

corpo'rale adj corporal

corporati'vismo m corporatism

corpora'tura f build

corporazi'one f corporation

cor'poreo adj bodily

cor'poso adj full-bodied

corpu'lento adj stout

cor'puscolo m corpuscle

corre'dare vt equip

corre'dino m (per neonato) layette

cor'redo m (nuziale) trousseau

cor'reggere vt correct; lace (bevanda)

corre'lare vt correlate

cor'rente adj running; (in vigore) current; (frequente) everyday; (inglese ecc) fluent ●f current; (d'aria) draught; **essere al** ~ be up to date. ~'**mente** adv (parlare) fluently

'**correre** vi run; (affrettarsi) hurry; Sport race; (notizie:) circulate; ~ **dietro a** run after ●vt run; ~ **un pericolo** run a risk; **lascia** ~I don't bother!

corre|tta'mente adv correctly. **cor'retto** pp di **correggere** ●adj correct; (caffè) with a drop of alcohol. ~**zi'one** f correction

cor'rida f bullfight

corri'doio m corridor; (Aeron) aisle

corri'|dore, -'trice mf racer; (a piedi) runner

corri'era f coach, bus

corri'ere m courier; (posta) mail; (spedizioniere) carrier

corri'mano m bannister

corrispet'tivo m amount due

corrispon'den|te adj corresponding ●mf correspondent. ~**za** f correspondence; **scuola/corsi per** ~**za** correspondence course; **vendite per** ~**za** mail-order [shopping]. **corri-**

'**spondere** vi correspond; (stanza:) communicate; **corrispondere a** (contraccambiare) return

corri'sposto adj (amore) reciprocated

corrobo'rare vt strengthen; fig corroborate

cor'roder|e vt, ~**si** vr corrode

cor'rompere vt corrupt; (con denaro) bribe

corrosi'one f corrosion. **corro'sivo** adj corrosive

cor'roso pp di corrodere

cor'rotto pp di corrompere ●adj corrupt

corrucci'a|rsi vr be vexed. ~**to** adj upset

corru'gare vt wrinkle; ~ **la fronte** knit one's brows

corruzi'one f corruption; (con denaro) bribery

'**corsa** f running; (rapida) dash; Sport race; (di treno ecc) journey; **di** ~ at a run; **fare una** ~ run

cor'sia f gangway; (di ospedale) ward; (Auto) lane; (di supermercato) aisle

cor'sivo m italics pl

'**corso** pp di correre ●m course; (strada) main street; (Comm) circulation; **lavori in** ~ work in progress; **nel** ~ **di** during. ~ **d'acqua** watercourse

'**corte** f [court]yard; (Jur, regale) court; **fare la** ~ **a qcno** court sb. ~ **d'appello** court of appeal

cor'teccia f bark

corteggia'mento m courtship

corteggi'a|re vt court. ~**tore** m admirer

cor'teo m procession

cor'te|se adj courteous. ~'**sia** f courtesy; **per** ~**sia** please

cortigi'ano, -a mf courtier ●f courtesan

cor'tile m courtyard

cor'tina f curtain; (schermo) screen

'corto *adj* short; **essere a ∼ di** be short of. **∼ circuito** *m* short [circuit]

cortome'traggio *m Cinema* short

cor'vino *adj* jet-black

'corvo *m* raven

'cosa *f* thing; (*faccenda*) matter; *inter, rel* what; **[che] ∼** what; **nessuna ∼** nothing; **ogni ∼** everything; **per prima ∼** first of all; **tante cose** so many things; (*auguro*) all the best

'cosca *f* clan

'coscia *f* thigh; (*Culin*) leg

cosci'en|te *adj* conscious. **∼za** *f* conscience; (*consapevolezza*) consciousness

co'scritto *m* conscript. **∼zi'one** *f* conscription

così *adv* so; (*in questo modo*) like this, like that; (*perciò*) therefore; **le cose stanno ∼** that's how things are; **fermo ∼!** hold it; **proprio ∼!** exactly!; **basta ∼!** that will do!; **ah, è ∼?** it's like that, is it?; **∼ ∼** so-so; **e ∼ via** and so on; **per ∼ dire** so to speak; **più di ∼** any more; **una ∼ cara ragazza!** such a nice girl!; **è stato ∼ generoso da aiutarti** he was kind enough to help you ● *conj* (*allora*) so ● *adj inv* (*tale*) like that; **una ragazza ∼** a girl like that

cosicché *conj* and so

cosid'detto *adj* so-called

co'smesi *f* cosmetics

co'smetico *adj & m* cosmetic

cosmico *adj* cosmic

cosmo *m* cosmos

cosmopo'lita *adj* cosmopolitan

co'spargere *vt* sprinkle; (*disseminare*) scatter

co'spetto *m* **al ∼ di** in the presence of

co'spicuo *adj* conspicuous; (*somma ecc*) considerable

cospi'ra|re *vi* conspire. **∼tore**, **∼trice** *mf* conspirator. **∼zi'one** *f* conspiracy

'costa *f* coast; (*Anat*) rib

costà *adv* there

co'stan|te *adj & f* constant. **∼za** *f* constancy

co'stare *vi* cost; **quanto costa? how much is it?**

co'stata *f* chop

costeggi'are *vt* (*per mare*) coast; (*per terra*) skirt

co'stei *pers pron* ▷ **COSTUI**

costellazi'one *f* constellation

coster'nato *adj* dismayed. **∼zi'one** *f* consternation

costi'er|a *f* stretch of coast. **∼o** *adj* coastal

costi'pa|to *adj* constipated. **∼zi'one** *f* constipation; (*raffreddore*) bad cold

costitu'ir|e *vt* constitute; (*formare*) form; (*nominare*) appoint. **∼si** *vr* (*Jur*) give oneself up

costituzio'nale *adj* constitutional. **costituzi'one** *f* constitution; (*fondazione*) setting up

'costo *m* cost; **ad ogni ∼** at all costs; **a nessun ∼** on no account

'costola *f* rib; (*di libro*) spine

costo'letta *f* cutlet

co'storo *pron* ▷ **COSTUI**

co'stoso *adj* costly

co'stretto *pp di* **costringere**

co'strin|gere *vt* compel; (*stringere*) constrict. **∼t'tivo** *adj* coercive

costru'|ire *vt* build. **∼t'tivo** *adj* constructive. **∼zi'one** *f* construction

co'stui, **co'stei**, *pl* **co'storo** *pron* (*soggetto*) he, she, *pl* they; (*complemento*) him, her, *pl* them

co'stume *m* (*usanza*) custom; (*condotta*) morals *pl*; (*indumento*) costume. **∼ da bagno** swim-suit; (*da uomo*) swimming trunks

co'tenna *f* pigskin; (*della pancetta*) rind

coto'letta *f* cutlet

co'tone m cotton. ~ **idrofilo** cotton wool, absorbent cotton *Am*

'cottimo m **lavorare a** ~ a do piece-work

'cotto pp di **cuocere** ● adj done; (□: *infatuato*) in love; (□: *sbronzo*) drunk; **ben** ~ (*carne*) well done

'cotton fi'oc® m inv cotton bud

cot'tura f cooking

co'vare vt hatch; sicken for (*malattia*); harbour (*odio*) ● vi smoulder

'covo m den

co'vone m sheaf

'cozza f mussel

coz'zare vi ~ **contro** bump into. **'cozzo** m fig clash

C.P. abbr (Casella Postale) PO Box

'crampo m cramp

'cranio m skull

cra'tere m crater

cra'vatta f tie; (*a farfalla*) bow-tie

cre'anza f politeness; **mala** ~ bad manners

cre'a|re vt create; (*causare*) cause. ~**tività** f creativity. ~**tivo** adj creative. ~**to** m creation. ~**tore**, ~**trice** mf creator. ~**zi'one** f creation

crea'tura f creature; (*bambino*) baby; **povera** ~! poor thing!

cre'den|te mf believer. ~**za** f belief; (*Comm*) credit; (*mobile*) sideboard. ~**zi'ali** fpl credentials

'creder|e vt believe; (*pensare*) think ● vi ~ **e in** believe in; **credo di sì** I think so; **non ti credo** I don't believe you. ~**si** vr think oneself to be. **cre'dibile** adj credible. **credibilità** f credibility

'credi|to m credit; (*stima*) esteem; **comprare a** ~**to** buy on credit. ~**tore**, ~**trice** mf creditor

credulità f credulity

'credu|lo adj credulous. ~**lone**, **-a** mf simpleton

'crema f cream; (*di uova e latte*) custard. ~ **idratante** moisturizer. ~ **pasticciera** egg custard. ~ **solare** suntan lotion

cre'ma|re vt cremate. ~**'torio** m crematorium. ~**zi'one** f cremation

'crème cara'mel f crème caramel

creme'ria f dairy (*also selling ice cream and cakes*)

'crepa f crack

cre'paccio m cleft; (*di ghiacciaio*) crevasse

crepacu'ore m heart-break

crepa'pelle: **a** ~ adv fit to burst; **ridere a** ~ split one's sides with laughter

cre'pare vi crack; (□: *morire*) kick the bucket; ~ **dal ridere** laugh fit to burst

crepa'tura f crevice

crêpe f inv pancake

crepi'tare vi crackle

cre'puscolo m twilight

cre'scendo m crescendo

'cresc|ere vi grow; (*aumentare*) increase ● vt (*allevare*) bring up; (*aumentare*) increase. ~**ita** f growth; (*aumento*) increase. ~**i'uto** pp di **crescere**

'cresi|ma f confirmation. ~**'mare** vt confirm

'crespo adj frizzy ● m crêpe

'cresta f crest; (*cima*) peak

'creta f clay

'Creta f Crete

cre'tino, **-a** adj stupid ● mf idiot

cric m inv jack

cri'ceto m hamster

crimi'nal|e adj & mf criminal. ~**ità** f crime. **'crimine** m crime

crimi'noso adj criminal

'crin|e m horsehair. ~**i'era** f mane

'cripta f crypt

crisan'temo m chrysanthemum

'crisi f inv crisis; (*Med*) fit

cristal'lino m crystalline

cristalliz'zar|e vt, ~**si** vr crystallize; *fig*: (parola, espressione:) become part of the language

cri'stallo *m* crystal

Cristia'nesimo *m* Christianity

cristi'ano, -a *adj & mf* Christian

'Cristo *m* Christ; **un povero c~** a poor beggar

cri'terio *m* criterion; (*buon senso*) [common] sense

'criti|ca *f* criticism; (*recensione*) review. **criti'care** *vt* criticize. **~co** *adj* critical ● *m* critic. **~cone, -a** *mf* faultfinder

crivel'lare *vt* riddle (**di** with)

cri'vello *m* sieve

Cro'azia *f* Croatia

croc'cante *adj* crisp ● *m* type of crunchy nut biscuit

croc'chetta *f* croquette

'croce *f* cross; **a occhio e ~** roughly. **C~ Rossa** Red Cross

croce'via *m inv* crossroads *sg*

croci'ata *f* crusade

cro'cicchio *m* crossroads *sg*

croci'era *f* cruise; (*Archit*) crossing

croci'fi|ggere *vt* crucify. **~ssi'one** *f* crucifixion. **~sso** *pp di* **crocifiggere** ● *adj* crucified ● *m* crucifix

crogio'larsi *vr* bask

crogi[u]'olo *m* crucible; *fig* melting pot

crol'lare *vi* collapse; (*prezzi:*) slump. **'crollo** *m* collapse; (*dei prezzi*) slump

cro'mato *adj* chromium-plated. **'cromo** *m* chrome. **cromo'soma** *m* chromosome

'cronaca *f* chronicle; (*di giornale*) news; (*Radio, TV*) commentary; **fatto di ~** news item. **~ nera** crime news

'cronico *adj* chronic

cro'nista *mf* reporter

crono'logico *adj* chronological

crono'metrare *vt* time

cro'nometro *m* chronometer

'crosta *f* crust; (*di formaggio*) rind; (*di ferita*) scab; (*quadro*) daub

cro'staceo *m* shellfish

cro'stata *f* tart

cro'stino *m* croûton

crucci'arsi *vr* worry. **'cruccio** *m* worry

cruci'ale *adj* crucial

cruci'verba *m inv* crossword [puzzle]

cru'del|e *adj* cruel. **~tà** *f inv* cruelty

'crudo *adj* raw; (*rigido*) harsh

cru'ento *adj* bloody

cru'miro *m* blackleg, scab

'crusca *f* bran

cru'scotto *m* dashboard

'Cuba *f* Cuba

cu'betto *m* **~ di ghiaccio** ice cube

'cubico *adj* cubic

cubi'tal|e *adj* **a caratteri ~i** in enormous letters

'cubo *m* cube

cuc'cagna *f* abundance; (*baldoria*) merry-making; **paese della ~** land of plenty

cuc'cetta *f* (*su un treno*) couchette; (*Naut*) berth

cucchia'ino *m* teaspoon

cucchi'a|io *m* spoon; **al ~io** (*dolce*) creamy. **~i'ata** *f* spoonful

'cuccia *f* dog's bed; **fa la ~!** lie down!

cuccio'lata *f* litter

'cucciolo *m* puppy

cu'cina *f* kitchen; (*il cucinare*) cooking; (*cibo*) food; (*apparecchio*) cooker; **far da ~** cook; **libro di ~** cook[ery] book. **~ a gas** gas cooker

cuci'n|are *vt* cook. **~ino** *m* kitchenette

cu'ci|re *vt* sew; **macchina per ~re** sewing-machine. **~to** *m* sewing. **~'tura** *f* seam

cucù *m inv* cuckoo

'cuculo *m* cuckoo

'cuffia f bonnet; (da bagno) bathing-cap; (ricevitore) headphones pl

cu'gino, -a mf cousin

'cui pron rel (persona: con prep) who, whom fml; (cose, animali: con prep) which; (tra articolo e nome) whose; **la persona con ~ ho parlato** the person [who] I spoke to; **la ditta per ~ lavoro** the company I work for, the company for which I work; **l'amico il ~ libro è stato pubblicato** the friend whose book was published; **in ~** (dove) where; (quando) that; **per ~** (perciò) so; **la città in ~ vivo** the city I live in, the city where I live; **il giorno in ~ l'ho visto** the day [that] I saw him

culi'nari|a f cookery. **~o** adj culinary

'culla f cradle. **cul'lare** vt rock

culmi'na|nte adj culminating. **~re** vi culminate. **'culmine** m peak

'culto m cult; (Relig) religion; (adorazione) worship

cul'tu|ra f culture. **~ra generale** general knowledge. **~rale** adj cultural

cultu'ris|mo m body-building

cumula'tivo adj cumulative; **biglietto ~** group ticket

'cumulo m pile; (mucchio) heap; (nuvola) cumulus

'cuneo m wedge

cu'netta f gutter

cu'ocere vt/i cook; fire (ceramica)

cu'oco, -a mf cook

cu'oio m leather. **~ capelluto** scalp

cu'ore m heart; **cuori** pl (carte) hearts; **nel profondo del ~** in one's heart of hearts; **di [buon] ~** (persona) kind-hearted; **nel ~ della notte** in the middle of the night; **stare a ~ a qcno** be very important to sb

cupi'digia f greed

'cupo adj gloomy; (suono) deep

'cupola f dome

'cura f care; (amministrazione) management; (Med) treatment; **a ~ di** edited by; **in ~** under treatment. **~ dimagrante** diet. **cu'rante** adj **medico curante** GP, doctor

cu'rar|e vt take care of; (Med) treat; (guarire) cure; edit (testo). **~si** vr take care of oneself; (Med) follow a treatment; **~si di** (badare a) mind

cu'rato m parish priest

cura'tore, -'trice mf trustee; (di testo) editor

'curia f curia

curio's|are vi be curious; (mettere il naso) pry (in into); (nei negozi) look around. **~ità** f inv curiosity. **curi'oso** adj curious; (strano) odd

cur'sore m (Comput) cursor

'curva f curve; (stradale) bend. **~ a gomito** U-bend. **cur'vare** vt/i curve; (strada:) bend. **cur'varsi** vr bend. **'curvo** adj curved; (piegato) bent

cusci'netto m pad; (Mech) bearing

cu'scino m cushion; (guanciale) pillow. **~ d'aria** air cushion

'cuspide f spire

cu'stode m caretaker. **~e giudiziario** official receiver. **~ia** f care; (Jur) custody; (astuccio) case. **custo'dire** vt keep; (badare) look after

cu'taneo adj skin attrib

'cute f skin

Dd

da prep from; (con verbo passivo) by; (moto a luogo) to; (moto per luogo) through; (stato in luogo) at; (continuativo) for; (causale) with; (in qualità di) as; (con caratteristica) with; (come) like; (temporale) since, for

da si traduce con **for** quando si tratta di un periodo di tempo e con **since** quando si riferisce al momento in cui qualcosa è cominciato. Nota che in inglese si usa il passato prossimo invece del presente: **aspetto da mesi** I've been waiting for months; **aspetto da lunedì** I've been waiting since Monday

••••▸ **da Roma a Milano** from Rome to Milan; **staccare un quadro dalla parete** take a picture off the wall; **i bambini dai 5 ai 10 anni** children between 5 and 10; **vedere qcsa da vicino/lontano** see sth from up close/from a distance; **scritto da** written by; **andare dal panettiere** go to the baker's; **passo da te più tardi** I'll come over to your place later; **passiamo da qui** let's go this way; **un appuntamento dal dentista** an appointment at the dentist's; **il treno passa da Venezia** the train goes through Venice; **dall'anno scorso** since last year; **vivo qui da due anni** I've been living here for two years; **da domani** from tomorrow; **piangere dal dolore** cry with pain; **ho molto da fare** I have a lot to do; **occhiali da sole** sunglasses; **qualcosa da mangiare** something to eat; **un uomo dai capelli scuri** a man with dark hair; **è un oggetto da poco** it's not worth much; **l'ho fatto da solo** I did it by myself; **si è fatto da sé** he is a self-made man; **non è da lui** it's not like him

dac'capo adv again; (dall'inizio) from the beginning

dacché conj since

'dado m dice; (Culin) stock cube; (Techn) nut

daf'fare m work

'dagli = DA + GLI. **'dai** = DA + I

'dai int come on!

'daino m deer; (pelle) buckskin

dal = DA + IL. **'dalla** = DA + LA. **'dalle** = DA + LE. **'dallo** = DA + LO

'dalia f dahlia

dal'tonico adj colour-blind

'dama f lady; (nei balli) partner; (gioco) draughts sg

dami'gella f (di sposa) bridesmaid

damigi'ana f demijohn

dam'meno adv non essere ∼ (di qcno) be no less good (than sb)

da'naro m = DENARO

dana'roso adj (🗊: ricco) loaded

da'nese adj Danish ●mf Dane ●m (lingua) Danish

Dani'marca f Denmark

dan'na|re vt damn; **far ∼re qcno** drive sb mad. **∼to** adj damned. **∼zi'one** f damnation

danneggia'mento m damage. **∼'are** vt damage; (nuocere) harm

'danno m damage; (a persona) harm. **dan'noso** adj harmful

'danza f dance; (il danzare) dancing. **dan'zare** vi dance

dapper'tutto adv everywhere

dap'poco adj worthless

dap'prima adv at first

'dardo m dart

dar|e vt give; take (esame); have (festa); ∼ qcsa a qcno give sb sth; ∼ **da mangiare a qcno** give sb something to eat; ∼ **il benvenuto a qcno** welcome sb; ∼ **la buonanotte a qcno** say good night to sb; ∼ **del tu/del lei a qcno** address sb as "tu"/"lei"; ∼ **del cretino a qcno** call sb an idiot; ∼ **qcsa per scontato** take

sth for granted; **cosa danno alla TV stasera?** what's on TV tonight? ● vi
~ **nell'occhio** be conspicuous; ~ **alla testa** go to one's head; ~ **su** (finestra, casa): look on to; ~ **sui** o **ai nervi a qcno** get on sb's nerves ● m (Comm) debit. ~**si** vr (scambiarsi) give each other; ~**si da fare** get down to it; **si è dato tanto da fare!** he went to so much trouble; ~**si a** (cominciare) take up; ~**si al bere** take to drink; ~**si per** (malato) pretend to be; ~**si per vinto** give up; **può** ~**si** maybe

'**darsena** f dock

'**data** f date. ~ **di emissione** date of issue. ~ **di nascita** date of birth. ~ **di scadenza** cut-off date

da'ta|re vt date; **a** ~**re da** as from. ~**to** adj dated

'**dato** adj given; (dedito) addicted; ~ **che** given that ● m datum. ~ **di fatto** well-established fact; **dati** pl data. **da'tore** m giver. **datore, datrice** mf di lavoro employer

'**dattero** m date

dattilogra'f|are vt type. ~**ia** f typing. **datti'lografo, -a** mf typist

dat'torno adv **togliersi** ~ clear off

da'vanti adv before; (dirimpetto) opposite; (di fronte) in front ● adj inv front ● m front; ~ **a** prep in front of

da'vanzo adv more than enough

dav'vero adv really; **per** ~ in earnest; **dici** ~? honestly?

'**dazio** m duty; (ufficio) customs pl

d.C. abbr (dopo Cristo) AD

'**dea** f goddess

debel'lare vt defeat

debili'ta|nte adj weakening. ~**re** vt weaken. ~**rsi** vr become weaker

debita'mente adv duly

'**debito** adj due; **a tempo** ~**to** in due course ● m debt. ~**tore, ~'trice** mf debtor

'**debo|le** adj weak; (luce) dim; (suono) faint ● m weak point; (prefe-

renza) weakness. ~'**lezza** f weakness

debor'dare vi overflow

debosci'ato adj debauched

debut'ta|nte m (attore) actor making his début ● f actress making her début. ~**re** vi make one's début. **de'butto** m début

deca'den|te adj decadent. ~'**tismo** m decadence. ~**za** f decline; (Jur) loss. **deca'dere** vi lapse. **decadi'mento** m (delle arti) decline

decaffei'nato adj decaffeinated ● m decaffeinated coffee

decan'tare vt (lodare) praise

decapi'ta|re vt decapitate; behead (condannato). ~**zi'one** f decapitation; beheading

decappot'tabile adj convertible

de'ce|dere vi (morire) die. ~'**duto** adj deceased

decele'rare vt decelerate

decen'nale adj ten-yearly. **de'cennio** m decade

de'cen|te adj decent. ~**te'mente** adv decently. ~**za** f decency

decentra'mento m decentralization

de'cesso m death; **atto di** ~ death certificate

de'cider|e vt decide; settle (questione). ~**si** vr make up one's mind

deci'frare vt decipher; (documenti cifrati) decode

deci'male adj decimal

deci'mare vt decimate

'**decimo** adj tenth

de'cina f (Math) ten; **una** ~ **di** (circa dieci) about ten

decisa'mente adv definitely

decisio'nale adj decision-making

deci|si'one f decision. ~'**sivo** adj decisive. **de'ciso** pp di **decidere** ● adj decided

decla'ma|re vt/i declaim. ~'**torio** adj (stile) declamatory

declas'sare vt downgrade

decli'na|re vt decline; ~**re ogni responsabilità** disclaim all responsibility ● vi go down; (*tramontare*) set. ~**zi'one** f declension. **de'clino** m decline; **in declino** on the decline

decodificazi'one f decoding

decol'lare vi take off

décolle'té m inv décolleté

de'collo m take-off

decolo'ra|nte m bleach. ~**re** vt bleach

decolorazi'one f bleaching

decom'po|rre vt, ~**rsi** vr decompose. ~**sizi'one** f decomposition

deconcen'trarsi vr become distracted

deconge'lare vt defrost

decongestio'nare vt relieve congestion in

deco'ra|re vt decorate. ~**tivo** adj decorative. ~**to** adj (*ornato*) decorated. ~**tore**, ~**trice** mf decorator. ~**zi'one** f decoration

de'coro m decorum

decorosa'mente adv decorously. **decoroso** adj dignified

decor'renza f ~ **dal...** starting from...

de'correre vi pass; ~ **da** with effect from. **de'corso** pp di **decorrere** ● m passing; (*Med*) course

de'crepito adj decrepit

decre'scente adj decreasing. **de'crescere** vi decrease; (*prezzi:*) go down; (*acque:*) subside

decre'tare vt decree. **de'creto** m decree. **decreto legge** decree which has the force of law

'dedalo m maze

'dedica f dedication

dedi'car|e vt dedicate. ~**si** vr dedicate oneself

'dedi|to adj ~ **a** given to; (*assorto*) engrossed in; (*addicted to*) (*vizi*) ~**zi'one** f dedication

de'dotto pp di **dedurre**

dedu'cibile adj (*tassa*) allowable

de'du|rre vt deduce; (*sottrarre*) deduct. ~**t'tivo** adj deductive. ~**zi'one** f deduction

defal'care vt deduct

defe'rire vt (*Jur*) remit

defezi|o'nare vi (*abbandonare*) defect. ~**'one** f defection

defici'en|te adj (*mancante*) deficient; (*Med*) mentally deficient ● mf mental defective ~**za** f deficiency; (*lacuna*) gap; (*Med*) mental deficiency

'defici|t m inv deficit. ~**'tario** adj (*bilancio*) deficit attrib

defi'larsi vr (*scomparire*) slip away

défilé m inv fashion show

defi'ni|re vt define; (*risolvere*) settle. ~**tiva'mente** adv for good. ~**'tivo** adj definitive. ~**to** adj definite. ~**zi'one** f definition; (*soluzione*) settlement

deflazi'one f deflation

deflet'tore m (*Auto*) quarterlight

deflu'ire vi (*liquidi:*) flow away; (*persone:*) stream out

de'flusso m (*di marea*) ebb

defor'mar|e vt deform (*arto*); fig distort. ~**si** vr lose its shape. **de'form|e** adj deformed. ~**ità** f deformity

defor'ma|to adj warped. ~**zi'one** f (*di fatti*) distortion

defrau'dare vt defraud

de'funto, **-a** adj & mf deceased

degene'ra|re vi degenerate. ~**to** adj degenerate. ~**zi'one** f degeneration. **de'genere** adj degenerate

de'gen|te mf patient. ~**za** f confinement

'degli = **DI + GLI**

deglu'tire vt swallow

de'gnare vt ~ **qcno di uno sguardo** deign to look at sb

'degno adj worthy; (*meritevole*) deserving

degrada'mento m degradation

degra'da|re vt degrade. **~rsi** vr lower oneself; (città): fall into disrepair. **~zi'one** f degradation

de'grado m damage; **~ ambientale** m environmental damage

degu'sta|re vt taste. **~zi'one** f tasting

'dei = DI + I. **'del** = DI + IL

dela'tore, -'trice mf [police] informer. **~zi'one** f informing

'delega f proxy

dele'ga|re vt delegate. **~to** m delegate. **~zi'one** f delegation

dele'terio adj harmful

del'fino m dolphin; (stile di nuoto) butterfly [stroke]

de'libera f bylaw

delibe'ra|re vt/i deliberate; **~ su/in** rule on/in. **~to** adj deliberate

delicata'mente adv delicately

delica'tezza f delicacy; (fragilità) frailty; (tatto) tact

deli'cato adj delicate

delimi'tare vt delimit

deline'a|re vt outline. **~rsi** vr be outlined; fig take shape. **~to** adj defined

delin'quen|te mf delinquent. **~za** f delinquency

deli'rante adj (Med) delirious; (assurdo) insane

deli'rare vi be delirious. **de'lirio** m delirium; fig frenzy

de'litt|o m crime. **~u'oso** adj criminal

de'lizi|a f delight. **~'are** vt delight. **~'oso** adj delightful; (cibo) delicious

'della = DI + LA. **'delle** = DI + LE. **'dello** = DI + LO

delocaliz'zare vt relocate

'delta m inv delta

delta'plano m hang-glider; fare **~** go hang-gliding

delucidazi'one f clarification

delu'dente adj disappointing

de'lu|dere vt disappoint. **~si'one** f disappointment. **de'luso** adj disappointed

demar'ca|re vt demarcate. **~zi'one** f demarcation

de'men|te adj demented. **~za** f dementia. **~zi'ale** (assurdo) zany

demilitariz'za|re vt demilitarize. **~zi'one** f demilitarization

demistificazi'one f debunking

demo'cra|tico adj democratic. **~'zia** f democracy

democristi'ano, -a adj & mf Christian Democrat

demogra'fia f demography. **de·mo'grafico** adj demographic

demo'li|re vt demolish. **~zi'one** f demolition

'demone m demon. **de'monio** m demon

demoraliz'zar|e vt demoralize. **~si** vr become demoralized

de'mordere vi give up

demoti'vato adj demotivated

de'nari mpl (nelle carte) diamonds

de'naro m money

deni'gra|re vt denigrate. **~'torio** adj denigratory

denomi'na|re vt name. **~'tore** m denominator. **~zi'one** f denomination; **~zione di origine controllata** guarantee of a wine's quality

deno'tare vt denote

densità f inv density. **'denso** adj dense

den'ta|le adj dental. **~rio** adj dental. **~'ta** f bite. **~'tura** f teeth pl

'dente m tooth; (di forchetta) prong; **al ~** (Culin) slightly firm, ~ **del giudizio** wisdom tooth. **~ di latte** milk tooth. **denti'era** f false teeth pl

denti'fricio m toothpaste

den'tista mf dentist

'dentro adv in, inside; (in casa) indoors; da **~** from within; qui **~** in here ● prep in, inside; (di tempo) within, by ●m inside

denu'dar|e vt bare. **~si** vr strip

de'nunci|a, de'nunzia f denunciation; (alla polizia) report; (dei redditi) [income] tax return. **~'are** vt denounce; (accusare) report

denutrizi'one f malnutrition

deodo'rante adj & m deodorant

dépendance f inv outbuilding

depe'ri|bile adj perishable. **~'mento** m wasting away; (di merci) deterioration. **~re** vi waste away

depi'la|re vt depilate. **~rsi** vr shave (gambe); pluck (sopracciglia). **~'torio** m depilatory

deplo'rabile adj deplorable

deplo'r|are vt deplore; (dolersi di) grieve over. **~evole** adj deplorable

de'porre vt put down; lay (uova); (togliere da una carica) depose; (testimoniare) testify

depor'ta|re vt deport. **~to, -a** mf deportee. **~zi'one** f deportation

deposi'tar|e vt deposit; (lasciare in custodia) leave; (in magazzino) store. **~io, -a** mf (di segreto) repository. **~si** vr settle

de'posito m deposit; (luogo) warehouse; (Mil) depot. **~to bagagli** left-luggage office. **~zi'one** f deposition; (da una carica) removal

depra'va|re vt deprave. **~to** adj depraved

depre'ca|bile adj appalling. **~re** vt deprecate

depre'dare vt plunder

depressi'one f depression. **de'presso** pp di **deprimere** ●adj depressed

deprez'zar|e vt depreciate. **~si** vr depreciate

depri'mente adj depressing

de'primer|e vt depress. **~si** vr become depressed

depu'ra|re vt purify. **~'tore** m purifier

depu'ta|re vt delegate. **~to, -a** mf Member of Parliament, MP

deragli'a|mento m derailment

deragli'are vi go off the lines; **far ~** derail

'derby m inv Sport local Derby

deregolamentazi'one f deregulation

dere'litto adj derelict

dere'tano m backside, bottom

de'ri|dere vt deride. **~si'one** f derision. **~'sorio** adj derisory

deri'va|re vi **~re da** (provenire) derive from ●vt derive; (sviare) divert. **~zi'one** f derivation; (di fiume) diversion

dermato'lo'gia f dermatology. **derma'tologo, -a** mf dermatologist

'deroga f dispensation. **dero'gare** vi **derogare a** depart from

der'rat|a f merchandise. **~e alimentari** foodstuffs

deru'bare vt rob

descrit'tivo adj descriptive. **de'scritto** pp di **descrivere**

des'cri|vere vt describe. **~'vibile** adj describable. **~zi'one** f description

de'serto adj uninhabited ●m desert

deside'rabile adj desirable

deside'rare vt wish; (volere) want; (intensamente) long for; **desidera?** can I help you?; **lasciare a ~** leave a lot to be desired

desi'de'rio m wish; (brama) desire; (intenso) longing. **~'roso** adj desirous; (bramoso) longing

desi'gnare vt designate; (fissare) fix

de'sistere vi **~ da** desist from

'desktop 'publishing m desktop publishing

deso'la|re vt distress. **~to** desolate; (spiacente) sorry. **~zi'one** f desolation

'despota m despot

de'star|e vt waken; fig awaken. **~si**

vr waken; *fig* awaken

desti'na|re *vt* destine; (*nominare*) appoint; (*assegnare*) assign; (*indirizzare*) address. **~'tario** *m* addressee. **~zi'one** *f* destination; *fig* purpose

de'stino *m* destiny; (*fato*) fate

destitu|'ire *vt* dismiss. **~zi'one** *f* dismissal

'desto *adj liter* awake

'destra *f* (*parte*) right; (*mano*) right hand; **prendere a ~** turn right

destreggi'ar|e *vi*, **~si** *vr* manoeuvre

de'strezza *f* dexterity, skill

'destro *adj* right; (*abile*) skilful

detei'nato *adj* tannin-free

dete'n|ere *vt* hold; (*polizia:*) detain. **~uto, -a** *mf* prisoner. **~zi'one** *f* detention

deter'gente *adj* cleaning; (*latte, crema*) cleansing ● *m* detergent; (*per la pelle*) cleanser

deteriora'mento *m* deterioration

deterio'rar|e *vt* deteriorate. **~si** *vr* deteriorate

determi'nante *adj* decisive

determi'na|re *vt* determine. **~rsi** *vr* **~rsi a** resolve to. **~'tezza** *f* determination. **~'tivo** *adj* (*Gram*) definite. **~to** *adj* (*risoluto*) determined; (*particolare*) specific. **~zi'one** *f* determination; (*decisione*) decision

deter'rente *adj & m* deterrent

deter'sivo *m* detergent. **~ per i piatti** washing-up liquid

dete'stare *vt* detest, hate

deto'nare *vt* detonate

de'tra|rre *vt* deduct (**da** from). **~zi'one** *f* deduction

detri'mento *m* detriment; **a ~ di** to the detriment of

de'trito *m* debris

'detta *f* **a ~ di** according to

dettagli'ante *mf* retailer

dettagli'a|re *vt* detail. **~ta'mente** *adv* in detail

det'taglio *m* detail; **al ~** (*Comm*) retail

det'ta|re *vt* dictate. **~to m, ~'tura** *f* dictation

'detto *adj* said; (*chiamato*) called; (*soprannominato*) nicknamed; **~ fatto** no sooner said than done ● *m* saying

detur'pare *vt* disfigure

deva'sta|re *vt* devastate. **~to** *adj* devastated

devi'a|re *vi* deviate ● *vt* divert. **~zi'one** *f* deviation; (*stradale*) diversion

devitaliz'zare *vt* deaden (*dente*)

devo'lu|to *pp di* **devolvere** ● *adj* devolved. **~zi'one** *f* devolution

de'volvere *vt* devolve

de'vo|to *adj* devout; (*affezionato*) devoted. **~zi'one** *f* devotion

di *prep* of; (*partitivo*) some; (*scritto da*) by; (*parlare, pensare ecc*) about; (*con causa, mezzo*) with; (*con provenienza*) from; (*in comparazioni*) than; (*con infinito*) to; **la casa di mio padre/dei miei genitori** my father's house/my parents' house; **compra del pane** buy some bread; **hai del pane?** do you have any bread?; **un film di guerra** a war film; **piangere di dolore** cry with pain; **coperto di neve** covered with snow; **sono di Genova** I'm from Genoa; **uscire di casa** leave one's house; **più alto di te** taller than you; **è ora di partire** it's time to go; **crede di aver ragione** he thinks he's right; **dire di sì** say yes; **di domenica** on Sundays; **di sera** in the evening; **una pausa di un'ora** an hour's break; **un corso di due mesi** a two-month course

dia'bet|e *m* diabetes. **~ico, -a** *adj & mf* diabetic

dia'bolico adj diabolical

dia'dema m diadem; (di donna) tiara

di'afano adj diaphanous

dia'framma m diaphragm; (divisione) screen

di'agnos|i f inv diagnosis. **∼ti'care** vt diagnose

diago'nale adj & f diagonal

dia'gramma m diagram

dia'letto m dialect

Dialetto As Italy was not unified until 1861, standard Italian was slow to become widely used except by the cultural elite. As a result dialects are used by many Italians, with 60% using their dialect regularly. Ranging from Neapolitan and Sicilian to Milanese and Venetian, they vary considerably from each other. Tuscan dialects are the closest to standard Italian.

---

di'alogo m dialogue

dia'mante m diamond

di'ametro m diameter

di'amine int che **∼**... what on earth...

diaposi'tiva f slide

di'ario m diary

diar'rea f diarrhoea

di'avolo m devil

di'batt|ere vt debate. **∼ersi** vr struggle. **∼ito** m debate; (meno formale) discussion

dica'stero m office

di'cembre m December

dice'ria f rumour

dichia'ra|re vt state; (ufficialmente) declare. **∼rsi** vr **si dichiara innocente** he says he's innocent. **∼zi'one** f statement; (documento, di guerra) declaration

dician'nove adj & m nineteen

dicias'sette adj & m seventeen

dici'otto adj & m eighteen

dici'tura f wording

didasca'lia f (di film) subtitle; (di illustrazione) caption

di'dattico adj didactic; (televisione) educational

di'dentro adv inside

didi'etro adv behind ● m hum hindquarters pl

di'eci adj & m ten

die'cina = DECINA

'diesel adj & f inv diesel

di'esis m inv sharp

di'eta f diet; **essere a ∼** be on a diet. **die'tetico** adj diet. **die'tista** mf dietician. **die'tologo, -a** mf dietician

di'etro adv behind ● prep behind; (dopo) after ● adj back; (di zampe) hind ● m back; **le stanze di ∼** the back rooms

dietro'front m inv about-turn; fig U-turn

di'fatti adv in fact

di'fen|dere vt defend. **∼dersi** vr defend oneself. **∼siva** f **stare sulla ∼siva** be on the defensive. **∼'sivo** adj defensive. **∼'sore** m defender; **avvocato ∼sore** defence counsel

di'fes|a f defence; **prendere le ∼e di qcno** come to sb's defence. **∼o** pp di **difendere**

difet't|are vi be defective; **∼are di** lack. **∼ivo** adj defective

di'fet|to m defect; (morale) fault, flaw; (mancanza) lack; (in tessuto, abito) flaw; **essere in ∼to** be at fault; **far ∼to** be lacking. **∼'toso** adj defective; (abito) flawed

diffa'ma|re vt (con parole) slander; (per iscritto) libel. **∼'torio** adj slanderous; (per iscritto) libellous. **∼zi'one** f slander; (scritta) libel

diffe'ren|te adj different. **∼za** f difference; **a ∼za di** unlike; **non fare ∼za** make no distinction (**fra** between). **∼zi'ale** adj & m differential

differenzi'ar|e vt differentiate. **~si** vr ~si da differ from

diffe'ri|re vt postpone ●vi be different. **~ta f** in **~ta** (TV) prerecorded

dif'ficil|e adj difficult; (duro) hard; (improbabile) unlikely ●m difficulty. **~mente** adv with difficulty

difficoltà f inv difficulty

dif'fida f warning

diffi'd|are vi **~are di** distrust ●vt warn. **~ente** adj mistrustful. **~enza** f mistrust

dif'fonder|e vt spread; diffuse (calore, luce ecc). **~si** vr spread. **diffusi'one** f diffusion; (di giornale) circulation

dif'fu|so pp di **diffondere** ●adj common; (malattia) widespread; (luce) diffuse

difi'lato adv straight; (subito) straightaway

'diga f dam; (argine) dike

dige'ribile adj digestible

dige|'rire vt digest; 🖐 stomach. **~sti'one** f digestion. **~'stivo** adj digestive ●m digestive; (dopo cena) liqueur

digi'tale adj digital; (delle dita) finger attrib ●f (fiore) foxglove

digitaliz'zare vt digitize

digi'tare vt key in

digiu'nare vi fast

digi'uno m **essere ~** have an empty stomach ●m fast; a **~** (bere ecc) on an empty stomach

digni|tà f dignity. **~'tario** m dignitary. **~'toso** adj dignified

digressi'one f digression

digri'gnare vi **~ i denti** grind one's teeth

dila'gare vi flood; fig spread

dilani'are vt tear to pieces

dilapi'dare vt squander

dila'ta|re vt, **~rsi** vr dilate; (metallo, gas:) expand

dilazio'nabile adj postponable

dilazi|o'nare vt delay. **~'one** f delay

dilegu'ar|e vt disperse. **~si** vr disappear

di'lemma m dilemma

dilet'tante mf amateur

dilet'tare vt delight

di'letto, -a adj beloved ●m delight ●mf (persona) beloved

dili'gen|te adj diligent; (lavoro) accurate. **~za** f diligence

dilu'ire vt dilute

dilun'gar|e vt prolong. **~si** vr **~si su** dwell on (argomento)

diluvi'are vi pour [down]. **di'luvio** m downpour; fig flood

dima'gran|te adj slimming. **~i'mento** m weight loss. **~ire** vi slim

dime'nar|e vt wave; wag (coda). **~si** vr be agitated

dimensi'one f dimension; (misura) size

dimenti'canza f forgetfulness; (svista) oversight

dimenti'car|e vt, **~si** vr **~ [di]** forget. **dimentico** adj **dimentico di** (che non ricorda) forgetful of

di'messo pp di **dimettere** ●adj humble; (trasandato) shabby; (voce) low

dimesti'chezza f familiarity

di'metter|e vt dismiss; (da ospedale ecc) discharge. **~si** vr resign

dimez'zare vt halve

diminu'ire vt/i diminish; (in maglia) decrease. **~'tivo** adj & m diminutive. **~zi'one** f decrease; (riduzione) reduction

dimissi'oni fpl resignation sg; **dare le ~** resign

di'mo|ra f residence. **~'rare** vi reside

dimo'strante mf demonstrator

dimo'stra|re vt demonstrate; (provare) prove; (*mostrare*) show. **∼rsi** vr prove [to be]. **∼tivo** adj demonstrative. **∼zi'one** f demonstration; (*Math*) proof

di'namico, -a adj dynamic. **dina'mismo** m dynamism

dinami'tardo adj attentato **∼** bomb attack

dina'mite f dynamite

'dinamo f inv dynamo

di'nanzi adv in front ● prep **∼ a** in front of

dina'stia f dynasty

dini'ego m denial

dinocco'lato adj lanky

dino'sauro m dinosaur

din'torn|i mpl outskirts; **nei ∼i di** in the vicinity of. **∼o** adv around

'dio m (pl **'dei**) god; **D∼** God

di'ocesi f diocese

dipa'nare vt wind into a ball; *fig* unravel

diparti'mento m department

dipen'den|te adj depending ● mf employee. **∼za** f dependence; (*edificio*) annexe

di'pendere vi **∼ da** depend on; (*provenire*) derive from; **dipende** it depends

di'pinger|e vt paint; (*descrivere*) describe. **∼si** vr (*truccarsi*) make up. di'**pinto** pp di **dipingere** ● adj painted ● m painting

di'plom|a m diploma. **∼'marsi** vr graduate

diplo'matico adj diplomatic ● m diplomat; (*pasticcino*) millefeuille (*with alcohol*)

diplo'mato mf person with school-leaving qualification ● adj qualified

diploma'zia f diplomacy

di'porto m imbarcazione da **∼** pleasure craft

dira'dar|e vt thin out; make less frequent (*visite*). **∼si** vr thin out; (*nebbia:*) clear

dira'ma|re vt issue ● vi, **∼rsi** vr branch out; (*diffondersi*) spread. **∼zi'one** f (*di strada*) fork

'dire vt say; (*raccontare, riferire*) tell; **∼ quello che si pensa** speak one's mind; **voler ∼** mean; **volevo ben ∼!** I wondered!; **∼ di sì/no** say yes/ no; **si dice che...** rumour has it that...; **come si dice "casa" in inglese?** what's the English for "casa"?; **che ne dici di...?** how about...?; **non c'è che ∼** there's no disputing that; **e ∼ che...** to think that...; **a dir poco/tanto** at least/ most ● vi **∼ bene/male di** speak highly/ill of; **dica pure** how can I help you?; **dici sul serio?** are you serious?

diretta'mente adv directly

diret'tissima f per **∼** (*Jur*) omitting normal procedure

diret'tissimo m fast train

diret'tiva f directive

di'retto pp di **dirigere** ● adj direct. **∼ a** (*intoso*) meant for. **essere ∼ a** be heading for. **in diretta** (*trasmissione*) live ● m (*treno*) through train

diret'to|re, -'trice mf manager; manageress; (*di scuola*) headmaster; headmistress. **∼tore d'orchestra** conductor

direzi'one f direction; (*di società*) management; (*Sch*) headmaster's/ headmistress's office (*primary school*)

diri'gen|te adj ruling ● mf executive; (*Pol*) leader. **∼za** f management. **∼zi'ale** adj managerial

di'riger|e vt direct; conduct (*orchestra*); run (*impresa*). **∼si** vr **∼si verso** head for

dirim'petto adv opposite ● prep **∼ a** facing

di'ritto¹, dritto adj straight; (*destro*) right ● adv straight; **andare ∼** go straight on ● m right side; (*Tennis*) forehand

di'ritt|o² m right; (*Jur*) law. **∼i** pl

d'autore royalties
dirit'tura f straight line; fig honesty. ~ **d'arrivo** Sport home straight
diroc'cato adj tumbledown
dirom'pente adj fig explosive
dirot'ta|re vt reroute (treno, aereo); (illegalmente) hijack; divert (traffico) • vi alter course. ~'**tore**, ~'**trice** mf hijacker
di'rotto adj (pioggia) pouring; (pianto) uncontrollable; **piovere a** ~ rain heavily
di'rupo m precipice
dis'abile mf disabled person
disabi'tato adj uninhabited
disabitu'arsi vr ~ **a** get out of the habit of
disac'cordo m disagreement
disadat'tato, -a adj maladjusted • mf misfit
disa'dorno adj unadorned
disa'gevole adj (scomodo) uncomfortable
disagi'ato adj poor; (vita) hard
di'sagio m discomfort; (difficoltà) inconvenience; (imbarazzo) embarrassment; **sentirsi a** ~ feel uncomfortable; **disagi** pl (privazioni) hardships
disappro'va|re vt disapprove of. ~**zi'one** f disapproval
disap'punto m disappointment
disar'mante adj fig disarming
disar'mare vt/i disarm. **di'sarmo** m disarmament
disa'strato, -a adj devastated
di'sastro m disaster; (🔲: grande confusione) mess; (🔲: persona) disaster area. **disa'stroso** adj disastrous
disat'ten|to adj inattentive. ~**zi'one** f inattention; (svista) oversight
disatti'vare vt de-activate
disa'vanzo m deficit
disavven'tura f misadventure
dis'brigo m dispatch

dis'capito m **a** ~ **di** to the detriment of
dis'carica f scrap-yard
discen'den|te adj descending • mf descendant. ~**za** f descent; (discendenti) descendants pl
di'scendere vt/i descend; (dal treno) get off; (da cavallo) dismount; (sbarcare) land. ~ **da** (trarre origine da) be a descendant of
di'scepolo, -a mf disciple
di'scernere vt discern
di'sces|a f descent; (pendio) slope; ~**a in picchiata** (di aereo) nosedive; **essere in** ~**a** (strada:) go downhill. ~**a libera** (in sci) downhill race. **disce'sista** mf (sciatore) downhill skier. ~**o** pp di **discendere**
dis'chetto m (Comput) diskette
dischi'uder|e vt open; (svelare) disclose. ~**si** vr open up
disci'oglier|e vt, ~**si** vr dissolve; (fondersi) melt. **disci'olto** pp di **disciogliere**
disci'pli|na f discipline. ~'**nare** adj disciplinary ~'**nato** adj disciplined
'disco m disc; (Comput) disk; Sport discus; (Mus) record; **ernia del** ~ slipped disc. ~ **fisso** (Comput) hard disk. ~ **volante** flying saucer
discogra'fia f (insieme di incisioni) discography. **disco'grafico** adj (industria) recording; **casa discografica** recording company
'discolo mf rascal • adj unruly
discol'par|e vt clear. ~**si** vr clear oneself
disconnet'tersi vr go offline
disco'noscere vt disown (figlio)
discontinuità f (nel lavoro) irregularity. **discon'tinuo** adj intermittent; (rendimento) uneven
discor'dan|te adj discordant. ~**za** f mismatch
discor'dare vi (opinioni:) conflict. **dis'corde** adj clashing. **dis'cordia** f

discord; (*dissenso*) dissension

dis'cor|rere *vi* talk (**di** about). **~sivo** *adj* colloquial. **dis'corso** *pp di* **discorrere** ● *m* speech; (*conversazione*) talk

dis'costo *adj* distant ● *adv* far away; **stare ~** stand apart

disco'te|ca *f* disco; (*raccolta*) record library

discre'pan|te *adj* contradictory. **~za** *f* discrepancy

dis'cre|to *adj* discreet; (*moderato*) moderate; (*abbastanza buono*) fairly good. **~zi'one** *f* discretion; (*giudizio*) judgement; **a ~zione di** at the discretion of

discrimi'nante *adj* extenuating

discrimi'na|re *vt* discriminate. **~'torio** (*atteggiamento*) discriminatory. **~zi'one** *f* discrimination

discussi'one *f* discussion; (*alterco*) argument. **dis'cusso** *pp di* **discutere** ● *adj* controversial

dis'cutere *vt* discuss; (*formale*) debate; (*litigare*) argue; **~ sul prezzo** bargain. **discu'tibile** *adj* debatable; (*gusto*) questionable

disde'gnare *vt* disdain. **dis'degno** *m* disdain

dis'det|ta *f* retraction; (*sfortuna*) bad luck; (*Comm*) cancellation. **~o** *pp di* **disdire**

disdi'cevole *adj* unbecoming

dis'dire *vt* retract; (*annullare*) cancel

diseduca'tivo *adj* boorish

dise'gna|re *vt* draw; (*progettare*) design. **~'tore**, **~'trice** *mf* designer. **di'segno** *m* drawing; (*progetto, linea*) design

diser'bante *m* herbicide ● *adj* herbicidal

disere'da|re *vt* disinherit ● *mf* i **~ti** the dispossessed

diser'|tare *vt/i* desert; **~tare la scuola** stay away from school. **~'tore** *m* deserter. **~zi'one** *f* desertion

disfaci'mento *m* decay

dis'fa|re *vt* undo; strip (*letto*); (*smantellare*) take down; (*annientare*) defeat; **~re le valigie** unpack [one's bags]. **~rsi** *vr* fall to pieces; (*sciogliersi*) melt; **~rsi di** (*liberarsi di*) get rid of; **~rsi in lacrime** dissolve into tears. **~tta** *f* defeat. **~tto** *adj fig* worn out

disfat'tis|mo *m* defeatism. **~ta** *adj & mf* defeatist

disfunzi'one *f* disorder

dis'gelo *m* thaw

dis'grazi|a *f* misfortune; (*incidente*) accident; (*sfavore*) disgrace. **~ata'mente** *adv* unfortunately. **~'ato, -a** *adj* unfortunate ● *mf* wretch

disgre'gar|e *vt* break up. **~si** *vr* disintegrate

disgu'ido *m* **~ postale** mistake in delivery

disgu'st|are *vt* disgust. **~arsi** **~arsi di** be disgusted by. **dis'gusto** *m* disgust. **~oso** *adj* disgusting

disidra'ta|re *vt* dehydrate. **~to** *adj* dehydrated

disil'lu|dere *vt* disenchant. **~si'one** *f* disenchantment. **~so** *adj* disillusioned

disimbal'lare *vt* unpack

disimpa'rare *vt* forget

disimpe'gnar|e *vt* release; (*compiere*) fulfil; redeem (*oggetto dato in pegno*). **~si** *vr* disengage oneself; (*cavarsela*) manage. **disim'pegno** *m* (*locale*) vestibule

disincan'tato *adj* (*disilluso*) disillusioned

disinfe'sta|re *vt* disinfest. **~zi'one** *f* disinfestation

disinfet'tante *adj & m* disinfectant

disinfet't|are *vt* disinfect. **~zi'one** *f* disinfection

disinfor'mato *adj* uninformed

disini'bito *adj* uninhibited

disinne'scare *vt* defuse (*mina*). **di-**

sin'nesco m (di bomba) bomb disposal

disinse'rire vt disconnect

disinte'gra|re vt, ~rsi vr disintegrate. ~zi'one f disintegration

disinteres'sarsi vr ~ di take no interest in. disinte'resse m indifference; (oggettività) disinterestedness

disintossi'ca|re vt detoxify. ~rsi vr come off drugs. ~zi'one f giving up alcohol/drugs

disin'volto adj natural. disinvol'tura f confidence

disles'sia f dyslexia

disli'vello m difference in height; fig inequality

dislo'care vt (Mil) post

dismi'sura f excess; a ~ excessively

disobbedi'ente adj disobedient

disobbe'dire vt disobey

disoccu'pa|to, -a adj unemployed ● mf unemployed person. ~zi'o-ne f unemployment

disonestà f dishonesty. diso'nesto adj dishonest

disono'rare vt dishonour. diso'nore m dishonour

di'sopra adv above ● adj upper ● m top

disordi'na|re vt disarrange. ~ta-'mente adv untidily. ~to adj untidy; (sregolato) immoderate. di'sordine m disorder

disorganiz'za|re vt disorganize. ~to adj disorganized. ~zi'one f disorganization

disorienta'mento m disorientation

disorien'ta|re vt disorientate. ~rsi vr lose one's bearings. ~to adj fig bewildered

di'sotto adv below ● adj lower ● m bottom

dis'paccio m dispatch

dispa'rato adj disparate

'dispari adj odd. ~tà f inv disparity

dis'parte adv in ~ apart; stare in ~ stand aside

dis'pendi|o m (spreco) waste. ~'oso adj expensive

dis'pen|sa f pantry; (distribuzione) distribution; (mobile) cupboard; (Jur) exemption; (Relig) dispensation; (pubblicazione periodica) number. ~'sare vt distribute; (esentare) exonerate

dispe'ra|re vi despair (di of). ~rsi vr despair. ~ta'mente (piangere) desperately. ~to adj desperate. ~zi'one f despair

dis'per|dere vt, ~dersi vr disperse. ~si'one f dispersion; (di truppe) dispersal. ~'sivo adj disorganized. ~so pp di disperdere ● adj scattered; (smarrito) lost ● m missing soldier

dis'pet|to m spite; a ~to di in spite of. ~'toso adj spiteful

dispia'c|ere m upset; (rammarico) regret; (dolore) sorrow; (preoccupazione) worry ● vi mi dispiace I'm sorry; non mi dispiace I don't dislike it; se non ti dispiace if you don't mind. ~i'uto adj upset; (dolente) sorry

dispo'nibil|e adj available; (gentile) helpful. ~ità f availability; (gentilezza) helpfulness

dis'por|re vt arrange ● vi dispose; (stabilire) order; ~re di have at one's disposal. ~si vr line up

disposi'tivo m device

disposizi'one f disposition; (ordine) order; (libera disposizione) disposal. di-s'posto pp di disporre ● adj ready; (incline) disposed; essere ben disposto verso be favourably disposed towards

di'spotico adj despotic

dispregia'tivo adj disparaging

disprez'zare vt despise. dis'prezzo m contempt

'disputa f dispute

dispu'tar|e vi dispute; (gareggiare)

compete. ~**si** vr ~**si** qcsa contend for sth

dissacra'torio adj debunking

dissangua'mento m loss of blood

dissangua're vt, ~**rsi** vr bleed. ~**rsi** vr fig become impoverished. ~**to** adj bloodless; fig impoverished

dissa'pore m disagreement

dissec'car|e vt, ~**si** vr dry up

dissemi'nare vt disseminate; (notizie) spread

dis'senso m dissent; (disaccordo) disagreement

dissente'ria f dysentery

dissen'tire vi disagree (da with)

dissertazi'one f dissertation

disser'vizio m poor service

disse'sta|re vt upset; (Comm) damage. ~**to** adj (strada) uneven. **disse'sto** m ruin

disse'tante adj thirst-quenching

disse'ta|re vt ~**rsi** vr quench sb's thirst

dissi'dente adj & mf dissident

dis'sidio m disagreement

dis'simile adj unlike, dissimilar

dissimu'lare vt conceal; (fingere) dissimulate

dissi'pa|re vt dissipate; (sperperare) squander. ~**rsi** vr (nebbia:) clear; (dubbio:) disappear. ~**to** adj dissipated. ~**zi'one** f squandering

dissoci'ar|e vt, ~**si** vr dissociate

disso'dare vt till

dis'solto pp di dissolvere

disso'luto adj dissolute

dis'solver|e vt, ~**si** vr dissolve; (disperdere) dispel

disso'nanza f dissonance

dissua'|dere vt dissuade. ~**si'one** f dissuasion. ~**sivo** adj dissuasive

distac'car|e vt detach; Sport leave behind. ~**si** vr be detached. **di'stacco** m detachment; (separazione)

separation; Sport lead

di'stan|te adj far away; fig: (person) detached ●adv far away ~**za** f distance. ~**zi'are** vt space out; Sport outdistance

di'stare vi be distant; quanto dista? how far is it?

di'sten|dere vt stretch out (parte del corpo); (spiegare) spread; (deporre) lay. ~**dersi** vr stretch; (sdraiarsi) lie down; (rilassarsi) relax. ~**si'one** f stretching; (rilassamento) relaxation; (Pol) détente. ~**sivo** adj relaxing

di'steso, -a pp di distendere ●f expanse

distil'l|are vt/i distil. ~**azi'one** f distillation. ~**e'ria** f distillery

di'stinguer|e vt distinguish. ~**si** vr distinguish oneself. **distin'guibile** adj distinguishable

di'stinta f (Comm) list. ~ **di pagamento** receipt. ~ **di versamento** paying-in slip

distinta'mente adv individually; (chiaramente) clearly

distin'tivo adj distinctive ●m badge

di'stin|to, -a pp di distinguere ●adj distinct; (signorile) distinguished; ~**ti saluti** Yours faithfully. ~**zi'one** f distinction

di'stogliere vt ~ **da** remove from; (dissuadere) dissuade from. **di'stolto** pp di distogliere

di'storcere vt twist

distorsi'one f (Med) sprain; (alterazione) distortion

di'stra|rre vt distract; (divertire) amuse. ~**rsi** vr get distracted; (svagarsi) amuse oneself; non ti distrarre! pay attention!. ~**tta'mente** adv absently. ~**tto** pp di distrarre ●adj absent-minded; (disattento) inattentive. ~**zi'one** f absent-mindedness; (errore) inattention; (svago) amusement

d

di'stretto m district

distribu|'ire vt distribute; (disporre) arrange; deal (carte). ~**tore** m distributor; (di benzina) petrol pump; (automatico) slot-machine. ~**zi'one** f distribution

distri'car|e vt disentangle; ~**si** fig get out of it

di'stru|ggere vt destroy. ~**t'tivo** adj destructive; (critica) negative. ~**tto** pp di distruggere. ~**zi'one** f destruction

distur'bar|e vt disturb; (sconvolgere) upset. ~**si** vr trouble oneself. **di'sturbo** m bother; (indisposizione) trouble; (Med) problem; (Radio, TV) interference; **disturbi** pl (Radio, TV) static. **disturbi di stomaco** stomach trouble

disubbidi'en|te adj disobedient. ~**za** f disobedience

disubbi'dire vi ~ **a** disobey

disugu|agli'anza f disparity. ~**ale** adj unequal; (irregolare) irregular

di'suso m **cadere in** ~ fall into disuse

di'tale m thimble

di'tata f poke; (impronta) finger-mark

'dito m (pl **di'dita**) finger; (di vino) finger. ~ **del piede** toe

'ditta f firm

dit'tafono m dictaphone

ditta'tor|e m dictator. ~**i'ale** adj dictatorial. **ditta'tura** f dictatorship

dit'tongo m diphthong

di'urno adj daytime; **spettacolo** ~ matinée

'diva f diva

divaga're vi digress. ~**zi'one** f digression

divam'pare vi burst into flames; fig spread like wildfire

di'vano m sofa. ~ **letto** sofa bed

divari'care vt open

di'vario m discrepancy; **un** ~ **di**

opinioni a difference of opinion

dive'n|ire vi = DIVENTARE. ~**uto** pp di divenire

diven'tare vi become; (lentamente) grow; (rapidamente) turn

di'verbio m squabble

diver'gen|te adj divergent. ~**za** f divergence; ~**za di opinioni** difference of opinion. **di'vergere** vi diverge

diversa'mente adv otherwise; (in modo diverso) differently

diversifi'ca|re vt diversify. ~**rsi** vr differ. ~**zi'one** f diversification

diver|si'one f diversion. ~**sità** f inv difference. ~**sivo** m diversion. **di'verso** adj different; **diversi** pl (parecchi) several ● pron several [people]

diver'tente adj amusing. **diverti'mento** m amusement

diver'tir|e vt amuse. ~**si** vr enjoy oneself

divi'dendo m dividend

di'vider|e vt divide; (condividere) share. ~**si** vr (separarsi) separate

di'vieto m prohibition; ~ **di sosta** no parking

divinco'larsi vr wriggle

divinità f inv divinity. **di'vino** adj divine

di'visa f uniform; (Comm) currency

divisi'one f division

di'vismo m worship; (atteggiamento) superstar mentality

di'vi|so pp di dividere. ~**'sore** m divisor. ~**'sorio** adj dividing

'divo, -a mf star

divo'rar|e vt devour. ~**si** vr ~**si da** be consumed with

divorzi'a|re vi divorce. ~**to, -a** mf divorcee. **di'vorzio** m divorce

divul'ga|re vt divulge; (rendere popolare) popularize. ~**rsi** vr spread. ~**tivo** adj popular. ~**zi'one** f popularization

dizio'nario m dictionary

dizi'one f diction

do m (Mus) C

>
> **DOC** Italian wines which are grown in certain specified areas and which conform to certain regulations may be styled DOC (Denominazione di Origine Controllata). The classification DOCG (Denominazione di Origine Controllata e Garantita) is awarded to DOC wines of particular quality. Wines must conform to the DOC criteria for at least five years before they can be classified as DOCG.

'**doccia** f shower; (grondaia) gutter; **fare la ~** have a shower

do'cen|te adj teaching ● mf teacher; (Univ) lecturer. **~za** f (Univ) lecturer's qualification

'**docile** adj docile

documen'tar|e vt document. **~si** vr gather information (su about)

documen'tario adj & m documentary

documen'ta|to adj well-documented; (persona) well-informed. **~zi'one** f documentation

docu'mento m document

dodi'cesimo adj & m twelfth. '**dodici** adj & m twelve

do'gan|a f customs pl; (dazio) duty. **doga'nale** adj customs. **~i'ere** m customs officer

'**doglie** fpl labour pains

'**dogma** m dogma. **dog'matico** adj dogmatic. **~'tismo** m dogmatism

'**dolce** adj sweet; (clima) mild; (voce, consonante) soft; (acqua) fresh ● m (portata) dessert; (torta) cake; **non mangio dolci** I don't eat sweet things. **~'mente** adv sweetly. **dol'cezza** f sweetness; (di clima) mildness

dolce'vita adj inv (maglione) rollneck

dolci'ario adj confectionery

dolci'astro adj sweetish

dolcifi'cante m sweetener ● adj sweetening

dolci'umi mpl sweets

do'lente adj painful; (spiacente) sorry

do'le|re vi ache, hurt; (dispiacere) regret. **~rsi** vr regret; (protestare) complain; **~rsi di** be sorry for

'**dollaro** m dollar

'**dolo** m (Jur) malice; (truffa) fraud

Dolo'miti fpl **le ~** the Dolomites

do'lore m pain; (morale) sorrow. **do'loroso** adj painful

do'loso adj malicious

do'manda f question; (richiesta) request; (scritta) application; (Comm) demand; **fare una ~ (a qcno)** ask (sb) a question. **~ di impiego** job application

doman'dar|e vt ask; (esigere) demand; **~e qcsa a qcno** ask sb for sth. **~si** vr wonder

do'mani adv tomorrow; **~ sera** tomorrow evening ● m **il ~** the future; **a ~** see you tomorrow

do'ma|re vt tame; fig control (emozioni). **~tore** m tamer

domat'tina adv tomorrow morning

do'meni|ca f Sunday. **~cale** adj Sunday attrib

do'mestico, -a adj domestic ● m servant ● f maid

domicili'are adj **arresti domiciliari** (Jur) house arrest

domicili'arsi vr settle

domi'cilio m domicile; (abitazione) home; **recapitiamo a ~** we do home deliveries

domi'na|re vt dominate; (controllare) control ● vi rule over; (prevalere) be dominant. **~rsi** vr control oneself. **~'tore**, **~'trice** mf ruler; **~zi'one** f domination

do'minio m control; (*Pol*) dominion; (*ambito*) field; **di ~ pubblico** common knowledge

don m inv (*ecclesiastico*) Father

do'na|re vt give; donate (sangue, organo) ●vi **~re a** (*giovare esteticamente*) suit. **~'tore**, **~'trice** mf donor. **~zi'one** f donation

dondo'l|are vt swing; (*cullare*) rock ●vi sway. **~arsi** vr swing. **~io** m rocking. **'dondolo** m swing; **cavallo/sedia a dondolo** rocking-horse/chair

dongio'vanni m inv Romeo

'donna f woman. **~ di servizio** domestic help

don'naccia f pej whore

'dono m gift

'dopo prep after; (*a partire da*) since ●adv afterwards; (*più tardi*) later; (*in seguito*) later on; **~ di me** after me

dopo'barba m inv aftershave

dopo'cena m inv evening

dopodiché adv after which

dopodo'mani adv the day after tomorrow

dopogu'erra m inv post-war period

dopo'pranzo m inv afternoon

dopo'sci adj & nm inv après-ski

doposcu'ola m inv after-school activities pl

dopo-'shampoo m inv conditioner ●adj inv conditioning

dopo'sole m inv aftersun cream ●adj inv aftersun

dopo'tutto adv after all

doppi'aggio m dubbing

doppia'mente adv doubly

doppi'a|re vt double; Sport lap; Cinema dub. **~'tore**, **~'trice** mf dubber

'doppio adj & adv double. **~ clic** m (*Comput*) double click. **~ fallo** m Tennis double fault. **~ gioco** m double-dealing. **~ mento** m double chin. **~ senso** m double entendre. **doppi**

vetri mpl double glazing ●m double; Tennis doubles pl. **~ misto** Tennis mixed doubles

doppi'one m duplicate

doppio'petto adj double-breasted

dop'pista mf doubles player

do'ra|re vt gild; (*Culin*) brown. **~to** adj gilt; (*color oro*) golden. **~'tura** f gilding

dormicchi'are vi doze

dormigli'one, **-a** mf sleepyhead; fig lazy-bones

dor'mi|re vi sleep; (*essere addormentato*) be asleep; fig be asleep. **~ta** f good sleep. **~'tina** f nap. **~'torio** m dormitory

dormi'veglia m essere in **~** be half asleep

dor'sale adj dorsal ●f (*di monte*) ridge

'dorso m back; (*di libro*) spine; (*di monte*) crest; (*nel nuoto*) backstroke

do'saggio m dosage

do'sare vt dose; fig measure; **~ le parole** weigh one's words

dosa'tore m measuring jug

'dose f dose; **in buona ~** fig in good measure. **~ eccessiva** overdose

dossi'er m inv file

'dosso m (*dorso*) back; **levarsi di ~ gli abiti** take off one's clothes

do'ta|re vt endow; (*di accessori*) equip. **~to** adj (*persona*) gifted; (*fornito*) equipped. **~zi'one** f (*attrezzatura*) equipment; **in ~zione** at one's disposal

'dote f dowry; (*qualità*) gift

'dotto adj learned ●m scholar; (*Anat*) duct

dotto'rato m doctorate. **dot'tore**, **~'ressa** mf doctor

dot'trina f doctrine

'dove adv where; **di ~ sei?** where do you come from; **fin ~?** how far?;

per ~? which way?

do'vere vi (obbligo) have to, must; **devo andare** I have to go, I must go; **devo venire anch'io?** do I have to come too?; **avresti dovuto dirmelo** you should have told me, you ought to have told me; **devo sedermi un attimo** I must sit down for a minute, I need to sit down for a minute; **dev'essere successo qualcosa** something must have happened; **come si deve** properly ● vt (essere debitore di, derivare) owe; **essere dovuto** a be due to ● m duty; **per ~** out of duty. **dove'roso** adj only right and proper

do'vunque adv (dappertutto) everywhere; (in qualsiasi luogo) anywhere ● conj wherever

do'vuto adj due; (debito) proper

doz'zi|na f dozen. ~'nale adj cheap

dra'gare vt dredge

'drago m dragon

'dramm|a m drama. **dram'matico** adj dramatic. ~atiz'zare vt dramatize. ~a'turgo m playwright. **dram'mone** m (film) tear-jerker

drappeggi'are vt drape. **drap'peggio** m drapery

drap'pello m (Mil) squad; (gruppo) band

'drastico adj drastic

dre'nare vt drain

drib'blare vt (in calcio) dribble

'dritta f (mano destra) right hand; (Naut) starboard; (informazione) pointer, tip; **a ~ e a manca** left, right and centre

'dritto adj = DIRITTO¹ ● mf ① crafty so-and-so

driz'zar|e vt straighten; (rizzare) prick up. ~**si** vr straighten [up]; (alzarsi) raise

'dro|ga f drug. ~'gare vt drug. ~'garsi** vr take drugs. ~'gato, -a mf drug addict

drogh|e'ria f grocery. ~i'ere, -a mf grocer

'dubbi|o adj doubtful; (ambiguo) dubious ● m doubt; (sospetto) suspicion; **mettere in ~o** doubt; **essere fuori ~o** be beyond doubt; **essere in ~o** be doubtful. ~'oso adj doubtful

dubi'ta|re vi doubt; ~**re di** doubt; (diffidare) mistrust; **dubito che venga** I doubt whether he'll come. ~'tivo adj ambiguous

'duca, du'chessa mf duke; duchess

'due adj & m two

due'cento adj & m two hundred

du'ello m duel

due'mila adj & m two thousand

due'pezzi m inv (bikini) bikini

du'etto m duo; (Mus) duet

'duna f dune

'dunque conj therefore; (allora) well [then]

'duo m inv duo; (Mus) duet

du'omo m cathedral

dupli'ca|re vt duplicate. ~**to m** duplicate. **'duplice** adj double; **in duplice** in duplicate

dura'mente adv (lavorare) hard; (rimproverare) harshly

du'rante prep during

du'r|are vi last; (cibo) keep; (resistere) hold out. ~**ata** f duration. ~**a'turo, ~evole** adj lasting, enduring

du'rezza f hardness; (di carne) toughness; (di voce, padre) harshness

'duro, -a adj hard; (persona, carne) tough; (voce) harsh; (pane) stale ● mf tough person

du'rone m hardened skin

'duttile adj (materiale) ductile; (carattere) malleable

DVD m inv DVD

Ee

e, ed *conj* and

'ebano *m* ebony

eb'bene *conj* well [then]

eb'brezza *f* inebriation; (*euforia*) elation; **guida in stato di ~** drink-driving. **'ebbro** *adj* inebriated; (*di gioia*) ecstatic

'ebete *adj* stupid

ebollizi'one *f* boiling

e'braico *adj* Hebrew ●*m* (*lingua*) Hebrew. **e'breo, -a** *adj* Jewish ●*mf* Jew

eca'tombe *f* fare un'~ wreak havoc

ecc *abbr* (eccetera) etc

ecce'den|te *adj* (peso, bagaglio) excess. **~za** *f* excess; (d'avanzo) surplus; **avere qcsa in ~za** have an excess of sth; **bagagli in ~za** excess baggage. **~za di cassa** surplus. **ec-'cedere** *vt* exceed ●*vi* go too far; **eccedere nel bere** drink too much

eccel'len|te *adj* excellent. **~za** *f* excellence; (titolo) Excellency; **per ~za** par excellence. **ec'cellere** *vi* excel (**in** at)

ec'centrico, -a *adj* & *mf* eccentric

eccessiva'mente *adv* excessively. ●**ecces'sivo** *adj* excessive

ec'cesso *m* excess; **andare agli eccessi** go to extremes; **all'~** to excess. **~ di velocità** speeding

ec'cetera *adv* et cetera

ec'cetto *prep* except; **~ che** (a meno che) unless. **eccettu'are** *vt* except

eccezio'nal|e *adj* exceptional. **~'mente** *adv* exceptionally; (contrariamente alla regola) as an exception

eccezi'one *f* exception; (Jur) objection; **a ~ di** with the exception of

eccita'mento *m* excitement. **ecci-'tante** *adj* exciting; (sostanza) stimulant ●*m* stimulant

ecci'ta|re *vt* excite. **~rsi** *vr* get excited. **~to** *adj* excited

eccitazi'one *f* excitement

ecclesi'astico *adj* ecclesiastical ●*m* priest

'ecco *adv* (qui) here; (là) there; **~!** exactly!; **~ fatto** there we are; **~ la tua borsa** here is your bag; **~ [il] mio figlio** there is my son; **~mi** here I am; **~ tutto** that is all

ec'come *adv* & *int* and how!

echeggi'are *vi* echo

e'clissi *f inv* eclipse

'eco *f* (pl m echi) echo

ecogra'fia *f* scan

ecolo'gia *f* ecology. **eco'logico** *adj* ecological; (prodotto) environmentally friendly

e commerci'ale *f* ampersand

econo'mia *f* economy; (scienza) economics; **fare ~ia** economize (di on). **eco'nomico** *adj* economic; (a buon prezzo) cheap. **~ista** *mf* economist. **~iz'zare** *vt/i* economize; save (tempo, denaro). **e'conomo, -a** *adj* thrifty ●*mf* (di collegio) bursar

é'cru *adj inv* raw

ec'zema *m* eczema

ed *conj* vedi **e**

'edera *f* ivy

e'dicola *f* [newspaper] kiosk

edifi'cabile *adj* (area, terreno) classified as suitable for development

edifi'cante *adj* edifying

edifi'care *vt* build

edi'ficio *m* building; fig structure

e'dile *adj* building attrib

edi'lizi|a *f* building trade. **~o** *adj* building attrib

edi'tore, -'trice *adj* publishing ●*mf* publisher; (curatore) editor. **~to'ria** *f* publishing. **~tori'ale** *adj* publishing ●*m* editorial

edizi'one *f* edition; (di manifestazione)

performance. ~ **ridotta** abridg[e]ment. ~ **della sera** (di telegiornale) evening news

edu'ca|re vt educate; (allevare) bring up. ~'**tivo** adj educational. ~**to** adj polite. ~'**tore**, ~'**trice** mf educator. ~**zi'one** f education; (di bambini) upbringing; (buone maniere) [good] manners pl. ~**zione fisica** physical education

e'felide f freckle

effemi'nato adj effeminate

efferve'scente adj effervescent; (frizzante) fizzy; (aspirina) soluble

effettiva'mente adv è troppo tardi – ~ it's too late – so it is

effet'tivo adj actual; (efficace) effective; (personale) permanent; (Mil) regular ● m sum total

ef'fett|o m effect; (impressione) impression; **in** ~**i** in fact; ~**i personali** personal belongings. ~**u'are** vt carry out (controllo, sondaggio). ~**u'arsi** vr take place

effi'cac|e adj effective. ~**ia** f effectiveness

effici'en|te adj efficient. ~**za** f efficiency

ef'fimero adj ephemeral

effusi'one f effusion

E'geo m **l'**~ the Aegean [Sea]

E'gitto m Egypt. **egizi'ano, -a** agg & mf Egyptian

'egli pers pron he; ~ **stesso** he himself

ego'centrico, -a adj egocentric

ego'is|mo m selfishness. ~**ta** adj selfish ● mf selfish person. ~**tico** adj selfish

e'gregio adj distinguished; **E**~ **Signore** Dear Sir

eiaculazi'one f ejaculation

elabo'ra|re vt elaborate; process (dati). ~**to** adj elaborate. ~**zi'one** f elaboration; (di dati) processing. ~**zione [di] testi** word processing

elar'gire vt lavish

elastici'tà f elasticity. ~**z'zato** adj (stoffa) elasticated. **e'lastico** adj elastic; (tessuto) stretch; (orario, mente) flexible; (persona) easygoing ● m elastic; (fascia) rubber band

ele'fante m elephant

ele'gan|te adj elegant. ~**za** f elegance

e'leggere vt elect. **eleg'gibile** adj eligible

elemen'tare adj elementary; **scuola** ~ primary school

ele'mento m element; **elementi** pl (fatti) data; (rudimenti) elements

ele'mosina f charity; **chiedere l'**~ beg. **elemosi'nare** vt/i beg

elen'care vt list

e'lenco m list. ~ **abbonati** telephone directory. ~ **telefonico** telephone directory

elet'tivo adj (carica) elective. **e'letto, -a** pp di **eleggere** ● adj chosen ● m elected member

eletto'ra|le adj electoral. ~**to** m electorate

elet'tore, -'trice mf voter

elet'trauto m inv garage for electrical repairs

elettri'cista m electrician

elettri'cità f electricity. **e'lettrico** adj electric. ~**z'zante** adj (notizia, gara) electrifying. ~**z'zare** vt fig electrify. ~**z'zato** adj fig electrified

elettrocardio'gramma m electrocardiogram

e'lettrodo m electrode

elettrodo'mestico m [electrical] household appliance

elet'trone m electron

elet'tronico, -a adj electronic ● f electronics

ele'va|re vt raise; (promuovere) promote; (erigere) erect; (fig: migliorare) better; ~ **al quadrato/cubo** square/cube. ~**rsi** vr rise; (edificio:) stand.

~to *adj* high. ~zi'one *f* elevation

elezi'one *f* election

'elica *f* (Aeron, Naut) propeller; (*del ventilatore*) blade

eli'cottero *m* helicopter

elimi'na|re *vt* eliminate. ~'toria *f* Sport preliminary heat. ~zi'one *f* elimination

é'li|te *f inv* élite. ~'tista *adj* élitist

'ella *pers pron* she

el'metto *m* helmet

elogi'are *vt* praise

elo'quen|te *adj* eloquent; *fig* tell-tale. ~za *f* eloquence

e'lu|dere *vt* elude; evade (*sorveglianza*). ~'sivo *adj* elusive

el'vetico *adj* Swiss

emaci'ato *adj* emaciated

'e-mail *f* e-mail; indirizzo ~ e-mail address. ~ spazzatura junk e-mail

ema'na|re *vt* give off; pass (*legge*) • *vi* emanate

emanci'pa|re *vt* emancipate. ~rsi *vr* become emancipated. ~to *adj* emancipated. ~zi'one *f* emancipation

emargi'na|to *m* marginalized person. ~zi'one *f* marginalization

em'bargo *m* embargo

em'ble|ma *m* emblem. ~'matico *adj* emblematic

embrio'nale *adj* embryonic. embri'one *m* embryo

emen|da'mento *m* amendment. ~'dare *vt* amend

emer'gen|te *adj* emergent. ~za *f* emergency; in caso di ~za in an emergency

e'mergere *vi* emerge; (*sottomarino:*) surface; (*distinguersi*) stand out

e'merso *pp di* emergere

e'messo *pp di* emettere

e'mettere *vt* emit; give out (luce, suono); let out (grido); (*mettere in circolazione*) issue

emi'crania *f* migraine

emi'gra|re *vi* emigrate. ~to, -a *mf* immigrant. ~zi'one *f* emigration

emi'nen|te *adj* eminent. ~za *f* eminence

e'miro *m* emir

emis'fero *m* hemisphere

emis'sario *m* emissary

emissi'one *f* emission; (*di denaro*) issue; (*trasmissione*) broadcast

emit'tente *adj* issuing; (*trasmittente*) broadcasting • *f* transmitter

emorra'gia *f* haemorrhage

emor'roidi *fpl* piles

emotività *f* emotional make-up. emo'tivo *adj* emotional

emozio'na|nte *adj* exciting; (*commovente*) moving. ~re *vt* excite; (*commuovere*) move. ~rsi *vr* become excited; (*commuoversi*) be moved. ~to *adj* excited; (*commosso*) moved. emozi'one *f* emotion; (*agitazione*) excitement

'empio *adj* impious; (*spietato*) pitiless; (*malvagio*) wicked

em'pirico *adj* empirical

em'porio *m* emporium; (*negozio*) general store

emu'la|re *vt* emulate. ~zi'one *f* emulation

emulsi'one *f* emulsion

en'ciclica *f* encyclical

enciclope'dia *f* encyclopaedia

encomi'are *vt* commend. en'comio *m* commendation

en'demico *adj* endemic

endo've|na *f* intravenous injection. ~'noso *adj* intravenous; per via ~nosa intravenously

ener'getico *adj* (risorse, crisi) energy *attrib*; (*alimento*) energy-giving

ener'gia *f* energy. e'nergico *adj* energetic; (*efficace*) strong

'enfasi *f* emphasis

en'fati|co *adj* emphatic. ~z'zare *vt* emphasize

e'nigma m enigma. enig'matico adj enigmatic. enig'mistica f puzzles pl

E.N.I.T. m abbr (Ente Nazionale Italiano per il Turismo) Italian State Tourist Office

en'nesimo adj (Math) nth; Ⓣ umpteenth

e'norm|e adj enormous. ~e'mente adv massively. ~ità f inv enormity; (assurdità) absurdity

eno'teca f wine-tasting shop

'ente m board; (società) company; (filosofia) being

entità f inv entity; (gravità) seriousness; (dimensione) extent

entou'rage m inv entourage

en'trambi adj & pron both

en'tra|re vi go in, enter; ~re in go into; (stare in, trovar posto in) fit into; (arruolarsi) join; ~rci (avere a che fare) have to do with; tu che c'entri? what has it got to do with you? ~ta f entrance; ~te pl (Comm) takings; (reddito) income sg

'entro prep (tempo) within

entro'terra m inv hinterland

entusias'mante adj fascinating

entusias'mar|e vt arouse enthusiasm in. ~si vr be enthusiastic (per about)

entusi'as|mo m enthusiasm. ~ta adj enthusiastic ● mf enthusiast. ~tico adj enthusiastic

enume'ra|re vt enumerate. ~zi'one f enumeration

enunci'a|re vt enunciate. ~zi'one f enunciation

epa'tite f hepatitis

'epico adj epic

epide'mia f epidemic

epi'dermide f epidermis

Epifa'nia f Epiphany

epi'gramma m epigram

epiles'sia f epilepsy. epi'lettico, -a adj & mf epileptic

e'pilogo m epilogue

epi'sodi|co adj episodic; caso ~co one-off case. ~o m episode

'epoca f age; (periodo) period; a quell'~ in those days; auto d'~ vintage car

ep'pure conj [and] yet

epu'rare vt purge

equa'tore m equator. equatori'ale adj equatorial

equazi'one f equation

e'questre adj equestrian; circo ~ circus

equili'bra|re vt balance. ~to adj well-balanced. equi'librio m balance; (buon senso) common sense; (di bilancia) equilibrium

equili'brismo m fare ~ do a balancing act

e'quino adj horse attrib

equi'nozio m equinox

equipaggia'mento m equipment

equipaggi'a|re vt equip; (di persone) man

equi'paggio m crew; (Aeron) cabin crew

equipa'rare vt make equal

é'quipe f inv team

equità f equity

equitazi'one f riding

equiva'len|te adj & m equivalent. ~za f equivalence

equiva'lere vi ~ a be equivalent to

equivo'care vi misunderstand

e'quivoco adj equivocal; (sospetto) suspicious ● m misunderstanding

'equo adj fair, just

'era f era

'erba f grass; (aromatica, medicinale) herb. ~ cipollina chives pl. er'baccia f weed. er'baceo adj herbaceous

erbi'cida m weed-killer

erbo'rist|a mf herbalist. **~e'ria** f herbalist's shop

er'boso adj grassy

er'culeo adj (forza) herculean

e'red|e mf heir; heiress. **~ità** f inv inheritance; (Biol) heredity. **~i'tare** vt inherit. **~itarietà** f heredity. **~i'tario** adj hereditary

ere'sia f heresy. **e'retico, -a** adj heretical ● mf heretic

e're|tto pp di erigere ● adj erect. **~zi'one** f erection; (costruzione) building

er'gastolo m life sentence; (luogo) prison

'erica f heather

e'rigere vt erect; (fig: fondare) found

eri'tema m (cutaneo) inflammation; (solare) sunburn

er'metico adj hermetic; (a tenuta d'aria) airtight

'ernia f hernia

e'rodere vi erode

e'ro|e m hero. **~ico** adj heroic. **~ismo** m heroism

ero'ga|re vt distribute; (fornire) supply. **~zi'one** f supply

ero'ina f heroine; (droga) heroin

erosi'one f erosion

e'rotico adj erotic

er'rante adj wandering. **er'rare** vi wander; (sbagliare) be mistaken

er'rato adj (sbagliato) mistaken

erronea'mente adv mistakenly

er'rore m error; (di stampa) misprint; **essere in ~** be wrong

'erta f stare all'**~** be on the alert

eru'di|rsi vr get educated. **~to** adj learned

erut'tare vt (vulcano:) erupt ● vi (ruttare) belch. **eruzi'one** f eruption; (Med) rash

esage'ra|re vt exaggerate ● vi aggerate; (nel comportamento) go over

the top; **~re nel mangiare** eat too much. **~ta'mente** adv excessively. **~to** adj exaggerated; (prezzo) exorbitant ● **è un ~to** he exaggerates. **~zi'one** f exaggeration; **è costato un'~zione** it cost the earth

esa'lare vt/i exhale

esal'ta|re vt exalt; (entusiasmare) elate. **~to** adj (fanatico) fanatical ● m fanatic. **~zi'one** f exaltation; (in discorso) fervour

e'same m examination, exam; **dare un ~** take an exam; **prendere in ~** examine. **~ del sangue** blood test. **esami** pl di maturità ≈ A-levels

esami'na|re vt examine. **~tore, ~'trice** mf examiner

e'sangue adj bloodless

e'sanime adj lifeless

esaspe'rante adj exasperating

esaspe'ra|re vt exasperate. **~rsi** vr get exasperated. **~zi'one** f exasperation

esat|ta'mente adv exactly. **~'tezza** f exactness; (precisione) precision; (di risultato) accuracy

e'satto pp di esigere ● adj exact; (risposta, risultato) correct; (orologio) right; **hai l'ora esatta?** do you have the right time?; **sono le due esatte** it's two o'clock exactly

esat'tore m collector

esau'dire vt grant; fulfil (speranze)

esauri'ente adj exhaustive

esau'ri|re vt exhaust. **~rsi** vr exhaust oneself; (merci ecc:) run out. **~to** adj exhausted; (merci) sold out; (libro) out of print; **fare il tutto ~** (spettacolo:) play to a full house

'esca f bait

escande'scenz|a f outburst; **dare in ~e** lose one's temper

escla'ma|re vi exclaim. **~zi'one** f exclamation

es'clu|dere vt exclude (possibilità,

ipotesi). **∼si'one** f exclusion. **∼'siva** f exclusive right; **in ∼siva** exclusive. **∼siva'mente** adv exclusively. **∼'sivo** adj exclusive. **∼so** pp di **escludere** ● adj **non è ∼so che ci sia** it's not out of the question that he'll be there

escogi'tare vt contrive

escursi'one f excursion; (scorreria) raid; (di temperatura) range

ese'cra|bile adj abominable. **∼re** vt abhor

esecu'tivo adj & m executive. **∼'tore, ∼'trice** mf executor; (Mus) performer. **∼zi'one** f execution; (Mus) performance

esegu'ire vt carry out; (Jur) execute; (Mus) perform

e'sempio m example; **ad ∼ per ∼** for example; **dare l'∼ a** qcno set sb an example; **fare un ∼** give an example

esem'plare m specimen; (di libro) copy

esen'tar|e vt exempt. **∼si** vr free oneself. **e'sente** adj exempt. **esente da imposta** duty-free. **esente da IVA** VAT-exempt

esen'tasse adj duty-free

e'sequie fpl funeral rites

eser'cente mf shopkeeper

eserci'ta|re vt exercise; (addestrare) train; (fare uso di) exert; (professione) practise. **∼rsi** vr practise. **∼zi'one** f exercise; (Mil) drill

e'sercito m army

eser'cizio m exercise; (pratica) practice; (Comm) financial year; (azienda) business; **essere fuori ∼** be out of practice

esi'bi|re vt show off; produce (documenti). **∼rsi** vr (Theat) perform; fig show off. **∼zi'one** f (Theat) performance; (di documenti) production

esibizio'nis|mo m showing off

esi'gen|te adj exacting; (pignolo) fastidious. **∼za** f demand; (bisogno) need. **e'sigere** vt demand; (riscuotere) collect

e'siguo adj meagre

esila'rante adj exhilarating

'esile adj slender; (voce) thin

esili'a|re vt exile. **∼rsi** vr go into exile. **∼to, -a** adj exiled ● mf exile. **e'silio** m exile

e'simer|e vt release. **∼si** vr **∼si da** get out of

esi'sten|te adj existing. **∼za** f existence.

e'sistere vi exist

esi'tante adj hesitating; (voce) faltering

esi'ta|re vi hesitate. **∼zi'one** f hesitation

'esito m result; **avere buon ∼** be a success

'esodo m exodus

e'sofago m oesophagus

eso'nerare vt exempt. **e'sonero** m exemption

esor'bitante adj exorbitant

esorciz'zare vt exorcize

esordi'ente mf person making his/her début. **e'sordio** m opening; (di attore) début. **esor'dire** vi début

esor'tare vt (pregare) beg; (incitare) urge

e'sotico adj exotic

espa'drillas fpl espadrilles

es'pan|dere vt expand. **∼dersi** vr expand; (diffondersi) extend. **∼si'one** f expansion. **∼'sivo** adj expansive; (persona) friendly

espatri'are vi leave one's country. **es'patrio** m expatriation

espedi'ente m expedient; **vivere di ∼i** live by one's wits

es'pellere vt expel

esperi'enza f experience; **parlare per ∼enza** speak from experience. **∼'mento** m experiment

es'perto, -a adj & mf expert

espi'a|re vt atone for. **~'torio** adj expiatory

espi'rare vt/i breathe out

espli'care vt carry on

esplicita'mente adv explicitly. **es'plicito** adj explicit

es'plodere vi explode ●vt fire

esplo'ra|re vt explore. **~'tore**, **~'trice** mf explorer; **giovane ~'tore** boy scout. **~zi'one** f exploration

esplo|si'one f explosion. **~'sivo** adj & m explosive

es'por|re vt expose; display (merci); (spiegare) expound; exhibit (quadri ecc). **~si** vr (compromettersi) compromise oneself; (al sole) expose oneself

espor'ta|re vt export. **~'tore**, **~'trice** mf exporter. **~zi'one** f export

esposizi'one f (mostra) exhibition; (in vetrina) display; (spiegazione ecc) exposition; (posizione, fotografia) exposure. **es'posto** pp di **esporre** ●adj exposed; **esposto a** (rivolto) facing ●m (Jur) statement

espressa'mente adv expressly; **non l'ha detto ~** he didn't put it in so many words

espres|si'one f expression. **~'sivo** adj expressive

es'presso pp di **esprimere** ●adj express ●m (lettera) express letter; (treno) express train; (caffè) espresso; **per ~** (spedire) [by] express [post]

es'primer|e vt express. **~si** vr express oneself

espropri'a|re vt dispossess. **~zi'one** f (Jur) expropriation. **es'proprio** m expropriation

espulsi'one f expulsion. **es'pulso** pp di **espellere**

es'senz|a f essence. **~i'ale** adj essential ●m important thing. **~ial'mente** adv essentially

'essere

● vi be; **c'è** there is; **ci sono** there are; **che ora è? – sono le dieci** what time is it? – it's ten o'clock; **sono io** who is it? – it's me; **ci sono!** (ho capito) I've got it!; **ci siamo!** (siamo arrivati) here we are at last!; **siamo in due** there are two of us; **questa camicia è da lavare** this shirt is to be washed; **non è da te** it's not like you; **~ di** (provenire da) be from; **~ per** (favorevole) be in favour of; **se fossi in te,...** if I were you,...; **sarà!** if you say so!; **come sarebbe a dire?** what are you getting at?

● v aux have; (in passivi) be; **siamo arrivati** we have arrived; **ci sono stato ieri** I was there yesterday; **sono nato a Torino** I was born in Turin; **è riconosciuto come...** he is recognized as...; **è stato detto che** it has been said that

● m being. **~ umano** human being. **~ vivente** living creature

essic'cato adj dried

'esso, -a pers pron he, she; (cosa, animale) it

est m east

'estasi f ecstasy; **andare in ~ per** go into raptures over

e'state f summer

e'sten|dere vt extend. **~dersi** vr spread; (allungarsi) stretch. **~si'one** f extension; (ampiezza) expanse; (Mus) range. **~'sivo** adj extensive

estenu'ante adj exhausting

estenu'a|re vt wear out; deplete (risorse, casse). **~rsi** vr wear oneself out

esteri'or|e adj & m exterior. **~'mente** adv externally; (di persone) outwardly

esterna'mente *adv* on the outside

ester'nare *vt* express, show

e'sterno *adj* external; **per uso ~** for external use only ● *m* (*allievo*) dayboy; (*Archit*) exterior; (*in film*) location shot

'estero *adj* foreign ● *m* foreign countries *pl*; **all'~** abroad

esterre'fatto *adj* horrified

e'steso *pp di* estendere ● *adj* extensive; (*diffuso*) widespread; **per ~**, (*scrivere*) in full

e'stetic|a *f* aesthetics *sg*. **~a'mente** *adv* aesthetically. **~o, -a** *adj* aesthetic; (*chirurgia, chirurgo*) plastic. **este'tista** *f* beautician

'estimo *m* estimate

e'stin|guere *vt* extinguish. **~guersi** *vr* die out. **~to, -a** *pp di* estinguere ● *mf* deceased. **~tore** *m* [fire] extinguisher. **~zi'one** *f* extinction; (*di incendio*) putting out

estir'pa|re *vt* uproot; extract (*dente*); *fig* eradicate (*crimine, malattia*). **~zi'one** *f* eradication; (*di dente*) extraction

e'stivo *adj* summer

e'stor|cere *vt* extort. **~si'one** *f* extortion. **~to** *pp di* estorcere

estradizi'one *f* extradition

e'straneo, -a *adj* extraneous; (*straniero*) foreign ● *mf* stranger

estrani'ar|e *vt* estrange. **~si** *vr* become estranged

e'stra|rre *vt* extract; (*sorteggiare*) draw. **~tto** *pp di* estrarre ● *m* extract; (*brano*) excerpt; (*documento*) abstract. **~tto conto** statement [of account], bank statement. **~zi'one** *f* extraction; (*sorte*) draw

estrema'mente *adv* extremely

estre'mis|mo *m* extremism. **~ta** *mf* extremist

estremità *f inv* extremity; (*di una corda*) end ● *fpl* (*Anat*) extremities

e'stremo *adj* extreme; (*ultimo*) last; **misure estreme** drastic measures; **l'E~ Oriente** the Far East ● *m* (*limite*) extreme. **estremi** *pl* (*di documento*) main points; (*di reato*) essential elements; **essere agli estremi** be at the end of one's tether

'estro *m* (*disposizione artistica*) talent; (*ispirazione*) inspiration; (*capriccio*) whim. **e'stroso** *adj* talented; (*capriccioso*) unpredictable

estro'mettere *vt* expel

estro'verso *adj* extroverted ● *m* extrovert

estu'ario *m* estuary

esube'ran|te *adj* exuberant. **~za** *f* exuberance

'esule *mf* exile

esul'tante *adj* exultant

esul'tare *vi* rejoice

esu'mare *vt* exhume

età *f inv* age; **raggiungere la maggiore ~** come of age; **un uomo di mezz'~** a middle-aged man

'etere *m* ether. **e'tereo** *adj* ethereal

eterna'mente *adv* eternally

eternità *f* eternity; **è un'~ che non la vedo** I haven't seen her for ages

e'terno *adj* eternal; (*questione, problema*) age-old; **in ~** ⓘ for ever

eterosessu'ale *mf* heterosexual

'etica *f* ethics

eti'chetta¹ *f* label; price-tag

eti'chetta² *f* etiquette

etichet'tare *vt* label

'etico *adj* ethical

eti'lometro *m* Breathalyzer®

Eti'opia *f* Ethiopia

'etnico *adj* ethnic

e'trusco *adj & mf* Etruscan

'ettaro *m* hectare

'etto, etto'grammo *m* hundred grams, ≈ quarter pound

eucari'stia *f* Eucharist

eufe'mismo m euphemism

eufo'ria f elation; (Med) euphoria. **eu'forico** adj elated; (Med) euphoric

'euro m inv Fin euro

Euro'city m international Intercity

eurodepu'tato m Euro MP, MEP

Eu'ropa f Europe. **euro'peo, -a** agg & mf European

eutana'sia f euthanasia

evacu'a|re vt evacuate. **~zi'one** f evacuation

e'vadere vt evade; (sbrigare) deal with ●vi ~ **da** escape from

evane'scente adj vanishing

evan'gel|ico adj evangelical. **evan-ge'lista** m evangelist

evapo'ra|re vi evaporate. **~zi'one** f evaporation

evasi'one f escape; (fiscale) evasion; fig escapism. **eva'sivo** adj evasive

e'vaso pp di **evadere** ●m fugitive

eva'sore m ~ **fiscale** tax evader

eveni'enza f eventuality

e'vento m event

eventu'al|e adj possible. **~ità** f inv eventuality

evi'den|te adj evident; **è ~te che** it is obvious that. **~te'mente** adv evidently. **~za** f evidence; **mettere in ~za** emphasize; **mettersi in ~za** make oneself conspicuous

evidenzi'a|re vt highlight. **~'tore** m (penna) highlighter

evi'tare vt avoid; (risparmiare) spare

evo'care vt evoke

evo'lu|to pp di **evolvere** ●adj evolved; (progredito) progressive; (civiltà, nazione) advanced; **una donna evoluta** a modern woman. **~zi'one** f evolution; (di ginnastica, aereo) circle

e'volver|e vt develop. **~si** vi evolve

ev'viva int hurray; **~ il Papa!** long live the Pope!; **gridare ~** cheer

ex+ pref ex+, former

'extra adj inv extra; (qualità) first-class ●m inv extra

extracomuni'tario adj non-EU

extrater'restre mf extra-terrestrial

Extravergine Olive oil which is obtained from the first pressing of the olives is called extravergine (extra virgin). It has a distinctive peppery flavour and is often a cloudy greenish colour. A less refined grade, suitable for cooking, is obtained by using chemical methods. This is called simply olio d'oliva.

Ff

fa¹ m inv (Mus) F

fa² adv ago; **due mesi ~** two months ago

fabbi'sogno m requirements pl

'fabbrica f factory

fabbri'cabile adj (area, terreno) that can be built on

fabbri'cante m manufacturer

fabbri'ca|re vt build; (produrre) manufacture; (fig: inventare) fabricate. **~to** m building. **~zi'one** f manufacturing; (costruzione) building

'fabbro m blacksmith

fac'cen|da f matter; **~e** pl (lavori domestici) housework sg. **~i'ere** m wheeler-dealer

fac'chino m porter

'facci|a f face; (di foglio) side; **~a a ~a** face to face; **~a tosta** cheek; **voltar ~a** change sides; **di ~a** (palazzo) opposite; **alla ~a di** (fam: a dispetto di) in spite of. **~'ata** f façade; (di foglio) side; (fig: esteriorità) outward appearance

fa'ceto *adj* facetious; **tra il serio e il ~** half joking

fa'chiro *m* fakir

'facile *adj* easy; (*affabile*) easygoing; **essere ~e alle critiche** be quick to criticize; **essere ~e al riso** laugh a lot; **~e a farsi** easy to do; **è ~e che piova** it's likely to rain. **~ità** *f* ease; (*disposizione*) aptitude; **avere ~ità di parola** express oneself well

facili'ta|re *vt* facilitate. **~zi'one** *f* facility; **~zioni** *pl* special terms

facil'mente *adv* (*con facilità*) easily; (*probabilmente*) probably

faci'lone *adj* slapdash. **~'ria** *f* slapdash attitude

faci'noroso *adj* violent

facoltà *f inv* faculty; (*potere*) power. **facolta'tivo** *adj* optional; **fermata facoltativa** request stop

facol'toso *adj* wealthy

'faggio *m* beech

fagi'ano *m* pheasant

fagio'lino *m* French bean

fagi'olo *m* bean; **a ~** (*arrivare, capitare*) at the right time

fagoci'tare *vt* gobble up (*società*)

fa'gotto *m* bundle; (*Mus*) bassoon

'faida *f* feud

fai da te *m* do-it-yourself, DIY

fal'cata *f* stride

'falce *f* scythe. **fal'cetto** *m* sickle. **~i'are** *vt* cut; *fig* mow down. **~ia'trice** *f* [lawn-]mower

'falco *m* hawk

fal'cone *m* falcon

'falda *f* stratum; (*di neve*) flake; (*di cappello*) brim; (*pendio*) slope

fale'gname *m* carpenter. **~'ria** *f* carpentry

'falla *f* leak

fal'lace *adj* deceptive

fallimen'tare *adj* disastrous; (*Jur*) bankruptcy. **falli'mento** *m* Fin bank-

ruptcy; *fig* failure

fal'li|re *vi Fin* go bankrupt; *fig* fail ●*vt* miss (*colpo*). **~to, -a** *adj* unsuccessful; *Fin* bankrupt ●*mf* failure; *Fin* bankrupt

'fallo *m* fault; (*errore*) mistake; *Sport* foul; (*imperfezione*) flaw; **senza ~** without fail

falò *m inv* bonfire

fal'sar|e *vt* alter; (*falsificare*) falsify. **~io, -a** *mf* forger; (*di documenti*) counterfeiter

falsifi'ca|re *vt* fake; (*contraffare*) forge. **~zi'one** *f* (*di documento*) falsification

falsità *f* falseness

'falso *adj* false; (*sbagliato*) wrong; (*opera d'arte ecc*) fake; (*gioielli, oro*) imitation ●*m* forgery; **giurare il ~** commit perjury

'fama *f* fame; (*reputazione*) reputation

'fame *f* hunger; **aver ~** be hungry; **fare la ~** barely scrape a living. **fa'melico** *adj* ravenous

famige'rato *adj* infamous

fa'miglia *f* family

famili'ar|e *adj* family attrib; (*ben noto*) familiar; (*senza cerimonie*) informal ●*mf* relative, relation **~ità** *f* familiarity; (*informalità*) informality. **~iz'zarsi** *vr* familiarize oneself

fa'moso *adj* famous

fa'nale *m* lamp; (*Auto*) light. **fanali posteriori** (*Auto*) rear lights

fa'natico, -a *adj* fanatical; **essere ~ di calcio** be a football fanatic ●*mf* fanatic. **fana'tismo** *m* fanaticism

fanci'ul|la *f* young girl. **~'lezza** *f* childhood. **~lo** *m* young boy

fan'donia *f* lie; **fandonie!** nonsense!

fan'fara *f* fanfare; (*complesso*) brass band

fanfaro'nata *f* brag. **fanfa'rone, -a** *mf* braggart

fan'ghiglia *f* mud. **'fango** *m* mud.

fan'goso *adj* muddy

fannul'lone, -a *mf* idler

fantasci'enza *f* science fiction

fanta'si|a *f* fantasy; (*immaginazione*) imagination; (*capriccio*) fancy; (*di tessuto*) pattern. ∼'oso *adj* (*stilista, ragazzo*) imaginative; (*resoconto*) improbable

fan'tasma *m* ghost

fantasti'c|are *vi* day-dream. ∼he'ria *f* day-dream. fan'tastico *adj* fantastic; (*racconto*) fantasy

'fante *m* infantryman; (*nelle carte*) jack. ∼'ria *m* infantry

fan'tino *m* jockey

fan'toccio *m* puppet

fanto'matico *adj* phantom *attrib*

fara'butto *m* trickster

fara'ona *f* (*uccello*) guinea-fowl

far'ci|re *vt* stuff; fill (*torta*). ∼to *adj* stuffed; (*dolce*) filled

far'dello *m* bundle; *fig* burden

'fare

• *vt* do; make (*dolce, letto ecc*); (*recitare la parte di*) play; (*trascorrere*) spend; ∼ una pausa/un sogno have a break/a dream; ∼ colpo su impress; ∼ paura a frighten; ∼ piacere a please; farla finita put an end to it; ∼ l'insegnante be a teacher; ∼ lo scemo play the idiot; ∼ una settimana al mare spend a week at the seaside; 3 più 3 fa 6 3 and 3 makes 6; quanto fa? – fanno 10 000 euro how much is it? – it's 10,000 euros; far ∼ qcsa a qcno get sb to do sth; (*costringere*) make sb do sth; ∼ vedere show; fammi parlare let me speak; niente a che ∼ con nothing to do with; non c'è niente da ∼ (*per problema*) there is nothing we/you/etc. can do; fa caldo/buio it's

warm/dark; non fa niente it doesn't matter; strada facendo on the way; farcela (*riuscire*) manage

• *vi* fai in modo di venire try and come; ∼ da act as; ∼ per make as if to; ∼ presto be quick; non fa per me it's not for me

• *m* way; sul far del giorno at daybreak.

• **farsi** *vr* (*diventare*) get; farsi avanti come forward; farsi i fatti propri mind one's own business; farsi la barba shave; farsi il ragazzo Ⅰ find a boyfriend; farsi male hurt oneself; farsi strada (*aver successo*) make one's way in the world

fa'retto *m* spot[light]

far'falla *f* butterfly

farfal'lino *m* (*cravatta*) bow tie

farfugli'are *vt* mutter

fa'rina *f* flour. fari'nacei *mpl* starchy food *sg*

fa'ringe *f* pharynx

fari'noso *adj* (*neve*) powdery; (*mela*) soft; (*patata*) floury

farma|'ceutico *adj* pharmaceutical. ∼'cia *f* pharmacy; (*negozio*) chemist's [shop]. ∼cia di turno duty chemist. ∼'cista *mf* chemist. 'farmaco *m* drug

Farmacia A *farmacia* in Italy sells medicines and health-related products, whereas a *profumeria* sells not only perfume, but also beauty and personal hygiene products. For film and developing services it is necessary to go to a shop specializing in photographic equipment.

'faro *m* (*Auto*) headlight; (*Aeron*) beacon; (*costruzione*) lighthouse

'farsa *f* farce

'fasci|a *f* band; (*zona*) area; (*ufficiale*)

sash; (benda) bandage. ~**'are** vt bandage; cling to (fianchi). ~**a'tura** f dressing; (azione) bandaging

fa'**scicolo** m file; (di rivista) issue; (libretto) booklet

'**fascino** m fascination

'**fascio** m bundle; (di fiori) bunch

fa'**scis|mo** m fascism. ~**ta** mf fascist

'**fase** f phase

fa'**stidi|o** m nuisance; (scomodo) inconvenience; **dar** ~**o a qcno** bother sb; ~**i** pl (preoccupazioni) worries; (disturbi) troubles. ~**oso** adj tiresome

'**fasto** m pomp. fa'**stoso** adj sumptuous

fa'**sullo** adj bogus

'**fata** f fairy

fa'**tale** adj fatal; (inevitabile) fated

fata'**l|ismo** m fatalism. ~**ista** mf fatalist. ~**ità** f inv fate; (caso sfortunato) misfortune. ~**'mente** adv inevitably

fa'**tica** f effort; (lavoro faticoso) hard work; (stanchezza) fatigue; **a** ~ with great difficulty; **è** ~ **sprecata** it's a waste of time; **fare** ~ **a fare qcsa** find it difficult to do sth; **fare** ~ **a finire qcsa** struggle to finish sth. fa-ti'**caccia** f pain

fati'**ca|re** vi toil; ~**re a** (stentare) find it difficult to. ~**ta** f effort; (sfacchinata) grind. fati'**coso** adj tiring; (difficile) difficult

'**fato** m fate

fat'**taccio** m hum foul deed

fat'**tezze** fpl features

fat'**tibile** adj feasible

'**fatto** pp di **fare** ● adj done, made; ~ **a mano** hand-made ● m fact; (azione) action; (avvenimento) event; **bada ai fatti tuoi!** mind your own business; **di** ~ in fact; **di** ~ **di** as regards

fat'**to|re** m (Math, causa) factor; (di fattoria) farm manager. ~**'ria** f farm; (casa) farmhouse

fatto'**rino** m messenger [boy]

fattuc'**chi'era** f witch

fat'**tura** f (stile) cut; (lavorazione) workmanship; (Comm) invoice

fattu'**ra|re** vt invoice; (adulterare) adulterate. ~**to** m turnover, sales pl. ~**zi'one** f invoicing, billing

'**fatuo** adj fatuous

fau'**tore** m supporter

'**fava** f broad bean

fa'**vella** f speech

fa'**villa** f spark

'**favo|la** f fable; (fiaba) story; (oggetto di pettegolezzi) laughing-stock; (meraviglia) dream. ~**'loso** adj fabulous

fa'**vore** m favour; **essere a** ~ **di** be in favour of; **per** ~ please; **di** ~ (condizioni, trattamento) preferential. ~**ggia'mento** m (Jur) aiding and abetting. favo'**revole** adj favourable. ~**vol'mente** adv favourably

favo'**ri|re** vt favour; (promuovere) promote; **vuol** ~**re?** (a cena, pranzo) will you have some?; (entrare) will you come in?. ~**to, -a** adj & mf favourite

'**fax** m inv fax. fa'**xare** vt fax

fazi'**one** f faction

faziosità f bias. fazi'**oso** m sectarian

fazzo'let'tino m ~ **[di carta]** [paper] tissue

fazzo'**letto** m handkerchief; (da testa) headscarf

feb'**braio** m February

'**febbre** f fever; **avere la** ~ have o run a temperature. ~ **da fieno** hay fever. feb'**brile** adj feverish

'**feccia** f dregs pl

'**fecola** f potato flour

fecon'**da|re** vt fertilize. ~**'tore** m fertilizer. ~**zi'one** f fertilization. ~**zione artificiale** artificial insemination. fe'**condo** adj fertile

'**fede** f faith; (fiducia) trust; (anello) wedding-ring; **in buona/mala** ~ in

f

good/bad faith; **prestar** ∼ **a** believe; **tener** ∼ **alla parola** keep one's word. **fe'dele** adj faithful ● mf believer; (seguace) follower. ∼**l'mente** adv faithfully. ∼**ltà** f faithfulness

'federa f pillowcase

fede'ra|le adj federal. ∼**lismo** m federalism. ∼**zi'one** f federation

fe'dina f avere la ∼ **penale sporca/pulita** have a/no criminal record

'fegato m liver; fig guts pl

'felce f fern

fe'lic|e adj happy; (fortunato) lucky. ∼**ità** f happiness

felici'ta|rsi vr ∼**rsi con** congratulate. ∼**zi'oni** fpl congratulations

'felpa f (indumento) sweatshirt

fel'pato adj brushed; (passo) stealthy

'feltro m felt; (cappello) felt hat

'femmin|a f female. **femmi'nile** adj feminine; (abbigliamento) women's; (sesso) female ● m feminine. ∼**ilità** f femininity. **femmi'nismo** m feminism

'femore m femur

'fend|ere vt split. ∼**i'tura** f split; (in roccia) crack

feni'cottero m flamingo

fenome'nale adj phenomenal. **fe-'nomeno** m phenomenon

'feretro m coffin

feri'ale adj weekday; **giorno** ∼ weekday

'ferie fpl holidays; (di università, tribunale ecc) vacation sg; **andare in** ∼ go on holiday

feri'mento m wounding

fe'ri|re vt wound; (in incidente) injure; fig hurt. ∼**rsi** vr injure oneself. ∼**ta** f wound. ∼**to** adj wounded ● m wounded person; (Mil) casualty

'ferma f (Mil) period of service

fermacapelli m inv hairslide

ferma'carte m inv paperweight

fermacra'vatta m inv tiepin

fer'maglio m clasp; (spilla) brooch; (per capelli) hair slide

ferma'mente adv firmly

fer'ma|re vt stop; (fissare) fix; (Jur) detain ● vi stop. ∼**rsi** vr stop. ∼**ta** f stop. ∼**ta dell'autobus** bus-stop. ∼**ta a richiesta** request stop

fermen'ta|re vi ferment. ∼**zi'one** f fermentation. **fer'mento** m ferment; (lievito) yeast

fer'mezza f firmness

'fermo adj still; (veicolo) stationary; (stabile) steady; (orologio) not working ● m (Jur) detention; (Mech) catch; **in stato di** ∼ in custody

fe'roc|e adj ferocious; (bestia) wild; (dolore) unbearable. ∼**e'mente** adv fiercely. ∼**ia** f ferocity

fer'raglia f scrap iron

ferra'gosto m 15 August (bank holiday in Italy); (periodo) August holidays pl

ferra'menta fpl ironmongery sg; **negozio di** ∼ ironmonger's

fer'ra|re vt shoe (cavallo). ∼**to** adj ∼**to in** (preparato in) well up in

'ferreo adj iron

'ferro m iron; (attrezzo) tool; (di chirurgo) instrument; **bistecca ai ferri** grilled steak; **di** ∼ (memoria) excellent; (alibi) cast-iron; **salute di** ∼ iron constitution. ∼ **battuto** wrought iron. ∼ **da calza** knitting needle. ∼ **di cavallo** horseshoe. ∼ **da stiro** iron

ferro'vecchio m scrap merchant

ferro'vi|a f railway. ∼**ario** adj railway. ∼**ere** m railwayman

'fertil|e adj fertile. ∼**ità** f fertility. ∼**iz'zante** m fertilizer

fer'vente adj blazing; fig fervent

'fervere vi (preparativi:) be well under way

'fervido adj fervent; ∼**i auguri** best wishes

fer'vore m fervour

fesse'ria f nonsense

'**fesso** pp di fendere ● adj cracked; (fig: sciocco) foolish ● m fig (idiota) fool; **far ~ qcno** con sb

fes'sura f crack; (per gettone ecc) slot

'**festa** f feast; (giorno festivo) holiday; (compleanno) birthday; (ricevimento) party; fig joy; **fare ~ a qcno** welcome sb; **essere in ~** be on holiday; **far ~** celebrate. **~'iolo** adj festive

festeggia'mento m celebration; (manifestazione) festivity

festeggi'are vt celebrate; (accogliere festosamente) give a hearty welcome to

fe'stino m party

festività fpl festivities. **fe'stivo** adj holiday; (lieto) festive. **festivi** mpl public holidays

fe'stoso adj merry

fe'tente adj evil smelling; fig revolting ● mf fig bastard

fe'ticcio m fetish

'**feto** m foetus

fe'tore m stench

'**fetta** f slice; **a fette** sliced. **~ bi-scottata** slices of crispy toast-like bread

fet'tuccia f tape; (con nome) name tape

feu'dale adj feudal. '**feudo** m feud

FFSS abbr (Ferrovie dello Stato) Italian state railways

fi'aba f fairy-tale. **fia'besco** adj fairy-tale

fi'acca f weariness; (indolenza) laziness; **battere la ~a** be sluggish. **fiac'care** vt weaken. **~o** adj weak; (indolente) slack; (stanco) weary; (partita) dull

fi'acco|la f torch. **~'lata** f torch-light procession

fi'ala f phial

fi'amma f flame; (Naut) pennant; **in fiamme** aflame. **andare in fiamme** go up in flames. **~ ossidrica** blowtorch

fiam'ma|nte adj flaming; **nuovo ~nte** brand new. **~ta** f blaze

fiammeggi'are vi blaze

fiam'mifero m match

fiam'mingo, -a adj Flemish ● mf Fleming ● m (lingua) Flemish

fiancheggi'are vt border; fig support

fi'anco m side; (di persona) hip; (di animale) flank; (Mil) wing; **al mio ~** by my side; **~ a ~** (lavorare) side by side

fi'asco m flask; fig fiasco; **fare ~** be a fiasco

fia'tare vi breathe; (parlare) breathe a word

fi'ato m breath; (vigore) stamina; **strumenti a ~** wind instruments; **senza ~** breathlessly; **tutto d'un ~** (bere, leggere) all in one go

'**fibbia** f buckle

'**fibra** f fibre; **fibre** pl (alimentari) roughage. **~ ottica** optical fibre

ficca'naso mf nosey parker

fic'car|e vt thrust; drive (chiodo ecc); (fam: mettere) shove. **~si** vr thrust oneself; (nascondersi) hide; **~si nei guai** get oneself into trouble

fiche f inv (gettone) chip

'**fico** m (albero) fig-tree; (frutto) fig. **~ d'India** prickly pear

'**fico, -a** fig mf cool sort ● adj cool

fidanza'mento m engagement

fidan'za|rsi vr get engaged. **~to, -a** mf (ufficiale) fiancé; fiancée

fi'da|rsi vr **~rsi di** trust. **~to** adj trustworthy

'**fido** m devoted follower; (Comm) credit

fi'duci|a f confidence; **degno di ~a** trustworthy; **persona di ~a** reliable person; **di ~a** (fornitore) usual. **~'oso** adj trusting

fi'ele m bile; fig bitterness

fie'nile m barn. **fi'eno** m hay

fi'era f fair

fie'rezza f (dignità) pride. **fi'ero** adj proud

fi'evole adj faint; (luce) dim

'fifa f 🔲 jitters; **aver ~** have the jitters

'figli|a f daughter; **~a unica** only child. **~'astra** f stepdaughter. **~'astro** m stepson. **~o** m son; (generico) child. **~o unico** only child

---

i

Figlio di papà With the rapid rise in living standards which took place in Italy after 1945, many more children grow up in affluent families than was previously the case, and *figli unici* (only children) are often the norm. Children, both young and grown-up, are often given considerable financial help by their parents, and are sometimes termed *figli di papà*, implying that they are also spoilt.

---

figli'occi|a f goddaughter. **~o** m godson

figli'o|la f girl. **~'lanza** f offspring. **~lo** m boy

'figo, -a ▷FICO, -A

fi'gura f figure; (aspetto esteriore) shape; (illustrazione) illustration; **far bella/brutta ~** make a good/bad impression; **mi hai fatto fare una brutta ~** you made me look a fool; **che ~!** how embarrassing!. **figu'raccia** f bad impression

figu'ra|re vt represent; (simboleggiare) symbolize; (immaginare) imagine ● vi (far figura) cut a dash; (in lista) appear. **~rsi** vr (immaginarsi) imagine; **~ti!** imagine that!; **posso? - [ma] ~ti!** may I? - of course!. **~'tivo** adj figurative

figu'rina f ≈ cigarette card

figu|ri'nista mf dress designer. **~'rino** m fashion sketch. **~'rone** m fare un **~rone** make an excellent impression

'fila f line; (di soldati ecc) file; (di oggetti) row; (coda) queue; **di ~** in succession; **far la ~** queue [up], stand in line Am

fi'lare vt spin; (Naut) pay out ● vi (andarsene) run away; (liquido:) trickle; **fila!** 🔲 scram!; **~ con** (🔲: amoreggiare) go out with

filar'monica f (orchestra) orchestra

fila'strocca f rigmarole; (per bambini) nursery rhyme

fi'la|to adj spun; (ininterrotto) running; (continuato) uninterrupted; **di ~to** (subito) immediately ● m yarn

fil di 'ferro m wire

fi'letto m (bordo) border; (di vite) thread; (Culin) fillet

fili'ale adj filial ● f (Comm) branch

fili'grana f filigree; (su carta) watermark

film m inv film. **~ giallo** thriller. **~ a lungo metraggio** feature film

fil'ma|re vt film. **~to** m short film. **fil'mino** m cine film

'filo m thread; (tessile) yarn; (metallico) wire; (di lama) edge; (venatura) grain; (di perle) string; (d'erba) blade; (di luce) ray; **con un ~ di voce** in a whisper; **fare il ~ a qcno** fancy sb; **perdere il ~** lose the thread. **~spinato** barbed wire

'filobus m inv trolleybus

filodiffusi'one f rediffusion

fi'lone m vein; (di pane) long loaf

filoso'fia f philosophy. **fi'losofo, -a** mf philosopher

fil'trare vt filter. **'filtro** m filter

'filza f string

fin ▷FINE, FINO¹

fi'nal|e adj final ● m end ● f Sport final. **fina'lista** mf finalist. **~ità** f inv finality; (scopo) aim. **~'mente** adv at last; (in ultimo) finally

fi'nanz|a f finance; **~i'ario** adj financial. **~i'ere** m financier; (guardia di finanza) customs officer. **~ia'mento**

m funding

finanzi'a|re *vt* fund, finance. ~**tore**, ~**trice** *mf* backer

finché *conj* until; (*per tutto il tempo che*) as long as

'fine *adj* fine; (*sottile*) thin; (*udito, vista*) keen; (*raffinato*) refined ●*f* end; **alla** ~ in the end; **alla fin** ~ after all; **in fin dei conti** when all's said and done; **senza** ~ endless ●*m* aim. ~ **settimana** weekend

fi'nestra *f* window. **fine'strella** *f* di aiuto (*Comput*) help box. **fine'strino** *m* (*Auto, Rail*) window

fi'nezza *f* fineness; (*sottigliezza*) thinness; (*raffinatezza*) refinement

'finger|e *vt* pretend; feign (*affetto ecc*). ~**si** *vr* pretend to be

fini'menti *mpl* finishing touches; (*per cavallo*) harness *sg*

fini'mondo *m* end of the world; *fig* pandemonium

fi'ni|re *vt/i* finish, end; (*smettere*) stop; (*diventare, andare a finire*) end up; ~**scila!** stop it!. ~**to** *adj* finished; (*abile*) accomplished. ~**tura** *f* finish

finlan'dese *adj* Finnish ●*mf* Finn ●*m* (*lingua*) Finnish

Fin'landia *f* Finland

'fino[1] *prep* ~ **a** till, until; (*spazio*) as far as; ~ **all'ultimo** to the last; **fin da** (*tempo*) since; (*spazio*) from; **fin qui** as far as here; **fin troppo** too much; ~ **a che punto** how far

'fino[2] *adj* fine; (*acuto*) subtle; (*puro*) pure

fi'nocchio *m* fennel; (🔲: *omosessuale*) poof

fi'nora *adv* so far, up till now

'finta *f* sham; *Sport* feint; **far** ~ **a** pretend to; **far** ~ **di niente** act as if nothing had happened; **per** ~ (*per scherzo*) for a laugh

'fint|o, -a *pp di* fingere ●*adj* false; (*artificiale*) artificial; **fare il** ~**o tonto** act dumb

finzi'one *f* pretence

fi'occo *m* bow; (*di neve*) flake; (*nappa*) tassel; **coi fiocchi** *fig* excellent. ~ **di neve** snowflake

fi'ocina *f* harpoon

fi'oco *adj* weak; (*luce*) dim

fi'onda *f* catapult

fio'raio, -a *mf* florist

fiorda'liso *m* cornflower

fi'ordo *m* fiord

fi'ore *m* flower; (*parte scelta*) cream; **fiori** *pl* (*nelle carte*) clubs; **a fior d'acqua** on the surface of the water; **fior di** (*abbondanza*) a lot of; **ha i nervi a fior di pelle** his nerves are on edge; **a fiori** flowery

fioren'tino *adj* Florentine

fio'retto *m* (*scherma*) foil; (*Relig*) act of mortification

fio'rire *vi* flower; (*albero:*) blossom; *fig* flourish

fio'rista *mf* florist

fiori'tura *f* (*di albero*) blossoming

fi'otto *m* **scorrere a fiotti** pour out; **piove a fiotti** the rain is pouring down

Fi'renze *f* Florence

'firma *f* signature; (*nome*) name

fir'ma|re *vt* sign. ~**tario, -a** *mf* signatory. ~**to** *adj* (*abito, borsa*) designer *attrib*

fisar'monica *f* accordion

fi'scale *adj* fiscal

fischi'are *vi* whistle ●*vt* whistle; (*in segno di disapprovazione*) boo

fischiet't|are *vt* whistle. ~**io** *m* whistling

fischi'etto *m* whistle. **'fischio** *m* whistle

'fisco *m* treasury; (*tasse*) taxation; **il** ~ the taxman

'fisica *f* physics

'fisico, -a *adj* physical ●*mf* physicist ●*m* physique

'fisima *f* whim

fisio|lo'gia f physiology. ~'logico adj physiological

fisiono'mia f features, face; (di paesaggio) appearance

fisiotera'pi|a f physiotherapy. ~sta mf physiotherapist

fis'sa|re vt fix, fasten; (guardare fissamente) stare at; arrange (appuntamento, ora). ~rsi vr (stabilirsi) settle; (fissare lo sguardo) stare; ~rsi su (ostinarsi) set one's mind on; ~rsi di fare qcsa become obsessed with doing sth. ~to m obsessive. ~zi'one f fixation; (ossessione) obsession

'fisso adj fixed; **un lavoro** ~ a regular job; **senza fissa dimora** of no fixed abode

fit'tizio adj fictitious

fitto¹ adj thick; ~ **di** full of ● m depth

fitto² m (affitto) rent; **dare a** ~ let; **prendere a** ~ rent; (noleggiare) hire

fiu'mana f swollen river; fig stream

fi'ume m river; fig stream

fiu'tare vt smell. **fi'uto** m [sense of] smell; fig nose

'flaccido adj flabby

fla'cone m bottle

fla'gello m scourge

fla'grante adj flagrant; **in** ~ in the act

fla'nella f flannel

'flash m inv Journ newsflash

'flauto m flute

'flebile adj feeble

'flemma f calm; (Med) phlegm

fles'sibil|e adj flexible. ~ità f flexibility

flessi'one f (del busto in avanti) forward bend

'flesso pp di flettere

flessu'oso adj supple

'flettere vt bend

flir'tare vi flirt

F.lli abbr (fratelli) Bros

'floppy disk m inv floppy disk

'florido adj flourishing

'floscio adj limp; (flaccido) flabby

'flotta f fleet. **flot'tiglia** f flotilla

flu'ente adj fluent

flu'ido m fluid

flu'ire vi flow

fluore'scente adj fluorescent

flu'oro m fluorine

'flusso m flow; (Med) flux; (del mare) flood[-tide]; ~ **e riflusso** ebb and flow

fluttu'ante adj fluctuating

fluttu'a|re vi (prezzi, moneta:) fluctuate. ~zi'one f fluctuation

fluvi'ale adj river

fo'bia f phobia

'foca f seal

fo'caccia f (pane) flat bread; (dolce) ≈ raisin bread

fo'cale adj (distanza, punto) focal. **focaliz'zare** vt get into focus (fotografia); focus (attenzione); define (problema)

'foce f mouth

foco'laio m (Med) focus; fig centre

foco'lare m hearth; (caminetto) fireplace; (Techn) furnace

fo'coso adj fiery

'foder|a f lining; (di libro) dust-jacket; (di poltrona ecc) loose cover. **fode'rare** vt line; cover (libro). ~o m sheath

'foga f impetuosity

'foggi|a f fashion; (maniera) manner; (forma) shape. ~'are vt mould

'foglia f leaf; (di metallo) foil

fogli'etto m (pezzetto di carta) piece of paper

'foglio m sheet; (pagina) leaf. ~ **elettronico** (Comput) spreadsheet. ~ **rosa** (Auto) provisional licence. ~

'fogna f sewer. ~'tura f sewerage

fo'lata f gust

fol'clo|re m folklore. ~'ristico adj

folk; (*bizzarro*) weird

folgo'ra|re *vi* (*splendere*) shine ● *vt* (*con un fulmine*) strike. ~**zi'one** *f* (*da fulmine, elettrica*) electrocution; (*idea*) brainwave

'folgore *f* thunderbolt

'folla *f* crowd

'folle *adj* mad; **in** ~ (*Auto*) in neutral

folle'mente *adv* madly

fol'lia *f* madness; **alla** ~ (*amare*) to distraction

'folto *adj* thick

fomen'tare *vt* stir up

fond'ale *m* (*Theat*) backcloth

fonda'men|ta *fpl* foundations. ~**'tale** *adj* fundamental. ~**to** *m* (*di principio, teoria*) foundation

fon'da|re *vt* establish; base (*ragionamento, accusa*). ~**to** *adj* (*ragionamento*) well-founded. ~**zi'one** *f* establishment; ~**zioni** *pl* (*di edificio*) foundations

fon'delli *mpl* **prendere qcno per i** ~ 🔲 pull sb's leg

fon'dente *adj* (*cioccolato*) dark

'fonder|e *vt/i* melt; (*colori*) blend. ~**si** *vr* melt; (*Comm*) merge

'fondi *mpl* (*denaro*) funds; (*di caffè*) grounds

'fondo *adj* deep; **è notte fonda** it's the middle of the night ● *m* bottom; (*fine*) end; (*sfondo*) background; (*indole*) nature; (*somma di denaro*) fund; (*feccia*) dregs *pl*; **andare a** ~ (*nave:*) sink; **da cima a** ~ from beginning to end; **in** ~ after all; **in** ~ **in** ~ deep down; **fino in** ~ right to the end; (*capire*) thoroughly. ~ **d'investimento** investment trust

fondo'tinta *m* foundation cream

fon'duta *f* ≈ fondue

fo'netic|a *f* phonetics. ~**o** *adj* phonetic

fon'tana *f* fountain

'fonte *f* spring; *fig* source ● *m* font

fo'raggio *m* forage

fo'rar|e *vt* pierce; punch (*biglietto*) ● *vi* puncture. ~**si** *vr* (*gomma, pallone:*) go soft

'forbici *fpl* scissors

forbi'cine *fpl* (*per le unghie*) nail scissors

'forca *f* (*patibolo*) gallows *pl*

for'cella *f* fork; (*per capelli*) hairpin

for'chet|ta *f* fork. ~**'tata** *f* (*quantità*) forkful

for'cina *f* hairpin

'forcipe *m* forceps *pl*

for'cone *m* pitchfork

fo'resta *f* forest. **fore'stale** *adj* forest *attrib*

foresti'ero, -a *adj* foreign ● *mf* foreigner

for'fait *m inv* fixed price; **dare** ~ (*abbandonare*) give up

'forfora *f* dandruff

'forgi|a *f* forge. ~**'are** *vt* forge

'forma *f* form; (*sagoma*) shape; (*Culin*) mould; (*da calzolaio*) last; **essere in** ~ be in good form; **a** ~ **di** in the shape of; **forme** *pl* (*del corpo*) figure *sg*; (*convenzioni*) appearances

formag'gino *m* processed cheese. **for'maggio** *m* cheese

for'mal|e *adj* formal. ~**ità** *f inv* formality. ~**iz'zarsi** *vr* stand on ceremony. ~**'mente** *adv* formally

for'ma|re *vt* form. ~**rsi** *vr* form; (*svilupparsi*) develop. ~**to** *m* size; (*di libro*) format; ~**to tessera** (*fotografia*) passportsize

format'tare *vt* format

formazi'one *f* formation; *Sport* line-up. ~ **professionale** vocational training

formico'l|are *vi* (*braccio ecc:*) tingle; ~**are di** be swarming with; **mi** ~**a la mano** I have pins and needles in my hand. ~**io** *m* swarming; (*di braccio ecc*) pins and needles *pl*

formi'dabile *adj* (*tremendo*) formidable; (*eccezionale*) tremendous

for'mina f mould

for'moso adj shapely

'formula f formula. **formu'lare** vt formulate; (esprimere) express

for'nace f furnace; (per laterizi) kiln

for'naio m baker; (negozio) bakery

for'nello m stove; (di pipa) bowl

for'ni|re vt supply (di with). ~'tore m supplier. ~'tura f supply

'forno m oven; (panetteria) bakery; **al ~** roast. ~ **a microonde** microwave [oven]

'foro m hole; (romano) forum; (tribunale) [law] court

'forse adv perhaps, maybe; **essere in ~** be in doubt

forsen'nato, -a adj mad ● mf madman/ madwoman

'forte adj strong; (colore) bright; (suono) loud; (resistente) tough; (spesa) considerable; (dolore) severe; (pioggia) heavy; (a tennis, calcio) good; (**I**: simpatico) great; (taglia) large ● adv strongly; (parlare) loudly; (velocemente) fast; (piovere) heavily ● m (fortezza) fort; (specialità) strong point

for'tezza f fortress; (forza morale) fortitude

fortifi'care vt fortify

for'tino m (Mil) blockhouse

for'tuito adj fortuitous; **incontro ~** chance encounter

for'tuna f fortune; (successo) success; (buona sorte) luck. **atterraggio di ~** forced landing; **aver ~** be lucky; **buona ~!** I good luck!; **di ~** makeshift; **per ~** luckily. **fortu'nato** adj lucky, fortunate; (impresa) successful. ~**ta'mente** adv fortunately

fo'runcolo m pimple; (grosso) boil

'forza f strength; (potenza) power; (fisica) force; **di ~** by force; **a ~ di** by dint of; **con ~** hard; ~**!** come on!; ~ **di volontà** will-power; **maggiore** circumstances beyond one's control; **la ~ pubblica** the police; **per ~** against one's will; (natu-

ralmente) of course; **farsi ~** bear up; **mare ~** 8 force 8 gale; **bella ~!** I big deal!. **le forze armate** the armed forces

for'za|re vt force; (scassare) break open; (sforzare) strain. ~**to** adj forced; (sorriso) strained ● m convict

forzi'ere m coffer

for'zuto adj strong

fo'schia f haze

'fosco adj dark

fos'fato m phosphate

'fosforo m phosphorus

'fossa f pit; (tomba) grave. ~ **biologica** cesspool. fos'sato m (di fortificazione) moat

fos'setta f dimple

'fossile m fossil

'fosso m ditch; (Mil) trench

'foto f inv **I** photo; **fare delle ~** take some photos

foto'camera f camera

foto'cellula f photocell

fotocomposizi'one f filmsetting, photocomposition

foto'copi|a f photocopy. ~**'are** vt photocopy. ~**a'trice** f photocopier

foto'finish m inv photo finish

fotogra'fare vt photograph. ~**'fia** f (arte) photography; (immagine) photograph; **fare ~fie** take photographs. **foto'grafico** adj photographic; **macchina fotografica** camera. fo'tografo, -a mf photographer

foto'gramma m frame

fotomo'dello, -a mf [photographer's] model

foto'manzo m photo story

fou'lard m inv scarf

fra prep (in mezzo a due) between; (in un insieme) among; (tempo, distanza) in; **detto ~ noi** between you and me; ~ **sé e sé** to oneself; ~ **l'altro** what's more; ~ **breve** soon; ~ **quindici giorni** in two weeks' time;

~ **tutti, siamo in venti** there are twenty of us altogether

fracas'sar|e vt smash. ~**si** vr shatter

fra'casso m din; (di cose che cadono) crash

'fradicio adj (bagnato) soaked; (guasto) rotten; **ubriaco** ~ blind drunk

'fragil|e adj fragile; fig frail. ~**ità** f fragility; fig frailty

'fragola f strawberry

fra'go|re m uproar; (di cose rotte) clatter; (di tuono) rumble. ~**'roso** adj uproarious; (tuono) rumbling; (suono) clanging

fra'gran|te adj fragrant. ~**za** f fragrance

frain'te|ndere vt misunderstand. ~**ndersi** vr be at cross-purposes. ~**so** pp di **fraintendere**

frammen'tario adj fragmentary

'frana f landslide. **fra'nare** vi slide down

franca'mente adv frankly

fran'cese adj French ● mf Frenchman; Frenchwoman ● m (lingua) French

fran'chezza f frankness

'Francia f France

'franco[1] adj frank; (Comm) free; **farla franca** get away with sth

'franco[2] m (moneta) franc

franco'bollo m stamp

fran'gente m (onda) breaker; (scoglio) reef; (fig: momento difficile) crisis; **in quel** ~ given the situation

'frangia f fringe

fra'noso adj subject to landslides

fran'toio m olive-press

frantu'mar|e vt, ~**si** vr shatter. **fran'tumi** mpl splinters; **andare in frantumi** be smashed to pieces

frappé m inv milkshake

frap'por|re vt interpose. ~**si** vr intervene

fra'sario m vocabulary; (libro) phrase book

'frase f sentence; (espressione) phrase. ~ **fatta** cliché

'frassino m ash[-tree]

frastagli'a|re vt make jagged. ~**to** adj jagged

frastor'na|re vt daze. ~**to** adj dazed

frastu'ono m racket

'frate m friar; (monaco) monk

fratel'la|nza f brotherhood. ~**stro** m half-brother

fra'tel|li mpl (fratello e sorella) brother and sister. ~**o** m brother

fraterniz'zare vi fraternize. **fra'terno** adj brotherly

frat'taglie fpl (di pollo ecc) giblets

frat'tanto adv in the meantime

frat'tempo m **nel** ~ meanwhile, in the meantime

frat'tu|ra f fracture. ~**'rare** vt, ~**'rarsi** vr break

fraudo'lento adj fraudulent

frazi'one f fraction; (borgata) hamlet

'freccia f arrow; (Auto) indicator. ~**'ata** f (osservazione pungente) cutting remark

fredda'mente adv coldly

fred'dare vt cool; (fig: con sguardo, battuta) cut down; (uccidere) kill

fred'dezza f coldness

'freddo m & adj cold; **aver** ~ be cold; **fa** ~ it's cold

freddo'loso adj sensitive to cold

fred'dura f pun

fre'ga|re vt rub; (🔲: truffare) cheat; (🔲: rubare) swipe. ~**rsene** 🔲 not give a damn; **chi se ne frega!** what the heck!. ~**si** vr rub (occhi). ~**ta** f rub. ~**'tura** f 🔲 (truffa) swindle; (delusione) letdown

'fregio m (Archit) frieze; (ornamento) decoration

'frem|ere vi quiver. ~**ito** m quiver

fre'na|re vt brake; (fig restrain; hold back (lacrime) •vi brake. ~**rsi** vr check oneself. ~**ta** f fare una ~**ta brusca** brake sharply

frene'sia f frenzy; (desiderio smodato) craze. **fre'netico** adj frenzied

'freno m brake; (fig check; **togliere il** ~ release the brake; **usare il** ~ apply the brake; **tenere a** ~ restrain. ~ **a mano** handbrake

frequen'tare vt frequent; attend (scuola ecc); mix with (persone)

fre'quen|te adj frequent; **di** ~**te** frequently. ~**za** f frequency; (assiduità) attendance

fre'schezza f freshness; (di temperatura) coolness

'fresco adj fresh; (temperatura) cool; **stai** ~**!** you're for it! •m coolness; **far** ~ be cool; **mettere/tenere in** ~ put/keep in a cool place

'fretta f hurry, haste; **aver** ~ be in a hurry; **far** ~ **a qcno** hurry sb; **in** ~ **e furia** in a great hurry. **frettolosa'mente** adv hurriedly. **fretto'loso** adj (persona) in a hurry; (lavoro) rushed, hurried

fri'abile adj crumbly

'friggere vt fry; **vai a farti** ~**!** get lost! •vi sizzle

friggi'trice f chip pan

frigidità f frigidity. **'frigido** adj frigid

fri'gnare vi whine

'frigo m inv fridge

frigo'bar m inv minibar

frigo'rifero adj refrigerating •m refrigerator

frit'tata f omelette

frit'tella f fritter; (▣: macchia d'unto) grease stain

'fritto pp di **friggere** •adj fried; **essere** ~ be done for •m fried food. ~ **misto** mixed fried fish/vegetables. **frit'tura** f fried dish

frivo'lezza f frivolity. **'frivolo** adj frivolous

frizio'nare vt rub. **frizi'one** f friction; (Mech) clutch; (di pelle) rub

friz'zante adj fizzy; (vino) sparkling; (aria) bracing

'frizzo m gibe

fro'dare vt defraud

'frode f fraud. ~ **fiscale** tax evasion

'frollo adj tender; (selvaggina) high; (persona) spineless; **pasta frolla** short[crust] pastry

'fronda f [leafy] branch; fig rebellion. **fron'doso** adj leafy

fron'tale adj frontal; (scontro) head-on

'fronte f forehead; (di edificio) front; **di** ~ opposite; **di** ~ **a** opposite, facing; (a paragone) compared with; **far** ~ **a** face •m (Mil, Pol) front. ~**ggi'are** vt face

fronti'era f frontier, border

fron'tone m pediment

'fronzolo m frill

'frotta f swarm; (di animali) flock

'frottola f fib; **frottole** pl nonsense sg

fru'gale adj frugal

fru'gare vi rummage •vt search

frul'la|re vt (Culin) whisk •vi (ali): whirr. ~**to** m ~**to di frutta** fruit drink with milk and crushed ice. ~**'tore** m [electric] mixer. **frul'lino** m whisk

fru'mento m wheat

frusci'are vi rustle

fru'scio m rustle; (radio, giradischi) background noise; (di acque) murmur

'frusta f whip; (frullino) whisk

fru'sta|re vt whip. ~**ta** f lash. **fru'stino** m riding crop

fru'stra|re vt frustrate. ~**to** adj frustrated. ~**zi'one** f frustration

'frutt|a f fruit; (portata) dessert. **frut'tare** vi bear fruit •vt yield. **frut'teto**

m orchard. **~i'vendolo, -a** *mf* greengrocer. **~o** *m* fruit; **Fin** yield; **~i di bosco** fruits of the forest. **~i di mare** seafood *sg*. **~u'oso** *adj* profitable

f.to *abbr* (firmato) signed

fu *adj* (defunto) late; **il ~ signor Rossi** the late Mr Rossi

fuci'la|re *vt* shoot. **~ta** *f* shot

fu'cile *m* rifle

fu'cina *f* forge

'fuga *f* escape; (perdita) leak; (Mus) fugue; **darsi alla ~** escape

fu'gace *adj* fleeting

fug'gevole *adj* short-lived

fuggi'asco, -a *mf* fugitive

fuggi'fuggi *m* stampede

fug'gi|re *vi* flee; (innamorati:) elope; fig fly. **~tivo, -a** *mf* fugitive

'fulcro *m* fulcrum

ful'gore *m* splendour

fu'liggine *f* soot

fulmi'nar|e *vt* strike by lightning; (con sguardo) look daggers at; (con scarica elettrica) electrocute. **~si** *vr* burn out. **'fulmine** *m* lightning. **ful'mineo** *adj* rapid

'fulvo *adj* tawny

fumai'olo *m* funnel; (di casa) chimney

fu'ma|re *vt/i* smoke; (in ebollizione) steam. **~'tore, ~'trice** *mf* smoker; **non fumatori** non-smoker, non-smoking

fu'metto *m* comic strip; **fumetti** *pl* comics

'fumo *m* smoke; (vapore) steam; fig hot air; **andare in ~** vanish. **fu-'moso** *adj* smoky; (discorso) vague

fu'nambolo, -a *mf* tightrope walker

'fune *f* rope; (cavo) cable

'funebre *adj* funeral; (cupo) gloomy

fune'rale *m* funeral

fu'nesto *adj* sad

'fungere *vi* **~ da** act as

Funghi Wild mushrooms are an Italian passion, and the most prized is the *porcino* (cep), which can be bought fresh or dried. However, many Italians are also avid mushroom-pickers and are expert at differentiating edible mushrooms (*funghi commestibili*) from poisonous ones. Local authorities often have a department controlling the picking and selling of mushrooms.

'fungo *m* mushroom; (Bot) fungus

funico'lare *f* funicular [railway]

funi'via *f* cableway

funzio'nal|e *adj* functional. **~ità** *f* functionality

funziona'mento *m* functioning

funzio'nare *vi* work, function; **~ da** (fungere da) act as

funzio'nario *m* official

funzi'one *f* function; (carica) office; (Relig) service; **entrare in ~** take up office

fu'oco *m* fire; (fisica, fotografia) focus; **far ~** fire; **dar ~ a** set fire to; **prendere ~** catch fire. **fuochi** *pl* **d'artificio** fireworks

fuorché *prep* except

fu'ori *adv* out; (all'esterno) outside; (all'aperto) outdoors; **andare di ~** (traboccare) spill over; **essere ~ di sé** be beside oneself; **essere in ~** (sporgere) stick out; **far ~** 🆒 do in; **~ luogo** (inopportuno) out of place; **~ mano** out of the way; **~ moda** old-fashioned; **~ pasto** between meals; **~ pericolo** out of danger; **~ questione** out of the question; **~ uso** out of use **•m** outside

fuori'bordo *m* speedboat (with outboard motor)

fuori'classe mf inv champion
fuorigi'oco m & adv offside
fuori'legge mf outlaw
fuori'serie adj custom-made • f (Auto) custom-built model
fuori'strada m off-road vehicle
fuorvi'are vt lead astray • vi go astray
furbe'ria f cunning. **fur'bizia** f cunning
'furbo adj cunning; (intelligente) clever; (astuto) shrewd; **bravo ~!** nice one!; **fare il ~** try to be clever
fu'rente adj furious
fur'fante m scoundrel
furgon'cino m delivery van. **fur-'gone** m van
furi|a f fury; (fretta) haste; **a ~a di** by dint of. **~'bondo**, **~'oso** adj furious
fu'rore m fury; (veemenza) frenzy; **far ~** be all the rage. **~ggi'are** vi be a great success
furtiva'mente adv covertly. **fur-'tivo** adj furtive
'furto m theft; (con scasso) burglary; **commettere un ~** steal. **~ d'iden-tità** identity theft
'fusa fpl **fare le ~** purr
fu'scello m (di legno) twig; (di paglia) straw; **sei un ~** you're as light as a feather
fu'seaux mpl leggings
fu'sibile m fuse
fusi'one f fusion; (Comm) merger
'fuso pp di **fondere** • adj melted • m spindle. **~ orario** time zone
fusoli'era f fuselage
fu'stagno m corduroy
fu'stino m (di detersivo) box
'fusto m stem; (tronco) trunk; (reci-piente di metallo) drum; (di legno) barrel
'futile adj futile
fu'turo adj & m future

Gg

gab'bar|e vt cheat. **~si** vr **~si di** make fun of
'gabbia f cage; (da imballaggio) crate. **~ degli imputati** dock. **~ toracica** rib cage
gabbi'ano m [sea]gull
gabi'netto m consulting room; (Pol) cabinet; (bagno) lavatory; (labora-torio) laboratory
'gaffe f inv blunder
gagli'ardo adj vigorous
gai'ezza f gaiety. **'gaio** adj cheerful
'gala f gala
ga'lante adj gallant. **~'ria** f gal-lantry. **galantu'omo** m (pl **galantuo-mini**) gentleman
ga'lassia f galaxy
gala'teo m [good] manners pl; (trat-tato) book of etiquette
gale'otto m (rematore) galley-slave; (condannato) convict
ga'lera f (nave) galley; ⊞ prison
'galla f (Bot) gall; **a ~** adv afloat; **ve-nire a ~** surface
galleggi'are vi float
galle'ria f tunnel; (d'arte) gallery; (Theat) circle; (arcata) arcade. **~ d'arte** art gallery
'Galles m Wales. **gal'lese** adj welsh • m Welshman; (lingua) Welsh • f Welshwoman
gal'letto m cockerel; **fare il ~** show off
gal'lina f hen
gal'lismo m machismo
'gallo m cock
gal'lone m stripe; (misura) gallon
galop'pare vi gallop. **ga'loppo** m gallop; **al galoppo** at a gallop
'gamba f leg; (di lettera) stem; **a**

quattro gambe on all fours; **essere in ~** (*essere forte*) be strong; (*capace*) be smart

gamba'letto m pop sock

gambe'retto m shrimp. **'gambero** m prawn; (*di fiume*) crayfish

'gambo m stem; (*di pianta*) stalk

'gamma f (*Mus*) scale; *fig* range

ga'nascia f jaw; **ganasce** pl del freno brake shoes

'gancio m hook

'ganghero m **uscire dai gangheri** *fig* get into a temper

'gara f competition; (*di velocità*) race; **fare a ~** compete

ga'rage m inv garage

ga'ran|te mf guarantor. **~'tire** vt guarantee; (*rendersi garante*) vouch for; (*assicurare*) assure. **~'zia** f guarantee; **in ~zia** under guarantee

gar'ba|re vi like; **non mi garba** I don't like it. **~to** adj courteous

'garbo m courtesy; (*grazia*) grace; **con ~** graciously

gareggi'are vi compete

garga'nella f **a ~** from the bottle

garga'rismo m gargle; **fare i gargarismi** gargle

ga'rofano m carnation

'garza f gauze

gar'zone m boy. **~ di stalla** stable-boy

gas m inv gas; **dare ~** (*Auto*) accelerate; **a tutto ~** flat out. **~ lacrimogeno** tear gas. **~ pl di scarico** exhaust fumes

gas'dotto m natural gas pipeline

ga'solio m diesel oil

ga'sometro m gasometer

gas's|are vt aerate; (*uccidere col gas*) gas. **~ato** adj gassy. **~oso, -a** adj gassy; (*bevanda*) fizzy ●f lemonade

'gastrico adj gastric. **ga'strite** f gastritis

gastro|no'mia f gastronomy. **~'nomico** adj gastronomic. **ga'stro-**

nomo, -a mf gourmet

'gatta f **una ~ da pelare** a headache

gatta'buia f hum clink

gat'tino, -a mf kitten

'gatto, -a mf cat. **~ delle nevi** snowmobile

gat'toni adv on all fours

gay adj inv gay

'gazza f magpie

gaz'zarra f racket

gaz'zella f gazelle; (*Auto*) police car

gaz'zetta f gazette

gaz'zosa f clear lemonade

'geco m gecko

ge'la|re vt/i freeze. **~ta** f frost

gela't|aio, -a mf ice-cream seller; (*negozio*) ice-cream shop. **~e'ria** f ice-cream parlour. **~i'era** f ice-cream maker

gela'ti|na f gelatine; (*dolce*) jelly. **~na di frutta** fruit jelly.

ge'lato adj frozen ●m ice-cream

'gelido adj freezing

'gelo m (*freddo intenso*) freezing cold; (*brina*) frost; *fig* chill

ge'lone m chilblain

gelosa'mente adv jealously

gelo'sia f jealousy. **ge'loso** adj jealous

'gelso m mulberry[-tree]

gelso'mino m jasmine

gemel'laggio m twinning

ge'mello, -a adj & mf twin; (*di polsino*) cuff-link; **Gemelli** pl (*Astr*) Gemini sg

'gem|ere vi groan; (*tubare*) coo. **~ito** m groan

'gemma f gem; (*Bot*) bud

'gene m gene

genealo'gia f genealogy

gene'ral|e[1] adj general; **spese ~i** overheads

gene'rale[2] m (*Mil*) general

generalità f (*qualità*) generality, general nature; ~ pl (dati personali) particulars

generaliz'za|re vt generalize. ~zi'one f generalization. general'mente adv generally

gene'ra|re vt give birth to; (causare) breed; (Techn) generate. ~'tore m (Techn) generator. ~zi'one f generation

'**genere** m kind; (Biol) genus; (Gram) gender; (letterario, artistico) genre; (prodotto) product; il ~ umano mankind; in ~ generally. generi pl alimentari provisions

ge'nerico adj generic; medico generico general practitioner

'**genero** m son-in-law

generosità f generosity. gene'roso adj generous

'**genesi** f inv genesis

ge'netico, -a adj genetic ●f genetics

gen'giva f gum

geni'ale adj ingenious; (congeniale) congenial

'**genio** m genius; andare a ~ be to one's taste. ~ civile civil engineering. ~ [militare] Engineers

geni'tale adj genital. genitali mpl genitals

geni'tore m parent

gen'naio m January

'**Genova** f Genoa

gen'taglia f rabble

'**gente** f people pl

gen'ti|le adj kind; G~e Signore (in lettere) Dear Sir. genti'lezza f kindness; per gentilezza (per favore) please. ~'mente adv kindly. ~u'omo (pl ~u'omini) m gentleman

genu'ino adj genuine; (cibo, prodotto) natural

geogra'fia f geography. geo'grafico adj geographical. ge'ografo, -a mf geographer

geolo'gia f geology. geo'logico adj geological. ge'ologo, -a mf geologist

ge'ometra mf surveyor

geome'tria f geometry

ge'ranio m geranium

gerar'chia f hierarchy

ge'rente m manager ●f manageress

'**gergo** m slang; (di professione ecc) jargon

geria'tria f geriatrics sg

Ger'mania f Germany

'**germe** m germ; (fig: principio) seed

germogli'are vi sprout. ger'moglio m sprout

gero'glifico m hieroglyph

'**gesso** m chalk; (Med, scultura) plaster

gestazi'one f gestation

gestico'lare vi gesticulate

gesti'one f management

ge'stir|e vi manage. ~si vr budget one's time and money

'**gesto** m gesture; (azione pl f gesta) deed

ge'store m manager

Gesù m Jesus. ~ bambino baby Jesus

gesu'ita m Jesuit

get'ta|re vt throw; (scagliare) fling; (emettere) spout; (Techn), fig cast; ~re via throw away. ~rsi vr throw oneself; ~rsi in (fiume) flow into. ~ta f throw

'**getto** m throw; (di liquidi, gas) jet; a ~ continuo in a continuous stream; di ~ straight off

getto'nato adj popular. get'tone m token; (per giochi) counter

'**ghetto** m ghetto

ghiacci'aio m glacier

ghiacci'a|re vt/i freeze. ~to adj frozen; (freddissimo) ice-cold

ghi'acci|o m ice; (Auto) black ice. ~'olo m icicle; (gelato) ice lolly

ghi'aia f gravel

ghi'anda f acorn

ghi'andola f gland

ghigliot'tina f guillotine

ghi'gnare vi sneer

ghi'ot|to adj greedy; (appetitoso) appetizing. ∼**tone, -a** mf glutton. ∼**tone'ria** f (qualità) gluttony; (cibo) tasty morsel

ghir'landa f (corona) wreath; (di fiori) garland

'ghiro m dormouse; **dormire come un ∼** sleep like a log

'ghisa f cast iron

già adv already; (un tempo) formerly; ∼**!** indeed!; **∼ da ieri** since yesterday

gi'acca f jacket. **∼ a vento** windcheater

giacché conj since

giac'cone m jacket

gia'cere vi lie

giaci'mento m deposit. **∼ di petrolio** oil deposit

gia'cinto m hyacinth

gi'ada f jade

giaggi'olo m iris

giagu'aro m jaguar

gial'lastro adj yellowish

gi'allo adj & m yellow; **[libro] ∼** thriller

Giap'pone m Japan. **giappo'nese** adj & mf Japanese

giardi'n|aggio m gardening. ∼**i'ere, -a** mf gardener ●f (Auto) estate car; (sottaceti) pickles pl

giar'dino m garden. **∼ d'infanzia** kindergarten. **∼ pensile** roofgarden. **∼ zoologico** zoo

giarretti'era f garter

giavel'lotto m javelin

gi'gan|te adj gigantic ●m giant. ∼**'tesco** adj gigantic

gigantogra'fia f blow-up

'giglio m lily

gilè m inv waistcoat

gin m inv gin

gineco|lo'gia f gynaecology. ∼**lo'gico** adj gynaecological. **gine'cologo, -a** mf gynaecologist

gi'nepro m juniper

gingil'larsi vr fiddle; (perder tempo) potter. **gin'gillo** m plaything; (ninnolo) knick-knack

gin'nasio m ≈ grammar school

gin'nast|a mf gymnast. ∼**ica** f gymnastics; (esercizi) exercises pl

ginocchi'ata f **prendere una ∼** bang one's knee

gi'nocchi|o m (pl m **ginocchi** o f **ginocchia**) knee; **in ∼o** on one's knees; **mettersi in ∼o** kneel down; (per supplicare) go down on one's knees. **∼'oni** adv kneeling

gio'ca|re vt/i play; (giocherellare) toy; (d'azzardo) gamble; (puntare) stake; (ingannare) trick. **∼rsi la carriera** throw one's career away. ∼**tore, ∼'trice** mf player; (d'azzardo) gambler

gio'cattolo m toy

giocherel'l|are vi toy; (nervosamente) fiddle. **∼one** adj skittish

gi'oco m game; (Techn) play; (d'azzardo) gambling; (scherzo) joke; (insieme di pezzi ecc) set; **fare il doppio ∼ con** double-cross sb

giocoli'ere m juggler

gio'coso adj playful

gi'oia f joy; (gioiello) jewel; (appellativo) sweetie

gioiell|e'ria f jeweller's [shop]. ∼**i'ere, -a** mf jeweller; (negozio) jeweller's. **gioi'ello** m jewel; **gioielli** pl jewellery

gioi'oso adj joyous

gio'ire vi **∼ per** rejoice at

Gior'dania f Jordan

giorna'laio, -a mf newsagent

gior'nale m [news]paper; (diario) journal. **∼ di bordo** logbook. **∼ radio** news bulletin

g

giornali'ero adj daily ●m (per sciare) day pass

giorna'lino m comic

giorna'lis|mo m journalism. ~ta mf journalist

giornal'mente adv daily

gior'nata f day; in ~ today

gi'orno m day; al ~ per day; al ~ d'oggi nowadays; di ~ by day; un ~ sì, un ~ no every other day

gi'ostra f merry-go-round

giova'mento m trarre ~ da derive benefit from

gi'ova|ne adj young; (giovanile) youthful ●m young man ●f young woman. ~'nile adj youthful. ~'notto m young man

gio'var|e vi ~e a be useful to; (far bene a) be good for. ~si vr ~si di avail oneself of

giovedì m inv Thursday. ~ grasso last Thursday before Lent

gioventù f youth; (i giovani) young people pl

giovi'ale adj jovial

giovi'nezza f youth

gira'dischi m inv record-player

gi'raffa f giraffe; Cinema boom

gi'randola f (fuoco d'artificio) Catherine wheel; (giocattolo) windmill; (banderuola) weathercock

gi'ra|re vt turn; (andare intorno, visitare) go round; (Comm) endorse; Cinema shoot ●vi turn; (aerei, uccelli): circle; (andare in giro) wander; ~re al largo steer clear. ~rsi vr turn [round]; mi gira la testa I'm dizzy

girar'rosto m spit

gira'sole m sunflower

gi'rata f turn; (Comm) endorsement; (in macchina ecc) ride; fare una ~ (a piedi) go for a walk; (in macchina) go for a ride

gira'volta f spin; fig U-turn

gi'rello m (per bambini) babywalker; (Culin) topside

gi'revole adj revolving

gi'rino m tadpole

'giro m turn; (circolo) circle; (percorso) round; (viaggio) tour; (passeggiata) short walk; (in macchina) drive; (in bicicletta) ride; (circolazione di denaro) circulation; nel ~ di un mese within a month; senza giri di parole without beating about the bush; a ~ di posta by return mail. ~ d'affari (Comm) turnover. giri pl al minuto rpm. ~ turistico sightseeing tour. ~ vita waist measurement

giro'collo m choker; a ~ crewneck

gi'rone m round

gironzo'lare vi wander about

girova'gare vi wander about. gi'rovago m wanderer

'gita f trip; andare in ~ go on a trip. ~ scolastica school trip. gi'tante mf tripper

giù adv down; (sotto) below; (dabbasso) downstairs; a testa in ~ (a capofitto) headlong; essere ~ be down; (di salute) be run down; ~ di corda down; ~ di lì, su per ~ more or less; non andare ~ a qcno stick in sb's craw

gi'ub|ba f jacket; (Mil) tunic. ~'botto m bomber jacket

giudi'care vt judge; (ritenere) consider

gi'udice m judge. ~ conciliatore justice of the peace. ~ di gara umpire. ~ di linea linesman

giu'dizi|o m judg[e]ment; (opinione) opinion; (senno) wisdom; (processo) trial; (sentenza) sentence; mettere ~o become wise. ~'oso adj sensible

gi'ugno m June

giu'menta f mare

gi'ungere vi arrive; ~ a (riuscire) succeed in ●vt (unire) join

gi'ungla f jungle

gi'unta f addition; (Mil) junta; per ~ in addition. ~ comunale district council

gi'unto pp di giungere ● m (Mech) joint

giun'tura f joint

giuo'care, giu'oco = GIO-CARE, GIOCO

giura'mento m oath; prestare ~ take the oath

giu'ra|re vt/i swear. ~to, -a adj sworn ● mf juror

giu'ria f jury

giu'ridico adj legal

giurisdizi'one f jurisdiction

giurispru'denza f jurisprudence

giu'rista mf jurist

giustifi'ca|re vt justify. ~zi'one f justification

giu'stizi|a f justice. ~'are vt execute. ~'ere m executioner

gi'usto adj just, fair; (adatto) right; (esatto) exact ● m (uomo retto) just man; (cosa giusta) right ● adv exactly; ~ ora just now

glaci'ale adj glacial

gla'diolo m gladiolus

'glassa f (Culin) icing

gli def art mpl (before vowel and s + consonant, gn, ps, z) the; ▸IL ● pron (a lui) [to] him; (a esso) [to] it; (a loro) [to] them

glice'rina f glycerine

'glicine m wisteria

gli'e|lo, -a pron [to] him/her/them; (forma di cortesia) [to] you; ~ chiedo I'll ask him/her/them/you; gliel'ho prestato I've lent it to him/her/them/you. ~ne (di ciò) [of] it; ~ne ho dato un po' I gave him/her/them/you some

glo'bal|e adj global; fig overall. ~izza'zione f globalization. ~'mente adv globally

'globo m globe. ~ oculare eyeball. ~ terrestre globe

'globulo m globule; (Med) corpuscle. ~ bianco white corpuscle. ~ rosso red corpuscle

'gloria f glory. ~'arsi vr ~arsi di be proud of. ~'oso adj glorious

glos'sario m glossary

glu'cosio m glucose

'gluteo m buttock

'gnorri m fare lo ~ play dumb

'gobb|a f hump. ~o, -a adj hunchbacked ● mf hunchback

'gocci|a f drop; (di sudore) bead; è stata l'ultima ~ it was the last straw. ~o'lare vi drip. ~o'lio m dripping

go'der|e vi (sessualmente) come; ~e di enjoy. ~sela have a good time. ~si vr ~si qcsa enjoy sth

godi'mento m enjoyment

goffa'mente adv awkwardly. 'goffo adj awkward

'gola f throat; (ingordigia) gluttony; (Geog) gorge; (di camino) flue; avere mal di ~ have a sore throat; far ~ a qcno tempt sb

golf m inv jersey; Sport golf

'golfo m gulf

golosità f inv greediness; (cibo) tasty morsel. go'loso adj greedy

'golpe m inv coup

gomi'tata f nudge

'gomito m elbow; alzare il ~ raise one's elbow

go'mitolo m ball

'gomma f rubber; (colla, da masticare) gum; (pneumatico) tyre. ~ da masticare chewing gum

gommapi'uma f foam rubber

gom'mista m tyre specialist

gom'mone m [rubber] dinghy

'gondol|a f gondola. ~i'ere m gondolier

gonfa'lone m banner

gonfi'abile adj inflatable

gonfi'ar|e vi swell ● vt blow up; pump up (pneumatico); (esagerare) exaggerate. ~si vr swell; (acque): rise. 'gonfio adj swollen; (pneumatico) inflated. **gonfi'ore** m swelling

gongo'la|nte _adj_ overjoyed. **~re** _vi_ be overjoyed

'gonna _f_ skirt. **~ pantalone** culottes _pl_

goo'glare _vt/i_ google

gorgogli'are _vi_ gurgle

go'rilla _m inv_ gorilla; (_guardia del corpo_) bodyguard

'gotico _adj & m_ Gothic

gover'nante _f_ housekeeper

gover'na|re _vt_ govern; (_dominare_) rule; (_dirigere_) manage; (_curare_) look after. **~tore** _m_ governor

go'verno _m_ government; (_dominio_) rule; **al ~ in** power

gps _m_ gps

gracchi'are _vi_ caw; _fig:_ (_persona:_) screech

graci'dare _vi_ croak

'gracile _adj_ delicate

gra'dasso _m_ braggart

grada'mente _adv_ gradually

gradazi'one _f_ gradation. **~ alcoolica** alcohol[ic] content

gra'devol|e _adj_ agreeable.

gradi'mento _m_ liking; **indice di ~** (_Radio, TV_) popularity rating; **non è di mio ~** it's not to my liking

gradi'nata _f_ flight of steps; (_di stadio_) stand; (_di teatro_) tiers _pl_

gra'dino _m_ step

gra'di|re _vt_ like; (_desiderare_) wish. **~to** _adj_ pleasant; (_bene accetto_) welcome

'grado _m_ degree; (_rango_) rank; **di buon ~** willingly; **essere in ~ di fare qcsa** be in a position to do sth (_essere capace a_) be able to do sth

gradu'ale _adj_ gradual

gradu'a|re _vt_ graduate. **~to** _adj_ graded; (_provvisto di scala graduata_) graduated ●_m_ (_Mil_) non-commissioned officer. **~toria** _f_ list. **~zi'one** _f_ graduation

'graffa _f_ clip

graf'fetta _f_ staple

graffi'a|re _vt_ scratch. **~'tura** _f_ scratch

'graffio _m_ scratch

gra'fia _f_ [hand]writing; (_ortografia_) spelling

'grafic|a _f_ graphics; **~a pubblicitaria** commercial art. **~a'mente** _adv_ graphically. **~o** _adj_ graphic ●_m_ graph; (_persona_) graphic designer

gra'migna _f_ weed

gram'matica _f_ grammar

'grammo _m_ gram[me]

gran _adj_ ▷**GRANDE**

'grana _f_ grain; (_formaggio_) parmesan; (🄵: _seccatura_) trouble; (🄵: _soldi_) readies _pl_

gra'naio _m_ barn

gra'nat|a _f_ (_Mil_) grenade; (_frutto_) pomegranate. **~i'ere** _m_ (_Mil_) grenadier

Gran Bre'tagna _f_ Great Britain

'granchio _m_ crab; (_errore_) blunder; **prendere un ~** make a blunder

grandango'lare _m_ wide-angle lens

'grande (_a volte_ **gran**) _adj_ (_ampio_) large; (_grosso_) big; (_alto_) tall; (_largo_) wide; (_fig: senso morale_) great; (_grandioso_) grand; (_adulto_) grown-up; **ho una gran fame** I'm very hungry; **fa un gran caldo** it is very hot; **in ~** on a large scale; **in gran parte** to a great extent; **un gran ballo** a grand ball ●_mf_ (_persona adulta_) grown-up; (_persona eminente_) great man/woman. **~ggi'are** _vi_ **~ggiare su** tower over; (_darsi arie_) show off

gran'dezza _f_ greatness; (_ampiezza_) largeness; (_larghezza_) width, breadth; (_dimensione_) size; (_fasto_) grandeur; (_prodigalità_) lavishness; **a ~ naturale** life-size

grandi'nare _vi_ hail; **grandina** it's hailing. **'grandine** _f_ hail

grandiosità _f_ grandeur. **grandi'oso** _adj_ grand

gran'duca _m_ grand duke

gra'nello m grain; (di frutta) pip
gra'nita f crushed ice drink
gra'nito m granite
'grano m grain; (frumento) wheat
gran'turco m maize
'granulo m granule
'grappa f grappa; (morsa) cramp
'grappolo m bunch. ~ d'uva
bunch of grapes
gras'setto m bold [type]
gras'sezza f fatness
'gras|so adj fat; (cibo) fatty; (unto)
greasy; (terreno) rich; (grossolano)
coarse ●m fat; (sostanza) grease.
~'soccio adj plump
'grata f grating. gra'tella, gra'ticola
f (Culin) grill
gra'tifica f bonus. ~zi'one f satisfaction
grati'na|re vt cook au gratin. ~to
adj au gratin
grati'tudine f gratitude. 'grato adj
grateful; (gradito) pleasant
gratta'capo m trouble
grattaci'elo m skyscraper
'gratta e 'vinci m inv scratch card
grat'tar|e vt scratch; (raschiare)
scrape; (grattugiare) grate; (🔟: rubare)
pinch ●vi grate. ~si vr scratch
oneself
grat'tugi|a f grater. ~'are vt grate
gratuita'mente adv free [of
charge]. gra'tuito adj free [of
charge]; (ingiustificato) gratuitous
gra'vare vt burden ●vi ~ su
weigh on
'grave adj (pesante) heavy; (serio)
serious; (difficile) hard; (voce, suono)
low; (fonetica) grave; essere ~ (ammalato) be seriously ill. ~'mente adv
seriously
gravi'danza f pregnancy. 'gravido
adj pregnant
gravità f seriousness; (Phys) gravity
gra'voso adj onerous
'grazi|a f grace; (favore) favour; (Jur)

pardon; entrare nelle ~e di qcno
get into sb's good books. ~'are vt
pardon
'grazie int thank you!, thanks!; ~
mille! many thanks!
grazi'oso adj charming; (carino)
pretty
'Grec|ia f Greece. g~o, -a agg &
mf Greek
'gregge m flock
'greggio adj raw ●m crude oil
grembi'ale, grembi'ule
m apron
'grembo m lap; (utero) womb;
fig bosom
gre'mi|re vt pack. ~rsi vr become
crowded (di with). ~to adj packed
'gretto adj stingy; (di vedute ristrette)
narrow-minded
'grezzo adj = GREGGIO
gri'dare vi shout; (di dolore) scream;
(animale:) cry ●vt shout
'grido m (pl m gridi o f grida) shout;
(di animale) cry; l'ultimo ~ the latest
fashion
'grigio adj & m grey
'griglia f grill; alla ~ grilled
gril'letto m trigger
'grillo m cricket; (fig: capriccio) whim
'grinfia f fig clutch
'grin|ta f grit. ~'toso adj de-
termined
'grinza f wrinkle; (di stoffa) crease
grip'pare vi (Mech) seize
gris'sino m bread-stick
'gronda f eaves pl
gron'daia f gutter
gron'dare vi pour; (essere bagnato
fradicio) be dripping
'groppa f back
'groppo m knot
gros'sezza f size; (spessore)
thickness
gros'sista mf wholesaler
'grosso adj big, large; (spesso) thick;

(*grossolano*) coarse; (*grave*) serious ● *m* big part; (*massa*) bulk; **farla grossa** do a stupid thing

grosso|lanità *f inv* (*qualità*) coarseness; (*di errore*) grossness; (*azione, parola*) coarse thing. **~lano** *adj* coarse; (*errore*) gross

grosso'modo *adv* roughly

'grotta *f* cave, grotto

grovi'era *m* Gruyère

gro'viglio *m* tangle; *fig* muddle

gru *f inv* (*uccello, edilizia*) crane

'gruccia *f* (*stampella*) crutch; (*per vestito*) hanger

gru'gni|re *vi* grunt. **~to** *m* grunt

'grugno *m* snout

'grullo *adj* silly

'grumo *m* clot; (*di farina ecc*) lump. **gru'moso** *adj* lumpy

'gruppo *m* group; (*comitiva*) party. **~ sanguigno** blood group

gruvi'era *m* Gruyère

'gruzzolo *m* nest-egg

guada'gnare *vt* earn; gain (*tempo, forza ecc*). **gua'dagno** *m* gain; (*profitto*) profit; (*entrate*) earnings *pl*

gu'ado *m* ford; **passare a ~** ford

gua'ina *f* sheath; (*busto*) girdle

gu'aio *m* trouble; **che ~!** that's just brilliant!; **essere nei guai** be in a fix; **guai a te se lo tocchi!** don't you dare touch it!

gu'anci|a *f* cheek. **~'ale** *m* pillow

gu'anto *m* glove. **guanti** *pl* [**da boxe**] boxing gloves

guarda'coste *m inv* coastguard

guarda'linee *m inv* *Sport* linesman

guar'dar|e *vt* look at; (*osservare*) watch; (*badare a*) look after; (*dare su*) look out on ● *vi* look; (*essere orientato verso*) face. **~si** *vr* look at oneself; (*astenersi*) refrain from

guarda'rob|a *m inv* wardrobe; (*di locale pubblico*) cloakroom. **~i'ere, -a**

mf cloakroom attendant

gu'ardia *f* guard; (*poliziotto*) policeman; (*vigilanza*) watch; **essere di ~** be on guard; (*medico:*) be on duty; **fare la ~ a** keep guard over; **mettere in ~** qcno warn sb. **~ carceraria** prison warder. **~ del corpo** bodyguard. **~ di finanza** ≈ Fraud Squad. **~ forestale** forest ranger. **~ medica** duty doctor

guardi'ano, -a *mf* caretaker. **~ notturno** night watchman

guar'dingo *adj* cautious

guardi'ola *f* gatekeeper's lodge

guarigi'one *f* recovery

gua'rire *vt* cure ● *vi* recover; (*ferita:*) heal [up]

guarnigi'one *f* garrison

guar'ni|re *vt* trim; (*Culin*) garnish. **~zi'one** *f* trimming; (*Culin*) garnish; (*Mech*) gasket

gua'star|e *vt* spoil; (*rovinare*) ruin; break (*meccanismo*). **~si** *vr* spoil; (*andare a male*) go bad; (*tempo:*) change for the worse; (*meccanismo:*) break down. **gu'asto** *adj* broken; (*ascensore, telefono*) out of order; (*auto*) broken down; (*cibo, dente*) bad ● *m* breakdown; (*danno*) damage

guazza'buglio *m* muddle

guaz'zare *vi* wallow

gu'ercio *adj* cross-eyed

gu'err|a *f* war; (*tecnica bellica*) warfare. **~ mondiale** world war. **~eggi'are** *vi* wage war. **guer'resco** *adj* (*di guerra*) war; (*bellicoso*) warlike. **~i'ero** *m* warrior

guer'rigli|a *f* guerrilla warfare. **~'ero, -a** *mf* guerrilla

'gufo *m* owl

'guglia *f* spire

gu'id|a *f* guide; (*direzione*) guidance; (*comando*) leadership; (*Auto*) driving; (*tappeto*) runner. **~ a destra/sinistra** right-/left-hand drive. **~a telefonica** telephone directory. **~a**

turistica tourist guide. **gui'dare** vt guide; (Auto) drive; steer (nave). **~a'tore**, **~a'trice** mf driver
guin'zaglio m leash
guiz'zare vi dart; (luce:) flash. **gu'izzo** m dart; (di luce) flash
'guscio m shell
gu'stare vt taste ●vi like. **'gusto** m taste; (piacere) liking; **mangiare di gusto** eat well; **prenderci gusto** develop a taste for. **gu'stoso** adj tasty; fig delightful
guttu'rale adj guttural

Hh

habitué mf inv regular
ham'burger m inv hamburger
'handicap m inv handicap
handicap'pa|re vt handicap. **~to**, **-a** mf disabled person ●adj disabled
'hascisc m hashish
henné m henna
hi-fi m inv hi-fi
'hippy adj hippy
hockey m hockey. **~ su ghiaccio** ice hockey. **~ su prato** hockey
hollywoodi'ano adj Hollywood
ho'tel m inv hotel

Ii

i def art mpl the; ▸IL
iber'na|re vi hibernate. **~zi'one** f hibernation
i'bisco m hibiscus
'ibrido adj & m hybrid

'iceberg m inv iceberg
i'cona f icon
Id'dio m God
i'dea f idea; (opinione) opinion; (ideale) ideal; (indizio) inkling; (piccola quantità) hint; (intenzione) intention; **cambiare ~** change one's mind; **neanche per ~!** not on your life!; **chiarirsi le idee** get one's ideas straight. **~ fissa** obsession
ide'a|le adj & m ideal. **~lista** mf idealist. **~liz'zare** vt idealize
ide'a|re vt conceive. **~'tore**, **~'trice** mf originator
'idem adv the same
i'dentico adj identical
identifi'cabile adj identifiable
identifi'ca|re vt identify. **~zi'one** f identification
identità f inv identity
ideolo'gia f ideology. **ideo'logico** adj ideological
idi'oma m idiom. **idio'matico** adj idiomatic
idi'ota adj idiotic ●mf idiot. **idio'zia** f (cosa stupida) idiocy
idola'trare vt worship
idoleggi'are vt idolize. **'idolo** m idol
idoneità f suitability; (Mil) fitness; **esame di ~** qualifying examination. **i'doneo** adj **idoneo a** suitable for; (Mil) fit for
i'drante m hydrant
idra'ta|nte adj (crema, gel) moisturizing. **~zi'one** f moisturizing
i'draulico adj hydraulic ●m plumber
'idrico adj water attrib
idrocar'buro m hydrocarbon
idroe'lettrico adj hydroelectric
i'drofilo adj ▸COTONE
i'drogeno m hydrogen
i'ella f 🔲 bad luck; **portare ~** be bad luck. **iel'lato** adj 🔲 jinxed, plagued by bad luck

i'ena f hyena

i'eri adv yesterday; ~ l'altro, l'altro ~ the day before yesterday; ~ pomeriggio yesterday afternoon; il giornale di ~ yesterday's paper

ietta'tore, -'trice mf jinx. ~tura f (sfortuna) bad luck

igi'en|e f hygiene. ~ico adj hygienic. **igie'nista** mf hygienist

i'gnaro adj unaware

i'gnobile adj base; (non onorevole) dishonourable

igno'ran|te adj ignorant ● mf ignoramus. ~za f ignorance

igno'rare vt (non sapere) be unaware of; (trascurare) ignore

i'gnoto adj unknown

---

il def art m the

L'articolo determinativo in inglese non si usa quando si parla in generale: **Il latte fa bene** milk is good for you

••••▶ **il signor Magnetti** Mr Magnetti; **il dottor Piazza** Dr Piazza; **ha il naso storto** he has a bent nose; **mettiti il cappello** put your hat on; **il lunedì** on Mondays; **il 1986** 1986; **5 euro il chilo** 5 euros a kilo

---

'ilar|e adj merry. ~ità f hilarity

illazi'one f inference

illecita'mente adv illicitly. **il'lecito** adj illicit

ille'gal|e adj illegal. ~ità f illegality. ~'mente adv illegally

illeg'gibile adj illegible; (libro) unreadable

illegittimità f illegitimacy. **ille'gittimo** adj illegitimate

il'leso adj unhurt

illette'rato, -a adj & mf illiterate

illimi'tato adj unlimited

illivi'dire vt bruise ● vi (per rabbia)

---

become livid

il'logico adj illogical

il'luder|e vt deceive. ~si vr deceive oneself

illumi'na|re vt light [up]; fig enlighten; ~re a giorno floodlight. ~rsi vr light up. ~zi'one f lighting; fig enlightenment

Illumi'nismo m Enlightenment

illusi'one f illusion; **farsi illusioni** delude oneself

il'luso, -a pp di **illudere** ● adj deluded ● mf day-dreamer.

illu'stra|re vt illustrate. ~'tivo adj illustrative. ~'tore, ~'trice mf illustrator. ~zi'one f illustration

il'lustre adj distinguished

imbacuc'ca|re vt, ~rsi vr wrap up. ~to adj wrapped up

imbal'la|ggio m packing. ~re vt pack; (Auto) race

imbalsa'ma|re vt embalm; stuff (animale). ~to adj embalmed; (animale) stuffed

imbambo'lato adj vacant

imbaraz'zante adj embarrassing

imbaraz'za|re vt embarrass; (ostacolare) encumber. ~to adj embarrassed

imba'razzo m embarrassment; (ostacolo) hindrance; **trarre qcno d'**~ help sb out of a difficulty. ~ **di stomaco** indigestion

imbarca'dero m landing-stage

imbar'ca|re vt embark; (☐: rimorchiare) score. ~rsi vr embark. ~zi'one f boat. ~zione di salvataggio lifeboat. **im'barco** m embarkation; (banchina) landing-stage

imba'sti|re vt tack; fig sketch. ~'tura f tacking, basting

im'battersi vr ~ in run into

imbat'ti|bile adj unbeatable. ~uto adj unbeaten

imbavagli'are vt gag

imbe'cille adj stupid ● mf imbecile

129

imbellire | imminente

imbel'lire vt embellish

imbestia'li|re vi, ~**rsi** vr fly into a rage. ~**to** adj enraged

im'bever|e vt imbue (**di** with). ~**si** vr absorb

imbe'v|ibile adj undrinkable. ~**uto** adj ~**uto di** (acqua) soaked in; (nozioni) imbued with

imbian'c|are vt whiten • vi turn white. ~**hino** m house painter

imbizzar'rir|e vi, ~**si** vr become restless; (arrabbiarsi) get angry

imboc'ca|re vt feed; (entrare) enter; fig prompt. ~**tura** f opening; (ingresso) entrance; (Mus: di strumento) mouthpiece. **im'bocco** m entrance

imbo'scar|e vt hide. ~**si** vr (Mil) shirk military service

imbo'scata f ambush

imbottigli'a|re vt bottle. ~**rsi** vr get snarled up in a traffic jam. ~**to** adj (vino, acqua) bottled

imbot'ti|re vt stuff; pad (giacca); (Culin) fill. ~**rsi** vr ~**rsi di** (fig. di pasticche) stuff oneself with. ~**ta** f quilt. ~**to** adj (spalle) padded; (cuscino) stuffed; (panino) filled. ~**tura** f stuffing; (di panino) padding; (Culin) filling

imbra'nato adj clumsy

imbrat'tar|e vt mark. ~**si** vr dirty oneself

imbroc'car|e vt hit; ~**la giusta** hit the nail on the head

imbrogli|'are vt muddle; (raggirare) cheat. **im'broglio** m tangle; (pasticcio) mess; (inganno) trick. ~**one, -a** mf cheat

imbronci'a|re vi, ~**rsi** vr sulk. ~**to** adj sulky

imbru'nire vi get dark; **all'**~ at dusk

imbrut'tire vt make ugly • vi become ugly

imbu'care vt post, mail; (nel biliardo) pot

imbur'rare vt butter

im'buto m funnel

IMC m abbr (**indice di massa corporea**) BMI

imi'ta|re vt imitate. ~**tore**, ~**trice** mf imitator. ~**zi'one** f imitation

immaco'lato adj immaculate

immagazzi'nare vt store

immagi'na|re vt imagine; (supporre) suppose; **s'immagini!** imagine that!. ~**rio** adj imaginary. ~**zi'one** f imagination. **im'magine** f image

imman'cabile adj unfailing. ~**mente** adv without fail

im'mane adj huge; (orribile) terrible

imma'nente adj immanent

immangi'abile adj inedible

immatrico'la|re vt register. ~**rsi** vr (studente) matriculate. ~**zi'one** f registration; (di studente) matriculation

immaturità f immaturity. **imma'turo** adj unripe; (persona) immature; (precoce) premature

immedesi'ma|rsi vr ~**rsi in** identify oneself with. ~**zi'one** f identification

immedia|ta'mente adv immediately. ~**tezza** f immediacy. **imme-di'ato** adj immediate

immemo'rabile adj immemorial

immens|a'mente adv enormously. ~**ità** f immensity. **im-'menso** adj immense

immensu'rabile adj immeasurable

im'merger|e vt immerse. ~**si** vr plunge; (sommergibile:) dive; ~**si in** immerse oneself in

immersi'one f immersion; (di sommergibile) dive. **im'merso** pp di **immergere**

immi'gra|nte adj & mf immigrant. ~**re** vi immigrate. ~**to, -a** mf immigrant. ~**zi'one** f immigration

immi'nen|te adj imminent. ~**za** f imminence

immischi'ar|e vt involve. ∼**si** vr ∼**si in meddle in

immis'sario m tributary

immissi'one f insertion

im'mobile adj motionless

im'mobili mpl real estate. ∼'**are** adj società ∼**are** building society, savings and loan Am

immobili|tà f immobility. ∼**z'zare** vt immobilize; (Comm) tie up

immo'lare vt sacrifice

immondez'zaio m rubbish tip. **immon'dizia** f filth; (spazzatura) rubbish. **im'mondo** adj filthy

immo'ral|e adj immoral. ∼**ità** f immorality

immorta'lare vt immortalize. **immor'tale** adj immortal

immoti'vato adj (gesto) unjustified

im'mun|e adj exempt; (Med) immune. ∼**ità** f immunity. ∼**iz'zare** vt immunize. ∼**izzazi'one** f immunization

immunodefici'enza f immunodeficiency

immuso'ni|rsi vr sulk. ∼**to** adj sulky

immu'ta|bile adj unchangeable. ∼**to** adj unchanging

impacchet'tare vt wrap up

impacci'a|re vt hamper; (disturbare) inconvenience; (imbarazzare) embarrass. ∼**to** adj embarrassed; (goffo) awkward. **im'paccio** m embarrassment; (ostacolo) hindrance; (situazione difficile) awkward situation

im'pacco m compress

impadro'nirsi vr ∼ **di** take possession of; (fig: imparare) master

impa'gabile adj priceless

impagi'na|re vt paginate. ∼**zi'one** f pagination

impagli'are vt stuff (animale)

impa'lato adj fig stiff

impalca'tura f scaffolding; fig

structure

impalli'dire vi turn pale; (fig: perdere d'importanza) pale into insignificance

impa'nare vt roll in breadcrumbs

impanta'narsi vr get bogged down

impape'rarsi, impappi'narsi vr falter, stammer

impa'rare vt learn

impareggi'abile adj incomparable

imparen'ta|rsi vr ∼ **con** become related to. ∼**to** adj related

'impari adj unequal; (dispari) odd

impar'tire vt impart

imparzi'al|e adj impartial. ∼**ità** f impartiality

impas'sibile adj impassive

impa'sta|re vt (Culin) knead; blend (colori). **im'pasto** m (Culin) dough; (miscuglio) mixture

im'patto m impact

impau'ri|re vt frighten. ∼**si** vr become frightened

im'pavido adj fearless

impazi'en|te adj impatient; ∼**te di fare qcsa** eager to do sth. ∼**tirsi** vr lose patience. ∼**za** f impatience

impaz'zata f **all'**∼ full speed

impaz'zire vi go mad; (maionese): separate; **far** ∼ **qcno** drive sb mad; ∼ **per** be crazy about; **da** ∼ (mal di testa) blinding

impec'cabile adj impeccable

impedi'mento m hindrance; (ostacolo) obstacle

impe'dire vt ∼ **di** prevent from; (impacciare) hinder; (ostruire) obstruct; ∼ **a qcno di fare qcsa** prevent sb [from] doing sth

impe'gna|re vt (dare in pegno) pawn; (vincolare) bind; (prenotare) reserve; (assorbire) take up. ∼**rsi** vr apply oneself; ∼**rsi a fare qcsa** commit oneself to doing sth. ∼**tiva**

f referral. ~'**tivo** *adj* binding; (*lavoro*) demanding. ~**ato** *adj* engaged; (*Pol*) committed. **im'pegno** *m* engagement; (*Comm*) commitment; (*zelo*) care

impel'lente *adj* pressing

impen'na|rsi *vr* (*cavallo:*) rear; *fig* bristle. ~**ta** *f* sharp rise; (*di cavallo*) rearing; (*di moto*) wheelie

impen'sa|bile *adj* unthinkable. ~**to** *adj* unexpected

impensie'rir|e *vt*, ~**si** *vr* worry

impe'ra|nte *adj* prevailing. ~**re** *vi* reign; (*tendenza:*) prevail

impera'tivo *adj* & *m* imperative

impera'tore, -'**trice** *m* emperor ● *f* empress

impercet'tibile *adj* imperceptible

imperdo'nabile *adj* unforgivable

imper'fe|tto *adj* & *m* imperfect. ~**zi'one** *f* imperfection

imperi'a|le *adj* imperial. ~'**lismo** *m* imperialism

imperi'oso *adj* imperious; (*impellente*) urgent

impe'rizia *f* lack of skill

imperme'abile *adj* waterproof ● *m* raincoat

imperni'ar|e *vt* pivot; (*fondare*) base. ~**si** *vr* ~**si su** be based on

im'pero *m* empire; (*potere*) rule

imperscru'tabile *adj* inscrutable

imperso'nale *adj* impersonal

imperso'nare *vt* personify; (*interpretare*) act [the part of]

imper'territo *adj* undaunted

imperti'nen|te *adj* impertinent. ~**za** *f* impertinence

imperver'sare *vi* rage

im'pervio *adj* inaccessible

'**impet|o** *m* impetus; (*impulso*) impulse; (*slancio*) transport. ~**u'oso** *adj* impetuous; (*vento*) blustering

impet'tito *adj* stiff

impian'tare *vt* install; set up

(*azienda*)

impi'anto *m* plant; (*sistema*) system; (*operazione*) installation. ~ **radio** (*Auto*) car stereo system

impia'strare *vt* plaster; (*sporcare*) dirty. **impi'astro** *m* poultice; (*persona noiosa*) bore; (*pasticcione*) cack-handed person

impic'car|e *vt* hang. ~**si** *vr* hang oneself

impicci|'arsi *vr* meddle. **im'piccio** *m* hindrance; (*seccatura*) bother. ~'**one**, -**a** *mf* nosey parker

impie'ga|re *vt* employ; (*usare*) use; spend (*tempo, denaro*); *Fin* invest; **l'autobus ha ~to un'ora** it took the bus an hour. ~**rsi** *vr* get [oneself] a job

impie'gatizio *adj* clerical

impie'gato, -**a** *mf* employee. ~ **di banca** bank clerk. **impi'ego** *m* employment; (*posto*) job; *Fin* investment

impieto'sir|e *vt* move to pity. ~**si** *vr* be moved to pity

impie'trito *adj* petrified

impigli'ar|e *vt* entangle. ~**si** *vr* get entangled

impi'grir|e *vt* make lazy. ~**si** *vr* get lazy

impli'car|e *vt* implicate; (*sottintendere*) imply. ~**rsi** *vr* become involved. ~**zi'one** *f* implication

implicita'mente *adv* implicitly. **im'plicito** *adj* implicit

implo'rar|e *vt* implore. ~**zi'one** *f* entreaty

impolve'rar|e *vt* cover with dust. ~**rsi** *vr* get covered with dust. ~**to** *adj* dusty

imponde'rabile *adj* imponderable; (*causa, evento*) unpredictable

impo'nen|te *adj* imposing. ~**za** *f* impressiveness

impo'nibile *adj* taxable ● *m* taxable income

impopo'lar|e adj unpopular. ~ità f unpopularity

im'por|re vt impose; (ordinare) order. ~si vr assert oneself; (aver successo) be successful; ~si di (prefiggersi di) set oneself the task of

impor'tan|te adj important ● m important thing. ~za f importance

impor'ta|re vt import; (comportare) cause ● vi matter; (essere necessario) be necessary. **non ~l** it doesn't matter! **non me ne ~** I couldn't care less!. ~tore, ~'trice mf importer. ~zi'one f importation; (merce importata) import

im'porto m amount

importu'nare vt pester. impor'tuno adj troublesome; (inopportuno) untimely

imposizi'one f imposition; (imposta) tax

imposses'sarsi vr ~ di seize

impos'sibil|e adj impossible ● m fare l'~e do absolutely all one can. ~ità f impossibility

im'posta¹ f tax; ~ sul reddito income tax; ~ sul valore aggiunto value added tax

im'posta² f (di finestra) shutter

impo'sta|re vt (progettare) plan; (basare) base; (Mus) pitch; (imbucare) post, mail; set out (domanda, problema). ~zi'one f planning; (di voce) pitching

im'posto pp di **imporre**

impo'store, -a mf impostor

impo'ten|te adj powerless; (Med) impotent. ~za f powerlessness; (Med) impotence

impove'rir|e vt impoverish. ~si vr become poor

imprati'cabile adj impracticable; (strada) impassable

imprati'chir|e vt train. ~si vr ~si in o a get practice in

impre'care vi curse

impreci's|abile adj indeterminable. ~ato adj indeterminate. ~i'one f inaccuracy. impre'ciso adj inaccurate

impre'gnar|e vt impregnate; (imbevere) soak; fig imbue. ~si vr become impregnated with

imprendi'tor|e, -'trice mf entrepreneur. ~i'ale adj entrepreneurial

imprepa'rato adj unprepared

im'presa f undertaking; (gesta) exploit; (azienda) firm

impre'sario m impresario; (appaltatore) contractor

imprescin'dibile adj inescapable

impressio'na|bile adj impressionable. ~nte adj impressive; (spaventoso) frightening

impressio'nare vt impress; (spaventare) frighten; expose (foto). ~o'narsi vr be affected; (spaventarsi) be frightened. ~one f impression; (sensazione) sensation; (impronta) mark; far ~one a qcno upset sb

impressio'nis|mo m impressionism. ~ta mf impressionist

im'presso pp di **imprimere** ● adj printed

impre'stare vt lend

impreve'dibile adj unexpected

imprevi'dente adj improvident

impre'visto adj unforeseen ● m unforeseen event

imprigiona'mento m imprisonment. ~'nare vt imprison

im'primere vt impress; (stampare) print; (comunicare) impart

impro'babil|e adj unlikely, improbable. ~ità f improbability

improdut'tivo adj unproductive

im'pronta f impression; fig mark. ~ digitale fingerprint. ~ ecologica carbon footprint. ~ del piede footprint

impro'perio m insult; **improperi**

pl abuse *sg*

im'proprio *adj* improper

improvvi'sa|re *vt/i* improvise. ∼**rsi** *vr* turn oneself into a. ∼**ta** *f* surprise. ∼**zi'one** *f* improvisation

improv'viso *adj* sudden; **all'**∼ unexpectedly

impru'den|te *adj* imprudent. ∼**za** *f* imprudence

impu'gna|re *vt* grasp; (*Jur*) contest. ∼**'tura** *f* grip; (*manico*) handle

impulsività *f* impulsiveness. **im-pul'sivo** *adj* impulsive

im'pulso *m* impulse; **agire d'**∼ act on impulse

impune'mente *adv* with impunity. **impu'nito** *adj* unpunished

impun'tura *f* stitching

impurità *f inv* impurity. **im'puro** *adj* impure

impu'tabile *adj* attributable (**a** to)

impu'ta|re *vt* attribute; (*accusare*) charge. ∼**to, -a** *m/f* accused. ∼**zi'one** *f* charge

imputri'dire *vi* rot

in *prep* in; (*moto a luogo*) to; (*su*) on; (*entro*) within; (*mezzo*) by; (*con materiale*) made of; **essere in casa/ufficio** be at home/at the office; **in mano/tasca** in one's hand/pocket; **andare in Francia/campagna** go to France/the country; **salire in treno** get on the train; **versa la birra nel bicchiere** pour the beer into the glass; **in alto** up there; **in giornata** within the day; **nel 1997** in 1997; **una borsa in pelle** a bag made of leather, a leather bag; **in macchina** (*viaggiare, venire*) by car; **in contanti** [in] cash; **in vacanza** on holiday; **se fossi in te** if I were you; **siamo in sette** there are seven of us

inabbor'dabile *adj* unapproachable

i'nabile *adj* incapable; (*fisicamente*) unfit. ∼**ità** *f* incapacity

inabi'tabile *adj* uninhabitable

inacces'sibile *adj* inaccessible; (*persona*) unapproachable

inaccet'tabile *adj* unacceptable. ∼**ità** *f* unacceptability

inacer'bi|re *vt* embitter; exacerbate (*rapporto*). ∼**si** *vr* grow bitter

inaci'di|re *vt* turn sour. ∼**si** *vr* go sour; (*persona:*) become bitter

ina'datto *adj* unsuitable

inadegu'ato *adj* inadequate

inadempi'ente *mf* defaulter. ∼**'mento** *m* nonfulfilment

inaffer'rabile *adj* elusive

ina'la|re *vt* inhale. ∼**'tore** *m* inhaler. ∼**zi'one** *f* inhalation

inalbe'rar|e *vt* hoist. ∼**si** *vr* (*cavallo:*) rear [up]; (*adirarsi*) lose one's temper

inalte'ra|bile *adj* unchangeable; (*colore*) fast. ∼**to** *adj* unchanged

inami'da|re *vt* starch. ∼**to** *adj* starched

inammis'sibile *adj* inadmissible

inamo'vibile *adj* irremovable

inani'mato *adj* inanimate; (*senza vita*) lifeless

inappa'gabile *adj* unsatisfiable. ∼**to** *adj* unfulfilled

inappe'tenza *f* lack of appetite

inappli'cabile *adj* inapplicable

inappun'tabile *adj* faultless

inar'car|e *vt* arch; raise (*sopracciglia*). ∼**si** *vr* (*legno:*) warp; (*ripiano:*) sag; (*linea:*) curve

inari'dir|e *vt* parch; empty of feelings (*persona*). ∼**si** *vr* dry up; (*persona:*) become empty of feelings

inartico'lato *adj* inarticulate

inaspettata'mente *adv* unexpectedly. **inaspet'tato** *adj* unexpected

inaspri'mento *m* embitterment; (*di conflitto*) worsening

ina'sprir|e *vt* embitter. ∼**si** *vr* become embittered

inattac'cabile *adj* unassailable; (*ir-*

reprensibile) irreproachable

inatten'dibile *adj* unreliable. **inat-'teso** *adj* unexpected

inattività *f* inactivity. **inat'tivo** *adj* inactive

inattu'abile *adj* impracticable

inau'dito *adj* unheard of

inaugu'rale *adj* inaugural; **viaggio** ∼ maiden voyage

inaugu'ra|re *vt* inaugurate; open (mostra), unveil (statua); christen (lavastoviglie ecc). ∼**zi'one** *f* inauguration; (*di mostra*) opening; (*di statua*) unveiling

inavver't|enza *f* inadvertence. ∼**ita'mente** *adv* inadvertently

incagli'ar|si *vr* ground ● *vt* hinder. ∼**si** *vr* run aground

incalco'labile *adj* incalculable

incal'li|rsi *vr* grow callous; (*abituarsi*) become hardened. ∼**to** *adj* callous; (*abituato*) hardened

incal'za|nte *adj* (*ritmo*) driving; (*richiesta*) urgent. ∼**re** *vt* pursue; *fig* press

incame'rare *vt* appropriate

incammi'nar|e *vt* get going; (*fig: guidare*) set off. ∼**si** *vr* set out

incana'lar|e *vt* canalize; *fig* channel. ∼**si** *vr* converge on

incande'scen|te *adj* incandescent; (*discussione*) burning

incan'ta|re *vt* enchant. ∼**rsi** *vr* stand spellbound; (*inceppparsi*) jam. ∼**'tore**, ∼**'trice** *n* enchanter ● *f* enchantress

incan'tesimo *m* spell

incan'tevole *adj* enchanting

in'canto *m* spell; *fig* delight; (*asta*) auction; **come per** ∼ as if by magic

incanu'ti|re *vt* turn white. ∼**to** *adj* white

inca'pac|e *adj* incapable. ∼**ità** *f* incapability

incapo'nirsi *vr* be set on (**a fare** on doing)

incap'pare *vi* ∼ **in** run into

incappucci'arsi *vr* wrap up

incapricci'arsi *vr* ∼ **di** take a fancy to

incapsu'lare *vt* seal; crown (dente)

incarce'ra|re *vt* imprison. ∼**zi'one** *f* imprisonment

incari'ca|re *vt* charge. ∼**rsi** *vr* take upon oneself; **me ne incarico io** I will see to it. ∼**to, -a** *adj* in charge ● *mf* representative. **in'carico** *m* charge; **per incarico di** on behalf of

incar'na|re *vt* embody. ∼**rsi** *vr* become incarnate

incarta'mento *m* documents *pl*. **incar'tare** *vt* wrap [in paper]

incas'sa|re *vt* pack; (*Mech*) embed; box in (mobile, frigo); (*riscuotere*) cash; take (colpo). ∼**to** *adj* set; (*fiume*) deeply embanked. **in'casso** *m* collection; (*introito*) takings *pl*

incasto'na|re *vt* set. ∼**'tura** *f* setting. ∼**to** *adj* embedded; (*anello*) inset (**di** with)

inca'strar|e *vt* fit in; (🅸: *in situazione*) corner. ∼**si** *vr* fit in. **in'castro** *m* joint; **a incastro** (*pezzi*) interlocking

incate'nare *vt* chain

incatra'mare *vt* tar

incatti'vire *vt* turn nasty

in'cauto *adj* imprudent

inca'va|re *vt* hollow out. ∼**to** *adj* hollow. ∼**'tura** *f* hollow. **in'cavo** *m* hollow; (*scanalatura*) groove

incendi'ar|e *vt* set fire to; *fig* inflame. ∼**si** *vr* catch fire. ∼**io, -a** *adj* incendiary; *fig:* (*discorso*) inflammatory; *fig:* (*bellezza*) sultry ● *mf* arsonist. **in'cendio** *m* fire. **incendio doloso** *m* arson

incene'ri|re *vt* burn to ashes; (*cremare*) cremate. ∼**rsi** *vr* be burnt to ashes. ∼**'tore** *m* incinerator

in'censo *m* incense

incensu'rato *adj* blameless; **essere** ∼ (*Jur*) have a clean record

incenti'vare vt motivate. **incen'tivo** m incentive

incen'trarsi vr ~ **su** centre on

incep'par|e vt block; fig hamper. **~si** vr jam

ince'rata f oilcloth

incerot'tato adj with a plaster on

incer'tezza f uncertainty. **in'certo** adj uncertain ●m uncertainty

inces'sante adj unceasing. **~'mente** adv incessantly

in'cest|o m incest. **~u'oso** adj incestuous

in'cetta f buying up; **fare ~ di** stockpile

inchi'esta f investigation

inchi'nar|e vt, **~si** vr bow. **in'chino** m bow; (di donna) curtsy

inchio'dare vt nail; nail down (coperchio); **~ a letto** (malattia:) confine to bed

inchi'ostro m ink

inciam'pare vi stumble; **~ in** (imbattersi) run into. **inci'ampo** m hindrance

inciden'tale adj incidental

inci'den|te m (episodio) incident; (infortunio) accident. **~za** f incidence

in'cidere vt cut; (arte) engrave; (registrare) record ●vi **~ su** (gravare) weigh upon

in'cinta adj pregnant

incipi'ente adj incipient

incipri'ar|e vt powder. **~si** vr powder one's face

in'circa adv **all'~** more or less

incisi'one f incision; (arte) engraving; (acquaforte) etching; (registrazione) recording

inci'sivo adj incisive ●m (dente) incisor

in'ciso m **per ~** incidentally

incita'mento m incitement. **inci'tare** vt incite

inci'vil|e adj uncivilized; (maleducato) impolite. **~tà** f barbarism; (maleduca-

zione) rudeness

incle'men|te adj harsh

incli'nabile adj reclining

incli'na|re vt tilt ●vi **~re** a be inclined to. **~rsi** vr list. **~to** adj tilted; (terreno) sloping. **~zi'one** f slope, inclination. **in'cline** adj inclined

in'clu|dere vt include; (allegare) enclose. **~si'one** f inclusion. **~'sivo** adj inclusive. **~so** pp di **includere** ●adj included; (compreso) inclusive; (allegato) enclosed

incoe'ren|te adj (contraddittorio) inconsistent. **~za** f inconsistency

in'cognit|a f unknown quantity. **~o** adj unknown ●m **in ~o** incognito

incol'lar|e vt stick; (con colla liquida) glue. **~si** vr stick to; **~si a qcno** stick close to sb

incolle'ri|rsi vr lose one's temper. **~to** adj enraged

incol'mabile adj (differenza) unbridgeable; (vuoto) unfillable

incolon'nare vt line up

inco'lore adj colourless

incol'pare vt blame

in'colto adj uncultivated; (persona) uneducated

in'colume adj unhurt

incom'ben|te adj impending. **~za** f task

in'combere vi **~ su** hang over; (spettare) a be incumbent on

incominci'are vt/i begin, start

incomo'dar|e vt inconvenience. **~si** vr trouble. **in'comodo** adj uncomfortable; (inopportuno) inconvenient ●m inconvenience

incompa'rabile adj incomparable

incompe'ten|te adj incompetent. **~za** f incompetence

incompi'uto adj unfinished

incom'pleto adj incomplete

incompren'si|bile adj incomprehensible. **~'one** f lack of understanding; (*malinteso*) misunderstanding. **incom'preso** *adj* misunderstood

inconce'pibile *adj* inconceivable

inconclu'dente *adj* inconclusive; (*persona*) ineffectual

incondizio|nata'mente *adv* unconditionally. ∼'nato *adj* unconditional

inconfes'sabile *adj* unmentionable

inconfon'dibile *adj* unmistakable

incongru'ente *adj* inconsistent

in'congruo *adj* inadequate

inconsa'pevol|e *adj* unaware; (*inconscio*) unconscious. ∼'mente *adv* unwittingly

inconscia'mente *adv* unconsciously. **in'conscio** *adj & m* (*Psych*) unconscious

inconsi'sten|te *adj* insubstantial; (*notizia ecc*) unfounded. ∼za *f* (*di ragionamento*, *prove*) flimsiness

inconsu'eto *adj* unusual

incon'sulto *adj* rash

incontami'nato *adj* uncontaminated

inconte'nibile *adj* irrepressible

inconten'tabile *adj* insatiable; (*esigente*) hard to please

inconti'nen|te *adj* incontinent. ∼za *f* incontinence

incon'trar|e *vt* meet; encounter, meet with (*difficoltà*). ∼si *vr* meet (con qcno sb)

incon'trario: **all'∼** *adv* the other way around; (*in modo sbagliato*) the wrong way around

incontra'sta|bile *adj* incontrovertible. ∼to *adj* undisputed

in'contro *m* meeting; *Sport* match. ∼ **al vertice** summit meeting ● *prep* ∼ **a** towards; **andare** ∼ **a qcno** go to meet sb; *fig* meet sb half way

inconveni'ente *m* drawback

incoraggia'mento *m* encouragement. ∼'ante *adj* encouraging

∼'are *vt* encourage

incornici'a|re *vt* frame. ∼'tura *f* framing

incoro'na|re *vt* crown. ∼zi'one *f* coronation

incorpo'rar|e *vt* incorporate; (*mescolare*) blend. ∼si *vr* blend; (*territori:*) merge

incorreg'gibile *adj* incorrigible

in'correre *vi* ∼ **in** incur; ∼ **nel pericolo di...** run the risk of...

incorrut'tibile *adj* incorruptible

incosci'en|te *adj* unconscious; (*irresponsabile*) reckless ● *mf* irresponsible person. ∼za *f* unconsciousness; recklessness

inco'stan|te *adj* changeable; (*persona*) fickle. ∼za *f* changeableness; (*di persona*) fickleness

incre'dibile *adj* unbelievable, incredible

incredulità *f* incredulity. **in'credulo** *adj* incredulous

incremen'tare *vt* increase; (*intensificare*) step up. **incre'mento** *m* increase. **incremento demografico** population growth

incresci'oso *adj* regrettable

incre'spar|e *vt* ruffle; wrinkle (*tessuto*); make frizzy (*capelli*); ∼**e la fronte** frown. ∼si *vr* (*acqua:*) ripple; (*tessuto:*) wrinkle; (*capelli:*) go frizzy

incrimi'na|re *vt* indict; *fig* incriminate. ∼zi'one *f* indictment

incri'na|re *vt* crack; *fig* affect (*amicizia*). ∼rsi *vr* crack; (*amicizia:*) be affected. ∼'tura *f* crack

incroci'a|re *vt* cross ● *vi* (*Aeron, Naut*) cruise. ∼rsi *vr* cross. ∼'tore *m* cruiser

in'crocio *m* crossing; (*di strade*) crossroads *sg*

incrol'labile *adj* indestructible

incro'sta|re *vt* encrust. ∼zi'one *f* encrustation

incuba|'trice *f* incubator. ∼zi'one

f incubation

'incubo *m* nightmare

in'cudine *f* anvil

incu'rabile *adj* incurable

incu'rante *adj* careless

incurio'sir|e *vt* make curious. ∼**si** *vr* become curious

incursi'one *f* raid. ∼ **aerea** air raid

incurva'mento *m* bending

incur'va|re *vt*, ∼**rsi** *vr* bend. ∼**tura** *f* bending

in'cusso *pp di* **incutere**

incusto'dito *adj* unguarded

in'cutere *vt* arouse

'indaco *m* indigo

indaffa'rato *adj* busy

inda'gare *vt/i* investigate

in'dagine *f* research; (*giudiziaria*) investigation. ∼ **di mercato** market survey

indebi'tar|e *vt*, ∼**si** *vr* get into debt

in'debito *adj* undue

indeboli'mento *m* weakening

indebo'lir|e *vt*, ∼**si** *vr* weaken

inde'cen|te *adj* indecent. ∼**za** *f* indecency; (*vergogna*) disgrace

indeci'frabile *adj* indecipherable

indecisi'one *f* indecision. **inde'ciso** *adj* undecided

inde'fesso *adj* tireless

indefi'ni|bile *adj* indefinable. ∼**to** *adj* indefinite

indefor'mabile *adj* crushproof

in'degno *adj* unworthy

indelica'tezza *f* indelicacy; (*azione*) tactless act. **indeli'cato** *adj* indiscreet; (*grossolano*) indelicate

in'denn|e *adj* uninjured; (*da malattia*) unaffected. ∼**ità** *f inv* allowance; (*per danni*) compensation. ∼**ità di trasferta** travel allowance. ∼**iz'zare** *vt* compensate. **inden'nizzo** *m* compensation

indero'gabile *adj* binding

indeside'ra|bile *adj* undesirable. ∼**to** *adj* (*figlio, ospite*) unwanted

indetermi'na|bile *adj* indeterminable. ∼**'tezza** *f* vagueness. ∼**to** *adj* indeterminate

'India *f* India. **i∼'ano, -a** *adj & mf* Indian; **in fila i∼ana** in single file

indiavo'lato *adj* possessed; (*vivace*) wild

indi'ca|re *vt* show, indicate; (*col dito*) point at; (*far notare*) point out; (*consigliare*) advise. ∼**'tivo** *adj* indicative ● *m* (*Gram*) indicative. ∼**'tore** *m* indicator; (*Techn*) gauge; (*prontuario*) directory. ∼**zi'one** *f* indication; (*istruzione*) direction

'indice *m* (*dito*) forefinger; (*lancetta*) pointer; (*di libro, statistica*) index; (*fig: segno*) sign

indietreggi'are *vi* draw back; (*Mil*) retreat

indi'etro *adv* back, behind; **all'∼** backwards; **avanti e ∼** back and forth; **essere ∼** be behind; (*mentalmente*) be backward; (*con pagamenti*) be in arrears; (*di orologio*) be slow; **fare marcia ∼** reverse; **rimandare ∼** send back; **rimanere ∼** be left behind; **torna ∼!** come back!

indi'feso *adj* undefended; (*inerme*) helpless

indiffe'ren|te *adj* indifferent; **mi è ∼te** it is all the same to me. ∼**za** *f* indifference

in'digeno, -a *adj* indigenous ● *mf* native

indi'gen|te *adj* needy. ∼**za** *f* poverty

indigesti'one *f* indigestion. **indi'gesto** *adj* indigestible

indi'gna|re *vt* make indignant. ∼**rsi** *vr* be indignant. ∼**to** *adj* indignant. ∼**zi'one** *f* indignation

indimenti'cabile *adj* unforgettable

indipen'den|te *adj* independent.

~te'mente adv independently; ~te-
mente dal tempo regardless of the
weather, whatever the weather. ~za
f independence

in'dire vt announce

indiretta'mente adv indirectly.
indi'retto adj indirect

indiriz'zar|e vt address; (mandare)
send; (dirigere) direct. ~si vr direct
one's steps. indi'rizzo m address; (direzione) direction

indisci'pli|na f lack of discipline.
~'nato adj undisciplined

indi'scre|to adj indiscreet. ~zi'one
f indiscretion

indi'scusso adj unquestioned

indiscu'tibil|e adj unquestionable.
~'mente adv unquestionably

indispen'sabile adj essential, in-
dispensable

indispet'tir|e vt irritate. ~si vr get
irritated

indi'spo|rre vt antagonize. ~sto
pp di indisporre ● adj indisposed.
~sizi'one f indisposition

indisso'lubile adj indissoluble

indistin'guibile adj indiscernible

indistinta'mente adv without exception. indi'stinto adj indistinct

indistrut'tibile adj indestructible

indistur'bato adj undisturbed

in'divia f endive

individu'a|le adj individual. ~'lista
mf individualist. ~'lità f individuality.
~re vt individualize; (localizzare) locate; (riconoscere) single out

indi'viduo m individual

indivi'sibile adj indivisible. indi-
'viso adj undivided

indizi'a|re vt throw suspicion on.
~to, -a adj suspected ● mf suspect.
in'dizio m sign; (Jur) circumstantial
evidence

'indole f nature

indolenzi'mento m stiffness

indolen'zi|rsi vr go stiff.

~to adj stiff

indo'lore adj painless

indo'mani m l'~ the following day

indo'nesia f Indonesia

indo'rare vt gild

indos'sa|re vt wear; (mettere ad-
dosso) put on. ~'tore, ~'trice
mf model

in'dotto pp di indurre

indottri'nare vt indoctrinate

indovi'n|are vt guess; (predire)
foretell. ~ato adj successful; (scelta)
well-chosen. ~ello m riddle. indo-
'vino, -a mf fortune-teller

indubbia'mente adv undoubt-
edly. in'dubbio adj undoubted

indugi'ar|e vi, ~si vr linger. in'du-
gio m delay

indul'gen|te adj indulgent. ~za f
indulgence

in'dul|gere vi ~gere a indulge in.
~to pp di indulgere ● m (Jur) pardon

indu'mento m garment; indumenti pl clothes

induri'mento m hardening

indu'rir|e vt, ~si vr harden

in'durre vt induce

in'dustri|a f industry. ~'ale adj in-
dustrial ● mf industrialist

industrializ'za|re vt industrialize.
~to adj industrialized. ~zi'one f in-
dustrialization

industri'arsi vr try one's hardest.
~'oso adj industrious

induzi'one f induction

inebe'tito adj stunned

inebri'ante adj intoxicating, exciting

i'nedia f starvation

i'nedito adj unpublished

ineffi'cace adj ineffective

ineffici'en|te adj inefficient. ~za f
inefficiency

ineguagli'abile adj incomparable

inegu'ale adj unequal;

(superficie) uneven

inelut'tabile *adj* inescapable

ine'rente *adj* ~ a concerning

i'nerme *adj* unarmed; *fig* defenceless

inerpi'carsi *vr* ~ su clamber up; (pianta:) climb up

i'ner|te *adj* inactive; (*Phys*) inert. ~**zia** *f* inactivity; (*Phys*) inertia

inesat'tezza *f* inaccuracy. **ine-'satto** *adj* inaccurate; (*erroneo*) incorrect; (*non riscosso*) uncollected

inesau'ribile *adj* inexhaustible

inesi'sten|te *adj* non-existent. ~**za** *f* non-existence

insperi'enza *f* inexperience. **ine-'sperto** *adj* inexperienced

inespli'cabile *adj* inexplicable

ine'sploso *adj* unexploded

inesti'mabile *adj* inestimable

inetti'tudine *f* ineptitude. **i'netto** *adj* inept; **inetto a** unsuited to

ine'vaso *adj* (pratiche) pending; (corrispondenza) unanswered

inevi'tabil|e *adj* inevitable. ~**mente** *adv* inevitably

i'nezia *f* trifle

infagot'tar|e *vt* wrap up. ~**si** *vr* wrap [oneself] up

infal'libile *adj* infallible

infa'ma|re *vt* defame. ~**'torio** *adj* defamatory

in'fam|e *adj* infamous; (🔒: orrendo) awful, shocking. ~**ia** *f* infamy

infan'garsi *vr* get muddy

infan'tile *adj* children's; (ingenuità) childlike; *pej* childish

in'fanzia *f* childhood; (bambini) children *pl*; **prima** ~ infancy

infar'cire *vi* pepper (discorso) (di with)

infari'na|re *vt* flour; ~**re di** sprinkle with. ~**'tura** *f fig* smattering

in'farto *m* coronary

infasti'dir|e *vt* irritate. ~**si** *vr* get irritated

infati'cabile *adj* untiring

in'fatti *conj* as a matter of fact; (veramente) indeed

infatu'a|rsi *vr* become infatuated (**di** with). ~**to** *adj* infatuated. ~**zi'one** *f* infatuation

infe'condo *adj* infertile

infe'del|e *adj* unfaithful. ~**tà** *f* unfaithfulness; ~ *pl* affairs

infe'lic|e *adj* unhappy; (inappropriato) unfortunate; (cattivo) bad. ~**ità** *f* unhappiness

infel'tri|rsi *vr* get matted. ~**to** *adj* matted

inferi'or|e *adj* (più basso) lower; (qualità) inferior ●*mf* inferior. ~**ità** *f* inferiority

inferme'ria *f* infirmary; (di nave) sick-bay

infermi'er|a *f* nurse. ~**e** *m* [male] nurse

infermità *f* sickness. ~ **mentale** mental illness. **in'fermo, -a** *adj* sick ●*mf* invalid

infer'nale *adj* infernal; (epaventoso) hellish

in'ferno *m* hell; **va all'~!** go to hell!

infero'cirsi *vr* become fierce

inferri'ata *f* grating

infervo'rar|e *vt* arouse enthusiasm in. ~**si** *vr* get excited

infe'stare *vt* infest

infet'ta|re *vt* infect. ~**rsi** *vr* become infected. ~**ivo** *adj* infectious. **in'fetto** *adj* infected. **infezi'one** *f* infection

infiac'chir|e *vt/i*, ~**si** *vr* weaken

infiam'mabile *adj* [in]flammable

infiam'ma|re *vt* set on fire; (Med, fig) inflame. ~**rsi** *vr* catch fire; (Med) become inflamed. ~**zi'one** *f* (Med) inflammation

in'fido *adj* treacherous

infie'rire *vi* (imperversare) rage; ~ **su**

attack furiously

in'figger|e vt drive. ~**si** vr ~**si in** penetrate

infi'lar|e vt thread; (mettere) insert; (indossare) put on. ~**si** vr slip on (vestito); ~**si in** (introdursi in) slip into

infil'tra|rsi vr infiltrate. ~**zi'one** f infiltration; (d'acqua) seepage; (Med: iniezione) injection

infil'zare vt pierce; (infilare) string; (conficcare) stick

'infimo adj lowest

in'fine adv finally; (insomma) in short

infinità f infinity; **un'~** di masses of. **infi'nito** adj infinite; (Gram) infinitive ● m infinite; (Gram) infinitive; (Math) infinity; all'**infinito** endlessly

infinocchi'are vt 🗓 hoodwink

infischi'arsi vr ~ di not care about; **me ne infischio** 🗓 I couldn't care less

in'fisso pp di infiggere ● m fixture; (di porta, finestra) frame

infit'tir|e vt/i. ~**si** vr thicken

inflazi'one f inflation

infles'sibil|e adj inflexible. ~**ità** f inflexibility

inflessi'one f inflexion

in'fli|ggere vt inflict. ~**tto** pp di infliggere

influ'en|te adj influential. ~**za** f influence; (Med) influenza

influen'za|bile adj (mente, opinione) impressionable. ~**re** vt influence. ~**to** adj (malato) with the flu

influ'ire vi ~ su influence

in'flusso m influence

info'carsi vr catch fire; (viso:) go red; (discussione:) become heated

infol'tire vt/i thicken

infon'dato adj unfounded

in'fondere vt instil

infor'care vt fork up; get on (bici); put on (occhiali)

infor'male adj informal

infor'ma|re vt inform. ~**rsi** vr inquire (di about)

infor'matic|a f computing, IT. ~**o** adj computer attrib

infor'ma|tivo adj informative. **infor'mato** adj informed; **male informato** ill-informed. ~**tore**, ~**trice** mf (di polizia) informer. ~**zi'one** f information (solo sg); **un'~zione** a piece of information

in'forme adj shapeless

infor'nare vt put into the oven

infortu'narsi vr have an accident.

infor'tu|nio m accident. ~**nio sul lavoro** industrial accident

infos'sa|rsi vr sink; (guance, occhi:) become hollow. ~**to** adj sunken, hollow

infradici'ar|e vt drench. ~**si** vr get drenched; (diventare marcio) rot

infra'dito m pl (scarpe) flip-flops

in'frang|ere vt break; (in mille pezzi) shatter. ~**ersi** vr break. ~'**gibile** adj unbreakable

in'franto pp di infrangere ● adj shattered; (cuore) broken

infra'rosso adj infra-red

infrastrut'tura f infrastructure

infrazi'one f offence

infred'da'tura f cold

infreddo'li|rsi vr feel cold. ~**to** adj cold

infrut'tuoso adj fruitless

infuo'ca|re vt make red-hot. ~**to** adj burning

infu'ori adv all'~ outwards; **all'~ di** except

infuri'a|re vi rage. ~**rsi** vr fly into a rage. ~**to** adj blustering

infusi'one f infusion. **in'fuso** pp di infondere ● m infusion

Ing. abbr ingegnere

ingabbi'are vt cage; (fig: mettere in prigione) jail

ingaggi'are vt engage; sign up

(calciatori ecc); begin (lotta, battaglia). **in'gaggio** m engagement; (di calciatore) signing [up]

ingan'nar|e vt deceive; (essere infedele a) be unfaithful to. ~**si** vr deceive oneself; **se non m'inganno** if I am not mistaken

ingan'nevole adj deceptive. **in'ganno** m deceit; (frode) fraud

ingarbugli'a|re vt entangle; (confondere) confuse. ~**rsi** vr get entangled; (confondersi) become confused. ~**to** adj confused

inge'gnarsi vr do one's best

in'gegnere m engineer. **ingegne'ria** f engineering

in'gegno m brains pl; (genio) genius; (abilità) ingenuity. ~**sa'mente** adv ingeniously

ingelo'sir|e vt make jealous. ~**si** vr become jealous

in'gente adj huge

ingenua'mente adv naïvely. ~**ità** f naïvety. **in'genuo** adj ingenuous; (credulone) naïve

inge'renza f interference

inge'rire vt swallow

inges'sa|re vt put in plaster. ~**tura** f plaster

Inghil'terra f England

inghiot'tire vt swallow

in'ghippo m trick

ingial'li|re vi, ~**rsi** vr turn yellow. ~**to** adj yellowed

ingigan'tir|e vt magnify ● vi, ~**si** vr grow to enormous proportions

inginocchi'a|rsi vr kneel [down]. ~**to** adj kneeling. ~**toio** m prie-dieu

ingiù adv down; **all'~** downwards; **a testa ~** head downwards

ingiun|gere vt order. ~**zi'one** f injunction. ~**zione di pagamento** final demand

ingi'uri|a f insult; (torto) wrong; (danno) damage. ~**'are** vt insult; (fare

un torto a) wrong. ~**oso** adj insulting

ingiu'stizia f injustice. **ingi'usto** adj unjust, unfair

in'glese adj English ● m Englishman; (lingua) English ● f Englishwoman

ingoi'are vt swallow

ingol'far|e vt flood (motore). ~**si** vr fig get involved; (motore) flood

ingom'bra|nte adj cumbersome. ~**re** vt clutter up; fig cram (mente)

in'gombro m encumbrance; **essere d'~** be in the way

ingor'digia f greed. **in'gordo** adj greedy

ingor'gar|e vt block. ~**si** vr be blocked [up]. **in'gorgo** m blockage; (del traffico) jam

ingoz'zar|e vt gobble up; (nutrire eccessivamente) stuff; fatten (animali)

ingra'naggio m gear; fig mechanism. ~**re** vt engage ● vi be in gear

ingrandi'mento m enlargement

ingran'di|re vt enlarge; (esagerare) magnify. ~**rsi** vr become larger; (aumentare) increase

ingras'sar|e vt fatten up; (Mech) grease ● vi, ~**si** vr put on weight

ingrati'tudine f ingratitude. **in'grato** adj ungrateful; (sgradevole) thankless

ingredi'ente m ingredient

in'gresso m entrance; (accesso) admittance; (sala) hall; ~ **gratuito/libero** admission free; **vietato l'~** no entry; no admittance

ingros'sar|e vt make big; (gonfiare) swell ● vi, ~**si** vr grow big; (gonfiare) swell

in'grosso: **all'~** adv wholesale; (pressappoco) roughly

ingua'ribile adj incurable

'inguine m groin

ingurgi'tare vt gulp down

ini'bi|re vt inhibit; (vietare) forbid.

~to adj inhibited. **~zi'one** f inhibition; (divieto) prohibition

iniet'tar|e vt inject. **~si** vr **~si di sangue** (occhi): become bloodshot. **iniezi'one** f injection

inimic'arsi vr make an enemy of. **inimi'cizia** f enmity

inimi'tabile adj inimitable

ininter|rotta'mente adv continuously. **~rotto** adj continuous

iniquità f iniquity. **i'niquo** adj iniquitous

inizi'are vt begin; (avviare) open; **~ qcno a qcsa** initiate sb in sth
● vi begin

inizia'tiva f initiative; **prendere l'~** take the initiative

inizi'a|to, -a adj initiated ● mf initiate; **gli ~ti** the initiated. **~tore, ~trice** mf initiator. **~zi'one** f initiation

i'nizio m beginning, start; **dare ~ a** start; **avere ~** get under way

innaffi'a|re vt water. **~toio** m watering-can

innal'zar|e vt raise; (erigere) erect. **~si** vr rise

innamo'ra|rsi vr fall in love (di with). **~ta** f girl-friend. **~to** adj in love ● m boy-friend

in'nanzi adv (stato in luogo) in front; (di tempo) ahead; (avanti) forward; (prima) before; **d'ora ~** from now on ● prep (prima) before; **~ a** in front of. **~'tutto** adv first of all; (soprattutto) above all

in'nato adj innate

innatu'rale adj unnatural

inne'gabile adj undeniable

innervo'sir|e vt make nervous. **~si** vr get irritated

inne'scare vt prime. **in'nesco** m primer

inne'stare vt graft; (Mech) engage; (inserire) insert. **in'nesto** m graft; (Mech) clutch; (Electr) connection

inne'vato adj covered in snow

'inno m hymn. **~ nazionale** national anthem

inno'cen|te adj innocent **~te'mente** adv innocently

in'nocuo adj innocuous

inno'va|re vt make changes in. **~'tivo** adj innovative. **~tore** adj trail-blazing. **~zi'one** f innovation

innume'revole adj innumerable

ino'doro adj odourless

inoffen'sivo adj harmless

inol'trar|e vt forward. **~si** vr advance

inol'trato adj late

i'noltre adv besides

inon'da|re vt flood. **~zi'one** f flood

inope'roso adj idle

inoppor'tuno adj untimely

inorgo'glir|e vt make proud. **~si** vr become proud

inorri'dire vt horrify ● vi be horrified

inosser'vato adj unobserved; (non rispettato) disregarded; **passare ~** go unnoticed

inossi'dabile adj stainless

'inox m inv (acciaio) stainless

inqua'dra|re vt frame; fig put in context (scrittore, problema). **~rsi** vr fit into. **~'tura** f framing

inqualifi'cabile adj unspeakable

inquie'tar|e vt worry. **~si** vr get worried; (impazientirsi) get cross. **in-qui'eto** adj restless; (preoccupato) worried. **inquie'tudine** f anxiety

inqui'lino, -a mf tenant

inquina'mento m pollution

inqui'na|re vt pollute. **~to** adj polluted

inqui'rente adj (Jur) (magistrato) examining; **commissione ~** commission of enquiry

inqui'si|re vt/i investigate. **~to** adj under investigation. **~'tore, ~'trice**

adj inquiring ●*mf* inquisitor. ~**zi'one** *f* inquisition

insabbi'are *vt* shelve

insa'lat|a *f* salad. ~**a belga** endive. ~**i'era** *f* salad bowl

insa'lubre *adj* unhealthy

insa'nabile *adj* incurable

insangui'na|re *vt* cover with blood. ~**to** *adj* bloody

insa'po|re *adj* tasteless. ~**'rire** *vt* flavour

insa'puta *f* all'~ di unknown to

insazi'abile *adj* insatiable

insce'nare *vt* stage

inscin'dibile *adj* inseparable

insedia'mento *m* installation

insedi'ar|e *vt* install. ~**si** *vr* install oneself

in'segna *f* sign; (*bandiera*) flag; (*decorazione*) decoration; (*emblema*) insignia *pl*; (*stemma*) symbol. ~ **luminosa** neon sign

insegna'mento *m* teaching. inse-'gnante *adj* teaching ●*mf* teacher

inse'gnare *vt/i* teach; ~ **qcsa a qcno** teach sb sth

insegui'mento *m* pursuit

insegu'i|re *vt* pursue. ~**'tore**, ~**'trice** *mf* pursuer

insemi'na|re *vt* inseminate. ~**zi'one** *f* insemination. ~**zione artificiale** artificial insemination

insena'tura *f* inlet

insen'sato *adj* senseless; (*folle*) crazy

insen'sibil|e *adj* insensitive; (*braccio ecc*) numb. ~**ità** *f* insensitivity

inseri'mento *m* insertion

inse'rir|e *vt* insert; place (*annuncio*); (*Electr*) connect. ~**si** *vr* ~**si in** get into. in'**serto** *m* file; (*in un film ecc*) insert

inservi'ente *mf* attendant

inserzi'o|ne *f* insertion; (*avviso*) advertisement. ~**'nista** *mf* advertiser

insetti'cida *m* insecticide

in'setto *m* insect

insicu'rezza *f* insecurity. insi'curo *adj* insecure

in'sidi|a *f* trick; (*tranello*) snare. ~**'are** *vt/i* lay a trap for. ~**'oso** *adj* insidious

insi'eme *adv* together; (*contemporaneamente*) at the same time ●*prep* ~ **a** [together] with ●*m* whole; (*completo*) outfit; (*Theat*) ensemble; (*Math*) set; **nell'**~ as a whole; **tutto** ~ all together; (*bere*) at one go

in'signe *adj* renowned

insignifi'cante *adj* insignificant

insi'gnire *vt* decorate

insin'dacabile *adj* final

insinu'ante *adj* insinuating

insinu'a|re *vt* insinuate. ~**rsi** *vr* penetrate; ~**rsi in** *fig* creep into

in'sipido *adj* insipid

insi'sten|te *adj* insistent. ~**te-'mente** *adv* repeatedly. ~**za** *f* insistence. in'**sistere** *vi* insist; (*perseverare*) persevere

insoddisfa'cente *adj* unsatisfactory

insoddi'sfa|tto *adj* unsatisfied; (*scontento*) dissatisfied. ~**zi'one** *f* dissatisfaction

insoffe'ren|te *adj* intolerant. ~**za** *f* intolerance

insolazi'one *f* sunstroke

inso'len|te *adj* rude, insolent. ~**za** *f* rudeness, insolence; (*commento*) insolent remark

in'solito *adj* unusual

inso'lubile *adj* insoluble

inso'luto *adj* unsolved; (*non pagato*) unpaid

insol'venza *f* insolvency

in'somma *adv* in short; ~**!** well really!; (*così così*) so so

in'sonne *adj* sleepless. ~**ia** *f* insomnia

insonno'lito *adj* sleepy

insonoriz'zato adj soundproofed

insoppor'tabile adj unbearable

insor'genza f onset

in'sorgere vi revolt, rise up; (sorgere) arise; (difficoltà) crop up

insormon'tabile adj (ostacolo, difficoltà) insurmountable

in'sorto pp di insorgere● adj rebellious ● m rebel

insospet'tabile adj unsuspected

insospet'tir|e vt make suspicious ● vi, **∼si** vr become suspicious

insoste'nibile adj untenable; (insopportabile) unbearable

insostitu'ibile adj irreplaceable

inspe'ra|bile adj una sua vittoria è **∼bile** there is no hope of him winning. **∼to** adj unhoped-for

inspie'gabile adj inexplicable

inspi'rare vt breathe in

in'stabil|e adj unstable; (tempo) changeable. **∼ità** f instability; (di tempo) changeability

instal'la|re vt install. **∼rsi** vr settle in. **∼zi'one** f installation

instau'ra|re vt found. **∼rsi** vr become established. **∼zi'one** f foundation

instra'dare vt direct

insù adv all'**∼** upwards

insuc'cesso m failure

insudici'ar|e vt dirty. **∼si** vr get dirty

insuffici'en|te adj insufficient; (inadeguato) inadequate ● m (Sch) fail. **∼za** f insufficiency; (inadeguatezza) inadequacy; (Sch) fail. **∼za cardiaca** heart failure. **∼za di prove** lack of evidence

insu'lare adj insular

insu'lina f insulin

in'sulso adj insipid; (sciocco) silly

insul'tare vt insult. **in'sulto** m insult

insupe'rabile adj insuperable; (eccezionale) incomparable

insussi'stente adj groundless

intac'care vt nick; (corrodere) corrode; draw on (capitale); (danneggiare) damage

intagli'are vt carve. **in'taglio** m carving

intan'gibile adj untouchable

in'tanto adv meanwhile; (per ora) for the moment; (avversativo) but; **∼ che** while

intarsi'a|re vt inlay. **∼to** adj **∼to di** inset with. **in'tarsio** m inlay

inta'sa|re vt clog; block (traffico). **∼rsi** vr get blocked. **∼to** adj blocked

inta'scare vt pocket

in'tatto adj intact

intavo'lare vt start

inte'gra|le adj whole; **edizione ∼le** unabridged edition; **pane ∼le** wholemeal bread. **∼nte** adj integral. **'integro** adj complete; (retto) upright

inte'gra|re vt integrate; (aggiungere) supplement. **∼rsi** vr integrate. **∼'tivo** adj (corso) supplementary. **∼zi'one** f integration

integrità f integrity

intelaia'tura f framework

intel'letto m intellect

intellettu'al|e adj & mf intellectual. **∼'mente** adv intellectually

intelli'gen|te adj intelligent. **∼te'mente** adv intelligently. **∼za** f intelligence

intelli'gibile adj intelligible

intempe'ranza f intemperance

intem'perie fpl bad weather

inten'den|te m superintendent. **∼za f ∼za di finanza** inland revenue office

in'tender|e vt (comprendere) understand; (udire) hear; (avere intenzione) intend; (significare) mean. **∼sela con** have an understanding with. **∼si** vr (capirsi) understand each other; **∼si di** (essere esperto) have a good knowledge of

intendi|'mento m understanding; (*intenzione*) intention. ~'tore, ~'trice mf connoisseur

intene'rir|e vt soften; (*commuovere*) touch. ~si vr be touched

intensifi'car|e vt, ~si vr intensify

intensità f intensity. **inten'sivo** adj intensive. **in'tenso** adj intense

inten'tare vt start up; ~ causa contro qcno bring o institute proceedings against sb

in'tento adj engrossed (a in) ● m purpose

intenzio|'nale adj intentional. **intenzi'one** f intention; senza ~ne unintentionally; avere ~ne di fare qcsa intend to do sth, have the intention of doing sth

intenzio'nato adj essere ~ a fare qcsa have the intention of doing sth

intera'gire vi interact

intera'mente adv completely

intera|t'tivo adj interactive. ~zi'one f interaction

interca'lare[1] m stock phrase

interca'lare[2] vt insert

intercambi'abile adj interchangeable

interca'pedine f cavity

inter'ce|dere vi intercede. ~ssi'one f intercession

intercet'ta|re vt intercept; tap (telefono). ~zi'one f interception. ~zione telefonica telephone tapping

inter'city m inv inter-city

intercontinen'tale adj intercontinental

inter'correre vi (tempo:) elapse; (esistere) exist

inter'detto pp di interdire ● adj astonished; (proibito) forbidden; rimanere ~ be taken aback

inter'di|re vt forbid; (Jur) deprive of civil rights. ~zi'one f prohibition

interessa'mento m interest

interes'sante adj interesting; essere in stato ~ be pregnant

interes'sa|re vt interest; (riguardare) concern ● vi ~re a matter to. ~rsi vr ~rsi a take an interest in. ~rsi di take care of. ~to, -a mf interested party ● adj interested; essere ~to pej have an interest

inte'resse m interest; fare qcsa per ~ do sth out of self-interest

inter'faccia f (Comput) interface

interfe'renza f interference

interfe'ri|re vi interfere

interiezi'one f interjection

interi'ora fpl entrails

interi'ore adj interior

inter'ludio m interlude

intermedi'ario, -a adj & mf intermediary

inter'medio adj in-between

inter'mezzo m (Mus, Theat) intermezzo

intermit'ten|te adj intermittent; (luce) flashing. ~za f luce a ~za flashing light

interna'mento m internment; (in manicomio) committal

inter'nare vt intern; (in manicomio) commit [to a mental institution]

internazio'nale adj international

'Internet f Internet, internet

in'terno adj internal; (Geog) inland; (interiore) inner; (politica) national; alunno ~ boarder ● m interior; (di condominio) flat; (Teleph) extension; Cinema interior shot; all'~ inside

in'tero adj whole, entire; (intatto) intact; (completo) complete; per ~ in full

interpel'lare vt consult

inter'por|re vt place (ostacolo). ~si vr come between

interpre'ta|re vt interpret; (Mus) perform. ~zi'one f interpretation;

(*Mus*) performance. **in'terprete** *mf* interpreter; (*Mus*) performer

inter'ra|re *vt* (*seppellire*) bury; plant (pianta). ~**to** *m* basement

interro'ga|re *vt* question; (*Sch*) test; examine (studenti). ~**tivo** *adj* interrogative; (*sguardo*) questioning; **punto** ~**tivo** question mark ●*m* question. ~**torio** *adj & m* questioning. ~**zi'one** *f* question; (*Sch*) oral [test]

inter'romper|e *vt* interrupt; (*sospendere*) stop; cut off (collegamento). ~**si** *vr* break off

interrut'tore *m* switch

interruzi'one *f* interruption; **senza** ~ non-stop. ~ **di gravidanza** termination of pregnancy

interse'care *vt*, ~**carsi** *vr* intersect. ~**zi'one** *f* intersection

interur'ba|na *f* long-distance call. ~**o** *adj* inter-city: **telefonata** ~**a** long-distance call

interval'lare *vt* space out. inter-**'vallo** *m* interval; (*spazio*) space; (*Sch*) break. **intervallo pubblicitario** commercial break

interve'nire *vi* intervene; (*Med: operare*) operate; ~ **a** take part in. **inter'vento** *m* intervention; (*presenza*) presence; (*chirurgico*) operation; **pronto intervento** emergency services

inter'vista *f* interview

intervi'sta|re *vt* interview. ~**'tore**, ~**'trice** *mf* interviewer

in'tes|a *f* understanding; **cenno d'**~**a** acknowledgement. ~**o** *pp di* **intendere** ●*adj* **resta** ~**o che...** needless to say,...; ~**il** agreed!; ~**o** a meant to

inte'sta|re *vt* head; write one's name and address at the top of (lettera); (*Comm*) register. ~**rsi** *vr* ~**rsi a fare qcsa** take it into one's head to do sth. ~**tario, -a** *mf* holder. ~**zi'one** *f* heading; (*su carta da lettere*)

letterhead

inte'stino *adj* (*lotte*) internal ●*m* intestine

intima'mente *adv* intimately

inti'ma|re *vt* order; ~**re l'alt a** **qcno** order sb to stop. ~**zi'one** *f* order

intimida'torio *adj* threatening. ~**zi'one** *f* intimidation

intimi'dire *vt* intimidate

intimità *f* cosiness. **'intimo** *adj* intimate; (*interno*) innermost; (*amico*) close ●*m* (*amico*) close friend; (*dell'animo*) heart

intimo'ri|re *vt* frighten. ~**rsi** *vr* get frightened. ~**to** *adj* frightened

in'tingere *vt* dip

in'tingolo *m* sauce; (*pietanza*) stew

intiriz'zi|re *vt* numb. ~**rsi** *vr* grow numb. ~**to** *adj* **essere** ~**to** (*dal freddo*) be perished

intito'lar|e *vt* entitle; (*dedicare*) dedicate. ~**si** *vr* be called

intolle'rabile *adj* intolerable

intona'care *vt* plaster. **in'tonaco** *m* plaster

into'na|re *vt* start to sing; tune (strumento); (*accordare*) match. ~**rsi** *vr* match. ~**to** *adj* (*persona*) able to sing in tune; (*colore*) matching

intonazi'one *f* (*inflessione*) intonation; (*ironica*) tone

inton'ti|re *vt* daze; (*gas:*) make dizzy ●*vi* be dazed. ~**to** *adj* dazed

intop'pare *vi* ~ **in** run into

in'toppo *m* obstacle

in'torno *adv* around ●*prep* ~ **a** around; (*circa*) about

intorpi'di|re *vt* numb. ~**rsi** *vr* become numb. ~**to** *adj* torpid

intossi'ca|re *vt* poison. ~**rsi** *vr* be poisoned. ~**zi'one** *f* poisoning

intralci'are *vt* hamper

in'tralcio *m* hitch; **essere d'**~ be a hindrance (a to)

intrallaz'zare vi intrigue. **intral-lazzo** m racket

intramon'tabile adj timeless

intransi'gen|te adj uncompromising. **~za** f intransigence

intransi'tivo adj intransitive

intrappo'lato adj rimanere ~ be trapped

intrapren'den|te adj enterprising. **~za** f initiative

intra'prendere vt undertake

intrat'tabile adj very difficult

intratte'n|ere vt entertain. **~ersi** vr linger. **~l'mento** m entertainment

intrave'dere vt catch a glimpse of; (presagire) foresee

intrecci'ar|e vt interweave; plait (capelli, corda). **~si** vr intertwine; (aggrovigliarsi) become tangled; **~e le mani** clasp one's hands

in'treccio m (trama) plot

intri'cato adj tangled

intri'gante adj scheming; (affascinante) intriguing

intri'ga|re vt entangle; (incuriosire) intrigue ●vi intrigue, scheme. **~rsi** vr meddle. **in'trigo** m plot; **intrighi** pl intrigues

in'triso adj ~ **di** soaked in

intri'stirsi vr grow sad

intro'du|rre vt introduce; (inserire) insert; **~rre a** (iniziare a) introduce to. **~rsi** vr get in (in to). **~t'tivo** adj (pagine, discorso) introductory. **~zi'one** f introduction

in'troito m income, revenue; (incasso) takings pl

intro'metter|e vt introduce. **~si** vr interfere; (interporsi) intervene. **intromissi'one** f intervention

intro'vabile adj that can't be found; (prodotto) unobtainable

intro'verso, -a adj introverted ● mf introvert

intrufo'larsi vr sneak in

in'truglio m concoction

intrusi'one f intrusion. **in'truso, -a** mf intruder

intu'i|re vt perceive

intui'tivo adj intuitive. **in'tuito** m intuition. **~zi'one** f intuition

inuguagli'anza f inequality

inu'mano adj inhuman

inu'mare vt inter

inumi'dir|e vt dampen; moisten (labbra). **~si** vr become damp

i'nutil|e adj useless; (superfluo) unnecessary. **~ità** f uselessness

inutiliz'za|bile adj unusable. **~to** adj unused

inva'dente adj intrusive

in'vadere vt invade; (affollare) overrun

invali'd|are vt invalidate; **~ità** f disability; (Jur) invalidity. **in'valido, -a** adj invalid; (handicappato) disabled ● mf disabled person

in'vano adv in vain

invari'abile adj invariable

invari'ato adj unchanged

invasi'one f invasion. **in'vaso** pp di invadere. **inva'sore** adj invading ● m invader

invecchia'mento m (di vino) maturation

invecchi'are vt/i age

in'vece adv instead; (anzi) but; **~ di** instead of

inve'ire vi **~ contro** inveigh against

inven'd|ibile adj unsaleable. **~uto** adj unsold

inven'tare vt invent

inventari'are vt make an inventory of. **inven'tario** m inventory

inven|'tivo, -a adj inventive ●f inventiveness. **~'tore, ~'trice** mf inventor. **~zi'one** f invention

inver'nale adj wintry. **in'verno** m winter

invero'simile adj improbable

inversi'one f inversion; (Mech) reversal. **in'verso** adj inverse; (opposto) opposite ● m opposite

inverte'brato adj & m invertebrate.

inver'ti|re vt reverse; (capovolgere) turn upside down.

investi'ga|re vt investigate. ∼**tore** m investigator. ∼**zi'one** f investigation

investi'mento m investment; (incidente) crash

inve'sti|re vt invest; (urtare) collide with; (travolgere) run over; ∼**re qcno di** invest sb with. ∼**'tura** f investiture

invi'a|re vt send. ∼**to, -a** mf envoy; (di giornale) correspondent

invidi|a f envy. ∼**'are** vt envy. ∼**'oso** adj envious

invigo'rir|e vt invigorate. ∼**si** vr become strong

invin'cibile adj invincible

in'vio m dispatch; (Comput) enter

invipe'ri|rsi vr get nasty. ∼**to** adj furious

invi'sibil|e adj invisible. ∼**ità** f invisibility

invi'tante adj (piatto, profumo) enticing

invi'ta|re vt invite. ∼**to, -a** mf guest. **in'vito** m invitation

invo'ca|re vt invoke; (implorare) beg. ∼**zi'one** f invocation

invogli'ar|e vt tempt; (indurre) induce. ∼**si** vr ∼**si di** take a fancy to

involon|taria'mente adv involuntarily. ∼**'tario** adj involuntary

invol'tino m (Culin) beef olive

in'volto m parcel; (fagotto) bundle

in'volucro m wrapping

invulne'rabile adj invulnerable

inzacche'rare vt splash with mud

inzup'par|e vt soak; (intingere) dip. ∼**si** vr get soaked

'io pers pron I; **chi è? - [sono] io** who is it? - [it's] me; **l'ho fatto io**

[stesso] I did it myself ● m l'∼ the ego

i'odio m iodine

l'onio m lo ∼ the Ionian [Sea]

i'osa: a ∼ adv in abundance

iperat'tivo adj hyperactive

ipermer'cato m hypermarket

iper'metrope adj long-sighted

ipertensi'one f high blood pressure

ip'no|si f hypnosis. ∼**tico** adj hypnotic. ∼**'tismo** m hypnotism. ∼**tiz'zare** vt hypnotize

ipoca'lorico adj low-calorie

ipocon'driaco, -a adj & mf hypochondriac

ipocri'sia f hypocrisy. **i'pocrita** adj hypocritical ● mf hypocrite

ipo'te|ca f mortgage. ∼**'care** vt mortgage

i'potesi f inv hypothesis; (caso, eventualità) eventuality. **ipo'tetico** adj hypothetical. **ipotiz'zare** vt hypothesize

'ippico, -a adj horse attrib ● f riding

ippoca'stano m horse-chestnut

ip'podromo m racecourse

ippo'potamo m hippopotamus

'ira f anger. ∼**'scibile** adj irascible

i'rato adj irate

'iride f (Anat) iris; (arcobaleno) rainbow

Ir'lan|da f Ireland. ∼**da del Nord** Northern Ireland. **i∼'dese** adj Irish ● m Irishman; (lingua) Irish ● f Irishwoman

iro'nia f irony. **i'ronico** adj ironic[al]

irradi'a|re vt/i radiate. ∼**zi'one** f radiation

irraggiun'gibile adj unattainable

irragio'nevole adj unreasonable; (speranza, timore) irrational; (assurdo) absurd

irrazio'nal|e adj irrational. ∼**ità** f irrationality

irre'a|le *adj* unreal. **~'listico** *adj* unrealistic. **~liz'zabile** *adj* unattainable. **~ltà** *f* unreality

irrecupe'rabile *adj* irrecoverable

irrego'lar|e *adj* irregular. **~ità** *f inv* irregularity

irremo'vibile *adj fig* adamant

irrepa'rabile *adj* irreparable

irrepe'ribile *adj* not to be found; **sarò ~** I won't be contactable

irrepren'sibile *adj* irreproachable

irrepri'mibile *adj* irrepressible

irrequi'eto *adj* restless

irresi'stibile *adj* irresistible

irrespon'sabil|e *adj* irresponsible. **~ità** *f* irresponsibility

irrever'sibile *adj* irreversible

irricono'scibile *adj* unrecognizable

irri'ga|re *vt* irrigate; (*fiume:*) flow through. **~zi'one** *f* irrigation

irrigidi'mento *m* stiffening

irrigi'dir|e *vt*, **~si** *vr* stiffen

irrile'vante *adj* unimportant

irrimedi'abile *adj* irreparable

irripe'tibile *adj* unrepeatable

irri'sorio *adj* derisive; (*differenza, particolare, somma*) insignificant

irri'ta|bile *adj* irritable. **~nte** *adj* aggravating

irri'ta|re *vt* irritate. **~rsi** *vr* get annoyed. **~to** *adj* irritated; (*gola*) sore. **~zi'one** *f* irritation

irrobu'stir|e *vt* fortify. **~si** *vr* get stronger

ir'rompere *vi* burst (**in** into)

irro'rare *vt* sprinkle

irru'ente *adj* impetuous

irruzi'one *f* **fare ~ in** burst into

i'scritto, -a *pp di* iscrivere ● *adj* registered ● *mf* member; **per ~** in writing

i'scriver|e *vt* register. **~si** *vr* **~si a**

register at, enrol at (*scuola*); join (*circolo ecc*). **iscrizi'one** *f* registration; (*epigrafe*) inscription

i'sla|mico *adj* Islamic. **~'mismo** *m* Islam

I'slan|da *f* Iceland. **i~'dese** *adj* Icelandic ● *mf* Icelander

'isola *f* island. **le isole britanniche** the British Isles. **~ pedonale** pedestrian precinct. **~ spartitraffico** traffic island

iso'lante *adj* insulating ● *m* insulator

iso'la|re *vt* isolate; (*Electr, Mech*) insulate; (*acusticamente*) soundproof. **~to** *adj* isolated ● *m* (*di appartamenti*) block

ispes'sir|e *vt*, **~si** *vr* thicken

ispetto'rato *m* inspectorate. **ispet'tore** *m* inspector. **ispezio'nare** *vt* inspect. **ispezi'one** *f* inspection

'ispido *adj* bristly

ispi'ra|re *vt* inspire; suggest (idea, soluzione). **~rsi** *vr* **~rsi a** be based on. **~to** *adj* inspired. **~zi'one** *f* inspiration; (*idea*) idea

Isra'el|e *m* Israel. **i~i'ano, -a** *agg & mf* Israeli

istan'taneo, -a *adj* instantaneous ● *f* snapshot

i'stante *m* instant; **all'~** instantly

i'stanza *f* petition

i'sterico *adj* hysterical. **iste'rismo** *m* hysteria

isti'ga|re *vt* instigate; **~re qcno al male** incite sb to evil. **~zi'one** *f* instigation

istin'tivo *adj* instinctive. **i'stinto** *m* instinct; **d'istinto** instinctively

istitu'ire *vt* institute; (*fondare*) found; initiate (manifestazione)

isti'tu|to *m* institute; (*universitario*) department; (*Sch*) secondary school. **~to di bellezza** beauty salon. **~'tore, ~'trice** *mf* (*insegnante*) tutor;

(*fondatore*) founder

istituzio'nale *adj* institutional. **istituzi'one** *f* institution

'istrice *m* porcupine

istru'i|re *vt* instruct; (*addestrare*) train; (*informare*) inform; (*Jur*) prepare. **~to** *adj* educated

istrut't|ivo *adj* instructive. **~ore, ~rice** *mf* instructor; **giudice ~ore** examining magistrate. **~oria** *f* (*Jur*) investigation. **istruzi'one** *f* education; (*indicazione*) instruction

l'tali|a *f* Italy. **i~'ano, -a** *adj & mf* Italian

Italo- Descendants of those who emigrated from Italy are often referred to as *italo-americani, italo-brasiliani*, etc. Massive emigration started in the 1870s, mainly from the north of Italy to South America. Buenos Aires and Sao Paulo have the highest concentrations of Italians outside Italy. Subsequently more and more southern Italians emigrated to the United States.

itine'rario *m* route, itinerary

itte'rizia *f* jaundice

'ittico *adj* fishing *attrib*

I.V.A. *f abbr* (imposta sul valore aggiunto) VAT

---

jack *m inv* jack

jazz *m* jazz. **jaz'zista** *mf* jazz player

jeep *f inv* jeep

'jolly *m inv* (*carta da gioco*) joker

ju'niores *mfpl Sport* juniors

---

ka'jal *m inv* kohl

kara'oke *m inv* karaoke

kara'te *m* karate

kg *abbr* (chilogrammo) kg

km *abbr* (chilometro) km

---

l' *def art mf* (*before vowel*) the; ▷**IL**

la *def art f* the; ▷**IL** ● *pron* (*oggetto, riferito a persona*) her; (*riferito a cosa, animale*) it; (*forma di cortesia*) you ● *m inv* (*Mus*) A

là *adv* there; **di là** (*in quel luogo*) in there; (*da quella parte*) that way; **eccolo là!** there he is!; **farsi più in là** (*far largo*) make way; **là dentro** in there; **là fuori** out there; **[ma] va là!** come off it!; **più in là** (*nel tempo*) later on; (*nello spazio*) further on

'labbro *m* (*pl f* (*Anat*) **labbra**) lip

labi'rinto *m* labyrinth; (*di sentieri ecc*) maze

labora'torio *m* laboratory; (*di negozio, officina ecc*) workshop

labori'oso *adj* industrious; (*faticoso*) laborious

labu'rista *adj* Labour ● *mf* member of the Labour Party

'lacca *f* lacquer; (*per capelli*) hairspray. **lac'care** *vt* lacquer

'laccio *m* noose; (*lazo*) lasso; (*trappola*) snare; (*stringa*) lace

lace'rante *adj* (*grido*) earsplitting

lace'ra|re *vt* tear; lacerate (*carne*).

∼rsi vr tear. **∼zi'one** f laceration.
'**lacero** adj torn; (cencioso) ragged
'**lacri|ma** f tear; (goccia) drop.
∼'mare vi weep. **∼'mevole** adj tear-jerking
lacri'mogeno adj gas **∼** tear gas
la'cuna f gap. **lacu'noso** adj (prepa-razione, resoconto) incomplete
la'custre adj lake attrib

Ladino Ladin (ladino in Italian) is a direct descendant of the Latin spoken in the valleys in north eastern Italy. Western Ladin is spoken in Alto Adige alongside German, and Eastern Ladin (also called Friulian) in Friuli-Venezia Giulia. Numbers of speakers are shrinking as gradually German or Italian predominate.

'**ladro, -a** m/f thief; **al ∼!** stop thief!; **∼'cinio** m theft. **la'druncolo** m petty thief
'**lager** m inv concentration camp
laggiù adv down there; (lontano) over there
'**lagna** f (□: persona) moaning Minnie; (film) bore
la'gna|nza f complaint. **∼rsi** vr moan; (protestare) complain (di about)
'**lago** m lake
la'guna f lagoon
'**laico, -a** adj lay; (vita) secular ● m layman ● f laywoman
'**lama** f blade ● m inv llama
lambic'carsi vr **∼ il cervello** rack one's brains
lam'bire vt lap
lamé m inv lamé
lamen'tar|e vt lament. **∼si** vr moan. **∼si di** complain about
lamen'te|la f complaint. **∼vole** adj mournful; (pietoso) pitiful. **la'mento** m moan
la'metta f **∼ [da barba]** razor blade

lami'era f sheet metal
'**lamina** f foil. **∼ d'oro** gold leaf
lami'na|re vt laminate. **∼to** adj laminated ● m laminate; (tessuto) lamé
'**lampa|da** f lamp. **∼da abbron-zante** sunlamp. **∼da a pila** torch. **∼'dario** m chandelier. **∼'dina** f light bulb
lam'pante adj clear
lampeggi'a|re vi flash. **∼'tore** m (Auto) indicator
lampi'one m street lamp
'**lampo** m flash of lightning; (luce) flash; **lampi** pl lightning sg. **∼ di genio** stroke of genius. [cerniera] **∼** zip [fastener], zipper Am
lam'pone m raspberry
'**lana** f wool; **di ∼** woollen. **∼ d'ac-ciaio** steel wool. **∼ vergine** new wool. **∼ di vetro** glass wool
lan'cetta f pointer; (di orologio) hand
'**lancia** f spear; (Naut) launch
lanci'ar|e vt throw; (da un aereo) drop; launch (missile, prodotto); give (grido); **∼e uno sguardo a** glance at. **∼si** vr fling oneself; (intraprendere) launch out
lanci'nante adj piercing
'**lancio** m throwing; (da aereo) drop; (di missile, prodotto) launch. **∼ del disco** discus [throwing]. **∼ del gia-vellotto** javelin [throwing]
'**landa** f heath
lani'ero adj wool
lani'ficio m woollen mill
lan'terna f lantern; (faro) lighthouse
la'nugine f down
lapi'dare vt stone; fig demolish
lapi'dario adj (conciso) terse
'**lapide** f tombstone; (commemorativa) memorial tablet
'**lapis** m inv pencil
'**lapsus** m inv lapse, error

'lardo m lard

larga'mente adv widely

lar'ghezza f breadth; fig liberality. ~ **di vedute** broadmindedness

'largo adj wide; (ampio) broad; (abito) loose; (liberale) liberal; (abbondante) generous; **stare alla larga** keep away; ~ **di manica** fig generous; ~ **di spalle/vedute** broad-shouldered/-minded ● m width; andare al ~ (Naut) go out to sea; **fare** ~ make room; **farsi** ~ make one's way; **al** ~ **di** off the coast of

'larice m larch

la'ringe f larynx. **larin'gite** f laryngitis

'larva f larva; (persona emaciata) shadow

la'sagne fpl lasagna sg

lasciapas'sare m inv pass

lasci'ar|e vt leave; (rinunciare) give up; (rimetterci) lose; (smettere di tenere) let go [of]; (concedere) let; ~**e di fare qcsa** (smettere) stop doing sth; **lascia perdere!** forget it!; **lascialo venire** let him come. ~**si** vr (reciproco) leave each other; ~**si andare** let oneself go

'lascito m legacy

'laser adj & m inv [raggio] ~ laser [beam]

lassa'tivo adj & m laxative

'lasso m ~ **di tempo** period of time

las'sù adv up there

'lastra f slab; (di ghiaccio) sheet; (Phot, di metallo) plate; (radiografia) X-ray [plate]

lastri'ca|re vt pave. ~**to, 'lastrico** m pavement

la'tente adj latent

late'rale adj side attrib; (Med, Techn ecc) lateral; **via** ~ side street

late'rizi mpl bricks

lati'fondo m large estate

la'tino adj & m Latin

lati'tan|te adj in hiding ● mf fugitive [from justice]

lati'tudine f latitude

'lato adj (ampio) broad; **in senso** ~ broadly speaking ● m side; (aspetto) aspect; **a** ~ **di** beside; **dal** ~ **mio** (punto di vista) for my part; **d'altro** ~ fig on the other hand

la'tra|re vi bark. ~**to** m barking

la'trina f latrine

'latta f tin, can

lat'taio, -a m milkman ● f milkwoman

lat'tante adj breast-fed ● mf suckling

'latt|e m milk. ~**e acido** sour milk. ~**e condensato** condensed milk. ~**e detergente** cleansing milk. ~**e in polvere** powdered milk. ~**e scremato** skimmed milk. ~**eo** adj milky. ~**e'ria** f dairy. ~**i'cini** mpl dairy products. ~**i'era** f milk jug

lat'tina f can

lat'tuga f lettuce

'laure|a f degree; **prendere la** ~ graduate. ~**'ando, -a** mf final-year student

laure'a|rsi vr graduate. ~**to, -a** agg & mf graduate

'lauro m laurel

'lauto adj lavish; ~ **guadagno** handsome profit

'lava f lava

la'vabile adj washable

la'vabo m wash-basin

la'vaggio m washing. ~ **automatico** (per auto) carwash. ~ **a secco** dry-cleaning

la'vagna f slate; (Sch) blackboard

la'van|da f wash; (Bot) lavender; **fare una** ~**da gastrica** have one's stomach pumped. ~**daia** f washerwoman. ~**de'ria** f laundry. ~**deria automatica** launderette

lavan'dino m sink; (⊞ persona) bottomless pit

lavapi'atti mf inv dishwasher

la'var|e vt wash; ~**e i piatti** wash up. ~**si** vr wash, have a wash; ~**si i denti** brush one's teeth; ~**si le mani** wash one's hands

lava'secco mf inv dry-cleaner's

lavasto'viglie f inv dishwasher

la'vata f wash; **dare una** ~ have a wash; ~ **di capo** fig scolding

lava'tivo, -a mf idler

lava'trice f washing-machine

lavo'rante mf worker

lavo'ra|re vi work ● vt work; knead (pasta ecc); till (la terra); ~**re a maglia** knit. ~**tivo** adj working. ~**to** adj (pietra, legno) carved; (cuoio) tooled; (metallo) wrought. ~**tore, ~trice** mf worker ● adj working. ~**zi'one** f manufacture; (di terra) working; (artigianale) workmanship; (del terreno) cultivation. **lavo'rio** m intense activity

la'voro m work; (faticoso, sociale) labour; (impiego) job; (Theat) play; **mettersi al** ~ set to work (**su** on). ~ **a maglia** knitting. ~ **nero** moonlighting. ~ **straordinario** overtime. ~ **a tempo pieno** full-time job. **lavori** pl **di casa** housework. **lavori** pl **in corso** roadworks. **lavori** pl **stradali** roadworks

le def art fpl the; ▷**IL** ● pers pron (oggetto) them; (a lei) her; (forma di cortesia) you

le'al|e adj loyal. ~'**mente** adv loyally. ~**tà** f loyalty

'lebbra f leprosy

'lecca 'lecca m inv lollipop

leccapi'edi mf inv pej bootlicker

lec'ca|re vt lick; fig suck up to. ~**rsi** vr lick; (fig: agghindarsi) doll oneself up; **da** ~**rsi i baffi** mouth-watering. ~**ta** f lick

leccor'nia f delicacy

'lecito adj lawful; (permesso) permissible

'ledere vt damage; (Med) injure

'lega f league; (di metalli) alloy; **far** ~ **con qcno** take up with sb

le'gaccio m string; (delle scarpe) shoelace

le'gal|e adj legal ● m lawyer. ~**ità** f legality. ~**iz'zare** vt authenticate; (rendere legale) legalize. ~'**mente** adv legally

le'game m tie; (amoroso) liaison; (connessione) link

lega'mento m (Med) ligament

le'gar|e vt tie; tie up (persona); tie together (due cose); (unire, rilegare) bind; alloy (metalli); (connettere) connect ● vi (far lega) get on well. ~**si** vr bind oneself; ~**si a qcno** become attached to sb

le'gato m legacy; (Relig) legate

lega'tura f tying; (di libro) binding

le'genda f legend

'legge f law; (parlamentare) act; **a norma di** ~ by law

le'genda f legend; (didascalia) caption. **leggen'dario** adj legendary

'leggere vt/i read

legge'r|ezza f lightness; (frivolezza) frivolity; (incostanza) fickleness. ~'**mente** adv slightly

leg'gero adj light; (bevanda) weak; (lieve) slight; (frivolo) frivolous; (incostante) fickle

leg'gibile adj (scrittura) legible; (stile) readable

'leggio m lectern; (Mus) music stand

legife'rare vi legislate

legio'nario m legionary. **legi'one** f legion

legisla'|tivo adj legislative. ~**tore** m legislator. ~'**tura** f legislature. ~**zi'one** f legislation

legittimità f legitimacy. **le'gittimo** adj legitimate; (giusto) proper; **legit'tima difesa** self-defence

'legna f firewood

'legname m timber

'legno m wood; **di** ~ wooden. ~ **compensato** plywood. **le'gnoso**

adj woody

le'gume m pod

'lei pers pron (soggetto) she; (oggetto, con prep) her; (forma di cortesia) you; **lo ha fatto ~ stessa** she did it herself

'lembo m edge; (di terra) strip

'lena f vigour

le'nire vt soothe

lenta'mente adv slowly

'lente f lens. **~ a contatto** contact lens. **~ d'ingrandimento** magnifying glass

len'tezza f slowness

len'ticchia f lentil

len'tiggine f freckle

'lento adj slow; (allentato) slack; (abito) loose

'lenza f fishing-line

len'zuolo m (pl f lenzuola) m sheet

le'one m lion; (Astr) Leo

leo'pardo m leopard

'lepre f hare

'lercio adj filthy

'lesbica f lesbian

lesi'nare vt grudge • vi be stingy

lesio'nare vt damage. **lesi'one** f lesion

'leso pp di ledere • adj injured

les'sare vt boil

'lessico m vocabulary

'lesso adj boiled • m boiled meat

'lesto adj quick; (mente) sharp

le'tale adj lethal

le'targ|ico adj lethargic. **~o** m lethargy; (di animali) hibernation

le'tizia f joy

'lettera f letter; **alla ~** literally; **~ maiuscola** capital letter; **~ minuscola** small letter; **lettere** pl (letteratura) literature sg; (Univ) Arts; **dottore in lettere** BA, Bachelor of Arts

lette'rale adj literal

lette'rario adj literary

lette'rato adj well-read

lettera'tura f literature

let'tiga f stretcher

let'tino m cot; (Med) couch

'letto m bed. **~ a castello** bunkbed. **~ a una piazza** single bed. **~ a due piazze** double bed. **~ matrimoniale** double bed

letto'rato m (corso) ≈ tutorial

let'tore, -'trice mf reader; (Univ) language assistant • m (Comput) disk drive. **~ CD-ROM** CD-Rom drive. **~ MP3** MP3 player

let'tura f reading

leuce'mia f leukaemia

'leva f lever; (Mil) call-up; **far ~** lever. **~ del cambio** gear lever

le'vante m East; (vento) east wind

le'va|re vt (alzare) raise; (togliere) take away; (rimuovere) take off; (estrarre) pull out; **~re di mezzo qcsa** get sth out of the way. **~rsi** vr rise; (da letto) get up; **~rsi di mezzo, ~rsi dai piedi** get out of the way. **~ta** f rising; (di posta) collection

leva'taccia f **fare una ~** get up at the crack of dawn

leva'toio adj **ponte ~** drawbridge

levi'ga|re vt smooth; (con carta vetro) rub down. **~to** adj (superficie) polished

levri'ero m greyhound

lezi'one f lesson; (Univ) lecture; (rimprovero) rebuke

lezi'oso adj (stile, modi) affected

lì pers pron mpl them

lì adv there; **fin lì** as far as there; **giù di lì** thereabouts; **lì per lì** there and then

Li'bano m Lebanon

'libbra f (peso) pound

li'beccio m south-west wind

li'bellula f dragon-fly

libe'rale adj liberal; (generoso) generous • mf liberal

libe'ra|re vt free; release (prigioniero); vacate (stanza); (salvare) rescue. **~rsi** vr (stanza:) become vacant; (*Teleph*) become free; (*da impegno*) get out of it; **~rsi** di get rid of. **~tore**, **~trice** *adj* liberating ●*mf* liberator. **~zi'one** *f* liberation; **la L~zione** Liberation Day

'liber|o *adj* free; (*strada*) clear. **~o docente** qualified university lecturer. **~o professionista** selfemployed person. **~tà** *f inv* freedom; (*di prigioniero*) release. **~tà provvisoria** (*Jur*) bail; **~tà** *pl* (*confidenze*) liberties

'liberty *m* & *adj inv* Art Nouveau

'Libi|a *f* Libya. **l~co**, **-a** *adj* & *mf* Libyan

li'braio *m* bookseller

libre'ria *f* (*negozio*) bookshop; (*mobile*) bookcase; (*biblioteca*) library

li'bretto *m* booklet; (*Mus*) libretto. **~ degli assegni** cheque book. **~ di circolazione** logbook. **~ d'istruzioni** instruction booklet. **~ di risparmio** bankbook. **~ universitario** student record of exam results

'libro *m* book. **~ giallo** thriller. **~ paga** payroll

lice'ale *mf* secondary-school student ●*adj* secondary-school *attrib*

li'cenza *f* licence; (*permesso*) permission; (*Mil*) leave; (*Sch*) school-leaving certificate; **essere in ~** be on leave

licenzia'mento *m* dismissal

licenzi'a|re *vt* dismiss, sack Ⓘ. **~rsi** *vr* (*da un impiego*) resign; (*accomiatarsi*) take one's leave

li'ceo *m* secondary school. **~ classico** *secondary school emphasizing humanities*. **~ scientifico** *secondary school emphasizing science*

Liceo There are two main types of secondary school in Italy: the *licei*, which offer an academic syllabus, and the *istituti*, which have a more vocational syllabus, offering subjects like accountancy, electronics, and catering. *Licei* may specialize in particular

subjects such as science, languages or classical studies.

'lido *m* beach

li'eto *adj* glad; (*evento*) happy; **molto ~!** pleased to meet you!

li'eve *adj* light; (*debole*) faint; (*trascurabile*) slight

lievi'tare *vi* rise ●*vt* leaven. **li'evito** *m* yeast. **lievito in polvere** baking powder

'lifting *m inv* face-lift

'ligio *adj* **essere ~ al dovere** have a sense of duty

'lilla[1] (*colore*) lilac

'lillà[2] *m inv* (*Bot*) lillac

'lima *f* file

limacci'oso *adj* slimy

li'mare *vt* file

li'metta *f* nail-file

limi'ta|re *m* threshold ●*vt* limit. **~rsi** *vr* **~rsi a fare qcsa** restrict oneself to doing sth; **~rsi in qcsa** cut down on sth. **~'tivo** *adj* limiting. **~zi'one** *f* limitation

'limite *m* limit; (*confine*) boundary. **~ di velocità** speed limit

li'mitrofo *adj* neighbouring

limo'nata *f* (*bibita*) lemonade; (*succo*) lemon juice

li'mone *m* lemon; (*albero*) lemon tree

'limpido *adj* clear; (*occhi*) limpid

'lince *f* lynx

linci'are *vt* lynch

'lindo *adj* neat; (*pulito*) clean

'linea *f* line; (*di autobus, aereo*) route; (*di metro*) line; (*di abito*) cut; (*di auto, mobile*) design; (*fisico*) figure; **è caduta la ~** I've been cut off; **in ~** (*Comput*) on line; **mantenere la ~** keep one's figure; **mettersi in ~** line up; **nave di ~** liner; **volo di ~** scheduled flight. **~ d'arrivo** finishing line. **~ continua** unbroken line

linea'menti *mpl* features

line'are adj linear; (discorso) to the point; (ragionamento) consistent

line'etta f (tratto lungo) dash; (d'unione) hyphen

lin'gotto m ingot

lingu|a f tongue; (linguaggio) language. **∼'accia** f (persona) backbiter. **∼'aggio** m language. **∼'etta** f (di scarpa) tongue; (di strumento) reed; (di busta) flap

lingu'ist|a mf linguist. **∼ica** f linguistics sg. **∼ico** adj linguistic

lino m (Bot) flax; (tessuto) linen

li'noleum m linoleum

liofiliz'za|re vt freeze-dry. **∼to** adj freeze-dried

liposuzi'one f liposuction

lique'far|e vt, **∼si** vr liquefy; (sciogliersi) melt

liqui'da|re vt liquidate; settle (conto); pay off (debiti); clear (merce); (🔢: uccidere) get rid of. **∼zi'one** f liquidation; (di conti) settling; (di merce) clearance sale

'liquido adj & m liquid

liqui'rizia f liquorice

li'quore m liqueur; **liquori** pl (bevande alcooliche) liquors

'lira f lira; (Mus) lyre

'lirico, -a adj lyrical; (poesia) lyric; (cantante, musica) opera attrib ● f lyric poetry; (Mus) opera

lisci'are vt smooth; (accarezzare) stroke. **'liscio** adj smooth; (capelli) straight; (liquore) neat; (acqua minerale) still; **passarla liscia** get away with it

'liso adj worn [out]

'lista f list; (striscia) strip. **∼ di attesa** waiting list; **in ∼ di attesa** (Aeron) stand-by. **∼ elettorale** electoral register. **∼ nera** blacklist. **∼ di nozze** wedding list. **li'stare** vt edge; (Comput) list

li'stino m list. **∼ prezzi** price list

Lit. abbr (lire italiane) Italian lire

'lite f quarrel; (baruffa) row; (Jur) lawsuit

liti'gare vi quarrel. **li'tigio** m quarrel. **litigi'oso** adj quarrelsome

lito'rale adj coastal ● m coast

'litro m litre

li'turgico adj liturgical

li'vella f level. **∼ a bolla d'aria** spirit level

livel'lar|e vt level. **∼si** vr level out

li'vello m level; **passaggio a ∼** level crossing; **sotto/sul ∼ del mare** below/above sea level

'livido adj livid; (per il freddo) blue; (per una botta) black and blue ● m bruise

Li'vorno f Leghorn

'lizza f lists pl; **essere in ∼ per qcsa** be in the running for sth

lo def art m (before s + consonant, gn, ps, z) the; ▶ **IL** ● pron (riferito a persona) him; (riferito a cosa) it; **non lo so l** don't know

'lobo m lobe

lo'cal|e adj local ● m (stanza) room; (treno) local train; **∼i** pl (edifici) premises. **∼e notturno** night-club. **∼ità** f inv locality

localiz'zare vt localize; (trovare) locate

localizzazi'one f localization

lo'cand|a f bill, poster

loca'tario, -a mf tenant. **∼'tore, ∼'trice** m landlord ● f landlady. **∼zi'one** f tenancy

locomo'tiva f locomotive. **∼zi'one** f locomotion; **mezzi di ∼** means of transport

'loculo m burial niche

lo'custa f locust

locuzi'one f expression

lo'dare vt praise. **'lode** f praise; **laurea con lode** first-class degree

'loden m inv (cappotto) loden coat

'lodola f lark

'loggia f loggia; (*massonica*) lodge

loggi'one m gallery, the gods

'logica f logic

logica'mente adv (*in modo logico*) logically; (*ovviamente*) of course

'logico adj logical

lo'gistica f logistics sg

logo'ra|re vt wear out; (*sciupare*) waste. **~rsi** vr wear out; (*persona:*) wear oneself out. **logo'rio** m wear and tear. **'logoro** adj worn-out

lom'baggine f lumbago

Lombar'dia f Lombardy

lom'bata f loin. **'lombo** m (*Anat*) loin

lom'brico m earthworm

'Londra f London

lon'gevo adj long-lived

longi'lineo adj tall and slim

longi'tudine f longitude

lontana'mente adv distantly; (*vagamente*) vaguely; **neanche ~** not for a moment

lonta'nanza f distance; (*separazione*) separation; **in ~** in the distance

lon'tano adj far; (*distante*) distant; (*nel tempo*) far-off, distant; (*parente*) distant; (*vago*) vague; (*assente*) absent; **più ~** further ● adv far [away]; **da ~** from a distance

'lontra f otter

lo'quace adj talkative

'lordo adj dirty; (*somma, peso*) gross

'loro¹ pron pl (*soggetto*) they; (*oggetto*) them; (*forma di cortesia*) you; **sta a ~** it is up to them

'loro² (**il ~** m, **la ~** f, **i ~** mpl, **le ~** fpl) poss adj their; (*forma di cortesia*) your; **un ~ amico** a friend of theirs; (*forma di cortesia*) a friend of yours ● poss pron theirs; (*forma di cortesia*) yours; **i ~** (*famiglia*) their folk

losanga f lozenge; **a losanghe** diamond-shaped

'losco adj suspicious

'lott|a f fight, struggle; (*contrasto*) conflict; *Sport* wrestling. **lot'tare** vi fight, struggle; *Sport, fig* wrestle. **~a'tore** m wrestler

lotte'ria f lottery

'lotto m [national] lottery; (*porzione*) lot; (*di terreno*) plot

lozi'one f lotion

lubrifi'ca|nte adj lubricating ● m lubricant. **~re** vt lubricate

luc'chetto m padlock

lucci'ca|nte adj sparkling. **~re** vi sparkle. **lucci'chio** m sparkle

'luccio m pike

'lucciola f glow-worm

'luce f light; **far ~ su** shed light on; **dare alla ~** give birth to. **~ della luna** moonlight. **luci** pl **di posizione** sidelights. **~ del sole** sunlight

lu'cen|te adj shining. **~'tezza** f shine

lucer'nario m skylight

lu'certola f lizard

lucida'labbra m inv lip gloss

luci'da|re vt polish. **~'trice** f [floor-]polisher. **'lucido** adj shiny; (*pavimento, scarpe*) polished; (*chiaro*) clear; (*persona, mente*) lucid; (*occhi*) watery ● m shine. **lucido [da scarpe]** [shoe] polish

lucra'tivo adj lucrative

'luglio m July

lu'gubre adj gloomy

'lui pron (*soggetto*) he; (*oggetto, con prep*) him; **lo ha fatto ~ stesso** he did it himself

lu'maca f (*mollusco*) snail; *fig* slowcoach

'lume m lamp; (*luce*) light; **a ~ di candela** by candlelight

luminosità f brightness. **lumi'noso** a luminous; (*stanza, cielo ecc*) bright

'luna f moon; **chiaro di ~** moonlight. **~ di miele** honeymoon

luna park *m inv* fairground

lu'nario *m* almanac; **sbarcare il ~** make both ends meet

lu'natico *a* moody

lunedì *m inv* Monday

lu'netta *f* half-moon [shape]

lun'gaggine *f* slowness

lun'ghezza *f* length. **~ d'onda** wavelength

'lungi *adv* l**ero [ben] ~ dall'immaginare che...** I never dreamt for a moment that...

lungimi'rante *adj* far-sighted

'lungo *adj* long; (*diluito*) weak; (*lento*) slow; **saperla lunga** be shrewd ●*m* length; **di gran lunga** by far; **andare per le lunghe** drag on ●*prep* (*durante*) throughout; (*per la lunghezza di*) along

lungofi'ume *m* riverside

lungo'lago *m* lakeside

lungo'mare *m* sea front

lungome'traggio *m* feature film

lu'notto *m* rear window

lu'ogo *m* place; (*punto preciso*) spot; (*passo d'autore*) passage; **aver ~** take place; **dar ~ a** give rise to; **del ~** (*usanze*) local. **~ pubblico** public place

luogote'nente *m* (*Mil*) lieutenant

lu'petto *m* Cub [Scout]

'lupo *m* wolf

'luppolo *m* hop

'lurido *adj* filthy. **luri'dume** *m* filth

lusin'g|are *vt* flatter. **~arsi** *vr* flatter oneself; (*illudersi*) fool oneself. **~hi'ero** *a* flattering

lus'sa|re *vt*, **~rsi** *vr* dislocate. **~zi'one** *f* dislocation

Lussem'burgo *m* Luxembourg

'lusso *m* luxury; **di ~** luxury *attrib*

lussu'oso *adj* luxurious

lussu'ria *f* lust

lu'strare *vt* polish

'lustro *adj* shiny ●*m* sheen; *fig* prestige; (*quinquennio*) five-year period

'lutt|o *m* mourning; **~o stretto** deep mourning. **~u'oso** *a* mournful

....

Mm

m *abbr* (metro) m

ma *conj* but; (*eppure*) yet; **ma!** (*dubbio*) I don't know; (*indignazione*) really!; **ma davvero?** really?; **ma sì!** why not!; (*certo che sì*) of course!

'macabro *adj* macabre

macché *int* of course not!

macche'roni *mpl* macaroni *sg*

macche'ronico *adj* (*italiano*) broken

'macchia¹ *f* stain; (*di diverso colore*) spot; (*piccola*) speck; **senza ~** spotless

'macchia² *f* (*boscaglia*) scrub

macchi'a|re *vt*, **~rsi** *vr* stain. **~to** *adj* (*caffè*) with a dash of milk; **~to di** (*sporco*) stained with

'macchina *f* machine; (*motore*) engine; (*automobile*) car. **~ da cucire** sewing machine. **~ da presa** cine camera. **~ da scrivere** typewriter. **~ fotografica (digitale)** (digital) camera

macchinal'mente *adv* mechanically

macchi'nare *vt* plot

macchi'nario *m* machinery

macchi'netta *f* (*per i denti*) brace

macchi'nista *m* (*Rail*) enginedriver; (*Naut*) engineer; (*Theat*) stagehand

macchi'noso *adj* complicated

mace'donia *f* fruit salad

Mace'donia f Macedonia

macel'la|io m butcher. ~**re** vt slaughter, butcher. **macelle'ria** f butcher's [shop]. **ma'cello** m (*mattatoio*) slaughterhouse; (*fig* shambles sg; **andare al macello** *fig* go to the slaughter

mace'rar|e vt macerate; *fig* distress. ~**si** vr be consumed

ma'cerie fpl rubble sg; (*rottami*) debris sg

ma'cigno m boulder

'macina f millstone

macinacaffè m inv coffee mill

macina'pepe m inv pepper mill

maci'na|re vt mill. ~**to** adj ground ● m (*carne*) mince. **maci'nino** m mill; (*hum*) old banger

maciul'lare vt (*stritolare*) crush

macrobiotic|a f negozio di ~**a** health-food shop. ~**o** adj macrobiotic

macu'lato adj spotted

'madido adj ~ **di** moist with

Ma'donna f Our Lady

mador'nale adj gross

'madre f mother. ~**lingua** adj inv inglese English native speaker. ~**lingua** f native land. ~**perla** f mother-of-pearl

ma'drina f godmother

maestà f majesty

maestosità f majesty. **mae'stoso** adj majestic

mae'strale m northwest wind

mae'stranza f workers pl

mae'stria f mastery

ma'estro, -a mf teacher ● m master; (*Mus*) maestro. ~ **di cerimonie** master of ceremonies ● adj (*principale*) chief; (*di grande abilità*) skilful

'mafi|a f Mafia. ~**oso** adj of the Mafia ● m member of the Mafia, Mafioso

Mafia The Mafia developed in Sicily in the nineteenth century, where it continues to wield considerable power in opposition to the authorities. Strictly speaking, the term Mafia applies only to Sicily, and its equivalents in other regions (Camorra in Naples and 'ndrangheta in Calabria) are separate organizations, although often working in collaboration with each other.

ma'gagna f fault

ma'gari adv (*forse*) maybe ● int I wish! ● conj (*per esprimere desiderio*) if only; (*anche se*) even if

magazzi'niere m storesman, warehouseman. **magaz'zino** m warehouse; (*emporio*) shop; **grande magazzino** department store

'maggio m May

maggio'lino m May bug

maggio'rana f marjoram

maggio'ranza f majority

maggio'rare vt increase

maggior'domo m butler

maggi'ore adj (*di dimensioni, numero*) bigger, larger; (*superlativo*) biggest, largest; (*di età*) older; (*superlativo*) oldest; (*di importanza, musica*) major; (*superlativo*) greatest; **la maggior parte di** most; **la maggior parte del tempo** most of the time ● pron (*di dimensioni*) the bigger, the larger; (*superlativo*) the biggest, the largest; (*di età*) the older; (*superlativo*) the oldest; (*di importanza*) the major; (*superlativo*) the greatest ● m (*Mil*) major; (*Aeron*) squadron leader. **maggio'renne** adj of age ● mf adult

maggiori'tario adj (*sistema*) first-past-the-post attrib. ~**'mente** adv [all] the more; (*più di tutto*) most

'Magi mpl **i re** ~ the Magi

ma'gia f magic; (*trucco*) magic trick. **magica'mente** adv magically. **'ma-**

gico *adj* magic

magi'stero *m* (*insegnamento*) teaching; (*maestria*) skill; **facoltà di ~** arts faculty

magi'stra|le *adj* masterly; **istituto ~e** teachers' training college

magi'stra|to *m* magistrate. **~'tura** *f* magistrature. **la ~tura** the Bench

'magli|a *f* stitch; (*lavoro ai ferri*) knitting; (*tessuto*) jersey; (*di rete*) mesh; (*di catena*) link; (*indumento*) vest; **fare la ~a** knit. **~a diritta** knit. **~a rosa** (*ciclismo*) ≈ yellow jersey. **~a rovescia** purl. **~e'ria** *f* knitwear. **~'etta** *f* **~etta [a maniche corte]** tee-shirt. **~'ficio** *m* knitwear factory. **ma'glina** *f* (*tessuto*) jersey

magli'one *m* sweater

'magma *m* magma

ma'gnanimo *adj* magnanimous

ma'gnate *m* magnate

ma'gnesi|a *f* magnesia. **~o** *m* magnesium

ma'gne|te *m* magnet. **~tico** *adj* magnetic. **~tismo** *m* magnetism

magne'tofono *m* tape recorder

magnifi|ca'mente *adv* magnificently. **~'cenza** *f* magnificence; (*generosità*) munificence. **ma'gnifico** *adj* magnificent; (*generoso*) munificent

ma'gnolia *f* magnolia

ma'gone *m* avere il ~ be down; **mi è venuto il ~** I've got a lump in my throat

'magr|a *f* low water. **ma'grezza** *f* thinness. **~o** *adj* thin; (*carne*) lean; (*scarso*) meagre

'mai *adv* never; (*inter, talvolta*) ever; **caso ~** if anything; **caso ~ tornasse** in case he comes back; **come ~?** why?; **cosa ~?** what on earth?; **~ più** never again; **più che ~** more than ever; **quando ~?** whenever?; **quasi ~** hardly ever

mai'ale *m* pig; (*carne*) pork

mai'olica *f* majolica

maio'nese *f* mayonnaise

'mais *m* maize

mai'uscol|a *f* capital [letter]. **~o** *adj* capital

mal ▷**MALE**

'mala *f* la ~ ✕ the underworld

mala'fede *f* bad faith

malaf'fare *m* **gente di ~** shady characters *pl*

mala'lingua *f* backbiter

mala'mente *adv* (*ridotto*) badly

malan'dato *adj* in bad shape; (*di salute*) in poor health

ma'lanimo *m* ill will

ma'lanno *m* misfortune; (*malattia*) illness; **prendersi un ~** catch something

mala'pena: **a ~** *adv* hardly

ma'laria *f* malaria

mala'ticcio *adj* sickly

ma'lato, -a *adj* ill, sick; (*pianta*) diseased ●*mf* sick person. **~ di mente** mentally ill person. **malat'tia** *f* disease, illness; **ho preso due giorni di malattia** I had two days off sick. **malattia venerea** venereal disease

malaugu'rato *adj* ill-omened. **mala'urio** *m* bad o ill omen

mala'vita *f* underworld

mala'voglia *f* unwillingness; **di ~** unwillingly

malcapi'tato *adj* wretched

malce'lato *adj* ill-concealed

mal'concio *adj* battered

malcon'tento *m* discontent

malco'stume *m* immorality

mal'destro *adj* awkward; (*inesperto*) inexperienced

maldi'cen|te *adj* slanderous. **~za** *f* slander

maldi'sposto *adj* ill-disposed

'male *adv* badly; **funzionare ~** not work properly; **star ~** be ill; **star ~ a qcno** (*vestito ecc*.) not suit sb; **ri-**

manerci ~ be hurt; **non c'è** ~! not bad at all! ● *m* evil; (*dolore*) pain; (*malattia*) illness; (*danno*) harm. **distinguere il bene dal** ~ know right from wrong; **andare a** ~ go off; **aver** ~ a have a pain in; **dove hai** ~? where does it hurt?; **far** ~ a qcno (*provocare dolore*) hurt sb; (*cibo:*) be bad for sb; **le cipolle mi fanno** ~ onions don't agree with me; **mi fa** ~ **la schiena** my back is hurting; **mal d'auto** car-sickness. **mal di denti** toothache. **mal di gola** sore throat. **mal di mare** sea-sickness; **avere il mal di mare** be sea-sick. **mal di pancia** stomach ache. **mal di testa** headache

male'detto *adj* cursed; (*orribile*) awful

male'di|re *vt* curse. ~**zi'one** *f* curse; ~**zi'one!** damn!

maledu|'cato *adj* ill-mannered. ~**cazi'one** *f* rudeness

male'fatta *f* misdeed

ma'lefico *adj* (*azione*) evil; (*nocivo*) harmful

maleodo'rante *adj* foul-smelling

ma'lessere *m* indisposition; *fig* uneasiness

ma'levolo *adj* malevolent

malfa'mato *adj* of ill repute

mal'fat|to *adj* badly done; (*malformato*) ill-shaped. ~**'tore** *m* wrongdoer

mal'fermo *adj* unsteady; (*salute*) poor

malfor'ma|to *adj* misshapen. ~**zi'one** *f* malformation

mal'grado *prep* in spite of ● *conj* although

ma'lia *f* spell

mali'gn|are *vi* malign. ~**ità** *f* malice; (*Med*) malignancy. **ma'ligno** *adj* malicious; (*perfido*) evil; (*Med*) malignant

malinco'ni|a *f* melancholy. **malin'conico** *adj* melancholy

malincu'ore: **a** ~ *adv* reluctantly

malinfor'mato *adj* misinformed

malintenzio'nato, -a *mf* miscreant

malin'teso *adj* mistaken ● *m* misunderstanding

ma'lizi|a *f* malice; (*astuzia*) cunning; (*espediente*) trick. ~**'oso** *adj* malicious; (*birichino*) mischievous

malle'abile *adj* malleable

malme'nare *vt* ill-treat

mal'messo *adj* (*vestito male*) shabbily dressed; (*casa*) poorly furnished; (*fig: senza soldi*) hard up]

malnu'tri|to *adj* undernourished. ~**zi'one** *f* malnutrition

'malo *adj* in ~ **modo** badly

ma'locchio *m* evil eye

ma'lora *f* ruin; **della** ~ awful; **andare in** ~ go to ruin

ma'lore *m* illness; **essere colto da** ~ be suddenly taken ill

malri'dotto *adj* (*persona*) in a sorry state

mal'sano *adj* unhealthy

'malta *f* mortar

mal'tempo *m* bad weather

'malto *m* malt

maltrat|ta'mento *m* ill-treatment. ~**'tare** *vt* ill-treat

malu'more *m* bad mood; **di** ~ in a bad mood

mal'vagi|o *adj* wicked. ~**tà** *f* wickedness

malversazi'one *f* embezzlement

mal'visto *adj* unpopular (**da** with)

malvi'vente *m* criminal

malvolenti'eri *adv* unwillingly

malvo'lere *vt* **farsi** ~ make oneself unpopular

'mamma *f* mummy, mum; ~ **mia!** good gracious!

mam'mella *f* breast

mam'mifero *m* mammal

'mammola *f* violet

ma'nata f handful; (colpo) slap

'manca f ▷ **MANCO**

manca'mento m avere un ~ faint

man'can|te adj missing; ~za f lack; (assenza) absence; (insufficienza) shortage; (fallo) fault; (imperfezione) defect; **sento la sua ~za** I miss him

man'care vi be lacking; (essere assente) be missing; (venir meno) fail; (morire) pass away; ~ **di** be lacking in; ~ **a** fail to keep (promessa); **mi manca casa** I miss home; **mi manchi** I miss you; **mi è mancato il tempo** I didn't have [the] time; **mi manca un euro** I'm one euro short; **quanto manca alla partenza?** how long before we leave?; **è mancata la corrente** there was a power failure; **sentirsi ~** feel faint; **sentirsi ~ il respiro** be unable to breathe [properly] ●vt miss (bersaglio); **è mancato poco che cadesse** he nearly fell

'manche f inv heat

man'chevole adj defective

'mancia f tip

manci'ata f handful

man'cino adj left-handed

'manco, -a adj left ●f left hand ●adv (nemmeno) not even

man'dante mf (di delitto) instigator

manda'rancio m clementine

man'dare vt send; (emettere) give off; utter (suono); ~ **a chiamare** send for; ~ **avanti la casa** run the house; ~ **giù** (ingoiare) swallow

manda'rino m (Bot) mandarin

man'data f consignment; (di serratura) turn; **chiudere a doppia ~** double lock

man'dato m (incarico) mandate; (Jur) warrant; (di pagamento) money order. ~ **di comparizione [in giudizio]** subpoena. ~ **di perquisizione** search warrant

man'dibola f jaw

mando'lino m mandolin

'mandor|la f almond; **a ~la** (occhi) almond-shaped. ~**lato** m nut brittle (type of nougat). ~**lo** m almond[-tree]

'mandria f herd

maneg'gevole adj easy to handle. **maneggi'are** vt handle

ma'neggio m handling; (intrigo) plot; (scuola di equitazione) riding school

ma'netta f hand lever; **manette** pl handcuffs

man'forte m dare ~ **a qcno** support sb

manga'nello m truncheon

manga'nese m manganese

mange'reccio adj edible

mangia'dischi® m inv type of portable record player

mangia'fumo adj inv **candela ~** air-purifier in the form of candle

mangia'nastri m inv cassette player

mangi'a|re vt/i eat; (consumare) eat up; (corrodere) eat away; take (scacchi, carte ecc) ●m eating; (cibo) food; (pasto) meal. ~**rsi** vr ~**rsi le parole** mumble; ~**rsi le unghie** bite one's nails

mangi'ata f big meal; **farsi una bella ~ di...** feast on...

man'gime m fodder

mangiucchi'are vt nibble

'mango m mango

ma'nia f mania; ~ **di grandezza** delusions of grandeur ●mf maniac

'manica f sleeve; (fam: gruppo) band; **a maniche lunghe** long-sleeved; **essere in maniche di camicia** be in shirt sleeves

'Manica f la ~ the [English] Channel

manica'retto m tasty dish

mani'chetta f hose

mani'chino m dummy

'manico m handle; (*Mus*) neck

mani'comio m mental home; (**fig**: *confusione*) tip

mani'cotto m muff; (*Mech*) sleeve

mani'cure f manicure ●*mf inv* (*persona*) manicurist

mani'e|ra f manner; **in ~ra che** so that. **~'rato** *adj* affected; (*stile*) mannered. **~'rismo** m mannerism

manifat'tura f manufacture; (*fabbrica*) factory

manife'stante *mf* demonstrator

manife'sta|re vt show; (*esprimere*) express ●vi demonstrate. **~rsi** vr show oneself. **~zi'one** f show; (*espressione*) expression; (*sintomo*) manifestation; (*dimostrazione pubblica*) demonstration

mani'festo *adj* evident ●m poster; (*dichiarazione pubblica*) manifesto

ma'niglia f handle; (*sostegno, in autobus ecc*) strap

manipo'la|re vt handle; (*massaggiare*) massage; (*alterare*) adulterate; (*fig*) manipulate. **~tore**, **~trice** *mf* manipulator. **~zi'one** f handling; (*massaggio*) massage; (*alterazione*) adulteration; *fig* manipulation

mani'scalco m smith

man'naia f axe; (*da macellaio*) cleaver

man'naro *adj* lupo m **~** werewolf

'mano f hand; (*strato di vernice ecc*) coat; **alla ~** informal; **fuori ~** out of the way; **man ~** little by little; **man ~ che** as; **sotto ~** to hand

mano'dopera f labour

ma'nometro m gauge

mano'mettere vt tamper with; (*violare*) violate

ma'nopola f knob; (*guanto*) mitten; (*su pullman*) handle

mano'scritto *adj* handwritten ●m manuscript

mano'vale m labourer

mano'vella f handle; (*Techn*) crank

ma'no|vra f manoeuvre; (*Rail*)

shunting; **fare le ~vre** (*Auto*) manoeuvre. **~'vrabile** *adj fig* easy to manipulate. **~'vrare** vt operate; *fig* manipulate (*persona*) ●vi manoeuvre

manro'vescio m slap

man'sarda f attic

mansi'one f task; (*dovere*) duty

mansu'eto *adj* meek; (*animale*) docile

man'tel|la f cape. **~o** m cloak; (*soprabito, di animale*) coat; (*di neve*) mantle

mante'ner|e vt keep; (*in buono stato, sostentare*) maintain. **~si** vr **~si in forma** keep fit. **manteni'mento** m maintenance

'mantice m bellows *pl*; (*di automobile*) hood

'manto m cloak; (*coltre*) mantle

manto'vana f (*di tende*) pelmet

manu'al|e *adj* & m manual. **~e d'uso** user manual. **~'mente** *adv* manually

ma'nubrio m handle; (*di bicicletta*) handlebars *pl*; (*per ginnastica*) dumb-bell

manu'fatto *adj* manufactured

manutenzi'one f maintenance

'manzo m steer; (*carne*) beef

'mappa f map

mappa'mondo m globe

mar ▷MARE

ma'rasma m *fig* decline

mara'to|na f marathon. **~'neta** *mf* marathon runner

'marca f mark; (*Comm*) brand; (*fabbricazione*) make; (*scontrino*) ticket. **~ da bollo** revenue stamp

mar'ca|re vt mark; *Sport* score. **~ta'mente** *adv* markedly. **~to** *adj* (*tratto, accento*) strong. **~'tore** m (*nel calcio*) scorer

mar'chese, -a m marquis ●f marchioness

marchi'are vt brand

'marchio m brand; (*caratteristica*) mark. **~ di fabbrica** trademark. **~**

m

registrato registered trademark

'marcia f march; (Auto) gear; Sport walk; **mettere in** (~) put into gear; **mettersi in** ~ start off; **fare** ~ **indietro** reverse; fig back-pedal. ~ **funebre** funeral march. ~ **nuziale** wedding march

marciapi'ede m pavement; (di stazione) platform

marci'a|re vi march; (funzionare) go, work. ~**tore**, ~**trice** mf walker

'marcio adj rotten ● m rotten part; fig corruption. **mar'cire** vi go bad, rot

'marco m (moneta) mark

'mare m sea; (luogo di mare) seaside; **sul** ~ (casa) at the seaside; (città) on the sea; **in alto** ~ on the high seas. ~ **Adriatico** Adriatic Sea. **mar Ionio** Ionian Sea. **mar Mediterraneo** Mediterranean. **mar Tirreno** Tyrrhenian Sea

ma'rea f tide; **una** ~ **di** hundreds of; **alta** ~ high tide; **bassa** ~ low tide

mareggi'ata f [sea] storm

mare'moto m tidal wave, seaquake

maresci'allo m marshal; (sottufficiale) warrantofficer

marga'rina f margarine

marghe'rita f marguerite. **margheri'tina** f daisy

margi'nale adj marginal

'margine m margin; (orlo) brink; (bordo) border. ~ **di errore** margin of error. ~ **di sicurezza** safety margin

ma'rina f navy; (costa) seashore; (quadro) seascape. ~ **mercantile** merchant navy. ~ **militare** navy

mari'naio m sailor

mari'na|re vt marinate. ~**ta** f marinade. ~**to** adj (Culin) marinated

ma'rino adj sea attrib, marine

mario'netta f puppet

ma'rito m husband

ma'rittimo adj maritime

mar'maglia f rabble

marmel'lata f jam; (di agrumi) marmalade

mar'mitta f pot; (Auto) silencer. ~ **catalitica** catalytic converter

'marmo m marble

mar'mocchio m 🔲 brat

mar'mor|eo adj marble. ~**iz'zato** adj marbled

mar'motta f marmot

Ma'rocco m Morocco

ma'roso m breaker

mar'rone adj brown ● m brown; (castagna) chestnut; **marroni** pl **canditi** marrons glacés

mar'sina f tails pl

mar'supio m (borsa) bumbag

martedì m inv Tuesday. ~ **grasso** Shrove Tuesday

martel'la|re vt hammer ● vi throb. ~**ta** f hammer blow

martel'letto m (di giudice) ● gavel

mar'tello m hammer; (di battente) knocker. ~ **pneumatico** pneumatic drill

marti'netto m (Mech) jack

'martire mf martyr. **mar'tirio** m martyrdom

'martora f marten

martori'are vt torment

mar'xis|mo m Marxism. ~**ta** agg & mf Marxist

marza'pane m marzipan

marzi'ale adj martial

marzi'ano, -a mf Martian

'marzo m March

mascal'zone m rascal

ma'scara m inv mascara

mascar'pone m full-fat cream cheese

ma'scella f jaw

'mascher|a f mask; (costume) fancy dress; (Cinema, Theat) usher; (maschere f; (nella commedia dell'arte) stock character. ~**a antigas** gas mask. ~**a**

di bellezza face pack. ~**a ad ossigeno** oxygen mask. ~**a'mento** *m* masking; (*Mil*) camouflage. **masche'rare** *vt* mask. ~**arsi** *vr* put on a mask; ~**arsi da** dress up as. ~**ata** *f* masquerade

maschi'accio *m* tomboy

ma'schile *adj* masculine; (*sesso*) male ● *m* masculine [gender].
~**lista** *adj* sexist. '**maschio** *adj* male; (*virile*) manly ● *m* male; (*figlio*) son.

masco'lino *adj* masculine

ma'scotte *f inv* mascot

maso'chismo *m* masochism. ~**ta** *adj* & *mf* masochist

'**massa** *f* mass; (*Electr*) earth, ground *Am*; **comunicazioni di** ~ mass media

massa'crare *vt* massacre. **mas'sacro** *m* massacre; *fig* mess

massaggi'are *vt* massage. **mas'saggio** *m* massage. ~**tore**, ~**trice** *m* masseur ● *f* masseuse

mas'saia *f* housewife

masse'rizie *fpl* household effects

mas'siccio *adj* massive; (*oro ecc*) solid; (*corporatura*) heavy ● *m* massif

'**massima** *f* maxim; (*temperatura*) maximum. ~**o** *adj* greatest; (*quantità*) maximum, greatest ● **il** ~**o** the maximum; **al** ~**o** at [the] most, as a maximum

'**masso** *m* rock

mas'sone *m* [Free]mason. ~'**ria** Freemasonry

ma'stello *m* wooden box for the grape or olive harvest

masteriz'zare *vt* (*Comput*) burn

masterizza'tore *m* (*Comput*) burner

masti'care *vt* chew; (*borbottare*) mumble

'**mastice** *m* mastic; (*per vetri*) putty

ma'stino *m* mastiff

masto'dontico *adj* gigantic

'**mastro** *m* master; **libro** ~ ledger

mastur'barsi *vr* masturbate. ~**zi'one** *f* masturbation

ma'tassa *f* skein

mate'matica *f* mathematics, maths. ~**o**, **-a** *adj* mathematical ● *mf* mathematician

materas'sino *m* ~ **gonfiabile** air bed

mate'rasso *m* mattress. ~ **a molle** spring mattress

ma'teria *f* matter; (*materiale*) material; (*di studio*) subject. ~ **prima** raw material

materi'ale *adj* material; (*grossolano*) coarse ● *m* material. ~**lismo** *m* materialism. ~**lista** *adj* materialistic ● *mf* materialist. ~**liz'zarsi** *vr* materialize. ~**l'mente** *adv* physically

maternità *f* motherhood; **ospedale di** ~ maternity hospital

ma'terno *adj* maternal; **lingua materna** mother tongue

ma'tita *f* pencil

ma'trice *f* matrix; (*origini*) roots *pl*; (*Comm*) counterfoil

ma'tricola *f* (*registro*) register; (*Univ*) fresher

ma'trigna *f* stepmother

matrimoni'ale *adj* matrimonial; **vita** ~ married life. **matri'monio** *m* marriage; (*cerimonia*) wedding

ma'trona *f* matron

'**matta** *f* (*nelle carte*) joker

matta'toio *m* slaughterhouse

matte'rello *m* rolling-pin

mat'tina *f* morning; **la** ~**na in the morning.** ~'**nata** *f* morning; (*Theat*) matinée. ~**no** *m* morning

'**matto**, **-a** *adj* mad, crazy; (*Med*) insane; (*falso*) false; (*opaco*) matt; ~ **da legare** barking mad; **avere una voglia matta di** be dying for ● *mf* madman; madwoman

mat'tone *m* brick; (*libro*) bore

matto'nella *f* tile

mattu'tino *adj* morning *attrib*

m

matu'rare vt ripen. **maturità** f maturity; (Sch) school-leaving certificate. **ma'turo** adj mature; (frutto) ripe

---

> *i*
>
> **Maturità** The Italian secondary school-leaving exam is called the *Esame di Maturità*. Candidates are examined by a committee consisting of external examiners and their own teachers, and the exams may be oral or written, depending on the subject. Candidates are tested on a wide range of subjects, including philosophy and history of art.

---

mauso'leo m mausoleum

maxi+ pref maxi+

'mazza f club; (martello) hammer; (di baseball, cricket) bat. ~ **da golf** golf-club. **maz'zata** f blow

maz'zetta f (di banconote) bundle

'mazzo m bunch; (carte da gioco) pack

me pers pron me; **me lo ha dato** he gave it to me; **fai come me** do as I do; **è più veloce di me** he is faster than me o faster than I am

me'andro m meander

M.E.C. m abbr (Mercato Comune Europeo) EEC

mec'canica f mechanics sg

meccanica'mente adv mechanically

mec'canico adj mechanical ●m mechanic. **mecca'nismo** m mechanism

mèche fpl [farsi] fare le ~ have one's hair streaked

me'dagli|a f medal. ~**'one** m medallion; (gioiello) locket

me'desimo adj same

'medi|a f average; (Sch) average mark; (Math) mean; **essere nella** ~**a** be in the mid-range. ~**'ano** m middle ●m (calcio) half-back

medi'ante prep by

medi'a|re vt act as intermediary in. ~**'tore**, ~**'trice** mf mediator; (Comm) middleman

medica'mento m medicine

medi'ca|re vt treat; dress (ferita). ~**zi'one** f medication; (di ferita) dressing

medi'c|ina f medicine. ~**ina legale** forensic medicine. ~**i'nale** adj medicinal ●m medicine

'medico adj medical ●m doctor. ~ **generico** general practitioner. ~ **legale** forensic scientist. ~ **di turno** duty doctor

medie'vale adj medieval

'medio adj average; (punto) middle; (statura) medium ●m (dito) middle finger

medi'ocre adj mediocre; (scadente) poor

medio'evo m Middle Ages pl

medi'ta|re vt meditate; (progettare) plan; (considerare attentamente) think over ●vi meditate. ~**zi'one** f meditation

mediter'raneo adj Mediterranean; **il [mar] M**~ the Mediterranean [Sea]

me'dusa f jellyfish

me'gafono m megaphone

mega'lomane mf megalomaniac

me'gera f hag

'meglio adv better; **tanto** ~, ~ **così** so much the better ●adj better; (superlativo) best ●mf best ●f avere la ~ **su** have the better of; **fare qcsa alla [bell'e]** ~ do sth as best one can ●m **fare del proprio** ~ do one's best; **fare qcsa il** ~ **possibile** make an excellent job of sth; **al** ~ to the best of one's ability

'mela f apple. ~ **cotogna** quince

mela'grana f pomegranate

mela'nina f melanin

melan'zana f aubergine,

eggplant *Am*

me'lassa *f* molasses *sg*

me'lenso *adj* (persona, film) dull

mel'lifluo *adj* (parole) honeyed; (voce) sugary

'melma *f* slime. **mel'moso** *adj* slimy

melo *m* apple[-tree]

melo'di|a *f* melody. **me'lodico** *adj* melodic. **∼oso** *adj* melodious

melo'dram|ma *m* melodrama. **∼'matico** *adj* melodramatic

melo'grano *m* pomegranate tree

me'lone *m* melon

'membro *m* member; (*pl f* **membra** (*Anat*)) limb

memo'rabile *adj* memorable

'memore *adj* mindful; (*riconoscente*) grateful

me'mori|a *f* memory; (*oggetto ricordo*) souvenir. **imparare a ∼a** learn by heart. **∼a tampone** (*Comput*) buffer. **∼a volatile** (*Comput*) volatile memory; **memorie** *pl* (*biografiche*) memoirs. **∼'ale** *m* memorial. **∼z'zare** *vt* memorize; (*Comput*) save, store

mena'dito: a ∼ *adv* perfectly

me'nare *vt* lead; (🔲: picchiare) hit

mendi'ca|nte *mf* beggar. **∼re** *vt/i* beg

me'ningi *fpl* **spremersi le ∼** rack one's brains

menin'gite *f* meningitis

'meno *adv* less; (*superlativo*) least; (*in operazioni, con temperatura*) minus; **far qcsa alla ∼ peggio** do sth as best one can; **fare a ∼ di qcsa** do without sth; **non posso fare a ∼ di ridere** I can't help laughing; **∼ male!** thank goodness!; **sempre ∼** less and less; **venir ∼** (*svenire*) faint; **venir ∼ a qcno** (*coraggio*:) fail sb; **sono le tre ∼ un quarto** it's a quarter to three; **che tu venga o ∼** whether you're coming or not; **quanto ∼** at least ● *adj inv* less; (*con*

nomi plurali) fewer ● *m* least; (*Math*) minus sign; **il ∼ possibile** as little as possible; **per lo ∼** at least ● *prep* except (for) ● *conj* **a ∼ che** unless

meno'ma|re *vt* (incidente:) maim. **∼to** *adj* disabled

meno'pausa *f* menopause

'mensa *f* table; (*Mil*) mess; (*Sch, Univ*) refectory

men'sil|e *adj* monthly ● *m* (*stipendio*) [monthly] salary; (*rivista*) monthly. **∼ità** *f inv* monthly salary. **∼'mente** *adv* monthly

'mensola *f* bracket; (*scaffale*) shelf

'menta *f* mint. **∼ peperita** peppermint

men'tal|e *adj* mental. **∼ità** *f inv* mentality

'mente *f* mind; **a ∼ fredda** in cold blood; **venire in ∼ a qcno** occur to sb

men'tina *f* mint

men'tire *vi* lie

'mento *m* chin

'mentre *conj* (*temporale*) while; (*invece*) whereas

menu *m inv* menu. **∼ fisso** set menu. **∼ a tendina** (*Comput*) pull-down menu

menzio'nare *vt* mention. **menzi'one** *f* mention

men'zogna *f* lie

mera'viglia *f* wonder; **a ∼** marvellously; **che ∼!** how wonderful!; **con mia grande ∼** much to my amazement; **mi fa ∼ che...** I am surprised that...

meravigli'ar|e *vt* surprise. **∼si** *vr* **∼si di** be surprised at

meravigli'oso *adj* marvellous

mer'can|te *m* merchant. **∼teggi'are** *vi* trade; (*sul prezzo*) bargain. **∼zia** *f* merchandise, goods *pl* ● *m* merchant ship

mer'cato *m* market; *Fin* market[-place]. **a buon ∼** (comprare) cheap[ly]; (articolo) cheap. ∼ **dei cambi** foreign exchange market. ∼ **coperto** covered market. ∼ **libero** free market. ∼ **nero** black market

'**merce** f goods pl

mercé / **alla** ∼ **di** at the mercy of

merce'nario adj & m mercenary

merce'ria f haberdashery; (negozio) haberdasher's

mercoledì m inv Wednesday. ∼ **delle Ceneri** Ash Wednesday

mer'curio m mercury

me'**renda** f afternoon snack; **far** ∼ have an afternoon snack

meri'diana f sundial

meri'diano adj midday ●m meridian

meridio'nale adj southern ●mf southerner. **meridi'one** m south

me'rin|ga f meringue. ∼'**gata** f meringue pie

meri'tare vt deserve. **meri'tevole** adj deserving

'**meri|to** m merit; (valore) worth; **in** ∼**to a** as to; **per** ∼**to di** thanks to. ∼'**torio** adj meritorious

mer'letto m lace

'**merlo** m blackbird

mer'luzzo m cod

'**mero** adj mere

meschine'ria f meanness. me-'**schino** adj wretched; (gretto) mean ●m wretch

mesco|la'mento m mixing. ∼'**lanza** f mixture

mesco'la|re vt mix; shuffle (carte); (confondere) mix up; blend (tè, tabacco ecc). ∼**rsi** vr mix; (immischiarsi) meddle. ∼**ta** f (a carte) shuffle; (Culin) stir

'**mese** m month

me'**setto** m **un** ∼ about a month

'**messa**¹ f Mass

'**messa**² f (il mettere) putting. ∼ **in moto** (Auto) starting. ∼ **in piega** (di capelli) set. ∼ **a punto** adjustment.

∼ **in scena** production. ∼ **a terra** earthing, grounding Am

messag'gero m messenger. mes-'**saggio** m message

'**messe** f harvest

Mes'sia m Messiah

messi'cano, -a adj & mf Mexican

'**Messico** m Mexico

messin'scena f staging; fig act

'**messo** pp di **mettere** ●m messenger

mesti'ere m trade; (lavoro) job; **essere del** ∼ be an expert

'**mesto** adj sad

'**mestola** f (di cuoco) ladle

mestru'a|le adj menstrual. ∼**zi'one** f menstruation. ∼**zi'oni** pl period

'**meta** f destination; fig aim

metà f inv half; (centro) middle; **a** ∼ **strada** half-way; **fare a** ∼ **con qcn** go halves with sb

metabo'lismo m metabolism

meta'done m methadone

meta'fora f metaphor. **meta'forico** adj metaphorical

me'**talli|co** adj metallic. ∼**z'zato** adj (grigio) metallic

me'**tall|o** m metal. ∼**ur'gia** f metallurgy

metalmec'canico adj engineering ●m engineering worker

me'**tano** m methane. ∼'**dotto** m methane pipeline

meta'nolo m methanol

me'**teora** f meteor. **meteo'rite** m meteorite

meteoro'lo|gia f meteorology. ∼'**logico** adj meteorological

me'**ticcio, -a** m/f half-caste

metico'loso adj meticulous

me'**tod|ico** adj methodical. '**metodo** m method. ∼**olo'gia** f methodology

me'**traggio** m length (in metres)

'metrico, -a adj metric; (in poesia) metrical •f metrics sg

'metro m metre; (nastro) tape measure •f inv (⊞: metropolitana) tube Br; subway

me'tronomo m metronome

metro'notte mf inv night security guard

me'tropoli f inv metropolis. ~'tana f subway, underground Br. ~'tano adj metropolitan

'metter|e vt put; (indossare) put on; (⊞: installare) put in; ~e al mondo bring into the world; ~e da parte set aside; ~e fiducia inspire trust; ~e qcsa in chiaro make sth clear; ~e in mostra display; ~e a posto tidy up; ~e in vendita put up for sale; ~e su set up (casa, azienda); ci ho messo un'ora it took me an hour; mettiamo che... let's suppose that... ~si vr (indossare) put on; (diventare) turn out; ~si a start to; ~si con qcno (⊞: formare una coppia) start to go out with sb; ~si a letto go to bed; ~si a sedere sit down; ~si in viaggio set out

'mezza f è la ~ it's half past twelve; sono le quattro e ~ it's half past four

mezza'luna f half moon; (simbolo islamico) crescent; (coltello) two-handled chopping knife

mezza'manica f a ~ (maglia) short-sleeved

mez'zano adj middle

mezza'notte f midnight

mezz'asta f a ~ adv at half mast

'mezzo adj half; di mezza età middle-aged; ~ bicchiere half a glass; una mezza idea a vague idea; sono le quattro e ~ it's half past four. mezz'ora f half an hour. mezza pensione f half board. mezza stagione f una giacca di mezza stagione a spring/autumn jacket ●adv (a metà) half ●m (metà) half; (centro)

middle; (per raggiungere un fine) means sg; uno e ~ one and a half; tre anni e ~ three and a half years; in ~ a in the middle of; nel giusto ~ the happy medium; levare di ~ clear away; per ~ di by means of; a ~ posta by mail; via di ~ fig half-way house; (soluzione) middle way. mezzi mpl (denaro) means pl. mezzi pubblici public transport. mezzi di trasporto [means of] transport

mezzo'busto a ~ adj (foto, ritratto) half-length

mezzo'fondo m middle-distance running

mezzogi'orno m midday; (sud) South. il M~ Southern Italy. ~ in punto high noon

mi[1] pers pron me; (refl) myself; mi ha dato un libro he gave me a book; mi lavo le mani I wash my hands; eccomi here I am

mi[2] m (Mus) E

'mica[1] f mica

'mica[2] adv ⊞ (per caso) by any chance; hai ~ visto Paolo? have you seen Paul, by any chance?; non è ~ bello it is not at all nice; ~ male not bad

'miccia f fuse

micidi'ale adj deadly

'micio m pussy-cat

'microbo m microbe

micro'cosmo m microcosm

micro'fiche f inv microfiche

micro'film m inv microfilm

mi'crofono m microphone

microorga'nismo m microorganism

microproces'sore m microprocessor

micro'scopi|o m microscope

micro'solco m (disco) long-playing record

mi'dollo m (pl f midolla, (Anat)) marrow; fino al ~ through and

m

through. ~ **spinale** spinal cord

mi'ele m honey

'mie, mi'ei ▷ MIO

mi'et|ere vt reap. ~i'trice f (Mech) harvester. ~i'tura f harvest

migli'aio m (pl f **migliaia**) thousand. **a migliaia** in thousands

'miglio m (Bot) millet; (misura: pl f **miglia**) mile

migliora'mento m improvement

miglio'rare vt/i improve

migli'ore adj better; (superlativo) the best ● mf **il/la** ~ **il/la** the best

'mignolo m little finger; (del piede) little toe

mi'gra|re vi migrate. ~**zi'one** f migration

'mila ▷ MILLE

Mi'lano f Milan

miliar'dario, -a m millionaire; (plurimiliardario) billionaire ● f millionairess; billionairess. **mili'ardo** m billion

mili'are adj **pietra** f ~ milestone

milio'nario, -a m millionaire ● f millionairess

mili'one m million

milio'nesimo adj millionth

mili'tante adj & mf militant

mili'tare vi ~ **in** be a member of (partito ecc) ● adj military ● m soldier; **fare il** ~ do one's military service. ~ **di leva** national serviceman

'milite m soldier. **mil'izia** f militia

'mille adj & m (pl f **mila**) a o one thousand; **due/tre mila** two/three thousand; ~ **grazie!** thanks a lot!

mille'foglie m inv (Culin) vanilla slice

mil'lennio m millennium

millepi'edi m inv centipede

mil'lesimo adj & m thousandth

milli'grammo m milligram

mil'limetro m millimetre

mi'mare vt mimic (persona)

● vi mime

mi'metico adj camouflage attrib

mimetiz'zar|e vt camouflage. ~**si** vr camouflage oneself

'mim|ica f mime. ~**ico** adj mimic. ~**o** m mime

mi'mosa f mimosa

'mina f mine; (di matita) lead

mi'naccia f threat

minacci'|are vt threaten. ~**'oso** adj threatening

mi'nare vt mine; fig undermine

mina'tor|e m miner. ~**io** adj threatening

mine'ra|le adj & m mineral. ~**rio** adj mining attrib

mi'nestra f soup. **mine'strone** m vegetable soup; (🄸: insieme confuso) hotchpotch

mini+ pref mini+

minia'tura f miniature. **miniaturiz'zato** adj miniaturized

mini'era f mine

mini'golf m miniature golf

mini'gonna f miniskirt

minima'mente adv minimally

mini'market m inv minimarket

minimiz'zare vt minimize

'minimo adj least, slightest; (il più basso) lowest; (salario, quantità ecc) minimum ● m minimum

mini'stero m ministry; (governo) government

mi'nistro m minister. **M~ del Tesoro** Finance Minister

mino'ranza f minority attrib

Minoranza linguistica Minoranze linguistiche (linguistic minorities) are protected by the Italian constitution. As well as dialects of Italian, and the related languages Sardinian and Ladin, other languages spoken.

They include German in Alto Adige; French in Valdaosta; Greek, Albanian, and Serbo-Croat in the rural south; Slovenian in the north-east and Catalan in Alghero.

mino'rato, -a adj disabled ●mf disabled person

mi'nore adj (gruppo, numero) smaller; (superlativo) smallest; (distanza) shorter; (superlativo) shortest; (prezzo) lower; (superlativo) lowest; (di età) younger; (superlativo) youngest; (di importanza) minor; (superlativo) least important ●mf younger; (superlativo) youngest; (Jur) minor; **i minori** di 14 anni children under 14. **mino-'renne** adj under age ●mf minor

minori'tario adj minority attrib

minu'etto m minuet

mi'nuscolo, -a adj tiny ●f small letter

mi'nuta f rough copy

mi'nuto[1] adj minute; (persona) delicate; (ricerca) detailed; (pioggia, neve) fine; **al ~** (Comm) retail

mi'nuto[2] m (di tempo) minute; **spaccare il ~** be dead on time

mi'nuzia f trifle. **~oso** adj detailed; (persona) meticulous

'mio (il **mio** m, la **mia** f, i **miei** mpl, le **mie** fpl) adj poss my; **questa macchina è mia** this car is mine; **~ padre** my father; **un ~ amico** a friend of mine ●poss pron mine; **i miei** (genitori ecc) my folks

'miope adj short-sighted. **mio'pia** f short-sightedness

'mira f aim; (bersaglio) target; **prendere la ~** take aim

mi'racolo m miracle. **~sa'mente** adv miraculously. **miraco'loso** adj miraculous

mi'raggio m mirage

mi'rar|e vi [take] aim. **~si** vr (guardarsi) look at oneself

mi'riade f myriad

mi'rino m sight; (Phot) view-finder

mir'tillo m blueberry

mi'santropo, -a mf misanthropist

mi'scela f mixture; (di caffè, tabacco ecc) blend. **~tore** m (di acqua) mixer tap

miscel'lanea f miscellany

'mischia f scuffle; (nel rugby) scrum

mischi'ar|e vt mix; shuffle (carte da gioco). **~si** vr mix; (immischiarsi) interfere

misco'noscere vt not appreciate

mi'scuglio m mixture

mise'rabile adj wretched

misera'mente adv (finire) miserably; (vivere) in abject poverty

mi'seria f poverty; (infelicità) misery; **guadagnare una ~** earn a pittance; **porca ~!** hell!

miseri'cordi|a f mercy. **~oso** adj merciful

'misero adj (miserabile) wretched; (povero) poor; (scarso) paltry

mi'sfatto m misdeed

mi'sogino m misogynist

mis'saggio m vision mixer

'missile m missile

missio'nario, -a mf missionary. **missi'one** f mission

misteri'oso adj mysterious. **mi-'stero** m mystery

'mistic|a f mysticism. **~'cismo** f mysticism. **~co** adj mystic[al] ●mf mystic

mistifi'ca|re vt distort (verità). **~zi'one** f (della verità) distortion

'misto adj mixed; **scuola mista** mixed or co-educational school ●m mixture; **~ lana/cotone** wool/cotton mix

mi'sura f measure; (dimensione) measurement; (taglia) size; (limite) limit; **su ~** (abiti) made to measure; (mobile) custom-made; **a ~** (andare, calzare) perfectly. **~ di sicurezza** safety measure. **mi-**

m

su'rare *vt* measure; try on (indumenti); (*limitare*) limit. **misu'rarsi con** (*gareggiare*) compete with. **misu'rato** *adj* measured. **misu'rino** *m* measuring spoon

'**mite** *adj* mild; (*prezzo*) moderate

'**mitico** *adj* mythical

miti'gar|e *vt* mitigate. **∼si** *vr* calm down; (*clima*) become mild

'**mito** *m* myth. **∼lo'gia** *f* mythology. **∼'logico** *adj* mythological

'**mitra** *f* (*Relig*) mitre ● *m inv* (*Mil*) machine-gun

mitragli'a|re *vt* machine-gun; **∼re di domande** fire questions at. **∼'trice** *f* machine-gun

mit'tente *mf* sender

mo' *m* **a ∼ di** by way of (*esempio, consolazione*)

'**mobbing** *m* harassment

'**mobile**¹ *adj* mobile; (*volubile*) fickle; (*che si può muovere*) movable; **beni mobili** personal estate; **squadra ∼** flying squad

'**mobile**² *m* piece of furniture; **mobili** *pl* furniture *sg*. **mo'bilia** *f* furniture. **∼li'ficio** *m* furniture factory

mo'bilio *m* furniture

mobilità *f* mobility

mobili'ta|re *vt* mobilize. **∼zi'one** *f* mobilization

mocas'sino *m* moccasin

'**moccolo** *m* candle-end; (*moccio*) snot

'**moda** *f* fashion; **di ∼** in fashion; **alla ∼** (*musica, vestiti*) up-to-date; **fuori ∼** unfashionable

modalità *f inv* formality; **∼ d'uso** instruction

mo'della *f* model. **model'lare** *vt* model

model'li|no *m* model. **∼sta** *mf* designer

mo'dello *m* model; (*stampo*) mould; (*di carta*) pattern; (*modulo*) form

'**modem** *m inv* modem

mode'ra|re *vt* moderate; (*diminuire*) reduce. **∼rsi** *vr* control oneself. **∼ta'mente** *adv* moderately **∼to** *adj* moderate. **∼'tore**, **∼'trice** *mf* (*in tavola rotonda*) moderator. **∼zi'one** *f* moderation

modern|a'mente *adv* (*in modo moderno*) in a modern style. **∼iz'zare** *vt* modernize. **mo'derno** *adj* modern

mo'dest|ia *f* modesty. **∼o** *adj* modest

'**modico** *adj* reasonable

'**modifica** *f* modification

modifi'ca|re *vt* modify. **∼zi'one** *f* modification

mo'dista *f* milliner

'**modo** *m* way; (*garbo*) manners *pl*; (*occasione*) chance; (*Gram*) mood; **ad ogni ∼** anyhow; **di ∼ che** so that; **fare in ∼ di** try to; **in che ∼** (*inter*) how; **in qualche ∼** somehow; **in questo ∼** like this; **∼ di dire** idiom; **per ∼ di dire** so to speak

modu'la|re *vt* modulate. **∼zi'one** *f* modulation. **∼zione di frequenza** frequency modulation

'**modulo** *m* form; (*lunare, di comando*) module. **∼ continuo** continuous paper

'**mogano** *m* mahogany

'**mogio** *adj* dejected

'**moglie** *f* wife

'**mola** *f* millstone; (*Mech*) grindstone

mo'lare *m* molar

'**mole** *f* mass; (*dimensione*) size

mo'lecola *f* molecule

mole'stare *vt* bother; (*più forte*) molest. **mo'lestia** *f* nuisance. **mo'lesto** *adj* bothersome

'**molla** *f* spring; **molle** *pl* tongs

mol'lare *vt* let go; (⏢: *lasciare*) leave; ⏢ give (*ceffone*); (*Naut*) cast off ● *vi* cease; **mollala!** ⏢ stop that!

'**molle** *adj* soft; (*bagnato*) wet

mol'letta *f* (*per capelli*) hair-grip; (*per bucato*) clothes-peg; **mollette** *pl*

(*per ghiaccio ecc*) tongs

mol'lezz|a f softness; **~e** pl fig luxury

mol'lica f crumb

'molo m pier; (*banchina*) dock

mol'teplic|e adj manifold; (*numeroso*) numerous. **~ità** f multiplicity

moltipli'ca|re vt, **~rsi** vr multiply. **~tore** m multiplier. **~trice** f calculating machine. **~zi'one** f multiplication

molti'tudine f multitude

'molto

● adj a lot of; (*con negazione e interrogazione*) much, a lot of; (*con nomi plurali*) many, a lot of; **non ~ tempo** not much time, not a lot of time

● adv very; (*con verbi*) a lot; (*con avverbi*) much; **~ stupido** very stupid; **mangiare ~** eat a lot; **~ più veloce** much faster; **non mangiare ~** not eat much

● pron a lot; (*molto tempo*) a lot of time; (*con negazione e interrogazione*) much, a lot; (*plurale*) many; **non ne ho ~** I don't have much; **non ne ho molti** I don't have many, I don't have a lot; **non ci metterò ~** I won't be long; **fra non ~** before long; **molti** (*persone*) a lot of people; **eravamo in molti** there were a lot of us

---

momentanea'mente adv momentarily; **è ~ assente** he's not here at the moment. **momen'taneo** adj momentary

mo'mento m moment; **a momenti** (*a volte*) sometimes; (*fra un momento*) in a moment; **dal ~ che** since; **per il ~** for the time being; **da un ~ all'altro** (cambiare idea ecc) from one moment to the next; (aspettare qcno ecc) at any moment

'monac|a f nun. **~o** m monk

'Monaco m Monaco ●f (*di Baviera*) Munich

mo'narc|a m monarch. **monar'chia** f monarchy

mona'stero m (*di monaci*) monastery; (*di monache*) convent. **mo'nastico** adj monastic

monche'rino m stump

'monco adj maimed; (*fig: troncato*) truncated; **~ di un braccio** one-armed

mon'dano adj worldly; **vita mondana** social life

mondi'ale adj world attrib; **di fama ~** world-famous

'mondo m world; **il bel ~** fashionable society; **un ~** (*molto*) a lot

mondovisi'one f in ~ transmitted worldwide

mo'nello, -a mf urchin

mo'neta f coin; (*denaro*) money; (*denaro spicciolo*) [small] change. **~ estera** foreign currency. **~ legale** legal tender. **~ unica** single currency. **mone'tario** adj monetary

mongolfi'era f hot air balloon

mo'nile m jewel

'monito m warning

moni'tore m monitor

monoco'lore adj (Pol) one-party

mono'dose adj inv individually packaged

monogra'fia f monograph

mono'gramma m monogram

mono'kini m inv monokini

mono'lingue adj monolingual

monolo'cale m studio apartment

mo'nologo m monologue

mono'pattino m (child's) scooter

mono'poli|o m monopoly. **~o di Stato** state monopoly. **~z'zare** vt monopolize

mono'sci m inv monoski

monosil'labico adj monosyllabic. **mono'sillabo** m monosyllable

monoto'nia f monotony. **mo'no-**

tono *adj* monotonous

mono'uso *adj* disposable

monsi'gnore *m* monsignor

mon'sone *m* monsoon

monta'carichi *m inv* hoist

mon'taggio *m* (*Mech*) assembly; *Cinema* editing; **catena di ~** production line

mon'ta|gna *f* mountain; (*zona*) mountains *pl*. **montagne** *pl* **russe** big dipper. **~'gnoso** *adj* mountainous. **~'naro, -a** *mf* highlander. **~no** *adj* mountain *attrib*

mon'tante *m* (*di finestra, porta*) upright

mon'ta|re *vt/i* mount; get on (*veicolo*); (*aumentare*) rise; (*Mech*) assemble; frame (*quadro*); (*Culin*) whip; edit (*film*); (*a cavallo*) ride; *fig* blow up; **~rsi la testa** get big-headed. **~to, -a** *mf* poser. **~'tura** *f* (*Mech*) assembling; (*di occhiali*) frame; (*di gioiello*) mounting; *fig* exaggeration

'monte *m* mountain; **a ~** up-stream; **andare a ~** be ruined; **mandare a ~ qcsa** ruin sth. **~ di pietà** pawnshop

Monte'negro *m* Montenegro

monte'premi *m inv* jackpot

mon'tone *m* ram; **carne di ~** mutton

montu'oso *adj* mountainous

monumen'tale *adj* monumental. **monu'mento** *m* monument

mo'quette *f* fitted carpet

'mora *f* (*del gelso*) mulberry; (*del rovo*) blackberry

mo'ral|e *adj* moral ●*f* morals *pl*; (*di storia*) moral ●*m* morale. **mora'lista** *mf* moralist. **~ità** *f* morality; (*condotta*) morals *pl*. **~iz'zare** *vt/i* moralize. **~'mente** *adv* morally

morbi'dezza *f* softness

'morbido *adj* soft

mor'billo *m* measles *sg*

'morbo *m* disease. **~sità** *f* (*qualità*)

morbidity

mor'boso *adj* morbid

mor'dente *adj* biting. 'mordere *vt* bite; (*corrodere*) bite into. **mordic-chi'are** *vt* gnaw

mor'fina *f* morphine. **morfi'nomane** *mf* morphine addict

mori'bondo *adj* dying; (*istituzione*) moribund

morige'rato *adj* moderate

mo'rire *vi* die; *fig* die out; **fa un freddo da ~** it's freezing cold, it's perishing; **~ di noia** be bored to death

mor'mone *mf* Mormon

mormo'r|are *vt/i* murmur; (*brontolare*) mutter. **~io** *m* murmuring; (*lamentela*) grumbling

'moro *adj* dark ●*m* Moor

mo'roso *adj* in arrears

'morsa *f* vice; *fig* grip

'morse *adj* **alfabeto ~** Morse code

mor'setto *m* clamp

morsi'care *vt* bite. 'morso *m* bite; (*di cibo, briglia*) bit; **i morsi della fame** hunger pangs

morta'della *f* mortadella (*type of salted pork*)

mor'taio *m* mortar

mor'tal|e *adj* mortal; (*simile a morte*) deadly; **di una noia ~e** deadly. **~ità** *f* mortality. **~'mente** *adv* (*ferito*) fatally; (*offeso*) mortally

morta'retto *m* firecracker

'morte *f* death

mortifi'ca|re *vt* mortify. **~rsi** *vr* be mortified. **~to** *adj* mortified. **~zi'one** *f* mortification

'morto, -a *pp di* **morire** ●*adj* dead; **~ di freddo** frozen to death; **stanco ~** dead tired ●*m* dead man ●*f* dead woman

mor'torio *m* funeral

mo'saico *m* mosaic

'mosca *f* fly. **~ cieca** blindman's buff

'**Mosca** f Moscow

mo'**scato** adj muscat; **noce mo-scata** nutmeg ● m muscatel

mosce'**rino** m midge

mo'**schea** f mosque

moschi'**cida** adj fly attrib

'**moscio** adj limp; **avere l'erre mo-scia** not be able to say one's r's properly

mo'**scone** m bluebottle; (barca) pedalo

'**moss|a** f movement; (passo) move. ~**o** pp di **muovere** ● adj (mare) rough; (capelli) wavy; (fotografia) blurred

mo'**starda** f mustard

'**mostra** f show; (d'arte) exhibition; **far ~ di** pretend; **in ~** on show; **mettersi in ~** make oneself conspicuous

mo'**stra|re** vt show; (indicare) point out; (spiegare) explain. ~**rsi** vr show oneself; (apparire) appear

'**mostro** m monster; (fig: persona) genius; **~ sacro** fig sacred cow

mostru|osa'**mente** adv tremendously. ~'**oso** adj monstrous; (incredibile) enormous

mo'**tel** m inv motel

moti'**va|re** vt cause; (Jur) justify. ~**to** adj (persona) motivated. ~**zi'one** f motivation; (giustificazione) justification

mo'**tivo** m reason; (movente) motive; (in musica, letteratura) theme; (disegno) motif

'**moto** m motion; (esercizio) exercise; (gesto) movement; (sommossa) rising ● f inv (motocicletta) motor bike; **mettere in ~** start (motore)

moto'**carro** m three-wheeler

motoci'**cl|etta** f motor cycle. ~**ismo** m motorcycling. ~**ista** mf motor-cyclist

moto'**cros|s** m motocross. ~'**sista** mf scrambler

moto'**lancia** f motor launch

moto'**nave** f motor vessel

mo'**tore** adj motor ● m motor, engine. **~ di ricerca** (Comput) search engine. moto'**retta** f motor scooter. moto'**rino** m moped. **motorino d'avviamento** starter

motoriz'**za|to** adj (Mil) motorized. ~**zi'one** f (ufficio) vehicle licensing office

moto'**scafo** m motorboat

motove'**detta** f patrol vessel

'**motto** m motto; (facezia) witticism; (massima) saying

mouse m inv (Comput) mouse

mo'**vente** m motive

movimen'**ta|re** vt enliven. ~**to** adj lively. movi'**mento** m movement; **essere sempre in movimento** be always on the go

mozi'**one** f motion

mozzafi'**ato** adj inv nail-biting

moz'**zare** vt cut off; dock (coda); **~ il fiato a qcno** take sb's breath away

mozza'**rella** f mozzarella (mild, white cheese)

mozzi'**cone** m (di sigaretta) stub

'**mozzo** m (Mech) hub; (Naut) ship's boy ● adj (coda) truncated; (testa) severed

'**mucca** f cow. **morbo della ~ pazza** mad cow disease

'**mucchio** m heap, pile; **un ~ di** fig lots of

'**muco** m mucus

'**muffa** f mould; **fare la ~** go mouldy. **muf'fire** vi go mouldy

muf'**fole** fpl mittens

mug'**gi|re** vi (mucca:) moo, low; (toro:) bellow

mu'**ghetto** m lily of the valley

mugo'**lare** vi whine; (persona:) moan. mugo'**lio** m whining

mulat'**tiera** f mule track

mu'**latto, -a** mf mulatto

muli'**nello** m (d'acqua) whirl-pool;

m

(di vento) eddy; *(giocattolo)* windmill

mu'lino *m* mill. **~ a vento** windmill

'mulo *m* mule

'multa *f* fine. **mul'tare** *vt* fine

multico'lore *adj* multicoloured

multi'lingue *adj* multilingual

multi'media *mpl* multimedia

multimedi'ale *adj* multimedia *attrib*

multimiliar'dario, -a *mf* multi-millionaire

multinazio'nale *f* multinational

'multiplo *adj & m* multiple

multiproprietà *f inv* time-share

multi'uso *(utensile)* all-purpose

'mummia *f* mummy

'mungere *vt* milk

munici'pal|e *adj* municipal. **~ità** *f inv* town council. **muni'cipio** *m* town hall

mu'nifico *adj* munificent

mu'nire *vt* fortify; **~ di** *(provvedere)* supply with

munizi'oni *fpl* ammunition *sg*

'munto *pp di* **mungere**

mu'over|e *vt* move; *(suscitare)* arouse. **~si** *vr* move

mura *fpl (cinta di città)* walls

mu'raglia *f* wall

mu'rale *adj* mural; *(pittura)* wall *attrib*

mur'a|re *vt* wall up. **~tore** *m* bricklayer; *(con pietre)* mason; *(operaio edile)* builder. **~tura** *f (di pietra)* masonry, stonework; *(di mattoni)* brickwork

mu'rena *f* moray eel

'muro *m* wall; *(di nebbia)* bank; **a ~** *(armadio)* built-in. **~ portante** load-bearing wall. **~ del suono** sound barrier

'muschio *m (Bot)* moss

musco'la|re *adj* muscular. **~tura** *f* muscles *pl*. **'muscolo** *m* muscle

mu'seo *m* museum

museru'ola *f* muzzle

'musi|ca *f* music. **~cal** *m inv* musical. **~cale** *adj* musical. **~'cista** *mf* musician.

'muso *m* muzzle; *(pej: di persona)* mug; *(di aeroplano)* nose; **fare il ~** sulk. **mu'sone, -a** *mf* sulker

'mussola *f* muslin

musul'mano, -a *mf* Moslem

'muta *f (cambio)* change; *(di penne)* moult; *(di cani)* pack; *(per immersione subacquea)* wetsuit

muta'mento *m* change

mu'tan|de *fpl* pants; *(da donna)* knickers. **~'doni** *mpl (da uomo)* long johns; *(da donna)* bloomers

mu'tare *vt* change

mu'tevole *adj* changeable

muti'la|re *vt* mutilate. **~to, -a** *mf* disabled person. **~to di guerra** disabled ex-serviceman

mu'tismo *m* dumbness; *fig* obstinate silence

'muto *adj* dumb; *(silenzioso)* silent; *(fonetica)* mute

'mutu|a *f (cassa f)* **~** sickness benefit fund. **~'ato, -a** *mf ≈* NHS patient

'mutuo[1] *adj* mutual

'mutuo[2] *m* loan; *(per la casa)* mortgage; **fare un ~** take out a mortgage. **~ ipotecario** mortgage

Nn

n° *abbr (numero)* No

'nacchera *f* castanet

'nafta *f (naphtha)*; *(per motori)* diesel oil

'naia *f (cobra)*; *(⚠: servizio militare)* national service

'nailon *m* nylon

'nano, -a *adj & mf* dwarf

napole'tano, -a adj & mf Neapolitan

'Napoli f Naples

'nappa f tassel; (pelle) soft leather

nar'ciso m narcissus

nar'cotico adj & m narcotic

na'rice f nostril

nar'ra|re vt tell. ~'**tivo, -a** adj narrative. ●f fiction. ~'**tore,** ~'**trice** mf narrator. ~**zi'one** f narration; (racconto) story

na'sale adj nasal

'nasc|ere vi (venire al mondo) be born; (germogliare) sprout; (sorgere) rise; ~**ere da** fig arise from. ~**ita** f birth. ~**i'turo** m unborn child

na'sconder|e vt hide. ~**si** vr hide

nascon'di|glio m hiding-place. ~**no** m hide-and-seek. **na'scosto** pp di **nascondere** ●adj hidden; **di nascosto** secretly

na'sello m (pesce) hake

'naso m nose

'nastro m ribbon; (di registratore ecc) tape. ~ **adesivo** adhesive tape. ~ **isolante** insulating tape. ~ **trasportatore** conveyor belt

na'tal|e adj (paese) of one's birth. N~**e** m Christmas; ~**i** pl parentage. ~**ità** f [number of] births. **nata'lizio** adj (del Natale) Christmas attrib; (di nascita) of one's birth

na'tante adj floating ●m craft

'natica f buttock

na'tio adj native

Natività f Nativity. **na'tivo, -a** agg & mf native

'nato pp di **nascere** ●adj born; **uno scrittore** ~ a born writer; **nata Rossi** née Rossi

NATO f Nato, NATO

na'tura f nature; **pagare in** ~ pay in kind. ~ **morta** still life

natu'ra|le adj natural; **al** ~**le** (alimento) plain, natural; (al naturale) naturally; ~**le!** naturally, of course. ~**lezza** f naturalness. ~**liz'zare** vt naturalize. ~**l'mente** adv naturally

natu'rista mf naturalist

naufra'gare vi be wrecked; (persona:) be shipwrecked. **nau'fragio** m shipwreck; fig wreck. **'naufrago, -a** mf survivor

'nause|a f nausea; **avere la** ~**a** feel sick. ~**ante** adj nauseating. ~**are** vt nauseate

'nautic|a f navigation. ~**o** adj nautical

na'vale adj naval

'nave f ship. ~ **cisterna** tanker. ~ **da guerra** warship. ~ **spaziale** spaceship

na'vetta f shuttle

navi'cella f ~ **spaziale** nose cone

navi'gabile adj navigable

navi'ga|re vi sail; ~**re in Internet** surf the Net. ~'**tore,** ~'**trice** mf navigator. ~**zi'one** f navigation

na'viglio m fleet; (canale) canal

nazio'na|le adj national ●f Sport national team. ~'**lismo** m nationalism. ~'**lista** mf nationalist ~**lità** f inv nationality.

nazionaliz'zare vt nationalize. **nazi'one** f nation

na'zista adj & mf Nazi

N.B. abbr (nota bene) N.B.

---

ne

Spesso non si traduce: **Ne ho cinque** I've got five (of them)

● pers pron (di lui) about him; (di lei) about her; (di loro) about them; (di ciò) about it; (da ciò) from that; (di un insieme) of it; (di un gruppo) of them

····▶ **non ne conosco nessuno** I don't know any of them; **ne ho**

I have some; **non ne ho più** I don't have any left

● adv from there; **ne vengo ora** I've just come from there; **me ne vado** I'm off

né conj **né... né...**neither... nor...; **non ne ho il tempo né la voglia** I don't have either the time or the inclination; **né tu né io vogliamo andare** neither you nor I want to go; **né l'uno né l'altro** neither [of them/us]

ne'anche adv (neppure) not even; (senza neppure) without even ● conj (e neppure) neither... nor; **non parlo inglese, e lui ~** I don't speak English, neither does he o and he doesn't either

'nebbi|a f mist; (in città, su strada) fog. **~oso** adj misty; foggy

necessaria'mente adv necessarily. **neces'sario** adj necessary

necessità f inv necessity; (bisogno) need

necessi'tare vi **~ di** need; (essere necessario) be necessary

necro'logio m obituary

ne'fando adj wicked

ne'fasto adj ill-omened

ne'ga|re vt deny; (rifiutare) refuse; **essere ~to per qcsa** be no good at sth. **~tivo, -a** adj negative ● nf negative. **~zi'one** f negation; (diniego) denial; (Gram) negative

ne'gletto adj neglected

'negli = IN + GLI

negli'gen|te adj negligent. **~za** f negligence

negozi'abile adj negotiable

negozi'ante mf dealer; (bottegaio) shopkeeper

negozi'a|re vt negotiate ● vi **~re in** trade in. **~ti** mpl negotiations

ne'gozio m shop

'negro, -a adj black ● mf black; (scrittore) ghost writer

'nei = IN + I. **nel** = IN + IL.
'nella = IN + LA. **'nelle** = IN + LE.
'nello = IN + LO

'nembo m nimbus

ne'mico, -a adj hostile ● mf enemy

nem'meno conj not even

'nenia f dirge; (per bambini) lullaby; (piagnucolio) wail

'neo+ pref neo+

neofa'scismo m neofascism

neo'litico adj Neolithic

'neon m neon

neo'nato, -a adj newborn ● mf newborn baby

neozelan'dese adj New Zealand
● mf New Zealander

nep'pure conj not even

'nerb|o m (forza) strength; fig backbone. **~o'ruto** adj brawny

ne'retto m (Typ) bold [type]

'nero adj black; (①: arrabbiato) fuming ● m black; **mettere ~ su bianco** put in writing

nerva'tura f nerves pl; (Bot) veining; (di libro) band

'nervo m nerve; (Bot) vein; **avere i nervi** be bad-tempered; **dare ai nervi a qcno** get on sb's nerves. **~sismo** m nerviness

ner'voso adj nervous; (irritabile) bad-tempered; **avere il ~** be irritable; **esaurimento** m **~** nervous breakdown

'nespol|a f medlar. **~o** m medlar[-tree]

'nesso m link

nes'suno adj no, not... any; (qualche) any; **non ho nessun problema** I don't have any problems, I have no problems; **non lo trovo da nessuna parte** I can't find it anywhere; **in nessun modo** on no account ● pron nobody, no one, not... anybody, not... anyone; (qualcuno) anybody, anyone; **hai delle domande? – nessuna** do you have any questions? –

none; ~ **di voi** none of you; ~ **dei due** (di voi due) neither of you; **non ho visto** ~ **dei tuoi amici** I haven't seen any of your friends; **c'è** ~? is anybody there?

net'tare vt clean

net'tezza f cleanliness. ~ **urbana** cleansing department

'netto adj clean; (chiaro) clear; (Comm) net; **di** ~ just like that

nettur'bino m dustman

neu'tral|e adj & m neutral. ~**ità** f neutrality. ~**iz'zare** vt neutralize. **'neutro** adj neutral; (Gram) neuter ● m (Gram) neuter

neu'trone m neutron

'neve f snow

nevi'care vi snow; ~**ca** it is snowing. ~**'cata** f snowfall. **ne'vischio** m sleet. **ne'voso** adj snowy

nevral'gia f neuralgia

ne'vro|si f inv neurosis. ~**tico** adj neurotic

'nibbio m kite

'nicchia f niche

nicchi'are vi shilly-shally

'nichel m nickel

nichi'lista adj & mf nihilist

nico'tina f nicotine

nidi'ata f brood. **'nido** m nest; (giardino d'infanzia) crèche

ni'ente pron nothing, not... anything; (qualcosa) anything; **non ho fatto** ~ **di male** I didn't do anything wrong, I did nothing wrong; **grazie! – di** ~! thank you! – don't mention it!; **non serve a** ~ it is no use; **vuoi** ~? do you want anything?; **da** ~ (poco importante) minor; (di poco valore) worthless ● adj inv ⊞ **non ho** ~ **fame** I'm not the slightest bit hungry ● adv **non fa** ~ (non importa) it doesn't matter; **per** ~ at all; (litigare) over nothing; ~ **af-fatto!** no way! ● m **un bel** ~ absolutely nothing

nientedi'meno, niente'meno adv ~ **che** no less than ● int fancy that!

'ninfa f nymph

nin'fea f water-lily

'ninnolo m plaything; (fronzolo) knick-knack

ni'pote m (di zii) nephew; (di nonni) grandson, grandchild ● f (di zii) niece; (di nonni) granddaughter, grandchild

'nitido adj neat; (chiaro) clear

ni'trato m nitrate

ni'tri|re vi neigh. ~**to** m (di cavallo) neigh

no adv no; (con congiunzione) not; **dire di no** say no; **credo di no** I don't think so; **perché no?** why not?; **io no** not me; **fa freddo, no?** it's cold, isn't it?

'nobil|e adj noble ● m noble, nobleman ● f noble, noblewoman. ~**i'are** adj noble. ~**tà** f nobility

'nocca f knuckle

nocci'ol|a f hazelnut. ~**o** m (albero) hazel

'nocciolo m stone; fig heart

'noce f walnut ● m (albero, legno) walnut. ~ **moscata** nutmeg. ~**'pesca** f nectarine

no'civo adj harmful

'nodo m knot; fig lump; (Comput) node; **fare il** ~ **della cravatta** do up one's tie. **no'doso** adj knotty

'noi pers pron (soggetto) we; (oggetto, con prep) us; **chi è? – siamo** ~ who is it? – it's us

'noia f boredom; (fastidio) bother; (persona) bore; **dar** ~ annoy

noi'altri pers pron we

noi'oso adj boring; (fastidioso) tiresome

noleggi'are vt hire; (dare a noleggio) hire out; charter (nave, aereo). **no'leggio** m hire; (di nave, aereo) charter. **'nolo** m hire; (Naut) freight; **a nolo** for hire '**nomade** adj nomadic ●mf nomad

'**nome** m name; (Gram) noun; **a ~ di** in the name of; **di ~** by name. **~ di famiglia** surname. **~ da ragazza** maiden name. **no'mea** f reputation

nomencla'tura f nomenclature

no'mignolo m nickname

'**nomina** f appointment. **nomi'nale** adj nominal; (Gram) noun attrib

nomi'na|re vt name; (menzionare) mention; (eleggere) appoint. **~'tivo** adj nominative; (Comm) registered ●m nominative; (nome) name

---

non adv not; **~ ti amo** I do not love you; **~ c'è di che** not at all

Per formare il negativo dei verbi regolari si usa l'ausiliare do: **Non mi piace** I don' like it

---

nonché conj (tanto meno) let alone; (anche) as well as

noncu'ran|te adj nonchalant; (negligente) indifferent. **~za** f nonchalance; (negligenza) indifference

nondi'meno conj nevertheless

'**nonna** f grandmother

'**nonno** m grandfather; **nonni** pl grandparents

non'nulla m inv trifle

'**nono** adj & m ninth

nono'stante prep in spite of ● conj although

nonvio'lento adj nonviolent

nord m north; **del ~** northern

nor'd-est m northeast; **a ~** north-easterly

'**nordico** adj northern

nordocciden'tale adj north-western

nordorien'tale adj northeastern

nor'd-ovest m northwest; **a ~** northwesterly

'**norma** f rule; (istruzione) instruction; **a ~ di legge** according to law; **è**

buona ~ it's advisable

nor'mal|e adj normal. **~ità** f normality. **~iz'zare** vt normalize. **~'mente** adv normally

norve'gese adj & mf Norwegian. **Nor'vegia** f Norway

nossi'gnore adv no way

nostal'gia f (di casa, patria) homesickness; (del passato) nostalgia; **aver ~ be** homesick; **aver ~ di qcno** miss sb. **no'stalgico, -a** adj nostalgic ● mf reactionary

no'strano adj local; (fatto in casa) home-made

'**nostro** (il nostro m, la nostra f, i nostri mpl, le nostre fpl) poss adj our; quella macchina **è nostra** that car is ours; **~ padre** our father; **un ~ amico** a friend of ours ● poss pron ours

'**nota** f (segno) sign; (comunicazione, commento, musica) note; (conto) bill; (lista) list; **degno di ~** noteworthy; **prendere ~** take note. **note** pl caratteristiche distinguishing marks

no'tabile adj & m notable

no'taio m notary

no'ta|re vt (segnare) mark; (annotare) note down; (osservare) notice; **far ~re qcsa** point sth out. **~zi'one** f marking; (annotazione) notation

'**notes** m inv notepad

no'tevole adj (degno di nota) remarkable; (grande) considerable

no'tifica f notification. **notifi'care** vt notify; (Comm) advise. **~zi'one** f notification

no'tizi|a f una **~a** a piece of news; (informazione) a piece of information; **le ~e** the news sg. **~'ario** m news sg

'**noto** adj [well-]known; **rendere ~** (far sapere) announce

notorietà f fame; **raggiungere la ~** become famous. **no'torio** adj well-known; pej notorious

not'tambulo m night-bird

not'tata f night; far ~ stay up all night

'notte f night; di ~ at night; ~ bianca sleepless night. ~**tempo** adv at night

not'turno adj nocturnal; (servizio ecc) night

no'vanta adj & m ninety

novan't|enne adj & mf ninety-year-old. ~**esimo** adj ninetieth. ~**ina** f about ninety. **'nove** adj & m nine. **no-ve'cento** adj & m nine hundred. **il Novecento** the twentieth century

no'vella f short story

novel'lino, -a adj inexperienced ●mf novice, beginner. **no'vello** adj new

no'vembre m November

novità f inv novelty; (notizie) news sg; **l'ultima** ~ (moda) the latest fashion

novizi'ato m (Relig) novitiate; (tirocinio) apprenticeship

nozi'one f notion; **nozioni** pl rudiments

'nozze fpl marriage sg; (cerimonia) wedding sg. ~ **d'argento** silver wedding [anniversary]. ~ **d'oro** golden wedding [anniversary]

'nub|e f cloud. ~**e tossica** toxic cloud. ~**i'fragio** m cloudburst

'nubile adj unmarried ●f unmarried woman

'nuca f nape

nucle'are adj nuclear

'nucleo m nucleus; (unità) unit

nu'dista mf nudist. ~**tà** f inv nudity

'nudo adj naked; (spoglio) bare; **a occhio** ~ to the naked eye

'nugolo m large number

'nulla pron = NIENTE

nulla'osta m inv permit

nullità f inv (persona) nonentity

'nullo adj (Jur) null and void

nume'ra|bile adj countable. ~**le** adj & m numeral

nume'ra|re vt number. ~**zi'one** f

numbering. **nu'merico** adj numerical

'numero m number; (romano, arabo) numeral; (di scarpe ecc) size; **dare i numeri** be off one's head. ~ **cardinale** cardinal [number]. ~ **decimale** decimal. ~ **ordinale** ordinal [number]. ~ **di telefono** phone number. ~ **verde** Freephone®. **nume'roso** adj numerous

'nunzio m nuncio

nu'ocere vi ~ a harm

nu'ora f daughter-in-law

nuo'ta|re vi swim; fig wallow. **nuo'to** m swimming. ~**trice** mf swimmer

nu'ov|a f (notizia) news sg. ~**a'mente** adv again. ~**o** adj new; **di** ~**o** again; **rimettere a** ~**o** give a new lease of life to

nutri'ente adj nourishing. ~**mento** m nourishment

nu'tri|re vt nourish; harbour (sentimenti). ~**rsi** eat; ~**rsi di** fig live on. ~**tivo** adj nourishing. ~**zi'one** f nutrition

'nuvola f cloud. **nuvo'loso** adj cloudy

nuzi'ale adj nuptial; (vestito, anello ecc) wedding attrib

Oo

o conj or; ~ **l'uno** ~ **l'altro** one or the other, either

O abbr (ovest) W

'oasi f inv oasis

obbedi'ente ecc = UBBIDIENTE ecc

obbli'ga|re vt force, oblige; ~**rsi** vr ~**rsi a** undertake to. ~**to** adj obliged. ~**torio** adj compulsory. ~**zi'one** f obligation; (Comm) bond. **'obbligo** m obligation; (dovere) duty;

avere obblighi verso be under an obligation to; **d'obbligo** obligatory

obbligatoria'mente adv fare qcsa ~ be obliged to do sth

ob'bro|brio m disgrace. ~'brioso adj disgraceful

obe'lisco m obelisk

obe'rare vt overburden

obesità f obesity. **o'beso** adj obese

obiet'tare vt/i object; ~ su object to

obiettivi'tà f objectivity. **obiet'tivo** adj objective ●m objective; (scopo) object

obie|t'tore m objector. ~ttore di coscienza conscientious objector. ~zi'one f objection

obi'torio m mortuary

o'blio m oblivion

o'bliquo adj oblique; fig underhand

oblite'rare vt obliterate

oblò m inv porthole

'oboe m oboe

obso'leto adj obsolete

'oca f (pl oche) goose

occasio'nal|e adj occasional. ~'mente** adv occasionally

occasi'one f occasion; (buon affare) bargain; (motivo) cause; (opportunità) chance; **d'~** secondhand

occhi'aia f eye socket; **occhiaie** pl shadows under the eyes

occhi'ali mpl glasses, spectacles. ~ da sole sunglasses. ~ da vista glasses, spectacles

occhi'ata f look; **dare un'~** have a look at

occhieggi'are vt ogle ●vi peep

occhi'ello m buttonhole; (asola) eyelet

'occhio m eye; ~! watch out!; **a quattr'occhi** in private; **tenere d'~** qcno keep an eye on sb; **a ~ [e croce]** roughly; **chiudere un'~** turn a blind eye; **dare nell'~** attract attention; **pagare o spendere un ~**

pay an arm and a leg. ~ **nero** (pesto) black eye. ~ **di pernice** (callo) corn. ~**lino** m fare l'~**lino** a qcno wink at sb

occiden'tale adj western ●mf westerner. **occi'dente** m west

oc'clu|dere vt obstruct. ~**si'one** f occlusion

occor'ren|te adj necessary ●m the necessary. ~**za** f need; **all'~za** if need be

oc'correre vi be necessary

occulta'mento m ~ **di prove** concealment of evidence

occul't|are vt hide. ~**ismo** m occult. **oc'culto** adj hidden; (magico) occult

occu'pante mf occupier; (abusivo) squatter

occu'pa|re vt occupy; spend (tempo); take up (spazio); (dar lavoro a) employ. ~**rsi** vr occupy oneself; (trovare lavoro) find a job; ~**rsi di** (badare) look after. ~**to** adj engaged; (persona) busy; (posto) taken. ~**zi'one** f occupation

o'ceano m ocean. ~ **Atlantico** Atlantic [Ocean]. ~ **Pacifico** Pacific [Ocean]

'ocra f ochre

ocu'lare adj ocular; (testimone, bagno) eye attrib

ocula'tezza f care. **ocu'lato** adj (scelta) wise

ocu'lista mf optician; (per malattie) ophthalmologist

od conj or

'ode f ode

odi'are vt hate

odi'erno adj of today; (attuale) present

'odi|o m hatred; **avere in ~o** hate. ~**'oso** adj hateful

odo'ra|re vt smell; (profumare) perfume ●vi ~**re di** smell of. ~**to** m sense of smell. **o'dore** m smell; (pro-

fumo) scent; **c'è odore di...** there's a smell of...; **sentire odore di** smell; **odori** *pl* (*Culin*) herbs. **odo'roso** *adj* fragrant

of'fender|e *vt* offend; (*ferire*) injure. **~si** *vr* take offence

offen'siv|a *f* (*Mil*) offensive. **~o** *adj* offensive

offe'rente *mf* offerer; (*in aste*) bidder

of'fert|a *f* offer; (*donazione*) donation; (*Comm*) supply; (*nelle aste*) bid; in **~a speciale** on special offer. **~o** *pp di offrire*

of'fes|a *f* offence. **~o** *pp di offendere* ● *adj* offended

offi'ciare *vt* officiate

offi'cina *f* workshop; **~** [**mecca'nica**] garage

of'frir|e *vt* offer. **~si** *vr* offer oneself; (*occasione*:) present itself; **~si di fare qcsa** offer to do sth

offu'scar|e *vt* darken; *fig* dull (*memoria, bellezza*); blur (*vista*). **~si** *vr* darken; *fig*: (*memoria, bellezza*:) fade away; (*vista*:) become blurred

of'talmico *adj* ophthalmic

oggettività *f* objectivity. **ogget'tivo** *adj* objective

og'getto *m* object; (*argomento*) subject; **oggetti** *pl* **smarriti** lost property, lost and found *Am*

'oggi *adv* & *m* today; (*al giorno d'oggi*) nowadays; **da ~ in poi** from today on; **~ a otto** a week today; **dall'~ al domani** overnight; **al giorno d'~** nowadays. **~gi'orno** *adv* nowadays

'ogni *adj inv* every; (*qualsiasi*) any; **~ tre giorni** every three days; **ad ~ costo** at any cost; **ad ~ modo** anyway; **~ cosa** everything; **~ tanto** now and then; **~ volta che** whenever

o'gnuno *pron* everyone, everybody; **~ di voi** each of you

'ola *f inv* Mexican wave

O'lan|da *f* Holland. **o~'dese** *adj*

Dutch ● *m* Dutchman; (*lingua*) Dutch ● *f* Dutchwoman

ole'andro *m* oleander

ole'at|o *adj* oiled; **carta ~a** greaseproof paper

oleo'dotto *m* oil pipeline. **ole'oso** *adj* oily

ol'fatto *m* sense of smell

oli'are *vt* oil

oli'era *f* cruet

olim'piadi *fpl* Olympic Games. **o'limpico** *adj* Olympic. **olim'pionico** *adj* (*primato, squadra*) Olympic

'olio *m* oil; **sott'~** in oil; **colori a ~** oils; **quadro a ~** oil painting. **~ di mais** corn oil. **~ d'oliva** olive oil. **~ di semi** vegetable oil. **~ solare** suntan oil

o'liv|a *f* olive. **oli'vastro** *adj* olive. **oli'veto** *m* olive grove. **~o** *m* olive tree

'olmo *m* elm

oltraggi'are *vt* offend. **ol'traggio** *m* offence

ol'tranza *f* **ad ~** to the bitter end

'oltre *adv* (*di luogo*) further; (*di tempo*) longer ● *prep* (*di luogo*) over; (*di tempo*) later than; (*più di*) more than; (*in aggiunta*) besides; **~ a** (*eccetto*) except, apart from; **per ~ due settimane** for more than two weeks. **~'mare** *adv* overseas. **~'modo** *adv* extremely

oltrepas'sare *vt* go beyond; (*eccedere*) exceed

o'maggio *m* homage; (*dono*) gift; **in ~ con** free with; **omaggi** *pl* (*saluti*) respects

ombeli'cale *adj* umbilical. **ombe'lico** *m* navel

'ombr|a *f* (*zona*) shade; (*immagine oscura*) shadow; **all'~a** in the shade. **~eggi'are** *vt* shade

om'brello *m* umbrella. **ombrel'lone** *m* beach umbrella

om'bretto *m* eye-shadow

om'broso *adj* shady

ome'lette *f inv* omelette

ome'lia *f* (*Relig*) sermon

omeopa'tia *f* homoeopathy. **omeo'patico** *adj* homoeopathic ●*m* homoeopath

omertà *f* conspiracy of silence

o'messo *pp di* omettere

o'mettere *vt* omit

OMG *m abbr* (organismo modificato geneticamente) GMO

omi'cid|a *adj* murderous ●*mf* murderer. ~**io** *m* murder. ~**io colposo** manslaughter

omissi'one *f* omission

omogeneiz'zato *adj* homogenized. **omo'geneo** *adj* homogeneous

omolo'gare *vt* approve

o'monimo, -a *mf* namesake ●*m* (*parola*) homonym

omosessu'al|e *adj & mf* homosexual. ~**ità** *f* homosexuality

On. *abbr* (onorevole) MP

'oncia *f* ounce

'onda *f* wave; **andare in** ~ *Radio* go on the air. **onde** *pl* **corte** short wave. **onde** *pl* **lunghe** long wave. **onde** *pl* **medie** medium wave. **on'data** *f* wave

ondeggi'are *vi* wave; (*barca:*) roll

ondula|'torio *adj* undulating. ~**zi'one** *f* undulation; (*di capelli*) wave

'oner|e *m* burden. ~**'oso** *adj* onerous

onestà *f* honesty; (*rettitudine*) integrity. **o'nesto** *adj* honest; (*giusto*) just

'onice *f* onyx

onnipo'tente *adj* omnipotent

onnipre'sente *adj* ubiquitous; *Rel* omnipresent

ono'mastico *m* name-day

ono'ra|re *vt* honour. ~**re** *vt* (*fare onore a*) be a credit to; honour (*promessa*). ~**rio** *adj* honorary ●*m* fee. ~**rsi** *vr* ~**rsi di** be proud of

o'nore *m* honour; **in** ~ **di** (*festa, ri-*

cevimento*) in honour of; **fare** ~ **a** do justice to (*pranzo*); **farsi** ~ **in** excel in

ono'revole *adj* honourable ●*mf* Member of Parliament

onorifi'cenza *f* honour; (*decorazione*) decoration. **ono'rifico** *adj* honorary

O.N.U. *f abbr* (Organizzazione delle Nazioni Unite) UN

o'paco *adj* opaque; (*colori ecc*) dull; (*fotografia, rossetto*) matt

o'pale *f* opal

'opera *f* (*lavoro*) work; (*azione*) deed; (*Mus*) opera; (*teatro*) opera house; (*ente*) institution; **mettere in** ~ put into effect; **mettersi all'** ~ get to work; **opere** *pl* **pubbliche** public works. ~ **d'arte** work of art. ~ **lirica** opera

ope'raio, -a *adj* working ●*mf* worker; ~ **specializzato** skilled worker

ope'ra|re *vt* (*Med*) operate on; **farsi** ~**re** have an operation ●*vi* operate; (*agire*) work. ~**tivo**, ~**torio** *adj* operating *attrib*. ~**tore**, ~**trice** *mf* operator; (*TV*) cameraman. ~**tore turistico** tour operator. ~**zi'one** *f* operation; (*Comm*) transaction

ope'retta *f* operetta

ope'roso *adj* industrious

opini'one *f* opinion. ~ **pubblica** public opinion, vox pop

'oppio *m* opium

oppo'nente *adj* opposing ●*mf* opponent

op'por|re *vt* oppose; (*obiettare*) object; ~**re resistenza** offer resistance. ~**si** *vr* ~**si a** oppose

opportu'ni|smo *m* expediency. ~**sta** *mf* opportunist. ~**tà** *f inv* opportunity; (*l'essere opportuno*) timeliness. **oppor'tuno** *adj* opportune; (*adeguato*) appropriate; **il momento opportuno** the right moment

opposi'tore *m* opposer. ~**zi'one** *f*

opposition; **d'~zione** (giornale, partito) opposition

op'posto pp di **opporre** ●adj opposite; (opinioni) opposing ●m opposite; **all'~** on the contrary

oppres|si'one f oppression. **~'sivo** adj oppressive. **op'presso** pp di **opprimere** ●adj oppressed; **~'sore** m oppressor

oppri'me|nte adj oppressive. **op'primere** vt oppress; (gravare) weigh down

op'pure conj otherwise, or [else]; **lunedì ~ martedì** Monday or Tuesday

op'tare vi **~ per** opt for

opu'lento adj opulent

o'puscolo m booklet; (pubblicitario) brochure

opzio'nale adj optional. **opzi'one** f option

'ora'¹ f time; (unità) hour; **di buon'~** early; **che ~ è?, che ore sono?** what time is it?; **mezz'~** half an hour; **a ore** (lavorare, pagare) by the hour; **50 km all'~** 50 km an hour; **a un'~ di macchina** one hour by car. **~ d'arrivo** arrival time. **l'~ esatta** (Teleph) speaking clock. **~ legale** daylight saving time. **~ di punta, ore pl di punta** peak time; (per il traffico) rush hour

'ora'² adv now; (tra poco) presently; **~ come ~** at the moment; **d'~ in poi** from now on; **per ~** for the time being, for now; **è ~ di finirla!** that's enough now! ●conj (dunque) now [then]; **~ che ci penso,...** now that I come to think about it,...

'orafo m goldsmith

o'rale adj & m oral; **per via ~** by mouth

ora'mai adv = ORMAI

o'rario adj (tariffa) hourly; (segnale) time attrib; (velocità) per hour ●m time; (tabella dell'orario) timetable, schedule Am; **essere in ~** be on

time; **in senso ~** clockwise. **~ di chiusura** closing time. **~ flessibile** flexitime. **~ di sportello** banking hours. **~ d'ufficio** business hours. **~ di visita** (Med) consulting hours

o'rata f gilthead

ora'tore, -'trice mf speaker

ora'torio, -a adj oratorical ●m (Mus) oratorio ●f oratory. **orazi'one** f (Relig) prayer

'orbita f orbit; (Anat) [eye-]socket

or'chestra f orchestra; (parte del teatro) pit

orche'stra|le adj orchestral ●mf member of an/the orchestra. **~re** vt orchestrate

orchi'dea f orchid

'orco m ogre

'orda f horde

or'digno m device; (arnese) tool. **~ esplosivo** explosive device

ordi'nale adj & m ordinal

ordina'mento m order; (leggi) rules pl.

ordi'nanza f bylaw; **d'~** (soldato) on duty

ordi'nare vt (sistemare) arrange; (comandare) order; (prescrivere) prescribe; (Relig) ordain

ordi'nario adj ordinary; (grossolano) common; (professore) with tenure; **di ordinaria amministrazione** routine ●m ordinary; (Univ) professor

ordi'nato adj (in ordine) tidy

ordinazi'one f order; **fare un'~** place an order

'ordine m order; (di avvocati, medici) association; **mettere in ~** put in order; **di prim'~** first-class; **di terz'~** (film, albergo) third- rate; **di ~ pratico/economico** of a practical/economic nature; **fino a nuovo ~** until further notice; **parola d'~** password. **~ del giorno** agenda. **ordini sacri** pl Holy Orders

or'dire vt (tramare) plot

orec'chino m ear-ring

o'recchi|o m (pl f orecchie) ear; avere ~o have a good ear; **mi è giunto all'~o che...** I've heard that...; ~'oni pl (Med) mumps sg

o'refice m jeweller. ~'ria f (arte) goldsmith's art; (negozio) goldsmith's [shop]

'orfano, -a adj orphan ● mf orphan. ~'trofio m orphanage

orga'netto m barrel-organ; (a bocca) mouth-organ; (fisarmonica) accordion

or'ganico adj organic ● m personnel

orga'nismo m organism; (corpo umano) body

orga'nista mf organist

organiz'za|re vt organize. ~rsi vr get organized. ~'tore, ~'trice mf organizer. ~zi'one f organization

'organo m organ

or'gasmo m orgasm

'orgia f orgy

or'gogli|o m pride. ~'oso adj proud

orien'tale adj eastern; (cinese ecc) oriental

orienta'mento m orientation; **perdere l'~** lose one's bearings; **senso dell'~** sense of direction

orien'ta|re vt orientate. ~rsi vr find one's bearings; (tendere) tend

ori'ente m east. **l'Estremo O~** the Far East. **il Medio O~** the Middle East

o'rigano m oregano

origi'na|le adj original; (eccentrico) odd ● m original. ~lità f originality. ~re vt/i originate. ~rio adj (nativo) native

o'rigine f origin; **in ~** originally; **aver ~ da** originate from; **dare ~ a** give rise to

o'rina f urine. **ori'nale** m chamberpot. **ori'nare** vi urinate

ori'undo adj native

orizzon'tale adj horizontal

orizzon'tare vt = ORIENTARE. oriz'zonte m horizon

or'la|re vt hem. ~'tura f hem. 'orlo m edge; (di vestito ecc) hem

'orma f track; (di piede) footprint; (impronta) mark

or'mai adv by now; (passato) by then; (quasi) almost

ormeggi'are vt moor

ormo'nale adj hormonal. **or'mone** m hormone

ornamen'tale adj ornamental. **orna'mento** m ornament

or'na|re vt decorate. ~rsi vr deck oneself. ~to adj (stile) ornate

ornitolo'gia f ornithology

'oro m gold; **d'~** gold; fig golden

orologi'aio, -a mf clockmaker, watchmaker

oro'logio m watch; (da tavolo, muro ecc) clock. **~ a pendolo** grandfather clock. **~ a polso** wrist-watch. **~ a sveglia** alarm clock

o'roscopo m horoscope

or'rendo adj awful, dreadful

or'ribile adj horrible

orripi'lante adj horrifying

or'rore m horror; **avere qcsa in ~** hate sth

orsacchi'otto m teddy bear

'orso m bear; (persona scontrosa) hermit. **~ bianco** polar bear

or'taggio m vegetable

or'tensia f hydrangea

or'tica f nettle

ortícol'tura f horticulture. **'orto** m vegetable plot

orto'dosso adj orthodox

ortogo'nale adj perpendicular

orto|gra'fia f spelling. ~'grafico adj spelling attrib

orto'lano *m* market gardener; (*negozio*) greengrocer's

orto'pe|dia *f* orthopaedics *sg*. **~'pedico** *adj* orthopaedic ● *m* orthopaedist

orzai'olo *m* sty

or'zata *f* barley-water

o'sare *vt/i* dare; (*avere audacia*) be daring

oscenità *f inv* obscenity. **o'sceno** *adj* obscene

oscil'la|re *vi* swing; (*prezzi ecc*.) fluctuate; *Tech* oscillate; (*fig: essere indeciso*) vacillate. **~zi'one** *f* swinging; (*di prezzi*) fluctuation; *Tech* oscillation

oscura'mento *m* darkening; (*di vista, mente*) dimming; (*totale*) black-out

oscu'r|are *vt* darken; *fig* obscure. **~arsi** *vr* get dark. **~ità** *f* darkness. **o'scuro** *adj* dark; (*triste*) gloomy; (*incomprensibile*) obscure

ospe'dal|e *m* hospital. **~i'ero** *adj* hospital *attrib*

ospi'ta|le *adj* hospitable. **~lità** *f* hospitality. **~re** *vt* give hospitality to. **'ospite** *m* (*chi ospita*) host; (*chi viene ospitato*) guest ● *f* hostess; guest

o'spizio *m* [old people's] home

ossa'tura *f* bone structure; (*di romanzo*) structure, framework. **'osseo** *adj* bone *attrib*

ossequi'|are *vt* pay one's respects to. **os'sequio** *m* homage; **ossequi** *pl* respects. **~'oso** *adj* obsequious

osser'van|te *adj* (*cattolico*) practising. **~za** *f* observance

osser'va|re *vt* observe; (*notare*) notice; keep (*ordine, silenzio*). **~'tore**, **~'trice** *mf* observer. **~'torio** *m* (*Astr*) observatory; (*Mil*) observation post. **~zi'one** *f* observation; (*rimprovero*) reproach

ossessio'na|nte *adj* haunting; (*persona*) nagging. **~re** *vt* obsess; (*infastidire*) nag. **ossessi'one** *f* obses-

sion. **osses'sivo** *adj* obsessive. **os-'sesso** *adj* obsessed

os'sia *conj* that is

ossi'dabile *adj* liable to tarnish

ossi'dar|e *vt*, **~si** *vr* oxidize

'ossido *m* oxide. **~ di carbonio** carbon monoxide

os'sidrico *adj* **fiamma ossidrica** blowlamp

ossige'nar|e *vt* oxygenate; (*decolorare*) bleach; *fig* put back on its feet (*azienda*). **~si** *vr* **~si i capelli** dye one's hair blonde. **os'sigeno** *m* oxygen

'osso *m* ((*Anat*): *pl f* **ossa**) bone; (*di frutto*) stone

osso'buco *m* marrowbone

os'suto *adj* bony

ostaco'lare *vt* hinder, obstruct. **o'stacolo** *m* obstacle; *Sport* hurdle

o'staggio *m* hostage; **prendere in ~** take hostage

o'stello *m* **~ della gioventù** youth hostel

osten'ta|re *vt* show off; **~re indifferenza** pretend to be indifferent. **~zi'one** *f* ostentation

oste'ria *f* inn

o'stetrico, **-a** *adj* obstetric ● *mf* obstetrician

'ostia *f* host; (*cialda*) wafer

'ostico *adj* tough

o'stil|e *adj* hostile. **~ità** *f inv* hostility

osti'na|rsi *vr* persist (a in). **~to** *adj* obstinate. **~zi'one** *f* obstinacy

'ostrica *f* oyster

ostru'ire *vt* obstruct. **~zi'one** *f* obstruction

otorinolaringoi'atra *mf* ear, nose and throat specialist

ottago'nale *adj* octagonal. **ot'tagono** *m* octagon

ot'tan|ta *adj* & *m* eighty. **~'tenne**

adj & mf eighty-year-old. ~**'tesimo** *adj* eightieth. ~**'tina** *f* about eighty

ot'tav|a *f* octave. ~**o** *adj* eighth

otte'nere *vt* obtain; (*più comune*) get; (*conseguire*) achieve

'ottico, -a *adj* optic[al] ● *mf* optician ● *f* (*scienza*) optics *sg*; (*di lenti ecc*) optics *pl*

otti'ma|le *adj* optimum. ~**'mente** *adv* very well

otti'mis|mo *m* optimism. ~**ta** *mf* optimist. ~**tico** *adj* optimistic

'ottimo *adj* very good ● *m* optimum

'otto *adj & m* eight

ot'tobre *m* October

otto'cento *adj & m* eight hundred; l'O~ the nineteenth century

ot'tone *m* brass

ottu'ra|re *vt* block; fill (*dente*). ~**rsi** *vr* clog. ~**'tore** *m* (*Phot*) shutter. ~**zi'one** *f* stopping; (*di dente*) filling

ot'tuso *pp di* **ottundere** ● *adj* obtuse

o'vaia *f* ovary

o'vale *adj & m* oval

o'vatta *f* cotton wool

ovazi'one *f* ovation

over'dose *f inv* overdose

'ovest *m* west

o'vi|le *m* sheep-fold. ~**no** *adj* sheep *attrib*

ovo'via *f* two-seater cable car

ovulazi'one *f* ovulation

o'vunque *adv* = **DOVUNQUE**

ov'vero *conj* or; (*cioè*) that is

ovvia'mente *adv* obviously

ovvi'are *vi* ~ a qcsa counter sth. **'ovvio** *adj* obvious

ozi'are *vi* laze around. **'ozio** *m* idleness. **ozi'oso** *adj* idle; (*questione*) pointless

o'zono *m* ozone; **buco nell'**~ hole in the ozone layer

Pp

pa'ca|re *vt* quieten. ~**to** *adj* quiet

pac'chetto *m* packet; (*postale*) parcel, package; (*di sigarette*) pack, packet. ~ **software** software package

'pacchia *f* 🔢 bed of roses

pacchi'ano *adj* garish

'pacco *m* parcel; (*involto*) bundle. ~ **regalo** gift-wrapped package

paccot'tiglia *f* junk, rubbish

'pace *f* peace; **darsi** ~ forget it; **fare** ~ **con** qcno make it up with sb; **lasciare in** ~ qcno leave sb in peace

pachi'stano, -a *mf & adj* Pakistani

pacifi'ca|re *vt* reconcile; (*mettere pace*) pacify. ~**zi'one** *f* reconciliation

pa'cifico *adj* pacific; (*calmo*) peaceful; **il P**~ the Pacific

paci'fis|mo *m* pacifism. ~**ta** *mf* pacifist

pa'dano *adj* **pianura padana** Po Valley

pa'del|la *f* frying-pan; (*per malati*) bedpan

padi'glione *m* pavilion

'padr|e *m* father; ~**i** *pl* (*antenati*) forefathers. **pa'drino** *m* godfather. ~**e'nostro** *m* **il** ~**enostro** the Lord's Prayer. ~**e'terno** *m* God Almighty

padro'nanza *f* mastery. ~ **di sé** self-control

pa'drone, -a *mf* master; mistress; (*datore di lavoro*) boss; (*proprietario*) owner. ~**ggi'are** *vt* master

pae'sag|gio *m* scenery; (*pittura*) landscape. ~**'gista** *mf* landscape architect

pae'sano, -a *adj* country ● *mf* villager

pa'ese m (*nazione*) country; (*territorio*) land; (*villaggio*) village; **il Bel P~** Italy; **va' a quel ~!** get lost!; **Paesi** pl **Bassi** Netherlands

paf'futo adj plump

'paga f pay, wages pl

pa'gabile adj payable

pa'gaia f paddle

paga'mento m payment; **a ~** (*parcheggio*) which you have to pay to use. **~ anticipato** (*Comm*) advance payment. **~ alla consegna** cash on delivery, COD

pa'gano, -a adj & mf pagan

pa'gare vt/i pay; **~ da bere a qcno** buy sb a drink

pa'gella f [school] report

'pagina f page. **Pagine** pl **Gialle®** Yellow Pages. **~ web** (*Comput*) web page

'paglia f straw

pagliac'cetto m (*per bambini*) rompers pl

pagliac'ciata f farce

pagli'accio m clown

pagli'aio m haystack

paglie'riccio m straw mattress

pagli'etta f (*cappello*) boater; (*per pentole*) steel wool

pagli'uzza f wisp of straw; (*di metallo*) particle

pa'gnotta f [round] loaf

pail'lette f inv sequin

'paio m (*pl* **paia**) pair; **un ~** (*circa due*) a couple; **un ~ di** (*scarpe, forbici*) a pair of

'Pakistan m Pakistan

'pala f shovel; (*di remo, elica*) blade; (*di ruota*) paddle

pala'fitta f pile-dwelling

pala'sport m inv indoor sports arena

pa'late fpl **a ~** (*fare soldi*) hand over fist

pa'lato m palate

palaz'zetto m **~ dello sport** indoor sports arena

palaz'zina f villa

pa'lazzo m palace; (*edificio*) building. **~ delle esposizioni** exhibition centre. **~ di giustizia** law courts pl, courthouse. **~ dello sport** indoor sports arena

'palco m (*pedana*) platform; (*Theat*) box. **~['scenico]** m stage

pale'sar|e vt disclose. **~si** vr reveal oneself. **pa'lese** adj evident

Pale'sti|na f Palestine. **~'nese** mf Palestinian

pa'lestra f gymnasium, gym; (*ginnastica*) gymnastics pl

pa'letta f spade; (*per focolare*) shovel. **~ [della spazzatura]** dustpan

pa'letto m peg

'palio m (*premio*) prize. **il P~** horse-race held at Siena

paliz'zata f fence

'palla f ball; (*proiettile*) bullet; (🔤: *bugia*) porkie; **che palle!** 🔤 this is a pain in the arse!. **~ di neve** snowball. **~ al piede** fig millstone round one's neck

pallaca'nestro f basketball

palla'mano f handball

pallanu'oto f water polo

palla'volo f volley-ball

palleggi'are vi (*calcio*) practise ball control; Tennis knock up

pallia'tivo m palliative

'pallido adj pale

pal'lina f (*di vetro*) marble

pal'lino m **avere il ~ del calcio** be crazy about football

pallon'cino m balloon; (*lanterna*) Chinese lantern; (🔤: *etilometro*) Breathalyzer®

pal'lone m ball; (*calcio*) football; (*aerostato*) balloon

pal'lore m pallor

pal'loso adj 🔤 boring

pal'lottola f pellet; (proiettile) bullet

'palm|a f (Bot) palm. ~o m (Anat) palm; (misura) hand's-breadth; restare con un ~o di naso feel disappointed

pal'mare m palmtop

'palo m pole; (di sostegno) stake; (in calcio) goalpost; **fare il** ~ (ladro:) keep a lookout. ~ **della luce** lamppost

palom'baro m diver

pal'pare vt feel

'palpebra f eyelid

palpi'ta|re vi throb; (fremere) quiver. ~**zi'one** f palpitation. **'palpito** m throb; (del cuore) beat

pa'lude f marsh, swamp

palu'doso adj marshy

pa'lustre adj marshy; (piante, uccelli) marsh attrib

'pampino m vine leaf

'panca f bench; (in chiesa) pew

pancarré m sliced bread

pan'cetta f (Culin) bacon; (di una certa età) paunch

pan'chetto m [foot]stool

pan'china f garden seat; (in calcio) bench

'pancia f belly; **mal di** ~ stomachache; **metter su** ~ develop a paunch; **a** ~ **in giù** lying face down

panci'olle: stare in ~ lounge about

panci'one m (persona) pot belly

panci'otto m waistcoat

pande'monio m pandemonium

pan'doro m sponge cake eaten at Christmas

'pane m bread; (pagnotta) loaf; (di burro) block. ~ **a cassetta** sliced bread. **pan grattato** breadcrumbs pl. ~ **di segale** rye bread. **pan di Spagna** sponge cake. ~ **tostato** toast

panett|e'ria f bakery; (negozio) baker's [shop]. ~**i'ere, -a** mf baker

panet'tone m kind of Christmas cake

'panfilo m yacht

pan'forte m nougat-like delicacy from Siena

'panico m panic; **lasciarsi prendere dal** ~ panic

pani'ere m basket; (cesta) hamper

pani'ficio m bakery; (negozio) baker's [shop]

pa'nino m [bread] roll. ~ **imbottito** filled roll. ~ **al prosciutto** ham roll. ~**'teca** f sandwich bar

'panna f cream. ~ **da cucina** [single] cream. ~ **montata** whipped cream

'panne f (Mech) **in** ~ broken down; **restare in** ~ break down

pan'nello m panel. ~ **solare** solar panel

'panno m cloth; **panni** pl (abiti) clothes

pan'nocchia f (di granoturco) cob

panno'lino m (per bambini) nappy; (da donna) sanitary towel

pano'ram|a m panorama; fig overview. ~**ico** adj panoramic

pantacol'lant mpl leggings

pantalon'cini m ~ [corti] shorts

panta'loni mpl trousers, pants Am

pan'tano m bog

pan'tera f panther; (auto della polizia) high-speed police car

pan'tofo|la f slipper

pan'zana f fib

pao'nazzo adj purple

'papa m Pope

papà m inv dad[dy]

pa'pale adj papal

papa'lina f skull-cap

papa'razzo m paparazzo

pa'pato m papacy

pa'pavero m poppy

'paper|a f (errore) slip of the tongue. ~**o** m gosling

papil'lon m inv bow tie

pa'piro m papyrus

'pappa f (per bambini) pap

pappa'gallo m parrot

pappa'molle mf wimp

'para f suole pl di ~ crêpe soles

pa'rabola f parable; (curva) parabola. ~ **satellitare** satellite dish

para'bolico adj parabolic

para'brezza m inv windscreen, windshield Am

paracadu'tar|e vt parachute. ~**si** vr parachute

paraca'du|te m inv parachute. ~**'tista** mf parachutist

para'carro m roadside post

paradi'siaco adj heavenly

para'diso m paradise. ~ **terrestre** Eden, earthly paradise

parados'sale adj paradoxical. pa-ra'dosso m paradox

para'fango m mudguard

paraf'fina f paraffin

parafra'sare vt paraphrase

para'fulmine m lightning-conductor

pa'raggi mpl neighbourhood sg

parago'na|bile adj comparable (a to). ~**re** vt compare. **para'gone** m comparison; **a paragone di** in comparison with

para'grafo m paragraph

pa'ra|lisi f inv paralysis. ~**'litico, -a** adj & mf paralytic. ~**liz'zare** vt paralyse

paral'lel|a f parallel line. ~**a'mente** adv in parallel. ~**o** agg & m parallel; ~**e** pl parallel bars. ~**o'gramma** m parallelogram

para'lume m lampshade

para'medico m paramedic

pa'rametro m parameter

para'noia f paranoia

para'occhi mpl blinkers. **parao'recchie** mpl earmuffs

Paraolim'piadi fpl Paralympic Games

para'petto m parapet

para'piglia m turmoil

para'plegico, -a adj & mf para-plegic

pa'rar|e vt (addobbare) adorn; (ripa-rare) shield; save (tiro, pallone); ward off, parry (schiaffo, pugno) ●vi (mi-rare) lead up to. ~**si** vr (abbigliarsi) dress up; (da pioggia, pugni) protect oneself; ~**si dinanzi a qcno** appear in front of sb

para'sole m inv parasol

paras'sita adj parasitic ●m parasite

parasta'tale adj government-controlled

pa'rata f parade; (in calcio) save; (in scherma, pugilato) parry

para'urti m inv (Auto) bumper, fender Am

para'vento m screen

par'cella f bill

parcheggi'a|re vt park. **par'cheg-gio** m parking; (posteggio) carpark, parking lot Am. ~**'tore, ~'trice** mf parking attendant. ~**tore abusivo** person extorting money for guarding cars

par'chimetro m parking-meter

'parco¹ adj sparing; (moderato) moderate

'parco² m park. ~ **a tema** theme park. ~ **di divertimenti** fun-fair. ~ **giochi** playground. ~ **naturale** wild-life park. ~ **nazionale** national park. ~ **regionale** [regional] wildlife park

pa'recchi adj a good many ●pron several

pa'recchio adj quite a lot of ●pron quite a lot ●adv rather; (parecchio tempo) quite a time

pareggi'a|re vt level; (eguagliare) equal; (Comm) balance ●vi draw

pa'reggio m (Comm) balance; Sport draw

paren'tado m relatives pl; (vincolo di sangue) relationship

pa'rente mf relative. ~ **stretto**

close relation

paren'tela f relatives pl; (vincolo di sangue) relationship

pa'rentesi f inv parenthesis; (segno grafico) bracket; (fig: pausa) break. ∼ pl graffe curly brackets. ∼ quadre square brackets. ∼ tonde round brackets

pa'reo m sarong

pa'rere[1] m opinion; a mio ∼ in my opinion

pa'rere[2] vi seem; (pensare) think; che te ne pare? what do you think of it?; pare di sì it seems so

pa'rete f wall; (in alpinismo) face. ∼ divisoria partition wall

'pari adj inv equal; (numero) even; andare di ∼ passo keep pace; arrivare a ∼ draw; (copiare, ripetere) word for word ● mf inv equal; ragazza alla ∼ au pair [girl] ● m (titolo nobiliare) peer

Pa'rigi f Paris

pa'riglia f pair

pari'tà f equality; Tennis deuce. ∼'tario adj parity attrib

parlamen'tare adj parliamentary ● mf Member of Parliament ● vi discuss. **parla'mento** m Parliament. il Parlamento europeo the European Parliament

par'lare vt/i speak, talk; (confessare) talk; ∼ bene/male di qcno speak well/ill of somebody; non parliamone più let's forget about it; non se ne parla nemmeno! don't even mention it!. ∼to adj (lingua) spoken. ∼'torio m parlour; (in prigione) visiting room

parlot'tare vi mutter. **parlot'tio** m muttering

parmigi'ano m Parmesan

paro'dia f parody

pa'rola f word; (facoltà) speech; parole pl (di canzone) words, lyrics; rivolgere la ∼ a address; dare a qcno la propria ∼ give sb one's

word; **in parole povere** crudely speaking. **parole pl incrociate** cross-word [puzzle] sg. ∼ **d'ordine** password. **paro'laccia** f swear-word

par'quet m inv (pavimento) parquet flooring

par'rocchia f parish. ∼'ale adj parish attrib. ∼'ano, -a mf parishioner. **'parr'oco** m parish priest

par'rucca f wig

parrucchi'ere, -a mf hairdresser

parruc'chino m toupée, hairpiece

parsi'monia f thrift

'parso pp di parere

'parte f part; (lato) side; (partito) party; (porzione) share; **a ∼** apart from; **in ∼** in part; **la maggior ∼** di the majority of; **d'altra ∼** on the other hand; **da ∼** aside; (in disparte) to one side; **farsi da ∼** stand aside; **da ∼ di** from; (per conto di) on behalf of; **è gentile da ∼ tua** it is kind of you; **fare una brutta ∼ a** qcno behave badly towards sb; **da che ∼ è...?** whereabouts is...?; **da una ∼..., dall'altra...** on the one hand..., on the other hand...; **dall'altra ∼ di** on the other side of; **da nessuna ∼** nowhere; **da tutte le parti** (essere) everywhere; **da questa ∼** (in questa direzione) this way; **da un anno a questa ∼** for about a year now; **essere dalla ∼ di** qcno be on sb's side; **essere in ∼ in causa** be involved; **prendere ∼ a** take part in. **∼ civile** plaintiff

parteci'pante mf participant

parteci'pa|re vi ∼re a participate in, take part in; (condividere) share in. ∼zi'one f participation; (annuncio) announcement; Fin shareholding; (presenza) presence. **par'tecipe** adj participating

parteggi'are vi ∼ per side with

par'tenza f departure; Sport start; **in ∼ per** leaving for

parti'cella f particle

parti'cipio m participle

partico'lar|e adj particular; (*privato*) private ●m detail, particular; **fin nei minimi ~i** down to the smallest detail. **~eggia'to** adj detailed. **~ità** f inv particularity; (*dettaglio*) detail

partigi'ano, -a adj & mf partisan

par'tire vi leave; (*aver inizio*) start; **a ~ da** [beginning] from

par'tita f game; (*incontro*) match; (*Comm*) lot; (*contabilità*) entry. **~ di calcio** football match. **~ a carte** game of cards

par'tito m party; (*scelta*) choice; (*occasione di matrimonio*) match

'parto m childbirth; **un ~ facile** an easy birth o labour; **dolori** pl **del ~** labour pains. **~ cesareo** Caesarian section. **~'rire** vt give birth to

par'venza f appearance

parzi'al|e adj partial. **~ità** f partiality. **~'mente** adv (*non completamente*) partially; **~mente scremato** semi-skimmed

pasco'lare vt graze. **'pascolo** m pasture

'Pasqua f Easter. **pa'squale** adj Easter attrib

'passa: **e ~** adv (*e oltre*) plus

pas'sabile adj passable

pas'saggio m passage; (*traversata*) crossing; Sport pass; (*su veicolo*) lift; **essere di ~** be passing through. **~ a livello** level crossing, grade crossing Am. **~ pedonale** pedestrian crossing

pas'sante mf passer-by ●m (*di cintura*) loop ●adj Tennis passing

passa'porto m passport

pas'sa|re vi pass; (*attraversare*) pass through; (*far visita*) call; (*andare*) go; (*essere approvato*) be passed; **~re alla storia** go down in history; **mi è ~to di mente** it slipped my mind; **~re per un genio/idiota** be taken for a genius/an idiot ●vt (*far scorrere*) pass over; (*sopportare*) go through; (*al tele-*

fono) put through; (*Culin*) strain; **~re di moda** go out of fashion; **le passo il signor Rossi** I'll put you through to Mr Rossi; **~rsela bene** be well off; **come te la passi?** how are you doing?. **~ta** f (*di vernice*) coat; (*spolverata*) dusting; (*occhiata*) look

passa'tempo m pastime

pas'sato adj past; **l'anno ~** last year; **sono le tre passate** it's past o after three o'clock ●m past; (*Culin*) purée; (*Gram*) past tense. **~ prossimo** (*Gram*) present perfect. **~ remoto** (*Gram*) [simple] past. **~ di verdure** cream of vegetable soup

passaver'dure m inv food mill

passeg'gero, -a adj passing ●mf passenger

passeggi'a|re vi walk, stroll. **~ta** f walk, stroll; (*luogo*) public walk; (*in bicicletta*) ride; **fare una ~ta** go for a walk

passeg'gino m pushchair, stroller Am

pas'seggio m walk; (*luogo*) promenade; **andare a ~** go for a walk; **scarpe da ~** walking shoes

passe-partout m inv master-key

passe'rella f gangway; (*Aeron*) boarding bridge; (*per sfilate*) catwalk

'passero m sparrow. **passe'rotto** m (*passero*) sparrow

pas'sibile adj **~ di** liable to

passio'nale adj passionate. **pas-si'one** f passion

pas'sivo adj passive ●m passive; (*Comm*) liabilities pl; **in ~** (*bilancio*) loss-making

pass magnetico m inv swipe card

'passo m step; (*orma*) footprint; (*andatura*) pace; (*brano*) passage; (*valico*) pass; **a due passi da qui** a stone's throw away; **a ~ d'uomo** at walking pace; **fare due passi** go for a stroll; **di pari ~** fig hand in hand. **~ carrabile**, **~ carraio** driveway

p

'past|a f (impasto per pane ecc) dough; (per dolci, pasticcini) pastry; (pastasciutta) pasta; (massa molle) paste; fig nature. ~a frolla shortcrust pastry. pa'stella f batter

Pasta A popular myth says that Marco Polo brought pasta back from China. Italians like to make their own pasta for special occasions (pasta fatta in casa), usually with eggs and sometimes with various fillings. Traditional pasta varies enormously from region to region, and sometimes the same name can be used for different types.

pastasci'utta f pasta
pa'stello m pastel
pa'sticca f pastille; (📱: pastiglia) pill
pasticc|e'ria f cake shop, patisserie; (pasticcini) pastries pl; (arte) confectionery
pasticci'are vi make a mess ● vt make a mess of
pasticci'ere, -a mf confectioner
pastic'cino m little cake
pa'sticci|o m (Culin) pie; (lavoro disordinato) mess. ~one, -a mf bungler ● adj bungling
pasti'ficio m pasta factory
pa'stiglia f (Med) pill, tablet; (di menta) sweet. ~ dei freni brake pad
'pasto m meal
pasto'rale adj pastoral. pa'store m shepherd; (Relig) pastor. pastore tedesco German shepherd
pastoriz'za|re vt pasteurize. ~zi'one f pasteurization
pa'stoso adj doughy; fig mellow
pa'stura f pasture; (per pesci) bait
pa'tacca f (macchia) stain; (fig: oggetto senza valore) piece of junk
pa'tata f potato. patate pl fritte chips Br, French fries. pata'tine fpl [potato] crisps, chips Am

pata'trac m inv (crollo) crash
pâté m inv pâté
pa'tella f limpet
pa'tema m anxiety
pa'tente f licence. ~ di guida driving licence
pater'na|le f scolding. ~lista m paternalist
paternità f paternity. pa'terno adj paternal; (affetto ecc) fatherly
pa'tetico adj pathetic. 'pathos m pathos
pa'tibolo m gallows sg
'patina f patina; (sulla lingua) coating
pa'ti|re vt/i suffer. ~to, -a adj suffering ● mf fanatic. ~to della musica music lover
patolo'gia f pathology. pato'logico adj pathological
'patria f native land
patri'arca m patriarch
pa'trigno m stepfather
patrimoni'ale adj property attrib. patri'monio m estate
patri'o|ta mf patriot
pa'trizio, -a adj & mf patrician
patro|ci'nare vt support. ~cinio m support
patro'nato m patronage. pa'trono m (Relig) patron saint; (Jur) counsel
'patta¹ f (di tasca) flap
'patta² f (pareggio) draw
patteggia'mento m bargaining. ~are vt/i negotiate
patti'naggio m skating. ~ su ghiaccio ice skating. ~ a rotelle roller skating
patti'na|re vi skate; (auto): skid. ~tore, ~trice mf skater. 'pattino m skate; (Aeron) skid. pattino da ghiaccio iceskate. pattino a rotelle roller skate; pattini mpl in linea roller blades®.
'patto m deal; (Pol) pact; a ~ che on condition that

pat'tuglia f patrol. ~ **stradale** patrol car; highway patrol

pattu'ire vt negotiate

pattumi'era f dustbin, trashcan Am

pa'ura f fear; (spavento) fright; **aver** ~ **be** afraid; **mettere** ~ **a** frighten. **pau'roso** adj (che fa paura) frightening; (che ha paura) fearful; (①: enorme) awesome

'pausa f pause; (nel lavoro) break; **fare una** ~ pause; (nel lavoro) have a break

pavimen'ta|re vt pave (strada). ~**zi'one** f (operazione) paving. **pavi'mento** m floor

pa'vone m peacock

pazien'tare vi be patient

pazi'ente adj & mf patient. ~**'mente** adv patiently. **pazi'enza** f patience

'pazza f madwoman. ~**'mente** adv madly

paz'z|esco adj foolish; (esagerato) crazy. ~**ia** f madness; (azione) [act of] folly. **'pazzo** adj mad; fig crazy ● m madman; **essere pazzo di/per** be crazy about; **darsi alla pazza gioia** live it up. **paz'zoide** adj whacky

'pecca f fault; **senza** ~ flawless. **peccami'noso** adj sinful

pec'ca|re vi sin; ~**re di** be guilty of (ingratitudine). ~**to** m sin; ~**to che...** it's a pity that...; **[che]** ~**to!** [what a] pity!. ~**'tore**, ~**'trice** mf sinner

'pece f pitch

'peco|ra f sheep. ~**ra nera** black sheep. ~**raio** m shepherd. ~**rella** f **cielo a** ~**relle** sky full of fluffy white clouds. ~**rino** m (formaggio) sheep's milk cheese

peculi'ar|e adj ~ **di** peculiar to. ~**ità** f inv peculiarity

pe'daggio m toll

pedago'gia f pedagogy. **peda'gogico** adj pedagogical

peda'lare vi pedal. **pe'dale** m pedal. **pedalò** m inv pedalo

pe'dana f footrest; Sport springboard

pe'dante adj pedantic. ~**'ria** f pedantry. **pedan'tesco** adj pedantic

pe'data f (in calcio) kick; (impronta) footprint

pede'rasta m pederast

pe'destre adj pedestrian

pedi'atra mf paediatrician. **pedia'tria** f paediatrics sg

pedi'cure mf inv chiropodist, podiatrist Am ● m pedicure

pedi'gree m inv pedigree

pe'dina f (nella dama) piece; fig pawn. ~**'mento** m shadowing. **pedi'nare** vt shadow

pe'dofilo, -a mf paedophile

pedo'nale adj pedestrian. **pe'done, -a** mf pedestrian

peeling m inv exfoliation treatment

'peggio adv worse; ~ **per te!** too bad!; **la persona** ~ **vestita** the worst dressed person ● adj worse, **niente di** ~ nothing worse ● m il ~ **è che...** the worst of it is that...; **pensare al** ~ think the worst ● f **alla** ~ at worst; **avere la** ~ get the worst of it; **alla meno** ~ as best I can

peggiora'mento m worsening

peggio'ra|re vt make worse, worsen ● vi get worse. ~**'tivo** adj pejorative

peggi'ore adj worse; (superlativo) worst ● mf **il/la** ~ the worst

'pegno m pledge; (nei giochi di società) forfeit; fig token

pelan'drone m slob

pe'la|re vt (spennare) pluck; (spellare) skin; (sbucciare) peel; (①: spillare denaro) fleece. ~**rsi** vr ① lose one's hair. ~**to** adj bald. ~**ti** mpl (pomodori) peeled tomatoes

pel'lame m skins pl

P

'pelle f skin; (cuoio) leather; (buccia) peel; avere la ~ d'oca have goose-flesh

pellegri'naggio m pilgrimage. **pelle'grino, -a** mf pilgrim

pelle'rossa mf Red Indian

pellette'ria f leather goods pl

pelli'cano m pelican

pellic'c|eria f furrier's [shop]. **pel-lic'ci|a** f fur; (indumento) fur coat. **~i'aio, -a** mf furrier

pel'licola f film. ~ [trasparente] cling film

'pelo m hair; (di animale) coat; (di lana) pile; per un ~ by the skin of one's teeth. **pe'loso** adj hairy

'peltro m pewter

pe'luche m: giocattolo di ~ soft toy

pe'luria f down

pelvico adj pelvic

'pena f (punizione) punishment; (sofferenza) pain; (dispiacere) sorrow; (disturbo) trouble; a mala ~ hardly; mi fa ~ I pity him; vale la ~ andare it is worth [while] going. ~ di morte death sentence

pe'nal|e adj criminal; diritto m ~e criminal law. **~ità** f inv penalty

penaliz'za|re vt penalize. **~zi'one** f (penalità) penalty

pe'nare vi suffer; (faticare) find it difficult

pen'daglio m pendant

pen'dant m inv fare ~ [con] match

pen'den|te adj hanging; (Comm) outstanding ● m (ciondolo) pendant; **~ti** pl drop earrings. **~za** f slope; (Comm) outstanding account

'pendere vi hang; (superficie:) slope; (essere inclinato) lean

pen'dio m slope; in ~ sloping

pendo'l|are adj pendulum ● mf commuter. **~ino** m (treno) special, first class only, fast train

'pendolo m pendulum

'pene m penis

pene'trante adj penetrating; (freddo) biting

pene'tra|re vt/i penetrate; (trafiggere) pierce ● vt (odore:) get into ● vi (entrare furtivamente) steal in. **~zi'one** f penetration

penicil'lina f penicillin

pe'nisola f peninsula

peni'ten|te adj & mf penitent. **~za** f penitence; (in gioco) forfeit. **~zi'ario** m penitentiary

'penna f pen; (di uccello) feather. ~ a feltro felt-tip[ped pen]. ~ a sfera ball-point [pen]

pen'nacchio m plume

penna'rello m felt-tip[ped pen]

pennel'la|re vt paint. **~ta** f brushstroke. **pen'nello** m brush; a pennello (alla perfezione) perfectly

pen'nino m nib

pen'none m flagpole

pen'nuto adj feathered

pe'nombra f half-light

pe'noso adj (Ⓘ: pessimo) painful

pen'sa|re vi think; penso di sì I think so; ~re a think of; remember to (chiudere il gas ecc); ci penso io I'll take care of it; ~re di fare qcsa think of doing sth; ~re tra sé e sé think to oneself ● vt think. **~ta** f idea

pensi'e|ro m thought; (mente) mind; (preoccupazione) worry; stare in ~ro per be anxious about. **~'roso** adj pensive

'pensi|le adj hanging; giardino ~le roof-garden ● m (mobile) wall unit. **~'lina** f bus shelter

pensio'nante mf boarder; (ospite pagante) lodger

pensio'nato, -a mf pensioner ● m (per anziani) [old folks'] home; (per studenti) hostel. **pensi'one** f pension; (albergo) boarding-house; (vitto e alloggio) board and lodging; andare in

pensione retire; **mezza pensione** half board. **pensione completa** full board

pen'soso adj pensive

pen'tagono m pentagon

Pente'coste f Whitsun

pen'ti|rsi vr ∼rsi di repent of; (*rammaricarsi*) regret. ∼'tismo m turning informant. ∼to m Mafioso turned informant

'pentola f saucepan; (*contenuto*) potful. ∼ **a pressione** pressure cooker

pe'nultimo adj penultimate

pe'nuria f shortage

penzo'l|are vi dangle. ∼**oni** adv dangling

pe'pa|re vt pepper. ∼**to** adj peppery

'pepe m pepper; **grano di** ∼ peppercorn. ∼ **in grani** whole peppercorns. ∼ **macinato** ground pepper

pepero'n|ata f peppers cooked in olive oil with onion, tomato and garlic. ∼'**cino** m chilli pepper. **pepe'rone** m pepper. **peperone verde** green pepper

pe'pita f nugget

per prep for; (*attraverso*) through; (*stato in luogo*) in, on; (*distributivo*) per; (*mezzo, entro*) by; (*causa*) with; (*in qualità di*) as; ∼ **strada** on the street; ∼ **la fine del mese** by the end of the month; **in fila** ∼ **due** in double file; **l'ho sentito** ∼ **telefono** I spoke to him on the phone; ∼ **iscritto** in writing; ∼ **caso** by chance; **ho aspettato** ∼ **ore** I've been waiting for hours; ∼ **tempo** in time; ∼ **sempre** forever; ∼ **scherzo** as a joke; **gridare** ∼ **il dolore** scream with pain; **vendere** ∼ **10 milioni** sell for 10 million; **uno** ∼ **volta** one at a time; **uno** ∼ **uno** one by one; **venti** ∼ **cento** twenty per cent; ∼ **fare qcsa** [in order to] do sth; **stare** ∼ be about to

'pera f pear; **farsi una** ∼ (⊞: **di** eroina) shoot up

per'cento adv per cent. **percentu'ale** f percentage

perce'pibile adj perceivable; (somma) payable

perce'pi|re vt perceive; (*riscuotere*) cash

perce't|tibile adj perceptible. ∼**zi'one** f perception

perché conj (*in interrogazioni*) why; (*per il fatto che*) because; (*affinché*) so that; ∼ **non vieni?** why don't you come?; **dimmi** ∼ tell me why; ∼ **no/sì!** because!; **la ragione** ∼ **l'ho fatto** the reason [that] I did it, the reason why I did it; **è troppo difficile** ∼ **lo possa capire** it's too difficult for me to understand ●m inv reason [why]; **senza un** ∼ without any reason

perciò conj so

per'correre vt cover (distanza); (*viaggiare*) travel. **per'corso** pp di **percorrere** ●m (*distanza*) distance; (*viaggio*) journey

per'coss|a f blow. ∼**o** pp di percuotere. **percu'otere** vt strike

percussi'o|ne f percussion; **strumenti** pl a ∼**ne** percussion instruments. ∼'**nista** mf percussionist

per'dente mf loser

'perder|e vt lose; (sprecare) waste; (non prendere) miss; fig: ruin (vizio); ∼**e tempo** waste time ● vi (recipiente): leak; **lascia** ∼**e!** forget it!. ∼**si** vr get lost; (reciproco) lose touch

perdigi'orno mf inv idler

'perdita f loss; (spreco) waste; (falla) leak; **a** ∼ **d'occhio** as far as the eye can see. ∼ **di tempo** waste of time. **perdi'tempo** m time-waster

perdo'nare vt forgive; (scusare) excuse. **per'dono** m forgiveness; (Jur) pardon

perdu'rare vi last; (perseverare) persist

perduta'mente adv hopelessly. **per'duto** pp di **perdere** ●adj lost; (rovinato) ruined

pe'renne adj everlasting; (Bot) perennial. ~'mente adv perpetually

peren'torio adj peremptory

per'fetto adj perfect ● m (Gram) perfect [tense]

perfezio'nar|e vt perfect; (migliorare) improve. ~**si** vr improve oneself; (specializzarsi) specialize

perfezi'o|ne f perfection; **alla** ~**ne** to perfection. ~**'nista** mf perfectionist

per'fidia f wickedness; (atto) wicked act. **'perfido** adj treacherous; (malvagio) perverse

per'fino adv even

perfo'ra|re vt pierce; punch (schede); (Mech) drill. ~**'tore, ~'trice** mf punch-card operator ● m perforator. ~**zi'one** f perforation; (di schede) punching

per'formance f inv performance

perga'mena f parchment

perico'lante adj precarious; (azienda) shaky

pe'rico|lo m danger; (rischio) risk; **mettere in** ~**lo** endanger. ~**'loso** adj dangerous

perife'ria f periphery; (di città) outskirts pl; fig fringes pl

peri'feric|a f peripheral; (strada) ring road. ~**o** adj (quartiere) outlying

pe'rifrasi f inv circumlocution

pe'rimetro m perimeter

peri'odico m periodical ● adj periodical; (vento, mal di testa) (Math) recurring. **pe'riodo** m period; (Gram) sentence. **periodo di prova** trial period

peripe'zie fpl misadventures

pe'rire vi perish

pe'ri|to, -a adj skilled ● mf expert

perito'nite f peritonitis

pe'rizia f skill; (valutazione) survey

'perla f pearl. **per'lina** f bead

perlo'meno adv at least

perlu'stra|re vt patrol. ~**zi'one** f patrol; **andare in** ~**zione** go on patrol

perma'loso adj touchy

perma'ne|nte adj permanent ● f perm; **farsi [fare] la** ~**nte** have a perm. ~**nza** f permanence; (soggiorno) stay; **in** ~**nza** permanently. ~**re** vi remain

perme'are vt permeate

per'messo pp di **permettere** ● m permission; (autorizzazione) permit; (Mil) leave; **[è]** ~**?** (posso entrare?) may I come in?; (posso passare?) excuse me. ~ **di lavoro** work permit

per'mettere vt allow, permit; **potersi** ~ qcsa (finanziariamente) afford sth; **come si permette?** how dare you?

permutazi'one f exchange; (Math) permutation

per'nic|e f partridge. ~**i'oso** adj pernicious

'perno m pivot

pernot'tare vi stay overnight

'pero m pear-tree

però conj but; (tuttavia) however

pero'rare vt plead

perpendico'lare adj & f perpendicular

perpe'trare vt perpetrate

perpetu'are vt perpetuate. **per'petuo** adj perpetual

perplessità f inv perplexity; (dubbio) doubt. **per'plesso** adj perplexed

perqui'si|re vt search. ~**zi'one** f search. ~**zione domiciliare** search of the premises

persecu'|tore, -'trice mf persecutor. ~**zi'one** f persecution

persegu'ire vt pursue

persegui'tare vt persecute

perseve'ra|nza f perseverance. ~**re** vi persevere

persi'ano, -a adj Persian ● f (di finestra) shutter. **'persico** adj Persian

per'sino adv = PERFINO

persi'sten|te adj persistent. **∼za** f persistence. **per'sistere** vi persist

'perso pp di perdere ●adj lost; **a tempo ∼** in one's spare time

per'sona f person; (un tale) somebody; **di ∼, in ∼** in person, personally; **per ∼** per person, a head; **per interposta ∼** through an intermediary; **persone** pl people

perso'naggio m personality; (Theat) character

perso'nal|e adj personal ●m staff. **∼e di terra** ground crew. **∼ità** f inv personality. **∼iz'zare** vt customize (auto ecc); personalize (penna ecc)

personifi'ca|re vt personify. **∼zi'one** f personification

perspi'cace adj shrewd

persua'|dere vt convince; impress (critici); **∼dere qcno a fare qcsa** persuade sb to do sth. **∼si'one** f persuasion. **∼sivo** adj persuasive. **persu'aso** pp di persuadere

per'tanto conj therefore

'pertica f pole

perti'nente adj relevant

per'tosse f whooping cough

pertur'ba|re vt perturb. **∼rsi** vr be perturbed. **∼zi'one** f disturbance. **∼zione atmosferica** atmospheric disturbance

per'va|dere vt pervade. **∼so** pp di pervadere

perve'nire vi reach; **far ∼ qcsa a qcno** send sth to sb

pervers|i'one f perversion. **∼ità** f perversity. **per'verso** adj perverse

perver'ti|re vt pervert. **∼to** adj perverted ●m pervert

per'vinca m (colore) blue with a touch of purple

p.es. abbr (per esempio) e.g.

pesa f weighing; (bilancia) weighing machine; (per veicoli) weighbridge

pe'sante adj heavy; (stomaco) overfull ●adv (vestirsi) warmly. **∼'mente** adv (cadere) heavily. **pesan'tezza** f heaviness

pe'sar|e vt/i weigh; **∼e su** fig lie heavy on; **∼e le parole** weigh one's words. **∼si** vr weigh oneself

'pesca' f (frutto) peach

'pesca² f fishing; **andare a ∼** go fishing. **∼ subacquea** underwater fishing. **pe'scare** vt fish for; (prendere) catch; (fig: trovare) fish out. **∼'tore** m fisherman

'pesce m fish. **∼ d'aprile!** April Fool!. **∼ grosso** fig big fish. **∼ piccolo** fig small fry. **∼ rosso** goldfish. **∼ spada** swordfish. **Pesci** pl (Astr) Pisces

pesce'cane m shark

pesche'reccio m fishing boat

pesc|he'ria f fishmonger's [shop]. **∼hi'era** f fish-pond. **∼i'vendolo** m fishmonger

'pesco m peach-tree

'peso m weight; **essere di ∼ per qcno** be a burden to sb; **di poco ∼** (senza importanza) not very important

pessi'mis|mo m pessimism. **∼ta** mf pessimist ●adj pessimistic. **'pes'simo** adj very bad

pe'staggio m beating-up. **pe'stare** vt tread on; (schiacciare) crush; (picchiare) beat; crush (aglio, prezzemolo)

'peste f plague; (persona) pest

pe'stello m pestle

pesti'cida m pesticide

pesti'len|za f pestilence; (fetore) stench. **∼zi'ale** adj noxious

'pesto adj ground; **occhio ∼** black eye ●m basil and garlic sauce

'petalo m petal

pe'tardo m banger

petizi'one f petition; **fare una ∼** draw up a petition

petro|li'era f [oil] tanker. **∼'lifero** adj oil-bearing. **pe'trolio** m oil

pettego'lare vi gossip. **∼'lezzo** m piece of gossip; **far ∼lezzi** gossip

pet'tegolo, -a adj gossipy ●mf

P

gossip

petti'na|re vt comb. **~rsi** vr comb one's hair. **~'tura** f combing; (acconciatura) hair-style. **'pettine** m comb

'petting m petting

petti'nino m (fermaglio) comb

petti'rosso m robin

'petto m chest; (seno) breast; a doppio ~ double-breasted

petto'rale m (in gare sportive) number. **~'rina** f (di salopette) bib. **~'ruto** adj (donna) full-breasted; (uomo) broad-chested

petu'lante adj impertinent

'pezza f cloth; (toppa) patch; (rotolo di tessuto) roll

pez'zente mf tramp; (avaro) miser

'pezzo m piece; (parte) part; un ~ (di tempo) some time; (di spazio) a long way; al ~ (costare) each; fare a pezzi tear to shreds. ~ **grosso** bigwig

pia'cente adj attractive

---

pia|ce|re

● m pleasure; (favore) favour; a ~re as much as one likes; per ~re! please!; ~re [di conoscerla]! pleased to meet you!; con ~re with pleasure

● vi la Scozia mi piace I like Scotland; mi piacciono i dolci I like sweets; ti piace? do you like it?; faccio come mi pare e piace I do as I please; lo spettacolo è piaciuto the show was a success.

Nota che il soggetto in italiano corrisponde al complemento oggetto in inglese, mentre il complemento indiretto in italiano corrisponde al soggetto in inglese: **Non mi piace** I don't like it

---

pia'vole adj pleasant

piaci'mento m a ~ as much as you like

pia'dina f unleavened bread

pi'aga f sore; scourge; (persona noiosa) pain; (fig: ricordo doloroso) wound

piagni'steo m whining

piagnuco'lare v whimper

pi'alla f plane. **pial'lare** vt plane

pi'ana f plane. **pianeggi'ante** adj level

piane'rottolo m landing

pia'neta m planet

pi'angere vi cry; (disperatamente) weep ● vt (lamentare) lament; (per un lutto) mourn

pianifi'ca|re vt plan. **~zi'one** f planning

pia'nista mf (Mus) pianist

pi'ano adj flat; (a livello) flush; (regolare) smooth; (facile) easy ● adv slowly; (con cautela) gently; **andarci** ~ go carefully ● m plain; (di edificio) floor; (livello) plane; (progetto) plan; (Mus) piano; di primo ~ first-rate; primo ~ (Phot) close-up; in primo ~ in the foreground. ~ **regolatore** town plan. ~ **di studi** syllabus

piano'forte m piano. ~ **a coda** grand piano

piano'terra m inv ground floor

pi'anta f plant; (del piede) sole; (disegno) plan; di sana ~ (totalmente) entirely; in ~ **stabile** permanently. ~ **stradale** road map. **~gi'one** f plantation

pian'tar|e vt plant; (conficcare) drive; (ﬁ: abbandonare) dump; **piantala!** ﬁ stop it!. **~si** vr plant oneself; (ﬁ: lasciarsi) leave each other

pianter'reno m ground floor

pi'anto pp di piangere ● m crying; (disperato) weeping; (lacrime) tears pl

pian'to'nare vt guard. **~'tone** m guard

pia'nura f plain

p'iastra f plate; (lastra) slab; (Culin) griddle. ~ **elettronica** circuit board. ~ **madre** (Comput) motherboard

pia'strella f tile

pia'strina f (Mil) identity disc; (Med) platelet; (Comput) chip

piatta'forma f platform. ~ **di lancio** launch pad

piat'tino m saucer

pi'atto adj flat ● m plate; (da portata, vivanda) dish; (portata) course; (parte piatta) flat; (di giradischi) turntable; **piatti** pl (Mus) cymbals; **lavare i piatti** do the washing-up. ~ **fondo** soup plate. ~ **piano** [ordinary] plate

pi'azza f square; (Comm) market; **letto a una** ~ single bed; **letto a due piazze** double bed; **far** ~ **pulita** make a clean sweep. ~**forte** m stronghold. **piaz'zale** m large square. ~**mento** m (in classifica) placing

piaz'za|re vt place. ~**rsi** vr Sport be placed. ~**rsi secondo** come second. ~**to** adj (cavallo) placed; **ben** ~**to** (robusto) well built

piaz'zista m salesman

piaz'zuola f ~ **di sosta** pull-in

pic'cante adj hot; (pungente) sharp; (salace) spicy

pic'carsi vr (risentirsi) take offence; ~ **di** (vantarsi) claim to

'picche fpl (in carte) spades

picchet'tare vt stake; (scioperanti:) picket. **pic'chetto** m picket

picchi'a|re vt beat, hit ● vi (bussare) knock; (Aeron) nosedive; ~**re in testa** (motore:) knock. ~**ta** f beating; (Aeron) nosedive; **scendere in** ~**ta** nosedive

picchiet'tare vt tap; (punteggiare) spot

'picchio m woodpecker

pic'cino adj tiny; (gretto) mean; (di poca importanza) petty ● m little one, child

picci'one m pigeon

'picco m peak; **a** ~ vertically; **colare a** ~ sink

'piccolo, -a adj small, little; (di età) young; (di statura) short; (gretto) petty ● mf child; **da** ~ as a child

pic'co|ne m pickaxe. ~**zza** f ice axe

pic'nic m inv picnic

pi'docchio m louse

piè m inv **a** ~ **di pagina** at the foot of the page; **saltare a** ~ **pari** skip

pi'ede m foot; **a piedi** on foot; **andare a piedi** walk; **a piedi nudi** barefoot; **in** ~ **libero** free; **in piedi** standing; **alzarsi in piedi** stand up; **ai piedi di** (montagna) at the foot of; **prendere** ~ fig gain ground; (moda:) catch on; **mettere in piedi** (allestire) set up

piedi'stallo m pedestal

pi'e|ga f (piegatura) fold; (di gonna) pleat; (di pantaloni) crease; (grinza) wrinkle; (andamento) turn; **non fare una** ~ (ragionamento:) be flawless

pie'ga|re vt fold; (flettere) bend ● vi bend. ~**rsi** vr bend. ~**rsi a** fig yield to. ~**tura** f folding

pieghet'tare vt pleat. ~**to** adj pleated. **pie'ghevole** adj pliable; (tavolo) folding ● m leaflet

piemon'tese adj Piedmontese

pi'en|a f (di fiume) flood; (folla) crowd. ~**o** adj full; (massiccio) solid; **in** ~**a estate** in the middle of summer; **a** ~**i voti** (diplomarsi) ≈ with A-grades, with first class honours ● m (colmo) height; (carico) full load; **in** ~**o** (completamente) fully; **fare il** ~**o** (di benzina) fill up

pie'none m **c'era il** ~ the place was packed

'piercing m inv body piercing

pietà f pity; (misericordia) mercy; **senza** ~ (persona) pitiless; (spietatamente) pitilessly; **avere** ~ **di qcno** take pity on sb; **far** ~ (far pena) be pitiful

pie'tanza f dish

pie'toso adj pitiful, merciful; (*pessimo*) terrible

pi'etr|a f stone. ~a dura semi-precious stone. ~a preziosa precious stone. ~a dello scandalo cause of the scandal. pie'trame m stones pl. ~ifi'care vt petrify. pie'trina f flint. pie'troso adj stony

pigi'ama m pyjamas pl

'pigia 'pigia m inv crowd, crush. pigi'are vt press

pigi'one f rent; dare a ~ let, rent out; prendere a ~ rent

pigli'are vt (🔲 : *afferrare*) catch. 'piglio m air

pig'mento m pigment

'pigna f cone

pi'gnolo adj pedantic

pigo'lare vi chirp. pigo'lio m chirping

pi'grizia f laziness. 'pigro adj lazy; (*intelletto*) slow

'pila f pile; (*Electr*) battery; (🔲 : *lampadina tascabile*) torch; (*vasca*) basin; a pile battery powered

pi'lastro m pillar

'pillola f pill; prendere la ~ be on the pill

pi'lone m pylon; (*di ponte*) pier

pi'lota mf pilot ● m (Auto) driver. pi'lotare vt pilot; drive (auto)

pinaco'teca f art gallery

pi'neta f pine-wood

ping-'pong m table tennis, ping-pong 🔲

'pingue adj fat. ~'edine f fatness

pingu'ino m penguin; (*gelato*) choc ice on a stick

'pinna f fin; (*per nuotare*) flipper

'pino m pine[-tree]; ~ marittimo cluster pine. pi'nolo m pine kernel

'pinta f pint

'pinza f pliers pl; (*Med*) forceps pl

pin'za|re vt (*con pinzatrice*) staple. ~'trice f stapler

pin'zette fpl tweezers pl

pinzi'monio m sauce for crudités

'pio adj pious; (*benefico*) charitable

pi'oggia f rain; (*fig: di pietre, insulti*) hail, shower; sotto la ~ in the rain. ~ acida acid rain

pi'olo m (*di scala*) rung

piom'ba|re vi fall heavily; ~re su fall upon ● vt fill (dente). ~'tura f (*di dente*) filling. piom'bino m (*sigillo*) [lead] seal; (*da pesca*) sinker; (*in gonne*) weight

pi'ombo m lead; (*sigillo*) [lead] seal; a ~ plumb; senza ~ (*benzina*) lead-free

pioni'ere, -a mf pioneer

pi'oppo m poplar

pio'vano adj acqua piovana rainwater

pi'ov|ere vi rain; ~e it's raining; ~iggi'nare vi drizzle. pio'voso adj rainy

'pipa f pipe

pipì f fare [la] ~ pee

pipi'strello m bat

pi'ramide f pyramid

pi'ranha m inv piranha

pi'rat|a m pirate. ~a della strada road-hog ● adj inv pirate. ~e'ria f piracy

pi'rofil|la f (*tegame*) oven-proof dish. ~o adj heat-resistant

pi'romane mf pyromaniac

pi'roscafo m steamer. ~ di linea liner

pi'scina f swimming pool. ~ coperta indoor swimming pool. ~ scoperta outdoor swimming pool

pi'sello m pea; (🔲 : *pene*) willie

piso'lino m nap; fare un ~ have a nap

'pista f track; (*Aeron*) runway; (*orma*) footprint; (*sci*) slope, piste. ~ d'atterraggio airstrip. ~ da ballo dance floor. ~ ciclabile cycle track

pi'stacchio m pistachio

pi'stola f pistol; (*per spruzzare*) spray-gun. ~ **a spruzzo** paint spray

pi'stone m piston

pi'tone m python

pit'to|re, -'trice mf painter. ~**'resco** adj picturesque. **pit'torico** adj pictorial

pit'tu|ra f painting. ~**'rare** vt paint

---

più

● adv more; (*superlativo*) most

Il comparativo e il superlativo di aggettivi di una sillaba o che terminano in -y si formano con i suffissi -er e -est: **più breve** shorter **il più giovane** the youngest

~ **importante** more important; **il ~ importante** the most important; ~ **caro** more expensive; **il ~ caro** the most expensive; **di ~** more; **una coperta in ~** an extra blanket; **non ho ~ soldi** I don't have any more money; **non vive ~ a Milano** he doesn't live in Milan any longer; ~ **o meno** more or less; **il ~ lentamente possibile** as slowly as possible; **per di ~** what's more; **mai ~!** never again!; ~ **di** more than; **sempre ~** more and more; (*Math*) plus

● adj more; (*superlativo*) most; ~ **tempo** more time; **la classe con ~ alunni** the class with most pupils; ~ **volte** several times

● m most; (*Math*) plus sign; **il ~ è fatto** the worst is over; **parlare del ~ e del meno** make small talk; **i ~** the majority

---

piuccheper'fetto m pluperfect

pi'uma f feather. **piu'maggio** m plumage. **piu'mino** m (*di cigni*) down; (*copriletto*) eiderdown; (*per cipria*) powder-puff; (*per spolverare*) feather duster; (*giacca*) down jacket. **piu-'mone®** m duvet

piut'tosto adv rather; (*invece*) instead

pi'vello m 🄵 greenhorn

'pizza f pizza; *Cinema* reel.

pizzai'ola f slices of beef in tomato sauce, oregano and anchovies

pizze'ria f pizza restaurant

pizzi'c|are vt pinch; (*pungere*) sting; (*di sapore*) taste sharp; (🄵: *sorprendere*) catch; (*Mus*) pluck ● vi scratch; (*cibo:*) be spicy **'pizzico** m, ~**otto** m pinch

'pizzo m lace; (*di montagna*) peak

pla'car|e vt placate; assuage (*fame, dolore*). ~**si** vr calm down

'placca f plate; (*commemorativa, dentale*) plaque; (*Med*) patch

plac'ca|re vt plate. ~**to** adj ~**to d'argento** silver-plated. ~**to d'oro** gold-plated. ~**tura** f plating

pla'centa f placenta

'placido adj placid

plagi'are vt plagiarize; pressure (*persona*). **'plagio** m plagiarism

plaid m inv tartan rug

pla'nare vi glide

'plancia f (*Naut*) bridge; (*passerella*) gangplank

pla'smare vt mould

'plastic|a f (*arte*) plastic art; (*Med*) plastic surgery; (*materia*) plastic. ~**o** adj plastic ● m plastic model

'platano m plane[-tree]

pla'tea f stalls pl; (*pubblico*) audience

'platino m platinum

plau'sibil|e adj plausible. ~**ità** f plausibility

ple'baglia f pej mob

pleni'lunio m full moon

'plettro m plectrum

pleu'rite f pleurisy

'plico m packet; **in ~ a parte** under separate cover

plissé adj inv plissé; (gonna) accordeon-pleated

plo'tone m platoon; (di ciclisti) group. ~ **d'esecuzione** firing-squad

'plumbeo adj leaden

plu'ral|e adj & m plural; **al ~e** in the plural. ~**ità** f majority

pluridiscipli'nare adj multidisciplinary

plurien'nale adj ~ **esperienza** many years' experience

pluripar'titico adj (Pol) multi-party

plu'tonio m plutonium

pluvi'ale adj rain attrib

pneu'matico adj pneumatic ● m tyre

pneu'monia f pneumonia

po' ▷**POCO**

po'chette f inv clutch bag

po'chino m **un ~ a** little bit

'poco

● adj little; (tempo) short; (con nomi plurali) few

● adv (con verbi) not much; (con avverbi) not very; **parla ~** he doesn't speak much; **lo conosco ~** I don't know him very well

poco + aggettivo spesso si traduce con un aggettivo specifico: ~ **probabile** unlikely, ~ **profondo** shallow

● pron little; (poco tempo) a short time; (plurale) few

● m little; **un po'** a little [bit]; **un po' di** a little, some; **a ~ a ~** little by little; **fra ~** soon; **per ~** (a poco prezzo) cheap; (quasi) nearly; **lo ~ fa** a little while ago; **sono arrivato da ~** I have just arrived; **un bel po'** quite a lot

---

po'dere m farm

pode'roso adj powerful

'podio m dais; (Mus) podium

po'dis|mo m walking. ~**ta** mf walker

po'e|ma m poem. ~**sia** f poetry; (componimento) poem. ~**ta** m poet. ~**tessa** f poetess. ~**tico** adj poetic

poggiapi'edi m inv footrest

poggi'a|re vt lean; (posare) place ● vi ~**re su** be based on. ~'**testa** m inv head-rest

poggi'olo m balcony

'poi adv (dopo) then; (più tardi) later [on]; (finalmente) finally. **d'ora in ~** from now on; **questa ~!** well!

poiché conj since

pois m inv **a ~** polka-dot

'poker m poker

po'lacco, -a adj Polish ● mf Pole ● m (lingua) Polish

po'lar|e adj polar. ~**iz'zare** vt polarize

'polca f polka

po'lemi|ca f controversy. ~**ca-'mente** adv controversially. ~**co** adj controversial. ~**z'zare** vi engage in controversy

po'lenta f cornmeal porridge

poli'clinico m general hospital

poli'estere m polyester

polio[mie'lite] f polio[myelitis]

'polipo m polyp

polisti'rolo m polystyrene

poli'tecnico m polytechnic

po'litic|a f politics sg; (linea di condotta) policy; **fare ~a** be in politics. ~**iz'zare** vt politicize. ~**o, -a** adj political ● mf politician

poliva'lente adj catch-all

poli'zi|a f police. ~**a giudiziaria** ≈ Criminal Investigation Department. ~**a stradale** traffic police. ~**'esco** adj police attrib; (romanzo, film) detective attrib. ~'**otto** m policeman

'polizza f policy

pol'la|io m chicken run; (🄸: *luogo chiassoso*) mad house. ∼me m poultry. ∼**'strello** m spring chicken. ∼stro m cockerel

'pollice m thumb; (*unità di misura*) inch

'polline m pollen; **allergia al** ∼ hay fever

polli'vendolo, -a mf poulterer

'pollo m chicken; (🄸: *semplicione*) simpleton

polmo|'nare adj pulmonary. **pol'mone** m lung. ∼**'nite** f pneumonia

'polo m pole; *Sport* polo; (*maglietta*) polo top. ∼ **nord** North Pole. ∼ **sud** South Pole

Po'lonia f Poland

'polpa f pulp

pol'paccio m calf

polpa'strello m fingertip

pol'pet|ta f meatball. ∼**'tone** m meat loaf

'polpo m octopus

pol'sino m cuff

'polso m pulse; (*Anat*) wrist; *fig* authority; **avere** ∼ be strict

pol'tiglia f mush

pol'trire vi lie around

pol'tron|a f armchair; (*Theat*) seat in the stalls. ∼**e** adj lazy

'polve|re f dust; (*sostanza polverizzata*) powder; **in** ∼**re** powdered; **sapone in** ∼**re** soap powder. ∼**rina** f (*medicina*) powder. ∼**riz'zare** vt pulverize; (*nebulizzare*) atomize. ∼**'rone** m cloud of dust. ∼**roso** adj dusty

po'mata f ointment, cream

po'mello m knob; (*guancia*) cheek

pomeridi'ano adj afternoon attrib; **alle tre pomeridiane** at three in the afternoon. **pome'riggio** m afternoon

'pomice f pumice

'pomo m (*oggetto*) knob. ∼ **d'Adamo** Adam's apple

pomo'doro m tomato

'pompa f pump; (*sfarzo*) pomp. **pompe** *pl* **funebri** (*funzione*) funeral. **pom'pare** vt pump; (*gonfiare d'aria*) pump up; (*fig: esagerare*) exaggerate; **pompare fuori** pump out

pom'pelmo m grapefruit

pompi'ere m fireman; **i pompieri** the fire brigade

pom'poso adj pompous

ponde'rare vt ponder

po'nente m west

'ponte m bridge; (*Naut*) deck; (*impalcatura*) scaffolding; **fare il** ∼ make a long weekend of it

pon'tefice m pontiff

pontifi'ca|re vi pontificate. ∼**to** m pontificate

ponti'ficio adj papal

pon'tile m jetty

popò f *inv* 🄸 pooh

popo'lano adj of the people

popo'la|re adj popular; (*comune*) common ●vt populate. ∼**rsi** vr get crowded. ∼**rità** f popularity. ∼**zi'one** f population. **'popolo** m people. **popo'loso** adj populous

'poppa f (*Naut*) stern; (*mammella*) breast; **a** ∼ astern

pop'pa|re vt suck. ∼**ta** f (*pasto*) feed. ∼**'toio** m [feeding-]bottle

popu'lista mf populist

por'cata f load of rubbish; **porcate** *pl* (🄸: *cibo*) junk food

porcel'lana f porcelain

porcel'lino m piglet. ∼ **d'India** guinea-pig

porche'ria f dirt; (*cosa orrenda*) piece of filth; (*robaccia*) rubbish

por'ci|le m pigsty. ∼**no** adj pig attrib ●m (*fungo*) edible mushroom. **'porco** m pig; (*carne*) pork

'porgere vt give; (*offrire*) offer; **porgo distinti saluti** (*in lettera*) I remain, yours sincerely

porno|gra'fia f pornography. ∼**'grafico** adj pornographic '**poro** m pore. **po'roso** adj porous

'**porpora** f purple

'**por|re** vt put; (collocare) place; (supporre) suppose; ask (domanda); present (candidatura); **poniamo il caso che...** let us suppose that...; ~**re fine o termine a** put an end to. ~**si** vr put oneself; ~**si a sedere** sit down; ~**si in cammino** set out

'**porro** m (Bot) leek; (verruca) wart

'**porta** f door; Sport goal; (di città) gate; (Comput) port. ~ **a ~** door-to-door; **mettere alla ~** show sb the door. ~ **di servizio** tradesmen's entrance

portaba'gagli m inv porter; (di treno ecc) luggage rack; (Auto) boot, trunk Am; (sul tetto di un'auto) roof rack

portabot'tiglie m inv bottle rack, wine rack

porta'cenere m inv ashtray

portachi'avi m inv keyring

porta'cipria m inv compact

portadocu'menti m inv document wallet

porta'erei f inv aircraft carrier

portafi'nestra f French window

porta'foglio m inv wallet; (per documenti) portfolio; (ministero) ministry

portafor'tuna m inv lucky charm ● adj inv lucky

portagi'oie m inv jewellery box

por'tale m door

portama'tite m inv pencil case

porta'mento m carriage; (condotta) behaviour

porta'mina m inv propelling pencil

portamo'nete m inv purse

portaom'brelli m inv umbrella stand

porta'pacchi m inv roof rack; (su bicicletta) luggage rack

porta'penne m inv pencil case

por'ta|re vt (verso chi parla) bring; (lontano da chi parla) take; (sorreggere) (Math) carry; (condurre) lead; (indossare) wear; (avere) bear. ~**rsi** vr (trasferirsi) move; (comportarsi) behave; ~**rsi bene/male gli anni** look young/old for one's age

portari'viste m inv magazine rack

porta'sci m inv ski rack

portasiga'rette m inv cigarette-case

por'ta|ta f (di pranzo) course; (Auto) carrying capacity; (di arma) range; (fig: abilità) capability; **a ~ta di mano** within reach. **por'tatile** agg & m portable. ~**to** adj (indumento) worn; (dotato) gifted; **essere ~to per qcsa** have a gift for sth; **essere ~to a** (tendere a) be inclined to. ~**tore, ~trice** mf bearer; **al ~tore** to the bearer. ~**tore di handicap** disabled person

portatovagli'olo m napkin ring

portau'ovo m inv egg-cup

porta'voce m inv spokesman ● f inv spokeswoman

por'tento m marvel; (persona dotata) prodigy

'**portico** m portico

porti'er|a f door; (tendaggio) door curtain. ~**e** m porter, doorman; Sport goalkeeper. ~**e di notte** night porter

porti'n|aio, -a mf caretaker. ~**e'ria** f concierge's room; (di ospedale) porter's lodge

'**porto** pp di **porgere** ● m harbour; (complesso) port; (vino) port [wine]; (spesa di trasporto) carriage; **andare in ~** succeed. ~ **d'armi** gun licence

Porto'gallo m Portugal. **p~hese** adj & mf Portuguese

por'tone m main door

portu'ale m docker

porzi'one f portion

'**posa** f laying; (riposo) rest; (Phot) exposure; (atteggiamento) pose; **mettersi in ~** pose

po'sa|re vt put; (giù) put [down] ● vi (poggiare) rest; (per un ritratto) pose.

~**rsi** vr alight; (sostare) rest; (Aeron) land. ~**ta** f piece of cutlery; ~**te** pl cutlery sg. ~**to** adj settable

po'scritto m postscript

posi'tivo adj positive

posizio'nare vt position

posizi'one f position; **farsi una** ~ get ahead

posolo'gia f dosage

po'spo|rre vt place after; (posticipare) postpone. ~**sto** pp di **posporre**

posse'd|ere vt possess, own. ~**i'mento** m possession

posses|s'ivo adj possessive. **pos-'sesso** m ownership; (bene) possession. ~**'sore** m owner

pos'sibil|e adj possible; **il più presto** ~ **e** as soon as possible ●m **fare [tutto] il** ~ do one's best. ~**ità** f inv possibility; (occasione) chance ●pl (mezzi) means

possi'dente mf land-owner

'**posta** f post, mail; (ufficio postale) post office; (al gioco) stake; **spese di** ~ postage; **per** ~ by post, by mail; **a bella** ~ on purpose; **Poste e Telecomunicazioni** pl [Italian] Post Office. ~ **elettronica** e-mail. ~ **prioritaria** ≈ first-class mail. ~ **vocale** voice-mail

posta'giro m postal giro

po'stale adj postal

postazi'one f position

postda'tare vt postdate (assegno)

posteggi'a|re vt/i park. ~**tore**, ~**trice** mf parking attendant. **po-'steggio** m car-park, parking lot Am; (di taxi) taxi-rank

'**posteri** mpl descendants. ~**ore** adj rear; (nel tempo) later. ~**tà** f posterity

po'sticcio adj artificial; (baffi, barba) false ●m hair-piece

postici'pare vt postpone

po'stilla f note; (Jur) rider

po'stino m postman, mailman Am

'**posto** pp di **porre** ●m place; (spazio)

room; (impiego) job; (Mil) post; (sedile) seat; **a/fuori** ~ in/out of place; **prendere** ~ take up room; **sul** ~ on-site; **essere a** ~ (casa, libri) be tidy; **fare** ~ a make room for; **al** ~ **di** (invece di) in place of, instead of. ~ **di blocco** checkpoint. ~ **di guida** driving seat. ~ **di lavoro** workstation. **posti** pl in piedi standing room. ~ **di polizia** police station

post-'partum adj post-natal

'**postumo** adj posthumous ●m after-effect

po'tabile adj drinkable; **acqua** ~ drinking water

po'tare vt prune

po'tassio m potassium

po'ten|te adj powerful; (efficace) potent. ~**za** f power; (efficacia) potency. ~**zi'ale** adj & m potential

po'tere m power; **al** ~ in power ●vi can, be able to; **posso entrare?** may I come in?; **posso fare qualche cosa?** can I do something?; **che tu possa essere felice!** may you be happy!; **non ne posso più** (sono stanco) I can't go on; (sono stufo) I can't take any more; **può darsi** perhaps; **può darsi che sia vero** perhaps it's true; **potrebbe aver ragione** he could be right, he might be right; **avresti potuto telefonare** you could have phoned, you might have phoned; **spero di poter venire** I hope to be able to come

potestà f power

'**pover|o, -a** adj poor; (semplice) plain ●m poor man ●f poor woman; **i** ~**i** the poor. ~**tà** f poverty

'**pozza** f pool. **poz'zanghera** f puddle

'**pozzo** m well; (minerario) pit. ~ **petrolifero** oil-well

PP.TT. abbr (Poste e Telegrafi) [Italian] Post Office

prali'nato adj (mandorla, gelato)

praline-coated

pram'matica f essere di ∼ be customary

pran'zare vi dine; (a mezzogiorno) lunch. 'pranzo m dinner; (a mezzogiorno) lunch. **pranzo di nozze** wedding breakfast

---

Pranzo Pranzo is traditonally the day's main meal and school timetables and hours of business are geared to a break between one and four o'clock. It starts with a *primo* (usually pasta), followed by a *secondo* (main course). Gradually Italians, especially city-dwellers, are adopting a more northern European timetable and making less of *pranzo*.

'**prassi** f standard procedure

prate'ria f grassland

'**prati**|**ca** f practice; (esperienza) experience; (documentazione) file; **avere** ∼**ca di qcsa** be familiar with sth; **far** ∼**ca** gain experience. ∼'**cabile** adj practicable; (strada) passable. ∼**ca-**'**mente** adv practically. ∼'**cante** mf apprentice; (Relig) [regular] church-goer

prati'ca|re vt practise; (frequentare) associate with; (fare) make

praticità f practicality. '**pratico** adj practical; (esperto) experienced; **essere pratico di qcsa** know about sth

'**prato** m meadow; (di giardino) lawn

pre'ambolo m preamble

preannunci'are vt give advance notice of

preavvi'sare vt forewarn. **preav-**'**viso** m warning

pre'cario adj precarious

precauzi'one f precaution; (cautela) care

prece'den|te adj previous ● m precedent. ∼**te'mente** adv previously.

∼**za** f precedence; (di veicoli) right of way; **dare la** ∼**za** give way. **pre'ce-dere** vt precede

pre'cetto m precept

precipi'ta|re vt ∼**re le cose** precipitate events ● vi fall headlong; (situazione, eventi) come to a head. ∼**rsi** vr (gettarsi) throw oneself; (affrettarsi) rush; ∼**rsi a fare qcsa** rush to do sth. ∼**zi'one** f (fretta) haste; (atmosferica) precipitation. **precipi-**'**toso** adj hasty; (avventato) reckless; (caduta) headlong

preci'pizio m precipice; **a** ∼ headlong

precisa'mente adv precisely

preci'sa|re vt specify; (spiegare) clarify. ∼**zi'one** f clarification

precisi'one f precision. **pre'ciso** adj precise; (ore) sharp; (identico) identical

pre'clu|dere vt preclude. ∼**so** pp di **precludere**

pre'coc|e adj precocious; (prematuro) premature

precon'cetto adj preconceived ● m prejudice

pre'corr|ere vt ∼**ere i tempi** be ahead of one's time

precur'sore m precursor

'**preda** f prey; (bottino) booty; **essere in** ∼ **al panico** be panic-stricken; **in** ∼ **alle fiamme** engulfed in flames. **pre'dare** vt plunder. ∼'**tore** m predator

predeces'sore mf predecessor

pre'del|la f platform. ∼'**lino** m step

predesti'na|re vt predestine. ∼**to** adj (Relig) predestined, preordained

predetermi'nato adj predetermined, preordained

pre'detto pp di **predire**

'**predica** f sermon; fig lecture

predi'care vt preach

predi'le|tto, -a pp di **prediligere** ● adj favourite ● mf pet. ∼**zi'one** f predilection. **predi'ligere** vt prefer

pre'dire vt foretell

predi'spo|rre vt arrange. ~**rsi** vr ~**rsi a** prepare oneself for. ~**si-zi'one** f predisposition; (al disegno ecc) bent (a for). ~**sto** pp di **predisporre**

predizi'one f prediction

predomi'na|nte adj predominant. ~**re** vi predominate. **predo'minio** m predominance

pre'done m robber

prefabbri'cato adj prefabricated ● m prefabricated building

prefazi'one f preface

prefe'renz|a f preference; **di** ~**a** preferably. ~**i'ale** adj preferential; **corsia** ~**iale** bus and taxi lane

prefe'ribil|e adj preferable. ~**mente** adv preferably

prefe'ri|re vt prefer. ~**to, -a** agg & mf favourite

pre'fet|to m prefect. ~**'tura** f prefecture

pre'figgersi vr be determined

pre'fisso pp di **prefiggere** ● m prefix; (Teleph) (dialling) code

pre'gare vt/i pray; (supplicare) beg; **farsi** ~ need persuading

pre'gevole adj valuable

preghi'era f prayer; (richiesta) request

pregi'ato adj esteemed; (prezioso) valuable. **'pregio** m esteem; (valore) value; (di persona) good point; **di pregio** valuable

pregiudi'ca|re vt prejudice; (danneggiare) harm. ~**to** adj prejudiced ● m (Jur) previous offender

pregiu'dizio m prejudice; (danno) detriment

'prego int (non c'è di che) don't mention it!; (per favore) please; ~? I beg your pardon?

pregu'stare vt look forward to

pre'lato m prelate

prela'vaggio m prewash

preleva'mento m withdrawal. **prele'vare** withdraw (denaro); collect (merci); (Med) take. **preli'evo** m (di soldi) withdrawal. **prelievo di sangue** blood sample

prelimi'nare adj preliminary ● m **preliminari** pl preliminaries

pre'ludio m prelude

prema'man inv maternity dress ● adj maternity attrib

prema'turo, -a adj premature ● mf premature baby

premedi'ta|re vt premeditate. ~**zi'one** f premeditation

'premere vt press; (Comput) hit (tasto) ● vi ~ **a** (importare) matter to; **mi preme sapere** I need to know; ~ **su** press on; push (pulsante)

pre'messa f introduction

pre'me|sso pp di **premettere**. ~**sso che** bearing in mind that. ~**ttere** vt put forward; (mettere prima) put before.

premi'a|re vt give a prize to; (ricompensare) reward. ~**zi'one** f prize giving

premi'nente adj pre-eminent

'premio m prize; (ricompensa) reward; (Comm) premium. ~ **di consolazione** booby prize

premoni|'tore adj (sogno, segno) premonitory. ~**zi'one** f premonition

premu'ni|re vt fortify. ~**si** vr take protective measures; ~**si di** provide oneself with; ~**si contro** protect oneself against

pre'mu|ra f (fretta) hurry; (cura) care. ~**roso** adj thoughtful

prena'tale adj antenatal

'prender|e vt take; (afferrare) seize; catch (treno, malattia, palla, pesce); have (cibo, bevanda); (far pagare) charge; (assumere) take on; (ottenere) get; (occupare) take up; ~**e informazioni** make inquiries; ~**e a calci/**

p

pugni kick/punch; **quanto prende?** what do you charge?; **~e una persona per un'altra** mistake a person for someone else ● vi (voltare) turn; (attecchire) take root; (rapprendersi) set; **~e a destra/sinistra** turn right/left; **~e a fare qcsa** start doing sth. **~si** vr **~si a pugni** come to blows; **~si cura di** take care of (ammalato)

prendi'sole m inv sundress

preno'ta|re vt book, reserve. **~to** adj booked, reserved **~zi'one** f booking, reservation

preoccu'pante adj alarming

preoccu'pa|re vt worry. **~rsi** vr **~rsi** worry (**di** about); **~rsi di fare qcsa** take the trouble to do sth. **~to** adj (ansioso) worried. **~zi'one** f worry; (apprensione) concern

prepa'gato adj prepaid

prepa'ra|re vt prepare. **~rsi** vr get ready. **~tivi** mpl preparations. **~to** m (prodotto) preparation. **~'torio** adj preparatory. **~zi'one** f preparation

prepensiona'mento m early retirement

preponde'ran|te adj predominant. **~za** f prevalence

pre'porre vt place before

preposizi'one f preposition

pre'posto pp di preporre ● adj **~ a** (addetto a) in charge of

prepo'ten|te adj overbearing ● mf bully

preroga'tiva f prerogative

'presa f taking; (conquista) capture; (stretta) hold; (di cemento ecc) setting; (Electr) socket; (pizzico) pinch; **essere alle prese con** be struggling with; **a ~ rapida** (cemento, colla) quick-setting; **fare ~ su qcno** influence sb. **~ d'aria** air vent. **~ multipla** adaptor

pre'sagio m omen. **presa'gire** vt foretell

'presbite adj long-sighted

presbi'terio m presbytery

pre'scelto adj selected

pre'scindere vi **~ da** leave aside; **a ~ da** apart from

presco'lare adj **in età ~** pre-school

pre'scri|tto pp di prescrivere

pre'scri|vere vt prescribe. **~zi'one** f prescription; (norma) rule

preselezi'one f **chiamare qcno in ~** call sb via the operator

presen'ta|re vt present; (far conoscere) introduce; show (documento); (inoltrare) submit. **~rsi** vr present oneself; (farsi conoscere) introduce oneself; (a ufficio) attend; (alla polizia ecc) report; (come candidato) stand, run; (occasione:) occur; **~rsi bene/male** (persona:) make a good/bad impression; (situazione:) look good/bad. **~tore, ~trice** mf presenter; (di notizie) announcer. **~zi'one** f presentation; (per conoscersi) introduction

pre'sente adj present; (attuale) current; (questo) this; **aver ~** remember ● m present; **i presenti** those present ● f **allegato alla ~** (in lettera) enclosed

presenti'mento m foreboding

pre'senza f presence; (aspetto) appearance; **in ~ di, alla ~ di** in the presence of; **di bella ~** personable. **~ di spirito** presence of mind

presenzi'are vi **~ a** attend

pre'sepe m, **pre'sepio** m crib

Presepe The presepe (also called presepio) is a traditional nativity scene made with ceramic or wooden figures. Most homes have small ones and large-scale models are assembled in churches during Advent. Presepi from Naples, sometimes made of porcelain, are particularly prized.

preser'va|re vt preserve; (proteggere) protect (**da** from). ~'**tivo** m condom. ~**zi'one** f preservation

'preside m headmaster; (Univ) dean ●f headmistress; (Univ) dean

presi'den|te m chairman; (Pol) president ●f chairwoman; (Pol) president. ~ **del consiglio [dei ministri]** Prime Minister. ~ **della repubblica** President of the Republic. ~**za** f presidency; (di assemblea) chairmanship

presidi'are vt garrison. **pre'sidio** m garrison

presi'edere vt preside over

'preso pp di **prendere**

'pressa f (Mech) press

pres'sante adj urgent

pressap'poco adv about

pres'sare vt press

pressi'one f pressure. ~ **del sangue** blood pressure

'presso prep near; (a casa) with; (negli indirizzi) care of, c/o; (lavorare) for ●**pressi** mpl: **nel pressi di...** In the neighbourhood o vicinity of...

pressoché adv almost

pressuriz'za|re vt pressurize. ~**to** adj pressurized

prestabi'li|re vt arrange in advance. ~**to** adj agreed

prestam'pato adj printed ●m (modulo) form

pre'stante adj good-looking

pre'star|e vt lend; ~**e attenzione** pay attention; ~**e aiuto** lend a hand; **farsi** ~**e** borrow (**da** from). ~**si** vr (frase:) lend itself; (persona:) offer

prestazi'one f performance; **prestazioni** pl (servizi) services

prestigia'tore, -'trice mf conjurer

pre'stigi|o m prestige; **gioco di** ~**o** conjuring trick. ~**'oso** m pres-

tigious

'prestito m loan; **dare in** ~ lend; **prendere in** ~ borrow

'presto adv soon; (di buon'ora) early; (in fretta) quickly; **a** ~ see you soon; **al più** ~ as soon as possible; ~ **o tardi** sooner or later

pre'sumere vt presume; (credere) think

presu'mibile adj è ~ **che...** presumably,...

pre'sunto adj (colpevole) presumed

presun'tu'oso adj presumptuous. ~**zi'one** f presumption

presup'po|rre vt suppose; (richiedere) presuppose. ~**sizi'one** f presupposition. ~**sto** m essential requirement

'prete m priest

preten'dente mf pretender ●m (corteggiatore) suitor

pre'ten|dere vt (sostenere) claim; (esigere) demand ●vi ~**dere a** claim to; ~**dere di** (esigere) demand to. ~**si'one** f pretension. ~**zi'oso** adj pretentious

pre'tes|a f pretension; (esigenza) claim; **senza** ~**e** unpretentious. ~**o** pp di **pretendere**

pre'testo m pretext

pre'tore m magistrate

pre'tura f magistrate's court

preva'le|nte adj prevalent. ~**nte'mente** adv primarily. ~**nza** f prevalence. ~**re** vi prevail

pre'valso pp di **prevalere**

preve'dere vt foresee; forecast (tempo); (legge ecc:) provide for

preve'nire vt precede; (evitare) prevent; (avvertire) forewarn

preven'ti'vare vt estimate; (aspettarsi) budget for. ~**'tivo** adj preventive ●m (Comm) estimate

preve'n|uto adj forewarned; (mal

disposto) prejudiced. ~**zi'one** *f* prevention; (*preconcetto*) prejudice

previ'den|te *adj* provident. ~**za** *f* foresight. ~**za sociale** social security, welfare *Am.* ~**zi'ale** *adj* provident

'previo *adj* ~ **pagamento** on payment

previsi'one *f* forecast; **in** ~ **di** in anticipation of

pre'visto *pp di* **prevedere** ● *adj* foreseen ● *m* **più/meno/prima del** ~ more/less/earlier than expected

prezi'oso *adj* precious

prez'zemolo *m* parsley

'prezzo *m* price. ~ **di fabbrica** factory price. ~ **all'ingrosso** wholesale price. **[a] metà** ~ half price

prigi'on|e *f* prison; (*pena*) imprisonment. **prigio'nia** *f* imprisonment. ~**i'ero, -a** *adj* imprisoned ● *mf* prisoner

'prima *adv* before; (*più presto*) earlier; (*in primo luogo*) first; ~, **finiamo questo** let's finish this first; ~ **o poi** sooner or later; **quanto** ~ as soon as possible ● *prep* ~ **di** before; ~ **d'ora** before now ● *conj* ~ **che** before ● *f* first class; (*Theat*) first night; (*Auto*) first [gear]

pri'mario *adj* primary; (*principale*) principal

pri'mat|e *m* primate. ~**o** *m* supremacy; *Sport* record

prima've|ra *f* spring. ~**rile** *adj* spring attrib

primeggi'are *vi* excel

primi'tivo *adj* primitive; (*originario*) original

pri'mizie *fpl* early produce *sg*

'primo *adj* first; (*fondamentale*) principal; (*precedente di due*) former; (*iniziale*) early; (*migliore*) best ● *m* first; **primi m** (*i primi giorni*) the beginning; **in un** ~ **tempo** at first. **prima copia** master copy

Primo In Italy, lunch invariably includes a *primo*, or first course, before the main course. The most common *primi* are pasta (traditional in the Centre and South) and risotto (traditional in the North), but a *primo* may also consist of soup (often containing small pasta shapes) or *gnocchi* (potato dumplings).

primordi'ale *adj* primordial

'primula *f* primrose

princi'pale *adj* main ● *m* head, boss ⒤

princi'pato *m* principality. **'principe** *m* prince. ~**'pessa** *f* princess

principi'ante *mf* beginner

prin'cipio *m* beginning; (*concetto*) principle; (*causa*) cause; **per** ~ on principle

pri'ore *m* prior

priori|tà *f inv* priority. ~**'tario** *adj* having priority

'prisma *m* prism

pri'va|re *vt* deprive. ~**rsi** *vr* deprive oneself

privatizzazi'one *f* privatization. **pri'vato, -a** *adj* private ● *mf* private citizen

privazi'one *f* deprivation

privilegi'are *vt* privilege; (*considerare più importante*) favour. **privi'legio** *m* privilege

'privo *adj* ~ **di** devoid of; (*mancante*) lacking in

pro *prep* for ● *m* advantage; **a che** ~? what's the point?

pro'babil|e *adj* probable. ~**ità** *f inv* probability. ~**'mente** *adv* probably

pro'ble|ma *m* problem. ~**'matico** *adj* problematic

pro'boscide *f* trunk

procacci'ar|e *vt*, ~**si** *vr* obtain

pro'cace *adj* (*ragazza*) provocative

pro'ced|ere *vi* proceed; (*iniziare*)

start; **~ere contro** (*Jur*) start legal proceedings against. **~i'mento** *m* process; (*Jur*) proceedings *pl.* **proce'dura** *f* procedure

proces'sare *vt* (*Jur*) try

processi'one *f* procession

pro'cesso *m* process; (*Jur*) trial

proces'sore *m* processor

processu'ale *adj* trial

pro'cinto *m* **essere in ~ di** be about to

procla'ma *m* proclamation

procla'ma|re *vt* proclaim. **~zi'one** *f* proclamation

procreazi'one *f* procreation

pro'cura *f* power of attorney; **per ~** by proxy

procu'ra|re *vt/i* procure; (*causare*) cause; (*cercare*) try. **~tore** *m* attorney. **P~tore Generale** Attorney General. **~tore legale** lawyer. **~tore della repubblica** public prosecutor

'**prode** *adj* brave. **pro'dezza** *f* bravery

prodi'gar|e *vt* lavish. **~si** *vr* do one's best

pro'digi|o *m* prodigy. **~'oso** *adj* prodigious

pro'dotto *pp di* **produrre** ● *m* product. **prodotti agricoli** farm produce *sg.* **~ derivato** by-product. **~ interno lordo** gross domestic product. **~ nazionale lordo** gross national product

pro'du|rre *vt* produce. **~rsi** *vr* (attore:) play; (accadere) happen. **~t-tività** *f* productivity. **~t'tivo** *adj* productive. **~t'tore, ~t'trice** *mf* producer. **~zi'one** *f* production

Prof. *abbr* (Professore) Prof.

profa'na|re *vt* desecrate

profe'rire *vt* utter

Prof.essa *abbr* (Professoressa) Prof.

profes'sare *vt* profess; practise (professione)

professio'nale *adj* professional

professi'o|ne *f* profession; **libera ~ne** profession. **~'nismo** *m* professionalism. **~'nista** *mf* professional

profes'sor|e, -'essa *mf* (Sch) teacher; (Univ) lecturer; (titolare di cattedra) professor

pro'fe|ta *m* prophet

pro'ficuo *adj* profitable

profi'lar|e *vt* outline; (ornare) border; (Aeron) streamline. **~si** *vr* stand out

profi'lattico *adj* prophylactic ● *m* condom

pro'filo *m* profile; (breve studio) outline; **di ~** in profile

profit'tare *vi* **~ di** (avvantaggiarsi) profit by; (approfittare) take advantage of. **pro'fitto** *m* profit; (vantaggio) advantage

profond|a'mente *adv* deeply, profoundly. **~ità** *f inv* depth

pro'fondo *adj* deep; *fig* profound; (cultura) great

'**profugo, -a** *mf* refugee

profu'mar|e *vt* perfume. **~si** *vr* put on perfume

profu'mato *adj* (fiore) fragrant; (fazzoletto ecc) scented

profume'ria *f* perfumery. **pro'fumo** *m* perfume, scent

profusi'one *f* profusion; **a ~** in profusion. **pro'fuso** *pp di* **profondere** ● *adj* profuse

proget'tare *vt* plan. **~'tista** *mf* designer. **pro'getto** *m* plan; (di lavoro importante) project. **progetto di legge** bill

prog'nosi *f inv* prognosis; **in ~ riservata** on the danger list

pro'gramma *m* programme; (Comput) program. **~ scolastico** syllabus

program'ma|re *vt* programme; (Comput) program. **~'tore, ~'trice** *mf* [computer] programmer. **~zi'one** *f* programming

progre'dire *vi* [make] progress

progres|si'one *f* progression.

~'sivo adj progressive. pro'gresso m progress

proi'bi|re vt forbid. ~'tivo adj prohibitive. ~to adj forbidden. ~zi'one f prohibition

proie|t'tare vt project; show (film). ~t'tore m projector; (Auto) headlight

proi'ettile m bullet

proiezi'one f projection

'prole f offspring. prole'tario agg & m proletarian

prolife'rare vi proliferate. pro'lifico adj prolific

pro'lisso adj verbose, prolix

'prologo m prologue

pro'lunga f (Electr) extension

prolun'gar|e vt prolong; (allungare) lengthen; extend (contratto, scadenza). ~si vr continue; ~si su (dilungarsi) dwell upon

prome'moria m memo; (per se stessi) reminder, note; (formale) memorandum

pro'me|ssa f promise. ~sso pp di promettere. ~ttere vt/i promise

promet'tente adj promising

promi'nente adj prominent

promiscuità f promiscuity. pro'miscuo adj promiscuous

promon'torio m promontory

pro'mo|sso pp di promuovere ● adj (Sch) who has gone up a year; (Univ) who has passed an exam. ~'tore, ~'trice mf promoter

promozio'nale adj promotional. promozi'one f promotion

promul'gare vt promulgate

promu'overe vt promote; (Sch) move up a class

proni'pote m (di bisnonno) great-grandson; (di prozio) great-nephew ● f (di bisnonno) great-granddaughter; (di prozio) great-niece

pro'nome m pronoun

pronosti'care vt forecast. pro'nostico m forecast

pron'tezza f readiness; (rapidità) quickness

'pronto adj ready; (rapido) quick; ~! (Teleph) hello!; tenersi ~ be ready (per for); pronti, via! (in gare) ready! steady! go!. ~ soccorso first aid; (in ospedale) accident and emergency

prontu'ario m handbook

pro'nuncia f pronunciation

pronunci'a|re vt pronounce; (dire) utter; deliver (discorso). ~rsi vr (su un argomento) give one's opinion. ~to adj pronounced; (prominente) prominent

pro'nunzia ecc = PRONUNCIA ecc

propa'ganda f propaganda

propa'ga|re vt propagate. ~rsi vr spread. ~zi'one f propagation

prope'deutico adj introductory

pro'pen|dere vi ~dere per be in favour of. ~so pp di propendere ● adj essere ~so a fare qcsa be inclined to do sth

propi'nare vt administer

pro'pizio adj favourable

proponi'mento m resolution

pro'por|re vt propose; (suggerire) suggest. ~si vr set oneself (obiettivo, meta); ~si di intend to

proporzio'na|le adj proportional. ~re vt proportion. proporzi'one f proportion

pro'posito m purpose; a ~ by the way; a ~ di with regard to; di ~ (apposta) on purpose

proposizi'one f clause; (frase) sentence

pro'post|a f proposal. ~o pp di proporre

proprietà f inv property; (diritto) ownership; (correttezza) propriety. ~ immobiliare property. ~ privata private property. proprie'taria f owner; (di casa affittata) landlady. pro'prie'tario m owner; (di casa affittata) landlord '**proprio** adj one's [own]; (caratteristico) typical; (appropriato) proper ●adv just; (veramente) really; **non** ~ not really, not exactly; (affatto) not... at all ●pron one's own ●m one's [own]; **lavorare in** ~ be one's own boss; **mettersi in** ~ set up on one's own

propul|si'one f propulsion. ~'sore m propeller

'**proroga** f extension

proro'ga|bile adj extendable. ~re vt extend

pro'rompere vi burst out

'**prosa** f prose. **pro'saico** adj prosaic

pro'scio|gliere vt release; (Jur) acquit. ~lto pp di prosciogliere

prosciu'gar|e vt dry up; (bonificare) reclaim. ~si vi dry up

prosci'utto m ham. ~ **cotto** cooked ham. ~ **crudo** Parma ham

pro'scri|tto, -a pp di proscrivere ●mf exile

prosecuzi'one f continuation

prosegui'mento m continuation; **buon** ~! (viaggio) have a good journey!; (festa) enjoy the rest of the party!

prosegu'ire vt continue ●vi go on, continue

prospe'r|are vi prosper. ~ità f prosperity. '**prospero** adj prosperous; (favorevole) favourable. ~'oso adj flourishing; (ragazza) buxom

prospet'tar|e vt show. ~si vr seem

prospet'tiva f perspective; (panorama) view; fig prospect. **pro'spetto** m (vista) view; (facciata) façade; (tabella) table

prospici'ente adj facing

prossima'mente adv soon

prossimità f proximity

'**prossimo, -a** adj near; (seguente) next; (molto vicino) close; **l'anno** ~ next year ●m neighbour

prosti'tu|ta f prostitute. ~zi'one f prostitution

protago'nista mf protagonist

pro'teggere vt protect; (favorire) favour

prote'ina f protein

pro'tender|e vt stretch out. ~si vr (in avanti) lean out. **pro'teso** pp di protendere

pro'te|sta f protest; (dichiarazione) protestation. ~'stante adj & mf Protestant. ~'stare vt/i protest

prote|t'tivo adj protective. ~tto pp di proteggere. ~t'tore, ~t'trice mf protector; (sostenitore) patron ●m (di prostituta) pimp. ~zi'one f protection

protocol'lare adj (visita) protocol ●vt register

proto'collo m protocol; (registro) register; **carta** ~ official stamped paper

pro'totipo m prototype

pro'tra|rre vt protract; (differire) postpone. ~rsi vr go on, continue. ~tto pp di protrarre

protube'ran|te adj protuberant. ~za f protuberance

'**prova** f test; (dimostrazione) proof; (tentativo) try; (di abito) fitting; Sport heat; (Theat) rehearsal; (bozza) proof; **in** ~ (assumere) for a trial period; **mettere alla** ~ put to the test. ~ **generale** dress rehearsal

pro'var|e vt test; (dimostrare) prove; (tentare) try; try on (abiti ecc); (sentire) feel; (Theat) rehearse. ~si vr try

proveni'enza f origin. **prove'nire** vi provenire **da** come from

pro'vento m proceeds pl

prove'nuto pp di provenire

pro'verbio m proverb

pro'vetta f test-tube; **bambino in** ~ test-tube baby

pro'vetto adj skilled

'**provider** m inv ISP, Internet Service Provider

pro'vinci|a f province; (strada) B road, secondary road. ~'ale adj provincial; strada ~ale B road

pro'vino m specimen; Cinema screen test

provo'ca|nte adj provocative. ~re vt provoke; (causare) cause. ~'tore, ~'trice mf trouble-maker. ~'torio adj provocative. ~zi'one f provocation

provve'd|ere vi ~ere a provide for. ~i'mento m measure; (previdenza) precaution

provvi'denz|a f providence. ~i'ale adj providential

provvigi'one f commission

provvi'sorio adj provisional

prov'vista f supply

pro'zio, -a m great-uncle ● f great-aunt

'prua f prow

pru'den|te adj prudent. ~za f prudence; per ~za as a precaution

'prudere vi itch

'prugn|a f plum. ~a secca prune. ~o m plum[-tree]

pru'rito m itch.

pseu'donimo m pseudonym

psica'na|lisi f psychoanalysis. ~'lista mf psychoanalyst. ~liz'zare vt psychoanalyse

'psiche f psyche

psichi'a|tra mf psychiatrist. ~'tria f psychiatry. ~trico adj psychiatric

'psichico adj mental

psico|lo'gia f psychology. ~'logico adj psychological. psi'cologo, -a mf psychologist

psico'patico, -a m psychopath

PT abbr (Posta e Telecomunicazioni) PO

pubbli'ca|re vt publish. ~zi'one f publication. ~zioni pl (di matrimonio) banns

pubbli'cista mf Journ correspondent

pubblicità f inv publicity; (annuncio) advertisement, advert; fare ~ a qcsa advertise sth; piccola ~ small advertisements. **pubbli'tario** adj advertising

'pubblico adj public; scuola pubblica state school ● m public; (spettatori) audience; grande ~ general public. Pubblica Sicurezza Police. ~ ufficiale civil servant

'pube m pubis

pubertà f puberty

pu'dico adj modest

pue'rile adj children's; pej childish

pugi'lato m boxing. **'pugile** m boxer

pugna'la|re vt stab. ~ta f stab. pu'gnale m dagger

'pugno m fist; (colpo) punch; (manciata) fistful; (numero limitato) handful; dare un ~ a punch

'pulce f flea; (microfono) bug

pul'cino m chick; (nel calcio) junior

pu'ledra f filly

pu'ledro m colt

pu'li|re vt clean. ~re a secco dryclean. ~to adj clean. ~'tura f cleaning. ~'zia f (il pulire) cleaning; (l'essere pulito) cleanliness; ~zie pl housework; fare le ~zie do the cleaning

'pullman m inv bus, coach; (urbano) bus

pul'mino m minibus

'pulpito m pulpit

pul'sante m button; (Electr) [push-]button. ~ di accensione on-/off switch

pul'sa|re vi pulsate. ~zi'one f pulsation

pul'viscolo m dust

'puma m inv puma

pun'gente adj prickly; (insetto) stinging; (odore ecc) sharp

'pung|ere vt prick; (insetto:) sting. ~igli'one m sting

pu'ni|re vt punish. ~'tivo adj punitive. **~zi'one** f punishment; *Sport* free kick

'punta f point; (estremità) tip; (di monte) peak; (un po') pinch; *Sport* forward; **doppie punte** (di capelli) split ends

pun'tare vt point; (spingere con forza) push; (scommettere) bet; (⊞: appuntare) fasten ● vi **~ su** fig rely on; **~ verso** (dirigersi) head for; **~ a** aspire to

punta'spilli m inv pincushion

pun'tat|a f (di una storia) instalment; (televisiva) episode; (al gioco) stake, bet; (breve visita) flying visit; **a ~e** serialized, in instalments

punteggia'tura f punctuation

pun'teggio m score

puntel'lare vt prop. **pun'tello** m prop

pun'tiglio m spite; (ostinazione) obstinacy. **~'oso** adj punctilious, pernickety pej

pun'tin|a f (da disegno) drawing pin, thumb tack Am; (di giradischi) stylus. **~o** m dot; **a ~o** perfectly; (cotto) to a T

'punto m point; (Med, in cucito,) stitch; (in punteggiatura) full stop; **in che ~?** where, exactly?; **due punti** colon; **in ~** sharp; **mettere a ~** put right; fig fine tune; tune up (motore); **essere sul ~ di fare qcsa** be about to do sth, be on the point of doing sth. **~ esclamativo** exclamation mark. **~ interrogativo** question mark. **~ nero** (Med) blackhead. **~ di riferimento** landmark; (per la qualità) benchmark. **~ di vendita** point of sale. **~ e virgola** semicolon. **~ di vista** point of view

puntu'al|e adj punctual. **~ità** f punctuality. **~'mente** adv punctually

pun'tura f (di insetto) sting; (di ago ecc) prick; (Med) puncture; (iniezione) injection; (fitta) stabbing pain

punzecchi'are vt prick; fig tease

'pupa f doll. **pu'pazzo** m puppet.

pupazzo di neve snowman

pup'illa f (Anat) pupil

pu'pillo, -a mf (di professore) favourite

purché conj provided

'pure adv too, also; (concessivo) fate **~!** please do! (tuttavia) yet; (anche se) even if; **pur di** just to

purè m inv purée. **~ di patate** creamed potatoes

pu'rezza f purity

'purga f purge. **pur'gante** m laxative. **pur'gare** vt purge

purga'torio m purgatory

purifi'care vt purify

puri'tano, -a adj & mf Puritan

'puro adj pure; (vino ecc) undiluted; **per ~ caso** purely by chance

puro'sangue adj & m thoroughbred

pur'troppo adv unfortunately

pus m pus. **'pustola** f pimple

puti'ferio m uproar

putre'far|e vi, **~si** vr putrefy

pu'trido adj putrid

'puzza f = **puzzo**

puz'zare vi stink; **~ di bruciato** fig smell fishy

'puzzo m stink, bad smell. **~la** f polecat. **~'lente** adj stinking

p.zza abbr (piazza) Sq.

Qq

qua adv here; **da un anno in ~** for the last year; **da quando in ~?** since when?; **di ~** this way; **di ~ di** on this side of; **~ dentro** in here; **~ sotto** under here; **~ vicino** near here; **~ e là** here and there

qua'derno m exercise book; (per

appunti) notebook

quadrango'lare *adj* (forma) quadrangular. **qua'drangolo** *m* quadrangle

qua'drante *m* quadrant; (*di orologio*) dial

qua'dra|re *vt* square; (*contabilità*) balance ● *vi* fit in. **~to** *adj* square; (*equilibrato*) level-headed ● *m* square; (*pugilato*) ring; **al ~to** squared

quadret'tato *adj* squared; (*carta*) graph *attrib*. **qua'dretto** *m* square; (*piccolo quadro*) small picture; **a quadretti** (*tessuto*) check

quadrien'nale *adj* (*che dura quattro anni*) four-year

quadri'foglio *m* four-leaf clover

quadri'latero *m* quadrilateral

quadri'mestre *m* four-month period

'quadro *m* picture, painting; (*quadrato*) square; (*fig: scena*) sight; (*tabella*) table; (*Theat*) scene; (*Comm*) executive **quadri** *pl* (*carte*) diamonds; (*a quadri*) (*tessuto, giacca, motivo*) check. **quadri** *pl* **direttivi** senior management

quaggiù *adv* down here

'quaglia *f* quail

'qualche *adj* (*alcuni*) a few, some; (*un certo*) some; (*in interrogazioni*) any; **ho ~ problema** I have a few problems, I have some problems; **~ tempo fa** some time ago; **~ libro italiano?** have you any Italian books?; **posso pren·dere ~ libro?** can I take some books?; **in ~ modo** somehow; **in ~ posto** somewhere; **~ volta** sometimes; **~ cosa =** QUALCOSA

qual'cos|a *pron* something; (*in interrogazioni*) anything; **~'altro** something else; **vuoi ~'altro?** would you like anything else?; **~a di strano** something strange; **vuoi ~a da mangiare?** would you like something to eat?

qual'cuno *pron* someone, somebody; (*in interrogazioni*) anyone, anybody; (*alcuni*) some; (*in interrogazioni*) any; **c'è ~?** is anybody in?; **qualcun altro** someone else, somebody else; **c'è qualcun altro che aspetta?** is anybody else waiting?; **ho letto ~ dei suoi libri** I've read some of his books; **conosci ~ dei suoi amici?** do you know any of his friends?

'quale *adj* (*indeterminato*) what; (*come*) as, like; **~ macchina è la tua?** which car is yours?; **~ motivo avrà di parlare così?** what reason would he have to speak like that?; **~ onore!** what an honour!; **città quali Venezia** towns like Venice; **~ che sia la tua opinione** whatever you may think ● *pron inter* which [one]; **~ preferisci?** which [one] do you prefer? ● *pron rel* **il/la ~** (*persona*) who; (*animale, cosa*) that, which; (*oggetto: con prep*) whom; (*animale, cosa*) which; **ho incontrato tua madre, la ~ mi ha detto...** I met your mother, who told me...; **l'ufficio nel ~ lavoro** the office in which I work; **l'uomo con il ~ parlavo** the man to whom I was speaking ● *adv* (*come*) as

qua'lifica *f* qualification; (*titolo*) title

qualifi'ca|re *vt* qualify; (*definire*) define. **~rsi** *vr* be placed. **~'tivo** *adj* qualifying. **~to** *adj* (*operaio*) semiskilled. **~zi'one** *f* qualification

qualità *f inv* quality; (*specie*) kind; **in ~ di** in one's capacity as. **qualita'tivo** *adj* qualitative

qua'lora *conj* in case

qual'siasi, qua'lunque *adj* any; (*non importa quale*) whatever; (*ordinario*) ordinary; **dammi una penna ~** give me any pen [whatsoever]; **farei ~ cosa** I would do anything; **~ cosa io faccia** whatever I do; **~ persona** anyone; **in ~ caso** in any case; **~ uno** any one, whichever; **l'uomo qualunque** the man in the street

qualunqu'ismo *m* lack of political views

'**quando** *conj & adv* when; **da ∼ ti ho visto** since I saw you; **da ∼ esci con lui?** how long have you been going out with him?; **da ∼ in qua?** since when?; **∼ ... ∼ ...** sometimes..., sometimes...

quantifi'care *vt* quantify

quantità *f inv* quantity; **una ∼ di** (*gran numero*) a great deal of. **quanti'tivo** *m* amount ●*adj* quantitative

'**quanto**
●*adj inter* how much; (*con nomi plurali*) how many; (*in esclamazione*) what a lot of; **∼ tempo?** how long?; **quanti anni hai?** how old are you?
●*adj rel* as much... as; (*con nomi plurali*) as many... as; **prendi ∼ denaro ti serve** take as much money as you need; **prendi quanti libri vuoi** take as many books as you like
●*pron inter* how much; (*quanto tempo*) how long; (*plurale*) how many; **quanti ne abbiamo oggi?** what date is it today?, what's the date today?
●*pron rel* as much as; (*quanto tempo*) as long as; (*plurale*) as many as; **prendine ∼/quanti ne vuoi** take as much/as many as you like; **stai ∼ vuoi** stay as long as you like; **questo è ∼** that's it
●*adv inter* how much; (*quanto tempo*) how long; **∼ sei alto?** how tall are you?; **∼ hai aspettato?** how long did you wait for?; **∼ costa?** how much is it?; **∼ mi dispiace!** I'm so sorry!; **∼ è bello!** how nice!
●*adv rel* as much as; **lavoro ∼ posso** I work as much as I can; **è tanto intelligente ∼ bello** he's as intelligent as he's good-looking; **in ∼** (*in qualità di*) as; (*poiché*) since; **in ∼ a me** as far as I'm concerned; **per ∼** however; **per ∼ ne sappia** as far as I know; **per ∼ mi riguarda** as far as I'm concerned; **∼ a** as for; **∼ prima** (*al più presto*) as soon as possible

quan'tunque *conj* although
qua'ranta *adj & m* forty
quaran'tena *f* quarantine
quaran'tenne *adj* forty-year-old. **∼io** *m* period of forty years
quaran't|esimo *adj* fortieth. **∼ina** *f* **una ∼ina** about forty
qua'resima *f* Lent
quar'tetto *m* quartet
quarti'ere *m* district; (*Mil*) quarters *pl*. **∼ generale** headquarters
quarto *adj* fourth ●*m* fourth; (*quarta parte*) quarter; **le sette e un ∼** a quarter past seven. **quarti** *pl* **di finale** quarterfinals. **∼ d'ora** quarter of an hour. **quar'tultimo, -a** *mf* fourth from the end
quarzo *m* quartz
'**quasi** *adv* almost, nearly; **∼ mai** hardly ever; **∼ ∼** (*come se*) as if; **∼ sto a casa** I'm tempted to stay home
quassù *adv* up here
'**quatto** *adj* crouching; (*silenzioso*) silent
quat'tordici *adj & m* fourteen
quat'trini *mpl* money *sg*
quattro *adj & m* four; **dirne ∼ a qcno** give sb a piece of one's mind; **farsi in ∼** (*per qcno/per fare qcsa*) go to a lot of trouble (for sb/to do sth); **in ∼ e quattr'otto** in a flash. **∼ per ∼** *m inv* (*Auto*) four-wheel drive [vehicle]
quat'trocchi: a ∼ *adv* in private
quattro|'cento *adj & m* four hundred; **il Q∼cento** the

fifteenth century

quattro'mila adj & m four thousand

'quell|o adj that; (pl those); **quell'al-bero** that tree; **quegli alberi** those trees; **quel cane** that dog; **quei cani** those dogs ● pron that [one]; (pl those [ones]); ~o **li** that one over there; ~o **che** the one that; (ciò che) what; **quelli che** the ones that, those that; ~o **a destra** the one on the right

'quercia f oak

que'rela f [legal] action

quere'lare vt bring an action against

que'sito m question

questio'nario m questionnaire

quest'ione f question; (faccenda) matter; (litigio) quarrel; **in ~ in** doubt; **è fuori ~** it's out of the question

'quest|o adj this; (pl these) ● pron this [one]; (pl these [ones]); ~o **qui**, ~o **qua** this one here; ~o **è quello che ha detto** that's what he said; **per ~o** for this or that reason. **quest'oggi** today

que'store m chief of police

que'stura f police headquarters

qui adv here; **da ~ in poi** from now on; **fin ~** (di tempo) up till now, until now; ~ **dentro** in here; ~ **sotto** under here; ~ **vicino** near here ● m ~ **pro quo** misunderstanding

quie'scienza f trattamento di ~ retirement package

quie'tanza f receipt

quie'tar|e vt calm. ~**si** vr quieten down

qui'et|e f quiet; **disturbo della ~e pubblica** breach of the peace. ~**o** adj quiet

'quindi adv then ● conj therefore

'quindi|ci adj & m fifteen. ~**'cina** f **una ~cina** about fifteen; **una ~cina di giorni** two weeks pl

quinquen'nale adj (che dura cinque anni) five-year. **quin'quennio** m [period of] five years

quin'tale m a hundred kilograms

'quinte fpl (Theat) wings

quin'tetto m quintet

'quinto adj fifth

quin'tuplo adj quintuple

'quota f quota; (rata) instalment; (altitudine) height; (Aeron) altitude, height; (ippica) odds pl; **perdere ~** lose altitude; **prendere ~** gain altitude. ~ **di iscrizione** entry fee

quo'ta|re vt (Comm) quote. ~**to** adj quoted; **essere ~to in Borsa** be quoted on the Stock Exchange. ~**zi'one** f quotation

quotidi|ana'mente adv daily. ~**'ano** adj daily; (ordinario) everyday ● m daily [paper]

quozi'ente m quotient. ~ **d'intel-ligenza** intelligence quotient, IQ

Rr

ra'barbaro m rhubarb

'rabbia f rage; (ira) anger; (Med) rabies sg; **che ~!** what a nuisance!; **mi fa ~** it makes me angry

rab'bino m rabbi

rabbiosa'mente adv furiously. **rabbi'oso** adj hot-tempered; (Med) rabid; (violento) violent

rabbo'nir|e vt pacify. ~**si** vr calm down

rabbrivi'dire vi shudder; (di freddo) shiver

rabbui'arsi vr become dark

raccapez'zar|e vt put together. ~**si** vr see one's way ahead

raccapricci'ante adj horrifying

raccatta'palle m inv ball boy ●f inv ball girl

raccat'tare vt pick up

rac'chetta f racket. ~ **da ping pong** table-tennis bat. ~ **da sci** ski pole. ~ **da tennis** tennis racket

racchi'udere vt contain

rac'coglilere vt pick; (da terra) pick up; (mietere) harvest; (collezionare) collect; (radunare) gather; win (voti ecc); (dare asilo a) take in. ~**ersi** vr gather; (concentrarsi) collect one's thoughts. ~'**mento** m concentration. ~'**tore**, ~'**trice** mf collector ●m (cartella) ringbinder

rac'colto, -**a** pp di **raccogliere** ● adj (rannicchiato) hunched; (intimo) cosy; (concentrato) engrossed ● m (mietitura) harvest ●f collection; (di scritti) compilation; (del grano ecc) harvesting; (adunata) gathering

raccoman'dabile adj recommendable; **poco** ~ (persona) shady

raccoman'dalre vt recommend; (affidare) entrust. ~**rsi** vr (implorare) beg. ~**ta** f registered letter; ~**ta con ricevuta di ritorno** recorded delivery. ~**espresso** f next-day delivery of recorded items. ~**zi'one** f recommendation

raccon'tare vt tell. **rac'conto** m story

raccorci'are vt shorten

raccor'dare vt join. **rac'cordo** m connection; (stradale) feeder. **raccordo anulare** ring road. **raccordo ferroviario** siding

ra'chitico adj rickety; (poco sviluppato) stunted

racimo'lare vt scrape together

'racket m inv racket

'radar m inv radar

raddol'cirle vt sweeten; fig soften. ~**si** vr become milder; (carattere:) mellow

raddoppi'are vt double. **rad'doppio** m doubling

raddriz'zare vt straighten

'raderle vt shave; graze (muro); ~**e al suolo** raze. ~**si** vr shave

radi'are vt strike off; ~ **dall'albo** strike off

radia'tore m radiator. ~**zi'one** f radiation

'radica f briar

radi'cale adj radical ●m (Gram) root; (Pol) radical

ra'dicchio m chicory

ra'dice f root

'radio f inv radio; **via** ~ by radio. ~ **a transistor** transistor radio ●m (Chem) radium.

radioama'tore, -'**trice** mf [radio] ham

radioascolta'tore, -'**trice** mf listener

radioat'tività f radioactivity. ~'**tivo** adj radioactive

radio'cro|naca f radio commentary; **fare la** ~**naca di** commentate on. ~'**nista** mf radio reporter

radiodiffusi'one f broadcasting

radio'fonico adj radio attrib

radiogra|'fare vt X-ray. ~'**fia** f X-ray [photograph]; (radiologia) radiography; **fare una** ~**fia** (paziente:) have an X-ray; (dottore:) take an X-ray

radio'lina f transistor

radi'ologo, -**a** mf radiologist

radi'oso adj radiant

radio'sveglia f radio alarm

radio'taxi m inv radio taxi

radiote'lefono m radiotelephone; (privato) cordless [phone]

radiotelevi'sivo adj broadcasting attrib

'rado adj sparse; (non frequente) rare; **di** ~ seldom

radu'nar|e vt, ~**si** vr gather [together]; Sport rally. **ra'duno** m meeting; Sport rally

ra'dura f clearing

r

'**rafano** m horseradish

raf'fermo adj stale

'**raffica** f gust; (di armi da fuoco) burst; (di domande) barrage

raffigu'ra|re vt represent. ~**zi'one** f representation

raffi'na|re vt refine. ~**ta'mente** adv elegantly. ~**to** adj refined. **raffine'ria** f refinery

rafforza'mento m reinforcement; (di muscolatura) strengthening. ~**re** vt reinforce. ~**tivo** m (Gram) intensifier

raffredda'mento m (processo) cooling

raffred'da|re vt cool. ~**arsi** vr get cold; (prendere un raffreddore) catch a cold. ~**ore** m cold. ~**ore da fieno** hay fever

raf'fronto m comparison

'**rafia** f raffia

Rag. abbr ragioniere

ra'gaz|za f girl; (fidanzata) girlfriend. ~**za alla pari** au pair [girl]. ~'**zata** f prank. ~**zo** m boy; (fidanzato) boyfriend

ragge'lar|e vt fig freeze. ~**si** vr fig turn to ice

raggi'ante adj radiant; ~ **di successo** flushed with success

raggi'era f a ~ with a pattern like spokes radiating from a centre

'**raggio** m ray; (Math) radius; (di ruota) spoke; ~ **d'azione** range. ~ **laser** laser beam

raggi'rare vt trick. **raggiro** m trick

raggi'un|gere vt reach; (conseguire) achieve. ~**gibile** adj (luogo) within reach

raggomito'lar|e vt wind. ~**si** vr curl up

raggranel'lare vt scrape together

raggrin'zir|e vt, ~**si** vr wrinkle

raggrup'pa|mento m (gruppo) group; (azione) grouping. ~**pare** vt group together

ragguagli'are vt compare; (informare) inform. **raggu'aglio** m comparison; (informazione) information

ragguar'devole adj considerable

'**ragia** f resin; **acqua** ~ turpentine

ragiona'mento m reasoning; (discussione) discussion. **ragio'nare** vi reason; (discutere) discuss

ragi'one f reason; (ciò che è giusto) right; **a** ~ **o a torto** rightly or wrongly; **aver** ~ be right; **perdere la** ~ go out of one's mind

ragione'ria f accountancy

ragio'nevol|e adj reasonable. ~'**mente** adv reasonably

ragioni'ere, -a mf accountant

ragli'are vi bray

ragna'tela f cobweb. '**ragno** m spider

ragù m inv meat sauce

RAI f abbr (Radio Audizioni Italiane) Italian public broadcasting company

ralle'gra|re vt gladden. ~**rsi** vr rejoice; (per evento) cheer up; ~**rsi con qcno** congratulate sb. ~'**menti** mpl congratulations

rallenta'mento m slowing down

rallen'ta|re vt/i slow down; (allentare) slacken. ~**rsi** vr slow down. ~'**tore** m speed bump; **al** ~'**tore** in slow motion

raman'zina f reprimand

ra'marro m type of lizard

ra'mato adj copper[-coloured]

'**rame** m copper

ramifi'ca|re vi, ~**rsi** vr branch out; (strada:) branch. ~**zi'one** f ramification

rammari'carsi vr ~ **di** regret; (lamentarsi) complain (**di** about). **ram'marico** m regret

rammen'dare vt darn. **ram'mendo** m darning

rammen'tar|e vt remember; ~**e qcsa a qcno** (richiamare alla memoria) remind sb of sth. ~**si** vr remember

rammol'li|re vt soften. ~**rsi** vr go

soft. ~to, -a mf wimp

'**ramo** m branch. ~'**scello** m twig

'**rampa** f (di scale) flight. ~ d'accesso slip road. ~ di lancio launch[ing] pad

ram'**pante** adj giovane ~ yuppie

rampi'**cante** adj climbing ●m (Bot) creeper

ram'**pollo** m hum brat; (discendente) descendant

ram'**pone** m harpoon; (per scarpe) crampon

'**rana** f frog, (nel nuoto) breaststroke; uomo ~ frogman

ran'**core** m resentment

ran'**dagio** adj stray

'**rango** m rank

rannicchi'**arsi** vr huddle up

rannuvo'**larsi** vr cloud over

ra'**nocchio** m frog

ranto'**lare** vi wheeze. '**rantolo** m wheeze; (di moribondo) deathrattle

'**rapa** f turnip

ra'**pace** adj rapacious; (uccello) predatory

ra'**pare** vt crop

'**rapida** f rapids pl. ~'**mente** adv rapidly

rapidità f speed

'**rapido** adj swift ●m (treno) express [train]

rapi'**mento** m kidnapping

ra'**pina** f robbery; (a mano armata) armed robbery. ~ in banca bank robbery. rapi'**nare** vt rob. ~'**tore** m robber

ra'**pire** vt abduct; (a scopo di riscatto) kidnap; (estasiare) ravish. ~'**tore**, ~'**trice** mf kidnapper

rappacifi'**care** vt pacify. ~rsi vr be reconciled. ~zi'**one** f reconciliation

rappor'**tare** vt reproduce (disegno); (confrontare) compare

rap'**porto** m report; (connessione) re

lation; (legame) relationship; (Math, Techn) ratio; rap'**porti** pl relationship; essere in buoni rapporti be on good terms. ~ di amicizia friendship. ~ di lavoro working relationship. rapporti pl sessuali sexual intercourse

rap'**prendersi** vr set; (latte:) curdle

rappre'**saglia** f reprisal

rappresen'**tan|te** mf representative. ~te di commercio sales representative. ~za f delegation; (Comm) agency; spese pl di ~za entertainment expenses; di ~za (appartamento ecc) company

rappresen'**ta|re** vt represent; (Theat) perform. ~'**tivo** adj representative. ~zi'**one** f representation; (spettacolo) performance

rap'**preso** pp di rapprendersi

rapso'**dia** f rhapsody

'**raptus** m inv fit of madness

rara'**mente** adv rarely, seldom

rare'**fa|re** vt, ~rsi vr rarefy. ~tto adj rarefied

rarità f inv rarity. '**raro** adj rare

ra'**sar|e** vt shave; trim (siepe ecc). ~si vr shave

raschi'**are** vt scrape; (togliere) scrape off

rasen'**tare** vt go close to. ra'**sente** prep very close to

'**raso** pp di radere ●adj smooth; (colmo) full to the brim; (barba) close-cropped; ~ terra close to the ground; un cucchiaio ~ a level spoonful ●m satin

ra'**soio** m razor

ras'**segna** f review; (mostra) exhibition; (musicale, cinematografica) festival; passare in ~ review; (Mil) inspect

rasse'**gna|re** vt present. ~rsi vr resign oneself. ~to adj (persona, aria, tono) resigned. ~zi'**one** f resignation

rassere'**nar|e** vt clear; fig cheer up.

r

~**si** vr become clear; fig cheer up

rasset'tare vt tidy up; (riparare) mend

rassicu'ra|nte adj reassuring. ~**re** vt reassure. ~**zi'one** f reassurance

rasso'dare vt harden; fig strengthen

rassomigli'a|nza f resemblance. ~**re** vi ~**re** a resemble

rastrella'mento m (di fieno) raking; (perlustrazione) combing. **rastrel'lare** vt rake; (perlustrare) comb

rastrelli'era f rack; (per biciclette) bicycle rack; (scolapiatti) [plate] rack. **ra'strello** m rake

'rata f instalment; **pagare a rate** pay by instalments. **rate'ale** adj by instalments; **pagamento rateale** payment by instalments

rate'are, rateiz'zare vt divide into instalments

ra'tifica f (Jur) ratification

ratifi'care vt (Jur) ratify

'ratto m abduction; (roditore) rat

rattop'pare vt patch. **rat'toppo** m patch

rattrap'pir|e vt make stiff. ~**si** vr become stiff

rattri'star|e vt sadden. ~**si** vr become sad

rau'cedine f hoarseness. **'rauco** adj hoarse

rava'nello m radish

ravi'oli mpl ravioli sg

ravve'dersi vr mend one's ways

ravvici'na'mento m reconciliation; (Pol) rapprochement

ravvici'nar|e vt bring closer; (riconciliare) reconcile. ~**si** vr be reconciled

ravvi'sare vt recognize

ravvi'var|e vt revive; fig brighten up. ~**si** vr revive

'rayon m rayon

razio'cinio m rational thought; (buon senso) common sense

razio'nal|e adj rational. ~**ità** f (ra-

ziocinio) rationality; (di ambiente) functional nature. ~**iz'zare** vt rationalize (programmi, metodi, spazio). ~'**mente** adv rationally

razio'nare vt ration. **razi'one** f ration

'razza f race; (di cani ecc) breed; (genere) kind; **che ~ di idiota!** ⚠ what an idiot!

raz'zia f raid

razzi'ale adj racial

raz'zis|mo m racism. ~**ta** adj & mf racist

'razzo m rocket. **~ da segnalazione** flare

razzo'lare vi (polli): scratch about

re m inv king; (Mus) D

rea'gire vi react

re'ale adj real; (di re) royal

rea'lis|mo m realism. ~**ta** mf realist; (fautore del re) royalist

realistica'mente adv realistically. **rea'listico** adj realistic

'reality tv f reality tv

realiz'zabile adj feasible

realiz'zar|e vt (attuare) carry out, realize; (Comm) make; score (gol, canestro); (rendersi conto di) realize. ~**rsi** vr come true; (nel lavoro ecc) fulfil oneself. ~**zi'one** f realization; (di sogno, persona) fulfilment. ~**zione scenica** production

rea'lizzo m (vendita) proceeds pl; (riscossione) yield

real'mente adv really

realtà f inv reality. **~ virtuale** virtual reality

re'ato m crime

reat'tivo adj reactive

reat'tore m reactor; (Aeron) jet [aircraft]

reazio'nario, -a adj & mf reactionary

reazi'one f reaction. **~ a catena** chain reaction

'rebus m inv rebus; (enigma) puzzle

recapi'tare vt deliver. **re'capito** m address; (consegna) delivery. **recapito a domicilio** home delivery. **recapito telefonico** contact telephone number

re'car|e vt bear; (produrre) cause. **∼si** vr go

re'cedere vi recede; fig give up

recensi'one f review

recen's|ire vt review. **∼ore** m reviewer

re'cente adj recent; **di ∼** recently. **∼'mente** adv recently

recessi'one f recession

re'cesso m recess

re'cidere vt cut off

reci'divo, -a adj (Med) recurrent ● mf repeat offender

recin|'tare vt close off. **re'cinto** m enclosure; (per animali) pen; (per bambini) play-pen. **∼zi'one** f (muro) wall; (rete) wire fence; (cancellata) railings pl

recipi'ente m container

re'ciproco adj reciprocal

re'ciso pp di recidere

'recita f performance. **reci'tare** vt recite; (Theat) act; play (ruolo). **∼zi'one** f recitation; (Theat) acting

recla'mare vi protest ● vt claim

ré'clame f inv advertising; (avviso pubblicitario) advertisement

re'clamo m complaint; **ufficio reclami** complaints department

recli'na|bile adj reclining; **sedile ∼bile** reclining seat. **∼re** vt tilt (sedile); lean (capo)

reclusi'one f imprisonment. **re'cluso, -a** adj secluded ● mf prisoner

'recluta f recruit

reclu|ta'mento m recruitment. **∼'tare** vt recruit

'record m inv record ● adj inv (cifra) record attrib

recrimi'na|re vi recriminate

recupe'rare vt recover. **re'cupero** m recovery; **corso di recupero** add-

itional classes; **minuti di recupero** Sport injury time

redargu'ire vt rebuke

re'datto pp di redigere

redat'tore, -'trice mf editor; (di testo) writer

redazi'one f (ufficio) editorial office; (di testi) editing

red'dizio adj profitable

'reddito m income. **∼ imponibile** taxable income

re'den|to pp di redimere. **∼'tore** m redeemer. **∼zi'one** f redemption

re'digere vt write; draw up (documento)

re'dimer|e vt redeem. **∼si** vr redeem oneself

'redini fpl reins

'reduce adj **∼ da** back from ● mf survivor

refe'rendum m inv referendum

refe'renza f reference

refet'torio m refectory

refrat'tario adj refractory; **essere ∼ a** have no aptitude for

refrige'ra|re vt refrigerate. **∼zi'one** f refrigeration

refur'tiva f stolen goods pl

rega'lare vt give

re'galo m present, gift

re'gata f regatta

reg'gen|te mf regent. **∼za** f regency

'regger|e vt (sorreggere) bear; (tenere in mano) hold; (dirigere) run; (governare) govern; (Gram) take ● vi (resistere) hold out; (durare) last; fig stand. **∼si** vr stand

'reggia f royal palace

reggi'calze m inv suspender belt

reggi'mento m regiment

reggi'petto, reggi'seno m bra

re'gia f (Cinema) direction; (Theat) production

re'gime m regime; (dieta) diet;

(*Mech*) speed
re'gina f queen
'regio adj royal
regio'na|le adj regional. ~'lismo m (parola) regionalism
regi'one f region
re'gista mf (*Cinema*) director; (*Theat, TV*) producer
regi'stra|re vt register; (*Comm*) enter; (*incidere su nastro*) tape, record; (*su disco*) record. ~'tore m recorder; (*magnetofono*) tape-recorder. ~ di cassa cash register. ~zi'one f registration; (*Comm*) entry; (*di programma*) recording
re'gistro m register; (*ufficio*) registry. ~ di cassa ledger
re'gnare vi reign
'regno m kingdom; (*sovranità*) reign. R~ Unito United Kingdom
'regola f rule; essere in ~ be in order; (*persona:*) have one's papers in order. **rego'labile** adj (*meccanismo*) adjustable. ~'mento m regulation; (*Comm*) settlement
rego'lar|e adj regular ●vt regulate; (*ridurre, moderare*) limit; (*sistemare*) settle. ~si vr (*agire*) act; (*moderarsi*) control oneself. ~ità f regularity. ~iz'zare vt settle (debito)
rego'la|ta f darsi una ~ta pull oneself together. ~'tore, ~'trice adj piano ~tore urban development plan
'regolo m ruler
regres'sivo adj regressive. **re-'gresso** m decline
reinseri'mento m (*di persona*) reintegration
reinser'irsi vr (*in ambiente*) reintegrate
reinte'grare vt restore
relativa'mente adv relatively; ~ a as regards. **rela'tivo** adj relative
rela'tore, -'trice mf (*in una conferenza*) speaker

re'lax m relaxation
relazi'one f relation[ship]; (*rapporto amoroso*) [love] affair; (*resoconto*) report; **pubbliche relazioni** pl public relations
rele'gare vt relegate
religi'o|ne f religion. ~so, -a adj religious ●m monk ●f nun
re'liqui|a f relic. ~'ario m reliquary
re'litto m wreck
re'ma|re vi row. ~'tore, ~'trice mf rower
remini'scenza f reminiscence
remissi'one f remission; (*sottomissione*) submissiveness. **remis'sivo** adj submissive
'remo m oar
'remora f senza remore without hesitation
re'moto adj remote
remune'ra|re vt remunerate. ~zi'one f remuneration
'render|e vt (*restituire*) return; (*esprimere*) render; (*fruttare*) yield; (*far diventare*) make. ~si vr become; ~si conto di qcsa realize sth; ~si utile make oneself useful
rendi'conto m report
rendi'mento m rendering; (*produzione*) yield
'rendita f income; (*dello Stato*) revenue
'rene m kidney. ~ artificiale kidney machine
'reni fpl (*schiena*) back
reni'tente adj essere ~ a (*consigli di qcno*) be unwilling to accept
'renna f reindeer (*pl inv*); (*pelle*) buckskin
'reo, -a adj guilty ●mf offender
re'parto m department; (*Mil*) unit
repel'lente adj repulsive
repen'taglio m mettere a ~ risk
repen'tino adj sudden
reper'ibile adj available; non è ~

(*perduto*) it's not to be found

repe'rire vt trace (*fondi*)

re'perto m ~ **archeologico** find

reper'torio m repertory; (*elenco*) index; **immagini** pl **di** ~ archive footage

'replica f reply; (*obiezione*) objection; (*copia*) replica; (Theat) repeat performance. **repli'care** vt reply; (Theat) repeat

repor'tage m inv report

repres'si|one f repression. ~'**vo** adj repressive. **re'presso** pp di **reprimere**. **re'primere** vt repress

re'pubbli|ca f republic. ~'**cano**, -**a** adj & mf republican

repu'tare vt consider

reputazi'one f reputation

requi'sito m requirement

requisi'toria f (*arringa*) closing speech

'resa f surrender; (Comm) rendering. ~ **dei conti** rendering of accounts

'residence m inv residential hotel

resi'den|te adj & mf resident. ~**za** f residence; (*soggiorno*) stay. ~**ziale** adj residential; **zona** ~**ziale** residential district

re'siduo adj residual ●m remainder

'resina f resin

resi'sten|te adj resistant; ~**te all'acqua** water-resistant. ~**za** f resistance; (*fisica*) stamina; (Electr) resistor; **la R~za** the Resistance

re'sistere vi ~ [**a**] resist; (*a colpi, scosse*) stand up to; ~ **alla pioggia/al vento** be rain-/wind-resistant

'reso pp di **rendere**

reso'conto m report

re'spin|gere vt repel; (*rifiutare*) reject; (*bocciare*) fail. ~**to** pp di **respingere**

respi'ra|re vt/i breathe. ~**tore** m respirator; (*a tubo*) snorkel; ~'**torio** adj respiratory; ~**zi'one** f breathing; (Med) respiration. ~**zione**

bocca a bocca mouth-to-mouth resuscitation, kiss of life. **re'spiro** m breath; (*il respirare*) breathing; fig respite

respon'sabil|e adj responsible (**di** for); (Jur) liable ●m/f person responsible. ~**e della produzione** production manager. ~**ità** f inv responsibility; (Jur) liability. ~**iz'zare** vt give responsibility to

re'sponso m response

'ressa f crowd

re'stante adj remaining ●m remainder

re'stare vi = RIMANERE

restau'ra|re vt restore. ~'**tore**, ~'**trice** m/f restorer. ~**zi'one** f restoration. **re'stauro** m (*riparazione*) repair

re'stio adj restive; ~ **a** reluctant to

restitu|'ire vt return; (*reintegrare*) restore. ~**zi'one** f return; (Jur) restitution

'resto m remainder; (*saldo*) balance; (*denaro*) change; **resti** pl (*avanzi*) remains; **del** ~ besides

re'stringer|e vt contract; take in (*vestiti*); (*limitare*) restrict; shrink (*stoffa*). ~**si** vr contract; (*farsi più vicini*) close up; (*stoffa*) shrink. **re'stringi'mento** m (*di tessuto*) shrinkage

restrit'tivo adj restrictive. ~**zi'one** f restriction

resurrezi'one f resurrection

resusci'tare vt/i revive

re'tata f round-up

'rete f net; (*sistema*) network; (*televisiva*) channel; (*in calcio*) goal; fig trap; (*per la spesa*) string bag. ~ **locale** (Comput) local [area] network. ~ **stradale** road network. ~ **televisiva** television channel

reti'cen|te adj reticent. ~**za** f reticence

retico'lato m grid; (*rete metallica*) wire netting. **re'ticolo** m network

re'torico, -a adj rhetorical; **domanda retorica** rhetorical question

r

● *f* rhetoric

retribu|'ire *vt* remunerate. **∼zi'one** *f* remuneration

'retro *adv* behind; **vedi ∼** see over ● *m inv* back. **∼ di copertina** outside back cover

retroat'tivo *adj* retroactive

retro'ce|dere *vi* retreat ● *vt* (*Mil*) demote; *Sport* relegate. **∼ssi'one** *f Sport* relegation

retroda'tare *vt* backdate

re'trogrado *adj* retrograde; *fig* old-fashioned; (*Pol*) reactionary

retrogu'ardia *f* (*Mil*) rearguard

retro'marcia *f* reverse [gear]

retro'scena *m inv* (*Theat*) back-stage; *fig* background details *pl*

retrospet'tivo *adj* retrospective

retro'stante *adj* **il palazzo ∼** the building behind

retrovi'sore *m* rear-view mirror

'retta¹ *f* (*Math*) straight line; (*di collegio, pensionato*) fee

'retta² *f* **dar ∼ a qcno** take sb's advice

rettango'lare *adj* rectangular. **ret'tangolo** *m* rectangle

ret'tifi|ca *f* rectification. **∼'care** *vt* rectify

'rettile *m* reptile

retti'lineo *adj* rectilinear; (*retto*) upright ● *m Sport* back straight

'retto *pp di* **reggere** ● *adj* straight; *fig* upright; (*giusto*) correct; **angolo ∼** right angle

ret'tore *m* (*Relig*) rector; (*Univ*) principal, vice-chancellor

reu'matico *adj* rheumatic

reuma'tismi *mpl* rheumatism

reve'rendo *adj* reverend

rever'sibile *adj* reversible

revisio'nare *vt* revise; (*Comm*) audit; (*Auto*) overhaul. **revisi'one** *f* revision; (*Comm*) audit; (*Auto*) overhaul. **revi'sore** *m* (*di conti*) auditor; (*di bozze*) proof-reader; (*di traduzioni*) revisor

re'vival *m inv* revival

'revoca *f* repeal. **revo'care** *vt* repeal

riabili'ta|re *vt* rehabilitate. **∼zi'one** *f* rehabilitation

riabitu'ar|e *vt* reaccustom. **∼si** *vr* reaccustom oneself

riac'cender|e *vt* rekindle (fuoco). **∼si** *vr* (luce:) come back on

riacqui'stare *vt* buy back; regain (libertà, prestigio); recover (vista, udito)

riagganci'are *vt* replace (ricevitore); **∼ la cornetta** hang up ● *vi* hang up

riallac'ciare *vt* refasten; reconnect (corrente); renew (amicizia)

rial'zare *vt* raise ● *vi* rise. **ri'alzo** *m* rise

riani'mar|e *vt* (*Med*) resuscitate; (*ridare forza a*) revive; (*ridare coraggio a*) cheer up. **∼si** *vr* regain consciousness; (*riprendere forza*) revive; (*riprendere coraggio*) cheer up

riaper'tura *f* reopening

ria'prir|e, **∼si** *vr* reopen

rias'sumere *vt* summarize

riassun'tivo *adj* summarizing. **rias'sunto** *pp di* **riassumere** ● *m* summary

ria'ver|e *vt* get back; regain (salute, vista). **∼si** *vr* recover

riavvicina'mento *m* reconciliation

riavvici'nar|e *vt* reconcile (paesi, persone). **∼si** *vr* (riconciliarsi) be reconciled, make it up

riba'dire *vt* (confermare) reaffirm

ri'balta *f* flap; (*Theat*) footlights *pl*; *fig* limelight

ribal'tar|e *vt/i*, **∼si** *vr* tip over; (*Naut*) capsize

ribas'sare *vt* lower ● *vi* fall. **ri'basso** *m* fall; (sconto) discount

ri'battere *vt* (a macchina) retype; (controbattere) deny ● *vi* answer back

ribel'l|arsi *vr* rebel. **ri'belle** *adj*

rebellious ●*mf* rebel. ∼'**ione** *f* rebellion

'**ribes** *m inv* (*rosso*) redcurrant; (*nero*) blackcurrant

ribol'lire *vi* ferment; *fig* seethe

ri'brezzo *m* disgust; far ∼ a disgust

rica'dere *vi* fall back; (*nel peccato ecc*) lapse; (*pendere*) hang [down]; ∼ su (*riversarsi*) fall on. rica'duta *f* relapse

rical'care *vt* trace

rica'ma|re *vt* embroider. ∼to *adj* embroidered

ri'cambi mpl spare parts

ricambi'are *vt* return; reciprocate (*sentimento*); ∼ qcsa a qcno repay sb for sth. ri'cambio *m* replacement; (*Biol*) metabolism; pezzo di ricambio spare [part]

ri'camo *m* embroidery

ricapito'la|re *vt* sum up. ∼zi'one *f* summary, recap [t]

ri'carica *f* (*di sveglia*) rewinding; (*Teleph*) top-up card

ricari'care *vt* reload (*macchina fotografica, fucile, camion*); recharge (*batteria*); (*Comput*) reboot

ricat'ta|re *vt* blackmail. ∼'tore, ∼'trice *mf* blackmailer. ri'catto *m* blackmail

rica'va|re *vt* get; (*ottenere*) obtain; (*dedurre*) draw. ∼to *m* proceeds *pl*. ri'cavo *m* proceeds *pl*

'ricca *f* rich woman. ∼'mente *adv* lavishly

ric'chezza *f* wealth; *fig* richness

'riccio *adj* curly ●*m* curl; (*animale*) hedgehog. ∼ di mare sea-urchin. ∼lo *m* curl. ∼'luto *adj* curly. ric'ci'uto *adj* (*barba*) curly

'ricco *adj* rich ●*m* rich man

ri'cerca *f* search; (*indagine*) investigation; (*scientifica*) research; (*Sch*) project

ricer'ca|re *vt* search for; (*fare ricer-*

che su) research. ∼ta *f* wanted woman. ∼'tezza *f* refinement. ∼to *adj* sought-after; (*raffinato*) refined; (*affettato*) affected ●*m* (*dalla polizia*) wanted man

ricetrasmit'tente *f* transceiver

ri'cetta *f* prescription; (*Culin*) recipe

ricet'tacolo *m* receptacle

ricet'tario *m* (*di cucina*) recipe book

ricetta'tore, -'trice *mf* fence, receiver of stolen goods. ∼zi'one *f* receiving (*stolen goods*)

rice'vente *adj* (*apparecchio, stazione*) receiving ●*mf* receiver

ri'cev|ere *vt* receive; (*dare il benvenuto*) welcome; (*di albergo*) accommodate. ∼i'mento *m* receiving; (*accoglienza*) welcome; (*trattenimento*) reception

ricevi'tor|e *m* receiver. ∼ia *f* ∼ia del lotto agency authorized to sell lottery tickets

rice'vuta *f* receipt

ricezi'one *f* (*Radio, TV*) reception

richia'mare *vt* (*al telefono*) call back; (*far tornare*) recall; (*rimproverare*) rebuke; (*attirare*) draw; ∼ alla mente call to mind. richi'amo *m* recall; (*attrazione*) call

richi'edere *vt* ask for; (*di nuovo*) ask again for; ∼ a qcno di fare qcsa ask o request sb to do sth. richi'esta *f* request; (*Comm*) demand

ri'chiud|ere *vt* close again. ∼si *vr* (*ferita:*) heal

rici'claggio *m* recycling

rici'clare *vt* recycle (*carta, vetro*); launder (*denaro sporco*)

'ricino *m* olio di ∼ castor oil

ricognizi'one *f* reconnaissance

ri'colmo *adj* full

ricominci'are *vt/i* start again

ricompa'rire *vi* reappear

ricom'pen|sa *f* reward. ∼'sare *vt* reward

ricom'por|re *vt* (*riscrivere*) rewrite;

r

(ricostruire) reform; (*Typ*) reset. **~si** *vr* regain one's composure

riconcili'a|re *vt* reconcile. **~rsi** *vr* be reconciled. **~zi'one** *f* reconciliation

ricono'scen|te *adj* grateful. **~za** *f* gratitude

rico'nosc|ere *vt* recognize; (*ammettere*) acknowledge. **~i'mento** *m* recognition; (*ammissione*) acknowledgement; (*per la polizia*) identification. **~i'uto** *adj* recognized

riconside'rare *vt* rethink

rico'prire *vt* re-cover; (*rivestire*) coat; (*di insulti*) shower (**di** with); hold (*carica*)

ricor'dar|e *vt* remember; (*richiamare alla memoria*) recall; (*far ricordare*) remind; (*rassomigliare*) look like. **~si** *vr* **~si [di]** remember. **ri'cordo** *m* memory; (*oggetto*) memento; (*di viaggio*) souvenir; **ricordi** *pl* (*memorie*) memoirs

ricor'ren|te *adj* recurrent. **~za** *f* recurrence; (*anniversario*) anniversary

ri'correre *vi* recur; (*accadere*) occur; (*data*): fall; **~ a** have recourse to; (*rivolgersi a*) turn to. **ri'corso** *pp di* **ricorrere ● m** recourse; (*Jur*) appeal

ricostitu'ente *m* tonic

ricostitu'ire *vt* re-establish

ricostru'|ire *vt* reconstruct. **~zi'one** *f* reconstruction

ricove'ra|re *vt* give shelter to; **~re in ospedale** admit to hospital, hospitalize. **~to, -a** *mf* hospital patient. **ri'covero** *m* shelter; (*ospizio*) home

ricre'a|re *vt* re-create; (*ristorare*) restore. **~rsi** *vr* amuse oneself. **~'tivo** *adj* recreational. **~zi'one** *f* recreation; (*Sch*) break

ri'credersi *vr* change one's mind

ricupe'rare *vt* recover; rehabilitate (*tossicodipendente*); **~ il tempo perduto** make up for lost time. **ri'cupero** *m* recovery; (*di tossicodipendente*) rehabilitation; (*salvataggio*) res-

cue; **[minuti** *mpl* **di] ricupero** injury time

ri'curvo *adj* bent

ri'dare *vt* give back, return

ri'dente *adj* (*piacevole*) pleasant

'ridere *vi* laugh; **~ di** (*deridere*) laugh at

ri'detto *pp di* **ridire**

ridicoliz'zare *vt* ridicule. **ri'dicolo** *adj* ridiculous

ridimensio'nare *vt* reshape; *fig* see in the right perspective

ri'dire *vt* repeat; (*criticare*) find fault with

ridon'dante *adj* redundant

ri'dotto *pp di* **ridurre ● m** (*Theat*) foyer **● *adj*** reduced

ri'du|rre *vt* reduce. **~rsi** *vr* diminish. **~rsi a** be reduced to. **~'ttivo** *adj* reductive. **~zi'one** *f* reduction; (*per cinema, teatro*) adaptation

rieducazi'one *f* (*di malato*) rehabilitation

riem'pi|re *vt* fill [up]; fill in (*moduli ecc*). **~rsi** *vr* fill [up]. **~'tivo** *adj* filling **● m** filler

rien'tranza *f* recess

rien'trare *vi* go/come back in; (*tornare*) return; (*piegare indentro*) recede; **~ in** (*far parte*) fall within. **ri'entro** *m* return; (*di astronave*) re-entry

riepilo'gare *vt* recapitulate. **rie'pilogo** *m* roundup

riesami'nare *vt* reappraise

riesu'mare *vt* exhume

rievo'ca|re *vt* commemorate. **~zi'one** *f* commemoration

rifaci'mento *m* remake

ri'fa|re *vt* do again; (*creare*) make again; (*riparare*) repair; (*imitare*) imitate; make (*letto*). **~rsi** *vr* (*rimettersi*) recover; (*vendicarsi*) get even; **~rsi una vita/carriera** make a new life/career for oneself; **~rsi di** make up for. **~tto** *pp di* **rifare**

riferi'mento *m* reference

rife'rir|e vt report; **~e a** attribute to ● vi make a report. **~si** vr **~si a** refer to

rifi'lare vt (tagliare a filo) trim; (🅱️: affibbiare) saddle

rifi'ni|re vt finish off. **~'tura** f finish

rifiu'tare vt refuse. **rifi'uto** m refusal; **rifiuti** pl (immondizie) rubbish sg. **rifiuti** pl urbani urban waste sg

riflessi'one f reflection; (osservazione) remark. **rifles'sivo** adj thoughtful; (Gram) reflexive

ri'flesso pp di **riflettere** ● m (luce) reflection; (Med) reflex; **per ~** indirectly

ri'fletter|e vt reflect ● vi think. **~si** vr be reflected

riflet'tore m reflector; (proiettore) searchlight

ri'flusso m ebb

rifocil'lar|e vt restore. **~si** vr liter, hum take some refreshment

ri'fondere vt refund

ri'forma f reform; (Relig) reformation; (Mil) medical exemption

rifor'ma|re vt re-form; (migliorare) reform; (Mil) declare unfit for military service. **~to** adj (chiesa) Reformed. **~'tore**, **~'trice** mf reformer. **~'torio** m reformatory. **rifor'mista** adj reformist

riforni'mento m supply; (scorta) stock; (di combustibile) refuelling; **stazione** f **di ~** petrol station

rifor'nir|e vt **~e di** provide with. **~si** vr restock, stock up (**di** with)

ri'fra|ngere vt refract. **~tto** pp di rifrangere. **~zi'one** f refraction

rifug'gire vi **~ da** fig shun

rifugi'a|rsi vr take refuge. **~to**, **-a** mf refugee. **~to economico** economic refugee

ri'fugio m shelter; (nascondiglio) hideaway

'riga f line; (fila) row; (striscia) stripe; (scriminatura) parting; (regolo) rule; **a**

righe (stoffa) striped; (quaderno) ruled; **mettersi in ~** line up

ri'gagnolo m rivulet

ri'gare vt rule (foglio) ● vi **~ dritto** behave well

rigatti'ere m junk dealer

rigene'rare vt regenerate

riget'tare vt throw back; (respingere) reject; (vomitare) throw up. **ri'getto** m rejection

ri'ghello m ruler

rigida'mente adv rigidly. **~ità** f rigidity; (di clima) severity; (severità) strictness. **'rigido** adj rigid; (freddo) severe; (severo) strict

rigi'rar|e vt turn again; (ripercorrere) go round; fig twist (argomentazione) ● vi walk about. **~si** vr turn round; (nel letto) turn over. **ri'giro** m (imbroglio) trick

'rigo m line; (Mus) staff

ri'goglio m in bloom. **~'oso** adj luxuriant

ri'gonfio adj swollen

ri'gore m rigours pl; **a ~** strictly speaking; **calcio di ~** penalty [klck]; **area di ~** penalty area; **essere di ~** be compulsory

rigo'roso adj (severo) strict; (scrupoloso) rigorous

riguada'gnare vt regain (quota, velocità)

riguar'dar|e vt look at again; (considerare) regard; (concernere) concern; **per quanto riguarda** with regard to. **~si** vr take care of oneself. **ri-gu'ardo** m care; (considerazione) consideration; **nei riguardi di** towards; **riguardo a** with regard to

ri'gurgito m regurgitation

rilanci'are vt throw back (palla); (di nuovo) throw again; increase (offerta); revive (moda); relaunch (prodotto) ● vi (a carte) raise the stakes

rilasci'ar|e vt (concedere) grant; (liberare) release; issue (documento). **~si** vr relax. **ri'lascio** m release; (di *documento*) issue

rilassa'mento *m* relaxation

rilas'sa|re *vt*, **~rsi** *vr* relax. **~to** *adj* (*ambiente*) relaxed

rile'ga|re *vt* bind (*libro*). **~to** *adj* bound. **~tura** *f* binding

ri'leggere *vt* reread

ri'lento: a **~** *adv* slowly

rileva'mento *m* survey; (*Comm*) buyout

rile'vante *adj* considerable

rile'va|re *vt* (*trarre*) get; (*mettere in evidenza*) point out; (*notare*) notice; (*topografia*) survey; (*Comm*) take over; (*Mil*) relieve. **~zi'one** *f* (*statistica*) survey

rili'evo *m* relief; (*Geog*) elevation; (*topografia*) survey; (*importanza*) importance; (*osservazione*) remark; **mettere in ~ qcsa** point sth out

rilut'tan|te *adj* reluctant. **~za** *f* reluctance

'rima *f* rhyme

riman'dare *vt* (*posporre*) postpone; (*mandare indietro*) send back; (*mandare di nuovo*) send again; (*far ridare un esame*) make resit an examination. **ri'mando** *m* return; (*in un libro*) cross-reference

rima'nen|te *adj* remaining ● *m* remainder. **~za** *f* remainder

rima'ne|re *vi* stay, remain; (*essere d'avanzo*) be left; (*venirsi a trovare*) be; (*restare stupito*) be astonished; (*restare d'accordo*) agree

rimar'chevole *adj* remarkable

ri'mare *vt/i* rhyme

rimargi'nar|e *vt*, **~si** *vr* heal

ri'masto *pp di* **rimanere**

rimbal'zare *vi* rebound; (*proiettile:*) ricochet; **far ~** bounce. **rim'balzo** *m* rebound; (*di proiettile*) ricochet

rimbam'bi|re *vi* be in one's dotage ● *vt* stun. **~to** *adj* in one's dotage

rimboc'care *vt* turn up; roll up (*maniche*); tuck in (*coperte*)

rimbom'bare *vi* resound

rimbor'sare *vt* reimburse, repay. **rim'borso** *m* reimbursement, repayment. **rimborso spese** reimbursement of expenses

rimedi'are *vi* **~ a** remedy; make up for (*errore*); (*procurare*) scrape up. **ri'medio** *m* remedy

rimesco'lare *vt* mix [up]; shuffle (*carte*); (*rivangare*) rake up

ri'messa *f* (*locale per veicoli*) garage; (*per aerei*) hangar; (*per autobus*) depot; (*di denaro*) remittance; (*di merci*) consignment

ri'messo *pp di* **rimettere**

ri'metter|e *vt* put back; (*restituire*) return; (*affidare*) entrust; (*perdonare*) remit; (*rimandare*) put off; (*vomitare*) bring up. **~si** *vr* (*ristabilirsi*) recover; (*tempo:*) clear up; **~si a** start again

'rimmel® *m inv* mascara

rimoder'nare *vt* modernize

rimon'tare *vt* (*risalire*) go up; (*Mech*) reassemble ● *vi* remount; **~ a** (*risalire*) go back to

rimorchi'a|re *vt* tow; Ⓤ pick up (*ragazza*). **~'tore** *m* tug[boat]. **ri'morchio** *m* tow; (*veicolo*) trailer

ri'morso *m* remorse

rimo'stranza *f* complaint

rimozi'one *f* removal; (*da un incarico*) dismissal. **~ forzata** illegally parked vehicles removed at owner's expense

rim'pasto *m* (*Pol*) reshuffle

rimpatri'are *vt/i* repatriate. **rim'patrio** *m* repatriation

rim'pian|gere *vt* regret. **~to** *pp di* **rimpiangere** ● *m* regret

rimpiaz'zare *vt* replace

rimpiccio'lire *vi* become smaller

rimpinz'ar|e *vt* **~e di** stuff with. **~si** *vr* stuff oneself

rimprove'rare *vt* reproach; **~ qcsa a qcno** reproach sb for sth.

rim'provero m reproach

rimune'ra|re vt remunerate. **∼tivo** adj remunerative. **∼zi'one** f remuneration

ri'muovere vt remove

ri'nascere vi be reborn

rinascimen'tale adj Renaissance. **Rinasci'mento** m Renaissance

ri'nascita f rebirth

rincal'zare vt (sostenere) support; (rimboccare) tuck in. **rin'calzo** m support; **rincalzi** pl (Mil) reserves

rincantucci'arsi vr hide oneself away in a corner

rinca'rare vt increase the price of ● vi become more expensive. **rin'caro** m price increase

rinca'sare vi return home

rinchi'uder|e vt shut up. **∼si** vr shut oneself up

rin'correre vt run after

rin'cors|a f run-up. **∼o** pp di rincorrere

rin'cresc|ere vi mi rincresce di non... I'm sorry o I regret that I can't...; **se non ti ∼e** if you don't mind. **∼i'mento** m regret. **∼i'uto** pp di rincrescere

rincreti'nire vi be stupid

rincu'lare vi (arma:) recoil; (cavallo:) shy. **rin'culo** m recoil

rincuo'rar|e vt encourage. **∼si** vr take heart

rinfacci'are vt ∼ qcsa a qcno throw sth in sb's face

rinfor'zar|e vt strengthen; (rendere più saldo) reinforce. **∼si** vr become stronger. **rin'forzo** m reinforcement; fig support

rinfran'care vt reassure

rinfre'scante adj cooling

rinfre'scar|e vt cool; (rinnovare) freshen up ● vi get cooler. **∼si** vr freshen [oneself] up. **rin'fresco** m light refreshment; (ricevimento) party

rin'fusa f alla ∼ at random

ringhi'era f railing; (di scala) banisters pl

ringiova'nire vt rejuvenate (pelle, persona); (vestito:) make look younger ● vi become young again; (sembrare) look young again

ringrazi|a'mento m thanks pl. **∼'are** vt thank

rinne'ga|re vt disown. **∼to, -a** mf renegade

rinnova'mento m renewal; (di edifici) renovation

rinno'var|e vt renew; renovate (edifici). **∼si** vr be renewed; (ripetersi) recur, happen again. **rin'novo** m renewal

rinoce'ronte m rhinoceros

rino'mato adj renowned

rinsal'dare vt consolidate

rinsa'vire vi come to one's senses

rinsec'chi|re vi shrivel up. **∼to** adj shrivelled up

rinta'narsi vr hide oneself away; (animale:) retreat into its den

rintoc'care vi (campana:) toll; (orologio:) strike. **rin'tocco** m toll; (di orologio) stroke

rinton'ti|re vt stun. **∼to** adj dazed

rintracci'are vt trace

rintro'nare vt stun ● vi boom

ri'nuncia f renunciation

rinunci|a|re vi ∼re a renounce, give up. **∼'tario** adj defeatist

ri'nunzia, rinunzi'are = RINUNCIA, RINUNCIARE

rinveni'mento m (di reperti) discovery; (di refurtiva) recovery. **rinve-'nire** vt find ● vi (riprendere i sensi) come round; (ridiventare fresco) revive

rinvi'are vt put off; (mandare indietro) return; (in libro) refer; ∼ **a giudizio** indict

rin'vio m Sport goal kick; (in libro) cross-reference; (di appuntamento) postponement; (di merce) return

rio'nale adj local. **ri'one** m district

riordi'nare vt tidy [up]; (ordinare di nuovo) reorder; (riorganizzare) re-organize

riorganiz'zare vt reorganize

ripa'gare vt repay

ripa'ra|re vt protect; (aggiustare) repair; (porre rimedio) remedy ● vi ~re a make up for. **~rsi** vr take shelter. **~to** adj (luogo) sheltered. **~zi'one** f repair; fig reparation. **ri'paro** m shelter; (rimedio) remedy

ripar'ti|re vt (dividere) divide ● vi leave again. **~zi'one** f division

ripas'sa|re vt recross; (rivedere) revise ● vi pass again. **ri'passo** m (di lezione) revision

ripensa'mento m second thoughts pl

ripen'sare vi changing one's mind; **~ a** think of; ripensaci! think again!

riper'correre vt go back over

riper'cosso pp di ripercuotere

ripercu'oter|e vt strike again. **~si** vr (suono:) reverberate; **~si su** (avere conseguenze) impact on. **ripercussi'one** f repercussion

ripe'scare vt fish out (oggetti)

ripe'tente mf student repeating a year

ripet'er|e vt repeat. **~ersi** vr (evento:) recur. **~izi'one** f repetition; (di lezione) revision; (lezione privata) private lesson. **~uta'mente** adv repeatedly

ri'piano m (di scaffale) shelf; (terreno pianeggiante) terrace

ri'picc|a f fare qcsa per **~a** do sth out of spite. **~o** m spite

'ripido adj steep

ripie'gar|e vt refold; (abbassare) lower ● vi (indietreggiare) retreat. **~si** vr bend; (sedile:) fold. **ripi'ego** m expedient; (via d'uscita) way out

ripi'eno adj full; (Culin) stuffed ● m filling; (Culin) stuffing

ri'porre vt put back; (mettere da parte) put away; (collocare) place; re-

peat (domanda)

ripor'tar|e vt (restituire) bring/take back; (riferire) report; (subire) suffer; (Math) carry; win (vittoria); transfer (disegno). **~si** vr go back; (riferirsi) refer

ripo'sante adj (colore) restful, soothing

ripo'sa|re vi rest ● vt put back. **~rsi** vr rest. **~to** adj (mente) fresh. **ri'poso** m rest; andare a riposo retire; riposo! (Mil) at easel; giorno di riposo day off

ripo'stiglio m cupboard

ri'posto pp di riporre

ri'prender|e vt take again; (prendere indietro) take back; (riconquistare) recapture; (ricuperare) recover; (ricominciare) resume; (rimproverare) reprimand; take in (cucitura); Cinema shoot. **~si** vr recover; (correggersi) correct oneself

ri'presa f resumption; (ricupero) recovery; (Theat) revival; Cinema shot; (Auto) acceleration; (Mus) repeat. **~ aerea** bird's-eye view

ripresen'tar|e vt resubmit (domanda, certificato). **~si** vr go/come back again; (come candidato) run again; (occasione:) arise again

ri'preso pp di riprendere

ripristi'nare vt restore

ripro'dotto pp di riprodurre

ripro'du|rre vt, **~rsi** vr reproduce. **~t'tivo** adj reproductive. **~zi'one** f reproduction

ripro'mettersi vr intend

ri'prova f confirmation

ripudi'are vt repudiate

ripu'gnan|te adj repugnant. **~za** f disgust. **ripu'gnare** vi **ripugnare a** disgust

ripu'li|re vt clean [up]; fig polish

ripuls|i'one f repulsion. **~'ivo** adj repulsive

ri'quadro m square; (pannello) panel

ri'sacca f undertow

risa'lire vt go back up ●vi ~ a (nel tempo) go back to; (essere datato a) date back to, go back to

risal'tare vi stand out. ri'salto m prominence; (rilievo) relief

risa'nare vt heal; (bonificare) reclaim

risa'puto adj well-known

risarci'mento m compensation. risar'cire vt indemnify

ri'sata f laugh

riscalda'mento m heating. ~ autonomo central heating (for one flat)

riscal'dar|e vt heat; warm (persona). ~si vr warm up

riscat'tar|e vt ransom. ~si vr redeem oneself. ri'scatto m ransom; (morale) redemption

rischia'rar|e vt light up; brighten (colore). ~si vr light up; (cielo:) clear up

rischi|'are vt risk ●vi run the risk. 'rischio m risk. ~'oso adj risky

risciac'quare vt rinse

riscon'trare vt (confrontare) compare; (verificare) check; (rilevare) find. ri'scontro m comparison; check; (Comm: risposta) reply

ri'scossa f revolt; (riconquista) recovery

riscossi'one f collection

ri'scosso pp di riscuotere

riscu'oter|e vt shake; (percepire) draw; (ottenere) gain; cash (assegno). ~si vr rouse oneself

risen'ti|re vt hear again; (provare) feel ●vi ~re di feel the effect of. ~rsi vr (offendersi) take offence. ~to adj resentful

ri'serbo m reserve; mantenere il ~ remain tight-lipped

ri'serva f reserve; (di caccia, pesca) preserve; Sport substitute, reserve. ~ di caccia game reserve. ~ naturale wildlife reserve

riser'va|re vt reserve; (prenotare)

book; (per occasione) keep. ~rsi vr (ripromettersi) plan for oneself (cambiamento). ~'tezza f reserve. ~to adj reserved

ri'siedere vi ~ a live in/at

'riso¹ m (cereale) rice

'riso² pp di ridere ●m (pl f risa) laughter; (singolo) laugh. ~'lino m giggle

ri'solto pp di risolvere

risolu'tezza f determination. riso'luto adj resolute, determined. ~zi'one f resolution

ri'solver|e vt resolve; (Math) solve. ~si vr (decidersi) decide; ~si in turn into

riso|na|nza f resonance; aver ~nza arouse great interest. ~re vi resound; (rimbombare) echo

ri'sorgere vi rise again

risorgi'mento m revival; (storico) Risorgimento

ri'sorsa f resource; (espediente) resort

ri'sorto pp di risorgere

ri'sotto m risotto

ri'sparmi mpl (soldi) savings

risparmi|'a|re vt save; (salvare) spare. ~'tore, ~'trice mf saver ri'sparmio m saving

rispecchi'are vt reflect

rispet'tabil|e adj respectable. ~ità f respectability

rispet'tare vt respect; farsi ~ command respect

rispet'tivo adj respective

ri'spetto m respect; ~ a as regards; (in confronto a) compared to

rispet'tosa'mente adv respectfully. ~'toso adj respectful

risplen'dente adj shining. ri'splendere vi shine

rispon'den|te adj ~te a in keeping with. ~za f correspondence

ri'spondere vi answer; (rimbeccare) answer back; (obbedire) respond; ~ a reply to; ~ **di** (rendersi responsabile) answer for

ri'spost|a f answer, reply; (reazione) response. ~o pp di rispondere

'rissa f brawl. ris'soso adj pugnacious

ristabi'lir|e vt re-establish. ~si vi (in salute) recover

rista'gnare vi stagnate; (sangue:) coagulate. ri'stagno m stagnation

ri'stampa f reprint; (azione) reprinting. ristam'pare vt reprint

risto'rante m restaurant

risto'ra|re vt refresh. ~rsi vi liter take some refreshment; (riposarsi) take a rest. ~'tore, ~'trice mf (proprietario di ristorante) restaurateur; (fornitore) caterer ● adj refreshing. ri'storo m refreshment; (sollievo) relief

ristret'tezza f narrowness; (povertà) poverty

ri'stretto pp di restringere ● adj narrow; (condensato) condensed; (limitato) restricted; di idee ristrette narrow-minded

ristruttu'rare vt restructure (ditta); refurbish (casa)

risucchi'are vt suck in. ri'succhio m whirlpool; (di corrente) undertow

risul'ta|re vi result; (riuscire) turn out. ~to m result

risuo'nare vi echo; (Phys) resonate

risurrezi'one f resurrection

risusci'tare vt resuscitate; fig revive ● vi return to life

risvegli'ar|e vt reawaken (interesse). ~si vi wake up; (natura:) awake; (desiderio:) be aroused. ri'sveglio m waking up (dell'interesse) revival; (del desiderio) arousal

ri'svolto m lapel; (di pantaloni) turn-up, cuff Am; (di manica) cuff; (di tasca) flap; (di libro) inside flap

ritagli'are vt cut out. ri'taglio m cutting; (di stoffa) scrap

ritar'da|re vi be late; (orologio:) be

slow ● vt delay; slow down (progresso); (differire) postpone. ~'tario, -a mf late-comer

ri'tardo m delay; essere in ~ be late; (volo:) be delayed

ri'tegno m reserve

rite'n|ere vt retain; deduct (somma); (credere) believe. ~uta f deduction

riti'ra|re vt throw back (palla); (prelevare) withdraw; (riscuotere) draw; collect (pacco). ~rsi vr withdraw; (stoffa:) shrink; (da attività) retire; (marea:) recede. ~ta f retreat; (WC) toilet. ri'tiro m withdrawal; (Relig) retreat; (da attività) retirement. ritiro bagagli baggage reclaim

'ritmo m rhythm

'rito m rite; di ~ customary

ritoc'care vt touch up

ritor'nare vi return; (andare venire indietro) go/come back; (ricorrere) recur; (ridiventare) become again

ritor'nello m refrain

ri'torno m return

ritorsi'one f retaliation

ri'trarre vt withdraw; (distogliere) turn away; (rappresentare) portray

ritrat'ta|re vt deal with again; retract (dichiarazione). ~zi'one f withdrawal, retraction

ritrat'tista mf portrait painter. ri'tratto pp di ritrarre ● m portrait

ritro'sia f shyness. ri'troso adj backward; (timido) shy; a ritroso backwards; ritroso a reluctant to

ritro'va|re vt find [again]; regain (salute). ~rsi vr meet; (di nuovo) meet again; (capitare) find oneself; (raccapezzarsi) see one's way. ~to m discovery. ri'trovo m meeting-place; (notturno) night-club

'ritto adj upright; (diritto) straight

ritu'ale adj & m ritual

riunifi'ca|re vt reunify. ~rsi vr be reunited. ~zi'one f reunification

riuni'one *f* meeting; (*fra amici*) reunion

riu'nir|e *vt* (*unire*) join together; (*radunare*) gather. **~si** *vr* be re-united; (*adunarsi*) meet

riu'sci|re *vi* (*aver successo*) succeed; (*in matematica ecc*) be good (**in** a); (*aver esito*) turn out; **le è riuscito simpatico** she found him likeable. **~ta** *f* result; (*successo*) success

'riva *f* shore; (*di fiume*) bank

ri'val|e *mf* rival. **~ità** *f inv* rivalry

rive'dere *vt* see again; revise (*lezione*); (*verificare*) check

rive'la|re *vt* reveal. **~rsi** *vr* (*dimostrarsi*) turn out. **~'tore** *adj* revealing ● *m* (*Techn*) detector. **~zi'one** *f* revelation

ri'vendere *vt* resell

rivendi'ca|re *vt* claim. **~zi'one** *f* claim

ri'vendi|ta *f* (*negozio*) shop. **~'tore**, **~'trice** *mf* retailer. **~tore autorizzato** authorized dealer

ri'verbero *m* reverberation; (*bagliore*) glare

rive'renza *f* reverence; (*inchino*) curtsy; (*di uomo*) bow

rive'rire *vt* respect; (*ossequiare*) pay one's respects to

river'sar|e *vt* pour. **~si** *vr* (*fiume*) flow

rivesti'mento *m* covering

rive'sti|re *vt* (*rifornire di abiti*) clothe; (*ricoprire*) cover; (*internamente*) line; hold (*carica*). **~rsi** *vr* get dressed again; (*per una festa*) dress up

rivi'era *f* coast; **la ~ ligure** the Italian Riviera

ri'vincita *f Sport* return match; (*vendetta*) revenge

rivis'suto *pp di* rivivere

ri'vista *f* review; (*pubblicazione*) magazine; (*Theat*) revue; **passare in ~** review

ri'vivere *vi* come to life again; (*riprendere le forze*) revive ● *vt* relive

ri'volger|e *vt* turn; (*indirizzare*) address; **~e da** (*distogliere*) turn away from. **~si** *vt* turn round; **~si a** (*indirizzarsi*) turn to

ri'volta *f* revolt

rivol'tante *adj* disgusting

rivol'tar|e *vt* turn [over]; (*mettendo l'interno verso l'esterno*) turn inside out; (*sconvolgere*) upset. **~si** *vr* (*ribellarsi*) revolt

rivol'tella *f* revolver

ri'volto *pp di* rivolgere

rivoluzio'nare *vt* revolutionize. **~io, -a** *adj & mf* revolutionary. **rivoluzi'one** *f* revolution; (*fig: disordine*) chaos

riz'zar|e *vt* raise; (*innalzare*) erect; prick up (*orecchie*). **~si** *vr* stand up; (*capelli:*) stand on end; (*orecchie:*) prick up

'roaming *m inv* (*Teleph*) **~ [internazionale]** roaming

'roba *f* stuff; (*personale*) belongings *pl*, stuff; (*faccenda*) thing; (🔲: *droga*) drugs *pl*. **~ da mangiare** things to eat

ro'baccia *f* rubbish

ro'bot *m inv* robot. **~ da cucina** food processor

robu'stezza *f* sturdiness, robustness; (*forza*) strength. **ro'busto** *adj* sturdy, robust; (*forte*) strong

'rocca *f* fortress. **~'forte** *f* stronghold

roc'chetto *m* reel

'roccia *f* rock

ro'da|ggio *m* running in. **~re** *vt* run in

'roder|e *vt* gnaw; (*corrodere*) corrode. **~si** *vr* **~si da** be consumed with. **rodi'tore** *m* rodent

rodo'dendro *m* rhododendron

ro'gnone *m* (*Culin*) kidney

'rogo *m* (*supplizio*) stake; (*per*

r

cadaveri) pyre

'Roma f Rome

Ro'ma'nia f Romania

ro'manico adj Romanesque

ro'mano, -a adj & mf Roman

romanti'cismo m romanticism. **ro'mantico** adj romantic

ro'man|za f romance. **~'zato** pp romanticized; **~'zesco** adj fictional; (stravagante) wild, unrealistic. **~zi'ere** m novelist

ro'manzo adj Romance ●m novel. **~ giallo** thriller

'rombo m rumble; (Math) rhombus; (pesce) turbot

'romper|e vt break; break off (relazione); **non ~e [le scatole]!** (🔲: seccare) don't be a pain [in the neck]!. **~si** vr break; **~si una gamba** break one's leg

rompi'capo m nuisance; (indovinello) puzzle

rompi'collo m daredevil; **a ~ at** breakneck speed

rompighi'accio m ice-breaker

rompi'scatole mf inv 🔲 pain

'ronda f rounds pl

ron'della f (Mech) washer

'rondine f swallow

ron'done m swift

ron'fare vi snore

ron'zino m jade

ron'zio m buzz

'rosa f rose. **~ dei venti** wind rose ●adj & m pink. **ro'saio** m rose-bush

ro'sario m rosary

ro'sato adj rosy ●m (vino) rosé

'roseo adj pink

ro'seto m rose garden

rosma'rino m rosemary

'roso pp di rodere

roso'lare vt brown

roso'lia f German measles

ro'sone m rosette; (apertura) rose-window

'rospo m toad

ros'setto m (per labbra) lipstick

'rosso adj & m red; **passare con il ~** jump a red light. **~ d'uovo** [egg] yolk. **ros'sore** m redness; (della pelle) flush

rosticce'ria f shop selling cooked meat and other prepared food

ro'tabile adj strada **~** carriageway

ro'taia f rail; (solco) rut

ro'ta|re vt/i rotate. **~zi'one** f rotation

rote'are vt/i roll

ro'tella f small wheel; (di mobile) castor

roto'lar|e vt/i roll. **~si** vr roll [about]. **'rotolo** m roll; **andare a rotoli** go to rack and ruin

rotondità f roundness; **~** pl (curve femminili) curves. **ro'tondo, -a** adj round ●f (spiazzo) terrace

ro'tore m rotor

'rotta¹ f (Naut), (Aeron) course; **far ~ per** make course for; **fuori ~ off** course

'rotta² f **a ~ di collo** at breakneck speed; **essere in ~ con** be on bad terms with

rot'tame m scrap; fig wreck

'rotto pp di rompere ●adj broken; (stracciato) torn

rot'tura f break

'rotula f kneecap

rou'lette f inv roulette

rou'lotte f inv caravan, trailer Am

rou'tine f inv routine; **di ~** (operazioni, controlli) routine

ro'vente adj scorching

'rovere m (legno) oak

rovesci'ar|e vt knock over; (sottosopra) turn upside down; (rivoltare) turn inside out; spill (liquido); overthrow (governo); reverse (situazione). **~si** vr (capovolgersi) overturn; (riversarsi) pour. **ro'vescio** m (contrario) reverse; **alla rovescia** (capovolto) upside down;

(*con l'interno all'esterno*) inside out ● *m* reverse; (*nella maglia*) purl; (*di pioggia*) downpour; *Tennis* backhand

ro'vina *f* ruin; (*crollo*) collapse

rovi'na|re *vt* ruin; (*guastare*) spoil ● *vi* crash. ~rsi *vr* be ruined. ~to *adj* (*oggetto*) ruined. rovi'noso *adj* ruinous

rovi'stare *vt* ransack

'rovo *m* bramble

'rozzo *adj* rough

R.R. *abbr* (*ricevuta di ritorno*) return receipt for registered mail

'ruba *f* andare a ~ sell like hot cakes

ru'bare *vt* steal

rubi'netto *m* tap, faucet *Am*

ru'bino *m* ruby

ru'brica *f* column; (*in programma televisivo*) TV report; (*quaderno con indice*) address book. ~ telefonica telephone and address book

'rude *adj* rough

'rudere *m* ruin

rudimen'tale *adj* rudimentary. rudi'menti *mpl* rudiments

ruffi'an|a *f* procuress. ~o *m* pimp; (*adulatore*) bootlicker

'ruga *f* wrinkle

'ruggine *f* rust; fare la ~ go rusty

rug'gi|re *vi* roar. ~to *m* roar

rugi'ada *f* dew

ru'goso *adj* wrinkled

rul'lare *vi* roll; (*Aeron*) taxi

rul'lino *m* film

rul'lio *m* rolling; (*Aeron*) taxiing

rum *m inv* rum

ru'meno, -a *adj* & *mf* Romanian

ru'mor|e *m* noise; *fig* rumour. ~eggi'are *vi* rumble. rumo'roso *adj* noisy; (*sonoro*) loud

ru'olo *m* roll; (*Theat*) role; di ~ on the staff

ru'ota *f* wheel; andare a ~ libera free-wheel. ~ di scorta spare wheel

'rupe *f* cliff

ru'rale *adj* rural

ru'scello *m* stream

'ruspa *f* bulldozer

rus'sare *vi* snore

'Russ|ia *f* Russia. r~o, -a *adj* & *mf* Russian; (*lingua*) Russian

'rustico *adj* rural; (*carattere*) rough

rut'tare *vi* belch. 'rutto *m* belch

'ruvido *adj* coarse

ruzzo'l|are *vi* tumble down. ~one *m* tumble; cadere ruzzoloni tumble down

Ss

'sabato *m* Saturday

'sabbi|a *f* sand. ~e *pl* mobili quicksand. ~'oso *a* sandy

sabo'ta|ggio *m* sabotage. ~re *vt* sabotage. ~tore, ~trice *mf* saboteur

'sacca *f* bag. ~ da viaggio travelling-bag

sacca'rina *f* saccharin

sac'cente *adj* pretentious ● *mf* know-all

saccheggi'a|re *vt* sack; *hum* raid (*frigo*)

sac'chetto *m* bag

'sacco *m* sack; (*Anat*) sac; mettere nel ~ *fig* swindle; un ~ (*moltissimo*) a lot; un ~ di (*gran quantità*) lots of. ~ a pelo sleeping-bag

sacer'dote *m* priest

sacra'mento *m* sacrament

sacrifi'ca|re *vt* sacrifice. ~rsi *vr* sacrifice oneself. ~to *adj* (*non valorizzato*) wasted. sacri'ficio *m* sacrifice

sa'crilego *adj* sacrilegious

'sacro *adj* sacred ● *m* (*Anat*) sacrum

sacro'santo adj sacrosanct

'sadico, -a adj sadistic ●mf sadist. sa'dismo m sadism

sa'etta f arrow

sa'fari m inv safari

'saga f saga

sa'gace adj shrewd

sag'gezza f wisdom

saggi'are vt test

'saggio[1] m (scritto) essay; (prova) proof; (di metallo) assay; (campione) sample; (esempio) example

'saggio[2] adj wise

sag'gistica f non-fiction

Sagit'tario m (Astr) Sagittarius

sa'goma f shape; (profilo) outline. sago'mato adj shaped

'sagra f festival

sagre|'stano m sacristan. ~'stia f sacristy

'sala f hall; (stanza) room; (salotto) living room. ~ **d'attesa** waiting room. ~ **da ballo** ballroom. ~ **macchine** engine room. ~ **operatoria** operating theatre. ~ **parto** delivery room. ~ **da pranzo** dining room

sa'lame m salami

sala'moia f brine

sa'lare vt salt

sa'lario m wages pl

sa'lasso m essere un ~ fig cost a fortune

sala'tini mpl savouries (eaten with aperitifs)

sa'lato adj salty; (costoso) dear

sal'ciccia f = SALSICCIA

sal'dar|e vt weld; set (osso); pay off (debito); settle (conto); ~**e a stagno** solder. ~**si** vr (Med: osso) knit

salda'trice f welder; (a stagno) soldering iron

salda'tura f weld; (azione) welding; (di osso) knitting

'saldo adj firm; (resistente) strong ●m

settlement; (svendita) sale; (Comm) balance

'sale m salt. ~ **fine** table salt. ~ **grosso** cooking salt. **sali** pl **e tabacchi** tobacconist's shop

'salice m willow. ~ **piangente** weeping willow

sali'ente adj outstanding; **i punti salienti di un discorso** the main points of a speech

sali'era f salt-cellar

sa'lina f salt-works sg

sa'li|re vi go/come up; (levarsi) rise; (su treno ecc) get on; (in macchina) get in ●vt go/come up (scale). ~**ta** f climb; (aumento) rise; **in ~ta** uphill

sa'liva f saliva

'salma f corpse

'salmo m psalm

sal'mone m & adj inv salmon

sa'lone m hall; (salotto) living room; (di parrucchiere) salon. ~ **di bellezza** beauty parlour

salo'pette f inv dungarees pl

salot'tino m bower

sa'lotto m drawing room; (soggiorno) sitting room; (mobili) [three-piece] suite

sal'pare vt/i sail; ~ **l'ancora** weigh anchor

'salsa f sauce

sal'sedine f saltiness

sal'siccia f sausage

sal'ta|re vi jump; (venir via) come off; (balzare) leap; (esplodere) blow up; ~**re fuori** spring from nowhere; (oggetto cercato): turn up; **è ~to fuori che...** it emerged that...; ~**re fuori con...** come out with...; ~**re in mente** spring to mind ●vt jump [over]; skip (pasti, lezioni); (Culin) sauté. ~**to** adj (Culin) sautéed

saltel'lare vi hop; (di gioia) skip

saltim'banco m acrobat

'salto m jump; (balzo) leap; (dislivello) drop; (omissione, lacuna) gap; **fare un**

~ **da** drop in on. ~ **in alto** high jump. ~ **con l'asta** pole-vault. ~ **in lungo** long jump. ~ **pagina** (*Comput*) page down

saltuaria'mente *adv* occasionally. **saltu'ario** *adj* desultory; **lavoro saltuario** casual work

sa'lubre *adj* healthy

salume'ria *f* delicatessen. **sa'lumi** *mpl* cold cuts

salu'tare *vt* greet; (*congedandosi*) say goodbye to; (*portare i saluti a*) give one's regards to; (*Mil*) salute ● *adj* healthy

sa'lute *f* health; ~! (*dopo uno starnuto*) bless you!; (*a un brindisi*) your health!

sa'luto *m* greeting; (*di addio*) goodbye; (*Mil*) salute; **saluti** *pl* (*ossequi*) regards

'salva *f* salvo; **sparare a salve** fire blanks

salvada'naio *m* money box

salva'gente *m* lifebelt; (*a giubbotto*) life jacket; (*ciambella*) rubber ring; (*spartitraffico*) traffic island

salvaguar'dare *vt* safeguard. **salvagu'ardia** *f* safeguard

sal'var|e *vt* save; (*proteggere*) protect. ~**si** *vr* save oneself

salva'slip *m inv* panty-liner

salva|'taggio *m* rescue; (*Naut*) salvage; (*Comput*) saving; **battello di** ~**taggio** lifeboat

sal'vezza *f* safety; (*Relig*) salvation

'salvia *f* sage

salvi'etta *f* serviette

'salvo *adj* safe ● *prep* except [for] ● *conj* ~ **che** (*a meno che*) unless; (*eccetto che*) except that

samari'tano, -a *adj* & *mf* Samaritan

sam'buco *m* elder

san *m* S~ **Francesco** Saint Francis

sa'nare *vt* heal

sana'torio *m* sanatorium

san'cire *vt* sanction

'sandalo *m* sandal

sangu|e *m* blood; **al** ~**e** (*carne*) rare; **farsi cattivo** ~**e per** worry about. ~**e freddo** composure; **a** ~**e freddo** in cold blood. ~**'igno** *adj* blood

sangui'naccio *m* (*Culin*) black pudding

sangui'nante *adj* bleeding

sangui'nar|e *vi* bleed. ~**io** *adj* bloodthirsty

sangui'noso *adj* bloody

sangui'suga *f* leech

sanità *f* soundness; (*salute*) health. ~ **mentale** mental health

sani'tario *adj* sanitary; **Servizio S**~ Health Service

'sano *adj* sound; (*salutare*) healthy; ~ **di mente** sane; ~ **come un pesce** as fit as a fiddle

San Sil'vestro *m* New Year's Eve

santifi'care *vt* sanctify

'santo *adj* holy; (*con nome proprio*) saint ● *m* saint. **san'tone** *m* guru. **santu'ario** *m* sanctuary

sanzi'one *f* sanction

sa'pere *vt* know; (*essere capace di*) be able to; (*venire a sapere*) hear; **saperla lunga** know a thing or two ● *vi* ~ **di** know about; (*aver sapore di*) taste of; (*aver odore di*) smell of; **saperci fare** have the know-how ● *m* knowledge

sapi'en|te *adj* expert ● *m* (*uomo colto*) sage. ~**za** *f* wisdom

sa'pone *m* soap. ~ **da bucato** washing soap. **sapo'netta** *f* bar of soap

sa'pore *m* taste. **sapori'ta'mente** *adv* soundly. **sapo'rito** *adj* tasty

sapu'tello, -a *adj* & *m* 🔲 know-all, know-it-all *Am*

saraci'nesca *f* roller shutter

sar'cas|mo *m* sarcasm. ~**tico** *adj* sarcastic

Sar'degna *f* Sardinia

sar'dina f sardine

'sardo, -a adj & mf Sardinian

> *i* Sardo Sardo is Sardinia's traditional language. It is considered to be an independent language because of its many differences from Italian and its long independent history. Sardinian preserves many features derived from Latin which were lost in Italian, e.g. the k-sound in words like *chelu* (Italian *cielo*).

sar'donico adj sardonic

'sarto, -a m tailor • f dressmaker. ~**'ria** f tailor's; dressmaker's; (arte) couture

'sasso m stone; (ciottolo) pebble

sassofo'nista mf saxophonist. **sas'sofono** m saxophone

sas'soso adj stony

sa'tellite adj inv & nm satellite

sati'nato adj glossy

'satira f satire. **sa'tirico** adj satirical

satu'ra|re vt saturate. ~**zi'one** f saturation. **'saturo** adj saturated; (pieno) full

'sauna f sauna

savoi'ardo m (biscotto) sponge finger

sazi'ar|e vt satiate. ~**si** vr ~**si di** fig grow tired of

sazietà f **mangiare a** ~ eat one's fill. **'sazio** adj satiated

sbaciucchi'ar|e vt smother with kisses. ~**si** vr kiss and cuddle

sbada'ta|ggine f carelessness; **è stata una** ~**ggine** it was careless. ~**'mente** adv carelessly. **sba'dato** adj careless

sbadigli'are vi yawn. **sba'diglio** m yawn

sba'fa|re vt sponge. **'sbafo** m sponging; **a** ~ without paying

sbagli'ar|e vi make a mistake; (aver torto) be wrong • vt make a mistake in; ~**e strada** go the wrong way; ~**e numero** get the number wrong; (Teleph) dial a wrong number. ~**si** vr make a mistake. **'sbaglio** m mistake; **per sbaglio** by mistake

sbal'l|are vt unpack; ⏺ screw up (conti) • vi ⏺ go crazy. ~**ato** adj (squilibrato) unbalanced

sballot'tare vt toss about

sbalor'di|re vt stun • vi be stunned. ~**'tivo** adj amazing. ~**to** adj stunned

sbal'zare vt throw; (da una carica) dismiss • vi bounce; (saltare) leap. **'sbalzo** m bounce; (sussulto) jolt; (di temperatura) sudden change; **a sbalzi** in spurts; **a sbalzo** (lavoro a rilievo) embossed

sban'care vt bankrupt; ~ **il banco** break the bank

sbanda'mento m (Auto) skid; (Naut) list; fig going off the rails

sban'da|re vi (Auto) skid; (Naut) list. ~**rsi** vr (disperdersi) disperse. ~**ta** f skid; (Naut) list. ~**to, -a** adj mixed-up • mf mixed-up person

sbandie'rare vt wave; fig display

sbarac'care vt/i clear up

sbaragli'are vt rout. **sba'raglio** m rout; **mettere allo sbaraglio** rout

sbaraz'zar|e vt clear. ~**si** vr ~**si di** get rid of

sbaraz'zino, -a adj mischievous • mf scamp

sbar'bar|e vt, ~**si** vr shave

sbar'care vt/i disembark; ~ **il lunario** make ends meet. **'sbarco** m landing; (di merci) unloading

'sbarra f bar; (di passaggio a livello) barrier. ~**'mento** m barricade. **sbar'rare** vt bar; (ostruire) block; cross (assegno); (spalancare) open wide

sbatacchi'are vt/i 🔲 bang

'sbatter|e vt bang; slam; bang (porta); (urtare) knock; (Culin) beat;

flap (ali); shake (tappeto) ● *vi* bang; (porta:) slam, bang. ~**si** *vr* ✗ rush around; ~**sene** di qcsa not give a damn about sth. **sbat'tuto** *adj* tossed; (*Culin*) beaten; *fig* run down

sba'va|re *vi* dribble; (colore:) smear. ~**'tura** *f* smear; **senza** ~**ture** *fig* faultless

sbelli'carsi *vr* ~ **dalle risa** split one's sides [with laughter]

'**sberla** *f* slap

sbia'di|re *vt/i*, ~**rsi** *vr* fade. ~**to** *adj* faded; *fig* colourless

sbian'car|e *vt/i*, ~**si** *vr* whiten

sbi'eco *adj* slanting; **di** ~ on the slant; (guardare) sidelong; **guardare** qcno di ~ look askance at sb; **tagliare di** ~ cut on the bias

sbigot'ti|re *vt* dismay ● *vi*, ~**rsi** *vr* be dismayed. ~**to** *adj* dismayed

sbilanci'ar|e *vt* unbalance ● *vi* (*perdere l'equilibrio*) overbalance. ~**si** *vr* lose one's balance

sbizzar'rirsi *vr* satisfy one's whims

sbloc'care *vt* unblock; (*Mech*) release; decontrol (prezzi)

sboc'care *vi* ~ **in** (fiume:) flow into; (strada:) lead to; (folla:) pour into

sboc'cato *adj* foul-mouthed

sbocci'are *vi* blossom

'**sbocco** *m* flowing; (foce) mouth; (*Comm*) outlet

sbolo'gnare *vt* 🄸 get rid of

'**sbornia** *f* **prendere una** ~ get drunk

sbor'sare *vt* pay out

sbot'tare *vi* burst out

sbotto'nar|e *vt* unbutton. ~**si** *vr* (🄸: confidarsi) open up; ~**si la camicia** unbutton one's shirt

sbra'carsi *vr* put on something more comfortable; ~ **dalle risate** 🄸 kill oneself laughing

sbracci'a|rsi *vr* wave one's arms. ~**to** *adj* bare-armed; (abito)

sleeveless

sbrai'tare *vi* bawl

sbra'nare *vt* tear to pieces

sbricio'lar|e *vt*, ~**si** *vr* crumble

sbri'ga|re *vt* expedite; (occuparsi di) attend to. ~**rsi** *vr* be quick. ~**'tivo** *adj* quick

sbrindel'lare *vt* tear to shreds. ~**to** *adj* in rags

sbro'dare *vt* stain

'**bronz|a** *f* **prendersi una** ~**a** get tight. **sbron'zarsi** *vr* get tight. ~**o** *adj* (ubriaco) tight

sbruffo'nata *f* boast. **sbruf'fone, -a** *mf* boaster

sbu'care *vi* come out

sbucci'ar|e *vt* peel; shell (piselli). ~**si** *vr* graze oneself

sbuf'fare *vi* snort; (per impazienza) fume. '**sbuffo** *m* puff

'**scabbia** *f* scabies *sg*

sca'broso *adj* rough; *fig* difficult; (scena) indecent

scacci'are *vt* chase away

'**scacc|o** *m* check; ~**hi** *pl* (gioco) chess; (pezzi) chessmen; **dare** ~**o matto** a checkmate; **una** ~**hi** (tessuto) checked. ~**hi'era** *f* chess-board

sca'dente *adj* shoddy

sca'de|nza *f* expiry; (*Comm*) maturity; (di progetto) deadline; **a breve/lunga** ~**nza** short-/long-term. ~**re** *vi* expire; (valore:) decline; (debito:) be due. **sca'duto** *adj* out-of-date

sca'fandro *m* diving suit; (di astronauta) spacesuit

scaf'fale *m* shelf; (libreria) bookshelf

sca'fista *m* motor-boat operator; (pej) refugee smuggler (using motorboat)

'**scafo** *m* hull

scagion'are *vt* exonerate

'**scaglia** *f* scale; (di sapone) flake; (scheggia) chip

scagli'ar|e *vt* fling. ~**si** *vr* fling oneself; ~**si contro** *fig* rail against

scaglio|o'nare vt space out. **~'one** m group; **a ~oni** in groups. **~one di reddito** tax bracket

'**scala** f staircase; (portatile) ladder; (Mus, misura, fig) scale; **scale** pl stairs. **~ mobile** escalat-or; (dei salari) cost of living index

sca'la|re vt climb; layer (capelli); (detrarre) deduct. **~ta** f climb; (dell'Everest ecc) ascent; **fare delle ~te** go climbing. **~'tore, ~'trice** mf climber

scalca'gnato adj down at heel

scalci'are vi kick

scalci'nato adj shabby

scalda'bagno m water heater

scalda'muscoli m inv leg-warmer

scal'dar|e vt heat. **~si** vr warm up; (eccitarsi) get excited

scal'fi|re vt scratch. **~t'tura** f scratch

scali'nata f flight of steps. **sca'lino** m step; (di scala a pioli) rung

scalma'narsi vr get worked up

'**scalo** m slipway; (Aeron, Naut) port of call; **fare ~ a** call at; (Aeron) land at

sca'lo|gna f bad luck. **~'gnato** adj unlucky

scalop'pina f escalope

scal'pello m chisel

'**scalpo** m scalp

scal'pore m noise; **far ~** fig cause a sensation

scal'trezza f shrewdness. '**scaltro** adj shrewd

scal'zare vt bare the roots of (albero); fig undermine; (da una carica) oust

'**scalzo** adj & adv barefoot

scambi|'are vt exchange; **~are qcno per qualcun altro** mistake sb for somebody else. **~'evole** adj reciprocal

'**scambio** m exchange; (Comm) trade; **libero ~** free trade

scamosci'ato adj suede

scampa'gnata f trip to the country

scampa'nato adj (gonna) flared

scampanel'lata f [loud] ring

scam'pare vt save; (evitare) escape. **~'scampo** m escape

'**scampolo** m remnant

scanala'tura f groove

scandagli'are vt sound

scanda'listico adj sensational

scandaliz'zare vt scandalize. **~iz'zarsi** vr be scandalized

'**scanda|lo** m scandal. **~'loso** adj (somma) ecc scandalous; (fortuna) outrageous

Scandi'navia f Scandinavia. **scandi'navo, -a** adj & mf Scandi-navian

scan'dire vt scan (verso); pro-nounce clearly (parole)

scan'nare vt slaughter

'**scanner** m inv scanner

scanneriz'zare vt (Comput) scan

scan'sar|e vt shift; (evitare) avoid. **~si** vr get out of the way

scansi'one f (Comput) scanning

'**scanso** m **a ~ di** in order to avoid; **a ~ di equivoci** to avoid any misun-derstanding

scanti'nato m basement

scanto'nare vi turn the corner; (svignarsela) sneak off

scanzo'nato adj easy-going

scapac'cione m smack

scape'strato adj dissolute

'**scapito** m loss

'**scapola** f shoulder-blade

'**scapolo** m bachelor

scappa'mento m (Auto) exhaust

scap'pa|re vi escape; (andarsene) dash [off]; (sfuggire) slip; **mi ~ da ridere** I want to burst out laughing. **~ta** f short visit. **~tella** f escapade; (infedeltà) fling. **~toia** f way out

scappel'lotto m cuff

scarabocchi'are vt scribble

scara'bocchio m scribble

scara'faggio m cockroach

scara'muccia f skirmish

scaraven'tare vt hurl

scarce'rare vt release [from prison]

scardi'nare vt unhinge

'scarica f discharge; (di arma da fuoco) volley; (fig) shower

scari'ca|re vt discharge; unload (arma, merci); (Comput) download; fig unburden. **~rsi** vr (fiume:) flow; (orologio, batteria:) run down; fig unwind. **~'tore** m loader; (di porto) docker. **'scarico** adj unloaded; (vuoto) empty; (orologio) run down; (batteria) flat; fig untroubled ● m unloading; (di rifiuti) dumping; (di acqua) draining; (di sostanze inquinanti) discharge; (luogo) [rubbish] dump; (Auto) exhaust; (idraulico) drain; (tubo) waste pipe

scarlat'tina f scarlet fever

scar'latto adj scarlet

'scarno adj thin; (stile) bare

sca'ro|gna f ⊤ bad luck. **~'gnato** adj ⊤ unlucky

'scarpa f shoe. **scarpe** pl **da ginnastica** trainers, gym shoes

scar'pata f slope; (burrone) escarpment

scarpi'nare vi hike

scar'pone m boot. **scarponi** pl **da sci** ski boot. **scarponi** pl **da trekking** walking boots

scarroz'zare vt/i drive around

scarseggi'are vi be scarce; **~ di** (mancare) be short of

scar'sezza f scarcity, shortage. **scarsità** f shortage. **'scarso** adj scarce; (manchevole) short

scarta'mento m (Rail) gauge. **~ ridotto** narrow gauge

scar'tare vt discard; unwrap (pacco); (respingere) reject ● vi (deviare) swerve. **'scarto** m scrap; (in carte) discard; (deviazione) swerve; (distacco) gap

scas'sa|re vt break. **~to** adj ⊤ clapped out

scassi'nare vt force open

scassina'tore, -'trice mf burglar. **'scasso** m (furto) house-breaking

scate'na|re vt fig stir up. **~rsi** vr break out; fig: (temporale:) break; (⊤: infiammarsi) get excited. **~to** adj crazy

'scatola f box; (di latta) can, tin Br; **in ~** (cibo) canned, tinned Br

scat'tare vi go off; (balzare) spring up; (adirarsi) lose one's temper; take (foto). **'scatto** m (balzo) spring; (d'ira) outburst; (di telefono) unit; (dispositivo) release; **a scatti** jerkily; **di scatto** suddenly

scatu'rire vi spring

scaval'care vt jump over (muretto); climb over (muro); (fig: superare) overtake

sca'vare vt dig (buca); dig up (tesoro); excavate (città sepolta). **'scavo** m excavation

'scegliere vt choose, select

scelle'rato adj wicked

'scelt|a f choice; (di articoli) range; **...a ~a** (in menu) choice of...; **prendine uno a ~a** take your choice o pick; **di prima ~a** top-grade, choice. **~o** pp di **scegliere** ● adj select; (merce ecc) choice

sce'mare vt/i diminish

sce'menza f silliness; (azione) silly thing to do/say. **'scemo** adj silly

'scempio m havoc; (fig: di paesaggio) ruination; **fare ~ di** play havoc with

'scena f scene; (palcoscenico) stage; **entrare in ~** go/come on; fig enter the scene; **fare ~** put on an act; **fare una ~** make a scene; **andare in ~** (Theat) be staged, be put on. **sce'nata** f row, scene

sce'nata f row, scene

'scendere vi go/come down; (da treno, autobus) get off; (da macchina) get out; (strada) slope; (notte, prezzi:)

fall •vt go/come down (scale)

sceneggi'a|re vt dramatize. **∼to m** television serial. **∼'tura** f screenplay

'scenico adj scenic

scervel'la|rsi vr rack one's brains. **∼to** adj brainless

'sceso pp di scendere

scetti'cismo m scepticism. **'scet- tico, -a** adj sceptical •mf sceptic

'scheda f card. **∼ elettorale** ballot-paper. **∼ di espansione** (Comput) expansion card. **∼ telefonica** phonecard. **sche'dare** vt file. **sche'dario** m file; (mobile) filing cabinet

sche'dina f ≈ pools coupon; **gio- care la ∼** do the pools

'scheggi|a f fragment; (di legno) splinter. **∼'arsi** vr chip; (legno:) splinter

'scheletro m skeleton

'schema m diagram; (abbozzo) outline. **sche'matico** adj schematic

'scherma f fencing

scher'mirsi vr protect oneself

'schermo m screen; **grande ∼** big screen

scher'nire vt mock. **'scherno** m mockery

scher'zare vi joke; (giocare) play

'scherzo m joke; (trucco) trick; (ef- fetto) play; (Mus) scherzo; **fare uno ∼ a qcno** play a joke on sb. **scher'zoso** adj playful

schiaccia'noci m inv nutcrackers pl

schiacci'ante adj damning

schiacci'are vt crush; Sport smash; press (pulsante); crack (noce)

schiaffeggi'are vt slap. **schi'affo** m slap; **dare uno schiaffo a** slap

schiamaz'zare vi make a racket; (galline:) cackle

schian'tar|e vt break. **∼si** vr crash •vi **schianto dalla fatica** I'm wiped out. **'schianto** m crash; ① knock-out; (divertente) scream

schia'rir|e vt clear; (sbiadire) fade

•vi, **∼si** vr brighten up; **∼si la gola** clear one's throat

schiavitù f slavery. **schi'avo, -a** mf slave

schi'ena f back; **mal di ∼** back-ache. **schie'nale** m (di sedia) back

schi'er|a f (Mil) rank; (moltitudine) crowd. **∼a'mento** m lining up

schie'rar|e vt draw up. **∼si** vr draw up; **∼si con** (parteggiare) side with

schiet'tezza f frankness. **schi'etto** adj frank; (puro) pure

schi'fezza f una ∼ rubbish. **schifil- 'toso** adj fussy. **'schifo** m disgust; **mi fa schifo** it makes me sick. **schi'foso** adj disgusting; (di cattiva qualità) rubbishy

schioc'care vt crack; snap (dita). **schi'occo** m (di frusta) crack; (di bacio) smack; (di dita, lingua) click

schi'uder|e vt, **∼si** vr open

schi'u|ma f foam; (di sapone) lather; (feccia) scum. **∼ma da barba** shaving foam. **∼'mare** vt skim •vi foam

schi'uso pp di schiudere

schi'var|e vt avoid. **'schivo** adj bashful

schizo'frenico adj schizophrenic

schiz'zare vt squirt; (inzaccherare) splash; (abbozzare) sketch •vi spurt; **∼ via** scurry away

schizzi'noso adj squeamish

'schizzo m squirt; (di fango) splash; (abbozzo) sketch

sci m inv ski; (sport) skiing. **∼ d'acqua** water-skiing

'scia f wake; (di fumo ecc) trail

sci'abola f sabre

scia'callo m jackal; fig profiteer

sciac'quar|e vt rinse. **∼si** vr rinse oneself. **sci'acquo** m mouthwash

scia'gu|ra f disaster. **∼'rato** adj un-fortunate; (scellerato) wicked

scialac'quare vt squander

scia'lare vi squander

sci'albo adj pale; fig dull

sci'alle *m* shawl

scia'luppa *f* dinghy. ~ **di salva-taggio** lifeboat

sci'ame *m* swarm

sci'ampo *m* shampoo

scian'cato *adj* lame

sci'are *vi* ski

sci'arpa *f* scarf

sci'atica *f* (*Med*) sciatica

scia'tore, -'trice *mf* skier

sci'atto *adj* slovenly; (*stile*) careless. **sciat'tone, -a** *mf* slovenly person

scienti'fico *adj* scientific

sci'enz|a *f* science; (*sapere*) know-ledge. ~**i'ato, -a** *mf* scientist

'scimmi|a *f* monkey. ~**ot'tare** *vt* ape

scimpanzé *m inv* chimpan-zee, chimp

scimu'nito *adj* idiotic

'scinder|e *vt*, **~si** *vr* split

scin'tilla *f* spark. **scintil'lante** *adj* sparkling. **scintil'lare** *vi* sparkle

scioc'ca|nte *adj* shocking. **~re** *vt* shock

scioc'chezza *f* foolishness; (*assur-dità*) nonsense. **sci'occo** *adj* foolish

sci'oglier|e *vt* untie; (*liberare*) re-lease; (*liquefare*) melt; dissolve (*con-tratto, qcsa nell'acqua*); loosen up (*muscoli*). **~si** *vr* release oneself; (*li-quefarsi*) melt; (*contratto*): be dis-solved; (*pastiglia*): dissolve

scioglilingua *m inv* tongue-twister

scio'lina *f* wax

sciol'tezza *f* agility; (*disinvol-tura*) ease

sci'olto *pp di* **sciogliere** ● *adj* loose; (*agile*) agile; (*disinvolto*) easy; **versi sciolti** blank verse *sg*

sciope'ra|nte *mf* striker. **~re** *vi* go on strike, strike. **sci'opero** *m* strike. **sciopero a singhiozzo** on-off strike

sciori'nare *vt fig* show off

sci'pito *adj* insipid

scip'pa|re *vt* ① snatch. **~'tore, ~'trice** *mf* bag snatcher. **'scippo** *m* bag-snatching

sci'rocco *m* sirocco

sciro'ppato *adj* (*frutta*) in syrup. **sci'roppo** *m* syrup

'scisma *m* schism

scissi'one *f* division

'scisso *pp di* **scindere**

sciu'par|e *vt* spoil; (*sperperare*) waste. **~si** *vr* get spoiled; (*deperire*) wear oneself out. **sciu'pio** *m* waste

scivo'l|are *vi* slide; (*involontariamente*) slip. **'scivolo** *m* slide; (*Techn*) chute. **~oso** *adj* slippery

scoc'care *vt* shoot ● *vi* (*scintilla*): shoot out; (*ora*): strike

scocci'a|re *vt* (*dare noia a*) bother. **~rsi** *vr* be bothered. **~to** *adj* ① narked. **~'tore, ~'trice** *mf* bore. **~'tura** *f* nuisance

sco'della *f* bowl

scodinzo'lare *vi* wag its tail

scogli'era *f* cliff; (*a fior d'acqua*) reef. **'scoglio** *m* rock; (*fig: ostacolo*) stum-bling block

scoi'attolo *m* squirrel

scola'|pasta *m inv* colander. **~pi'atti** *m inv* dish drainer

sco'lara *f* schoolgirl

sco'la|re *vt* drain; strain (*pasta, ver-dura*) ● *vi* drip

sco'la|ro *m* schoolboy. **~'resca** *f* pupils *pl*. **~'stico** *adj* school *attrib*

scol'la|re *vt* cut away the neck of (*abito*); (*staccare*) unstick. **~to** *adj* low-necked. **~'tura** *f* neckline

'scolo *m* drainage

scolo'ri|re *vt*, **~rsi** *vr* fade. **~to** *adj* faded

scol'pire *vt* carve; (*imprimere*) engrave

scombi'nare *vt* upset

scombus'so|lare *vt* muddle up

scom'mess|a *f* bet. **~o** *pp di*

scommettere. ~~scom'mettere~~ vt bet

scomo'dar|e vt, ~si vr trouble. **scomodità** f discomfort. **'scomodo** adj uncomfortable

scompa'rire vi disappear; (morire) pass on. **scom'parsa** f disappearance; (morte) passing, death. **scom'parso, -a** pp di **scomparire** ●mf departed

scomparti'mento m compartment. **scom'parto** f compartment

scom'penso m imbalance

scompigli'are vt disarrange. **scom'piglio** m confusion

scom'po|rre vt take to pieces; (fig: turbare) upset. ~rsi vr get flustered. ~sto pp di **scomporre** ●adj (sguaiato) unseemly; (disordinato) untidy

sco'muni|ca f excommunication. ~'care vt excommunicate

sconcer'ta|re vt disconcert; (rendere perplesso) bewilder. ~to adj disconcerted; bewildered

scon'cezza f obscenity. **'sconcio** adj dirty ●m è uno **sconcio che...** it's a disgrace that...

sconclusio'nato adj incoherent

scon'dito adj unseasoned; (insalata) with no dressing

sconfes'sare vt disown

scon'figgere vt defeat

sconfi'na|re vi cross the border; (in proprietà privata) trespass. ~to adj unlimited

scon'fitt|a f defeat. ~o pp di **sconfiggere**

scon'forto m dejection

sconge'lare vt thaw out (cibo), defrost

scongi|u'rare vt beseech; (evitare) avert. ~'uro m **fare gli scongiuri** touch wood, knock on wood Am

scon'nesso pp di **sconnettere** ●adj fig incoherent. **scon'nettere** vt disconnect

sconosci'uto, -a adj unknown

●mf stranger

sconquas'sare vt smash; (sconvolgere) upset

sconside'rato adj inconsiderate

sconsigli'a|bile adj not advisable. ~re vt advise against

sconso'lato adj disconsolate

scon'ta|re vt discount; (dedurre) deduct; (pagare) pay off; serve (pena). ~to adj discount; (ovvio) expected; ~to **del 10%** with 10% discount

scon'tento adj displeased ●m discontent

'sconto m discount; **fare uno ~** give a discount

scon'trarsi vr clash; (urtare) collide

scon'trino m ticket; (di cassa) receipt

'scontro m clash; (urto) collision

scon'troso adj unsociable

sconveni'ente adj unprofitable; (scorretto) unseemly

sconvol'gente adj mind-blowing

scon'vol|gere vt upset; (mettere in disordine) disarrange. ~gi'mento m upheaval. ~to pp di **sconvolgere** ●adj distraught

'scopa f broom. **sco'pare** vt sweep

scoperchi'are vt take the lid off (pentola); take the roof off (casa)

sco'pert|a f discovery. ~o pp di **scoprire** ●adj uncovered; (senza riparo) exposed; (conto) overdrawn; (spoglio) bare

'scopo m aim; **allo ~ di** in order to

scoppi'are vi burst; fig break out. **scoppiet'tare** vi crackle. **'scoppio** m burst; (di guerra) outbreak; (esplosione) explosion

sco'prire vt discover; (togliere la copertura a) uncover

scoraggi'a|re vt discourage. ~rsi vr lose heart

scor'butico adj peevish

scorcia'toia f short cut

'scorcio m (di epoca) end; (di cielo)

patch; (*in arte*) foreshortening; **di ~** (vedere) from an angle. **~ panoramico** panoramic view

scor'da|re *vt*, **~rsi** *vr* forget. **~to** *adj* (*Mus*) out of tune

'scorgere *vt* make out; (*notare*) notice

'scoria *f* waste; (*di metallo, carbone*) slag; **scorie** *pl* **radioattive** radioactive waste

scor'nato *adj fig* hangdog. **'scorno** *m* humiliation

scorpi'one *m* scorpion; (*Astr*) **S ~** Scorpio

scorraz'zare *vi* run about

'scorrere *vt* (*dare un'occhiata*) glance through ● *vi* run; (*scivolare*) slide; (*fluire*) flow; (*Comput*) scroll. **scor're-vole** *adj* **porta scorrevole** sliding door

scor'ria *f* raid

scorret'tezza *f* (*mancanza di educazione*) bad manners *pl*. **scor'retto** *adj* incorrect; (*sconveniente*) improper

scorri'banda *f* raid; *fig* excursion

'scors|a *f* glance. **~o** *pp di* **scorrere** ● *adj* last

scor'soio *adj* **nodo ~** noose

'scor|ta *f* escort; (*provvista*) supply. **~'tare** *vt* escort

scor'te|se *adj* discourteous. **~'sia** *f* discourtesy

scorti'ca|re *vt* skin. **~'tura** *f* graze

'scorto *pp di* **scorgere**

'scorza *f* peel; (*crosta*) crust; (*corteccia*) bark

sco'sceso *adj* steep

'scossa *f* shake; (*Electr, fig*) shock; **prendere la ~** get an electric shock. **~ elettrica** electric shock. **~ sismica** earth tremor

'scosso *pp di* **scuotere** ● *adj* shaken; (*sconvolto*) upset

sco'stante *adj* off-putting

sco'sta|re *vt* push away. **~rsi** *vr* stand aside

scostu'mato *adj* dissolute; (*maleducato*) ill-mannered

scot'tante *adj* dangerous

scot'ta|re *vt* scald ● *vi* burn; (*bevanda:*) be too hot; (*sole, pentola:*) be very hot. **~rsi** *vr* burn oneself; (*al sole*) get sunburnt; *fig* get one's fingers burnt. **~'tura** *f* burn; (*da liquido*) scald; **~tura solare** sunburn; *fig* painful experience

'scotto *adj* overcooked

sco'vare *vt* (*scoprire*) discover

'Scoz|ia *f* Scotland. **~'zese** *adj* Scottish ● *mf* Scot

scredi'tare *vt* discredit

scre'mare *vt* skim

screpo|la're *vt*, **~rsi** *vr* crack. **~to** *adj* (*labbra*) chapped. **~'tura** *f* crack

screzi'ato *adj* speckled

'screzio *m* disagreement

scribac|chi'are *vt* scribble. **~'chino, -a** *mf* scribbler; (*impiegato*) penpusher

scric|chio'l|are *vi* creak. **~io** *m* creaking

'scricciolo *m* wren

'scrigno *m* casket

scrimina'tura *f* parting

'scrit|ta *f* writing; (*su muro*) graffiti. **~to** *pp di* **scrivere** ● *adj* written ● *m* writing; (*lettera*) letter. **~'toio** *m* writing-desk. **~'tore, ~'trice** *mf* writer. **~'tura** *f* writing; (*Relig*) scripture

scrittu'rare *vt* engage

scriva'nia *f* desk

scri'vere *vt* write; (*descrivere*) write about; **~ a macchina** type

scroc'c|are *vt* **~are a scrocco** eat as a sponge off. **'scrocco** *m* 🗍 **a scrocco** 🗍 without paying. **~one, -a** *mf* sponger

'scrofa *f* sow

scrol'lar|e *vt* shake; **~e le spalle** shrug one's shoulders. **~si** *vr* shake oneself; **~si qcsa di dosso** shake sth off

s

scrosci'are vi roar; (pioggia:) pelt down. **'scroscio** m roar; (di pioggia) pelting

scro'star|e vt scrape. **∼si** vr peel off

'scrupo|lo m scruple; (diligenza) care; **senza scrupoli** unscrupulous, without scruples. **∼'loso** adj scrupulous

scru'ta|re vt scan; (indagare) search. **∼'tore** m (alle elezioni) returning officer

scruti'nare vt scrutinize. **scru'tinio** m (di voti alle elezioni) poll; (Sch) assessment of progress

scu'cire vt unstitch

scude'ria f stable

scu'detto m Sport championship shield

'scudo m shield

sculacci'are vt spank. **∼'ata** f spanking. **∼'one** m spanking

sculet'tare vi wiggle one's hips

scul'tore, -'trice m sculptor • f sculptress. **∼'tura** f sculpture

scu'ola f school. **∼ elementare** primary school. **∼ guida** driving school. **∼ materna** day nursery. **∼ media [inferiore]** secondary school (10-13). **∼ [media] superiore** secondary school (13-18)

scu'oter|e vt shake. **∼si** vr (destarsi) rouse oneself; **∼si di dosso** shake off

'scure f axe

scu'reggia f 🔲 fart. **scureggi'are** vi 🔲 fart

scu'rire vt/i darken

'scuro adj dark • m darkness; (imposta) shutter

'scusa f excuse; (giustificazione) apology; **chiedere ∼** apologize; **chiedo ∼!** I'm sorry!

scu'sar|e vt excuse. **∼si** vr **∼si apologize (di** for); **[mi] scusi!** excuse me!; (chiedendo perdono) [I'm] sorry!

sdebi'tarsi vr repay a kindness

sde'gna|re vt despise. **∼rsi** vr get angry. **∼to** adj indignant. **'sdegno** m disdain. **sde'gnoso** adj disdainful

sdolci'nato adj sentimental

sdoppi'are vt halve

sdrai'arsi vr lie down. **'sdraio** m [**sedia a**] **sdraio** deckchair

sdrammatiz'zare vi provide some comic relief

sdruccio'levole adj slippery

---

se

● conj if; (interrogativo) whether, if; **se mai** (caso mai) if need be; **se mai telefonasse,...** should he call,..., if he calls,...; **se no** otherwise, or else; **se non altro** at least, if nothing else; **se pure** (sebbene) even though; (anche se) even if; **non so se sia vero** I don't know whether it's true, I don't know if it's true; **come se** as if; **se lo avessi saputo prima!** if only I had known before!; **e se andassimo fuori a cena?** how about going out for dinner?

● m inv if

---

sé pers pron oneself; (lui) himself; (lei) herself; (esso, essa) itself; (loro) themselves; **l'ha fatto da sé** he did it himself; **ha preso i soldi con sé** he took the money with him; **si sono tenuti le notizie per sé** they kept the news to themselves

seb'bene conj although

'secca f shallows pl; **in ∼** (nave) aground

sec'cante adj annoying

sec'ca|re vt dry; (importunare) annoy • vi dry up. **∼rsi** vr dry up; (irritarsi) get annoyed; (annoiarsi) get bored. **∼'tore, ∼'trice** mf nuisance. **∼'tura** f bother

secchi'ello m pail

'secchio m bucket. ~ della spazzatura rubbish bin, trash can Am

'secco, -a adj dry; (disseccato) dried; (magro) thin; (brusco) curt; (preciso) sharp ●m (siccità) drought; lavare a ~ dry-clean

secessi'one f secession

seco'lare adj age-old; (laico) secular. 'secolo m century; (epoca) age

se'cond|a f (Rail, Sch) second class; (Auto) second [gear]. ~o adj second ●m second; (secondo piatto) main course ●prep according to; ~o me in my opinion

secrezi'one f secretion

'sedano m celery

seda'tivo adj & m sedative

'sede f seat; (centro) centre; (Relig) see; (Comm) head office. ~ sociale registered office

seden'tario adj sedentary

se'der|e vi sit. ~si vr sit down ●m (deretano) bottom

'sedia f chair. ~ a dondolo rocking chair. ~ a rotelle wheelchair

sedi'cente adj self-styled

'sedici adj & m sixteen

se'dile m seat

sedizi'o|ne f sedition. ~so adj seditious

se'dotto pp di sedurre

sedu'cente adj seductive

se'durre vt seduce

se'dut|a f session; (di posa) sitting. ~ stante adv here and now

seduzi'one f seduction

'sega f saw

'segala f rye

se'gare vt saw

'seggio m seat. ~ elettorale polling station

seg'gio|la f chair. ~lino m seat; (da bambino) child's seat. ~lone m (per bambini) high chair

seggio'via f chair lift

seghe'ria f sawmill

se'ghetto m hacksaw

seg'mento m segment

segna'lar|e vt signal; (annunciare) announce; (indicare) point out. ~si vr distinguish oneself

se'gna|le m signal; (stradale) sign. ~le acustico beep. ~le orario time signal. ~letica f signals pl. ~letica stradale road signs pl

se'gnar|e vt mark; (prendere nota) note; (indicare) indicate; Sport score. ~si vr cross oneself. 'segno m sign; (traccia, limite) mark; (bersaglio) target; far segno (col capo) nod; (con la mano) beckon. segno zodiacale birth sign

segre'gare vt segregate. ~zi'one f segregation

segretari'ato m secretariat

segre'tario, -a mf secretary. ~ comunale town clerk

segrete'ria f [administrative] office; (segretariato) secretariat. ~ telefonica answering machine

segre'tezza f secrecy

se'greto adj & m secret; in ~ in secret

segu'ace mf follower

segu'ente adj following, next

se'gugio m bloodhound

segu'ire vt/i follow; (continuare) continue

segui'tare vt/i continue

'seguito m retinue; (sequela) series; (continuazione) continuation; di ~ in succession; in ~ later on; in ~ a following; al ~ owing to; fare ~ a follow up

'sei adj & m six. sei'cento adj & m six hundred; il Seicento the seventeenth century. sei'mila adj & m six thousand

sel'ciato m paving

selet'tivo adj selective. selezio'nare vt select. selezi'one f selection

s

'sella f saddle. **sel'lare** vt saddle

seltz m soda water

'selva f forest

selvag'gina f game

sel'vaggio, -a adj wild; (primitivo) savage ● mf savage

sel'vatico adj wild

se'maforo m traffic lights pl

se'mantica f semantics sg

sem'brare vi seem; (assomigliare) look like; **che te ne sembra?** what do you think?; **mi sembra che...** I think...

'seme m seed; (di mela) pip; (di carte) suit; (sperma) semen

se'mestre m half-year

semi'cerchio m semicircle

semifi'nale f semifinal

semi'freddo m ice cream and sponge dessert

'semina f sowing

semi'nare vt sow; Ⓕ shake off (inseguitori)

semi'nario m seminar; (Relig) seminary

seminter'rato m basement

se'mitico adj Semitic

sem'mai conj in case ● adv è lui, ~, che... if anyone, it's him who...

'semola f bran. **semo'lino** m semolina

'semplice adj simple; **in parole semplici** in plain words. **~'cemente** adv simply. **~cità** f simplicity. **~fi'care** vt simplify

'sempre adv always; (ancora) still; **per ~** for ever

sempre'verde adj & m evergreen

'senape f mustard

se'nato m senate. **sena'tore** m senator

se'nile adj senile. **~ità** f senility

'senno m sense

'seno m breast; (Math) sine

sen'sato adj sensible

sensazi|o'nale adj sensational. **~'one** f sensation

sen'sibile adj sensitive; (percepibile) perceptible; (notevole) considerable. **~ità** f sensitivity. **~iz'zare** vt make more aware (a of)

sensi'tivo, -a adj sensory ● mf sensitive person; (medium) medium

'senso m sense; (significato) meaning; (direzione) direction; **non ha ~** it doesn't make sense; **perdere i sensi** lose consciousness. **~ dell'umorismo** sense of humour. **~ unico** (strada) one-way; **~ vietato** no entry

sensu'alle adj sensual. **~ità** f sensuality

sen'tenz|a f sentence; (massima) saying. **~i'are** vi pass judgment

senti'ero m path

sentimen'tale adj sentimental. **senti'mento** m feeling

senti'nella f sentry

sen'ti|re vt feel; (udire) hear; (ascoltare) listen to; (gustare) taste; (odorare) smell ● vi feel; (udire) hear; **~re caldo/freddo** feel hot/cold. **~rsi** vr feel; **~rsi di fare qcsa** feel like doing sth; **~rsi bene** feel well; **~rsi poco bene** feel unwell. **~to** adj sincere

sen'tore m inkling

'senza prep without; **~ correre** without running; **senz'altro** certainly; **~ ombrello** without an umbrella

senza'tetto m inv i **~** the homeless

sepa'ra|re vt separate. **~rsi** vr separate; (amici:) part; **~rsi da** be separated from. **~ta'mente** adv separately. **~zi'one** f separation

se'pol|cro m sepulchre. **~to** pp di seppellire. **~'tura** f burial

seppel'lire vt bury

'seppia f cuttle fish; **nero di ~** sepia

sep'pure *conj* even if

se'quenza *f* sequence

seque'strare *vt* (*rapire*) kidnap; (*Jur*) impound; (*confiscare*) confiscate. **se'questro** *m* impounding; (*di persona*) kidnap[ping]

'sera *f* evening; **di ∼** in the evening. **se'rale** *adj* evening. **se'rata** *f* evening; (*ricevimento*) party

ser'bare *vt* keep; harbour (*odio*); cherish (*speranza*)

serba'toio *m* tank. **∼ d'acqua** water tank; (*per una città*) reservoir

'Serbia *f* Serbia

'serbo, -a *adj* & *mf* Serbian ● *m* (*lingua*) Serbian

sere'nata *f* serenade

serenità *f* serenity. **se'reno** *adj* serene; (*cielo*) clear

ser'gente *m* sergeant

seria'mente *adv* seriously

'serie *f inv* series; (*complesso*) set; *Sport* division; **fuori ∼** custom-built; **produzione in ∼** mass production; **di ∼ B** second-rate

serietà *f* seriousness. **'serio** *adj* serious; (*degno di fiducia*) reliable; **sul serio** seriously; (*davvero*) really

ser'mone *m* sermon

'serpe *f liter* viper. **∼ggi'are** *vi* meander; (*diffondersi*) spread

ser'pente *m* snake

'serra *f* greenhouse; **effetto ∼** greenhouse effect

ser'randa *f* shutter

ser'ra|re *vt* shut; (*stringere*) tighten; (*incalzare*) press on. **∼'tura** *f* lock

'server *m inv* (*Comput*) server

ser'vir|e *vt* serve; (*al ristorante*) wait on ● *vi* serve; (*essere utile*) be of use; **non serve** it's no good. **∼si** *vr* (*di cibo*) help oneself; **∼si da** buy from; **∼si di** use

servitù *f* servitude; (*personale di servizio*) servants *pl*

ser'vizio *m* service; (*da caffè ecc*) set;

(*di cronaca, sportivo*) report; **servizi** *pl* bathroom; **essere di ∼** be on duty; **fare ∼** (*autobus ecc*) run; **fuori ∼** (*bus*) not in service; (*ascensore*) out of order; **∼ compreso** service charge included. **∼ in camera** room service. **∼ civile** civilian duties done instead of national service. **∼ militare** military service. **∼ pubblico** utility company. **∼ al tavolo** waiter service

'servo, -a *mf* servant

servo'sterzo *m* power steering

ses'san|ta *adj* & *m* sixty. **∼'tina** *f* **una ∼tina** about sixty

sessi'one *f* session

'sesso *m* sex

sessu'al|e *adj* sexual. **∼ità** *f* sexuality

'sesto¹ *adj* sixth

'sesto² *m* (*ordine*) order

'seta *f* silk

setacci'are *vt* sieve. **se'taccio** *m* sieve

'sete *f* thirst; **avere ∼** be thirsty

'setta *f* sect

set'tan|ta *adj* & *m* seventy. **∼'tina** *f* **una ∼tina** about seventy

'sette *adj* & *m* seven. **∼cento** *agg* & *m* seven hundred; **il S∼cento** the eighteenth century

set'tembre *m* September

settentri|o'nale *adj* northern ● *mf* northerner. **∼'one** *m* north

setti'ma|na *f* week. **∼'nale** *agg* & *m* weekly

'settimo *adj* seventh

set'tore *m* sector

severità *f* severity. **se'vero** *adj* severe; (*rigoroso*) strict

se'vizi|a *f* torture; **se'vizie** *pl* torture *sg*. **∼'are** *vt* torture

sezio'nare *vt* divide; (*Med*) dissect. **sezi'one** *f* section; (*reparto*) department; (*Med*) dissection

sfaccen'dato *adj* idle

sfacchi'na|re *vi* toil. **∼ta** *f*

drudgery

sfaccia|taggine f insolence. **~'ato** adj cheeky, fresh Am

sfa'celo m ruin; **in ~** in ruins

sfal'darsi vr flake off

sfa'mar|e vt feed. **~si** vr satisfy one's hunger

sfar'zoso adj sumptuous

sfa'sato adj [1] confused; (motore) which needs tuning

sfascia'r|e vt unbandage; (fracassare) smash. **~rsi** vr fall to pieces. **~to** adj beat-up

sfa'tare vt explode

sfati'cato adj lazy

sfavil'lare vi sparkle

sfavo'revole adj unfavourable

sfavo'rire vt disadvantage

sfer|a f sphere. **~ico** adj spherical

sfer'rare vt unshoe (cavallo); (scagliare) land

sfer'zare vt whip

sfian'carsi vr wear oneself out

sfi'bra|re vt exhaust. **~to** adj exhausted

'sfida f challenge. **sfi'dare** vt challenge

sfi'duci|a f mistrust. **~'ato** adj discouraged

sfigu'rare vt disfigure • vi (far cattiva figura) look out of place

sfilacci'ar|e vt, **~si** vr fray

sfi'la|re vt unthread; (togliere di dosso) take off • vi (truppe:) march past; (in parata) parade. **~rsi** vr come unthreaded; (collant:) ladder; take off (pantaloni). **~ta** f parade; (sfilza) series. **~ta di moda** fashion show

sfilza f (di errori) string

'sfinge f sphinx

sfi'nito adj worn out

sfio'rare vt skim; touch on (argomento)

sfio'rire vi wither; (bellezza:) fade

'sfitto adj vacant

'sfizio m whim, fancy; **togliersi uno ~** satisfy a whim

sfo'cato adj out of focus

sfoci'are vi **~ in** flow into

sfode'ra|re vt draw (pistola, spada). **~to** adj unlined

sfo'gar|e vt vent. **~si** vr give vent to one's feelings

sfoggi'are vt/i show off. **'sfoggio** m show, display; **fare sfoggio di** show off

'sfoglia f sheet of pastry; **pasta ~** puff pastry

sfogli'are vt leaf through

'sfogo m outlet; fig outburst; (Med) rash; **dare ~ a** give vent to

sfolgo'rare vi blaze

sfol'lare vt clear • vi (Mil) be evacuated

sfol'tire vt thin [out]

sfon'dare vt break down • vi (aver successo) make a name for oneself

'sfondo m background

sfor'ma|re vt pull out of shape (tasche). **~rsi** vr lose its shape; (persona:) lose one's figure. **~to** m (Culin) flan

sfor'nito adj **~ di** (negozio) out of

sfor'tuna f bad luck. **~ta'mente** adv unfortunately. **sfortu'nato** adj unlucky

sfor'zar|e vt force. **~si** vr try hard. **'sforzo** m effort; (tensione) strain

sfot'tere vt [x] tease

sfracel'larsi vr smash

sfrat'tare vt evict. **'sfratto** m eviction

sfrecci'are vi flash past

sfregi'a|re vt slash. **~to** adj scarred

'sfregio m slash

sfre'na|rsi vr run wild. **~to** adj wild

sfron'tato adj shameless

sfrutta'mento m exploitation.

sfrut'tare vt exploit

sfug'gente adj elusive; (mento) receding

sfug'gi|re vi escape; ~re a escape [from]; **mi sfugge** it escapes me; **mi è sfuggito di mano** I lost hold of it ● vt avoid. ~**ta** f di ~**ta** in passing

sfu'ma|re vi (svanire) vanish; (colore:) shade off ● vt soften (colore). ~**tura** f shade

sfuri'ata f outburst [of anger]

sga'bello m stool

sgabuz'zino m cupboard

sgam'bet'tare vi kick one's legs; (camminare) trot. **sgam'betto** m fare lo sgambetto a qcno trip sb up

sganasci'arsi vr ~ **dalle risa** roar with laughter

sganci'ar|e vt unhook; (Rail) uncouple; drop (bombe); 🅕 cough up (denaro). ~**si** vr become unhooked; fig get away

sanghe'rato adj ramshackle

sgar'bato adj rude. **'sgarbo** m discourtesy

sgargi'ante adj garish

sgar'rare vi be wrong; (da regola) stray from the straight and narrow. **'sgarro** m mistake, slip

sgattaio'lare vi sneak away; ~ **via** decamp

sghignaz'zare vi laugh scornfully, sneer

sgoccio'lare vi drip

sgo'larsi vr shout oneself hoarse

sgomb[e]'rare vt clear [out]. **'sgombro** adj clear ● m (trasloco) removal; (pesce) mackerel

sgomen'tar|e vt dismay. ~**si** vr be dismayed. **sgo'mento** m dismay

sgomi'nare vt defeat

sgom'mata f screech of tyres

sgonfi'ar|e vt deflate. ~**si** vr go down. **'sgonfio** adj flat

'sgorbio m scrawl; (fig: vista sgradevole) sight

sgor'gare vi gush [out] ● vt flush out, unblock (lavandino)

sgoz'zare vt ~ **qcno** cut sb's throat

sgra'd|evole adj disagreeable. ~**ito** adj unwelcome

sgrammati'cato adj ungrammatical

sgra'nare vt shell (piselli); open wide (occhi)

sgran'chir|e vt, ~**si** vr stretch

sgranocchi'are vt munch

sgras'sare vt remove the grease from

sgrazi'ato adj ungainly

sgreto'lar|e vt, ~**si** vr crumble

sgri'da|re vt scold. ~**ta** f scolding

sgros'sare vt rough-hew (marmo); fig polish

sguai'ato adj coarse

sgual'cire vt crumple

sgu'ardo m look; (breve) glance

sguazzare vi splash; (nel fango) wallow

sguinzagli'are vt unleash

sgusci'are vt shell ● vi (sfuggire) slip away; ~ **fuori** slip out

shake'rare vt shake

---

si

● pers pron (riflessivo) oneself; (lui) himself; (lei) herself; (esso, essa) itself; (loro) themselves; (reciproco) each other; (tra più di due) one another; (impersonale) you, one; **lavarsi** wash [oneself]; **si è lavata** she washed [herself]; **lavarsi le mani** wash one's hands; **si è lavata le mani** she washed her hands; **si è mangiato un pollo intero** he ate an entire chicken by himself; **incontrarsi** meet each other; **la gente si aiuta a vicenda** people help one another; **non**

si sa mai you never know, one never knows *fml*; **queste cose si dimenticano facilmente** these things are easily forgotten
● *m* (*chiave, nota*) B

sì *adv* yes

'sia[1] ▷**ESSERE**

'sia[2] *conj* ~...~... (*entrambi*) both...and...; (*o l'uno o l'altro*) either...or...; ~ **che venga**, ~ **che non venga** whether he comes or not; **scegli** ~ **questo** ○ **quello** choose either this one or that one; **voglio** ~ **questo che quello** I want both this one and that one

sia'mese *adj* Siamese

sibi'lare *vi* hiss

si'cario *m* hired killer

sicché *conj* (*perciò*) so [that]; (*allora*) then

siccità *f* drought

sic'come *conj* as

Si'cili|a *f* Sicily. **s~'ano, -a** *adj & mf* Sicilian

si'cura *f* safety catch; (*di portiera*) child-proof lock. **~'mente** *adv* definitely

sicu'rezza *f* certainty; (*salvezza*) safety; **uscita di** ~ emergency exit. ~ **delle frontiere** homeland security

si'curo *adj* safe; (*certo*) sure; (*saldo*) steady; (*Comm*) sound ● *adv* certainly ● *m* safety; **al** ~ safe; **andare sul** ~ play [it] safe; **di** ~ definitely; **di** ~, **sarà arrivato** he must have arrived

siderur'gia *f* iron and steel industry

'sidro *m* cider

si'epe *f* hedge

si'ero *m* serum

sieroposi'tivo *adj* HIV positive

si'esta *f* afternoon nap

si'fone *m* siphon

Sig. *abbr* (*signore*) Mr

Sig.a *abbr* (*signora*) Mrs, Ms

siga'retta *f* cigarette

'sigaro *m* cigar

Sigg. *abbr* (*signori*) Messrs

sigil'lare *vt* seal. **si'gillo** *m* seal

'sigla *f* initials pl. ~ **musicale** signature tune. **si'glare** *vt* initial

Sig.na *abbr* (*signorina*) Miss, Ms

signifi'ca|re *vt* mean. ~'**tivo** *adj* significant. ~**to** *m* meaning

si'gnora *f* lady; (*davanti a nome proprio*) Mrs; (*non sposata*) Miss; (*in lettere ufficiali*) Dear Madam; **il signor Vené e** ~ Mr and Mrs Vené

si'gnore *m* gentleman; (*Relig*) lord; (*davanti a nome proprio*) Mr; (*in lettere ufficiali*) Dear Sir. **signo'rile** *adj* gentlemanly; (*di lusso*) luxury

signo'rina *f* young lady; (*seguito da nome proprio*) Miss

silenzia'tore *m* silencer

si'lenzi|o *m* silence. ~'**oso** *adj* silent

silhou'ette *f* silhouette

si'licio *m* **piastrina di** ~ silicon chip

sili'cone *m* silicone

'sillaba *f* syllable

silu'rare *vt* torpedo. **si'luro** *m* torpedo

simboleggi'are *vt* symbolize

sim'bolico *adj* symbolic[al]

'simbolo *m* symbol

similarità *f inv* similarity

'simil|e *adj* similar; (*tale*) such; ~**e a** like ~ *m* (*il prossimo*) fellow man. ~'**mente** *adv* similarly. ~'**pelle** *f* Leatherette®

simme'tria *f* symmetry. **sim'metrico** *adj* symmetric[al]

simpa'ti|a *f* liking; (*compenetrazione*) sympathy; **prendere qcno in** ~**a** take a liking to sb. **sim'patico** *adj* nice. ~**iz'zante** *mf* well-wisher. ~**iz'zare** *vt* ~**izzare con** take a liking to; ~**izzare per qcsa/qcno** lean towards sth/sb

simposio | slogare

sim'posio m symposium

simu'la|re vt simulate; feign (amicizia, interesse). ~zi'one f simulation

simul'taneo adj simultaneous

sina'goga f synagogue

sincerità f sincerity. sin'cero adj sincere

'sincope f syncopation; (Med) fainting fit

sincron'ia f synchronization

sincroniz'zare vt synchronize

sinda'ca|le adj [trade] union, [labor] union Am. ~'lista mf trade unionist, labor union member Am. ~re vt inspect. ~to m [trade] union, [labor] union Am; (associazione) syndicate

'sindaco m mayor

'sindrome f syndrome

sinfo'nia f symphony. sin'fonico adj symphonic

singhi|oz'zare vi (di pianto) sob. ~'ozzo m hiccup; (di pianto) sob

singo'lar|e adj singular ●m singular. ~'mente adv individually; (stranamente) peculiarly

'singolo adj single ●m individual; Tennis singles pl

si'nistra f left; a ~ on the left; girare a ~ turn to the left; con la guida a ~ (auto) with left-hand drive

sini'strato adj injured

si'nistr|o, -a adj left[-hand]; (avverso) sinister ●m accident ●f left [hand]; (Pol) left [wing]

'sino prep = FINO¹

si'nonimo adj synonymous ●m synonym

sin'tassi f syntax

'sintesi f inv synthesis; (riassunto) summary

sin'teti|co adj synthetic; (conciso) summary. ~z'zare vt summarize

sintetizza'tore m synthesizer

sinto'matico adj symptomatic.

'sintomo m symptom

sinto'nia f tuning; in ~ on the same wavelength

sinu'oso adj (strada) winding

si'pario m curtain

si'rena f siren

'Siri|a f Syria. s~'ano, -a adj & mf Syrian

si'ringa f syringe

'sismico adj seismic

si'stem|a m system. ~a operativo (Comput) operating system

siste'ma|re vt (mettere) put; tidy up (casa, camera); (risolvere) sort out; (procurare lavoro a) fix up with a job; (trovare alloggio a) find accommodation for; (sposare) marry off; (□: punire) sort out. ~rsi vr settle down; (trovare un lavoro) find a job; (trovare alloggio) find accommodation; (sposarsi) marry. ~tico adj systematic. ~zi'one f arrangement; (di questione) settlement; (lavoro) job; (alloggio) accommodation; (matrimonio) marriage

'sito m site. ~ web web site

situ'are vt place

situazi'one f situation

ski-'lift m inv ski tow

slacci'are vt unfasten

slanci'a|rsi vr hurl oneself. ~to adj slender. 'slancio m impetus; (impulso) impulse

sla'vato adj fair

'slavo adj Slav[onic]

sle'al|e adj disloyal. ~tà f disloyalty

sle'gare vt untie

'slitta f sledge, sleigh. ~'mento m (di macchina) skid; (fig: di riunione) postponement

'slitta|re vi (Auto) skid; (riunione:) be put off. ~ta f skid

slit'tino m toboggan

'slogan m inv slogan

slo'ga|re vt dislocate. ~rsi vr ~rsi una caviglia sprain one's ankle. ~'tura f dislocation

sloggi'are vi move out

Slo'vacchia f Slovakia

Slo'venia f Slovenia

smacchi'a|re vt clean. ~'tore m stain remover

'**smacco** m humiliating defeat

smagli'ante adj dazzling

smagli'a|rsi vr (calza:) run. ~'tura f run

smalizi'ato adj cunning

smal'ta|re vt enamel; glaze (ceramica); varnish (unghie). ~to adj enamelled

smalti'mento m disposal; (di merce) selling off. ~ rifiuti waste disposal; (di grassi) burning off

smal'tire vt burn off; (merce) sell off; fig get through (corrispondenza); ~ la sbornia sober up

'**smalto** m enamel; (di ceramica) glaze; (per le unghie) nail varnish

smantel|la'mento m dismantling. ~'lare vt dismantle

smarri'mento m loss; (psicologico) bewilderment

smar'ri|re vt lose; (temporaneamente) mislay. ~rsi vr get lost; (turbarsi) be bewildered

smasche'rar|e vt unmask. ~si vr (tradirsi) give oneself away

smemo'rato, -a adj forgetful ● mf scatterbrain

smen'ti|re vt deny. ~ta f denial

sme'raldo m & adj emerald

smerci'are vt sell off

smerigli'ato adj emery; vetro ~ frosted glass. **sme'riglio** m emery

'**smesso** pp di smettere ● adj (abiti) cast-off

'**smett|ere** vt stop; stop wearing (abiti); ~ila! stop it!

smidol'lato adj spineless

sminu'ir|e vt diminish. ~si vr fig belittle oneself

sminuz'zare vt crumble; (fig: analizzare) analyse in detail

smista'mento m clearing; (postale) sorting. **smi'stare** vt sort; (Mil) post

smisu'rato adj boundless; (esorbitante) excessive

smobili'ta|re vt demobilize. ~zi'one f demobilization

smo'dato adj immoderate

smog m smog

'**smoking** m inv dinner jacket, tuxedo Am

smon'ta|re vt take to pieces; (scoraggiare) dishearten ● vi (da veicolo) get off; (da cavallo) dismount; (dal servizio) go off duty. ~si vr lose heart

'**smorfi|a** f grimace; (moina) simper; fare ~e make faces. ~'oso adj affected

'**smorto** adj pale; (colore) dull

smor'zare vt dim (luce); tone down (colori); deaden (suoni); quench (sete)

'**smosso** pp di smuovere

smotta'mento m landslide

sms m inv (short message service) text message

'**smunto** adj emaciated

smu'over|e vt shift; (commuovere) move. ~si vr move; (commuoversi) be moved

smus'sar|e vt round off; (fig: attenuare) tone down. ~si vr go blunt

snatu'rato adj inhuman

snel'lir|e vt slim down. ~si vr slim [down]. '**snello** adj slim

sner'va|re vt enervate. ~rsi vr get exhausted

sni'dare vt drive out

snif'fare vt snort

snob'bare vt snub. **sno'bismo** m snobbery

snoccio'lare vt stone; fig blurt out

sno'da|re vt (sciogliere) loosen. ~rsi vr come untied; (strada:) wind. ~to adj (persona) double-jointed; (dita) flexible

so'ave adj gentle

sobbal'zare vi jerk; (trasalire) start. **sob'balzo** m jerk; (trasalimento) start

sobbar'carsi vr ~ a undertake

sob'borgo m suburb

sobil'la|re vt stir up

'sobrio adj sober

soc'chiu|dere vt half-close. ~**so** pp di socchiudere ● adj (occhi) half-closed; (porta) ajar

soc'cor|rere vt assist. ~**so** pp di soccorrere ● m assistance; soccorsi pl rescuers; (dopo disastro) relief workers. ~**so stradale** breakdown service

socialdemo'cra|tico, -a adj Social Democratic ● mf Social Democrat. ~**zia** f Social Democracy

soci'ale adj social

socia'li|smo m Socialism. ~**sta** agg & mf Socialist. ~**z'zare** vi socialize

società f inv society; (Comm) company. ~ **per azioni** plc. ~ **a responsabilità limitata** limited liability company

soci'evole adj sociable

'socio, -a mf member; (Comm) partner

sociolo'gia f sociology. **socio'lo-gico** adj sociological

'soda f soda

soddisfa'cente adj satisfactory

soddi'sfa|re vt/i satisfy; meet (richiesta); make amends for (offesa). ~**tto** pp di soddisfare ● adj satisfied. ~**zi'one** f satisfaction

'sodo adj hard; fig firm; (uovo) hard-boiled ● adv hard; **dormire** ~ sleep soundly

sofà m inv sofa

soffe'ren|te adj ill

soffer'marsi vr pause; ~ **su** dwell on the

sof'ferto pp di soffrire

soffi'a|re vt blow; reveal (segreto); (rubare) pinch 𝕋 ● vi blow. ~**ta** f fig ⊠ tip-off

'soffice adj soft

'soffio m puff; (Med) murmur

sof'fitt|a f attic. ~**o** m ceiling

soffo'ca|nte adj suffocating. ~**re** vt/i suffocate; (con cibo) choke; fig stifle

sof'friggere vt fry lightly

sof'frire vt/i suffer; (sopportare) bear; ~ **di** suffer from

sof'fritto pp di soffriggere

sof'fuso adj (luce) soft

sofisti'ca|re vt (adulterare) adulterate ● vi (sottilizzare) quibble. ~**to** adj sophisticated

sogget'tivo adj subjective

sog'getto m subject ● adj subject; **essere** ~ **a** be subject to

soggezi'one f subjection; (rispetto) awe

sogghi'gnare vi sneer

soggio'gare vt subdue

soggior'nare vi stay. **soggi'orno** m stay; (stanza) living room

soggi'ungere vt add

'soglia f threshold

sogli'ola f sole

so'gna|re vt/i dream; ~**re a occhi aperti** daydream. ~**tore, ~'trice** mf dreamer. **'sogno** m dream; **fare un sogno** have a dream; **neanche per sogno!** not at all!

'soia f soya

sol m (Mus) G

so'laio m attic

sola'mente adv only

so'lar|e adj (energia, raggi) solar; (crema) sun attrib. ~**ium** m inv solarium

sol'care vt plough. **'solco** m furrow; (di ruota) track; (di nave) wake; (di disco) groove

sol'dato m soldier

'soldo m non ha un ~ he hasn't got a penny; **senza un** ~ penniless;

soldi pl (denaro) money sg

'sole m sun; (luce del sole) sun[light]; **al ~** in the sun; **prendere il ~** sunbathe

soleggi'ato adj sunny

so'lenn|e adj solemn. **~ità** f solemnity

so'lere vi be in the habit of; **come si suol dire** as they say

sol'fato m sulphate

soli'da|le adj in agreement. **~rietà** f solidarity

solidifi'car|e vt/i, **~si** vr solidify

solidità f solidity; (di colori) fastness. **'solido** adj solid; (robusto) sturdy; (colore) fast **●** m solid

so'lista adj **●** mf soloist

solita'mente adv usually

soli'tario adj solitary; (isolato) lonely **●** m (brillante) solitaire; (gioco di carte) patience, solitaire

'solito adj usual; **essere ~ fare** qcsa be in the habit of doing sth **●** m usual; **di ~** usually

soli'tudine f solitude

solleci'ta|re vt speed up; urge (persona). **~zi'one** f (richiesta) request; (preghiera) entreaty

sol'leci|to adj prompt **●** m reminder. **~'tudine** f promptness; (interessamento) concern

solle'one m noonday sun; (periodo) dog days of summer

solleti'care vt tickle

solleva'mento m **~ pesi** weightlifting

solle'var|e vt lift; (elevare) raise; (confortare) comfort. **~si** vr rise; (riaversi) recover

solli'evo m relief

'solo, -a adj alone; (isolato) lonely; (unico) only; (Mus) solo; **da ~** by myself/yourself/himself etc **●** m f **il ~, la sola** the only one **●** m (Mus) solo **●** adv only

sol'stizio m solstice

sol'tanto adv only

so'lubile adj soluble; (caffè) instant

soluzi'one f solution; (Comm) payment

sol'vente adj & m solvent; **~ per unghie** nail polish remover

so'maro m ass; (Sch) dunce

so'matico adj somatic

somigli'an|te adj similar. **~za** f resemblance

somigli'ar|e vi **~e a** resemble. **~si** vr be alike

'somma f sum; (Math) addition

som'mare vt add; (totalizzare) add up

som'mario adj & m summary

som'mato adj **tutto ~** all things considered

sommeli'er m inv wine waiter

som'mer|gere vt submerge. **~'gibile** m submarine. **~so** pp di **sommergere**

som'messo adj soft

sommini'stra|re vt administer. **~zi'one** f administration

sommità f inv summit

'sommo adj highest; fig supreme **●** m summit

som'mossa f rising

sommozza'tore m frogman

so'naglio m bell

so'nata f sonata; fig 🔢 beating

'sonda f (Mech) drill; (Med, spaziale). **son'daggio** m drilling; (Med, spaziale) probe; (indagine) survey. **sondaggio d'opinioni** opinion poll. **son'dare** vt sound; (investigare) probe

sonnambu'lismo m sleepwalking. **son'nambulo, -a** mf sleepwalker

sonnecchi'are vi doze

son'nifero m sleeping-pill

'sonno m sleep; **aver ~** be sleepy. **~'lenza** f sleepiness

so'noro adj resonant; (rumoroso) loud; (onde, scheda) sound attrib

sontu'oso adj sumptuous

sopo'rifero adj soporific

sop'palco m platform

soppe'rire vi ~ **a qcsa** provide for sth

soppe'sare vt weigh up

soppor'ta|re vt support; (tollerare) stand; bear (dolore)

soppressi'one f removal; (di legge) abolition; (di diritti, pubblicazione) suppression; (annullamento) cancellation. **sop'presso** pp di **sopprimere**

sop'primere vt get rid of; abolish (legge); suppress (diritti, pubblicazione); (annullare) cancel

'sopra adv on top; (più in alto) higher [up]; (al piano superiore) upstairs; (in testo) above; **mettilo lì** ~ put it up there; **di** ~ upstairs; **pensarci** ~ think about it; **vedi** ~ see above ● prep ~ **[a]** on; (senza contatto, oltre) over; (riguardo a) about; **è** ~ **al tavolo, è** ~ **il tavolo** it's on the table; **il quadro è appeso** ~ **al camino** the picture is hanging over the fireplace; **il ponte passa** ~ **all'autostrada** the bridge crosses over the motorway; **è caduto** ~ **il tetto** it fell on the roof; **l'uno** ~ **l'altro** one on top of the other; (senza contatto) one above the other; **abita** ~ **di me** he lives upstairs from me; **i bambini** ~ **i dieci anni** children over ten; **20°** ~ **lo zero** 20° above zero; ~ **il livello del mare** above sea level; **rifletti** ~ **quello che è successo** think about what happened ● m **il [di]** ~ the top

so'prabito m overcoat

soprac'ciglio m (pl f **sopracciglia**) eyebrow

sopracco'per|ta f bedspread; (di libro) [dust-]jacket. ~**'tina** f book jacket

soprad'detto adj above-mentioned

sopraele'vata f elevated railway

sopraf'fa|re vt overwhelm. ~**tto** pp di **sopraffare**. ~**zi'one** f abuse of power

sopraf'fino adj excellent; (gusto, udito) highly refined

sopraggi'ungere vi (persona:) turn up; (accadere) happen

soprallu'ogo m inspection

sopram'mobile m ornament

soprannatu'rale adj & m supernatural

sopran'nome m nickname

so'prano mf soprano

soprappensi'ero adv lost in thought

sopras'salto m **di** ~ with a start

soprasse'dere vi ~ **a** postpone

soprat'tutto adv above all

sopravvalu'tare vt overvalue

soprav|ve'nire vi turn up; (accadere) happen. ~**'vento** m fig upper hand

sopravvi|s'suto pp di **sopravvivere**. ~**'venza** f survival. **sopravvi'vere** vi survive; **sopravvivere a** outlive (persona)

soprinten'den|te mf supervisor; (di museo ecc) keeper. ~**za** f supervision; (ente) board

so'pruso m abuse of power

soq'quadro m **mettere a** ~ turn upside down

sor'betto m sorbet

'sordido adj sordid; (avaro) stingy

sor'dina f mute; **in** ~ on the quiet

sordità f deafness. **'sordo, -a** adj deaf; (rumore, dolore) dull ● mf deaf person. **sordo'muto, -a** adj deaf-and-dumb

so'rel|la f sister. ~**'lastra** f stepsister

sor'gente f spring; (fonte) source

'sorgere vi rise; fig arise

sormon'tare vt surmount

sorni'one adj sly

sorpas'sa|re vt surpass; (*eccedere*) exceed; overtake (veicolo). **~to** adj old-fashioned. **sor'passo** m overtaking

sorpren'dente adj surprising; (*straordinario*) remarkable

sor'prendere vt surprise; (*cogliere in flagrante*) catch

sor'pres|a f surprise; di **~a** by surprise. **~o** pp di **sorprendere**

sor're|ggere vt support; (*tenere*) hold up. **~ggersi** vr support oneself. **~tto** pp di **sorreggere**

sor'ri|dere vi smile. **~so** pp di **sorridere** ●m smile

sorseggi'are vt sip. **'sorso** m sip; (*piccola quantità*) drop

'sorta f sort; di **~** whatever; ogni **~** di all sorts of

'sorte f fate; (*caso imprevisto*) chance; tirare a **~** draw lots. **sor'teggio** m draw

sorti'legio m witchcraft

sor'ti|re vi come out. **~ta** f (*Mil*) sortie; (*battuta*) witticism

'sorto pp di **sorgere**

sorvegli'an|te mf keeper; (*controllore*) overseer. **~za** f watch; (*Mil ecc*) surveillance

sorvegli'are vt watch over; (*controllare*) oversee; (*polizia*): keep under surveillance

sorvo'lare vt fly over; *fig* skip

'sosia m inv double

so'spen|dere vt hang; (*interrompere*) stop; (*privare di una carica*) suspend. **~si'one** f suspension

so'speso pp di **sospendere** ●adj (*impiegato, alunno*) suspended; **~** a hanging from; **~** a un filo *fig* hanging by a thread ●m in **~** pending; (*emozionato*) in suspense

sospet'tare vt suspect. **so'spetto** adj suspicious; persona sospetta suspicious person ●m suspicion; (*persona*) suspect. **~'toso** adj suspicious

so'spin|gere vt drive. **~to** pp di **sospingere**

sospi'rare vi sigh ●vt long for. **so'spiro** m sigh

'sosta f stop; (*pausa*) pause; senza **~** non-stop; "divieto di **~**" "no parking"

sostan'tivo m noun

so'stanz|a f substance; **~e** pl (*patrimonio*) property sg. **~i'oso** adj substantial; (*cibo*) nourishing

so'stare vi stop; (*fare una pausa*) pause

so'stegno m support

soste'ner|e vt support; (*sopportare*) bear; (*resistere*) withstand; (*affermare*) maintain; (*nutrire*) sustain; sit (*esame*); **~e le spese** meet the costs. **~si** vr support oneself

sosteni'tore, -'trice mf supporter

sostenta'mento m maintenance

soste'nuto adj (*stile*) formal; (*prezzi, velocità*) high

sostitu'ir|e vt substitute (a for), replace (con with). **~si** vr **~si a** replace

sosti'tu|to, -ta mf replacement, stand-in ●m (*surrogato*) substitute. **~zi'one** f substitution

sot'tana f petticoat; (*di prete*) cassock

sotter'raneo adj underground ●m cellar

sotter'rare vt bury

sottigli'ezza f slimness; *fig* subtlety

sot'til|e adj thin; (*udito, odorato*) keen; (*osservazione, distinzione*) subtle. **~iz'zare** vi split hairs

sottin'te|ndere vt imply. **~so** pp di **sottintendere** ●m allusion; senza **~si** openly ●adj implied

'sotto adv below; (*più in basso*) lower [down]; (*al di sotto*) underneath; (*al piano di sotto*) downstairs; è li **~** it's underneath; ~ ~ deep down; (di nascosto) on the quiet; **di** ~ downstairs; **mettersi** ~ fig get down to it; **mettere** ~ (🅘: investire) knock down • prep ~ [a] under; (al di sotto di) under[neath]; **abita** ~ **di me** he lives downstairs from me; **i bambini** ~ **i dieci anni** children under ten; **20°** ~ **zero** 20° below zero; ~ **il livello del mare** below sea level; ~ **la pioggia** in the rain; ~ **calmante** under sedation; ~ **condizione che...** on condition that...; ~ **giuramento** under oath; ~ **sorveglianza** under surveillance; ~ **Natale/gli esami** around Christmas/exam time; **al di** ~ **di** under; **andare** ~ **i 50 all'ora** do less than 50km an hour • **m il** [di] ~ the bottom

sotto'banco adv under the counter

sottobicchi'ere m coaster

sotto'bosco m undergrowth

sotto'braccio adv arm in arm

sotto'fondo m background

sottoline'are vt underline; fig stress

sot'tolio adv in oil

sotto'mano adv within reach

sottoma'rino adj & m submarine

sotto'messo pp di **sottomettere**

sotto'metter|e vt subject; subdue (popolo). ~**si** vr submit. **sottomissi'one** f submission

sottopas'saggio m underpass; (pedonale) subway

sotto'por|re vt submit; (costringere) subject. ~**si** vr submit oneself; ~**si a** undergo. **sotto'posto** pp di **sottoporre**

sotto'scala m cupboard under the stairs

sotto'scritto pp di **sottoscrivere** • m undersigned

sotto'scri|vere vt sign; (approvare) sanction, subscribe to. ~**zi'one** f (petizione) petition; (approvazione) sanction; (raccolta di denaro) appeal

sotto'sopra adv upside down

sotto'stante adj **la strada** ~ the road below

sottosu'olo m subsoil

sottosvilup'pato adj underdeveloped

sotto'terra adv underground

sotto'titolo m subtitle

sottovalu'tare vt underestimate

sotto'veste f slip

sotto'voce adv in a low voice

sottovu'oto adj vacuum-packed

sot'tra|rre vt remove; embezzle (fondi); (Math) subtract. ~**rsi a** ~**rsi a** escape from; avoid (responsabilità). ~**tto** pp di **sottrarre**. ~**zi'one** f removal; (di fondi) embezzlement; (Math) subtraction

sottuffici'ale m non-commissioned officer; (Naut) petty officer

sou'brette f inv showgirl

so'vietico, -a adj & mf Soviet

sovraccari'care vt overload. **sovrac'carico** adj overloaded (**di** with) • m overload

sovrannatu'rale adj & m = **SOPRANNATURALE**

so'vrano, -a adj sovereign; fig supreme • mf sovereign

sovrap'por|re vt superimpose. ~**si** vr overlap

sovra'stare vt dominate; fig: (pericolo): hang over

sovrinten'den|te, ~za = **SOPRINTENDENTE, SOPRINTENDENZA**

sovru'mano adj superhuman

sovvenzi'one f subsidy

sovver'sivo adj subversive

'sozzo adj filthy

S.p.A. abbr (società per azioni) plc

spac'ca|re vt split; chop (legna). ~**rsi** vr split. ~**'tura** f split

spacci'a|re vt deal in, push (droga). ~**re qcsa per qcsa** pass sth off as sth. ~rsi vr ~rsi per pass oneself off as. ~'tore, ~'trice mf (di droga) pusher; (di denaro falso) distributor of forged bank notes. 'spaccio m (di droga) dealing; (negozio) shop

'spacco m split

spac'cone, -a mf boaster

'spada f sword. ~c'cino m swordsman

spae'sato adj disorientated

spa'ghetti mpl spaghetti sg

spa'ghetto m ([I]: spavento) fright

'Spagna f Spain

spa'gnolo, -a adj Spanish ●mf Spaniard ●m (lingua) Spanish

'spago m string; dare ~ a qcno encourage sb

spal'ato adj odd

spalan'ca|re vt, ~rsi vr open wide. ~to adj wide open

spa'lare vt shovel

'spall|a f shoulder; (di comico) straight man; (di schiena) back; alle ~e di qcno (ridere) behind sb's back. ~eggi'are vt back up

spal'letta f parapet

spalli'era f back; (di letto) headboard; (ginnastica) wall bars pl

spal'lina f strap; (imbottitura) shoulder pad

spal'mare vt spread

'spander|e vt spread; (versare) spill. ~si vr spread

spappo'lare vt crush

spa'ra|re vt/i shoot; (fig) ~rle grosse talk big. ~toria f shooting

sparecchi'are vt clear

spa'reggio m (Comm) deficit; Sport play-off

'sparg|ere vt scatter; (diffondere) spread; shed (lacrime, sangue). ~ersi vr spread. ~i'mento m scattering; ~imento di sangue bloodshed

spa'ri|re vi disappear; ~scii get lost!. ~zi'one f disappearance

spar'lare vi ~ di run down

'sparo m shot

sparpagli'ar|e vt, ~si vr scatter

'sparso pp di spargere ●adj scattered; (sciolto) loose

spar'tire vt share out; (separare) separate

sparti'traffico m inv traffic island; (di autostrada) central reservation, median strip Am

spartizi'one f division

spa'ruto adj gaunt; (gruppo) small; (peli, capelli) sparse

sparvi'ero m sparrow-hawk

'spasimo m spasm

spa'smodico adj spasmodic

spas'sar|si vr amuse oneself; ~sela have a good time

spassio'nato adj dispassionate

'spasso m fun; essere uno ~ be hilarious; andare a ~ go for a walk. spas'soso adj hilarious

'spatola f spatula

spau'racchio m scarecrow; fig bugbear. spau'rire vt frighten

spa'valdo adj defiant

spaventa'passeri m inv scarecrow

spaven'tar|e vt frighten. ~si vr be frightened. spa'vento m fright. spaven'toso adj frightening; ([I]: enorme) incredible

spazi'ale adj spatial; (cosmico) space attrib

spazi'are vt space out ●vi range

spazien'tirsi vr lose patience

'spazi|o m space. ~'oso adj spacious

spaz'z|are vt sweep; ~are via sweep away; ([I]: mangiare) devour. ~a'tura f rubbish. ~ino m road sweeper; (netturbino) dustman

'spazzo|la f brush; (di tergicristallo) blade. ~'lare vt brush. ~'lino m small brush. ~lino da denti toothbrush. ~'lone m scrubbing brush

specchi'arsi vr look at oneself in the mirror; (riflettersi) be mirrored; ~ **in qcno** model oneself on sb

specchi'etto m ~ **retrovisore** driving mirror

'specchio m mirror

speci'a|le adj special ●m (TV) special [programme]. ~**lista** mf specialist. ~**lità** f inv specialty

specializ'za|re vt, ~**rsi** vr specialize. ~**to** adj skilled

special'mente adv especially

'specie f inv species; (tipo) kind; **fare** ~ **a** surprise

specifi'care vt specify. **spe'cifico** adj specific

specu'lare[1] vi speculate; ~ **su** (indagare) speculate on; (Fin) speculate in

specu'lare[2] adj mirror attrib

specula'tore, -'trice mf speculator. ~**zi'one** f speculation

spe'di|re vt send. ~**to** pp di spedire ●adj quick; (parlata) fluent. ~**zi'one** f dispatch; (Comm) consignment; (scientifica) expedition

'spegner|e vt put out; turn off (gas, luce); switch off (motore); slake (sete). ~**si** vr go out; (morire) pass away

spelacchi'ato adj (tappeto) threadbare; (cane) mangy

spe'lar|e vt skin (coniglio). ~**si** vr (cane:) moult

speleolo'gia f potholing

spel'lar|e vt skin; fig fleece. ~**si** vr peel off

spe'lonca f cave; fig hole

spendacci'one, -a mf spendthrift

'spendere vt spend; ~ **fiato** waste one's breath

spen'nare vt pluck; Ⓘ fleece (cliente)

spennel'lare vt brush

spensie|ra'tezza f lightheartedness. ~**'rato** adj carefree

'spento pp di spegnere ●adj off; (gas) out; (smorto) dull

spe'ranza f hope; **pieno di ~** hopeful; **senza ~** hopeless

spe'rare vt hope for; (aspettarsi) expect ●vi ~ **in** trust in; **spero di sì** I hope so

'sper|dersi vr get lost. ~**'duto** adj lost; (isolato) secluded

spergi'uro, -a mf perjurer ●m perjury

sperimen'ta|le adj experimental. ~**re** vt experiment with; test (resistenza, capacità, teoria). ~**zi'one** f experimentation

'sperma m sperm

spe'rone m spur

sperpe'rare vt squander. **'sperpero** m waste

'spes|a f expense; (acquisto) purchase; **andare a far** ~**e** go shopping; **fare la** ~**a** do the shopping; **fare le** ~**e di** pay for. ~**e** pl bancarie bank charges. ~**e a carico del destinatario** carriage forward. **spe'sato** adj all-expenses-paid. ~**o** pp di spendere

'spesso[1] adj thick

'spesso[2] adv often

spes'sore m thickness; (fig: consistenza) substance

spet'tabile adj (Comm) abbr (**Spett.**) S~ **ditta Rossi** Messrs Rossi

spettaco'lare adj spectacular. **spet'tacolo** m spectacle; (rappresentazione) show. ~**'loso** adj spectacular

spet'tare vi ~ **a** be up to; (diritto:) be due to

spetta'tore, -'trice mf spectator; **spettatori** pl audience sg

spette'golare vi gossip

spet'trale adj ghostly. **'spettro** m ghost; (Phys) spectrum

'spezie fpl spices

spez'zar|e vt, ~**si** vr break

spezza'tino m stew

spez'zato m coordinated jacket and trousers

spezzet'tare vt break into small pieces

'spia f spy; (della polizia) informer; (di porta) peep-hole; **fare la ~** sneak. **~ [luminosa]** light. **~ dell'olio** oil [warning] light

spiacci'care vt squash

spia'ce|nte adj sorry. **~vole** adj unpleasant

spi'aggia f beach

spia'nare vt level; (rendere liscio) smooth; roll out (pasta); raze to the ground (edificio)

spian'tato adj fig penniless

spi'are vt spy on; wait for (occasione ecc)

spiattel'lare vt blurt out; shove (oggetto)

spi'azzo m (radura) clearing

spic'ca|re vt **~re un salto** jump; **~re il volo** take flight • vi stand out. **~to** adj marked

'spicchio m (di agrumi) segment; (di aglio) clove

spicci'a|rsi vr hurry up. **~'tivo** adj speedy

'spicciolo adj (comune) banal; (denaro, 5 euro) in change. **spiccioli** pl change sg

'spicco m relief; **fare ~** stand out

'spider f inv open-top sports car

spie'dino m kebab. **spi'edo** m spit; **allo spiedo** on a spit, spit-roasted

spie'ga|re vt explain; open out (cartina); unfurl (vele). **~rsi** vr explain oneself; (vele, bandiere:) unfurl. **~zi'one** f explanation

spiegaz'zato adj crumpled

spie'tato adj ruthless

spiffe'rare vt blurt out • vi (vento:) whistle. **'spiffero** m draught

'spiga f spike; (Bot) ear

spigli'ato adj self-possessed

'spigolo m edge; (angolo) corner

'spilla f brooch. **~ da balia** safety pin. **~ di sicurezza** safety pin

spil'lare vt tap

'spillo m pin. **~ di sicurezza** safety pin; (in arma) safety catch

spi'lorcio adj stingy

'spina f thorn; (di pesce) bone; (Electr) plug. **~ dorsale** spine

spi'naci mpl spinach

spi'nale adj spinal

spi'nato adj (filo) barbed; (pianta) thorny

spi'nello m Ⓘ joint

'spinger|e vt push; fig drive. **~si** vr (andare) proceed

spi'noso adj thorny

'spint|a f push; (violenta) thrust; fig spur. **~o** pp di **spingere**

spio'naggio m espionage

spio'vente adj sloping

spi'overe vi liter stop raining; (ricadere) fall; (scorrere) flow down

'spira f coil

spi'raglio m small opening; (soffio d'aria) breath of air; (raggio di luce) gleam of light

spi'rale adj spiral • f spiral; (negli orologi) hairspring; (anticoncezionale) coil

spi'rare vi (soffiare) blow; (morire) pass away

spiri't|ato adj possessed; (espressione) wild. **'spirito** m spirit; (arguzia) wit; (intelletto) mind; **fare dello spirito** be witty; **sotto spirito** in brandy. **~o'saggine** f witticism. **spi'ritoso** adj witty

spiritu'ale adj spiritual

splen|dere vi shine. **~dido** adj splendid. **~dore** m splendour

'spoglia f (di animale) skin; **spoglie** pl (salma) mortal remains; (bottino) spoils

spogli'a|re vt strip; (svestire) undress; (fare lo spoglio di) go through. **~rello** m strip-tease. **~rsi** vr strip, undress. **~'toio** m dressing room; Sport changing room; (guardaroba) cloakroom, checkroom Am. 'spoglio adj undressed; (albero, muro) bare ●m (scrutinio) perusal

'spola f shuttle; fare la ~ shuttle

spol'pare vt flesh; fig fleece

spolve'rare vt dust; 🔲 devour (cibo)

'sponda f shore; (di fiume) bank; (bordo) edge

sponsoriz'zare vt sponsor

spon'taneo adj spontaneous

spopo'lar|e vt depopulate ● vi (avere successo) draw the crowds. ~si vr become depopulated

sporadica'mente adv sporadically. spo'radico adj sporadic

spor'c|are vt dirty; (macchiare) soil. ~arsi vr get dirty. ~izia f dirt. 'sporco adj dirty; avere la coscienza sporca have a guilty conscience ●m dirt

spor'gen|te adj jutting. ~za f projection

'sporger|e vt stretch out; ~e querela contro take legal action against ●vi jut out. ~si vr lean out

sport m inv sport

'sporta f shopping basket

spor'tello m door; (di banca ecc) window. ~ automatico cash dispenser

spor'tivo, -a adj sports attrib; (persona) sporty ●m sportsman ●f sportswoman

'sporto pp di sporgere

'sposa f bride. ~'lizio m wedding

spo'sa|re vt marry; fig espouse. ~rsi vr get married; (vino): go (con with). ~to adj married. 'sposo m bridegroom; sposi pl [novelli] newlyweds

spossa'tezza f exhaustion. spos'sato adj exhausted, worn out

spo'sta|re vt move; (differire) postpone; (cambiare) change. ~rsi vr move. ~to, -a adj ill-adjusted ●mf

(disadattato) misfit

'spranga f bar. spran'gare vt bar

'sprazzo m (di colore) splash; (di luce) flash; fig glimmer

spre'care vt waste. ~ spreco m waste

spre'g|evole adj despicable. ~ia-'tivo adj pejorative. 'spregio m contempt

spregiudi'cato adj unscrupulous

'spremer|e vt squeeze. ~si vr ~si le meningi rack one's brains

spremia'grumi m lemon squeezer

spre'muta f juice. ~ d'arancia fresh orange [juice]

sprez'zante adj contemptuous

sprigio'nar|e vt emit. ~si vr burst out

spriz'zare vt/i spurt; be bursting with (salute, gioia)

sprofon'dar|e vi sink; (crollare) collapse. ~si vr ~si in sink into; fig be engrossed in

'sprone m spur; (sartoria) yoke

sproporzio'nato adj disproportionate. ~'one f disproportion

sproposi'tato adj full of blunders; (enorme) huge. spro'posito m blunder; (eccesso) excessive amount

sprovve'duto adj unprepared; ~ di lacking in

sprov'visto adj ~ di out of; lacking in (fantasia, pazienza); alla sprovvista unexpectedly

spruz'za|re vt sprinkle; (vaporizzare) spray; (inzaccherare) spatter. ~'tore m spray; 'spruzzo m spray; (di fango) splash

spudo'ra'tezza f shamelessness. ~'rato adj shameless

'spugna f sponge; (tessuto) towelling. spu'gnoso adj spongy

'spuma f foam; (schiuma) froth; (Culin) mousse. spu'mante m sparkling wine. spumeggi'are vi foam

spun'ta|re vt break the point of;

trim (capelli); ~**rla** *fig* win ● *vi*
(pianta:) sprout; (capelli:) begin to
grow; (*sorgere*) rise; (*apparire*) appear.
~**rsi** *vr* get blunt. ~**ta** *f* trim

spun'tino *m* snack

'**spunto** *m* cue; *fig* starting point;
dare ~ **a** give rise to

spur'gar|e *vt* purge. ~**si** *vr* (*Med*)
expectorate

spu'tare *vt/i* spit; ~ **sentenze** pass
judgment. '**sputo** *m* spit

'**squadra** *f* team, squad; (*di polizia
ecc*) squad; (*da disegno*) square. **squa-
'drare** *vt* square; (*guardare*) look up
and down

squa'dr|iglia *f*, ~**one** *m* squadron

squagli'ar|e *vt*, ~**si** *vr* melt; ~**sela**
(⊡: *svignarsela*) steal out

squalifi|ca *f* disqualification.
~'**care** *vt* disqualify

'**squallido** *adj* squalid. **squal'lore** *m*
squalor

'**squalo** *m* shark

'**squama** *f* scale; (*di pelle*) flake

squa'm|are *vt* scale. ~**arsi** *vr*
(pelle:) flake off. ~'**moso** *adj* scaly;
(pelle) flaky

squarcia'gola: a ~ *adv* at the top of
one's voice

squarci'are *vt* rip. '**squarcio** *m* rip;
(*di ferita, in nave*) gash; (*di cielo*) patch

squattri'nato *adj* penniless

squilib'ra|re *vt* unbalance. ~**to**, ~**a**
adj unbalanced ● *mf* lunatic. **squi'li-
brio** *m* imbalance

squil'la|nte *adj* shrill. ~**re** *vi* (cam-
pana:) peal; (tromba:) blare; (tele-
fono:) ring. '**squillo** *m* blare; (*Teleph*)
ring ● *f* (*ragazza*) call girl

squi'sito *adj* exquisite

sradi'care *vt* uproot; eradicate
(vizio, male)

sragio'nare *vi* rave

srego'lato *adj* inordinate; (*dissoluto*)
dissolute

s.r.l. *abbr* (società a responsabilità li-

mitata) Ltd

sroto'lare *vt* uncoil

SS *abbr* (strada statale) national road

'**stabile** *adj* stable; (*permanente*) lasting; (saldo) steady; (*Theat*) repertory
company ● *m* (*edifi-
cio*) building

stabili'mento *m* factory; (*industriale*) plant; (*edificio*) establishment.
~ **balneare** lido

stabi'li|re *vt* establish; (*decidere*) de-
cide. ~**rsi** *vr* settle. ~**tà** *f* stability

stabiliz'za|re *vt* stabilize. ~**rsi** *vr*
stabilize. ~'**tore** *m* stabilizer

stac'car|e *vt* detach; pronounce
clearly (parole); (*separare*) separate;
turn off (corrente) ● *vi* (⊡: *finire di lavorare*) knock off. ~**si** *vr* come off;
~**si da** break away from (partito, famiglia)

stacci'onata *f* fence

'**stacco** *m* gap

'**stadio** *m* stadium

'**staffa** *f* stirrup

staf'fetta *f* dispatch rider

stagio'nale *adj* seasonal

stagio'na|re *vt* season (legno);
mature (formaggio). ~**to** *adj* (legno)
seasoned; (formaggio) matured

stagi'one *f* season; **alta/bassa** ~
high/low season

stagli'arsi *vr* stand out

sta'gna|nte *adj* stagnant. ~**re** *vt*
(saldare) solder; (*chiudere ermeticamente*)
seal ● *vi* stagnate. '**stagno** *adj* water-
tight ● *m* (metallo) tin

sta'gnola *f* tinfoil

'**stal|la** *f* stable; (*per buoi*) cowshed.
~**i'ere** *m* groom

stal'lone *m* stallion

sta'mani, **stamat'tina** *adv* this
morning

stam'becco *m* ibex

stam'berga *f* hovel

'**stampa** *f* (*Typ*) printing; (*giornali,
giornalisti*) press; (*riproduzione*) print

stam'pa|nte f printer. ~**nte laser** laser printer. ~**re** vt print. ~'**tello** m block letters pl

stam'pella f crutch

'**stampo** m mould; **di vecchio** ~ (persona) of the old school

sta'nare vt drive out

stan'car|e vt tire; (annoiare) bore. ~**si** vr get tired

stan'chezza f tiredness. '**stanco** adj tired; **stanco di** fed up with. **stanco morto** dead tired, exhausted

'**standard** adj & m inv standard. ~**iz'zare** vt standardize

'**stan|ga** f bar; (persona) beanpole. ~'**gata** f fig blow; (🔲: nel calcio) big kick. **stan'ghetta** f (di occhiali) leg

sta'notte adv tonight; (la notte scorsa) last night

'**stante** prep on account of; **a se** ~ separate

stan'tio adj stale

stan'tuffo m piston

'**stanza** f room; (metrica) stanza

stanzi'are vt allocate

stap'pare vt uncork

'stare

● vi (rimanere) stay; (abitare) live; (con gerundio) be; **sto solo cinque minuti** I'll stay only five minutes; **sto in piazza Peyron** I live in Peyron Square; **sto dormendo** he's sleeping; ~ **a** (attenersi) keep to; (spettare) be up to; ~ **bene** (economicamente) be well off; (di salute) be well; (addirsi) suit; ~ **dietro a** (seguire) follow; (sorvegliare) keep an eye on; (corteggiare) run after; ~ **in piedi** stand; ~ **per** be about to; **come stai/sta?** how are you?; **lasciar** ~ leave alone; **starci** (essere contento) go into; (essere d'accordo) agree; **il 3 nel 12 ci sta 4 volte** 3 into 12

---

goes 4; **non sa** ~ **agli scherzi** he can't take a joke; ~ **sulle proprie** keep oneself to oneself.
● **starsene** vr (rimanere) stay

---

starnu'tire vi sneeze. **star'nuto** m sneeze

sta'sera adv this evening, tonight

sta'tale adj state attrib ● mf state employee ● f main road

'**statico** adj static

sta'tista m statesman

sta'tistic|a f statistics sg. ~**o** adj statistical

'**stato** pp di essere, stare ● m state; (posizione sociale) position; (Jur) status. ~ **d'animo** frame of mind. ~ **civile** marital status. **S~ Maggiore** (Mil) General Staff. **Stati** pl **Uniti [d'America]** United States [of America]

'**statua** f statue

statuni'tense adj United States attrib, US attrib ● mf citizen of the United States, US citizen

sta'tura f height; **di alta** ~ tall; **di bassa** ~ short

sta'tuto m statute

stazio'nario adj stationary

stazi'one f station; (città) resort. ~ **balneare** seaside resort. ~ **ferroviaria** train station. ~ **di servizio** service station. ~ **termale** spa

'**stecca** f stick; (di ombrello) rib; (da biliardo) cue; (Med) splint; (di sigarette) carton; (di reggiseno) stiffener

stec'cato m fence

stec'chito adj skinny; (rigido) stiff; (morto) stone cold dead

'**stella** f star; **salire alle stelle** (prezzi:) rise sky-high. ~ **alpina** edelweiss. ~ **cadente** shooting star. ~ **filante** streamer. ~ **di mare** starfish

stel'lare adj stellar

'**stelo** m stem; **lampada** f **a** ~

standard lamp

'**stemma** *m* coat of arms

stempi'ato *adj* bald at the temples

sten'dardo *m* standard

sten'der|e *vt* spread out; (*appendere*) hang out; (*distendere*) stretch [out]; (*scrivere*) write down. ~si *vr* stretch out

stendibianche'ria *m inv*, sten-di'toio *m* clothes horse

stenodatti|logra'fia *f* shorthand typing

stenogra'f|are *vt* take down in shorthand. ~ia *f* shorthand

sten'ta|re *vi* ~re a find it hard to. ~to *adj* laboured. 'stento *m* effort; a stento with difficulty; stenti *pl* hardships, privations

'sterco *m* dung

'stereo['fonico] *adj* stereo[phonic]

stereoti'pato *adj* stereotyped; (*sorriso*) insincere. stere'otipo *m* stereotype

'steril|e *adj* sterile; (*terreno*) barren. ~ità *f* sterility. ~iz'zare *vt* sterilize. ~izzazi'one *f* sterilization

ster'lina *f* pound; lira ~ [pound] sterling

stermi'nare *vt* exterminate

stermi'nato *adj* immense

ster'minio *m* extermination

ste'roide *m* steroid

ster'zare *vi* steer. 'sterzo *m* steering

'steso *pp di* stendere

'stesso *adj* same; io ~ myself; tu ~ yourself; me ~ myself; se ~ himself; in quel momento ~ at that very moment; dalla stessa regina by the Queen herself; coi miei stessi occhi with my own eyes ●*pron* lo ~ the same one; (*la stessa cosa*) the same; fa lo ~ it's all the same; ci vado lo ~ I'll go just the same

ste'sura *f* drawing up; (*documento*) draft

stick *m* colla a ~ glue stick; deodorante a ~ stick deodorant

'stigma *m* stigma. ~te *fpl* stigmata

sti'lare *vt* draw up

'stil|e *m* style. sti'lista *mf* stylist. ~iz'zato *adj* stylized

stil'lare *vi* ooze

stilo'grafic|a *f* fountain pen. ~o *adj* penna ~a fountain pen

'stima *f* esteem; (*valutazione*) estimate. sti'mare *vt* esteem; (*valutare*) estimate; (*ritenere*) consider

stimo'la|nte *adj* stimulating ●*m* stimulant. ~re *vt* stimulate; (*incitare*) incite

'stimolo *m* stimulus; (*fitta*) pang

'stinco *m* shin

'stinger|e *vt/i* fade. ~si *vr* fade. 'stinto *pp di* stingere

sti'par|e *vt* cram. ~si *vr* crowd together

stipendi'ato *adj* salaried ●*m* salaried worker. sti'pendio *m* salary

'stipite *m* doorpost

stipu'la|re *vt* stipulate. ~zi'one *f* stipulation; (*accordo*) agreement

stira'mento *m* sprain

sti'ra|re *vt* iron; (*distendere*) stretch. ~rsi *vr* (*distendersi*) stretch; pull (*muscolo*). ~'tura *f* ironing. 'stiro *m* ferro da stiro iron

'stirpe *f* stock

stiti'chezza *f* constipation. 'stitico *adj* constipated

'stiva *f* (*Naut*) hold

sti'vale *m* boot. stivali *pl* di gomma Wellington boots

'stizza *f* anger

stiz'zi|re *vt* irritate. ~rsi *vr* become irritated. ~to *adj* irritated. stiz'zoso *adj* peevish

stocca'fisso *m* stockfish

stoc'cata *f* stab; (*battuta pungente*) gibe

'**stoffa** f material; fig stuff

'**stola** f stole

'**stolto** adj foolish

stoma'chevole adj revolting

sto'maco m stomach; **mal di ~** stomach-ache

sto'na|re vt/i sing/play out of tune ●vi (non intonarsi) clash. **~to** adj out of tune; (discordante) clashing; (confuso) bewildered. **~'tura** f false note; (discordanza) clash

'**stoppia** f stubble

stop'pino m wick

stop'poso adj tough

storcer|e vt, **~si** vr twist

stor'di|re vt stun; (intontire) daze. **~rsi** vr dull one's senses. **~to** adj stunned; (intontito) dazed; (sventato) heedless

'**storia** f history; (racconto, bugia) story; (pretesto) excuse; **fare [delle] storie** make a fuss

'**storico, -a** adj historical; (di importanza storica) historic ●mf historian

stori'one m sturgeon

'**stormo** m flock

'**storno** m starling

storpi'a|re vt cripple; mangle (parole). **~'tura** f deformation. '**storpio, -a** adj crippled ●mf cripple

'**stort|a** f (distorsione) sprain; **prendere una ~a alla caviglia** sprain one's ankle. **~o** pp di **storcere** ●adj crooked; (ritorto) twisted; (gambe) bandy; fig wrong

sto'viglie fpl crockery sg

'**strabico** adj cross-eyed

strabili'ante adj astonishing

stra'bismo m squint

straboc'care vi overflow

stra'carico adj overloaded

stracci'are vt (▣: vincere) thrash. **~'ato** adj torn; (persona) in rags; (prezzi) slashed; **a un prezzo ~ato** dirt cheap. '**straccio** adj torn ●m rag; (strofinaccio) cloth. **~'one**

m tramp

stra'cotto adj overdone; (▣: innamorato) head over heels ●m stew

'**strada** f road; (di città) street; **essere fuori ~** be on the wrong track; **fare ~** lead the way; **farsi ~** make one's way. **~ a senso unico** one-way street. **~ senza uscita** blind alley. **stra'dale** adj road attrib

strafalci'one m blunder

stra'fare vi overdo things

stra'foro: di ~ adv on the sly

strafot'ten|te adj arrogant. **~za** f arrogance

'**strage** f slaughter

'**stralcio** m (parte) extract

stralu'na|re vt **~re gli occhi** open one's eyes wide. **~to** adj (occhi) staring; (persona) distraught

stramaz'zare vi fall heavily

strambe'ria f oddity. '**strambo** adj strange

strampa'lato adj odd

stra'nezza f strangeness

strango'lare vt strangle

strani'ero, -a adj foreign ●mf foreigner

'**strano** adj strange

straordi'naria'mente adv extraordinarily. **~'nario** adj extraordinary; (notevole) remarkable; (edizione) special; **lavoro ~nario** overtime; **treno ~nario** special train

strapaz'zar|e vt ill-treat; scramble (uova). **~si** vr tire oneself out. **stra'pazzo** m strain; **da strapazzo** fig worthless

strapi'eno adj overflowing

strapi'ombo m projection; **a ~** sheer

strap'par|e vt tear; (per distruggere) tear up; pull out (dente, capelli); (sradicare) pull up; (estorcere) wring. **~si** vr get torn; (allontanarsi) tear oneself away. '**strappo** m tear; (strattone) jerk; (▯: *passaggio*) lift; **fare uno strappo alla regola** make an exception to the rule. **~ muscolare** muscle strain

strapun'tino *m* folding seat

strari'pare *vi* flood

strasci'c|are *vt* trail; shuffle (piedi); drawl (parole). **'strascico** *m* train; *fig* after-effect

strass *m inv* rhinestone

strata'gemma *m* stratagem

strate'gia *f* strategy. **stra'tegico** *adj* strategic

'strato *m* layer; (*di vernice ecc*) coat; (*roccioso, sociale*) stratum. **~'sfera** *f* stratosphere. **~'sferico** *adj* stratospheric

stravac'carsi *vr* ▯ slouch

strava'gan|te *adj* extravagant; (*eccentrico*) eccentric. **~za** *f* extravagance; (*eccentricità*) eccentricity

stra'vecchio *adj* ancient

strave'dere *vt* **~ per** worship

stravizi'are *vi* indulge oneself. **stra'vizio** *m* excess

stra'volg|ere *vt* twist; (*turbare*) upset. **~i'mento** *m* twisting. **stra'volto** *adj* distraught; (▯: *stanco*) done in

strazi'a|nte *adj* heartrending; (*dolore*) agonizing. **~re** *vt* grate on (orecchie); break (cuore). **'strazio** *m* agony; **che strazio!** ▯ it's awful!

'strega *f* witch. **stre'gare** *vt* bewitch. **stre'gone** *m* wizard

'stregua *f* **alla ~ di** like

stre'ma|re *vt* exhaust. **~to** *adj* exhausted

'strenuo *adj* strenuous

strepi|'tare *vi* make a din. **'strepito** *m* noise. **~'toso** *adj* noisy; *fig* resounding

stres'sa|nte *adj* (*lavoro, situazione*) stressful. **~to** *adj* stressed [out]

'stretta *f* grasp; (*dolore*) pang; **essere alle strette** be in dire straits.

~ di mano handshake

stret'tezza *f* narrowness; **stret'tezze** *pl* (*difficoltà finanziarie*) financial difficulties

'stret|to *pp di* **stringere** ● *adj* narrow; (*serrato*) tight; (*vicino*) close; (*dialetto*) broad; (*rigoroso*) strict; **lo ~ necessario** the bare minimum ● *m* (*Geog*) strait. **~'toia** *f* bottleneck; (▯: *difficoltà*) tight spot

stri'a|to *adj* striped. **~'tura** *f* streak

stri'dente *adj* strident

'stridere *vi* squeak; *fig* clash. **stri'dore** *m* screech

'stridulo *adj* shrill

strigli'a|re *vt* groom. **~ta** *f* grooming; *fig* dressing down

stril'l|are *vi t* scream. **'strillo** *m* scream

strimin'zito *adj* skimpy; (*magro*) skinny

strimpel'lare *vt* strum

'strin|ga *f* lace; (*Comput*) string. **~'gato** *adj* *fig* terse

'stringer|e *vt* press; (*serrare*) squeeze; (*tenere stretto*) hold tight; take in (abito); (*comprimere*) be tight; (*restringere*) tighten; **~ e la mano a** shake hands with ● *vi* (*premere*) press. **~si** *vr* (*accostarsi*) draw close (**a** to); (*avvicinarsi*) squeeze up

'striscia *f* strip; (*riga*) stripe. **strisce** *pl* [**pedonali**] zebra crossing *sg*

strisci'a|re *vi* crawl; (*sfiorare*) graze ● *vt* drag (piedi). **~si** *vr* **~si a** rub against. **'striscio** *m* graze; (*Med*) smear; **colpire di striscio** graze

strisci'one *m* banner

strito'lare *vt* grind

striz'zare *vt* squeeze; (*torcere*) wring [out]; **~ l'occhio** wink

'strofa *f* strophe

strofi'naccio *m* cloth; (*per spolverare*) duster

strofi'nare *vt* rub

strombaz'zare *vt* boast about ● *vi* hoot

strombaz'zata *f* hoot

stron'care *vt* cut off; (*reprimere*) crush; (*criticare*) tear to shreds

stropicci'are *vt* rub; crumple (vestito)

stroz'za|re *vt* strangle. ~**tura** *f* strangling; (*di strada*) narrowing

strozzi'naggio *m* loan-sharking

stroz'zino *m pej* usurer; (*truffatore*) shark

strug'gente *adj* all-consuming

strumen'tale *adj* instrumental

strumentaliz'zare *vt* make use of

stru'mento *m* instrument; (*arnese*) tool. ~ **a corda** string instrument. ~ **musicale** musical instrument

strusci'are *vt* rub

'strutto *m* lard

strut'tura *f* structure. **struttu'rale** *adj* structural

struttu'rare *vt* structure

strutturazi'one *f* structuring

'struzzo *m* ostrich

stuc'ca|re *vt* stucco

stuc'chevole *adj* nauseating

'stucco *m* stucco

stu'den|te, -'t'essa *mf* student; (*di scuola*) schoolboy; schoolgirl. ~**tesco** *m* student; (*di scolaro*) school attrib

studi'ar|e *vt* study. ~**si** *vr* ~**si di** try to

'studi|o *m* studying; (*stanza, ricerca*) study; (*di artista, TV ecc*) studio; (*di professionista*) office. ~'**oso, -a** *adj* studious ● *mf* scholar

'stufa *f* stove. ~ **elettrica** electric fire

stu'fa|re *vt* (*Culin*) stew; (*dare fastidio*) bore. ~**rsi** *vr* get bored. ~**to** *m* stew

'stufo *adj* bored; **essere** ~ **di** be fed up with

stu'oia *f* mat

stupefa'cente *adj* amazing ● *m* drug

stu'pendo *adj* stupendous

stupi'd|aggine *f* (*azione*) stupid thing; (*cosa da poco*) nothing. ~**ata** *f* stupid thing. ~**ità** *f* stupidity. '**stupido** *adj* stupid

stu'pir|e *vt* astonish ● *vi*, ~**si** *vr* be astonished. **stu'pore** *m* amazement

stu'pra|re *vt* rape. ~'**tore** *m* rapist. '**stupro** *m* rape

sturalavan'dini *m inv* plunger

stu'rare *vt* uncork; unblock (lavandino)

stuzzi'care *vt* prod [at]; pick (denti); poke (fuoco); (*molestare*) tease; whet (appetito)

stuzzi'chino *m* (*Culin*) appetizer

su *prep* on; (*senza contatto*) over; (*riguardo a*) about; (*circa, intorno a*) about, around; **le chiavi sono sul tavolo** the keys are on the table; **il quadro è appeso sul camino** the picture is hanging over the fireplace; **un libro sull'antico Egitto** a book on *o* about Ancient Egypt; **costa sui 25 euro** it costs about 25 euros; **decidere sul momento** decide at the time; **su commissione** on commission; **su due piedi** on the spot; **uno su dieci** one out of ten ● *adv* (*sopra*) up; (*al piano di sopra*) upstairs; (*addosso*) on; **ho su il cappotto** I've got my coat on; **in su** (*guardare*) up; **dalla vita in su** from the waist up; **su!** come on!

su'bacqueo *adj* underwater

subaffit'tare *vt* sublet. **subaf'fitto** *m* sublet

subal'terno *adj* & *m* subordinate

sub'buglio *m* turmoil

sub'conscio *adj* & *m* subconscious

'subdolo *adj* devious

suben'trare *vi* (*circostanze:*) come up; ~ **a** take the place of

su'bire *vt* undergo; (*patire*) suffer

subis'sare vt fig ~ di overwhelm with

'subito adv at once; ~ dopo straight after

su'blime adj sublime

subodo'rare vt suspect

subordi'nato, -a adj & mf subordinate

subur'bano adj suburban

suc'cedere vi (accadere) happen; ~e a succeed; (venire dopo) follow; ~e al trono succeed to the throne. ~si vr happen one after the other

successi'one f succession; in ~ in succession

succes|siva'mente adv subsequently. ~'sivo adj successive

suc'ces|so pp di succedere ● m success; (esito) outcome; (disco ecc) hit

succes'sore m successor

succhi'are vt suck [up]

suc'cinto adj (conciso) concise; (abito) scanty

'succo m juice; fig essence; ~ di frutta fruit juice. **suc'coso** adj juicy

succu'lento adj succulent

succur'sale f branch [office]

sud m south; del ~ southern

su'da|re vi sweat; (faticare) sweat blood; ~re freddo be in a cold sweat. ~ta f sweat. ~'ticcio adj sweaty. ~to adj sweaty

sud'detto adj above-mentioned

'suddito, -a mf subject

suddi'vi|dere vt subdivide. ~si'one f subdivision

su'd-est m southeast

'sudici|o adj filthy. ~'ume m filth

su'dore m sweat; fig sweat

su'd-ovest m southwest

suffici'en|te adj sufficient; (presuntuoso) conceited ● m bare essentials pl; (Sch) pass mark. ~za f sufficiency; (presunzione) conceit; (Sch) pass; a ~za enough

suf'fisso m suffix

suf'fragio m vote. ~ universale universal suffrage

suggeri'mento m suggestion

sugge'ri|re vt suggest; (Theat) prompt. ~'tore, ~'trice mf (Theat) prompter

suggestiona'bile adj suggestible

suggestio'na|re vt influence suggesti'one f influence

sugge'stivo adj suggestive; (musica ecc) evocative

'sughero m cork

'sugli = SU + GLI

'sugo m (di frutta) juice; (di carne) gravy; (salsa) sauce; (sostanza) substance

'sui = SU + I

sui'cid|a adj suicidal ● mf suicide. **suici'darsi** vr commit suicide. ~io m suicide

su'ino adj carne suina pork ● m swine

sul = SU + IL. **'sullo** = SU + LO. **'sulla** = SU + LA. **'sulle** = SU + LE

sul'ta|na f sultana. ~'nina adj uva ~nina sultana. ~no m sultan

'sunto m summary

'suo, -a poss adj il ~, i suoi his; (di cosa, animale) its; (forma di cortesia) your; la sua, le sue her; (di cosa, animale) its; (forma di cortesia) your; questa macchina è sua this car is his/hers; ~ padre his/her/your father; un ~ amico a friend of his/hers/yours ● poss pron il ~, i suoi his; (di cosa, animale) its; (forma di cortesia) yours; la sua, le sue hers; (di cosa animale) its; (forma di cortesia) yours; i suoi his/her folk

su'ocera f mother-in-law

su'ocero m father-in-law

su'ola f sole

su'olo m ground; (terreno) soil

suo'na|re vt/i (Mus) play; ring (campanello); sound (allarme, clacson);

(orologio:) strike. ~'tore, ~'trice mf player. suone'ria f alarm; (di cellulare) ringtone. su'ono m sound

su'ora f nun; Suor Maria Sister Maria

superal'colico m spirit • adj bevande di superalcoliche spirits

supera'mento m (di timidezza) overcoming; (di esame) success (di in)

supe'rare vt surpass; (eccedere) exceed; (vincere) overcome; overtake (veicolo); pass (esame)

su'perbo adj haughty; (magnifico) superb

superdo'tato adj highly gifted

superfici'al|e adj superficial • mf superficial person. ~ità f superficiality. super'ficie f surface; (area) area

su'perfluo adj superfluous

superi'or|e adj superior; (di grado) senior; (più elevato) higher; (sovrastante) upper; (al di sopra) above • mf superior. ~ità f superiority

superla'tivo adj & m superlative

supermer'cato m supermarket

super'sonico adj supersonic

su'perstite adj surviving • mf survivor

superstizi'o|ne f superstition. ~so adj superstitious

super'strada f toll-free motorway

supervisi'one f supervision. ~'sore m supervisor

su'pino adj supine

suppel'lettili fpl furnishings

suppergiù adv about

supplemen'tare adj supplementary

supple'mento m supplement; ~ rapido express train supplement

sup'plen|te adj temporary • mf (Sch) supply teacher. ~za f temporary post

'suppli|ca f plea; (domanda) petition. ~'care vt beg

sup'plire vt replace • vi ~ a (com-

pensare) make up for

sup'plizio m torture

sup'porre vt suppose

sup'porto m support

supposizi'one f supposition

sup'posta f suppository

sup'posto pp di supporre

supre'mazia f supremacy. su'premo adj supreme

sur'fare vi ~ in Internet surf the Net

surge'la|re vt deep-freeze. ~ti mpl frozen food sg. ~to adj frozen

surrea'lis|mo m surrealism. ~ta mf surrealist

surriscal'dare vt overheat

surro'gato m substitute

suscet'tibil|e adj touchy. ~ità f touchiness

susci'tare vt stir up; arouse (ammirazione ecc)

su'sin|a f plum. ~o m plumtree

su'spense f suspense

sussegu'ente adj subsequent. ~irsi vr follow one after the other

sussidi'ar|e vt subsidize. ~io adj subsidiary. sus'sidio m subsidy; (aiuto) aid. sussidio di disoccupazione unemployment benefit

sus'siego m haughtiness

sussi'stenza f subsistence. sus'sistere vi subsist; (essere valido) hold good

sussul'tare vi start. sus'sulto m start

sussur'rare vt whisper. sus'surro m whisper

sva'gar|e vt amuse. ~si vr amuse oneself. 'svago m relaxation; (divertimento) amusement

svali'giare vt rob; burgle (casa)

svalu'ta|re vt devalue; fig underestimate. ~rsi vr lose value. ~zi'one f devaluation

svam'pito adj absent-minded

sva'nire vi vanish

svantaggi'a|to adj at a disadvantage; (bambino, paese) disadvantaged. **svan'taggio** m disadvantage; **essere in svantaggio** Sport be losing; **~oso** adj disadvantageous

svapo'rare vi evaporate

svari'ato adj varied

sva'sato adj flared

'svastica f swastika

sve'dese adj & m (lingua) Swedish ●mf Swede

'sveglia f (orologio) alarm [clock]; **~!** get up!; **mettere la ~** set the alarm [clock]

svegli'ar|e vt wake up; fig awaken. **~si** vr wake up. **'sveglio** adj awake; (di mente) quick-witted

sve'lare vt reveal

svel'tezza f speed; fig quick-wittedness

svel'tir|e vt quicken. **~si** vr (persona:) liven up. **'svelto** adj quick; (slanciato) svelte; **alla svelta** quickly

'svend|ere vt undersell. **~ita** f [clearance] sale

sve'nire vi faint

sven'ta|re vt foil. **~to** adj thoughtless ●mf thoughtless person

'sventola f slap

svento'lare vt/i wave

sven'trare vt disembowel; fig demolish (edificio)

sven'tura f misfortune. **sventu'rato** adj unfortunate

sve'nuto pp di **svenire**

svergo'gnato adj shameless

sver'nare vi winter

sve'stir|e vt undress

'Svezia f Sweden

svez'zare vt wean

svi'ar|e vt divert; (corrompere) lead astray. **~si** vr fig go astray

svico'lare vi turn down a side

street; (dalla questione ecc) evade the issue; (da una persona) dodge out of the way

svi'gnarsela vr slip away

svi'lire vt debase

svilup'par|e vt, **~si** vr develop. **svi'luppo** m development; **paese in via di sviluppo** developing country

svinco'lar|e vt release; clear (merce). **~si** vr free oneself. **'svincolo** m clearance; (di autostrada) exit

svisce'ra|re vt gut; fig dissect. **~to** adj passionate; (ossequioso) obsequious

'svista f oversight

svi'tare vt unscrew. **~to** adj (ⅠⅠ: matto) cracked, nutty

'Svizzer|a f Switzerland. **s~o, -a** adj & mf Swiss

> **Svizzera** Italian is one of the four national languages of Switzerland, but is spoken widely only in the canton of Ticino in the south of the country, and to a lesser extent in Grisons. Around half a million people in Switzerland have Italian as their first language. Their language rights are protected by the Swiss constitution. *i*

svogli|a'tezza f half-hearted-ness. **~'ato** adj lazy

svolaz'za|nte adj (capelli) windswept. **~re** vi flutter

'svolger|e vt unwind; unwrap (pacco); (risolvere) solve; (portare a termine) carry out; (sviluppare) develop. **~si** vr (accadere) take place. **svolgi'mento** m course; (sviluppo) development

'svolta f turning; fig turning-point. **svol'tare** vi turn

'svolto pp di **svolgere**

svuo'tare vt empty [out]

Tt

tabac'c|aio, -a mf tobacconist. ~**he'ria** f tobacconist's. **ta'bacco** m tobacco

Tabaccheria By law, cigarettes and other tobacco products can be sold only in *tabaccherie*, which must be licensed by the State. They can be recognized by a sign with a large T. As well as tobacco, *tabaccherie* have a monopoly on postage stamps, lottery tickets, and other items controlled by the State.

ta'bel|la f table; (*lista*) list. ~**la dei prezzi** price list. ~**lina** f (*Math*) multiplication table. ~**lone** m wall chart. ~**lone del canestro** backboard

taber'nacolo m tabernacle

tabù adj & m inv taboo

tabu'lato m [data] printout

'tacca f notch; **di mezza** ~ (*attore, giornalista*) second-rate

tac'cagno adj □ stingy

tac'cheggio m shoplifting

tac'chetto m Sport stud

tac'chino m turkey

tacci'are vt ~ **qcno di qcsa** accuse sb of sth

'tacco m heel; **alzare i tacchi** take to one's heels; **scarpe senza** ~ flat shoes. **tacchi** pl **a spillo** stiletto heels

taccu'ino m notebook

ta'cere vi be silent ●vt say nothing about; **mettere a** ~ **qcsa** (*scandalo*) hush sth up

ta'chimetro m speedometer

'tacito adj silent; (*inespresso*) tacit.

taci'turno adj taciturn

ta'fano m horsefly

taffe'ruglio m scuffle

'taglia f (*riscatto*) ransom; (*ricompensa*) reward; (*statura*) height; (*misura*) size. ~ **unica** one size

taglia'carte m inv paperknife

taglia'erba m inv lawn-mower

tagliafu'oco adj inv **porta** ~ fire door; **striscia** ~ fire break

tagli'ando m coupon; **fare il** ~ ≈ put one's car in for its MOT

tagli'ar|e vt cut; (*attraversare*) cut across; (*interrompere*) cut off; (*togliere*) cut out; carve (*carne*); mow (*erba*); **farsi** ~**e i capelli** have a haircut ●vi cut. ~**si** vr cut oneself; ~**si i capelli** have a haircut

taglia'telle fpl tagliatelle sg, thin, flat strips of egg pasta

taglieggi'are vt extort money from

tagli'e|nte adj sharp ●m cutting edge. ~**re** m chopping board

'taglio m cut; (*il tagliare*) cutting; (*di stoffa*) length; (*parte tagliente*) edge. ~ **cesareo** Caesarean section

tagli'ola f trap

tagliuz'zare vt cut

tail'leur m inv [lady's] suit

'talco m talcum powder

'tale adj such a; (*con nomi plurali*) such; **c'è un** ~ **disordine** there is such a mess; **non accetto tali scuse** I won't accept such excuses; **il rumore era** ~ **che non si sentiva nulla** there was so much noise you couldn't hear yourself think; **il** ~ **giorno** on such and such a day; **quel tal signore** that gentleman; **il** ~ **quale** just like ●pron **un** ~ someone; **quel** ~ that man; **il tal dei tali** such and such a person

ta'lento m talent

tali'smano m talisman

tallo'nare vt be hot on the heels of

talloncino | targa

tallon'cino m coupon

tal'lone m heel

tal'mente adv so

ta'lora adv = TALVOLTA

'talpa f mole

tal'volta adv sometimes

tamburel'lare vi (con le dita) drum; (pioggia:) beat, drum. **tambu'rello** m tambourine. **tambu'rino** m drummer. **tam'buro** m drum

tampona'mento m (Auto) collision; (di ferita) dressing; (di falla) plugging. ~ **a catena** pile-up. **tampo'nare** vt (urtare) crash into; (otturare) plug. **tam'pone** m swab; (per timbri) pad; (per mestruazioni) tampon; (Comput) (per tergi) buffer

'tana f den

'tanfo m stench

'tanga m inv tanga

tan'gen|te adj tangent ● f tangent; (somma) bribe. ~**'topoli** f widespread corruption in Italy in the early 90s. ~**zi'ale** f orbital road

tan'gibile adj tangible

'tango m tango

tan'tino: un ~ adv a little [bit]

'tanto adj [so] much; (con nomi plurali) [so] many, [such] a lot of; ~ **tempo** [such] a long time; **non ha tanta pazienza** he doesn't have much patience; ~ **tempo quanto ti serve** as much time as you need; **non è ~ intelligente quanto suo padre** he's not as intelligent as his father; **tanti amici quanti parenti** as many friends as relatives ● pron much; (plurale) many; (tanto tempo) a long time; **è un uomo come tanti** he's just an ordinary man; **tanti** (molte persone) many people; **non ci vuole così ~** it doesn't take that long; ~ **quanto** as much as; **tanti quanti** as many as ● conj (comunque) anyway, in any case ● adv (così) so; (con verbi) so much; ~ **debole** so weak; **è ~ ingenuo da crederle** he's naive enough to be-

lieve her; **di** ~ **in** ~ every now and then; ~ **l'uno come l'altro** both; ~ **quanto** as much as; **tre volte** ~ three times as much; **una volta** ~ once in a while; **tant'è** so much so; ~ **per cambiare** for a change

'tappa f stop; (parte di viaggio) stage

tappa'buchi m inv stopgap

tap'par|e vt plug; cork (bottiglia); ~**e la bocca a qcno** 🔲 shut sb up. ~**si** vr ~**si gli occhi** cover one's eyes; ~**si il naso** hold one's nose

tappa'rella f 🔲 roller blind

tappe'tino m mat; (Comput) mouse mat

tap'peto m carpet; (piccolo) rug; **mandare qcno al** ~ knock sb down

tappez'z|are vt paper (pareti); (rivestire) cover. ~**e'ria** f tapestry; (di carta) wallpaper; (arte) upholstery. ~**i'ere** m upholsterer; (imbianchino) decorator

'tappo m plug; (di sughero) cork; (di metallo, per penna) top; (🔲: persona piccola) dwarf. ~ **di sughero** cork

'tara f (difetto) flaw; (ereditaria) hereditary defect; (peso) tare

ta'rantola f tarantula

ta'ra|re vt calibrate (strumento). ~**to** adj (Comm) discounted; (Techn) calibrated; (Med) with a hereditary defect; (🔲) crazy

tarchi'ato adj stocky

tar'dare vi be late ● vt delay

'tard|i adv late; **al più** ~**i** at the latest; **più** ~**i** later [on]; **sul** ~**i** late in the day; **far** ~**i** (essere in ritardo) be late; (con gli amici) stay up late; **a più** ~**i** see you later. **tar'divo** adj late; (bambino) retarded. ~**o** adj slow; (tempo) late

'targ|a f plate; (Auto) numberplate. ~**a di circolazione** numberplate. **tar'gato** adj **un'auto targata...** a car with the registration number.... ~**'hetta** f (su porta) nameplate; (sulla *valigia*) name tag

ta'rif|fa f tariff. **∼'fario** m price list

'tarlo m woodworm

'tarma f moth

ta'rocco m tarot; **ta'rocchi** pl tarot

tartagli'are vi stutter

'tartaro adj & m tartar

tarta'ruga f tortoise; (*di mare*) turtle; (*per pettine ecc*) tortoiseshell

tartas'sare vt harass

tar'tina f canapé

tar'tufo m truffle

'tasca f pocket; (*in borsa*) compartment; **da ∼** pocket attrib. **∼ da pasticciere** icing bag

ta'scabile adj pocket attrib ●m paperback

tasca'pane m inv haversack

ta'schino m breast pocket

'tassa f tax; (*d'iscrizione ecc*) fee; (*doganale*) duty. **∼ di circolazione** road tax. **∼ d'iscrizione** registration fee

tas'sametro m taximeter

tas'sare vt tax

tassa|tiva'mente adv without question

tassazi'one f taxation

tas'sello m wedge; (*di stoffa*) gusset

tassì m inv taxi. **tas'sista** mf taxi driver

'tasso[1] m yew; (*animale*) badger

'tasso[2] m rate. **∼ di cambio** exchange rate. **∼ di interesse** interest rate

ta'stare vt feel; (*sondare*) sound; **∼ il terreno** fig test the water

tasti'e|ra f keyboard. **∼'rista** mf keyboarder

'tasto m key; (*tatto*) touch. **∼ delicato** fig touchy subject. **∼ funzione** (*Comput*) function key. **∼ tabulatore** tab key

'tattica f tactics pl

'tattico adj tactical

'tatto m (*senso*) touch; (*accortezza*)

tact; **aver ∼** be tactful

tatu'a|ggio m tattoo. **∼re** vt tattoo

'tavola f table; (*illustrazione*) plate; (*asse*) plank. **∼ calda** snackbar

tavo'lato m boarding; (*pavimento*) wood floor

tavo'letta f bar; (*medicinale*) tablet; **andare a ∼** (*Auto*) drive flat out

tavo'lino m small table

'tavolo m table. **∼ operatorio** (*Med*) operating table

tavo'lozza f palette

'tazza f cup; (*del water*) bowl. **∼ da caffè/tè** coffee-cup/teacup

taz'zina f **∼ da caffè** espresso coffee cup

T.C.I. abbr (Touring Club Italiano) Italian Touring Club

te pers pron you; **te l'ho dato** I gave it to you

tè m inv tea

TEAM f abbr (Tessera Europea di Assicurazione Malattia) EHIC

tea'trale adj theatrical

te'atro m theatre. **∼ all'aperto** open-air theatre. **∼ di posa** Cinema set. **∼ tenda** marquee for theatre performances

'tecnico, -a adj technical ●mf technician ●f technique

tecno|lo'gia f technology. **∼'logico** adj technological

te'desco, -a adj & mf German

tedi'oso adj tedious

te'game m saucepan

'teglia f baking tin

'tegola f tile; fig blow

tei'era f teapot

tek m teak

'tela f cloth; (*per quadri, vele*) canvas; (*Theat*) curtain. **∼ cerata** oilcloth. **∼ di lino** linen

te'laio m (*di bicicletta, finestra*) frame; (*Auto*) chassis; (*per tessere*) loom

t

tele'camera *f* television camera

teleco|man'dato *adj* remote-controlled, remote control *attrib*. ∼'mando *m* remote control

Telecom Italia *f* Italian State telephone company

telecomunicazi'oni *fpl* telecommunications

tele'cro|naca *f* [television] commentary. ∼naca diretta live [television] coverage. ∼'nista *mf* television commentator

tele'ferica *f* cableway

telefo'na|re *vt/i* [tele]phone, ring. ∼ta *f* call. ∼ta interurbana long-distance call

telefonica'mente *adv* by [tele-]phone

tele'fo|nico *adj* [tele]phone *attrib*. ∼'nino *m* mobile [phone]. ∼'nista *mf* operator

te'lefono *m* [tele]phone. ∼ senza filo cordless [phone]. ∼ interno internal telephone. ∼ satellitare satphone. ∼ a schede cardphone

telegior'nale *m* television news *sg*

tele'grafico *adj* telegraphic; (risposta) monosyllabic; **sii telegrafico** keep it brief

tele'gramma *m* telegram

telela'voro *m* teleworking

tele'matica *f* data communications, telematics

teleno'vela *f* soap opera

teleobiet'tivo *m* telephoto lens

telepa'tia *f* telepathy

telero'manzo *m* television serial

tele'scopio *m* telescope

teleselezi'one *f* subscriber trunk dialling, STD; **chiamare in** ∼ dial direct

telespetta'tore, -'trice *mf* viewer

tele'text® *m* Teletext®

televisi'one *f* television; **guardare la** ∼ watch television

televi'sivo *adj* television *attrib*; **operatore** ∼ television cameraman; **apparecchio** ∼ television set

televi'sore *m* television [set]

'tema *m* theme; (*Sch*) essay. **te'matica** *f* main theme

teme'rario *adj* reckless

te'mere *vt* be afraid of, fear ● *vi* be afraid, fear

temperama'tite *m inv* pencil-sharpener

tempera'mento *m* temperament

tempe'ra|re *vt* temper; sharpen (matita). ∼to *adj* temperate. ∼'tura *f* temperature. ∼tura ambiente room temperature

tempe'rino *m* penknife

tem'pe|sta *f* storm. ∼sta di neve snowstorm. ∼sta di sabbia sandstorm

tempe|stiva'mente *adv* quickly. ∼'stivo *adj* timely. ∼'stoso *adj* stormy

'tempia *f* (*Anat*) temple

'tempio *m* (*Relig*) temple

tem'pismo *m* timing

'tempo *m* time; (*atmosferico*) weather; (*Mus*) tempo; (*Gram*) tense; (*di film*) part; (*di partita*) half; **a suo** ∼ in due course; ∼ **fa** some time ago; **un** ∼ once; **ha fatto il suo** ∼ it's superannuated. ∼ **supplementare** *Sport* extra time, overtime *Am*. ∼'rale *adj* temporal ● *m* [thunder] storm. ∼ranea'mente *adv* temporarily. ∼'raneo *adj* temporary. ∼'reg-gi'are *vi* play for time

tem'prare *vt* temper

te'nac|e *adj* tenacious. ∼ia *f* tenacity

te'naglia *f* pincers *pl*

'tenda *f* curtain; (*per campeggio*) tent; (*tendone*) awning. ∼ **a ossigeno** oxygen tent

ten'denz|a *f* tendency. ∼ial'mente *adv* by nature

'tendere vt (allargare) stretch [out]; (tirare) tighten; (porgere) hold out; fig lay (trappola) ●vi ~ a aim at; (essere portato a) tend to

'tendine m tendon

ten'do|ne m awning; (di circo) tent. ~**poli** f inv tent city

tene'broso adj gloomy

te'nente m lieutenant

tenera'mente adv tenderly

te'ner|e vt hold; (mantenere) keep; (gestire) run; (prendere) take; (seguire) follow; (considerare) consider ●vi hold; ~**ci a**, ~**e a** be keen on; ~**e per** support (squadra). ~**si** vr hold on (a a to); (in una condizione) keep oneself; (seguire) stick to; ~**si indietro** stand back

tene'rezza f tenderness. **'tenero** adj tender

'tenia f tapeworm

'tennis m tennis. ~ **da tavolo** table tennis. **ten'nista** mf tennis player

te'nore m standard; (Mus) tenor; a ~ **di legge** by law. ~ **di vita** standard of living

tensi'one f tension; (Electr) voltage; **alta** ~ high voltage

ten'tacolo m tentacle

ten'ta|re vt attempt; (sperimentare) try; (indurre in tentazione) tempt. ~**tivo** m attempt. ~**zi'one** f temptation

tenten'nare vi waver

'tenue adj fine; (debole) weak; (esiguo) small; (leggero) slight

te'nuta f (capacità) capacity; (Sport: resistenza) stamina; (possedimento) estate; (divisa) uniform; (abbigliamento) clothes pl; a ~ **d'aria** airtight. ~ **di strada** road holding

teolo'gia f theology. **teo'logico** adj theological. **te'ologo** m theologian

teo'rema m theorem

teo'ria f theory

teorica'mente adv theoretically.

te'orico adj theoretical

te'pore m warmth

'teppa f mob. **tep'pismo** m hooliganism. **tep'pista** m hooligan

tera'peutico adj therapeutic. **tera'pia** f therapy

tergicri'stallo m windscreen wiper, windshield wiper Am

tergilu'notto m rear windscreen wiper

tergiver'sare vi hesitate

'tergo m a ~ behind

ter'male adj thermal; **stazione** ~ spa. **'terme** fpl thermal baths

'termico adj thermal

termi'na|le adj & m terminal; **malato** ~ **le** terminally ill person. ~**re** vt/i finish, end. **'termine** m (limite) limit; (fine) end; (condizione, espressione) term

terminolo'gia f terminology

'termite f termite

termoco'perta f electric blanket

ter'mometro m thermometer

'termos m inv thermos®

termosi'fone m radiator; (sistema) central heating

ter'mostato m thermostat

'terra f earth; (regione) land; (terreno) ground; (argilla, clay; (cosmetico) dark face powder (for impression of tan); a ~ (sulla costa) ashore; (installazioni) onshore; **per** ~ on the ground; **sotto** ~ underground. ~**'cotta** f terracotta; **vasellame di** ~**cotta** earthenware. ~**pi'eno** m embankment

ter'razz|a f, ~**o** m balcony

terremo'tato, -a adj (zona) affected by an earthquake ●mf earthquake victim. **terre'moto** m earthquake

ter'reno adj earthly ●m ground; (suolo) soil; (proprietà terriera) land; **perdere/guadagnare** ~ lose/gain ground. ~ **di gioco** playing field

t

ter'restre adj terrestrial; esercito ∼ land forces pl

ter'ribil|e adj terrible. ∼'mente adv terribly

ter'riccio m potting compost

terrifi'cante adj terrifying

territori'ale adj territorial. **terri'torio** m territory

ter'rore m terror

terro'ris|mo m terrorism. ∼ta mf terrorist

terroriz'zare vt terrorize

'terso adj clear

ter'zetto m trio

terzi'ario adj tertiary

'terzo adj third; di terz'ordine (locale, servizio) third-rate; la terza età the third age ●adj m third; terzi pl (Jur) third party sg. **ter'zultimo, -a** agg & mf third from last

'tesa f brim

'teschio m skull

'tesi f inv thesis

'teso pp di tendere ●adj taut; fig tense

tesor|e'ria f treasury. ∼i'ere m treasurer

te'soro m treasure; (tesoreria) treasury

'tessera f card; (abbonamento all'autobus) season ticket

'tessere vt weave; hatch (complotto)

tesse'rino m travel card

'tessile adj textile. **tessili** mpl textiles; (operai) textile workers

tessi'tore, -'trice mf weaver

tes'suto m fabric; (Anat) tissue

'testa f head; (cervello) brain; essere in ∼ a be ahead of; in ∼ Sport in the lead; ∼ o croce? heads or tails?

testa-'coda m inv fare un ∼ spin right round

testa'mento m will; T∼ (Relig) Testament

testar'daggine f stubbornness. **te'stardo** adj stubborn

te'stata f head; (intestazione) heading; (colpo) butt

'teste mf witness

te'sticolo m testicle

testi'mon|e mf witness. ∼e oculare eye witness

testi'monial mf inv celebrity promoting brand of cosmetics

testimoni'anza f testimony. ∼'are vt testify to ●vi give evidence

'testo m text; far ∼ be an authority

te'stone, -a mf blockhead

testu'ale adj textual

'tetano m tetanus

'tetro adj gloomy

tetta'rella f teat

'tetto m roof. ∼ apribile sunshine roof. **tet'toia** f roofing. **tet'tuccio** m tettuccio apribile sun-roof

'Tevere m Tiber

ti pers pron you; (riflessivo) yourself; ti ha dato un libro he gave you a book; lavati le mani wash your hands; eccoti! here you are!; sbrigati! hurry up!

ti'ara f tiara

ticchet't|are vi tick. ∼io m ticking

'ticchio m tic; (ghiribizzo) whim

'ticket m inv (per farmaco, esame) amount paid by National Health patients

tiepida'mente adv half-heartedly. **ti'epido** adj lukewarm

ti'fare vi ∼ per shout for. **'tifo** m (Med) typhus; fare il tifo per fig be a fan of

tifoi'dea f typhoid

ti'fone m typhoon

ti'foso, -a mf fan

'tiglio m lime

ti'grato adj gatto ∼ tabby [cat]

'tigre f tiger

'tilde mf tilde

tim'ballo m (Culin) pie

tim'brare vt stamp; ∼ **il cartellino** clock in/out

'timbro m stamp; (di voce) tone

timida'mente adv timidly, shyly. **timi'dezza** f timidity, shyness. **'timido** adj timid, shy

'timo m thyme

ti'mon|e m rudder. ∼**i'ere** m helmsman

ti'more m fear; (soggezione) awe

'timpano m eardrum; (Mus) kettledrum

ti'nello m dining-room

'tinger|e vt dye; (macchiare) stain. ∼**si** vi (viso, cielo:) be tinged (di with); ∼**si i capelli** have one's hair dyed; (da solo) dye one's hair

'tino m, **ti'nozza** f tub

'tint|a f dye; (colore) colour; **in** ∼**a unita** plain. ∼**a'rella** f Ⓘ suntan

tintin'nare vi tinkle

'tinto pp di tingere. ∼**'ria** f (negozio) cleaner's. **tin'tura** f dyeing; (colorante) dye.

'tipico adj typical

'tipo m type; (individuo) guy

tipogra'fia f printery; (arte) typography. **tipo'grafico** adj typographic[al]. **ti'pografo** m printer

tip tap m tap dancing

ti'raggio m draught

tiramisù m inv dessert made of coffee-soaked sponge, eggs, Marsala, cream and cocoa powder

tiran'nia f tyranny. **ti'ranno, -a** adj tyrannical ● mf tyrant

ti'rar|e vt pull; (gettare) throw; kick (palla); (sparare) fire; (tracciare) draw; (stampare) print ● vi pull; (vento:) blow; (abito:) be tight; (sparare) fire; ∼**e avanti** get by; ∼**e su** (crescere) bring up; (da terra) pick up. ∼**si** vr ∼**si indietro** fig back out

tiras'segno m target shooting; (alla fiera) rifle range

ti'rata f tug; **in una** ∼ in one go

tira'tore m shot. ∼ **scelto** marksman

tira'tura f printing; (di giornali) circulation; (di libri) [print] run

'tirchio adj mean

tiri'tera f spiel

'tiro m (traino) draught; (lancio) throw; (sparo) shot; (scherzo) trick. ∼ **con l'arco** archery. ∼ **alla fune** tug-of-war. ∼ **a segno** rifle-range

tiro'cinio m apprenticeship

ti'roide f thyroid

Tir'reno m **il [mar]** ∼ the Tyrrhenian Sea

ti'sana f herb[al] tea

tito'lare adj regular ● mf principal; (proprietario) owner; (calcio) regular player

'titolo m title; (accademico) qualification; (Comm) security; **a** ∼ **di** as; **a** ∼ **di favore** as a favour. **titoli** pl di studio qualifications

titu'ba|nte adj hesitant. ∼**nza** f hesitation. ∼**re** vi hesitate

tivù f inv Ⓘ TV, telly

'tizio m fellow

tiz'zone m brand

toc'cante adj touching

toc'ca|re vt touch; touch on (argomento); (tastare) feel; (riguardare) concern ● vi ∼**re a** (capitare) happen to; **mi tocca aspettare** I'll have to wait; **tocca a te** it's your turn; (pagare da bere) it's your round

tocca'sana m inv cure-all

'tocco m touch; (di pennello, orologio) stroke; (di pane ecc) chunk ● adj Ⓘ crazy, touched

'toga f toga; (accademica, di magistrato) gown

'toglier|e vt take off (coperta); take away (bambino da scuola, sete); (Math) take out, remove (dente); ∼**e qcsa di mano a qcno** take sth away from sb; ∼**e qcno dei guai** get sb out of trouble; **ciò non toglie**

che... nevertheless... ~**si** vr take off (abito); ~**si la vita** take one's [own] life

toilette f inv, **to'letta** f toilet; (mobile) dressing table

tolle'ra|nte adj tolerant. ~**nza** f tolerance. ~**re** vt tolerate

'**tolto** pp di **togliere**

to'maia f upper

'**tomba** f grave, tomb

tom'bino m manhole cover

'**tombola** f bingo; (caduta) tumble

'**tomo** m tome

to'naca f habit

tonalità f inv (Mus) tonality

'**tondo** adj round ●m circle

'**tonico** adj & m tonic

tonifi'care v brace

tonnel'la|ggio m tonnage. ~**ta** f ton

'**tonno** m tuna [fish]

'**tono** m tone

ton'sil|la f tonsil. ~'lite f tonsillitis

'**tonto** adj 🗓 thick

top m inv (indumento) sun-top

to'pazio m topaz

'**topless** m inv in ~ topless

'**topo** m mouse. ~ **di biblioteca** fig bookworm

to'ponimo m place name

'**toppa** f patch; (serratura) keyhole

to'race m chest

'**torba** f peat

'**torbido** adj cloudy; fig troubled

'**torcer|e** v twist; wring [out] (biancheria). ~**si** vr twist

'**torchio** m press

'**torcia** f torch

torci'collo m stiff neck

'**tordo** m thrush

to'rero m bullfighter

To'rino f Turin

tor'menta f snowstorm

tormen'tare vt torment.

tor'mento m torment

torna'conto m benefit

tor'nado m tornado

tor'nante m hairpin bend

tor'nare vi return, go/come back; (ridiventare) become again; (conto:) add up; ~ **a sorridere** become happy again

tor'neo m tournament

'**tornio** m lathe

'**torno** m togliersi di ~ get out of the way

'**toro** m bull; (Astr) T~Taurus

tor'pedin|e f torpedo

tor'pore m torpor

'**torre** f tower; (scacchi) castle. ~ **di controllo** control tower

torrefazi'one f roasting

tor'ren|te m torrent, mountain stream; (fig: di lacrime) flood. ~**zi'ale** adj torrential

tor'retta f turret

'**torrido** adj torrid

torri'one m keep

tor'rone m nougat

'**torso** m torso; (di mela, pera) core; **a ~ nudo** bare-chested

'**torsolo** m core

'**torta** f cake; (crostata) tart

tortel'lini mpl tortellini, small packets of pasta stuffed with pork, ham, Parmesan and nutmeg

torti'era f baking tin

tor'tino m pie

'**torto** pp di **torcere** ●adj twisted ●m wrong; (colpa) fault; **aver ~** be wrong; **a ~** wrongly

'**tortora** f turtle-dove

tortu'oso adj winding; (ambiguo) tortuous

tor'tu|ra f torture. ~'**rare** vt torture

'**torvo** adj grim

to'sare vt shear

tosa'tura f shearing

To'scana f Tuscany

'**tosse** f cough

'**tossico** adj toxic ●m poison. **tossi**-'**comane** mf drug addict

tos'sire vi cough

tosta'pane m inv toaster

to'stare vt toast (pane); roast (caffè)

'**tosto** adv (subito) soon ●adj 🔲 cool

tot adj inv **una cifra ~** such and such **a figure** ●m **un ~** so much

to'tale adj & m total. **~ità** f entirety; **la ~ità dei presenti** all those present

totali'tario adj totalitarian

totaliz'zare vt total; score (punti)

total'mente adv totally

'**totano** m squid

toto'calcio m ≈ [football] pools pl

tournée f inv tour

to'vaglia f tablecloth. **~etta** f **~etta [all'americana]** place mat. **~olo** m napkin

'**tozzo** adj squat

tra = FRA

trabal'la|nte adj staggering; (sedia) rickety. **~re** vi stagger; (veicolo:) jolt

tra'biccolo m 🔲 contraption; (auto) jalopy

traboc'care vi overflow

traboc'chetto m trap

tracan'nare vt gulp down

'**trace|a** f track; (orma) footstep; (striscia) trail; (residuo) trace; fig sign. **~are** vt trace; sketch out (schema); draw (linea). **~ato** m (schema) layout

tra'chea f windpipe

tra'colla f shoulder-strap; **borsa a ~** shoulder-bag

tra'collo m collapse

tradi'mento m betrayal

tra'di|re vt betray; be unfaithful to (moglie, marito). **~tore**, **~trice** mf traitor

tradizio'na|le adj traditional.

~lista mf traditionalist. **~l'mente** adv traditionally. **tradizi'one** f tradition

tra'dotto pp di **tradurre**

tra'du|rre vt translate. **~t'tore**, **~t'trice** mf translator. **~ttore elettronico** electronic phrasebook. **~zi'one** f translation

tra'ente mf (Comm) drawer

trafe'lato adj breathless

traffi'ca|nte mf dealer. **~nte di droga** [drug] pusher. **~re** vi (affaccendarsi) busy oneself; **~re in** pej traffic in. '**traffico** m traffic; (Comm) trade

tra'figgere vt stab; (straziare) pierce

tra'fila f fig rigmarole

trafo'rare vt bore, drill. **tra'foro** m boring; (galleria) tunnel

trafu'gare vt steal

tra'gedia f tragedy

traghet'tare vt ferry. **tra'ghetto** m ferrying; (nave) ferry

tragica'mente adv tragically. '**tragico** adj tragic

tra'gitto m journey; (per mare) crossing

tragu'ardo m finishing post; (meta) goal

traiet'toria f trajectory

trai'nare vt drag; (rimorchiare) tow

tralasci'are vt interrupt; (omettere) leave out

'**tralcio** m (Bot) shoot

tra'liccio m trellis

tram m inv tram, streetcar Am

'**trama** f weft; (di film ecc) plot

traman'dare vt hand down

tra'mare vt weave; (macchinare) plot

tram'busto m turmoil

trame'stio m bustle

tramez'zino m sandwich

tra'mezzo m partition

'**tramite** prep through ●m link; **fare da ~** act as go-between

tramon'tana f north wind

tramon'tare vi set; (declinare) decline. **tra'monto** m sunset; (declino) decline

tramor'tire vt stun • vi faint

trampo'lino m springboard; (per lo sci) ski-jump

'trampolo m stilt

tramu'tare vt transform

'trancia f shears pl; (fetta) slice

tra'nello m trap

trangugi'are vt gulp down

'tranne prep except

tranquilla'mente adv peacefully

tranquil'lante m tranquillizer

tranquilli'tà f calm; (di spirito) tranquillity. ~z'zare vt reassure. tran'quillo adj quiet; (pacifico) peaceful; (coscienza) easy

transat'lantico adj transatlantic • m ocean liner

tran'sa|tto pp di transigere. ~zi'one f (Comm) transaction

trans'senna f (barriera) barrier

trans'genico adj genetically modified, transgenic

tran'sigere vi reach an agreement; (cedere) yield

transi'ta|bile adj passable. ~re vi pass

transi'tivo adj transitive

'transi|to m transit; diritto di ~to right of way; "divieto di ~to" "no thoroughfare". ~'torio adj transitory. ~zi'one f transition

tranvi'ere m tram driver

'trapano m drill

trapas'sare vt go [right] through • vi (morire) pass away

tra'passo m passage

tra'pezio m trapeze; (Math) trapezium

trapi|an'tare vt transplant. ~'anto m transplant

'trappola f trap

tra'punta f quilt

'trarre vt draw; (ricavare) obtain; ~ in inganno deceive

trasa'lire vi start

trasan'dato adj shabby

trasbor'dare vt transfer; (Naut) tran[s]ship • vi change. tra'sbordo m trans[s]hipment

tra'scendere vt transcend • vi (eccedere) go too far

trasci'nar|e vt drag; (entusiasmo:) carry away. ~si vr drag oneself

tra'scorrere vt spend • vi pass

tra'scri|tto pp di trascrivere. ~vere vt transcribe. ~zi'one f transcription

trascu'ra|bile adj negligible. ~re vt neglect; (non tenere conto di) disregard. ~'tezza f negligence. ~to adj negligent; (curato male) neglected; (nel vestire) slovenly

trasecu'lato adj amazed

trasferi'mento m transfer; (trasloco) move

trasfe'ri|re vt transfer. ~rsi vr move

tra'sferta f transfer; (indennità) subsistence allowance; Sport away match; giocare in ~ play away

trasfigu'rare vt transfigure

trasfor'ma|re vt transform; (in rugby) convert. ~'tore m transformer. ~zi'one f transformation; (in rugby) conversion

trasfor'mista mf quick-change artist

trasfusi'one f transfusion

trasgre'dire vt disobey; (Jur) infringe

trasgredi'trice f transgressor

trasgres|si'one f infringement. ~'sore m transgressor

tra'slato adj metaphorical

traslo'car|e vt move • vi, ~si vr move house. tra'sloco m removal

tra'smesso pp di trasmettere

tra'smett|ere vt pass on; (Radio, TV) broadcast; (Med, Techn) transmit. ∼i'tore m transmitter

trasmis'si|bile adj transmissible. ∼'one f transmission; (Radio, TV) programme

trasmit'tente m transmitter •f broadcasting station

traso'gna|re vi day-dream

traspa'ren|te adj transparent. ∼za f transparency; in ∼za against the light. traspa'rire vi show [through]

traspi'ra|re vi perspire; fig transpire. ∼zi'one f perspiration

tra'sporre vt transpose

traspor'tare vt transport; lasciarsi ∼ da get carried away by. tra'sporto m transport; (passione) passion

trastul'lar|e vt amuse. ∼si vr amuse oneself

trasu'dare vt ooze with •vi sweat

trasver'sale adj transverse

trasvo'la|re vt fly over •vi ∼re su fig skim over. ∼ta f crossing [by air]

'tratta f illegal trade; (Comm) draft

trat'tabile adj or near offer

tratta'mento m treatment. ∼ di riguardo special treatment

trat'ta|re vt treat; (commerciare in) deal in; (negoziare) negotiate •vi ∼re di deal with. ∼rsi vr di che si tratta? what is it about?; si tratta di... it's about.... ∼'tive fpl negotiations. ∼to m treaty; (opera scritta) treatise

tratteggi'are vt outline; (descrivere) sketch

tratte'ner|e vt (far restare) keep; hold (respiro, in questura); hold back (lacrime, riso); (frenare) restrain; (da paga) withhold; sono stato trattenuto (ritardato) I got held up. ∼si vr restrain oneself; (fermarsi) stay; ∼si su (indugiare) dwell on. tratteni'mento m entertainment; (ricevimento) party

tratte'nuta f deduction

trat'tino m dash; (in parole composte) hyphen

'tratto pp di trarre •m (di spazio, tempo) stretch; (di penna) stroke; (linea) line; (brano) passage; tratti pl features; a tratti at intervals; ad un ∼ suddenly

trat'tore m tractor

tratto'ria f restaurant

'trauma m trauma. trau'matico adj traumatic

tra'vaglio m labour; (angoscia) anguish

trava'sare vt decant

'trave f beam

tra'versa f crossbar; è una ∼ di Via Roma it's off Via Roma

traver'sa|re vt cross. ∼ta f crossing

traver'sie fpl misfortunes

traver'sina f (Rail) sleeper

tra'vers|o adj crosswise •adv di ∼o crossways; andare di ∼o (cibo:) go down the wrong way; camminare di ∼o not walk in a straight line. ∼one m (in calcio) cross

travesti'mento m disguise

trave'sti|re vt disguise. ∼rsi vr disguise oneself. ∼to adj disguised •m transvestite

travi'are vt lead astray

travi'sare vt distort

tra'vol|gere vt sweep away; (sopraffare) overwhelm. ∼to pp di tra'volgere

trazi'one f traction. ∼ anteriore/posteriore front-/rear-wheel drive

tre adj & m three

trebbi'a|re vt thresh

'treccia f plait, braid

tre'cento adj & m three hundred; il T∼ the fourteenth century

tredi'cesima f Christmas bonus of one month's pay

'tredici adj & m thirteen

'tregua f truce; fig respite

tre'mare vi tremble; (di freddo) shiver

tremenda'mente adv terribly. **tre'mendo** adj terrible; **ho una fame tremenda** I'm very hungry

tremen'tina f turpentine

tre'mila adj & m three thousand

'tremito m tremble

tremo'lare vi shake; (luce:) flicker. **tre'more** m trembling

tre'nino m miniature railway

'treno m train

'tren|ta adj & m thirty; **~ta e lode** top marks. **~tatré giri** m inv LP. **~tenne** adj & mf thirty-year-old. **~tesimo** adj & m thirtieth. **~tina** f **una ~tina di** about thirty

trepi'dare vi be anxious. **'trepido** adj anxious

treppi'ede m tripod

'tresca f intrigue; (amorosa) affair

tri'angolo m triangle

tri'bale adj tribal

tribo'la|re vi suffer; (fare fatica) go through trials and tribulations. **~zi'one** f tribulation

tribù f inv tribe

tri'buna f tribune; (per uditori) gallery; Sport stand. **~ coperta** stand

tribu'nale m court

tribu'tare vt bestow

tribu'tario adj tax attrib. **tri'buto** m tribute; (tassa) tax

tri'checo m walrus

tri'ciclo m tricycle

trico'lore adj three-coloured ● m (bandiera) tricolour

tri'dente m trident

trien'nale adj (ogni tre anni) three-yearly; (lungo tre anni) three-year. **tri'ennio** m three-year period

tri'foglio m clover

trifo'lato adj sliced and cooked with olive oil, parsley and garlic

'triglia f mullet

trigonome'tria f trigonometry

tri'mestre m quarter; (Sch) term

'trina f lace

trin'ce|a f trench

trincia'pollo m inv poultry shears pl

trinci'are vt cut up

Trinità f Trinity

'trio m trio

trion'fa|le adj triumphal. **~nte** adj triumphant. **~re** vi triumph; **~re su** triumph over. **tri'onfo** m triumph

tripli'care vt triple. **'triplice** adj triple; **in triplice [copia]** in triplicate. **'triplo** adj treble ● m **il triplo (di)** three times as much (as)

'trippa f tripe; (🔟: pancia) belly

'triste adj sad; (luogo) gloomy. **tri-'stezza** f sadness. **~o** adj wicked; (meschino) miserable

trita'carne m inv mincer

tri'ta|re vt mince. **'trito** adj **trito e ritrito** well-worn, trite

'trittico m triptych

tritu'rare vt chop finely

triumvi'rato m triumvirate

tri'vella f drill. **trivel'lare** vt drill

trivi'ale adj vulgar

tro'feo m trophy

'trogolo m (per maiali) trough

'troia f sow; (🗙 donna) whore

'tromba f trumpet; (Auto) horn; (delle scale) well. **~ d'aria** whirlwind

trom'b|etta f toy trumpet. **~one** m trombone

trom'bosi f thrombosis

tron'care vt sever; truncate (parola)

'tronco adj truncated; **licenziare in ~** fire on the spot ● m trunk; (di strada) section. **tron'cone** m stump

troneggi'are vi **~ su** tower over

'trono m throne

tropi'cale adj tropical. **'tropico** m tropic

'troppo adj too much; (con nomi plurali) too many ● pron too much; (plurale) too many; (troppo tempo) too long; **troppi** (troppa gente) too many people ● adv too; (con verbi) too much; ~ **stanco** too tired; **ho mangiato** ~ I ate too much; **hai fame?** – **non** ~ are you hungry? – not very

'trota f trout

trot'tare vi trot. **trotterel'lare** vi trot along; (bimbo:) toddle

'trotto m trot; **andare al** ~ trot

'trottola f [spinning] top; (movimento) spin

troupe f inv ~ **televisiva** camera crew

tro'va|re vt find; (scoprire) find out; (incontrare) meet; (ritenere) think; **andare a** ~**re** go and see. ~**rsi** vr find oneself; (luogo:) be; (sentirsi) feel. ~**ta** f bright idea. ~**ta pubblicitaria** advertising gimmick

truc'ca|re vt make up; (falsificare) fix ⊠. ~**rsi** vr make up

'trucco m (cosmetico) make-up; (imbroglio) trick

'truce adj fierce; (delitto) appalling

truci'dare vt slay

truciolo m shaving

trucu'lento adj truculent

'truffa f fraud. **truf'fare** vt swindle. ~**'tore**, ~**'trice** mf swindler

'truppa f troops pl; (gruppo) group

tu pers pron you; **sei tu?** is that you?; **l'hai fatto tu?** did you do it yourself?; **a tu per tu** in private; **darsi del tu** use the familiar tu

'tuba f tuba; (cappello) top hat

tuba'tura f piping

tubazi'oni fpl piping sg, pipes

tuberco'losi f tuberculosis

tu'betto m tube

tu'bino m (vestito) shift

'tubo m pipe; (Anat) canal; **non ho**

capito un ~ ⊠ I understood zilch. ~ **di scappamento** exhaust [pipe]

tuf'fa|re vt plunge. ~**rsi** vr dive. ~**'tore**, ~**'trice** mf diver

'tuffo m dive; (bagno) dip; **ho avuto un** ~ **al cuore** my heart missed a beat. ~ **di testa** dive

'tufo m tufa

tu'gurio m hovel

tuli'pano m tulip

'tulle m tulle

tume'fa|tto adj swollen. ~**zi'one** f swelling. **'tumido** adj swollen

tu'more m tumour

tumulazi'one f burial

tu'mult|o m turmoil; (sommossa) riot. ~**u'oso** adj uproarious

'tunica f tunic

Tuni'sia f Tunisia

'tunnel m inv tunnel

'tuo (il ~ m, la tua f, i ~i mpl, le tue fpl) poss adj your; **è tua questa macchina?** is this car yours?; **un** ~ **amico** a friend of yours; ~ **padre** your father ● poss pron yours; **i tuoi** your folks

tuo'nare vi thunder. **tu'ono** m thunder

tu'orlo m yolk

tu'racciolo m stopper; (di sughero) cork

tu'rar|e vt stop; cork (bottiglia). ~**si** vr become blocked; ~**si il naso** hold one's nose

turba'mento m disturbance; (sconvolgimento) upsetting. ~ **della quiete pubblica** breach of the peace

tur'bante m turban

tur'ba|re vt upset. ~**rsi** vr get upset. ~**to** adj upset

tur'bina f turbine

turbi'nare vi whirl. **'turbine** m whirl. **turbine di vento** whirlwind

turbo'lenza f turbulence

turboreat'tore m turbo-jet

tur'chese adj & mf turquoise

Tur'chia f Turkey

tur'chino adj & m deep blue

'turco, -a adj Turkish ●mf Turk ●m (lingua) Turkish; fig double Dutch; fumare come un ~ smoke like a chimney

tu'ri|smo m tourism. ~ culturale heritage tourism. ~ta mf tourist. ~tico adj tourist attrib

'turno m turn; a ~ in turn; di ~ on duty; fare a ~ take turns. ~ di notte night shift

'turpe adj base

'tuta f overalls pl; Sport tracksuit. ~ da lavoro overalls pl. ~ mimetica camouflage. ~ spaziale spacesuit. ~ subacquea wetsuit

tu'tela f (Jur) guardianship; (protezione) protection. tute'lare vt protect

tu'tina f sleepsuit; (da danza) leotard

tu'tore, -'trice mf guardian

'tutta f mettercela ~ per fare qcsa go flat out for sth

tutta'via conj nevertheless

'tutto adj whole; (con nomi plurali) all; (ogni) every; tutta la classe the whole class, all the class; tutti gli alunni all the pupils; a tutta velocità at full speed; ho aspettato ~ il giorno I waited all day [long]; in ~ il mondo all over the world; noi tutti all of us; era tutta contenta she was delighted; tutti e due both; tutti e tre all three ●pron all; (tutta la gente) everybody; (tutte le cose) everything; (qualunque cosa) anything; l'ho mangiato ~ I ate it all; le ho lavate tutte I washed them all; raccontami ~ tell me everything; lo sanno tutti everybody knows; è capace di ~ he's capable of anything; ~ compreso all in; del ~ quite; in ~ altogether ●adv completely; tutt'a un tratto all at once; tutt'altro not at all; tutt'altro che anything but ●m whole. ~'fare a inv & nmf [impiegato] ~ general handyman; donna

~ general maid

tut'tora adv still

tutù m inv tutu, ballet dress

tv f inv TV

Uu

ubbidi'en|te adj obedient. ~za f obedience. ubbi'dire vi ~ (a) obey

ubi'ca|to adj located. ~zi'one f location

ubria'car|e vt get drunk. ~si vr get drunk; ~si di fig become intoxicated with

ubria'chezza f drunkenness; in stato di ~ inebriated

ubri'aco, -a adj drunk ●mf drunk

ubria'cone m drunkard

uc'cell|era f aviary. uc'cello m bird; (✗: pene) cock

uc'cider|e vt kill. ~si vr kill oneself

ucci'si|one f killing. uc'ciso pp di uccidere. ~'sore m killer

u'dente adj i non udenti the hearing-impaired

u'dibile adj audible

udi'enza f audience; (colloquio) interview; (Jur) hearing

u'di|re vt hear. ~'tivo adj auditory. ~to m hearing. ~'tore, ~'trice mf listener; (Sch) unregistered student (allowed to attend lectures). ~'torio m audience

uffici'al|e adj official ●m officer; (funzionario) official; pubblico ~e public official. ~iz'zare vt make official

uf'ficio m office; (dovere) duty. ~ di collocamento employment office. ~ informazioni information office. ~ del personale personnel department. ~sa'mente adv unofficially

uffici'oso adj unofficial

'ufo[1] m inv ufo

'ufo[2]: a ∼ adv without paying

uggi'oso adj boring

uguagli'a|nza f equality. ∼re vt make equal; (essere uguale) equal; (livellare) level. ∼rsi vr ∼rsi a compare oneself to

ugu'al|e adj equal; (lo stesso) the same; (simile) like. ∼'mente adv equally; (malgrado tutto) all the same

'ulcera f ulcer

uli'veto m olive grove

ulteri'or|e adj further. ∼'mente adv further

ultima'mente adv lately

ulti'ma|re vt complete. ∼tum m inv ultimatum

ulti'missime fpl stop press sg

'ultimo adj last; (notizie ecc) latest; (più lontano) farthest; fig ultimate ● m last; fino all'∼ to the last; per ∼ at the end; l'∼ piano the top floor

ultrà mf inv Sport fanatical supporter

ultramo'derno adj ultramodern

ultra'rapido adj extra-fast

ultrasen'sibile adj ultrasensitive

ultra's|onico adj ultrasonic. ∼u'ono m ultrasound

ultravio'letto adj ultraviolet

ulu'la|re vi howl. ∼to m howling

umana'mente adv (trattare) humanely; ∼ impossibile not humanly possible

uma'nesimo m humanism

umanità f humanity. umani'tario adj humanitarian. u'mano adj human; (benevolo) humane

umidifica'tore m humidifier

umidità f dampness; (di clima) humidity. 'umido adj damp; (clima) humid; (mani, occhi) moist ● m dampness; in umido (Culin) stewed

'umile adj humble

umili'a|nte adj humiliating. ∼re vt humiliate. ∼rsi vr humble oneself.

∼zi'one f humiliation. umil'mente adv humbly. umiltà f humility

u'more m humour; (stato d'animo) mood; di cattivo/buon ∼ in a bad/ good mood

umo'ri|smo m humour. ∼ta mf humorist. ∼tico adj humorous

---

un in def art

Un/una si traduce con one quando si tratta di un numero

a;
····▸ (davanti a vocale o h muta)
an; ▷**UNO**

---

una indef art f a; ▷**UN**

u'nanim|e adj unanimous. ∼e'mente adv unanimously. ∼ità f unanimity; all'∼ità unanimously

unci'nato adj hooked; (parentesi) angle

un'cino m hook

'undici adj & m eleven

'unger|e vt grease, (sporcare) get greasy; (Relig) anoint; (blandire) flatter. ∼si vr (con olio solare) oil oneself; ∼si le mani get one's hands greasy

unghe'rese adj & mf Hungarian. Unghe'ria f Hungary

'unghi|a f nail; (di animale) claw. ∼'ata f (graffio) scratch

ungu'ento m ointment

unica'mente adv only. 'unico adj only; (singolo) single; (incomparabile) unique

unifi'ca|re vt unify. ∼zi'one f unification

unifor'mar|e vt level. ∼si vr conform (a to)

uni'form|e adj & f uniform. ∼ità f uniformity

unilate'rale adj unilateral

uni'one f union; (armonia) unity. U∼ Europea European Union. U∼ Monetaria **Europea** European Monetary Union. **~ sindacale** trade union

u'ni|re vt unite; (collegare) join; blend (colori ecc). **~rsi** vr unite; (collegarsi) join

'unisex adj inv unisex

unità f inv unity; (Math, Mil) unit; (Comput) drive. **~rio** adj unitary

u'nito adj united; (tinta) plain

univer'sa|le adj universal. **~'mente** adv universally

università f inv university. **~rio, -a** adj university attrib ● mf (insegnante) university lecturer; (studente) undergraduate

Università Italy's first university was founded in Bologna in 1088, and they are still run on traditional lines. Oral exams are the norm. Students study for a number of exams, which can be taken in a flexible order. For this reason Italian students often combine study with a job. The drop-out rate is high.

uni'verso m universe

uno, -a indef art (before s + consonant, gn, ps, z) a
● pron one; a ~ a ~ one by one; l'~ e l'altro both [of them]; né l'~ né l'altro neither [of them]; ~ di noi one of us; ~ fa quello che può you do what you can
● adj a, one
● m (numerale) one; (un tale) some man;
● f some woman

'unt|o pp di ungere ● adj greasy ● m grease. **~u'oso** adj greasy. unzi'one f l'Estrema Unzione Extreme Unction

u'omo m (pl uomini) man. **~ d'affari** business man. **~ di fiducia** right-hand man. **~ di Stato** statesman

u'ovo m (pl f uova) egg. **~ in camicia** poached egg. **~ alla coque** boiled egg. **~ di Pasqua** Easter egg. **~ sodo** hard-boiled egg. **~ strapazzato** scrambled egg

ura'gano m hurricane

u'ranio m uranium

urba'n|esimo m urbanization. **~ista** mf town planner. **~istica** f town planning. **~istico** adj urban. urbanizzazi'one f urbanization. ur'bano adj urban; (cortese) urbane

ur'gen|te adj urgent. **~te'mente** adv urgently. **~za** f urgency; in caso d'~za in an emergency; d'~za (misura, chiamata) emergency

'urgere vi be urgent

u'rina f urine. uri'nare vi urinate

ur'lare vi yell; (cane, vento:) howl. 'urlo m (pl m urli, f urla) shout; (di cane, vento) howling

'urna f urn; (elettorale) ballot box; andare alle urne go to the polls

urrà int hurrah!

ur'tar|e vt knock against; (scontrarsi) bump into; fig irritate. **~si** vr collide; fig clash

'urto m knock; (scontro) crash; (contrasto) conflict; fig clash; d'~ (misure, terapia) shock

usa e getta adj inv (rasoio, siringa) disposable

u'sanza f custom; (moda) fashion

u'sa|re vt use; (impiegare) employ; (esercitare) exercise; **~re fare qcsa** be in the habit of doing sth ● vi (essere di moda) be fashionable; non si usa più it is out of fashion; it's not used any more. **~to** adj used; (non nuovo) second-hand

u'scente adj (presidente) outgoing

usci'ere m usher. 'uscio m door

u'sci|re vi come out; (andare fuori) go out; (sfuggire) get out; (essere sorteggiato) come up; (giornale:) come out; **~re da** (Comput) exit from, quit; **~re di strada** leave the road. **~ta** f exit, way out; (spesa) outlay; (di auto-

strada) junction; (*battuta*) witty remark;
essere in libera ~ta be off duty.
~ta di servizio back door. **~ta di sicurezza** emergency exit

usi'gnolo *m* nightingale

'uso *m* use; (*abitudine*) custom; (*usanza*) usage; **fuori ~** out of use; **per ~ esterno** for external use only

U.S.S.L. *f abbr* (*Unità Socio-Sanitaria Locale*) local health centre

ustio'na|rsi *vr* burn oneself ●*adj* burnt. **usti'one** *f* burn

usu'ale *adj* usual

usufru'ire *vi* **~ di** take advantage of

u'sura *f* usury

usur'pare *vt* usurp

u'tensile *m* tool; (*Culin*) utensil; **cassetta degli utensili** tool box

u'tente *mf* user. **~ finale** end user

u'tenza *f* use; (*utenti*) users *pl*. **~ finale** end users

ute'rino *adj* uterine. **'utero** *m* womb

'util|e *adj* useful ●*m* (*Comm*) profit.
~ità *f* usefulness; (*Comput*) utility.
~i'taria *f* (*Auto*) small car. **~i'tario** *adj* utilitarian

utiliz'za|re *vt* utilize. **~zi'one** *f* utilization. **uti'lizzo** *m* use

uto'pistico *adj* Utopian

'uva *f* grapes *pl*; **chicco d'~** grape.
~ passa raisins *pl*. **~ sultanina** currants *pl*

. . . .

Vv

. . . .

va'cante *adj* vacant

va'canza *f* holiday; (*posto vacante*) vacancy. **essere in ~** be on holiday

'vacca *f* cow. **~ da latte** dairy cow

vacc|i'nare *vt* vaccinate. **~ina-zi'one** *f* vaccination. **vac'cino** *m*

vaccine

vacil'la|nte *adj* tottering; (*oggetto*) wobbly; (*luce*) flickering; *fig* wavering. **~re** *vi* totter; (*oggetto*): wobble; (*luce*): flicker; *fig* waver

'vacuo *adj* (*vano*) vain; *fig* empty ●*m* vacuum

vagabon'dare *vi* wander. **vaga-'bondo, -a** *adj* (*cane*) stray; **gente vagabonda** tramps *pl* ●*mf* tramp

va'gare *vi* wander

vagheggi'are *vt* long for

va'gi|na *f* vagina. **~'nale** *adj* vaginal

va'gi|re *vi* whimper

'vaglia *m inv* money order. **~ bancario** bank draft. **~ postale** postal order

vagli'are *vt* sift; *fig* weigh

'vago *adj* vague

vagon'cino *m* (*di funivia*) car

va'gone *m* (*per passeggeri*) carriage; (*per merci*) wagon. **~ letto** sleeper. **~ ristorante** restaurant car

vai'olo *m* smallpox

va'langa *f* avalanche

va'lente *adj* skilful

va'ler|e *vi* be worth; (*contare*) count; (*regola*): apply (**per** to); (*essere valido*) be valid; **far ~ i propri diritti** assert one's rights; **farsi ~e** assert oneself; **non vale!** that's not fair!
●*vt* **~re** qcsa a qcno (*procurare*) earn sb sth; **~ne la pena** be worth it; **vale la pena di vederlo** it's worth seeing; **~si di** avail oneself of

valeri'ana *f* valerian

va'levole *adj* valid

vali'care *vt* cross. **'valico** *m* pass

validità *f* validity; **con ~ illimitata** valid indefinitely

'valido *adj* valid; (*efficace*) efficient; (*contributo*) valuable

valige'ria *f* (*fabbrica*) leather factory; (*negozio*) leather goods shop

va'ligia f suitcase; **fare le valigie** pack one's bags. ~ **diplomatica** diplomatic bag

val'lata f valley. **'valle** f valley; **a valle** downstream

val'lett|a f (TV) assistant. ~**o** m valet; (TV) assistant

val'lone m (valle) deep valley

va'lor|e m value; (merito) merit; (coraggio) valour; ~**i** pl (Comm) securities; **di** ~**e** (oggetto) valuable; **oggetti** pl **di** ~**e** valuables; **senza** ~**e** worthless. ~**iz'zare** vt (mettere in valore) use to advantage; (aumentare di valore) increase the value of; (migliorare l'aspetto di) enhance

valo'roso adj courageous

'valso pp di **valere**

va'luta f currency. ~ **estera** foreign currency

valu'ta|re vt value; weigh up (situazione). ~**rio** adj (mercato, norme) currency. ~**zi'one** f valuation

'valva f valve. **'valvola** f valve; (Electr) fuse

vam'pata f blaze; (di calore) blast; (al viso) flush

vam'piro m vampire

vana'mente adv in vain

van'da|lico adj atto ~**lico** act of vandalism. ~**'lismo** m vandalism. **'vandalo** m vandal

vaneggi'are vi rave

'vanga f spade. **van'gare** vt dig

van'gelo m Gospel; ([🔒]: verità) gospel [truth]

vanifi'care vt nullify

va'niglia f vanilla. ~**'ato** adj (zucchero) vanilla attrib

vanità f vanity. **vani'toso** adj vain

'vano adj vain ● m (stanza) room; (spazio vuoto) hollow

van'taggi|o m advantage; Sport lead; Tennis advantage; **trarre** ~**o da qcsa** derive benefit from sth. ~**'oso** adj advantageous

van't|are vt praise; (possedere) boast. ~**arsi** vr boast. ~**e'ria** f boasting. **'vanto** m boast

'vanvera f **a** ~ at random; **parlare a** ~ talk nonsense

va'por|e m steam; (di benzina, cascata) vapour; **a** ~**e** steam attrib; **al** ~**e** (Culin) steamed. ~**e acqueo** steam, water vapour; **battello a** ~**e** steamboat. **vapo'retto** m ferry. ~**i'era** f steam engine

vaporiz'za|re vt vaporize. ~**'tore** m spray

vapo'roso adj (vestito) filmy; **capelli vaporosi** big hair sg

va'rare vt launch

var'care vt cross. **'varco** m passage; **aspettare al varco** lie in wait

vari'abil|e adj variable ● f variable. ~**ità** f variability

vari'a|nte f variant. ~**re** vt/i vary; ~**re di umore** change one's mood. ~**zi'one** f variation

va'rice f varicose vein

vari'cella f chickenpox

vari'coso adj varicose

varie'gato adj variegated

varietà f inv variety ● m inv variety show

'vario adj varied; (al pl, parecchi) various; **vari** pl (molti) several; **varie ed eventuali** any other business

vario'pinto adj multicoloured

'varo m launch

va'saio m potter

'vasca f tub; (piscina) pool; (lunghezza) length. ~ **da bagno** bath

va'scello m vessel

va'schetta f tub

vase'lina f Vaseline®

vasel'lame m china. ~ **d'oro/ d'argento** gold/silver plate

'vaso m pot; (da fiori) vase; (Anat) vessel; (per cibi) jar. ~ **da notte** chamber pot

vas'soio m tray

vastità f vastness. **'vasto** adj vast; **di vaste vedute** broad-minded

Vati'cano m Vatican

ve pers pron you; **ve l'ho dato** I gave it to you

vecchia f old woman. **vecchi'aia** f old age. **'vecchio** adj old ●mf old man; **i vecchi** old people

'vece f in ∼ di in place of; **fare le veci di qcno** take sb's place

ve'dente adj **i non vedenti** the visually handicapped

ve'der|e vt/i see; **far** ∼**e** show; **farsi** ∼**e** show one's face; **non vedo l'ora di...** I can't wait to.... ∼**si** vr see oneself; (reciproco) see each other

ve'detta f lookout; (Naut) patrol vessel

'vedovo, -a m widower ●f widow

ve'duta f view

vee'mente adj vehement

vege'ta|le adj & m vegetable. ∼**li'ano** adj & mf vegan. ∼**re** vi vegetate. ∼**ri'ano, -a** adj & mf vegetarian. ∼**zi'one** f vegetation

'vegeto adj ▷vivo

veg'gente mf clairvoyant

'veglia f watch; **fare la** ∼ keep watch. ∼ **funebre** vigil

vegli'|are vi be awake; ∼**are su** watch over. ∼**'one** m ∼**one di Capodanno** New Year's Eve celebration

ve'icolo m vehicle

'vela f sail; (Sport) sailing; **far** ∼ set sail

ve'la|re vt veil; (fig: nascondere) hide. ∼**rsi** vr (vista:) mist over; (voce:) go husky. ∼**ta'mente** adv indirectly. ∼**to** adj veiled; (occhi) misty; (collant) sheer

'velcro® velcro®

veleggi'are vi sail

ve'leno m poison. **vele'noso** adj poisonous

veli'ero m sailing ship

ve'lina f (carta) ∼ tissue paper;

(copia) carbon copy

ve'lista m yachtsman ●f yachtswoman

ve'livolo m aircraft

vellei'tario adj unrealistic

'vello m fleece

vellu'tato adj velvety. **vel'luto** m velvet. **velluto a coste** corduroy

'velo m veil; (di zucchero, cipria) dusting; (tessuto) voile

ve'loc|e adj fast. ∼**e'mente** adv quickly. **velo'cista** mf (Sport) sprinter. ∼**ità** f inv speed; (Auto: marcia) gear. ∼**iz'zare** vt speed up

ve'lodromo m cycle track

'vena f vein; **essere in** ∼ **di** be in the mood for

ve'nale adj venal; (persona) mercenary, venal

ve'nato adj grainy

vena'torio adj hunting attrib

vena'tura f (di legno) grain; (di foglia, marmo) vein

ven'demmi|a f grape harvest. ∼**are** vt harvest

'vender|e vt sell. ∼**si** vr sell oneself; "**vendesi**" "for sale"

ven'detta f revenge

vendi'car|e vt avenge. ∼**rsi** vr get one's revenge. ∼**'tivo** adj vindictive

'vendi|ta f sale; **in** ∼**ta** on sale. ∼**ta all'asta** sale by auction. ∼**ta al dettaglio** retailing. ∼**ta all'ingrosso** wholesaling. ∼**ta al minuto** retailing. ∼**tore, ∼trice** mf seller. ∼**tore ambulante** hawker, pedlar

vene'ra|bile, ∼**ndo** adj venerable

vene'ra|re vt revere

venerdì m inv Friday. **V**∼ **Santo** Good Friday

'Venere f Venus. **ve'nereo** adj venereal

Ve'nezi|a f Venice. **v**∼**'ano, -a** agg & mf Venetian ●f (persiana) Venetian blind; (Culin) sweet bun

veni'ale adj venial

ve'nire vi come; (riuscire) turn out; (costare) cost; (in passivi) be; ~ **a sapere** learn; ~ **in mente** occur; ~ **meno** (svenire) faint; ~ **meno a un contratto** go back on a contract; ~ **via** come away; (staccarsi) come off; **vieni a prendermi** come and pick me up

ven'taglio m fan

ven'tata f gust [of wind]; fig breath

ven'te|nne adj & mf twenty-year-old. ~**simo** adj & m twentieth. '**venti** adj & m twenty

venti'la|re vt air. ~'**tore** m fan. ~**zi'one** f ventilation

ven'tina f una ~ (circa venti) about twenty

ventiquat'trore f inv (valigia) overnight case

'**vento** m wind; **farsi** ~ fan oneself

ven'tosa f sucker

ven'toso adj windy

'**ventre** m stomach. **ven'triloquo** m ventriloquist

ven'tura f fortune

ven'turo adj next

ve'nuta f coming

vera'mente adv really

ve'randa f veranda

ver'bal|e adj verbal ● m (di riunione) minutes pl. ~'**mente** adv verbally

'**verbo** m verb. ~ **ausiliare** auxiliary [verb]

'**verde** adj green ● m green; (vegetazione) greenery; (semaforo) green light. ~ **oliva** olive green. ~'**rame** m verdigris

ver'detto m verdict

ver'dura f vegetables pl; **una** ~ a vegetable

'**verga** f rod

vergi'n|ale adj virginal. '**vergine** f virgin; (Astr) V~ Virgo ● adj virgin; (cassetta) blank. ~**ità** f virginity

ver'gogna f shame; (timidezza) shyness

vergo'gn|arsi vr feel ashamed; (essere timido) feel shy. ~**oso** adj ashamed; (timido) shy; (disonorevole) shameful

ve'rifica f check. **verifi'cabile** adj verifiable

verifi'car|e vt check. ~**si** vr come true

ve'rismo m realism

verit|à f truth. ~**i'ero** adj truthful

'**verme** m worm. ~ **solitario** tapeworm

ver'miglio adj & m vermilion

'**vermut** m inv vermouth

ver'nacolo m vernacular

ver'nic|e f paint; (trasparente) varnish; (pelle) patent leather; fig veneer; "**vernice fresca**" "wet paint". ~**i'are** vt paint; (con vernice trasparente) varnish. ~**ia'tura** f painting; (strato) paintwork; fig veneer

'**vero** adj true; (autentico) real; (perfetto) perfect; **è** ~? is that so?; **sei stanca**, ~? you're tired, aren't you ● m truth; (realtà) life

verosimigli'anza f probability. **vero'simile** adj probable

ver'ruca f wart; (sotto la pianta del piede) verruca

versa'mento m payment; (in banca) deposit

ver'sante m slope

ver'sa|re vt pour; (spargere) shed; (rovesciare) spill; pay (denaro). ~**rsi** vr spill; (sfociare) flow

ver'satil|e adj versatile. ~**ità** f versatility

ver'setto m verse

versi'one f version; (traduzione) translation; "~ **integrale**" "unabridged version"

'**verso**[1] m verse; (grido) cry; (gesto) gesture; (senso) direction; (modo) manner; **non c'è** ~ **di** there is no way of

'**verso**[2] prep towards; (nei pressi di)

round about; ~ **dove?** which way?

'vertebra f vertebra

'vertere vi ~ **su** focus on

verti'cal|e adj vertical; (in parole crociate) down ● m vertical ● f handstand. ~**mente** adv vertically

'vertice m summit; (Math) vertex; **conferenza al ~** summit conference

ver'tigine f dizziness; (Med) vertigo. **vertigini** fpl giddy spells

vertigi|nosa'mente adv dizzily. ~**'noso** adj dizzy; (velocità) breakneck; (prezzi) sky-high; (scollatura) plunging

ve'scica f bladder; (sulla pelle) blister

'vescovo m bishop

'vespa f wasp

vespasi'ano m urinal

'vespro m vespers pl

ves'sillo m standard

ve'staglia f dressing gown

'vest|e f dress; (rivestimento) covering; **in ~e di** in the capacity of. ~**i'ario** m clothing

ve'stibolo m hall

ve'stigio m (pl m vestigi, pl f vestigia) trace

ve'sti|re vt dress. ~**rsi** vr get dressed. ~**ti** pl clothes. ~**to** adj dressed ● m (da uomo) suit; (da donna) dress

vete'rano, -a adj & mf veteran

veteri'naria f veterinary science

veteri'nario adj veterinary ● m veterinary surgeon

'veto m inv veto

ve'tra|io m glazier. ~**ta** f big window; (in chiesa) stained-glass window; (porta) glass door. ~**to** adj glazed. **vetre'ria** f glass works

ve'tri|na f [shop-]window; (mobile) display cabinet. ~**'nista** mf window dresser

vetri'olo m vitriol

'vetro m glass; (di finestra, porta) pane. ~**'resina** f fibreglass

'vetta f peak

vet'tore m vector

vetto'vaglie fpl provisions

vet'tura f coach; (ferroviaria) carriage; (Auto) car. **vettu'rino** m coachman

vezzeggi'a|re vt fondle. ~**'tivo** m pet name. **vezzi** pl (moine) affectation sg. **vez'zoso** adj charming; pej affected

vi pers pron you; (riflessivo) yourselves; (reciproco) each other; (tra più persone) one another; **vi ho dato un libro** I gave you a book; **lavatevi le mani** wash your hands; **eccovi** here you are! ● adv = **ci**

'via[1] f street, road; fig way; (Anat) tract; **in ~ di** in the course of; **per ~ di** on account of; **~ che** as; **per ~ aerea** by airmail

'via[2] adv away; (fuori) out; **andar ~** go away; **e così ~** and so on; **e ~ dicendo** and whatnot ● int ~! go away!; Sport go!; (andiamo) come on! ● m starting signal

viabilità f road conditions pl; (rete) road network; (norme) road and traffic laws pl

via'card f inv motorway card

viaggi'a|re vi travel. ~**'tore, ~'trice** mf traveller

vi'aggio m journey; (breve) trip; **buon ~!** safe journey!, have a good trip!; **fare un ~** go on a journey. **~ di nozze** honeymoon

vi'ale m avenue; (privato) drive

vi'bra|nte adj vibrant. ~**re** vi vibrate; (fremere) quiver. ~**zi'one** f vibration

vi'cario m vicar

'vice mf deputy. ~**diret'tore** m assistant manager

vi'cenda f event; **a ~** (fra due) each other; (a turno) in turn[s]

vice'versa adv vice versa

vici'na|nza f nearness; ~**nze** pl (paraggi) neighbourhood. ~**to** m neighbourhood; (*vicini*) neighbours *pl*

vi'cino, -a *adj* near; (*accanto*) next ● *adv* near, close. ~ a *prep* near [to] ● *mf* neighbour. ~ di casa nextdoor neighbour

'**vicolo** *m* alley

'**video** *m* video. ~'camera *f* camcorder. ~cas'setta *f* video cassette

videoci'tofono *m* video entry phone

video'clip *m inv* video clip

videogi'oco *m* video game

videoregistra'tore *m* video-recorder

video'teca *f* video library

video'tel® *m* ≈ Videotex®

videote'lefono *m* videophone

videotermi'nale *m* visual display unit, VDU

vidi'mare *vt* authenticate

vie'tare *vt* forbid; sosta ~ta no parking; ~to fumare no smoking

vi'gente *adj* in force. '**vigere** *vi* be in force

vigi'la|nte *adj* vigilant. ~nza *f* vigilance. ~re *vt* keep an eye on ● *vi* keep watch

'**vigile** *adj* watchful ● *m* ≈ [urbano] policeman. ~ del fuoco fireman

vi'gilia *f* eve

vigliacche'ria *f* cowardice. vi'gli'acco, -a *adj* cowardly ● *mf* coward

'**vigna** *f*, vi'gneto *m* vineyard

vi'gnetta *f* cartoon

vi'gore *m* vigour; entrare in ~ come into force. vigo'roso *adj* vigorous

'**vile** *adj* cowardly; (*abietto*) vile

'**villa** *f* villa

vil'laggio *m* village. ~ turistico holiday village

vil'lano *adj* rude ● *m* boor; (*contadino*) peasant

villeggi'a|nte *mf* holiday-maker. ~re *vi* spend one's holidays. ~'tura

f holiday[s] [*pl*]

vil'l|etta *f* small detached house. ~ino *m* detached house

viltà *f* cowardice

'**vimine** *m* wicker

'**vinc|ere** *vt* win; (*sconfiggere*) beat; (*superare*) overcome. ~ita *f* win; (*somma vinta*) winnings *pl*. ~i'tore, ~i'trice *mf* winner

vinco'la|nte *adj* binding. ~re *vt* bind; (*Comm*) tie up. '**vincolo** *m* bond

vi'nicolo *adj* wine *attrib*

vinil'pelle® *f* Leatherette®

'**vino** *m* wine. ~ spumante sparkling wine. ~ da taglio blending wine. ~ da tavola table wine

'**vinto** *pp di* vincere

vi'ola *f* (*Bot*) violet; (*Mus*) viola. viola *adj* & *m inv* purple

vio'la|re *vt* violate. ~zi'one *f* violation. ~zione di domicilio breaking and entering

violen'tare *vt* rape

vio'len|to *adj* violent. ~za *f* violence. ~za carnale rape

vio'letta *f* violet

vio'letto *adj* & *m* (*colore*) violet

violi'nista *mf* violinist. vio'lino *m* violin. violon'cello *m* cello

vi'ottolo *m* path

'**vipera** *f* viper

vi'ra|ggio *m* (*Phot*) toning; (*Aeron, Naut*) turn. ~re *vi* turn

'**virgol|a** *f* comma. ~ette *fpl* inverted commas

vi'ril|e *adj* virile; (*da uomo*) manly. ~ità *f* virility; manliness

virtù *f inv* virtue; in ~ di (*legge*) under. virtu'ale *adj* virtual. virtu'oso *adj* virtuous ● *m* virtuoso

viru'lento *adj* virulent

'**virus** *m inv* virus

visa'gista *mf* beautician

visce'rale *adj* visceral; (*odio*) deep-seated; (*reazione*) gut

'**viscere** m internal organ ●*fpl* guts

'**vischi|o** m mistletoe. ~'**oso** adj viscous; (*appiccicoso*) sticky

vi'**scont|e** m viscount. ~'**essa** f viscountess

vi'**scoso** adj viscous

vi'**sibile** adj visible

visi'**bilio** m profusion; andare in ~ go into ecstasies

visibilità f visibility

visi'**era** f (*di elmo*) visor; (*di berretto*) peak

visio'**nare** vt examine; Cinema screen. visi'**one** f vision; prima visione Cinema first showing

'**visit|a** f visit; (*breve*) call; (*Med*) examination. ~**a di controllo** (*Med*) checkup. visi'**tare** vt visit; (*brevemente*) call on; (*Med*) examine; ~**a'tore**, ~**a'trice** mf visitor

vi'**sivo** adj visual

'**viso** m face

vi'**sone** m mink

'**vispo** adj lively

vis'**suto** pp di vivere ●adj experienced

'**vist|a** f sight; (*veduta*) view; **a ~ d'occhio** (*crescere*) visibly; (*estendersi*) as far as the eye can see; in ~**a di** in view of. ~**o** pp di vedere ●m visa. vi'**stoso** adj showy; (*notevole*) considerable

visu'**al|e** adj visual. ~**izza'tore** m (*Comput*) display, VDU. ~**izzazi'one** f (*Comput*) display

'**vita** f life; (*durata della vita*) lifetime; (*Anat*) waist; **a ~** for life; essere in ~ be alive

vi'**tal|e** adj vital. ~**ità** f vitality

vita'**lizio** adj life attrib ●m [life] annuity

vita'**min|a** f vitamin. ~**iz'zato** adj vitamin-enriched

'**vite** f (*Mech*) screw; (*Bot*) vine

vi'**tello** m calf; (*Culin*) veal; (*pelle*) calfskin

vi'**ticcio** m tendril

viticol'**t|ore** m wine grower. ~**ura** f wine growing

'**vitreo** adj vitreous; (*sguardo*) glassy

'**vittima** f victim

'**vitto** m food; (*pasti*) board. ~ **e alloggio** board and lodging

vit'**toria** f victory

vittori'**oso** adj victorious

vi'**uzza** f narrow lane

'**viva** int hurrah!; ~ **la Regina!** long live the Queen!

vl'**vac|e** adj vivacious, (*mente*) lively; (*colore*) bright. ~**ità** f vivacity; (*di mente*) liveliness; (*di colore*) brightness. ~**iz'zare** vt liven up

vi'**vaio** m nursery; (*per pesci*) pond; fig breeding ground

viva'**mente** adv (ringraziare) warmly

vi'**vanda** f food; (*piatto*) dish

vi'**vente** adj living ●mpl **i viventi** the living

'**vivere** vi live; ~ **di** live on ●vt (*passare*) go through ●m life

'**viveri** mpl provisions

'**vivido** adj vivid

vivisezi'**one** f vivisection

'**vivo** adj alive; (*vivente*) living; (*vivace*) lively; (*colore*) bright; ~ **e vegeto** alive and kicking; farsi ~ keep in touch; (*arrivare*) turn up ●m **dal ~** (*trasmissione*) live; (*disegnare*) from life; **i vivi** the living

vizi'**are** vt spoil (*bambino ecc*); (*guastare*) vitiate. ~'**ato** adj spoilt; (*aria*) stale. '**vizio** m vice; (*cattiva abitudine*) bad habit; (*difetto*) flaw. ~'**oso** adj dissolute; (*difettoso*) faulty; **circolo** ~'**oso** vicious circle

vocabo'**lario** m dictionary; (*lessico*) vocabulary. vo'**cabolo** m word

vo'**cale** adj vocal ●f vowel. vo'**calico** adj (*corde*) vocal; (*suono*) vowel attrib

vocazi'one f vocation

'voce f voice; (diceria) rumour; (di bilancio, dizionario) entry

voci'are vi (spettegolare) gossip ● m buzz of conversation

vocife'rare vi shout

'vog|a f rowing; (lena) enthusiasm; (moda) vogue; **essere in** ~**a** be in fashion. **vo'gare** vi row. ~**a'tore** m oarsman; (attrezzo) rowing machine

'vogli|a f desire; (volontà) will; (della pelle) birthmark; **aver** ~**a di fare qcsa** feel like doing sth

'voi pers pron you; **siete** ~? is that you?; **l'avete fatto** ~? did you do it yourself?. ~**a'ltri** pers pron you

vo'lano m shuttlecock; (Mech) flywheel

vo'lante adj flying; (foglio) loose ● m steering-wheel

volan'tino m leaflet

vo'la|re vi fly. ~**ta** f Sport final sprint; **di** ~**ta** in a rush

vo'latile adj (liquido) volatile ● m bird

volée f inv Tennis volley

vo'lente adj ~ **o nolente** whether you like it or not

volenti'eri adv willingly; ~! with pleasure!

vo'lere vt want; (chiedere di) ask for; (aver bisogno di) need; **vuole che lo faccia io** he wants me to do it; **fai come vuoi** do as you like; **se tuo padre vuole, ti porto al cinema** if your father agrees, I'll take you to the cinema; **vorrei un caffè** I'd like a coffee; **la vuoi smettere?** will you stop that!; **senza** ~ without meaning to; **voler bene/male a qcno** love/have something against sb; **voler dire** mean; **ci vuole il latte** we need milk; **ci vuole tempo/pazienza** it takes time/patience; **volerne a** have a grudge against; **vuole ... vuoi ...** either... or...; **vo'leri** pl wishes

vol'gar|e adj vulgar; (popolare) common. ~**ità** f inv vulgarity. ~**iz'zare** vt popularize. ~**mente** adv (grossolanamente) vulgarly, coarsely; (comunemente) commonly

'volger|e vt/i turn. ~**si** vr turn [round]; ~**si a** (dedicarsi) take up

voli'era f aviary

voli'tivo adj strong-minded

'volo m flight; **al** ~ (fare qcsa) quickly; (prendere qcsa) in mid-air; **alzarsi in** ~ (uccello:) take off; **in** ~ airborne. ~ **di linea** scheduled flight. ~ **nazionale** domestic flight. ~ **a vela** gliding.

volontà f inv will; (desiderio) wish; **a** ~ (mangiare) as much as you like. **volontaria'mente** adv voluntarily. **volon'tario** adj voluntary ● m volunteer

volonte'roso adj willing

'volpe f fox

volt m inv volt

'volta f time; (turno) turn; (curva) bend; (Archit) vault; **4 volte 4** 4 times 4; **a volte** sometimes; **c'era una** ~... once upon a time, there was...; **una** ~ once; **due volte** twice; **tre/quattro volte** three/four times; **una** ~ **per tutte** once and for all; **uno per** ~ one at a time; **uno alla** ~ one at a time; **alla** ~ **di** in the direction of

volta'faccia m inv volte-face

vol'taggio m voltage

vol'ta|re vt/i turn; (rigirare) turn round; (rivoltare) turn over. ~**rsi** vr turn [round]

volta'stomaco m nausea

volteggi'are vi circle; (ginnastica) vault

'volto pp di **volgere** ● m face; **mi ha mostrato il suo vero** ~ he revealed his true colours

vo'lubile adj fickle

vo'lum|e m volume. ~**i'noso** adj voluminous

voluta'mente *adv* deliberately

voluttu|osità *f* voluptuousness. **∼'oso** *adj* voluptuous

vomi'tare *vt* vomit, be sick. **'vomito** *m* vomit

'vongola *f* clam

vo'race *adj* voracious

vo'ragine *f* abyss

'vortice *m* whirl; (*gorgo*) whirlpool; (*di vento*) whirlwind

'vostro (**il ∼** *m*, **la vostra** *f*, **i vostri** *mpl*, **le vostre** *fpl*) *poss adj* your; **è vostra questa macchina?** is this car yours?; **un ∼ amico** a friend of yours; **∼ padre** your father ●*poss pron* yours; **i vostri** your folks

vo'ta|nte *mf* voter. **∼re** *vi* vote. **∼zi'one** *f* voting; (*Sch*) marks *pl*. **'voto** *m* vote; (*Sch*) mark; (*Relig*) vow

vs. *abbr* (*Comm*) (vostro) yours

vul'canico *adj* volcanic. **vul'cano** *m* volcano

vulne'rabil|e *adj* vulnerable. **∼ità** *f* vulnerability

vuo'tare *vt*, **vuo'tarsi** *vr* empty

vu'oto *adj* empty; (*non occupato*) vacant; **∼ di** (*sprovvisto*) devoid of ●*m* empty space; (*Phys*) vacuum; *fig* void; **assegno a ∼** dud cheque; **sotto ∼** (*prodotto*) vacuum-packed; **∼ a perdere** no deposit. **∼ d'aria** air pocket

W *abbr* (viva) long live

'wafer *m inv* (*biscotto*) wafer

walkie-'talkie *m inv* walkie-talkie

watt *m inv* watt

WC *m* WC

'Web *m inv* Web

'webmaster *m* webmaster

'western *adj inv* cowboy *attrib* ●*m* Cinema western

X, x *adj* raggi *pl* **X** X-rays; **il giorno X** D-day

xenofo'bia *f* xenophobia. **xe'nofobo, -a** *adj* xenophobic ●*mf* xenophobe

xi'lofono *m* xylophone

yacht *m inv* yacht

yen *m inv* Fin yen

'yoga *m* yoga; (*praticante*) yogi

'yogurt *m inv* yoghurt. **∼i'era** *f* yoghurt-maker

zaba[gl]i'one *m* zabaglione (*dessert made from eggs, wine or marsala and sugar*)

zaf'fata *f* whiff; (*di fumo*) cloud

zaffe'rano *m* saffron

zaf'firo *m* sapphire

'zaino *m* rucksack

'zampa *f* leg; **a quattro zampe** (*animale*) four-legged; (*carponi*) on

v
w
x
y
z

all fours

zampil'la|nte adj spurting. ~re vi spurt. **zam'pillo** m spurt

zam'pogna f bagpipe

zam'pone fpl stuffed pig's trotter with lentils

'zanna f fang; (di elefante) tusk

zan'zar|a f mosquito. ~i'era f (velo) mosquito net; (su finestra) insect screen

'zappa f hoe. **zap'pare** vt hoe

'zattera f raft

zatte'roni mpl (scarpe) wedge shoes

za'vorra f ballast; fig dead wood

'zazzera f mop of hair

'zebra f zebra; **zebre** pl (passaggio pedonale) zebra crossing

'zecca[1] f mint; **nuovo di** ~ brand-new

'zecca[2] f (parassita) tick

zec'chino m sequin; **oro** ~ pure gold

ze'lante adj zealous. **'zelo** m zeal

'zenit m zenith

'zenzero m ginger

'zeppa f wedge

'zeppo adj packed full; **pieno** ~ **di** crammed o packed with

zer'bino m doormat

'zero m zero, nought; (in calcio) nil; Tennis love; **due a** ~ (in partite) two nil

'zeta f zed, zee Am

'zia f aunt

zibel'lino m sable

'zigomo m cheek-bone

zig'zag m inv zigzag; **andare a** ~ zigzag

zim'bello m decoy; (oggetto di scherno) laughing-stock

'zinco m zinc

'zingaro, -a mf gypsy

'zio m uncle

zi'tel|la f spinster; pej old maid. ~'lona f pej old maid

zit'tire vi fall silent ● vt silence. **'zitto** adj silent; **sta' zitto!** keep quiet!

ziz'zania f (discordia) discord

'zoccolo m clog; (di cavallo) hoof; (di terra) clump; (di parete) skirting board, baseboard Am; (di colonna) base

zodi'acale adj of the zodiac. **zo-'diaco** m zodiac

'zolfo m sulphur

'zolla f clod; (di zucchero) lump

zol'letta f sugar lump

'zombi mf inv fig zombie

'zona f zone; (area) area. ~ **di depressione** area of low pressure. ~ **disco** area for parking discs only. ~ **pedonale** pedestrian precinct. ~ **verde** green belt

'zonzo adv **andare a** ~ stroll about

zoo m inv zoo

zoolo'gia f zoology. **zoo'logico** adj zoological. **zo'ologo, -a** mf zoologist

zoo sa'fari m inv safari park

zoppi'ca|nte adj limping; fig shaky. ~re vi limp; (essere debole) be shaky. **'zoppo, -a** adj lame ● mf cripple

zoti'cone m boor

'zucca f marrow; (🔲: testa) head; (🔲: persona) thickie

zucche'r|are vt sugar. ~i'era f sugar bowl. ~i'ficio m sugar refinery. **zucche'rino** adj sugary ● m sugar lump

'zucchero m sugar. ~ **di canna** cane sugar. ~ **vanigliato** vanilla sugar. ~ **a velo** icing sugar. **zucche-'roso** adj honeyed

zuc'chin|a f, ~o m courgette, zucchini Am

'zuffa f scuffle

zufo'lare vt/i whistle

zu'mare vi zoom

'zuppa f soup. ~ **inglese** trifle

zup'petta f **fare** ~ **[con]** dunk

zuppi'era f soup tureen

'zuppo adj soaked

Phrasefinder/Frasi utili

Key phrases	Frasi chiave
yes, please	sì, grazie
no, thank you	no, grazie
sorry!	scusa
excuse me	mi scusi
you're welcome	prego
I'm sorry, I don't understand	scusi, non capisco

Meeting people	**Incontri**
hello/goodbye	ciao/arrivederci
how do you do?	come sta?
how are you?	come stai?
nice to meet you	piacere

1

Asking questions	Fare domande
do you speak English/Italian?	parli inglese/italiano?
what's your name?	come ti chiami?
where are you from?	di dove sei?
where is...?	dov'è...?
can I have...?	posso avere... ?
would you like...?	vuoi...?
do you mind if...?	le dispiace se...?

About you	Presentarsi
my name is...	mi chiamo...
I'm English/Italian/American	sono inglese/italiano/-a/americano/-a
I don't speak Italian/English very well	non parlo molto bene l'italiano/l'inglese
I'm here on holiday	sono qui in vacanza
I live near York/Pisa	abito vicino a York/Pisa

Emergencies	Emergenze
can you help me, please?	mi può aiutare, per favore?
I'm lost	mi sono perso/-a
I'm ill	sto male
call an ambulance	chiami un'ambulanza
watch out!	attenzione!

Reading signs	Segnali e cartelli
no entry	vietato l'ingresso
no smoking	vietato fumare
fire exit	uscita di sicurezza
for sale	in vendita/vendesi
push	spingere
pull	tirare
press	premere

Going Places/In viaggio

By rail and underground | In treno e sul metrò

where can I buy a ticket?	dove si fanno i biglietti?
what time is the next train to Milan/New York?	a che ora è il prossimo treno per Milano/New York?
do I have to change?	devo cambiare?
can I take my bike on the train?	posso portare la bicicletta sul treno?
which platform for the train to Bath/Florence?	da quale binario parte il treno per Bath/Firenze?
a single/return, (*Amer*) round trip to Baltimore/Turin, please	un biglietto di sola andata/di andata e ritorno per Baltimora/Torino, per favore
I'd like an all-day ticket	vorrei un biglietto giornaliero
I'd like to reserve a seat	vorrei prenotare un posto
is there a student/senior citizen discount?	c'è uno sconto per studenti/anziani?
is this the train for Rome/Manchester?	è questo il treno per Roma/Manchester?
what time does the train arrive in Naples/London?	a che ora arriva il treno a Napoli/Londra?
have I missed the train?	ho perso il treno?
which line do I need to take for the Colosseum/London Eye?	che linea si prende per il Colosseo/London Eye?

3

YOU WILL HEAR:	SENTIRAI:
il treno è in arrivo sul binario 2	the train is arriving at platform 2
c'è un treno per Roma alle 10	there's a train to Rome at 10 o'clock
il treno è in ritardo/orario	the train is delayed/on time
la prossima fermata è ...	the next stop is...
il suo biglietto non è valido	your ticket isn't valid

MORE USEFUL WORDS:	ALTRE PAROLE UTILI:
underground station, (*Amer*) subway station	stazione di metropolitana
timetable	orario
connection	coincidenza
express train	treno espresso
local train	treno locale
high-speed train	treno ad alta velocità

DID YOU KNOW...?	LO SAPEVI...?
In an Italian train station, before you get on the train you must validate your ticket, i.e. have it stamped in the special yellow machine on the platform to make it valid for your journey. You risk a fine if you forget to do this.	Dall'aeroporto di Heathrow è possibile raggiungere il centro di Londra in meno di venti minuti grazie all'Heathrow Express.

At the airport · All'aeroporto

when's the next flight to Paris/Rome?	quand'è il prossimo volo per Parigi/Roma?
what time do I have to check in?	a che ora si fa il check-in?
where do I check in?	dov'è il check-in?
I'd like to confirm my flight	vorrei confermare il mio volo
I'd like a window seat/an aisle seat	vorrei un posto accanto al finestrino/di corridoio
I want to change/cancel my reservation	vorrei cambiare/annullare la mia prenotazione
can I carry this in my hand luggage, (Amer) carry-on luggage?	posso portare questo nel bagaglio a mano?
my luggage hasn't arrived	il mio bagaglio non è arrivato

YOU WILL HEAR:	SENTIRAI:
il volo BA7057 è in ritardo/cancellato	flight BA7057 is delayed/cancelled
presentarsi all'uscita 29	please go to gate 29
la sua carta d'imbarco, per favore	your boarding card, please

MORE USEFUL WORDS:	ALTRE PAROLE UTILI:
arrivals	arrivi
departures	partenze
baggage claim	ritiro bagagli

5

Asking how to get there | Chiedere e dare indicazioni

how do I get to the airport?	come si arriva all'aeroporto?
how long will it take to get there?	quanto ci vuole per arrivarci?
how far is it from here?	quanto dista da qui?
which bus do I take for the cathedral?	quale autobus devo prendere per andare al duomo?
where does this bus go?	dove va questo autobus?
does this bus/train go to...?	questo autobus/treno va a...?
where should I get off?	può dirmi dove devo scendere?
how much is it to the town centre?	quant'è la tariffa per il centro?
what time is the last bus?	che ora è l'ultimo autobus?
where's the nearest underground station, (Amer) subway station?	dov'è la metropolitana più vicina?
is this the turning for...?	si svolta qui per...?
can you call me a taxi?	può chiamarmi un taxi, per favore?

YOU WILL HEAR:	SENTIRAI:
prenda la prima a destra	take the first turning on the right
dopo il semaforo/la chiesa svolti a sinistra	turn left at the traffic lights/just past the church

Disabled travellers | Viaggiatori disabili

I'm disabled	sono disabile
is there wheelchair access?	c'è l'accesso per sedia a rotelle?
are guide dogs permitted?	sono ammessi i cani guida per non vedenti?

On the road   Sulla strada

where's the nearest petrol station, (*Amer*) gas station?	dov'è la stazione di servizio più vicina?
what's the best way to get there?	qual è la strada migliore per arrivarci?
I've got a puncture, (*Amer*) flat tire	ho bucato
I'd like to hire, (*Amer*) rent a bike/car	vorrei noleggiare una bicicletta/una macchina
where can I park around here?	c'è un parcheggio qui vicino?
there's been an accident	c'è stato un incidente
my car's broken down	ho la macchina in panne
the car won't start	la macchina non parte
where's the nearest garage?	dov'è l'officina più vicina?
pump number six, please	pompa numero sei, grazie
fill it up, please	il pieno, per favore
can I wash my car here?	c'è l'autolavaggio?
can I park here?	posso parcheggiare qui?
there's a problem with the brakes/lights	i freni/fari hanno qualcosa che non va
the clutch/gearstick isn't working	la frizione/leva del cambio non funziona
take the third exit off the roundabout, (*Amer*) traffic circle	alla rotatoria prenda la terza uscita
turn right at the next junction	al prossimo incrocio svolti a destra
slow down	rallenta
I can't drink – I'm driving	non posso bere, devo guidare
can I buy a road map here?	vendete cartine stradali?

YOU WILL HEAR: SENTIRAI:

favorisca la patente	can I see your driving licence?
deve compilare la denuncia di sinistro	you need to fill out an accident report
questa strada è a senso unico	this road is one-way
qui non si può parcheggiare	you can't park here

MORE USEFUL WORDS: ALTRE PAROLE UTILI:

diesel	gasolio
unleaded	senza piombo/verde
motorway, (*Amer*) expressway	autostrada
toll	pedaggio
satnav, (*Amer*) GPS	navigatore satellitare
speed camera	autovelox
roundabout	rotatoria
crossroads	crocevia
dual carriageway, (*Amer*) divided highway	strada a due carreggiate
exit	uscita
traffic lights	semaforo
driver	conducente

DID YOU KNOW...? LO SAPEVI...?

In Italy, all drivers are required to wear a reflective vest and to use a reflective triangle warning sign if they need to stop at the roadside.	Il pedaggio per circolare e sostare in auto nel centro di Londra, nei giorni lavorativi, si può pagare presso le stazioni di servizio o le edicole.

COMMON ITALIAN ROAD SIGNS

Alt polizia	Stop for police check
Consentito ai soli mezzi autorizzati	Authorized vehicles only
Passo carrabile	No blocking of passageway
Lavori in corso	Roadworks ahead
Zona pedonale	Pedestrian zone
Rallentare	Slow down
Zona rimozione	Tow-away zone
ZTL (Zona traffico limitato)	Traffic restricted area
Postazione fissa di misuratore della velocità	Speed cameras ahead
Passaggio a livello	Train crossing

SEGNALI STRADALI COMUNI NEI PAESI ANGLOFONI

Cattle	Animali domestici vaganti
Contraflow	Doppio senso di circolazione
Ford	Guado
Get in lane	Immettersi in corsia
Give way	Dare precedenza
Keep clear	Lasciare libero il passaggio
No overtaking, (*Amer*) Do not pass	Divieto di sorpasso
Pedestrians crossing	Attraversamento pedonale
Red route – no stopping	Divieto di sosta e fermata
Reduce speed now	Rallentare
Stop	Stop

Keeping in touch/Comunicazioni

On the phone   Al telefono

where can I buy a phone card?	dove si comprano le schede telefoniche?
may I use your phone?	posso usare il telefono?
do you have a mobile, (*Amer*) cell phone?	hai il cellulare?
what is your phone number?	qual è il tuo numero di telefono?
what is the area code for Venice/ Sheffield?	qual è il prefisso di Venezia/ Sheffield?
I want to make a phone call	vorrei fare una telefonata
I'd like to reverse the charges, (*Amer*) call collect	vorrei fare una telefonata a carico del destinatario
the line's engaged/busy	è occupato
there's no answer	non risponde nessuno
hello, this is Natalie	pronto, sono Natalie
is Riccardo there, please?	c'è Riccardo, per favore?
who's calling?	chi parla?
sorry, wrong number	ha sbagliato numero
just a moment, please	un attimo, prego
would you like to hold?	vuole attendere in linea?
it's a business/personal call	è una chiamata di lavoro/personale
I'll put you through to him/her	le passo la comunicazione
s/he cannot come to the phone at the moment	in questo momento non può venire al telefono
please tell him/her I called	gli/le dica che ho chiamato
I'd like to leave a message for him/her	vorrei lasciare un messaggio

I'll try again later	riproverò più tardi
please tell him/her that Maria called	gli/le dica che ha chiamato Maria
can he/she ring me back?	mi può richiamare?
my home number is...	il mio numero è...
my business number is...	il mio numero al lavoro è...
my fax number is...	il mio numero di fax è...
we were cut off	è caduta la linea
I'll call you later	ti chiamo più tardi
I need to top up my phone	mi serve una ricarica per il cellulare
the battery's run out	ho la batteria scarica
I'm running low on credit	sto esaurendo il credito
send me a text	mandami un sms/messaggino
there's no signal here	non c'è campo
you're breaking up	la linea è molto disturbata
could you speak a little louder?	puoi parlare più forte?

YOU WILL HEAR:	SENTIRAI:
pronto?	hello
chiamami sul cellulare	call me on my mobile, (*Amer*) cell phone
vuole lasciare un messaggio?	would you like to leave a message?

MORE USEFUL WORDS:	ALTRE PAROLE UTILI:
text message	SMS/messaggino
top-up card	ricarica
phone box, (*Amer*) phone booth	cabina telefonica
dial	comporre il numero
directory enquiries	elenco abbonati

Writing Corrispondenza

what's your address?	qual è il tuo indirizzo?
where is the nearest post office?	dov'è l'ufficio postale più vicino?
could I have a stamp for the UK/Italy, please?	mi dà un francobollo per la Gran Bretagna/l'Italia, per favore?
I'd like to send a parcel	vorrei spedire un pacco
where is the nearest postbox, (Amer) mailbox?	dov'è la buca delle lettere più vicina?
dear Isabella/Fred	cara Isabella/caro Fred
dear Sir or Madam	gentili Signori
yours sincerely	distinti saluti
yours faithfully	cordialmente
best wishes	cari saluti

YOU WILL HEAR:	SENTIRAI:
vuole spedirla per posta prioritaria?	would you like to send it first class?
c'è qualcosa di valore?	is it valuable?

MORE USEFUL WORDS:	ALTRE PAROLE UTILI:
letter	lettera
postcode, (Amer) ZIP code	codice di avviamento postale/CAP
airmail	posta aerea
postcard	cartolina
fragile	fragile
urgent	urgente
registered post, (Amer) mail	raccomandata

On line   Internet

are you on the Internet?	siete su Internet?
what's your e-mail address?	qual è il tuo indirizzo email?
I'll e-mail it to you on Tuesday	te lo mando per email martedì
I looked it up on the Internet	l'ho cercato su Internet
the information is on their website	le informazioni si trovano sul sito web
my e-mail address is anna dot rossi at rapido dot com	il mio indirizzo email è: anna punto rossi chiocciola rapido punto com
can I check my e-mail here?	posso controllare l'email qui?
I have broadband/dial-up	ho la linea veloce/connessione dial-up
do you have wireless internet access?	avete accesso internet wireless?
I'll send you the file as an attachment	ti mando il file in allegato

YOU WILL SEE:	VEDRAI:
ricerca	search
fare doppio click sull'icona	double-click on the icon
apri l'applicazione	open (up) the application
scarica il file	download file

MORE USEFUL WORDS:	ALTRE PAROLE UTILI:
subject (*of an email*)	oggetto
password	password
social networking site	sito di social network
search engine	motore di ricerca
mouse	mouse
keyboard	tastiera

13

Meeting up — Appuntamenti

what shall we do this evening?	cosa facciamo stasera?
do you want to go out tonight?	ti va di uscire stasera?
where shall we meet?	dove ci diamo appuntamento?
I'll see you outside the café at 6 o'clock	ci vediamo davanti al bar alle 6
see you later	a più tardi
I can't today, I'm busy	oggi non posso, sono impegnato
I'm sorry, I've got something planned	mi dispiace, ho già altri programmi
let's meet for a coffee in town	troviamoci al centro per un caffè
would you like to see a show/film, (Amer) movie?	ti va di andare a teatro/al cinema?
what about next week instead?	che ne dici se facciamo la prossima settimana?
shall we go for something to eat?	andiamo a mangiare qualcosa?

YOU WILL HEAR:	SENTIRAI:
piacere	nice to meet you
posso offrirti qualcosa da bere?	can I buy you a drink?

MORE USEFUL WORDS:	ALTRE PAROLE UTILI:
bar	bar
bar (serving counter in a bar/pub)	banco
meal	pasto
snack	spuntino
date	appuntamento
cigarette	sigaretta

Food and Drink/Mangiare e bere

Booking a table / Prenotare un ristorante

can you recommend a good restaurant?	può consigliarmi un buon ristorante?
I'd like to reserve a table for four	vorrei prenotare un tavolo per quattro
a reservation for tomorrow evening at eight o'clock	una prenotazione per domani sera alle otto
I booked a table for two	ho prenotato un tavolo per due

Ordering / Per Ordinare

could we see the menu/wine list, please?	possiamo avere il menù/la carta dei vini, per favore?
do you have a vegetarian menu?	avete un menù vegetariano?
could we have some more bread?	possiamo avere dell'altro pane?
could I have the bill, (*Amer*) check?	il conto, per favore
what would you recommend?	che cosa consiglia?
I'd like a black/white coffee	vorrei un caffè/un caffè macchiato

YOU WILL HEAR:	IL CAMERIERE CHIEDE …
Volete ordinare?	Are you ready to order?
Prendete un antipasto?	Would you like a starter?
Che cosa prendete come secondo?	What will you have for the main course?
Posso consigliare …	I can recommend …
Altro?	Anything else?
Buon appetito!	Enjoy your meal!
Il servizio non è compreso	Service is not included.

The menu   Il menu

starters	antipasti		antipasti	starters
melon	melone		antipasto di mare	seafood starter
omelette	frittata		antipasto di terra	assorted hams etc
soup	zuppa			
salad	insalata		prosciutto crudo	cured ham
			zuppa	soup

fish	pesce		pesce	fish
cod	merluzzo		acciughe	anchovies
hake	nasello		calamari	squid
halibut	ippoglosso		cozze	mussels
herring	aringa		dentice	sea bream
monk fish	squadro		frutti di mare	seafood
mussels	cozze		gamberetti	shrimp
oysters	ostriche		gamberi	prawns
plaice	platessa		merluzzo	cod
prawns	gamberi		nasello	hake
red mullet	triglie		ostriche	oysters
salmon	salmone		pesce spada	swordfish
seafood	frutti di mare		platessa	plaice
sea bass	spigola		rombo	turbot
shrimp	gamberetti		salmone	salmon
sole	sogliola		sogliola	sole
squid	calamari		spigola	sea bass
trout	trota		tonno	tuna
tuna	tonno		triglie	red mullet
turbot	rombo		trota	trout

meat	carne		carne	meat
beef	manzo		agnello	lamb
chicken	pollo		anatra	duck

duck	anatra	bistecca	steak
goose	oca	cinghiale	wild boar
hare	lepre	coniglio	rabbit
lamb	agnello	fegato	liver
liver	fegato	lepre	hare
pork	maiale	maiale	pork
rabbit	coniglio	manzo	beef
steak	bistecca	oca	goose
veal	vitello	pollo	chicken
wild boar	cinghiale	vitello	veal

vegetables	**verdure**	**verdure**	**vegetables**
artichokes	carciofi	asparagi	asparagus
asparagus	asparagi	carciofi	artichokes
aubergines	melanzane	carote	carrots
beans	fagioli	cavolfiore	cauliflower
cabbage	cavolo	cavolo	cabbage
carrots	carote	cipolle	onions
cauliflower	cavolfiore	fagioli	beans
celery	sedano	fagiolini	green beans
courgettes	zucchini	funghi	mushrooms
green beans	fagiolini	insalata	salad
mushrooms	funghi	melanzane	aubergines
onions	cipolle	patate	potatoes
peas	piselli	peperoni	peppers
peppers	peperoni	piselli	peas
potatoes	patate	sedano	celery
salad	insalata	zucchini	courgettes

the way it's cooked	**cottura**	**cottura**	**the way it's cooked**
boiled	lesso	al forno	cooked in the oven
fried	fritto	al pomodoro	in tomato sauce
grilled	alla griglia		

17

griddled	alla piastra		al ragù	in a meat sauce
puree	purè		al sangue	rare
roast	arrosto		alla griglia	grilled
stewed	in umido		arrosto	roast
rare	al sangue		ben cotta	well done
medium	cotta al punto giusto		cotta al punto giusto	medium
well done	ben cotta		fritto	fried
			in umido	stewed
			lesso	boiled

desserts	**dolci**		**dolci**	**desserts**
cream	panna		crostata	tart
fruit	frutta		frutta	fruit
ice cream	gelato		gelato	ice cream
pie	torta		panna	cream
tart	crostata		torta	pie

sundries	**contorni, salse, ecc.**		**contorni, salse, ecc.**	**sundries**
bread	pane		aceto	vinegar
butter	burro		burro	butter
cheese	formaggio		condimento	seasoning
herbs	erbe		erbe	herbs
mayonnaise	maionese		formaggio	cheese
mustard	senape		maionese	mayonnaise
olive oil	olio d'oliva		olio d'oliva	olive oil
pepper	pepe		pane	bread
rice	riso		pepe	pepper
salt	sale		riso	rice
sauce	salsa		sale	salt
seasoning	condimento		salsa	sauce
vinegar	aceto		senape	mustard

drinks	bevande		bevande	drinks
beer	birra		acqua minerale	mineral water
bottle	bottiglia		bibite analcoliche	soft drinks
carbonated	gassato		birra	beer
coffee	caffè		bottiglia	bottle
decaffeinated coffee	decaffeinato		caffè	coffee
espresso	espresso		decaffeinato	decaffeinated coffee
half-bottle	mezza bottiglia		espresso	espresso
liqueur	liquore		gassato	carbonated
mineral water	acqua minerale		liquore	liqueur
red wine	vino rosso		mezza bottiglia	half-bottle
soft drinks	bibite analcoliche		naturale	still
sparkling wine	spumante		spumante	sparkling wine
still	naturale		vino	wine
table wine	vino da tavola		vino bianco	white wine
white wine	vino bianco		vino da tavola	table wine
wine	vino		vino rosso	red wine

19

Places to stay/Dove alloggiare

Camping | In campeggio

can we pitch our tent here?	possiamo montare la tenda qui?
can we park our caravan here?	possiamo parcheggiare la roulotte qui?
what are the facilities like?	che attrezzature ci sono?
how much is it per night?	quant'è a notte?
where do we park the car?	dov'è il parcheggio?
we're looking for a campsite	stiamo cercando un campeggio
this is a list of local campsites	questo è l'elenco dei campeggi della zona
we go on a camping holiday every year	andiamo in campeggio tutti gli anni

At the hotel | In albergo

I'd like a double/single room with bath	vorrei una camera doppia/singola con bagno
we have a reservation in the name of Morris	abbiamo prenotato a nome Morris
we'll be staying three nights, from Friday to Sunday	ci fermiamo tre notti, da venerdì a domenica
how much does the room cost?	quant'è la camera?
I'd like to see the room, please	vorrei vedere la camera, per favore
what time is breakfast?	a che ora è la colazione?
can I leave this in your safe?	posso lasciare questo nella cassaforte?
bed and breakfast	camera e prima colazione
we'd like to stay another night	vorremmo fermarci un'altra notte
please call me at 7:30	mi chiami alle 7:30, per favore
are there any messages for me?	ci sono messaggi per me?

★★★

Hostels | Ostelli

could you tell me where the youth hostel is?	mi sa dire dov'è l'ostello della gioventù?
what time does the hostel close?	a che ora chiude l'ostello?
I'm staying in a hostel	alloggio in un ostello
the hostel we're staying in is great value	l'ostello in cui alloggiamo è molto conveniente
I know a really good hostel in Dublin	conosco un ottimo ostello a Dublino
I'd like to go backpacking in Australia	mi piacerebbe girare l'Australia con zaino e sacco a pelo

Rooms to let | In affitto

I'm looking for a room with a reasonable rent	vorrei affittare una camera a prezzo modico
I'd like to rent an apartment for a few weeks	vorrei affittare un appartamento per qualche settimana
where do I find out about rooms to let?	dove posso informarmi su camere in affitto?
what's the weekly rent?	quant'è l'affitto alla settimana?
I'm staying with friends at the moment	al momento alloggio presso amici
I rent an apartment on the outskirts of town	affitto un appartamento in periferia
the room's fine—I'll take it	la camera mi piace, la prendo
the deposit is one month's rent in advance	la caparra è di un mese d'affitto

Shopping and money/Spese e soldi

At the bank — In banca

I'd like to change some money	vorrei cambiare dei soldi
I want to change some euros into pounds	vorrei cambiare degli euro in sterline
do you take Eurocheques?	accettate Eurochèque?
what's the exchange rate today?	quant'è il tasso di cambio oggi?
I prefer traveller's cheques, (*Amer*) traveler's checks to cash	preferisco i traveller's cheque al contante
I'd like to transfer some money from my account	vorrei fare un bonifico
I'll get some money from the cash machine	prenderò dei soldi dal bancomat®
I'm with another bank	ho il conto in un'altra banca

Finding the right shop — Il negozio giusto

where's the main shopping district?	dov'è la zona commerciale principale?
where's a good place to buy sunglasses/shoes?	qual è il posto migliore per comprare occhiali da sole/scarpe?
where can I buy batteries/postcards?	dove posso comprare pile/cartoline?
where's the nearest chemist/bookshop?	dov'è la farmacia/libreria più vicina?
is there a good food shop around here?	c'è un buon negozio di generi alimentari qui vicino?
what time do the shops open/close?	a che ora aprono/chiudono i negozi?
where can I hire a car?	dove posso noleggiare una macchina?
where did you get those?	dove le/li hai comprate/-i?
I'm looking for presents for my family	sto cercando dei regali per la mia famiglia
we'll do all our shopping on Saturday	faremo la spesa sabato
I love shopping	adoro fare spese

Are you being served? — Nei negozi

how much does that cost?	quanto costa quello?
can I try it on?	posso provarlo?
can you keep it for me?	me lo mette da parte?
could you wrap it for me, please?	me lo incarta, per favore?
can I pay by credit card/cheque, (Amer) check?	posso pagare con la carta di credito/un assegno?
do you have this in another colour, (Amer) color?	c'è in altri colori?
could I have a bag, please?	mi dà un sacchetto, per favore?
I'm just looking	sto solo dando un'occhiata
I'll think about it	ci devo pensare
I'd like a receipt, please	mi dà lo scontrino, per favore?
I need a bigger/smaller size	mi serve la taglia più grande/piccola
I take a size 10/a medium	porto la 42/la media
it doesn't suit me	non mi sta bene
I'm sorry, I don't have any change/anything smaller	mi dispiace, non ho spiccioli/biglietti più piccoli
that's all, thank you	nient'altro, grazie

Changing things — Cambiare un acquisto

can I have a refund?	rimborsare i soldi?
can you mend it for me?	può ripararlo?
can I speak to the manager?	posso parlare con il direttore?
it doesn't work	non funziona
I'd like to change it, please	vorrei cambiarlo, per favore
I bought this here yesterday	l'ho comprato qui ieri

Currency Convertor		Convertitore di valute	
€/$	£/$	£/$	€/$
0.25		0.25	
0.50		0.50	
0.75		0.75	
1		1	
1.5		1.5	
2		2	
3		3	
5		5	
10		10	
20		20	
30		30	
40		40	
50		50	
100		100	
200		200	
1000		1000	

Sport and leisure/Sport e tempo libero

Keeping fit | Tenersi in forma

where can we play tennis/badminton?	dove si può giocare a tennis/badminton?
I'm looking for a swimming pool/golf course	sto cercando una piscina/un campo da golf
is there a hotel gym?	c'è una palestra in albergo?
are there any yoga/pilates classes here?	ci sono corsi di yoga/pilates?
I would like to go cycling/riding	mi piacerebbe andare in bici/a cavallo
I love swimming/football	mi piace nuotare/il calcio
where can I get tickets for the match, (*Amer*) game on Saturday?	dove si comprano i biglietti per la partita di sabato?

Going out | Uscire

what's on at the theatre/cinema?	cosa danno a teatro/al cinema?
how much are the tickets?	quanto costano i biglietti?
what time does the concert/performance start?	a che ora inizia il concerto/lo spettacolo?
I'd like to book tickets for tonight	vorrei prenotare dei biglietti per stasera
we'd like to go to a club	vorremmo andare in qualche locale

25

Good timing/L'Ora giusta

Telling the time   Dire l'ora

could you tell me the time?	mi dica che ore sono?
what time is it?	che ora è?
it's 2 o'clock	sono le due
at about 8 o'clock	verso le otto
at 9 o'clock tomorrow	domani mattina alle nove
from 10 o'clock onwards	dalle dieci in poi
at 8 a.m./p.m.	alle otto di mattina/di sera
at 5 o'clock in the morning/afternoon	alle cinque del mattino/di sera
it's five past/quarter past/half past one	è l'una e cinque/e un quarto/e mezza
it's twenty-five to/quarter to/five to one	è l'una meno venticinque/meno un quarto/meno cinque
a quarter /three quarters of an hour	un quarto/tre quarti d'ora

Days and dates   Giorni, mesi e date

Sunday, Monday, Tuesday, Wednesday, Thursday, Friday, Saturday	domenica, lunedì, martedì, mercoledì, giovedì, venerdì, sabato
January, February, March, April, May, June, July, August, September, October, November, December	gennaio, febbraio, marzo, aprile, maggio, giugno, luglio, agosto, settembre, ottobre, novembre, dicembre
what's the date?	quanti ne abbiamo oggi?
it's the second of June	è il due giugno
we meet up every Monday	ci incontriamo ogni lunedì
she comes on Tuesdays	viene di martedì
we're going away in August	saremo via ad agosto
it was the first of April	era il primo aprile
on November 8th	l'otto novembre

Public holidays and special days	Festività
Bank holiday	festa civile
Bank holiday Monday	festa civile che cade di lunedì
long weekend	ponte
New Year's Day (Jan 1)	Capodanno (1 gennaio)
Epiphany (Jan 6)	Epifania (la Befana: 6 gennaio)
St Valentine's Day (Feb 14)	San Valentino (14 febbraio)
Shrove Tuesday/Pancake Day	martedì grasso
Ash Wednesday	mercoledì delle Ceneri
St Joseph's Day (Mar 19)	San Giuseppe (19 marzo)
Mother's Day	Festa della mamma
Palm Sunday	domenica delle Palme
Maundy Thursday	giovedì grasso
Good Friday	venerdì santo
Easter Day	Pasqua
Easter Monday	lunedì dell'Angelo (pasquetta)
Anniversary of the liberation of Italy in 1945	anniversario della Liberazione (25 aprile)
May Day (May 1)	Festa del lavoro (1 maggio)
Father's Day	Festa del papà
Independence Day (Jul 4)	anniversario dell'Indipendenza (4 luglio)
Assumption (Aug 15)	Assunzione (ferragosto: 15 agosto)
Halloween (Oct 31)	vigilia d'Ognissanti
All Saints' Day (Nov 1)	Ognissanti (1 novembre)
Thanksgiving	giorno del Ringraziamento
Christmas Eve (Dec 24)	vigilia di Natale (24 dicembre)
Christmas Day (Dec 25)	Natale (25 dicembre)
Boxing Day (Dec 26)	Santo Stefano (26 dicembre)
New Year's Eve (Dec 31)	San Silvestro (31 dicembre)

Health and Beauty/Salute e bellezza

At the doctor's Dal medico

can I see a doctor?	potrei vedere un medico?
I don't feel well	non mi sento bene
it hurts here	mi fa male qui
I have a migraine/stomachache	ho l'emicrania/il mal di stomaco
are there any side effects?	ci sono effetti collaterali?
I have a sore ankle/wrist/knee	mi fa male la caviglia/il polso/il ginocchio

YOU WILL HEAR: SENTIRAI:

deve prendere un appuntamento	you need to make an appointment
si accomodi	please take a seat
ha la Tessera Europea di Assicurazione Malattia (TEAM)?	do you have a European Health Insurance Card (EHIC)?
ha l'assistenza medica?	do you have Health Insurance?
devo misurarle la pressione	I need to take your blood pressure

MORE USEFUL WORDS: ALTRE PAROLE UTILI:

nurse	infermiere/a
antibiotics	antibiotici
medicine	medicina
infection	infezione
treatment	cura
rest	riposo

At the pharmacy In farmacia

can I have some painkillers?	mi dà un antidolorifico/analgesico?
I have asthma/hay fever/eczema	soffro d'asma/di rinite allergica/d'eczema
I've been stung by a wasp/bee	mi ha punto una vespa/un'ape
I've got a cold/cough/the flu	ho il raffreddore/la tosse/l'influenza
I need something for diarrhoea/stomachache	vorrei qualcosa per la diarrea/il mal di stomaco
I'm pregnant	sono incinta

YOU WILL HEAR:	SENTIRAI
ha già preso questo farmaco?	have you taken this medicine before?
le sue medicine sono pronte tra dieci minuti	your prescription will be ready in ten minutes
da assumere durante i pasti/tre volte al giorno?	take at mealtimes/three times a day?
è allergico/-a a qualcosa?	are you allergic to anything?
sta prendendo qualche altro farmaco?	are you taking any other medication?

MORE USEFUL WORDS:	ALTRE PAROLE UTILI:
plasters, (Amer) Band-Aid™	cerotti
insect repellent	insettifugo
contraception	anticoncezionali
sun cream	solare
aftersun	doposole
dosage	dosi

At the hairdresser's/ beauty salon — Dal parrucchiere/ dall'estetista

I'd like a cut and blow dry	taglio e asciugatura spazzola e phon
just a trim please	solo una spuntatina, per favore
a grade 3 back and sides	9 mm sia sui lati che dietro
I'd like my hair washed first please	mi faccia lo shampoo prima, per favore
can I have a manicure/pedicure/ facial?	fate la manicure/pedicure/pulizia del viso?
how much is a head/back massage?	quant'è il massaggio alla testa/ schiena?
can I see a price list?	potrei vedere il listino prezzi?
do you offer reflexology/ aromatherapy treatments?	fate riflessologia/aromaterapia?

YOU WILL HEAR: — SENTIRAI:

vuole l'asciugatura a spazzola e phon?	would you like your hair blow-dried?
da che lato porta la riga?	where is your parting?
le faccio un taglio scalato?	would you like your hair layered?

MORE USEFUL WORDS: — ALTRE PAROLE UTILI:

dry/greasy/fine/flyaway/frizzy hair	capelli secchi/grassi/sottili/ sfibrati/crespi
highlights	colpi di sole
extensions	allungamento capelli/extensions
sunbed	lettino solare
leg/arm/bikini wax	ceretta gambe/braccia/inguine

At the dentist's   Dal dentista

I have toothache	ho mal di denti
I'd like an emergency appointment	vorrei un appuntamento d'urgenza
I have cracked a tooth	mi si è spezzato un dente
my gums are bleeding	mi sanguinano le gengive

YOU WILL HEAR: SENTIRAI:

apra bene la bocca	open your mouth
bisogna fare un'otturazione	you need a filling
devo farle una radiografia	we need to take an X-ray
sciacqui bene	please rinse

MORE USEFUL WORDS: ALTRE PAROLE UTILI:

anaesthetic	anestesia
root canal treatment	devitalizzazione del dente
injection	iniezione
floss	filo interdentale

Weights & measures/ Pesi e misure

Length/Lunghezza

inches/pollici	0.39	3.9	7.8	11.7	15.6	19.7	39
cm/centimetri	1	10	20	30	40	50	100

Distance/Distanze

miles/miglia	0.62	6.2	12.4	18.6	24.9	31	62
km/chilometri	1	10	20	30	40	50	100

Weight/Pesi

pounds/libbre	2.2	22	44	66	88	110	220
kg/chilogrammi	1	10	20	30	40	50	100

Capacity/Capacità

gallons/galloni	0.22	2.2	4.4	6.6	8.8	11	22
litres/litri	1	10	20	30	40	50	100

Temperature/Temperatura

°C	0	5	10	15	20	25	30	37	38	40
°F	32	41	50	59	68	77	86	98.4	100	104

Clothing and shoe sizes/Taglie e numeri di scarpe

Women's clothing sizes/Abbigliamento femminile

UK	8	10	12	14	16	18
US	6	8	10	12	14	16
Continent	36	38	40	42	44	46

Men's clothing sizes/Abbigliamento maschile

UK/US	36	38	40	42	44	46
Continent	46	48	50	52	54	56

Men's and women's shoes/Scarpe da uomo e da donna

UK women	4	5	6	7	7.5	8			
UK men			6	7	8	9	10	11	
US	6.5	7.5	8.5	9.5	10.5	11.5	12.5	13.5	14.5
Continent	37	38	39	40	41	42	43	44	45

Aa

a /ə/, accentato /eɪ/ indef art; davanti a una vocale **an**

> un *m*, una *f*; (before s + consonant, gn, ps and z) uno; (before feminine noun starting with a vowel) un'; **a tiger is a feline** la tigre è un felino; **a knife and fork** un coltello e una forchetta; **a Mr Smith is looking for you** un certo signor Smith ti sta cercando

> (each) a; **£2 a kilo/a head** due sterline al chilo/a testa

when a refers to professions, it is not translated: **I am a lawyer** sono avvocato

A /eɪ/ *n* (Mus) la *m inv*

aback /ə'bæk/ *adv* **be taken ~** essere preso in contropiede

abandon /ə'bændən/ *vt* abbandonare; (give up) rinunciare a ●*n* abbandono *m*. **~ed** *adj* abbandonato

abashed /ə'bæʃt/ *adj* imbarazzato

abate /ə'beɪt/ *vi* calmarsi

abattoir /'æbətwɑː(r)/ *n* mattatoio *m*

abbey /'æbɪ/ *n* abbazia *f*

abbreviat|e /ə'briːvɪeɪt/ *vt* abbreviare. **~ion** *n* abbreviazione *f*

abdicat|e /'æbdɪkeɪt/ *vi* abdicare ●*vt* rinunciare a. **~ion** *n* abdicazione *f*

abdom|en /'æbdəmən/ *n* addome *m*. **~inal** *adj* addominale

abduct /əb'dʌkt/ *vt* rapire. **~ion** *n* rapimento *m*

abhor /əb'hɔː(r)/ *vt* (*pt/pp* abhorred) aborrire. **~rence** *n* orrore *m*

abid|e /ə'baɪd/ *vt* (*pt/pp* abided) (tolerate) sopportare ●**abide by** *vi* rispettare. **~ing** *adj* perpetuo

ability /ə'bɪlətɪ/ *n* capacità *f inv*

abject /'æbdʒekt/ *adj* (poverty) degradante; (apology) umile; (coward) abietto

ablaze /ə'bleɪz/ *adj* in fiamme; **be ~ with light** risplendere di luci

able /'eɪbl/ *adj* capace, abile; **be ~ to do sth** poter fare qcsa; **were you ~ to...?** sei riuscito a...? **~-'bodied** *adj* robusto; (Mil) abile

ably /'eɪblɪ/ *adv* abilmente

abnormal /æb'nɔːml/ *adj* anormale. **~ity** *n* anormalità *f inv*. **~ly** *adv* in modo anormale

aboard /ə'bɔːd/ *adv & prep* a bordo

aboli|sh /ə'bɒlɪʃ/ *vt* abolire. **~tion** *n* abolizione *f*

abomina|ble /ə'bɒmɪnəbl/ *adj* abominevole

abort /ə'bɔːt/ *vt* fare abortire; *fig* annullare. **~ion** *n* aborto *m*; **have an ~ion** abortire. **~ive** *adj* (attempt) infruttuoso

abound /ə'baʊnd/ *vi* abbondare; **~ in** abbondare di

about /ə'baʊt/ *adv* (here and there) [di] qua e [di] là; (approximately) circa; **be ~** (illness, tourists:) essere in giro; **be up and ~** essere alzato; **leave sth lying ~** lasciare in giro qcsa ●*prep* (concerning) su; (in the region of) intorno a; (*time, price etc*) verso; **what is the book/the film ~?** di cosa parla il libro/il film?; **he wants to see you – what ~?** ti vuole vedere – a che proposito?; **talk/know ~** parlare/sapere di; **I know nothing ~ it** non ne so niente; **~ 5**

a

o'clock intorno le 5; **travel** ~ **the world** viaggiare per il mondo; **be** ~ **to do sth** stare per fare qcsa; **how** ~ **going to the cinema?** e se andassimo al cinema?

about: ~-'**face** *n*, ~-'**turn** *n* dietro front *m inv*

above /ə'bʌv/ *adv & prep* sopra; ~ **all** soprattutto

above: ~-'**board** *adj* onesto. ~-'**mentioned** *adj* suddetto

abrasive /ə'breɪsɪv/ *adj* abrasivo; (remark) caustico ● *n* abrasivo *m*

abreast /ə'brest/ *adv* fianco a fianco; **come** ~ **of** allinearsi con; **keep** ~ **of** tenersi al corrente di

abroad /ə'brɔːd/ *adv* all'estero

abrupt /ə'brʌpt/ *adj* brusco

abscess /'æbsɪs/ *n* ascesso *m*

abscond /əb'skɒnd/ *vi* fuggire

absence /'æbsəns/ *n* assenza *f*; (lack) mancanza *f*

absent[1] /'æbsənt/ *adj* assente

absent[2] /æb'sent/ *vt* ~ **oneself** essere assente

absentee /æbsən'tiː/ *n* assente *mf*

absent-minded /æbsənt'maɪndɪd/ *adj* distratto

absolute /'æbsəluːt/ *adj* assoluto; **an** ~ **idiot** un perfetto idiota. ~**ly** *adv* assolutamente; (Ⅰ: indicating agreement) esattamente

absolve /əb'zɒlv/ *vt* assolvere

absorb /əb'sɔːb/ *vt* assorbire; ~**ed in** assorto in. ~**ent** *adj* assorbente

absorption /əb'sɔːpʃn/ *n* assorbimento *m*; (in activity) concentrazione *f*

abstain /əb'steɪn/ *vi* astenersi (from da)

abstemious /əb'stiːmɪəs/ *adj* moderato

abstention /əb'stenʃn/ *n* (Pol) astensione *f*

abstract /'æbstrækt/ *adj* astratto ● *n* astratto *m*; (summary) estratto *m*

absurd /əb'sɜːd/ *adj* assurdo. ~**ity** *n*

assurdità *f inv*

abundan|ce /ə'bʌndəns/ *n* abbondanza *f*. ~**t** *adj* abbondante

abuse[1] /ə'bjuːz/ *vt* (misuse) abusare di; (insult) insultare; (ill-treat) maltrattare

abuse[2] /ə'bjuːs/ *n* abuso *m*; (verbal) insulti *mpl*; (ill-treatment) maltrattamento *m*. ~**ive** *adj* offensivo

abysmal /ə'bɪzml/ *adj* Ⅰ: pessimo; (ignorance) abissale

abyss /ə'bɪs/ *n* abisso *m*

academic /ækə'demɪk/ *adj* teorico; (qualifications, system) scolastico; **be** ~ (person:) avere predisposizione allo studio ● *n* docente *mf* universitario, -a

academy /ə'kædəmɪ/ *n* accademia *f*; (of music) conservatorio *m*

accelerat|e /ək'seləreɪt/ *vt/i* accelerare. ~**ion** *n* accelerazione *f*. ~**or** *n* (Auto) acceleratore *m*

accent /'æksənt/ *n* accento *m*

accept /ək'sept/ *vt* accettare. ~**able** *adj* accettabile. ~**ance** *n* accettazione *f*

access /'ækses/ *n* accesso *m*. ~**ible** *adj* accessibile

accession /ək'seʃn/ *n* (to throne) ascesa *f* al trono

accessory /ək'sesərɪ/ *n* accessorio *m*; (Jur) complice *mf*

accident /'æksɪdənt/ *n* incidente *m*; (chance) caso *m*; **by** ~ per caso; (unintentionally) senza volere; **I'm sorry, it was an** ~ mi dispiace, non l'ho fatto apposta. ~**al** *adj* (meeting) casuale; (death) incidentale; (unintentional) involontario. ~**ally** *adv* per caso; (unintentionally) inavvertitamente

acclaim /ə'kleɪm/ *n* acclamazione *f* ● *vt* acclamare (as come)

accolade /'ækəleɪd/ *n* riconoscimento *m*

accommodat|e /ə'kɒmədeɪt/ *vt* ospitare; (oblige) favorire. ~**ing** *adj* accomodante. ~**ion** *n* (place to stay) sistemazione f

accompan|iment /əˈkʌmpənɪmənt/ n accompagnamento m. **~ist** n (Mus) accompagnatore, -trice mf

accompany /əˈkʌmpənɪ/ vt (pt/pp -ied) accompagnare

accomplice /əˈkʌmplɪs/ n complice mf

accomplish /əˈkʌmplɪʃ/ vt (achieve) concludere; realizzare (aim). **~ed** adj dotato; (fact) compiuto. **~ment** n realizzazione f; (achievement) risultato m; (talent) talento m

accord /əˈkɔːd/ n (treaty) accordo m; **with one ~** tutti d'accordo; **of his own ~** di sua spontanea volontà. **~ance** n **in ~ance with** in conformità di o a

according /əˈkɔːdɪŋ/ adv **~ to** secondo. **~ly** adv di conseguenza

accordion /əˈkɔːdɪən/ n fisarmonica f

accost /əˈkɒst/ vt abbordare

account /əˈkaʊnt/ n conto m; (report) descrizione f; (of eye-witness) resoconto m; **~s** pl (Comm) conti mpl; **on ~ of** a causa di; **on no ~** per nessun motivo; **on this ~** per questo motivo; **on my ~** per causa mia; **of no ~** di nessuna importanza; **take into ~** tener conto di ● **account for** vi (explain) spiegare; (person) render conto di; (constitute) costituire. **~ability** n responsabilità f inv. **~able** adj responsabile (for di)

accountant /əˈkaʊntənt/ n (bookkeeper) contabile mf; (consultant) commercialista mf

accumulat|e /əˈkjuːmjʊleɪt/ vt accumulare ● vi accumularsi. **~ion** n accumulazione f

accura|cy /ˈækərəsɪ/ n precisione f. **~te** adj preciso. **~tely** adv con precisione

accusation /ækjʊˈzeɪʃn/ n accusa f

accuse /əˈkjuːz/ vt accusare; **~ sb of doing sth** accusare qcno di fare

qcsa. **~d** n **the ~d** l'accusato m, l'accusata f

accustom /əˈkʌstəm/ vt abituare **(to a)**; **grow** or **get ~ed to** abituarsi a. **~ed** adj abituato

ace /eɪs/ n (Cards) asso m; (tennis) ace m inv

ache /eɪk/ n dolore m ● vi dolere, far male; **~ all over** essere tutto indolenzito

achieve /əˈtʃiːv/ vt ottenere (success); realizzare (goal, ambition). **~ment** n (feat) successo m

acid /ˈæsɪd/ adj acido ● n acido m. **~ity** n acidità f. **~ rain** n pioggia f acida

acknowledge /əkˈnɒlɪdʒ/ vt riconoscere; rispondere a (greeting); far cenno di aver notato (sb's presence); **~ receipt of** accusare ricevuta di. **~ment** n riconoscimento m; **send an ~ment of a letter** confermare il ricevimento di una lettera

acne /ˈæknɪ/ n acne f

acorn /ˈeɪkɔːn/ n ghianda f

acoustic /əˈkuːstɪk/ adj acustico. **~s** npl acustica fsg

acquaint /əˈkweɪnt/ vt **~ sb with** metter qcno al corrente di; **be ~ed with** conoscere (person); essere a conoscenza di (fact). **~ance** n (person) conoscente mf; **make sb's ~ance** fare la conoscenza di qcno

acquiesce /ækwɪˈes/ vi acconsentire (to, in a). **~nce** n acquiescenza f

acquire /əˈkwaɪə(r)/ vt acquisire

acquisit|ion /ækwɪˈzɪʃn/ n acquisizione f. **~ive** adj avido

acquit /əˈkwɪt/ vt (pt/pp acquitted) assolvere; **~ oneself well** cavarsela bene. **~tal** n assoluzione f

acre /ˈeɪkə(r)/ n acro m (= 4 047 m²)

acrid /ˈækrɪd/ adj acre

acrimon|ious /ækrɪˈməʊnɪəs/ adj aspro. **~y** n asprezza f

acrobat /ˈækrəbæt/ n acrobata mf. **~ic** adj acrobatico

a **across** /əˈkrɒs/ adv dall'altra parte; (wide) in larghezza; (not lengthwise) attraverso; (in crossword) orizzontale; come ~ sth imbattersi in qcsa; go ~ attraversare ● prep (crosswise) di traverso su; (on the other side of) dall'altra parte di

act /ækt/ n atto m; (in variety show) numero m; put on an ~ 🔲 fare scena ● vi agire; (behave) comportarsi; (Theat) recitare; (pretend) fingere; ~ as fare da ● vt recitare (role). ~ing adj (deputy) provvisorio ● n (Theat) recitazione f; (profession) teatro m. ~ing profession n professione f dell'attore

action /ˈækʃn/ n azione f; (Mil) combattimento m; (Jur) azione f legale; out of ~ (machine:) fuori uso; take ~ agire. ~ 'replay n replay m inv

active /ˈæktɪv/ adj attivo. ~ely adv attivamente. ~ity n attività f inv

actor /ˈæktə(r)/ n attore m. ~ress n attrice f

actual /ˈæktʃʊəl/ adj (real) reale. ~ly adv in realtà

acute /əˈkjuːt/ adj acuto; (shortage, hardship) estremo

ad /æd/ n 🔲 pubblicità f inv

AD abbr (Anno Domini) d.C.

adapt /əˈdæpt/ vt adattare (play) ● vi adattarsi. ~ability n adattabilità f. ~able adj adattabile

adaptation /ædæpˈteɪʃn/ n (Theat) adattamento m

adapter, adaptor /əˈdæptə(r)/ n adattatore m; (two-way) presa f multipla

add /æd/ vt aggiungere; (Math) addizionare ● vi addizionare. □ ~ up vt addizionare (figures) ● vi addizionare; ~ up to ammontare a; it doesn't ~ up fig non quadra

adder /ˈædə(r)/ n vipera f

addict /ˈædɪkt/ n tossicodipendente

mf; fig fanatico, -a mf

addict|ed /əˈdɪktɪd/ adj assuefatto (to a); ~ed to drugs tossicodipendente; he's ~ed to television è videodipendente. ~ion n dipendenza f; (to drugs) tossicodipendenza f. ~ive adj be ~ive dare assuefazione

addition /əˈdɪʃn/ n (Math) addizione f; (thing added) aggiunta f; in ~ in aggiunta. ~al adj supplementare. ~ally adv in più

additive /ˈædɪtɪv/ n additivo m

address /əˈdres/ n indirizzo m; (speech) discorso m; form of ~ formula f di cortesia ● vt indirizzare; (speak to) rivolgersi a (person); tenere un discorso a (meeting). ~ee n destinatario, -a mf

adept /ˈædept/ adj & n esperto, -a mf (at in)

adequate /ˈædɪkwət/ adj adeguato. ~ly adv adeguatamente

adhere /ədˈhɪə(r)/ vi aderire; ~ to attenersi a (principles, rules)

adhesive /ədˈhiːsɪv/ adj adesivo ● n adesivo m

adjacent /əˈdʒeɪsənt/ adj adiacente

adjective /ˈædʒɪktɪv/ n aggettivo m

adjourn /əˈdʒɜːn/ vt/i aggiornare (until a). ~ment n aggiornamento m

adjust /əˈdʒʌst/ vt modificare; regolare (focus, sound etc) ● vi adattarsi. ~able adj regolabile. ~ment n adattamento m; (Techn) regolamento m

administer /ədˈmɪnɪstə(r)/ vt amministrare; somministrare (medicine)

administrat|ion /ədmɪnɪˈstreɪʃn/ n amministrazione f; (Pol) governo m. ~or n amministratore, -trice f

admirable /ˈædmərəbl/ adj ammirevole

admiral /ˈædmərəl/ n ammiraglio m

admiration /ædməˈreɪʃn/ n ammirazione f

admire /ədˈmaɪə(r)/ vt ammirare.

~r n ammiratore, -trice mf

admission /əd'mɪʃn/ n ammissione f; (to hospital) ricovero m; (entry) ingresso m

admit /əd'mɪt/ vt (pt/pp **admitted**) (let in) far entrare; (to hospital) ricoverare; (acknowledge) ammettere • vi **to ~ to sth** ammettere qcsa. **~tance** n ammissione f; 'no **~tance**' 'vietato l'ingresso'. **~tedly** adv bisogna riconoscerlo

admonish /əd'mɒnɪʃ/ vt ammonire

ado /ə'du:/ n without more **~** senza ulteriori indugi

adolescen|ce /ædə'lesns/ n adolescenza f. **~t** adj & n adolescente mf

adopt /ə'dɒpt/ vt adottare; (Pol) scegliere (candidate). **~ion** n adozione f. **~ive** adj adottivo

ador|able /ə'dɔ:rəbl/ adj adorabile. **~ation** n adorazione f

adore /ə'dɔ:(r)/ vt adorare

adrenalin /ə'drenəlɪn/ n adrenalina f

Adriatic /eɪdrɪ'ætɪk/ adj & n the **~ [Sea]** il mare Adriatico, l'Adriatico m

adrift /ə'drɪft/ adj alla deriva; be **~** andare alla deriva; **come ~** staccarsi

adult /'ædʌlt/ n adulto, -a mf

adultery /ə'dʌltərɪ/ n adulterio m

advance /əd'vɑ:ns/ n avanzamento m; (Mil) avanzata f; (payment) anticipo m; **in ~** in anticipo • vi avanzare; (make progress) fare progressi • vt avanzare (theory); promuovere (cause); anticipare (money). **~ booking** n prenotazione f [in anticipo]. **~d** adj avanzato. **~ment** n promozione f

advantage /əd'vɑ:ntɪdʒ/ n vantaggio m; **take ~ of** approfittare di. **~ous** adj vantaggioso

advent /'ædvent/ n avvento m

adventur|e /əd'ventʃə(r)/ n avventura f. **~ous** adj avventuroso

adverb /'ædvɜ:b/ n avverbio m

adversary /'ædvəsərɪ/ n avversario, -a f

advers|e /'ædvɜ:s/ adj avverso. **~ity** n avversità f

advert /'ædvɜ:t/ n **[T]** = **advertisement**

advertise /'ædvətaɪz/ vt reclamizzare; mettere un annuncio per (job, flat) • vi fare pubblicità; (for job, flat) mettere un annuncio

advertisement /əd'vɜ:tɪsmənt/ n pubblicità f inv; (in paper) inserzione f, annuncio m

advertis|er /'ædvətaɪzə(r)/ n (in newspaper) inserzionista m, f. **~ing** n pubblicità f • attrib pubblicitario

advice /əd'vaɪs/ n consigli mpl; **piece of ~** consiglio m

advisable /əd'vaɪzəbl/ adj consigliabile

advis|e /əd'vaɪz/ vt consigliare; (inform) avvisare; **~e sb to do sth** consigliare a qcno di fare qcsa; **~e sb against sth** sconsigliare qcsa a qcno. **~er** n consulente mf. **~ory** adj consultivo

advocate¹ /'ædvəkət/ n (supporter) fautore, -trice mf

advocate² /'ædvəkeɪt/ vt propugnare

aerial /'eərɪəl/ adj aereo • n antenna f

aerobics /eə'rəʊbɪks/ n aerobica fsg

aero|drome /'eərədrəʊm/ n aerodromo m. **~plane** n aeroplano m

aerosol /'eərəsɒl/ n bomboletta f spray

aesthetic /i:s'θetɪk/ adj estetico

afar /ə'fɑ:(r)/ adv from **~** da lontano

affable /'æfəbl/ adj affabile

affair /ə'feə(r)/ n affare m; (scandal) caso m; (sexual) relazione f

affect /ə'fekt/ vt influire su; (emotionally) colpire; (concern) riguardare.

a

~**ation** n affettazione f. ~**ed** adj affettato

affection /əˈfekʃn/ n affetto m. ~**ate** adj affettuoso

affirm /əˈfɜːm/ vt affermare; (Jur) dichiarare solennemente

affirmative /əˈfɜːmətɪv/ adj affermativo ● n **in the** ~ affermativamente

afflict /əˈflɪkt/ vt affliggere. ~**ion** n afflizione f

affluen|ce /ˈæflʊəns/ n agiatezza f. ~**t** adj agiato

afford /əˈfɔːd/ vt **be able to** ~ **sth** potersi permettere qcsa. ~**able** adj abbordabile

affront /əˈfrʌnt/ n affronto m

afield /əˈfiːld/ adv **further** ~ più lontano

afloat /əˈfləʊt/ adj a galla

afraid /əˈfreɪd/ adj **be** ~ aver paura; **I'm** ~ **not** purtroppo no; **I'm** ~ **so** temo di sì; **I'm** ~ **I can't help you** mi dispiace, ma non posso esserle d'aiuto

afresh /əˈfreʃ/ adv da capo

Africa /ˈæfrɪkə/ n Africa f. ~**n** adj & n africano, -a mf

after /ˈɑːftə(r)/ adv dopo; **the day** ~ il giorno dopo; **be** ~ cercare ● prep dopo; ~ **all** dopotutto; **the day** ~ **tomorrow** dopodomani ● conj dopo che

after: ~-**effect** n conseguenza f. ~**math** /-mɑːθ/ n conseguenze fpl; **the** ~**math of war** il dopoguerra; **in the** ~**math of** nel periodo successivo a. ~**noon** n pomeriggio m; **good** ~**noon!** buon giorno!. ~**shave** n [lozione f] dopobarba m inv. ~**thought** n added as an ~**thought** aggiunto in un secondo momento; ~**wards** adv in seguito

again /əˈɡen/ adv di nuovo; **[then]** ~ (besides) inoltre; (on the other hand) d'altra parte; ~ **and** ~ continuamente

against /əˈɡenst/ prep contro

age /eɪdʒ/ n età f inv; (era) era f; ~**s** 🔟 secoli; **what** ~ **are you?** quanti anni hai?; **be under** ~ non avere l'età richiesta; **he's two years of** ~ ha due anni ● vt/i (pres p **ageing**) invecchiare

aged¹ /eɪdʒd/ adj ~ **two** di due anni

aged² /ˈeɪdʒɪd/ adj anziano ● **the** ~ pl gli anziani

agency /ˈeɪdʒənsɪ/ n agenzia f; **have the** ~ **for** essere un concessionario di

agenda /əˈdʒendə/ n ordine m del giorno; **on the** ~ all'ordine del giorno; fig in programma

agent /ˈeɪdʒənt/ n agente mf

aggravat|e /ˈæɡrəveɪt/ vt aggravare; (annoy) esasperare. ~**ion** n aggravamento m; (annoyance) esasperazione f

aggress|ion /əˈɡreʃn/ n aggressione f. ~**ive** adj aggressivo. ~**iveness** n aggressività f. ~**or** n aggressore m

aghast /əˈɡɑːst/ adj inorridito

agil|e /ˈædʒaɪl/ adj agile. ~**ity** n agilità f

agitat|e /ˈædʒɪteɪt/ vt mettere in agitazione; (shake) agitare ● vi fig ~ **for** creare delle agitazioni per. ~**ed** adj agitato. ~**ion** n agitazione f. ~**or** n agitatore, -trice mf

ago /əˈɡəʊ/ adv fa; **a long time/a month** ~ molto tempo/un mese fa

agonize /ˈæɡənaɪz/ vi angosciarsi (over per). ~**ing** adj angosciante

agony /ˈæɡənɪ/ n agonia f; (mental) angoscia f; **be in** ~ avere dei dolori atroci

agree /əˈɡriː/ vt accordarsi su; ~ **to do sth** accordarsi di fare qcsa; ~ **that** essere d'accordo [sul fatto] che ● vi essere d'accordo; (figures): concordare; (*reach agreement*) mettersi d'accordo; (*get on*) andare d'accordo; (*consent*) acconsentire (**to** a); it doesn't ∼ with me mi fa male; ∼ with sth (*approve of*) approvare qcsa

agreeable /əˈɡriːəbl/ adj gradevole; (*willing*) d'accordo

agreed /əˈɡriːd/ adj convenuto

agreement /əˈɡriːmənt/ n accordo m; in ∼ d'accordo

agricultural /æɡrɪˈkʌltʃərəl/ adj agricolo. ∼e n agricoltura f

aground /əˈɡraʊnd/ adv run ∼ (ship:) arenarsi

ahead /əˈhed/ adv avanti; be ∼ of essere davanti a; fig essere avanti rispetto a; draw ∼ passare davanti (**of** a); get ∼ (*in life*) riuscire; go ∼! fai pure!; look ∼ pensare all'avvenire; plan ∼ fare progetti per l'avvenire

aid /eɪd/ n aiuto m; in ∼ of a favore di ●vt aiutare

Aids /eɪdz/ n AIDS m

aim /eɪm/ n mira f; fig scopo m; take ∼ prendere la mira ●vt puntare (gun) (**at** contro) ●vi mirare; ∼ to do sth aspirare a fare qcsa. ∼less adj, ∼lessly adv senza scopo

air /eə(r)/ n aria f; be on the ∼ (*programme:*) essere in onda; put on ∼s darsi delle arie; by ∼ in aereo; (*airmail*) per via aerea ●vt arieggiare; far conoscere (views)

air: ∼-conditioned adj con aria condizionata. ∼-conditioning n aria f condizionata. ∼craft n aereo m. ∼craft carrier n portaerei f inv. ∼field n campo m d'aviazione. ∼force n aviazione f. ∼ freshener n deodorante m per l'ambiente. ∼gun n fucile m pneumatico. ∼ hostess n hostess f inv. ∼line n compagnia f aerea. ∼mail n posta f aerea. ∼plane n Am aereo m. ∼port n aeroporto m. ∼tight adj ermetico. ∼-traffic controller n controllore m

di volo

airy /ˈeərɪ/ adj (-ier, -iest) arieggiato; (*manner*) noncurante

aisle /aɪl/ n corridoio m; (*in supermarket*) corsia f; (*in church*) navata f

ajar /əˈdʒɑː(r)/ adj socchiuso

alarm /əˈlɑːm/ n allarme m; set the ∼ (*of alarm clock*) mettere la sveglia ●vt allarmare. ∼ clock n sveglia f

Albania /ælˈbeɪnɪə/ n Albania f

album /ˈælbəm/ n album m inv

alcohol /ˈælkəhɒl/ n alcol m. ∼ic adj alcolico ●n alcolizzato, -a mf. ∼ism n alcolismo m

alcove /ˈælkəʊv/ n alcova f

alert /əˈlɜːt/ adj sveglio; (*watchful*) vigile ●n segnale m d'allarme; be on the ∼ stare allerta ●vt allertare

algebra /ˈældʒɪbrə/ n algebra f

Algeria /ælˈdʒɪərɪə/ n Algeria f. ∼n adj & n algerino, -a mf

alias /ˈeɪlɪəs/ n pseudonimo m ●adv alias

alibi /ˈælɪbaɪ/ n alibi m inv

alien /ˈeɪlɪən/ adj straniero; fig estraneo ●n straniero, -a mf; (*from space*) alieno, -a f

alienate /ˈeɪlɪəneɪt/ vt alienare. ∼ion n alienazione f

alight¹ /əˈlaɪt/ vi scendere; (*bird:*) posarsi

alight² adj be ∼ essere in fiamme; set ∼ dar fuoco a

align /əˈlaɪn/ vt allineare. ∼ment n allineamento m; out of ∼ment non allineato

alike /əˈlaɪk/ adj simile; be ∼ rassomigliarsi ●adv in modo simile; look ∼ rassomigliarsi; summer and winter ∼ sia d'estate che d'inverno

alimony /ˈælɪmənɪ/ n alimenti mpl

alive /əˈlaɪv/ adj vivo; ∼ with brulicante di; ∼ to sensibile a; ∼ and kicking vivo e vegeto

alkali /ˈælkəlaɪ/ n alcali m

a

all /ɔːl/

● *adj* tutto; ~ the children, ~ children tutti i bambini; ~ day tutto il giorno; he refused ~ help ha rifiutato qualsiasi aiuto; for ~ that (*nevertheless*) ciononostante; in ~ sincerity in tutta sincerità; be ~ for essere favorevole a

● *pron* tutto; ~ of you/them tutti voi/loro; ~ of it tutto; ~ of the town tutta la città; in ~ in tutto; ~ in ~ tutto sommato; most of ~ più di ogni altra cosa; once and for ~ una volta per tutte

● *adv* completamente; ~ but quasi; ~ at once (*at the same time*) tutto in una volta; ~ at once, ~ of a sudden all'improvviso; ~ too soon troppo presto; ~ the same (*nevertheless*) ciononostante; ~ the better meglio ancora; she's not ~ that good an actress non è poi così brava come attrice; ~ in tutto; 🔲 esausto; thirty/three ~ (*in sport*) trenta/tre pari; ~ over (*finished*) tutto finito; (*everywhere*) dappertutto; it's ~ right (*I don't mind*) non fa niente; I'm ~ right (*not hurt*) non ho niente; ~ right! va bene!

allay /ə'leɪ/ *vt* placare (suspicions, anger)

allegation /ælɪ'geɪʃn/ *n* accusa *f*

allege /ə'ledʒ/ *vt* dichiarare. ~d *adj* presunto. ~dly *adv* a quanto si dice

allegiance /ə'liːdʒəns/ *n* fedeltà *f*

allergic /ə'lɜːdʒɪk/ *adj* allergico. ~y *n* allergia *f*

alleviate /ə'liːvɪeɪt/ *vt* alleviare

alley /'ælɪ/ *n* vicolo *m*; (*for bowling*) corsia *f*

alliance /ə'laɪəns/ *n* alleanza *f*

alligator /'ælɪgeɪtə(r)/ *n* alligatore *m*

allocat|e /'æləkeɪt/ *vt* assegnare; distribuire (resources). ~ion *f*, (*of resources*) distribuzione *f*

allot /ə'lɒt/ *vt* (*pt/pp* **allotted**) distribuire. ~ment *n* distribuzione *f*; (*share*) parte *f*; (*land*) piccolo lotto *m* di terreno

allow /ə'laʊ/ *vt* permettere; (*grant*) accordare; (*reckon on*) contare; (*agree*) ammettere; ~ for tener conto di; ~ sb to do sth permettere a qcno di fare qcsa; you are not ~ed to... è vietato...

allowance /ə'laʊəns/ *n* sussidio *m*; (*Am: pocket money*) paghetta *f*; (*for petrol etc*) indennità *f inv*; (*of luggage, duty free*) limite *m*; make ~s for essere indulgente verso (sb); tener conto di (sth)

alloy /'æloɪ/ *n* lega *f*

allusion /ə'luːʒn/ *n* allusione *f*

ally¹ /'ælaɪ/ *n* alleato, -a *mf*

ally² /ə'laɪ/ *vt* (*pt/pp* -**ied**) alleare; ~ oneself with allearsi con

almighty /ɔːl'maɪtɪ/ *adj* (🔲: *big*) mega *inv* ● *n* the A~ l'Onnipotente *m*

almond /'ɑːmənd/ *n* mandorla *f*; (*tree*) mandorlo *m*

almost /'ɔːlməʊst/ *adv* quasi

alone /ə'ləʊn/ *adj* solo; leave me ~! lasciami in pace!; let ~ (*not to mention*) figurarsi ● *adv* da solo

along /ə'lɒŋ/ *prep* lungo ● *adv* ~ with assieme a; all ~ tutto il tempo; come ~! (*hurry up*) vieni qui!; I'll be ~ in a minute arrivo tra un attimo; move ~ spostarsi; move ~! circolare!

alongside *adv* lungo bordo ● *prep* lungo; work ~ sb lavorare fianco a fianco con qcno

aloof /ə'luːf/ *adj* distante

aloud /ə'laʊd/ *adv* ad alta voce

alphabet /'ælfəbet/ *n* alfabeto *m*. ~ical *adj* alfabetico

Alps /ælps/ npl Alpi fpl

already /ɔːl'redɪ/ adv già

Alsatian /æl'seɪʃn/ n (dog) pastore m tedesco

also /'ɔːlsəʊ/ adv anche; ~, I need... [e] inoltre, ho bisogno di...

altar /'ɔːltə(r)/ n altare m

alter /'ɔːltə(r)/ vt cambiare; aggiustare (clothes) ● vi cambiare. ~ation n modifica f

alternate¹ /'ɔːltənət/ vi alternarsi ● vt alternare

alternate² /ɔːl'tɜːnət/ adj alterno; on ~ days a giorni alterni

alternative /ɔːl'tɜːnətɪv/ adj alternativo ● n alternativa f. ~ly adv alternativamente

although /ɔːl'ðəʊ/ conj benché, sebbene

altitude /'æltɪtjuːd/ n altitudine f

altogether /ɔːltə'geðə(r)/ adv (in all) in tutto; (completely) completamente; I'm not ~ sure non sono del tutto sicuro

aluminium /æljʊ'mɪnɪəm/ n, Am **aluminum** /ə'luːmɪnəm/ n alluminio m

always /'ɔːlweɪz/ adv sempre

am /æm/ ▶ BE

a.m. abbr (ante meridiem) del mattino

amalgamate /ə'mælgəmeɪt/ vt fondere ● vi fondersi

amass /ə'mæs/ vt accumulare

amateur /'æmətə(r)/ n non professionista mf; pej dilettante mf ● attrib dilettante; ~ dramatics filodrammatica f. ~ish adj dilettantesco

amaze /ə'meɪz/ vt stupire. ~d adj stupito. ~ment n stupore m

amazing /ə'meɪzɪŋ/ adj incredibile

ambassador /æm'bæsədə(r)/ n ambasciatore, -trice m

ambigu|ity /æmbɪ'gjuːətɪ/ n ambiguità f inv. ~ous adj ambiguo

ambiti|on /æm'bɪʃn/ n ambizione

f; (aim) aspirazione f. ~ous adj ambizioso

ambivalent /æm'bɪvələnt/ adj ambivalente

amble /'æmbl/ vi camminare senza fretta

ambulance /'æmbjʊləns/ n ambulanza f

ambush /'æmbʊʃ/ n imboscata f ● vt tendere un'imboscata a

amend /ə'mend/ vt modificare. ~ment n modifica f. ~s npl make ~s fare ammenda (for di, per)

amenities /ə'miːnətɪz/ npl comodità fpl

America /ə'merɪkə/ n America f. ~n adj & n americano, -a mf

amiable /'eɪmɪəbl/ adj amabile

amicable /'æmɪkəbl/ adj amichevole

ammonia /ə'məʊnɪə/ n ammoniaca f

ammunition /æmjʊ'nɪʃn/ n munizioni fpl

amnesty /'æmnəstɪ/ n amnistia f

among[st] /ə'mʌŋ[st]/ prep tra, fra

amount /ə'maʊnt/ n quantità f inv; (sum of money) importo m ● vi ~ to ammontare a; fig equivalere a

amphibi|an /æm'fɪbɪən/ n anfibio m. ~ous adj anfibio

amphitheatre /'æmfɪ-/ n anfiteatro m

ampl|e /'æmpl/ adj (large) grande; (proportions) ampio; (enough) largamente sufficiente

amplif|ier /'æmplɪfaɪə(r)/ n amplificatore m. **~y** vt (pt/pp **-ied**) amplificare (sound)

amputat|e /'æmpjʊteɪt/ vt amputare. **~ion** n amputazione f

amuse /ə'mjuːz/ vt divertire. **~ment** n divertimento m. **~ment arcade** n sala f giochi

amusing /ə'mjuːzɪŋ/ adj divertente

an /ən/, accentato /æn/ ▷A

anaem|ia /ə'niːmɪə/ n anemia f. **~ic** adj anemico

anaesthetic /ænəs'θetɪk/ n anestesia f

anaesthet|ist /ə'niːsθətɪst/ n anestesista mf

analogy /ə'nælədʒɪ/ n analogia f

analyse /'ænəlaɪz/ vt analizzare

analysis /ə'næləsɪs/ n analisi f inv

analyst /'ænəlɪst/ n analista mf

analytical /ænə'lɪtɪkl/ adj analitico

anarch|ist /'ænəkɪst/ n anarchico, -a mf. **~y** n anarchia f

anatom|ical /ænə'tɒmɪkl/ adj anatomico. **~ically** adv anatomicamente. **~y** n anatomia f

ancest|or /'ænsestə(r)/ n antenato, -a mf. **~ry** n antenati mpl

anchor /'æŋkə(r)/ n ancora f ● vi gettar l'ancora ● vt ancorare

anchovy /'æntʃəvɪ/ n acciuga f

ancient /'eɪnʃənt/ adj 🗓 vecchio

ancillary /æn'sɪlərɪ/ adj ausiliario

and /ænd/, accentato /ænd/ conj e; **two ~ two** due più due; **six hundred ~ two** seicentodue; **more ~ more** sempre più; **nice ~ warm** bello caldo; **try ~ come** cerca di venire; **go ~ get** vai a prendere

anecdote /'ænɪkdəʊt/ n aneddoto m

anew /ə'njuː/ adv di nuovo

angel /'eɪndʒl/ n angelo m. **~ic** adj angelico

anger /'æŋgə(r)/ n rabbia f ● vt far arrabbiare

angle¹ /'æŋgl/ n angolo m; fig angolazione f; **at an ~** storto

angle² vi pescare con la lenza; **~ for** fig cercare di ottenere. **~r** n pescatore, -trice mf

Anglican /'æŋglɪkən/ adj & n anglicano, -a mf

angr|y /'æŋgrɪ/ adj (**-ier, -iest**) arrabbiato; **get ~y** arrabbiarsi; **~y with** or **at sb** arrabbiato con qcno; **~y at** or **about sth** arrabbiato per qcsa. **~ily** adv rabbiosamente

anguish /'æŋgwɪʃ/ n angoscia f

animal /'ænɪml/ adj & n animale m

animate¹ /'ænɪmət/ adj animato

animate² /'ænɪmeɪt/ vt animare. **~d** adj animato; (person) vivace. **~ion** n animazione f

animosity /ænɪ'mɒsətɪ/ n animosità f inv

ankle /'æŋkl/ n caviglia f

annihilat|e /ə'naɪəleɪt/ vt annientare. **~ion** n annientamento m

anniversary /ænɪ'vɜːsərɪ/ n anniversario m

announce /ə'naʊns/ vt annunciare. **~ment** n annuncio m. **~r** n annunciatore, -trice mf

annoy /ə'nɔɪ/ vt dare fastidio a; **get ~ed** essere infastidito. **~ance** n seccatura f; (anger) irritazione f. **~ing** adj fastidioso

annual /'ænjʊəl/ adj annuale; (income) annuo ● n (Bot) pianta f annua; (children's book) almanacco m

annul /ə'nʌl/ vt (pt/pp **annulled**) annullare

anonymous /ə'nɒnɪməs/ adj anonimo

anorak /'ænəræk/ n giacca f a vento

another /ə'nʌðə(r)/ adj & pron; **[one]** un altro, un'altra; **in ~ way** diversamente; **one ~** l'un l'altro

answer /'ɑːnsə(r)/ n risposta f; (solution) soluzione f ● vt rispondere a (person, question, letter); esaudire (prayer); ~ **the door** aprire la porta; ~ **the telephone** rispondere al telefono ● vi rispondere; ~ **back** ribattere; ~ **for** rispondere di. ~**able** adj responsabile; **be** ~**able to sb** rispondere a qcno. ~**ing machine** n (Teleph) segreteria f telefonica

ant /ænt/ n formica f

antagonis|m /æn'tægənɪzm/ n antagonismo m. ~**tic** adj antagonistico

antagonize /æn'tægənaɪz/ vt provocare l'ostilità di

Antarctic /æn'tɑːktɪk/ n Antartico m ● adj antartico

antenatal /ænti'neɪtl/ adj prenatale

antenna /æn'tenə/ n antenna f

anthem /'ænθəm/ n inno m

anthology /æn'θɒlədʒɪ/ n antologia f

anthropology /ænθrə'pɒlədʒɪ/ n antropologia f

anti-'aircraft /ænti-/ adj antiaereo

antibiotic /æntɪbaɪ'ɒtɪk/ n antibiotico m

anticipat|e /æn'tɪsɪpeɪt/ vt prevedere; (forestall) anticipare. ~**ion** n anticipo m; (excitement) attesa f

anti'climax n delusione f

anti'clockwise adj & adv in senso antiorario

antidote /'æntɪdəʊt/ n antidoto m

'antifreeze n antigelo m

antiquated /'æntɪkweɪtɪd/ adj antiquato

antique /æn'tiːk/ adj antico ● n antichità f inv. ~ **dealer** n antiquario, -a mf

antiquity /æn'tɪkwətɪ/ n antichità f

anti'septic adj & n antisettico m

anti'social adj (behaviour) antisociale; (person) asociale

antlers /'æntləz/ npl corna fpl

anus /'eɪnəs/ n ano m

anxiety /æŋ'zaɪətɪ/ n ansia f

anxious /'æŋkʃəs/ adj ansioso. ~**ly** adv con ansia

---

any /'enɪ/

● adj (no matter which) qualsiasi, qualunque; ~ **colour/number you like** qualsiasi colore/numero ti piaccia; **we don't have** ~ **wine/biscuits** non abbiamo vino/biscotti; **for** ~ **reason** per qualsiasi ragione

> **any** Is often not translated: **have we** ~ **wine/biscuits?** abbiamo del vino/dei biscotti?

● pron (some) ne; (no matter which) uno qualsiasi; **I don't want** ~ [**of it**] non ne voglio [nessuno]; **there aren't** ~ non ce ne sono; **have we** ~? ne abbiamo?; **have you read** ~ **of her books?** hai letto qualcuno dei suoi libri?

● adv **I can't go** ~ **quicker** non posso andare più in fretta; **is it** ~ **better?** va un po' meglio?; **would you like** ~ **more?** ne vuoi ancora?; **I can't eat** ~ **more** non posso mangiare più niente

---

'anybody pron chiunque; (after negative) nessuno; **I haven't seen** ~ non ho visto nessuno

'anyhow adv ad ogni modo, comunque; (badly) non importa come

'anyone pron = **anybody**

'anything pron qualche cosa, qualcosa; (no matter what) qualsiasi cosa; (after negative) niente; **take/buy** ~ **you like** prendi/compra quello che vuoi; **I don't remember** ~ non mi ricordo niente; **he's** ~ **but stupid** è tutto, ma non stupido; **I'll do** ~ **but that** farò qualsiasi cosa, tranne quello

a

a

'anyway adv ad ogni modo, comunque

'anywhere adv dovunque; (after negative) da nessuna parte; **put it ~** mettilo dove vuoi; **I can't find it ~** non lo trovo da nessuna parte; **~ else** da qualch'altra parte; (after negative) da nessun'altra parte; **I don't want to go ~ else** non voglio andare da nessun'altra parte

apart /ə'pɑːt/ adv lontano; **live ~** vivere separati; **100 miles ~** lontani 100 miglia; **~ from** a parte; **you can't tell them ~** non si possono distinguere; **joking ~** scherzi a parte

apartment /ə'pɑːtmənt/ n (Am: flat) appartamento m; **in my ~** a casa mia

apathy /'æpəθɪ/ n apatia f

ape /eɪp/ n scimmia f ● vt scimmiottare

aperitif /ə'perɪtiːf/ n aperitivo m

aperture /'æpətʃə(r)/ n apertura f

apex /'eɪpeks/ n vertice m

apologetic /əpɒlə'dʒetɪk/ adj (air, remark) di scusa; **be ~** essere spiacente

apologize /ə'pɒlədʒaɪz/ vi scusarsi (for per)

apology /ə'pɒlədʒɪ/ n scusa f; fig a **~ for a dinner** una sottospecie di cena

apostle /ə'pɒsl/ n apostolo m

apostrophe /ə'pɒstrəfɪ/ n apostrofo m

appal /ə'pɔːl/ vt (pt/pp appalled) sconvolgere. **~ling** adj sconvolgente

apparatus /æpə'reɪtəs/ n apparato m

apparent /ə'pærənt/ adj evidente; (seeming) apparente. **~ly** adv apparentemente

apparition /æpə'rɪʃn/ n apparizione f

appeal /ə'piːl/ n appello m; (attraction) attrattiva f ● vi fare appello; **~ to** (be attractive to) attrarre. **~ing** adj attraente

appear /ə'pɪə(r)/ vi apparire; (seem) sembrare; (publication:) uscire; (Theat) esibirsi. **~ance** n apparizione f; (look) aspetto m; **to all ~ances** a giudicare dalle apparenze; **keep up ~ances** salvare le apparenze

appease /ə'piːz/ vt placare

appendicitis /əpendɪ'saɪtɪs/ n appendicite f

appendix /ə'pendɪks/ n (pl -ices /-ɪsiːz/) (of book) appendice f; (pl -es) (Anat) appendice f

appetite /'æpɪtaɪt/ n appetito m

applaud /ə'plɔːd/ vt/i applaudire. **~se** n applauso m

apple /'æpl/ n mela f. **~-tree** n melo m

appliance /ə'plaɪəns/ n attrezzo m; **[electrical] ~** elettrodomestico m

applicable /'æplɪkəbl/ adj **be ~ to** essere valido per; **not ~** (on form) non applicabile

applicant /'æplɪkənt/ n candidato, -a mf

application /æplɪ'keɪʃn/ n applicazione f; (request) domanda f; (for job) candidatura f. **~ form** n modulo m di domanda

applied /ə'plaɪd/ adj applicato

apply /ə'plaɪ/ vt (pt/pp -ied) applicare; **~ oneself** applicarsi ● vi applicarsi; (law:) essere applicabile; **~ to** (ask) rivolgersi a; **~ for** fare domanda per (job etc)

appoint /ə'pɔɪnt/ vt nominare; fissare (time). **~ment** n appuntamento m; (to job) nomina f; (job) posto m

appraisal /ə'preɪz(ə)l/ n valutazione f

appreciable /ə'priːʃəbl/ adj sensibile

appreciate /ə'priːʃɪeɪt/ vt apprezzare; (understand) comprendere ● vi (increase in value) aumentare di valore.

~**ion** n (gratitude) riconoscenza f; (enjoyment) apprezzamento m; (understanding) comprensione f; (in value) aumento m. ~**ive** adj riconoscente

apprehens|ion /æprɪˈhenʃn/ n arresto m; (fear) apprensione f. ~**ive** adj apprensivo

apprentice /əˈprentɪs/ n apprendista mf. ~**ship** n apprendistato m

approach /əˈprəʊtʃ/ n avvicinamento m; (to problem) approccio m; (access) accesso m; **make** ~**es** to fare degli approcci con • vi avvicinarsi • vt avvicinarsi a; (with request) rivolgersi a; affrontare (problem). ~**able** adj accessibile

appropriate¹ /əˈprəʊprɪət/ adj appropriato

appropriate² /əˈprəʊprɪeɪt/ vt appropriarsi di

approval /əˈpruːvl/ n approvazione f; **on** ~ in prova

approv|e /əˈpruːv/ vt approvare • vi ~**e of** approvare (sth); avere una buona opinione di (sb). ~**ing** adj (smile, nod) d'approvazione

approximate /əˈprɒksɪmət/ adj approssimativo. ~**ly** adv approssimativamente

approximation /əprɒksɪˈmeɪʃn/ n approssimazione f

apricot /ˈeɪprɪkɒt/ n albicocca f

April /ˈeɪprəl/ n aprile m; ~ **Fool's Day** il primo d'aprile

apron /ˈeɪprən/ n grembiule m

apt /æpt/ adj appropriato; **be** ~ **to do sth** avere tendenza a fare qcsa

aptitude /ˈæptɪtjuːd/ n disposizione f. ~ **test** n test m inv attitudinale

aquarium /əˈkweərɪəm/ n acquario m

Aquarius /əˈkweərɪəs/ n (Astr) Acquario m

aquatic /əˈkwætɪk/ adj acquatico

Arab /ˈærəb/ adj & n arabo, -a mf. ~**ian** adj arabo

Arabic /ˈærəbɪk/ adj arabo; ~ **numerals** numeri mpl arabici • n arabo m

arable /ˈærəbl/ adj coltivabile

arbitrary /ˈɑːbɪtrərɪ/ adj arbitrario

arbitrat|e /ˈɑːbɪtreɪt/ vi arbitrare. ~**ion** n arbitraggio m

arc /ɑːk/ n arco m

arcade /ɑːˈkeɪd/ n portico m; (shops) galleria f

arch /ɑːtʃ/ n arco m; (of foot) dorso m del piede

archaeological /ɑːkɪəˈlɒdʒɪkl/ adj archeologico

archaeolog|ist /ɑːkɪˈɒlədʒɪst/ n archeologo, -a mf. ~**y** n archeologia f

archaic /ɑːˈkeɪɪk/ adj arcaico

arch'bishop /ɑːtʃ-/ n arcivescovo m

architect /ˈɑːkɪtekt/ n architetto m. ~**ural** adj architettonico

architecture /ˈɑːkɪtektʃə(r)/ n architettura f

archives /ˈɑːkaɪvz/ npl archivi mpl

archway /ˈɑːtʃweɪ/ n arco m

Arctic /ˈɑːktɪk/ adj artico • n **the** ~ l'Artico

ardent /ˈɑːdənt/ adj ardente

arduous /ˈɑːdjʊəs/ adj arduo

are /ɑː(r)/ ▶**BE**

area /ˈeərɪə/ n area f; (region) zona f; (fig: field) campo m. ~ **code** n prefisso m [telefonico]

arena /əˈriːnə/ n arena f

Argentina /ɑːdʒənˈtiːnə/ n Argentina f

Argentinian /-ˈtɪnɪən/ adj & n argentino, -a mf

argue /ˈɑːgjuː/ vi litigare (about su); (debate) dibattere; **don't** ~! non discutere! • vt (debate) dibattere; (reason) ~ **that** sostenere che

argument /ˈɑːgjʊmənt/ n argomento m; (reasoning) ragionamento m; **have an** ~ litigare. ~**ative** adj polemico

a

arid /ˈærɪd/ adj arido

Aries /ˈeəriːz/ n (Astr) Ariete m

arise /əˈraɪz/ vi (pt arose, pp arisen) (opportunity, need, problem:) presentarsi; (result) derivare

aristocracy /ærɪˈstɒkrəsɪ/ n aristocrazia f

aristocrat /ˈærɪstəkræt/ n aristocratico, -a mf. ~ic adj aristocratico

arithmetic /əˈrɪθmətɪk/ n aritmetica f

arm /ɑːm/ n braccio m; (of chair) bracciolo m; ~s pl (weapons) armi fpl; ~ in ~ a braccetto; up in ~s 🔲 furioso (about per) ● vt armare

'armchair n poltrona f

armed /ɑːmd/ adj armato; ~ forces forze fpl armate; ~ robbery rapina f a mano armata

armour /ˈɑːmə(r)/ n armatura f. ~ed adj (vehicle) blindato

'armpit n ascella f

army /ˈɑːmɪ/ n esercito m; **join the ~** arruolarsi

aroma /əˈrəʊmə/ n aroma f. ~tic adj aromatico

arose /əˈrəʊz/ ▷ARISE

around /əˈraʊnd/ adv intorno; **all ~** tutt'intorno; **I'm not from ~ here** non sono di qui; **he's not ~** non c'è ● prep intorno a; in giro per (room, shops, world)

arouse /əˈraʊz/ vt svegliare; (sexually) eccitare

arrange /əˈreɪndʒ/ vt sistemare (furniture, books); organizzare (meeting); fissare (date, time); ~ **to do sth** combinare di fare qcsa. ~ment n (of furniture) sistemazione f; (Mus) arrangiamento m; (agreement) accordo; (of flowers) composizione f; **make ~ments** prendere disposizioni

arrears /əˈrɪəz/ npl arretrati mpl; **be in ~** essere in arretrato; **paid in ~** pagato a lavoro eseguito

arrest /əˈrest/ n arresto m; **under ~** in stato d'arresto ● vt arrestare

arrival /əˈraɪvl/ n arrivo m; **new ~s** pl nuovi arrivati mpl

arrive /əˈraɪv/ vi arrivare; ~ **at** fig raggiungere

arrogan|ce /ˈærəgəns/ n arroganza f. ~t adj arrogante

arrow /ˈærəʊ/ n freccia f

arse /ɑːs/ n 🔲 culo m

arsenic /ˈɑːsənɪk/ n arsenico m

arson /ˈɑːsn/ n incendio m doloso. ~ist n incendiario, -a mf

art /ɑːt/ n arte f; ~**s and crafts** pl artigianato m; **the A~s** pl l'arte f; **A~s degree** (Univ) laurea f in Lettere

artery /ˈɑːtərɪ/ n arteria f

'art gallery n galleria f d'arte

arthritis /ɑːˈθraɪtɪs/ n artrite f

artichoke /ˈɑːtɪtʃəʊk/ n carciofo m

article /ˈɑːtɪkl/ n articolo m; ~ **of clothing** capo m d'abbigliamento

articulate¹ /ɑːˈtɪkjʊlət/ adj (speech) chiaro; **be** ~ esprimersi bene

articulate² /ɑːˈtɪkjʊleɪt/ vt scandire (words). ~**d lorry** n autotreno m

artificial /ɑːtɪˈfɪʃl/ adj artificiale. ~**ly** adv artificialmente; (smile) artificiosamente

artillery /ɑːˈtɪlərɪ/ n artiglieria f

artist /ˈɑːtɪst/ n artista mf

as /æz/ conj come; (since) siccome; (while) mentre; **as he grew older** diventando vecchio; **as you get to know her** conoscendola meglio; **young as she is** per quanto sia giovane ● prep come; **as a friend** come amico; **as a child** da bambino; **as a foreigner** in quanto straniero; **disguised as** da travestito da ● adv anche; **as soon as I get home** [non] appena arrivo a casa; **as quick as you** veloce quanto te; **as quick as you** can più veloce che puoi; **as far as** (distance) fino a; **as far as I'm concerned** per quanto mi riguarda; **as long as** finché; (provided that) purché

asbestos /æz'bestəs/ n amianto m

ascend /ə'send/ vi salire ● vt salire a (throne)

Ascension /ə'senʃn/ n (Relig) Ascensione f

ascent /ə'sent/ n ascesa f

ascertain /æsə'teɪn/ vt accertare

ash[1] /æʃ/ n (tree) frassino m

ash[2] n cenere f

ashamed /ə'ʃeɪmd/ adj be/feel ~ vergognarsi

ashore /ə'ʃɔː(r)/ adv a terra; **go ~** sbarcare

ash: **~tray** n portacenere m. **A~ 'Wednesday** n mercoledì m inv delle Ceneri

Asia /'eɪʒə/ n Asia f. **~n** adj & n asiatico, -a mf. **~tic** adj asiatico

aside /ə'saɪd/ adv **take sb ~** prendere qcno a parte; **put sth ~** mettere qcsa da parte; **~ from you** Am a parte tu

ask /ɑːsk/ vt fare (question); (invite) invitare; **~ sb sth** domandare or chiedere qcsa a qcno; **~ sb to do sth** domandare or chiedere a qcno di fare qcsa ● vi **~ about sth** informarsi su qcsa; **~ after** chiedere [notizie] di (sb); **~ for** chiedere (sth); chiedere di (sb); **~ for trouble** 🔢 andare in cerca di guai. □ **~ in** vt **~ sb in** invitare qcno ad entrare. □ **~ out** vt **~ sb out** chiedere a qcno di uscire

askew /ə'skjuː/ adj & adv di traverso

asleep /ə'sliːp/ adj be ~ dormire; **fall ~** addormentarsi

asparagus /ə'spærəgəs/ n asparagi mpl

aspect /'æspekt/ n aspetto m

asphalt /'æsfælt/ n asfalto m

aspire /ə'spaɪə(r)/ vi **~ to** aspirare a

ass /æs/ n asino m

assassin /ə'sæsɪn/ n assassino, -a mf. **~ate** vt assassinare. **~ation** n as-

sassinio m

assault /ə'sɔːlt/ n (Mil) assalto m; (Jur) aggressione f ● vt aggredire

assemble /ə'sembl/ vi radunarsi ● vt radunare; (Techn) montare

assembly /ə'semblɪ/ n assemblea f; (Sch) assemblea f giornaliera di alunni e professori di una scuola; (Techn) montaggio m. **~ line** n catena f di montaggio

assent /ə'sent/ n assenso m ● vi acconsentire

assert /ə'sɜːt/ vt asserire; far valere (one's rights); **~ oneself** farsi valere. **~ion** n asserzione f. **~ive** adj **be ~ive** farsi valere

assess /ə'ses/ vt valutare; (for tax purposes) stabilire l'imponibile di. **~ment** n valutazione f; (of tax) accertamento m

asset /'æset/ n (advantage) vantaggio m; (person) elemento m prezioso. **~s** pl beni mpl; (on balance sheet) attivo msg

assign /ə'saɪn/ vt assegnare. **~ment** n (task) incarico m

assimilate /ə'sɪmɪleɪt/ vt assimilare; integrare (person)

assist /ə'sɪst/ vt/i assistere; **~ sb to do sth** assistere qcno nel fare qcsa. **~ance** n assistenza f. **~ant** adj **~ant manager** vicedirettore, -trice mf ● n assistente mf; (in shop) commesso, -a mf

associat|e[1] /ə'səʊʃɪeɪt/ vt associare (with a); **be ~ed with sth** (involved in) essere coinvolto in qcsa ● vi **~e with** frequentare. **~ion** n associazione f. **A~ion 'Football** n [gioco m del] calcio m

associate[2] /ə'səʊʃɪət/ adj associato ● n collega mf; (member) socio, -a mf

assort|ed /ə'sɔːtɪd/ adj assortito. **~ment** n assortimento m

assum|e /ə'sjuːm/ vt presumere; assumere (control); **~e office** entrare in carica; **~ing that you're right,...**

a

ammettendo che tu abbia ragione,...

assumption /ə'sʌmpʃn/ n supposizione f; **on the** ~ **that** partendo dal presupposto che; **the A**~ (Relig) l'Assunzione f

assurance /ə'ʃʊərəns/ n assicurazione f; (confidence) sicurezza f

assure /ə'ʃʊə(r)/ vt assicurare. ~d adj sicuro

asterisk /'æstərɪsk/ n asterisco m

asthma /'æsmə/ n asma f. ~tic adj asmatico

astonish /ə'stɒnɪʃ/ vt stupire. ~ing adj stupefacente. ~ment n stupore m

astound /ə'staʊnd/ vt stupire

astray /ə'streɪ/ adv go ~ smarrirsi; (morally) uscire dalla retta via; **lead** ~ traviare

astronaut /'æstrənɔːt/ n astronauta mf

astronomer /ə'strɒnəmə(r)/ n astronomo, -a mf. ~ical adj astronomico. ~y n astronomia f

astute /ə'stjuːt/ adj astuto

asylum /ə'saɪləm/ n [political] ~ asilo m politico; [lunatic] ~ manicomio m

at /ət/, accentato /æt/ prep a; **at the station/the market** alla stazione/al mercato; **at the office/the bank** in ufficio/banca; **at the beginning** all'inizio; **at John's** da john; **at the hairdresser's** dal parrucchiere; **at home** a casa; **at work** al lavoro; **at school** a scuola; **at a party/wedding** a una festa/un matrimonio; **at 1 o'clock** all'una; **at 50 km an hour** a 50 all'ora; **at Christmas/Easter** a Natale/Pasqua; **at times** talvolta; **two at a time** due alla volta; **good at languages** bravo nelle lingue; **at sb's request** su richiesta di qcno; **are you at all worried?** sei preoccupato?

ate /et/ ▷EAT

atheist /'eɪθɪɪst/ n ateo, -a mf

athlete /'æθliːt/ n atleta mf. ~ic adj atletico. ~ics n atletica fsg

Atlantic /ət'læntɪk/ adj & n **the** ~ [Ocean] l'[Oceano m] Atlantico m

atlas /'ætləs/ n atlante m

atmospher|e /'ætməsfɪə(r)/ n atmosfera f. ~ic adj atmosferico

atom /'ætəm/ n atomo m. ~ **bomb** n bomba f atomica

atomic /ə'tɒmɪk/ adj atomico

atrocious /ə'trəʊʃəs/ adj atroce; (meal, weather) abominevole

atrocity /ə'trɒsɪtɪ/ n atrocità f inv

attach /ə'tætʃ/ vt attaccare; attribuire (importance); **be** ~**ed to** fig essere attaccato a

attachment /ə'tætʃmənt/ n (affection) attaccamento m; (accessory) accessorio m; (to email) allegato m

attack /ə'tæk/ n attacco m; (physical) aggressione f ● vt attaccare; (physically) aggredire. ~er n assalitore, -trice mf; (critic) detrattore, -trice mf

attain /ə'teɪn/ vt realizzare (ambition); raggiungere (success, age, goal)

attempt /ə'tempt/ n tentativo m ● vt tentare

attend /ə'tend/ vt essere presente a; (go regularly to) frequentare; (doctor:) avere in cura ● vi essere presente; (pay attention) prestare attenzione. □ ~ **to** vt occuparsi di; (in shop) servire. ~**ance** n presenza f. ~**ant** n guardiano, -a mf

attention /ə'tenʃn/ n attenzione f; ~! (Mil) attenti!; **pay** ~ prestare attenzione; **need** ~ aver bisogno di attenzioni; (skin, hair, plant:) dover essere curato; (car, tyres:) dover essere riparato; **for the** ~ **of** all'attenzione di

attentive /ə'tentɪv/ adj (pupil, audience) attento

attic /'ætɪk/ n soffitta f

attitude /'ætɪtjuːd/ n atteggiamento m

attorney /ə'tɜ:nɪ/ n (Am: lawyer) avvocato m; **power of** ∼ delega f

attract /ə'trækt/ vt attirare. ∼**ion** n attrazione f; (feature) attrattiva f. ∼**ive** adj (person) attraente; (proposal, price) allettante

attribute¹ /'ætrɪbju:t/ n attributo m

attribute² /ə'trɪbju:t/ vt attribuire

aubergine /'əʊbəʒi:n/ n melanzana f

auction /'ɔ:kʃn/ n asta f ● vt vendere all'asta. ∼**eer** n banditore m

audacious /ɔ:'deɪʃəs/ adj sfacciato; (daring) audace. ∼**ty** n sfacciataggine f; (daring) audacia f

audible /'ɔ:dəbl/ adj udibile

audience /'ɔ:dɪəns/ n (Theat) pubblico m; (TV) telespettatori mpl; (Radio) ascoltatori mpl; (meeting) udienza f

audit /'ɔ:dɪt/ n verifica f del bilancio ● vt verificare

audition /ɔ:'dɪʃn/ n audizione f ● vi fare un'audizione

auditor /'ɔ:dɪtə(r)/ n revisore m di conti

auditorium /ɔ:dɪ'tɔ:rɪəm/ n sala f

augment /ɔ:g'ment/ vt aumentare

augur /'ɔ:gə(r)/ vi ∼ **well/ill** essere di buon/cattivo augurio

August /'ɔ:gəst/ n agosto m

aunt /ɑ:nt/ n zia f

au pair /əʊ'peə(r)/ n ∼ **[girl]** ragazza f alla pari

aura /'ɔ:rə/ n aura f

austere /ɒ'stɪə(r)/ adj austero. ∼**ity** n austerità f

Australia /ɒ'streɪlɪə/ n Australia f. ∼**n** adj & n australiano, -a mf

Austria /'ɒstrɪə/ n Austria f. ∼**n** adj & n austriaco, -a mf

authentic /ɔ:'θentɪk/ adj autentico. ∼**ate** vt autenticare. ∼**ity** n autenticità f

author /'ɔ:θə(r)/ n autore m

authoritative /ɔ:'θɒrɪtətɪv/ adj autorevole; (manner) autoritario

authority /ɔ:'θɒrətɪ/ n autorità f; (permission) autorizzazione f; **be in** ∼ **over** avere autorità su

authorization /ɔ:θəraɪ'zeɪʃn/ n autorizzazione f

authorize /'ɔ:θəraɪz/ vt autorizzare

autobiography /ɔ:tə-/ n autobiografia f

autograph /'ɔ:tə-/ n autografo m

automate /'ɔ:təmeɪt/ vt automatizzare

automatic /ɔ:tə'mætɪk/ adj automatico ● n (car) macchina f col cambio automatico; (washing machine) lavatrice f automatica. ∼**ally** adv automaticamente

automation /ɔ:tə'meɪʃn/ n automazione f

automobile /'ɔ:təməbi:l/ n automobile f

autonomous /ɔ:'tɒnəməs/ adj autonomo. ∼**y** n autonomia f

autopsy /'ɔ:tɒpsɪ/ n autopsia f

autumn /'ɔ:təm/ n autunno m. ∼**al** adj autunnale

auxiliary /ɔ:g'zɪlɪərɪ/ adj ausiliario ● n ausiliare m

avail /ə'veɪl/ n **to no** ∼ invano ● vi ∼ **oneself of** approfittare di

available /ə'veɪləbl/ adj disponibile; (book, record etc) in vendita

avalanche /'ævəlɑ:nʃ/ n valanga f

avarice /'ævərɪs/ n avidità f

avenue /'ævənju:/ n viale m; fig strada f

average /'ævərɪdʒ/ adj medio; (mediocre) mediocre ● n media f; **on** ∼ in media ● vt (sales, attendance) etc: raggiungere una media di. □ ∼ **out at** vi risultare in media

averse /ə'vɜ:s/ adj **not be** ∼**e to** sth non essere contro qcsa. ∼**ion** n avversione f (**to** per)

avert /ə'vɜ:t/ vt evitare (crisis); di-

a	
b	

stogliere (eyes)

aviation /eɪvɪˈeɪʃn/ n aviazione f

avid /ˈævɪd/ adj avido (**for** di); (reader) appassionato

avocado /ævəˈkɑːdəʊ/ n avocado m

avoid /əˈvɔɪd/ vt evitare. **~able** adj evitabile

await /əˈweɪt/ vt attendere

awake /əˈweɪk/ adj sveglio; **wide ~** completamente sveglio ● vt (pt awoke, pp awoken) svegliarsi

awaken /əˈweɪkn/ vt svegliare. **~ing** n risveglio m

award /əˈwɔːd/ n premio m; (medal) riconoscimento m; (of prize) assegnazione f ● vt assegnare; (hand over) consegnare

aware /əˈweə(r)/ adj **be ~ of** (sense) percepire; (know) essere conscio di; **become ~ of** accorgersi di, (learn) venire a sapere di: **be ~ that** rendersi conto che. **~ness** n percezione f; (knowledge) consapevolezza f

awash /əˈwɒʃ/ adj inondato (**with** di)

away /əˈweɪ/ adv via; **go/stay ~** andare/stare via; **he's ~ from his desk/the office** non è alla sua scrivania/in ufficio; **far ~** lontano; **four kilometres ~** a quattro chilometri; **play ~** (Sport) giocare fuori casa. **~ game** n partita f fuori casa

awe /ɔː/ n soggezione f

awful /ˈɔːfl/ adj terribile. **~ly** adv terribilmente; (pretty) estremamente

awkward /ˈɔːkwəd/ adj (movement) goffo; (moment, situation) imbarazzante; (time) scomodo. **~ly** adv (move) goffamente; (say) con imbarazzo

awning /ˈɔːnɪŋ/ n tendone m

awoke(n) /əˈwəʊk (ən)/ ▷ AWAKE

axe /æks/ n scure f ● vt (pres p axing) fare dei tagli a (budget); sopprimere (jobs); annullare (project)

axis /ˈæksɪs/ n (pl axes /-siːz/) asse m

axle /ˈæksl/ n (Techn) asse m

Bb

BA n abbr Bachelor of Arts

babble /ˈbæbl/ vi farfugliare; (stream): gorgogliare

baby /ˈbeɪbɪ/ n bambino, -a m/f; (🔳: darling) tesoro m

baby: **~ carriage** n Am carrozzina f. **~ish** adj bambinesco. **~-sit** vi fare da baby-sitter. **~-sitter** n baby-sitter mf

bachelor /ˈbætʃələ(r)/ n scapolo m; B**~ of Arts/Science** laureato, -a mf in lettere/in scienze

back /bæk/ n schiena f; (of horse, hand) dorso m; (of chair) schienale m; (of house, cheque, page) retro m; (in football) difesa f; **at the ~** in fondo; **in the ~** (Auto) dietro; **~ to front** (sweater) il davanti di dietro; **at the ~ of beyond** in un posto sperduto ● adj posteriore; (taxes, payments) arretrato ● adv indietro; (returned) di ritorno; **turn/move ~** tornare/ spostarsi indietro; **put it ~ here/ there** rimettilo qui/là; **~ at home** di ritorno a casa; **I'll be ~ in five minutes** torno fra cinque minuti; **I'm just ~** sono appena tornato; **when do you want the book ~?** quando rivuoi il libro?; **pay ~** ripagare (sb); restituire (money); **~ in power** di nuovo al potere ● vt (support) sostenere; (with money) finanziare; puntare su (horse); (cover the back of) rivestire il retro di ● vi (Auto) fare retromarcia. □ **~ down** vi battere in ritirata. □ **~ in** vi (Auto) entrare in retromarcia; (person:) entrare camminando all'indietro. □ **~ out** vi (Auto) uscire in retromarcia; (person:) uscire camminando all'indietro; *fig* tirarsi indietro (of da). □ ~ **up** *vt* sostenere; confermare (person's alibi); (*Comput*) fare una copia di salvataggio di; **be ~ed up** (traffic): essere congestionato ● *vi* (*Auto*) fare retromarcia

back: ~**ache** *n* mal *m* di schiena. ~**bone** *n* spina *f* dorsale. ~**date** *vt* retrodatare (cheque). ~**'door** *n* porta *f* di servizio

backer /'bækə(r)/ *n* sostenitore, -trice *mf*; (with money) finanziatore, -trice *mf*

back: ~**'fire** *vi* (*Auto*) avere un ritorno di fiamma; (fig: plan) fallire. ~**ground** *n* sfondo *m*; (environment) ambiente *m*. ~**hand** *n* (tennis) rovescio *m*

backing /'bækɪŋ/ *n* (support) supporto *m*; (material) riserva *f*; (*Mus*) accompagnamento *m*; ~ **group** gruppo *m* d'accompagnamento

back: ~**lash** *n* fig reazione *f* opposta. ~**log** *n* ~**log of work** lavoro *m* arretrato. ~**side** *n* 🖪 fondoschiena *m inv.* ~**slash** *n* (*Typ*) barra *f* retroversa. ~**stage** *adj* & *adv* dietro le quinte. ~**stroke** *n* dorso *m*. ~**-up** *n* rinforzi *mpl*; (*Comput*) riserva *f*

backward /'bækwəd/ *adj* (step) indietro; (child) lento nell'apprendimento; (country) arretrato ● *adv* ~**s** (also Am: ~) indietro; (fall, walk) all'indietro; ~**s and forwards** avanti e indietro

back: ~**water** *n* fig luogo *m* allo scarto. ~**'yard** *n* cortile *m*

bacon /'beɪkn/ *n* ≈ pancetta *f*

bacteria /bæk'tɪərɪə/ *npl* batteri *mpl*

bad /bæd/ *adj* (worse, worst) cattivo; (weather, habit, news, accident) brutto; (apple etc) marcio; **the light is** ~ non c'è una buona luce; **use** ~ **language** dire delle parolacce; **feel** ~ sentirsi male; (feel guilty) sentirsi in colpa; **have a** ~ **back** avere dei problemi alla schiena; **smoking is** ~ **for you** fumare fa male; **go** ~ an-

dare a male; **that's just too** ~! pazienza!; **not** ~ niente male

bade /bæd/ ▶ **BID**

badge /bædʒ/ *n* distintivo *m*

badger /'bædʒə(r)/ *n* tasso *m* ● *vt* tormentare

badly /'bædlɪ/ *adv* male; (hurt) gravemente; ~ **off** povero; ~ **behaved** maleducato; **need** ~ aver estremamente bisogno di

bad-'mannered *adj* maleducato

badminton /'bædmɪntən/ *n* badminton *m*

bad-'tempered *adj* irascibile

baffle /'bæfl/ *vt* confondere

bag /bæg/ *n* borsa *f*; (of paper) sacchetto *m*; **old** ~ 🖾 megera *f*; ~**s under the eyes** occhiaie *fpl*; ~**s of** 🖪 un sacco di

baggage /'bægɪdʒ/ *n* bagagli *mpl*

baggy /'bægɪ/ *adj* (clothes) ampio

'bagpipes *npl* cornamusa *fsg*

bail /beɪl/ *n* cauzione *f*; **on** ~ su cauzione ● **bail out** *vt* (*Naut*) aggottare; ~ **sb out** (*Jur*) pagare la cauzione per qcno ● *vi* (*Aeron*) paracadutarsi

bait /beɪt/ *n* esca *f* ● *vt* innescare; (fig: torment) tormentare

bake /beɪk/ *vt* cuocere al forno; (make) fare ● *vi* cuocersi al forno

baker /'beɪkə(r)/ *n* fornaio, -a *mf*, panettiere, -a *mf*; ~**'s [shop]** panetteria *f*. ~**y** *n* panificio *m*, forno *m*

balance /'bæləns/ *n* equilibrio *m*; (*Comm*) bilancio *m*; (outstanding sum) saldo *m*; [**bank**] ~ saldo *m*; **be** or **hang in the** ~ *fig* essere in sospeso ● *vt* bilanciare; equilibrare (budget); (*Comm*) fare il bilancio di (books) ● *vi* bilanciarsi; (*Comm*) essere in pareggio. ~**d** *adj* equilibrato. ~ **sheet** *n* bilancio *m* [d'esercizio]

balcony /'bælkənɪ/ *n* balcone *m*

bald /bɔːld/ *adj* (person) calvo; (tyre) liscio; (statement) nudo e crudo; **go**

~ perdere i capelli

bale /beɪl/ n balla f

ball[1] /bɔːl/ n palla f; (football) pallone m; (of yarn) gomitolo m; **on the ~** [T] sveglio

ball[2] (dance) ballo m

ballad /ˈbæləd/ n ballata f

ballast /ˈbæləst/ n zavorra f

ball-'bearing n cuscinetto m a sfera

ballerina /bæləˈriːnə/ n ballerina f [classica]

ballet /ˈbæleɪ/ n balletto m; (art form) danza f; **~ dancer** n ballerino, -a mf [classico, -a]

balloon /bəˈluːn/ n pallone m; (Aeron) mongolfiera f

ballot /ˈbælət/ n votazione f. **~-box** n urna f. **~-paper** n scheda f di votazione

ball: **~-point** ['pen] n penna f a sfera. **~room** n sala f da ballo

Baltic /ˈbɔːltɪk/ adj & n **the ~** [Sea] il [mar] Baltico

bamboo /bæmˈbuː/ n bambù m inv

ban /bæn/ n proibizione f ● vt (pt/pp banned) proibire; **~ from** espellere da (club); **she was ~ned** from driving le hanno ritirato la patente

banal /bəˈnɑːl/ adj banale. **~ity** n banalità f inv

banana /bəˈnɑːnə/ n banana f

band /bænd/ n (strip) nastro m; (Mus: pop group) complesso m; (Mus: brass) ~ banda f; (Mil) fanfara f ● **band together** vi riunirsi

bandage /ˈbændɪdʒ/ n benda f ● vt fasciare (limb)

b. & b. abbr bed and breakfast

bandit /ˈbændɪt/ n bandito m

band: **~stand** n palco m coperto [dell'orchestra]. **~wagon** n **jump on the ~wagon** fig seguire la corrente

bandy[1] /ˈbændɪ/ vt (pt/pp -ied)

scambiarsi (words). □ **~ about** vt far circolare

bandy[2] adj (-ier, -iest) **be ~** avere le gambe storte

bang /bæŋ/ n (noise) fragore m; (of gun, firework) scoppio m; (blow) colpo m ● adv ~ **in the middle of** [T] proprio nel mezzo di; **go ~** (gun:) sparare; (balloon:) esplodere ● int bum! ● vt battere (fist); battere su (table); sbattere (door, head) ● vi scoppiare; (door:) sbattere

banger /ˈbæŋə(r)/ n (firework) petardo m; ([T]: sausage) salsiccia f; **old ~** ([T]: car) macinino m

bangle /ˈbæŋgl/ n braccialetto m

banish /ˈbænɪʃ/ vt bandire

banisters /ˈbænɪstəz/ npl ringhiera fsg

bank[1] /bæŋk/ n (of river) sponda f; (slope) scarpata f ● vi (Aeron) inclinarsi in virata

bank[2] n banca f ● vt depositare in banca ● vi ~ **with** avere un conto [bancario] presso. □ **~ on** vt contare su

'bank card n carta f di assegno.

banker /ˈbæŋkə(r)/ n banchiere m

bank: **~ 'holiday** n giorno m festivo. **~ing** n bancario m. **~note** n banconota f

bankrupt /ˈbæŋkrʌpt/ adj fallito; **go ~** fallire ● n persona f che ha fatto fallimento ● vt far fallire. **~cy** n bancarotta f

banner /ˈbænə(r)/ n stendardo m; (of demonstrators) striscione m

banquet /ˈbæŋkwɪt/ n banchetto m

banter /ˈbæntə(r)/ n battute fpl di spirito

baptism /ˈbæptɪzm/ n battesimo m

Baptist /ˈbæptɪst/ adj & n battista mf

baptize /bæpˈtaɪz/ vt battezzare

bar /bɑː(r)/ n sbarra f; (Jur) ordine m degli avvocati; (of chocolate) tavoletta f; (café) bar m inv; (counter) banco m; (Mus) battuta f; ~ **of soap/gold** saponetta f/lingotto m; **behind** ~**s** ① dietro le sbarre ● vt (pt/pp **barred**) sbarrare (way); sprangare (door); escludere (person) ● prep tranne; ~ **none** in assoluto

barbarian /bɑːˈbeərɪən/ n barbaro, -a mf

barbar|ic /bɑːˈbærɪk/ adj barbarico. ~**ity** n barbarie f inv. ~**ous** adj barbaro

barbecue /ˈbɑːbɪkjuː/ n barbecue m inv; (party) grigliata f, barbecue m inv ● vt arrostire sul barbecue

barber /ˈbɑːbə(r)/ n barbiere m

bare /beə(r)/ adj nudo; (tree, room) spoglio; (floor) senza moquette ● vt scoprire; mostrare (teeth)

bare: ~**back** adv senza sella. ~**faced** adj sfacciato. ~**foot** adv scalzo. ~'**headed** adj a capo scoperto

barely /ˈbeəlɪ/ adv appena

bargain /ˈbɑːgɪn/ n (agreement) patto m; (good buy) affare m. **into the** ~ per di più ● vi contrattare; (haggle) trattare. □ ~ **for** vt (expect) aspettarsi

barge /bɑːdʒ/ n barcone m ● **barge in** vi ① (to room) piombare dentro; (into conversation) interrompere bruscamente. ~ **into** vt piombare dentro a (room); venire addosso a (person)

baritone /ˈbærɪtəʊn/ n baritono m

bark¹ /bɑːk/ n (of tree) corteccia f

bark² n abbaiamento m ● vi abbaiare

barley /ˈbɑːlɪ/ n orzo m

bar: ~**maid** n barista f. ~**man** n barista m

barmy /ˈbɑːmɪ/ adj ① strampalato

barn /bɑːn/ n granaio m

barometer /bəˈrɒmɪtə(r)/ n barometro m

baron /ˈbærn/ n barone m. ~**ess** n

baronessa f

baroque /bəˈrɒk/ adj & n barocco m

barracks /ˈbærəks/ npl caserma fsg

barrage /ˈbærɑːʒ/ n (Mil) sbarramento m; (fig: of criticism) sfilza f

barrel /ˈbærl/ n barile m, botte f; (of gun) canna f. ~**organ** n organetto m [a cilindro]

barren /ˈbærən/ adj sterile; (landscape) brullo

barricade /ˈbærɪˈkeɪd/ n barricata f ● vt barricare

barrier /ˈbærɪə(r)/ n barriera f; (Rail) cancello m; fig ostacolo m

barrister /ˈbærɪstə(r)/ n avvocato m

barter /ˈbɑːtə(r)/ vi barattare (for con)

base /beɪs/ n base f ● adj vile ● vt basare; **be** ~**d on** basarsi su

base: ~**ball** n baseball m. ~**ment** n seminterrato m

bash /bæʃ/ n colpo m [violento] ● vt colpire [violentemente]; (dent) ammaccare; ~**ed in** adj ammaccato

bashful /ˈbæʃfl/ adj timido

basic /ˈbeɪsɪk/ adj di base; (condition, requirement) basilare; (living conditions) povero; **my Italian is pretty** ~ il mio italiano è abbastanza rudimentale; **the** ~**s** (of language, science) i rudimenti; (essentials) l'essenziale m. ~**ally** adv fondamentalmente

basil /ˈbæzɪl/ n basilico m

basin /ˈbeɪsn/ n bacinella f; (washhand ~) lavabo m; (for food) recipiente m; (Geog) bacino m

basis /ˈbeɪsɪs/ n (pl -**ses** /-siːz/) base f

bask /bɑːsk/ vi crogiolarsi

basket /ˈbɑːskɪt/ n cestino m. ~**ball** n pallacanestro f

bass /beɪs/ adj basso; ~ **voice** voce f di basso ● n basso m

bastard /'bɑːstəd/ n (*illegitimate child*) bastardo, -a *mf*; ⊠ figlio *m* di puttana

bat[1] /bæt/ n mazza *f*; (*for table tennis*) racchetta *f*; **off one's own ~** 🔲 tutto da solo ● vt (*pt/pp* batted) battere; **she didn't ~ an eyelid** *fig* non ha battuto ciglio

bat[2] n (*Zool*) pipistrello *m*

batch /bætʃ/ n gruppo *m*; (*of goods*) partita *f*; (*of bread*) infornata *f*

bated /'beɪtɪd/ adj **with ~ breath** col fiato sospeso

bath /bɑːθ/ n (*pl* ~s /bɑːðz/) bagno *m*; (*tub*) vasca *f* da bagno; ~**s** *pl* piscina *f*; **have a ~** fare un bagno ● vt fare il bagno a

bathe /beɪð/ n bagno *m* ● vi fare il bagno ● vt lavare (*wound*). ~**r** n bagnante *mf*

bathing /'beɪðɪŋ/ n bagni *mpl*. ~**-cap** n cuffia *f*. ~**-costume** n costume *m* da bagno

bathroom n bagno *m*

battalion /bə'tælɪən/ n battaglione *m*

batter /'bætə(r)/ n (*Culin*) pastella *f*; ~**ed** adj (*car*) malandato; (*wife, baby*) maltrattato

battery /'bætərɪ/ n batteria *f*; (*of torch, radio*) pila *f*

battle /'bætl/ n battaglia *f*; *fig* lotta *f* ● vi *fig* lottare

battle: ~**field** n campo *m* di battaglia. ~**ship** n corazzata *f*

bawl /bɔːl/ vt/i urlare

bay[1] /beɪ/ n (*Geog*) baia *f*

bay[2] n **keep at ~** tenere a bada

bay[3] n (*Bot*) alloro *m*. ~**-leaf** n foglia *f* d'alloro

bayonet /'beɪənɪt/ n baionetta *f*

bay 'window n bay window *f inv* (*grande finestra sporgente*)

bazaar /bə'zɑː(r)/ n bazar *m inv*

BC abbr (*before Christ*) a.C.

be /biː/

● vi (*pres* am, are, is, are; *pt* was, were; *pp* been) essere; **he is a teacher** è insegnante, fa l'insegnante; **what do you want to be?** cosa vuoi fare?; **be quiet!** sta' zitto!; **I am cold/hot** ho freddo/caldo; **it's cold/hot, isn't it?** fa freddo/caldo, vero?; **how are you?** come stai?; **I am well** sto bene; **there is** c'è; **there are** ci sono; **I have been to Venice** sono stato a Venezia; **has the postman been?** è passato il postino?; **you're coming too, aren't you?** vieni anche tu, no?; **it's yours, is it?** è tuo, vero?; **was John there? – yes, he was** c'era John? – sì; **John wasn't there – yes he was!** John non c'era – sì che c'era!; **three and three are six** tre più tre fanno sei; **he is five** ha cinque anni; **that will be £10, please** fanno 10 sterline, per favore; **how much is it?** quanto costa?; **that's £5 you owe me** mi devi 5 sterline

● v aux **I am coming/reading** sto venendo/leggendo; **I'm staying** (*not leaving*) resto; **I am being lazy** sono pigro; **I was thinking of you** stavo pensando a te; **you are not to tell him** non devi dirglielo; **you are to do that immediately** devi farlo subito

● passive essere; **I have been robbed** sono stato derubato

beach /biːtʃ/ n spiaggia *f*. ~**wear** n abbigliamento *m* da spiaggia

bead /biːd/ n perlina *f*

beak /biːk/ n becco *m*

beaker /'biːkə(r)/ n coppa *f*

beam /biːm/ n trave *f*; (*of light*) raggio *m* ● vi irradiare; (*person:*) essere raggiante. ~**ing** adj raggiante

bean /biːn/ n fagiolo m; (of coffee) chicco m

bear[1] /beə(r)/ n orso m

bear[2] v (pt **bore**, pp **borne**) ●vt (endure) sopportare; mettere al mondo (child); (carry) portare; ~ **in mind** tenere presente ●vi ~ **left/right** andare a sinistra/a destra. □ ~ **with** vt aver pazienza con. **~able** adj sopportabile

beard /bɪəd/ n barba f. **~ed** adj barbuto

bearer /ˈbeərə(r)/ n portatore, -trice mf; (of passport) titolare mf

bearing /ˈbeərɪŋ/ n portamento m; (Techn) cuscinetto m [a sfera]; **have a ~ on** avere attinenza con; **get one's ~s** orientarsi

beast /biːst/ n bestia f; (fig: person) animale m

beat /biːt/ n battito m; (rhythm) battuta f; (of policeman) giro m d'ispezione ●v (pt **beat**, pp **beaten**) ●vt battere; picchiare (person); ~ **it!** darsela a gambe; **it ~s me why...** fig non capisco proprio perché. **beat up** vt picchiare

beating /ˈbiːtɪŋ/ n bastonata f; **get a ~ing** (with fists) essere preso a pugni; (team, player:) prendere una batosta

beautician /bjuːˈtɪʃn/ n estetista mf

beauti|ful /ˈbjuːtɪfl/ adj bello. **~fully** adv splendidamente

beauty /ˈbjuːtɪ/ n bellezza f. ~ **parlour** n istituto m di bellezza. ~ **spot** n neo m; (place) luogo m pittoresco

beaver /ˈbiːvə(r)/ n castoro m

became /bɪˈkeɪm/ ▷**BECOME**

because /bɪˈkɒz/ conj perché; ~ **you didn't tell me, I...** poiché non me lo hai detto,... ●adv ~ **of** a causa di

beckon /ˈbekn/ vt/i ~ [**to**] chiamare con un cenno

becom|e /bɪˈkʌm/ v (pt **became**, pp **become**) ●vt diventare ●vi diventare; **what has ~ of her?** che ne è di lei? **~ing** adj (clothes) bello

bed /bed/ n letto m; (of sea, lake) fondo m; (layer) strato m; (of flowers) aiuola f; **in ~** a letto; **go to ~** andare a letto; ~ **and breakfast** pensione f familiare in cui il prezzo della camera comprende la prima colazione. **~clothes** npl lenzuola fpl e coperte fpl. **~ding** n biancheria f per il letto, materasso e guanciali

bed: **~room** n camera f da letto. ~ **'sitter** n = camera f ammobiliata fornita di cucina. **~spread** n copriletto m. **~time** n l'ora f di andare a letto

bee /biː/ n ape f

beech /biːtʃ/ n faggio m

beef /biːf/ n manzo m. **~burger** n hamburger m inv

bee: **~hive** n alveare m. **~-line** n **make a ~line for** fig precipitarsi verso

been /biːn/ ▷**BE**

beer /bɪə(r)/ n birra f

beetle /ˈbiːtl/ n scarafaggio m

beetroot /ˈbiːtruːt/ n barbabietola f

before /bɪˈfɔː(r)/ prep prima di; **the day ~ yesterday** ieri l'altro; ~ **long** fra poco ●adv prima; **never ~ have I seen...** non ho mai visto prima...; ~ **that** prima; ~ **going** prima di andare ●conj (time) prima che; ~ **you go** prima che tu vada. **~hand** adv in anticipo

befriend /bɪˈfrend/ vt trattare da amico

beg /beg/ v (pt/pp **begged**) ●vi mendicare ●vt pregare; chiedere (favour, forgiveness)

began /bɪˈgæn/ ▷**BEGIN**

beggar /ˈbegə(r)/ n mendicante mf; **poor ~!** povero cristo!

begin /bɪˈgɪn/ vt/i (pt **began**, pp **begun**, pres p **beginning**) cominciare. **~ner** n principiante mf. **~ning**

n principio *m*

begrudge /bɪˈgrʌdʒ/ *vt* (envy) essere invidioso di; dare malvolentieri (money)

begun /bɪˈgʌn/ ▷BEGIN

behalf /bɪˈhɑːf/ *n* on ~ of a nome di; on my ~ a nome mio

behave /bɪˈheɪv/ *vi* comportarsi; ~ [oneself] comportarsi bene

behaviour /bɪˈheɪvjə(r)/ *n* comportamento *m*; (of prisoner, soldier) condotta *f*

behead /bɪˈhed/ *vt* decapitare

behind /bɪˈhaɪnd/ *prep* dietro; be ~ sth *fig* stare dietro qcsa ● *adv* dietro, indietro; (late) in ritardo; a long way ~ molto indietro ● *n* [] didietro *m*. ~hand *adv* indietro

beige /beɪʒ/ *adj* & *n* beige *m inv*

being /ˈbiːɪŋ/ *n* essere *m*; come into ~ nascere

belated /bɪˈleɪtɪd/ *adj* tardivo

belch /beltʃ/ *vi* ruttare ● *vt* ~ [out] eruttare (smoke)

belfry /ˈbelfrɪ/ *n* campanile *m*

Belgian /ˈbeldʒən/ *adj* & *n* belga *mf*

Belgium /ˈbeldʒəm/ *n* Belgio *m*

belief /bɪˈliːf/ *n* fede *f*; (opinion) convinzione *f*

believe /bɪˈliːv/ *vt/i* credere. ~r *n* (Relig) credente *mf*; be a great ~r in credere fermamente in

belittle /bɪˈlɪtl/ *vt* sminuire (person, achievements)

bell /bel/ *n* campana *f*; (on door) campanello *m*

belligerent /bɪˈlɪdʒərənt/ *adj* belligerante; (aggressive) bellicoso

bellow /ˈbeləʊ/ *vi* gridare a squarciagola; (animal:) muggire

bellows /ˈbeləʊz/ *npl* (for fire) soffietto *msg*

belly /ˈbelɪ/ *n* pancia *f*

belong /bɪˈlɒŋ/ *vi* appartenere (to a); (be member) essere socio (to di). ~ings *npl* cose *fpl*

beloved /bɪˈlʌvɪd/ *adj* & *n* amato, -a *mf*

below /bɪˈləʊ/ *prep* sotto; (with numbers) al di sotto di ● *adv* sotto, di sotto; (Naut) sotto coperta; see ~ guardare qui di seguito

belt /belt/ *n* cintura *f*; (area) zona *f*; (Techn) cinghia *f* ● *vi* ~ along ([]: rush) filare velocemente ● *vt* ([]: hit) picchiare

bench /bentʃ/ *n* panchina *f*; (work~) piano *m* da lavoro; the B~ (Jur) la magistratura

bend /bend/ *n* curva *f*; (of river) ansa *f* ● *v* (pt/pp bent) ● *vt* piegare ● *vi* piegarsi; (road:) curvare; ~ [down] chinarsi. □ ~ over *vi* inchinarsi

beneath /bɪˈniːθ/ *prep* sotto, al di sotto di; he thinks it's ~ him *fig* pensa che sia sotto al suo livello ● *adv* giù

beneficial /benɪˈfɪʃl/ *adj* benefico

beneficiary /benɪˈfɪʃərɪ/ *n* beneficiario, -a *mf*

benefit /ˈbenɪfɪt/ *n* vantaggio *m*; (allowance) indennità *f inv* ● *v* (pt/pp -fited, pres p -fiting) ● *vt* giovare a ● *vi* trarre vantaggio (from da)

benign /bɪˈnaɪn/ *adj* benevolo; (Med) benigno

bent /bent/ ▷BEND ● *adj* (person) ricurvo; (distorted) curvato; ([]: dishonest) corrotto; be ~ on doing sth essere ben deciso a fare qcsa ● *n* predisposizione *f*

bereave|d /bɪˈriːvd/ *n* the ~d *pl* i familiari del defunto. ~ment *n* lutto *m*

beret /ˈbereɪ/ *n* berretto *m*

berry /ˈberɪ/ *n* bacca *f*

berserk /bəˈsɜːk/ *adj* go ~ diventare una belva

berth /bɜːθ/ *n* (in bed) cuccetta *f*; (anchorage) ormeggio *m* ● *vi* ormeggiare

beside /bɪˈsaɪd/ *prep* accanto a; ~ oneself fuori di sé

besides /bɪˈsaɪdz/ *prep* oltre a

●*adv* inoltre

besiege /bɪ'siːdʒ/ *vt* assediare

best /best/ *adj* migliore; **the ~ part of a year** la maggior parte dell'anno; **~ before** (*Comm*) preferibilmente prima di ●*n* **the ~** il meglio; (*person*) il/la migliore; **at ~** a tutt'al più; **all the ~!** tanti auguri!; **do one's ~** fare del proprio meglio; **to the ~ of my knowledge** per quel che ne so; **make the ~ of it** cogliere il lato buono della cosa ●*adv* meglio, nel modo migliore; **as ~ I could** meglio che potevo. **~ 'man** *n* testimone *m*

bestow /bɪ'stəʊ/ *vt* conferire ('on a)

best'seller *n* bestseller *m inv*

bet /bet/ *n* scommessa *f* ●*vt/i* (*pt/pp* **bet** *or* **betted**) scommettere

betray /bɪ'treɪ/ *vt* tradire. **~al** *n* tradimento *m*

better /'betə(r)/ *adj* migliore, meglio; **get ~** migliorare; (*after illness*) rimettersi ●*adv* meglio; (*wealthier*) più ricco; **all the ~** tanto meglio; **the sooner the ~** prima è, meglio è; **I've thought ~ of it** ci ho ripensato; **you'd ~ stay** faresti meglio a restare; **I'd ~ not** è meglio che non lo faccia ●*vt* migliorare; **~ oneself** migliorare le proprie condizioni

between /bɪ'twiːn/ *prep* fra, tra; **~ you and me** detto fra di noi; **~ us** (*together*) tra me e te ●*adv* **[in] ~** in mezzo; (*time*) frattempo

beverage /'bevərɪdʒ/ *n* bevanda *f*

beware /bɪ'weə(r)/ *vi* guardarsi (**of** da); **~ of the dog!** attenti al cane!

bewilder /bɪ'wɪldə(r)/ *vt* disorientare; **~ed** perplesso. **~ment** *n* perplessità *f*

beyond /bɪ'jɒnd/ *prep* oltre; **~ reach** irraggiungibile; **~ doubt** senza alcun dubbio; **~ belief** da non credere; **it's ~ me** 𝕀 non riesco proprio a capire ●*adv* più in là

bias /'baɪəs/ *n* (*preference*) preferenza *f*; *pej* pregiudizio *m* ●*vt* (*pt/pp* **biased**) (*influence*) influenzare. **~ed** *adj* parziale

bib /bɪb/ *n* bavaglino *m*

Bible /'baɪbl/ *n* Bibbia *f*

biblical /'bɪblɪkl/ *adj* biblico

biceps /'baɪseps/ *n* bicipite *m*

bicker /'bɪkə(r)/ *vi* litigare

bicycle /'baɪsɪkl/ *n* bicicletta *f* ●*vi* andare in bicicletta

bid[1] /bɪd/ *n* offerta *f*; (*attempt*) tentativo *m* ●*vt/i* (*pt/pp* **bid**, *pres p* **bidding**) offrire; (*in cards*) dichiarare

bid[2] *vt* (*pt* **bade** *or* **bid**, *pp* **bidden** *or* **bid**, *pres p* **bidding**) *liter* (*command*) comandare; **~ sb welcome** dare il benvenuto a qcno

bidder /'bɪdə(r)/ *n* offerente *mf*

bide /baɪd/ *vt* **~ one's time** aspettare il momento buono

bifocals /baɪ'fəʊklz/ *npl* occhiali *mpl* bifocali

big /bɪg/ *adj* (**bigger, biggest**) grande; (*brother, sister*) più grande; (𝕀) generoso ●*adv* **talk ~** 𝕀 spararle grosse

bigam|ist /'bɪgəmɪst/ *n* bigamo, -a *mf*. **~y** *n* bigamia *f*

big-'headed *adj* 𝕀 gasato

bigot /'bɪgət/ *n* fanatico, -a *mf*. **~ed** *adj* di mentalità ristretta

bike /baɪk/ *n* 𝕀 bici *f inv*

bikini /bɪ'kiːni/ *n* bikini *m inv*

bile /baɪl/ *n* bile *f*

bilingual /baɪ'lɪŋgwəl/ *adj* bilingue

bill[1] /bɪl/ *n* fattura *f*; (*in restaurant etc*) conto *m*; (*poster*) manifesto *m*; (*Pol*) progetto *m* di legge; (*Am: note*) biglietto *m* di banca ●*vt* fatturare

bill[2] *n* (*beak*) becco *m*

'billfold *n* *Am* portafoglio *m*

billiards /'bɪljədz/ *n* biliardo *m*

billion /'bɪljən/ *n* (*thousand million*) miliardo *m*; (*old-fashioned Br: million million*) mille miliardi *mpl*

bin /bɪn/ n bidone m

bind /baɪnd/ vt (pt/pp bound) legare (to a); (bandage) fasciare; (Jur) obbligare.~ ing (promise, contract) vincolante ● n (of book) rilegatura f; (on ski) attacco m [di sicurezza]

binge /bɪndʒ/ n fam ~ fare baldoria; (eat a lot) abbuffarsi ● vi abbuffarsi (on di)

binoculars /bɪ'nɒkjʊləz/ npl [pair of] ~ binocolo msg

biograph|er /baɪ'ɒgrəfə(r)/ n biografo, -a mf. ~y n biografia f

biological /baɪə'lɒdʒɪkl/ adj biologico

biolog|ist /baɪ'ɒlədʒɪst/ n biologo, -a mf. ~y n biologia f

birch /bɜːtʃ/ n (tree) betulla f

bird /bɜːd/ n uccello m; (□: girl) ragazza f

Biro® /'baɪrəʊ/ n biro® f inv

birth /bɜːθ/ n nascita f

birth: ~ **certificate** n certificato m di nascita. ~**control** n controllo m delle nascite. ~**day** n compleanno m. ~**mark** n voglia f. ~**rate** n natalità f

biscuit /'bɪskɪt/ n biscotto m

bisect /baɪ'sekt/ vt dividere in due [parti]

bishop /'bɪʃəp/ n vescovo m; (in chess) alfiere m

bit¹ /bɪt/ n pezzo m; (smaller) pezzetto m; (for horse) morso m; (Comput) bit m inv; a ~ **of** un pezzo di (cheese, paper); un po' di (time, rain, silence); ~ **by** ~ poco a poco; **do one's** ~ fare la propria parte

bit² ▷**BITE**

bitch /bɪtʃ/ n cagna f; (✗) stronza f. ~y adj velenoso

bit|e /baɪt/ n morso m; (insect ~) puntura f; (mouthful) boccone m ● vt (pt **bit**, pp **bitten**) mordere; (insect:) pungere; ~**e one's nails** mangiarsi le unghie ● vi mordere; (insect:) pungere. ~**ing** adj (wind, criticism) pun-

gente; (remark) mordace

bitter /'bɪtə(r)/ adj amaro ● n Br birra f amara. ~**ly** adv amaramente; **it's** ~**ly** cold c'è un freddo pungente. ~**ness** n amarezza f

bizarre /bɪ'zɑː(r)/ adj bizzarro

black /blæk/ adj nero; **be** ~ **and blue** essere pieno di lividi ● n negro, -a mf ● vt boicottare (goods). □ ~ **out** vt cancellare ● vi (lose consciousness) perdere coscienza

black: ~**berry** n mora f. ~**bird** n merlo m. ~**board** n (Sch) lavagna f. ~**currant** n ribes m inv nero; ~ **eye** n occhio m nero. ~ '**ice** n ghiaccio m (sulla strada). ~**leg** n Br crumiro m. ~**list** vt mettere sulla lista nera. ~**mail** n ricatto m ● vt ricattare. ~**mailer** n ricattatore, -trice mf. ~**-out** n blackout m inv; **have a** ~**-out** (Med) perdere coscienza. ~**smith** n fabbro m

bladder /'blædə(r)/ n (Anat) vescica f

blade /bleɪd/ n lama f; (of grass) filo m

blame /bleɪm/ n colpa f ● vt dare la colpa a; ~ **sb for doing sth** dare la colpa a qcno per aver fatto qcsa; **no one is to** ~ non è colpa di nessuno. ~**less** adj innocente

bland /blænd/ adj (food) insipido; (person) insulso

blank /blæŋk/ adj bianco; (look) vuoto ● n spazio m vuoto; (cartridge) a salve. ~ '**cheque** n assegno m in bianco

blanket /'blæŋkɪt/ n coperta f

blare /bleə(r)/ vi suonare a tutto volume. □ ~ **out** vt far risuonare ● vi (music, radio:) strillare

blaspheme /blæs'fiːm/ vi bestemmiare

blasphem|ous /'blæsfəməs/ adj blasfemo. ~y n bestemmia f

blast /blɑːst/ n (gust) raffica f; (sound) scoppio m ● vt (with explosive) far saltare • int ⊠ maledizione!. ~ed adj ⊠ maledetto

blast-off n (of missile) lancio m

blatant /'bleɪtənt/ adj sfacciato

blaze /bleɪz/ n incendio m; a ~ of colour un'esplosione f di colori • vi ardere

blazer /'bleɪzə(r)/ n blazer m inv

bleach /bliːtʃ/ n decolorante m; (for cleaning) candeggina f • vt sbiancare; ossigenare (hair)

bleak /bliːk/ adj desolato; (fig: prospects, future) tetro

bleat /bliːt/ vi belare • n belato m

bleed /bliːd/ v (pt/pp bled) • vi sanguinare • vt spurgare (brakes, radiator)

bleep /bliːp/ n bip m • vi suonare • vt chiamare (col cercapersone) (doctor). ~er n cercapersone m inv

blemish /'blemɪʃ/ n macchia f

blend /blend/ n (of tea, coffee, whisky) miscela f; (of colours) insieme m • vt mescolare • vi (colours, sounds:) fondersi (with con). ~er n (Culin) frullatore m

bless /bles/ vt benedire. ~ed adj also ⊠ benedetto. ~ing n benedizione f

blew /bluː/ ▷ BLOW

blight /blaɪt/ n (Bot) ruggine f • vt far avvizzire (plants)

blind[1] /blaɪnd/ adj cieco; **the ~** npl i ciechi mpl; ~ **man/woman** cieco/cieca • vt accecare

blind[2] n [roller] ~ avvolgibile m; [Venetian] ~ veneziana f

blind: ~ **alley** n vicolo m cieco. ~fold adj be ~fold avere gli occhi bendati • n benda f • vt bendare gli occhi a. ~ly adv ciecamente. ~ness n cecità f

blink /blɪŋk/ vi sbattere le palpebre; (light:) tremolare

blinkers /'blɪŋkəz/ npl paraocchi mpl

bliss /blɪs/ n (Rel) beatitudine f; (happiness) felicità f. ~ful adj beato;

(happy) meraviglioso

blister /'blɪstə(r)/ n (Med) vescica f; (in paint) bolla f • vi (paint:) formare una bolla/delle bolle

blizzard /'blɪzəd/ n tormenta f

bloated /'bləʊtɪd/ adj gonfio

blob /blɒb/ n goccia f

bloc /blɒk/ n (Pol) blocco m

block /blɒk/ n blocco m; (building) isolato m; (building ~) cubo m (per giochi di costruzione); ~ **of flats** palazzo m • vt bloccare. □ ~ **up** vt bloccare

blockade /blɒ'keɪd/ n blocco m • vt bloccare

blockage /'blɒkɪdʒ/ n ostruzione f

block: ~**head** n ⊡ testone, -a mf. ~ **'letters** npl stampatello m

bloke /bləʊk/ n ⊡ tizio m

blonde /blɒnd/ adj biondo • n bionda f

blood /blʌd/ n sangue m

blood: ~ **bath** n bagno m di sangue. ~ **group** n gruppo m sanguigno. ~**hound** n segugio m. ~ **pressure** n pressione f del sangue. ~**shed** n spargimento m di sangue. ~**shot** adj iniettato di sangue. ~**stream** n sangue m. ~**thirsty** adj assetato di sangue

bloody /'blʌdɪ/ adj (-ier, -iest) insanguinato; ⊠ maledetto • adv ⊠ ~ **easy/difficult** facile/difficile da matti. ~-'**minded** adj scorbutico

bloom /bluːm/ n fiore m; **in ~** (flower:) sbocciato; (tree:) in fiore • vi fiorire; fig essere in forma smagliante

blossom /'blɒsəm/ n fiori mpl (d'albero); (single one) fiore m • vi sbocciare

blot /blɒt/ n also fig macchia f • blot out vt (pt/pp blotted) fig cancellare

blotch /blɒtʃ/ n macchia f. ~y adj chiazzato

'**blotting-paper** n carta f assorbente

blouse /blaʊz/ n camicetta f

blow¹ /bləʊ/ n colpo m

blow² v (pt blew, pp blown) ● vi (wind): soffiare; (fuse): saltare ● vt (🅸: squander) sperperare; ~ one's nose soffiarsi il naso. □ ~ away vt far volar via (papers) ● vi (papers): volare via. □ ~ down vt abbattere ● vi abbattersi al suolo. □ ~ out vt (extinguish) spegnere. □ ~ over vi (storm): passare; (fuss, trouble): dissiparsi. □ ~ up vt (inflate) gonfiare; (enlarge) ingrandire (photograph); (by explosion) far esplodere ● vi esplodere

blow: ~-dry vt asciugare col fon. ~lamp n fiamma f ossidrica

'blowtorch n fiamma f ossidrica

blue /bluː/ adj (pale) celeste; (navy) blu inv; (royal) azzurro; ~ with cold livido per il freddo ● n blu m inv; have the ~s essere giù [di tono]; out of the ~ inaspettatamente

blue: ~bell n giacinto m di bosco. ~berry n mirtillo m. ~bottle n moscone m. ~ film n film m inv a luci rosse. ~print n fig riferimento m

bluff /blʌf/ n bluff m inv ● vi bluffare

blunder /'blʌndə(r)/ n gaffe f inv ● vi fare una/delle gaffe

blunt /blʌnt/ adj spuntato; (person) reciso. ~ly adv schiettamente

blur /blɜː(r)/ n it's all a ~ fig è tutto un insieme confuso ● vt (pt/pp blurred) rendere confuso. ~red adj (vision, photo) sfocato

blurb /blɜːb/ n soffietto m editoriale

blurt /blɜːt/ vt ~ out spifferare

blush /blʌʃ/ n rossore m ● vi arrossire

BMI n abbr (body mass index) IMC m

boar /bɔː(r)/ n cinghiale m

board /bɔːd/ n tavola f; (for notices) tabellone m; (committee) assemblea f; (of directors) consiglio m; full ~ Br pensione f completa; half ~ Br mezza pensione f; ~ and lodging vitto e alloggio m; go by the ~ 🅸

andare a monte ● vt (Naut, Aeron) salire a bordo di ● vi (passengers): salire a bordo. □ ~ up vt sbarrare con delle assi. □ ~ with vt stare a pensione da.

boarder /'bɔːdə(r)/ n pensionante mf; (Sch) convittore, -trice mf

board: ~ing-house n pensione f. ~ing-school n collegio m

boast /bəʊst/ vi vantarsi (about di). ~ful adj vanaglorioso

boat /bəʊt/ n barca f; (ship) nave f

bob /bɒb/ n (hairstyle) caschetto m ● vi (pt/pp bobbed) (also ~ up and down) andare su e giù

'bob-sleigh n bob m inv

bode /bəʊd/ vi ~ well/ill essere di buono/cattivo auguro

bodily /'bɒdɪlɪ/ adj fisico ● adv (forcibly) fisicamente

body /'bɒdɪ/ n corpo m; (organization) ente m; (amount: of poems etc) quantità f. ~guard n guardia f del corpo. ~part n pezzo m del corpo. ~work n (Auto) carrozzeria f

bog /bɒg/ n palude f ● vt (pt/pp bogged) get ~ged down impantanarsi

boggle /'bɒgl/ vi the mind ~s non posso neanche immaginarlo

bogus /'bəʊgəs/ adj falso

boil¹ /bɔɪl/ n (Med) foruncolo m

boil² n bring/come to the ~ portare/arrivare ad ebollizione ● vt [far] bollire ● vi bollire; (fig: with anger) ribollire; the water or kettle's ~ing l'acqua bolle. boil down to vt fig ridursi a. □ ~ over vi strabboccare (bollendo). □ ~ up vt far bollire

boiler /'bɔɪlə(r)/ n caldaia f. ~suit n tuta f

boisterous /'bɔɪstərəs/ adj chiassoso

bold /bəʊld/ adj audace ● n (Typ) neretto m. ~ness n audacia f

bolster /'bəʊlstə(r)/ n cuscino m (lungo e rotondo) ● vt ~ [up] sostenere

bolt /bəʊlt/ n (for door) catenaccio m; (for fixing) bullone m ● vt fissare (con i bulloni) (**to** a); chiudere col chiavistello (door); ingurgitare (food) ● vi svignarsela; (horse:) scappar via ● adv ~ **upright** diritto come un fuso

bomb /bɒm/ n bomba f ● vt bombardare

bombard /bɒm'bɑːd/ vt also fig bombardare

bomb|er /'bɒmə(r)/ n (Aeron) bombardiere m; (person) dinamitardo m. ~**er jacket** giubbotto m, bomber m inv. ~**shell** n (fig: news) bomba f

bond /bɒnd/ n fig legame m; (Comm) obbligazione f ● vt (glue:) attaccare

bondage /'bɒndɪdʒ/ n schiavitù f

bone /bəʊn/ n osso m; (of fish) spina f ● vt disossare (meat); togliere le spine a (fish). ~**-'dry** adj secco

bonfire /'bɒn-/ n falò m inv. ~ **night** festa celebrata la notte del 5 novembre con fuochi d'artificio e falò

bonnet /'bɒnɪt/ n cuffia f; (of car) cofano m

bonus /'bəʊnəs/ n (individual) gratifica f; (production ~) premio m; (life insurance) dividendo m; **a** ~ fig qualcosa in più

bony /'bəʊnɪ/ adj (-ier, -iest) ossuto; (fish) pieno di spine

boo /buː/ interj (to surprise or frighten) bu! ● vt/i fischiare

boob /buːb/ n 🔲 (mistake) gaffe f inv; (breast) tetta f ● vi 🔲 fare una gaffe

book /bʊk/ n libro m; (of tickets) blocchetto m; **keep the** ~**s** (Comm) tenere la contabilità; **be in sb's bad/ good** ~**s** essere nel libro nero/nelle grazie di qcno ● vt (reserve) prenotare; (for offence) multare ● vi (reserve) prenotare

book: ~case n libreria f. ~**ing-office** n biglietteria f. ~**keeping** n contabilità f. ~**let** n opuscolo m. ~**maker** n allibratore m. ~**mark** n segnalibro m. ~**seller** n libraio, -a mf.

~**shop** n libreria f. ~**worm** n topo m di biblioteca

boom /buːm/ n (Comm) boom m inv; (upturn) impennata f; (of thunder, gun) rimbombo m ● vi (thunder, gun:) rimbombare; fig prosperare

boost /buːst/ n spinta f ● vt stimolare (sales); sollevare (morale); far crescere (hopes). ~**er** n (Med) dose f supplementare

boot /buːt/ n stivale m; (up to ankle) stivaletto m; (football) scarpetta f; (climbing) scarpone m; (Auto) portabagagli m inv ● vt (Comput) inizializzare

booth /buːð/ n (telophono, voting) cabina f; (at market) bancarella f

booze /buːz/ 🔲 n alcolici mpl. ~**-up** n bella bevuta f

border /'bɔːdə(r)/ n bordo m; (frontier) frontiera f; (in garden) bordura f ● vi ~ on confinare con; fig essere ai confini di (madness). ~**line** n linea f di demarcazione; ~**line case** caso m dubbio

bore¹ /bɔː(r)/ ▷ **BEAR**²

bore² vt (Techn) forare

bor|e³ n (of gun) calibro m; (person) seccatore, -trice mf; (thing) seccatura f ● vt annoiare. ~**edom** n noia f. **be** ~**ed** (to tears or to death) annoiarsi (da morire). ~**ing** adj noioso

born /bɔːn/ pp **be** ~ nascere; **I was** ~ **in** 1966 sono nato nel 1966 ● adj nato; **a** ~ **liar/actor** un bugiardo/ attore nato

borne /bɔːn/ ▷ **BEAR**²

borough /'bʌrə/ n municipalità f inv

borrow /'bɒrəʊ/ vt prendere a prestito (from da); **can I** ~ **your pen?** mi presti la tua penna?

boss /bɒs/ n direttore, -trice mf ● vt (also ~ **about**) comandare a bacchetta. ~**y** adj autoritario

botanical /bə'tænɪkl/ adj botanico

botan|ist /'bɒtənɪst/ n botanico, -a mf. ~**y** n botanica f

both /bəʊθ/ adj & pron tutti e due,

entrambi ● adv ~ **men and women**
entrambi uomini e donne; ~ **[of]
the children** tutti e due i bambini;
they are ~ **dead** sono morti entrambi; ~ **of them** tutti e due

bother /'bɒðə(r)/ n preoccupazione
f; (minor trouble) fastidio m; **it's no** ~
non c'è problema ● int 𝖳 che seccatura! ● vt (annoy) dare fastidio a; (disturb) disturbare ● vi preoccuparsi
(**about** di); **don't** ~ lascia perdere

bottle /'bɒtl/ n bottiglia f; (baby's)
biberon m inv ● vt imbottigliare. □ ~
up vt fig reprimere

bottle: ~**neck** n fig ingorgo m.
~**-opener** n apribottiglie m inv

bottom /'bɒtm/ adj ultimo; **the** ~
shelf l'ultimo scaffale in basso ● n (of
container) fondo m; (of river) fondale m;
(of hill) piedi mpl; (buttocks) sedere m;
at the ~ **of the page** in fondo alla
pagina; **get to the** ~ **of** fig vedere
cosa c'è sotto. ~**less** adj senza fondo

bough /baʊ/ n ramoscello m

bought /bɔːt/ ▷**BUY**

boulder /'bəʊldə(r)/ n masso m

bounce /baʊns/ vi rimbalzare; (𝖳:
cheque:) essere respinto ● vt far rimbalzare (ball)

bound¹ /baʊnd/ n balzo m ● vi
balzare

bound² ▷**BIND** ● adj ~ **for** (ship)
diretto a; **be** ~ **to do** (likely) dovere
fare per forza; (obliged) essere co-
stretto a fare

boundary /'baʊndərɪ/ n limite m

bouquet /bʊ'keɪ/ n mazzo m di
fiori; (of wine) bouquet m

bout /baʊt/ n (Med) attacco m;
(Sport) incontro m

bow¹ /bəʊ/ n (weapon) arco m; (Mus)
archetto m; (knot) nodo m

bow² /baʊ/ n inchino m ● vi inchinarsi ● vt piegare (head)

bow³ /baʊ/ n (Naut) prua f

bowl¹ /bəʊl/ n (for soup, cereal) sco-
della f; (of pipe) fornello m

bowl² n (ball) boccia f ● vt lanciare
● vi (Cricket) servire; (in bowls) lanciare.
□ ~ **over** vt buttar giù; (fig: leave
speechless) lasciar senza parole

bowler¹ /'bəʊlə(r)/ n (Cricket) lancia-
tore m; (Bowls) giocatore m di bocce

bowler² n ~ **[hat]** bombetta f

bowling /'bəʊlɪŋ/ n gioco m delle
bocce. ~**-alley** n pista f da bowling

bow-tie /bəʊ-/ n cravatta f a
farfalla

box¹ /bɒks/ n scatola f; (Theat)
palco m

box² vi (Sport) fare il pugile ● vt ~
sb's ears dare uno scappaccione
a qcno

box|er /'bɒksə(r)/ n pugile m. ~**ing**
n pugilato m. **B**~**ing Day** n [giorno m
di] Santo Stefano m

box: ~**-office** n (Theat) botteghino
m. ~**-room** n Br sgabuzzino m

boy /bɔɪ/ n ragazzo m; (younger) bambino m

'boy band n boy band f inv

boycott /'bɔɪkɒt/ n boicottaggio m
● vt boicottare

boy: ~**friend** n ragazzo m. ~**ish** adj
da ragazzino

bra /brɑː/ n reggiseno m

brace /breɪs/ n sostegno m; (dental)
apparecchio m; ~**s** npl bretelle fpl ● vt
~ **oneself** fig farsi forza (**for** per affrontare)

bracelet /'breɪslɪt/ n braccialetto m

bracken /'brækn/ n felce f

bracket /'brækɪt/ n mensola f;
(group) categoria f; (Typ) parentesi f
inv ● vt mettere fra parentesi

brag /bræg/ vi (pt/pp **bragged**) vantarsi (**about** di)

braid /breɪd/ n (edging) passamano m

brain /breɪn/ n cervello m; ~**s** pl fig
testa fsg

brain: ~**child** n invenzione f personale. ~**wash** vt fare il lavaggio del
cervello a. ~**wave** n lampo m

di genio

brainy /'breɪnɪ/ adj (**-ier, -iest**) intelligente
brake /breɪk/ n freno m ●vi frenare. **~-light** n stop m inv
bramble /'bræmbl/ n rovo m; (fruit) mora f
bran /bræn/ n crusca f
branch /brɑːntʃ/ n also fig ramo m; (Comm) succursale f ●vi (road): biforcarsi. □ **~ off** vi biforcarsi. □ **~ out** vi **~ out into** allargare le proprie attività nel ramo di
brand /brænd/ n marca f; (on animal) marchio m ●vt marcare (animal); fig tacciare (**as di**)
brandish /'brændɪʃ/ vt brandire
brandy /'brændɪ/ n brandy m inv
brash /bræʃ/ adj sfrontato
brass /brɑːs/ n ottone m; **the ~** (Mus) gli ottoni mpl; **top ~** 🔲 pezzi mpl grossi. **~ band** n banda f (di soli ottoni)
brassiere /'bræzɪə(r)/ n fml, Am reggipetto m
brat /bræt/ n pej marmocchio, -a mf
bravado /brə'vɑːdəʊ/ n bravata f
brave /breɪv/ adj coraggioso ●vt affrontare. **~ry** n coraggio m
brawl /brɔːl/ n rissa f ●vi azzuffarsi
brawn /brɔːn/ adj sfrontato
Brazil /brə'zɪl/ n Brasile m. **~ian** adj & n brasiliano, -a mf. **~ nut** n noce f del Brasile
breach /briːtʃ/ n (of law) violazione f; (gap) breccia f; (fig: in party) frattura f; **~ of contract** inadempienza f di contratto; **~ of the peace** violazione f della quiete pubblica ●vt recedere (contract)
bread /bred/ n pane m; **a slice of ~ and butter** una fetta di pane imburrato
breadcrumbs npl briciole fpl; (Culin) pangrattato m
breadth /bredθ/ n larghezza f

'bread-winner n quello, -a mf che porta i soldi a casa
break /breɪk/ n rottura f; (interval) intervallo m; (interruption) interruzione f; (🔲: chance) opportunità f inv ●v (pt broke, pp broken) ●vt rompere; (interrupt) interrompere; **~ one's arm** rompersi un braccio ●vi rompersi; (day): spuntare; (storm): scoppiare; (news): diffondersi; (boy's voice): cambiare. □ **~ away** vi scappare; fig chiudere (**from** con). □ **~ down** vi (machine, car): guastarsi; (emotionally): cedere (psicologicamente) ●vt sfondare (door); ripartire (figures). □ **~ into** vt introdursi (con la forza) in; forzare (car). □ **~ off** vt rompere (engagement) ●vi (part of whole): rompersi. □ **~ out** vi (fight, war): scoppiare. □ **~ up** vt far cessare (fight); disperdere (crowd) ●vi (crowd): disperdersi; (couple): separarsi; (Sch) iniziare le vacanze
'break|able /'breɪkəbl/ adj fragile. **~age** n rottura f. **~down** n (of car, machine) guasto m; (Med) esaurimento m nervoso; (of figures) analisi f inv. **~er** n (wave) frangente m
breakfast /'brekfəst/ n [prima] colazione f
break:~through n scoperta f. **~water** n frangiflutti m inv
breast /brest/ n seno m. **~-feed** vt allattare [al seno]. **~-stroke** n nuoto m a rana
breath /breθ/ n respiro m, fiato. **~less** adj senza fiato. **~-taking** adj mozzafiato. **~ test** n prova f [etilica] f del palloncino
breathalyse /'breθəlaɪz/ vt sottoporre alla prova [etilica] del palloncino. **~r®** n Br alcoltest m inv
breathe /briːð/ vt/i respirare. □ **~ in** vi inspirare ●vt respirare (scent, air). □ **~ out** vt/i espirare
breath|er /'briːðə(r)/ n pausa f. **~ing** n respirazione f
bred /bred/ ▷ BREED
breed /briːd/ n razza f ●v (pt/pp

b

bred/ • vt allevare; (give rise to) generare • vi riprodursi. ~er n allevatore, -trice mf. ~ing n allevamento m; fig educazione f

breez|e /briːz/ n brezza f. ~y adj ventoso

brew /bruː/ n infuso m • vt mettere in infusione (tea); produrre (beer) • vi fig (trouble:) essere nell'aria. ~er n birraio m. ~ery n fabbrica f di birra

bribe /braɪb/ n (money) bustarella f; (large sum of money) tangente f • vt corrompere. ~ry n corruzione f

brick /brɪk/ n mattone m. '~layer n muratore m • **brick up** vt murare

bridal /'braɪdl/ adj nuziale

bride /braɪd/ n sposa f. ~groom n sposo m. ~smaid n damigella f d'onore

bridge¹ /brɪdʒ/ n ponte m; (of nose) dorso m; (of spectacles) ponticello m • vt fig colmare (gap)

bridge² n (Cards) bridge m

bridle /'braɪdl/ n briglia f

brief¹ /briːf/ adj breve

brief² n istruzioni fpl; (Jur: case) causa f • vt dare istruzioni a; (Jur) affidare la causa a. ~case n cartella f

briefs /briːfs/ npl slip m inv

brigad|e /brɪ'geɪd/ n brigata f. ~ier n generale m di brigata

bright /braɪt/ adj (metal, idea) brillante; (day, room, future) luminoso; (clever) intelligente. ~ red rosso m acceso

bright|en /'braɪtn/ v ~en [up] • vt ravvivare; rallegrare (person) • vi (weather:) schiarirsi; (face:) illuminarsi; (person:) rallegrarsi. ~ly adv (shine) intensamente; (smile) allegramente. ~ness n luminosità f; (intelligence) intelligenza f

brilliance /'brɪljəns/ n luminosità f; (of person) genialità f

brilliant /'brɪljənt/ adj (very good) eccezionale; (very intelligent) brillante; (sunshine) splendente

brim /brɪm/ n bordo m; (of hat) tesa f • **brim over** vi (pt/pp brimmed) traboccare

brine /braɪn/ n salamoia f

bring /brɪŋ/ vt (pt/pp brought) portare (person, object). □ ~ about vt causare. □ ~ along vt portare [con sé]. □ ~ back vt restituire (sth borrowed); reintrodurre (hanging); fare ritornare in mente (memories). □ ~ down vt portare giù; fare cadere (government); fare abbassare (price). □ ~ off vt ~ sth off riuscire a fare qcsa. □ ~ on vt (cause) provocare. □ ~ out vt (emphasize) mettere in evidenza; pubblicare (book). □ ~ round vt portare; (persuade) convincere; far rinvenire (unconscious person). □ ~ up vt (vomit) rimettere; allevare (children); tirare fuori (question, subject)

brink /brɪŋk/ n orlo m

brisk /brɪsk/ adj svelto; (person) sbrigativo; (trade, business) redditizio; (walk) a passo spedito

bristl|e /'brɪsl/ n setola f • vi ~ing with pieno di. ~ly adj (chin) ispido

Brit|ain /'brɪtn/ n Gran Bretagna f. ~ish adj britannico; (ambassador) della Gran Bretagna • npl the ~ish il popolo britannico. ~on n cittadino, -a britannico, -a mf

brittle /'brɪtl/ adj fragile

broach /brəʊtʃ/ vt toccare (subject)

broad /brɔːd/ adj ampio; (hint) chiaro; (accent) marcato. **two metres** ~ largo due metri; in ~ **daylight** in pieno giorno. ~ **band** n banda f larga. ~ **beans** npl fave fpl

'broadcast n trasmissione f • vt/i (pt/pp -cast) trasmettere. ~er n giornalista mf radiotelevisivo, -a. ~ing n diffusione f radiotelevisiva; **be in** ~ing lavorare per la televisione/radio

broaden /'brɔːdn/ vt allargare • vi allargarsi

broadly /'brɔːdlɪ/ adv largamente; ~ [speaking] generalmente

broad'minded adj di larghe vedute

broccoli /'brɒkəlɪ/ n inv broccoli mpl

brochure /'brəʊʃə(r)/ n opuscolo m; (travel ~) dépliant m inv

broke /brəʊk/ ▷BREAK ● adj 🔢 al verde

broken /'brəʊkn/ ▷BREAK ● adj rotto; (fig: marriage) fallito. ~ English inglese m stentato. ~**-hearted** adj affranto

broker /'brəʊkə(r)/ n broker m inv

brolly /'brɒlɪ/ n 🔢 ombrello m

bronchitis /brɒŋ'kaɪtɪs/ n bronchite f

bronze /brɒnz/ n bronzo m ● attrib di bronzo

brooch /brəʊtʃ/ n spilla f

brood /bruːd/ n covata f; (hum: children) prole f ● vi fig rimuginare

brook /brʊk/ n ruscello m

broom /bruːm/ n scopa f. ~**stick** n manico m di scopa

broth /brɒθ/ n brodo m

brothel /'brɒθl/ n bordello m

brother /'brʌðə(r)/ n fratello m

brother: ~**-in-law** n (pl ~**s-in-law**) cognato m. ~**ly** adj fraterno

brought /brɔːt/ ▷BRING

brow /braʊ/ n fronte f; (of hill) cima f

'browbeat vt (pt -**beat**, pp -**beaten**) intimidire

brown /braʊn/ adj marrone; castano (hair) ● n marrone m ● vt rosolare (meat) ● vi (meat): rosolarsi. ~ **'paper** n carta f da pacchi

browse /braʊz/ vi (read) leggicchiare; (in shop) curiosare

bruise /bruːz/ n livido m; (on fruit) ammaccatura f ● vt ammaccare (fruit); ~ **one's arm** farsi un livido sul braccio. ~**d** adj contuso

brunette /bruː'net/ n bruna f

brunt /brʌnt/ n **bear the** ~ **of** sth subire maggiormente qcsa

brush /brʌʃ/ n spazzola f; (with long handle) spazzolone m; (for paint) pennello m; (bushes) boscaglia f; (fig: conflict) breve scontro m ● vt spazzolare (hair); lavarsi (teeth); scopare (stairs, floor). □ ~ **against** vt sfiorare. □ ~ **aside** vt fig ignorare. □ ~ **off** vt spazzolare; (with hands) togliere; ignorare (criticism). □ ~ **up** vt/i fig ~ **up [on]** rinfrescare

brusque /brʊsk/ adj brusco

Brussels /'brʌslz/ n Bruxelles f. ~ **sprouts** npl cavoletti mpl di Bruxelles

brutal /'bruːtl/ adj brutale. ~**ity** n brutalità f inv

brute /bruːt/ n bruto m. ~ **force** n forza f bruta

BSc n abbr Bachelor of Science

BSE n abbr (bovine spongiform encephalitis) encefalite f bovina spongiforme

bubble /'bʌbl/ n bolla f; (in drink) bollicina f

buck[1] /bʌk/ n maschio m del cervo; (rabbit) maschio m del coniglio ● vi (horse): saltare a quattro zampe. □ ~ **up** vt 🔢 tirarsi su; (hurry) sbrigarsi

buck[2] n Am 🔢 dollaro m

buck[3] n **pass the** ~ scaricare la responsabilità

bucket /'bʌkɪt/ n secchio m

buckle /'bʌkl/ n fibbia f ● vt allacciare ● vi (shelf): piegarsi; (wheel): storcersi

bud /bʌd/ n bocciolo m

Buddhis|m /'bʊdɪzm/ n buddismo m. ~**t** adj & n buddista mf

buddy /'bʌdɪ/ n 🔢 amico, -a m

budge /bʌdʒ/ vt spostare ● vi spostarsi

budgerigar /'bʌdʒərɪgɑː(r)/ n cocorita f

budget /'bʌdʒɪt/ n bilancio m; (allot-

ted to specific activity) budget m inv ● vi
(pt/pp **budgeted)** prevedere le spese;
~ **for sth** includere qcsa nelle spese
previste

buffalo /'bʌfələʊ/ n *(inv or pl* -es**)**
bufalo m

buffer /'bʌfə(r)/ n *(Rail)* respingente
m; **old** ~ ⚠ vecchio bacucco m; ~
zone n zona f cuscinetto

buffet¹ /'bʊfeɪ/ n buffet m inv

buffet² /'bʌfɪt/ vt *(pt/pp* **buffeted)**
sferzare

bug /bʌg/ n *(insect)* insetto m;
(Comput) bug m inv; *(⚠: device)* cimice
f ● vt *(pt/pp* **bugged)** ⚠ installare
delle microspie in *(room)*; mettere
sotto controllo *(telephone)*; *(⚠:
annoy)* scocciare

buggy /'bʌgɪ/ n **[baby]** ~ passeggino m

bugle /'bju:gl/ n tromba f

build /bɪld/ n *(of person)* corporatura
f ● vt/i *(pt/pp* **built)** costruire. □ ~ **on**
vt aggiungere *(extra storey)*; sviluppare *(previous work)*. □ ~ **up** vt ~
up one's strength rimettersi in
forza ● vi *(pressure, traffic:)* aumentare; *(excitement, tension:)* crescere

builder /'bɪldə(r)/ n *(company)* co-
struttore m; *(worker)* muratore m

building /'bɪldɪŋ/ n edificio m. ~
site n cantiere m *[di costruzione]*. ~
society n istituto m di credito immobiliare

build-up n *(of gas etc)* accumulo m;
fig battage m inv pubblicitario

built /bɪlt/ ▷**BUILD**. ~-**in** adj *(unit)* a
muro; *(fig: feature)* incorporato.
~-**up area** n *(Auto)* centro m abitato

bulb /bʌlb/ n bulbo m; *(Electr)* lampadina f

Bulgaria /bʌl'geərɪə/ n Bulgaria f

bulge /bʌldʒ/ n rigonfiamento m
● vi esser gonfio *(with* di); *(stomach,
wall:)* sporgere; *(eyes, with surprise:)*
uscire dalle orbite. ~**ing** adj gonfio;
(eyes) sporgente

bulk /bʌlk/ n volume m; *(greater part)*
grosso m; **in** ~ in grande quantità;
(loose) sfuso. ~**y** adj voluminoso

bull /bʊl/ n toro m

bulldog n bulldog m inv

bulldozer /'bʊldəʊzə(r)/ n bulldozer m inv

bullet /'bʊlɪt/ n pallottola f

bulletin /'bʊlɪtɪn/ n bollettino m. ~
board n *(Comput)* bacheca f elettronica

bullet-proof adj antiproiettile inv;
(vehicle) blindato

bullfight n corrida f. ~**er** n
torero m

bull: ~**ring** n arena f. ~'**s-eye** n
centro m del bersaglio; **score a**
~'**s-eye** fare centro

bully /'bʊlɪ/ n prepotente mf ● vt fare
il/la prepotente con. ~**ing** n prepo-
tenze fpl

bum¹ /bʌm/ n ⚠ sedere m

bum² n Am ⚠ vagabondo, -a mf
● **bum around** vi ⚠ vagabondare

bumble-bee /'bʌmbl-/ n cala-
brone m

bump /bʌmp/ n botta f; *(swelling)*
bozzo m, gonfiore m; *(in road)* protuberanza f ● vt sbattere. □ ~ **into** vt
sbattere contro; *(meet)* imbattersi in.
□ ~ **off** vt ⚠ far fuori

bumper /'bʌmpə(r)/ n *(Auto)* pa-
raurti m inv ● adj abbondante

bun /bʌn/ n focaccina f *(dolce)*; *(hair)*
chignon m inv

bunch /bʌntʃ/ n *(of flowers, keys)*
mazzo m; *(of bananas)* casco m; *(of
people)* gruppo m; ~ **of grapes** grappolo m d'uva

bundle /'bʌndl/ n fascio m; *(of
money)* mazzetta f; **a** ~ **of nerves** ⚠
un fascio di nervi ● vt ~ **[up]** affa-
stellare

bungalow /'bʌŋgələʊ/ n bungalow
m inv

bungle /'bʌŋgl/ vt fare un

bunk | butt

pasticcio di

bunk /bʌŋk/ n cuccetta f. **~-beds** npl letti mpl a castello

bunny /'bʌnɪ/ n ⊞ coniglietto m

buoy /bɔɪ/ n boa f

burden /'bɜːdn/ n carico m ● vt caricare. **~some** adj gravoso

bureau /'bjʊərəʊ/ n (pl **-x** /-əʊz/ or **~s**) (desk) scrivania f; (office) ufficio m

bureaucracy /bjʊə'rɒkrəsɪ/ n burocrazia f

bureaucrat /'bjʊərəkræt/ n burocrate mf. **~ic** adj burocratico

burger /'bɜːgə(r)/ n hamburger m inv

burglar /'bɜːglə(r)/ n svaligiatore, -trice mf. **~ alarm** n antifurto m inv

burgle /'bɜːgl/ vt svaligiare

burial /'berɪəl/ n sepoltura f. **~ ground** n cimitero m

burly /'bɜːlɪ/ adj (**-ier**, **-iest**) corpulento

burn /bɜːn/ n bruciatura f ● v (pt/pp **burnt** or **burned**) ● vt bruciare● vi bruciare. ▫ **~ down** v/i bruciare. ▫ **~ out** vi fig esaurirsi. **~er** n (on stove) bruciatore m ● (Comput) masterizzatore m

burnt /bɜːnt/ ▷ BURN

burp /bɜːp/ n ⊞ rutto m ● vi ⊞ ruttare

burrow /'bʌrəʊ/ n tana f ● vt scavare (hole)

bursar /'bɜːsə(r)/ n economo, -a mf. **~y** n borsa f di studio

burst /bɜːst/ n (of gunfire, energy, laughter) scoppio m; (of speed) scatto m ● v (pt/pp **burst**) ● vt far scoppiare ● vi scoppiare; **~ into tears** scoppiare in lacrime; **she ~ into the room** ha fatto irruzione nella stanza. ▫ **~ out** vi **~ out laughing/crying** scoppiare a ridere/piangere

bury /'berɪ/ vt (pt/pp **-ied**) seppellire; (hide) nascondere

bus /bʌs/ n autobus m inv, pullman m

inv; (long distance) pullman m inv, corriera f

bush /bʊʃ/ n cespuglio m; (land) boscaglia f. **~y** adj (**-ier**, **-iest**) folto

business /'bɪznɪs/ n affare m; (Comm) affari mpl; (establishment) attività f di commercio; **on ~** per affari; **he has no ~ to** non ha alcun diritto di; **mind one's own ~** farsi gli affari propri; **that's none of your ~** non sono affari tuoi. **~-like** adj efficiente. **~man** n uomo m d'affari. **~woman** n donna f d'affari

busker /'bʌskə(r)/ n suonatore, -trice mf ambulante

'bus station n stazione f degli autobus

'bus-stop n fermata f d'autobus

bust¹ /bʌst/ n busto m; (chest) petto m

bust² /bʌst/ adj ⊞ rotto; **go ~** fallire ● v (pt/pp **busted** or **bust**) ⊞ ● vt far scoppiare ● vi scoppiare

'bust-up n ⊞ lite f

busy /'bɪzɪ/ adj (**-ier**, **-iest**) occupato; (day, time) intenso; (street) affollato; (with traffic) pieno di traffico; **be ~ doing** essere occupato a fare ● vt **~ oneself** darsi da fare

'busybody n ficcanaso mf inv

but /bʌt/, atono /bət/ conj ma ● prep eccetto, tranne; **nobody ~ you** nessuno tranne te; **~ for** (without) se non fosse stato per; **the last ~ one** il penultimo; **the next ~ one** il secondo ● adv (only) soltanto; **there were ~ two** ce n'erano soltanto due

butcher /'bʊtʃə(r)/ n macellaio m; **~'s [shop]** macelleria f ● vt macellare; fig massacrare

butler /'bʌtlə(r)/ n maggiordomo m

butt /bʌt/ n (of gun) calcio m; (of cigarette) mozzicone m; (for water) barile m; (fig: target) bersaglio m ● vt dare una testata a; (goat:) dare una cornata a. ▫ **~ in** vi interrompere

butter /'bʌtə(r)/ n burro m ● vt imburrare. □ ~ **up** vt 🔢 ruffianarsi

butter: ~**cup** n ranuncolo m. ~**fingers** nsg 🔢 be a ~**fingers** avere le mani di pasta frolla. ~**fly** n farfalla f

button /'bʌtn/ n bottone m ● vt ~ [up] abbottonare ● vi abbottonarsi. ~**hole** n occhiello m, asola f

buy /baɪ/ n good/bad ~ buon/cattivo acquisto m ● vt (pt/pp bought) comprare; ~ sb a drink pagare da bere a qcno; I'll ~ this one (drink) questo, lo offro io. ~**er** n compratore, -trice mf

buzz /bʌz/ n ronzio m; give sb a ~ 🔢 (on phone) dare un colpo di telefono a qcno; (excite) mettere in fermento qcno ● vi ronzare ● vt ~ sb chiamare qcno col cicalino. □ ~ **off** vi 🔢 levarsi di torno

buzzer /'bʌzə(r)/ n cicalino m

---

by /baɪ/

● prep (near, next to) vicino a; (at the latest) per; by Mozart di Mozart; he was run over by a bus è stato investito da un autobus; by oneself da solo; by the sea al mare; by sea via mare; by car/bus in macchina/autobus; by day/night di giorno/notte; by the hour/metre a ore/metri; six metres by four sei metri per quattro; he won by six metres ha vinto di sei metri; I missed the train by a minute ho perso il treno per un minuto; I'll be home by six sarò a casa per le sei; by this time next week a quest'ora tra una settimana; he rushed by me mi è passato accanto di corsa

● adv she'll be here by and by sarà qui fra poco; by and large in complesso

---

bye[-**bye**] /baɪ['baɪ]/ int 🔢 ciao

by: ~-**election** n elezione f straordinaria indetta per coprire una carica rimasta vacante in Parlamento. ~-**law** n legge f locale. ~**pass** n circonvallazione f; (Med) by-pass m inv ● vt evitare. ~-**product** n sottoprodotto m. ~**stander** n spettatore, -trice mf

---

Cc

cab /kæb/ n taxi m inv; (of lorry, train) cabina f

cabaret /'kæbəreɪ/ n cabaret m inv

cabbage /'kæbɪdʒ/ n cavolo m

cabin /'kæbɪn/ n (of plane, ship) cabina f; (hut) capanna f

cabinet /'kæbɪnɪt/ n armadietto m; [display] ~ vetrina f; C~ (Pol) consiglio m dei ministri. ~-**maker** n ebanista mf

cable /'keɪbl/ n cavo m. ~ 'railway n funicolare f. ~ 'television n televisione f via cavo

cackle /'kækl/ vi ridacchiare

cactus /'kæktəs/ n (pl -ti /-taɪ/ or -tuses) cactus m inv

caddie /'kædɪ/ n portabastoni m inv

caddy /'kædɪ/ n [tea-]~ barattolo m del tè

cadet /kə'det/ n cadetto m

cadge /kædʒ/ vt/i 🔢 scroccare

café /'kæfeɪ/ n caffè m inv

cafeteria /kæfə'tɪərɪə/ n tavola f calda

caffeine /'kæfiːn/ n caffeina f

cage /keɪdʒ/ n gabbia f

cake /keɪk/ n torta f; (small) pasticcino m. ~**d** adj incrostato (with di)

calamity /kə'læmətɪ/ n calamità f inv

calcium /'kælsɪəm/ n calcio m

calculat|e /'kælkjʊleɪt/ *vt* calcolare. **~ing** *adj fig* calcolatore. **~ion** *n* calcolo *m*. **~or** *n* calcolatrice *f*

calendar /'kælɪndə(r)/ *n* calendario *m*

calf¹ /kɑːf/ *n* (*pl* calves) vitello *m*

calf² *n* (*pl* calves) (*Anat*) polpaccio *m*

calibre /'kælɪbə(r)/ *n* calibro *m*

call /kɔːl/ *n* grido *m*; (*Teleph*) telefonata *f*; (*visit*) visita *f*; **be on ~** (*doctor:*) essere di guardia ● *vt* chiamare; indire (strike); **be ~ed** chiamarsi ● *vi* chiamare; **~ [in** or **round]** passare. □ **~ back** *vt/i* richiamare. □ **~ for** *vt* (*ask for*) chiedere; (*require*) richiedere; (*fetch*) passare a prendere. □ **~ off** *vt* richiamare (dog); disdire (meeting); revocare (strike). □ **~ on** *vt* chiamare; (*appeal to*) fare un appello a; (*visit*) visitare. □ **~ out** *vt* chiamare ad alta voce (names) ● *vi* chiamare ad alta voce. □ **~ together** *vt* riunire. □ **~ up** *vt* (*Mil*) chiamare alle armi; (*Teleph*) chiamare

call: **~-box** *n* cabina *f* telefonica. **~centre** *n* call centre *m inv*. **~er** *n* visitatore, -trice *mf*; (*Teleph*) persona *f* che telefona. **~ing** *n* vocazione *f*

callous /'kæləs/ *adj* insensibile

calm /kɑːm/ *adj* calmo ● *n* calma *f*. □ **~ down** *vt* calmare ● *vi* calmarsi. **~ly** *adv* con calma

calorie /'kælərɪ/ *n* caloria *f*

calves /kɑːvz/ *npl* see **calf¹** *&2*

camcorder /'kæmkɔːdə(r)/ *n* videocamera *f*

came /keɪm/ ▷**COME**

camel /'kæml/ *n* cammello *m*

camera /'kæmərə/ *n* macchina *f* fotografica; (*TV*) telecamera *f*. **~man** *n* operatore *m* [televisivo], cameraman *m inv*

camouflage /'kæməflɑːʒ/ *n* mimetizzazione *f* ● *vt* mimetizzare

camp /kæmp/ *n* campeggio *f*; (*Mil*) campo *m* ● *vi* campeggiare; (*Mil*) accamparsi

campaign /kæm'peɪn/ *n* campagna *f* ● *vi* fare una campagna

camp: **~-bed** *n* letto *m* da campo. **~er** *n* campeggiatore, -trice *mf*; (*Auto*) camper *m inv*. **~ing** *n* campeggio *m*. **~site** *n* campeggio *m*

campus /'kæmpəs/ *n* (*pl* -puses) (*Univ*) città *f* universitaria, campus *m inv*

can¹ /kæn/ *n* (*for petrol*) latta *f*; (*tin*) scatola *f*; **~ of beer** lattina *f* di birra ● *vt* mettere in scatola

can² /kæn/, *atono* /kən/ *v aux* (*pres* can; *pt* could) (*be able to*) potere; (*know how to*) sapere; **I cannot** or **can't go** non posso andare; **he could not** or **couldn't go** non poteva andare; **she can't swim** non sa nuotare; **I ~ smell something burning** sento odor di bruciato

Canad|a /'kænədə/ *n* Canada *m*. **~ian** *adj e n* canadese *mf*

canal /kə'næl/ *n* canale *m*

Canaries /kə'neərɪz/ *npl* Canarie *fpl*

canary /kə'neərɪ/ *n* canarino *m*

cancel /'kænsl/ *v* (*pt/pp* cancelled) ● *vt* disdire (meeting, newspaper); revocare (contract, order); annullare (reservation, appointment, stamp). **~lation** *n* (*of meeting, contract*) revoca *f*; (*in hotel, restaurant, for flight*) cancellazione *f*

cancer /'kænsə(r)/ *n* cancro *m*; C**~** (*Astr*) Cancro *m*. **~ous** *adj* canceroso

candid /'kændɪd/ *adj* franco

candidate /'kændɪdət/ *n* candidato, -a *mf*

candle /'kændl/ *n* candela *f*. **~stick** *n* portacandele *m inv*

candour /'kændə(r)/ *n* franchezza *f*

candy /'kændɪ/ *n Am* caramella *f*; **a [piece of] ~** una caramella. **~floss** *n* zucchero *m* filato

cane /keɪn/ *n* (*stick*) bastone *m*; (*Sch*)

bacchetta f ● vt prendere a bacchettate (pupil)

canister /'kænɪstə(r)/ n barattolo m (di metallo)

cannabis /'kænəbɪs/ n cannabis f

cannibal /'kænɪbl/ n cannibale mf. **~ism** n cannibalismo m

cannon /'kænən/ n inv cannone m. **~-ball** n palla f di cannone

cannot /'kænɒt/ ▷CAN²

canoe /kə'nu:/ n canoa f ● vi andare in canoa

'**can-opener** n apriscatole m inv

canopy /'kænəpɪ/ n baldacchino f; (of parachute) calotta f

cantankerous /kæn'tæŋkərəs/ adj stizzoso

canteen /kæn'ti:n/ n mensa f; **~ of cutlery** servizio m di posate

canter /'kæntə(r)/ n andare a piccolo galoppo

canvas /'kænvəs/ n tela f; (painting) dipinto m su tela

canvass /'kænvəs/ vi (Pol) fare propaganda elettorale. **~ing** n sollecitazione f di voti

canyon /'kænjən/ n canyon m inv

cap /kæp/ n berretto m; (nurse's) cuffia f; (top, lid) tappo m ● vt (pt/pp capped) (fig do better than) superare

capability /keɪpə'bɪlətɪ/ n capacità f

capabl|e /'keɪpəbl/ adj capace; (skilful) abile; **be ~e of doing sth** essere capace di fare qcsa. **~y** adv con abilità

capacity /kə'pæsətɪ/ n capacità f; (function) qualità f; **in my ~ as** in qualità di

cape¹ /keɪp/ n (cloak) cappa f

cape² n (Geog) capo m

capital /'kæpɪtl/ n (town) capitale f; (money) capitale m; (letter) lettera f maiuscola. **~ city** n capitale f

capital|ism /'kæpɪtəlɪzm/ n capitalismo m. **~ist** adj & n capitalista mf.

~ize vi **~ize on** fig trarre vantaggio da. **~ 'letter** n lettera f maiuscola. **~ 'punishment** n pena f capitale

Capitol Situato su Capitol Hill, nella città di Washington, il Campidoglio (the Capitol) è la sede del Congresso (Congress) degli Stati Uniti d'America e per estensione indica il Congresso stesso.

capitulat|e /kə'pɪtjʊleɪt/ vi capitolare. **~ion** n capitolazione f

Capricorn /'kæprɪkɔ:n/ n (Astr) Capricorno m

capsize /kæp'saɪz/ vi capovolgersi ● vt capovolgere

capsule /'kæpsjʊl/ n capsula f

captain /'kæptɪn/ n capitano m ● vt comandare (team)

caption /'kæpʃn/ n intestazione f; (of illustration) didascalia f

captivate /'kæptɪveɪt/ vt incantare

captiv|e /'kæptɪv/ adj prigioniero; **hold/take ~e** tenere/fare prigioniero ● n prigioniero, -a mf. **~ity** n prigionia f; (animals) cattività f

capture /'kæptʃə(r)/ n cattura f ● vt catturare; attirare (attention)

car /kɑ:(r)/ n macchina f; **by ~** in macchina

carafe /kə'ræf/ n caraffa f

caramel /'kærəmel/ n (sweet) caramella f al mou; (Culin) caramello m

caravan /'kærəvæn/ n roulotte f inv; (horse-drawn) carovana f

carbohydrate /kɑ:bə'haɪdreɪt/ n carboidrato m

carbon /'kɑ:bən/ n carbonio m. **~ di'oxide** n anidride f carbonica. **~ 'footprint** n impronta f ecologica

carburettor /kɑ:bju'retə(r)/ n carburatore m

carcass /'kɑ:kəs/ n carcassa f

card /kɑ:d/ n (for birthday, Christmas etc) biglietto m di auguri; (playing ~)

carta f [da gioco]; (*membership* ~) tessera f; (*business* ~) biglietto m da visita; (*credit* ~) carta f di credito; (*Comput*) scheda ~

'**cardboard** n cartone m. ~ '**box** n scatola f di cartone; (*large*) scatolone m

cardigan /'kɑːdɪgən/ n cardigan m inv

cardinal /'kɑːdɪnl/ adj cardinale; ~ **number** numero m cardinale ● n (*Relig*) cardinale m

care /keə(r)/ n cura f; (*caution*) attenzione f; (*worry*) preoccupazione f; ~ **of** (*on letter abbr* c/o) presso; **take** ~ (*be cautious*) stare attento; **take** ~, **take** ~ ciao, stammi bene; **take** ~ **of** occuparsi di; **be taken into** ~ essere preso in custodia da un ente assistenziale ● vi ~ **about** interessarsi di; ~ **for** (*feel affection for*) volere bene a; (*look after*) aver cura di; **I don't** ~ **for chocolate** non mi piace il cioccolato; **I don't** ~ non me ne importa; **who** ~s? chi se ne frega?

career /kə'rɪə(r)/ n carriera f; (*profession*) professione f ● vi andare a tutta velocità

care: ~**free** adj spensierato. ~**ful** adj attento; (*driver*) prudente. ~**fully** adv con attenzione. ~**less** adj irresponsabile; (*in work*) trascurato; (*work*) fatto con poca cura; (*driver*) distratto. ~**lessly** adv negligentemente. ~**lessness** n trascuratezza f. ~**r** n persona f che accudisce a un anziano o a un malato

caress /kə'res/ n carezza f ● vt accarezzare

'**caretaker** n custode mf; (*in school*) bidello m

'**car ferry** n traghetto m (*per il trasporto di auto*)

cargo /'kɑːgəʊ/ n (pl -es) carico m

Caribbean /kærɪ'biːən/ n the ~ (*sea*) il Mar dei Caraibi ● adj caraibico

caricature /'kærɪkətjʊə(r)/ n caricatura f

carnage /'kɑːnɪdʒ/ n carneficina f

carnation /kɑː'neɪʃn/ n garofano m

carnival /'kɑːnɪvl/ n carnevale m

carol /'kærəl/ n [**Christmas**] ~ canzone f natalizia

carp[1] /kɑːp/ n inv carpa f

carp[2] vi ~ **at** trovare da ridire su

'**car park** n parcheggio m

carpent|er /'kɑːpɪntə(r)/ n falegname m. ~**ry** n falegnameria f

carpet /'kɑːpɪt/ n tappeto m; (*wall-to-wall*) moquette f inv ● vt mettere la moquette in (*room*)

carriage /'kærɪdʒ/ n carrozza f; (*of goods*) trasporto m; (*cost*) spese fpl di trasporto; (*bearing*) portamento m; ~**way** n strada f carrozzabile; **north-bound** ~**way** carreggiata f nord

carrier /'kærɪə(r)/ n (*company*) impresa f di trasporti; (*Aeron*) compagnia f di trasporto aereo; (*of disease*) portatore m. ~ **bag** n borsa f [per la spesa]

carrot /'kærət/ n carota f

carry /'kærɪ/ v (pt/pp -**ied**) ● vt portare; (*transport*) trasportare; **get carried away** [ⓘ] lasciarsi prender la mano e vi (*sound*) trasmettersi. □ ~ **off** vt portare via; vincere (*prize*). □ ~ **on** vi continuare; ([ⓘ]: *make scene*) fare delle storie; ~ **on with sth** continuare qcsa; ~ **on with sb** [ⓘ] intendersela con qcno ● vt mantenere (*business*). □ ~ **out** vt portare fuori; eseguire (*instructions, task*); mettere in atto (*threat*); effettuare (*experiment, survey*)

'**carry-cot** n porte-enfant m inv

cart /kɑːt/ n carretto m ● vt ([ⓘ]: *carry*) portare

carton /'kɑːtn/ n scatola f di cartone; (*for drink*) cartone m; (*of cream, yoghurt*) vasetto m; (*of cigarettes*) stecca f

cartoon /kɑːˈtuːn/ n vignetta f; (strip) vignette fpl; (film) cartone m animato; (in art) bozzetto m. **~ist** n vignettista mf. (for films) disegnatore, -trice mf di cartoni animati

cartridge /ˈkɑːtrɪdʒ/ n cartuccia f; (for film) bobina f; (of record player) testina f

carve /kɑːv/ vt scolpire; tagliare (meat)

case¹ /keɪs/ n caso m; **in any ~** in ogni caso; **in that ~** in questo caso; **just in ~** per sicurezza; **in ~ he comes** nel caso in cui venisse

case² n (container) scatola f; (crate) cassa f; (for spectacles) astuccio m; (suitcase) valigia f; (for display) vetrina f

cash /kæʃ/ n denaro m contante; (🔲: money) contanti mpl; **pay [in] ~** pagare in contanti; **~ on delivery** pagamento alla consegna ● vt incassare (cheque). **~ desk** n cassa f

cashier /kæˈʃɪə(r)/ n cassiere, -a mf

casino /kəˈsiːnəʊ/ n casinò m inv

casket /ˈkɑːskɪt/ n scrigno m; (Am: coffin) bara f

casserole /ˈkæsərəʊl/ n casseruola f; (stew) stufato m

cassette /kəˈset/ n cassetta f. **~ recorder** n registratore m (a cassette)

cast /kɑːst/ n (mould) forma f; (Theat) cast m inv; [plaster] **~** (Med) ingessatura f ● vt (pt/pp cast) dare (vote); (Theat) assegnare le parti di (play); fondere (metal); (throw) gettare; **an actor as** dare ad un attore il ruolo di; **~ a glance at** lanciare uno sguardo a. □ **~ off** vi (Naut) sganciare gli ormeggi ● vt (in knitting) diminuire. □ **~ on** vt (in knitting) avviare

castaway /ˈkɑːstəweɪ/ n naufrago, -a mf

caster /ˈkɑːstə(r)/ n (wheel) rotella f. **~ sugar** n zucchero m raffinato

cast 'iron n ghisa f

cast-'iron adj di ghisa; fig solido

castle /ˈkɑːsl/ n castello m;

(in chess) torre f

'cast-offs npl abiti mpl smessi

castrat|e /kæˈstreɪt/ vt castrare. **~ion** n castrazione f

casual /ˈkæʒʊəl/ adj (chance) casuale; (remark) senza importanza; (glance) di sfuggita; (attitude, approach) disinvolto; (chat) informale; (clothes) casual inv; (work) saltuario; **~ wear** abbigliamento m casual. **~ly** adv (dress) casual; (meet) casualmente

casualty /ˈkæʒʊəltɪ/ n (injured person) ferito m; (killed) vittima f. **~ [department]** n pronto soccorso m

cat /kæt/ n gatto m; pej arpia f

catalogue /ˈkætəlɒg/ n catalogo m ● vt catalogare

catalyst /ˈkætəlɪst/ n (Chem) & fig catalizzatore m

catapult /ˈkætəpʌlt/ n catapulta f; (child's) fionda f ● vt fig catapultare

catarrh /kəˈtɑː(r)/ n catarro m

catastroph|e /kəˈtæstrəfɪ/ n catastrofe f. **~ic** adj catastrofico

catch /kætʃ/ n (of fish) pesca f; (fastener) fermaglio m; (on door) fermo m; (on window) gancio m; (🔲: snag) trabello m ● v (pt/pp caught) ● vt acchiappare (ball); (grab) afferrare; prendere (illness, fugitive, train); **~ a cold** prendersi un raffreddore; **~ sight of** scorgere; **I caught him stealing** lo sorpreso mentre rubava; **~ one's finger in the door** chiudersi il dito nella porta; **~ sb's eye** or **attention** attirare l'attenzione di qcno ● vi (fire): prendere; (get stuck) impigliarsi. □ **~ on** vi (🔲: understand) afferrare; (become popular) diventare popolare. □ **~ up** vt raggiungere ● vi recuperare; (runner:) riguadagnare terreno; **~ up with** raggiungere (sb); mettersi in pari con (work)

catching /ˈkætʃɪŋ/ adj contagioso

catchphrase n tormentone m

catchy /ˈkætʃɪ/ adj (-ier, -iest)

orecchiabile

categor|ical /ˌkætɪˈgɒrɪkl/ adj categorico. **~y** n categoria f

cater /ˈkeɪtə(r)/ vi **~ for** provvedere a (needs); fig venire incontro alle esigenze di. **~ing** n (trade) ristorazione f; (food) rinfresco m

caterpillar /ˈkætəpɪlə(r)/ n bruco m

cathedral /kəˈθiːdrl/ n cattedrale f

Catholic /ˈkæθəlɪk/ adj & n cattolico, -a mf. **~ism** n cattolicesimo m

cat's eyes npl catarifrangente msg (inserito nell'asfalto)

cattle /ˈkætl/ npl bestiame msg

catwalk /ˈkætwɔːk/ n passerella f

caught /kɔːt/ ▷CATCH

cauliflower /ˈkɒlɪ-/ n cavolfiore m

cause /kɔːz/ n causa f • vt causare; **~ sb to do sth** far fare qcsa a qcno

caution /ˈkɔːʃn/ n cautela f; (warning) ammonizione f • vt mettere in guardia; (Jur) ammonire

cautious /ˈkɔːʃəs/ adj cauto

cavalry /ˈkævəlrɪ/ n cavalleria f

cave /keɪv/ n caverna f • **cave in** vi (roof:) crollare; (fig: give in) capitolare

cavern /ˈkævən/ n caverna f

caviare /ˈkævɪɑː(r)/ n caviale m

cavity /ˈkævɪtɪ/ n cavità f inv; (in tooth) carie f inv

CD n CD m inv. **~ player** n lettore m [di] compact

CD-Rom /siːdiːˈrɒm/ n CD-Rom m inv. **~ drive** n lettore m [di] CD-Rom

cease /siːs/ n **without ~** incessantemente • vt/i cessare. **~-fire** n cessate il fuoco m inv. **~less** adj incessante

cedar /ˈsiːdə(r)/ n cedro m

ceiling /ˈsiːlɪŋ/ n soffitto m; fig tetto m [massimo]

celebrat|e /ˈselɪbreɪt/ vt festeggiare (birthday, victory) • vi far festa. **~ed** adj celebre (**for** per). **~ion** n celebrazione f

celebrity /sɪˈlebrətɪ/ n celebrità f inv

celery /ˈselərɪ/ n sedano m

cell /sel/ n cella f; (Biol) cellula f

cellar /ˈselə(r)/ n scantinato m; (for wine) cantina f

cello /ˈtʃeləʊ/ n violoncello m

Cellophane® /ˈseləfeɪn/ n cellofan m inv

cellphone /ˈselfəʊn/ n cellulare m

cellular phone /seljʊləˈfəʊn/ n [telefono m] cellulare m

celluloid /ˈseljʊlɔɪd/ n celluloide f

Celsius /ˈselsɪəs/ adj Celsius

cement /sɪˈment/ n cemento m; (adhesive) mastice m • vt cementare; fig consolidare

cemetery /ˈsemɪtrɪ/ n cimitero m

censor /ˈsensə(r)/ n censore m • vt censurare. **~ship** n censura f

censure /ˈsenʃə(r)/ vt biasimare

census /ˈsensəs/ n censimento m

cent /sent/ n (of dollar) centesimo m; (of euro) cent m inv, centesimo m

centenary /senˈtiːnərɪ/ n, Am **centennial** /senˈtenɪəl/ n centenario m

center /ˈsentə(r)/ n Am = centre

centi|grade /ˈsentɪ-/ adj centigrado. **~metre** n centimetro m. **~pede** n centopiedi m inv

central /ˈsentrl/ adj centrale. **~ 'heating** n riscaldamento m autonomo. **~ize** vt centralizzare. **~ly** adv al centro; **~ly heated** con riscaldamento autonomo. **~ reser'vation** n (Auto) banchina f spartitraffico

centre /ˈsentə(r)/ n centro m • v (pt/pp centred) • vt centrare • vi **~ on** fig incentrarsi su. **~-'forward** n centravanti m inv

century /ˈsentʃərɪ/ n secolo m

cereal /ˈsɪərɪəl/ n cereale m

ceremon|ial /serɪˈməʊnɪəl/ adj da cerimonia • n cerimoniale m. **~ious** adj cerimonioso

ceremony /ˈserɪmənɪ/ n

cerimonia f

certain /'sɜ:tn/ adj certo; **for ~** di sicuro; **make ~** accertarsi ; **he is ~ to win** è certo di vincere; **it's not ~ whether he'll come** non è sicuro che venga. **~ly** adv certamente; **~ly not!** no di certo! **~ty** n certezza f; **it's a ~ty** è una cosa certa

certificate /sə'tɪfɪkət/ n certificato m

certify /'sɜ:tɪfaɪ/ vt (pt/pp -ied) certificare; (declare insane) dichiarare malato di mente

chafe /tʃeɪf/ vt irritare

chain /tʃeɪn/ n catena f ●vt incatenare (prisoner); attaccare con la catena (dog) (to a). □ ~ **up** vt legare alla catena (dog)

chain: ~ **re'action** n reazione f a catena. **~-smoker** n fumatore, -trice mf accanito, -a. ~ **store** n negozio m appartenente a una catena

chair /tʃeə(r)/ n sedia f; (Univ) cattedra f ●vt presiedere. **~-lift** n seggiovia f. **~man** n presidente m

chalet /'ʃæleɪ/ n chalet m inv; (in holiday camp) bungalow m inv

chalk /tʃɔ:k/ n gesso m. **~y** adj gessoso

challeng|e /'tʃælɪndʒ/ n sfida f; (Mil) intimazione f ●vt sfidare; (Mil) intimare il chi va là a; fig mettere in dubbio (statement). **~er** n sfidante mf. **~ing** adj (job) impegnativo

chamber /'tʃeɪmbə(r)/ n **C~ of Commerce** camera f di commercio

chambermaid n cameriera f [d'albergo]

champagne /ʃæm'peɪn/ n champagne m inv

champion /'tʃæmpɪən/ n (Sport) campione m; (of cause) difensore, difenditrice mf ●vt (defend) difendere; (fight for) lottare per. **~ship** n (Sport) campionato m

chance /tʃɑ:ns/ n caso m; (possibility) possibilità f inv; (opportunity) occasione

f; **by ~** per caso; **take a ~** provarci; **give sb a second ~** dare un'altra possibilità a qcno ●attrib fortuito ●vt **I'll ~ it** □ corro il rischio

chancellor /'tʃɑ:nsələ(r)/ n cancelliere m; (Univ) rettore m; **C~ of the Exchequer** ≈ ministro m del tesoro

chandelier /ʃændə'lɪə(r)/ n lampadario m

change /tʃeɪndʒ/ n cambiamento m; (money) resto m; (small coins) spiccioli mpl; **for a ~** tanto per cambiare; **a ~ of clothes** un cambio di vestiti; **the ~** [of life] la menopausa ●vt cambiare; (substitute) scambiare (for qcno); **~ one's clothes** cambiarsi [i vestiti]; **~ trains** cambiare treno ●vi cambiare; (~ clothes) cambiarsi; **all ~l** stazione terminale!

changeable /'tʃeɪndʒəbl/ adj mutevole; (weather) variabile

'changing-room n camerino m; (for sports) spogliatoio m

channel /'tʃænl/ n canale m; **the [English] C~** la Manica; **the C~ Islands** le isole del Canale ●vt (pt/pp channelled) **~ one's energies into sth** convogliare le proprie energie in qcsa

chant /tʃɑ:nt/ n cantilena f; (of demonstrators) slogan m inv di protesta ●vt cantare; (demonstrators:) gridare

chao|s /'keɪɒs/ n caos m. **~tic** adj caotico

chap /tʃæp/ n □ tipo m

chapel /'tʃæpl/ n cappella f

chaperon /'ʃæpərəʊn/ n chaperon f inv ●vt fare da chaperon a (sb)

chapter /'tʃæptə(r)/ n capitolo m

char¹ /tʃɑ:(r)/ n □ donna f delle pulizie

char² vt (pt/pp charred) (burn) carbonizzare

character /'kærɪktə(r)/ n carattere m; (in novel, play) personaggio m; **quite a ~** □ un tipo particolare

characteristic /kærɪktə'rɪstɪk/ adj

caratteristico ● n caratteristica f. **~ally** adv tipicamente

characterize /'kærɪktəraɪz/ vt caratterizzare

charade /ʃə'rɑːd/ n farsa f

charcoal /'tʃɑː-/ n carbonella f

charge /tʃɑːdʒ/ n (cost) prezzo m; (Electr, Mil) carica f; (Jur) accusa f; **free of ~** gratuito; **be in ~** essere responsabile (**of** di); **take ~** assumersi la responsabilità; **take ~ of** occuparsi di ● vt far pagare (fee); far pagare a (person); (Electr, Mil) caricare; (Jur) accusare (**with** di); **~ sb for sth** far pagare qcsa a qcno; **~ it to my account** lo addebiti sul mio conto ● vi (attack) caricare

charitable /'tʃærɪtəbl/ adj caritatevole; (kind) indulgente

charity /'tʃærɪtɪ/ n carità f; (organization) associazione f di beneficenza; **concert given for ~** concerto m di beneficenza; **live on ~** vivere di elemosina

charm /tʃɑːm/ n fascino m; (object) ciondolo m ● vt affascinare. **~ing** adj affascinante

chart /tʃɑːt/ n carta f nautica; (table) tabella f

charter /'tʃɑːtə(r)/ n **~ [flight]** [volo m] charter m inv ● vt noleggiare. **~ed accountant** n commercialista m

chase /tʃeɪs/ n inseguimento m ● vt inseguire. **chase away** o **off** vt cacciare via

chassis /'ʃæsɪ/ n (pl chassis /-sɪz/) telaio m

chastity /'tʃæstətɪ/ n castità f

chat /tʃæt/ n chiacchierata f; **have a ~ with** fare quattro chiacchere con ● vi (pt/pp chatted) chiacchierare; (Comput) chattare. **~ show** n talk show m inv

chatter /'tʃætə(r)/ n chiacchiere fpl ● vi chiacchierare; (teeth:) battere. **~box** n Ⓣ chiacchierone, -a mf

chauffeur /'ʃəʊfə(r)/ n autista mf

chauvin|ism /'ʃəʊvɪnɪzm/ n sciovinismo m. **~ist** n sciovinista mf. **male ~ist** n Ⓣ maschilista m

cheap /tʃiːp/ adj a buon mercato; (rate) economico; (vulgar) grossolano; (of poor quality) scadente ● adv a buon mercato. **~ly** adv a buon mercato

cheat /tʃiːt/ n imbroglione, -a mf; (at cards) baro m ● vt imbrogliare; **~ sb out of sth** sottrarre qcsa a qcno con l'inganno ● vi imbrogliare; (at cards) barare. ▫ **~ on** vt Ⓣ tradire (wife)

check¹ /tʃek/ adj (pattern) a quadri ● n disegno m a quadri

check² /tʃek/ n (of tickets) controllo m; (in chess) scacco m; (Am: bill) conto m; (Am: cheque) assegno m; (Am: tick) segnetto m; **keep a ~ on** controllare; **keep in ~** tenere sotto controllo ● vt verificare; controllare (tickets); (restrain) contenere; (stop) bloccare ● vi controllare; **~ on sth** controllare qcsa. ▫ **~ in** vi registrarsi all'arrivo (in albergo); (Aeron) fare il check-in ● vt registrare l'arrivo (in albergo). ▫ **~ out** vi (of hotel) saldare il conto ● vt (Ⓣ: investigate) controllare. ▫ **~ up** vi accertarsi; **~ up on** prendere informazioni su

check: ~-in n (in airport: place) banco m accettazione, check-in m inv; **~mate** int scacco matto! **~-out** n (in supermarket) cassa f. **~-up** n (Med) visita f di controllo, check-up m inv

cheek /tʃiːk/ n guancia f; (impudence) sfacciataggine f. **~y** adj sfacciato

cheep /tʃiːp/ vi pigolare

cheer /tʃɪə(r)/ n evviva m inv; **three ~s** tre urrà; **~s!** salute!; (goodbye) arrivederci; (thanks) grazie! ● vt/i acclamare. ▫ **~ up** vt tirare su [di morale] ● vi tirarsi su [di morale]; **~ up!** su con la vita! **~ful** adj allegro. **~fulness** n allegria f. **~ing** n acclamazione f

cheerio /tʃɪərɪ'əʊ/ int Ⓣ arrivederci

'cheerless adj triste, tetro

cheese /tʃiːz/ n formaggio m. **~cake** n dolce m al formaggio

chef /ʃef/ n cuoco, -a mf, chef mf inv

chemical /'kemɪkl/ adj chimico ● n prodotto m chimico

chemist /'kemɪst/ n (pharmacist) farmacista mf; (scientist) chimico, -a mf; **~'s [shop]** farmacia f. **~ry** n chimica f

cheque /tʃek/ n assegno m. **~-book** n libretto m degli assegni. **~ card** n carta f assegni

cherish /'tʃerɪʃ/ vt curare teneramente; (love) avere caro; nutrire (hope)

cherry /'tʃerɪ/ n ciliegia f; (tree) ciliegio m

chess /tʃes/ n scacchi mpl

chessboard n scacchiera f

chest /tʃest/ n petto m; (box) cassapanca f

chestnut /'tʃesnʌt/ n castagna f; (tree) castagno m

chest of 'drawers n cassettone m

chew /tʃuː/ vt masticare. **~inggum** n gomma f da masticare

chic /ʃiːk/ adj chic inv

chick /tʃɪk/ n pulcino m; (🔲; girl) ragazza f

chicken /'tʃɪkn/ n pollo ● adj attrib (soup) di pollo ● **chicken out** vi 🔲 he **~ed** out gli è venuta fifa. **~pox** n varicella f

chicory /'tʃɪkərɪ/ n cicoria f

chief /tʃiːf/ adj principale ● n capo m. **~ly** adv principalmente

chilblain /'tʃɪlbleɪn/ n gelone m

child /tʃaɪld/ n (pl **~ren**) bambino, -a mf; (son/daughter) figlio, -a mf

child: ~birth n parto m. **~hood** n infanzia f. **~ish** adj infantile. **~less** adj senza figli. **~like** adj ingenuo

Chile /'tʃɪlɪ/ n Cile m. **~an** adj & n cileno, -a mf

chill /tʃɪl/ n freddo m; (illness) infreddatura f ● vt raffreddare

chilli /'tʃɪlɪ/ n (pl -es) **~ [pepper]** peperoncino m

chilly /'tʃɪlɪ/ adj freddo

chime /tʃaɪm/ vi suonare

chimney /'tʃɪmnɪ/ n camino m. **~-pot** n comignolo m. **~-sweep** n spazzacamino m

chimpanzee /tʃɪmpæn'ziː/ n scimpanzé m inv

chin /tʃɪn/ n mento m

china /'tʃaɪnə/ n porcellana f

Chin|a /'tʃaɪnə/ n Cina f. **~ese** adj & n cinese mf; (language) cinese m; the **~ese** pl i cinesi

chink[1] /tʃɪŋk/ n (slit) fessura f

chink[2] n (noise) tintinnio m

chip /tʃɪp/ n (fragment) scheggia f; (in china, paintwork) scheggiatura f; (Comput) chip m inv; (in gambling) fiche f inv; **~s** pl Br (Culin) patatine fpl fritte; Am (Culin) patatine fpl ● vt (pt/pp **chipped**) (damaged) scheggiare. □ **~ in** vi 🔲 intromettersi; (with money) contribuire. **~ped** adj (damaged) scheggiato

chiropod|ist /kɪ'rɒpədɪst/ n podiatra mf inv. **~y** n podiatria f

chirp /tʃɜːp/ vi cinguettare; (cricket:) fare cri cri. **~y** adj 🔲 pimpante

chisel /'tʃɪzl/ n scalpello m

chival|rous /'ʃɪvlrəs/ adj cavalleresco. **~ry** n cavalleria f

chives /tʃaɪvz/ npl erba f cipollina

chlorine /'klɔːriːn/ n cloro m

chock-a-block /tʃɒkə'blɒk/, **chock-full** /tʃɒk'fʊl/ adj pieno zeppo

chocolate /'tʃɒkələt/ n cioccolato m; (drink) cioccolata f; **a ~** un cioccolatino

choice /tʃɔɪs/ n scelta f ● adj scelto

choir /'kwaɪə(r)/ n coro m. **~boy** n corista m

choke /tʃəʊk/ n (Auto) aria f ● vt/i soffocare

cholera /'kɒlərə/ n colera m

cholesterol /kə'lestərɒl/ n colesterolo m

choose /tʃuːz/ vt/i (pt chose, pp chosen) scegliere; as you ~ come vuoi

chop /tʃɒp/ n (blow) colpo m (d'ascia); (Culin) costata f ● vt (pt/pp chopped) tagliare. □ ~ **down** vt abbattere (tree). □ ~ **off** vt spaccare

chop|per /'tʃɒpə(r)/ n accetta f; [] elicottero m. ~**py** adj increspato

chord /kɔːd/ n (Mus) corda f

chore /tʃɔː(r)/ n corvé f inv; [household] ~s faccende fpl domestiche

chorus /'kɔːrəs/ n coro m; (of song) ritornello m

chose, chosen /tʃəuz/, /'tʃəuzn/. ▷CHOOSE

Christ /kraɪst/ n Cristo m

christen /'krɪsn/ vt battezzare. ~**ing** n battesimo m

Christian /'krɪstʃən/ adj & n cristiano, -a mf. ~**ity** n cristianesimo m. ~ **name** n nome m di battesimo

Christmas /'krɪsməs/ n Natale m ● attrib di Natale. '~ **card** n biglietto m d'auguri di Natale. ~ **Day** n il giorno di Natale. ~ **Eve** n la vigilia di Natale. '~ **present** n regalo m di Natale. '~ **pudding** dolce m natalizio a base di frutta candita e liquore. '~ **tree** n albero m di Natale

chrome /krəum/ n, **chromium** /'krəumɪəm/ n cromo m

chromosome /'krəuməsəum/ n cromosoma m

chronic /'krɒnɪk/ adj cronico

chronicle /'krɒnɪkl/ n cronaca f

chronological /krɒnə'lɒdʒɪkl/ adj cronologico. ~**ly** adv (ordered) in ordine cronologico

chubby /'tʃʌbɪ/ adj (-ier, -iest) paffuto

chuck /tʃʌk/ vt [] buttare. □ ~ **out**

vt [] buttare via (object); buttare fuori (person)

chuckle /'tʃʌkl/ vi ridacchiare

chug /tʃʌg/ vi (pt/pp chugged) the train ~ged out of the station il treno è uscito dalla stazione sbuffando

chum /tʃʌm/ n amico, -a mf. ~**my** adj [] be ~**my** with essere amico di

chunk /tʃʌŋk/ n grosso pezzo m

church /tʃɜːtʃ/ n chiesa f. ~**yard** n cimitero m

churn /tʃɜːn/ vt churn out sfornare

chute /ʃuːt/ n scivolo m; (for rubbish) canale m di scarico

cider /'saɪdə(r)/ n sidro m

cigar /sɪ'gɑː(r)/ n sigaro m

cigarette /sɪgə'ret/ n sigaretta f

cine-camera /'sɪnɪ-/ n cinepresa f

cinema /'sɪnɪmə/ n cinema m inv

cinnamon /'sɪnəmən/ n cannella f

circle /'sɜːkl/ n cerchio m; (Theat) galleria f; in a ~ in cerchio ● vt girare intorno a; cerchiare (mistake) ● vi descrivere dei cerchi

circuit /'sɜːkɪt/ n circuito m; (lap) giro m. ~ **board** n circuito m stampato. ~**ous** adj ~**ous route** percorso m lungo e indiretto

circular /'sɜːkjulə(r)/ adj circolare ● n circolare f

circulat|e /'sɜːkjuleɪt/ vt far circolare ● vi circolare. ~**ion** n circolazione f; (of newspaper) tiratura f

circumcis|e /'sɜːkəmsaɪz/ vt circoncidere. ~**ion** n circoncisione f

circumference /sə'kʌmfərəns/ n conconferenza f

circumstance /'sɜːkəmstəns/ n circostanza f; ~**s** pl (financial) condizioni fpl finanziarie

circus /'sɜːkəs/ n circo m

cistern /'sɪstən/ n (tank) cisterna f; (of WC) serbatoio m

cite /saɪt/ vt citare

citizen /'sɪtɪzn/ n cittadino, -a mf;

(*of town*) abitante *mf.* **~ship** *n* cittadinanza *f*

citrus /'sɪtrəs/ *n* ~ **[fruit]** agrume *m*

city /'sɪtɪ/ *n* città *f inv*; **the C~** la City (*di Londra*)

---

i **City** La *City* è quella parte del centro di Londra dove un tempo si trovava l'antica città. Oggi è il centro finanziario della capitale britannica dove numerose banche e istituti finanziari hanno la propria sede centrale; molto spesso la *City* indica infatti le istituzioni finanziarie oltre che la zona della città.

---

civic /'sɪvɪk/ *adj* civico

civil /'ʃɪvl/ *adj* civile

civilian /sɪ'vɪljən/ *adj* civile; **in ~ clothes** in borghese ● *n* civile *mf*

civilization /sɪvɪlaɪ'zeɪʃn/ *n* civiltà *f inv*. **~e** *vt* civilizzare

civil: ~ 'servant *n* impiegato, -a *f* statale. **C~ 'Service** *n* pubblica amministrazione *f*

clad /klæd/ *adj* vestito (**in** di)

claim /kleɪm/ *n* richiesta *f*; (*right*) diritto *m*; (*assertion*) dichiarazione *f*; **lay ~ to sth** rivendicare qcsa ● *vt* richiedere; reclamare (*lost property*); rivendicare (*ownership*); ~ **that** sostenere che. **~ant** *n* richiedente *mf*

clairvoyant /kleə'vɔɪənt/ *n* chiaroveggente *mf*

clam /klæm/ *n* (*Culin*) vongola *f* ● **clam up** *vi* (*pt/pp* **clammed**) zittirsi

clamber /'klæmbə(r)/ *vi* arrampicarsi

clammy /'klæmɪ/ *adj* (**-ier, -iest**) appiccicaticcio

clamour /'klæmə(r)/ *n* (*protest*) rimostranza *f* ● *vi* ~ **for** chiedere a gran voce

clamp /klæmp/ *n* morsa *f* ● *vt* am-

morsare; (*Auto*) mettere i ceppi bloccaruote a. □ ~ **down** *vi* 🔢 essere duro; ~ **down on** reprimere

clan /klæn/ *n* clan *m inv*

clang /klæŋ/ *n* suono *m* metallico. **~er** *n* 🔢 gaffe *f inv*

clap /klæp/ *n* **give sb a ~** applaudire qcno; ~ **of thunder** tuono *m* ● *vt/i* (*pt/pp* **clapped**) applaudire; ~ **one's hands** applaudire. **~ping** *n* applausi *mpl*

clari|fication /klærɪfɪ'keɪʃn/ *n* chiarimento *m*. **~fy** *vt/i* (*pt/pp* **-ied**) chiarire

clarinet /klærɪ'net/ *n* clarinetto *m*

clarity /'klærətɪ/ *n* chiarezza *f*

clash /klæʃ/ *n* scontro *m*; (*noise*) fragore *m* ● *vi* scontrarsi; (*colours*) stonare; (*events*) coincidere

clasp /klɑːsp/ *n* chiusura *f* ● *vt* agganciare; (*hold*) stringere

class /klɑːs/ *n* classe *f*; (*lesson*) corso *m* ● *vt* classificare

classic /'klæsɪk/ *adj* classico ● *n* classico *m*; **~s** *pl* (*Univ*) lettere *fpl* classiche. **~al** *adj* classico

classi|fication /klæsɪfɪ'keɪʃn/ *n* classificazione *f*. **~fy** *vt* (*pt/pp* **-ied**) classificare

classroom *n* aula *f*

classy /'klɑːsɪ/ *adj* (**-ier, -iest**) 🔢 d'alta classe

clatter /'klætə(r)/ *n* fracasso *m* ● *vi* far fracasso

clause /klɔːz/ *n* clausola *f*; (*Gram*) proposizione *f*

claustrophob|ia /klɔːstrə'fəʊbɪə/ *n* claustrofobia *f*

claw /klɔː/ *n* artiglio *m*; (*of crab, lobster &* (*Techn*)) tenaglia *f* ● *vt* graffiare

clay /kleɪ/ *n* argilla *f*

clean /kliːn/ *adj* pulito, lindo ● *adv* completamente ● *vt* pulire (*shoes, windows*); ~ **one's teeth** lavarsi i denti; **have a coat ~ed** portare un cappotto in lavanderia. **clean up** vt pulire. ● vi far pulizia

cleaner /'kli:nə(r)/ n uomo m/donna f delle pulizie; (substance) detersivo m; [dry] ~'s lavanderia f, tintoria f

cleanliness /klenlɪnɪs/ n pulizia f

cleanse /klenz/ vt pulire. ~r n detergente m

cleansing cream /'klenz-/ n latte m detergente

clear /klɪə(r)/ adj chiaro; (conscience) pulito; (road) libero; (profit, majority) netto; (sky) sereno; (water) limpido; (glass) trasparente; **make sth ~** mettere qcsa in chiaro; **have I made myself ~?** mi sono fatto capire?; **five ~ days** cinque giorni buoni ● adv **stand ~ of** allontanarsi da; **keep ~ of** tenersi alla larga da ● vt sgombrare (room, street); sparecchiare (table); (acquit) scagionare; (authorize) autorizzare; scavalcare senza toccare (fence, wall); guadagnare (sum of money); passare (Customs); **~ one's throat** schiarirsi la gola ● vi (face, sky:) rasserenarsi; (fog:) dissiparsi. □ **~ away** vt metter via. □ **~ off** vi 🔢 filar via. □ **~ out** vt sgombrare ● vi 🔢 filar via. □ **~ up** vt (tidy) mettere a posto; chiarire (mystery) ● vi (weather:) schiarirsi

clearance /'klɪərəns/ n (space) spazio m libero; (authorization) autorizzazione f; (Customs) sdoganamento m. **~ sale** n liquidazione f

clear|ing /'klɪərɪŋ/ n radura f. **~ly** adv chiaramente. **~way** n (Auto) strada f con divieto di sosta

cleavage /'kli:vɪdʒ/ n (woman's) décolleté m inv

clench /klentʃ/ vt serrare

clergy /'klɜ:dʒɪ/ npl clero m. **~man** n ecclesiastico m

cleric /'klerɪk/ n ecclesiastico m. **~al** adj impiegatizio; (Relig) clericale

clerk /klɑ:k/, Am /klɜ:k/ n impie-

gato, -a mf; (Am: shop assistant) commesso, -a mf

clever /'klevə(r)/ adj intelligente; (skilful) abile

cliché /'kli:ʃeɪ/ n cliché m inv

click /klɪk/ vi scattare; (Comput) cliccare ● n (Comput) click m. **click on** vt (Comput) cliccare su

client /'klaɪənt/ n cliente mf

cliff /klɪf/ n scogliera f

climat|e /'klaɪmət/ n clima f. **~e change** n cambiamento m climatico. **~ic** adj climatico

climax /'klaɪmæks/ n punto m culminante

climb /klaɪm/ n salita f ● vt scalare (mountain); arrampicarsi su (ladder, tree) ● vi arrampicarsi; (rise) salire; (road:) salire. □ **~ down** vi scendere; (from ladder, tree) scendere; fig tornare sui propri passi

climber /'klaɪmə(r)/ n alpinista mf; (plant) rampicante m

clinch /klɪntʃ/ vt 🔢 concludere (deal) ● n (in boxing) clinch m inv

cling /klɪŋ/ vi (pt/pp clung) aggrapparsi; (stick) aderire. **~ film** n pellicola f trasparente

clinic /'klɪnɪk/ n ambulatorio m. **~al** adj clinico

clink /klɪŋk/ n tintinnio m; (🔢: prison) galera f ● vi tintinnare

clip[1] /klɪp/ n fermaglio m; (jewellery) spilla f ● vt (pt/pp **clipped**) attaccare

clip[2] /klɪp/ n (extract) taglio m ● vt obliterare (ticket). **~board** n fermabloc m inv. **~pers** npl (for hair) rasoio m; (for hedge) tosasiepi m inv; (for nails) tronchesina f. **~ping** n (from newspaper) ritaglio m

cloak /kləʊk/ n mantello m. **~room** n guardaroba m inv; (toilet) bagno m

clock /klɒk/ n orologio m; (🔢: speedometer) tachimetro m. □ **~ in** vi attaccare. □ **~ out** vi staccare

clock: **~wise** adj & adv in senso orario. **~work** n meccanismo m

clog /klɒɡ/ n zoccolo m ● vt (pt/pp clogged) ~ [up] intasare (drain); inceppare (mechanism) ● vi (drain): intasarsi

cloister /'klɔɪstə(r)/ n chiostro m

clone /kləʊn/ n clone m

close[1] /kləʊs/ adj vicino; (friend) intimo; (weather) afoso; **have a ~ shave** ≈ scamparla bella; **be ~ to sb** essere unito a qcno ● adv vicino; **~ by** vicino; **~ on five o'clock** quasi le cinque

close[2] /kləʊz/ n fine f ● vt chiudere ● vi chiudersi; (shop:) chiudere. **~ down** vt chiudere ● vi (TV station:) interrompere la trasmissione; (factory:) chiudere

closely /'kləʊslɪ/ adv da vicino; (watch, listen) attentamente

closet /'klɒzɪt/ n Am armadio m

close-up /'kləʊs-/ n primo piano m

closure /'kləʊʒə(r)/ n chiusura f

clot /klɒt/ n grumo m; (🅹: idiot) tonto, -a mf ● vi (pt/pp clotted) (blood:) coagularsi

cloth /klɒθ/ n (fabric) tessuto m; (duster etc) straccio m

clothe /kləʊð/ vt vestire

clothes /kləʊðz/ npl vestiti mpl, abiti mpl. **~-brush** n spazzola f per abiti. **~-line** n corda f stendibiancheria

clothing /'kləʊðɪŋ/ n abbigliamento m

cloud /klaʊd/ n nuvola f ● cloud over vi rannuvolarsi. **~burst** n acquazzone m

cloudy /'klaʊdɪ/ adj (-ier, -iest) nuvoloso; (liquid) torbido

clout /klaʊt/ n colpo m; (influence) impatto m (with su) ● vt 🅹 colpire

clove /kləʊv/ n chiodo m di garofano; **~ of garlic** spicchio m d'aglio

clover /'kləʊvə(r)/ n trifoglio m

clown /klaʊn/ n pagliaccio m ● vi **~ [about]** fare il pagliaccio

club /klʌb/ n club m inv; (weapon)

clava f; (Sport) mazza f; **~s** pl (Cards) fiori mpl ● v (pt/pp clubbed) vt bastonare. □ **~ together** vi unirsi

cluck /klʌk/ vi chiocciare

clue /kluː/ n indizio m; (in crossword) definizione f; **I haven't a ~** 🅹 non ne ho idea

clump /klʌmp/ n gruppo m

clumsiness /'klʌmzɪnɪs/ n goffaggine f

clumsy /'klʌmzɪ/ adj (-ier, -iest) maldestro; (tool) scomodo; (remark) senza tatto

clung /klʌŋ/ ▷CLING

cluster /'klʌstə(r)/ n gruppo m ● vi raggrupparsi (round intorno a)

clutch /klʌtʃ/ n stretta f; (Auto) frizione f; **be in sb's ~es** essere in balia di qcno ● vt stringere; (grab) afferrare ● vi **~ at** afferrare

clutter /'klʌtə(r)/ n caos m ● vt ~ [up] ingombrare

coach /kəʊtʃ/ n pullman m inv; (Rail) vagone m; (horse-drawn) carrozza f; (Sport) allenatore, -trice mf ● vt fare esercitare; (Sport) allenare

coal /kəʊl/ n carbone m

coalition /kəʊə'lɪʃn/ n coalizione f

coarse /kɔːs/ adj grossolano; (joke) spinto

coast /kəʊst/ n costa f ● vi (free-wheel) scendere a ruota libera. **~al** adj costiero. **~er** n (mat) sottobicchiere m inv

coast: ~guard n guardia f costiera. **~line** n litorale m

coat /kəʊt/ n cappotto m; (of animal) manto m; (of paint) mano f; **~ of arms** stemma f ● vt coprire; (with paint) ricoprire. **~-hanger** n gruccia f. **~-hook** n gancio m [appendiabiti]

coating /'kəʊtɪŋ/ n rivestimento m; (of paint) stato m

coax /kəʊks/ vt convincere con le moine

cobweb /'kɒb-/ n ragnatela f

cocaine /kə'keɪn/ n cocaina f

cock /kɒk/ n gallo m; (any male bird) maschio m ● vt sollevare il grilletto di (gun); ~ **its ears** (animal): drizzare le orecchie

cockerel /'kɒkərəl/ n galletto m

cock-'eyed adj 🆒 storto; (absurd) assurdo

cockney /'kɒknɪ/ (dialect) dialetto m londinese; (person) abitante mf dell'est di Londra

cock: ~**pit** n (Aeron) cabina f. ~**roach** /-rəʊtʃ/ n scarafaggio m. ~**tail** n cocktail m inv. ~-**up** n 🆇 **make a ~-up** fare un casino (of con)

cocky /'kɒkɪ/ adj (-ier, -iest) 🆒 presuntuoso

cocoa /'kəʊkəʊ/ n cacao m

coconut /'kəʊkənʌt/ n noce f di cocco

cocoon /kə'ku:n/ n bozzolo m

cod /kɒd/ n inv merluzzo m

COD abbr (cash on delivery) pagamento m alla consegna

code /kəʊd/ n codice m. ~**d** adj codificato

coedu'cational /kəʊ-/ adj misto

coerc|e /kəʊ'ɜːs/ vt costringere. ~**ion** n coercizione f

coffee /'kɒfɪ/ n caffè m inv

coffeepot n caffettiera f

coffin /'kɒfɪn/ n bara f

cog /kɒg/ n (Techn) dente m (di ruota)

coherent /kəʊ'hɪərənt/ adj coerente; (when speaking) logico

coil /kɔɪl/ n rotolo m; (Electr) bobina f; ~**s** pl spire fpl ● vt ~ [up] avvolgere

coin /kɔɪn/ n moneta f ● vt coniare (word)

coincide /kəʊɪn'saɪd/ vi coincidere

coinciden|ce /kəʊ'ɪnsɪdəns/ n coincidenza f. ~**tal** adj casuale. ~**tally** adv casualmente

coke /kəʊk/ n [carbone m] coke m

Coke® n Coca[-cola]® f

cold /kəʊld/ adj freddo; **I'm ~** ho freddo ● n freddo m; (Med) raffreddore m

cold-'blooded adj spietato

coleslaw /'kəʊlslɔː/ n insalata f di cavolo crudo, cipolle e carote in maionese

collaborat|e /kə'læbəreɪt/ vi collaborare; ~**e on sth** collaborare in qcsa. ~**ion** n collaborazione f; (with enemy) collaborazionismo m. ~**or** n collaboratore, -trice mf; (with enemy) collaborazionista mf

collaps|e /kə'læps/ n crollo m ● vi (person): svenire; (roof, building): crollare. ~**ible** adj pieghevole

collar /'kɒlə(r)/ n colletto m; (for animal) collare m. ~-**bone** n clavicola f

colleague /'kɒli:g/ n collega mf

collect /kə'lekt/ vt andare a prendere (person); ritirare (parcel, tickets); riscuotere (taxes); raccogliere (rubbish); (as hobby) collezionare ● vi riunirsi ● adv **call** ~ Am telefonare a carico del destinatario. ~**ed** adj controllato

collection /kə'lekʃn/ n collezione f; (in church) questua f; (of rubbish) raccolta f; (of post) levata f

collector /kə'lektə(r)/ n (of stamps etc) collezionista f

college /'kɒlɪdʒ/ n istituto m parauniversitario; **C~ of...** Scuola f di...

collide /kə'laɪd/ vi scontrarsi

collision /kə'lɪʒn/ n scontro m

colloquial /kə'ləʊkwɪəl/ adj colloquiale. ~**ism** n espressione f colloquiale

colon /'kəʊlən/ n due punti mpl; (Anat) colon m inv

colonel /'kɜːnl/ n colonnello m

colonial /kə'ləʊnɪəl/ adj coloniale

colon|ize /'kɒlənaɪz/ vt colonizzare. ~**y** n colonia f

colossal /kə'lɒsl/ adj colossale

colour /'kʌlə(r)/ n colore m; (com-

plexion) colorito *m*; **~s** *pl* (*flag*) bandiera *fsg*; **off~** 🔲 giù di tono ●*vt* colorare; **~ [in]** colorare ●*vi* (*blush*) arrossire

colour~: **~-blind** *adj* daltonico. **~ed** *adj* colorato; (*person*) di colore ●*n* (*person*) persona *f* di colore. **~ful** *adj* pieno di colore. **~less** *adj* incolore

column /'kɒləm/ *n* colonna *f*. **~ist** *n* giornalista *mf* che cura una rubrica

coma /'kəʊmə/ *n* coma *m inv*

comb /kəʊm/ *n* pettine *m*; (*for wearing*) pettinino *m* ●*vt* pettinare; (*fig: search*) setacciare; **~ one's hair** pettinarsi i capelli

combat /'kɒmbæt/ *n* combattimento *m* ●*vt* (*pt/pp* combated) combattere

combination /kɒmbɪ'neɪʃn/ *n* combinazione *f*

combine¹ /kəm'baɪn/ *vt* unire; **~ a job with being a mother** conciliare il lavoro con il ruolo di madre ●*vi* (*chemical elements*) combinarsi

combine² /'kɒmbaɪn/ *n* (*Comm*) associazione *f*. **~ harvester** *n* mietitrebbia *f*

combustion /kəm'bʌstʃn/ *n* combustione *f*

come /kʌm/ *vi* (*pt* came, *pp* come) venire; **where do you ~ from?** da dove vieni?; **~ to** (*reach*) arrivare a; **that ~s to £10** fanno 10 sterline; **~ into money** ricevere dei soldi; **~ true/open** verificarsi/aprirsi; **~ first** arrivare primo; *fig* venire prima di tutto; **~ in two sizes** esistere in due misure; **the years to ~** gli anni a venire; **how ~?** 🔲 come mai? **come about** *vi* succedere. **~ across** *vi* **~ across as being** 🔲 dare l'impressione di essere ●*vt* (*find*) imbattersi in. □ **~ along** *vi* venire; (*job, opportunity*) presentarsi; (*progress*) andare bene. □ **~ apart** *vi* smontarsi; (*break*) rompersi. □ **~ away** *vi* venir via; (*button, fastener*) staccarsi. □ **~ back** *vi* ritornare. □ **~ by**

vi passare ●*vt* (*obtain*) avere. □ **~ down** *vi* scendere; **~ down to** (*reach*) arrivare a. **come in** *vi* entrare; (*in race*) arrivare; (*tide:*) salire. □ **~ in for** *vt* **~ in for criticism** essere criticato. □ **~ off** *vi* staccarsi; (*take place*) esserci; (*succeed*) riuscire. □ **~ on** *vi* (*make progress*) migliorare; **~ on!** (*hurry*) dai!; (*indicating disbelief*) ma va làl. □ **~ out** *vi* venir fuori; (*book, sun:*) uscire; (*stain:*) andar via. □ **~ over** *vi* venire. □ **~ round** *vi* venire; (*after fainting*) riaversi; (*change one's mind*) farsi convincere. □ **~ to** *vi* (*after fainting*) riaversi. □ **~ up** *vi* salire; (*sun:*) sorgere; (*plant:*) crescere; **something came up** (*I was prevented*) ho avuto un imprevisto. □ **~ up with** *vt* tirar fuori

'come-back *n* ritorno *m*

comedian /kə'miːdɪən/ *n* comico *m*

comedy /'kɒmədɪ/ *n* commedia *f*

comet /'kɒmɪt/ *n* cometa *f*

comfort /'kʌmfət/ *n* benessere *m*; (*consolation*) conforto *m* ●*vt* confortare

comfortabl|e /'kʌmfətəbl/ *adj* comodo; **be ~e** (*person:*) stare comodo; (*fig: in situation*) essere a proprio agio; (*financially*) star bene. **~y** *adv* comodamente

'comfort station *n Am* bagno *m* pubblico

comic /'kɒmɪk/ *adj* comico ●*n* comico, -a *mf*; (*periodical*) fumetto *m*. **~al** *adj* comico. **~ strip** *n* striscia *f* di fumetti

coming /'kʌmɪŋ/ *n* venuta *f*; **~s and goings** viavai *m*

comma /'kɒmə/ *n* virgola *f*

command /kə'mɑːnd/ *n* comando *m*; (*order*) ordine *m*; (*mastery*) padronanza *f* ●*vt* ordinare; comandare (*army*)

commandeer /kɒmən'dɪə(r)/ *vt* requisire

command|er /kə'mɑːndə(r)/ *n* comandante *m*. **~ing** *adj* (*view*) imponente; (lead) dominante. ~ing officer n comandante m. ~ment n comandamento m

commemorat|e /kə'meməreit/ vt commemorare. ~ion n commemorazione f. ~ive adj commemorativo

commence /kə'mens/ vt/i cominciare. ~ment n inizio m

commend /kə'mend/ vt complimentarsi con (**on** per); (recommend) raccomandare (**to** a). ~able adj lodevole

comment /'kɒment/ n commento m ●vi fare commenti (**on** su)

commentary /'kɒmantri/ n commento m; [running] ~ (**on** radio, (TV)) cronaca f diretta

commentat|e /'kɒmanteit/ vt ~ **on** (TV, Radio) fare la cronaca di. ~or n cronista mf

commerce /'kɒmɜːs/ n commercio m

commercial /kə'mɜːʃl/ adj commerciale ●n (TV) pubblicità f inv. ~ize vt commercializzare

commiserate /kə'mizəreit/ vi esprimere il proprio rincrescimento (**with** a)

commission /kə'miʃn/ n commissione f; **receive one's** ~ (Mil) essere promosso ufficiale; **out of** ~ fuori uso ●vt commissionare

commissionaire /kəmiʃə'neə(r)/ n portiere m

commit /kə'mit/ vt (pt/pp committed) commettere; (to prison, hospital) affidare (**to** a); impegnare (funds); ~ **oneself** impegnarsi. ~ment n impegno m; (involvement) compromissione f. ~ted adj impegnato

committee /kə'miti/ n comitato m

commodity /kə'mɒdəti/ n prodotto m

common /'kɒmən/ adj comune; (vulgar) volgare ●n prato m pubblico; **have in** ~ avere in comune; **House of C~s** Camera f dei Comuni. ~er n

persona f non nobile

common: ~**law** n diritto m consuetudinario. ~**ly** adv comunemente. **C~ 'Market** n Mercato m Comune. ~**place** adj banale. ~**room** n sala f dei professori/degli studenti. ~ **'sense** n buon senso m

commotion /kə'məuʃn/ n confusione f

communicate /kə'mju:nikeit/ vt/i comunicare

communication /kəmju:nɪ'keiʃn/ n comunicazione f; (of disease) trasmissione f; **be in** ~ **with sb** essere in contatto con qcno; ~**s** pl (technology) telecomunicazioni fpl. ~ **cord** n fermata f d'emergenza

communicative /kə'mju:nikətiv/ adj comunicativo

Communion /kə'mju:niən/ n [Holy] ~ comunione f

Communis|m /'kɒmjunizm/ n comunismo m. ~**t** adj & n comunista mf

community /kə'mju:nəti/ n comunità f. ~ **centre** n centro m sociale

commute /kə'mju:t/ vi fare il pendolare ●vt (Jur) commutare. ~**r** n pendolare mf

compact¹ /kəm'pækt/ adj compatto

compact² /'kɒmpækt/ n portacipria *f inv*. ~ **disc** *n* compact disc *m inv*

companion /kəmˈpænjən/ *n* compagno, -a *mf*. ~**ship** *n* compagnia *f*

company /ˈkʌmpəni/ *n* compagnia *f*; (*guests*) ospiti *mpl*. ~ **car** *n* macchina *f* della ditta

comparable /ˈkɒmpərəbl/ *adj* paragonabile

comparative /kəmˈpærətɪv/ *adj* comparativo; (*relative*) relativo ● *n* (*Gram*) comparativo *m*. ~**ly** *adv* relativamente

compare /kəmˈpeə(r)/ *vt* paragonare (with/to a) ● *vi* essere paragonato

comparison /kəmˈpærɪsn/ *n* paragone *m*

compartment /kəmˈpɑːtmənt/ *n* compartimento *m*; (*Rail*) scompartimento *m*

compass /ˈkʌmpəs/ *n* bussola *f*. ~**es** *npl*, **pair of** ~**es** compasso *msg*

compassion /kəmˈpæʃn/ *n* compassione *f*. ~**ate** *adj* compassionevole

compatible /kəmˈpætəbl/ *adj* compatibile

compel /kəmˈpel/ *vt* (*pt/pp* **compelled**) costringere. ~**ling** *adj* (*reason*) inconfutabile

compensat|e /ˈkɒmpənseɪt/ *vt* risarcire ● *vi* ~**e** for *fig* compensare di. ~**ion** *n* risarcimento *m*; (*fig: comfort*) consolazione *f*

compère /ˈkɒmpeə(r)/ *n* presentatore, -trice *mf*

compete /kəmˈpiːt/ *vi* competere; (*take part*) gareggiare

competen|ce /ˈkɒmpɪtəns/ *n* competenza *f*. ~**t** *adj* competente

competition /kɒmpəˈtɪʃn/ *n* concorrenza *f*; (*contest*) gara *f*

competitive /kəmˈpetɪtɪv/ *adj* competitivo; ~ **prices** prezzi *mpl* concorrenziali

competitor /kəmˈpetɪtə(r)/ *n*

concorrente *mf*

complacen|cy /kəmˈpleɪsənsɪ/ *n* compiacimento *m*. ~**t** *adj* compiaciuto

complain /kəmˈpleɪn/ *vi* lamentarsi (about di); (*formally*) reclamare; ~ of (*Med*) accusare. ~**t** *n* lamentela *f*; (*formal*) reclamo *m*; (*Med*) disturbo *m*

complement[1] /ˈkɒmplɪmənt/ *n* complemento *m*

complement[2] /ˈkɒmplɪment/ *vt* complementare; ~ **each other** complementarsi a vicenda. ~**ary** *adj* complementare

complete /kəmˈpliːt/ *adj* completo; (*utter*) finito ● *vt* completare; compilare (form). ~**ly** *adv* completamente

completion /kəmˈpliːʃn/ *n* fine *f*

complex /ˈkɒmpleks/ *adj* complesso ● *n* complesso *m*

complexion /kəmˈplekʃn/ *n* carnagione *f*

complexity /kəmˈpleksɪtɪ/ *n* complessità *f inv*

complicat|e /ˈkɒmplɪkeɪt/ *vt* complicare. ~**ed** *adj* complicato. ~**ion** *n* complicazione *f*

compliment /ˈkɒmplɪmənt/ *n* complimento *m*; ~**s** *pl* omaggi *mpl* ● *vt* complimentare. ~**ary** *adj* complimentoso; (*given free*) in omaggio

comply /kəmˈplaɪ/ *vi* (*pt/pp* -ied) ~ **with** conformarsi a

component /kəmˈpəʊnənt/ *adj* & *n* ~ [part] componente *m*

compose /kəmˈpəʊz/ *vt* comporre; ~ **oneself** ricomporsi; **be** ~**d of** essere composto da. ~**d** *adj* (*calm*) composto. ~**r** *n* compositore, -trice *mf*

composition /kɒmpəˈzɪʃn/ *n* composizione *f*; (*essay*) tema *m*

compost /ˈkɒmpɒst/ *n* composta *f*

composure /kəmˈpəʊʒə(r)/ *n* calma *f*

compound /ˈkɒmpaʊnd/ *adj* composto. ~ **fracture** *n* frattura *f* esposta. ~ '**interest** n interesse m composto ● n (Chem) composto m; (Gram) parola f composta; (enclosure) recinto m

comprehen|d /kɒmprɪˈhend/ vt comprendere. ~**sible** adj comprensibile. ~**sion** n comprensione f

comprehensive /kɒmprɪˈhensɪv/ adj a m comprensivo; ~ [**school**] scuola f media in cui gli allievi hanno capacità d'apprendimento diverse. ~ in**surance** n (Auto) polizza f casco

compress[1] /ˈkɒmpres/ n compressa f

compress[2] /kəmˈpres/ vt comprimere; ~**ed air** aria f compressa

comprise /kəmˈpraɪz/ vt comprendere; (form) costituire

compromise /ˈkɒmprəmaɪz/ n compromesso m ● vt compromettere ● vi fare un compromesso

compuls|ion /kəmˈpʌlʃn/ n desiderio m irresistibile. ~**ive** adj (Psych) patologico. ~**ive eating** voglia f ossessiva di mangiare. ~**ory** adj obbligatorio

compute /kəmˈpjuːt/ vt calcolare

comput|er /kəmˈpjuːtə(r)/ n computer m inv. ~**erize** vt computerizzare. ~**ing** n informatica f

comrade /ˈkɒmreɪd/ n camerata m; (Pol) compagno, -a mf. ~**ship** n cameratismo m

con[1] /kɒn/ ▷**PRO**

con[2] n 🄸 fregatura f ● vt (pt/pp **conned**) 🄸 fregare

concave /ˈkɒnkeɪv/ adj concavo

conceal /kənˈsiːl/ vt nascondere

concede /kənˈsiːd/ vt (admit) ammettere; (give up) rinunciare a; lasciar fare (goal)

conceit /kənˈsiːt/ n presunzione f. ~**ed** adj presuntuoso

conceivable /kənˈsiːvəbl/ adj concepibile

conceive /kənˈsiːv/ vt (Biol) concepire ● vi aver figli. □ ~ **of** vt fig

concepire

concentrat|e /ˈkɒnsəntreɪt/ vt concentrare ● vi concentrarsi. ~**ion** n concentrazione f. ~**ion camp** n campo m di concentramento

concept /ˈkɒnsept/ n concetto m. ~**ion** n concezione f; (idea) idea f

concern /kənˈsɜːn/ n preoccupazione f; (Comm) attività f inv ● vt (be about, affect) riguardare; (worry) preoccupare; **be** ~**ed about** essere preoccupato per; ~ **oneself with** preoccuparsi di; **as far as I am** ~**ed** per quanto mi riguarda. ~**ing** prep riguardo a

concert /ˈkɒnsət/ n concerto m. ~**ed** adj collettivo

concertina /kɒnsəˈtiːnə/ n piccola fisarmonica f

concerto /kənˈtʃeətəʊ/ n concerto m

concession /kənˈseʃn/ n concessione f; (reduction) sconto m. ~**ary** adj (reduced) scontato

concise /kənˈsaɪs/ adj conciso

conclu|de /kənˈkluːd/ vt concludere ● vi concludersi. ~**ding** adj finale

conclusion /kənˈkluːʒn/ n conclusione f; **in** ~ per concludere

conclusive /kənˈkluːsɪv/ adj definitivo. ~**ly** adv in modo definitivo

concoct /kənˈkɒkt/ vt confezionare; fig inventare. ~**ion** n mistura f; (drink) intruglio m

concrete /ˈkɒnkriːt/ adj concreto ● n calcestruzzo m

concussion /kənˈkʌʃn/ n commozione f cerebrale

condemn /kənˈdem/ vt condannare; dichiarare inagibile (building). ~**ation** n condanna f

condensation /kɒndenˈseɪʃn/ n condensazione f

condense /kənˈdens/ vt condensare; (Phys) condensare ● vi condensarsi. ~**d milk** n latte m condensato

condescend /kɒndɪ'send/ vi degnarsi. **~ing** adj condiscendente

condition /kən'dɪʃn/ n condizione f; **on ~ that** a condizione che ● vt (Psych) condizionare. **~al** adj (acceptance) condizionato; (Gram) condizionale ● n (Gram) condizionale m. **~er** n balsamo m; (for fabrics) ammorbidente m

condolences /kən'dəʊlənsɪz/ npl condoglianze fpl

condom /'kɒndəm/ n preservativo m

condo[minium] /'kɒndə (' mɪnɪəm)/ n Am condominio m

condone /kən'dəʊn/ vt passare sopra a

conduct¹ /'kɒndʌkt/ n condotta f

conduct² /kən'dʌkt/ vt condurre; dirigere (orchestra); (of bus) bigliettaio m; (Phys) conduttore m. **~ress** n bigliettaia f

cone /kəʊn/ n cono m; (Bot) pigna f; (Auto) birillo m ● **cone off** vt be **~d off** (Auto) essere chiuso da birilli

confederation /kənfedə'reɪʃn/ n confederazione f

conference /'kɒnfərəns/ n conferenza f

confess /kən'fes/ vt confessare ● vi confessare; (Relig) confessarsi. **~ion** n confessione f. **~ional** n confessionale m. **~or** n confessore m

confetti /kən'fetɪ/ n coriandoli mpl

confide /kən'faɪd/ vt confidare. □ **~ in** vt ~ in sb fidarsi di qcno

confidence /'kɒnfɪdəns/ n (trust) fiducia f; (self-assurance) sicurezza f di sé; (secret) confidenza f; **in ~** in confidenza. **~ trick** n truffa f

confident /'kɒnfɪdənt/ adj fiducioso; (self-assurance) sicuro di sé. **~ly** adv con aria fiduciosa

confidential /kɒnfɪ'denʃl/ adj confidenziale

configur|ation /kənfɪɡə'reɪʃn/ n configurazione f. **~e** vt configurare

confine /kən'faɪn/ vt rinchiudere; (limit) limitare; **be ~d to bed** essere confinato a letto. **~d** adj (space) limitato. **~ment** n detenzione f; (Med) parto m

confirm /kən'fɜːm/ vt confermare; (Relig) cresimare. **~ation** n conferma f; (Relig) cresima f. **~ed** adj incallito; **~ed bachelor** scapolo m impenitente

confiscat|e /'kɒnfɪskeɪt/ vt confiscare. **~ion** n confisca f

conflict¹ /'kɒnflɪkt/ n conflitto m

conflict² /kən'flɪkt/ vi essere in contraddizione. **~ing** adj contraddittorio

conform /kən'fɔːm/ vi (person:) conformarsi; (thing:) essere conforme (**to** a). **~ist** n conformista mf

confounded /kən'faʊndɪd/ adj 🆃 maledetto

confront /kən'frʌnt/ vt affrontare; **the problems ~ing us** i problemi che dobbiamo affrontare. **~ation** n confronto m

confus|e /kən'fjuːz/ vt confondere. **~ing** adj che confonde. **~ion** n confusione f

congeal /kən'dʒiːl/ vi (blood:) coagularsi

congest|ed /kən'dʒestɪd/ adj congestionato. **~ion** n congestione f

congratulat|e /kən'ɡrætjʊleɪt/ vt congratularsi con (**on** per). **~ions** npl radunarsi.

congregat|e /'kɒnɡrɪɡeɪt/ vi radunarsi. **~ion** n (Relig) assemblea f

congress /'kɒnɡres/ n congresso m. **~man** n Am (Pol) membro m del congresso

conifer /'kɒnɪfə(r)/ n conifera f

conjugat|e /'kɒndʒʊɡeɪt/ vt coniugare. **~ion** n coniugazione f

conjunction /kən'dʒʌŋkʃn/ n congiunzione f; **in ~ with** insieme a

conjur|e /'kʌndʒə(r)/ vi **~ing**

tricks npl giochi mpl di prestigio. ~or n prestigiatore, -trice mf. □ ~ **up** vt evocare (image); tirar fuori dal nulla (meal)

conk /kɒŋk/ vi ~ **out** 🖪 (machine:) guastarsi; (person:) crollare

'con-man n 🖪 truffatore m

connect /kə'nekt/ vt collegare; **be ~ed with** avere legami con; (be related to) essere imparentato con; **be well ~ed** aver conoscenze influenti ● vi essere collegato (**with** a); (train:) fare coincidenza

connection /kə'nekʃn/ n (between ideas) nesso m; (in travel) coincidenza f; (Electr) collegamento m; **in ~ with** con riferimento a. ~**s** pl (people) conoscenze fpl

connoisseur /kɒnə'sɜː(r)/ n intenditore, -trice mf

conquer /'kɒŋkə(r)/ vt conquistare; fig superare (fear). ~**or** n conquistatore m

conquest /'kɒŋkwest/ n conquista f

conscience /'kɒnʃəns/ n coscienza f

conscientious /kɒnʃɪ'enʃəs/ adj coscienzioso. ~ **ob'jector** n obiettore m di coscienza

conscious /'kɒnʃəs/ adj conscio; (decision) meditato; [**fully**] ~ cosciente; **be/become ~ of** sth rendersi conto di qcsa. ~**ly** adv consapevolmente. ~**ness** n consapevolezza f; (Med) conoscenza f

conscript¹ /'kɒnskrɪpt/ n coscritto m

conscript² /kən'skrɪpt/ vt (Mil) chiamare alle armi. ~**ion** n coscrizione f, leva f

consecrate /'kɒnsɪkreɪt/ vt consacrare. ~**ion** n consacrazione f

consecutive /kən'sekjʊtɪv/ adj consecutivo

consensus /kən'sensəs/ n consenso m

consent /kən'sent/ n consenso m ● vi acconsentire

consequen|ce /'kɒnsɪkwəns/ n conseguenza f; (importance) importanza f. ~**t** adj conseguente. ~**tly** adv di conseguenza

conservation /kɒnsə'veɪʃn/ n conservazione f. ~**ist** n fautore, -trice mf della tutela ambientale

conservative /kən'sɜːvətɪv/ adj conservativo; (estimate) ottimistico. **C~** (Pol) adj conservatore ● n conservatore, -trice mf

conservatory /kən'sɜːvətrɪ/ n spazio m chiuso da vetrate adiacente alla casa

conserve /kən'sɜːv/ vt conservare

consider /kən'sɪdə(r)/ vt considerare; ~ **doing** sth considerare la possibilità di fare qcsa. ~**able** adj considerevole. ~**ably** adv considerevolmente

consider|ate /kən'sɪdərət/ adj pieno di riguardo. ~**ately** adv con riguardo. ~**ation** n considerazione f; (thoughtfulness) attenzione f; (respect) riguardo m; (payment) compenso m; **take** sth **into ~ation** prendere qcsa in considerazione. ~**ing** prep considerando

consign /kən'saɪn/ vt affidare. ~**ment** n consegna f

consist /kən'sɪst/ vi ~ **of** consistere di

consisten|cy /kən'sɪstənsɪ/ n coerenza f; (density) consistenza f. ~**t** adj coerente; (loyalty) costante. ~**tly** adv coerentemente; (late, loyal) costantemente

consolation /kɒnsə'leɪʃn/ n consolazione f. ~ **prize** n premio m di consolazione

console /kən'səʊl/ vt consolare

consolidate /kən'sɒlɪdeɪt/ vt consolidare

consonant /'kɒnsənənt/ n consonante f

conspicuous /kən'spɪkjʊəs/ adj facilmente distinguibile

conspiracy /kən'spɪrəsɪ/ n cospirazione f

conspire /kən'spaɪə(r)/ vi cospirare

constable /'kʌnstəbl/ n agente m [di polizia]

constant /'kɒnstənt/ adj costante. ~ly adv costantemente

constellation /kɒnstə'leɪʃn/ n costellazione f

consternation /kɒnstə'neɪʃn/ n costernazione f

constipat|ed /'kɒnstɪpeɪtɪd/ adj stitico. ~ion n stitichezza f

constituency /kən'stɪtjʊənsɪ/ n area f elettorale di un deputato nel Regno Unito

constituent /kən'stɪtjʊənt/ n costituente m; (Pol) elettore, -trice f

constitut|e /'kɒnstɪtjuːt/ vt costituire. ~ion n costituzione f. ~ional adj costituzionale

construct /kən'strʌkt/ vt costruire. ~ion n costruzione f; under ~ion in costruzione. ~ive adj costruttivo

consul /'kɒnsl/ n console m. ~ar adj consolare. ~ate n consolato m

consult /kən'sʌlt/ vt consultare. ~ant n consulente mf; (Med) specialista mf. ~ation n consultazione f; (Med) consulto m

consume /kən'sjuːm/ vt consumare. ~r n consumatore, -trice m/f. ~r goods npl beni mpl di consumo. ~er organization n organizzazione f per la tutela dei consumatori

consummate /'kɒnsəmeɪt/ vt consumare

consumption /kən'sʌmpʃn/ n consumo m

contact /'kɒntækt/ n contatto m; (person) conoscenza f ● vt mettersi in contatto con. ~ 'lenses npl lenti fpl a contatto

contagious /kən'teɪdʒəs/ adj contagioso

contain /kən'teɪn/ vt contenere; ~ oneself controllarsi. ~er n recipiente m; (for transport) container m inv

contaminat|e /kən'tæmɪneɪt/ vt contaminare. ~ion n contaminazione f

contemplat|e /'kɒntəmpleɪt/ vt contemplare; (consider) considerare; ~e doing sth considerare di fare qcsa. ~ion n contemplazione f

contemporary /kən'tempərərɪ/ adj & n contemporaneo, -a mf

contempt /kən'tempt/ n disprezzo m; beneath ~ più che vergognoso; ~ of court oltraggio m alla Corte. ~ible adj spregevole. ~uous adj sprezzante

contend /kən'tend/ vi ~ with occuparsi di ● vt (assert) sostenere. ~er n concorrente mf

content¹ /'kɒntent/ n contenuto m

content² /kən'tent/ adj soddisfatto ● vt ~ oneself accontentarsi (with di). ~ed adj soddisfatto. ~edly adv con aria soddisfatta

contentment /kən'tentmənt/ n soddisfazione f

contents /'kɒntents/ npl contenuto m

contest¹ /'kɒntest/ n gara f

contest² /kən'test/ vt contestare (statement); impugnare (will); (Pol) (candidates): contendersi; (one candidate): aspirare a. ~ant n concorrente mf

context /'kɒntekst/ n contesto m

continent /'kɒntɪnənt/ n continente m; the C~ l'Europa f continentale

continental /kɒntɪ'nentl/ adj continentale. ~ breakfast n prima colazione f a base di pane, burro, marmellata, croissant, ecc. ~ quilt n piumone m

contingency /kən'tɪndʒənsɪ/ n eventualità f inv

continual /kən'tɪnjʊəl/ adj

continuo
continuation /kəntɪnjʊˈeɪʃn/ n
continuazione f
continue /kənˈtɪnjuː/ vt continuare;
~ **doing** or **to do sth** continuare a
fare qcsa; **to be ~d** continua • vi
continuare. **~d** adj continuo
continuity /kɒntrˈnjuːətɪ/ n continuità f
continuous /kənˈtɪnjʊəs/ adj
continuo
contort /kənˈtɔːt/ vt contorcere.
~ion n contorsione f. **~ionist** n
contorsionista mf
contour /ˈkɒntʊə(r)/ n contorno m;
(line) curva f di livello
contraband /ˈkɒntrəbænd/ n contrabbando m
contracep|tion /kɒntrəˈsepʃn/ n
contraccezione f. **~tive** n contraccettivo m
contract¹ /ˈkɒntrækt/ n contratto m
contract² /kənˈtrækt/ vi (get smaller)
contrarsi • vt contrarre (illness).
~ion n contrazione f. **~or** n imprenditore, -trice mf
contradict /kɒntrəˈdɪkt/ vt contraddire. **~ion** n contraddizione f.
~ory adj contraddittorio
contraption /kənˈtræpʃn/ n 🄸
aggeggio m
contrary¹ /ˈkɒntrərɪ/ adj contrario
• adv ~ **to** contrariamente a • n
contrario m; **on the ~** al contrario
contrary² /kənˈtreərɪ/ adj disobbediente
contrast¹ /ˈkɒntrɑːst/ n contrasto m
contrast² /kənˈtrɑːst/ vt confrontare • vi contrastare. **~ing** adj contrastante
contraven|e /kɒntrəˈviːn/ vt trasgredire. **~tion** n trasgressione f
contribut|e /kənˈtrɪbjuːt/ vt/i contribuire. **~ion** n contribuzione f;
(what is contributed) contributo m. **~or**

n contributore, -trice mf
contrive /kənˈtraɪv/ vt escogitare;
~ **to do sth** riuscire a fare qcsa
control /kənˈtrəʊl/ n controllo m;
~s pl (of car, plane) comandi mpl; **get
out of ~** sfuggire al controllo • vt
(pt/pp **controlled**) controllare; **~
oneself** controllarsi
controvers|ial /kɒntrəˈvɜːʃl/ adj
controverso. **~y** n controversia f
convalesce /kɒnvəˈles/ vi essere in
convalescenza
convector /kənˈvektə(r)/ n ~
[heater] convettore m
convene /kənˈviːn/ vt convocare
• vi riunirsi
convenience /kənˈviːnɪəns/ n
convenienza f; [public] ~ gabinetti
mpl pubblici; **with all modern ~s**
con tutti i comfort
convenient /kənˈviːnɪənt/ adj comodo; **be ~ for sb** andar bene per
qcno; **if it is ~ [for you]** se ti va
bene. **~ly** adv comodamente; **~ly
located** in una posizione comoda
convent /ˈkɒnvənt/ n convento m
convention /kənˈvenʃn/ n convenzione f; (assembly) convegno m. **~al**
adj convenzionale
converge /kənˈvɜːdʒ/ vi convergere
conversation /kɒnvəˈseɪʃn/ n
conversazione f. **~al** adj di conversazione. **~alist** n conversatore,
-trice mf
converse¹ /kənˈvɜːs/ vi conversare
converse² /ˈkɒnvɜːs/ n inverso m.
~ly adv viceversa
conversion /kənˈvɜːʃn/ n conversione f
convert¹ /ˈkɒnvɜːt/ n convertito,
-a mf
convert² /kənˈvɜːt/ vt convertire
(into in); sconsacrare (church).
~ible adj convertibile • n (Auto) macchina f decappottabile
convex /ˈkɒnveks/ adj convesso

convey /kən'veɪ/ vt portare; trasmettere (idea, message). ~**or belt** n nastro m trasportatore

convict¹ /'kɒnvɪkt/ n condannato, -a mf

convict² /kən'vɪkt/ vt giudicare colpevole. ~**ion** n condanna f; (belief) convinzione f; **previous** ~**ion** precedente m penale

convinc|e /kən'vɪns/ vt convincere. ~**ing** adj convincente

convoluted /'kɒnvəlu:tɪd/ adj contorto

convoy /'kɒnvɔɪ/ n convoglio m

convuls|e /kən'vʌls/ vt sconvolgere; **be** ~**ed with laughter** contorcersi dalle risa. ~**ion** n convulsione f

coo /ku:/ vi tubare

cook /kʊk/ n cuoco, -a mf ● vt cucinare; **is it** ~**ed?** è cotto?; ~ **the books** 🔲 truccare i libri contabili ● vi (food): cuocere; (person:) cucinare. ~**book** n libro m di cucina

cooker /'kʊkə(r)/ n cucina f; (apple) mela f da cuocere. ~**y** n cucina f. ~**y book** n libro m di cucina

cookie /'kʊkɪ/ n Am biscotto m

cool /ku:l/ adj fresco; (calm) calmo; (unfriendly) freddo ● n fresco m ● vt rinfrescare ● vi rinfrescarsi. ~**-box** n borsa f termica. ~**ness** n freddezza f

coop /ku:p/ n stia f ● vt ~ **up** rinchiudere

co-operat|e /kəʊ'ɒpəreɪt/ vi cooperare. ~**ion** n cooperazione f

co-operative /kəʊ'ɒpərətɪv/ adj cooperativo ● n cooperativa f

co-opt /kəʊ'ɒpt/ vt eleggere

co-ordinat|e /kəʊ'ɔ:dɪneɪt/ vt coordinare. ~**ion** n coordinazione f

cop /kɒp/ n 🔲 poliziotto m

cope /kəʊp/ vi 🔲 farcela; **can she** ~ **by herself?** ce la fa da sola?; ~ **with** farcela con

copious /'kəʊpɪəs/ adj abbondante

copper¹ /'kɒpə(r)/ n rame m; ~**s** pl

monete fpl da uno o due pence ● attrib di rame

copper² n 🔲 poliziotto m

copy /'kɒpɪ/ n copia f ● vt (pt/pp -ied) copiare

copyright n diritti mpl d'autore

coral /'kɒrəl/ n corallo m

cord /kɔ:d/ n corda f; (thinner) cordoncino m; (fabric) velluto m a coste; ~**s** pl pantaloni mpl di velluto a coste

cordial /'kɔ:dɪəl/ adj cordiale ● n analcolico m

cordon /'kɔ:dn/ n cordone m (di persone) ● **cordon off** vt mettere un cordone (di persone) intorno a

core /kɔ:(r)/ n (of apple, pear) torsolo m; (fig: of organization) cuore m; (of problem, theory) nocciolo m

cork /kɔ:k/ n sughero m; (for bottle) turacciolo m. ~**screw** n cavatappi m inv

corn¹ /kɔ:n/ n grano m; (Am: maize) granturco m

corn² n (Med) callo m

corned beef /kɔ:nd'bi:f/ n manzo m sotto sale

corner /'kɔ:nə(r)/ n angolo m; (football) calcio m d'angolo, corner m inv ● vt bloccare; (Comm) accaparrarsi (market)

cornet /'kɔ:nɪt/ n (Mus) cornetta f; (for ice-cream) cono m

corn: ~**flour** n, Am ~**starch** n farina f di granturco

corny /'kɔ:nɪ/ adj (-ier, -iest) (🔲: joke, film) scontato; (person) banale; (sentimental) sdolcinato

coronary /'kɒrənərɪ/ adj coronario ● n [**thrombosis**] trombosi f coronarica

coronation /kɒrə'neɪʃn/ n incoronazione f

coroner /'kɒrənə(r)/ n coroner m inv (nel diritto britannico, ufficiale incaricato delle indagini su morti sospette)

corporal¹ /'kɔ:pərəl/ n (Mil)

caporale *m*

corporal² *adj* corporale; ∼ **punish-ment** punizione *f* corporale

corporate /ˈkɔːpərət/ *adj* (decision, policy, image) aziendale; ∼ **life** la vita in un'azienda

corporation /kɔːpəˈreɪʃn/ *n* ente *m*; (*of town*) consiglio *m* comunale

corps /kɔː(r)/ *n* (*pl* **corps** /kɔːz/) corpo *m*

corpse /kɔːps/ *n* cadavere *m*

corpulent /ˈkɔːpjʊlənt/ *adj* cor-pulento

correct /kəˈrekt/ *adj* corretto; be ∼ (*person:*) aver ragione; ∼! esatto! •*vt* correggere. ∼**ion** *n* correzione *f*. ∼**ly** *adv* correttamente

correspond /kɒrɪˈspɒnd/ *vi* corri-spondere (**to** a); (*two things:*) corri-spondere; (*write*) scriversi. ∼**ence** *n* corrispondenza *f*. ∼**ent** *n* corrispon-dente *mf*. ∼**ing** *adj* corrispondente. ∼**ingly** *adv* in modo corrispondente

corridor /ˈkɒrɪdɔː(r)/ *n* corridoio *m*

corro|de /kəˈrəʊd/ *vt* corrodere •*vi* corrodersi. ∼**sion** *n* corrosione *f*

corrugated /ˈkɒrəɡeɪtɪd/ *adj* ondu-lato. ∼ **iron** *n* lamiera *f* ondulata

corrupt /kəˈrʌpt/ *adj* corrotto •*vt* corrompere. ∼**ion** *n* corruzione *f*

corset /ˈkɔːsɪt/ *n* & -**s** *pl* busto *m*

Corsica /ˈkɔːsɪkə/ *n* Corsica *f*. ∼**n** *adj* & *n* corso, -a *f*

cosmetic /kɒzˈmetɪk/ *adj* cosmetico •*n* ∼**s** *pl* cosmetici *mpl*

cosmic /ˈkɒzmɪk/ *adj* cosmico

cosmopolitan /kɒzməˈpɒlɪtən/ *adj* cosmopolita

cosmos /ˈkɒzmɒs/ *n* cosmo *m*

cosset /ˈkɒsɪt/ *vt* coccolare

cost /kɒst/ *n* costo *m*; ∼**s** *pl* (*Jur*) spese *fpl* processuali; at all ∼**s** a tutti i costi; I learnt to my ∼ ho imparato a mie spese •*vt* (*pt/pp* cost) costare; it ∼ me £20 mi è co-stato 20 sterline •*vt* (*pt/pp* costed)

∼ **[out]** stabilire il prezzo di

costly /ˈkɒstlɪ/ *adj* (**-ier, -iest**) costoso

costume /ˈkɒstjuːm/ *n* costume *m*. ∼ **jewellery** *n* bigiotteria *f*

cosy /ˈkəʊzɪ/ *adj* (**-ier, -iest**) (pub, chat) intimo; **it's nice and ∼ in here** si sta bene qui

cot /kɒt/ *n* lettino *m*; (*Am:* camp-bed) branda *f*

cottage /ˈkɒtɪdʒ/ *n* casetta *f*. ∼ 'cheese *n* fiocchi *mpl* di latte

cotton /ˈkɒtn/ *n* cotone *m* ●attrib di cotone ●**cotton on** *vi* 🄸 capire

cotton 'wool *n* cotone *m* idrofilo

couch /kaʊtʃ/ *n* divano *m*. ∼ **po-tato** *n* pantofolaio, -a *m*

cough /kɒf/ *n* tosse *f* •*vi* tossire. ▫ ∼ **up** *vt/i* sputare; (🄸: *pay*) sborsare

'cough mixture *n* sciroppo *m* per la tosse

council /ˈkaʊnsl/ *n* consiglio *m*. ∼ **house** *n* casa *f* popolare

councillor /ˈkaʊnsələ(r)/ *n* consi-gliere, -a *mf*

counsel /ˈkaʊnsl/ *n* consigli *mpl*; (*Jur*) avvocato *m* •*vt* (*pt/pp* coun-selled) consigliare a (person). ∼**lor** *n* consigliere, -a *mf*

count¹ /kaʊnt/ *n* (*nobleman*) conte *m*

count² *n* conto *m*; **keep** ∼ tenere il conto •*vt/i* contare. ▫ ∼ **on** *vt* contare su

countdown /'kaʊntdaʊn/ n conto m alla rovescia

counter¹ /'kaʊntə(r)/ n banco m; (in games) gettone m

counter² adv ~ to contro, in contrasto a; **go** ~ **to sth** andare contro qcsa ● vt/i opporre (measure, effect); parare (blow)

counter'act vt neutralizzare

'counter-attack n contrattacco m

'counterfeit /-fɪt/ adj contraffatto ● n contraffazione f ● vt contraffare

'counterfoil n matrice f

counter-pro'ductive adj controproduttivo

countess /'kaʊntɪs/ n contessa f

countless /'kaʊntlɪs/ adj innumerevole

country /'kʌntrɪ/ n nazione f, paese m; (native land) patria f; (countryside) campagna f; **in the** ~ in campagna; **go to the** ~ andare in campagna; (Pol) indire le elezioni politiche. ~**man** n uomo m di campagna; (fellow ~man) compatriota m. ~**side** n campagna f

county /'kaʊntɪ/ n contea f (unità amministrativa britannica)

coup /kuː/ n (Pol) colpo m di stato

couple /'kʌpl/ n coppia f; **a** ~ **of** un paio di

coupon /'kuːpɒn/ n tagliando m; (for discount) buono m sconto

courage /'kʌrɪdʒ/ n coraggio m. ~**ous** adj coraggioso

courgette /kʊə'ʒet/ n zucchino m

courier /'kʊrɪə(r)/ n corriere m; (for tourists) guida f

course /kɔːs/ n (Sch) corso m; (Naut) rotta f; (Culin) portata f; (for golf) campo m; ~ **of treatment** (Med) serie f inv di cure; **of** ~ naturalmente; **in the** ~ **of** durante; **in due** ~ a tempo debito

court /kɔːt/ n tribunale m; (Sport)

campo m; **take sb to** ~ citare qcno in giudizio ● vt fare la corte a (woman); sfidare (danger); ~**ing couples** coppiette fpl

courteous /'kɜːtɪəs/ adj cortese

courtesy /'kɜːtəsɪ/ n cortesia f

court: ~ **martial** n (pl ~**s martial**) corte f marziale ~**-martial** vt (pt ~**-martialled**) portare davanti alla corte marziale; ~**yard** n cortile m

cousin /'kʌzn/ n cugino, -a mf

cove /kəʊv/ n insenatura f

cover /'kʌvə(r)/ n copertura f; (of cushion, to protect sth) fodera f; (of book, magazine) copertina f; **take** ~ mettersi al riparo; **under separate** ~ a parte ● vt coprire; foderare (cushion); (Journ) fare un servizio su. □ ~ **up** vt coprire; fig soffocare (scandal)

coverage /'kʌvərɪdʒ/ n (Journ) it got a lot of ~ i media gli hanno dedicato molto spazio

cover: ~ **charge** n coperto m. ~**ing** n copertura f; (for floor) rivestimento m; ~**ing letter** lettera f d'accompagnamento

covet /'kʌvɪt/ vt bramare

cow /kaʊ/ n vacca f, mucca f

coward /'kaʊəd/ n vigliacco, -a mf. ~**ice** n vigliaccheria f. ~**ly** adj da vigliacco

'cowboy n cowboy m inv; 🄸 buffone m

cower /'kaʊə(r)/ vi acquattarsi

coy /kɔɪ/ adj falsamente timido; (flirtatiously) civettuolo; **be** ~ **about sth** essere evasivo su qcsa

crab /kræb/ n granchio m

crack /kræk/ n (in wall) crepa f; (in china, glass, bone) incrinatura f; (noise) scoppio m; (🄸: joke) battuta f; **have a** ~ (try) fare un tentativo ● adj (🄸: best) di prim'ordine ● vt incrinare (china, glass); schiacciare (nut); decifrare (code); 🄸 risolvere (problem); ~ **a joke** 🄸 fare una battuta ● vi (china, glass:) incrinarsi; (whip:) schioccare. ▫ ~ **down** vi 🔲 prendere seri provvedimenti. ▫ ~ **down on** vt 🔲 prendere seri provvedimenti contro

cracker /'krækə(r)/ n (biscuit) cracker m inv; (firework) petardo m; [Christmas] ~ tubo m di cartone colorato contenente una sorpresa

crackle /'krækl/ vi crepitare

cradle /'kreɪdl/ n culla f

craft¹ /krɑːft/ n inv (boat) imbarcazione f

craft² n mestiere m; (technique) arte f. **~sman** n artigiano m

crafty /'krɑːftɪ/ adj (-ier, -iest) astuto

cram /kræm/ v (pt/pp crammed) ● vt stipare (into in) ● vi (for exams) sgobbare

cramp /kræmp/ n crampo m. **~ed** adj (room) stretto; (handwriting) appiccicato

cranberry /'krænbərɪ/ n (Culin) mirtillo m rosso

crane /kreɪn/ n (at docks, bird) gru f inv ● vt ~ **one's neck** allungare il collo

crank¹ /kræŋk/ n tipo, -a mf strampalato, -a

crank² n (Techn) manovella f. **~shaft** n albero m a gomiti

cranky /'kræŋkɪ/ adj strampalato; (Am: irritable) irritabile

cranny /'krænɪ/ n fessura f

crash /kræʃ/ n (noise) fragore m; (Aeron, Auto) incidente m; (Comm) crollo m ● vi schiantarsi (into contro); (plane:) precipitare ● vt schiantare (car)

crash: ~ **course** n corso m intensivo. **~-helmet** n casco m

crate /kreɪt/ n (for packing) cassa f

crater /'kreɪtə(r)/ n cratere m

crav|e /kreɪv/ vt morire dalla voglia di. **~ing** n voglia f smodata

crawl /krɔːl/ n (swimming) stile m libero; **do the** ~ nuotare a stile libero; **at a** ~ a passo di lumaca ● vi andare carponi; ~ **with** brulicare di. **~er lane** n (Auto) corsia f riservata al traffico lento

crayon /'kreɪən/ n pastello m a cera; (pencil) matita f colorata

craze /kreɪz/ n mania f

crazy /'kreɪzɪ/ adj (-ier, -iest) matto; **be** ~ **about** andar matto per

creak /kriːk/ n scricchiolio m ● vi scricchiolare

cream /kriːm/ n crema f; (fresh) panna f ● adj (colour) [bianco] panna inv ● vt (Culin) sbattere. ~ '**cheese** n formaggio m cremoso. **~y** adj cremoso

crease /kriːs/ n piega f ● vt stropicciare ● vi stropicciarsi. **~-resistant** adj che non si stropiccia

creat|e /kriː'eɪt/ vt creare. **~ion** n creazione f. **~ive** adj creativo. **~or** n creatore, -trice mf

creature /'kriːtʃə(r)/ n creatura f

crèche /kreʃ/ n asilo m nido

credibility /kredə'bɪlətɪ/ n credibilità f

credible /'kredəbl/ adj credibile

credit /'kredɪt/ n credito m; (honour) merito m; **take the** ~ **for** prendersi il merito di ● vt (pt/pp credited) accreditare; ~ **sb with sth** (Comm) accreditare qcsa a qcno; fig attribuire qcsa a qcno. **~able** adj lodevole

credit: ~ **card** n carta f di credito. **~or** n creditore, -trice mf

creed /kriːd/ n credo m inv

creek /kriːk/ n insenatura f; (Am: stream) torrente m

creep /kriːp/ vi (pt/pp crept) muoversi furtivamente ● n 🔲 tipo m viscido. ~ **er** n pianta f rampicante. **~y** adj che fa venire i brividi

cremat|e /krɪ'meɪt/ vt cremare. **~ion** n cremazione f

crematorium /kremə'tɔːrɪəm/ n

crematorio m

crept /krept/ ▷CREEP

crescent /ˈkresənt/ n mezzaluna f

crest /krest/ n cresta f; (coat of arms) cimiero m

Crete /kriːt/ n Creta f

crevice /ˈkrevɪs/ n crepa f

crew /kruː/ n equipaggio m; (gang) équipe f inv. ~ **cut** n capelli mpl a spazzola. ~ **neck** n girocollo m

crib[1] /krɪb/ n (for baby) culla f

crib[2] vt/i (pt/pp cribbed) 🗊 copiare

crick /krɪk/ n ~ **in the neck** torcicollo m

cricket[1] /ˈkrɪkɪt/ n (insect) grillo m

cricket[2] n cricket m. ~**er** n giocatore m di cricket

crime /kraɪm/ n crimine m; (criminality) criminalità f

criminal /ˈkrɪmɪnl/ adj criminale; (law, court) penale ● n criminale mf

crimson /ˈkrɪmzn/ adj cremisi inv

cringe /krɪndʒ/ vi (cower) acquattarsi; (at bad joke etc) fare una smorfia

crinkle /ˈkrɪŋkl/ vt spiegazzare ● vi spiegazzarsi

cripple /ˈkrɪpl/ n storpio, -a mf ● vt storpiare; fig danneggiare. ~**d** adj (person) storpio; (ship) danneggiato

crisis /ˈkraɪsɪs/ n (pl -ses /-siːz/) crisi f inv

crisp /krɪsp/ adj croccante; (air) frizzante; (style) incisivo. ~**bread** n crostini mpl di pane. ~**s** npl patatine fpl

criterion /kraɪˈtɪərɪən/ n (pl -ria /-rɪə/) criterio m

critic /ˈkrɪtɪk/ n critico, -a mf. ~**al** adj critico. ~**ally** adv in modo critico; ~**ally ill** gravemente malato

criticism /ˈkrɪtɪsɪzm/ n critica f; **he doesn't like** ~ non ama le critiche

criticize /ˈkrɪtɪsaɪz/ vt criticare

croak /krəʊk/ vi gracchiare; (frog:) gracidare

Croatia /krəʊˈeɪʃə/ n Croazia f

crochet /ˈkrəʊʃeɪ/ n lavoro m all'uncinetto ● vt fare all'uncinetto. ~**hook** n uncinetto m

crockery /ˈkrɒkərɪ/ n terrecotte fpl

crocodile /ˈkrɒkədaɪl/ n coccodrillo m. ~ **tears** lacrime fpl di coccodrillo

crocus /ˈkrəʊkəs/ n (pl -es) croco m

crook /krʊk/ n (🗊: criminal) truffatore, -trice mf

crooked /ˈkrʊkɪd/ adj storto; (limb) storpiato; (🗊: dishonest) disonesto

crop /krɒp/ n raccolto m; fig quantità f inv ● v (pt/pp cropped) ● vt coltivare. □ ~ **up** vi 🗊 presentarsi

croquet /ˈkrəʊkeɪ/ n croquet m

croquette /krəʊˈket/ n crocchetta f

cross /krɒs/ adj (annoyed) arrabbiato; **talk at** ~ **purposes** fraintendersi ● n croce f; (Bot, Zool) incrocio m ● vt sbarrare (cheque); incrociare (road, animals). ~ **oneself** farsi il segno della croce; ~ **one's arms** incrociare le braccia; ~ **one's legs** accavallare le gambe; **keep one's fingers** ~**ed for sb** tenere le dita incrociate per qcno; **it** ~**ed my mind** mi è venuto in mente ● vi (go across) attraversare; (lines:) incrociarsi. □ ~ **out** vt depennare

cross: ~**bar** n (of goal) traversa f; (on bicycle) canna f. ~**ex'amine** vt sottoporre a controinterrogatorio. ~**-'eyed** adj strabico. ~**fire** n fuoco m incrociato. ~**ing** n (for pedestrians) passaggio m pedonale; (sea journey) traversata f. ~**'reference** n rimando m. ~**roads** n incrocio m. ~**'section** n sezione f; (of community) campione m. ~**word** n ~**word [puzzle]** parole fpl crociate

crouch /kraʊtʃ/ vi accovacciarsi

crow /krəʊ/ n corvo m; **as the** ~ **flies** in linea d'aria ● vi cantare. ~**bar** n piede m di porco

crowd /kraʊd/ n folla f ● vt affollare ● vi affollarsi. ~**ed** adj affollato

crown /kraʊn/ n corona f ● vt incoronare; incapsulare (tooth)

crucial /'kru:ʃl/ adj cruciale

crucifix /'kru:sɪfɪks/ n crocifisso m

crucif|ixion /kru:sɪ'fɪkʃn/ n crocifissione f. **~y** vt (pt/pp -ied) crocifiggere

crude /kru:d/ adj (oil) greggio; (language) crudo; (person) rozzo

cruel /kru:əl/ adj (crueller, cruellest) crudele (to verso). **~ly** adv con crudeltà. **~ty** n crudeltà f

cruis|e /kru:z/ n crociera f ● vi fare una crociera; (car:) andare a velocità di crociera. **~er** n (Mil) incrociatore m; (motor boat) motoscafo m. **~ing speed** n velocità m inv di crociera

crumb /krʌm/ n briciola f

crumb|le /'krʌmbl/ vt sbriciolare ● vi sbriciolarsi; (building, society:) sgretolarsi. **~ly** adj friabile

crumple /'krʌmpl/ vt spiegazzare ● vi spiegazzarsi

crunch /krʌntʃ/ n **①** when it comes to the **~** quando si viene al dunque ● vt sgranocchiare ● vi (snow:) scricchiolare

crusade /kru:'seɪd/ n crociata f. **~r** n crociato m

crush /krʌʃ/ n (crowd) calca f; have a **~ on sb** essersi preso una cotta per qcno ● vt schiacciare; sgualcire (clothes)

crust /krʌst/ n crosta f

crutch /krʌtʃ/ n gruccia f; (Anat) inforcatura f

crux /krʌks/ n fig punto m cruciale

cry /kraɪ/ n grido m; have a **~** farsi un pianto; a **far ~ from** fig tutta un'altra cosa rispetto a ● vi (pt/pp cried) (weep) piangere; (call) gridare

crypt /krɪpt/ n cripta f. **~ic** adj criptico

crystal /'krɪstl/ n cristallo m; (glassware) cristalli mpl. **~lize** vi (become clear) concretizzarsi

cub /kʌb/ n (animal) cucciolo m; C**~**

[Scout] lupetto m

Cuba /'kju:bə/ n Cuba f

cubby-hole /'kʌbɪ-/ n (compartment) scomparto m; (room) ripostiglio m

cub|e /kju:b/ n cubo m. **~ic** adj cubico

cubicle /'kju:bɪkl/ n cabina f

cuckoo /'kʊku:/ n cuculo m. **~ clock** n orologio m a cucù

cucumber /'kju:kʌmbə(r)/ n cetriolo m

cuddl|e /'kʌdl/ vt coccolare ● vi **~e up to** starsene accoccolati insieme a ● n have a **~e** (child:) farsi coccolare; (lovers:) abbracciarsi. **~y** adj tenerone; (wanting cuddles) coccolone. **~y 'toy** n peluche m inv

cue¹ /kju:/ n segnale m; (Theat) battuta f d'entrata

cue² n (in billiards) stecca f. **~ ball** n pallino m

cuff /kʌf/ n polsino m; (Am: turn-up) orlo m; (blow) scapaccione m; **off the ~** improvvisando ● vt dare una pacca a. **~-link** n gemello m

cul-de-sac /'kʌldəsæk/ n vicolo m cieco

culinary /'kʌlɪnərɪ/ adj culinario

cull /kʌl/ vt scegliere (flowers); (kill) selezionare e uccidere

culminat|e /'kʌlmɪneɪt/ vi culminare. **~ion** n culmine m

culprit /'kʌlprɪt/ n colpevole mf

cult /kʌlt/ n culto m

cultivate /'kʌltɪveɪt/ vt coltivare; fig coltivarsi (person)

cultural /'kʌltʃərəl/ adj culturale

culture /'kʌltʃə(r)/ n cultura f. **~d** adj colto

cumbersome /'kʌmbəsəm/ adj ingombrante

cunning /'kʌnɪŋ/ adj astuto ● n astuzia f

cup /kʌp/ n tazza f; (prize, of bra) coppa f

cupboard /'kʌbəd/ n armadio m.

~love ☐ amore m interessato

curator /kjʊəˈreɪtə(r)/ n direttore, -trice mf (di museo)

curb /kɜːb/ vt tenere a freno

curdle /ˈkɜːdl/ vi coagularsi

cure /kjʊə(r)/ n cura f ● vt curare; (salt) mettere sotto sale; (smoke) affumicare

curfew /ˈkɜːfjuː/ n coprifuoco m

curiosity /kjʊərɪˈɒsəti/ n curiosità f

curious /ˈkjʊərɪəs/ adj curioso. ~ly adv (strangely) curiosamente

curl /kɜːl/ n ricciolo m ● vt arricciare ● vi arricciarsi. □ ~ **up** vi raggomitolarsi

curler /ˈkɜːlə(r)/ n bigodino m

curly /ˈkɜːlɪ/ adj (-ier, -iest) riccio

currant /ˈkʌrənt/ n (dried) uvetta f

currency /ˈkʌrənsɪ/ n valuta f; (of word) ricorrenza f; **foreign** ~ valuta f estera

current /ˈkʌrənt/ adj corrente ● n corrente f. ~ **affairs** or **events** npl attualità fsg. ~ly adv attualmente

curriculum /kəˈrɪkjʊləm/ n programma m di studi. ~ **vitae** n curriculum vitae m inv

curry /ˈkʌrɪ/ n curry m inv; (meal) piatto m cucinato nel curry ● vt (pt/pp -ied) ~ **favour with sb** cercare d'ingraziarsi qcno

curse /kɜːs/ n maledizione f; (oath) imprecazione f ● vt maledire ● vi imprecare

cursory /ˈkɜːsərɪ/ adj sbrigativo

curt /kɜːt/ adj brusco

curtain /ˈkɜːtn/ n tenda f; (Theat) sipario m

curtsy /ˈkɜːtsɪ/ n inchino m ● vi (pt/pp -ied) fare l'inchino

curve /kɜːv/ n curva f ● vi curvare; ~ **to the right/left** curvare a destra/sinistra. ~d adj curvo

cushion /ˈkʊʃn/ n cuscino m ● vt attutire; (protect) proteggere

cushy /ˈkʊʃɪ/ adj (-ier, -iest) ☐

facile

custard /ˈkʌstəd/ n (liquid) crema f pasticciera

custody /ˈkʌstədɪ/ n (of child) custodia f; (imprisonment) detenzione f preventiva

custom /ˈkʌstəm/ n usanza f; (Jur) consuetudine f; (Comm) clientela f. ~ary adj (habitual) abituale; **it's ~ary to...** è consuetudine.... ~er n cliente mf

customs /ˈkʌstəmz/ npl dogana f. ~ **officer** n doganiere m

cut /kʌt/ n (with knife etc, of clothes) taglio m; (reduction) riduzione f; (in public spending) taglio m ● vt/i (pt/pp **cut**, pres p **cutting**) tagliare; (reduce) ridurre; ~ **one's finger** tagliarsi il dito; ~ **sb's hair** tagliare i capelli a qcno ● vi (with cards) alzare. □ ~ **back** vt tagliare (hair); potare (hedge); (reduce) ridurre. □ ~ **down** vt abbattere (tree); (reduce) ridurre. □ ~ **off** vt tagliar via; (disconnect) interrompere; fig isolare; **I was ~ off** (Teleph) la linea è caduta. □ ~ **out** vt ritagliare; (delete) eliminare; **be ~ out for** ☐ essere tagliato per; ~ **it out!** ☐ dacci un taglio!. □ ~ **up** vt (slice) tagliare a pezzi

cute /kjuːt/ adj ☐ (in appearance) carino; (clever) acuto

cutlery /ˈkʌtlərɪ/ n posate fpl

cutlet /ˈkʌtlɪt/ n cotoletta f

'cut-price adj a prezzo ridotto; (shop) che fa prezzi ridotti

'cut-throat adj spietato

cutting /ˈkʌtɪŋ/ adj (remark) tagliente ● n (from newspaper) ritaglio m; (of plant) talea f

CV n abbr curriculum vitae

cycl|e /ˈsaɪkl/ n ciclo m; (bicycle) bicicletta f, bici f inv ☐ ● vi andare in bicicletta. ~ing n ciclismo m. ~ist n ciclista mf

cylind|er /ˈsɪlɪndə(r)/ n cilindro m. ~rical adj cilindrico

cynic /'sınık/ n cinico, -a mf. **~al** adj cinico. **~ism** n cinismo m

Cyprus /'saıprəs/ n Cipro m

Czech /tʃek/ adj ceco; **~ Republic** Repubblica f Ceca ● n ceco, -a mf

Dd

dab /dæb/ n colpetto m; a **~** of un pochino di ● vt (pt/pp **dabbed**) toccare leggermente (eyes). □ **~ on** vt mettere un po' di (paint etc)

daddy-'long-legs n zanzarone m [dei boschi]; (Am: spider) ragno m

daffodil /'dæfədıl/ n giunchiglia f

daft /dɑːft/ adj sciocco

dagger /'dægə(r)/ n stiletto m

dahlia /'deılıə/ n dalia f

Dáil Eireann Dáil Eireann è la camera bassa del Parlamento della Repubblica di Irlanda. È composto di 166 deputati (o TD) in rappresentanza di 41 collegi elettorali. I deputati sono infatti eletti col sistema proporzionale e la Costituzione ne prevede uno per ogni 20.000-30.000 cittadini. *i*

---

daily /'deılı/ adj giornaliero ● adv giornalmente ● n (newspaper) quotidiano m; (🔲: cleaner) donna f delle pulizie

dainty /'deıntı/ adj (-ier, -iest) grazioso; (movement) delicato

dairy /'deərı/ n caseificio m; (shop) latteria f. **~ cow** n mucca f da latte. **~ products** npl latticini mpl

daisy /'deızı/ n margheritina f; (larger) margherita f

dam /dæm/ n diga f ● vt (pt/pp

dammed) costruire una diga su

damag|e /'dæmıdʒ/ n danno m (to a); **~es** pl (Jur) risarcimento msg ● vt danneggiare; fig nuocere a. **~ing** adj dannoso

dame /deım/ n liter dama f; Am 🔲 donna f

damn /dæm/ adj 🔲 maledetto ● adv (lucky, late) maledettamente ● n I **don't give a ~** 🔲 non me ne frega un accidente ● vt dannare. **~ation** n dannazione f ● int 🔲 accidenti!

damp /dæmp/ adj umido ● n umidità f ● vt inumidire

dance /dɑːns/ n ballo m ● vt/i ballare. **~-hall** n sala f da ballo. **~ music** n musica f da ballo

dancer /'dɑːnsə(r)/ n ballerino, -a mf

dandelion /'dændılaıən/ n dente m di leone

dandruff /'dændrʌf/ n forfora f

Dane /deın/ n danese mf; **Great ~** danese m

danger /'deındʒə(r)/ n pericolo m; **in/out of ~** in/fuori pericolo. **~ous** adj pericoloso. **~ously** adv pericolosamente; **~ously ill** in pericolo di vita

dangle /'dæŋgl/ vi penzolare ● vt far penzolare

Danish /'deınıʃ/ adj & n danese m. **~ 'pastry** n dolce m a base di pasta sfoglia contenente pasta di mandorle, mele ecc

dare /deə(r)/ vt/i osare; (challenge) sfidare (to a); **~ [to] do sth** osare fare qcsa; **I ~ say!** molto probabilmente! ● n sfida f. **~devil** n spericolato, -a mf

daring /'deərıŋ/ adj audace ● n audacia f

dark /dɑːk/ adj buio; **~ blue/brown** blu/marrone scuro; **it's getting ~** sta cominciando a fare buio; **~ horse** fig (in race, contest) vincitore m imprevisto; (fig much known about) misterioso m; **keep sth ~** fig tenere qcsa nascosto ● n **after ~** col buio;

in the ~ al buio; **keep sb in the** ~ fig tenere qcno all'oscuro

dark|en /'dɑːkn/ vt oscurare ●vi oscurarsi. ~**ness** n buio m

'**dark-room** n camera f oscura

darling /'dɑːlɪŋ/ adj adorabile; **my** ~ **Joan** carissima Joan ●n tesoro m

darn /dɑːn/ vt rammendare. ~**ing-needle** n ago m da rammendo

dart /dɑːt/ n dardo m; (in sewing) pince f inv; ~**s** sg (game) freccette fpl ●vi lanciarsi

dartboard /'dɑːtbɔːd/ n bersaglio m [per freccette]

dash /dæʃ/ n (Typ) trattino m; (in Morse) linea f; **a** ~ **of milk** un goccio di latte; (make a) ~ **for** lanciarsi verso ●vi **I must** ~ devo scappare ●vt far svanire (hopes). □ ~ **off** vi scappar via ●vt (write quickly) buttare giù. □ ~ **out** vi uscire di corsa

'**dashboard** n cruscotto m

data /'deɪtə/ npl & sg dati mpl. ~**base** n base [di] dati f, database m inv. ~**comms** n telematica f. ~ **processing** n elaborazione f [di] dati

date[1] /deɪt/ n (fruit) dattero m

date[2] n data f; (meeting) appuntamento m; **to** ~ fino ad oggi; **out of** ~ (not fashionable) fuori moda; (expired) scaduto; (information) non aggiornato; **make a** ~ **with sb** dare un appuntamento a qcno; **be up to** ~ essere aggiornato ●vt/i datare; (go out with) uscire con. □ ~ **back to** vi risalire a

dated /'deɪtɪd/ adj fuori moda; (language) antiquato

daub /dɔːb/ vt imbrattare (walls)

daughter /'dɔːtə(r)/ n figlia f. ~**-in-law** n (pl ~**s-in-law**) nuora f

dawdle /'dɔːdl/ vi bighellonare; (over work) cincischiarsi

dawn /dɔːn/ n alba f; **at** ~ all'alba ●vi albeggiare; **it** ~**ed on me** fig mi è apparso chiaro

day /deɪ/ n giorno m; (whole day) gior-

nata f; (period) epoca f; **these** ~**s** oggigiorno; **in those** ~**s** a quei tempi; **it's had its** ~ ha fatto il suo tempo

day: ~**break** n at ~**break** allo spuntar del giorno. ~**-dream** n sogno m ad occhi aperti ●vi sognare ad occhi aperti. ~**light** n luce f del giorno. ~**time** n giorno m; **in the** ~**time** di giorno

daze /deɪz/ n **in a** ~ stordito; fig sbalordito. ~**d** adj stordito; fig sbalordito

dazzle /'dæzl/ vt abbagliare

dead /ded/ adj morto; (numb) intorpidito; ~ **body** morto m; ~ **centre** pieno centro m ●adv ~ **tired** stanco morto; ~ **slow/easy** lentissimo/facilissimo; **you're** ~ **right** hai perfettamente ragione; **stop** ~ fermarsi di colpo; **be** ~ **on time** essere in perfetto orario ●n **the** ~ pl i morti; **in the** ~ **of night** nel cuore della notte

deaden /'dedn/ vt attutire (sound); calmare (pain)

dead: ~ '**end** n vicolo m cieco. ~**line** n scadenza f. ~**lock** n reach ~**lock** fig giungere a un punto morto

deadly /'dedlɪ/ adj (-**ier, -iest**) mortale; (🄵 dreary) barboso; ~ **sins** peccati mpl capitali

deaf /def/ adj sordo; ~ **and dumb** sordomuto. ~**-aid** n apparecchio m acustico

deaf|en /'defn/ vt assordare; (permanently) render sordo. ~**ening** adj assordante. ~**ness** n sordità f

deal /diːl/ n (agreement) accordo m; (in business) accordo m, affare m; **whose** ~? (in cards) a chi tocca dare le carte?; **a good** or **great** ~ molto; **get a raw** ~ 🄵 ricevere un trattamento ingiusto ●vt (pt/pp **dealt** /delt/) (in cards) dare; ~ **sb a blow** dare un colpo a qcno. □ ~ **in** vi trattare in. □ ~ **out** vt (hand out) distribuire. □ ~ **with** v (*handle*) occuparsi di; trattare con (*company*); (*be about*) trattare di; **that's been ~t with** è stato risolto

deal|er /'di:lə(r)/ n commerciante mf; (*in drugs*) spacciatore, -trice mf. **~ings** npl **have ~ings with** avere o che fare con

dean /di:n/ n decano m; (*Univ*) ≈ preside mf di facoltà

dear /dɪə(r)/ adj caro; (*in letter*) Caro; (*formal*) Gentile ●n caro, -a mf ●int **oh ~!** Dio mio!. **~ly** adv (*love*) profondamente; (*pay*) profumatamente

death /deθ/ n morte f. **~ certificate** n certificato m di morte. **~ duty** n tassa f di successione

death trap n trappola f mortale

debatable /dɪ'beɪtəbl/ adj discutibile

debate /dɪ'beɪt/ n dibattito m ●vt discutere; (*in formal debate*) dibattere ●vi **~ whether to...** considerare se...

debauchery /dɪ'bɔːtʃərɪ/ n dissolutezza f

debit /'debɪt/ n debito m ●vt (pt/pp **debited**) (*Comm*) addebitare (sum)

debris /'debriː/ n macerie fpl

debt /det/ n debito m; **be in ~** avere dei debiti. **~or** n debitore, -trice mf

decade /'dekeɪd/ n decennio m

decaden|ce /'dekədəns/ n decadenza f. **~t** adj decadente

decay /dɪ'keɪ/ n (also fig) decadenza f; (rot) decomposizione f; (of tooth) carie f inv ●vi imputridire; (rot) decomporsi; (tooth): cariarsi

deceased /dɪ'siːst/ adj defunto ●n **the ~d** il defunto; la defunta

deceit /dɪ'siːt/ n inganno m. **~ful** adj falso

deceive /dɪ'siːv/ vt ingannare

December /dɪ'sembə(r)/ n dicembre m

decency /'diːsənsɪ/ n decenza f

decent /'diːsənt/ adj decente; (respectable) rispettabile; **very ~ of you** molto gentile da parte tua. **~ly** adv decentemente; (kindly) gentilmente

decept|ion /dɪ'sepʃn/ n inganno m. **~ive** adj ingannevole. **~ively** adv ingannevolmente; **it looks ~ively easy** sembra facile, ma non lo è

decibel /'desɪbel/ n decibel m inv

decide /dɪ'saɪd/ vt decidere ●vi decidere (**on** di)

decided /dɪ'saɪdɪd/ adj risoluto. **~ly** adv risolutamente; (without doubt) senza dubbio

decimal /'desɪml/ adj decimale ●n numero m decimale. **~ 'point** n virgola f

decipher /dɪ'saɪfə(r)/ vt decifrare

decision /dɪ'sɪʒn/ n decisione f

decisive /dɪ'saɪsɪv/ adj decisivo

deck[1] /dek/ vt abbigliare

deck[2] n (Naut) ponte m; **on ~** in coperta; **top ~** (of bus) piano m di sopra; **~ of cards** mazzo m. **~chair** n [sedia f a] sdraio f inv

declaration /deklə'reɪʃn/ n dichiarazione f

declare /dɪ'kleə(r)/ vt dichiarare; **anything to ~?** niente da dichiarare?

decline /dɪ'klaɪn/ n declino m ●vt also (Gram) declinare ●vi (decrease) diminuire; (health): deperire; (say no) rifiutare

decode /diː'kəʊd/ vt decifrare; (Comput) decodificare

decompose /diːkəm'pəʊz/ vi decomporsi

décor /'deɪkɔː(r)/ n decorazione f; (including furniture) arredamento m

decorat|e /'dekəreɪt/ vt decorare; (paint) pitturare; (wallpaper) tappezzare. **~ion** n decorazione f. **~ive** adj decorativo. **~or** n **painter and ~or** imbianchino m

decoy[1] /'diːkɔɪ/ n esca f

d

decoy² /dɪˈkɔɪ/ vt adescare

decrease¹ /ˈdiːkriːs/ n diminuzione f

decrease² /dɪˈkriːs/ vt/i diminuire

decree /dɪˈkriː/ n decreto m ● vt (pt/pp decreed) decretare

decrepit /dɪˈkrepɪt/ adj decrepito

dedicat|e /ˈdedɪkeɪt/ vt dedicare. ~ed adj (person) scrupoloso. ~ion n dedizione f; (in book) dedica f

deduce /dɪˈdjuːs/ vt dedurre (from da)

deduct /dɪˈdʌkt/ vt dedurre

deduction /dɪˈdʌkʃn/ n deduzione f

deed /diːd/ n azione f; (Jur) atto m di proprietà

deem /diːm/ vt ritenere

deep /diːp/ adj profondo; go off the ~ end 🄵 arrabbiarsi

deepen /ˈdiːpn/ vt approfondire; scavare più profondamente (trench) ● vi approfondirsi; (fig: mystery:) infittirsi

deep-'freeze n congelatore m

deeply /ˈdiːpli/ adv profondamente

deer /dɪə(r)/ n inv cervo m

deface /dɪˈfeɪs/ vt sfigurare (picture); deturpare (monument)

default /dɪˈfɔːlt/ n (non-payment) morosità f; (failure to appear) contumacia f; win by ~ (Sport) vincere per abbandono dell'avversario; in ~ of per mancanza di ● adj ~ drive (Comput) lettore m di default ● vi (not pay) venir meno a un pagamento

defeat /dɪˈfiːt/ n sconfitta f ● vt sconfiggere; (frustrate) vanificare (attempts); that ~s the object questo fa fallire l'obiettivo

defect¹ /dɪˈfekt/ vi (Pol) fare defezione

defect² /ˈdiːfekt/ n difetto m. ~ive adj difettoso

defence /dɪˈfens/ n difesa f. ~less adj indifeso

defend /dɪˈfend/ vt difendere; (justify) giustificare. ~ant n (Jur) imputato, -a mf

defensive /dɪˈfensɪv/ adj difensivo ● n difensiva f; on the ~ sulla difensiva

defer /dɪˈfɜː(r)/ v (pt/pp deferred) ● vt (postpone) rinviare ● vi ~ to sb rimettersi a qcno

deferen|ce /ˈdefərəns/ n deferenza f. ~tial adj deferente

defian|ce /dɪˈfaɪəns/ n sfida f; in ~ce of sfidando. ~t adj (person) ribelle; (gesture, attitude) di sfida. ~tly adv con aria di sfida

deficien|cy /dɪˈfɪʃənsɪ/ n insufficienza f. ~t adj insufficiente; be ~t in mancare di

deficit /ˈdefɪsɪt/ n deficit m inv

define /dɪˈfaɪn/ vt definire

definite /ˈdefɪnɪt/ adj definito; (certain) (answer, yes) definitivo; (improvement, difference) netto; he was ~ about it è stato chiaro in proposito. ~ly adv sicuramente

definition /defɪˈnɪʃn/ n definizione f

definitive /dɪˈfɪnətɪv/ adj definitivo

deflat|e /dɪˈfleɪt/ vt sgonfiare. ~ion n (Comm) deflazione f

deflect /dɪˈflekt/ vt deflettere

deform|ed /dɪˈfɔːmd/ adj deforme. ~ity n deformità f inv

defrost /diːˈfrɒst/ vt sbrinare (fridge); scongelare (food)

deft /deft/ adj abile

defuse /diːˈfjuːz/ vt disinnescare; calmare (situation)

defy /dɪˈfaɪ/ v (pt/pp -ied) (challenge) sfidare; resistere a (attempt); (not obey) disobbedire a

degenerate¹ /dɪˈdʒenəreɪt/ vi degenerare; ~ into fig degenerare in

degenerate² /dɪˈdʒenərət/ adj degenerato

degree /dɪˈɡriː/ n grado m; (Univ)

laurea f; **20 ~s** 20 gradi; **not to the same ~** non allo stesso livello

deign /deɪn/ vi **~ to do sth** degnarsi di fare qcsa

deity /ˈdiːɪtɪ/ n divinità f inv

dejected /dɪˈdʒektɪd/ adj demoralizzato

delay /dɪˈleɪ/ n ritardo m; **without ~** senza indugio ● vt ritardare; **be ~ed** (person): essere trattenuto; (train, aircraft): essere in ritardo ● vi indugiare

delegate¹ /ˈdelɪɡət/ n delegato, -a mf

delegat|e² /ˈdelɪɡeɪt/ vt delegare. **~ion** n delegazione f

delet|e /dɪˈliːt/ vt cancellare. **~ion** n cancellatura f

deliberate¹ /dɪˈlɪbərət/ adj deliberato; (slow) posato; **~ly** adv deliberatamente; (slowly) in modo posato

deliberat|e² /dɪˈlɪbəreɪt/ vt/i deliberare. **~ion** n deliberazione f

delicacy /ˈdelɪkəsɪ/ n delicatezza f; (food) prelibatezza f

delicate /ˈdelɪkət/ adj delicato

delicatessen /delɪkəˈtesn/ n negozio m di specialità gastronomiche

delicious /dɪˈlɪʃəs/ adj delizioso

delight /dɪˈlaɪt/ n piacere m ● vt deliziare ● vi **~ in** dilettarsi con. **~ed** adj lieto. **~ful** adj delizioso

deli|rious /dɪˈlɪrɪəs/ adj **be ~rious** delirare; (fig: very happy) essere pazzo di gioia. **~rium** n delirio m

deliver /dɪˈlɪvə(r)/ vt consegnare; recapitare (post, newspaper); tenere (speech); dare (message); tirare (blow); (set free) liberare; **~ a baby** far nascere un bambino. **~ance** n liberazione f. **~y** n consegna f; (of post) distribuzione f; (Med) parto m; **cash on ~y** pagamento m alla consegna

delude /dɪˈluːd/ vt ingannare; **~ oneself** illudersi

deluge /ˈdeljuːdʒ/ n diluvio m ● vt

(fig: with requests etc) inondare

delusion /dɪˈluːʒn/ n illusione f

de luxe /dəˈlʌks/ adj di lusso

delve /delv/ vi **into** (into pocket etc) frugare in; (into notes, the past) fare ricerche in

demand /dɪˈmɑːnd/ n richiesta f; (Comm) domanda f; **in ~** richiesto; **on ~** a richiesta ● vt esigere (of/from sb). **~ing** adj esigente

demented /dɪˈmentɪd/ adj demente

demister /diːˈmɪstə(r)/ n (Auto) sbrinatore m

demo /ˈdeməʊ/ n (pl **~s**) ◫ manifestazione f; **~ disk** (Comput) demodisk m inv

democracy /dɪˈmɒkrəsɪ/ n democrazia f

democrat /ˈdeməkræt/ n democratico, -a mf. **~ic** adj democratico

demo|lish /dɪˈmɒlɪʃ/ vt demolire. **~lition** n demolizione f

demon /ˈdiːmən/ n demonio m

demonstrat|e /ˈdemənstreɪt/ vt dimostrare; fare una dimostrazione sull'uso di (appliance) ● vi (Pol) manifestare. **~ion** n dimostrazione f; (Pol) manifestazione f

demonstrator /ˈdemənstreɪtə(r)/ n (Pol) manifestante mf; (for product) dimostratore, -trice mf

demoralize /dɪˈmɒrəlaɪz/ vt demoralizzare

demote /dɪˈməʊt/ vt retrocedere di grado; (Mil) degradare

demure /dɪˈmjʊə(r)/ adj schivo

den /den/ n tana f; (room) rifugio m

denial /dɪˈnaɪəl/ n smentita f

denim /ˈdenɪm/ n [tessuto m] jeans m; **~s** pl [blue]jeans mpl

Denmark /ˈdenmɑːk/ n Danimarca f

denounce /dɪˈnaʊns/ vt denunciare

dens|e /dens/ adj denso; (crowd, forest) fitto; (stupid) ottuso. **~ely** adv (populated) densamente; **~ely wooded** fittamente ricoperto di alberi. **~ity** n densità f inv; (of forest) fittezza f

dent /dent/ n ammaccatura f ● vt ammaccare; **~ed** adj ammaccato

dental /'dentl/ adj dei denti; (treatment) dentistico; (hygiene) dentale. **~ surgeon** n odontoiatra mf, medico m dentista

dentist /'dentist/ n dentista mf. **~ry** n odontoiatria f

dentures /'dentʃəz/ npl dentiera fsg

deny /dɪ'naɪ/ vt (pt/pp -ied) negare; (officially) smentire; **~ sb sth** negare qcsa a qcno

deodorant /diː'əʊdərənt/ n deodorante m

depart /dɪ'pɑːt/ vi (plane, train:) partire; (liter: person) andare via; (deviate) allontanarsi (**from** da)

department /dɪ'pɑːtmənt/ n reparto m; (Pol) ministero m; (of company) sezione f; (Univ) dipartimento m. **~ store** n grande magazzino m

departure /dɪ'pɑːtʃə(r)/ n partenza f; (from rule) allontanamento f; **new ~** svolta f

depend /dɪ'pend/ vi dipendere (**on** da); (rely) contare (**on** su); **it all ~s** dipende; **~ing on what he says** a seconda di quello che dice. **~able** adj fidato. **~ant** n persona f a carico. **~ence** n dipendenza f. **~ent** adj dipendente (**on** da)

depict /dɪ'pɪkt/ vt (in writing) dipingere; (with picture) rappresentare

deplete /dɪ'pliːt/ vt ridurre; **totally ~d** completamente esaurito

deplor|able /dɪ'plɔːrəbl/ adj deplorevole. **~e** vt deplorare

deploy /dɪ'plɔɪ/ vt (Mil) spiegare ● vi schierarsi

deport /dɪ'pɔːt/ vt deportare. **~ation** n deportazione f

depose /dɪ'pəʊz/ vt deporre

deposit /dɪ'pɒzɪt/ n deposito m;

(against damage) cauzione f; (first instalment) acconto m ● vt (pt/pp deposited) depositare. **~ account** n libretto m di risparmio; (without instant access) conto m vincolato

depot /'depəʊ/ n deposito m; Am (Rail) stazione f ferroviaria

depress /dɪ'pres/ vt deprimere; (press down) premere. **~ed** adj depresso; **~ed area** zona f depressa. **~ing** adj deprimente. **~ion** n depressione f

deprivation /deprɪ'veɪʃn/ n privazione f

deprive /dɪ'praɪv/ vt **~ sb of sth** privare qcno di qcsa. **~d** adj (area, childhood) disagiato

depth /depθ/ n profondità f inv; **in ~** (study, analyse) in modo approfondito; **in the ~s of winter** in pieno inverno; **be out of one's ~** (in water) non toccare il fondo; fig sentirsi in alto mare

deputize /'depjʊtaɪz/ vi **~ for** fare le veci di

deputy /'depjʊtɪ/ n vice mf; (temporary) sostituto, -a mf ● attrib **~ leader** ≈ vicesegretario, -a mf; **~ chairman** vicepresidente mf

derail /dɪ'reɪl/ vt **be ~ed** (train:) essere deragliato. **~ment** n deragliamento m

derelict /'derɪlɪkt/ adj abbandonato

deri|de /dɪ'raɪd/ vt deridere. **~sion** n derisione f

derisory /dɪ'raɪsərɪ/ adj (laughter) derisorio; (offer) irrisorio

derivation /derɪ'veɪʃn/ n derivazione f

derivative /dɪ'rɪvətɪv/ adj derivato ● n derivato m

derive /dɪ'raɪv/ vt (obtain) derivare; **be ~d from** (word:) derivare da

derogatory /dɪ'rɒgətrɪ/ adj (comments) peggiorativo

descend /dɪ'send/ vi scendere ● vt scendere da; **be ~ed from** discendere da. **~ant** n discendente mf

descent /dɪˈsent/ n discesa f; (lineage) origine f

describe /dɪˈskraɪb/ vt descrivere

descrip|tion /dɪˈskrɪpʃn/ n descrizione f; **they had no help of any ~tion** non hanno avuto proprio nessun aiuto. **~tive** adj descrittivo; (vivid) vivido

desecrat|e /ˈdesɪkreɪt/ vt profanare. **~ion** n profanazione f

desert[1] /ˈdezət/ n deserto m ● adj deserto; **~ island** isola f deserta

desert[2] /dɪˈzɜːt/ vt abbandonare ● vi disertare. **~ed** adj deserto. **~er** n (Mil) disertore m. **~ion** n (Mil) diserzione f; (of family) abbandono m

deserts /dɪˈzɜːts/ npl **get one's just ~** ottenere ciò che ci si merita

deserv|e /dɪˈzɜːv/ vt meritare. **~ing** adj meritevole; **~ing cause** opera f meritoria

design /dɪˈzaɪn/ n progettazione f; (fashion, appearance) design m; (pattern) modello m; (aim) proposito m ● vt progettare; disegnare (clothes, furniture, model); **be ~ed for** essere fatto per

designat|e /ˈdezɪgneɪt/ vt designare. **~ion** n designazione f

designer /dɪˈzaɪnə(r)/ n progettista mf; (of clothes) stilista mf; (Theat: of set) scenografo, -a mf

desirable /dɪˈzaɪərəbl/ adj desiderabile

desire /dɪˈzaɪə(r)/ n desiderio m ● vt desiderare

desk /desk/ n scrivania f; (in school) banco m; (in hotel) reception f inv; (cash ~) cassa f. **~top 'publishing** n desktop publishing m, editoria f da tavolo

desolat|e /ˈdesələt/ adj desolato. **~ion** n desolazione f

despair /dɪˈspeə(r)/ n disperazione f; **in ~** disperato; (say) per disperazione ● vi **I ~ of that boy** quel ra-

gazzo mi fa disperare

desperat|e /ˈdespərət/ adj disperato; **be ~** (criminal:) essere un disperato; **be ~e for sth** morire dalla voglia di. **~ely** adv disperatamente; **he said ~ely** ha detto, disperato. **~ion** n disperazione f; **in ~ion** per disperazione

despicable /dɪˈspɪkəbl/ adj disprezzevole

despise /dɪˈspaɪz/ vt disprezzare

despite /dɪˈspaɪt/ prep malgrado

despondent /dɪˈspɒndənt/ adj abbattuto

despot /ˈdespɒt/ n despota m

dessert /dɪˈzɜːt/ n dolce m. **~ spoon** n cucchiaio m da dolce

destination /destɪˈneɪʃn/ n destinazione f

destiny /ˈdestɪnɪ/ n destino m

destitute /ˈdestɪtjuːt/ adj bisognoso

destroy /dɪˈstrɔɪ/ vt distruggere. **~er** n (Naut) cacciatorpediniere m

destruc|tion /dɪˈstrʌkʃn/ n distruzione f. **~tive** adj distruttivo; (fig: criticism) negativo

detach /dɪˈtætʃ/ vt staccare. **~able** adj separabile. **~ed** adj fig distaccato; **~ed house** villetta f

detachment /dɪˈtætʃmənt/ n distacco m; (Mil) distaccamento m

detail /ˈdiːteɪl/ n particolare m, dettaglio m; **in ~** particolareggiatamente ● vt esporre con tutti i particolari; (Mil) assegnare. **~ed** adj particolareggiato, dettagliato

detain /dɪˈteɪn/ vt (police:) trattenere; (delay) far ritardare. **~ee** n detenuto, -a mf

detect /dɪˈtekt/ vt individuare; (perceive) percepire. **~ion** n scoperta f

detective /dɪˈtektɪv/ n investigatore, -trice mf. **~ story** n racconto m poliziesco

detector /dɪˈtektə(r)/ n (for metal) metal detector m inv

detention /dɪˈtenʃn/ n detenzione f; (Sch) punizione f

deter /dɪˈtɜː(r)/ vt (pt/pp deterred) impedire; ~ sb from doing sth impedire a qcno di fare qcsa

detergent /dɪˈtɜːdʒənt/ n detersivo m

deteriorat|e /dɪˈtɪərɪəreɪt/ vi deteriorarsi. ~ion n deterioramento m

determination /dɪtɜːmɪˈneɪʃn/ n determinazione f

determine /dɪˈtɜːmɪn/ vt (ascertain) determinare; ~ to (resolve) decidere di. ~d adj deciso

deterrent /dɪˈterənt/ n deterrente m

detest /dɪˈtest/ vt detestare. ~able adj detestabile

detonat|e /ˈdetəneɪt/ vt far detonare ● vi detonare. ~or n detonatore m

detour /ˈdiːtʊə(r)/ n deviazione f

detract /dɪˈtrækt/ vi ~ from sminuire (merit); rovinare (pleasure, beauty)

detriment /ˈdetrɪmənt/ n to the ~ of a danno di. ~al adj dannoso

devastat|e /ˈdevəsteɪt/ vt devastare. ~ed adj 🔲 sconvolto. ~ing adj devastante; (news) sconvolgente. ~ion n devastazione f

develop /dɪˈveləp/ vt sviluppare; contrarre (illness); (add to value of) valorizzare (area) ● vi svilupparsi; ~ into divenire. ~er n [property] ~er n imprenditore, -trice mf edile

development /dɪˈveləpmənt/ n sviluppo m; (of vaccine etc) messa f a punto

deviant /ˈdiːvɪənt/ adj deviato

deviat|e /ˈdiːvɪeɪt/ vi deviare. ~ion n deviazione f

device /dɪˈvaɪs/ n dispositivo m

devil /ˈdevl/ n diavolo m

devious /ˈdiːvɪəs/ adj (person) sub-

dolo; (route) tortuoso

devise /dɪˈvaɪz/ vt escogitare

devoid /dɪˈvɔɪd/ adj ~ of privo di

devolution /diːvəˈluːʃn/ n (of power) decentramento m

devot|e /dɪˈvəʊt/ vt dedicare. ~ed adj (daughter etc) affezionato; be ~ed to sth consacrarsi a qcsa. ~ee n appassionato, -a mf

devotion /dɪˈvəʊʃn/ n dedizione f; ~s pl (Relig) devozione fsg

devour /dɪˈvaʊə(r)/ vt divorare

devout /dɪˈvaʊt/ adj devoto

dew /djuː/ n rugiada f

dexterity /dekˈsterətɪ/ n destrezza f

diabet|es /daɪəˈbiːtiːz/ n diabete m. ~ic adj diabetico ● n diabetico, -a mf

diabolical /daɪəˈbɒlɪkl/ adj diabolico

diagnose /daɪəgˈnəʊz/ vt diagnosticare

diagnosis /daɪəgˈnəʊsɪs/ n (pl -oses /-siːz/) diagnosi f inv

diagonal /daɪˈægənl/ adj diagonale ● n diagonale f

diagram /ˈdaɪəgræm/ n diagramma m

dial /ˈdaɪəl/ n (of clock, machine) quadrante m; (Teleph) disco m combinatore ● v (pt/pp dialled) ● vi (Teleph) fare il numero; ~ direct chiamare in teleselezione ● vt fare (number)

dialect /ˈdaɪəlekt/ n dialetto m

dialling /ˈdaɪəlɪŋ/ ~ code n prefisso m. ~ tone n segnale m di linea libera

dialogue /ˈdaɪəlɒg/ n dialogo m

'dial tone n Am (Teleph) segnale m di linea libera

diameter /daɪˈæmɪtə(r)/ n diametro m

diamond /ˈdaɪəmənd/ n diamante m, brillante m; (shape) losanga f; ~s pl (in cards) quadri mpl

diaper /ˈdaɪəpə(r)/ n Am pannolino m

diaphragm /'daɪəfræm/ n diaframma m

diarrhoea /daɪə'rɪːə/ n diarrea f

diary /'daɪərɪ/ n (for appointments) agenda f; (for writing in) diario m

dice /daɪs/ n inv dadi mpl ● vt (Culin) tagliare a dadini

dictat|e /dɪk'teɪt/ vt/i dettare. ~ion n dettato m

dictator /dɪk'teɪtə(r)/ n dittatore m. ~ial adj dittatoriale. ~ship n dittatura f

dictionary /'dɪkʃənrɪ/ n dizionario m

did /dɪd/ ▷**DO**

didn't /'dɪdnt/ = did not

die /daɪ/ vi (pres p dying) morire (of di); **be dying to do sth** 🔢 morire dalla voglia di fare qcsa. □ ~ **down** vi calmarsi; (fire, flames:) spegnersi. □ ~ **out** vi estinguersi; (custom:) morire

diesel /'diːzl/ n diesel m

diet /'daɪət/ n regime m alimentare; (restricted) dieta f; **be on a** ~ essere a dieta ● vi essere a dieta

differ /'dɪfə(r)/ vi differire; (disagree) non essere d'accordo

difference /'dɪfrəns/ n differenza f; (disagreement) divergenza f

different /'dɪfrənt/ adj diverso, differente; (various) diversi; **be** ~ **from** essere diverso da

differently /'dɪfrəntlɪ/ adv in modo diverso; ~ **from** diversamente da

difficult /'dɪfɪkəlt/ adj difficile. ~y n difficoltà f inv

diffuse¹ /dɪ'fjuːs/ adj diffuso; (wordy) prolisso

diffuse² /dɪ'fjuːz/ vt (Phys) diffondere

dig /dɪg/ n (poke) spinta f; (remark) frecciata f; (Archaeol) scavo m; ~s pl 🔢 camera fsg ammobiliata ● vt/i (pt/pp **dug**, pres p **digging**) scavare

(hole); vangare (garden); (thrust) conficcare; ~ **sb in the ribs** dare una gomitata a qcno. □ ~ **out** vt fig tirar fuori. □ ~ **up** vt scavare (garden, street, object); sradicare (plant); (fig: find) scovare

digest¹ /'daɪdʒest/ n compendio m

digest² /daɪ'dʒest/ vt digerire. ~**ible** adj digeribile. ~**ion** n digestione f

digger /'dɪgə(r)/ n (Techn) scavatrice f

digit /'dɪdʒɪt/ n cifra f; (finger) dito m

digital /'dɪdʒɪtl/ adj digitale; ~ **camera** fotocamera f digitale. ~ **clock** orologio m digitale

digitize /'dɪdʒɪtaɪz/ vt digitalizzare

dignified /'dɪgnɪfaɪd/ adj dignitoso

dignitary /'dɪgnɪtərɪ/ n dignitario m

dignity /'dɪgnɪtɪ/ n dignità f

digress /daɪ'gres/ vi divagare. ~**ion** n digressione f

dike /daɪk/ n diga f

dilapidated /dɪ'læpɪdeɪtɪd/ adj cadente

dilate /daɪ'leɪt/ vi dilatarsi

dilemma /dɪ'lemə/ n dilemma m

dilute /daɪ'luːt/ vt diluire

dim /dɪm/ adj (dimmer, dimmest) debole (light); (dark) scuro; (prospect, chance) scarso; (indistinct) impreciso; (🔢: stupid) tonto ● vt/i (pt/pp **dimmed**) affievolire. ~**ly** adv (see, remember) indistintamente; (shine) debolmente

dime /daɪm/ n Am moneta f da dieci centesimi

dimension /daɪ'menʃn/ n dimensione f

diminish /dɪ'mɪnɪʃ/ vt/i diminuire

dimple /'dɪmpl/ n fossetta f

din /dɪn/ n baccano m

dine /daɪn/ vi pranzare. ~**r** n (Am: restaurant) tavola f calda; **the last** ~**r in the restaurant** l'ultimo cliente nel ristorante

dinghy /ˈdɪŋgɪ/ n dinghy m; (inflatable) canotto m pneumatico

dingy /ˈdɪndʒɪ/ adj (-ier, -iest) squallido e tetro

dinner /ˈdɪnə(r)/ n cena f; (at midday) pranzo m. **~-jacket** n smoking m inv

dinosaur /ˈdaɪnəsɔː(r)/ n dinosauro m

dint /dɪnt/ n **by ~ of** a forza di

dip /dɪp/ n (in ground) inclinazione f; (Culin) salsina f; **go for a ~** andare a fare una nuotata ● v (pt/pp dipped) ● vt (in liquid) immergere; abbassare (head, headlights) ● vi (land): formare un avvallamento. □ **~ into** vt scorrere (book)

diphthong /ˈdɪfθɒŋ/ n dittongo m

diploma /dɪˈpləʊmə/ n diploma m

diplomacy /dɪˈpləʊməsɪ/ n diplomazia f

diplomat /ˈdɪpləmæt/ n diplomatico, -a mf. **~ic** adj diplomatico. **~ically** adv con diplomazia

'dip-stick n (Auto) astina f dell'olio

dire /ˈdaɪə(r)/ adj (situation, consequences) terribile

direct /dɪˈrekt/ adj diretto ● adv direttamente ● vt (aim) rivolgere (attention, criticism); (control) dirigere; fare la regia di (film, play); **~ sb** (show the way) indicare la strada a qcno; **~ sb to do sth** ordinare a qcno di fare qcsa. **~ 'current** n corrente m continua

direction /dɪˈrekʃn/ n direzione f; (of play, film) regia f; **~s** pl indicazioni fpl

directly /dɪˈrektlɪ/ adv direttamente; (at once) immediatamente ● conj [non] appena

director /dɪˈrektə(r)/ n (Comm) direttore, -trice mf; (of play, film) regista mf

directory /dɪˈrektərɪ/ n elenco m; (Teleph) elenco m [telefonico]; (of streets) stradario m

dirt /dɜːt/ n sporco m; **~ cheap** 🔢 a [un] prezzo stracciato

dirty /ˈdɜːtɪ/ adj (-ier, -iest) sporco; **~ trick** brutto scherzo m; **~ word** parolaccia f ● vt (pt/pp -ied) sporcare

dis|a'bility /dɪs-/ n infermità f inv. **~abled** adj invalido

disad'vantage n svantaggio m; **at a ~tage** in una posizione di svantaggio. **~taged** adj svantaggiato. **~tageous** adj svantaggioso

disa'gree vi non essere in disaccordo; **~ with** (food): far male a

disa'greeable adj sgradevole

disa'greement n disaccordo m; (quarrel) dissidio m

disap'pear vi scomparire. **~ance** n scomparsa f

disap'point vt deludere; **I'm ~ed** sono deluso. **~ing** adj deludente. **~ment** n delusione f

disap'proval n disapprovazione f

disap'prove vi disapprovare; **~ of sb/sth** disapprovare qcno/qcsa

dis'arm vt disarmare ● vi (Mil) disarmarsi. **~ament** n disarmo m. **~ing** adj (frankness etc) disarmante

disar'ray n in **~** in disordine

disast|er /dɪˈzɑːstə(r)/ n disastro m. **~rous** adj disastroso

dis'band vt sciogliere; smobilitare (troops) ● vi sciogliersi; (regiment:) essere smobilitato

disbe'lief n incredulità f; **in ~** con incredulità

disc /dɪsk/ n disco m; (CD) compact disc m inv

discard /dɪˈskɑːd/ vt scartare; (throw away) eliminare; scaricare (boyfriend)

discern /dɪˈsɜːn/ vt discernere. **~ible** adj discernibile. **~ing** adj perspicace

'discharge¹ n (Electr) scarica f; (dismissal) licenziamento m; (Mil) congedo m; (Med: of blood) emissione f; (of cargo) scarico m

dis'charge² vt scaricare (battery, cargo); (dismiss) licenziare; (Mil) congedare; (Jur) assolvere (accused); dimettere (patient) ●vi (Electr) scaricarsi

disciple /dɪˈsaɪpl/ n discepolo m

disciplinary /ˈdɪsɪplɪnərɪ/ adj disciplinare

discipline /ˈdɪsɪplɪn/ n disciplina f ●vt disciplinare; (punish) punire

'disc jockey n disc jockey m inv

dis'claim vt disconoscere. ~er n rifiuto m

dis'clos|e vt svelare. ~ure n rivelazione f

disco /ˈdɪskəʊ/ n discoteca f

dis'colour vt scolorire ●vi scolorirsi

dis'comfort n scomodità f; fig disagio m

disconcert /dɪskənˈsɜːt/ vt sconcertare

discon'nect vt disconnettere

disconsolate /dɪsˈkɒnsələt/ adj sconsolato

discon'tent n scontentezza f. ~ed adj scontento

discon'tinue vt cessare, smettere; (Comm) sospendere la produzione di; ~d line fine f serie

'discord n discordia f; (Mus) dissonanza f. ~ant adj ~ant note nota f discordante

'discount¹ n sconto m

dis'count² vt (not believe) non credere a; (leave out of consideration) non tener conto di

dis'courage vt scoraggiare; (dissuade) dissuadere

dis'courteous adj scortese

dis'cover /dɪˈskʌvə(r)/ vt scoprire. ~y n scoperta f

dis'credit n discredito m ●vt (pt/pp discredited) screditare

discreet /dɪˈskriːt/ adj discreto

discrepancy /dɪˈskrepənsɪ/ n discrepanza f

discretion /dɪˈskreʃn/ n discrezione f

discriminat|e /dɪˈskrɪmɪneɪt/ vi discriminare (against contro); ~e between distinguere tra. ~ing adj esigente. ~ion n discriminazione f; (quality) discernimento m

discus /ˈdɪskəs/ n disco m

discuss /dɪˈskʌs/ vt discutere; (examine critically) esaminare. ~ion n discussione f

disdain /dɪsˈdeɪn/ n sdegno f ●vt sdegnare. ~ful adj sdegnoso

disease /dɪˈziːz/ n malattia f. ~d adj malato

disem'bark vi sbarcare

disen'tangle vt districare

dis'figure vt deformare

dis'grace n vergogna f; I am in ~ sono caduto in disgrazia; it's a ~ è una vergogna ●vt disonorare. ~ful adj vergognoso

disgruntled /dɪsˈɡrʌntld/ adj malcontento

disguise /dɪsˈɡaɪz/ n travestimento m; in ~ travestito ●vt contraffare (voice); dissimulare (emotions); ~d as travestito da

disgust /dɪsˈɡʌst/ n disgusto m; in ~ con aria disgustata ●vt disgustare. ~ing adj disgustoso

dish /dɪʃ/ n piatto m; do the ~es lavare i piatti ● **dish out** vt (serve) servire; (distribute) distribuire. □ ~ **up** vt servire

'dishcloth n strofinaccio m

dis'honest adj disonesto. ~y n disonestà f

dis'honour n disonore m ●vt disonorare (family); non onorare (cheque). ~able adj disonorevole. ~ably adv in modo disonorevole

'dishwasher n lavapiatti f inv

disil'lusion vt disilludere. ~ment n disillusione f

disin'fect vt disinfettare. ~ant n

disinfettante m.

dis'integrate vi disintegrarsi

dis'interested adj disinteressato

dis'jointed adj sconnesso

disk /dɪsk/ n (Comput) disco m; (diskette) dischetto m

dis'like n avversione f; **your likes and** ∼s i tuoi gusti • vt l ∼ him/it non mi piace; **I don't** ∼ him/it non mi dispiace

dislocate /'dɪsləkeɪt/ vt slogare; ∼ one's shoulder slogarsi una spalla

dis'lodge vt sloggiare

dis'loyal adj sleale. ∼ty n slealtà f

dismal /'dɪzməl/ adj (person) abbacchiato; (news, weather) deprimente; (performance) mediocre

dismantle /dɪs'mæntl/ vt smontare (tent, machine); fig smantellare

dis'may n sgomento m. ∼ed adj sgomento

dis'miss vt licenziare (employee); (reject) scartare (idea, suggestion). ∼al n licenziamento m

dis'mount vi smontare

diso'bedien|ce n disubbidienza f. ∼t adj disubbidiente

diso'bey vt disubbidire a (rule) • vi disubbidire

dis'order n disordine m; (Med) disturbo m. ∼ly adj disordinato; (crowd) turbolento; ∼ly conduct turbamento m della quiete pubblica

dis'organized adj disorganizzato

dis'orientate vt disorientare

dis'own vt disconoscere

disparaging /dɪ'spærɪdʒɪŋ/ adj sprezzante

dispatch /dɪ'spætʃ/ n (Comm) spedizione f; (Mil, report) dispaccio m; with ∼ con prontezza • vt spedire; (kill) spedire al creatore

dispel /dɪ'spel/ vt (pt/pp dispelled) dissipare

dispensable /dɪ'spensəbl/ adj dispensabile

dispense /dɪ'spens/ vt distribuire; ∼ with fare a meno di; dispensing chemist farmacista mf; (shop) farmacia f. ∼r n (device) distributore m

dispers|al /dɪ'spɜːsl/ n dispersione f. ∼e vt disperdere • vi disperdersi

dispirited /dɪ'spɪrɪtɪd/ adj scoraggiato

display /dɪ'spleɪ/ n mostra f; (Comm) esposizione f; (of feelings) manifestazione f; pej ostentazione f; (Comput) display m inv • vt mostrare; esporre (goods); manifestare (feeling); (Comput) visualizzare

dis'please vt non piacere a; be ∼d with essere scontento di

dis'pleasure n malcontento m

disposable /dɪ'spəʊzəbl/ adj (throwaway) usa e getta; (income) disponibile

disposal /dɪ'spəʊzl/ n (getting rid of) eliminazione f; be at sb's ∼ essere a disposizione di qcno

disproportionate /dɪsprə'pɔːʃə-nət/ adj sproporzionato

dis'prove vt confutare

dispute /dɪ'spjuːt/ n disputa f; (industrial) contestazione f • vt contestare (statement)

disqualifi'cation n squalifica f; (from driving) ritiro m della patente

dis'qualify vt (pt/pp -ied) escludere; (Sport) squalificare; ∼ sb from driving ritirare la patente a qcno

disre'gard n mancanza f di considerazione • vt ignorare

dis'reputable adj malfamato

disre'spect n mancanza f di rispetto. ∼ful adj irrispettoso

disrupt /dɪs'rʌpt/ vt creare scompiglio in; sconvolgere (plans). ∼ion n scompiglio m; (of plans) sconvolgimento m. ∼ive adj (person, behaviour) indisciplinato

dissatis'faction n malcontento m

dis'satisfied adj scontento

dissect /dɪˈsekt/ vt sezionare. ∼ion n dissezione f

dissent /dɪˈsent/ n dissenso m ● vi dissentire

dissertation /dɪsəˈteɪʃn/ n tesi f inv

dissident /ˈdɪsɪdənt/ n dissidente mf

dis'similar adj dissimile (to da)

dissolute /ˈdɪsəluːt/ adj dissoluto

dissolve /dɪˈzɒlv/ vt dissolvere ● vi dissolversi

dissuade /dɪˈsweɪd/ vt dissuadere

distance /ˈdɪstəns/ n distanza f; It's a short ∼ from here to the station la stazione non è lontana da qui; in the ∼ in lontananza; from a ∼ da lontano

distant /ˈdɪstənt/ adj distante; (relative) lontano

dis'taste n avversione f. ∼ful adj spiacevole

distil /dɪˈstɪl/ vt (pt/pp distilled) distillare. ∼lation n distillazione f. ∼lery n distilleria f

distinct /dɪˈstɪŋkt/ adj chiaro; (different) distinto. ∼ion n distinzione f; (Sch) massimo m dei voti. ∼ive adj caratteristico. ∼ly adv chiaramente

distinguish /dɪˈstɪŋgwɪʃ/ vt/i distinguere; ∼ oneself distinguersi. ∼ed adj rinomato; (appearance) distinto; (career) brillante

distort /dɪˈstɔːt/ vt distorcere. ∼ion n distorsione f

distract /dɪˈstrækt/ vt distrarre. ∼ed adj assente; (①: worried) preoccupato. ∼ing adj che distoglie. ∼ion n distrazione f; (despair) disperazione f; drive sb to ∼ portare qcno alla disperazione

distraught /dɪˈstrɔːt/ adj sconvolto

distress /dɪˈstres/ n angoscia f; (pain) sofferenza f; (danger) difficoltà f ● vt sconvolgere; (sadden) affliggere. ∼ing adj penoso; (shocking) sconvolgente. ∼ signal n segnale m di richiesta di soccorso

distribut|e /dɪˈstrɪbjuːt/ vt distribuire. ∼ion n distribuzione f. ∼or n distributore m

district /ˈdɪstrɪkt/ n regione f; (Admin) distretto m. ∼ nurse n infermiere, -a mf che fa visite a domicilio

dis'trust n sfiducia f ● vt non fidarsi di. ∼ful adj diffidente

disturb /dɪˈstɜːb/ vt disturbare; (emotionally) turbare; spostare (papers). ∼ance n disturbo m; ∼ances (pl: rioting etc) disordini mpl. ∼ed adj turbato; [mentally] ∼ed malato di mente. ∼ing adj inquietante

dis'used adj non utilizzato

ditch /dɪtʃ/ n fosso m ● vt (①: abandon) abbandonare (plan, car); piantare (lover)

dither /ˈdɪðə(r)/ vi titubare

divan /dɪˈvæn/ n divano m

dive /daɪv/ n tuffo m; (Aeron) picchiata f; (①: place) bettola f ● vi tuffarsi; (when in water) immergersi; (Aeron) scendere in picchiata; (①: rush) precipitarsi

diver /ˈdaɪvə(r)/ n (from board) tuffatore, -trice mf; (scuba) sommozzatore, -trice mf; (deep sea) palombaro m

diver|ge /daɪˈvɜːdʒ/ vi divergere. ∼gent adj divergente

diverse /daɪˈvɜːs/ adj vario

diversify /daɪˈvɜːsɪfaɪ/ vt/i (pt/pp -ied) diversificare

diversion /daɪˈvɜːʃn/ n deviazione f; (distraction) diversivo m

diversity /daɪˈvɜːsətɪ/ n varietà f

divert /daɪˈvɜːt/ vt deviare (traffic); distogliere (attention)

divide /dɪˈvaɪd/ vt dividere (by per); six ∼d by two sei diviso due ● vi dividersi

dividend /ˈdɪvɪdend/ n dividendo m; pay ∼s fig ripagare

divine /dɪˈvaɪn/ adj divino

diving /ˈdaɪvɪŋ/ n (from board) tuffi mpl; (scuba) immersione m. **~-board** n trampolino m. **~ mask** n maschera f [subacquea]. **~suit** n muta f; (deep sea) scafandro m

division /dɪˈvɪʒn/ n divisione f; (in sports league) serie f

divorce /dɪˈvɔːs/ n divorzio m ●vt divorziare da. **~d** adj divorziato; **get ~d** divorziare

divorcee /dɪvɔːˈsiː/ n divorziato, -a mf

divulge /daɪˈvʌldʒ/ vt rendere pubblico

DIY n abbr do-it-yourself

dizziness /ˈdɪzɪnɪs/ n giramenti mpl di testa

dizzy /ˈdɪzɪ/ adj (-ier, -iest) vertiginoso; **I feel ~** mi gira la testa

---

do¹ /duː/

3 sing pres tense **does**; past tense **did**; past participle **done**

●vt fare; (🄳: cheat) fregare; **be done** (Culin) essere cotto; **well done** bravo; (Culin) ben cotto; **do the flowers** sistemare i fiori; **do the washing up** lavare i piatti; **do one's hair** farsi i capelli

●vi (be suitable) andare; (be enough) bastare; **this will do** questo va bene; **that will do!** basta così; **do well/badly** cavarsela bene/male; **how is he doing?** come sta?

●v aux (used to form questions and negatives; often not translated) **do you speak Italian?** parli italiano?; **you don't like him, do you?** non ti piace, vero?; (expressing astonishment) non dirmi che ti piace!; **yes, I do** sì; (emphatic) invece sì; **no, I don't** no; **I don't smoke** non fumo; **don't**

you/doesn't he? vero?; **so do I** anch'io; **do come in, John** entra, John; **how do you do?** piacere. □ **~ away with** vt abolire (rule). □ **~ for** vt done for 🄳 rovinato. □ **~ in** vt (🄳: kill) uccidere; farsi male a (back); **done in** 🄳 esausto. □ **~ up** vt (fasten) abbottonare; (renovate) rimettere a nuovo; (wrap) avvolgere. □ **~ with** vt **I could do with a spanner** mi ci vorrebbe una chiave inglese. □ **~ without** vt fare a meno di

do² /duː/ n (pl dos or do's) 🄳 festa f

docile /ˈdəʊsaɪl/ adj docile

dock¹ /dɒk/ n (Jur) banco m degli imputati

dock² n (Naut) bacino m ●vi entrare in porto; (spaceship) congiungersi. **~er** n portuale m. **~s** npl porto m. **~yard** n cantiere m navale

doctor /ˈdɒktə(r)/ n dottore m, dottoressa f ●vt alterare (drink); castrare (cat). **~ate** n dottorato m

doctrine /ˈdɒktrɪn/ n dottrina f

document /ˈdɒkjʊmənt/ n documento m. **~ary** adj documentario ●n documentario m

dodge /dɒdʒ/ n 🄳 trucco m ●vt schivare (blow); evitare (person) ●vi scansarsi; **~ out of the way** scansarsi

dodgems /ˈdɒdʒəmz/ npl autoscontro msg

dodgy /ˈdɒdʒɪ/ adj (-ier, -iest) (🄳: dubious) sospetto

doe /dəʊ/ n femmina f (di daino, renna, lepre); (rabbit) coniglia f

does /dʌz/ ▷DO

doesn't /ˈdʌznt/ = does not

dog /dɒg/ n cane m ●vt (pt/pp dogged) (illness, bad luck) perseguitare

dogged /ˈdɒgɪd/ adj ostinato

'dog house n **in the ~** 🄳 in disgrazia

dogma /ˈdɒgmə/ n dogma m. ~**tic** adj dogmatico

do-it-yourself /ˈduːɪtjəˈself/ n fai da te m, bricolage m. ~ **shop** n negozio m di bricolage

dole /dəʊl/ n sussidio m di disoccupazione; **be on the** ~ essere disoccupato ● **dole out** vt distribuire

doleful /ˈdəʊlfl/ adj triste

doll /dɒl/ n bambola f ● **doll oneself up** vt 🎓 mettersi in ghingheri

dollar /ˈdɒlə(r)/ n dollaro m

dollop /ˈdɒləp/ n 🎓 cucchiaiata f

dolphin /ˈdɒlfɪn/ n delfino m

dome /dəʊm/ n cupola f

domestic /dəˈmestɪk/ adj domestico; (Pol) interno; (Comm) nazionale

domesticated /dəˈmestɪkeɪtɪd/ adj (animal) addomesticato

domestic flight n volo m nazionale

dominant /ˈdɒmɪnənt/ adj dominante

dominat|e /ˈdɒmɪneɪt/ vt/i dominare. ~**ion** n dominio m

domineering /dɒmɪˈnɪərɪŋ/ adj autoritario

dominion /dəˈmɪnjən/ n Br (Pol) dominion m inv

donat|e /dəʊˈneɪt/ vt donare. ~**ion** n donazione f

done /dʌn/ ▷**DO**

donkey /ˈdɒŋkɪ/ n asino m; ~**'s years** 🎓 secoli mpl. ~**-work** n sgobbata f

donor /ˈdəʊnə(r)/ n donatore, -trice mf

doodle /ˈduːdl/ vi scarabocchiare

doom /duːm/ n fato m; (ruin) rovina f ● vt **be** ~**ed [to failure]** essere destinato al fallimento; ~**ed** (ship) destinato ad affondare

door /dɔː(r)/ n porta f; (of car) portiera f; **out of** ~**s** all'aperto

door: ~**mat** n zerbino m. ~**step** n gradino m della porta. ~**way** n vano

m della porta

dope /dəʊp/ n 🎓 (drug) droga f leggera; (information) indiscrezioni fpl; (idiot) idiota mf ● vt drogare; (Sport) dopare

dormant /ˈdɔːmənt/ adj latente; (volcano) inattivo

dormitory /ˈdɔːmɪtərɪ/ n dormitorio m

dormouse /ˈdɔː-/ n ghiro m

dosage /ˈdəʊsɪdʒ/ n dosaggio m

dose /dəʊs/ n dose f

dot /dɒt/ n punto m; **at 8 o'clock on the** ~ alle 8 in punto

dot-com /dɒtˈkɒm/ n azienda f legata a Internet

dote /dəʊt/ vi ~ **on** stravedere per

dotty /ˈdɒtɪ/ adj (-**ier**, -**iest**) 🎓 tocco; (idea) folle

double /ˈdʌbl/ adj doppio ● adv cost ~ costare il doppio; **see** ~ vedere doppio; ~ **the amount** la quantità doppia ● n doppio m; (person) sosia m inv; ~**s** pl (Tennis) doppio m; **at the** ~ di corsa ● vt raddoppiare; (fold) piegare in due ● vi raddoppiare. □ ~ **back** vi (go back) fare dietro front. □ ~ **up** vi (bend) piegarsi in due (**with** per); (share) dividere una stanza

double: ~'**bass** n contrabbasso m. ~ '**bed** n letto m matrimoniale. ~ '**chin** n doppio mento m. ~'**click** vt/i cliccare due volte, fare doppio clic (**on** su). ~'**cross** vt ingannare. ~'**decker** n autobus m inv a due piani. ~ '**Dutch** n 🎓 ostrogoto m. ~ '**glazing** n doppiovetro m

doubly /ˈdʌblɪ/ adv doppiamente

doubt /daʊt/ n dubbio m ● vt dubitare di. ~**ful** adj dubbio; (having doubts) in dubbio. ~**fully** adv con aria dubbiosa. ~**less** adv indubbiamente

dough /dəʊ/ n pasta f; (for bread) impasto m; 🎓 (money) quattrini mpl. ~**nut** n bombolone m, krapfen m inv

dove /dʌv/ n colomba f. ~**tail** n

(*Techn*) incastro *m* a coda di rondine

down[1] /daʊn/ *n* (*feathers*) piumino *m*

down[2] *adv* giù; **go/come ~** scendere; **~ there** laggiù; **sales are ~** le vendite sono diminuite; **£50 ~** 50 sterline d'acconto; **~ 10%** ridotto del 10%; **~ with...!** abbasso...! ● *prep* **walk ~ the road** camminare per strada; **~ the stairs** giù per le scale; **fall ~ the stairs** cadere giù dalle scale; **get that ~ you!** butta giù!; **be ~ the pub** ⊞ essere al pub ● *vt* bere tutto d'un fiato (*drink*)

down: ~-and-'out *n* spiantato, -a *mf*. **~cast** *adj* abbattuto. **~fall** *n* caduta *f*; (*of person*) rovina *f*. **~'hearted** *adj* scoraggiato. **~'hill** *adv* in discesa; **go ~hill** essere in declino. **~load** *vt* scaricare. **~ payment** *n* deposito *m*. **~pour** *n* acquazzone *m*. **~right** *adj* (*absolute*) totale; (*lie*) bell'e buono; (*idiot*) perfetto ● *adv* (*completely*) completamente. **~stairs** *adv* al piano di sotto ● *adj* del piano di sotto. **~'stream** *adv* a valle. **~-to-'earth** *adj* (*person*) con i piedi per terra. **~town** *adv* Am in centro. **~ward[s]** *adj* verso il basso; (*slope*) in discesa ● *adv* verso il basso

---

Downing Street È una via del centro di Londra, nel quartiere di Westminster. Al numero 10 si trova la residenza ufficiale del Primo Ministro britannico e al numero 11 quella del *Chancellor of the Exchequer* (il Cancelliere dello Scacchiere, equivalente del Ministro delle Finanze e del Tesoro). Le espressioni *Downing Street* o *Number 10* sono spesso usate dalla stampa per indicare il Primo Ministro.

---

dowry /'daʊrɪ/ *n* dote *f*

doze /dəʊz/ *n* sonnellino *m* ● *vi* sonnecchiare. □ **~ off** *vi* assopirsi

dozen /'dʌzn/ *n* dozzina *f*; **~s of books** libri a dozzine

Dr *abbr* doctor

drab /dræb/ *adj* spento

draft[1] /drɑːft/ *n* abbozzo *m*; (*Comm*) cambiale *f*; Am (*Mil*) leva *f* ● *vt* abbozzare; Am (*Mil*) arruolare

draft[2] *n* Am = **draught**

drag /dræg/ *n* ⊞ scocciatura *f*; **in ~** ⊞ (*man*) travestito da donna ● *vt* (*pt/pp* **dragged**) trascinare; dragare (*river*). □ **~ on** *vi* (*time, meeting:*) trascinarsi

dragon /'drægən/ *n* drago *m*. **~-fly** *n* libellula *f*

drain /dreɪn/ *n* tubo *m* di scarico; (*grid*) tombino *m*; **the ~s** *pl* le fognature ● *vt* essere a ~ on sb's finances prosciugare le finanze di qcno ● *vt* drenare (*land, wound*); scolare (*liquid, vegetables*); svuotare (*tank, glass, person*) ● *vi* ~ **[away]** andar via

drama /'drɑːmə/ *n* arte *f* drammatica; (*play*) opera *f* teatrale; (*event*) dramma *m*

dramatic /drə'mætɪk/ *adj* drammatico

dramat|ist /'dræmətɪst/ *n* drammaturgo, -a *mf*. **~ize** *vt* adattare per il teatro; *fig* drammatizzare

drank /dræŋk/ ▷ **DRINK**

drape /dreɪp/ *n* Am tenda *f* ● *vt* appoggiare (**over** su)

drastic /'dræstɪk/ *adj* drastico; **~ally** *adv* drasticamente

draught /drɑːft/ *n* corrente *f* [d'aria]; **~s** *sg* (*game*) [gioco *m* della] dama *fsg*

draught beer *n* birra *f* alla spina

draughty /'drɑːftɪ/ *adj* pieno di correnti d'aria; **it's ~** c'è corrente

draw /drɔː/ *n* (*attraction*) attrazione *f*; (*Sport*) pareggio *m*; (*in lottery*) sorteggio *m* ● *v* (*pt* **drew**, *pp* **drawn**) ● *vt* tirare; (*attract*) attirare; disegnare (*picture*); tracciare (*line*); ritirare (*money*); **~ lots** tirare a sorte ● *vt* (tea:) essere in infusione; (Sport) pareggiare; ~ **near** avvicinarsi. □ ~ **back** vt tirare indietro; ritirare (hand); tirare (curtains) ● vi (recoil) tirarsi indietro. □ ~ **in** vt ritirare (claws etc) ● vi (train): arrivare; (days:) accorciarsi. □ ~ **out** vt (pull out) tirar fuori; ritirare (money) ● vi (train): partire; (days:) allungarsi. □ ~ **up** vt redigere (document); accostare (chair); raddrizzare to one's full height farsi grande ● vi (stop) fermarsi

draw: ~**back** n inconveniente m. ~**bridge** n ponte m levatoio

drawer /drɔː(r)/ n cassetto m

drawing /'drɔːɪŋ/ n disegno m

drawing: ~ **pin** n puntina f. ~ **room** n salotto m

drawl /drɔːl/ n pronuncia f strascicata

drawn /drɔːn/ ▷ DRAW

dread /dred/ n terrore m ● vt aver il terrore di

dreadful /'dredful/ adj terribile. ~**ly** adv terribilmente

dream /driːm/ n sogno m ● attrib di sogno ● vt/i (pt/pp **dreamt** /dremt/ or **dreamed**) sognare (**about/of** di)

dreary /'drɪərɪ/ adj (-ier, -iest) tetro; (boring) monotono

dredge /dredʒ/ vt/i dragare

dregs /dregz/ npl feccia fsg

drench /drentʃ/ vt get ~**ed** inzupparsi; ~**ed** zuppo

dress /dres/ n (woman's) vestito m; (clothing) abbigliamento m ● vt vestire; (decorate) adornare; (Culin) condire; (Med) fasciare; ~ **oneself**, get ~**ed** vestirsi ● vi vestirsi. □ ~ **up** vi mettersi elegante; (in disguise) travestirsi (**as** da)

dress circle n (Theat) prima galleria f

dressing /'dresɪŋ/ n (Culin) condimento m; (Med) fasciatura f

dressing: ~**-gown** n vestaglia f.

~**-room** n (in gym) spogliatoio m; (Theat) camerino m. ~**-table** n toilette f inv

dress: ~**maker** n sarta f. ~ **rehearsal** n prova f generale

drew /druː/ ▷ DRAW

dribble /'drɪbl/ vi sgocciolare; (baby:) sbavare; (Sport) dribblare

dried /draɪd/ adj (food) essiccato

drier /'draɪə(r)/ n asciugabiancheria m inv

drift /drɪft/ n movimento m lento; (of snow) cumulo m; (meaning) senso m ● vi (off course) andare alla deriva; (snow): accumularsi; (fig: person): procedere senza meta. □ ~ **apart** vi (people:) allontanarsi l'uno dall'altro

drill /drɪl/ n trapano m; (Mil) esercitazione f ● vt trapanare; (Mil) fare esercitare ● vi (Mil) esercitarsi; ~ **for oil** trivellare in cerca di petrolio

drink /drɪŋk/ n bevanda f; (alcoholic) bicchierino m; **have a** ~ bere qualcosa; **a** ~ **of water** un po' d'acqua ● vt/i (pt **drank**, pp **drunk**) bere. □ ~ **up** vt finire ● vi finire il bicchiere

drink|able /'drɪŋkəbl/ adj potabile. ~**er** n bevitore, -trice mf

'drinking-water n acqua f potabile

drip /drɪp/ n gocciolamento m; (drop) goccia f; (Med) flebo f inv; (🔲: person) mollaccione, -a mf ● vi (pt **dripped**) gocciolare. ~**-dry** adj che non si stira. ~**ping** n (from meat) grasso m d'arrosto ● adj ~**ping** [**wet**] fradicio

drive /draɪv/ n (in car) giro m; (entrance) viale m; (energy) grinta f; (Psych) pulsione f; (organized effort) operazione f; (Techn) motore m; (Comput) lettore m ● v t (pt **drove**, pp **driven**) ● vt portare (person by car); guidare (car); (Sport: hit) mandare; (Techn) far funzionare; ~ **sb mad** far diventare matto qcno ● vi guidare. □ ~ **at** **what are you driving at?** dove vuoi arrivare? **drive away** vt portare via in macchina; (*chase*) cacciare ● vi andare via in macchina. □ ~ **in** vt piantare (nail) ● vi arrivare [in macchina]. □ ~ **off** vt portare via in macchina; (*chase*) cacciare ● vi andare via in macchina. □ ~ **on** vi proseguire (in macchina). □ ~ **up** vi arrivare (in macchina)

drivel /ˈdrɪvl/ n 🔟 sciocchezze fpl

driver /ˈdraɪvə(r)/ n guidatore, -trice mf; (of train) conducente mf

driving /ˈdraɪvɪŋ/ adj (rain) violento; (force) motore ● n guida f

driving: ~ **licence** n patente f di guida. ~ **test** n esame m di guida

drizzle /ˈdrɪzl/ n pioggerella f ● vi piovigginare

drone /drəʊn/ n (bee) fuco m; (sound) ronzio m

droop /druːp/ vi abbassarsi; (flowers:) afflosciarsi

drop /drɒp/ n (of liquid) goccia f; (fall) caduta f; (in price, temperature) calo m ● v (pt/pp dropped) ● vt far cadere; sganciare (bomb); (omit) omettere; (give up) abbandonare ● vi cadere; (price, temperature, wind:) calare; (ground:) essere in pendenza. □ ~ **in** vi passare. □ ~ **off** vi depositare (person) ● vi cadere; (fall asleep) assopirsi. □ ~ **out** vi cadere; (of race, society) ritirarsi; ~ **out of school** lasciare la scuola

'drop-out n persona f contro il sistema sociale

drought /draʊt/ n siccità f

drove /drəʊv/ ▷ **DRIVE**

drown /draʊn/ vi annegare ● vt annegare; coprire (noise); **he was** ~ed è annegato

drowsy /ˈdraʊzɪ/ adj sonnolento

drudgery /ˈdrʌdʒərɪ/ n lavoro m pesante e noioso

drug /drʌg/ n droga f; (Med) farmaco m; **take** ~**s** drogarsi ● vt (pt/pp drugged) drogare

drug: ~ **addict** n tossicomane, -a

mf. ~ **dealer** n spacciatore, -trice mf [di droga]. ~**gist** n Am farmacista m. ~**store** n Am negozio m di generi vari, inclusi medicinali, che funge anche da bar; (dispensing) farmacia f

drum /drʌm/ n tamburo m; (for oil) bidone m; (Mus) (pl: sing also) batteria f ● v (pt/pp drummed) ● vi suonare il tamburo; (in pop-group) suonare la batteria ● vt ~ **sth into sb** ripetere qcsa a qcno cento volte. ~**mer** n percussionista mf; (in pop-group) batterista mf. ~**stick** n bacchetta f; (of chicken, turkey) coscia f

drunk /drʌŋk/ ▷ **DRINK** ● adj ubriaco; **get** ~ ubriacarsi ● n ubriaco, -a mf

drunk|ard /ˈdrʌŋkəd/ n ubriacone, -a mf. ~**en** adj ubriaco; ~**en driving** guida f in stato di ebbrezza

dry /draɪ/ adj (drier, driest) asciutto; (climate, country) secco ● vt/i (pt/pp dried) asciugare; ~ **one's eyes** asciugarsi le lacrime. □ ~ **up** vi seccarsi; (fig: source:) prosciugarsi; (🔟: be quiet) stare zitto; (do dishes) asciugare i piatti

dry: ~-**'clean** vt pulire a secco. ~-**'cleaner's** n (shop) tintoria f. ~**ness** n secchezza f

DTD n abbr (digital type definition) DTD f

dual /ˈdjuːəl/ adj doppio

dual 'carriageway n strada f a due carreggiate

dub /dʌb/ vt (pt/pp dubbed) doppiare (film); (name) soprannominare

dubious /ˈdjuːbɪəs/ adj dubbio; **be** ~ avere dei dubbi riguardo

duchess /ˈdʌtʃɪs/ n duchessa f

duck /dʌk/ n anatra f ● vt (in water) immergere; ~ **one's head** abbassare la testa ● vi abbassarsi. ~**ling** n anatroccolo m

duct /dʌkt/ n condotto m; (Anat) dotto m

dud /dʌd/ 🔟 adj (Mil) disattivato; (coin) falso; (cheque) a vuoto ● n (*banknote*) banconota *f* falsa

due /dju:/ *adj* dovuto; **be ~** (*train:*) essere previsto; **the baby is ~ next week** il bambino dovrebbe nascere la settimana prossima; **~ to** (*owing to*) a causa di; **be ~ to** (*causally*) essere dovuto a; **I'm ~ to...** dovrei...; **in ~ course** a tempo debito ● *adv* **~ north** direttamente a nord

duel /dju:əl/ *n* duello *m*

dues /dju:z/ *npl* quota *f* [di iscrizione]

duet /dju:'et/ *n* duetto *m*

dug /dʌg/ ▷**DIG**

duke /dju:k/ *n* duca *m*

dull /dʌl/ *adj* (*overcast, not bright*) cupo; (*not shiny*) opaco; (*sound*) soffocato; (*boring*) monotono; (*stupid*) ottuso ● *vt* intorpidire (mind); attenuare (pain)

dumb /dʌm/ *adj* muto; (**I**: *stupid*) ottuso. **~founded** *adj* sbigottito. ▫ **~ down** vt semplificare il livello di

dummy /'dʌmɪ/ *n* (*tailor's*) manichino *m*; (*for baby*) succhiotto *m*; (*model*) riproduzione *f*

dump /dʌmp/ *n* (*for refuse*) scarico *m*; (**I**: *town*) mortorio *m*; **be down in the ~s** **I** essere depresso ● *vt* scaricare; (**I**: *put down*) lasciare; (**I**: *get rid of*) liberarsi di

dumpling /'dʌmplɪŋ/ *n* gnocco *m*

dunce /dʌns/ *n* zuccone, -a *mf*

dung /dʌŋ/ *n* sterco *m*

dungarees /dʌŋɡə'ri:z/ *npl* tuta *fsg*

dungeon /'dʌndʒən/ *n* prigione *f* sotterranea

duplicate[1] /'dju:plɪkət/ *adj* doppio ● *n* duplicato *m*; (*document*) copia *f*; **in ~** in duplicato

duplicate[2] /'dju:plɪkeɪt/ *vt* fare un duplicato di; (*research:*) essere una ripetizione di (work)

durable /'djʊərəbl/ *adj* resistente; durevole (basis, institution)

duration /djʊ'reɪʃn/ *n* durata *f*

duress /djʊə'res/ *n* costrizione *f*; **under ~** sotto minaccia

during /'djʊərɪŋ/ *prep* durante

dusk /dʌsk/ *n* crepuscolo *m*

dust /dʌst/ *n* polvere *f* ● *vt* spolverare; (*sprinkle*) cospargere (cake) (with di) ● *vi* spolverare

dust: **~bin** *n* pattumiera *f*. **~er** *n* strofinaccio *m*. **~jacket** *n* sopraccoperta *f*. **~man** *n* spazzino *m*. **~pan** *n* paletta *f* per la spazzatura

dusty /'dʌstɪ/ *adj* (-ier, -iest) polveroso

Dutch /dʌtʃ/ *adj* olandese; **go ~** **I** fare alla romana ● *n* (*language*) olandese *m*; **the ~** *pl* gli olandesi. **~man** *n* olandese *m*

duty /'dju:tɪ/ *n* dovere *m*; (*task*) compito *m*; (*tax*) dogana *f*; **be on ~** essere di servizio. **~-free** *adj* esente da dogana

duvet /'du:veɪ/ *n* piumone *m*

DVD *n* DVD *m inv*

dwarf /dwɔ:f/ *n* (*pl* -s *or* dwarves) nano, -a *mf* ● *vt* rimpicciolire

dwell /dwel/ *vi* (*pt/pp* dwelt) *liter* dimorare. ▫ **~ on** *vt fig* soffermarsi su. **~ing** *n* abitazione *f*

dwindle /'dwɪndl/ *vi* diminuire

dye /daɪ/ *n* tintura *f* ● *vt* (*pres p* dyeing) tingere

dying /'daɪɪŋ/ ▷**DIE**[2]

dynamic /daɪ'næmɪk/ *adj* dinamico

dynamite /'daɪnəmaɪt/ *n* dinamite *f*

dynamo /'daɪnəməʊ/ *n* dinamo *f inv*

dynasty /'dɪnəstɪ/ *n* dinastia *f*

d
e

····················

Ee

····················

each /i:tʃ/ *adj* ogni ● *pron* ognuno; **£1 ~** una sterlina ciascuno; **they love/hate ~ other** si amano/odiano; **we lend ~ other money** ci prestiamo i soldi

eager /'iːgə(r)/ adj ansioso (to do di fare); (pupil) avido di sapere. ~ly adv (wait) ansiosamente; (offer) premurosamente. ~ness n premura f

eagle /'iːgl/ n aquila f

ear[1] /ɪə(r)/ n (of corn) spiga f

ear[2] n orecchio m. ~ache n mal m d'orecchi. ~drum n timpano m

earl /ɜːl/ n conte m

early /'ɜːlɪ/ adj (-ier, -iest) (before expected time) in anticipo; (spring) prematuro; (reply) pronto; (works, writings) primo; **be here ~!** sii puntuale!; **you're ~!** sei in anticipo!; **~ morning walk** passeggiata f mattutina; **in the ~ morning** la mattina presto; **in the ~ spring** all'inizio della primavera; **~ retirement** prepensionamento m ● adv presto; (ahead of time) in anticipo; **~ in the morning** la mattina presto

earn /ɜːn/ vt guadagnare; (deserve) meritare

earnest /'ɜːnɪst/ adj serio ● n **in ~** sul serio. ~ly adv con aria seria

earnings /'ɜːnɪŋz/ npl guadagni mpl; (salary) stipendio m

ear: ~phones npl cuffia fsg. ~ring n orecchino m. ~shot n **within ~shot** a portata d'orecchio; **he is out of ~shot** non può sentire

earth /ɜːθ/ n terra f; **where/what on ~?** dove/che diavolo? ● vt (Electr) mettere a terra

'earthquake n terremoto m

earwig /'ɪəwɪg/ n forbicina f

ease /iːz/ n a proprio agio; **at ~!** (Mil) riposo!; **ill at ~** a disagio; **with ~** con facilità ● vt calmare (pain); alleviare (tension, shortage); (slow down) rallentare; (loosen) allentare ● vi (pain, situation, wind): calmarsi

easel /'iːzl/ n cavalletto m

easily /'iːzɪlɪ/ adv con facilità; **~ the best** certamente il meglio

east /iːst/ n est m; **to the ~ of** a est

di ● adj dell'est ● adv verso est

Easter /'iːstə(r)/ n Pasqua f. **~ egg** n uovo m di Pasqua

east|**erly** /'iːstəlɪ/ adj da levante. **~ern** adj orientale. **~ward[s]** /-wəd[z]/ adv verso est

easy /'iːzɪ/ adj (-ier, -iest) facile; **take it** slow o things **~** prendersela con calma; **take it ~!** (don't get excited) calma!; **go ~ with** andarci piano con

easy: **~ chair** n poltrona f. **~going** adj conciliante; **too ~going** troppo accomodante

eat /iːt/ vt/i (pt **ate**, pp **eaten**) mangiare. □ **~ into** vt intaccare. □ **~ up** vt mangiare tutto (food); fig inghiottire (profits)

eaves /iːvz/ npl cornicione msg. **~drop** vi (pt/pp **-dropped**) origliare; **~drop on** ascoltare di nascosto

ebb /eb/ n (tide) riflusso m; **at a low ~** fig a terra ● vi rifluire; fig declinare

ebony /'ebənɪ/ n ebano m

eccentric /ɪk'sentrɪk/ adj & n eccentrico, -a mf

echo /'ekəʊ/ n (pl **-es**) eco f or m ● v (pt/pp **echoed**, pres p **echoing**) vt echeggiare; ripetere (words) ● vi risuonare (with di)

eclipse /ɪ'klɪps/ n (Astr) eclissi f inv ● vt fig eclissare

ecolog|**ical** /iːkə'lɒdʒɪkl/ adj ecologico. **~y** n ecologia f

e-commerce /iː'kɒmɜːs/ n e-commerce m inv, commercio m elettronico

economic /iːkə'nɒmɪk/ adj economico; **~ refugee** rifugiato, -a mf economico. **-a. ~al** adj economico. **~ally** adv economicamente; (thriftily) in economia. **~s** n economia f

economist /ɪ'kɒnəmɪst/ n economista mf

economize /ɪ'kɒnəmaɪz/ vi economizzare (on su)

economy /ɪˈkɒnəmɪ/ *n* economia *f*

ecstasy /ˈekstəsɪ/ *n* estasi *f inv*; (*drug*) ecstasy *f*

eczema /ˈeksɪmə/ *n* eczema *m*

edge /edʒ/ *n* bordo *m*; (*of knife*) filo *m*; (*of road*) ciglio *m*; **on** ~ con i nervi tesi; **have the** ~ **on** 🔢 avere un vantaggio su • *vt* bordare. □ ~ **forward** *vi* avanzare lentamente

edgeways /ˈedʒweɪz/ *adv* di fianco; **I couldn't get a word in** ~ non ho potuto infilare neanche mezza parola nel discorso

edgy /ˈedʒɪ/ *adj* nervoso

edible /ˈedɪbl/ *adj* commestibile; **this pizza's not** ~ questa pizza è immangiabile

> **Edinburgh Festival** La più importante manifestazione culturale britannica, fondata nel 1947 e tenuta annualmente nella capitale scozzese, in agosto. Il festival offre spettacoli di musica, teatro, danza, ecc. e attira ogni anno moltissimi visitatori. Un settore sempre molto interessante è quello del cosiddetto *Fringe*, ossia gli eventi fuori dal programma ufficiale. *i*

edit /ˈedɪt/ *vt* (*pt/pp* **edited**) far la revisione di (text); curare l'edizione di (anthology, dictionary); dirigere (newspaper); montare (film); editare (tape); ~**ed by** (book) a cura di

edition /ɪˈdɪʃn/ *n* edizione *f*

editor /ˈedɪtə(r)/ *n* (*of anthology, dictionary*) curatore, -trice *mf*; (*of newspaper*) redattore, -trice *mf*; (*of film*) responsabile *mf* del montaggio

editorial /edɪˈtɔːrɪəl/ *adj* redazionale • *n* (*Journ*) editoriale *m*

educate /ˈedjʊkeɪt/ *vt* istruire; educare (mind); **be** ~**d at Eton** essere educato a Eton. ~**d** *adj* istruito

education /edjʊˈkeɪʃn/ *n* istru-

zione *f*; (*culture*) cultura *f*, educazione *f*. ~**al** *adj* istruttivo; (*visit*) educativo; (*publishing*) didattico

eel /iːl/ *n* anguilla *f*

eerie /ˈɪərɪ/ *adj* (**-ier, -iest**) inquietante

effect /ɪˈfekt/ *n* effetto *m*; **in** ~ in effetti; **take** ~ (*law*:) entrare in vigore; (*medicine*:) fare effetto • *vt* effettuare

effective /ɪˈfektɪv/ *adj* efficace; (*striking*) che colpisce; (*actual*) di fatto; ~ **from** in vigore a partire da. ~**ly** *adv* efficacemente; (*actually*) di fatto. ~**ness** *n* efficacia *f*

effeminate /ɪˈfemɪnət/ *adj* effeminato

efficiency /ɪˈfɪʃənsɪ/ *n* efficienza *f*; (*of machine*) rendimento *m*

efficient /ɪˈfɪʃənt/ *adj* efficiente. ~**ly** *adv* efficientemente

effort /ˈefət/ *n* sforzo *m*; **make an** ~ sforzarsi. ~**less** *adj* facile. ~**lessly** *adv* con facilità

e.g. *abbr* (*exempli gratia*) per es.

egg[1] /eg/ *vt* ~ **on** 🔢 incitare

egg[2] *n* uovo *m*. ~**cup** *n* portauovo *m inv*. ~**head** *n* 🔢 intellettuale *mf*. ~**shell** *n* guscio *m* d'uovo. ~**timer** *n* clessidra *f* per misurare il tempo di cottura delle uova

ego /ˈiːgəʊ/ *n* ego *m*. ~**centric** *adj* egocentrico. ~**ism** *n* egoismo *m*. ~**ist** *n* egoista *mf*. ~**tism** *n* egotismo *m*. ~**tist** *n* egotista *mf*

Egypt /ˈiːdʒɪpt/ *n* Egitto *m*. ~**ian** *adj* & *n* egiziano, -a *mf*

EHIC *n* abbr (**European Health Insurance Card**) TEAM *f*

eiderdown /ˈaɪdə-/ *n* (*quilt*) piumino *m*

eigh|t /eɪt/ *adj* otto • *n* otto *m*. ~**teen** *adj* diciotto. ~**teenth** *adj* diciottesimo

eighth /eɪtθ/ *adj* ottavo • *n* ottavo *m*

eightieth /ˈeɪtɪɪθ/ *adj* ottantesimo

eighty /ˈeɪtɪ/ *adj* ottanta

either /ˈaɪðə(r)/ *adj* & *pron* ~ [of

them] l'uno o l'altro; **I don't like ~ [of them]** non mi piace né l'uno né l'altro; **on ~ side** da tutte e due le parti ● *adv* **I don't ~** nemmeno io; **I don't like John or his brother ~** non mi piace John e nemmeno suo fratello ● *conj* **~ John or his brother will be there** ci saranno o John o suo fratello; **I don't like ~ John or his brother** non mi piacciono né John né suo fratello; **~ you go to bed or else...** o vai a letto o altrimenti ...

eject /ɪ'dʒekt/ *vt* eiettare (pilot); espellere (tape, drunk)

eke /iːk/ *vt* **~ out** far bastare; (*increase*) arrotondare; **~ out a living** arrangiarsi

elaborate¹ /ɪ'læbərət/ *adj* elaborato

elaborate² /ɪ'læbəreɪt/ *vi* entrare nei particolari (**on** di)

elapse /ɪ'læps/ *vi* trascorrere

elastic /ɪ'læstɪk/ *adj* elastico ● *n* elastico *m.* **~ 'band** elastico *m*

elated /ɪ'leɪtɪd/ *adj* esultante

elbow /'elbəʊ/ *n* gomito *m*

elder¹ /'eldə(r)/ *n* (*tree*) sambuco *m*

eld|er² *adj* maggiore ● the ~ il/la maggiore. **~erly** *adj* anziano. **~est** *adj* maggiore ● the ~est il/la maggiore

elect /ɪ'lekt/ *adj* **the president ~** il futuro presidente ● *vt* eleggere; **~ to do sth** decidere di fare qcsa. **~ion** *n* elezione *f*

elector /ɪ'lektə(r)/ *n* elettore, -trice *mf.* **~al** *adj* elettorale; **~al roll** liste *fpl* elettorali. **~ate** *n* elettorato *m*

electric /ɪ'lektrɪk/ *adj* elettrico

electrical /ɪ'lektrɪkl/ *adj* elettrico; **~ engineering** elettrotecnica *f*

electric 'blanket *n* termocoperta *f*

electrician /ɪlek'trɪʃn/ *n* elettricista *m*

electricity /ɪlek'trɪsəti/ *n*

elettricità *f*

electrify /ɪ'lektrɪfaɪ/ *vt* (*pt/pp* **-ied**) elettrificare; *fig* elettrizzare. **~ing** *adj* *fig* elettrizzante

electrocute /ɪ'lektrəkjuːt/ *vt* fulminare; (*execute*) giustiziare sulla sedia elettrica

electrode /ɪ'lektrəʊd/ *n* elettrodo *m*

electron /ɪ'lektrɒn/ *n* elettrone *m*

electronic /ɪlek'trɒnɪk/ *adj* elettronico. **~ mail** *n* posta *f* elettronica. **~s** *n* elettronica *f*

elegance /'elɪɡəns/ *n* eleganza *f*

elegant /'elɪɡənt/ *adj* elegante

element /'elɪmənt/ *n* elemento *m*. **~ary** *adj* elementare

elephant /'elɪfənt/ *n* elefante *m*

elevat|e /'elɪveɪt/ *vt* elevare. **~ion** *n* elevazione *f*; (*height*) altitudine *f*; (*angle*) alzo *m*

elevator /'elɪveɪtə(r)/ *n* Am ascensore *m*

eleven /ɪ'levn/ *adj* undici ● *n* undici *m.* **~th** *adj* undicesimo; **at the ~th hour** 🛈 all'ultimo momento

elf /elf/ *n* (*pl* **elves**) elfo *m*

eligible /'elɪdʒəbl/ *adj* eleggibile; **~ for** aver diritto a

eliminate /ɪ'lɪmɪneɪt/ *vt* eliminare

élite /er'liːt/ *n* fior fiore *m*

ellip|se /ɪ'lɪps/ *n* ellisse *f.* **~tical** *adj* ellittico

elm /elm/ *n* olmo *m*

elope /ɪ'ləʊp/ *vi* fuggire [per sposarsi]

eloquen|ce /'eləkwəns/ *n* eloquenza *f.* **~t** *adj* eloquente. **~tly** *adv* con eloquenza

else /els/ *adv* altro; **who ~?** e chi altro?; **he did of course, who ~?** l'ha fatto lui e chi, se no?; **nothing ~** nient'altro; **or ~** altrimenti; **someone ~** qualcun altro; **somewhere ~** da qualche altra parte; **anyone ~** chiunque altro; (*as ques-*

tion) nessun'altro?; **anything** ~ qualunque altra cosa; *(as question)* altro?. ~**where** *adv* altrove

elude /ɪ'luːd/ *vt* eludere; *(avoid)* evitare; **the name** ~**s me** il nome mi sfugge

elusive /ɪ'luːsɪv/ *adj* elusivo

emaciated /ɪ'meɪsɪeɪtɪd/ *adj* emaciato

e-mail /'iːmeɪl/ *n* posta *f* elettronica ● *vt* spedire via posta elettronica. ~ **address** *n* indirizzo *m* e-mail

embankment /ɪm'bæŋkmənt/ *n* argine *m*; *(Rail)* massicciata *f*

embargo /em'baːkɡəʊ/ *n* *(pl* -**es)** embargo *m*

embark /em'baːk/ *vi* imbarcarsi; ~ **on** intraprendere. ~**ation** *n* imbarco *m*

embarrass /em'bærəs/ *vt* imbarazzare. ~**ed** *adj* imbarazzato. ~**ing** *adj* imbarazzante. ~**ment** *n* imbarazzo *m*

embassy /'embəsɪ/ *n* ambasciata *f*

embedded /ɪm'bedɪd/ *adj* *(in concrete)* cementato; *(traditions, feelings)* radicato

embellish /ɪm'belɪʃ/ *vt* abbellire

embers /'embəz/ *npl* braci *fpl*

embezzle /ɪm'bezl/ *vt* appropriarsi indebitamente di. ~**ment** *n* appropriazione *f* indebita

emblem /'embləm/ *n* emblema *m*

embrace /ɪm'breɪs/ *vt* abbracciare ● *vi* abbracciarsi

embroider /ɪm'brɔɪdə(r)/ *vt* ricamare *(design)*; *fig* abbellire. ~**y** *n* ricamo *m*

embryo /'embrɪəʊ/ *n* embrione *m*

emerald /'emərəld/ *n* smeraldo *m*

emer|ge /ɪ'mɜːdʒ/ *vi* emergere; *(come into being: nation)* nascere; *(sun, flowers)* spuntare fuori. ~**gence** *n* emergere *m* *(of new country)* nascita *f*

emergency /ɪ'mɜːdʒənsɪ/ *n* emergenza *f*; **in an** ~ in caso di emer-

genza. ~ **exit** *n* uscita *f* di sicurezza

emigrant /'emɪɡrənt/ *n* emigrante *mf*

emigrat|e /'emɪɡreɪt/ *vi* emigrare. ~**ion** *n* emigrazione *f*

eminent /'emɪnənt/ *adj* eminente. ~**ly** *adv* eminentemente

emission /ɪ'mɪʃn/ *n* emissione *f*; *(of fumes)* esalazione *f*

emit /ɪ'mɪt/ *vt* *(pt/pp* **emitted)** emettere; esalare *(fumes)*

emotion /ɪ'məʊʃn/ *n* emozione *f*. ~**al** *adj* denso di emozione; *(person, reaction)* emotivo; **become** ~**al** avere una reazione emotiva

emotive /ɪ'məʊtɪv/ *adj* emotivo

emperor /'empərə(r)/ *n* imperatore *m*

emphasis /'emfəsɪs/ *n* enfasi *f*; **put the** ~ **on sth** accentuare qcsa

emphasize /'emfəsaɪz/ *vt* accentuare *(word, syllable)*; sottolineare *(need)*

emphatic /ɪm'fætɪk/ *adj* categorico

empire /'empaɪə(r)/ *n* impero *m*

empirical /em'pɪrɪkl/ *adj* empirico

employ /em'plɔɪ/ *vt* impiegare; *fig* usare *(tact)*. ~**ee** *n* impiegato, -a *mf*. ~**er** *n* datore *m* di lavoro. ~**ment** *n* occupazione *f*; *(work)* lavoro *m*. ~**ment agency** *n* ufficio *m* di collocamento

empower /em'paʊə(r)/ *vt* autorizzare; *(enable)* mettere in grado

empress /'emprɪs/ *n* imperatrice *f*

empty /'emptɪ/ *adj* vuoto; *(promise, threat)* vano ● *v* *(pt/pp* -**ied)** ● *vt* vuotare *(container)* ● *vi* vuotarsi

emulate /'emjʊleɪt/ *vt* emulare

emulsion /ɪ'mʌlʃn/ *n* emulsione *f*

enable /ɪ'neɪbl/ *vt* ~ **sb** to mettere qcno in grado di

enact /ɪ'nækt/ *vt* *(Theat)* rappresentare; decretare *(law)*

enamel /ɪ'næml/ *n* smalto *m* ● *vt* *(pt/pp* **enamelled)** smaltare

enchant /ɪnˈtʃɑːnt/ vt incantare. ~ing adj incantevole. ~ment n incanto m

encircle /ɪnˈsɜːkl/ vt circondare

enclave /ˈenkleɪv/ n enclave f inv; fig territorio m

enclos|e /ɪnˈkləʊz/ vt circondare (land); (in letter) allegare (with a). ~ed adj (space) chiuso; (in letter) allegato. ~ure n (at zoo) recinto m; (in letter) allegato m

encore /ˈɒŋkɔː(r)/ n & int bis m inv

encounter /ɪnˈkaʊntə(r)/ n incontro m; (battle) scontro m ● vt incontrare

encourag|e /ɪnˈkʌrɪdʒ/ vt incoraggiare; promuovere (the arts, independence). ~ement n incoraggiamento m; (of the arts) promozione f. ~ing adj incoraggiante; (smile) di incoraggiamento

encroach /ɪnˈkrəʊtʃ/ vt ~ on invadere (land, privacy); abusare di (time); interferire con (rights)

encyclop[a]ed|ia /ɪnsaɪkləˈpiːdɪə/ n enciclopedia f. ~ic adj enciclopedico

end /end/ n fine f; (of box, table, piece of string) estremità f; (of town, room) parte f; (purpose) fine m; in the ~ alla fine; at the ~ of May alla fine di maggio; at the ~ of the street/garden in fondo alla strada/al giardino; on ~ (upright) in piedi; for days on ~ per giorni e giorni; for six days on ~ per sei giorni di fila; put an ~ to sth mettere fine a qcsa; make ~s meet 🄕 sbarcare il lunario; no ~ of 🄕 un sacco di ● vt/i finire. ~ up vi finire; ~ up doing sth finire col fare qcsa

endanger /ɪnˈdeɪndʒə(r)/ vt rischiare (one's life); mettere a repentaglio (sb else, success of sth)

endear|ing /ɪnˈdɪərɪŋ/ adj accattivante. ~ment n term of ~ment vezzeggiativo m

endeavour /ɪnˈdevə(r)/ n tentativo m ● vi sforzarsi (to to)

ending /ˈendɪŋ/ n fine f; (Gram) desinenza f

endless /ˈendlɪs/ adj interminabile; (patience) infinito. ~ly adv continuamente; (patient) infinitamente

endorse /ɪnˈdɔːs/ vt girare (cheque); (sports personality:) fare pubblicità a (product); approvare (plan). ~ment n (of cheque) girata f; (of plan) conferma f; (on driving licence) registrazione f su patente di un'infrazione

endur|e /ɪnˈdjʊə(r)/ vt sopportare ● vi durare. ~ing adj duraturo

enemy /ˈenəmɪ/ n nemico, -a mf ● attrib nemico

energetic /enəˈdʒetɪk/ adj energico

energy /ˈenədʒɪ/ n energia f

enforce /ɪnˈfɔːs/ vt far rispettare (law). ~d adj forzato

engage /ɪnˈgeɪdʒ/ vt assumere (staff); (Theat) ingaggiare; (Auto) ingranare (gear) ● vi (Techn) ingranare; ~ in impegnarsi in. ~d adj (in use, busy) occupato; (person) impegnato; (to be married) fidanzato; get ~d fidanzarsi (to con); ~d tone (Teleph) segnale m di occupato. ~ment n fidanzamento m; (appointment) appuntamento m; (Mil) combattimento m; ~ment ring anello m di fidanzamento

engine /ˈendʒɪn/ n motore m; (Rail) locomotiva f. ~-driver n macchinista m

engineer /endʒɪˈnɪə(r)/ n ingegnere m; (service, installation) tecnico m; (Naut, Am (Rail) macchinista m ● vt fig architettare. ~ing n ingegneria f

England /ˈɪŋglənd/ n Inghilterra f

English /ˈɪŋglɪʃ/ adj inglese; the ~ Channel la Manica ● n (language) inglese m; the ~ pl gli inglesi. ~man n inglese m. ~woman n inglese f

engrav|e /ɪnˈgreɪv/ vt incidere.

~ing *n* incisione *f*

engulf /ɪnˈɡʌlf/ *vt* (fire, waves:) inghiottire

enhance /ɪnˈhɑːns/ *vt* accrescere (beauty, reputation); migliorare (performance)

enigma /ɪˈnɪɡmə/ *n* enigma *m*. ~**tic** *adj* enigmatico

enjoy /ɪnˈdʒɔɪ/ *vt* godere di (good health); ~ **oneself** divertirsi; **I** ~ **cooking/painting** mi piace cucinare/dipingere; ~ **your meal** buon appetito. ~**able** *adj* piacevole. ~**ment** *n* piacere *m*

enlarge /ɪnˈlɑːdʒ/ *vt* ingrandire ● *vi* ~ **upon** dilungarsi su. ~**ment** *n* ingrandimento *m*

enlighten /ɪnˈlaɪtn/ *vt* illuminare. ~**ed** *adj* progressista. ~**ment** *n* **The E**~**ment** l'Illuminismo *m*

enlist /ɪnˈlɪst/ *vt* (Mil) reclutare; ~ **sb's help** farsi aiutare da qcno ● *vi* (Mil) arruolarsi

enliven /ɪnˈlaɪvn/ *vt* animare

enormity /ɪˈnɔːmətɪ/ *n* enormità *f*

enormous /ɪˈnɔːməs/ *adj* enorme. ~**ly** *adv* estremamente; (grateful) infinitamente

enough /ɪˈnʌf/ *adj* & *n* abbastanza; **I didn't bring** ~ **clothes** non ho portato abbastanza vestiti; **have you had** ~**?** (to eat/drink) hai mangiato/bevuto abbastanza?; **is that** ~**?** ne ho abbastanza?; **is that** ~**?** basta?; **that's** ~**!** basta così; **£50 isn't** ~ 50 sterline non sono sufficienti ● *adv* abbastanza; **you're not working fast** ~ non lavori abbastanza in fretta; **funnily** ~ stranamente

enquir|e /ɪnˈkwaɪə(r)/ *vi* domandare; ~**e about** chiedere informazioni su. ~**y** *n* domanda *f*; (investigation) inchiesta *f*

enrage /ɪnˈreɪdʒ/ *vt* fare arrabbiare

enrol /ɪnˈrəʊl/ *vi* (pt/pp -rolled) (for exam, in club) iscriversi (for, in a).

~**ment** *n* iscrizione *f*

ensu|e /ɪnˈsjuː/ *vi* seguire; **the** ~**ing discussion** la discussione che ne è seguita

ensure /ɪnˈʃʊə(r)/ *vt* assicurare; ~ **that** (person:) assicurarsi che; (measure:) garantire che

entail /ɪnˈteɪl/ *vt* comportare; **what does it** ~**?** in che cosa consiste?

entangle /ɪnˈtæŋɡl/ *vt* **get** ~**d in** rimanere impigliato in; *fig* rimanere coinvolto in

enter /ˈentə(r)/ *vt* entrare in; iscrivere (horse, runner in race); cominciare (university); partecipare a (competition); (Comput) immettere (data); (write down) scrivere ● *vi* entrare; (Theat) entrare in scena; (register as competitor) iscriversi; (take part) partecipare (in a)

enterpris|e /ˈentəpraɪz/ *n* impresa *f*; (quality) iniziativa *f*. ~**ing** *adj* intraprendente

entertain /entəˈteɪn/ *vt* intrattenere; (invite) ricevere; nutrire (ideas, hopes); prendere in considerazione (possibility) ● *vi* intrattenersi; (have guests) ricevere. ~**er** *n* artista *mf*. ~**ing** *adj* (person) di gradevole compagnia; (evening, film, play) divertente. ~**ment** *n* (amusement) intrattenimento *m*

enthral /ɪnˈθrɔːl/ *vt* (pt/pp enthralled) **be** ~**led** essere affascinato (by da)

enthusias|m /ɪnˈθjuːzɪæzm/ *n* entusiasmo *m*. ~**t** *n* entusiasta *mf*. ~**tic** *adj* entusiastico

entice /ɪnˈtaɪs/ *vt* attirare. ~**ment** *n* (incentive) incentivo *m*

entire /ɪnˈtaɪə(r)/ *adj* intero. ~**ly** *adv* del tutto; **I'm not** ~**ly satisfied** non sono completamente soddisfatto. ~**ty** /-tɪ/ **in its** ~**ty** nell'insieme

entitlement /ɪnˈtaɪtlmənt/ *n* diritto *m*

entity /ˈentətɪ/ *n* entità *f*

entrance¹ /'entrəns/ n entrata f; (Theat) entrata f in scena; (right to enter) ammissione f; 'no ~' 'ingresso vietato'. ~ **examination** n esame m di ammissione. ~ **fee** n **how much is the ~ fee?** quanto costa il biglietto di ingresso?

entrance² /ɪn'trɑːns/ vt estasiare

entrant /'entrənt/ n concorrente mf

entreat /ɪn'triːt/ vt supplicare

entrenched /ɪn'trentʃt/ adj (ideas, views) radicato

entrust /ɪn'trʌst/ vt ~ sb with sth, ~ sth to sb affidare qcsa a qcno

entry /'entrɪ/ n ingresso m; (way in) entrata f; (in directory etc) voce f; (in appointment diary) appuntamento m; no ~ ingresso vietato; (Auto) accesso vietato. ~ **form** n modulo m di ammissione. ~ **visa** n visto m di ingresso

enumerate /ɪ'njuːmərеɪt/ vt enumerare

envelop /ɪn'veləp/ vt (pt/pp enveloped) avviluppare

envelope /'envələʊp/ n busta f

enviable /'envɪəbl/ adj invidiabile

envious /'envɪəs/ adj invidioso. ~ly adv con invidia

environment /ɪn'vaɪrənmənt/ n ambiente m

environmental /ɪnvaɪrən'mentl/ adj ambientale. ~**ist** n ambientalista mf. ~**ly** adv ~**ly friendly** che rispetta l'ambiente

envisage /ɪn'vɪzɪdʒ/ vt prevedere

envoy /'envɔɪ/ n inviato, -a f

envy /'envɪ/ n invidia f ● vt (pt/pp -ied) ~ **sb sth** invidiare qcno per qcsa

enzyme /'enzaɪm/ n enzima m

epic /'epɪk/ adj epico ● n epopea f

epidemic /epɪ'demɪk/ n epidemia f

epilep|sy /'epɪlepsɪ/ n epilessia f. ~**tic** /-'leptɪk/ adj epilettico, -a ● n

epilogue /'epɪlɒg/ n epilogo m

episode /'epɪsəʊd/ n episodio m

epitaph /'epɪtɑːf/ n epitaffio m

epitom|e /ɪ'pɪtəmɪ/ n epitome f. ~**ize** vt essere il classico esempio di

epoch /'iːpɒk/ n epoca f

equal /'iːkwl/ adj (parts, amounts) uguale; (~ **height**) della stessa altezza; **be ~ to the task** essere all'altezza del compito ● n pari m inv ● vt (pt/pp **equalled**) (be same in quantity as) essere pari a; (rival) uguagliare; **5 plus 5 ~s 10** 5 più 5 [è] uguale a 10. ~**ity** n uguaglianza f

equalize /'iːkwəlaɪz/ vi (Sport) pareggiare. ~**r** n (Sport) pareggio m

equally /'iːkwəlɪ/ adv (divide) in parti uguali; ~ **intelligent** della stessa intelligenza; ~,... allo stesso tempo...

equator /ɪ'kweɪtə(r)/ n equatore m

equilibrium /iːkwɪ'lɪbrɪəm/ n equilibrio m

equinox /'iːkwɪnɒks/ n equinozio m

equip /ɪ'kwɪp/ vt (pt/pp **equipped**) equipaggiare; attrezzare (kitchen, office). ~**ment** n attrezzatura f

equivalent /ɪ'kwɪvələnt/ adj equivalente; **be ~ to** equivalere a ● n equivalente m

equivocal /ɪ'kwɪvəkl/ adj equivoco

era /'ɪərə/ n età f; (geological) era f

eradicate /ɪ'rædɪkeɪt/ vt eradicare

erase /ɪ'reɪz/ vt cancellare. ~**r** n gomma f [da cancellare]; (for blackboard) cancellino m

erect /ɪ'rekt/ adj eretto ● vt erigere. ~**ion** n erezione f

ero|de /ɪ'rəʊd/ vt (water:) erodere; (acid:) corrodere. ~**sion** n erosione f; (by acid) corrosione f

erotic /ɪ'rɒtɪk/ adj erotico.

err /ɜː(r)/ vi errare; (sin) peccare

errand /'erənd/ n commissione f

erratic /ɪ'rætɪk/ adj irregolare; (person, moods) imprevedibile; (exchange rate) incostante

erroneous /ɪˈrəʊnɪəs/ adj erroneo

error /ˈerə(r)/ n errore m; **in ~** per errore

erudit|e /ˈeruːdaɪt/ adj erudito. **~ion** n erudizione f

erupt /ɪˈrʌpt/ vi eruttare; (spots:) spuntare; (fig: in anger) dare in escandescenze. **~ion** n eruzione f; fig scoppio m

escalat|e /ˈeskəleɪt/ vi intensificarsi ● vt intensificare. **~ion** n escalation f inv. **~or** n scala f mobile

escapade /ˈeskəpeɪd/ n scappatella f

escape /ɪˈskeɪp/ n fuga f; (from prison) evasione f; **have a narrow ~** cavarsela per un pelo ● vi (prisoner:) evadere (**from** da); sfuggire (**from** sb alla sorveglianza di qcno); (animal:) scappare; (gas:) fuoriuscire ● vt **~ notice** passare inosservato; **the name ~s me** mi sfugge il nome

escapism /ɪˈskeɪpɪzm/ n evasione f [dalla realtà]

escort[1] /ˈeskɔːt/ n accompagnatore, -trice mf; (Mil etc) scorta f

escort[2] /ɪˈskɔːt/ vt accompagnare; (Mil etc) scortare

Eskimo /ˈeskɪməʊ/ n esquimese mf

especial /ɪˈspeʃl/ adj speciale. **~ly** adv specialmente; (kind) particolarmente

espionage /ˈespɪənɑːʒ/ n spionaggio m

essay /ˈeseɪ/ n saggio m; (Sch) tema f

essence /ˈesns/ n essenza f; **in ~** in sostanza

essential /ɪˈsenʃl/ adj essenziale ● npl **the ~s** l'essenziale m. **~ly** adv essenzialmente

establish /ɪˈstæblɪʃ/ vt stabilire; (contact, lead); fondare (firm); (prove) accertare; **~ oneself as** affermarsi come. **~ment** n (firm) azienda f; **the E~ment** l'ordine m costituito

estate /ɪˈsteɪt/ n tenuta f; (possessions) patrimonio m; (housing) quar-

tiere m residenziale. **~ agent** n agente m immobiliare. **~ car** n giardiniera f

esteem /ɪˈstiːm/ n stima f ● vt stimare; (consider) giudicare

estimate[1] /ˈestɪmət/ n valutazione f; (Comm) preventivo m; **at a rough ~** a occhio e croce

estimate[2] /ˈestɪmeɪt/ vt stimare. **~ion** n (esteem) stima f; **in my ~ion** (judgement) a mio giudizio

estuary /ˈestjʊərɪ/ n estuario m

etc /etˈsetərə/ abbr (et cetera) ecc

etching /ˈetʃɪŋ/ n acquaforte f

eternal /ɪˈtɜːnl/ adj eterno

eternity /ɪˈtɜːnətɪ/ n eternità f

ethic /ˈeθɪk/ n etica f. **~al** adj etico. **~s** n etica f

ethnic /ˈeθnɪk/ adj etnico

etiquette /ˈetɪket/ n etichetta f

EU n abbr (European Union) UE f

euphemis|m /ˈjuːfəmɪzm/ n eufemismo m. **~tic** adj eufemistico

euphoria /juːˈfɔːrɪə/ n euforia f

euro /ˈjʊərəʊ/ n euro m inv

Euro- /ˈjʊərəʊ-/ pref **~cheque** n eurochèque m inv. **~dollar** n eurodollaro m

Europe /ˈjʊərəp/ n Europa f

European /jʊərəˈpɪən/ adj europeo; **~ Union** Unione f Europea ● n europeo, -a mf

Euro-sceptic /jʊərəʊˈskeptɪk/ adj euroscettico ● n euroscettico, -a mf

evacuat|e /ɪˈvækjʊeɪt/ vt evacuare (building, area). **~ion** n evacuazione f

evade /ɪˈveɪd/ vt evadere (taxes); evitare (the enemy, authorities); **~ the issue** evitare l'argomento

evaluat|e /ɪˈvæljʊeɪt/ vt valutare. **~ion** n valutazione f

evange|lical /iːvænˈdʒelɪkl/ adj evangelico. **~list** n evangelista m

evaporat|e /ɪˈvæpəreɪt/ vi evaporare; fig svanire. **~ion** n evaporazione f

evasion /ɪ'veɪʒn/ n evasione f

evasive /ɪ'veɪsɪv/ adj evasivo

eve /iːv/ n liter vigilia f

even /'iːvn/ adj (level) piatto; (same, equal) uguale; (regular) regolare; (number) pari; **get ~ with** vendicarsi di; **now we're ~** adesso siamo pari • adv anche, ancora; **~ if** anche se; **~ so** con tutto ciò; **not ~** nemmeno; **~ bigger/hotter** ancora più grande/caldo • vt **~ the score** (Sport) pareggiare. □ **~ out** vi livellarsi. □ **~ up** vt livellare

evening /'iːvnɪŋ/ n sera f; (whole evening) serata f; **this ~** stasera; **in the ~** la sera. **~ class** n corso m serale. **~ dress** n abito m scuro; (woman's) abito m da sera

event /ɪ'vent/ n avvenimento m; (function) manifestazione f; (Sport) gara f; **in the ~ of** nell'eventualità di; **in the ~** alla fine. **~ful** adj movimentato

eventual /ɪ'ventjʊəl/ adj **the ~ winner was...** alla fine il vincitore è stato.... **~ity** n eventualità f. **~ly** adv alla fine; **~ly!** finalmente!

ever /'evə(r)/ adv mai; **I haven't ~...** non ho mai...; **for ~** per sempre; **hardly ~** quasi mai; **~ since** da quando; (since that time) da allora; **~ so** 🆅 veramente

'**evergreen** n sempreverde m

ever'lasting adj eterno

every /'evrɪ/ adj ogni; **~ one** ciascuno; **~ other day** un giorno si un giorno no

every: **~body** pron tutti pl. **~day** adj quotidiano, di ogni giorno. **~one** pron tutti pl; **~thing** pron tutto; **~where** adv dappertutto; (wherever) dovunque

evict /ɪ'vɪkt/ vt sfrattare. **~ion** n sfratto m

eviden|ce /'evɪdəns/ n evidenza f; (Jur) testimonianza f; **give ~ce** te-

stimoniare. **~t** adj evidente. **~tly** adv evidentemente

evil /'iːvl/ adj cattivo • n male m

evocative /ɪ'vɒkətɪv/ adj evocativo; **be ~ of** evocare

evoke /ɪ'vəʊk/ vt evocare

evolution /iːvə'luːʃn/ n evoluzione f

evolve /ɪ'vɒlv/ vt evolvere • vi evolversi

ewe /juː/ n pecora f

exact /ɪg'zækt/ adj esatto • vt esigere. **~ing** adj esigente. **~itude** n esattezza f. **~ly** adv esattamente; **not ~ly** non proprio. **~ness** n precisione f

exaggerat|e /ɪg'zædʒəreɪt/ vt/i esagerare. **~ion** n esagerazione f

exam /ɪg'zæm/ n esame m

examination /ɪgzæmɪ'neɪʃn/ n esame m; (of patient) visita f

examine /ɪg'zæmɪn/ vt esaminare; visitare (patient). **~r** n (Sch) esaminatore, -trice mf

example /ɪg'zɑːmpl/ n esempio m; **for ~** per esempio; **make an ~ of sb** punire qcno per dare un esempio; **be an ~ to sb** dare il buon esempio a qcno

exasperat|e /ɪg'zæspəreɪt/ vt esasperare. **~ion** n esasperazione f

excavat|e /'ekskəveɪt/ vt scavare; (Archaeol) fare gli scavi di. **~ion** n scavo m

exceed /ɪk'siːd/ vt eccedere. **~ingly** adv estremamente

excel /ɪk'sel/ v (pt/pp **excelled**) • vi eccellere • vt **~ oneself** superare se stessi

excellen|ce /'eksələns/ n eccellenza f. **E~cy** n (title) Eccellenza f. **~t** adj eccellente

except /ɪk'sept/ prep eccetto, tranne; **~ for** eccetto, tranne; **~ that...** eccetto che... • vt eccettuare. **~ing** prep eccetto, tranne

exception /ɪkˈsepʃn/ n eccezione f; **take ~ to** fare obiezioni a. **~al** adj eccezionale. **~ally** adv eccezionalmente

excerpt /ˈeksɜːpt/ n estratto m

excess /ɪkˈses/ n eccesso m; **in ~ of** oltre. **~ baggage** n bagaglio m in eccedenza. **~ 'fare** n supplemento m

excessive /ɪkˈsesɪv/ adj eccessivo. **~ly** adv eccessivamente

exchange /ɪksˈtʃeɪndʒ/ n scambio m; (Teleph) centrale f; (Comm) cambio m; **in ~** in cambio (for di) ● vt scambiare (for con); cambiare (money). **~ rate** n tasso m di cambio

excise[1] /ˈeksaɪz/ n dazio m; **~ duty** dazio m

excise[2] /ekˈsaɪz/ vt recidere

excitable /ɪkˈsaɪtəbl/ adj eccitabile

excit|e /ɪkˈsaɪt/ vt eccitare. **~ed** adj eccitato; **get ~ed** eccitarsi. **~edly** adv tutto eccitato. **~ement** n eccitazione f. **~ing** adj eccitante; (story, film) appassionante; (holiday) entusiasmante

exclaim /ɪkˈskleɪm/ vt/i esclamare

exclamation /ekskləˈmeɪʃn/ n esclamazione f. **~ mark** n, Am **~ point** n punto m esclamativo

exclu|de /ɪkˈskluːd/ vt escludere. **~ding** pron escluso. **~sion** n esclusione f

exclusive /ɪkˈskluːsɪv/ adj (rights, club) esclusivo; (interview) in esclusiva; **~ of...** ...escluso. **~ly** adv esclusivamente

excruciating /ɪkˈskruːʃɪeɪtɪŋ/ adj atroce (pain); (Ⅱ: very bad) spaventoso

excursion /ɪkˈskɜːʃn/ n escursione f

excusable /ɪkˈskjuːzəbl/ adj perdonabile

excuse[1] /ɪkˈskjuːs/ n scusa f

excuse[2] /ɪkˈskjuːz/ vt scusare; **~ from** esonerare da; **~ me!** (to get attention) scusi!; (to get past) permesso!,

scusi!; (indignant) come ha detto?

ex-di'rectory adj be **~** non figurare sull'elenco telefonico

execute /ˈeksɪkjuːt/ vt eseguire; (put to death) giustiziare; attuare (plan)

execution /eksɪˈkjuːʃn/ n esecuzione f; (of plan) attuazione f. **~er** n boia m inv

executive /ɪgˈzekjutɪv/ adj esecutivo ● n dirigente mf; (Pol) esecutivo m

executor /ɪgˈzekjutə(r)/ n (Jur) esecutore, -trice mf

exempt /ɪgˈzempt/ adj esente ● vt esentare (from da). **~ion** n esenzione f

exercise /ˈeksəsaɪz/ n esercizio m; (Mil) esercitazione f; **physical ~s** ginnastica f; **take ~** fare del moto ● vt esercitare (muscles, horse); portare a spasso (dog); mettere in pratica (skills) ● vi esercitarsi. **~ book** n quaderno m

exert /ɪgˈzɜːt/ vt esercitare; **~ oneself** sforzarsi. **~ion** n sforzo m

exhale /eksˈheɪl/ vt/i esalare

exhaust /ɪgˈzɔːst/ n (Auto) scappamento m; (pipe) tubo m di scappamento; **~ fumes** fumi mpl di scarico m ● vt esaurire. **~ed** adj esausto. **~ing** adj estenuante; (climate, person) sfibrante. **~ion** n esaurimento m. **~ive** adj fig esauriente

exhibit /ɪgˈzɪbɪt/ n oggetto m esposto; (Jur) reperto m ● vt esporre; fig dimostrare

exhibition /eksɪˈbɪʃn/ n mostra f; (of strength, skill) dimostrazione f. **~ist** n esibizionista m

exhibitor /ɪgˈzɪbɪtə(r)/ n espositore, -trice mf

exhort /ɪgˈzɔːt/ vt esortare

exile /ˈeksaɪl/ n esilio m; (person) esule mf ● vt esiliare

exist /ɪgˈzɪst/ vi esistere. **~ence** n esistenza f; **in ~** esistente; **be in**

~ence esistere. ~ing adj attuale

exit /ˈeksɪt/ n uscita f; (Theat) uscita f di scena ● vi (Theat) uscire di scena; (Comput) uscire

exorbitant /ɪɡˈzɔːbɪtənt/ adj esorbitante

exotic /ɪɡˈzɒtɪk/ adj esotico

expand /ɪkˈspænd/ vt espandere ● vi espandersi; (Comm) svilupparsi; (metal:) dilatarsi; (de-) **on** (: fig: explain better) approfondire

expanse /ɪkˈspæns/ n estensione f. ~ion n espansione f; (Comm) sviluppo m; (of metal) dilatazione f. ~ive adj espansivo

expatriate /eksˈpætrɪət/ n espatriato, -a mf

expect /ɪkˈspekt/ vt aspettare (letter, baby); (suppose) pensare; (demand) esigere; **I ~ so** penso di si; **be ~ing** essere in stato interessante

expectan|cy /ɪkˈspektənsɪ/ n aspettativa f. ~t adj in attesa; ~t **mother** donna f incinta. ~tly adv con impazienza

expectation /ekspekˈteɪʃn/ n aspettativa f, speranza f

expedient /ɪkˈspiːdɪənt/ adj conveniente ● n espediente m

expedition /ekspɪˈdɪʃn/ n spedizione f. ~ary adj (Mil) di spedizione

expel /ɪkˈspel/ vt (pt/pp expelled) espellere

expend /ɪkˈspend/ vt consumare. ~able adj sacrificabile

expenditure /ɪkˈspendɪtʃə(r)/ n spesa f

expense /ɪkˈspens/ n spesa f; business ~s pl spese fpl; **at my ~** a mie spese; **at the ~ of** fig a spese di

expensive /ɪkˈspensɪv/ adj caro, costoso. ~ly adv costosamente

experience /ɪkˈspɪərɪəns/ n esperienza f ● vt provare (sensation); avere (problem). ~d adj esperto

experiment /ɪkˈsperɪmənt/ n esperimento ● vi sperimentare. ~al

adj sperimentale

expert /ˈekspɜːt/ adj & n esperto, -a mf. ~ly adv abilmente

expertise /ekspɜːˈtiːz/ n competenza f

expire /ɪkˈspaɪə(r)/ vi scadere

expiry /ɪkˈspaɪərɪ/ n scadenza f. ~ **date** n data f di scadenza

explain /ɪkˈspleɪn/ vt spiegare

explana|tion /ekspləˈneɪʃn/ n spiegazione f. ~tory adj esplicativo

explicit /ɪkˈsplɪsɪt/ adj esplicito. ~ly adv esplicitamente

explode /ɪkˈspləʊd/ vi esplodere ● vt fare esplodere

exploit[1] /ˈeksplɔɪt/ n impresa f

exploit[2] /ɪkˈsplɔɪt/ vt sfruttare. ~ation n sfruttamento m

explora|tion /ekspləˈreɪʃn/ n esplorazione f. ~tory adj esplorativo

explore /ɪkˈsplɔː(r)/ vt esplorare; fig studiare (implications). ~r n esploratore, -trice mf

explos|ion /ɪkˈspləʊʒn/ n esplosione f. ~ive adj & n esplosivo m

export /ˈekspɔːt/ n esportazione f ● vt /-ˈspɔːt/ esportare. ~er n esportatore, -trice mf

expos|e /ɪkˈspəʊz/ vt esporre; (reveal) svelare; smascherare (traitor etc). ~ure n esposizione f; (Med) esposizione f prolungata al freddo/caldo; (of crimes) smascheramento m; **24 ~ures** (Phot) 24 pose

express /ɪkˈspres/ adj espresso ● adv (send) per espresso ● n (train) espresso m ● vt esprimere; ~ **oneself** esprimersi. ~ion n espressione f. ~ive adj espressivo. ~ly adv espressamente

expulsion /ɪkˈspʌlʃn/ n espulsione f

exquisite /ekˈskwɪzɪt/ adj squisito

extend /ɪkˈstend/ vt prolungare (visit, road); prorogare (visa, contract); ampliare (building, knowledge); (*stretch out*) allungare; tendere (hand) ●*vi* (garden, knowledge:) estendersi

extension /ɪkˈstenʃn/ *n* prolungamento *m*; (*of visa, contract*) proroga *f*; (*of treaty*) ampliamento *m*; (*part of building*) annesso *m*; (*length of cable*) prolunga *f*; (*Teleph*) interno *m*; ~ **226** interno 226

extensive /ɪkˈstensɪv/ *adj* ampio, vasto. **~ly** *adv* ampiamente

extent /ɪkˈstent/ *n* (*scope*) portata *f*; **to a certain ~** fino a un certo punto; **to such an ~ that...** fino al punto che...

exterior /ɪkˈstɪərɪə(r)/ *adj & n* esterno *m*

exterminat|e /ɪkˈstɜːmɪneɪt/ *vt* sterminare. **~ion** *n* sterminio *m*

external /ɪkˈstɜːnl/ *adj* esterno; **for ~ use only** (*Med*) per uso esterno. **~ly** *adv* esternamente

extinct /ɪkˈstɪŋkt/ *adj* estinto. **~ion** *n* estinzione *f*

extinguish /ɪkˈstɪŋgwɪʃ/ *vt* estinguere. **~er** *n* estintore *m*

extort /ɪkˈstɔːt/ *vt* estorcere. **~ion** *n* estorsione *f*

extortionate /ɪkˈstɔːʃənət/ *adj* esorbitante

extra /ˈekstrə/ *adj* in più; (*train*) straordinario; **an ~ £10** 10 sterline extra, 10 sterline in più ●*adv* in più; (*especially*) più; **pay ~** pagare in più, pagare extra; **strong/busy** fortissimo/occupatissimo ●*n* (*Theat*) comparsa *f*. **~s** *pl* extra *mpl*

extract[1] /ˈekstrækt/ *n* estratto *m*

extract[2] /ɪkˈstrækt/ *vt* estrarre (tooth, oil); strappare (secret); ricavare (truth). **~or** [**fan**] *n* aspiratore *m*

extradit|e /ˈekstrədaɪt/ *vt* (*Jur*) estradare. **~ion** *n* estradizione *f*

extraordinar|y /ɪkˈstrɔːdɪnərɪ/ *adj* straordinario. **~ily** *adv* straordinariamente

extravagan|ce /ɪkˈstrævəgəns/ *n* (*with money*) prodigalità *f*; (*of behaviour*) stravaganza *f*. **~t** *adj* spendaccione; (*bizarre*) stravagante; (*claim*) esagerato

extrem|e /ɪkˈstriːm/ *adj* estremo ●*n* estremo *m*; **in the ~e** al massimo. **~ely** *adv* estremamente. **~ist** *n* estremista *mf*

extricate /ˈekstrɪkeɪt/ *vt* districare

extrovert /ˈekstrəvɜːt/ *n* estroverso, -a *mf*

exuberant /ɪgˈzjuːbərənt/ *adj* esuberante

exude /ɪgˈzjuːd/ *vt* also *fig* trasudare

exult /ɪgˈzʌlt/ *vi* esultare

eye /aɪ/ *n* occhio *m*; (*of needle*) cruna *f*; **keep an ~ on** tener d'occhio; **see ~ to ~** aver le stesse idee ●*vt* (*pt/pp* **eyed**, *pres p* **ey[e]ing**) guardare

eye: **~ball** *n* bulbo *m* oculare. **~ brow** *n* sopracciglio *m* (*pl* sopracciglia *f*). **~lash** *n* ciglio *m* (*pl* ciglia *f*). **~lid** *n* palpebra *f*. **~opener** *n* rivelazione *f*. **~shadow** *n* ombretto *m*. **~sight** *n* vista *f*. **~sore** *n* 🔢 pugno *m* nell'occhio. **~witness** *n* testimone *mf* oculare

Ff

fable /ˈfeɪbl/ *n* favola *f*

fabric /ˈfæbrɪk/ *n* also *fig* tessuto *m*

fabulous /ˈfæbjʊləs/ *adj* 🔢 favoloso

façade /fəˈsɑːd/ *n* (*of building, person*) facciata *f*

face /feɪs/ *n* faccia *f*, viso *m*; (*grimace*) smorfia *f*; (*surface*) faccia *f*; (*of clock*) quadrante *m*; **pull ~s** far boccacce; **in the ~ of** di fronte a; **on the ~ of it** in apparenza ●*vt* essere di fronta a; (*confront*) affrontare; ~

north (house:) dare a nord; ~ the fact that arrendersi al fatto che. □ ~ up to vt accettare (facts); affrontare (person)

face: ~flannel n ≈ guanto m di spugna. ~less adj anonimo. ~lift n plastica f facciale

facetious /fəˈsiːʃəs/ adj spiritoso. ~ remarks spiritosaggini mpl

facial /ˈfeɪʃl/ adj facciale ● n trattamento m di bellezza al viso

facile /ˈfæsaɪl/ adj semplicistico

facilitate /fəˈsɪlɪteɪt/ vt rendere possibile; (make easier) facilitare

facilit|y /fəˈsɪlətɪ/ n facilità f; ~ies pl (of area, in hotel etc) attrezzature fpl

fact /fækt/ n fatto m; in ~ infatti

faction /ˈfækʃn/ n fazione f

factor /ˈfæktə(r)/ n fattore m

factory /ˈfæktərɪ/ n fabbrica f

factual /ˈfæktʃʊəl/ adj be ~ attenersi ai fatti. ~ly (inaccurate) dal punto di vista dei fatti

faculty /ˈfækltɪ/ n facoltà f inv

fad /fæd/ n capriccio m

fade /feɪd/ vi sbiadire; (sound, light:) affievolirsi; (flower:) appassire. ~ in vt cominciare in dissolvenza (picture). □ ~ out vt finire in dissolvenza (picture)

fag /fæg/ n (chore) fatica f; (🔢: cigarette) sigaretta f; (Am 🔢: homosexual) frocio m. ~ end n 🔢 cicca f

Fahrenheit /ˈfærənhaɪt/ adj Fahrenheit

fail /feɪl/ vi (attempt:) fallire; (eyesight, memory:) indebolirsi; (engine, machine:) guastarsi; (marriage:) andare a rotoli; (in exam) essere bocciato; ~ to do sth non fare qcsa; I tried but I ~ed ho provato ma non ci sono riuscito ● vt non superare (exam); bocciare (candidate); (disappoint) deludere; words ~ me mi mancano le parole

failing /ˈfeɪlɪŋ/ n difetto m ● prep ~ that altrimenti

failure /ˈfeɪljə(r)/ n fallimento m; (mechanical) guasto m; (person) incapace mf

faint /feɪnt/ adj leggero; (memory) vago; feel ~ sentirsi mancare ● n svenimento m ● vi svenire

faint: ~hearted adj timido. ~ly adv (slightly) leggermente

fair[1] /feə(r)/ n fiera f

fair[2] adj (hair, person) biondo; (skin) chiaro; (weather) bello; (just) giusto; (quite good) discreto; (Sch) abbastanza bene; a ~ amount abbastanza ● adv play ~ fare un gioco pulito. ~ly adv con giustizia; (rather) discretamente, abbastanza. ~ness n giustizia f. ~ play n fair play m inv. ~ trade n commercio m equo e solidale

fairy /ˈfeərɪ/ n fata f; ~ story, ~tale n fiaba f

faith /feɪθ/ n fede f; (trust) fiducia f; in good/bad ~ in buona/mala fede

faithful /ˈfeɪθfl/ adj fedele. ~ly adv fedelmente; yours ~ly distinti saluti. ~ness n fedeltà f

fake /feɪk/ adj falso ● n falsificazione f; (person) impostore m ● vt falsificare; (pretend) fingere

falcon /ˈfɔːlkən/ n falcone m

fall /fɔːl/ n caduta f; (in prices) ribasso m; (Am: autumn) autunno m; have a ~ fare una caduta ● vi (pt fell, pp fallen) cadere; (night:) scendere; ~ in love innamorarsi. □ ~ about vi (with laughter) morire dal ridere. ~ back on vt 🔢 innamorarsi di (person); cascarci (sth, trick). □ ~ down vi cadere; (building:) crollare. □ ~ in vi caderci dentro; (collapse) crollare; (Mil) mettersi in riga; ~ in with concordare con (plan). □ ~ off vi cadere; (diminish) diminuire. □ ~ out vi (quarrel) litigare; his hair is ~ing out perde i capelli. □ ~ over vi cadere. □ ~ through vi (plan:) andare a monte

fallacy /ˈfæləsɪ/ n errore m

fallible /ˈfæləbl/ adj fallibile

'fall-out n pioggia f radioattiva

false /fɔːls/ adj falso; ~ **bottom** doppio fondo m; ~ **start** (Sport) falsa partenza f. ~**hood** n menzogna f. ~**ness** n falsità f

false 'teeth npl dentiera f

falsify /ˈfɔːlsɪfaɪ/ vt (pt/pp -ied) falsificare

falter /ˈfɔːltə(r)/ vi vacillare; (making speech) esitare

fame /feɪm/ n fama f

familiar /fəˈmɪljə(r)/ adj familiare; be ~ **with** (know) conoscere. ~**ity** n familiarità f. ~**ize** vt familiarizzare; ~**ize oneself with** familiarizzarsi con

family /ˈfæməlɪ/ n famiglia f

family: ~ **'planning** n pianificazione f familiare. ~ **'tree** n albero m genealogico

famine /ˈfæmɪn/ n carestia f

famished /ˈfæmɪʃt/ adj be ~ 🄵 avere una fame da lupo

famous /ˈfeɪməs/ adj famoso

fan[1] /fæn/ n ventilatore m; (handheld) ventaglio m ●vt (pt/pp fanned) far vento a; ~ **oneself** sventagliarsi; fig ~ **the flames** soffiare sul fuoco. □ ~ **out** vi spiegarsi a ventaglio

fan[2] n (admirer) ammiratore, -trice m/f; (Sport) tifoso m; (of Verdi etc) appassionato, -a m/f

fanatic /fəˈnætɪk/ n fanatico, -a m/f. ~**al** adj fanatico. ~**ism** n fanatismo m

'fan belt n cinghia f per ventilatore

fanciful /ˈfænsɪfl/ adj fantasioso

fancy /ˈfænsɪ/ n fantasia f; I've taken a real ~ to him mi è molto simpatico; as the ~ takes you come ti pare ●adj [a] fantasia ●vt (pt/pp -ied) (believe) credere; (🄵: want) aver voglia di; **he fancies you** 🄵 gli piaci; ~ **that!** ma guarda un po'! ~ **'dress** n costume m (per maschera)

fanfare /ˈfænfeə(r)/ n fanfara f

fang /fæŋ/ n zanna f; (of snake) dente m

fantas|ize /ˈfæntəsaɪz/ vi fantasticare. ~**tic** adj fantastico. ~**y** n fantasia f

far /fɑː(r)/ adv lontano; (much) molto; **by** ~ di gran lunga; ~ **away** lontano; as ~ as the church fino alla chiesa; **how** ~ **is it from here?** quanto dista da qui?; **as** ~ **as I know** per quanto io sappia ●adj (end, side) altro; **the F~ East** l'Estremo Oriente m

farc|e /fɑːs/ n farsa f. ~**ical** adj ridicolo

fare /feə(r)/ n tariffa f; (food) vitto m. ~**-dodger** n passeggero, -a m/f senza biglietto

farewell /feəˈwel/ int liter addio! ●n addio m

far-'fetched adj improbabile

farm /fɑːm/ n fattoria f ●vi fare l'agricoltore ●vt coltivare (land). ~**er** n agricoltore m

farm: ~**house** n casa f colonica. ~**ing** n agricoltura f. ~**yard** n aia f

far: ~**-'reaching** adj di larga portata. ~**'sighted** adj fig prudente; (Am: long-sighted) presbite

farther /ˈfɑːðə(r)/ adv più lontano ●adj at the ~ end of all'altra estremità di

fascinat|e /ˈfæsɪneɪt/ vt affascinare. ~**ing** adj affascinante. ~**ion** n fascino m

fascis|m /ˈfæʃɪzm/ n fascismo m. ~**t** n fascista m/f ●adj fascista

fashion /ˈfæʃn/ n moda f; (manner) maniera f ●vt modellare. ~**able** adj di moda; **be** ~**able** essere alla moda. ~**ably** adv alla moda

fast[1] /fɑːst/ adj veloce; (colour) indelebile; **be** ~ (clock:) andare avanti ●adv velocemente; (firmly) saldamente; ~**er!** più in fretta!; **be** ~ **asleep** dormire profondamente

fast² *n* digiuno *m* • *vi* digiunare

fasten /ˈfɑːsn/ *vt* allacciare; chiudere (window); (*stop flapping*) mettere un fermo a *vi* allacciarsi. **~er** *n*, **~ing** *n* chiusura *f*

fat /fæt/ *adj* (**fatter, fattest**) (person, cheque) grasso • *n* grasso *m*

fatal /ˈfeɪtl/ *adj* mortale; (error) fatale. **~ism** *n* fatalismo *m*. **~ist** *n* fatalista *mf*. **~ity** *n* morte *f*. **~ly** *adv* mortalmente

fate /feɪt/ *n* destino *m*. **~ful** *adj* fatidico

father /ˈfɑːðə(r)/ *n* padre *m*; **F~ Christmas** Babbo *m* Natale • *vt* generare (child)

father: ~hood *n* paternità *f*. **~-in-law** *n* (*pl* **~s-in-law**) suocero *m*. **~ly** *adj* paterno

fathom /ˈfæðəm/ *n* (*Naut*) braccio *m* • *vt* ~ **[out]** comprendere

fatigue /fəˈtiːg/ *n* fatica *f*.

fatten /ˈfætn/ *vt* ingrassare (animal). **~ing** *adj* **cream** is **~ing** la panna fa ingrassare

fatty /ˈfætɪ/ *adj* grasso • *n* □ ciccione, -a *mf*

fatuous /ˈfætjʊəs/ *adj* fatuo

faucet /ˈfɔːsɪt/ *n* Am rubinetto *m*

fault /fɔːlt/ *n* difetto *m*; (*Geol*) faglia *f*; (*Tennis*) fallo *m*; **be at ~** avere torto; **find ~ with** trovare da ridire su; **it's your ~** è colpa tua • *vt* criticare. **~less** *adj* impeccabile

faulty /ˈfɔːltɪ/ *adj* difettoso

favour /ˈfeɪvə(r)/ *n* favore *m*; **be in ~ of sth** essere a favore di qcsa; **do sb a ~** fare un piacere a qcno • *vt* (*prefer*) preferire. **~able** *adj* favorevole

favourit|e /ˈfeɪv(ə)rɪt/ *adj* preferito • *n* preferito, -a *mf*; (*Sport*) favorito, -a *mf*. **~ism** *n* favoritismo *m*

fawn /fɔːn/ *adj* fulvo • *n* (animal) cerbiatto *m*

fax /fæks/ *n* (document, machine) fax *m inv*; **by ~** per fax • *vt* faxare. **~ ma-**

chine *n* fax *m inv*. **~-modem** *n* modem-fax *m inv*, fax-modem *m inv*

fear /fɪə(r)/ *n* paura *f*; **no ~!** □ vai tranquillo! • *vt* temere • *vi* ~ **for sth** temere per qcsa

fear|ful /ˈfɪəfl/ *adj* pauroso; (*awful*) terribile. **~less** *adj* impavido. **~some** *adj* spaventoso

feas|ibility /fiːzɪˈbɪlɪtɪ/ *n* praticabilità *f*. **~ible** *adj* fattibile; (*possible*) probabile

feast /fiːst/ *n* festa *f*; (*banquet*) banchetto *m* • *vi* banchettare; ~ **on** godersi

feat /fiːt/ *n* impresa *f*

feather /ˈfeðə(r)/ *n* piuma *f*

feature /ˈfiːtʃə(r)/ *n* (quality) caratteristica *f*; (*Journ*) articolo *m*; **~s** (*pl: of face*) lineamenti *mpl* • *vt* (film): avere come protagonista • *vi* (*on a list etc*) comparire. ~ **film** *n* lungometraggio *m*

February /ˈfebrʊərɪ/ *n* febbraio *m*

fed /fed/ ▷**FEED** • *adj* **be ~ up** □ essere stufo (**with** di)

federal /ˈfed(ə)rəl/ *adj* federale

federation /fedəˈreɪʃn/ *n* federazione *f*

fee /fiː/ *n* tariffa *f*; (lawyer's, doctor's) onorario *m*; (*for membership, school*) quota *f*

feeble /ˈfiːbl/ *adj* debole; (excuse) fiacco

feed /fiːd/ *n* mangiare *m*; (*for baby*) pappa *f* • *v* (*pt/pp* **fed**) • *vt* dar da mangiare a (animal); (support) nutrire; ~ **sth into sth** inserire qcsa in qcsa • *vi* mangiare

'feedback *n* controreazione *f*; (*of information*) reazione *f*, feedback *m*

feel /fiːl/ *v* (*pt/pp* **felt**) • *vt* sentire; (experience) provare; (think) pensare; (touch: searching) tastare; (touch: for texture) toccare • *vi* ~ **soft/hard** essere duro/morbido al tatto; ~ **hot/hungry** aver caldo/fame; ~ **ill** sentirsi male; **I don't ~ like it** non ne ho voglia; **how do you ~ about it?** (opinion) che te ne pare?; **it doesn't ~ right** non mi sembra giusto. **~er** n (of animal) antenna f; **put out ~ers** fig tastare il terreno; **~ing** n sentimento m; (awareness) sensazione f

feet /fiːt/ ▷**FOOT**

feign /feɪn/ vt simulare

fell[1] /fel/ vt (knock down) abbattere

fell[2] ▷**FALL**

fellow /ˈfeləʊ/ n (of society) socio m; (🔲: man) tipo m

fellow 'countryman n compatriota m

felony /ˈfeləni/ n delitto m

felt[1] /felt/ ▷**FEEL**

felt[2] n feltro m. **~[-tipped] 'pen** /[ˈtɪpt]/ n pennarello m

female /ˈfiːmeɪl/ adj femminile; **the ~ antelope** l'antilope femmina ● n femmina f

femin|ine /ˈfemmɪn/ adj femminile ● n (Gram) femminile m. **~inity** n femminilità f. **~ist** adj & n femminista mf

fenc|e /fens/ n recinto m; (🔲: person) ricettatore m ● vi (Sport) tirar di scherma. □ **~ in** vt chiudere in un recinto. **~er** n schermidore m. **~ing** n steccato m; (Sport) scherma f

fend /fend/ vi **~ for oneself** badare a se stesso. □ **~ off** vt parare; difendersi da (criticisms)

fender /ˈfendə(r)/ n parafuoco m inv; (Am: on car) parafango m

fennel /ˈfenl/ n finocchio m

ferment[1] /ˈfɜːment/ n fermento m

ferment[2] /fəˈment/ vi fermentare ● vt far fermentare. **~ation** n fermentazione f

fern /fɜːn/ n felce f

feroc|ious /fəˈrəʊʃəs/ adj feroce. **~ity** n ferocia f

ferret /ˈferɪt/ n furetto m ● **ferret out** vt scovare

ferry /ˈferɪ/ n traghetto m ● vt traghettare

fertil|e /ˈfɜːtaɪl/ adj fertile. **~ity** n fertilità f

fertilize /ˈfɜːtɪlaɪz/ vt fertilizzare (land, ovum). **~r** n fertilizzante m

fervent /ˈfɜːvənt/ adj fervente

fervour /ˈfɜːvə(r)/ n fervore m

fester /ˈfestə(r)/ vi suppurare

festival /ˈfestɪvl/ n (Mus, Theat) festival m; (Relig) festa f

festive /ˈfestɪv/ adj festivo; **~e season** periodo m delle feste natalizie. **~ities** vt andare/venire a prendere; (be sold for) raggiungere [il prezzo di]

fetch /fetʃ/ vt andare/venire a prendere; (be sold for) raggiungere [il prezzo di]

fetching /ˈfetʃɪŋ/ adj attraente

fête /feɪt/ n festa f ● vt festeggiare

fetish /ˈfetɪʃ/ n feticcio m

fetter /ˈfetə(r)/ vt incatenare

feud /fjuːd/ n faida f

feudal /ˈfjuːdl/ adj feudale

fever /ˈfiːvə(r)/ n febbre f. **~ish** adj febbricitante; fig febbrile

few /fjuː/ adj pochi; **every ~ days** ogni due o tre giorni; **a ~ people** alcuni; **~er reservations** meno prenotazioni; **the ~est number** il numero più basso ● pron pochi; **~ of us** pochi di noi; **a ~** alcuni; **quite a ~ parecchi; **~er than last year** meno dell'anno scorso

fiancé /frˈɒnseɪ/ n fidanzato m. **~e** n fidanzata f

fiasco /frˈæskəʊ/ n fiasco m

fib /fɪb/ n storia f; **tell a ~** raccontare una storia

fibre /ˈfaɪbə(r)/ n fibra f. **~glass** n fibra f di vetro

fickle /ˈfɪkl/ adj incostante

fiction /ˈfɪkʃn/ n [works of] **~** narrativa f; (fabrication) finzione f. **~al** adj immaginario

fictitious /fɪkˈtɪʃəs/ adj fittizio

fiddle /'fɪdl/ n 🎻 violino m; (cheating) imbroglio m ● vi gingillarsi (with con) ● vt 🎻 truccare (accounts)

fidget /'fɪdʒɪt/ vi agitarsi. **~y** adj agitato

field /fiːld/ n campo m

field: ~-glasses npl binocolo msg. **F~** 'Marshal n feldmaresciallo m. **~work** n ricerche fpl sul terreno

fiend /fiːnd/ n demonio m

fierce /fɪəs/ adj feroce. **~ness** n ferocia f

fiery /'faɪərɪ/ adj (-ier, -iest) focoso

fifteen /fɪf'tiːn/ adj & n quindici m. **~th** adj quindicesimo

fifth /fɪfθ/ adj quinto

fiftieth /'fɪftɪɪθ/ adj cinquantesimo

fifty /'fɪftɪ/ adj cinquanta

fig /fɪg/ n fico m

fight /faɪt/ n lotta f; (brawl) zuffa f; (argument) litigio m; (boxing) incontro m ● v (pt/pp fought) ● vt also fig combattere ● vi combattere; (brawl) azzuffarsi; (argue) litigare. **~er** n combattente mf; (Aeron) caccia m inv. **~ing** n combattimento m

figment /'fɪgmənt/ n it's a ~ of your imagination questo è tutta una tua invenzione

figurative /'fɪgjərətɪv/ adj (sense) figurato; (art) figurativo

figure /'fɪgə(r)/ n (digit) cifra f; (carving, sculpture, illustration, form) figura f; (body shape) linea f; ~ of speech modo m di dire ● vi (appear) figurare ● vt (Am: think) pensare. □ ~ out vt dedurre; capire (person)

figurehead n figura f simbolica

file¹ /faɪl/ n scheda f; (set of documents) incartamento m; (folder) cartellina f; (Comput) file m inv ● vt archiviare (documents)

file² n (line) fila f; **in single ~** in fila

file³ n (Techn) lima f ● vt limare

filing cabinet /'faɪlɪŋkæbɪnət/ n schedario m, classificatore m

fill /fɪl/ n **eat one's ~** mangiare a sazietà ● vt riempire; otturare (tooth) ● vi riempirsi. □ ~ **in** vt compilare (form). □ ~ **out** vt compilare (form). □ ~ **up** vi (room, tank:) riempirsi; (Auto) far il pieno ● vt riempire

fillet /'fɪlɪt/ n filetto m ● vt (pt/pp filleted) disossare

filling /'fɪlɪŋ/ n (Culin) ripieno m; (of tooth) piombatura f. **~ station** n stazione f di rifornimento

film /fɪlm/ n (Cinema) film m inv; (Phot) pellicola f; [cling] ~ pellicola f per alimenti ● vt/i filmare. **~ star** n star f inv, divo, -a mf

filter /'fɪltə(r)/ n filtro m ● vt filtrare. □ ~ **through** vi (news:) trapelare. **~ tip** n filtro m; (cigarette) sigaretta f col filtro

filth /fɪlθ/ n sudiciume m. **~y** adj (-ier, -iest) sudicio; (word) sconcio

fin /fɪn/ n pinna f

final /'faɪnl/ adj finale; (conclusive) decisivo ● n (Sport) finale f. **~s** pl (Univ) esami mpl finali

finale /fɪ'nɑːlɪ/ n finale m

final|ist /'faɪnlɪst/ n finalista mf. **~ity** n finalità f

final|ize /'faɪnlaɪz/ vt mettere a punto (text); definire (agreement). **~ly** adv (at last) finalmente; (at the end) alla fine; (to conclude) per finire

finance /'faɪnæns/ n finanza f ● vt finanziare

financial /far'nænʃl/ adj finanziario

find /faɪnd/ n scoperta f ● vt (pt/pp found) trovare; (establish) scoprire; ~ sb guilty (Jur) dichiarare qcno colpevole. □ ~ **out** vt scoprire ● vi (enquire) informarsi

findings /'faɪndɪŋz/ npl conclusioni fpl

fine¹ /faɪn/ n (penalty) multa f ● vt multare

fine² adj bello; (slender) fine; **he's ~** (in health) sta bene. **~ arts** npl belle arti fpl. ● adv bene; **that's cutting it**

~ non ci lascia molto tempo ● *int*
[va] bene. ~**ly** *adv* (cut) finemente

finger /ˈfɪŋgə(r)/ *n* dito *m* (*pl* dita *f*)
● *vt* tastare

finger: ~**nail** *n* unghia *f*. ~**print** *n*
impronta *f* digitale. ~**tip** *n* punta *f*
del dito; **have sth at one's ~tips**
sapere qcsa a menadito; (*close at
hand*) avere qcsa a portata di mano

finish /ˈfɪnɪʃ/ *n* fine *f*; (*finishing line*)
traguardo *m*; (*of product*) finitura *f*;
have a good ~ (runner:) avere un
buon finale ● *vt* finire; ~ **reading** finire di leggere ● *vi* finire

finite /ˈfaɪnaɪt/ *adj* limitato

Finland /ˈfɪnlənd/ *n* Finlandia *f*

Finn /fɪn/ *n* finlandese *mf*. ~**ish** *adj*
finlandese ● *n* (*language*) finnico *m*

fiord /fjɔːd/ *n* fiordo *m*

fir /fɜː(r)/ *n* abete *m*

fire /ˈfaɪə(r)/ *n* fuoco *m*; (*forest, house*)
incendio *m*; **be on ~** bruciare; **catch
~** prendere fuoco; **set ~ to** dar
fuoco a; **under ~** sotto il fuoco ● *vt*
cuocere (pottery); sparare (shot); tirare (gun); (囗: *dismiss*) buttar fuori
● *vi* sparare (**at a**)

fire: ~ **alarm** *n* allarme *m* antincen-
dio. ~**arm** *n* arma *f* da fuoco. ~
brigade *n* vigili *mpl* del fuoco.
~**engine** *n* autopompa *f*.
~**escape** *n* uscita *f* di sicurezza. ~
extinguisher *n* estintore *m*. ~**man**
n pompiere *m*, vigile *m* del fuoco.
~**place** *n* caminetto *m*. ~**side** *n* **by
or at the ~side** accanto al fuoco.
~**wood** *n* legna *f* (*da ardere*). ~**work**
n fuoco *m* d'artificio

firm¹ /fɜːm/ *n* ditta *f*, azienda *f*

firm² *adj* fermo; (soil) compatto;
(*stable, properly fixed*) solido; (*resolute*)
risoluto. ~**ly** *adv* (hold) stretto; (say)
con fermezza

first /fɜːst/ *adj & n* primo, -a *mf*; **at ~**
all'inizio; **who's ~?** chi è il primo?;
from the ~ [fin] dall'inizio ● *adv* (arrive, leave) per primo; (*beforehand*)

prima; (*in listing*) prima di tutto, in-
nanzitutto

first: ~ **aid** *n* pronto soccorso *m*.
~**-'aid kit** *n* cassetta *f* di pronto
soccorso. ~**-class** *adj* di prim'ordine;
(Rail) di prima classe ● *adv* (travel) in
prima classe. ~ **'floor** *n* primo piano
m; (*Am*: *ground floor*) pianterreno *m*.
~**ly** *adv* in primo luogo. ~ **name** *n*
nome *m* di battesimo. ~**-rate** *adj*
ottimo

fish /fɪʃ/ *n* pesce *m* ● *vt/i* pescare.
□ ~ **out** *vt* tirar fuori

fish: ~**erman** *n* pescatore *m*. ~
finger *n* bastoncino *m* di pesce

fishing /ˈfɪʃɪŋ/ *n* pesca *f*. ~ **boat** *n*
peschereccio *m*. ~**-rod** *n* canna *f*
da pesca

fish: ~**monger** /-mʌŋgə(r)/ *n* pesci-
vendolo *m*. ~**y** *adj* (囗: *suspicious*) sospetto

fission /ˈfɪʃn/ *n* (*Phys*) fissione *f*

fist /fɪst/ *n* pugno *m*

fit¹ /fɪt/ *n* (attack) attacco *m*; (*of rage*)
accesso *m*; (*of generosity*) slancio *m*

fit² *adj* (**fitter, fittest**) (suitable)
adatto; (healthy) in buona salute;
(Sport) in forma; **be ~ to do sth** essere in grado di fare qcsa; ~ **to eat**
buono da mangiare; **keep ~** tenersi
in forma

fit³ *n* (*of clothes*) taglio *m*; **it's a good
~** (coat) etc: ti/le sta bene ● *v* (*pt/pp*
fitted) ● *vi* (be the right size) andare
bene; **it won't ~** (*no room*) non ci
sta ● *vt* (*fix*) applicare (**to a**); (install)
installare; **it doesn't ~ me** (coat
etc:) non mi sta bene. ~ **with** fornire
di. □ ~ **in** *vi* (person:) adattarsi; **it
won't ~ in** (*no room*) non c'è spazio
(*in schedule, vehicle*) trovare un
buco per

fit|ful /ˈfɪtfl/ *adj* irregolare. ~**fully**
adv (sleep) a sprazzi. ~**ments** *npl* (*in
house*) impianti *mpl* fissi. ~**ness** *n*
(*suitability*) capacità *f*; [physical]
~**ness** forma *f*, fitness *m*

fitting /ˈfɪtɪŋ/ adj appropriato ● n (of clothes) prova f; (Techn) montaggio m; ~s pl accessori mpl. ~ **room** n camerino m

five /faɪv/ adj & n cinque m. ~r n 🔲 biglietto m da cinque sterline

fix /fɪks/ n (🔲: drugs) pera f; **be in a** ~ 🔲 essere nei guai ● vt fissare; (repair) aggiustare; preparare (meal). □~ **up** vt fissare (meeting)

fixed /fɪkst/ adj fisso

fixture /ˈfɪkstʃə(r)/ n (Sport) incontro m; ~s **and fittings** impianti mpl fissi

fizz /fɪz/ vi frizzare

fizzle /ˈfɪzl/ vi ~ **out** finire in nulla

fizzy /ˈfɪzɪ/ adj gassoso. ~ **drink** n bibita f gassata

flabbergasted /ˈflæbəgɑːstɪd/ adj be ~ rimanere a bocca aperta

flabby /ˈflæbɪ/ adj floscio

flag[1] /flæg/ n bandiera f ● **flag down** vt (pt/pp flagged) far segno di fermarsi a (taxi)

flag[2] vi (pt/pp flagged) cedere

'flag-pole n asta f della bandiera

flagrant /ˈfleɪgrənt/ adj flagrante

flair /fleə(r)/ n (skill) talento m; (style) stile m

flake /fleɪk/ n fiocco m ● vi ~ [off] cadere in fiocchi

flaky /ˈfleɪkɪ/ adj a scaglie. ~ **pastry** n pasta f sfoglia

flamboyant /flæmˈbɔɪənt/ adj (personality) brillante; (tie) sgargiante

flame /fleɪm/ n fiamma f

flammable /ˈflæməbl/ adj infiammabile

flan /flæn/ n [fruit] ~ crostata f

flank /flæŋk/ n fianco m ● vt fiancheggiare

flannel /ˈflæn(ə)l/ n flanella f; (for washing) ~ guanto m di spugna; ~s (trousers) pantaloni mpl di flanella

flap /flæp/ n (of pocket, envelope) ri-

svolto m; (of table) ribalta f; **in a** ~ 🔲 in grande agitazione ● vi sbattere; 🔲 agitarsi ● vt ~ **its wings** battere le ali

flare /fleə(r)/ n fiammata f; (device) razzo m ● **flare up** vi (rash:) venire fuori; (fire:) fare una fiammata; (person, situation:) esplodere. ~d adj (garment) svasato

flash /flæʃ/ n lampo m; **in a** ~ 🔲 in un attimo ● vi lampeggiare; ~ **past** passare come un bolide ● vt lanciare (smile); ~ **one's head-lights** lampeggiare; ~ **a torch** at puntare una torcia su

flash: ~**back** n scena f retrospettiva. ~**light** n (Phot) flash m inv; (Am: torch) torcia f [elettrica]. ~**y** adj vistoso

flask /flɑːsk/ n fiasco m; (vacuum ~) termos m inv

flat /flæt/ adj (flatter, flattest) piatto; (refusal) reciso; (beer) sgasato; (battery) scarico; (tyre) a terra; **A** ~ (Mus) la bemolle ● n appartamento m; (Mus) bemolle m; (puncture) gomma f a terra

flat: ~**ly** adv (refuse) categoricamente. ~ **rate** n tariffa f unica

flatten /ˈflætn/ vt appiattire

flatter /ˈflætə(r)/ vt adulare. ~**ing** adj (comments) lusinghiero; (colour, dress) che fa sembrare più bello. ~**y** n adulazione f

flaunt /flɔːnt/ vt ostentare

flavour /ˈfleɪvə(r)/ n sapore m ● vt condire; **chocolate** ~**ed** al sapore di cioccolato. ~**ing** n condimento m

flaw /flɔː/ n difetto m. ~**less** adj perfetto

flea /fliː/ n pulce m. ~ **market** n mercato m delle pulci

fleck /flek/ n macchiolina f

fled /fled/ ▷**FLEE**

flee /fliː/ vt/i (pt/pp fled) fuggire (from da)

fleec|e /fliːs/ n pelliccia f ● vt 🔲

spennare. ~**y** adj (lining) felpato

fleet /fliːt/ n flotta f; (of cars) parco m

fleeting /ˈfliːtɪŋ/ adj catch a ~ glance of sth intravedere qcsa; for a ~ moment per un attimo

flesh /fleʃ/ n carne f; **in the** ~ in persona. ~**y** adj carnoso

flew /fluː/ ▷**FLY**²

flex¹ /fleks/ vt flettere (muscle)

flex² n (Electr) filo m

flexib|ility /fleksɪˈbɪlɪtɪ/ n flessibilità f. ~**le** adj flessibile

'flexitime /ˈfleksɪ-/ n orario m flessibile

flick /flɪk/ vt dare un buffetto a; ~ sth off sth togliere qcsa da qcsa con un colpetto. □ ~ **through** vt sfogliare

flicker /ˈflɪkə(r)/ vi tremolare

flight¹ /flaɪt/ n (fleeing) fuga f; take ~ darsi alla fuga

flight² n (flying) volo m; ~ **of stairs** rampa f

flight recorder n registratore m di volo

flimsy /ˈflɪmzɪ/ adj (-ier, -iest) (material) leggero; (shelves) poco robusto; (excuse) debole

flinch /flɪntʃ/ vi (wince) sussultare; (draw back) ritirarsi; ~ **from a task** fig sottrarsi a un compito

fling /flɪŋ/ n have a ~ (🔒 affair) aver un'avventura ●vt (pt/pp flung) gettare

flint /flɪnt/ n pietra f focaia; (for lighter) pietrina f

flip /flɪp/ v (pt/pp flipped) ●vt dare un colpetto a; buttare in aria (coin) ●vi 🔒 uscire dai gangheri; (go mad) impazzire. □ ~ **through** vt sfogliare

flippant /ˈflɪpənt/ adj irriverente

flipper /ˈflɪpə(r)/ n pinna f

flirt /flɜːt/ n civetta f ●vi flirtare

flit /flɪt/ vi (pt/pp flitted) volteggiare

float /fləʊt/ n galleggiante m; (in pro-

cession) carro m; (money) riserva f di cassa ●vi galleggiare; (Fin) fluttuare

flock /flɒk/ n gregge m; (of birds) stormo m ●vi affollarsi

flog /flɒg/ vt (pt/pp flogged) bastonare; (🔒 sell) vendere

flood /flʌd/ n alluvione f; (of river) straripamento m; (fig: of replies, letters, tears) diluvio m; **be in** ~ (river:) essere straripato ●vt allagare ●vi (river:) straripare

'floodlight n riflettore m ●vt (pt/pp floodlit) illuminare con riflettori

floor /flɔː(r)/ n pavimento m; (storey) piano m; (for dancing) pista f ●vt (baffle) confondere; (knock down) stendere (person)

floor polish n cera f per il pavimento

flop /flɒp/ n 🔒 (failure) tonfo m; (Theat) fiasco m ●vi (pt/pp flopped) (🔒 fail) far fiasco. □ ~ **down** vi accasciarsi

floppy /ˈflɒpɪ/ adj floscio. ~ **'disk** n floppy disk m inv. ~ **[disk] drive** n lettore di floppy m

floral /ˈflɔːrəl/ adj floreale

florid /ˈflɒrɪd/ adj (complexion) florido; (style) troppo ricercato

florist /ˈflɒrɪst/ n fioraio, -a mf

flounder¹ /ˈflaʊndə(r)/ vi dibattersi; (speaker:) impappinarsi

flounder² n (fish) passera f di mare

flour /ˈflaʊə(r)/ n farina f

flourish /ˈflʌrɪʃ/ n gesto m drammatico; (scroll) ghirigoro m ●vi prosperare ●vt brandire

flout /flaʊt/ vt fregarsene di (rules)

flow /fləʊ/ n flusso m ●vi scorrere; (hang loosely) ricadere

flower /ˈflaʊə(r)/ n fiore m ●vi fiorire

flower: ~-**bed** n aiuola f. ~**y** adj fiorito

flown /fləʊn/ ▷**FLY**²

flu /fluː/ n influenza f

fluctuat|e /ˈflʌktjʊeɪt/ vi fluttuare.
~ion n fluttuazione f

fluent /ˈfluːənt/ adj spedito; speak
~ Italian parlare correntemente l'i-
taliano. **~ly** adv speditamente

fluff /flʌf/ n peluria f. **~y** adj (**-ier,
-iest**) vaporoso; (toy) di peluche

fluid /ˈfluːɪd/ adj fluido• n fluido m

flung /flʌŋ/ ▷ **FLING**

fluorescent /flʊəˈresnt/ adj fluore-
scente

flush /flʌʃ/ n (blush) [vampata f di]
rossore m• vi arrossire• vt lavare
con un getto d'acqua; **~ the toilet**
tirare l'acqua• adj a livello (**with** di);
(🔲: affluent) a soldi

flute /fluːt/ n flauto m

flutter /ˈflʌtə(r)/ n battito m• vi
svolazzare

flux /flʌks/ n **in a state of ~** in uno
stato di flusso

fly[1] /flaɪ/ n (pl **flies**) mosca f

fly[2] v (pt **flew**, pp **flown**)• vi volare;
(go by plane) andare in aereo; (flag):
sventolare; (rush) precipitarsi; **~
open** spalancarsi• vt pilotare
(plane); trasportare [in aereo]
(troops, supplies); volare con (Alita-
lia etc)

fly[3] n & **flies** pl (on trousers) patta f

flying /ˈflaɪɪŋ/ **~ 'buttress** n arco
m rampante. **~ 'colours: with ~
colours** a pieni voti. **~ 'saucer** n
disco m volante. **~ 'start** n **get off
to a ~ start** fare un'ottima partenza. **~ 'visit** n visita f lampo

fly: **~leaf** n risguardo m. **~over** n
cavalcavia m inv

foal /fəʊl/ n puledro m

foam /fəʊm/ n schiuma f; (synthetic)
gommapiuma® f• vi spumare; **~ at
the mouth** fare la bava alla bocca. **~
'rubber** n gommapiuma® f

fob /fɒb/ vt (pt/pp **fobbed**) **~ sth off**
affibbiare qcsa (**on sb** a qcno); **~ sb
off** liquidare qcno

focal /ˈfəʊkl/ adj focale

focus /ˈfəʊkəs/ n fuoco m; **in ~** a
fuoco; **out of ~** sfocato• v (pt/pp
focused or **focussed**)• vt fig concen-
trare (on su)• vi **~ on** (Phot) mettere
a fuoco; fig concentrarsi (on su)

fodder /ˈfɒdə(r)/ n foraggio m

foe /fəʊ/ n nemico, -a mf

foetus /ˈfiːtəs/ n (pl **-tuses**) feto m

fog /fɒg/ n nebbia f

foggy /ˈfɒgɪ/ adj (**foggier, foggiest**)
nebbioso; **it's ~** c'è nebbia

'fog-horn n sirena f da nebbia

foil[1] /fɔɪl/ n lamina f di metallo

foil[2] vt (thwart) frustrare

foil[3] n (sword) fioretto m

foist /fɔɪst/ vt appioppare (**on sb** a
qcno)

fold[1] /fəʊld/ n (for sheep) ovile m

fold[2] n piega f• vt piegare; **~ one's
arms** incrociare le braccia• vi piegarsi; (fail) collassare. ◻ **~ up** vt ripiegare (chair)• vi essere pieghevole;
(business): collassare

fold|er /ˈfəʊldə(r)/ n cartella f. **~ing**
adj pieghevole

folk /fəʊk/ npl gente f; **my ~s** (family) i miei; **hello there ~s** ciao
a tutti

folklore n folclore m

follow /ˈfɒləʊ/ vt/i seguire; **it
doesn't ~** non è necessariamente
così; **~ suit** fig fare lo stesso; **as ~s**
come segue. ◻ **~ up** vt fare seguito
a (letter)

follow|er /ˈfɒləʊə(r)/ n seguace mf.
~ing adj seguente• n m seguito m;
(supporters) seguaci mpl• prep in seguito a

folly /ˈfɒlɪ/ n follia f

fond /fɒnd/ adj affezionato; (hope)
vivo; **be ~ of** essere appassionato di
(music); **I'm ~ of...** (food, person)
mi piace moltissimo...

fondle /ˈfɒndl/ vt coccolare

fondness /ˈfɒndnɪs/ n affetto m;
(for things) amore m

font /fɒnt/ n fonte f battesimale; (Typ) carattere m di stampa

food /fuːd/ n cibo m; (for animals, groceries) mangiare m; **let's buy some ~** compriamo qualcosa da mangiare

food processor n tritatutto m inv elettrico

fool[1] /fuːl/ n sciocco, -a mf; **she's no ~** non è una stupida; **make a ~ of oneself** rendersi ridicolo ●vt prendere in giro ●vi **~ around** giocare; (husband, wife:) avere l'amante

fool[2] n (Culin) crema f

'fool|hardy adj temerario. **~ish** adj stolto. **~ishly** adv scioccamente. **~ishness** n scioccheza f. **~proof** adj facilissimo

foot /fʊt/ n (pl feet) piede m; (of animal) zampa f; (measure) piede m (= 30,48 cm); **on ~** a piedi; **on one's feet** in piedi; **put one's ~ in it** 🅣 fare una gaffe

foot: **~-and-'mouth disease** n afta f epizootica. **~ball** n calcio m; (ball) pallone m. **~baller** n giocatore m di calcio. **~bridge** n passerella f. **~hills** npl colline fpl pedemontane. **~hold** n punto m d'appoggio. **~ing** n lose one's **~ing** perdere l'appiglio; **on an equal ~ing** in condizioni di parità. **~man** n valletto m. **~note** n nota f a piè di pagina. **~path** n sentiero m. **~print** n orma f. **~step** n passo m; follow in sb's **~steps** fig seguire l'esempio di qcno. **~wear** n calzature fpl

for /fə(r)/, accentato /fɔː(r)/
● prep per; **~ this reason** per questa ragione; **I have lived here ~ ten years** vivo qui da dieci anni; **~ supper** per cena; **~ all that** nonostante questo; **what ~?** a che scopo?; **send ~ a doctor** chiamare un dottore; **fight ~ a cause** lottare per una causa; **go ~ a walk**

andare a fare una passeggiata; **there's no need ~ you to go** non c'è bisogno che tu vada; **it's not ~ me to say** non sta a me dirlo; **now you're ~ it** ora sei nei pasticci
● conj poiché, perché

forage /'fɒrɪdʒ/ n foraggio m ●vi **~ for** cercare

forbade /fə'bæd/ ▷**FORBID**

forbear|ance /fɔː'beərəns/ n pazienza f. **~ing** adj tollerante

forbid /fə'bɪd/ vt (pt forbade, pp forbidden) proibire. **~ding** adj (prospect) che spaventa; (stern) severo

force /fɔːs/ n forza f; **in ~** in vigore; (in large numbers) in massa; **come into ~** entrare in vigore; **the [armed] ~s** pl le forze armate ●vt forzare; **~ sth on sb** (decision) imporre qcsa a qcno; (drink) costringere qcno a fare qcsa

forced /fɔːst/ adj forzato

force: **~-'feed** vt (pt/pp -**fed**) nutrire a forza. **~ful** adj energico

forceps /'fɔːseps/ npl forcipe m

forcible /'fɔːsɪbl/ adj forzato

ford /fɔːd/ n guado m ●vt guadare

fore /fɔː(r)/ n **to the ~** in vista; **come to the ~** salire alla ribalta

fore: **~arm** n avambraccio m. **~boding** /-'bəʊdɪŋ/ n presentimento m. **~cast** n previsione f ●vt (pt/pp -**cast**) prevedere. **~court** n cortile m anteriore. **~finger** n [dito m] indice m. **~front** n be in the **~front** essere all'avanguardia. **~gone** adj be a **~gone conclusion** essere una cosa scontata. **~ground** n primo piano m. **~head** /'fɒrɪhed/, /'fɔːhed/ n fronte f

foreign /'fɒrən/ adj straniero; (trade) estero; (not belonging) estraneo; **he is ~** è uno straniero. **~ currency** n valuta f estera. **~er** n straniero, -a mf. **~ language** n lingua f straniera

fore: ~man n caporeparto m.
~most adj principale ● adv first and
~most in primo luogo

'**forerunner** n precursore m

fore'see vt (pt -saw, pp -seen) prevedere. ~**able** adj in the ~**able future** in futuro per quanto si possa
prevedere

'**foresight** n previdenza f

forest /'forist/ n foresta f. ~**er** n
guardia f forestale

fore'stall vt prevenire

forestry /'foristri/ n silvicoltura f

'**foretaste** n pregustazione f

fore'tell vt (pt/pp -told) predire

forever /fə'revə(r)/ adv per sempre;
he's ~ **complaining** si lamenta
sempre

fore'warn vt avvertire

foreword /'fɔːwɜːd/ n prefazione f

forfeit /'fɔːfit/ n (in game) pegno m;
(Jur) penalità f ● vt perdere

forgave /fə'geiv/ ▷ FORGIVE

forge[1] /fɔːdʒ/ vi ~ **ahead** (runner:)
lasciarsi indietro gli altri; fig farsi
strada

forge[2] n fucina f ● vt fucinare; (counterfeit) contraffare. ~**r** n contraffattore m. ~**ry** n contraffazione f

forget /fə'get/ vt/i (pt -got, pp
-gotten, pres p -getting) dimenticare; dimenticarsi di (language,
skill). ~**ful** adj smemorato. ~**fulness**
n smemoratezza f. ~**-me-not** n nonti-scordar-di-mé m inv. ~**table** adj
(day, film) da dimenticare

forgive /fə'giv/ vt (pt -gave, pp
-given) ~ **sb for sth** perdonare
qcno per qcsa. ~**ness** n perdono m

forgo /fɔː'gəʊ/ vt (pt -went, pp
-gone) rinunciare a

forgot(ten) /fə'gɒt(n)/ ▷ FORGET

fork /fɔːk/ n forchetta f; (for digging)
forca f; (in road) bivio m ● vi (road:)
biforcarsi; ~ **right** prendere a de-

stra. □ ~ **out** vt 🔢 sborsare

fork-lift 'truck n elevatore m

forlorn /fə'lɔːn/ adj (look) perduto;
(place) derelitto; ~ **hope** speranza
f vana

form /fɔːm/ n forma f; (document)
modulo m; (Sch) classe f ● vt formare;
formulare (opinion) ● vi formarsi

formal /'fɔːml/ adj formale. ~**ity** n
formalità f inv. ~**ly** adv in modo formale; (officially) ufficialmente

format /'fɔːmæt/ n formato m ● vt
formattare (disk, page)

formation /fɔː'meiʃn/ n formazione f

former /'fɔːmə(r)/ adj precedente;
(PM, colleague) ex; the ~, the latter il primo, l'ultimo. ~**ly** adv precedentemente; (in olden times) in
altri tempi

formidable /'fɔːmidəbl/ adj formidabile

formula /'fɔːmjulə/ n (pl -ae /-liː/ or
-s) formula f

formulate /'fɔːmjuleɪt/ vt formulare

forsake /fə'seik/ vt (pt -sook /-sʊk/,
pp -saken) abbandonare

fort /fɔːt/ n (Mil) forte m

forth /fɔːθ/ adv back and ~ avanti e
indietro; **and so** ~ e così via

forth: ~'**coming** adj prossimo; (communicative) communicativo; **no response was** ~ non arrivava nessuna
risposta. ~**right** adj schietto.
~'**with** adv immediatamente

fortieth /'fɔːtiəθ/ adj quarantesimo

fortnight /'fɔːt-/ Br n quindicina f.
~**ly** adj bimensile ● adv ogni due settimane

fortress /'fɔːtris/ n fortezza f

fortunate /'fɔːtʃənət/ adj fortunato;
that's ~! meno male!. ~**ly** adv fortunatamente

fortune /'fɔːtʃuːn/ n fortuna f.
~**-teller** n indovino, -a mf

forty /ˈfɔːtɪ/ adj & n quaranta m

forum /ˈfɔːrəm/ n foro m

forward /ˈfɔːwəd/ adv avanti; (towards the front) in avanti ● adj in avanti; (presumptuous) sfacciato ● n (Sport) attaccante m ● vt inoltrare (letter); spedire (goods). ∼s adv avanti

fossil /ˈfɒsl/ n fossile m. ∼ized adj fossile; (ideas) fossilizzato

foster /ˈfɒstə(r)/ vt allevare (child). ∼-child n figlio, -a mf in affidamento. ∼-mother n madre f affidataria

fought /fɔːt/ ▷FIGHT

foul /faʊl/ adj (smell, taste) cattivo; (air) viziato; (language) osceno; (mood, weather) orrendo; ∼ play n (Jur) delitto m e n (Sport) fallo m ● vt inquinare (water); (Sport) commettere un fallo contro; (nets, rope:) impigliarsi in. ∼-smelling adj puzzo

found[1] /faʊnd/ ▷FIND

found[2] vt fondare

foundation /faʊnˈdeɪʃn/ n (basis) fondamento m; (charitable) fondazione f; ∼s pl (of building) fondamenta fpl; lay the ∼-stone porre la prima pietra

founder[1] /ˈfaʊndə(r)/ n fondatore, -trice mf

founder[2] vi (ship:) affondare

fountain /ˈfaʊntɪn/ n fontana f. ∼-pen n penna f stilografica

four /fɔː(r)/ adj & n quattro m

four: ∼some /ˈfɔːsəm/ n quartetto m. ∼teen adj & n quattordici m. ∼teenth adj quattordicesimo

fourth /fɔːθ/ adj quarto m

fowl /faʊl/ n pollame m

fox /fɒks/ n volpe f ● vt (puzzle) ingannare

foyer /ˈfɔɪeɪ/ n (Theat) ridotto m; (in hotel) salone m d'ingresso

fraction /ˈfrækʃn/ n frazione f

fracture /ˈfræktʃə(r)/ n frattura f ● vt fratturare ● vi fratturarsi

fragile /ˈfrædʒaɪl/ adj fragile

fragment /ˈfrægmənt/ n frammento m. ∼ary adj frammentario

fragran|ce /ˈfreɪɡrəns/ n fragranza f. ∼t adj fragrante

frail /freɪl/ adj gracile

frame /freɪm/ n (of picture, door, window) cornice f; (of spectacles) montatura f; (Anat) ossatura f; (structure, of bike) telaio m; ∼ of mind stato m d'animo ● vt incorniciare (picture); fig formulare; (﹅: incriminate) montare. ∼work n struttura f

France /frɑːns/ n Francia f

frank[1] /fræŋk/ vt affrancare (letter)

frank[2] adj franco. ∼ly adv francamente

frantic /ˈfræntɪk/ adj frenetico; be ∼ with worry essere agitatissimo. ∼ally adv freneticamente

fraternal /frəˈtɜːnl/ adj fraterno

fraud /frɔːd/ n frode f; (person) impostore m. ∼ulent adj fraudolento

fraught /frɔːt/ adj ∼ with pieno di

fray[1] /freɪ/ n mischia f

fray[2] vi sfilacciarsi

freak /friːk/ n fenomeno m; (person) scherzo m di natura; (﹅: weird person) tipo m strambo ● adj anomale. ∼ish adj strambo

freckle /ˈfrekl/ n lentiggine f. ∼d adj lentigginoso

free /friː/ adj (freer, freest) libero; (ticket, copy) gratuito; (lavish) generoso; ∼ of charge gratuito; set ∼ liberare ● vt (pt/pp freed) liberare

free: ∼dom n libertà f. ∼hold n proprietà f (fondiaria) assoluta. ∼ˈkick n calcio m di punizione. ∼lance adj & adv indipendente. ∼ly adv liberamente; (generously) generosamente; I ∼ly admit that... devo ammettere che.... ∼mason n massone m. ∼-range adj ∼-range egg uovo m di gallina ruspante. ∼style n stile m libero. ∼way n Am autostrada f

freez|e /friːz/ vt (pt froze, pp frozen) gelare; bloccare (wages) ● vi (water:) gelare; **it's ~ing** si gela; **my hands are ~ing** ho le mani congelate

freez|er /ˈfriːzə(r)/ n freezer m inv, congelatore m. **~ing** adj gelido ● n **below ~ing** sotto zero

freight /freɪt/ n carico m. **~er** n nave f da carico. **~ train** n Am treno m merci

French /frentʃ/ adj francese ● n (language) francese m; **the ~** pl i francesi mpl

French: ~ 'fries npl patate fpl fritte. **~man** n francese m. **~ 'window** n porta-finestra f. **~woman** n francese f

frenzied /ˈfrenzɪd/ adj frenetico

frenzy /ˈfrenzɪ/ n frenesia f

frequency /ˈfriːkwənsɪ/ n frequenza f

frequent[1] /ˈfriːkwənt/ adj frequente. **~ly** adv frequentemente

frequent[2] /frɪˈkwent/ vt frequentare

fresh /freʃ/ adj fresco; (new) nuovo; (Am: cheeky) sfacciato. **~ly** adv di recente

freshen /ˈfreʃn/ vi (wind:) rinfrescare. □ **~ up** vt dare una rinfrescata a ● vi rinfrescarsi

freshness /ˈfreʃnɪs/ n freschezza f

fret /fret/ vi (pt/pp fretted) inquietarsi. **~ful** adj irritabile

friction /ˈfrɪkʃn/ n frizione f

Friday /ˈfraɪdeɪ/ n venerdì m inv

fridge /frɪdʒ/ n frigo m

fried /fraɪd/ ▷ FRY ● adj fritto; **~ egg** uovo m fritto

friend /frend/ n amico, -a mf. **~ly** adj (-ier, -iest) (relations, match) amichevole; (neighbourhood, smile) piacevole; (software) di facile uso; **be ~ly with** essere amico di. **~ship** n amicizia f

frieze /friːz/ n fregio m

fright /fraɪt/ n paura f; **take ~** spaventarsi

frighten /ˈfraɪtn/ vt spaventare. **~ed** adj spaventato; **be ~ed** aver paura (of di). **~ing** adj spaventoso

frightful /ˈfraɪtfl/ adj terribile

frigid /ˈfrɪdʒɪd/ adj frigido. **~ity** n freddezza f; (Psych) frigidità f

frill /frɪl/ n (dress) con tanti volant. **~y** adj (dress) con tanti volant

fringe /frɪndʒ/ n frangia f; (of hair) frangetta f; (fig: edge) margine m. **~ benefits** npl benefici mpl supplementari

fritter /ˈfrɪtə(r)/ n frittella f ● fritter away vt sprecare

frivol|ity /frɪˈvɒlətɪ/ n frivolezza f. **~ous** adj frivolo

fro /frəʊ/ ▷ TO

frock /frɒk/ n abito m

frog /frɒg/ n rana f. **~man** n uomo m rana

frolic /ˈfrɒlɪk/ vi (pt/pp frolicked) (lambs:) sgambettare; (people:) folleggiare

from /frɒm/ prep da; **~ Monday** da lunedì; **~ that day** da quel giorno; **he's ~ London** è di Londra; **this is a letter ~ my brother** questa è una lettera di mio fratello; **documents ~ the 16th century** documenti del XVI secolo; **made ~** fatto con; **she felt ill ~ fatigue** si sentiva male dalla stanchezza; **~ now on** d'ora in poi

front /frʌnt/ n parte f anteriore; (fig: organization etc) facciata f; (of garment) davanti m; (sea~) lungomare m; (Mil, Pol, Meteorol) fronte m. **in ~ of** davanti a; **in** or **at the ~** davanti; **to the ~** avanti ● adj davanti; (page, row, wheel) anteriore

frontal /ˈfrʌntl/ adj frontale

front 'door n porta f d'entrata

frontier /ˈfrʌntɪə(r)/ n frontiera f

frost /frɒst/ n gelo m; (hoar~) brina f

~**bite** n congelamento m. ~**bitten** adj congelato

frost|ed /'frɒstɪd/ adj ~**ed glass** vetro m smerigliato. ~**ily** adv gelidamente. ~**ing** n Am (Culin) glassa f. ~**y** adj also fig gelido

froth /frɒθ/ n schiuma f ● vi far schiuma. ~**y** adj schiumoso

frown /fraʊn/ n cipiglio m ● vi aggrottare le sopracciglia. □ ~ **on** vt disapprovare

froze /frəʊz/ ▷**FREEZE**

frozen /'frəʊzn/ ▷**FREEZE** ● adj (corpse, hand) congelato; (Culin) gelido; **I'm** ~ sono gelato. ~ **food** n surgelati mpl

frugal /'fru:gl/ adj frugale

fruit /fru:t/ n frutto m; (collectively) frutta f; **eat more** ~ mangia più frutta. ~ **cake** n dolce m con frutta candita

fruition /fru:'ɪʃn/ n **come to** ~ dare dei frutti

fruit: ~**less** adj infruttuoso. ~ '**salad** n macedonia f [di frutta]

frustrat|e /frʌ'streɪt/ vt frustrare; rovinare (plans). ~**ing** adj frustrante. ~**ion** n frustrazione f

fry¹ vt/i (pt/pp **fried**) friggere

fry² /fraɪ/ n inv **small** ~ fig pesce m piccolo

frying pan n padella f

fudge /fʌdʒ/ n caramella f a base di zucchero, burro e latte

fuel /'fju:əl/ n carburante m; fig nutrimento m ● vt fig alimentare

fugitive /'fju:dʒɪtɪv/ n fuggiasco, -a mf

fulfil /fʊl'fɪl/ vt (pt/pp -**filled**) soddisfare (conditions, need); realizzare (dream, desire); ~ **oneself** realizzarsi. ~**ling** adj soddisfacente. ~**ment** n **sense of** ~**ment** senso m di appagamento

full /fʊl/ adj pieno (**of** di); (detailed) esauriente; (bus, hotel) completo;

(skirt) ampio; **at** ~ **speed** a tutta velocità; **in** ~ **swing** in pieno fervore ● **in** ~ per intero

full: ~ '**moon** n luna f piena. ~-**scale** adj (model) in scala reale; (alert) di massima gravità. ~ '**stop** n punto m. ~-**time** adj & adv a tempo pieno

fully /'fʊlɪ/ adv completamente; (in detail) dettagliatamente; ~ **booked** (hotel, restaurant) tutto prenotato

fumble /'fʌmbl/ vi ~ **in** rovistare in; ~ **with** armeggiare con; ~ **for one's keys** rovistare alla ricerca delle chiavi

fume /fju:m/ vi (be angry) essere furioso

fumes /fju:mz/ npl fumi mpl; (from car) gas mpl di scarico

fumigate /'fju:mɪgeɪt/ vt suffumicare

fun /fʌn/ n divertimento m; **for** ~ per ridere; **make** ~ **of** prendere in giro; **have** ~ divertirsi

function /'fʌŋkʃn/ n funzione f; (event) cerimonia f ● vi funzionare; ~ **as** (serve as) funzionare da. ~**al** adj funzionale

fund /fʌnd/ n fondo m; fig pozzo m. ~**s** pl fondi mpl ● vt finanziare

fundamental /fʌndə'mentl/ adj fondamentale

funeral /'fju:nərəl/ n funerale m

funeral directors n impresa f di pompe funebri

'**funfair** n luna park m inv

fungus /'fʌŋgəs/ n (pl -**gi** /-gaɪ/) fungo m

funnel /'fʌnl/ n imbuto m; (on ship) ciminiera f

funnily /'fʌnɪlɪ/ adv comicamente; (oddly) stranamente; ~ **enough** strano a dirsi

funny /'fʌnɪ/ adj (-**ier**, -**iest**) buffo; (odd) strano. ~ **business** n affare m losco

fur /fɜː(r)/ n pelo m; (for clothing) pelliccia f; (in kettle) deposito m. **~ 'coat** n pelliccia f

furious /'fjʊərɪəs/ adj furioso

furnace /'fɜːnɪs/ n fornace f

furnish /'fɜːnɪʃ/ vt ammobiliare (flat); fornire (supplies). **~ed** adj **~ed room** stanza f ammobiliata. **~ings** npl mobili mpl

furniture /'fɜːnɪtʃə(r)/ n mobili mpl

furrow /'fʌrəʊ/ n solco m

furry /'fɜːrɪ/ adj (animal) peloso; (toy) di peluche

further /'fɜːðə(r)/ adj (additional) ulteriore; **at the ~ end** all'altra estremità; **until ~ notice** fino a nuovo avviso ● adv più lontano; **~,...** inoltre,...; **~ off** più lontano ● vt promuovere

further'more adv per di più

furthest /'fɜːðɪst/ adj più lontano ● adv più lontano

furtive /'fɜːtɪv/ adj furtivo

fury /'fjʊərɪ/ n furore m

fuse¹ /fjuːz/ n (of bomb) detonatore m; (cord) miccia f

fuse² n (Electr) fusibile m ● vt fondere; (Electr) far saltare ● vi fondersi; (Electr) saltare; **the lights have ~d** sono saltate le luci. **~-box** n scatola f dei fusibili

fuselage /'fjuːzəlɑːʒ/ n (Aeron) fusoliera f

fusion /'fjuːʒn/ n fusione f

fuss /fʌs/ n storie fpl; **make a ~** fare storie; **make a ~ of** colmare di attenzioni ● vi fare storie

fussy /'fʌsɪ/ adj (-ier, -iest) (person) difficile da accontentare; (clothes etc) pieno di fronzoli

futil|e /'fjuːtaɪl/ adj inutile. **~ity** n futilità f

future /'fjuːtʃə(r)/ adj & n futuro; **in ~** in futuro. **~ perfect** futuro m anteriore

futuristic /fjuːtʃə'rɪstɪk/ adj futuristico

fuzz /fʌz/ n **the ~** (■: police) la pula

fuzzy /'fʌzɪ/ adj (-ier, -iest) (hair) crespo; (photo) sfuocato

Gg

gab /gæb/ n 🆄 **have the gift of the ~** avere la parlantina

gabble /'gæb(ə)l/ vi parlare troppo in fretta

gad /gæd/ vi (pt/pp gadded) **~ about** andarsene in giro

gadget /'gædʒɪt/ n aggeggio m

Gaelic /'geɪlɪk/ adj & n gaelico m

gaffe /gæf/ n gaffe f inv

gag /gæg/ n bavaglio m; (joke) battuta f ● vt (pt/pp gagged) imbavagliare

gaily /'geɪlɪ/ adv allegramente

gain /geɪn/ n guadagno m; (increase) aumento m ● vt acquisire; **~ weight** aumentare di peso; **~ access** accedere ● vi (clock): andare avanti. **~ful** adj **~ful employment** lavoro m remunerativo

gait /geɪt/ n andatura f

gala /'gɑːlə/ n gala f; **swimming ~** manifestazione f di nuoto ● attrib di gala

galaxy /'gæləksɪ/ n galassia f

gale /geɪl/ n bufera f

gall /gɔːl/ n (impudence) impudenza f

gallant /'gælənt/ adj coraggioso; (chivalrous) galante. **~ry** n coraggio m

'gall-bladder n cistifellea f

gallery /'gælərɪ/ n galleria f

galley /'gælɪ/ n (ship's kitchen) cambusa f; **~ [proof]** bozza f in colonna

gallivant /'gælɪvænt/ vi 🔢 andare in giro

gallon /'gælən/ n gallone m (= 4,5 l; Am = 3,7 l)

gallop /'gæləp/ n galoppo m ●vi galoppare

gallows /'gæləʊz/ n forca f

galore /gə'lɔː(r)/ adv a bizzeffe

galvanize /'gælvənaɪz/ vt (Techn) galvanizzare; fig stimolare (**into** a)

gambl|e /'gæmbl/ n (risk) azzardo m ●vi giocare; (on Stock Exchange) speculare; ~**e on** (rely) contare su. ~**er** n giocatore, -trice m f [d'azzardo]. ~**ing** n gioco m [d'azzardo]

game /geɪm/ n gioco m; (match) partita f; (animals, birds) selvaggina f; (Sch) ≈ ginnastica f ●adj (brave) coraggioso; **are you ~?** ti va?; **be ~ for** essere pronto per. ~**keeper** n guardacaccia m inv

gammon /'gæmən/ n coscia f di maiale

gamut /'gæmət/ n fig gamma f

gander /'gændə(r)/ n oca f maschio

gang /gæŋ/ n banda f; (of workmen) squadra f ● **gang up** vi far comunella (**on** contro)

gangling /'gæŋglɪŋ/ adj spilungone

gangmaster /'gæŋmɑːstə(r)/ n caporale m (di manodopera abusiva)

gangrene /'gæŋgriːn/ n cancrena f

gangster /'gæŋstə(r)/ n gangster m inv

gangway /'gæŋweɪ/ n passaggio m; (Aeron, Naut) passerella f

gaol /dʒeɪl/ n carcere m ●vt incarcerare. ~**er** n carceriere m

gap /gæp/ n spazio m; (in ages, between teeth) scarto m; (in memory) vuoto m; (in story) punto m oscuro

gap|e /geɪp/ vi stare a bocca aperta; (be wide open) spalancarsi; ~**e at** guardare a bocca aperta. ~**ing** adj aperto

---

gap year In Gran Bretagna il gap year è l'anno di intervallo che gli studenti si prendono tra la fine della scuola secondaria e l'università. Molti studenti utilizzano questo periodo sabbatico per intraprendere attività completamente diverse da ciò che hanno studiato o che studieranno e alcuni lo utilizzano per lavorare e mettere da parte qualche risparmio. Altri, infine, ne approfittano per viaggiare all'estero e conoscere il mondo.

garage /'gærɑːʒ/ n garage m inv; (for repairs) meccanico m; (for petrol) stazione f di servizio

garbage /'gɑːbɪdʒ/ n immondizia f; (nonsense) idiozie fpl. ~ **can** n Am bidone m dell'immondizia

garden /'gɑːdn/ n giardino m; [public] ~**s** pl giardini mpl pubblici ●vi fare giardinaggio. ~ **centre** n negozio m di piante e articoli da giardinaggio. ~**er** n giardiniere, -a mf. ~**ing** n giardinaggio m

gargle /'gɑːgl/ n gargarismo m ●vi fare gargarismi

gargoyle /'gɑːgɔɪl/ n gargouille f inv

garish /'geərɪʃ/ adj sgargiante

garland /'gɑːlənd/ n ghirlanda f

garlic /'gɑːlɪk/ n aglio m. ~ **bread** n pane m condito con aglio

garment /'gɑːmənt/ n indumento m

garnish /'gɑːnɪʃ/ n guarnizione f ●vt guarnire

garrison /'gærɪsn/ n guarnigione f

garter /'gɑːtə(r)/ n giarrettiera f; (for socks) reggicalze m inv da uomo

gas /gæs/ n gas m inv; (Am 🔢: petrol) benzina f ●v (pt/pp **gassed**) ●vt asfissiare ●vi 🔢 blaterare. ~ **cooker** n cucina f a gas. ~ **fire** n stufa f a gas

gash /gæʃ/ n taglio m ●vt tagliare

gasket /'gæskɪt/ n (Techn) guarnizione f

gas: ~ **mask** n maschera f antigas. ~**-meter** n contatore m del gas

gasoline /'gæsəli:n/ n Am benzina f

gasp /gɑ:sp/ vi avere il fiato mozzato

'gas station n Am distributore m di benzina

gastric /'gæstrık/ adj gastrico. ~ **'flu** n influenza f gastro-intestinale. ~ **'ulcer** n ulcera f gastrica

gate /geıt/ n cancello m; (at airport) uscita f

gate: ~**crash** vt entrare senza invito a. ~**crasher** n intruso, -a mf. ~**way** n ingresso m

gather /'gæðə(r)/ vt raccogliere; (conclude) dedurre; (in sewing) arricciare; ~ **speed** acquistare velocità; ~ **together** radunare (people, belongings); (obtain gradually) acquistare ● vi (people:) radunarsi. ~**ing** n family ~**ing** ritrovo m di famiglia

gaudy /'gɔ:dı/ adj (-ier, -iest) pacchiano

gauge /geıdʒ/ n calibro m; (Rail) scartamento m; (device) indicatore m ● vt misurare; fig stimare

gaunt /gɔ:nt/ adj (thin) smunto

gauze /gɔ:z/ n garza f

gave /geıv/ ▷**GIVE**

gawky /'gɔ:kı/ adj (-ier, -iest) sgraziato

gawp /gɔ:p/ vi ~ [at] 🔲 guardare con aria da ebete

gay /geı/ adj gaio; (homosexual) omosessuale; (bar, club) gay

gaze /geız/ n sguardo m fisso ● vi guardare; ~ **at** fissare

GB abbr (Great Britain) GB

gear /gıə(r)/ n equipaggiamento m; (Techn) ingranaggio m; (Auto) marcia f; **in** ~ con la marcia innestata; **change** ~ cambiare marcia ● vt finalizzare (**to** a)

gearbox n (Auto) scatola f del cambio

geese /gi:s/ ▷**GOOSE**

gel /dʒel/ n gel m inv

gelatine /'dʒelətın/ n gelatina f

gelignite /'dʒelıgnaıt/ n gelatina esplosiva f

gem /dʒem/ n gemma f

Gemini /'dʒemınaı/ n (Astr) Gemelli mpl

gender /'dʒendə(r)/ n (Gram) genere m

gene /dʒi:n/ n gene m

genealogy /dʒi:nı'ælədʒı/ n genealogia f

general /'dʒenrəl/ adj generale ● n generale m; **in** ~ in generale. ~ **e'lection** n elezioni fpl politiche

generaliz|ation /dʒenrəlaı'zeıʃn/ n generalizzazione f. ~**e** vi generalizzare

generally /'dʒenrəlı/ adv generalmente

general prac'titioner n medico m generico

generate /'dʒenəreıt/ vt generare

generation /dʒenə'reıʃn/ n generazione f

generator /'dʒenəreıtə(r)/ n generatore m

generosity /dʒenə'rɒsıtı/ n generosità f

generous /'dʒenərəs/ adj generoso. ~**ly** adv generosamente

genetic /dʒı'netık/ adj genetico. ~ **engineering** n ingegneria f genetica. ~**s** n genetica f

Geneva /dʒı'ni:və/ n Ginevra f

genial /'dʒi:nıəl/ adj gioviale

genitals /'dʒenıtlz/ npl genitali mpl

genitive /'dʒenıtıv/ adj & n ~ [**case**] genitivo m

genius /'dʒi:nıəs/ n (pl -**uses**) genio m

genocide /'dʒenəsaıd/ n genocidio m

genre /'ʒæıg.rə/ n genere m [letterario]

gent /dʒent/ n 🔲 signore m; the ~**s**

sg il bagno per uomini

genteel /dʒen'tiːl/ *adj* raffinato

gentle /'dʒentl/ *adj* delicato;
(breeze, tap, slope) leggero

gentleman /'dʒentlmən/ *n* signore
m; (well-mannered) gentiluomo *m*

gent|leness /'dʒentlnɪs/ *n* delica-
tezza *f*. **~ly** *adv* delicatamente

genuine /'dʒenjʊm/ *adj* genuino.
~ly *adv* (sorry) sinceramente

geograph|ical /dʒɪə'græfɪkl/ *adj*
geografico. **~y** *n* geografia *f*

geological /dʒɪə'lɒdʒɪkl/ *adj* geo-
logico

geolog|ist /dʒɪ'ɒlədʒɪst/ *n* geologo,
-a *mf*. **~y** *n* geologia *f*

geranium /dʒə'reɪnɪəm/ *n* ge-
ranio *m*

geriatric /dʒerɪ'ætrɪk/ *adj* geria-
trico; **~ ward** *n* reparto *m* geriatria.
~s *n* geriatria *f*

germ /dʒɜːm/ *n* germe *m*; **~s** *pl* mi-
crobi *mpl*

German /'dʒɜːmən/ *n* & *adj* tedesco,
-a *mf*; (language) tedesco *m*

Germanic /dʒə'mænɪk/ *adj* ger-
manico

German 'measles *n* rosolia *f*

Germany /'dʒɜːmənɪ/ *n* Germania *f*

germinate /'dʒɜːmɪneɪt/ *vi* germogliare

gesticulate /dʒe'stɪkjʊleɪt/ *vi* ge-
sticolare

gesture /'dʒestʃə(r)/ *n* gesto *m*

---

get /get/ *verb*

past tense/past participle **got**, *past
participle Am* **gotten**, *pres participle*
getting

● *vt* (receive) ricevere; (obtain) ottenere; trovare (job); (buy, catch,
fetch) prendere; (transport, deliver
to airport etc) portare; (reach on

telephone) trovare; (**1**: understand)
comprendere; preparare (meal);
~ sb to do sth far fare qcsa a
qcno

● *vi* (become) **~ tired/bored/angry**
stancarsi/annoiarsi/arrabbiarsi;
I'm ~ting hungry mi sta ve-
nendo fame; **~ dressed/married**
vestirsi/sposarsi; **~ sth ready**
preparare qcsa; **~ nowhere** non
concludere nulla; **this is ~ting
us nowhere** questo non ci è di
nessun aiuto; **~ to** (reach) arrivare a. □ **~ at** *vi* (criticize) criticare, **I see what you're ~ting
at** ho capito cosa vuoi dire; **what
are you ~ting at?** dove vuoi andare a parare?. □ **~ away** *vi*
(leave) andarsene; (escape) scappare. □ **~ back** *vi* tornare ● *vt*
(recover) riavere; **~ one's own
back** rifarsi. □ **~ by** *vi* passare;
(manage) cavarsela. □ **~ down** *vi*
scendere; **~ down to work**
mettersi al lavoro ● *vt* (depress)
buttare giù. □ **~ in** *vi* entrare
● *vt* mettere dentro (washing); far
venire (plumber). □ **~ off** *vi*
scendere; (from work) andarsene;
(Jur) essere assolto; **~ off the
bus/one's bike** scendere dal
pullman/dalla bici ● *vt* (remove)
togliere. □ **~ on** *vi* salire; (be on
good terms) andare d'accordo;
(make progress) andare avanti; (in
life) riuscire; **~ on the bus/one's
bike** salire sul pullman/sulla bici;
how are you ~ting on? come
va?. □ **~ out** *vi* uscire; (of car)
scendere; **~ out!** fuori!; **~ out
of** (avoid doing) evitare ● *vt* togliere
(cork, stain). □ **~ over** *vi* andare
al di là ● *vt* *fig* riprendersi da (illness). □ **~ round** *vt* aggirare
(rule); rigirare (person) ● *vi* **I
never ~ round to it** non mi
sono mai deciso a farlo. □ **~
through** *vi* (on telephone) prendere

la linea. □~ **up** vi alzarsi; (climb)
salire; ~ **up a hill** salire su una
collina

geyser /'giːzə(r)/ n scaldabagno m;
(Geol) geyser m inv

ghastly /'gɑːstlɪ/ adj (-ier, -iest) terribile; **feel** ~ sentirsi da cani

gherkin /'gɜːkɪn/ n cetriolino m

ghetto /'getəʊ/ n ghetto m

ghost /ɡəʊst/ n fantasma m. ~**ly** adj
spettrale

giant /'dʒaɪənt/ n gigante m ●adj
gigante

gibberish /'dʒɪbərɪʃ/ n stupidaggini fpl

gibe /dʒaɪb/ n malignità f inv

giblets /'dʒɪblɪts/ npl frattaglie fpl

giddiness /'gɪdmɪs/ n vertigini fpl

giddy /'gɪdɪ/ adj (-ier, -iest) vertiginoso; **feel** ~ avere le vertigini

gift /gɪft/ n dono m; (to charity) donazione f. ~**ed** adj dotato. ~-**wrap** vt
impacchettare in carta da regalo

gig /gɪg/ n (Mus) Ⅱ concerto m

gigantic /dʒaɪˈgæntɪk/ adj gigantesco

giggle /'gɪgl/ n risatina f ●vi ridacchiare

gild /gɪld/ vt dorare

gills /gɪlz/ npl branchia fsg

gilt /gɪlt/ adj dorato ●n doratura f.
~-**edged stock** n investimento m
sicuro

gimmick /'gɪmɪk/ n trovata f

gin /dʒɪn/ n gin m inv

ginger /'dʒɪndʒə(r)/ adj rosso fuoco
inv; (cat) rosso ●n zenzero m. ~ **ale**
n, ~ **beer** n bibita f allo zenzero.
~**bread** n panpepato m

gipsy /'dʒɪpsɪ/ n = **gypsy**

giraffe /dʒɪˈrɑːf/ n giraffa f

girder /'gɜːdə(r)/ n (Techn) trave f

girl /gɜːl/ n ragazza f; (child)
femmina f. ~ **band** n girl band f inv.
~**friend** n amica f; (of boy) ragazza f.

~**ish** adj da ragazza

giro /'dʒaɪrəʊ/ n bancogiro m;
(cheque) sussidio m di disoccupazione

girth /gɜːθ/ n circonferenza f

gist /dʒɪst/ n the ~ la sostanza

give /gɪv/ v ●v (pt gave,
pp given) ●vt dare; (as present) regalare (**to** a); fare (lecture, present,
shriek); donare (blood); ~ **birth** partorire ●vi (to charity) fare delle donazioni; (yield) cedere. □ ~ **away** vt dar
via; (betray) tradire; (distribute) assegnare; ~ **away the bride** portare la
sposa all'altare. □ ~ **back** vt restituire. □ ~ **in** vt consegnare ●vi
(yield) arrendersi. □ ~ **off** vt emanare. □ ~ **over** vi rinunciare. □ ~
up vt rinunciare a; ~ **oneself**
up arrendersi ●vi rinunciare. □ ~
way vi cedere; (Auto) dare la precedenza; (collapse) crollare

given /'gɪvn/ ▷**GIVE** ●adj ~ **name**
nome m di battesimo

glacier /'glæsɪə(r)/ n ghiacciaio m

glad /glæd/ adj contento (**of** di).
~**den** vt rallegrare

gladly /'glædlɪ/ adv volentieri

glamour /'glæmə(r)/ n fascino m

glance /glɑːns/ n sguardo m ●vi ~
at dare un'occhiata a. □ ~ **up** vi alzare gli occhi

gland /glænd/ n glandola f

glare /gleə(r)/ n bagliore m; (look)
occhiataccia f ●vi ~ **at** dare un'occhiataccia a

glaring /'gleərɪŋ/ adj sfolgorante;
(mistake) madornale

glass /glɑːs/ n vetro m; (for drinking)
bicchiere m. ~**es** (pl: spectacles) occhiali mpl. ~**y** adj vitreo

glaze /gleɪz/ n smalto m ●vt mettere
i vetri a (door, window); smaltare
(pottery); (Culin) spennellare. ~**d** adj
(eyes) vitreo

gleam /gli:m/ n luccichio m ● vi luccicare

glean /gli:n/ vt racimolare (information)

glee /gli:/ n gioia f. **~ful** adj gioioso

glib /glɪb/ adj pej insincero

glid|e /glaɪd/ vi scorrere; (through the air) planare. **~er** n aliante m

glimmer /'glɪmə(r)/ n barlume m ● vi emettere un barlume

glimpse /glɪmps/ n catch a **~** of intravedere ● vt intravedere

glint /glɪnt/ vi luccicare

glisten /'glɪsn/ vi luccicare

glitter /'glɪtə(r)/ vi brillare

gloat /gləʊt/ vi gongolare (**over** su)

global /'gləʊbl/ adj mondiale. **~ization** n globalizzazione f

globe /gləʊb/ n globo m; (map) mappamondo m

gloom /glu:m/ n oscurità f; (sadness) tristezza f. **~ily** adv (sadly) con aria cupa

gloomy /'glu:mɪ/ adj (-ier, -iest) cupo

glorif|y /'glɔːrɪfaɪ/ vt (pt/pp -ied) glorificare; **a ~ied waitress** niente più che una cameriera

glorious /'glɔːrɪəs/ adj splendido; (deed, hero) glorioso

glory /'glɔːrɪ/ n gloria f; (splendour) splendore m; (cause for pride) vanto m ● vi (pt/pp -ied) **~ in** vantarsi di

gloss /glɒs/ n lucentezza f. **~ gloss over** vt sorvolare su

glossary /'glɒsərɪ/ n glossario m

glossy /'glɒsɪ/ adj (-ier, -iest) lucido; **~ [magazine]** rivista f femminile

glove /glʌv/ n guanto m. **~ compartment** n (Auto) cruscotto m

glow /gləʊ/ n splendore m; (in cheeks) rossore m; (of candle) luce f soffusa ● vi risplendere; (candle:) brillare; (person:) avvampare. **~ing** adj ardente; (account) entusiastico

~worm n lucciola f

glucose /'glu:kəʊs/ n glucosio m

glue /glu:/ n colla f ● vt (pres p gluing) incollare

glum /glʌm/ adj (glummer, glummest) tetro

glutton /'glʌtən/ n ghiottone, -a mf. **~ous** adj ghiotto. **~y** n ghiottoneria f

gnarled /nɑːld/ adj nodoso

gnash /næʃ/ vt **~ one's teeth** digrignare i denti

gnaw /nɔː/ vt rosicchiare

go[1] /gəʊ/ n (pl goes) energia f; (attempt) tentativo m; **on the go** in movimento; **at one go** in una sola volta; **it's your go** tocca a te; **make a go of it** riuscire

---

go[2] /gəʊ/

3 sing pres tense **goes**, past tense **went**, past participle **gone**

● vi andare; (leave) andar via; (vanish) sparire; (become) diventare; (be sold) vendersi; **go and see** andare a vedere; **go swimming/shopping** andare a nuotare/fare spese; **where's the time gone?** come ha fatto il tempo a volare così?; **it's all gone** è finito; **be going to do** stare per fare; **I'm not going to** non ne ho nessuna intenzione; **to go** (🇺🇸) hamburgers etc) da asporto; **a coffee to go** un caffè da portar via. □ **~ about** vi andare in giro. □ **~ away** vi andarsene. □ **~ back** vi ritornare. □ **~ by** vi passare. □ **~ down** vi scendere; (sun:) tramontare; (ship:) affondare; (swelling:) diminuire. □ **~ for** vt andare a prendere; andare a cercare (doctor); (choose) optare per; (🇺🇸: attack) aggredire; **he's** not the kind I go for non è il genere che mi attira. ▫ ~ **in** vi entrare. ▫ ~ **in for** vt partecipare a (competition); darsi a (tennis). ▫ ~ **off** vi andarsene; (alarm:) scattare; (gun, bomb:) esplodere; (food, milk:) andare a male; go well riuscire. ▫ ~ **on** vi andare avanti; what's going on? cosa succede? go on at vt 🔟 scocciare. ▫ ~ **out** vi uscire; (light, fire:) spegnersi. ▫ ~ **over** vi andare ● vt (check) controllare. ▫ ~ **round** vi andare in giro; (visit) andare; (turn) girare; is there enough to go round? ce n'è abbastanza per tutti? go through vi (bill, proposal:) passare ● vt (suffer) subire; (check) controllare; (read) leggere. ▫ ~ **under** vi passare sotto; (ship, swimmer:) andare sott'acqua; (fail) fallire. ▫ ~ **up** vi salire; (Theat: curtain:) aprirsi. ▫ ~ **with** vt accompagnare. ▫ ~ **without** vt fare a meno di (supper, sleep) ● vi fare senza

goad /gəʊd/ vt spingere (into a); (taunt) pronare

'go-ahead adj (person, company) intraprendente ● n okay m

goal /gəʊl/ n porta f; (point scored) gol m inv; (in life) obiettivo m; score a ~ segnare. ~ie 🔟, ~keeper n portiere m. ~post n palo m

goat /gəʊt/ n capra f

gobble /'gɒbl/ vt ~ [down, up] tranguiare

God, god /gɒd/ n Dio m, dio m

god: ~child n figlioccio, -a mf. ~daughter n figlioccia f. ~dess n dea f. ~father n padrino m. ~forsaken adj dimenticato da Dio. ~mother n madrina f. ~send n manna f. ~son n figlioccio m

going /'gəʊɪŋ/ adj (price, rate) corrente; ~ **concern** azienda f florida

● n it's hard ~ è una faticaccia; while the ~ is good finché si può. ~s-'on npl avvenimenti mpl

gold /gəʊld/ n oro m ● adj d'oro

golden /'gəʊldn/ adj dorato. ~ 'handshake n buonuscita f (al termine di un rapporto di lavoro). ~ **mean** n giusto mezzo m. ~ 'wedding n nozze fpl d'oro

gold: ~fish n inv pesce m rosso. ~mine n miniera f d'oro. ~plated adj placcato d'oro. ~smith n orefice m

golf /gɒlf/ n golf m

golf: ~club n circolo m di golf; (implement) mazza f da golf. ~course n campo m di golf. ~er n giocatore, -trice mf di golf

gondola /'gɒndələ/ n gondola f. ~lier n gondoliere m

gone /gɒn/ ▷go

gong /gɒŋ/ n gong m inv

good /gʊd/ adj (better, best) buono; (child, footballer, singer) bravo; (holiday, film) bello; ~ at bravo in; a ~ deal of anger molta rabbia; as ~ as (almost) quasi; ~ morning, ~ afternoon buon giorno; ~ evening buona sera; ~ night buonanotte; have a ~ time divertirsi ● n bene m; for ~ per sempre; do ~ far del bene; do sb ~ far bene a qcno; it's no ~ è inutile; be up to no ~ combinare qualcosa

goodbye /gʊd'baɪ/ int arrivederci

good: ~-for-nothing n buono, -a mf a nulla. G~ 'Friday n Venerdì m Santo

good-'looking adj bello

goodness /'gʊdnɪs/ n bontà f; my ~! santo cielo!; thank ~! grazie al cielo!

goods /gʊdz/ npl prodotti mpl. ~ train n treno m merci

good'will n buona volontà f; (Comm) avviamento m

goody /'gʊdɪ/ n (🄸: person) buono m. ~-**goody** n santarellino, -a mf

gooey /'guːɪ/ adj appiccicaticcio; fig sdolcinato

google /'guːgl/ vt/i googlare

goose /guːs/: ~-**flesh** n, ~-**pimples** npl pelle fsg d'oca

gooseberry /'gʊzbərɪ/ n uva f spina

gore¹ /ɡɔː(r)/ n sangue m

gore² vt incornare

gorge /ɡɔːdʒ/ n (Geog) gola f ● vt ~ oneself ingozzarsi

gorgeous /'ɡɔːdʒəs/ adj stupendo

gorilla /ɡə'rɪlə/ n gorilla m inv

gorse /ɡɔːs/ n ginestrone m

gory /'ɡɔːrɪ/ adj (-ier, -iest) cruento

gosh /ɡɒʃ/ int 🄸 caspita

gospel /'ɡɒspl/ n vangelo m. ~ truth n sacrosanta verità f

gossip /'ɡɒsɪp/ n pettegolezzi mpl; (person) pettegolo, -a mf ● vi pettegolare. ~y adj pettegolo

got /ɡɒt/ ▷ **GET**; **have** ~ avere; **have** ~ **to** do sth dover fare qcsa

gotten /'ɡɒtn/ Am see get

gouge /ɡaʊdʒ/ vt ~ **out** cavare

gourmet /'ɡʊəmeɪ/ n buongustaio, -a mf

govern /'ɡʌv(ə)n/ vt/i governare; (determine) determinare

government /'ɡʌvnmənt/ n governo m. ~al adj governativo

governor /'ɡʌvənə(r)/ n governatore m; (of school) membro m del consiglio di istituto; (of prison) direttore, -trice mf; (🄸: boss) capo m

gown /ɡaʊn/ n vestito m; (Jur, Univ) toga f

GP n abbr general practitioner

GPS abbr (Global Positioning System) GPS m

grab /ɡræb/ vt (pt/pp grabbed) ~ [hold of] afferrare

grace /ɡreɪs/ n grazia f; (before meal)

benedicite m inv; **with good** ~ volentieri; **three days'** ~ tre giorni di proroga. ~**ful** adj aggraziato. ~**fully** adv con grazia

gracious /'ɡreɪʃəs/ adj cortese; (elegant) lussuoso

grade /ɡreɪd/ n livello m; (Comm) qualità f; (Sch) voto m; (Am Sch: class) classe f; **Am** = gradient ● vt (Comm) classificare; (Sch) dare il voto a. ~ **crossing** n Am passaggio m a livello

gradient /'ɡreɪdɪənt/ n pendenza f

gradual /'ɡrædʒʊəl/ adj graduale. ~**ly** adv gradualmente

graduate¹ /'ɡrædʒʊət/ n laureato, -a mf

graduate² /'ɡrædʒʊeɪt/ vi (Univ) laurearsi

graduation /ɡrædʒʊ'eɪʃn/ n laurea f

graffiti /ɡrə'fiːtɪ/ npl graffiti mpl

graft /ɡrɑːft/ n (Bot, Med) innesto m; (Med: organ) trapianto m; (🄸: hard work) duro lavoro m; (🄸: corruption) corruzione f ● vt innestare; trapiantare (organ)

grain /ɡreɪn/ n (of sand, salt) granello m; (of rice) chicco m; (cereals) cereali mpl; (in wood) venatura f; **it goes against the** ~ fig è contro la mia/sua natura

gram /ɡræm/ n grammo m

grammar /'ɡræmə(r)/ n grammatica f. ~ **school** n ≈ liceo m

grammatical /ɡrə'mætɪkl/ adj grammaticale

grand /ɡrænd/ adj grandioso; 🄸 eccellente

'grandchild n nipote mf

'granddaughter n nipote f

grandeur /'ɡrændʒə(r)/ n grandiosità f

'grandfather n nonno m. ~ **clock** n pendolo m (che poggia a terra)

grandiose /'ɡrændɪəʊs/ adj

grandioso

grand: ~**mother** n nonna f. ~**parents** npl nonni mpl. ~ **pi'ano** n pianoforte m a coda. ~**son** n nipote m. ~**stand** n tribuna f

granite /'grænɪt/ n granito m

granny /'grænɪ/ n 🄸 nonna f

grant /grɑ:nt/ n (money) sussidio m; (Univ) borsa f di studio ● vt accordare; (admit) ammettere; **take sth for** ~**ed** dare per scontato qcsa

granule /'grænju:l/ n granello m

grape /greɪp/ n acino m; ~**s** pl uva fsg

grapefruit /'greɪp-/ n inv pompelmo m

graph /grɑ:f/ n grafico m

graphic /'græfɪk/ adj grafico; (vivid) vivido. ~**s** n grafica f

grapple /'græpl/ vi ~ **with** also fig essere alle prese con

grasp /grɑ:sp/ n stretta f; (understanding) comprensione f ● vt afferrare. ~**ing** adj avido

grass /grɑ:s/ n erba f; **at the** ~ **roots** alla base. ~**hopper** n cavalletta f. ~**land** n prateria f

grassy /'grɑ:sɪ/ adj erboso

grate¹ /greɪt/ n grata f

grate² vt (Culin) grattugiare ● vi stridere

grateful /'greɪtfl/ adj grato. ~**ly** adv con gratitudine

grater /'greɪtə(r)/ n (Culin) grattugia f

gratif|y /'grætɪfaɪ/ vt (pt/pp -ied) appagare. ~**ied** adj appagato. ~**ying** adj appagante

grating /'greɪtɪŋ/ n grata f

gratitude /'grætɪtju:d/ n gratitudine f

gratuitous /grə'tju:ɪtəs/ adj gratuito

gratuity /grə'tju:ɪtɪ/ n gratifica f

grave¹ /greɪv/ adj grave

grave² n tomba f

gravel /'grævl/ n ghiaia f

grave: ~**stone** n lapide f. ~**yard** n cimitero m

gravitate /'grævɪteɪt/ vi gravitare

gravity /'grævɪtɪ/ n gravità f

gravy /'greɪvɪ/ n sugo m della carne

gray /greɪ/ adj Am = **grey**

graze¹ /greɪz/ vi (animal): pascolare

graze² n escoriazione f ● vt (touch lightly) sfiorare; (scrape) escoriare; sbucciarsi (knee)

grease /gri:s/ n grasso m ● vt ungere. ~**proof** '**paper** n carta f oleata

greasy /'gri:sɪ/ adj (-ier, -iest) untuoso; (hair, skin) grasso

great /greɪt/ adj grande; (🄸: marvellous) eccezionale

great: **G**~ '**Britain** n Gran Bretagna f. ~-'**grandfather** n bisnonno m. ~-'**grandmother** n bisnonna f

great|ly /'greɪtlɪ/ adv enormemente. ~**ness** n grandezza f

Greece /gri:s/ n Grecia f

greed /gri:d/ n avidità f; (for food) ingordigia f

greedy /'gri:dɪ/ adj (-ier, -iest) avido; (for food) ingordo

Greek /gri:k/ adj e n greco, -a mf; (language) greco m

green /gri:n/ adj verde; (fig: inexperienced) immaturo ● n verde m; ~**s** pl verdura f; **the G**~**s** pl (Pol) i verdi. ~ **belt** n zona f verde intorno a una città. ~ **card** n (Auto) carta f verde

---

Green Card Negli Stati Uniti è un documento ufficiale che concede a qualsiasi persona priva della cittadinanza americana il permesso di risiedere e lavorare indefinitivamente negli Stati Uniti. Nel Regno Unito, invece, è un documento che i conducenti o proprietari di autoveicoli devono richiedere alla propria compagnia di assicurazione per convalidare la polizza in occasione di viaggi all'estero.

greenery /ˈgriːnəri/ n verde m

green: ~**grocer** n fruttivendolo, -a mf. ~**house** n serra f. ~**house effect** n effetto m serra. ~ **light** n verde m

greet /griːt/ vt salutare; (welcome) accogliere. ~**ing** n saluto m; (welcome) accoglienza f. ~**ings card** n biglietto m d'auguri

gregarious /grɪˈgeəriəs/ adj gregario; (person) socievole

grenade /grɪˈneɪd/ n granata f

grew /gruː/ ▷GROW

grey /greɪ/ adj grigio; (hair) bianco • n grigio m. ~**hound** n levriero m

grid /grɪd/ n griglia f; (on map) reticolato m; (Electr) rete f

grief /griːf/ n dolore m; **come to** ~ (plans:) naufragare

grievance /ˈgriːvəns/ n lamentela f

grieve /griːv/ vt addolorare • vi essere addolorato

grill /grɪl/ n graticola f; (for grilling) griglia f; **mixed** ~ grigliata f mista • vt/i cuocere alla griglia; (interrogate) sottoporre al terzo grado

grille /grɪl/ n grata f

grim /grɪm/ adj (grimmer, grimmest) arcigno; (determination) accanito

grimace /grɪˈmeɪs/ n smorfia f • vi fare una smorfia

grime /graɪm/ n sudiciume m

grimy /ˈgraɪmɪ/ adj (-ier, -iest) sudicio

grin /grɪn/ n sorriso m • vi (pt/pp grinned) fare un gran sorriso

grind /graɪnd/ n (🔲: hard work) sfacchinata f • vt (pt/pp ground) macinare; affilare (knife); (Am: mince) tritare; ~ **one's teeth** digrignare i denti

grip /grɪp/ n presa f; fig controllo m; (bag) borsone m; **get a** ~ **on oneself** controllarsi • vt (pt/pp gripped) afferrare; (tyres:) far presa su; tenere avvinto (attention)

grisly /ˈgrɪzlɪ/ adj (-ier, -iest) raccapricciante

gristle /ˈgrɪsl/ n cartilagine f

grit /grɪt/ n graniglia f; (for roads) sabbia f; (courage) coraggio m • vt (pt/pp gritted) spargere sabbia su (road); ~ **one's teeth** serrare i denti

groan /grəʊn/ n gemito m • vi gemere

grocer /ˈgrəʊsə(r)/ n droghiere, -a mf; ~'**s** [shop] drogheria f. ~**ies** npl generi mpl alimentari

groggy /ˈgrɒgɪ/ adj (-ier, -iest) stordito; (unsteady) barcollante

groin /grɔɪn/ n (Anat) inguine m

groom /gruːm/ n sposo m; (for horse) stalliere m • vt strigliare (horse); fig preparare; **well-**~**ed** ben curato

groove /gruːv/ n scanalatura f

grope /grəʊp/ vi brancolare; ~ **for** cercare a tastoni

gross /grəʊs/ adj obeso; (coarse) volgare; (glaring) grossolano; (salary, weight) lordo • n inv grossa f. ~**ly** adv (very) enormemente

grotesque /grəʊˈtesk/ adj grottesco

ground[1] /graʊnd/ ▷GRIND

ground[2] n terra f; (Sport) terreno m; (reason) ragione f; ~**s** pl (park) giardini mpl; (of coffee) fondi mpl • vt (ship:) arenarsi • vt bloccare a terra (aircraft); Am (Electr) mettere a terra

ground: ~ **floor** n pianterreno m. ~**ing** n base f. ~**less** adj infondato. ~**sheet** n telone m impermeabile. ~**work** n lavoro m di preparazione

group /gruːp/ n gruppo m • vt raggruppare • vi raggrupparsi

grouse[1] /graʊs/ n inv gallo m

cedrone

grouse² /graʊs/ vi 🔲 brontolare

grovel /'grɒvl/ vi (pt/pp grovelled) strisciare. **~ling** adj leccapiedi inv

grow /grəʊ/ v (pt grew, pp grown) ● vi crescere; (become) diventare; (unemployment, fear:) aumentare; (town:) ingrandirsi ● vt coltivare; ~ one's hair farsi crescere i capelli. □ ~ **up** vi crescere; (town:) svilupparsi

growl /graʊl/ n grugnito m ● vi ringhiare

grown /grəʊn/ ▷GROW ● adj adulto. **~-up** adj & n adulto, -a mf

growth /grəʊθ/ n crescita f; (increase) aumento m; (Med) tumore m

grub /grʌb/ n larva f; (🔲: food) mangiare m

grubby /'grʌbɪ/ adj (-ier, -iest) sporco

grudg|e /grʌdʒ/ n rancore m; bear sb a ~e portare rancore a qcno ● vt dare a malincuore. **~ing** adj reluttante. **~ingly** adv a malincuore

gruelling /'gru:əlɪŋ/ adj estenuante

gruesome /'gru:səm/ adj macabro

gruff /grʌf/ adj burbero

grumble /'grʌmbl/ vi brontolare (at contro)

grumpy /'grʌmpɪ/ adj (-ier, -iest) scorbutico

grunt /grʌnt/ n grugnito m ● vi fare un grugnito

guarant|ee /gærən'ti:/ n garanzia f ● vt garantire. **~or** n garante mf

guard /gɑ:d/ n guardia f; (security) guardiano m; (on train) capotreno m; (Techn) schermo m protettivo; **be on ~** essere di guardia ● vt sorvegliare; (protect) proteggere. □ ~ **against** vt guardarsi da. **~-dog** n cane m da guardia

guarded /'gɑ:dɪd/ adj guardingo

guardian /'gɑ:dɪən/ n (of minor) tutore, -trice mf

guerrilla /gə'rɪlə/ n guerrigliero, -a mf. **~ warfare** n guerriglia f

guess /ges/ n supposizione f ● vt indovinare ● vi indovinare; (Am: suppose) supporre. **~work** n supposizione f

guest /gest/ n ospite mf; (in hotel) cliente mf. **~-house** n pensione f

guffaw /gʌ'fɔ:/ n sghignazzata f ● vi sghignazzare

guidance /'gaɪdəns/ n guida f; (advice) consigli mpl

guide /gaɪd/ n guida f; [Girl] G~ giovane esploratrice f ● vt guidare. **~book** n guida f turistica

guide: ~-dog n cane m per ciechi. **~lines** npl direttive fpl

guild /gɪld/ n corporazione f

guile /gaɪl/ n astuzia f

guillotine /'gɪləti:n/ n ghigliottina f; (for paper) taglierina f

guilt /gɪlt/ n colpa f. **~ily** adv con aria colpevole

guilty /'gɪltɪ/ adj (-ier, -iest) colpevole; **have a ~ conscience** avere la coscienza sporca

guinea-pig /'gɪnɪ-/ n porcellino m d'India; (fig: used for experiments) cavia f

guitar /gɪ'tɑ:(r)/ n chitarra f. **~ist** n chitarrista mf

gulf /gʌlf/ n (Geog) golfo m; fig abisso m

gull /gʌl/ n gabbiano m

gullet /'gʌlɪt/ n esofago m; (throat) gola f

gullible /'gʌlɪbl/ adj credulone

gully /'gʌlɪ/ n burrone m; (drain) canale m di scolo

gulp /gʌlp/ n azione f di deglutire; (of food) boccone m; (of liquid) sorso m ● vi deglutire. □ ~ **down** vt trangugiare (food); scolarsi (liquid)

gum¹ /gʌm/ n (Anat) gengiva f

gum² /gʌm/ n (chewing gum) gomma f da masticare, chewing gum m inv ● vt (pt/pp gummed)

ingommare (**to a**)

gun /gʌn/ n pistola f; (*rifle*) fucile m; (*cannon*) cannone m ● **gun down** vt (*pt/pp* **gunned**) freddare

gun: ~**fire** n spari mpl; (*of cannon*) colpi mpl [di cannone]. ~**man** uomo m armato

gun: ~**powder** n polvere f da sparo. ~**shot** n colpo m [di pistola]

gurgle /ˈɡɜːɡl/ vi gorgogliare; (baby:) fare degli urletti

gush /ɡʌʃ/ vi sgorgare; (*enthuse*) parlare con troppo entusiasmo (**over** di). □ ~ **out** vi sgorgare. ~**ing** adj eccessivamente entusiastico

gust /ɡʌst/ n (*of wind*) raffica f

gusto /ˈɡʌstəʊ/ n **with** ~ con trasporto

gusty /ˈɡʌstɪ/ adj ventoso

gut /ɡʌt/ n intestino m; ~**s** pl pancia f; (🔢: *courage*) fegato m ● vt (*pt/pp* **gutted**) (*Culin*) svuotare delle interiora; ~**ted by fire** sventrato da un incendio

gutter /ˈɡʌtə(r)/ n canale m di scolo; (*on roof*) grondaia f, fig bassifondi mpl

guttural /ˈɡʌtərəl/ adj gutturale

guy /ɡaɪ/ n 🔢 tipo m, tizio m

guzzle /ˈɡʌzl/ vt ingozzarsi con (*food*); **he's** ~**d the lot** si è sbafato tutto

gym /dʒɪm/ n 🔢 palestra f; (*gymnastics*) ginnastica f

gymnasium /dʒɪmˈneɪzɪəm/ n palestra f

gymnast /ˈdʒɪmnæst/ n ginnasta mf. ~**ics** n ginnastica f

gymslip /(Sch) ≈ grembiule m (da bambina)

gynaecolog|ist /ɡaɪnɪˈkɒlədʒɪst/ n ginecologo, -a mf. ~**y** n ginecologia f

gypsy /ˈdʒɪpsɪ/ n zingaro, -a mf

gyrate /dʒaɪˈreɪt/ vi roteare

Hh

haberdashery /hæbəˈdæʃərɪ/ n merceria f; Am negozio m d'abbigliamento da uomo

habit /ˈhæbɪt/ n abitudine f; (*Relig: costume*) tonaca f; **be in the** ~ **of doing sth** avere l'abitudine di fare qcsa

habitable /ˈhæbɪtəbl/ adj abitabile

habitat /ˈhæbɪtæt/ n habitat m inv

habitation /hæbɪˈteɪʃn/ n **unfit for human** ~ inagibile

habitual /həˈbɪtjʊəl/ adj abituale; (*smoker, liar*) inveterato. ~**ly** adv regolarmente

hack¹ /hæk/ n (*writer*) scribacchino, -a mf

hack² vt tagliare; ~ **to pieces** tagliare a pezzi

hackneyed /ˈhæknɪd/ adj trito [e ritrito]

had /hæd/ ▷**HAVE**

haddock /ˈhædək/ n inv eglefino m

haemorrhage /ˈhemərɪdʒ/ n emorragia f

haemorrhoids /ˈhemərɔɪdz/ npl emorroidi fpl

hag /hæg/ n **old** ~ vecchia befana f

haggard /ˈhægəd/ adj sfatto

hail¹ /heɪl/ vt salutare; far segno a (*taxi*) ● vi ~ **from** provenire da

hail² /heɪl/ n grandine f ● vi grandinare. ~**stone** n chicco m di grandine. ~**storm** n grandinata f

hair /heə(r)/ n capelli mpl; (*on body, of animal*) pelo m

hair: ~**brush** n spazzola f per capelli. ~**cut** n taglio m di capelli; **have a** ~ farsi tagliare i capelli. ~**do** n 🔢 pettinatura f. ~**dresser** n parrucchiere, -a mf. ~**dryer** n fon m *inv;* (with hood) casco m [asciugaca-pelli]. **~grip** n molletta f. **~pin** n forcina f. **~pin 'bend** n tornante m, curva f a gomito. **~raising** adj terrificante. **~style** n acconciatura f

hairy /'heərɪ/ adj (-ier, -iest) peloso; (🔟 frightening) spaventoso

half /hɑːf/ n (pl halves) metà f inv; **cut in ~** tagliare a metà; **one and a ~** uno e mezzo; **a dozen** mezza dozzina; **~ an hour** mezz'ora • adj mezzo; [at] **~ price** [a] metà prezzo • adv a metà; **~ past two** le due e mezza

half: ~-'hearted adj esitante. **~ 'mast** n at ~ mast a mezz'asta. **~-'term** n vacanza f di metà trimestre. **~-'time** n (Sport) intervallo m. **~'way** adj the **~way mark/stage** il livello intermedio • adv a metà strada; **get ~way** fig arrivare a metà

hall /hɔːl/ n (entrance) ingresso m; (room) sala f; (mansion) residenza f di campagna; **~ of residence** (Univ) casa f dello studente

'hallmark n marchio m di garanzia; fig marchio m

hallo /hə'ləʊ/ int ciao!; (on telephone) pronto!; **say ~ to** salutare

Hallowe'en /hæləʊ'iːn/ n vigilia f d'Ognissanti e notte delle streghe, celebrata soprattutto dai bambini

hallucination /həluːsɪ'neɪʃn/ n allucinazione f

halo /'heɪləʊ/ n (pl -es) aureola f; (Astr) alone m

halt /hɔːlt/ n alt m inv; **come to a ~** fermarsi; (traffic:) bloccarsi • vi fermarsi; **~!** alt! • vt fermare. **~ing** adj esitante

halve /hɑːv/ vt dividere a metà; (reduce) dimezzare

ham /hæm/ n prosciutto m; (Theat) attore, -trice mf da strapazzo

hamburger /'hæmbɜːgə(r)/ n hamburger m inv

hammer /'hæmə(r)/ n martello m

• vt martellare • vi ~ **at/on** picchiare a

hammock /'hæmək/ n amaca f

hamper[1] /'hæmpə(r)/ n cesto m; [gift] ~ cestino m

hamper[2] vt ostacolare

hamster /'hæmstə(r)/ n criceto m

hand /hænd/ n mano f; (of clock) lancetta f; (writing) scrittura f; (worker) manovale m; **at ~, to ~** a portata di mano; **on the one ~** da un lato; **on the other ~** d'altra parte; **out of ~** incontrollabile; (summarily) su due piedi; **give sb a ~** dare una mano a qcno • vt porgere. **~ down** vt tramandare. **~ in** vt consegnare. **~ out** vt distribuire. **~ over** vt passare; (to police) consegnare

hand: ~bag n borsa f (da signora). **~brake** n freno a mano. **~cuffs** npl manette fpl. **~ful** n manciata f; **be [quite] a ~ful** 🔟 essere difficile da tenere a freno

handicap /'hændɪkæp/ n handicap m inv. **~ped** adj mentally/physically **~ped** mentalmente/fisicamente handicappato

handi|craft /'hændɪkrɑːft/ n artigianato m. **~work** n opera f

handkerchief /'hæŋkətʃɪf/ n (pl ~s & -chieves) fazzoletto m

handle /'hændl/ n manico m; (of door) maniglia f; **fly off the** 🔟 perdere le staffe • vt maneggiare; occuparsi di (problem, customer); prendere (difficult person); trattare (subject). **~bars** npl manubrio m

hand: ~-out n (at lecture) foglio m informativo; (🔟 money) elemosina f. **~shake** n stretta f di mano

handsome /'hænsəm/ adj bello; (fig: generous) generoso

handwriting n calligrafia f

handy /'hændɪ/ adj (-ier, -iest) utile; (person) abile; **have/keep ~** avere/tenere a portata di mano. **~man** n tuttofare m inv

hang /hæŋ/ vt (pt/pp **hung**) appendere (picture); (pt/pp **hanged**) impiccare (criminal); ~ **oneself** impiccarsi ● vi (pt/pp **hung**) pendere; (hair:) scendere ● n **get the** ~ **of it** 🔲 afferrare. □ ~ **about** vi gironzolare. □ ~ **on** vi tenersi stretto; (🔲: wait) aspettare; (Teleph) restare in linea. □ ~ **on to** vt tenersi stretto a; (keep) tenere. □ ~ **out** vi spuntare; **where does he usually** ~ **out?** 🔲 dove bazzica di solito? ● vt stendere (washing). □ ~ **up** vt appendere; (Teleph) riattaccare ● vi essere appeso; (Teleph) riattaccare

hangar /'hæŋə(r)/ n (Aeron) hangar m inv

hanger /'hæŋə(r)/ n gruccia f. ~-**on** n leccapiedi mf

hang: ~-**glider** n deltaplano m. ~**over** n 🔲 postumi mpl da sbornia. ~-**up** n 🔲 complesso m

hanky /'hæŋkɪ/ n 🔲 fazzoletto m

haphazard /hæp'hæzəd/ adj a casaccio

happen /'hæpn/ vi capitare, succedere; **as it** ~**s** per caso; **I** ~**ed to meet him** mi è capitato di incontrarlo; **what has** ~**ed to him?** cosa gli è capitato?; (become of) che fine ha fatto? ~**ing** n avvenimento m

happi|ly /'hæpɪlɪ/ adv felicemente; (fortunately) fortunatamente. ~**ness** n felicità f

happy /'hæpɪ/ adj (-ier, -iest) contento, felice. ~-**go-'lucky** adj spensierato

harass /'hærəs/ vt perseguitare. ~**ed** adj stressato. ~**ment** n persecuzione f; **sexual** ~**ment** molestie fpl sessuali

harbour /'hɑːbə(r)/ n porto ● vt dare asilo a; nutrire (grudge)

hard /hɑːd/ adj duro; (question, problem) difficile; ~ **of hearing** duro d'orecchi; **be** ~ **on sb** (person:) essere duro con qcno ● adv (work) duramente; (pull, hit, rain,

snow) forte; ~ **hit by unemployment** duramente colpito dalla disoccupazione; **take sth** ~ non accettare qcsa; **think** ~! pensaci bene!; **try** ~ mettercela tutta; **try** ~**er** metterci più impegno; ~ **done by** 🔲 trattato ingiustamente

hard: hard-boiled adj (egg) sodo. ~ **disk** n hard disk m inv, disco m rigido

harden /'hɑːdn/ vi indurirsi

hard: ~-'**headed** adj (businessman) dal sangue freddo. ~**line** adj duro

hard|ly /'hɑːdlɪ/ adv appena; ~**ly ever** quasi mai. ~**ness** n durezza f. ~**ship** n avversità f inv

hard: ~ '**shoulder** n (Auto) corsia f d'emergenza. ~**ware** n ferramenta fpl; (Comput) hardware m inv. ~-'**working** adj **be** ~-**working** essere un gran lavoratore

hardy /'hɑːdɪ/ adj (-ier, -iest) dal fisico resistente; (plant) che sopporta il gelo

hare /heə(r)/ n lepre f. ~-**brained** adj 🔲 (scheme) da scervellati

hark /hɑːk/ vi ~ **back to** fig ritornare su

harm /hɑːm/ n male m; (damage) danni mpl; **out of** ~'s **way** in un posto sicuro; **it won't do any** ~ non farà certo male ● vt far male a; (damage) danneggiare. ~**ful** adj dannoso. ~**less** adj innocuo

harmonica /hɑː'mɒnɪkə/ n armonica f [a bocca]

harmonious /hɑː'məʊnɪəs/ adj armonioso. ~**ly** adv in armonia

harness /'hɑːnɪs/ n finimenti mpl; (of parachute) imbracatura f ● vt bardare (horse); sfruttare (resources)

harp /hɑːp/ n arpa f ● **harp on** vi 🔲 insistere (about su). ~**ist** n arpista mf

harpoon /hɑː'puːn/ n arpione m

harpsichord /'hɑːpsɪkɔːd/ n clavicembalo m

h

harrowing /ˈhærəʊɪŋ/ adj straziante

harsh /hɑːʃ/ adj duro; (light) abbagliante. **~ness** n durezza f

harvest /ˈhɑːvɪst/ n raccolta f; (of grapes) vendemmia f; (crop) raccolto m ● vt raccogliere

has /hæz/ ▷ HAVE

hassle /ˈhæsl/ n rottura f ● vt rompere le scatole a

haste /heɪst/ n fretta f

hast|y /ˈheɪstɪ/ adj (-ier, -iest) frettoloso; (decision) affrettato. **~ily** adv frettolosamente

hat /hæt/ n cappello m

hatch¹ /hætʃ/ n (for food) sportello m passavivande; (Naut) boccaporto m

hatch² vi **~[out]** rompere il guscio; (egg) schiudersi ● vt covare; tramare (plot)

'hatchback n tre/cinque porte m inv; (door) porta f del bagagliaio

hatchet /ˈhætʃɪt/ n ascia f

hate /heɪt/ n odio m ● vt odiare. **~ful** adj odioso

hatred /ˈheɪtrɪd/ n odio m

haught|y /ˈhɔːtɪ/ adj (-ier, -iest) altezzoso. **~ily** adv altezzosamente

haul /hɔːl/ n (fish) pescata f; (loot) bottino m; (pull) tirata f ● vt tirare; trasportare (goods) ● vi **~ on** tirare. **~age** n trasporto m. **~ier** n autotrasportatore m

haunt /hɔːnt/ n ritrovo m ● vt frequentare; (linger in the mind) perseguitare; **this house is ~ed** questa casa è abitata da fantasmi

---

have /hæv/

● vt (3 sg pres tense **has**; pt/pp **had**) avere; fare (breakfast, bath, walk etc); **~ a drink** bere qualcosa; **~ lunch/dinner** pranzare/cenare; **~ a rest** riposarsi; **I had my hair cut** mi sono tagliata i capelli; **we had the**

house painted abbiamo fatto tinteggiare la casa; **I had it made** l'ho fatto fare; **~ to do** sth dover fare qcsa; **~ him telephone me tomorrow** digli di telefonarmi domani; **he has** or **he's got two houses** ha due case; **you've got the money, ~n't you?** hai i soldi, no?

● v aux avere; (with verbs of motion & some others) essere; **I ~ seen him** l'ho visto; **he has never been there** non ci è mai stato. □ **~ on** vt (be wearing) portare; (dupe) prendere in giro; **I've got something on tonight** ho un impegno stasera. □ **~ out** vt **~ it out with sb** chiarire le cose con qcno

● npl the **~s** and the **~-nots** i ricchi e i poveri

---

haven /ˈheɪvn/ n fig rifugio m

haversack /ˈhævə-/ n zaino m

havoc /ˈhævək/ n strage f; **play ~ with** fig scombussolare

hawk /hɔːk/ n falco m

hay /heɪ/ n fieno m. **~ fever** n raffreddore m da fieno. **~stack** n pagliaio m

'haywire adj **go ~** dare i numeri; (plans:) andare all'aria

hazard /ˈhæzəd/ n (risk) rischio m ● vt rischiare; **~ a guess** azzardare un'ipotesi. **~ous** adj rischioso. **~ [warning] lights** npl (Auto) luci fpl d'emergenza

haze /heɪz/ n foschia f

hazel /ˈheɪz(ə)l/ n nocciolo m; (colour) [color m] nocciola m. **~-nut** n nocciola f

hazy /ˈheɪzɪ/ adj (-ier, -iest) nebbioso; (fig: person) confuso; (memories) vago

he /hiː/ pron lui; **he's tired** è stanco; **I'm going but he's not** io vengo, ma lui no

head /hed/ n testa f; (of firm) capo

m; (of primary school) direttore, -trice mf; (of secondary school) preside mf; (on beer) schiuma f; **be off one's** ~ essere fuori di testa; **have a good** ~ **for business** avere il senso degli affari; **have a good** ~ **for heights** non soffrire di vertigini; **10 pounds a** ~ 10 sterline a testa; **20** ~ **of cattle** 20 capi di bestiame; ~ **first** a capofitto; ~ **over heels in love** innamorato pazzo; ~**s or tails?** testa o croce? ● vt essere a capo di; essere in testa a (list); colpire di testa (ball) ● vi ~ **for** dirigersi verso.

head: ~**ache** n mal m di testa. ~**er** /'hedə(r)/ n rinvio m di testa; (dive) tuffo m di testa. ~**ing** n (in list etc) titolo m. ~**lamp** n (Auto) fanale m. ~**land** n promontorio m. ~**line** n titolo m. ~**long** adj & adv a capofitto. ~**master** n (of primary school) direttore m; (of secondary school) preside m. ~**mistress** n (of primary school) direttrice f; (of secondary school) preside f. ~**on** adj (collision) frontale ● adv frontalmente. ~**phones** npl cuffie fpl. ~**quarters** npl sede fsg; (Mil) quartier m generale msg. ~**strong** adj testardo

heady /'hedɪ/ adj che dà alla testa

heal /hiːl/ vt/i guarire

health /helθ/ n salute f

health|y /'helθɪ/ adj (-ier, -iest) sano. ~**ily** adv in modo sano

heap /hiːp/ n mucchio m; ~**s of** 🔢 un sacco di ● vt ~ [**up**] ammucchiare; ~**ed teaspoon** un cucchiaino abbondante

hear /hɪə(r)/ vt/i (pt/pp **heard**) sentire; ~, ~! bravo! ~ **from** vi aver notizie di. □ ~ **of** vi sentir parlare di; **he would not** ~ **of it** non ne ha voluto sentir parlare

hearing /'hɪərɪŋ/ n udito m; (Jur) udienza f. ~**-aid** n apparecchio m acustico

'hearsay n **from** ~ per sentito dire

hearse /hɜːs/ n carro m funebre

heart /hɑːt/ n cuore m; ~**s** pl (in cards) cuori mpl; **by** ~ a memoria

heart: ~**ache** n pena f. ~ **attack** n infarto m. ~**-break** n afflizione f. ~**-breaking** adj straziante. ~**-burn** n mal m di stomaco. ~**felt** adj di cuore

hearth /hɑːθ/ n focolare m

heart|ily /'hɑːtɪlɪ/ adv di cuore; (eat) con appetito; **be** ~**ily sick of sth** non poterne più di qcsa. ~**less** adj spietato. ~**-searching** n esame m di coscienza. ~**-to-**~ n conversazione f a cuore aperto ● adj a cuore aperto. ~**y** adj caloroso; (meal) copioso; (person) gioviale

heat /hiːt/ n calore m; (Sport) prova f eliminatoria ● vt scaldare ● vi scaldarsi. ~**ed** adj (swimming pool) riscaldato; (discussion) animato. ~**er** n (for room) stufa f; (for water) boiler m inv; (Auto) riscaldamento m

heath /hiːθ/ n brughiera f

heathen /'hiːðn/ adj & n pagano, -a mf

heather /'heðə(r)/ n erica f

heating /'hiːtɪŋ/ n riscaldamento m

heat: ~**-stroke** n colpo m di sole. ~ **wave** n ondata f di calore

heave /hiːv/ vt tirare; (lift) tirare su; (🔢: throw) gettare; emettere (sigh) ● vi tirare

heaven /'hev(ə)n/ n paradiso m; ~ **help you if...** Dio ti scampi se...; H~**s!** santo cielo!. ~**ly** adj celeste; 🔢 delizioso

heav|y /'hevɪ/ adj (-ier, -iest) pesante; (traffic) intenso; (rain, cold) forte; **be a** ~**y smoker/drinker** essere un gran fumatore/bevitore. ~**ily** adv pesantemente; (smoke, drink etc) molto. ~**yweight** n peso m massimo

Hebrew /'hiːbruː/ adj ebreo

heckle /'hekl/ vt interrompere di continuo. ~**r** n disturbatore, -trice mf

hectic /'hektɪk/ adj frenetico

hedge /hedʒ/ n siepe f ● vi fig essere

evasivo. ∿**hog** n riccio m
heed /hi:d/ n to prestare
ascolto a ● vt prestare ascolto a.
∿**less** adj noncurante
heel¹ /hi:l/ n tallone m, (of shoe)
tacco m; **take to one's** ∿**s** 🆃 darsela a gambe
heel² vi ∿ **over** (Naut) inclinarsi
hefty /'heftɪ/ adj (-ier, -iest) massiccio
heifer /'hefə(r)/ n giovenca f
height /haɪt/ n altezza f; (of plane)
altitudine f; (of season, fame) culmine
m. ∿**en** vt fig accrescere
heir /eə(r)/ n erede mf. ∿**ess** n eredi-
tiera f. ∿**loom** n cimelio m di famiglia
held /held/ ▷**HOLD**²
helicopter /'helɪkɒptə(r)/ n elicot-
tero m
hell /hel/ n inferno m; **go to** ∿! 🆇
va' al diavolo! ● int porca miseria!
hello /hə'ləʊ/ int & n = hallo
helm /helm/ n timone m; **at the** ∿
fig al timone
helmet /'helmɪt/ n casco m
help /help/ n aiuto m; (employee)
aiuto m domestico; **that's no** ∿ non
è d'aiuto ● vt aiutare; ∿ **oneself to**
sth servirsi di qcsa; ∿ **yourself** (at
table) serviti pure; **I could not** ∿
laughing non ho potuto trattenermi
dal ridere; **it cannot be** ∿**ed** non
c'è niente da fare; **I can't** ∿ **it** non
ci posso far niente ● vi aiutare
help|er /'helpə(r)/ n aiutante mf.
∿**ful** adj (person) di aiuto; (advice)
utile. ∿**ing** n porzione f. ∿**less** adj
(unable to manage) incapace; (powerless)
impotente
hem /hem/ n orlo m ● vt (pt/pp
hemmed) orlare. □ ∿ **in** vt intrappolare
hemisphere /'hemɪ-/ n emisfero m
hen /hen/ n gallina f; (any female bird)
femmina f

hence /hens/ adv (for this reason)
quindi. ∿**forth** adv d'ora innanzi
henpecked adj tiranneggiato dalla
moglie
her /hɜ:(r)/ poss adj il suo m, la sua f,
i suoi mpl, le sue fpl; ∿ **mother/**
father sua madre/suo padre ● pers
pron (direct object) la; (indirect object) le;
(after prep) lei; **I know** ∿ la conosco;
give ∿ **the money** dalle i soldi;
give it to ∿ daglielo; **I came with**
∿ sono venuto con lei; **it's** ∿ è lei;
I've seen ∿ l'ho vista; **I've seen** ∿,
but not him ho visto lei, ma non lui
herb /hɜ:b/ n erba f
herbal /'hɜ:b(ə)l/ adj alle erbe; ∿
tea tisana f
herd /hɜ:d/ n gregge m ● vt (tend)
sorvegliare; (drive) far muovere; fig
ammassare
here /hɪə(r)/ adv qui, qua; **in** ∿ qui
dentro; **come/bring** ∿ vieni/porta
qui; ∿ **is...,** ∿ **are...** ecco...; ∿ **you**
are! ecco qua!. ∿**after** adv in futuro. ∿**by** adv con la presente
heredit|ary /hə'redɪtərɪ/ adj eredi-
tario. ∿**y** n eredità f
here|sy /'herəsɪ/ n eresia f. ∿**tic** n
eretico, -a mf
here'with adv (Comm) con la
presente
heritage /'herɪtɪdʒ/ n eredità f. ∿
'tourism n turismo m culturale
hernia /'hɜ:nɪə/ n ernia f
hero /'hɪərəʊ/ n (pl -es) eroe m
heroic /hɪ'rəʊɪk/ adj eroico
heroin /'herəʊɪn/ n eroina f (droga)
hero|ine /'herəʊɪn/ n eroina f.
∿**ism** n eroismo m
heron /'herən/ n airone m
herring /'herɪŋ/ n aringa f
hers /hɜ:z/ poss pron il suo m, la sua f,
i suoi mpl, le sue fpl; **a friend of** ∿
un suo amico; **friends of** ∿ dei suoi
amici; **that is** ∿ quello è suo; (as opposed to mine) quello è il suo

her'self *pers pron (reflexive)* si; *(emphatic)* lei stessa; *(after prep)* sé, se stessa; **she poured a drink** si è versata da bere; **she told me so** me lo ha detto lei stessa; **she's proud of ~** è fiera di sé; **by ~** da sola

hesitant /'hezɪtənt/ *adj* esitante. **~ly** *adv* con esitazione

hesitat|e /'hezɪteɪt/ *vi* esitare. **~ion** *n* esitazione *f*

hetero'sexual /hetərəʊ-/ *adj* eterosessuale

hexagon /'heksəgən/ *n* esagono *m*. **~al** *adj* esagonale

hey /heɪ/ *int* ehi

heyday /'heɪ-/ *n* tempi *mpl* d'oro

hi /haɪ/ *int* ciao!

hibernat|e /'haɪbəneɪt/ *vi* andare in letargo. **~ion** *n* letargo *m*

hiccup /'hɪkʌp/ *n* singhiozzo *m*; (□: *hitch*) intoppo *m* ● *vi* fare un singhiozzo

hide[1] /haɪd/ *n (leather)* pelle *f* (di *animale*)

hide[2] *vt (pt* hid, *pp* hidden) nascondere ● *vi* nascondersi. **~-and-'seek** *n* **play ~-and-seek** giocare a nascondino

hideous /'hɪdɪəs/ *adj* orribile

'hide-out *n* nascondiglio *m*

hiding[1] /'haɪdɪŋ/ *n* (□: *beating*) bastonata *f*; *(defeat)* batosta *f*

hiding[2] *n* **go into ~** sparire dalla circolazione

hierarchy /'haɪərɑːkɪ/ *n* gerarchia *f*

hieroglyphics /haɪərə'glɪfɪks/ *npl* geroglifici *mpl*

hi-fi /'haɪfaɪ/ *n* stereo *m*, hi-fi *m inv* ● *adj* □ ad alta fedeltà

high /haɪ/ *adj* alto; *(meat)* che comincia ad andare a male; *(wind)* forte; *(on drugs)* fatto; **it's ~ time we did something about it** è ora di fare qualcosa in proposito ● *adv* in alto; **~ and low** in lungo e in largo

● *n* massimo *m*; *(temperature)* massima *f*; **be on a ~** □ essere fatto

high: ~er education *n* formazione *f* universitaria. **~-'handed** *adj* dispotico. **~ heels** *npl* tacchi *mpl* alti

highlight /'haɪlaɪt/ *n fig* momento *m* clou; **~s** *pl (in hair)* mèche *fpl* ● *vt (emphasize)* evidenziare. **~er** *n (marker)* evidenziatore *m*

highly /'haɪlɪ/ *adv* molto; **speak ~ of** lodare; **think ~ of** avere un'alta opinione di. **~-'strung** *adj* nervoso

high: ~-rise *adj (building)* molto alto ● *n* edificio *m* molto alto. **~ school** *n* ≈ scuola *f* superiore. **~ street** *n* strada *f* principale. **~way code** *n* codice *m* stradale

---

High School Negli Stati Uniti indica la scuola superiore, generalmente per studenti di età compresa tra i 14 e i 18 anni. In Gran Bretagna il termine è usato solo nella denominazione di alcune scuole. *i*

---

hijack /'haɪdʒæk/ *vt* dirottare ● *n* dirottamento *m*. **~er** *n* dirottatore, -trice *mf*

hike /haɪk/ *n* escursione *f* a piedi ● *vi* fare un'escursione a piedi. **~r** *n* escursionista *mf*

hilarious /hɪ'leərɪəs/ *adj* esilarante

hill /hɪl/ *n* collina *f*; *(mound)* collinetta *f*; *(slope)* altura *f*

hill: ~side *n* pendio *m*. **~y** *adj* collinoso

hilt /hɪlt/ *n* impugnatura *f*; **to the ~** *(support)* fino in fondo; *(mortgaged)* fino al collo

him /hɪm/ *pron (direct object)* lo; *(indirect object)* gli; *(with prep)* lui; **I know ~** lo conosco; **give ~ the money** dagli i soldi; **give it to ~** daglielo; **I spoke to ~** gli ho parlato; **it's ~** è lui; **she loves ~** lo ama; **she loves ~, not you** ama lui, non te. **~'self** *pers pron (reflexive)* si;

(*emphatic*) lui stesso; (*after prep*) sé, se stesso; **he poured ~ a drink** si è versato da bere; **he told me so** ~self me lo ha detto lui stesso; **he's proud of ~self** è fiero di sé; **by** ~self da solo

hind|er /'hɪndə(r)/ *vt* intralciare. ~**rance** *n* intralcio *m*

hindsight /'haɪnd-/ *n* **with ~** con il senno del poi

Hindu /'hɪmduː/ *n* indù *mf inv* ● *adj* indù. ~**ism** *n* induismo *m*

hinge /hɪndʒ/ *n* cardine *m* ● *vi* ~ **on** *fig* dipendere da

hint /hɪnt/ *n* (*clue*) accenno *m*; (*advice*) suggerimento *m*; (*indirect suggestion*) allusione *f*; (*trace*) tocco *m* ● *vt* ~ **that...** far capire che... ● *vi* ~ **at** alludere a

hip /hɪp/ *n* fianco *m*

hippie /'hɪpɪ/ *n* hippy *mf inv*

hippopotamus /hɪpə'pɒtəməs/ *n* (*pl* -**muses** *or* -**mi** /-maɪ/) ippopotamo *m*

hire /'haɪə(r)/ *vt* affittare; assumere (person); ~ **[out]** affittare ● *n* noleggio *m*; **'for ~'** 'affittasi'. ~ **car** *n* macchina *f* a noleggio. ~ **purchase** *n* acquisto *m* rateale

his /hɪz/ *poss adj* il suo *m*, la sua *f*, i suoi *mpl*, le sue *fpl*; ~ **mother/father** sua madre/suo padre ● *poss pron* il suo *m*, la sua *f*, i suoi *mpl*, le sue *fpl*; **a friend of ~** un suo amico; **friends of ~** dei suoi amici; **that is ~** questo è suo; (*as opposed to mine*) questo è il suo

hiss /hɪs/ *n* sibilo *m*; (*of disapproval*) fischio *m* ● *vt* fischiare ● *vi* sibilare; (*in disapproval*) fischiare

historian /hɪ'stɔːrɪən/ *n* storico, -a *mf*

history /'hɪstərɪ/ *n* storia *f*; **make ~** passare alla storia

hit /hɪt/ *n* (*blow*) colpo *m*; (□: *success*) successo *m*; **score a direct ~** (*missile:*) colpire in pieno ● *vt/i* (*pt/pp* hit,

pres p hitting) colpire; ~ **one's head on the table** battere la testa contro il tavolo; **the car ~ the wall** la macchina ha sbattuto contro il muro; ~ **the roof** □ perdere le staffe. □ ~ **off** *vt* ~ **it off** andare d'accordo. □ ~ **on** *vt fig* trovare

hitch /hɪtʃ/ *n* intoppo *m*; **technical** ~ problema *m* tecnico ● *vt* attaccare; ~ **a lift** chiedere un passaggio. □ ~ **up** *vt* tirarsi su (trousers). ~**-hike** *vi* fare l'autostop. ~**-hiker** *n* autostoppista *mf*

hither /'hɪðə(r)/ *adv* ~ **and thither** di qua e di là. ~**'to** *adv* finora

hit-or-'miss *adj* on a very ~ **basis** all'improvvista

hive /haɪv/ *n* alveare *m*; ~ **of industry** fucina *f* di lavoro ● **hive off** *vt* (*Comm*) separare

hoard /hɔːd/ *n* provvista *f*; (*of money*) gruzzolo *m* ● *vt* accumulare

hoarding /'hɔːdɪŋ/ *n* palizzata *f*; (*with advertisements*) tabellone *m* per manifesti pubblicitari

hoarse /hɔːs/ *adj* rauco. ~**ly** *adv* con voce rauca. ~**ness** *n* raucedine *f*

hoax /həʊks/ *n* scherzo *m*; (*false alarm*) falso allarme *m*. ~**er** *n* burlone, -a *mf*

hob /hɒb/ *n* piano *m* di cottura

hobble /'hɒbl/ *vi* zoppicare

hobby /'hɒbɪ/ *n* hobby *m inv*. ~**-horse** *n fig* fissazione *f*

hockey /'hɒkɪ/ *n* hockey *m*

hoe /həʊ/ *n* zappa *f*

hog /hɒg/ *n* maiale *m* ● *vt* (*pt/pp* hogged) □ monopolizzare

hoist /hɔɪst/ *n* montacarichi *m inv*; (□: *push*) spinta *f* in su ● *vt* sollevare; innalzare (flag); levare (anchor)

hold[1] /həʊld/ *n* (Aeron, Naut) stiva *f*

hold[2] *n* presa *f*; (*fig: influence*) ascendente *m*; **get ~ of** trovare; procurarsi (information) ● *v* (*pt/pp* held) ● *vt* tenere; (*container:*) contenere; essere titolare di (licence, passport);

trattenere (breath, suspect); mantenere vivo (interest); (civil servant etc:) occupare (position); (retain) mantenere; ~ **sb's hand** tenere qcno per mano; ~ **one's tongue** tenere la bocca chiusa; ~ **sb responsible** considerare qcno responsabile. ~ **that** (believe) ritenere che ● vi tenere; (weather, luck:) durare; (offer:) essere valido; (Teleph) restare in linea; **I don't ~ with the idea that...** 🗌 non sono d'accordo sul fatto che... 🗌 ~ **back** vt rallentare ● vi esitare. 🗌 ~ **down** vt tenere a bada (sb). 🗌 ~ **on** vi (wait) attendere; (Teleph) restare in linea. 🗌 ~ **on to** vt aggrapparsi a; (keep) tenersi. 🗌 ~ **out** vt porgere (hand); fig offrire (possibility) ● vi (resist) resistere. 🗌 ~ **up** vt tenere su; (delay) rallentare; (rob) assalire; ~ **one's head up** fig tenere la testa alta

'hold: ~**all** n borsone m. ~**er** n titolare mf; (of record) detentore, -trice mf; (container) astuccio m. ~**-up** n ritardo m; (attack) rapina f a mano armata

hole /həʊl/ n buco m

holiday /'hɒlɪdeɪ/ n vacanza f; (public) giorno m festivo; (day off) giorno m di ferie; **go on** ~ andare in vacanza ● vi andare in vacanza. ~**-maker** n vacanziere mf

holiness /'həʊlɪnɪs/ n santità f; **Your H~** Sua Santità

Holland /'hɒlənd/ n Olanda f

hollow /'hɒləʊ/ adj cavo; (promise) a vuoto; (voice) assente; (cheeks) infossato ● n cavità f inv; (in ground) affossamento m

holly /'hɒlɪ/ n agrifoglio m

holocaust /'hɒləkɔːst/ n olocausto m

holster /'həʊlstə(r)/ n fondina f

holy /'həʊlɪ/ adj (-ier, -est) santo; (water) benedetto. **H~ Ghost** or **Spirit** n Spirito m Santo. **H~ Scriptures** npl sacre scritture fpl. **H~ Week** n settimana f santa

homage /'hɒmɪdʒ/ n omaggio m; **pay ~ to** rendere omaggio a

home /həʊm/ n casa f; (for children) istituto m; (for old people) casa f di riposo; (native land) patria f ● adv **at ~** a casa; (football) in casa; **feel at ~** sentirsi a casa propria; **come/go** venire/andare a casa; **drive a nail ~** piantare un chiodo a fondo ● adj domestico; (movie, video) casalingo; (team) ospitante; (Pol) nazionale

home: ~ **ad'dress** n indirizzo m di casa. ~**land** n patria f; ~**land se'curity** n sicurezza f delle frontiere. ~**less** adj senza tetto

homely /'həʊmlɪ/ adj (-ier, -iest) semplice; (atmosphere) familiare; (Am: ugly) bruttino

home: ~**'made** adj fatto in casa. **H~ Office** n Br ministero m degli interni. ~**sick** adj **be** ~**sick** avere nostalgia (for di). ~ **'town** n città f inv natia. ~**work** n (Sch) compiti mpl

homicide /'hɒmɪsaɪd/ n (crime) omicidio m

homoeopath|ic /həʊmɪəʊ'pæθɪk/ adj omeopatico. ~**y** n omeopatia f

homogeneous /hɒmə'dʒiːnɪəs/ adj omogeneo

homo'sexual adj & n omosessuale f

honest /'ɒnɪst/ adj onesto; (frank) sincero. ~**ly** adv onestamente; (frankly) sinceramente; ~**ly!** ma insomma!. ~**y** n onestà f; (frankness) sincerità f

honey /'hʌnɪ/ n miele m; (🗌: darling) tesoro m

honey: ~**comb** n favo m. ~**moon** n luna f di miele. ~**suckle** n caprifoglio m

honorary /'ɒnərərɪ/ adj onorario

honour /'ɒnə(r)/ n onore m ● vt onorare. ~**able** adj onorevole. ~**ably** adv con onore. ~**s degree** n ≈ diploma m di laurea

hood /hʊd/ n cappuccio m; (of pram)

tettuccio *m*; (*over cooker*) cappa *f*; Am (*Auto*) cofano *m*

hoodlum /ˈhuːdləm/ *n* teppista *m*

'hoodwink *vt* ⓣ infinocchiare

hoof /huːf/ *n* (*pl* ~s *or* hooves) zoccolo *m*

hook /hʊk/ *n* gancio *m*; (*for fishing*) amo *m*; off the ~ (*Teleph*) staccato; *fig* fuori pericolo ● *vt* agganciare ● *vi* agganciarsi

hook|ed /hʊkt/ *adj* (nose) adunco ~ed on (ⓣ: *drugs*) dedito a; be ~ed on skiing essere un fanatico dello sci. ~er *n* Am ⊠ battona *f*

hookey /ˈhʊkɪ/ *n* play ~ Am ⓣ marinare la scuola

hooligan /ˈhuːlɪɡən/ *n* teppista *mf*. ~ism *n* teppismo *m*

hoop /huːp/ *n* cerchio *m*

hooray /hʊˈreɪ/ *int* & *n* = hurrah

hoot /huːt/ *n* colpo *m* di clacson; (*of siren*) ululato *m*; (*of owl*) grido *m* ● *vi* (owl:) gridare; (car:) clacsonare; (siren:) ululare; (*jeer*) fischiare. ~er *n* (*of factory*) sirena *f*; (*Auto*) clacson *m inv*

hoover® /ˈhuːvə(r)/ *n* aspirapolvere *m inv* ● *vt* passare l'aspirapolvere su (carpet); passare l'aspirapolvere in (room)

hop /hɒp/ *n* saltello *m* ● *vi* (*pt/pp* hopped) saltellare; ~ it! ⓣ tela!. □ ~ in *vi* ⓣ saltar su

hope /həʊp/ *n* speranza *f* ● *vi* sperare (for in); I ~ so/not spero di sì/no ● *vt* ~ that sperare che

hope|ful /ˈhəʊpfl/ *adj* pieno di speranza; (*promising*) promettente; be ~ful that avere buone speranze che. ~fully *adv* con speranza; (it is hoped) se tutto va bene. ~less *adj* senza speranze; (useless) impossibile; (incompetent) incapace. ~lessly *adv* disperatamente; (inefficient, lost) completamente. ~lessness *n* disperazione *f*

horde /hɔːd/ *n* orda *f*

horizon /həˈraɪzn/ *n* orizzonte *m*

horizontal /hɒrɪˈzɒntl/ *adj* orizzontale

hormone /ˈhɔːməʊn/ *n* ormone *m*

horn /hɔːn/ *n* corno *m*; (*Auto*) clacson *m inv*

horoscope /ˈhɒrəskəʊp/ *n* oroscopo *m*

horribl|e /ˈhɒrɪbl/ *adj* orribile. ~y *adv* spaventosamente

horrid /ˈhɒrɪd/ *adj* orrendo

horrific /həˈrɪfɪk/ *adj* raccapricciante; (accident, prices, story) terrificante

horrify /ˈhɒrɪfaɪ/ *vt* (*pt/pp* -ied) far inorridire; I was horrified ero sconvolto. ~ing *adj* terrificante

horror /ˈhɒrə(r)/ *n* orrore *m*. ~ film *n* film *m* dell'orrore

horse /hɔːs/ *n* cavallo *m*.

horse: ~back *n* on ~back a cavallo. ~power *n* cavallo *m* [vapore]. ~-racing *n* corse *fpl* di cavalli. ~shoe *n* ferro *m* di cavallo

horti'cultural /hɔːtɪ-/ *adj* di orticoltura

'horticulture *n* orticoltura *f*

hose /həʊz/ *n* (pipe) manichetta *f* ● **hose down** *vt* lavare con la manichetta

hospice /ˈhɒspɪs/ *n* (*for the terminally ill*) ospedale *m* per i malati in fase terminale

hospitabl|e /hɒˈspɪtəbl/ *adj* ospitale. ~y *adv* con ospitalità

hospital /ˈhɒspɪtl/ *n* ospedale *m*

hospitality /hɒspɪˈtælətɪ/ *n* ospitalità *f*

host¹ /həʊst/ *n* a ~ of una moltitudine di

host² *n* ospite *m*

host³ *n* (*Relig*) ostia *f*

hostage /ˈhɒstɪdʒ/ *n* ostaggio *m*; hold sb ~ tenere qcno in ostaggio

hostel /ˈhɒstl/ *n* ostello *m*

hostess /ˈhəʊstɪs/ *n* padrona *f* di

casa; (Aeron) hostess f inv

hostile /'hɒstaɪl/ adj ostile

hostilit|y /hɒ'stɪlətɪ/ n ostilità f; ~ies pl ostilità fpl

hot /hɒt/ adj (hotter, hottest) caldo; (spicy) piccante; **I am** or **feel** ~ ho caldo; **it is** ~ fa caldo

'hotbed n fig focolaio m

hotchpotch /'hɒtʃpɒtʃ/ n miscuglio m

'hot-dog n hot dog m inv

hotel /həʊ'tel/ n albergo m. ~ier n albergatore, -trice mf

hot: ~**house** n serra f. ~**plate** n piastra f riscaldante o~'**water bottle** n borsa f dell'acqua calda

hound /haʊnd/ n cane m da caccia o vt fig perseguire

hour /'aʊə(r)/ n ora f. ~**ly** adj ad ogni ora; (pay, rate) a ora o adv ogni ora

house[1] /haʊs/: ~**boat** n casa f galleggiante. ~**breaking** n furto m con scasso. ~**hold** n casa f, famiglia f. ~**holder** n capo m di famiglia. ~**keeper** n governante f di casa. ~**keeping** n governo m della casa; (money) soldi mpl per le spese di casa. ~**plant** n pianta f da appartamento. ~**trained** adj che non sporca in casa. ~**warming party** n festa f di inaugurazione della nuova casa. ~**wife** n casalinga f. ~**work** n lavoro m domestico

house[1] /haʊs/ n casa f; (Pol) camera f; (Theat) sala f; **at my** ~ a casa mia, da me

house[2] /haʊz/ vt alloggiare (person)

housing /'haʊzɪŋ/ n alloggio m. ~ **estate** n zona f residenziale

hovel /'hɒvl/ n tugurio m

hover /'hɒvə(r)/ vi librarsi; (linger) indugiare. ~**craft** n hovercraft m inv

how /haʊ/ adv come; ~ **are you?** come stai?; ~ **about a coffee/ going on holiday?** che ne diresti di un caffè/di andare in vacanza?; ~

do you do? molto lieto!; ~ **old are you?** quanti anni hai?; ~ **long** quanto tempo; ~ **many** quanti; ~ **much** quanto; ~ **often** ogni quanto; **and** ~**!** eccome!; ~ **odd!** che strano!

how'ever adv (nevertheless) comunque; ~ **small** per quanto piccolo

howl /haʊl/ n ululato m o vi ululare; (cry, with laughter) singhiozzare. ~**er** n 🔲 strafalcione m

HP n abbr hire purchase; n abbr (horse power) C.V.

hub /hʌb/ n mozzo m; fig centro m

'hub-cap n coprimozzo m

huddle /'hʌdl/ vi ~ **together** rannicchiarsi

hue[1] /hju:/ n colore m

hue[2] n ~ **and cry** clamore m

huff /hʌf/ n **be in/go into a** ~ fare il broncio

hug /hʌɡ/ n abbraccio m o vt (pt/pp hugged) abbracciare; (keep close to) tenersi vicino a

huge /hju:dʒ/ adj enorme

hull /hʌl/ n (Naut) scafo m

hullo /hə'ləʊ/ int = hallo

hum /hʌm/ n ronzio m o v (pt/pp hummed) v cant icchiare o vi (motor:) ronzare; fig fervere (di attività); ~ **and haw** esitare

human /'hju:mən/ adj umano o n essere m umano. ~ '**being** n essere m umano

humane /hju:'meɪn/ adj umano

humanitarian /hju:mænɪ'teərɪən/ adj & n umanitario, -a mf

humanit|y /hju:'mænətɪ/ n umanità f. ~**ies** pl (Univ) dottrine fpl umanistiche

humbl|e /'hʌmbl/ adj umile o vt umiliare

'humdrum adj noioso

humid /'hju:mɪd/ adj umido. ~**ifier** n umidificatore m. ~**ity** /-'mɪdətɪ/ n umidità f

humiliat|e /hjuːˈmɪlɪeɪt/ vt umiliare. **~ion** n umiliazione f

humility /hjuːˈmɪlɪtɪ/ n umiltà f

humorous /ˈhjuːmərəs/ adj umoristico. **~ly** adv con spirito

humour /ˈhjuːmə(r)/ n umorismo m; (mood) umore m; **have a sense of ~** avere il senso dell'umorismo • vt compiacere

hump /hʌmp/ n protuberanza f; (of camel, hunchback) gobba f

hunch /hʌntʃ/ n (idea) intuizione f
'hunch|back n gobbo, -a mf. **~ed** adj **~ed up** incurvato

hundred /ˈhʌndrəd/ adj **one/a ~** cento • n cento m; **~s of** centinaia di. **~th** adj centesimo • n centesimo m. **~weight** n cinquanta chili m

hung /hʌŋ/ ▷HANG

Hungarian /hʌŋˈɡeərɪən/ n & adj ungherese mf; (language) ungherese m

Hungary /ˈhʌŋɡərɪ/ n Ungheria f

hunger /ˈhʌŋɡə(r)/ n fame f. **~-strike** n sciopero m della fame m

hungr|y /ˈhʌŋɡrɪ/ adj (-ier, -iest) affamato; **be ~y** aver fame. **~ily** adv con appetito

hunk /hʌŋk/ n (grosso) pezzo m

hunt /hʌnt/ n caccia f • vt andare a caccia di (animal); dare la caccia a (criminal) • vi andare a caccia; **~ for** cercare. **~er** n cacciatore m. **~ing** n caccia f

hurl /hɜːl/ vt scagliare

hurrah /hʊˈrɑː/, **hurray** /hʊˈreɪ/ int urrà! • n urrà m

hurricane /ˈhʌrɪkən/ n uragano m

hurried /ˈhʌrɪd/ adj affrettato; (job) fatto in fretta. **~ly** adv in fretta

hurry /ˈhʌrɪ/ n fretta f; **be in a ~** aver fretta • vi (pt/pp **-ied**) affrettarsi. □ **~ up** vi sbrigarsi • vt fare sbrigare (person); accelerare (things)

hurt /hɜːt/ vt (pt/pp **hurt**) far male a; (offend) ferire • vi far male; **my leg ~s** mi fa male la gamba.

~ful adj fig offensivo

hurtle /ˈhɜːtl/ vi **~ along** andare a tutta velocità

husband /ˈhʌzbənd/ n marito m

hush /hʌʃ/ n silenzio m • **hush up** mettere a tacere. **~ed** adj (voice) sommesso. **~-'hush** adj ⊞ segretissimo

husky /ˈhʌskɪ/ adj (-ier, -iest) (voice) rauco

hustle /ˈhʌsl/ vt affrettare • n attività f incessante; **~ and bustle** trambusto m

hut /hʌt/ n capanna f

hybrid /ˈhaɪbrɪd/ adj ibrido • n ibrido m

hydrant /ˈhaɪdrənt/ n [fire] **~** idrante m

hydraulic /haɪˈdrɔːlɪk/ adj idraulico

hydroe'lectric /haɪdrəʊ-/ adj idroelettrico

hydrofoil /ˈhaɪdrə-/ n aliscafo m

hydrogen /ˈhaɪdrədʒən/ n idrogeno m

hyena /haɪˈiːnə/ n iena f

hygien|e /ˈhaɪdʒiːn/ n igiene f. **~ic** adj igienico

hymn /hɪm/ n inno m. **~-book** n libro m dei canti

hypermarket /ˈhaɪpəmɑːkɪt/ n ipermercato m

hyphen /ˈhaɪfn/ n lineetta f. **~ate** vt unire con lineetta

hypno|sis /hɪpˈnəʊsɪs/ n ipnosi f. **~tic** adj ipnotico

hypno|tism /ˈhɪpnətɪzm/ n ipnotismo m. **~tist** n ipnotizzatore, -trice mf. **~tize** vt ipnotizzare

hypochondriac /haɪpə-ˈkɒndrɪæk/ adj ipocondriaco • n ipocondriaco, -a mf

hypocrisy /hɪˈpɒkrəsɪ/ n ipocrisia f

hypocrit|e /ˈhɪpəkrɪt/ n ipocrita mf. **~ical** adj ipocrita

hypodermic /haɪpəˈdɜːmɪk/ adj & n **~ [syringe]** siringa f ipodermica

hypothe|sis /haɪˈpɒθəsɪs/ n ipotesi f inv. ~**tical** adj ipotetico. ~**tically** adv in teoria; (speak) per ipotesi

hyster|ia /hɪˈstɪərɪə/ n isterismo m. ~**ical** adj isterico. ~**ically** adv istericamente; ~**ically funny** da morir dal ridere. ~**ics** npl attacco m isterico

I /aɪ/ pron io; **I'm tired** sono stanco; **he's going, but I'm not** lui va, ma io no

ice /aɪs/ n ghiaccio m • vt glassare (cake). □ ~ **over/up** vi ghiacciarsi

ice: ~**axe** n piccozza f per il ghiaccio. ~**berg** /-bɜːg/ n iceberg m inv. ~**box** n Am frigorifero m. ~'-**cream** n gelato m. ~'-**cube** n cubetto m di ghiaccio

Iceland /ˈaɪsland/ n Islanda f. ~**er** n islandese mf; ~**ic** /-ˈlændɪk/ adj & n islandese m

ice: ~**lolly** n ghiacciolo m. ~ **rink** n pista f di pattinaggio. ~ **skater** pattinatore, -trice mf sul ghiaccio. ~ **skating** pattinaggio m su ghiaccio

icicle /ˈaɪsɪkl/ n ghiacciolo m

icing /ˈaɪsɪŋ/ n glassa f. ~ **sugar** n zucchero m a velo

icon /ˈaɪkɒn/ n icona f

ic|y /ˈaɪsɪ/ adj (-**ier**, -**iest**) ghiacciato; fig gelido. ~**ily** adv gelidamente

idea /aɪˈdɪə/ n idea f; **I've no** ~! non ne ho idea!

ideal /aɪˈdɪəl/ adj ideale • n ideale m. ~**ism** n idealismo m. ~**ist** n idealista mf. ~**istic** adj idealistico. ~**ize** vt idealizzare. ~**ly** adv idealmente

identical /aɪˈdentɪkl/ adj identico

identi|fication /aɪdentɪfɪˈkeɪʃn/ n

identificazione f; (proof of identity) documento m di riconoscimento. ~**fy** vt (pt/pp -**ied**) identificare

identity /aɪˈdentətɪ/ n identità f inv. ~ **card** n carta f d'identità. ~ **theft** n furto m d'identità

ideolog|ical /aɪdɪəˈlɒdʒɪkl/ adj ideologico. ~**y** n ideologia f

idiom /ˈɪdɪəm/ n idioma m. ~**atic** adj idiomatico

idiot /ˈɪdɪət/ n idiota mf. ~**ic** adj idiota

idl|e /ˈaɪd(ə)l/ adj (lazy) pigro, ozioso; (empty) vano; (machine) fermo • vi oziare; (engine): girare a vuoto. ~**eness** n ozio m. ~**y** adv oziosamente

idol /ˈaɪdl/ n idolo m. ~**ize** vt idolatrare

idyllic /ɪˈdɪlɪk/ adj idillico

i.e. abbr (id est) cioè

if /ɪf/ conj se; **as if** come se

ignite /ɪɡˈnaɪt/ vt dar fuoco a • vi prender fuoco

ignition /ɪɡˈnɪʃn/ n (Auto) accensione f. ~ **key** n chiave f d'accensione

ignoramus /ɪɡnəˈreɪməs/ n ignorante mf

ignoran|ce /ˈɪɡnərəns/ n ignoranza f. ~**t** adj (lacking knowledge) ignaro; (rude) ignorante

ignore /ɪɡˈnɔː(r)/ vt ignorare

ill /ɪl/ adj ammalato; **feel** ~ **at ease** sentirsi a disagio • adv male m. ~**-advised** adj avventato. ~**-bred** adj maleducato

illegal /ɪˈliːɡl/ adj illegale

illegibl|e /ɪˈledʒɪbl/ adj illeggibile

illegitima|cy /ɪlɪˈdʒɪtɪməsɪ/ n illegittimità f. ~**te** adj illegittimo

illitera|cy /ɪˈlɪtərəsɪ/ n analfabetismo m. ~**te** adj & n analfabeta mf

illness /ˈɪlnɪs/ n malattia f

illogical /ɪˈlɒdʒɪkl/ adj illogico

h
i

illuminat|e /ɪˈluːmɪneɪt/ vt illuminare. ~ing adj chiarificatore. ~ion n illuminazione f

illusion /ɪˈluːʒn/ n illusione f; be under the ~ that avere l'illusione che

illustrat|e /ˈɪləstreɪt/ vt illustrare. ~ion n illustrazione f. ~or n illustratore, -trice mf

illustrious /ɪˈlʌstrɪəs/ adj illustre

ill 'will n malanimo m

image /ˈɪmɪdʒ/ n immagine f; (exact likeness) ritratto m

imagin|able /ɪˈmædʒɪnəbl/ adj immaginabile. ~ary adj immaginario

imaginat|ion /ɪmædʒɪˈneɪʃn/ n immaginazione f, fantasia f; ~ion è solo una tua idea. ~ive adj fantasioso. ~ively adv con fantasia or immaginazione

imagine /ɪˈmædʒɪn/ vt immaginare; (wrongly) inventare

im'balance n squilibrio m

imbecile /ˈɪmbəsiːl/ n imbecille mf

imitat|e /ˈɪmɪteɪt/ vt imitare. ~ion n imitazione f. ~or n imitatore, -trice mf

immaculate /ɪˈmækjʊlət/ adj immacolato. ~ly adv immacolatamente

imma'ture adj immaturo

immediate /ɪˈmiːdɪət/ adj immediato; (relative) stretto; in the ~ vicinity nelle immediate vicinanze. ~ly adv immediatamente; ~ly next to subito accanto a ● conj [non] appena

immense /ɪˈmens/ adj immenso

immers|e /ɪˈmɜːs/ vt immergere; be ~ed in fig essere immerso in. ~ion n immersione f. ~ion heater n scaldabagno m elettrico

immigrant /ˈɪmɪɡrənt/ n immigrante mf

imminent /ˈɪmɪnənt/ adj imminente

immobil|e /ɪˈməʊbaɪl/ adj immo-

bile. ~ize vt immobilizzare

immoderate /ɪˈmɒdərət/ adj smodato

immoral /ɪˈmɒrəl/ adj immorale. ~ity n immoralità f

immortal /ɪˈmɔːtl/ adj immortale. ~ity n immortalità f. ~ize vt immortalare

immune /ɪˈmjuːn/ adj immune (to/from da). ~ system n sistema m immunitario

immunity /ɪˈmjuːnəti/ n immunità f

immuniz|e /ˈɪmjʊnaɪz/ vt immunizzare

imp /ɪmp/ n diavoletto m

impact /ˈɪmpækt/ n impatto m

impair /ɪmˈpeə(r)/ vt danneggiare

impale /ɪmˈpeɪl/ vt impalare

impart /ɪmˈpɑːt/ vt impartire

im'parti|al adj imparziale. ~'ality n imparzialità f

im'passable adj impraticabile

im'passive adj impassibile

im'patien|ce n impazienza f. ~t adj impaziente. ~tly adv impazientemente

impeccabl|e /ɪmˈpekəbl/ adj impeccabile. ~y adv in modo impeccabile

impede /ɪmˈpiːd/ vt impedire

impediment /ɪmˈpedɪmənt/ n impedimento m; (in speech) difetto m

impending /ɪmˈpendɪŋ/ adj imminente

impenetrable /ɪmˈpenɪtrəbl/ adj impenetrabile

imperative /ɪmˈperətɪv/ adj imperativo ● n (Gram) imperativo m

imper'ceptible adj impercettibile

im'perfect adj imperfetto; (faulty) difettoso ● n (Gram) imperfetto m. ~ion n imperfezione f

imperial /ɪmˈpɪərɪəl/ adj imperiale. ~ism n imperialismo m. ~ist n imperialista mf

im'personal *adj* impersonale

impersonat|e /ɪm'pɜːsəneɪt/ *vt* impersonare. **~or** *n* imitatore, -trice *mf*

impertinen|ce /ɪm'pɜːtɪnəns/ *n* impertinenza *f*. **~t** *adj* impertinente

impervious /ɪm'pɜːvɪəs/ *adj* ~ **to** *fig* indifferente a

impetuous /ɪm'petjʊəs/ *adj* impetuoso. **~ly** *adv* impetuosamente

impetus /'ɪmpɪtəs/ *n* impeto *m*

implacable /ɪm'plækəbl/ *adj* implacabile

im'plant[1] *vt* trapiantare; *fig* inculcare

'implant[2] *n* trapianto *m*

implement[1] /'ɪmplɪmənt/ *n* attrezzo *m*

implement[2] /'ɪmplɪment/ *vt* mettere in atto. **~ation** /-'eɪʃn/ *n* attuazione *f*

implicat|e /'ɪmplɪkeɪt/ *vt* implicare. **~ion** *n* implicazione *f*; **by ~ion** implicitamente

implicit /ɪm'plɪsɪt/ *adj* implicito; (*absolute*) assoluto

implore /ɪm'plɔː(r)/ *vt* implorare

imply /ɪm'plaɪ/ *vt* (*pt/pp* **-ied**) implicare; **what are you ~ing?** che cosa vorresti insinuare?

impo'lite *adj* sgarbato

import[1] /'ɪmpɔːt/ *n* (*Comm*) importazione *f*

import[2] /ɪm'pɔːt/ *vt* importare

importan|ce /ɪm'pɔːtəns/ *n* importanza *f*. **~t** *adj* importante

importer /ɪm'pɔːtə(r)/ *n* importatore, -trice *mf*

impos|e /ɪm'pəʊz/ *vt* imporre (**on** a) ● *vi* imporsi; **~e on** abusare di. **~ing** *adj* imponente. **~ition** *n* imposizione *f*

impossi'bility *n* impossibilità *f*

im'possibl|e *adj* impossibile

impostor /ɪm'pɒstə(r)/ *n* impostore, -trice *mf*

impoten|ce /'ɪmpətəns/ *n* impotenza *f*. **~t** *adj* impotente

impound /ɪm'paʊnd/ *vt* confiscare

impoverished /ɪm'pɒvərɪʃt/ *adj* impoverito

im'practical *adj* non pratico

impregnable /ɪm'pregnəbl/ *adj* imprendibile

impregnate /'ɪmpregneɪt/ *vt* impregnare (**with** di); (*Biol*) fecondare

im'press *vt* imprimere; *fig* colpire (*positivamente*); **~ sth on sb** fare capire qcsa a qcno

impression /ɪm'preʃn/ *n* impressione *f*; (*imitation*) imitazione *f*. **~able** *adj* (child, mind) influenzabile. **~ism** *n* impressionismo *m*. **~ist** *n* imitatore, -trice *mf*; (*artist*) impressionista *mf*

impressive /ɪm'presɪv/ *adj* imponente

'imprint[1] *n* impressione *f*

im'print[2] *vt* imprimere; **~ed on my mind** impresso nella mia memoria

im'prison *vt* incarcerare. **~ment** *n* reclusione *f*

im'probable *adj* improbabile

impromptu /ɪm'promptjuː/ *adj* improvvisato

im'proper *adj* (use) improprio; (behaviour) scorretto. **~ly** *adv* scorrettamente

improve /ɪm'pruːv/ *vt/i* migliorare. **improve on** *vt* perfezionare. **~ment** *n* miglioramento *m*

improvis|e /'ɪmprəvaɪz/ *vt/i* improvvisare

impuden|ce /'ɪmpjʊdəns/ *n* sfrontatezza *f*. **~t** *adj* sfrontato

impuls|e /'ɪmpʌls/ *n* impulso *m*; **on [an] ~e** impulsivamente. **~ive** *adj* impulsivo

im'pur|e *adj* impuro. **~ity** *n* impurità *f inv*; **~ities** *pl* impurità *fpl*

in /ɪn/ *prep* in; (*with names of towns*) a;

in the garden in giardino; **in the street** in *or* per strada; **in bed/hospital** a letto/all'ospedale; **in the world** nel mondo; **in the rain** sotto la pioggia; **in the sun** al sole; **in this heat** con questo caldo; **in summer/winter** in estate/inverno; **in 1995** nel 1995; **in the evening** la sera; **he's arriving in two hours time** arriva fra due ore; **deaf in one ear** sordo da un orecchio; **in the army** nell'esercito; **in English/Italian** in inglese/italiano; **in ink/pencil** a penna/matita; **in red** (dressed, circled) di rosso; **the man in the raincoat** l'uomo con l'impermeabile; **in a soft/loud voice** a voce bassa/alta; **one in ten people** una persona su dieci; **in doing this, he...** nel far questo,...; **in itself** in sé; in that in quanto ● *adv* (*at home*) a casa; (*indoors*) dentro; **he's not in yet** non è ancora arrivato; **in there/here** li/qui dentro; **ten in all** dieci in tutto; **day in, day out** giorno dopo giorno; **have it in for sb** 🄣 avercela con qcno; **send him in** in fallo entrare; **come in** entrare; **bring in the washing** portare dentro i panni ● *adj* (🄣: *in fashion*) di moda ●*n* **the ins and outs** i dettagli

ina'bility *n* incapacità *f*

inac'cessible *adj* inaccessibile

in'accura|cy *n* inesattezza *f*. ~**te** *adj* inesatto

in'ac|tive *adj* inattivo. ~**'tivity** *n* inattività *f*

in'adequate *adj* inadeguato. ~**ly** *adv* inadeguatamente

inadvertently /ɪnəd'vɜːtəntlɪ/ *adv* inavvertitamente

inad'visable *adj* sconsigliabile

inane /ɪ'neɪn/ *adj* stupido

in'animate *adj* esanime

inap'propriate *adj* inadatto

inar'ticulate *adj* inarticolato

inat'tentive *adj* disattento

in'audib|le *adj* impercettibile

inaugurat|e /ɪ'nɔːgjʊreɪt/ *vt* inaugurare. ~**ion** *n* inaugurazione *f*

inborn /'ɪnbɔːn/ *adj* innato

inbred /ɪn'bred/ *adj* congenito

incalculable /ɪn'kælkjʊləbl/ *adj* incalcolabile

in'capable *adj* incapace

incapacitate /ɪnkə'pæsɪteɪt/ *vt* rendere incapace

incarnat|e /ɪn'kɑːnat/ *adj* **the devil ~e** il diavolo in carne e ossa

incendiary /ɪn'sendɪərɪ/ *adj* incendiario

incense[1] /'ɪnsens/ *n* incenso *m*

incense[2] /ɪn'sens/ *vt* esasperare

incentive /ɪn'sentɪv/ *n* incentivo *m*

incessant /ɪn'sesənt/ *adj* incessante

incest /'ɪnsest/ *n* incesto *m*

inch /ɪntʃ/ *n* pollice *m* (= 2.54 cm) ● *vi* ~ **forward** avanzare gradatamente

inciden|ce /'ɪnsɪdəns/ *n* incidenza *f*. ~**t** *n* incidente *m*

incidental /ɪnsɪ'dentl/ *adj* incidentale; ~ **expenses** spese *fpl* accessorie. ~**ly** *adv* incidentalmente; (*by the way*) a proposito

incinerat|e /ɪn'sɪnəreɪt/ *vt* incenerire. ~**or** *n* inceneritore *m*

incision /ɪn'sɪʒn/ *n* incisione *f*

incite /ɪn'saɪt/ *vt* incitare. ~**ment** *n* incitamento *m*

inclination /ɪnklɪ'neɪʃn/ *n* inclinazione *f*

incline[1] /ɪn'klaɪn/ *vt* inclinare; **be ~d to do sth** essere propenso a fare qcsa

incline[2] /'ɪnklaɪn/ *n* pendio *m*

inclu|de /ɪn'kluːd/ *vt* includere. ~**ding** *prep* incluso. ~**sion** *n* inclusione *f*

inclusive /ɪn'kluːsɪv/ *adj* incluso; ~ **of** comprendente; **be ~ of** comprendere ● *adv* incluso

incognito /ɪnkɒɡ'niːtəʊ/ *adv* incognito

inco'herent *adj* incoerente; (*be-*

cause drunk etc) incomprensibile

income /'ɪnkʌm/ n reddito m. ~ tax n imposta f sul reddito

'incoming adj in arrivo. ~ tide n marea f montante

in'comparable adj incomparabile

incom'patible adj incompatibile

in'competen|ce n incompetenza f. ~t adj incompetente

incom'plete adj incompleto

incompre'hensible adj incomprensibile

incon'ceivable adj inconcepibile

incon'clusive adj inconcludente

incongruous /ɪn'kʊŋgrʊəs/ adj contrastante

incon'siderate adj trascurabile

incon'sistency n incoerenza f

incon'sistent adj incoerente; be ~ with non essere coerente con. ~ly adv in modo incoerente

incon'spicuous adj non appariscente. ~ly adv modestamente

incon'venien|ce n scomodità f; (drawback) inconveniente m; put sb to ~ce dare disturbo a qcno. ~t adj scomodo; (time, place) inopportuno. ~tly adv in modo inopportuno

incorporate /ɪn'kɔːpəreɪt/ vt incorporare; (contain) comprendere

incor'rect adj incorretto. ~ly adv scorrettamente

increase¹ /'ɪnkriːs/ n aumento m; on the ~ in aumento

increas|e² /ɪn'kriːs/ vt/i aumentare. ~ing adj (impatience etc) crescente; (numbers) in aumento. ~ingly adv sempre più

in'credible adj incredibile

incredulous /ɪn'kredjʊləs/ adj incredulo

incriminate /ɪn'krɪmɪneɪt/ vt (Jur) incriminare

incubat|e /'ɪŋkjʊbeɪt/ vt incubare. ~ion n incubazione f. ~ion period n (Med) periodo m di incubazione.

~or n (for baby) incubatrice f

incur /ɪn'kɜː(r)/ vt (pt/pp incurred) incorrere; contrarre (debts)

in'curable adj incurabile

indebted /ɪn'detɪd/ adj obbligato (to verso)

in'decent adj indecente

inde'cision n indecisione f

inde'cisive adj indeciso. ~ness n indecisione f

indeed /ɪn'diːd/ adv (in fact) difatti; yes ~! sì, certamente!; ~ I am/do veramente!; very much ~ moltissimo; thank you very much ~ grazie infinite; ~? davvero?

inde'finable adj indefinibile

in'definite adj indefinito. ~ly adv indefinitamente; (postpone) a tempo indeterminato

indelible /ɪn'delɪbl/ adj indelebile

indemnity /ɪn'demnɪtɪ/ n indennità f inv

indent¹ /'ɪndent/ n (Typ) rientranza f dal margine

indent² /ɪn'dent/ vt (Typ) fare rientrare dal margine. ~ation n (notch) intaccatura f

inde'penden|ce n indipendenza f. ~t adj indipendente. ~tly adv indipendentemente

indescribable /ɪndɪ'skraɪbəbl/ adj indescrivibile

indestructible /ɪndɪ'strʌktəbl/ adj indistruttibile

indeterminate /ɪndɪ'tɜːmɪnət/ adj indeterminato

index /'ɪndeks/ n indice m

index: ~ finger n dito m indice. ~-linked adj (pension) legato al costo della vita

India /'ɪndɪə/ n India f. ~n adj indiano; (American) indiano [d'America] ● n indiano, -a mf; (American) indiano, -a mf [d'America]

indicat|e /'ɪndɪkeɪt/ vt indicare; (register) segnare ● vi (Auto) mettere la freccia. ~ion n indicazione f

indicative /ɪn'dɪkətɪv/ adj be ~ of essere indicativo di ●n (Gram) indicativo m

indicator /'ɪndɪkeɪtə(r)/ n (Auto) freccia f

indict /ɪn'daɪt/ vt accusare. ~ment n accusa f

in'differen|ce n indifferenza f. ~t adj indifferente; (not good) mediocre

indi'gestible adj indigesto. ~ion n indigestione f

indigna|nt /ɪn'dɪgnənt/ adj indignato. ~ntly adv con indignazione. ~tion n indignazione f

indi'rect adj indiretto. ~ly adv indirettamente

indi'screet adj indiscreto

indis'cretion n indiscrezione f

indiscriminate /ɪndɪ'skrɪmɪnət/ adj indiscriminato. ~ly adv senza distinzione

indi'spensable adj indispensabile

indis'posed /ɪndɪ'spəʊzd/ adj indisposto

indis'putable /ɪndɪ'spju:təbl/ adj indisputabile

indistinguishable /ɪndɪ'stɪŋgwɪʃəbl/ adj indistinguibile

individual /ɪndɪ'vɪdjʊəl/ adj individuale ●n individuo m. ~ity n individualità f

indoctrinate /ɪn'dɒktrɪneɪt/ vt indottrinare

indomitable /ɪn'dɒmɪtəbl/ adj indomito

indoor /'ɪndɔ:(r)/ adj interno; (shoes) per casa; (plant) da appartamento; (swimming pool etc) coperto. ~s adv dentro

induce /ɪn'dju:s/ vt indurre (to a); (produce) causare. ~ment n (incentive) incentivo m

indulge /ɪn'dʌldʒ/ vt soddisfare; viziare (child) ●vi ~ in concedersi. ~nce n lusso m; (leniency) indulgenza

f. ~nt adj indulgente

industrial /ɪn'dʌstrɪəl/ adj industriale; take ~ action scioperare. ~ist n industriale mf. ~ized adj industrializzato

industr|ious /ɪn'dʌstrɪəs/ adj industrioso. ~y n industria f; (zeal) operosità f

inebriated /ɪ'ni:brɪeɪtɪd/ adj ebbro

in'edible adj immangiabile

inef'fective adj inefficace

ineffectual /ɪnɪ'fektʃʊəl/ adj inutile; (person) inconcludente

inef'ficien|cy n inefficienza f. ~t adj inefficiente

in'eligible adj inadatto

inept /ɪ'nept/ adj inetto

ine'quality n ineguaglianza f

inert /ɪ'nɜ:t/ adj inerte. ~ia n inerzia f

inescapable /ɪnɪ'skeɪpəbl/ adj inevitabile

inevitabl|e /ɪn'evɪtəbl/ adj inevitabile. ~y adv inevitabilmente

ine'xact adj inesatto

inex'cusable adj imperdonabile

inex'pensive adj poco costoso

inex'perience n inesperienza f. ~d adj inesperto

inexplicable /ɪnɪk'splɪkəbl/ adj inesplicabile

in'fallible adj infallibile

infam|ous /'ɪnfəməs/ adj infame; (person) infamante. ~y n infamia f

infan|cy /'ɪnfənsɪ/ n infanzia f; in its ~cy fig agli inizi. ~t n bambino, -a mf piccolo, -a. ~tile adj infantile

infantry /'ɪnfəntrɪ/ n fanteria f

infatuat|ed /ɪn'fætʃʊeɪtɪd/ adj infatuato (with di). ~ion n infatuazione f

infect /ɪn'fekt/ vt infettare; become ~ed (wound:) infettarsi. ~ion adj infettivo

infer /ɪn'fɜ:(r)/ vt (pt/pp inferred) dedurre (from da); (imply) implicare.

~ence n deduzione f

inferior /ɪnˈfɪərɪə(r)/ adj inferiore; (goods) scadente; (in rank) subalterno ●n inferiore mf; (in rank) subalterno, -a mf

inferiority /ɪnfɪərɪˈɒrɪtɪ/ n inferiorità f. ~ **complex** n complesso m di inferiorità

in'fertile adj sterile. ~'tility n sterilità f

infest /ɪnˈfest/ vt be ~ed with essere infestato di

infi'delity n infedeltà f

infiltrate /ˈɪnfɪltreɪt/ vt infiltrare; (Pol) infiltrarsi ln

infinite /ˈɪnfɪnət/ adj infinito

infinitive /ɪnˈfɪnɪtɪv/ n (Gram) infinito m

infinity /ɪnˈfɪnətɪ/ n infinità f

infirm /ɪnˈfɜːm/ adj debole. ~ary n infermeria f. ~ity n debolezza f

inflame /ɪnˈfleɪm/ vt infiammare. ~d adj infiammato; become ~d infiammarsi

in'flammable adj infiammabile

inflammation /ɪnfləˈmeɪʃn/ n infiammazione f

inflate /ɪnˈfleɪt/ vt gonfiare. ~ion n inflazione f. ~ionary adj inflazionario

in'flexible adj inflessibile

inflict /ɪnˈflɪkt/ vt infliggere (on a)

influen|ce /ˈɪnflʊəns/ n influenza f ●vt influenzare. ~tial adj influente

influenza /ɪnflʊˈenzə/ n influenza f

influx /ˈɪnflʌks/ n affluenza f

inform /ɪnˈfɔːm/ vt informare; keep sb ~ed tenere qcno al corrente ●vi ~ against denunziare

in'for|mal adj informale; (agreement) ufficioso. ~mally adv in modo informale. ~'mality n informalità f inv

information /ɪnfəˈmeɪʃn/ n informazioni fpl; a piece of ~ un'informazione. ~ion highway n autostrada f telematica. ~ion

technology n informatica f. ~ive adj informativo; (film, book) istruttivo

informer /ɪnˈfɔːmə(r)/ n informatore, -trice mf; (Pol) delatore, -trice f

infra-'red /ɪnfrə-/ adj infrarosso

infringe /ɪnˈfrɪndʒ/ vt ~ on usurpare. ~ment n violazione f

infuriat|e /ɪnˈfjʊərɪeɪt/ vt infuriare. ~ing adj esasperante

ingenious /ɪnˈdʒiːnɪəs/ adj ingegnoso

ingenuity /ɪndʒɪˈnjuːətɪ/ n ingegnosità f

ingot /ˈɪŋgət/ n lingotto m

ingrained /ɪnˈgreɪnd/ adj (in person) radicato; (dirt) incrostato

ingratiate /ɪnˈgreɪʃɪeɪt/ vt ~ oneself with sb ingraziarsi qcno

in'gratitude n ingratitudine f

ingredient /ɪnˈgriːdɪənt/ n ingrediente m

ingrowing /ˈɪngrəʊɪŋ/ adj (nail) incarnito

inhabit /ɪnˈhæbɪt/ vt abitare. ~ant n abitante mf

inhale /ɪnˈheɪl/ vt aspirare, (Med) inalare ●vi inspirare; (when smoking) aspirare. ~r n (device) inalatore m

inherent /ɪnˈhɪərənt/ adj inerente

inherit /ɪnˈherɪt/ vt ereditare. ~ance n eredità f inv

inhibit /ɪnˈhɪbɪt/ vt inibire. ~ed adj inibito. ~ion n inibizione f

inho'spitable adj inospitale

initial /ɪˈnɪʃl/ adj iniziale ●n iniziale f ●vt (pt/pp initialled) siglare. ~ly adv all'inizio

initiat|e /ɪˈnɪʃɪeɪt/ vt iniziare. ~ion n iniziazione f

initiative /ɪˈnɪʃətɪv/ n iniziativa f

inject /ɪnˈdʒekt/ vt iniettare. ~ion n iniezione f

injur|e /ˈɪndʒə(r)/ vt ferire; (wrong) nuocere. ~y n ferita f; (wrong) torto m

in'justice *n* ingiustizia *f*; **do sb an ~** giudicare qcno in modo sbagliato

ink /ɪŋk/ *n* inchiostro *m*

inland /'ɪnlənd/ *adj* interno ● *adv* all'interno. **I~ Revenue** *n* fisco *m*

in-laws /'ɪnlɔːz/ *npl* 🄵 parenti *mpl* acquisiti

inlay /'ɪnleɪ/ *n* intarsio *m*

inlet /'ɪnlet/ *n* insenatura *f*; (*Techn*) entrata *f*

inmate /'ɪnmeɪt/ *n* (*of hospital*) degente *mf*; (*of prison*) carcerato, -a *mf*

inn /ɪn/ *n* locanda *f*

innate /ɪ'neɪt/ *adj* innato

inner /'ɪnə(r)/ *adj* interno. **~most** *adj* il più profondo. **~ tube** camera *f* d'aria

innocen|ce /'ɪnəsəns/ *n* innocenza *f*. **~t** *adj* innocente

innocuous /ɪ'nɒkjuəs/ *adj* innocuo

innovat|e /'ɪnəveɪt/ *vi* innovare. **~ion** *n* innovazione *f*. **~ive** *adj* innovativo. **~or** *n* innovatore, -trice *mf*

innuendo /ɪnjuː'endəʊ/ *n* (*pl* -es) insinuazione *f*

innumerable /ɪ'njuːmərəbl/ *adj* innumerevole

inoculat|e /ɪ'nɒkjʊleɪt/ *vt* vaccinare. **~ion** *n* vaccinazione *f*

inof'fensive *adj* inoffensivo

in'opportune *adj* inopportuno

input /'ɪnpʊt/ *n* input *m inv*, ingresso *m*

inquest /'ɪnkwest/ *n* inchiesta *f*

inquir|e /ɪn'kwaɪə(r)/ *vi* informarsi (**about** su); **~e into** far indagini su ● *vt* domandare. **~y** *n* domanda *f*; (*investigation*) inchiesta *f*

inquisitive /ɪn'kwɪzətɪv/ *adj* curioso

in'sane *adj* pazzo; *fig* insensato

in'sanity *n* pazzia *f*

insatiable /ɪn'seɪʃəbl/ *adj* insaziabile

inscri|be /ɪn'skraɪb/ *vt* iscrivere. **~ption** *n* iscrizione *f*

inscrutable /ɪn'skruːtəbl/ *adj* impenetrabile

insect /'ɪnsekt/ *n* insetto *m*. **~icide** *n* insetticida *m*

inse'cur|e *adj* malsicuro; (*fig*: person) insicuro. **~ity** *n* mancanza *f* di sicurezza

in'sensitive *adj* insensibile

in'separable *adj* inseparabile

insert¹ /'ɪnsɜːt/ *n* inserto *m*

insert² /ɪn'sɜːt/ *vt* inserire. **~ion** *n* inserzione *f*

inside /ɪn'saɪd/ *n* interno *m*. **~s** *npl* 🄵 pancia *f* ● *attrib* (*Auto*) **~ lane** *n* corsia *f* interna ● *adv* dentro; **~ out** a rovescio; (*thoroughly*) a fondo ● *prep* dentro; (*of time*) entro

insight /'ɪnsaɪt/ *n* intuito *m* (**into** per); **an ~ into** un quadro di

insig'nificant *adj* insignificante

insin'cer|e *adj* poco sincero. **~ity** *n* mancanza *f* di sincerità

insinuat|e /ɪn'sɪnjʊeɪt/ *vt* insinuare. **~ion** *n* insinuazione *f*

insipid /ɪn'sɪpɪd/ *adj* insipido

insist /ɪn'sɪst/ *vi* insistere (**on** per) ● *vt* **~ that** insistere che. **~ence** *n* insistenza *f*. **~ent** *adj* insistente

insolen|ce /'ɪnsələns/ *n* insolenza *f*. **~t** *adj* insolente

in'soluble *adj* insolubile

insomnia /ɪn'sɒmnɪə/ *n* insonnia *f*

inspect /ɪn'spekt/ *vt* ispezionare; controllare (ticket). **~ion** *n* ispezione *f*; (*of ticket*) controllo *m*. **~or** *n* ispettore, -trice *mf*; (*of tickets*) controllore *m*

inspiration /ɪnspə'reɪʃn/ *n* ispirazione *f*

inspire /ɪn'spaɪə(r)/ *vt* ispirare

insta'bility *n* instabilità *f*

install /ɪn'stɔːl/ *vt* installare. **~ation** *n* installazione *f*

instalment /ɪn'stɔːlmənt/ *n* (*Comm*) rata *f*; (*of serial*) puntata *f*; (*of publication*) fascicolo *m*

instance /'ɪnstəns/ n (case) caso m; (example) esempio m; **in the first ∼** in primo luogo; **for ∼** per esempio

instant /'ɪnstənt/ adj immediato; (Culin) espresso ● n istante m. **∼aneous** adj istantaneo

instead /ɪn'sted/ adv invece; **∼ of doing** anziché fare; **∼ of me** al mio posto; **∼ of going** invece di andare

instigat|e /'ɪnstɪgeɪt/ vt istigare. **∼ion** n istigazione f; **at his ∼ion** dietro suo suggerimento. **∼or** n istigatore, -trice mf

instinct /'ɪnstɪŋkt/ n istinto m. **∼ive** adj istintivo

institut|e /'ɪnstɪtjuːt/ n istituto m ● vt istituire (scheme); intentare (search); intentare (legal action). **∼ion** n istituzione f; (home for elderly) istituto m per anziani; (for mentally ill) istituto m per malati di mente

instruct /ɪn'strʌkt/ vt istruire; (order) ordinare. **∼ion** n istruzione f; **∼s** (orders) ordini mpl. **∼ive** adj istruttivo. **∼or** n istruttore, -trice mf

instrument /'ɪnstrʊmənt/ n strumento m. **∼al** adj strumentale; **be ∼al in** contribuire a. **∼alist** n strumentista mf

insu'bordi|nate adj insubordinato. **∼nation** n insubordinazione f

in'sufferable adj insopportabile

insuf'ficient adj insufficiente

insular /'ɪnsjʊlə(r)/ adj fig gretto

insulat|e /'ɪnsjʊleɪt/ vt isolare. **∼ing tape** n nastro m isolante. **∼ion** n isolamento m

insulin /'ɪnsjʊlɪn/ n insulina f

insult¹ /'ɪnsʌlt/ n insulto m

insult² /ɪn'sʌlt/ vt insultare

insur|ance /ɪn'ʃʊərəns/ n assicurazione f. **∼e** vt assicurare

intact /ɪn'tækt/ adj intatto

integral /'ɪntɪgrəl/ adj integrale

integrat|e /'ɪntɪgreɪt/ vt integrare ● vi integrarsi. **∼ion** n integrazione f

integrity /ɪn'tegrətɪ/ n integrità f

intellect /'ɪntəlekt/ n intelletto m. **∼ual** adj & n intellettuale mf

intelligen|ce /ɪn'telɪdʒəns/ n intelligenza f; (Mil) informazioni fpl. **∼t** adj intelligente

intelligible /ɪn'telɪdʒəbl/ adj intelligibile

intend /ɪn'tend/ vt destinare; (have in mind) aver intenzione di; **be ∼ed for** essere destinato a. **∼ed** adj (effect) voluto ● n my **∼ed** 🆒 il mio/la mia fidanzato, -a

intense /ɪn'tens/ adj intenso; (person) dai sentimenti intensi. **∼ly** adv intensamente; (very) estremamente

intensity /ɪn'tensətɪ/ n intensità f

intensive /ɪn'tensɪv/ adj intensivo. **∼ care** (for people in coma) rianimazione f; **∼ care [unit]** terapia f intensiva

intent /ɪn'tent/ adj intento; **∼ on** (absorbed in) preso da; **be ∼ on doing sth** essere intento a fare qcsa ● n intenzione f; **to all ∼s and purposes** a tutti gli effetti. **∼ly** adv attentamente

intention /ɪn'tenʃn/ n intenzione f. **∼al** adj intenzionale. **∼ally** adv intenzionalmente

inter'action n cooperazione f. **∼ve** adj interattivo

intercept /ɪntə'sept/ vt intercettare

'interchange n scambio m; (Auto) raccordo m [autostradale]

inter'changeable adj interscambiabile

'intercourse n (sexual) rapporti mpl [sessuali]

interest /'ɪntrəst/ n interesse m; **have an ∼ in** (Comm) essere cointeressato in; **be of ∼** essere interessante; **∼ rate** n tasso m di interesse ● vt interessare. **∼ed** adj interessato. **∼ing** adj interessante

interface /'ɪntəfeɪs/ n interfaccia f ● vt interfacciare ● vi interfacciarsi

io

interfere /ɪntə'fɪə(r)/ vi interferire; **~ with** interferire con. **~nce** n interferenza f

interior /ɪn'tɪərɪə(r)/ adj interiore ●n interno m. **~ designer** n arredatore, -trice mf

interlude /'ɪntəlu:d/ n intervallo m

intermediary /ɪntə'mi:dɪərɪ/ n intermediario, -a mf

interminable /ɪn'tɜ:mɪnəbl/ adj interminabile

intermittent /ɪntə'mɪtənt/ adj intermittente

intern /ɪn'tɜ:n/ vt internare

internal /ɪn'tɜ:nl/ adj interno. **I~ 'Revenue** (Am) n fisco m. **~ly** adv internamente; (deal with) all'interno

inter'national adj internazionale ●n (game) incontro m internazionale; (player) competitore, -trice mf in gare internazionali. **~ly** adv internazionalmente

Internet /'ɪntənet/ n Internet m

interpret /ɪn'tɜ:prɪt/ vt interpretare ●vi fare l'interprete. **~ation** n interpretazione f. **~er** n interprete mf

interrogate /ɪn'terəgeɪt/ vt interrogare. **~ion** n interrogazione f; (by police) interrogatorio m

interrogative /ɪntə'rɒgətɪv/ adj & n **~ [pronoun]** interrogativo m

interrupt /ɪntə'rʌpt/ vt/i interrompere. **~ion** n interruzione f

intersect /ɪntə'sekt/ vi intersecarsi ●vt intersecare. **~ion** n intersezione f; (of street) incrocio m

inter'twine vi attorcigliarsi

interval /'ɪntəvl/ n intervallo m; **bright ~s** pl schiarite fpl

intervene /ɪntə'vi:n/ vi intervenire. **~tion** n intervento m

interview /'ɪntəvju:/ n (Journ) intervista f; (for job) colloquio m [di lavoro] ●vt intervistare. **~er** n intervistatore, -trice mf

intestine /ɪn'testɪn/ n intestino m.

~al adj intestinale

intimacy /'ɪntɪməsɪ/ n intimità f

intimate¹ /'ɪntɪmət/ adj intimo. **~ly** adv intimamente

intimate² /'ɪntɪmeɪt/ vt far capire; (imply) suggerire

intimidate /ɪn'tɪmɪdeɪt/ vt intimidire. **~ion** n intimidazione f

into /'ɪntə/, di fronte a una vocale /'ɪntʊ/ prep dentro, in; **go ~ the house** andare dentro [casa] o in casa; **be ~** (🄵 like) essere appassionato di; **I'm not ~ that** questo non mi piace; **7 ~ 21 goes 3** il 7 nel 21 ci sta 3 volte; **translate ~ French** tradurre in francese; **get ~ trouble** mettersi nei guai

in'tolerable adj intollerabile

in'toleran|ce n intolleranza f. **~t** adj intollerante

intoxicat|ed /ɪn'tɒksɪkeɪtɪd/ adj inebriato. **~ion** n ebbrezza f

in'transitive adj intransitivo

intravenous /ɪntrə'vi:nəs/ adj endovenoso. **~ly** adv per via endovenosa

intrepid /ɪn'trepɪd/ adj intrepido

intricate /'ɪntrɪkət/ adj complesso

intrigue /ɪn'tri:g/ n intrigo m ●vt intrigare ●vi tramare. **~ing** adj intrigante

intrinsic /ɪn'trɪnsɪk/ adj intrinseco

introduce /ɪntrə'dju:s/ vt presentare; (bring in, insert) introdurre

introduct|ion /ɪntrə'dʌkʃn/ n introduzione f; (to person) presentazione f; (to book) prefazione f. **~ory** adj introduttivo

introvert /'ɪntrəvɜ:t/ n introverso, -a mf

intru|de /ɪn'tru:d/ vi intromettersi. **~der** n intruso, -a mf. **~sion** n intrusione f

intuit|ion /ɪntjʊ'ɪʃn/ n intuito m. **~ive** adj intuitivo

inundate /'ɪnəndeɪt/ vt (flood)

inondare (**with** di)

invade /ɪnˈveɪd/ vt invadere. ∼**r** n invasore m

invalid[1] /ˈɪnvəlɪd/ n invalido, -a mf

invalid[2] /ɪnˈvælɪd/ adj non valido. ∼**ate** vt invalidare

in'valuable adj prezioso; (priceless) inestimabile

in'variabl|e adj invariabile. ∼**y** adv invariabilmente

invasion /ɪnˈveɪʒn/ n invasione f

invent /ɪnˈvent/ vt inventare. ∼**ion** n invenzione f. ∼**ive** adj inventivo. ∼**or** n inventore, -trice mf

inventory /ˈɪnvəntrɪ/ n inventario m

invest /ɪnˈvest/ vt investire ● vi fare investimenti; ∼ **in** (☐: buy) comprarsi

investigat|e /ɪnˈvestɪgeɪt/ vt investigare. ∼**ion** n investigazione f

invest|ment /ɪnˈvestmənt/ n investimento m. ∼**or** n investitore, -trice mf

inveterate /ɪnˈvetərət/ adj inveterato

invidious /ɪnˈvɪdɪəs/ adj ingiusto; (position) antipatico

invincible /ɪnˈvɪnsəbl/ adj invincibile

in'visible adj invisibile

invitation /ɪnvɪˈteɪʃn/ n invito m

invit|e /ɪnˈvaɪt/ vt invitare; (attract) attirare. ∼**ing** adj invitante

invoice /ˈɪnvɔɪs/ n fattura f ● vt ∼ **sb** emettere una fattura a qcno

in'voluntar|y adj involontario

involve /ɪnˈvɒlv/ vt comportare; (affect, include) coinvolgere; (entail) implicare; **get** ∼**d with sb** legarsi a qcno; (romantically) legarsi sentimentalmente a qcno. ∼**d** adj complesso. ∼**ment** n coinvolgimento n

inward /ˈɪnwəd/ adj interno; (thoughts etc) interiore; ∼ **investment** (Comm) investimento m stra-

niero. ∼**ly** adv interiormente. ∼**[s]** adv verso l'interno

iodine /ˈaɪədiːn/ n iodio m

iota /aɪˈəʊtə/ n briciolo m

IOU n abbr (I owe you) pagherò m inv

IQ n abbr (intelligence quotient) Q.I.

Iran /ɪˈrɑːn/ n Iran m. ∼**ian** adj & n iraniano, -a mf

Iraq /ɪˈrɑːk/ n Iraq m. ∼**i** adj & n iracheno, -a mf

irate /aɪˈreɪt/ adj adirato

Ireland /ˈaɪələnd/ n Irlanda f

iris /ˈaɪrɪs/ n (Anat) iride f; (Bot) iris f inv

Irish /ˈaɪrɪʃ/ adj irlandese ● n the ∼ pl gli irlandesi mpl. ∼**man** n irlandese m. ∼**woman** n irlandese f

iron /ˈaɪən/ adj di ferro. **I∼ Curtain** cortina f di ferro ● n ferro m; (appliance) ferro m [da stiro] ● vt/i stirare. □ ∼ **out** vt eliminare stirando; fig appianare

'ironmonger /-mʌŋgə(r)/ n ∼**'s [shop]** negozio m di ferramenta

irony /ˈaɪrənɪ/ n ironia f

irrational /ɪˈræʃənl/ adj irrazionale

irrefutable /ɪrɪˈfjuːtəbl/ adj irrefutabile

irregular /ɪˈregjʊlə(r)/ adj irregolare. ∼**ity** n irregolarità f inv

irrelevant /ɪˈreləvənt/ adj non pertinente

irreparabl|e /ɪˈrepərəbl/ adj irreparabile. ∼**y** adv irreparabilmente

irreplaceable /ɪrɪˈpleɪsəbl/ adj insostituibile

irresistible /ɪrɪˈzɪstəbl/ adj irresistibile

irrespective /ɪrɪˈspektɪv/ adj ∼ **of** senza riguardo per

irresponsible /ɪrɪˈspɒnsɪbl/ adj irresponsabile

irreverent /ɪˈrevərənt/ adj irreverente

irrevocabl|e /ɪˈrevəkəbl/ adj irrevocabile. ∼**y** adv irrevocabilmente

irrigat|e /'ɪrɪɡeɪt/ vt irrigare. **~ion** n irrigazione f

irritable /'ɪrɪtəbl/ adj irritabile

irritat|e /'ɪrɪteɪt/ vt irritare. **~ing** adj irritante. **~ion** n irritazione f

is /ɪz/ ▶BE

Islam /'ɪzlɑːm/ n Islam m. **~ic** adj islamico

island /'aɪlənd/ n isola f; (in road) isola f spartitraffico. **~er** n isolano, -a mf

isolat|e /'aɪsəleɪt/ vt isolare. **~ed** adj isolato. **~ion** n isolamento f

Israel /'ɪzreɪl/ n Israele m. **~i** adj & n israeliano, -a mf

issue /'ɪʃuː/ n (outcome) risultato m; (of magazine) numero m; (of stamps etc) emissione f; (offspring) figli mpl; (matter, question) questione f; at ~ in questione; **take ~ with sb** prendere posizione contro qcno ● vt distribuire (supplies); rilasciare (passport); emettere (stamps, order); pubblicare (book); **be ~d with** sth ricevere qcsa ● vi **~ from** uscire da

it /ɪt/ pron (direct object) lo m, la f; (indirect object) gli m, le f; **it's broken** è rotto/rotta; **will it be enough?** basterà?; **it's hot** fa caldo; **it's raining** piove; **it's me** sono io; **who is it?** chi è?; **it's two o'clock** sono le due; **I doubt it** ne dubito; **take it with you** prendilo con te; **give it a wipe** dagli una pulita

Italian /ɪ'tæljən/ adj & n italiano, -a mf; (language) italiano m

Italy /'ɪtəlɪ/ n Italia f

itch /ɪtʃ/ n prurito m ● vi avere prurito, prudere; **be ~ing to** 🄸 avere una voglia matta di. **~y** adj che prude; **my foot is ~y** ho prurito al piede

item /'aɪtəm/ n articolo m; (on agenda, programme) punto m; (on invoice) voce f; **~ of news** notizia f. **~ize** vt dettagliare (bill)

itinerary /aɪ'tɪnərərɪ/ n itinerario m

itself /ɪt'self/ pron (reflexive) si; (emphatic) essa stessa; **the baby looked at ~ in the mirror** il bambino si è guardato nello specchio; **by ~** da solo; **the machine in ~ is simple** la macchina di per sé è semplice

ITV n abbr (Independent Television) stazione f televisiva privata britannica

ivory /'aɪvərɪ/ n avorio m

ivy /'aɪvɪ/ n edera f

>
> **The Ivy League** Il gruppo delle più antiche e rinomate università statunitensi, situate nel nordest del paese: Harvard, Yale, Columbia University, Cornell University, Dartmouth College, Brown University, Princeton University e la University of Pennsylvania. L'espressione deriva dall'edera che cresce sugli antichi edifici universitari.

Jj

jab /dʒæb/ n colpo m secco; (🄸: injection) puntura f ● vt (pt/pp jabbed) punzecchiare

jack /dʒæk/ n (Auto) cric m inv; (in cards) fante m, jack m inv ● **jack up** vt (Auto) sollevare (con il cric)

jackdaw /'dʒækdɔː/ n taccola f

jacket /'dʒækɪt/ n giacca f; (of book) sopraccoperta f. **~ po'tato** n patata f cotta al forno con la buccia

jackpot n premio m (di una lotteria); **win the ~** vincere alla lotteria; **hit the ~** fig fare un colpo grosso

jade /dʒeɪd/ n giada f ● attrib di giada

jagged /'dʒæɡɪd/ adj dentellato

jail /dʒeɪl/ = gaol

jam¹ /dʒæm/ n marmellata f

jam² n (Auto) ingorgo m; (🔲: difficulty) guaio m • v (pt/pp jammed) • vt (cram) pigiare; disturbare (broadcast); inceppare (mechanism, drawer etc); be ~med (roads:) essere congestionato • vi (mechanism:) incepparsi; (window, drawer:) incastrarsi

Jamaica /dʒə'meɪkə/ n Giamaica f. ~n adj & n giamaicano, -a mf

jangle /'dʒæŋgl/ vt far squillare • vi squillare

janitor /'dʒænɪtə(r)/ n (caretaker) custode m; (in school) bidello, -a mf

January /'dʒænjʊərɪ/ n gennaio m

Japan /dʒə'pæn/ n Giappone m. ~ese adj & n giapponese mf; (language) giapponese m

jar¹ /dʒɑː(r)/ n (glass) barattolo m

jar² vi (pt/pp jarred) (sound:) stridere

jargon /'dʒɑːgən/ n gergo m

jaundice /'dʒɔːndɪs/ n itterizia f. ~d adj fig inacidito

jaunt /dʒɔːnt/ n gita f

jaunty /'dʒɔːntɪ/ adj (-ier, -iest) sbarazzino

jaw /dʒɔː/ n mascella f; (bone) mandibola f

jay-walker /'dʒeɪwɔːkə(r)/ n pedone m distratto

jazz /dʒæz/ n jazz m • jazz up vt ravvivare. ~y adj vistoso

jealous /'dʒeləs/ adj geloso. ~y n gelosia f

jeans /dʒiːnz/ npl [blue] jeans mpl

jeep /dʒiːp/ n jeep f inv

jeer /dʒɪə(r)/ n scherno m • vi schernire; ~ at prendersi gioco di • vt (boo) fischiare

jelly /'dʒelɪ/ n gelatina f. ~fish n medusa f

jeopar|dize /'dʒepədaɪz/ vt mettere in pericolo. ~dy n in ~dy in pericolo

jerk /dʒɜːk/ n scatto m, scossa f • vt scattare • vi sobbalzare; (limb,

muscle:) muoversi a scatti. ~ily adv a scatti. ~y adj traballante

jersey /'dʒɜːzɪ/ n maglia f; (Sport) maglietta f; (fabric) jersey m

jest /dʒest/ n scherzo m; in ~ per scherzo • vi scherzare

Jesus /'dʒiːzəs/ n Gesù m

jet¹ /dʒet/ n (stone) giaietto m

jet² n (of water) getto m; (nozzle) becco m; (plane) aviogetto m, jet m inv

jet: ~-'black adj nero ebano. ~lag n scombussolamento m da fuso orario. ~-pro'pelled adj a reazione

jettison /'dʒetɪsn/ vt gettare a mare; fig abbandonare

jetty /'dʒetɪ/ n molo m

Jew /dʒuː/ n ebreo m

jewel /'dʒuːəl/ n gioiello m. ~ler n gioielliere m; ~ler's [shop] gioielleria f. ~lery n gioielli mpl

jiffy /'dʒɪfɪ/ n 🔲 in a ~ in un batter d'occhio

jigsaw /'dʒɪgsɔː/ n ~ [puzzle] puzzle m inv

jilt /dʒɪlt/ vt piantare

jingle /'dʒɪŋgl/ n (rhyme) canzoncina f pubblicitaria • vi tintinnare

job /dʒɒb/ n lavoro m; this is going to be quite a ~ 🔲 [questa] non sarà un'impresa facile; it's a good ~ that... meno male che.... ~ centre n ufficio m statale di collocamento. ~less adj senza lavoro

jockey /'dʒɒkɪ/ n fantino m

jocular /'dʒɒkjʊlə(r)/ adj scherzoso

jog /dʒɒg/ n colpetto m; at a ~ in un balzo; (Sport) go for a ~ andare a fare jogging • v (pt/pp jogged) • vt (hit) urtare; ~ sb's memory farlo ritornare in mente a qcno • vi (Sport) fare jogging. ~ging n jogging m

join /dʒɔɪn/ n giuntura f • vt raggiungere, unire; raggiungere (person); (become member of) iscriversi a; entrare in (firm) • vi (roads:) congiun-

joiner | just

448

gersi. ▫ ~ **in** vi partecipare. ▫ ~ **up** vi (Mil) arruolarsi ● vt unire

joiner /'dʒɔɪnə(r)/ n falegname m

joint /dʒɔɪnt/ adj comune ● n articolazione f; (in wood, brickwork) giuntura f; (Culin) arrosto m; (𝕀: bar) bettola f; (𝕏 drug) spinello m. ~**ly** adv unitamente

joist /dʒɔɪst/ n travetto m

jok|e /dʒəʊk/ n (trick) scherzo m; (funny story) barzelletta f ● vi scherzare. ~**er** n burlone, -a mf; (in cards) jolly m inv. ~**ing** n ~**ing apart** scherzi a parte. ~**ingly** adv per scherzo

jolly /'dʒɒlɪ/ adj (-ier, -iest) allegro ● adv 𝕀 molto

jolt /dʒəʊlt/ n scossa f, sobbalzo m ● vt far sobbalzare ● vi sobbalzare

jostle /'dʒɒsl/ vt spingere

jot /dʒɒt/ n nulla f ● **jot down** vt (pt/pp jotted) annotare. ~**ter** n taccuino m

journal /'dʒɜːnl/ n giornale m; (diary) diario m. ~**ese** n gergo m giornalistico. ~**ism** n giornalismo m. ~**ist** n giornalista mf

journey /'dʒɜːnɪ/ n viaggio m

jovial /'dʒəʊvɪəl/ adj gioviale

joy /dʒɔɪ/ n gioia f. ~**ful** adj gioioso. ~**ride** n 𝕀 giro m con una macchina rubata. ~**stick** n (Comput) joystick m inv

jubil|ant /'dʒuːbɪlənt/ adj giubilante. ~**ation** n giubilo m

jubilee /'dʒuːbɪliː/ n giubileo m

judge /dʒʌdʒ/ n giudice m ● vt giudicare; (estimate) valutare; (consider) ritenere ● vi giudicare (by da). ~**ment** n giudizio m; (Jur) sentenza f

judic|ial /dʒuː'dɪʃl/ adj giudiziario. ~**iary** n magistratura f. ~**ious** adj giudizioso

judo /'dʒuːdəʊ/ n judo m

jug /dʒʌɡ/ n brocca f; (small) bricco m

juggernaut /'dʒʌɡənɔːt/ n 𝕀

grosso autotreno m

juggle /'dʒʌɡl/ vi fare giochi di destrezza. ~**r** n giocoliere, -a mf

juice /dʒuːs/ n succo m

juicy /'dʒuːsɪ/ adj (-ier, -iest) succoso; (𝕀: story) piccante

juke-box /'dʒuːk-/ n juke-box m inv

July /dʒʊ'laɪ/ n luglio m

jumble /'dʒʌmbl/ n accozzaglia f ● vt ~ [up] mischiare. ~ **sale** n vendita f di beneficenza

jumbo /'dʒʌmbəʊ/ n ~ [**jet**] jumbo jet m inv

jump /dʒʌmp/ n salto m; (in prices) balzo m; (in horse racing) ostacolo m ● vi saltare; (with fright) sussultare; (prices): salire rapidamente; ~ **to conclusions** saltare alle conclusioni ● vt saltare; ~ **the gun** fig precipitarsi; ~ **the queue** non rispettare la fila. ▫ ~ **at** vt fig accettare con entusiasmo (offer). ▫ ~ **up** vi rizzarsi in piedi

jumper /'dʒʌmpə(r)/ n (sweater) golf m inv

jumpy /'dʒʌmpɪ/ adj nervoso

junction /'dʒʌŋkʃn/ n (of roads) incrocio m; (of motorway) uscita f; (Rail) nodo m ferroviario

June /dʒuːn/ n giugno m

jungle /'dʒʌŋɡl/ n giungla f

junior /'dʒuːnɪə(r)/ adj giovane; (in rank) subalterno; (Sport) junior inv ● n the ~ **s** (Sch) i più giovani. ~ **school** n scuola f elementare

junk /dʒʌŋk/ n cianfrusaglie fpl. ~ **food** n 𝕀 cibo m poco sano, porcherie fpl. ~ **mail** n posta f spazzatura

junkie /'dʒʌŋkɪ/ n 𝕏 tossico, -a mf

'**junk-shop** n negozio m di rigattiere

jurisdiction /dʒʊərɪs'dɪkʃn/ n giurisdizione f

juror /'dʒʊərə(r)/ n giurato, -a mf

jury /'dʒʊərɪ/ n giuria f

just /dʒʌst/ adj giusto ● adv (barely)

appena; (simply) solo; (exactly) esattamente; ~ **as tall** altrettanto alto; ~ **as I was leaving** proprio quando stavo andando via; **I've ~ seen her** l'ho appena vista; **it's ~ as well** meno male; ~ **at that moment** proprio in quel momento; ~ **listen!** ascolta!; **I'm ~ going** sto andando proprio ora

justice /ˈdʒʌstɪs/ n giustizia f; **do ~ to** rendere giustizia a; **J~ of the Peace** giudice m conciliatore

justifiabl|e /ˈdʒʌstɪfaɪəbl/ adj giustificabile

justi|fication /dʒʌstɪfɪˈkeɪʃn/ n giustificazione f. ~**fy** vt (pt/pp -**ied**) giustificare

jut /dʒʌt/ vi (pt/pp **jutted**) ~ **out** sporgere

juvenile /ˈdʒuːvənaɪl/ adj giovanile; (childish) infantile; (for the young) per i giovani ● n giovane m/f. ~ **delinquency** n delinquenza f giovanile

Kk

kangaroo /kæŋgəˈruː/ n canguro m

karate /kəˈrɑːtɪ/ n karate m

keel /kiːl/ n chiglia f. **keel over** vi capovolgersi

keen /kiːn/ adj (intense) acuto; (interest) vivo; (eager) entusiastico; (competition) feroce; (wind, knife) tagliente; ~ **on** entusiasta di; **she's ~ on him** le piace molto; **be ~ to do sth** avere voglia di fare qcsa. ~**ness** n entusiasmo m

keep /kiːp/ n (maintenance) mantenimento m; (of castle) maschio m; **for ~s** per sempre ● v (pt/pp **kept**) ● vt tenere; (not throw away) conservare; (detain) trattenere; mantenere (family,

promise); avere (shop); allevare (animals); rispettare (law, rules); ~ **sth hot** tenere qcsa in caldo; ~ **sb from doing sth** impedire a qcno di fare qcsa; ~ **sb waiting** far aspettare qcno; ~ **sth to oneself** tenere qcsa per sè; ~ **sth from sb** tenere nascosto qcsa a qcno ● vi (remain) rimanere; (food): conservarsi; ~ **calm** rimanere calmo; ~ **left/right** tenere la destra/la sinistra; ~ **[on] doing sth** continuare a fare qcsa. □ ~ **back** vt trattenere (person); ~ **sth back from sb** tenere nascosto qcsa a qcno ● vi tenersi indietro. □ ~ **in with** vt mantenersi in buoni rapporti con. □ ~ **on** vi [] assillare (**at sb** qcno). □ ~ **up** vi stare al passo ● vt (continue) continuare

kennel /ˈkenl/ n canile m; ~**s** pl (boarding) canile m; (breeding) allevamento m di cani

Kenya /ˈkenjə/ n Kenia m. ~**n** adj & n keniota m/f

kept /kept/ ▷**KEEP**

kerb /kɜːb/ n bordo m del marciapiede

kerosene /ˈkerəsiːn/ n Am cherosene m

ketchup /ˈketʃʌp/ n ketchup m

kettle /ˈketl/ n bollitore m; **put the ~ on** mettere l'acqua a bollire

key /kiː/ n also (Mus) chiave f; (of piano, typewriter) tasto m ● vt ~ **[in]** digitare (character); **could you ~ this?** puoi battere questo?

key: ~**board** n (Comput, Mus) tastiera f. ~**hole** n buco m della serratura. ~**-ring** n portachiavi m inv

khaki /ˈkɑːkɪ/ adj cachi inv ● n cachi m

kick /kɪk/ n calcio m; ([] thrill) piacere m; **for ~s** [] per spasso ● vt dar calci a; ~ **the bucket** [] crepare ● vi (animal): scalciare; (person): dare calci. □ ~ **off** vi (Sport) dare il calcio d'inizio; [] iniziare. □ ~ **up** vt ~ **up**

a row fare une scenata

'kick-off n (Sport) calcio m d'inizio

kid /kɪd/ n capretto m; (🔲: child) ragazzino, -a *mf* • v (pt/pp kidded) • vt 🔲 prendere in giro • vi 🔲 scherzare

kidnap /'kɪdnæp/ vt (pt/pp -napped) rapire, sequestrare. **~per** n sequestratore, -trice *mf*, rapitore, -trice *mf*. **~ping** n rapimento m, sequestro m [di persona]

kidney /'kɪdnɪ/ n rene m; (Culin) rognone m. **~ machine** n rene m artificiale

kill /kɪl/ vt uccidere; *fig* metter fine a; ammazzare (time). **~er** n assassino, -a *mf*. **~ing** n uccisione *f*; (murder) omicidio m; **make a ~ing** *fig* fare un colpo grosso

kiln /kɪln/ n fornace *f*

kilo /'kiːləʊ/ **~byte** n kilobyte m inv. **~gram** n chilogrammo m. **~metre** n chilometro m. **~watt** n chilowatt m inv

kilt /kɪlt/ n kilt m inv (gonnellino degli scozzesi)

kin /kɪn/ n congiunti *mpl*; next of ~ parente stretto; parenti *mpl* stretti

kind[1] /kaɪnd/ n genere m, specie *f*; (brand, type) tipo m; ~ of 🔲 alquanto; two of a ~ due della stessa specie

kind[2] adj gentile, buono; ~ to animals amante degli animali; ~ regards cordiali saluti

kindergarten /'kɪndəgɑːtn/ n asilo m infantile

kindle /'kɪndl/ vt accendere

kind|ly /'kaɪndlɪ/ adj (-ier, -iest) benevolo • adv gentilmente; (if you please) per favore. **~ness** n gentilezza *f*

king /kɪŋ/ n re m inv. **~dom** n regno m

king: ~fisher n martin m inv pescatore. **~-sized** adj (cigarette) king-size inv, lungo; (bed) matrimoniale

grande

kink /kɪŋk/ n nodo m. **~y** adj 🔲 bizzarro

kiosk /'kiːɒsk/ n chiosco m; (Teleph) cabina *f* telefonica

kipper /'kɪpə(r)/ n aringa *f* affumicata

kiss /kɪs/ n bacio m; ~ of life respirazione *f* bocca a bocca • vt baciare • vi baciarsi

kit /kɪt/ n equipaggiamento m, kit m inv; (tools) attrezzi *mpl*; (construction ~) pezzi *mpl* da montare, kit m inv • **kit out** vt (pt/pp kitted) equipaggiare. **~bag** n sacco m a spalla

kitchen /'kɪtʃɪn/ n cucina *f* • attrib di cucina. **~ette** n cucinino m

kitchen towel Scottex® m inv

kite /kaɪt/ n aquilone m

kitten /'kɪtn/ n gattino m

knack /næk/ n tecnica *f*; have the ~ for doing sth avere la capacità di fare qcsa

knead /niːd/ vt impastare

knee /niː/ n ginocchio m. **~cap** n rotula *f*

kneel /niːl/ vi (pt/pp knelt) ~ [down] inginocchiarsi; be ~ing essere inginocchiato

knelt /nelt/ ▷ KNEEL

knew /njuː/ ▷ KNOW

knickers /'nɪkəz/ *npl* mutandine *fpl*

knife /naɪf/ n (pl knives) coltello m • vt 🔲 accoltellare

knight /naɪt/ n cavaliere m; (in chess) cavallo m • vt nominare cavaliere

knit /nɪt/ vt/i (pt/pp knitted) lavorare a maglia; ~ one, purl one un diritto, un rovescio. **~ting** n lavorare m a maglia; (work) lavoro m a maglia. **~ting-needle** n ferro m da calza. **~wear** n maglieria *f*

knives /naɪvz/ ▷ KNIFE

knob /nɒb/ n pomello m; (of stick) pomo m; (of butter) noce *f*. **~bly** adj nodoso; (bony) spigoloso

knock /nɒk/ n colpo m; **there was a ~ at the door** hanno bussato alla porta ● vt bussare a (door); (🗊: *criticize*) denigrare; **~ a hole in sth** fare un buco in qcsa; **~ one's head** battere la testa (on contro) ● vi (at door) bussare. □ **~ about** vt malmenare ● vi 🗊 girovagare. □ **~ down** vt far cadere; (with fist) stendere con un pugno; (in car) investire; (demolish) abbattere; (🗊: *reduce*) ribassare (price). □ **~ off** vt (🗊: *steal*) fregare; (🗊: *complete quickly*) fare alla bell'e meglio ● vi (🗊: *cease work*) staccare. □ **~ out** vt eliminare; (make unconscious) mettere K.O.; (🗊: *anaesthetize*) addormentare. □ **~ over** vt rovesciare; (in car) investire

knock: ~er n battente m.
~-kneed /-'niːd/ adj con gambe storte. **~-out** n (in boxing) knock-out m inv

knot /nɒt/ n nodo m ● vt (pt/pp knotted) annodare

know /nəʊ/ v (pt knew, pp known) ● vt sapere; conoscere (person, place); (recognize) riconoscere; **get to ~ sb** conoscere qcno; **~ how to swim** sapere nuotare ● vi sapere; **did you ~ about this?** lo sapevi? ● n **in the ~** 🗊 al corrente

know: ~-all n 🗊 sapientone, -a mf. **~-how** n abilità f. **~ingly** adv (intentionally) consapevolmente; (smile etc) con un'aria d'intesa

knowledge /'nɒlɪdʒ/ n conoscenza f. **~able** adj ben informato

known /nəʊn/ ▷KNOW ● adj noto

knuckle /'nʌkl/ n nocca f ● **knuckle down** vi darci sotto (to con). □ **~ under** vi sottomettersi

Koran /kə'rɑːn/ n Corano m

Korea /kə'rɪə/ n Corea f. **~n** adj & n coreano, -a mf

kosher /'kəʊʃə(r)/ adj kasher inv

kudos /'kjuːdɒs/ n gloria f

Ll

lab /læb/ n laboratorio m

label /'leɪbl/ n etichetta f ● vt (pt/pp labelled) mettere un'etichetta a; fig etichettare (person)

laboratory /lə'bɒrətrɪ/ n laboratorio m

laborious /lə'bɔːrɪəs/ adj laborioso

labour /'leɪbə(r)/ n lavoro m; (workers) manodopera f; (Med) doglie fpl; **be in ~** avere le doglie; **L~** (Pol) partito m laburista ● attrib (Pol) laburista ● vi lavorare ● vt **~ the point** fig ribadire il concetto. **~er** n manovale m

lace /leɪs/ n pizzo m; (of shoe) laccio m ● attrib di pizzo ● vt allacciare (shoes); correggere (drink)

lacerate /'læsəreɪt/ vt lacerare

lack /læk/ n mancanza f ● vt mancare di; **I ~ the time** mi manca il tempo ● vi **be ~ing** mancare; **be ~ing in sth** mancare di qcsa

lad /læd/ n ragazzo m

ladder /'lædə(r)/ n scala f; (in tights) sfilatura f

laden /'leɪdn/ adj carico (with di)

ladle /'leɪdl/ n mestolo m ● vt **~ [out]** versare (col mestolo)

lady /'leɪdɪ/ n signora f; (title) Lady; **ladies [room]** bagno m per donne

lady: ~bird n, Am **~bug** n coccinella f. **~like** adj signorile

lag¹ /læg/ vi (pt/pp lagged) **~ behind** restare indietro

lag² /læg/ (pt/pp lagged) isolare (pipes)

lager /'lɑːgə(r)/ n birra f chiara

lagoon /lə'guːn/ n laguna f

laid /leɪd/ ▷LAY³

lain /leɪn/ ▷LIE²

lair /leə(r)/ n tana f

lake /leɪk/ n lago m

lamb /læm/ n agnello m

lame /leɪm/ adj zoppo; fig (argument) zoppicante; (excuse) traballante

lament /lə'ment/ n lamento m • vt lamentare • vi lamentarsi

lamentable /'læməntəbl/ adj deplorevole

lamp /læmp/ n lampada f; (in street) lampione m. **~post** n lampione m. **~shade** n paralume m

lance /lɑːns/ n fiocina f • vt (Med) incidere. **~-'corporal** n appuntato m

land /lænd/ n terreno m; (country) paese m; (as opposed to sea) terra f; **plot of ~** pezzo m di terreno • vt (Naut) sbarcare; (fam: obtain) assicurarsi; **be ~ed with sth** ⓣ ritrovarsi fra capo e collo qcsa • vi (Aeron) atterrare; (fall) cadere. □ **~ up** vi ⓣ finire

landing /'lændɪŋ/ n (Naut) sbarco m; (Aeron) atterraggio m; (top of stairs) pianerottolo m. **~-stage** n pontile m da sbarco. **~ strip** n pista f d'atterraggio di fortuna

land: **~lady** n proprietaria f; (of flat) padrona f di casa. **~lord** n proprietario m; (of flat) padrone m di casa. **~mark** n punto m di riferimento; fig pietra f miliare. **~scape** /-skeɪp/ n paesaggio m. **~slide** n frana f; (Pol) valanga f di voti

lane /leɪn/ n sentiero m; (Auto, Sport) corsia f

language /'læŋgwɪdʒ/ n lingua f; (speech, style) linguaggio m. **~ laboratory** n laboratorio m linguistico

lank /læŋk/ adj (hair) dritto

lanky /'læŋkɪ/ adj (-ier, -iest) allampanato

lantern /'læntən/ n lanterna f

lap¹ /læp/ n grembo m

lap² n (of journey) tappa f; (Sport) giro m • v (pt/pp lapped) • vi (water:) **~ against** lambire • vt (Sport) doppiare

lap³ vt (pt/pp lapped) **~ up** bere avidamente; bersi completamente (lies); credere ciecamente a (praise)

lapel /lə'pel/ n bavero m

lapse /læps/ n sbaglio m; (moral) sbandamento m [morale]; (of time) intervallo m • vi (expire) scadere; (morally) scivolare; **~ into** cadere in

laptop /'læptɒp/ n ~ [computer] computer m inv portabile, laptop m inv

lard /lɑːd/ n strutto m

larder /'lɑːdə(r)/ n dispensa f

large /lɑːdʒ/ adj grande; (number, amount) grande, grosso; **by and ~** in complesso; **at ~** in libertà; (in general) ampiamente. **~ly** adv ampiamente; **~ly because of** in gran parte a causa di

lark¹ /lɑːk/ n (bird) allodola f

lark² n (joke) burla f • **lark about** vi giocherellare

larva /'lɑːvə/ n (pl **-vae** /-viː/) larva f

laser /'leɪzə(r)/ n laser m inv. **~ printer** n stampante f laser

lash /læʃ/ n frustata f; (eyelash) ciglio m • vt (whip) frustare; (tie) legare fermamente. □ **~ out** vi attaccare; (spend) sperperare (on in)

lashings /'læʃɪŋz/ npl **~ of** ⓣ una marea di

lass /læs/ n ragazzina f

lasso /lə'suː/ n lazo m

last /lɑːst/ adj (final) ultimo; (recent) scorso; **~ year** l'anno scorso; **at ~** alla fine; **at ~!** finalmente!; **that's the ~ straw** ⓣ questa è l'ultima goccia • n ultimo, -a m/f; **the ~ but one** il penultimo • adv per ultimo; (last time) l'ultima volta • vi durare. **~ing** adj durevole. **~ly** adv infine

late /leɪt/ adj (delayed) in ritardo; (at a late hour) tardo; (deceased) defunto; **it's ~** (at night) è tardi; **in ~ November** alla fine di Novembre • adv tardi; **stay up ~** stare alzati fino a tardi.

∼comer n ritardatario, -a mf; (to political party etc) nuovo, -a arrivato, -a mf. **∼ly** adv recentemente. **∼ness** n ora f tarda; (delay) ritardo m

latent /'leɪtnt/ adj latente

later /'leɪtə(r)/ adj (train) che parte più tardi; (edition) più recente ● adv più tardi; **∼ on** più tardi, dopo

lateral /'lætərəl/ adj laterale

latest /'leɪtɪst/ adj ultimo; (most recent) più recente; **the ∼ [news]** le ultime notizie **in six o'clock at the ∼** alle sei al più tardi

lathe /leɪð/ n tornio m

lather /'lɑːðə(r)/ n schiuma f ● vt insaponare ● vi far schiuma

Latin /'lætɪn/ adj latino ● n latino m. **∼ A'merica** n America f Latina. **∼ A'merican** adj & n latino-americano, -a mf

latitude /'lætɪtjuːd/ n (Geog) latitudine f; fig libertà f d'azione

latter /'lætə(r)/ adj ultimo ● n **the ∼** quest'ultimo. **∼ly** adv ultimamente

Latvia /'lætvɪə/ n Lettonia f. **∼n** adj & n lettone mf

laugh /lɑːf/ n risata f ● vi ridere (at/about di); **∼ at sb** (mock) prendere in giro qcno. **∼able** adj ridicolo. **∼ing-stock** n zimbello m

laughter /'lɑːftə(r)/ n risata f

launch[1] /lɔːntʃ/ n (boat) varo m

launch[2] n lancio m; (of ship) varo m ● vt lanciare (rocket, product); varare (ship); sferrare (attack)

launder /'lɔːndə(r)/ vt lavare e stirare; **∼ money** fig riciclare denaro sporco. **∼ette** n lavanderia f automatica

laundry /'lɔːndrɪ/ n lavanderia f; (clothes) bucato m

lava /'lɑːvə/ n lava f

lavatory /'lævətrɪ/ n gabinetto m

lavish /'lævɪʃ/ adj copioso; (wasteful) prodigo; **on a ∼ scale** su vasta scala

● vt **∼ sth on sb** ricoprire qcno di qcsa. **∼ly** adv copiosamente

law /lɔː/ n legge f; **study ∼** studiare giurisprudenza, studiare legge; **∼ and order** ordine m pubblico

lawcourt n tribunale m

lawn /lɔːn/ n prato m [all'inglese]. **∼-mower** n tosaerbe m inv

'law suit n causa f

lawyer /'lɔːjə(r)/ n avvocato m

lax /læks/ adj negligente; (morals etc) lassista

laxative /'læksətɪv/ n lassativo m

lay[1] /leɪ/ adj laico; fig profano

lay[2] ▶ LIE[2]

lay[3] vt (pt/pp laid) porre, mettere; apparecchiare (table) ● vi (hen:) fare le uova. □ **∼ down** vt posare; stabilire (rules, conditions). □ **∼ off** vt licenziare (workers) ● vi (Ⅱ: stop) **lay off!** smettila! **lay out** vt (display, set forth) esporre; (plan) pianificare (garden); (spend) sborsare; (Typ) impaginare

lay: ∼about n fannullone, -a mf. **∼-by** n corsia f di sosta

layer /'leɪə(r)/ n strato m

lay: ∼man n profano m. **∼out** n disposizione f; (Typ) impaginazione f, layout m inv

laze /leɪz/ vi **∼ [about]** oziare

laziness /'leɪzɪnɪs/ n pigrizia f

lazy /'leɪzɪ/ adj (-ier, -iest) pigro. **∼-bones** n poltrone, -a mf

lead[1] /led/ n piombo m; (of pencil) mina f

lead[2] /liːd/ n guida f; (leash) giunzaglio m; (flex) filo m; (clue) indizio m; (Theat) parte f principale; (distance ahead) distanza f (over su); **in the ∼** in testa ● v (pt/pp led) vt condurre; dirigere (expedition, party etc); (induce) indurre; **∼ the way** mettersi in testa ● vi (be in front) condurre; (in race, competition) essere in testa; (at cards) giocare (per primo). □ **∼ away** vt portar via. □ **∼ to** vt portare a.

□ ~ **up to** vt preludere; **what's this
~ing up to?** dove porta questo?

leader /'li:də(r)/ n capo m; (of orchestra) primo violino m; (in newspaper)
articolo m di fondo. **~ship** n direzione f, leadership f inv; **show ~ship**
mostrare capacità di comando

leading /'li:dɪŋ/ adj principale; ~
lady/man attrice f/attore m principale; ~ **question** domanda f tendenziosa

leaf /li:f/ n (pl **leaves**) foglia f; (of
table) asse f ● **leaf through** vt sfogliare. **~let** n dépliant m inv; (advertising) dépliant m inv pubblicitario; (political) manifestino m

league /li:g/ n lega f; (Sport) campionato m; **be in ~ with** essere in
combutta con

leak /li:k/ n (hole) fessura f; (Naut)
falla f; (of gas & fig) fuga f ● vi colare;
(ship:) fare acqua; (liquid, gas:) fuoriuscire ● vt ~ **sth to sb** fig far trapelare qcsa a qcno. **~y** adj che perde;
(Naut) che fa acqua

lean[1] /li:n/ adj magro

lean[2] v (pt/pp **leaned** or **leant** /lent/)
● vt appoggiare (**against/on** contro/
su) ● vi appoggiarsi (**against/on**
contro/su); (not be straight) pendere;
be ~ing against essere appoggiato
contro; ~ **on sb** (depend on) appoggiarsi a qcno; (II: exert pressure on)
stare alle calcagne di qcno. □ ~
back vi sporgersi indietro. □ ~ **forward** vi piegarsi in avanti. □ ~ **out**
vi sporgersi. □ ~ **over** vi piegarsi

leaning /'li:nɪŋ/ adj pendente; **the**
L~ **Tower of Pisa** la torre di Pisa, la
torre pendente ● n tendenza f

leap /li:p/ n salto m ● vi (pt/pp **leapt**
/lept/ or **leaped**) saltare; **he leapt at
it** II l'ha preso al volo. **~-frog** n cavallina f. ~ **year** n anno m bisestile

learn /lɜ:n/ v (pt/pp **learnt** or
learned) ● vt imparare; ~ **to swim**
imparare a nuotare; **I have ~ed
that...** (heard) sono venuto a sapere

che... ● vi imparare

learn|ed /'lɜ:nɪd/ adj colto. **~er** n
also (Auto) principiante mf. **~ing** n
cultura f. **~ing curve** n curva f d'apprendimento

lease /li:s/ n contratto m d'affitto;
(rental) affitto m ● vt affittare

leash /li:ʃ/ n guinzaglio m

least /li:st/ adj più piccolo; (amount)
minore; **you've got ~ luggage** hai
meno bagagli di tutti ● n **the ~** il
meno; **at ~** almeno; **not in the ~**
niente affatto ● adv meno; **the ~
expensive wine** il vino meno caro

leather /'leðə(r)/ n pelle f; (of soles)
cuoio m ● attrib di pelle/cuoio. **~y** adj
(meat, skin) duro

leave /li:v/ n (holiday) congedo m;
(Mil) licenza f; **on ~** in congedo/
licenza f ● v (pt/pp **left**) ● vt lasciare;
uscire da (house, office); (forget) dimenticare; **there is nothing left**
non è rimasto niente ● vi andare via;
(train, bus:) partire. □ ~ **behind** vt
lasciare; (forget) dimenticare. □ ~
out vt omettere; (not put away) lasciare fuori

leaves /li:vz/ ▷ **LEAF**

Leban|on /'lebənən/ n Libano m
~ese /-'ni:z/ adj & n libanese mf

lecture /'lektʃə(r)/ n conferenza f;
(Univ) lezione f; (reproof) ramanzina f
● vi fare una conferenza (**on** qcsa);
(Univ) insegnare (**on sth** qcsa) ● vt ~
sb rimproverare qcno. ~ n conferenziere, -a mf; (Univ) docente m universitario, -a

led /led/ ▷ **LEAD**[2]

ledge /ledʒ/ n cornice f; (of window)
davanzale m

leek /li:k/ n porro m

leer /lɪə(r)/ n sguardo m libidinoso
● vi ~ [**at**] guardare in modo libidinoso

left[1] /left/ ▷ **LEAVE**

left[2] adj sinistro ● adv a sinistra ● n
also (Pol) sinistra f; **on the ~**

a sinistra;

left: ~·**handed** adj mancino. ~·**luggage office** n deposito m bagagli. ~**overs** npl rimasugli mpl. ~·**wing** adj (Pol) di sinistra

leg /leg/ n gamba f. (of animal) zampa f; (of journey) tappa f; (Culin: of chicken) coscia f; (: of lamb) cosciotto m

legacy /'legəsɪ/ n lascito m

legal /'li:gl/ adj legale; **take** ~ **action** intentare un'azione legale. ~**ly** adv legalmente

legality /lɪ'gælɪtɪ/ n legalità f

legalize /'li:gəlaɪz/ vt legalizzare

legend /'ledʒənd/ n leggenda f. ~**ary** adj leggendario

legib|le /'ledʒəbl/ adj leggibile. ~**ly** adv in modo leggibile

legislat|e /'ledʒɪsleɪt/ vi legiferare. ~**ion** n legislazione f

legitima|te /lɪ'dʒɪtɪmət/ adj legittimo; (excuse) valido

leisure /'leʒə(r)/ n tempo m libero; **at your** ~ con comodo. ~**ly** adj senza fretta

lemon /'lemən/ n limone m. ~**ade** n limonata f

lend /lend/ vt (pt/pp lent) prestare; ~ **a hand** fig dare una mano. ~**ing library** n biblioteca f per il prestito

length /leŋθ/ n lunghezza f. (piece) pezzo m; (of wallpaper) parte f; (of visit) durata f; **at** ~ a lungo; (at last) alla fine

length|en /'leŋθən/ vt allungare ● vi allungarsi. ~**ways** adv per lungo

lengthy /'leŋθɪ/ adj (-ier, -iest) lungo

lens /lenz/ n lente f; (Phot) obiettivo m; (of eye) cristallino m

lent /lent/ ▷LEND

Lent n Quaresima f

Leo /'li:əʊ/ n (Astr) Leone m

leopard /'lepəd/ n leopardo m

leotard /'li:ətɑ:d/ n body m inv

lesbian /'lezbɪən/ adj lesbico ● n lesbica f

less /les/ adj meno di; ~ **and** ~ sempre meno ● adv & prep meno ● n meno m

lessen /'lesn/ vt/i diminuire

lesson /'lesn/ n lezione f

lest /lest/ conj liter per timore che

let /let/ vt (pt/pp let, pres p letting) lasciare, permettere; (rent) affittare; ~ **alone** (not to mention) tanto meno; 'to ~' 'affittasi'; ~ **us go** andiamo; ~ **sb do sth** lasciare fare qcsa a qcno, permettere a qcno di fare qcsa; ~ **me know** fammi sapere; **just** ~ **him try!** che ci provi solamente!; ~ **oneself in for** sth 🔲 impelagarsi in qcsa. □ ~ **down** vt sciogliersi (hair); abbassare (blinds); (lengthen) allungare; (disappoint) deludere; **don't** ~ **me down** conto su di te. □ ~ **in** vt far entrare. □ ~ **off** vt far partire; (not punish) perdonare; ~ **sb off doing sth** abbonare qcsa a qcno. □ ~ **out** vt far uscire; (make larger) allargare; emettere (scream, groan). □ ~ **through** vt far passare. □ ~ **up** vi 🔲 diminuire

'let-down n delusione f

lethal /'li:θl/ adj letale

letharg|ic /lɪ'θɑ:dʒɪk/ adj apatico. ~**y** n apatia f

letter /'letə(r)/ n lettera f. ~-**box** n buca f per le lettere. ~-**head** n carta f intestata. ~**ing** n caratteri mpl

lettuce /'letɪs/ n lattuga f

'let-up n 🔲 pausa f

leukaemia /lu:'ki:mɪə/ n leucemia f

level /'levl/ adj piano; (in height, competition) allo stesso livello; (spoonful) raso; **draw** ~ **with sb** affiancare qcno ● n livello m; **on the** ~ 🔲 giusto ● vt (pt/pp levelled) livellare; (aim) puntare (at su)

level 'crossing n passaggio m a livello

lever /'li:və(r)/ n leva f ● **lever up** vt sollevare (con una leva). **~age** n azione f di una leva; fig influenza f

levy /'levɪ/ vt (pt/pp levied) imporre (tax)

lewd /lju:d/ adj osceno

liabil|ity /laɪə'bɪlətɪ/ n responsabilità f; (🔲: burden) peso m; **~ies** pl debiti mpl

liable /'laɪəbl/ adj responsabile (for di); **be ~ to** (rain, break etc) rischiare di; (tend to) tendere a

liaise /lɪ'eɪz/ vi 🔲 essere in contatto

liaison /lɪ'eɪzɒn/ n contatti mpl; (Mil) collegamento m; (affair) relazione f

liar /'laɪə(r)/ n bugiardo, -a mf

libel /'laɪbl/ n diffamazione f ● vt (pt/pp libelled) diffamare. **~lous** adj diffamatorio

liberal /'lɪb(ə)rəl/ adj (tolerant) di larghe vedute; (generous) generoso. **L~** adj (Pol) liberale n liberale m/f

liberat|e /'lɪbəreɪt/ vt liberare. **~ed** adj (woman) emancipata. **~ion** n liberazione f; (of women) emancipazione f. **~or** n liberatore, -trice mf

liberty /'lɪbətɪ/ n libertà f; **take the ~ of doing sth** prendersi la libertà di fare qcsa; **be at ~ to do sth** essere libero di fare qcsa

Libra /'li:brə/ n (Astr) Bilancia f

librarian /laɪ'breərɪən/ n bibliotecario, -a mf

library /'laɪbrərɪ/ n biblioteca f

Libya /'lɪbɪə/ n Libia f. **~n** adj & n libico, -a mf

lice /laɪs/ ▷**LOUSE**

licence /'laɪsns/ n licenza f; (for TV) canone m televisivo; (for driving) patente f; (freedom) sregolatezza f. **~-plate** n targa f

license /'laɪsns/ vt autorizzare; **be ~d** (car:) avere il bollo; (restaurant:) essere autorizzato alla vendita di alcolici

lick /lɪk/ n leccata f; **a ~ of paint**

una passata leggera di pittura ● vt leccare; (🔲: defeat) battere; leccarsi (lips)

lid /lɪd/ n coperchio m; (of eye) palpebra f

lie[1] /laɪ/ n bugia f; **tell a ~** mentire ● vi (pt/pp lied, pres p lying) mentire

lie[2] vi (pt lay, pp lain, pres p lying) (person:) sdraiarsi; (object:) stare; (remain) rimanere; **leave sth lying about** or **around** lasciare qcsa in giro. **~ down** vi sdraiarsi

lie-in n **have a ~** restare a letto fino a tardi

lieutenant /lef'tenənt/ n tenente m

life /laɪf/ n (pl **lives**) vita f

life: **~belt** n salvagente m. **~-boat** n lancia f di salvataggio; (on ship) scialuppa f di salvataggio. **~-buoy** n salvagente m. **~ coach** n life coach m/f inv. **~-guard** n bagnino m. **~-jacket** n giubbotto m di salvataggio. **~less** adj inanimato. **~like** adj realistico. **~long** adj di tutta la vita. **~-size[d]** adj in grandezza naturale. **~time** n vita f; **the chance of a ~time** un'occasione unica

lift /lɪft/ n ascensore m; (Auto) passaggio m ● vt sollevare; revocare (restrictions); (🔲: steal) rubare ● vi (fog:) alzarsi. □ **~ up** vt sollevare

'lift-off n decollo m (di razzo)

light[1] /laɪt/ adj (not dark) luminoso; **~ green** verde chiaro ● n luce f; (lamp) lampada f; **in the ~ of** fig alla luce di; **have you got a ~?** ha da accendere?; **come to ~** essere rivelato ● vt (pt/pp **lit** or **lighted**) accendere; (illuminate) illuminare. □ **~ up** vi (face:) illuminarsi

light[2] adj (not heavy) leggero ● adv **travel ~** viaggiare con poco bagaglio

'light-bulb n lampadina f

lighten[1] /'laɪtn/ vt illuminare

lighten[2] vt alleggerire (load)

lighter /'laɪtə(r)/ n accendino m
light: ~'**hearted** adj spensierato.
~**house** n faro m. ~**ly** adv leggermente; (accuse) con leggerezza; (without concern) senza dare importanza alla cosa; **get off** ~**ly** cavarsela a buon mercato
lightning /'laɪtnɪŋ/ n lampo m, fulmine m. ~**-conductor** n parafulmine m
lightweight adj leggero ● n (in boxing) peso m leggero
like¹ /laɪk/ adj simile ● prep come; ~ **this/that** così; **what's he** ~? com'è? ● conj (Ⅱ: as) come; (Am: as if) come se
like² vt piacere, gradire; **I should/would** ~ vorrei, gradirei; **I** ~ **him** mi piace; **I** ~ **this car** mi piace questa macchina; **I** ~ **dancing** mi piace ballare; **I** ~ **that!** Ⅱ questa mi è piaciuta! ● n ~**s and dislikes** pl gusti mpl
like|able /'laɪkəbl/ adj simpatico.
~**lihood** n probabilità f. ~**ly** adj (-ier, -iest) probabile ● adv probabilmente; **not** ~**ly!** Ⅱ neanche per sogno!
liken /'laɪkən/ vt paragonare (**to** a)
like|ness /'laɪknɪs/ n somiglianza f.
~**wise** adv lo stesso
liking /'laɪkɪŋ/ n gusto m; **is it to your** ~? è di suo gusto?; **take a** ~ **to sb** prendere qcno in simpatia
lilac /'laɪlək/ n lillà m ● adj color lillà
lily /'lɪlɪ/ n giglio m. ~ **of the valley** n mughetto m
limb /lɪm/ n arto m
lime¹ /laɪm/ n (fruit) cedro m; (tree) tiglio m
lime² n calce f. ~**light** n **be in the** ~**light** essere molto in vista.
~**stone** n calcare m
limit /'lɪmɪt/ n limite m; **that's the** ~! Ⅱ questo è troppo! ● vt limitare (**to** a). ~**ation** n limite m. ~**ed** adj ristretto; ~**ed company** società f

anonima
limousine /'lɪməzɪːn/ n limousine f inv
limp¹ /lɪmp/ n andatura f zoppicante; **have a** ~ zoppicare ● vi zoppicare
limp² adj floscio
line¹ /laɪn/ n linea f; (length of rope, cord) filo m; (of writing) riga f; (of poem) verso m; (row) fila f; (wrinkle) ruga f; (of business) settore m; (Am: queue) coda f; **in** ~ **with** in conformità con ● vt segnare; fiancheggiare (street). □ ~ **up** vi allinearsi ● vt allineare
line² vt foderare (garment)
lined¹ /laɪnd/ adj (face) rugoso; (paper) a righe
lined² adj (garment) foderato
linen /'lɪnɪn/ n lino m; (articles) biancheria f ● attrib di lino
liner /'laɪnə(r)/ n nave f di linea
linger /'lɪŋgə(r)/ vi indugiare
lingerie /'læɪə.ʒərɪ/ n biancheria f intima (da donna)
linguist /'lɪŋgwɪst/ n linguista mf
linguistic /lɪŋ'gwɪstɪk/ adj linguistico. ~**s** n linguistica fsg
lining /'laɪnɪŋ/ n (of garment) fodera f; (of brakes) guarnizione f
link /lɪŋk/ n (of chain) anello m; fig legame m ● vt collegare. □ ~ **up** vi unirsi (**with** a); (TV) collegarsi
lino /'laɪnəʊ/ n, **linoleum** /lɪ'nəʊlɪəm/ n linoleum m
lint /lɪnt/ n garza f
lion /'laɪən/ n leone m. ~**ess** n leonessa f
lip /lɪp/ n labbro m (pl labbra f); (edge) bordo m
lip: ~**-read** vi leggere le labbra; ~**-service** n **pay** ~**-service to** approvare soltanto a parole. ~**salve** n burro m [di] cacao. ~**stick** n rossetto m
liqueur /lɪ'kjʊə(r)/ n liquore m
liquid /'lɪkwɪd/ n liquido m ● adj

liquido

liquidat|e /'lıkwıdeıt/ vt liquidare. ~**ion** n liquidazione f; (Comm) go into ~**ion** andare in liquidazione

liquidize /'lıkwıdaız/ vt rendere liquido. ~**r** n (Culin) frullatore m

liquor /'lıkə(r)/ n bevanda f alcoolica

liquorice /'lıkərıs/ n liquirizia f

liquor store n Am negozio m di alcolici

lisp /lısp/ n pronuncia f con la lisca ● vi parlare con la lisca

list¹ /lıst/ n lista f ● vt elencare

list² vi (ship:) inclinarsi

listen /'lısn/ vi ascoltare; ~ **to** ascoltare. ~**er** n ascoltatore, -trice m f

listless /'lıstlıs/ adj svogliato

lit /lıt/ ▷**LIGHT**¹

literacy /'lıtərəsı/ n alfabetizzazione f

literal /'lıtərəl/ adj letterale. ~**ly** adv letteralmente

literary /'lıtərərı/ adj letterario

literate /'lıtərət/ adj be ~ saper leggere e scrivere

literature /'lıtrətʃə(r)/ n letteratura f

Lithuania /lıθjʊ'eınıə/ n Lituania f. ~**n** adj & n lituano, -a m f

litre /'li:tə(r)/ n litro m

litter /'lıtə(r)/ n immondizie fpl; (Zool) figliata f ● vt be ~**ed** with essere ingombrato di. ~**bin** n bidone m della spazzatura

little /'lıtl/ adj piccolo; (not much) poco ● adv & n poco m; a ~ un po'; a ~ **water** un po' d'acqua; a ~ **better** un po' meglio; ~ **by** ~ a poco a poco

live¹ /laıv/ adj vivo; (ammunition) carico; ~ **broadcast** trasmissione f in diretta; be ~ (Electr) essere sotto tensione; ~ **wire** n fig persona f dinamica ● adv (broadcast) in diretta

live² /lıv/ vi vivere; (reside) abitare; ~ **with** convivere con. □ ~ **down** vt far dimenticare. □ ~ **off** vt vivere alle spalle di. □ ~ **on** vt vivere di ● vi sopravvivere. □ ~ **up** vt ~ **it up** far la bella vita. □ ~ **up to** vt essere all'altezza di

liveli|hood /'laıvlıhʊd/ n mezzi mpl di sostentamento. ~**ness** n vivacità f

lively /'laıvlı/ adj (-ier, -iest) vivace

liver /'lıvə(r)/ n fegato m

lives /laıvz/ ▷**LIFE**

livestock /'laıvstɒk/ n bestiame m

livid /'lıvıd/ adj [] livido

living /'lıvıŋ/ adj vivo ● n **earn one's** ~ guadagnarsi da vivere; **the** ~ pl i vivi. ~**-room** n soggiorno m

lizard /'lızəd/ n lucertola f

load /ləʊd/ n carico m; ~**s of** [] un sacco di ● vt caricare. ~**ed** adj carico; ([]: rich) ricchissimo

loaf¹ /ləʊf/ n (pl **loaves**) pagnotta f

loaf² vi oziare

loan /ləʊn/ n prestito m; **on** ~ in prestito ● vt prestare

loath|e /ləʊð/ vt detestare. ~**ing** n disgusto m. ~**some** adj disgustoso

lobby /'lɒbı/ n atrio m; (Pol) gruppo m di pressione, lobby m inv

lobster /'lɒbstə(r)/ n aragosta f

local /'ləʊkl/ adj locale; **I'm not** ~ non sono del posto ● n abitante m f del luogo; ([]: public house) pub m locale. ~ **authority** n autorità f locale. ~ **call** n (Teleph) telefonata f urbana. ~ **government** n autorità f inv locale

locality /ləʊ'kælətı/ n zona f

local|ization /ləʊkəlaı'zeıʃn/ n localizzazione f. ~**ized** adj localizzato

locally /'ləʊkəlı/ adv localmente; (live, work) nei paraggi

locat|e /ləʊ'keıt/ vt situare; trovare (person); be ~**ed** essere situato. ~**ion** n posizione f; **filmed**

on ~**ion** girato in esterni

lock¹ /lɒk/ n (hair) ciocca f

lock² n (on door) serratura f; (on canal) chiusa f ● vt chiudere a chiave; (block-care (wheels)) ● vi chiudersi. □ ~ **in** vt chiudere dentro. □ ~ **out** vt chiudere fuori. □ ~ **up** vt (in prison) mettere dentro ● vi chiudersi

locker /'lɒkə(r)/ n armadietto m

locket /'lɒkɪt/ n medaglione m

lock: ~**-out** n serrata f. ~**smith** n fabbro m

locomotive /ləʊkə'məʊtɪv/ n locomotiva f

lodge /lɒdʒ/ n (porter's) portineria f; (masonic) loggia f ● vt presentare (claim, complaint); (with bank, solicitor) depositare; **be** ~**d** essersi conficcato ● vi essere a pensione (**with** da); (become fixed) conficcarsi. ~**r** n inquilino, -a mf

lodgings /'lɒdʒɪŋz/ npl camere fpl in affitto

loft /lɒft/ n soffitta f

lofty /'lɒftɪ/ adj (-ier, -iest) alto; (haughty) altezzoso

log /lɒg/ n ceppo m; (Auto) libretto m di circolazione; (Naut) giornale m di bordo ● vt (pt logged) registrare. □ ~ **on to** vt (Comput) connettersi a

logarithm /'lɒgərɪðm/ n logaritmo m

log-book n (Naut) giornale m di bordo; (Auto) libretto m di circolazione

loggerheads /'lɒgə-/ npl **be at** ~ Ⓣ essere in totale disaccordo

logic /'lɒdʒɪk/ n logica f. ~**al** adj logico. ~**ally** adv logicamente

logistics /lə'dʒɪstɪks/ npl logistica f

logo /'ləʊgəʊ/ n logo m inv

loin /lɔɪn/ n (Culin) lombata f

loiter /'lɔɪtə(r)/ vi gironzolare

loll|ipop /'lɒlɪpɒp/ n lecca-lecca m inv. ~**y** n lecca-lecca m; (Ⓣ: money)

quattrini mpl

London /'lʌndən/ n Londra f ● attrib londinese, di Londra. ~**er** n londinese mf

lone /ləʊn/ adj solitario. ~**liness** n solitudine f

lonely /'ləʊnlɪ/ adj (-ier, -iest) solitario; (person) solo

lone|r /'ləʊnə(r)/ n persona f solitaria. ~**some** adj solo

long¹ /lɒŋ/ adj lungo; **a** ~ **time** molto tempo; **a** ~ **way** distante; **in the** ~ **run** a lungo andare; (in the end) alla fin fine ● adv a lungo, lungamente; **how** ~ **is it?** quanto è lungo?; (in time) quanto dura?; **all day** ~ tutto il giorno; **no** ~ **ago** non molto tempo fa; **before** ~ fra breve; **he's no** ~**er here** non è più qui; **as or so** ~ **as** finché; (provided that) purché; **so** ~! Ⓣ ciao!; **will you be** ~? [ti] ci vuole molto?

long² vi ~ **for** desiderare ardentemente

long-'distance adj a grande distanza; (Sport) di fondo; (call) interurbano

longing /'lɒŋɪŋ/ adj desideroso ● n brama f. ~**ly** adv con desiderio

longitude /'lɒŋgɪtjuːd/ n (Geog) longitudine f

long: ~ **jump** n salto m in lungo. ~**-range** adj (Aeron, Mil) a lunga portata; (forecast) a lungo termine. ~**-sighted** adj presbite. ~**-term** adj a lunga scadenza. ~**-winded** /-'wɪndɪd/ adj prolisso

loo /luː/ n Ⓣ gabinetto m

look /lʊk/ n occhiata f; (appearance) aspetto m; [**good**] ~**s** pl bellezza f; **have a** ~ **at** dare un'occhiata a ● vi guardare; (seem) sembrare; ~ **here!** mi ascolti bene!; ~ **at** guardare; ~ **for** cercare; ~ **like** (resemble) assomigliare a. □ ~ **after** vt badare a. □ ~ **down** vi guardare in basso; ~ **down on sb** fig guardare dall'alto in basso qcno. □ **~ forward to** vt essere impaziente di. □ **~ in** vi passare da. □ **~ into** vt (examine) esaminare. □ **~ on to** vt (room): dare su. □ **~ out** vi guardare fuori; (take care) fare attenzione; **~ out for** cercare; **~ out!** attento! **look round** vi girarsi; (in shop, town etc) dare un'occhiata. □ **~ through** vt dare un'occhiata a (script, notes). □ **~ up** vi guardare in alto; **~ up to sb** fig rispettare qcno ●vt cercare [nel dizionario] (word); (visit) andare a trovare

'look-out n guardia f; (prospect) prospettiva f; **be on the ~ for** tenere gli occhi aperti per

loom /luːm/ vi apparire; fig profilarsi

loony /'luːniː/ adj & n 🔢 matto, -a mf. **~ bin** n manicomio m

loop /luːp/ n cappio m; (on garment) passante m. **~hole** n (in the law) scappatoia f

loose /luːs/ adj libero; (knot) allentato; (page) staccato; (clothes) largo; (morals) dissoluto; (inexact) vago; **be at a ~ end** non sapere cosa fare; **come ~** (knot): sciogliersi; **set ~** liberare. **~ 'change** n spiccioli mpl. **~ly** adv scorrevolmente; (defined) vagamente

loosen /'luːsn/ vt sciogliere

loot /luːt/ n bottino m ●vt/i depredare. **~er** n predatore, -trice mf. **~ing** n saccheggio m

lop /lɒp/ **~ off** vt (pt/pp lopped) potare

lop'sided adj sbilenco

lord /lɔːd/ n signore m; (title) Lord m; **House of L~s** Camera f dei Lords; **the L~'s Prayer** il Padrenostro; **good L~!** Dio mio!

lorry /'lɒriː/ n camion m inv; **~ driver** n camionista mf

lose /luːz/ v (pt/pp lost) ●vt perdere ●vi perdere; (clock): essere indietro; **get lost** perdersi; **get lost!** 🔢 va a quel paese! **~r** n perdente mf

loss /lɒs/ n perdita f; (Comm) **~es** perdite fpl; **be at a ~** essere perplesso; **be at a ~ for words** non trovare le parole

lost /lɒst/ ▷**LOSE** ●adj perduto. **~ 'property office** n ufficio m oggetti smarriti

lot¹ /lɒt/ (at auction) lotto m; **draw ~s** tirare a sorte

lot² n **the ~** il tutto; **a ~ of, ~s of** molto; **the ~ of you** tutti voi; **it has changed a ~** è cambiato molto

lotion /'ləʊʃn/ n lozione f

lottery /'lɒtəriː/ n lotteria f. **~ ticket** n biglietto m della lotteria

loud /laʊd/ adj sonoro, alto; (colours) sgargiante ●adv forte; **out ~** ad alta voce. **~'hailer** n megafono m. **~ly** adv forte. **~ 'speaker** n altoparlante m

lounge /laʊndʒ/ n salotto m; (in hotel) salone m ●vi poltrire. **~ suit** n vestito m da uomo, completo m da uomo

louse /laʊs/ n (pl **lice**) pidocchio m

lousy /'laʊziː/ adj (-ier, -iest) 🔢 schifoso

lout /laʊt/ n zoticone m. **~ish** adj rozzo

lovable /'lʌvəbl/ adj adorabile

love /lʌv/ n amore m; (Tennis) zero m; **in ~** innamorato (**with** di) ●vt amare (person, country); **I ~ watching tennis** mi piace molto guardare il tennis. **~affair** n relazione f [sentimentale]. **~ letter** n lettera f d'amore

lovely /'lʌvliː/ adj (-ier, -iest) bello; (in looks) bello, attraente; (in character) piacevole; (meal) delizioso; **have a ~ time** divertirsi molto

lover /'lʌvə(r)/ n amante mf

loving /'lʌvɪŋ/ adj affettuoso

low /ləʊ/ adj basso; (depressed) giù m ●adv basso; **feel ~** sentirsi giù ● n minimo m; (Meteorol) depressione f;

at an all-time ~ (prices etc) al livello minimo

lower /'ləʊə(r)/ adj & adv ▷ **LOW** •vt abbassare; ~ **oneself** abbassarsi

loyal /'lɔɪəl/ adj leale. ~**ty** n lealtà f; ~ **card** carta f fedeltà

lozenge /'lɒzɪndʒ/ n losanga f; (tablet) pastiglia f

LP n abbr long-playing record

Ltd abbr (Limited) s.r.l.

lubricat|e /'luːbrɪkeɪt/ vt lubrificare. ~**ion** n lubrificazione f

lucid /'luːsɪd/ adj (explanation) chiaro; (sane) lucido. ~**ity** n lucidità f; (of explanation) chiarezza f

luck /lʌk/ n fortuna f; **bad** ~ sfortuna f; **good** ~! buona fortuna! ~**ily** adv fortunatamente

lucky /'lʌkɪ/ adj (-ier, -iest) fortunato; **be** ~ essere fortunato; (thing:) portare fortuna. ~ **'charm** n portafortuna m inv

lucrative /'luːkrətɪv/ adj lucrativo

ludicrous /'luːdɪkrəs/ adj ridicolo. ~**ly** adv (expensive, complex) eccessivamente

lug /lʌg/ vt (pt/pp lugged) 🅸 trascinare

luggage /'lʌgɪdʒ/ n bagaglio m; ~-**rack** n portabagagli m inv. ~ **trolley** n carrello m portabagagli. ~-**van** n bagagliaio m

lukewarm /'luːk-/ adj tiepido; fig poco entusiasta

lull /lʌl/ n pausa f •vt ~ **to sleep** cullare

lullaby /'lʌləbaɪ/ n ninna nanna f

lumber /'lʌmbə(r)/ n cianfrusaglie fpl; (Am: timber) legname m •vt 🅸 ~ **sb with sth** affibbiare qcsa a qcno. ~ **jack** n taglialegna m inv

luminous /'luːmɪnəs/ adj luminoso

lump[1] /lʌmp/ n (of sugar) zolletta f; (swelling) gonfiore m; (in breast) nodulo m; (in sauce) grumo m •vt ~ **together** ammucchiare

lump[2] vt ~ **it** 🅸 **you'll just have to** ~ **it** che ti piaccia o no è così

lump sum n somma f globale

lumpy /'lʌmpɪ/ adj (-ier, -iest) grumoso

lunacy /'luːnəsɪ/ n follia f

lunar /'luːnə(r)/ adj lunare

lunatic /'luːnətɪk/ n pazzo, -a mf

lunch /lʌntʃ/ n pranzo m •vi pranzare

luncheon /'lʌntʃn/ n (formal) pranzo m. ~ **meat** n carne f in scatola. ~ **voucher** n buono m pasto

lung /lʌŋ/ n polmone m. ~ **cancer** n cancro m al polmone

lunge /lʌndʒ/ vi lanciarsi (at su)

lurch[1] /lɜːtʃ/ n **leave in the** ~ 🅸 lasciare nei guai

lurch[2] vi barcollare

lure /lʊə(r)/ n esca f; fig lusinga f •vt adescare

lurid /'lʊərɪd/ adj (gaudy) sgargiante; (sensational) sensazionalistico

lurk /lɜːk/ vi appostarsi

luscious /'lʌʃəs/ adj saporito; fig sexy inv

lush /lʌʃ/ adj lussureggiante

lust /lʌst/ n lussuria f •vi ~ **after** desiderare [fortemente]. ~**ful** adj lussurioso

lute /luːt/ n liuto m

luxuriant /lʌg'zʊərɪənt/ adj lussureggiante

luxurious /lʌg'zʊərɪəs/ adj lussuoso

luxury /'lʌkʃərɪ/ n lusso m •attrib di lusso

lying /'laɪɪŋ/ ▷ **LIE**[1] & [2] •n mentire m

lynch /lɪntʃ/ vt linciare

lyric /'lɪrɪk/ adj lirico. ~**al** adj lirico; (🅸: enthusiastic) entusiasta. ~**s** npl parole fpl

Mm

mac /mæk/ n ① impermeabile m

macaroni /mækə'rəʊni/ n maccheroni mpl

mace¹ /meɪs/ n (staff) mazza f

mace² n (spice) macis m o f

machine /mə'ʃiːn/ n macchina f
● vt (sew) cucire a macchina; (Techn) lavorare a macchina. ~-gun n mitragliatrice f

machinery /mə'ʃiːnəri/ n macchinario m

mackerel /'mækr(ə)l/ n inv sgombro m

mackintosh /'mækɪntɒʃ/ n impermeabile m

mad /mæd/ adj (madder, maddest) pazzo, matto; (①: angry) furioso (at con); like a ① come un pazzo; be ~ about sb/sth (①: keen on) andare matto per qcno/qcsa

madam /'mædəm/ n signora f

mad cow disease n morbo m della mucca pazza

madden /'mædən/ vt (make angry) far diventare matto

made /meɪd/ ▷MAKE; ~ to measure [fatto] su misura

mad|ly /'mædlɪ/ adv follemente; ~ly in love innamorato follemente. ~man n pazzo m. ~ness n pazzia f

madonna /mə'dɒnə/ n madonna f

magazine /mægə'ziːn/ n rivista f; (Mil, Phot) magazzino m

maggot /'mægət/ n verme m

magic /'mædʒɪk/ n magia f; (tricks) giochi mpl di prestigio ● adj magico; (trick) di prestigio. ~al adj magico

magician /mə'dʒɪʃn/ n mago, -a mf; (entertainer) prestigiatore, -trice m

magistrate /'mædʒɪstreɪt/ n

magistrato m

magnet /'mægnɪt/ n magnete m, calamita f. ~ic adj magnetico. ~ism n magnetismo m

magnification /mægnɪfɪ'keɪʃn/ n ingrandimento m

magnifice|nce /mæg'nɪfɪsəns/ n magnificenza f. ~t adj magnifico

magnify /'mægnɪfaɪ/ vt (pt/pp -ied) ingrandire; (exaggerate) ingigantire. ~ing glass n lente f d'ingrandimento

magnitude /'mægnɪtjuːd/ n grandezza f; (importance) importanza f

magpie /'mægpaɪ/ n gazza f

mahogany /mə'hɒgənɪ/ n mogano m ● attrib di mogano

maid /meɪd/ n cameriera f; old ~ pej zitella f

maiden /'meɪdn/ n (liter) fanciulla f ● adj (speech, voyage) inaugurale. ~ 'aunt n zia f zitella. ~ name n nome m da ragazza

mail /meɪl/ n posta f ● vt impostare. ~bag n sacco m postale. ~box n Am cassetta f delle lettere; (e-mail) casella f di posta elettronica. ~ing list n elenco m d'indirizzi per un mailing. ~man n Am postino m. ~ order n vendita f per corrispondenza. ~-order firm n ditta f di vendita per corrispondenza. ~shot n mailing m inv

maim /meɪm/ vt menomare

main¹ /meɪn/ n (water, gas, electricity) conduttura f principale

main² adj principale; the ~ thing is to... la cosa essenziale è di... ● n in the ~ nel complesso

main: ~land /-lænd/ n continente m. ~ly adv principalmente. ~ street n via f principale

maintain /meɪn'teɪn/ vt mantenere; (keep in repair) curare la manutenzione di; (claim) sostenere

maintenance /'meɪntənəns/ n mantenimento m; (care) manuten-

zione f; (allowance) alimenti mpl

maisonette /meɪzə'nɛt/ n appartamento m a due piani

majestic /mə'dʒɛstɪk/ adj maestoso

majesty /'mædʒəstɪ/ n maestà f; His/Her M~ Sua Maestà

major /'meɪdʒə(r)/ adj maggiore; ~ road strada f con diritto di precedenza ●n (Mil, Mus) maggiore m ● Am ~ **in** specializzarsi in

Majorca /mə'jɔːkə/ n Maiorca f

majority /mə'dʒɒrətɪ/ n maggioranza f; be in the ~ avere la maggioranza

make /meɪk/ n (brand) marca f ●v (pt/pp made) ● vt fare; (earn) guadagnare; rendere (happy, clear); prendere (decision); ~ sb laugh far ridere qcno; ~ sb do sth far fare qcsa a qcno; ~ it (to party, top of hill etc) farcela; **what time do you** ~ **it?** che ore fai? ● vi ~ **as if to** fare per. □ ~ **do** vi arrangiarsi. □ ~ **for** vt dirigersi verso. □ ~ **off** vi fuggire. □ ~ **out** vt (distinguish) distinguere; (write out) rilasciare (cheque); compilare (list); (claim) far credere. □ ~ **over** vt cedere. □ ~ **up** vt (constitute) comporre; (complete) (invent) inventare; (apply cosmetics to) truccare; fare (parcel); ~ **up one's mind** decidersi; ~ **it up** (after quarrel) riconciliarsi ● vi (after quarrel) fare la pace; ~ up for compensare; ~ up for lost time recuperare il tempo perso

'make-believe n finzione f

maker /'meɪkə(r)/ n fabbricante mf; M~ Creatore m

make: ~ **shift** adj di fortuna ●n espediente m. **~-up** n trucco m; (character) natura f

making /'meɪkɪŋ/ n have the ~s of aver la stoffa di

maladjusted /mælə'dʒʌstɪd/ adj disadattato

malaria /mə'leərɪə/ n malaria f

Malaysia /mə'leɪzɪə/ n Malesia f

male /meɪl/ adj maschile ●n maschio m. ~ **nurse** n infermiere m

malfunction /mæl'fʌŋkʃn/ n funzionamento m imperfetto ● vi funzionare male

malice /'mælɪs/ n malignità f; bear sb ~ voler del male a qcno

malicious /mə'lɪʃəs/ adj maligno

mallet /'mælɪt/ n martello m di legno

malnu'trition /mæl-/ n malnutrizione f

mal'practice n negligenza f

malt /mɔːlt/ n malto m

Malta /'mɔːltə/ n Malta f. **~ese** adj & n maltese mf

mammal /'mæml/ n mammifero m

mammoth /'mæməθ/ adj mastodontico ●n mammut m inv

man /mæn/ n (pl men) uomo m; (chess, draughts) pedina f ● vt (pt/pp manned) equipaggiare; essere di servizio a (counter, telephones)

manage /'mænɪdʒ/ vt dirigere; gestire (shop, affairs); (cope with) farcela; ~ **to do sth** riuscire a fare qcsa ● vi riuscire; (cope) farcela (on coll). **~able** adj (hair) docile; (size) maneggevole. **~ment** n gestione f; the ~ment la direzione

manager /'mænɪdʒə(r)/ n direttore m; (of shop, bar) gestore m; (Sport) manager m inv. **~ess** n direttrice f. **~ial** adj **~ial staff** personale m direttivo

mandate /'mændeɪt/ n mandato m. **~ory** adj obbligatorio

mane /meɪn/ n criniera f

mangle /'mæŋgl/ vt (damage) maciullare

man: **~'handle** vt malmenare. **~hole** n botola f. **~hood** n età f adulta; (quality) virilità f. **~hour** n ora f lavorativa. **~-hunt** n caccia f all'uomo

man|ia /'meɪnɪə/ n mania f. **~iac** n maniaco, -a mf

manicure /'mænɪkjʊə(r)/ n manicure f ● vt fare la manicure a

manifest /'mænɪfest/ adj manifesto ● vt ~ itself manifestarsi. ~ly adv palesemente

manifesto /mænɪ'festəʊ/ n manifesto m

manipulat|e /mə'nɪpjʊleɪt/ vt manipolare. ~ion n manipolazione f

man'kind n genere m umano

manly /'mænlɪ/ adj virile

'man-made adj artificiale. ~ fibre n fibra f sintetica

manner /'mænə(r)/ n maniera f; in this ~ in questo modo; have no ~s avere dei pessimi modi; good/bad ~s buone/cattive maniere fpl. ~ism n affettazione f

manor /'mænə(r)/ n maniero m

'manpower n manodopera f

mansion /'mænʃn/ n palazzo m

'manslaughter n omicidio m colposo

mantelpiece /'mæntl-/ n mensola f di caminetto

manual /'mænjʊəl/ adj manuale ● n manuale m

manufacture /mænjʊ'fæktʃə(r)/ vt fabbricare ● n manifattura f. ~r n fabbricante m

manure /mə'njʊə(r)/ n concime m

manuscript /'mænjʊskrɪpt/ n manoscritto m

many /'menɪ/ adj & pron molti; there are as ~ boys as girls ci sono tanti ragazzi quante ragazze; as ~ as 500 ben 500; as ~ as that così tanti; as ~ altrettanti; very ~, a good/great ~ moltissimi; ~ a time molte volte

map /mæp/ n carta f geografica; (of town) mappa f ● **map out** vt (pt/pp mapped) fig programmare

mar /mɑː(r)/ vt (pt/pp marred) rovinare

marathon /'mærəθən/ n maratona f

marble /'mɑːbl/ n marmo m; (for game) pallina f ● attrib di marmo

march n marcia f; (protest) dimostrazione f ● vi marciare ● vt far marciare; ~ sb off scortare qcno fuori

March /mɑːtʃ/ n marzo m

mare /meə(r)/ n giumenta f

margarine /mɑːdʒə'riːn/ n margarina f

margin /'mɑːdʒɪn/ n margine m. ~al adj marginale. ~ally adv marginalmente

marijuana /mærʊ'wɑːnə/ n marijuana f

marina /mə'riːnə/ n porticciolo m

marine /mə'riːn/ adj marino ● n (sailor) soldato m di fanteria marina

marionette /mærɪə'net/ n marionetta f

mark[1] /mɑːk/ n (currency) marco m

mark[2] n (stain) macchia f; (sign, indication) segno m; (Sch) voto m ● vt segnare; (stain) macchiare; (Sch) correggere; (Sport) marcare; ~ time (Mil) segnare il passo; fig non far progressi; ~ my words ricordati quello che dico. □ ~ out vt delimitare; fig designare

marked /mɑːkt/ adj marcato. ~ly adv notevolmente

marker /'mɑːkə(r)/ n (for highlighting) evidenziatore m; (Sport) marcatore m; (of exam) esaminatore, -trice mf

market /'mɑːkɪt/ n mercato m ● vt vendere al mercato; (launch) commercializzare; on the ~ sul mercato. ~ing n marketing m. ~ re'search n ricerca f di mercato

marksman /'mɑːksmən/ n tiratore m scelto

marmalade /'mɑːməleɪd/ n marmellata f d'arance

maroon /mə'ruːn/ adj marrone rossastro

marquee /mɑː'kiː/ n tendone m

marriage /'mærɪdʒ/ n

matrimonio *m*

married /'mærɪd/ *adj* sposato; (life) coniugale

marrow /'mærəʊ/ *n* (Anat) midollo *m*; (vegetable) zucca *f*

marr|y /'mærɪ/ *vt* (pt/pp **married**) sposare; **get ~ied** sposarsi ● *vi* sposarsi

marsh /mɑːʃ/ *n* palude *f*

marshal /'mɑːʃl/ *n* (steward) cerimoniere *m* ● *vt* (pt/pp **marshalled**) fig organizzare (arguments)

marshy /'mɑːʃɪ/ *adj* paludoso

martial /'mɑːʃl/ *adj* marziale

martyr /'mɑːtə(r)/ *n* martire *mf* ● *vt* martoriare. **~dom** *n* martirio *m*. **~ed** *adj* 🔟 da martire

marvel /'mɑːvl/ *n* meraviglia *f* ● *vi* (pt/pp **marvelled**) meravigliarsi (at di). **~lous** *adj* meraviglioso

Marxis|m /'mɑːksɪzm/ *n* marxismo *m*. **~t** *adj* & *n* marxista *mf*

marzipan /'mɑːzɪpæn/ *n* marzapane *m*

mascara /mæ'skɑːrə/ *n* mascara *m inv*

mascot /'mæskət/ *n* mascotte *f inv*

masculin|e /'mæskjʊlɪn/ *adj* maschile ● *n* (Gram) maschile *m*. **~ity** *n* mascolinità *f*

mash /mæʃ/ *vt* impastare. **~ed potatoes** *npl* purè *m inv* di patate

mask /mɑːsk/ *n* maschera *f* ● *vt* mascherare

masochis|m /'mæsəkɪzm/ *n* masochismo *m*. **~t** *n* masochista *mf*

mason /'meɪsn/ *n* muratore *m*

Mason *n* massone *m*. **~ic** *adj* massonico

masonry /'meɪsnrɪ/ *n* massoneria *f*

masquerade /mæskə'reɪd/ *n* fig mascherata *f* ● *vi* **~ as** (pose) farsi passare per

mass¹ /mæs/ *n* (Relig) messa *f*

mass² *n* massa *f*; **~es of** 🔟 un sacco di ● *vi* ammassarsi

massacre /'mæsəkə(r)/ *n* massacro *m* ● *vt* massacrare

massage /'mæsɑːʒ/ *n* massaggio *m* ● *vt* massaggiare; fig manipolare (statistics)

masseu|r /mæ'sɜː(r)/ *n* massaggiatore *m*. **~se** *n* massaggiatrice *f*

massive /'mæsɪv/ *adj* enorme

mass: ~ media *npl* mezzi *mpl* di comunicazione di massa, mass media *mpl*. **~-pro'duce** *vt* produrre in serie

mast /mɑːst/ *n* (Naut) albero *m*; (for radio) antenna *f*

master /'mɑːstə(r)/ *n* maestro *m*, padrone *m*; (teacher) professore *m*; (of ship) capitano *m*; **M~** (boy) signorino *m*

master: ~-key *n* passe-partout *m inv*. **~-mind** *n* cervello *m* ● *vt* ideare e dirigere. **~piece** *n* capolavoro *m*. **~stroke** *n* colpo *m* da maestro. **~y** *n* (of subject) padronanza *f*

masturbat|e /'mæstəbeɪt/ *vi* masturbarsi. **~ion** *n* masturbazione *f*

mat /mæt/ *n* stuoia *f*; (on table) sottopiatto *m*

match¹ /mætʃ/ *n* (Sport) partita *f*; (equal) uguale *mf*; (marriage) matrimonio *m*; (person to marry) partito *m*; **be a good ~** (colours): intonarsi bene; **be no ~ for** non essere dello stesso livello di ● *vt* (equal) uguagliare; (be like) andare bene con ● *vi* intonarsi

match² *n* fiammifero *m*. **~box** *n* scatola *f* di fiammiferi

matching /'mætʃɪŋ/ *adj* intonato

mate¹ /meɪt/ *n* compagno, -a *mf*; (assistant) aiuto *m*; (Naut) secondo *m*; (🔟: friend) amico, -a *mf* ● *vi* accoppiarsi ● *vt* accoppiare

mate² *n* (in chess) scacco *m* matto

material /mə'tɪərɪəl/ *n* materiale *m*; (fabric) stoffa *f*; **raw ~s** materie *fpl* prime ● *adj* materiale

maternal /mə'tɜːnl/ *adj* materno

maternity /mə'tɜːnətɪ/ *n* maternità *f*. **~ clothes** *npl* abiti *mpl* premaman.

~ **ward** *n* maternità *f inv*

mathematic|al /mæθə'mætɪkl/ *adj* matematico. ~**ian** *n* matematico, -a *mf*

mathematics /mæθ'mætɪks/ *n* matematica *fsg*

maths /mæθs/ *n* [1] matematica *fsg*

matinée /'mætɪneɪ/ *n* (*Theat*) matinée *m*

matricul|ate /mə'trɪkjʊleɪt/ *vi* immatricolarsi. ~**ion** *n* immatricolazione *f*

matrix /'meɪtrɪks/ *n* (*pl* **matrices** /-si:z/) *n* matrice *f*

matted /'mætɪd/ *adj* ~ **hair** capelli *mpl* tutti appiccicati tra loro

matter /'mætə(r)/ *n* (*affair*) faccenda *f*; (*question*) questione *f*; (*pus*) pus *m*; (*phys: substance*) materia *f*; **as a ~ of fact** a dire la verità; **what is the ~?** che cosa c'è? • *vi* importare; ~ **to sb** essere importante per qcno; **it doesn't ~** non importa. ~**-of-fact** *adj* pratico

mattress /'mætrɪs/ *n* materasso *m*

matur|e /mə'tʃʊə(r)/ *adj* maturo; (*Comm*) in scadenza • *vi* maturare • *vt* far maturare. ~**ity** *n* maturità *f*; (*Fin*) maturazione *f*

maul /mɔːl/ *vt* malmenare

mauve /məʊv/ *adj* malva

maxim /'mæksɪm/ *n* massima *f*

maximum /'mæksɪməm/ *adj* massimo; **ten minutes ~** dieci minuti al massimo • *n* (*pl* **-ima**) massimo *m*

may /meɪ/ *v aux* (*solo al presente*) potere; ~ **I come in?** posso entrare?; **if I ~ say so** se mi posso permettere; ~ **you both be very happy** siate felici; **I ~ as well stay** potrei anche rimanere; **it ~ be true** potrebbe esser vero; **she ~ be old, but...** sarà anche vecchia, ma...

May /meɪ/ *n* maggio *m*

maybe /'meɪbiː/ *adv* forse, può darsi

'May Day *n* il primo maggio

mayonnaise /meɪə'neɪz/ *n* maionese *f*

mayor /'meə(r)/ *n* sindaco *m*. ~**ess** *n* sindaco *m*; (*wife of mayor*) moglie *f* del sindaco

maze /meɪz/ *n* labirinto *m*

me /miː/ *pron* (*object*) mi; (*with preposition*) me; **she called me** mi ha chiamato; **she called me, not you** ha chiamato me, non te; **give me the money** dammi i soldi; **give it to me** dammelo; **he gave it to me** me lo ha dato; **it's ~** sono io

meadow /'medəʊ/ *n* prato *m*

meagre /'miːgə(r)/ *adj* scarso

meal¹ /miːl/ *n* pasto *m*

meal² *n* (*grain*) farina *f*

mean¹ /miːn/ *adj* avaro; (*unkind*) meschino

mean² *adj* medio *m* (*average*) media *f*; **Greenwich ~ time** ora *f* media di Greenwich

mean³ *vt* (*pt/pp* **meant**) voler dire; (*signify*) significare; (*intend*) intendere; **I ~ it** lo dico seriamente; ~ **well** avere buone intenzioni; **be meant for** (*present:*) essere destinato a; (*remark:*) essere riferito a

meander /mɪ'ændə(r)/ *vi* vagare

meaning /'miːnɪŋ/ *n* significato *m*. ~**ful** *adj* significativo. ~**less** *adj* senza senso

means /miːnz/ *n* mezzo *m*; ~ **of transport** mezzo *m* di trasporto; **by** ~ **of** per mezzo di; **by all** ~! certamente!; **by no** ~ niente affatto • *npl* (*resources*) mezzi *mpl*

meant /ment/ ▷**MEAN³**

'meantime *n* **in the** ~ nel frattempo • *adv* intanto

'meanwhile *adv* intanto

measles /'miːzlz/ *n* morbillo *m*

measly /'miːzlɪ/ *adj* [1] misero

measure /'meʒə(r)/ *n* misura *f* • *vt/i* misurare. □ ~ **up to** *vt fig* essere all'altezza di. ~**d** *adj* misurato.

~**ment** n misura f

meat /miːt/ n carne f. ~ **ball** n (Culin) polpetta f di carne. ~ **loaf** n polpettone m

mechan|ic /mɪˈkænɪk/ n meccanico m. ~**ical** adj meccanico; ~**ical engineering** ingegneria f meccanica. ~**ically** adv meccanicamente. ~**ics** n meccanica f ● npl meccanismo msg

mechan|ism /ˈmekənɪzm/ n meccanismo m. ~**ize** vt meccanizzare

medal /ˈmedl/ n medaglia f

medallist /ˈmedəlɪst/ n vincitore, -trice mf di una medaglia

meddle /ˈmedl/ vi immischiarsi (in di); (tinker) armeggiare (with con)

media /ˈmiːdɪə/ npl ▶**MEDIUM** ● npl the ~ i mass media

mediat|e /ˈmiːdɪeɪt/ vi fare da mediatore. ~**ion** n mediazione f. ~**or** n mediatore, -trice mf

medical /ˈmedɪkl/ adj medico ● n visita f medica. ~ **insurance** n assicurazione f sanitaria. ~ **student** n studente, -essa mf di medicina

medicat|ed /ˈmedɪkeɪtɪd/ adj medicato. ~**ion** n (drugs) medicinali mpl

medicinal /mɪˈdɪsɪnl/ adj medicinale

medicine /ˈmedsən/ n medicina f

medieval /medɪˈiːvl/ adj medievale

mediocr|e /miːdɪˈəʊkə(r)/ adj mediocre. ~**ity** n mediocrità f

meditat|e /ˈmedɪteɪt/ vi meditare (on su). ~**ion** n meditazione f

Mediterranean /medɪtəˈreɪnɪən/ n the ~ [Sea] il [mare m] Mediterraneo m ● adj mediterraneo

medium /ˈmiːdɪəm/ adj medio; (Culin) di media cottura ● n (pl media) mezzo m; (pl -s) (person) medium mf inv

medium-sized adj di taglia media

medley /ˈmedlɪ/ n miscuglio m; (Mus) miscellanea f

meek /miːk/ adj mite, mansueto.

~**ly** adv docilmente

meet /miːt/ v (pt/pp met) ● vt incontrare; (at station, airport) andare incontro a; (for first time) far la conoscenza di; (pay) pagare (bill); soddisfare (requirements) ● vi incontrarsi; (committee:) riunirsi; ~ **with** incontrare (problem); incontrarsi con (person) ● n raduno m [sportivo]

meeting /ˈmiːtɪŋ/ n riunione f, meeting m inv; (large) assemblea f; (by chance) incontro m

megabyte /ˈmegəbaɪt/ n megabyte m

megaphone /ˈmegəfəʊn/ n megafono m

melancholy /ˈmelənkəlɪ/ adj malinconico ● n malinconia f

mellow /ˈmeləʊ/ adj (wine) generoso; (sound, colour) caldo; (person) dolce ● vi (person:) addolcirsi

melodrama /ˈmelə-/ n melodramma m. ~**tic** adj melodrammatico

melody /ˈmelədɪ/ n melodia f

melon /ˈmelən/ n melone m

melt /melt/ vt sciogliere ● vi sciogliersi. □ ~ **down** vt fondere. ~**ing-pot** n fig crogiuolo m

member /ˈmembə(r)/ n membro m; ~ **countries** paesi mpl membri; M~ **of Parliament** deputato, -a mf; M~ **of the European Parliament** eurodeputato, -a mf. ~**ship** n iscrizione f; (members) soci mpl

membrane /ˈmembreɪn/ n membrana f

memo /ˈmeməʊ/ n promemoria m inv

memorable /ˈmemərəbl/ adj memorabile

memorandum /meməˈrændəm/ n promemoria m inv

memorial /mɪˈmɔːrɪəl/ n monumento m. ~ **service** n funzione f commemorativa

memorize /ˈmeməraɪz/ vt

memorizzare

memory /'memərɪ/ n also (Comput) memoria f; (thing remembered) ricordo m; **from ~ a** memoria; **in ~ of** in ricordo di

men /men/ ▷ **MAN**

menac|e /'menəs/ n minaccia f; (nuisance) piaga f ● vt minacciare. **~ing** adj minaccioso

mend /mend/ vt riparare; (darn) rammendare ● n **on the ~** in via di guarigione

'menfolk n uomini mpl

menial /'mi:nɪəl/ adj umile

meningitis /menɪn'dʒaɪtɪs/ n meningite f

menopause /'menə-/ n menopausa f

menstruat|e /'menstruent/ vi mestruare. **~ion** n mestruazione f

mental /mentl/ adj mentale; (⊞: mad) pazzo. **a'rithmetic** n calcolo m mentale. **~ illness** n malattia f mentale

mental|ity /men'tælətɪ/ n mentalità f inv. **~ly** adv mentalmente; **~ly ill** malato di mente

mention /'menʃn/ n menzione f ● vt menzionare; **don't ~ it** non c'è di che

menu /'menju:/ n menu m inv

MEP n abbr Member of the European Parliament

mercenary /'mɜːsɪnərɪ/ adj mercenario ● n mercenario m

merchandise /'mɜːtʃəndaɪz/ n merce f

merchant /'mɜːtʃənt/ n commerciante mf. **~ bank** n banca f d'affari. **~ 'navy** n marina f mercantile

merci|ful /'mɜːsɪfl/ adj misericordioso. **~fully** adv ⊞ grazie a Dio. **~less** adj spietato

mercury /'mɜːkjʊrɪ/ n mercurio m

mercy /'mɜːsɪ/ n misericordia f; **be at sb's ~** essere alla mercè di qcno,

essere in balia di qcno

mere /mɪə(r)/ adj solo. **~ly** adv solamente

merge /mɜːdʒ/ vi fondersi

merger /'mɜːdʒə(r)/ n fusione f

meringue /mə'ræŋ/ n meringa f

merit /'merɪt/ n merito m; (advantage) qualità f inv ● vt meritare

mermaid /'mɜːmeɪd/ n sirena f

merri|ly /'merɪlɪ/ adv allegramente. **~ment** n baldoria f

merry /'merɪ/ adj (-ier, -iest) allegro; **~ Christmas!** Buon Natale!

merry: **~-go-round** n giostra f. **~-making** n festa f

mesh /meʃ/ n maglia f

mesmerize /'mezməraɪz/ vt ipnotizzare. **~d** adj fig ipnotizzato

mess /mes/ n disordine m, casino m ⊞; (trouble) guaio m; (something dirty) sporco m; (Mil) mensa f; **make a ~ of** (botch) fare un pasticcio di ● **mess about** vi perder tempo; **~ about with** armeggiare con ● vt prendere in giro (person). □ **~ up** vt mettere in disordine, incasinare ⊞; (botch) mandare all'aria

message /'mesɪdʒ/ n messaggio m

messenger /'mesɪndʒə(r)/ n messaggero m

Messiah /mɪ'saɪə/ n Messia m

Messrs /'mesəz/ npl (on letter) **~ Smith** Spett. ditta Smith

messy /'mesɪ/ adj (-ier, -iest) disordinato; (in dress) sciatto

met /met/ ▷ **MEET**

metal /'metl/ n metallo m ● adj di metallo. **~lic** adj metallico

metaphor /'metəfə(r)/ n metafora f. **~ical** adj metaforico

meteor /'mi:tɪə(r)/ n meteora f. **~ic** adj fulmineo

meteorological /'mi:tɪərə'lɒdʒɪkl/ adj meteorologico

meteo|rologist /'mi:tɪə'rɒlədʒɪst/ n meteorologo, -a mf. **~rology** n meteorologia f

meter[1] /'mi:tə(r)/ n contatore m

meter[2] n Am = **metre**

method /'meθəd/ n metodo m

methodical /mɪ'θɒdɪkl/ adj metodico. **~ly** adv metodicamente

methylated /'meθɪleɪtɪd/ adj **~ spirit[s]** alcol m denaturato

meticulous /mɪ'tɪkjʊləs/ adj meticoloso. **~ly** adv meticolosamente

metre /'mi:tə(r)/ n metro m

metric /'metrɪk/ adj metrico

metropolis /mɪ'trɒpəlɪs/ n metropoli f inv

mew /mju:/ n miao m ●vi miagolare

Mexican /'meksɪkən/ adj & n messicano, -a mf. **'Mexico** n Messico m

miaow /mɪ'aʊ/ n miao m ●vi miagolare

mice /maɪs/ ▷ **MOUSE**

mickey /'mɪkɪ/ n take the **~** out of prendere in giro

micro /'maɪkrəʊ/: **~chip** n microchip m. **~computer** n microcomputer m. **~film** n microfilm m. **~phone** microfono m. **~processor** n microprocessore m. **~scope** n microscopio m. **~scopic** adj microscopico. **~wave** n microonda f; (oven) forno m a microonde

microbe /'maɪkrəʊb/ n microbo m

mid /mɪd/ adj **~ May** metà maggio; in **~ air** a mezz'aria

midday /mɪd'deɪ/ n mezzogiorno m

middle /'mɪdl/ adj di centro; the **M~ Ages** il medioevo; the **~ class[es]** la classe media; the **M~ East** il Medio Oriente ●n mezzo m; in the **~ of** (room, floor etc) in mezzo a; in the **~ of the night** nel pieno della notte, a notte piena

middle: **~aged** adj di mezza età. **~class** adj borghese. **~man** n (Comm) intermediario m

middling /'mɪdlɪŋ/ adj discreto

midge /mɪdʒ/ n moscerino m

midget /'mɪdʒɪt/ n nano, -a mf

Midlands /'mɪdləndz/ npl the **~** l'Inghilterra fsg centrale

'midnight n mezzanotte f

midriff /'mɪdrɪf/ n diaframma m

midst /mɪdst/ n in the **~ of** in mezzo a; in our **~** fra di noi, in mezzo a noi

mid: **~summer** n mezza estate f **~way** adv a metà strada. **~wife** n ostetrica f. **~'winter** n pieno inverno m

might[1] /maɪt/ v aux **I ~** potrei; will you come? – I **~** vieni? – può darsi; it **~** be true potrebbe essere vero; I **~** as well stay potrei anche restare; you **~** have drowned avresti potuto affogare; you **~** have said so! avresti potuto dirlo!

might[2] n potere m

mighty /'maɪtɪ/ adj (-ier, -iest) potente ●adv **I** molto

migraine /'mi:greɪn/ n emicrania f

migrant /'maɪgrənt/ adj migratore ●n (bird) migratore, -trice mf; (person: for work) emigrante mf

migrate /maɪ'greɪt/ vi migrare. **~ion** n migrazione f

Milan /mɪ'læn/ n Milano f

mild /maɪld/ adj (weather) mite; (person) dolce; (flavour) delicato; (illness) leggero

mildew /'mɪldju:/ n muffa f

mild|ly /'maɪldlɪ/ adv moderatamente; (say) dolcemente; **to put it ~ly** a dir poco, senza esagerazione. **~ness** n (of person, words) dolcezza f; (of weather) mitezza f

mile /maɪl/ n miglio m (= 1,6 km); **~s nicer** **I** molto più bello

mile|age /-ɪdʒ/ n chilometraggio m. **~stone** n pietra f miliare

militant /'mɪlɪtənt/ adj & n militante mf

military /'mɪlɪtrɪ/ adj militare. **~ service** n servizio m militare

militia /mɪ'lɪʃə/ n milizia f

milk /mɪlk/ n latte m • vt mungere

milk: ~**man** n lattaio m. ~ **shake** n frappé m inv

milky /'mɪlkɪ/ adj (-ier, -iest) latteo; (tea etc) con molto latte. M~ **Way** n (Astr) Via f Lattea

mill /mɪl/ n mulino m; (factory) fabbrica f; (for coffee etc) macinino m • vt macinare (grain). **mill about, mill around** vi brulicare

millennium /mɪ'lenɪəm/ n millennio m

miller /'mɪlə(r)/ n mugnaio m

million /'mɪljən/ n milione m; a ~ **pounds** un milione di sterline. ~**aire** n miliardario, -a mf

'millstone n fig peso m

mime /maɪm/ n mimo m • vt mimare

mimic /'mɪmɪk/ n imitatore, -trice mf • vt (pt/pp **mimicked**) imitare. ~**ry** n mimetismo m

mince /mɪns/ n carne f tritata • vt (Culin) tritare; **not** ~ **one's words** parlare senza mezzi termini

mince 'pie n pasticcino m a base di frutta secca

mincer /'mɪnsə(r)/ n tritacarne m inv

mind /maɪnd/ n mente f; (sanity) ragione f; **to my** ~ a mio parere; **give sb a piece of one's** ~ dire chiaro e tondo a qcno quello che si pensa; **make up one's** ~ decidersi; **have sth in** ~ avere qcsa in mente; **bear sth in** ~ tenere presente qcsa; **have something on one's** ~ essere preoccupato; **have a good** ~ **to** avere una gran voglia di; **I have changed my** ~ ho cambiato idea; **in two** ~s indeciso; **are you out of your** ~? sei diventato matto? • vt (look after) occuparsi di; **I don't** ~ **the noise** il rumore non mi dà fastidio; **I don't** ~ **what we do** non mi importa quello che facciamo; ~ **the**

step! attenzione al gradino! • vi **I don't** ~ non mi importa; **never** ~! non importa!; **do you** ~ **if...?** ti dispiace se...? **mind out** vi ~ **out!** [fai] attenzione!

mind|ful adj ~**ful of** attento a. ~**less** adj noncurante

mine¹ /maɪn/ poss pron il mio m, la mia f, i miei mpl, le mie fpl; **a friend of** ~ un mio amico; **friends of** ~ dei miei amici; **that is** ~ questo è mio; (as opposed to yours) questo è il mio

mine² n miniera f; (explosive) mina f • vt estrarre; (Mil) minare. ~ **detector** n rivelatore m di mine. ~**field** n campo m minato

mineral /'mɪnərəl/ n minerale m • adj minerale. ~ **water** n acqua f minerale

mingle /'mɪŋgl/ vi ~ **with** mescolarsi a

mini /'mɪnɪ/ n (skirt) mini f

miniature /'mɪnɪtʃə(r)/ adj in miniatura • n miniatura f

mini|bus /'mɪnɪ-/ n minibus m, pulmino m. ~**cab** n taxi m inv

minim|al /'mɪnɪməl/ adj minimo. ~**ize** vt minimizzare. ~**um** n (pl -ima) minimo m • adj minimo; **ten minutes** ~**um** minimo dieci minuti

mining /'maɪnɪŋ/ n estrazione f • adj estrattivo

miniskirt /'mɪnɪ-/ n minigonna f

minist|er /'mɪnɪstə(r)/ n ministro m; (Relig) pastore m. ~**erial** adj ministeriale

ministry /'mɪnɪstrɪ/ n (Pol) ministero m; **the** ~ (Relig) il ministero sacerdotale

mink /mɪŋk/ n visone m

minor /'maɪnə(r)/ adj minore • n minorenne mf

minority /maɪ'nɒrətɪ/ n minoranza f; (age) minore età f

mint¹ /mɪnt/ n 1 patrimonio m • adj in ~ **condition** in condizione perfetta

mint² n (herb) menta f

minus /'maɪnəs/ prep meno; (ℤ: without) senza ● n ~ [**sign**] meno m

minute¹ /'mɪnɪt/ n minuto m; in a ~ (shortly) in un minuto; ~s pl (of meeting) verbale msg

minute² /maɪ'njuːt/ adj minuto; (precise) minuzioso

mirac|le /'mɪrəkl/ n miracolo m. ~ulous adj miracoloso

mirage /'mɪrɑːʒ/ n miraggio m

mirror /'mɪrə(r)/ n specchio m ● vt rispecchiare

mirth /mɜːθ/ n ilarità f

misappre'hension n malinteso m; be under a ~ avere frainteso

misbe'have vi comportarsi male

mis'calcu|late vt/i calcolare male. ~lation n calcolo m sbagliato

'miscarriage n aborto m spontaneo; ~ of justice errore m giudiziario. **mis'carry** vi abortire

miscellaneous /mɪsə'leɪnɪəs/ adj assortito

mischief /'mɪstʃɪf/ n malefatta f, (harm) danno m

mischievous /'mɪstʃɪvəs/ adj (naughty) birichino; (malicious) dannoso

miscon'ception n concetto m erroneo

mis'conduct n cattiva condotta f

misde'meanour n reato m

miser /'maɪzə(r)/ n avaro m

miserab|le /'mɪzrəbl/ adj (unhappy) infelice; (wretched) miserabile; (fig: weather) deprimente. ~y adv (live, fail) miseramente; (say) tristemente

miserly /'maɪzəlɪ/ adj avaro; (amount) ridicolo

misery /'mɪzərɪ/ n miseria f; (ℤ: person) piagnone, -a mf

mis'fire vi (gun:) far cilecca; (plan etc:) non riuscire

'misfit n disadattato, -a mf

mis'fortune n sfortuna f

mis'guided adj fuorviato

mishap /'mɪshæp/ n disavventura f

misin'terpret vt fraintendere

mis'judge vt giudicare male; (estimate wrongly) valutare male

mis'lay vt (pt/pp -laid) smarrire

mis'lead vt (pt/pp -led) fuorviare. ~ing adj fuorviante

mis'manage vt amministrare male. ~ment n cattiva amministrazione f

'misprint n errore m di stampa

miss /mɪs/ n colpo m mancato ● vt (fail to hit or find) mancare; perdere (train, bus, class); (feel the loss of) sentire la mancanza di; I ~ed that part (failed to notice) mi è sfuggita quella parte ● vi but he ~ed (failed to hit) ma l'ha mancato. ▫ ~ **out** vt saltare, omettere

Miss n (pl -es) signorina f

misshapen /mɪs'ʃeɪpən/ adj malformato

missile /'mɪsaɪl/ n missile m

missing /'mɪsɪŋ/ adj mancante; (person) scomparso; (Mil) disperso; be ~ essere introvabile

mission /'mɪʃn/ n missione f

missionary /'mɪʃənrɪ/ n missionario, -a mf

mist /mɪst/ n (fog) foschia f ● mist up vi appannarsi, annebbiarsi

mistake /mɪ'steɪk/ n sbaglio m; by ~ per sbaglio ● vt (pt mistook, pp mistaken) sbagliare (road, house); fraintendere (meaning, words); ~ for prendere per

mistaken /mɪ'steɪkən/ adj sbagliato; be ~ sbagliarsi; ~ identity errore m di persona. ~ly adv erroneamente

mistletoe /'mɪsltəʊ/ n vischio m

mistress /'mɪstrɪs/ n padrona f; (teacher) maestra f; (lover) amante f

mis'trust n sfiducia f ● vt non aver fiducia in

misty /ˈmɪstɪ/ adj (-ier, -iest) nebbioso

misunder'stand vt (pt/pp **-stood**) fraintendere. **~ing** n malinteso m

misuse[1] /mɪsˈjuːz/ vt usare male

misuse[2] /mɪsˈjuːs/ n cattivo uso m

mite /maɪt/ n (child) piccino, -a mf

mitten /ˈmɪtn/ n manopola f, muffola m

mix /mɪks/ n (combination) mescolanza f; (Culin) miscuglio m; (ready-made) preparato m ● vt mischiare ● vi mischiarsi; (person:) inserirsi; **~ with** (associate with) frequentare. □ **~ up** vt mescolare (papers); (confuse, mistake for) confondere

mixed /mɪkst/ adj misto; **~ up** (person) confuso

mixer /ˈmɪksə(r)/ n (Culin) frullatore m, mixer m inv; **he's a good ~** è un tipo socievole

mixture /ˈmɪkstʃə(r)/ n mescolanza f; (medicine) sciroppo m; (Culin) miscela f

'mix-up n (confusion) confusione f; (mistake) pasticcio m

moan /məʊn/ n lamento m ● vi lamentarsi; (complain) lagnarsi

moat /məʊt/ n fossato m

mob /mɒb/ n folla f; (rabble) gentaglia f; (⬚: gang) banda f ● vt (pt/pp **mobbed**) assalire

mobile /ˈməʊbaɪl/ adj mobile ● n composizione f mobile. **~ 'home** n casa f roulotte. **~ [phone]** n [telefono m] cellulare m, telefonino m

mock /mɒk/ adj finto ● vt canzonare. **~ery** n derisione f

model /ˈmɒdl/ n modello m; [fashion] **~** indossatore, -trice mf, modello, -a mf ● adj (yacht, plane) in miniatura; (pupil, husband) esemplare, modello ● v (pt/pp **modelled**) ● vt indossare (clothes) ● vi fare l'indossatore, -trice mf; (for artist) posare

modem /ˈməʊdem/ n modem m inv

moderate[1] /ˈmɒdəreɪt/ vt mode-

rare ● vi moderarsi

moderate[2] /ˈmɒdərət/ adj moderato ● n (Pol) moderato, -a mf. **~ly** adv (drink, speak etc) moderatamente; (good, bad etc) relativamente

moderation /mɒdəˈreɪʃn/ n moderazione f; **in ~** con moderazione

modern /ˈmɒdn/ adj moderno. **~ize** vt modernizzare

modest /ˈmɒdɪst/ adj modesto. **~y** n modestia f

modif|ication /mɒdɪfɪˈkeɪʃn/ n modificazione f. **~y** vt (pt/pp **-fied**) modificare

module /ˈmɒdjuːl/ n modulo m

moist /mɔɪst/ adj umido

moisten /ˈmɔɪsn/ vt inumidire

moistur|e /ˈmɔɪstʃə(r)/ n umidità f. **~izer** n [crema f] idratante m

mole[1] /məʊl/ n (on face etc) neo m

mole[2] /məʊl/ n (Zool) talpa f

molecule /ˈmɒlɪkjuːl/ n molecola f

molest /məˈlest/ vt molestare

mollycoddle /ˈmɒlɪkɒdl/ vt tenere nella bambagia

molten /ˈməʊltən/ adj fuso

mom /mɒm/ n Am ⬚ mamma f

moment /ˈməʊmənt/ n momento m; **at the ~** in questo momento. **~arily** adv momentaneamente. **~ary** adj momentaneo

momentous /məˈmentəs/ adj molto importante

momentum /məˈmentəm/ n impeto m

monarch /ˈmɒnək/ n monarca m. **~y** n monarchia f

monast|ery /ˈmɒnəstrɪ/ n monastero m. **~ic** adj monastico

Monday /ˈmʌndeɪ/ n lunedì m inv

money /ˈmʌnɪ/ n denaro m

money-box n salvadanaio m

mongrel /ˈmʌŋɡrəl/ n bastardo m

monitor /ˈmɒnɪtə(r)/ n (Techn) monitor m inv ● vt controllare

monk /mʌŋk/ n monaco m

monkey /'mʌŋkɪ/ n scimmia f.
~**-nut** n nocciolina f americana.
~**-wrench** n chiave f inglese a
rullino

mono /'mɒnəʊ/ n mono m

monologue /'mɒnəlɒg/ n mono-
logo m

monopol|ize /mə'nɒpəlaɪz/ vt mo-
nopolizzare. ~**y** n monopolio m

monotone /'mɒnətəʊn/ n speak
in a ~ parlare con tono monotono

monoton|ous /mə'nɒtənəs/ adj
monotono. ~**y** n monotonia f

monsoon /mɒn'suːn/ n monsone m

monster /'mɒnstə(r)/ n mostro m

monstrous /'mɒnstrəs/ adj mo-
struoso

Montenegro /'mɒntɪ'niːgrəʊ/ n
Montenegro m

month /mʌnθ/ n mese m. ~**ly** adj
mensile ● adv mensilmente ● n (periodical) mensile m

monument /'mɒnjʊmənt/ n monumento m. ~**al** adj fig monumentale

moo /muː/ n muggito m ● vi (pt/pp
mooed) muggire

mood /muːd/ n umore m; **be in a
good/bad** ~ essere di buon/cattivo
umore; **be in the** ~ **for** essere in
vena di

moody /'muːdɪ/ adj (-ier, -iest) (variable) lunatico; (bad-tempered) di ma-
lumore

moon /muːn/ n luna f; **over the** ~
🅸 al settimo cielo

moon: ~light n chiaro m di luna
● vi 🅸 lavorare in nero. ~**lit** adj illu-
minato dalla luna

moor[1] /mʊə(r)/ n brughiera f

moor[2] vt (Naut) ormeggiare

mop /mɒp/ n straccio m (per i
pavimenti); ~ **of hair** zazzera f ● vt
(pt/pp mopped) lavare con lo straccio. □ ~ **up** vt (dry) asciugare con lo

straccio; (clean) pulire con lo straccio

mope /məʊp/ vi essere depresso

moped /'məʊped/ n ciclomotore m

moral /'mɒrəl/ adj morale ● n morale f. ~**ly** adv moralmente. ~**s** pl
moralità f

morale /mə'rɑːl/ n morale m

morality /mə'rælətɪ/ n moralità f

more /mɔː(r)/ adj adv; **a few** ~
books un po' più di libri; **some** ~
tea? ancora un po' di tè?; **there's
no** ~ **bread** non c'è più pane; **there
are no** ~ **apples** non ci sono più
mele; **one** ~ **word and...** ancora
una parola e... ● pron di più; **would
you like some** ~? ne vuoi ancora?;
no ~, **thank you** non ne voglio più,
grazie ● adv più; ~ **interesting** più
interessante; ~ **and quickly** sempre più veloce; ~ **than** più di; **I
don't love him any** ~ non lo amo
più; **once** ~ ancora una volta; ~ **or
less** più o meno; **the** ~ **I see him,
the** ~ **I like him** più lo vedo, più
mi piace

moreover /mɔːr'əʊvə(r)/ adv
inoltre

morgue /mɔːg/ n obitorio m

morning /'mɔːnɪŋ/ n mattino m,
mattina f; **in the** ~ del mattino; (tomorrow) domani mattina

Morocc|o /mə'rɒkəʊ/ n Marocco m
● adj ~**an** adj & n marocchino, -a mf

moron /'mɔːrɒn/ n 🅸 deficiente mf

morose /mə'rəʊs/ adj scontroso

Morse /mɔːs/ n ~ **[code]** (codice
m] Morse m

morsel /'mɔːsl/ n (food) boccone m

mortal /'mɔːtl/ adj & n mortale mf.
~**ity** n mortalità f. ~**ly** adv
(wounded, offended) a morte;
(afraid) da morire

mortar /'mɔːtə(r)/ n mortaio m

mortgage /'mɔːgɪdʒ/ n mutuo m;
(on property) ipoteca f ● vt ipotecare

mortuary /'mɔːtjʊərɪ/ n camera f
mortuaria

m

mosaic /məʊˈzeɪɪk/ n mosaico m

Moslem /ˈmʊzlɪm/ adj & n musulmano, -a mf

mosque /mɒsk/ n moschea f

mosquito /mɒsˈkiːtəʊ/ n (pl -es) zanzara f

moss /mɒs/ n muschio m. **~y** adj muschioso

most /məʊst/ adj (majority) la maggior parte di; for the ~ part per lo più ● adv più, maggiormente; (very) estremamente, molto; the ~ interesting day la giornata più interessante; a ~ interesting day una giornata estremamente interessante; the ~ beautiful woman in the world la donna più bella del mondo; ~ unlikely veramente improbabile ● pron ~ of them la maggior parte di loro; at [the] ~ al massimo; make the ~ of sfruttare al massimo; ~ of the time la maggior parte del tempo. **~ly** adv per lo più

MOT n revisione f obbligatoria di autoveicoli

motel /məʊˈtel/ n motel m inv

moth /mɒθ/ n falena f; [clothes-] ~ tarma f

mother /ˈmʌðə(r)/ n madre f; M~'s Day la festa della mamma ● vt fare da madre a

mother: ~-in-law n (pl ~s-in-law) suocera f. ~ly adj materno. ~-of-pearl n madreperla f. ~-to-be n futura mamma f. ~ tongue n madrelingua f

motif /məʊˈtiːf/ n motivo m

motion /ˈməʊʃn/ n moto m; (proposal) mozione f; (gesture) gesto m ● vt/i ~ [to] sb to come in fare segno a qcno di entrare. **~less** adj immobile. **~lessly** adv senza alcun movimento

motivat|e /ˈməʊtɪveɪt/ vt motivare. **~ion** n motivazione f

motive /ˈməʊtɪv/ n motivo m

motley /ˈmɒtlɪ/ adj disparato

motor /ˈməʊtə(r)/ n motore m; (car) macchina f ● adj a motore; (Anat) motore ● vi andare in macchina

motor: ~ bike n [] moto f inv. ~ boat n motoscafo m. ~ car n automobile f. ~ cycle n motocicletta f. **~cyclist** n motociclista m. **~ing** n automobilismo m. **~ist** n automobilista mf. **~way** n autostrada f

motto /ˈmɒtəʊ/ n (pl -es) motto m

mould[1] /məʊld/ n (fungus) muffa f

mould[2] n stampo m ● vt foggiare; fig formare. **~ing** n (Archit) cornice f

mouldy /ˈməʊldɪ/ adj ammuffito; ([]: worthless) ridicolo

moult /məʊlt/ vi (bird:) fare la muta; (animal:) perdere il pelo

mound /maʊnd/ n mucchio m; (hill) collinetta f

mount /maʊnt/ n (horse) cavalcatura f; (of jewel, photo, picture) montatura f ● vt montare a (horse); salire su (bicycle); incastonare (jewel); incorniciare (photo, picture) ● vi aumentare. □ ~ up vi aumentare

mountain /ˈmaʊntɪn/ n montagna f; ~ bike n mountain bike f inv

mountaineer /maʊntɪˈnɪə(r)/ n alpinista mf. **~ing** n alpinismo m

mountainous /ˈmaʊntɪnəs/ adj montagnoso

mourn /mɔːn/ vt lamentare ● vi ~ for piangere la morte di. ~ er n persona f che partecipa a un funerale. **~ful** adj triste. **~ing** n in ~ing in lutto

mouse /maʊs/ n (pl mice) topo m; (Comput) mouse m inv. **~trap** n trappola f [per topi]

mousse /muːs/ n (Culin) mousse f inv

moustache /məˈstɑːʃ/ n baffi mpl

mouth[1] /maʊð/ vt ~ sth dire qcsa silenziosamente muovendo solamente le labbra

mouth[2] /maʊθ/ n bocca f; (of river) foce f

mouth: ~ful n boccone m.

~-organ n armonica f [a bocca].
~wash n acqua f dentifricia

move /muːv/ n mossa f; (*moving house*) trasloco m; **on the ~** in movimento; **get a ~ on** 🄸 darsi una mossa ● vt muovere; (*emotionally*) commuovere; spostare (car); (*transfer*) trasferire; (*propose*) proporre; **~ house** traslocare ● vi muoversi; (*move house*) traslocare. □ **~ along** vi andare avanti ● vt muovere in avanti. □ **~ away** vi allontanarsi; (*move house*) trasferirsi ● vt allontanare. □ **~ forward** vi avanzare ● vt spostare avanti. □ **~ in** vi (*to a house*) trasferirsi. □ **~ off** vi (*vehicle:*) muoversi. □ **~ out** vi andare via. □ **~ over** vi spostarsi ● vt spostare. □ **~ up** vi muoversi; (*advance*) avanzare

movement /'muːvmənt/ n movimento m

movie /'muːvɪ/ n film m inv; **go to the ~s** andare al cinema

moving /'muːvɪŋ/ adj mobile; (*touching*) commovente

mow /məʊ/ v (*pt* mowed, *pp* mown *or* mowed) tagliare (lawn). □ **~ down** vt (*destroy*) sterminare

mower /'məʊə(r)/ n tosaerbe m inv

MP n abbr Member of Parliament

MP3 player n lettore m MP3

Mr /'mɪstə(r)/ n (*pl* Messrs) Signor m

Mrs /'mɪsɪz/ n Signora f

Ms /mɪz/ n Signora f (*modo m formale di rivolgersi ad una donna quando non si vuole connotarla come sposata o nubile*)

much /mʌtʃ/ adj, adv & pron molto; **~ as** per quanto; **I love you just as ~ as** before/him ti amo quanto prima/lui; **as ~ as £5 million** ben cinque milioni di sterline; **as ~ as that** così tanto; **very ~** tantissimo, moltissimo; **~ the same** quasi uguale

muck /mʌk/ n (*dirt*) sporco m; (*farming*) letame m; (🄸: *filth*) porcheria f. □ **~ about** vi 🄸 perder tempo; **~**

about with trafficare con. □ **~ up** vt 🄸 rovinare; (*make dirty*) sporcare

mud /mʌd/ n fango m

muddle /'mʌdl/ n disordine m; (*mix-up*) confusione f ● vt **~ [up]** confondere (dates)

muddy /'mʌdɪ/ adj (**-ier, -iest**) (path) fangoso; (shoes) infangato

muesli /'muːzlɪ/ n muesli m inv

muffle /'mʌfl/ vt smorzare (sound). **muffle up** vt (*for warmth*) imbaccuccare

muffler /'mʌflə(r)/ n sciarpa f; Am (*Auto*) marmitta f

mug[1] /mʌg/ n tazza f; (*for beer*) boccale m; (🄸: *face*) muso m; (🄸: *simpleton*) pollo m

mug[2] vt (*pt/pp* mugged) aggredire e derubare. **~ger** n assalitore, -trice mf. **~ging** n aggressione f per furto

muggy /'mʌgɪ/ adj (**-ier, -iest**) afoso

mule /mjuːl/ n mulo m

mull /mʌl/ vt **~ over** rimuginare su

multiple /'mʌltɪpl/ adj multiplo

multiplication /mʌltɪplɪ'keɪʃn/ n moltiplicazione f

multiply /'mʌltɪplaɪ/ v (*pt/pp* -**ied**) ● vt moltiplicare (**by** per) ● vi moltiplicarsi

mum[1] /mʌm/ adj **keep ~** 🄸 non aprire bocca

mum[2] n 🄸 mamma f

mumble /'mʌmbl/ vt/i borbottare

mummy[1] /'mʌmɪ/ n 🄸 mamma f

mummy[2] n (*Archaeol*) mummia f

mumps /mʌmps/ n orecchioni mpl

munch /mʌntʃ/ vt/i sgranocchiare

mundane /mʌn'deɪn/ adj (*everyday*) banale

municipal /mjuː'nɪsɪpl/ adj municipale

mural /'mjʊərəl/ n dipinto m murale

murder /'mɜːdə(r)/ n assassinio m ● vt assassinare; (🄸: *ruin*) massacrare. **~er** n assassino, -a mf. **~ous** adj omicida

murky /'mɜːkɪ/ adj (-ier, -iest)
oscuro

murmur /'mɜːmə(r)/ n mormorio m
● vt/i mormorare

muscle /'mʌsl/ n muscolo m
● **muscle in** vi ⊠ intromettersi
(on in)

muscular /'mʌskjʊlə(r)/ adj muscolare; (strong) muscoloso

muse /mjuːz/ vi meditare (on su)

museum /mjuːˈzɪəm/ n museo m

mushroom /'mʌʃrʊm/ n fungo m
● vi fig spuntare come funghi

music /'mjuːzɪk/ n musica f; (written)
spartito m.

musical /'mjuːzɪkl/ adj musicale;
(person) dotato di senso musicale
● n commedia f musicale. ● **box** n
carillon m inv. ~ **instrument** n strumento m musicale

musician /mjuːˈzɪʃn/ n musicista mf

Muslim /'mʊzlɪm/ adj & n musulmano, -a mf

mussel /'mʌsl/ n cozza f

must /mʌst/ v aux (solo al presente)
dovere; **you ~ not be late** non devi
essere in ritardo; **she ~ have finished by now** (probability) deve aver
finito ormai ● **n a ~** ⊞ una cosa da
non perdere

mustard /'mʌstəd/ n senape f

musty /'mʌstɪ/ adj (-ier, -iest)
stantio

mutation /mjuːˈteɪʃn/ n (Biol) mutazione f

mute /mjuːt/ adj muto

mutilat|e /'mjuːtɪleɪt/ vt mutilare.
~**ion** n mutilazione f

mutter /'mʌtə(r)/ vt/i borbottare

mutton /'mʌtn/ n carne f di
montone

mutual /'mjuːtjʊəl/ adj reciproco;
(⊞: common) comune. ~**ly** adv reciprocamente

muzzle /'mʌzl/ n (of animal) muso
m; (of firearm) bocca f; (for dog) muse-

ruola f ● vt fig mettere il bavaglio a

my /maɪ/ adj il mio m, la mia f, i miei
mpl, le mie fpl; **my mother/father**
mia madre/mio padre

myself /maɪˈself/ pron (reflexive) mi;
(emphatic) me stesso; (after prep) me;
I've seen it ~ l'ho visto io stesso;
by ~ da solo; **I thought to ~** ho
pensato tra me e me; **I'm proud of
~** sono fiero di me

mysterious /mɪˈstɪərɪəs/ adj misterioso. ~**ly** adv misteriosamente

mystery /'mɪstərɪ/ n mistero m; ~
[story] racconto m del mistero

mysti|c[al] /'mɪstɪk[l]/ adj mistico.
~**cism** n misticismo m

mystify /'mɪstɪfaɪ/ vt (pt/pp -ied)
disorientare

mystique /mɪˈstiːk/ n mistica f

myth /mɪθ/ n mito m. ~**ical** adj
mitico

mythology /mɪˈθɒlədʒɪ/ n mitologia f

Nn

nab /næb/ vt (pt/pp nabbed) ⊞
beccare

nag[1] /næg/ n (horse) ronzino m

nag[2] (pt/pp nagged) vt assillare ● vi
essere insistente ● n (person) brontolone, -a mf. ~**ging** adj (pain) persistente

nail /neɪl/ n chiodo m; (of finger, toe)
unghia f ● **nail down** vt inchiodare;
~ **sb down to a time/price** far fissare a qcno un'ora/un prezzo

nail polish n smalto m [per
unghie]

naked /'neɪkɪd/ adj nudo; **with the
~ eye** a occhio nudo

name /neɪm/ n nome m; **what's**

your ~? come ti chiami?; my ~ is Matthew mi chiamo Matthew; I know her by ~ la conosco di nome; by the ~ of Bates di nome Bates; call sb ~s 🔲 insultare qcno ●*vt* (*to position*) nominare; chiamare (baby); (*identify*) citare; be ~d after essere chiamato col nome di. ~less *adj* senza nome. ~ly *adv* cioè

namesake *n* omonimo, -a *mf*

nanny /'nænɪ/ *n* bambinaia *f*. ~-goat *n* capra *f*

nap /næp/ *n* pisolino *m*; have a ~ fare un pisolino ●*vi* (*pt/pp* napped) catch sb ~ping cogliere qcno alla sprovvista

napkin /'næpkɪn/ *n* tovagliolo *m*

Naples /'neɪplz/ *n* Napoli *f*

nappy /'næpɪ/ *n* pannolino *m*

narcotic /nɑː'kɒtɪk/ *adj & n* narcotico *m*

narrat|e /nə'reɪt/ *vt* narrare. ~ion *n* narrazione *f*

narrative /'nærətɪv/ *adj* narrativo ●*n* narrazione *f*

narrator /nə'reɪtə(r)/ *n* narratore, -trice *mf*

narrow /'nærəʊ/ *adj* stretto; (fig: views) ristretto; (margin, majority) scarso ●*vi* restringersi. ~ly *adv* ~ly escape death evitare la morte per un pelo. ~-'minded *adj* di idee ristrette

nasal /'neɪzl/ *adj* nasale

nasty /'nɑːstɪ/ *adj* (-ier, -iest) (smell, person, remark) cattivo; (injury, situation, weather) brutto; turn ~ (person:) diventare cattivo

nation /'neɪʃn/ *n* nazione *f*

national /'næʃənl/ *adj* nazionale ●*n* cittadino, -a *mf*

national 'anthem *n* inno *m* nazionale

nationalism /'næʃənəlɪzm/ *n* nazionalismo *m*

nationality /næʃə'nælɪtɪ/ *n* nazionalità *f inv*

'nation-wide *adj* su scala nazionale

native /'neɪtɪv/ *adj* nativo; (*innate*) innato ●*n* nativo, -a *mf*; (*local inhabitant*) abitante *mf* del posto; (*outside Europe*) indigeno, -a *mf*; she's a ~ of Venice è originaria di Venezia

native: ~ 'land *n* paese *m* nativo. ~ 'language *n* lingua *f* madre

Nativity /nə'tɪvətɪ/ *n* the ~ la Natività *f*. ~ play *n* rappresentazione *f* sulla nascita di Gesù

natter /'nætə(r)/ *vi* 🔲 chiacchierare

natural /'nætʃrəl/ *adj* naturale

natural 'history *n* storia *f* naturale

naturalist /'nætʃ(ə)rəlɪst/ *n* naturalista *mf*

naturally /'nætʃ(ə)rəlɪ/ *adv* (of course) naturalmente; (by nature) per natura

nature /'neɪtʃə(r)/ *n* natura *f*; by ~ per natura. ~ reserve *n* riserva *f* naturale

naughty /'nɔːtɪ/ *adj* (-ier, -iest) monello; (slightly indecent) spinto

nausea /'nɔːzɪə/ *n* nausea *f*

nautical /'nɔːtɪkl/ *adj* nautico. ~ mile *n* miglio *m* marino

naval /'neɪvl/ *adj* navale

nave /neɪv/ *n* navata *f* centrale

navel /'neɪvl/ n ombelico m

navigable /'nævɪgəbl/ adj navigabile

navigat|e /'nævɪgeɪt/ vi navigare; (Auto) fare da navigatore ● vt navigare su (river). **~ion** n navigazione f. **~or** n navigatore m

navy /'neɪvɪ/ n marina f ● **~ [blue]** adj blu marine inv ● n blu m inv marine

Neapolitan /nɪə'pɒlɪtən/ adj & n napoletano, -a mf

near /nɪə(r)/ adj vicino; (future) prossimo; **the ~est bank** la banca più vicina ● adv vicino; **draw ~** avvicinarsi; **~ at hand** a portata di mano ● prep vicino a; **he was ~ to tears** aveva le lacrime agli occhi ● vt avvicinarsi a

near: **~by** adj & adv vicino. **~ly** adv quasi; **it's not ~ly enough** non è per niente sufficiente. **~-sighted** adj Am miope

neat /ni:t/ adj (tidy) ordinato; (clever) efficace; (undiluted) liscio. **~ly** adv ordinatamente; (cleverly) efficacemente. **~ness** n (tidiness) ordine m

necessarily /nesə'serɪlɪ/ adv necessariamente

necessary /'nesəsərɪ/ adj necessario

necessit|ate /nɪ'sesɪteɪt/ vt rendere necessario. **~y** n necessità f inv

neck /nek/ n collo m; (of dress) colletto m; **~ and ~** testa a testa

necklace /'neklɪs/ n collana f

neckline n scollatura f

need /ni:d/ n bisogno m; **be in ~ of** avere bisogno di; **if ~ be** se ce ne fosse bisogno; **there is a ~ for** c'è bisogno di; **there is no ~ for that** non ce n'è bisogno; **there is no ~ for you to go** non c'è bisogno che tu vada ● vt aver bisogno di; **I ~ to know** devo saperlo; **it ~s to be done** bisogna farlo ● v aux **you ~ not go** non c'è bisogno che tu vada;

~ I come? devo [proprio] venire?

needle /'ni:dl/ n ago m; (for knitting) uncinetto m; (of record player) puntina f ● vt (fam: annoy) punzecchiare

needless /'ni:dlɪs/ adj inutile

'needlework n cucito m

needy /'ni:dɪ/ adj (-ier, -iest) bisognoso

negative /'negətɪv/ adj negativo ● n negazione f; (Phot) negativo m; **in the ~** (Gram) alla forma negativa

neglect /nɪ'glekt/ n trascuratezza f; state of ~ stato m di abbandono ● vt trascurare; **he ~ed to write** non si è curato di scrivere. **~ed** adj trascurato. **~ful** adj negligente; **be ~ful of** trascurare

negligen|ce /'neglɪdʒəns/ n negligenza f. **~t** adj negligente

negligible /'neglɪdʒəbl/ adj trascurabile

negotiable /nɪ'gəʊʃəbl/ adj (road) transitabile; (Comm) negoziabile; **not ~** (cheque) non trasferibile

negotiat|e /nɪ'gəʊʃɪeɪt/ vt negoziare; (Auto) prendere (bend) ● vi negoziare. **~ion** n negoziato m. **~or** n negoziatore, -trice mf

neigh /neɪ/ vi nitrire

neighbour /'neɪbə(r)/ n vicino, -a mf. **~hood** n vicinato m; **in the ~hood of** nei dintorni di; fig circa. **~ing** adj vicino. **~ly** adj amichevole

neither /'naɪðə(r)/ adj & pron nessuno dei due, né l'uno né l'altro ● adv **~... nor** né... né ● conj nemmeno, neanche; **~ do/did I** nemmeno io

neon /'ni:ɒn/ n neon m. **~ light** n luce f al neon

nephew /'nevju:/ n nipote m

nerve /nɜ:v/ n nervo m; (fam: courage) coraggio m; (fam: impudence) faccia f tosta; **lose one's ~** perdersi d'animo. **~-racking** adj logorante

nervous /'nɜ:vəs/ adj nervoso; **he makes me ~** mi mette in agitazione; **be a** ~ **wreck** avere i nervi a pezzi. ~ **breakdown** n esaurimento m nervoso. ~**ly** adv nervosamente. ~**ness** n nervosismo m; (before important event) tensione f

nervy /'nɜːvɪ/ adj (-ier, -iest) nervoso; (Am: impudent) sfacciato

nest /nest/ n nido m ● vi fare il nido. ~**egg** n gruzzolo m

nestle /'nesl/ vi accoccolarsi

net[1] /net/ n rete f ● vt (pt/pp netted) (catch) prendere (con la rete)

net[2] adj netto ● vt (pt/pp netted) incassare un utile netto di

'netball n sport m inv femminile, simile a pallacanestro

Netherlands /'neðələndz/ npl the ~ i Paesi mpl Bassi

netting /'netɪŋ/ n [wire] ~ reticolato m

nettle /'netl/ n ortica f

'network n rete f

neur|osis /njʊə'rəʊsɪs/ n (pl -oses /-siːz/) nevrosi f inv. ~**otic** adj nevrotico

neuter /'njuːtə(r)/ adj (Gram) neutro ● n (Gram) neutro m ● vt sterilizzare

neutral /'njuːtrəl/ adj neutro; (country, person) neutrale ● n in ~ (Auto) in folle. ~**ity** n neutralità f. ~**ize** vt neutralizzare

never /'nevə(r)/ adv [non...] mai; ([I] expressing disbelief) ma va; ~ **again** mai più; **well I** ~! ciò che avrebbe dettol. ~**-ending** adj interminabile

nevertheless /nevəðə'les/ adv tuttavia

new /njuː/ adj nuovo

new: ~**born** adj neonato. ~**comer** n nuovo, -a arrivato, -a mf. ~**fangled** /-'fæŋgld/ adj pej modernizzato

newly adv (recently) di recente; ~**-built** costruito di recente. ~**-weds** npl sposini mpl

news /njuːz/ n notizie fpl; (TV) tele-

giornale m; (Radio) giornale m radio; **piece of** ~ notizia f

news: ~**agent** n giornalaio, -a mf. ~**caster** n giornalista mf televisivo, -a/radiofonico, -a. ~**flash** n notizia f flash. ~**letter** n bollettino m d'informazione. ~**paper** n giornale m; (material) carta f di giornale. ~**reader** n giornalista mf televisivo, -a/radiofonico, -a

next /nekst/ adj prossimo; (adjoining) vicino; **who's** ~? a chi tocca?; ~ **door** accanto; ~ **to nothing** quasi niente; **the** ~ **day** il giorno dopo; ~ **week** la settimana prossima; **the week after** ~ fra due settimane ● adv dopo; **when will you see him** ~? quando lo rivedi la prossima volta?; ~ **to** accanto a ● n seguente mf; ~ **of kin** parente m prossimo

nib /nɪb/ n pennino m

nibble /'nɪbl/ vt/i mordicchiare

nice /naɪs/ adj (day, weather, holiday) bello; (person) gentile, simpatico; (food) buono; **it was** ~ **meeting you** è stato un piacere conoscerla. ~**ly** adv gentilmente; (well) bene. ~**ties** n nicchia f

niche /niːʃ/ n nicchia f

nick /nɪk/ n tacca f; (on chin etc) taglietto m; ([I]: prison) galera f; ([I]: police station) centrale f [di polizia]; **in the** ~ **of time** appena in tempo ● vt intaccare; ([I]: steal) fregare; ([I]: arrest) beccare; ~ **one's chin** farsi un taglietto nel mento

nickel /'nɪkl/ n nichel m; Am moneta f da cinque centesimi

'nickname n soprannome m ● vt soprannominare

nicotine /'nɪkətiːn/ n nicotina f

niece /niːs/ n nipote f

niggling /'nɪɡlɪŋ/ adj (detail) insignificante; (pain) fastidioso; (doubt) persistente

night /naɪt/ n notte f; (evening) sera f; **at ~** la notte, di notte; (in the evening) la sera, di sera; **Monday ~** lunedì notte/sera ● adj di notte

night: **~cap** n papalina f; (drink) bicchierino m bevuto prima di andare a letto. **~-club** n locale m notturno, night[-club] m inv. **~dress** n camicia f da notte. **~fall** n crepuscolo m. **~-gown**, 🅔 **~ie** /'naɪtɪ/ n camicia f da notte

night: **~-life** n vita f notturna. **~ly** adj di notte, di sera ● adv ogni notte, ogni sera. **~mare** n incubo m. **~-school** n scuola f serale. **~-time** n **at ~-time** di notte, la notte. **~-'watchman** n guardiano m notturno

nil /nɪl/ n nulla m; (Sport) zero m

nimbl|e /'nɪmbl/ adj agile. **~y** adv agilmente

nine /naɪn/ adj inv ove ● n nove m. **~'teen** adj diciannove inv ● n diciannove. **~'teenth** adj & n diciannovesimo, -a mf

ninetieth /'naɪntɪɪθ/ adj & n novantesimo, -a mf

ninety /'naɪntɪ/ adj novanta inv ● n novanta m

ninth /naɪnθ/ adj & n nono, -a mf

nip /nɪp/ n pizzicotto m; (bite) morso m ● vt pizzicare; (bite) mordere; **~ in the bud** fig stroncare sul nascere ● vi (🅔: run) fare un salto

nipple /'nɪpl/ n capezzolo m; (Am: on bottle) tettarella f

nippy /'nɪpɪ/ adj (-ier, -iest) 🅔 (cold) pungente; (quick) svelto

nitrogen /'naɪtrədʒn/ n azoto m

no /nəʊ/ adv no ● n (pl **noes**) no m inv ● adj nessuno; **I have no time** non ho tempo; **in no time** in un baleno; **'no parking'** 'sosta vietata'; **'no smoking'** 'vietato fumare'; **no one**

nessuno κ **nobody**

noble /'nəʊbl/ adj nobile. **~man** n nobile m

nobody /'nəʊbədɪ/ pron nessuno; **he knows ~** non conosce nessuno ● n **he's a ~** non è nessuno

nocturnal /nɒk'tɜ:nl/ adj notturno

nod /nɒd/ n cenno m del capo ● vi (pt/pp **nodded**) fare un cenno col capo; (in agreement) fare di sì col capo ● vt **~ one's head** fare di sì col capo. □ **~ off** vi assopirsi

noise /nɔɪz/ n rumore m; (loud) rumore m, chiasso m. **~less** adj silenzioso. **~lessly** adv silenziosamente

noisy /'nɔɪzɪ/ adj (-ier, -iest) rumoroso

nomad /'nəʊmæd/ n nomade mf. **~ic** adj nomade

nominat|e /'nɒmɪneɪt/ vt proporre come candidato; (appoint) designare. **~ion** n nomina f; (person nominated) candidato, -a mf

nonchalant /'nɒnʃələnt/ adj disinvolto

non-com'mittal adj che non si sbilancia

nondescript /'nɒndɪskrɪpt/ adj qualunque

none /nʌn/ pron (person) nessuno; (thing) niente; **~ of us** nessuno di noi; **~ of this** niente di questo; **there's ~ left** non ce n'è più ● adv **she's ~ too pleased** non è per niente soddisfatta; **I'm ~ the wiser** non ne so più di prima

nonentity /nɒ'nentətɪ/ n nullità f

non-ex'istent adj inesistente

nonplussed /nɒn'plʌst/ adj perplesso

nonsens|e /'nɒnsəns/ n sciocchezze fpl. **~ical** adj assurdo

non-'smoker n non fumatore, -trice mf; (compartment) scompartimento m non fumatori

non-'stop adj **~ 'flight** volo m diretto ● adv senza sosta; (fly) senza scalo

noodles /'nuːdlz/ *npl* taglierini *mpl*

nook /nʊk/ *n* cantuccio *m*

noon /nuːn/ *n* mezzogiorno *m*; **at** ~ a mezzogiorno

noose /nuːs/ *n* nodo *m* scorsoio

nor /nɔː(r)/ *adv* & *conj* né; ~ **do I** neppure io

norm /nɔːm/ *n* norma *f*

normal /'nɔːml/ *adj* normale. ~**ity** *n* normalità *f*. ~**ly** *adv* (*usually*) normalmente

north /nɔːθ/ *n* nord *m*; **to the** ~ a nord di ● *adj* del nord, settentrionale ● *adv* a nord

north: N~ **America** *n* America *f* del Nord. ~-**east** *adj* di nord-est, nordorientale ● *n* nord-est *m* ● *adv* a nord-est; (*travel*) verso nord-est

norther|ly /'nɔːðəlɪ/ *adj* (*direction*) nord; (*wind*) del nord. ~**n** *adj* del nord, settentrionale. N~**n Ireland** *n* Irlanda *f* del Nord

north: N~ **Sea** *n* Mare *m* del Nord. ~**ward[s]** /-wəd[z]/ *adv* verso nord. ~-**west** *adj* di nord-ovest, nordoccidentale ● *n* nord-ovest *m* ● *adv* a nord-ovest; (*travel*) verso nord-ovest

Nor|way /'nɔːweɪ/ *n* Norvegia *f*. ~**wegian** *adj* & *n* norvegese *mf*

nose /nəʊz/ *n* naso *m*

nose: ~**bleed** *n* emorragia *f* nasale. ~**dive** *n* (*Aeron*) picchiata *f*

nostalg|ia /nʊ'stældʒɪə/ *n* nostalgia *f*. ~**ic** *adj* nostalgico

nostril /'nɒstrəl/ *n* narice *f*

nosy /'nəʊzɪ/ *adj* (-**ier**, -**iest**) 🔲 ficcanaso *inv*

not /nɒt/ *adv* non; **he is** ~ **Italian** non è italiano; **I hope** ~ spero di no; ~ **all of us have been invited** non siamo stati tutti invitati; **if** ~ se no; ~ **at all** niente affatto; ~ **a bit** per niente; ~ **even** neanche; ~ **yet** non ancora; ~ **only...** but **also...** non solo... ma anche...

notabl|e /'nəʊtəbl/ *adj* (*remarkable*) notevole. ~**y** *adv* (*in particular*) in particolare

notary /'nəʊtərɪ/ *n* notaio *m*; ~ '**public** notaio *m*

notch /nɒtʃ/ *n* tacca *f* ● **notch up** *vt* (*score*) segnare

note /nəʊt/ *n* nota *f*; (*short letter, banknote*) biglietto *m*; (*memo, written comment etc*) appunto *m*; **of** ~ (*person*) di spicco; (*comments, event*) degno di nota; **make a** ~ **of** prendere nota di; **take** ~ **of** (*notice*) prendere nota di ● *vt* (*notice*) notare; (*write*) annotare. □ ~ **down** *vt* annotare

'**notebook** *n* taccuino *m*; (*Comput*) notebook *m inv*

noted /'nəʊtɪd/ *adj* noto, celebre (**for** per)

'**notepaper** *n* carta *f* da lettere

nothing /'nʌθɪŋ/ *pron* niente, nulla ● *adv* niente affatto. **for** ~ (*free, in vain*) per niente; (*with no reason*) senza motivo; ~ **but** nient'altro che; ~ **much** poco o nulla; ~ **interesting** niente di interessante; **it's** ~ **to do with you** non ti riguarda

notice /'nəʊtɪs/ *n* (*on board*) avviso *m*; (*review*) recensione *f*; (*termination of employment*) licenziamento *m*; [**advance**] ~ preavviso *m*; **two months** ~ due mesi di preavviso; **at short** ~ con breve preavviso; **until further** ~ fino nuovo avviso; **hand in one's** ~ (*employee*) dare le dimissioni; **give an employee** ~ dare il preavviso a un impiegato; **take no** ~ **of** non fare caso a; **take no** ~ **I** non farci caso! ● *vt* notare. ~**able** *adj* evidente. ~**ably** *adv* sensibilmente. ~-**board** *n* bacheca *f*

noti|fication /nəʊtɪfɪ'keɪʃn/ *n* notifica *f*. ~**fy** *vt* (*pt/pp* -**ied**) notificare

notion /'nəʊʃn/ *n* idea *f*, nozione *f*. ~**s** *pl* (*Am:* haberdashery) merceria *f*

notorious /nəʊ'tɔːrɪəs/ *adj* famigerato; **be** ~ **for** essere tristemente famoso per

n

notwith'standing prep malgrado ● adv ciononostante

nougat /'nu:ga:/ n torrone m

nought /nɔːt/ n zero m

noun /naʊn/ n nome m, sostantivo m

nourish /'nʌrɪʃ/ vt nutrire. ~**ing** adj nutriente. ~**ment** n nutrimento m

novel /'nɒvl/ adj insolito ● n romanzo m. ~**ist** n romanziere, -a mf. ~**ty** n novità f; ~**ties** pl (objects) oggettini mpl

November /nəʊ'vembə(r)/ n novembre m

novice /'nɒvɪs/ n novizio, -a mf

now /naʊ/ adv ora, adesso; by ~ ormai; just ~ proprio ora; right ~ subito; ~ and again, ~ and then ogni tanto; ~, ~! su! ● conj ~ [that] ora che, adesso che

'nowadays adv oggigiorno

nowhere /'nəʊ-/ adv in nessun posto, da nessuna parte

nozzle /'nɒzl/ n bocchetta f

nuance /'nju:æia.s/ n sfumatura f

nuclear /'nju:klɪə(r)/ adj nucleare

nucleus /'nju:klɪəs/ n (pl -lei /-lɪaɪ/) nucleo m

nude /nju:d/ adj nudo ● n nudo m; in the ~ nudo

nudge /nʌdʒ/ n colpetto m di gomito ● vt dare un colpetto col gomito a

nudism /'nju:dɪzm/ n nudismo m

nud|ist /'nju:dɪst/ n nudista mf. ~**ity** n nudità f

nuisance /'nju:sns/ n seccatura f; (person) piaga f; what a ~! che seccatura!

null /nʌl/ adj ~ and void nullo

numb /nʌm/ adj intorpidito; ~ with cold intirizzito dal freddo

number /'nʌmbə(r)/ n numero m; a ~ of people un certo numero di persone ● vt numerare; (include) annoverare. ~**-plate** n targa f

numeral /'nju:mərəl/ n numero m, cifra f

numerical /nju:'merɪkl/ adj numerico; in ~ order in ordine numerico

numerous /'nju:mərəs/ adj numeroso

nun /nʌn/ n suora f

nurse /nɜːs/ n infermiere, -a mf; children's ~ bambinaia f ● vt curare

nursery /'nɜːsərɪ/ n stanza f dei bambini; (for plants) vivaio m; [day] ~ asilo m. ~ **rhyme** n filastrocca f. ~ **school** n scuola f materna

nut /nʌt/ n noce f; (Techn) dado m; (🅸: head) zucca f; ~s npl frutta f secca; be ~s 🅸 essere svitato. ~**crackers** npl schiaccianoci m inv. ~**meg** n noce f moscata

nutrit|ion /nju:'trɪʃn/ n nutrizione f. ~**ious** adj nutriente

'nutshell n in a ~ fig in parole povere

nylon /'naɪlɒn/ n nailon m; ~s pl calze fpl di nailon ● attrib di nailon

Oo

oaf /əʊf/ n (pl oafs) zoticone, -a mf

oak /əʊk/ n quercia f ● attrib di quercia

OAP n abbr (old-age pensioner) pensionato, -a mf

oar /ɔː(r)/ n remo m. ~**sman** n vogatore m

oasis /əʊ'eɪsɪs/ n (pl oases /-si:z/) oasi f inv

oath /əʊθ/ n giuramento m; (swearword) bestemmia f

oatmeal /'əʊt-/ n farina f d'avena

oats /əʊts/ npl avena fsg; (Culin) [rolled] ~ fiocchi mpl di avena

obedien|ce /əˈbiːdɪəns/ n ubbidienza f. **~t** adj ubbidiente

obes|e /əˈbiːs/ adj obeso. **~ity** n obesità f

obey /əˈbeɪ/ vt ubbidire a; osservare (instructions, rules) ● vi ubbidire

obituary /əˈbɪtjʊərɪ/ n necrologio m

object¹ /ˈɒbdʒɪkt/ n oggetto m; (Gram) complemento m oggetto; **money is no ~** i soldi non sono un problema

object² /əbˈdʒekt/ vi (be against) opporsi (to a); **~ that...** obiettare che...

objection /əbˈdʒekʃn/ n obiezione f; **have no ~** non avere niente in contrario. **~able** adj discutibile; (person) sgradevole

objectiv|e /əbˈdʒektɪv/ adj oggettivo ● n obiettivo m. **~ely** adv obiettivamente. **~ity** n oggettività f

obligation /ɒblɪˈɡeɪʃn/ n obbligo m; **be under an ~** avere un obbligo; **without ~** senza impegno

obligatory /əˈblɪɡətrɪ/ adj obbligatorio

oblig|e /əˈblaɪdʒ/ vt (compel) obbligare; **much ~ed** grazie mille. **~ing** adj disponibile

oblique /əˈbliːk/ adj obliquo; fig indiretto ● n **[stroke]** barra f

obliterate /əˈblɪtəreɪt/ vt obliterare

oblivion /əˈblɪvɪən/ n oblio m

oblivious /əˈblɪvɪəs/ adj **be ~** essere dimentico (of, to di)

oblong /ˈɒblɒŋ/ adj oblungo ● n rettangolo m

obnoxious /əbˈnɒkʃəs/ adj detestabile

oboe /ˈəʊbəʊ/ n oboe m inv

obscen|e /əbˈsiːn/ adj osceno; (profits, wealth) vergognoso. **~ity** n oscenità f

obscur|e /əbˈskjʊə(r)/ adj oscuro ● vt oscurare; (confuse) mettere in

ombra. **~ity** n oscurità f

obsequious /əbˈsiːkwɪəs/ adj ossequioso

observatory /əbˈzɜːvətrɪ/ n osservatorio m

observe /əbˈzɜːv/ vt osservare; (notice) notare; (keep, celebrate) celebrare. **~r** n osservatore, -trice mf

obsess /əbˈses/ vt **be ~ed by** essere fissato con. **~ion** n fissazione f. **~ive** adj ossessivo

obsolete /ˈɒbsəliːt/ adj obsoleto; (word) desueto

obstacle /ˈɒbstəkl/ n ostacolo m

obstina|cy /ˈɒbstɪnəsɪ/ n ostinazione f. **~te** adj ostinato

obstruct /əbˈstrʌkt/ vt ostruire; (hinder) ostacolare. **~ion** n ostruzione f; (obstacle) ostacolo m. **~ive** adj **be ~ive** (person:) creare dei problemi

obtain /əbˈteɪn/ vt ottenere. **~able** adj ottenibile

obtrusive /əbˈtruːsɪv/ adj (object) stonato

obtuse /əbˈtjuːs/ adj ottuso

obvious /ˈɒbvɪəs/ adj ovvio. **~ly** adv ovviamente

occasion /əˈkeɪʒn/ n occasione f; (event) evento m; **on ~** talvolta; **on the ~ of** in occasione di

occasional /əˈkeɪʒənl/ adj saltuario; **he has the ~ glass of wine** ogni tanto beve un bicchiere di vino. **~ly** adv ogni tanto

occult /əˈkʌlt/ adj occulto

occupant /ˈɒkjʊpənt/ n occupante mf; (of vehicle) persona f a bordo

occupation /ɒkjʊˈpeɪʃn/ n occupazione f; (job) professione f. **~al** adj professionale

occupier /ˈɒkjʊpaɪə(r)/ n residente mf

occupy /ˈɒkjʊpaɪ/ vt (pt/pp occupied) occupare; (keep busy) tenere occupato

occur /əˈkɜː(r)/ vi (pt/pp occurred)

o

accadere; (*exist*) trovarsi: **it ~red to me that** mi è venuto in mente che. **~rence** n (*event*) fatto m

ocean /'əʊʃn/ n oceano m

octave /'ɒktɪv/ n (*Mus*) ottava f

October /ɒk'təʊbə(r)/ n ottobre m

octopus /'ɒktəpəs/ n (*pl* **-puses**) polpo m

odd /ɒd/ adj (*number*) dispari; (*not of set*) scompagnato; (*strange*) strano; **forty ~** quaranta e rotti; **~ jobs** lavoretti *mpl*; **the ~ one out** l'eccezione; **at ~ moments** a tempo perso; **have the ~ glass of wine** avere un bicchiere di vino ogni tanto

odd|ity /'ɒdɪtɪ/ n stranezza f. **~ly** adv stranamente; **~ly enough** strananamente. **~ment** n (*of fabric*) scampolo m

odds /ɒdz/ npl (*chances*) probabilità fpl; **at ~** in disaccordo; **~ and ends** cianfrusaglie fpl; **it makes no ~** non fa alcuna differenza

odour /'əʊdə(r)/ n odore m. **~less** adj inodore

of /ɒv/, /əv/ prep di; **a cup of tea/ coffee** una tazza di tè/caffè; **the hem of my skirt** l'orlo della mia gonna; **the summer of 1989** l'estate del 1989; **the two of us** noi due; **made of** di; **that's very kind of you** è molto gentile da parte tua; **a friend of mine** un mio amico; **a child of three** un bambino di tre anni; **the fourth of January** il quattro gennaio; **within a year of their divorce** a circa un anno dal loro divorzio; **half of it** la metà di; **the whole of the room** tutta la stanza

off /ɒf/ prep da; (*distant from*) lontano da; **take £10 ~ the price** ridurre il prezzo di 10 sterline; **~ the coast** presso la costa; **a street ~ the main road** una traversa della via principale; (*near*) a strada vicino alla via principale; **get ~ the ladder** scendere dalla scala; **get off the bus** uscire dall'autobus; **leave the lid ~**

the saucepan lasciare la pentola senza il coperchio ● adj (*button, handle*) staccato; (*light, machine*) spento; (*brake*) tolto; (*tap*) chiuso; **'off'** (*on appliance*) 'off'; **2 kilometres ~ a** due chilometri di distanza; **a long way ~** molto distante; (*time*) lontano; **~ and on** di tanto in tanto; **with his hat/coat ~** senza il cappello/cappotto; **with the light ~** a luce spenta; **20% ~** 20% di sconto; **be ~** (*leave*) andar via; (*Sport*) essere partito; (*food:*) essere andato a male; (*all gone*) essere finito; (*wedding, engagement:*) essere cancellato; **I'm ~ alcohol** ho smesso di bere; **be ~ one's food** non avere appetito; **she's ~ today** (*on holiday*) è in ferie oggi; (*ill*) è malata oggi; **I'm ~ home** vado a casa; **you'd be better ~ doing...** faresti meglio a fare...; **have a day ~** avere un giorno di vacanza; **drive/sail ~** andare via

'off-beat adj insolito

'off-chance n possibilità f remota

offence /ə'fens/ n (*illegal act*) reato m; **give ~** offendere; **take ~** offendersi (**at** per)

offend /ə'fend/ vt offendere. **~er** n (*Jur*) colpevole mf

offensive /ə'fensɪv/ adj offensivo ● n offensiva f

offer /'ɒfə(r)/ n offerta f ● vt offrire; opporre (*resistance*); **~ sb sth** offrire qcsa a qcno; **~ to do sth** offrirsi di fare qcsa. **~ing** n offerta f

off'hand adj (*casual*) spiccio ● adv su due piedi

office /'ɒfɪs/ n ufficio m; (*post, job*) carica f. **~ hours** pl orario m d'ufficio

officer /'ɒfɪsə(r)/ n ufficiale m; (*police*) agente m (di polizia)

official /ə'fɪʃl/ adj ufficiale ● n funzionario. **~a** mf; (*Sport*) dirigente m. **~ly** adv ufficialmente

'offing n **in the ~** in vista

'off-licence n negozio m per la vendita di alcolici

'offset vt (pt/pp -set, pres p -setting) controbilanciare

'offshore ● adj (wind) di terra; (company, investment) offshore. ● adv (sail) al largo; (relocate) all'estero (in paesi dove la manodopera costa meno); ~ **rig** n piattaforma f petrolifera, off-shore m inv

off'side adj (Sport) [in] fuori gioco; (wheel etc) (left) sinistro; (right) destro

'offspring n prole m

off'stage adv dietro le quinte

often /'ɒfn/ adv spesso; **how** ~ ogni quanto; **every so** ~ una volta ogni tanto

oh /əʊ/ int oh!; ~ **dear** oh Dio!

oil /ɔɪl/ n olio m; (petroleum) petrolio m; (for heating) nafta f ● vt oliare

oil: ~**field** n giacimento m di petrolio. ~**-painting** n pittura f a olio. ~ **refinery** n raffineria f di petrolio. ~ **rig** n piattaforma f per trivellazione subacquea

oily /'ɔɪlɪ/ adj (-ier, -iest) unto; fig untuoso

ointment /'ɔɪntmənt/ n pomata f

OK /əʊ'keɪ/ int va bene, o.k. ● adj **if that's OK with you** se ti va bene; **she's OK** (well) sta bene; **is the milk still OK?** il latte è ancora buono? ● adv (well) bene ● vt (anche **okay**) (pt/pp **okayed**) dare l'o.k.

old /əʊld/ adj vecchio; (girlfriend) ex; **how** ~ **is she?** quanti anni ha?; **she is ten years** ~ ha dieci anni

old: ~ **'age** n vecchiaia f. ~**'fash-ioned** adj antiquato

olive /'ɒlɪv/ n (fruit, colour) oliva f; (tree) olivo m, ulivo m; (colour) olivastro. ~ **branch** n fig ramoscello m d'olivo. ~ **'oil** n olio m di oliva

Olympic /ə'lɪmpɪk/ adj olimpico; ~**s,** the **Games** Olimpiadi fpl

omelette /'ɒmlɪt/ n omelette f inv

omission /ə'mɪʃn/ n omissione f

omit /ə'mɪt/ vt (pt/pp **omitted**) omettere

on /ɒn/ prep su; (on horizontal surface) su, sopra; ~ **Monday** lunedì; ~ **Mondays** di lunedì; ~ **the first of May** il primo maggio; ~ **arriving** all'arrivo; ~ **foot** a piedi; ~ **the right/left** a destra/sinistra; ~ **the radio/television** alla radio/ televisione; ~ **the bus/train** in autobus/treno ● adv (further on) dopo; (switched on) acceso; (in operation) in funzione; **he had his hat/coat** ~ portava il cappello/cappotto; **be** ~ (event:) esserci; ~ **and** ~ senza sosta; **go** ~ continuare

once /wʌns/ adv una volta; (formerly) un tempo; ~ **upon a time there was** c'era una volta; **at** ~ subito; (at the same time) contemporaneamente; ~ **and for all** una volta per tutte ● conj [non] appena. ~**-over** n 🔟 **give sb/sth the** ~**-over** (look, check) dare un'occhiata veloce a qcno/qcsa

---

one /wʌn/

● adj uno, una; **not** ~ **person** nemmeno una persona

● n uno m

● pron uno; (impersonal) si; ~ **another** l'un l'altro; ~ **by** ~ [a] uno a uno; ~ **never knows** non si sa mai

---

one: ~**self** pron (reflexive) si; (emphatic) sé, se stesso; **by** ~**self** da solo; **be proud of** ~**self** essere fieri di sé. ~**-way** adj (street) a senso unico; (ticket) di sola andata

onion /'ʌnjən/ n cipolla f

on-'line adj/adv su Internet

'onlooker n spettatore, -trice mf

only /'əʊnlɪ/ adj solo; ~ **child** figlio, -a mf unico, -a ● adv & conj solo, solamente; ~ **just** appena

'onset n (beginning) inizio m

onslaught /'ɒnslɔːt/ n attacco m

ooze /uːz/ vi fluire

opaque /əʊˈpeɪk/ adj opaco

open /ˈəʊpən/ adj aperto; (free to all) pubblico; (job) vacante; **in the ~ air** all'aperto ● **in the ~** all'aperto; fig alla luce del sole ● vt aprire ● vi aprirsi; (shop:) aprire; (flower:) sbocciare. □ **~ up** vt aprire ● vi aprirsi

opening /ˈəʊpənɪŋ/ n apertura f; (beginning) inizio m; (job) posto m libero; **~ hours** npl orario m d'apertura

openly /ˈəʊpənlɪ/ adv apertamente

open: **~-'minded** adj aperto; (broad-minded) di vedute larghe. **~-plan** adj a pianta aperta

---

> **Open University** Fondata nel 1969, è il sistema di università a distanza del Regno Unito. L'insegnamento viene impartito con vari mezzi: per corrispondenza, attraverso programmi radiotelevisivi trasmessi dalla BBC e anche via Internet. Gli studenti inviano per posta i compiti svolti a un tutore. Generalmente si seguono corsi part time della durata di quattro o cinque anni, anche se non ci sono limiti di tempo per completare gli studi.

---

opera /ˈɒpərə/ n opera f

opera-house n teatro m lirico

operate /ˈɒpəreɪt/ vt far funzionare (machine, lift); azionare (lever, brake); mandare avanti (business) ● vi (Techn) funzionare; (be in action) essere in funzione; (Mil, fig) operare; **~ on** (Med) operare

operatic /ɒpəˈrætɪk/ adj lirico, operistico

operation /ɒpəˈreɪʃn/ n operazione f; (Techn) funzionamento m; **in ~** (Techn) in funzione; **come into ~** fig entrare in funzione; (law:) entrare in vigore; **have an ~** (Med) subire un'operazione. **~al** adj operativo; (law etc) in vigore

operative /ˈɒpərətɪv/ adj operativo

operator /ˈɒpəreɪtə(r)/ n (user) operatore, -trice mf; (Teleph) centralinista mf

opinion /əˈpɪnjən/ n opinione f; **in my ~** secondo me. **~ated** adj dogmatico

opponent /əˈpəʊnənt/ n avversario, -a mf

opportune /ˈɒpətjuːn/ adj opportuno. **~ist** n opportunista mf. **~istic** adj opportunistico

opportunity /ɒpəˈtjuːnətɪ/ n opportunità f inv

oppose /əˈpəʊz/ vt opporsi a; **be ~ed to sth** essere contrario a qcsa; **as ~ed to** al contrario di. **~ing** adj avversario; (opposite) opposto

opposite /ˈɒpəzɪt/ adj opposto; (house) di fronte; **~ number** fig controparte f; **the ~ sex** l'altro sesso ● n contrario m ● adv di fronte ● prep di fronte a

opposition /ɒpəˈzɪʃn/ n opposizione f

oppress /əˈpres/ vt opprimere. **~ion** n oppressione f. **~ive** adj oppressivo; (heat) opprimente. **~or** n oppressore m

opt /ɒpt/ vi **~ for** optare per; **~ out** dissociarsi (of da)

optical /ˈɒptɪkl/ adj ottico; **~ illusion** illusione f ottica

optician /ɒpˈtɪʃn/ n ottico, -a mf

optimism /ˈɒptɪmɪzm/ n ottimismo m. **~t** n ottimista mf. **~tic** adj ottimistico

option /ˈɒpʃn/ n scelta f; (Comm) opzione f. **~al** adj facoltativo; **~al extras** pl optional m inv

or /ɔː(r)/ conj o, oppure; (after negative) né; **or [else]** se no; **in a year or two** fra un anno o due

oral /ˈɔːrəl/ adj orale ● n 🔲 esame m orale. **~ly** adv oralmente

orange /ˈɒrɪndʒ/ n arancia f; (colour) arancione m ● adj arancione. **~ade** n aranciata f. ~ **juice** n succo m d'arancia

orbit /'ɔːbɪt/ n orbita f ●vt orbitare. ~**al** adj ~**al road** tangenziale f

orchard /'ɔːtʃəd/ n frutteto m

orches|tra /'ɔːkɪstrə/ n orchestra f. ~**tral** adj orchestrale. ~**trate** vt orchestrare

orchid /'ɔːkɪd/ n orchidea f

ordain /ɔː'deɪn/ vt decretare; (Relig) ordinare

ordeal /ɔː'diːl/ n fig terribile esperienza f

order /'ɔːdə(r)/ n ordine m; (Comm) ordinazione f; **out of** ~ (machine) fuori servizio; **in** ~ **that** affinché; **in** ~ **to** per ●vt ordinare

orderly /'ɔːdəlɪ/ adj ordinato ●n (Mil) attendente m; (Med) inserviente m

ordinary /'ɔːdɪnərɪ/ adj ordinario

ore /ɔː(r)/ n minerale m grezzo

organ /'ɔːgən/ n (Anat, Mus) organo m

organic /ɔː'gænɪk/ adj organico; (without chemicals) biologico. ~**ally** adv organicamente; ~**ally grown** coltivato biologicamente

organism /'ɔːgənɪzm/ n organismo m

organist /'ɔːgənɪst/ n organista mf

organization /ɔːgənaɪ'zeɪʃn/ n organizzazione f

organize /'ɔːgənaɪz/ vt organizzare. ~**r** n organizzatore, -trice mf

orgasm /'ɔːgæzm/ n orgasmo m

orgy /'ɔːdʒɪ/ n orgia f

Orient /'ɔːrɪənt/ n Oriente m. **o~al** adj orientale ●n orientale mf

orient|ate /'ɔːrɪənteɪt/ vt ~**ate oneself** orientarsi. ~**ation** n orientamento m

origin /'ɒrɪdʒɪn/ n origine f

original /ə'rɪdʒɪn(ə)l/ adj originario; (not copied, new) originale ●n originale m; **in the** ~ in versione originale.

~**ity** n originalità f. ~**ly** adv originariamente

originat|e /ə'rɪdʒɪnеɪt/ vi ~**e in** avere origine in. ~**or** n ideatore, -trice mf

ornament /'ɔːnəmənt/ n ornamento m; (on mantelpiece etc) soprammobile m. ~**al** adj ornamentale. ~**ation** n decorazione f

ornate /ɔː'neɪt/ adj ornato

orphan /'ɔːfn/ n orfano, -a mf ●vt rendere orfano; **be** ~**ed** rimanere orfano. ~**age** n orfanotrofio m

orthodox /'ɔːθədɒks/ adj ortodosso

oscillate /'ɒsɪleɪt/ vi oscillare

osteopath /'ɒstɪəpæθ/ n osteopata mf

ostracize /'ɒstrəsaɪz/ vt bandire

ostrich /'ɒstrɪtʃ/ n struzzo m

other /'ʌðə(r)/ adj, pron e n altro a mf; **the** ~ **[one]** l'altro, -a mf; **the** ~ **two** gli altri due; **two** ~**s** altri due; ~ **people** gli altri; **any** ~ **questions?** altre domande?; **every** ~ **day** (alternate days) a giorni alterni; **the** ~ **day** l'altro giorno; **the** ~ **evening** l'altra sera; **someone/something or** ~ qualcuno/qualcosa ●adv ~ **than him** tranne lui; **somehow or** ~ in qualche modo; **somewhere or** ~ da qualche parte

otherwise adv altrimenti; (differently) diversamente

otter /'ɒtə(r)/ n lontra f

ouch /aʊtʃ/ int ahi!

ought /ɔːt/ v aux **I/we** ~ **to stay** dovrei/dovremmo rimanere; **he** ~ **not to have done it** non avrebbe dovuto farlo; **that** ~ **to be enough** questo dovrebbe bastare

ounce /aʊns/ n oncia f (= 28,35 g)

our /'aʊə(r)/ adj il nostro m, la nostra f, i nostri mpl, le nostre fpl; ~ **mother/father** nostra madre/nostro padre

ours /aʊəz/ poss pron il nostro m, la nostra f, i nostri mpl, le nostre fpl; a

friend of ~ un nostro amico;
friends of ~ dei nostri amici; **that
is** ~ quello è nostro; (as opposed to
yours) quello è il nostro

ourselves /auə'selvz/ pron (reflexive)
ci; (emphatic) noi, noi stessi; **we
poured** ~ **a drink** ci siamo versati
da bere; **we heard it** ~ l'abbiamo
sentito noi stessi; **we are proud of**
~ siamo fieri di noi; **by** ~ da soli

out /aut/ adv fuori; (not alight) spento;
be ~ (flower:) essere sbocciato;
(workers:) essere in sciopero; (calculation:) essere sbagliato; (Sport) essere fuori; (unconscious) aver perso i
sensi; (fig: not feasible) fuori questione;
the sun is ~ è uscito il sole; ~ **and
about in piedi; get** ~! 🗓 fuori!;
you should get ~ **more** dovresti
uscire più spesso; ~ **with it!** 🗓
sputa il rospo!; • prep ~ **of** fuori da;
~ **of date** non aggiornato; (passport) scaduto; ~ **of order** guasto;
~ **of print/stock** esaurito; ~ **of
bed/the room** fuori dal letto/dalla
stanza; ~ **of breath** senza fiato; ~
of danger fuori pericolo; ~ **of work**
disoccupato; **nine** ~ **of ten** nove su
dieci; **be** ~ **of sugar/bread** rimanere senza zucchero/pane; **go** ~ **of
the room** uscire dalla stanza

outbreak n (of war) scoppio m; (of
disease) insorgenza f

outburst n esplosione f

outcome n risultato m

outcry n protesta f

outdated adj sorpassato

out'do vt (pt -did, pp -done) superare

outdoor adj (life, sports) all'aperto;
~ **clothes** pl vestiti per uscire; ~
swimming pool piscina f scoperta

out'doors adv all'aria aperta; **go** ~
uscire [all'aria aperta]

outer adj esterno

outfit n equipaggiamento m;
(clothes) completo m; (🗓: organization)

organizzazione. ~**ter** n men's
~**ter's** negozio m di abbigliamento
maschile

'outgoing adj (president) uscente;
(mail) in partenza; (sociable) estroverso. ~**s** npl uscite fpl

out'grow vi (pt -grew, pp -grown)
diventare troppo grande per

outing /'autɪŋ/ n gita f

outlandish /aut'lændɪʃ/ adj stra-
vagante

outlaw n fuorilegge mf inv • vt dichiarare illegale

outlay n spesa f

outlet n sbocco m; fig sfogo m;
(Comm) punto m [di] vendita

outline n contorno m; (summary)
sommario m • vt tracciare il contorno
di; (describe) descrivere

out'live vt sopravvivere a

outlook n vista f; (future prospect)
prospettiva f; (attitude) visione f

outlying adj ~ **areas** n zone fpl
periferiche

out'number vt superare in
numero

out-patient n paziente mf
esterno, -a; ~**s' department** ambulatorio m

output n produzione f

outright¹ adj completo; (refusal) netto

out'right² adv completamente; (at
once) immediatamente; (frankly) francamente

outset n inizio m; **from the** ~ fin
dall'inizio

outside¹ adj esterno • n esterno m;
from the ~ dall'esterno; **at the** ~
al massimo

out'side² adv all'esterno, fuori; (out
of doors) fuori; **go** ~ andare fuori
• prep fuori da; (in front of) davanti a

outskirts npl sobborghi mpl

out'spoken adj schietto

out'standing adj eccezionale;

(landmark) prominente; (not settled) in sospeso

out'stretched adj allungato

out'strip vt (pt/pp -**stripped**) superare

'outward /-wəd/ adj esterno; (journey) di andata ● adv verso l'esterno. ~**ly** adv esternamente. ~**s** adv verso l'esterno

out'weigh vt aver maggior peso di

out'wit vt (pt/pp -**witted**) battere in astuzia

oval /ˈəʊvl/ adj ovale ● n ovale m

ovary /ˈəʊvərɪ/ n (Anat) ovaia f

ovation /əˈveɪʃn/ n ovazione f

oven /ˈʌvn/ n forno m. ~**-ready** adj pronto da mettere in forno

over /ˈəʊvə(r)/ prep sopra; (across) al di là di; (during) durante; (more than) più di; ~ **the phone** al telefono; ~ **the page** alla pagina seguente; **all** ~ **Italy** in tutta [l']Italia; (travel) per l'Italia ● adv (Math) col resto di; (ended) finito; ~ **again** un'altra volta; ~ **and** ~ più volte; ~ **and above** oltre a; ~ **here/there** qui/là; **all** ~ (everywhere) dappertutto; **it's all** ~ è tutto finito; **I ache all** ~ ho male dappertutto; **come/bring** ~ venire/portare; **turn** ~ girare

over- pref (too) troppo

overall[1] /ˈəʊvərɔːl/ n grembiule m; ~**s** pl tuta fsg [da lavoro]

overall[2] /əʊvərˈɔːl/ adj complessivo; (general) generale ● adv complessivamente

over'balance vi perdere l'equilibrio

over'bearing adj prepotente

'overboard adv (Naut) in mare

'overcast adj coperto

over'charge vt ~ **sb** far pagare più del dovuto a qcno ● vi far pagare più del dovuto

'overcoat n cappotto m

over'come vt (pt -**came**, pp -**come**)

vincere; **be** ~ **by** essere sopraffatto da

over'crowded adj sovraffollato

over'do vt (pt -**did**, pp -**done**) esagerare; (cook too long) stracuocere; ~ **it** (🔁: do too much) strafare

'overdose n overdose f inv

'overdraft n scoperto m; **have an** ~ avere il conto scoperto

over'draw vt (pt -**drew**, pp -**drawn**) ~ **one's account** andare allo scoperto; **be** ~**n by** (account:) essere [allo] scoperto di

over'due adj in ritardo

over'estimate vt sopravvalutare

'overflow[1] n (water) acqua f che deborda; (people) pubblico m in eccesso; (outlet) scarico m; ~ **car park** parcheggio m supplementare

over'flow[2] vi debordare

over'grown adj (garden) coperto di erbacce

'overhaul[1] n revisione f

over'haul[2] vt (Techn) revisionare

'overhead[1] adv in alto

'overhead[2] adj aereo; (railway) sopraelevato; (lights) da soffitto. ~**s** npl spese fpl generali

over'hear vt (pt/pp -**heard**) sentire per caso (conversation)

over'joyed adj felicissimo

'overland adj & adv via terra; ~ **route** via f terrestre

over'lap v (pt/pp -**lapped**) ● vi sovrapporsi ● vt sovrapporre

over'leaf adv sul retro

over'load vt sovraccaricare

over'look vt dominare; (fail to see, ignore) lasciarsi sfuggire

over'night[1] adv per la notte; **stay** ~ fermarsi a dormire

over'night[2] adj notturno; ~ **bag** piccola borsa f da viaggio; ~ **stay** sosta f per la notte

'overpass n cavalcavia m inv

over'pay vt (pt/pp -**paid**) strapagare

over'power vt sopraffare. ~ing adj insostenibile

over'priced adj troppo caro

overre'act vi avere una reazione eccessiva. ~ion n reazione f eccessiva

over'rid|e vt (pt -rode, pp -ridden) passare sopra a. ~ing adj prevalente

over'rule vt annullare (decision)

over'run vt (pt -ran, pp -run, pres p -running) invadere; oltrepassare (time); **be** ~ **with** essere invaso da

over'seas¹ adv oltremare

'overseas² adj d'oltremare

over'see vt (pt -saw, pp -seen) sorvegliare

over'shadow vt adombrare

over'shoot vt (pt/pp -shot) oltrepassare

'oversight n disattenzione f; **an** ~ una svista

over'sleep vi (pt/pp -slept) svegliarsi troppo tardi

over'step vt (pt/pp -stepped) ~ **the mark** oltrepassare ogni limite

overt /əʊ'vɜːt/ adj palese

over'tak|e vt/i (pt -took, pp -taken) sorpassare. ~ing n sorpasso m; **no** ~ing divieto di sorpasso

'overthrow¹ n (Pol) rovesciamento m

over'throw² vt (pt -threw, pp -thrown) (Pol) rovesciare

'overtime n lavoro m straordinario ● adv **work** ~ fare lo straordinario

overture /'əʊvətjʊə(r)/ n (Mus) preludio m; ~s pl fig approccio msg

over'turn vt ribaltare ● vi ribaltarsi

over'weight adj sovrappeso

overwhelm /-'welm/ vt sommergere (with di); (with emotion) confondere. ~ing adj travolgente; (victory, majority) schiacciante

over'work n lavoro m eccessivo ● vt far lavorare eccessivamente ● vi lavorare eccessivamente

ow|e /əʊ/ vt also fig dovere ([to] sb a qcno); ~**e sb sth** dovere qcsa a qcno. ~ing adj **be** ~ing (money:) essere da pagare ● prep ~ing **to** a causa di

owl /aʊl/ n gufo m

own¹ /əʊn/ adj proprio ● pron **a car of my** ~ una macchina per conto mio; **on one's** ~ da solo; **hold one's** ~ **with** tener testa a; **get one's** ~ **back** prendersi una rivincita

own² vt possedere; (confess) ammettere; **I don't** ~ **it** non mi appartiene. □ ~ **up** vi confessare (**to sth** qcsa)

owner /'əʊnə(r)/ n proprietario, -a mf. ~**ship** n proprietà f

oxygen /'ɒksɪdʒən/ n ossigeno m; ~ **mask** maschera f a ossigeno

oyster /'ɔɪstə(r)/ n ostrica f

ozone /'əʊzəʊn/ n ozono m. ~-'friendly adj che non danneggia l'ozono. ~ **layer** n fascia f d'ozono

• • • • • • • • • • • • • • •

Pp

pace /peɪs/ n passo m; (speed) ritmo m; **keep** ~ **with** camminare di pari passo con ● vi ~ **up and down** camminare avanti e indietro. ~**-maker** n (Med) pacemaker m; (runner) battistrada m

Pacific /pə'sɪfɪk/ adj & n **the** ~ [Ocean] l'oceano m Pacifico, il Pacifico

pacifist /'pæsɪfɪst/ n pacifista mf

pacify /'pæsɪfaɪ/ vt (pt/pp -ied) placare (person); pacificare (country)

pack /pæk/ n (of cards) mazzo m; (of hounds) muta f; (of wolves, thieves) branco m; (of cigarettes etc) pacchetto

_m_; a ~ of lies un mucchio di bugie
● _vt_ impacchettare (article); fare
(suitcase); mettere in valigia (swim-
suit etc); (_press down_) comprimere;
~ed [out] (crowded) pieno zeppo ● _vi_
fare i bagagli; **send** sb ~ing 🄸
mandare qcno a stendere. ▫ ~ **up** _vt_
impacchettare ● _vi_ 🄸 (machine:)
piantare in asso

package /ˈpækɪdʒ/ _n_ pacco _m_ ● _vt_
impacchettare. ~ **deal** offerta _f_
tutto compreso. ~ **holiday** _n_ vacanza _f_ organizzata. ~ **tour** viaggio
_m_ organizzato

packet /ˈpækɪt/ _n_ pacchetto _m_; **cost**
a 🄸 costare un sacco

pact /pækt/ _n_ patto _m_

pad[1] /pæd/ _n_ imbottitura _f_; (_for writ-
ing_) bloc-notes _m_, taccuino _m_; (🄸:
home) (piccolo) appartamento _m_ ● _vt_
(_pt/pp_ **padded**) imbottire. ▫ ~ **out**
_vt_ gonfiare

pad[2] _vi_ (_pt/pp_ **padded**) camminare
con passo felpato

paddle[1] /ˈpæd(ə)l/ _n_ pagaia _f_ ● _vt_
(_row_) spingere remando

paddle[2] _vi_ (_wade_) sguazzare

paddock /ˈpædək/ _n_ recinto _m_

padlock /ˈpædlɒk/ _n_ lucchetto _m_
● _vt_ chiudere con lucchetto

paediatrician /piːdɪəˈtrɪʃn/ _n_ pe-
diatra _mf_

page[1] /peɪdʒ/ _n_ pagina _f_

page[2] _n_ (_boy_) paggetto _m_; (_in hotel_)
fattorino _m_ ● _vt_ far chiamare (person)

pager /ˈpeɪdʒə(r)/ _n_ cercapersone
m inv

paid /peɪd/ ▷PAY ● _adj_ ~ **employment** lavoro _m_ remunerato; **put** ~
to mettere un termine a

pail /peɪl/ _n_ secchio _m_

pain /peɪn/ _n_ dolore _m_; **be in** ~ soffrire; **take** ~**s** darsi un gran d'affare;
~ **in the neck** 🄸 spina _f_ nel fianco

pain: ~**ful** _adj_ doloroso; (_laborious_)
penoso. ~**killer** _n_ calmante _m_.
~**less** _adj_ indolore

painstaking /ˈpeɪnzteɪkɪŋ/ _adj_ minuzioso

paint /peɪnt/ _n_ pittura _f_; ~**s** colori
mpl ● _vt/i_ pitturare; (artist:) dipingere.
~**brush** _n_ pennello _m_. ~**er** _n_ pittore,
-trice _mf_; (_decorator_) imbianchino _m_.
~**ing** _n_ pittura _f_; (_picture_) dipinto _m_.
~**work** _n_ pittura _f_

pair /peə(r)/ _n_ paio _m_; (_of people_)
coppia _f_; ~ **of trousers** paio _m_ di
pantaloni; ~ **of scissors** paio _m_ di
forbici

pajamas /pəˈdʒɑːməz/ _npl_ Am pigiama _msg_

Pakistan /pɑːkɪˈstɑːn/ _n_ Pakistan _m_.
~**i** _adj_ pakistano ● _n_ pakistano, -a _mf_

pal /pæl/ _n_ 🄸 amico, -a _mf_

palace /ˈpælɪs/ _n_ palazzo _m_

palatable /ˈpælətəbl/ _adj_ gradevole
(al gusto)

palate /ˈpælət/ _n_ palato _m_

pale /peɪl/ _adj_ pallido

Palestine /ˈpælɪstaɪn/ _n_ Palestina
_f_. ~**ian** _adj_ palestinese ● _n_ palestinese _mf_

palette /ˈpælɪt/ _n_ tavolozza _f_

palm /pɑːm/ _n_ palmo _m_; (tree) palma
_f_; P~ **Sunday** _n_ Domenica _f_ delle
Palme. **palm off** _vt_ ~ **sth off on sb**
rifilare qcsa a qcno

palpable /ˈpælpəbl/ _adj_ palpabile;
(_perceptible_) tangibile

palpitate /ˈpælpɪteɪt/ _vi_ palpitare.
~**ions** _npl_ palpitazioni _fpl_

pamper /ˈpæmpə(r)/ _vt_ viziare

pamphlet /ˈpæmflɪt/ _n_ opuscolo _m_

pan /pæn/ _n_ tegame _m_, pentola _f_;
(_for frying_) padella _f_; (_of scales_) piatto
_m_ ● _vt_ (_pt/pp_ **panned**) (🄸: criticize)
stroncare

pancake _n_ crêpe _f inv_, frittella _f_

panda /ˈpændə/ _n_ panda _m inv_. ~
car _n_ macchina _f_ della polizia

pandemonium /pændɪˈmoʊ-
mǝʊnɪəm/ _n_ pandemonio _m_

pander /ˈpændə(r)/ _vi_ ~ **to sb**

p

compiacere qcno

pane /peɪn/ n ~ [of glass] vetro m

panel /ˈpænl/ n pannello m; (group of people) giuria f; ~ **of experts** gruppo m di esperti. ~**ling** n pannelli mpl

pang /pæŋ/ n ~**s of hunger** morsi mpl della fame; ~**s of conscience** rimorsi mpl di coscienza

panic /ˈpænɪk/ n panico m • vi (pt/pp **panicked**) lasciarsi prendere dal panico. ~**-stricken** adj in preda al panico

panoram|a /pænəˈrɑːmə/ n panorama m. ~**ic** adj panoramico

pansy /ˈpænzɪ/ n viola f del pensiero; (Ⅱ: effeminate man) finocchio m

pant /pænt/ vi ansimare

panther /ˈpænθə(r)/ n pantera f

panties /ˈpæntɪz/ npl mutandine fpl

pantomime /ˈpæntəmaɪm/ n pantomima f

pantry /ˈpæntrɪ/ n dispensa f

pants /pænts/ npl (underwear) mutande fpl; (woman's) mutandine fpl; (trousers) pantaloni mpl

'pantyhose n Am collant m inv

paper /ˈpeɪpə(r)/ n carta f; (wallpaper) carta f da parati; (newspaper) giornale m; (exam) esame m; (treatise) saggio m; ~**s** pl (documents) documenti mpl; (for identification) documento m [d'identità]; **on** ~ in teoria, per iscritto; **put down on** ~ mettere per iscritto • attrib di carta • vt tappezzare

paper: ~**back** n edizione f economica. ~**clip** n graffetta f. ~**weight** n fermacarte m inv. ~**work** n lavoro m d'ufficio

parable /ˈpærəbl/ n parabola f

parachut|e /ˈpærəʃuːt/ n paracadute m • vi lanciarsi col paracadute. ~**ist** n paracadutista mf

parade /pəˈreɪd/ n (military) parata f militare • vi sfilare • vt (show off) far sfoggio di

paradise /ˈpærədaɪs/ n paradiso m

paraffin /ˈpærəfɪn/ n paraffina f

paragraph /ˈpærəɡrɑːf/ n paragrafo m

parallel /ˈpærəlel/ adj & adv parallelo. ~ **bars** npl parallele fpl. ~ **port** n (Comput) porta f parallela • n (Geog), fig parallelo m; (line) parallela f • vt essere paragonabile a

Paralympics /pærəˈlɪmpɪks/ npl **the P**~ le Paraolimpiadi fpl

paralyse /ˈpærəlaɪz/ vt also fig paralizzare

paralysis /pəˈræləsɪs/ n (pl -ses) /-siːz/ paralisi f inv

paramedic /pærəˈmedɪk/ n paramedico, -a mf

parameter /pəˈræmɪtə(r)/ n parametro m

paranoia /pærəˈnɔɪə/ n paranoia f

paraphernalia /pærəfəˈneɪlɪə/ n armamentario m

paraplegic /pærəˈpliːdʒɪk/ adj paraplegico • n paraplegico, -a mf

parasite /ˈpærəsaɪt/ n parassita mf

paratrooper /ˈpærətruːpə(r)/ n paracadutista m

parcel /ˈpɑːsl/ n pacco m

parch /pɑːtʃ/ vt disseccare; **be** ~**ed** (person:) morire dalla sete

pardon /ˈpɑːdn/ n perdono m; (Jur) grazia f; ~? prego?; **I beg your** ~? fml chiedo scusa?; **I do beg your** ~ (sorry) chiedo scusa! • vt perdonare; (Jur) graziare

parent /ˈpeərənt/ n genitore, -trice mf; ~**s** pl genitori mpl. ~**al** adj dei genitori

parenthesis /pəˈrenθəsɪs/ n (pl -ses) /-siːz/ parentesi f inv

Paris /ˈpærɪs/ n Parigi f

parish /ˈpærɪʃ/ n parrocchia f. ~**ioner** n parrocchiano, -a mf

park /pɑːk/ n parco m • vt/i (Auto) posteggiare, parcheggiare; ~ **oneself** Ⅱ installarsi

park-and-'ride n park

and ride *m inv*

parking /'pɑːkɪŋ/ *n* parcheggio *m*, posteggio *m*; **'no ~'** 'divieto di sosta'. **~-lot** *n Am* posteggio *m*, parcheggio *m*. **~-meter** *n* parchimetro *m*. **~ space** *n* posteggio *m*, parcheggio *m*

parliament /'pɑːləmənt/ *n* parlamento *m*. **~ary** *adj* parlamentare

> **Parliament** Il Parlamento britannico è l'organo legislativo del paese, suddiviso in due Camere: *House of Commons* e *House of Lords*. La prima è composta di 650 parlamentari, o MP's (*Members of Parliament*), eletti a suffragio popolare; la seconda è formata da oltre 1000 membri, tra i quali esponenti dell'aristocrazia, ex primi ministri e cittadini che in qualche modo si sono distinti. Ogni anno è il capo della monarchia ad aprire ufficialmente il Parlamento e l'anno legislativo. *i*

parlour /'pɑːlə(r)/ *n* salotto *m*

parochial /pə'rəʊkɪəl/ *adj* parrocchiale; *fig* ristretto

parody /'pærədɪ/ *n* parodia *f* ● *vt* (*pt/pp* **-ied**) parodiare

parole /pə'rəʊl/ *n* **on ~** in libertà condizionale ● *vt* mettere in libertà condizionale

parrot /'pærət/ *n* pappagallo *m*

parsley /'pɑːslɪ/ *n* prezzemolo *m*

parsnip /'pɑːsnɪp/ *n* pastinaca *f*

part /pɑːt/ *n* parte *f*; (*of machine*) pezzo *m*; **for my ~** per quanto mi riguarda; **on the ~ of** da parte di; **take sb's ~** prendere le parti di qcno; **take ~ in** prendere parte a ● *adv* in parte ● *vt* ~ **one's hair** farsi la riga ● *vi* ~ (*people:*) separare; ~ **with** separarsi da

partial /'pɑːʃl/ *adj* parziale; **be ~ to** aver un debole per. **~ly** *adv* parzialmente

particip|ant /pɑː'tɪsɪpənt/ *n* partecipante *mf*. **~ate** *vi* partecipare (**in** a). **~ation** *n* partecipazione *f*

particle /'pɑːtɪkl/ *n* (*Gram, Phys*) particella *f*

particular /pə'tɪkjʊlə(r)/ *adj* particolare; (*precise*) meticoloso; *pej* noioso; **in ~** in particolare. **~ly** *adv* particolarmente. **~s** *npl* particolari *mpl*

parting /'pɑːtɪŋ/ *n* separazione *f*; (*in hair*) scriminatura *f* ● *attrib* di commiato

partisan /pɑːtɪ'zæn/ *n* partigiano, -a *mf*

partition /pɑː'tɪʃn/ *n* (*wall*) parete *f* divisoria; (*Pol*) divisione *f* ● *vt* dividere (*in parti*). □ ~ **off** *vt* separare

partly /'pɑːtlɪ/ *adv* in parte

partner /'pɑːtnə(r)/ *n* (*Comm*) socio, -a *mf*; (*sport, in relationship*) compagno, -a *mf*. **~ship** *n* (*Comm*) società *f*

partridge /'pɑːtrɪdʒ/ *n* pernice *f*

part-'time *adj & adv* part time; **be or work ~** lavorare part time

party /'pɑːtɪ/ *n* ricevimento *m*, festa *f*; (*group*) gruppo *m*; (*Pol*) partito *m*; (*Jur*) parte *f* (in causa); **be ~ to** essere parte attiva in

pass /pɑːs/ *n* lasciapassare *m inv*; (*in mountains*) passo *m*; (*Sport*) passaggio *m*; (*Sch: mark*) [voto *m*] sufficiente *m*; **make a ~ at** 𝕀 fare delle avances a ● *vt* passare; (*overtake*) sorpassare; (*approve*) far passare; fare (*remark*); (*Jur*) pronunciare (*sentence*). ~ **the time** passare il tempo ● *vi* passare; (*in exam*) essere promosso. □ ~ **away** *vi* mancare. □ ~ **down** *vt* passare; *fig* trasmettere. □ ~ **out** *vi* 𝕀 svenire. □ ~ **round** *vt* far passare. □ ~ **through** *vt* attraversare. □ ~ **up** *vt* passare; (𝕀: *miss*) lasciar sfuggire

passable /'pɑːsəbl/ *adj* (*road*) praticabile; (*satisfactory*) passabile

passage /'pæsɪdʒ/ *n* passaggio *m*; (*corridor*) corridoio *m*; (*voyage*) traversata f

passenger /'pæsɪndʒə(r)/ n passeggero, -a mf. ~ **seat** n posto m accanto al guidatore

passer-by /pɑːsə'baɪ/ n (pl ~sby) passante mf

passion /'pæʃn/ n passione f. ~**ate** adj appassionato

passive /'pæsɪv/ adj passivo ● n passivo m. ~**ness** n passività f

Passover /'pɑːsəʊvə(r)/ n Pasqua f ebraica

pass: ~**port** n passaporto m. ~**word** n parola f d'ordine

past /pɑːst/ adj passato; (former) ex; in the ~ few days nei giorni scorsi; that's all ~ tutto questo è passato; the ~ week la settimana scorsa ● n passato m ● prep oltre; at ten ~ two alle due e dieci ● adv oltre; go/come ~ passare

pasta /'pæstə/ n pasta[sciutta] f

paste /peɪst/ n pasta f; (dough) impasto m; (adhesive) colla f ● vt incollare

pastel /'pæstl/ n pastello m ● attrib pastello

pasteurize /'pɑːstʃəraɪz/ vt pastorizzare

pastime /'pɑːstaɪm/ n passatempo m

pastry /'peɪstrɪ/ n pasta f; ~**ies** pasticcini mpl

pasture /'pɑːstʃə(r)/ n pascolo m

pasty¹ /'pæstɪ/ n ≈ pasticcio m

pasty² /'peɪstɪ/ adj smorto

pat /pæt/ n buffetto m; (of butter) pezzetto m ● adv have sth off ~ conoscere qcsa a menadito ● vt (pt/pp patted) dare un buffetto a; ~ **sb on the back** fig congratularsi con qcno

patch /pætʃ/ n toppa f; (spot) chiazza f; (period) periodo m; not a ~ **on** T molto inferiore a ● vt mettere una toppa su. □ ~ **up** vt riparare alla bell'e meglio; appianare (quarrel)

pâté /'pæteɪ/ n pâté m inv

patent /'peɪtnt/ adj palese ● n brevetto m ● vt brevettare. ~ **leather** shoes npl scarpe fpl di vernice. ~**ly** adv in modo palese

patern|al /pə'tɜːnl/ adj paterno. ~**ity** n paternità f

path /pɑːθ/ n (pl ~s /pɑːðz/) sentiero m; (orbit) traiettoria m; fig strada f

pathetic /pə'θetɪk/ adj patetico; (T: very bad) penoso

patience /'peɪʃns/ n pazienza f; (game) solitario m

patient /'peɪʃnt/ adj paziente ● n paziente mf. ~**ly** adv pazientemente

patio /'pætɪəʊ/ n terrazza f

patriot /'pætrɪət/ n patriota mf. ~**ic** adj patriottico. ~**ism** n patriottismo m

patrol /pə'trəʊl/ n pattuglia f ● vt/i pattugliare. ~ **car** n autopattuglia f

patron /'peɪtrən/ n patrono m; (of charity) benefattore, -trice mf; (of the arts) mecenate mf; (customer) cliente mf

patroniz|e /'pætrənaɪz/ vt frequentare abitualmente; fig trattare con condiscendenza. ~**ing** adj condiscendente. ~**ingly** adv con condiscendenza

pattern /'pætn/ n disegno m (stampato); (for knitting, sewing) modello m

paunch /pɔːntʃ/ n pancia f

pause /pɔːz/ n pausa f ● vi fare una pausa

pave /peɪv/ vt pavimentare; ~ the **way** preparare la strada (for a). ~**ment** n marciapiede m

paw /pɔː/ n zampa f ● vt T mettere le zampe addosso a

pawn¹ /pɔːn/ n (in chess) pedone m; fig pedina f

pawn² vt impegnare ● n in ~ in pegno. ~**broker** n prestatore, -trice mf su pegno. ~**shop** n monte m di pietà

pay /peɪ/ n paga f; **in the ~** of al soldo di ● v (pt/pp **paid**) ● vt pagare; prestare (attention); fare (compliment, visit); **~ cash** pagare in contanti ● vi pagare; (be profitable) rendere; **it doesn't ~** ... è fatica sprecata...; **~ for sth** pagare per qcsa. □ **~ back** vt ripagare. □ **~ in** vt versare. □ **~ off** vt saldare (debt) ● vi fig dare dei frutti. □ **~ up** vi pagare

payable /ˈpeɪəbl/ adj pagabile; **make ~ to** intestare a

payment /ˈpeɪmənt/ n pagamento m

PC n abbr (personal computer) PC m inv

pea /piː/ n pisello m

peace /piːs/ n pace f; **~ of mind** tranquillità f

peach /piːtʃ/ n pesca f; (tree) pesco m

peacock /ˈpiːkɒk/ n pavone m

peak /piːk/ n picco m; fig culmine m. **~ed 'cap** n berretto m a punta. **~ hours** npl ore fpl di punta

peal /piːl/ n (of bells) scampanio m; **~s of laughter** fragore m di risate

peanut /ˈpiːnʌt/ n nocciolina f [americana]; **~s** [T] miseria f

pear /peə(r)/ n pera f; (tree) pero m

pearl /pɜːl/ n perla f

peasant /ˈpeznt/ n contadino, -a mf

pebble /ˈpebl/ n ciottolo m

peck /pek/ n beccata f; (kiss) bacetto m ● vt beccare; (kiss) dare un bacetto a. **~ing order** n gerarchia f. □ **~ at** vt beccare

peculiar /prˈkjuːlɪə(r)/ adj strano; (special) particolare; **~ to** tipico di. **~ity** n stranezza f; (feature) particolarità f inv

pedal /ˈpedl/ n pedale m ● vi pedalare. **~ bin** n pattumiera f a pedale

pedantic /prˈdæntɪk/ adj pedante

pedestal /ˈpedɪstl/ n piedistallo m

pedestrian /prˈdestrɪən/ n pedone m ● adj fig scadente. **~ 'crossing** n passaggio m pedonale. **~ 'precinct** n zona f pedonale

pedigree /ˈpedɪɡriː/ n pedigree m inv; (of person) lignaggio m ● attrib (animal) di razza; con pedigree

peek /piːk/ vi [T] sbirciare

peel /piːl/ n buccia f ● vt sbucciare ● vi (nose) etc: spellarsi; (paint:) staccarsi

peep /piːp/ n sbirciata f ● vi sbirciare

peer¹ /pɪə(r)/ vi **~ at** scrutare

peer² n nobile m; **his ~s** pl (in rank) i suoi pari mpl; (in age) i suoi coetanei mpl. **~age** n nobiltà f

peg /peɡ/ n (hook) piolo m; (for tent) picchetto m; (for clothes) molletta f; **off the ~** [T] prêt-à-porter

pejorative /prˈdʒɒrətɪv/ adj peggiorativo

pelican /ˈpelɪkən/ n pellicano m

pellet /ˈpelɪt/ n pallottola f

pelt /pelt/ n bombardare ● vi ([T]: run fast) catapultarsi; **~ down** (rain:) venir giù a fiotti

pelvis /ˈpelvɪs/ n (Anat) bacino m

pen¹ /pen/ n (for animals) recinto m

pen² /pen/ n penna f; (ball-point) penna f a sfera

penal /ˈpiːnl/ adj penale. **~ize** vt penalizzare

penalty /ˈpenltɪ/ n sanzione f; (fine) multa f; (in football) **~ [kick]** [calcio m di] rigore m; **~ area** or **box** area f di rigore

penance /ˈpenəns/ n penitenza f

pence /pens/ ▷**PENNY**

pencil /ˈpensl/ n matita f. **~-sharpener** n temperamatite m inv

pendulum /ˈpendjʊləm/ n pendolo m

penetrat|e /ˈpenɪtreɪt/ vt/i penetrare. **~ing** adj acuto; (sound, stare) penetrante. **~ion** n penetrazione f

penguin /ˈpeŋɡwɪn/ n pinguino m

penicillin /penɪˈsɪlɪn/ n penicillina f

peninsula /pɪˈnɪnsjʊlə/ n penisola f

penis /ˈpiːnɪs/ n pene m

pen: ~**knife** n temperino m.
~**name** n pseudonimo m

penniless /ˈpenɪlɪs/ adj senza un soldo

penny /ˈpenɪ/ n (pl pence; single coins pennies) penny m; Am centesimo m; **spend a** ~ 🚻 andare in bagno

pension /ˈpenʃn/ n pensione f. ~**er** n pensionato, -a mf

pensive /ˈpensɪv/ adj pensoso

Pentecost /ˈpentɪkɒst/ n Pentecoste f

pent-up /ˈpentʌp/ adj represso

penultimate /pɪˈnʌltɪmət/ adj penultimo

people /ˈpiːpl/ npl persone fpl, gente fsg; (citizens) popolo msg; **a lot of** ~ una marea di gente; **the** ~ la gente; **English** ~ gli inglesi; ~ **say** si dice; **for four** ~ per quattro • vt popolare

pepper /ˈpepə(r)/ n pepe m; (vegetable) peperone m • vt (season) pepare

pepper: ~**corn** n grano m di pepe. ~ **mill** n macinapepe m inv. ~**mint** n menta f peperita; (sweet) caramella f alla menta. ~**pot** n pepiera f

per /pɜː(r)/ prep per; ~ **annum** all'anno; ~ **cent** percento

perceive /pəˈsiːv/ vt percepire; (interpret) interpretare

percentage /pəˈsentɪdʒ/ n percentuale f

perceptible /pəˈseptəbl/ adj percettibile; (difference) sensibile

percept|ion /pəˈsepʃn/ n percezione f. ~**ive** adj perspicace

perch /pɜːtʃ/ n pertica f • vi (bird:) appollaiarsi

percolator /ˈpɜːkəleɪtə(r)/ n caffettiera f a filtro

percussion /pəˈkʌʃn/ n percussione f. ~ **instrument** n strumento

m a percussione

perfect [1] /ˈpɜːfɪkt/ adj perfetto • n (Gram) passato m prossimo

perfect [2] /pəˈfekt/ vt perfezionare. ~**ion** n perfezione f; **to** ~**ion** alla perfezione. ~**ionist** n perfezionista mf

perfectly /ˈpɜːfɪktlɪ/ adv perfettamente

perform /pəˈfɔːm/ vt compiere, fare; eseguire (operation, sonata); recitare (role); mettere in scena (play) • vi (Theat) recitare; (Techn) funzionare. ~**ance** n esecuzione f; (at theatre, cinema) rappresentazione f; (Techn) rendimento m. ~**er** n artista mf

perfume /ˈpɜːfjuːm/ n profumo m

perhaps /pəˈhæps/ adv forse

peril /ˈperɪl/ n pericolo m. ~**ous** adj pericoloso

perimeter /pəˈrɪmɪtə(r)/ n perimetro m

period /ˈpɪərɪəd/ n periodo m; (menstruation) mestruazioni fpl; (Sch) ora f di lezione; (full stop) punto m fermo • attrib (costume) d'epoca; (furniture) in stile. ~**ic** adj periodico. ~**ical** n periodico m, rivista f

peripher|al /pəˈrɪfərəl/ adj periferico. ~**y** n periferia f

perish /ˈperɪʃ/ vi (rot) deteriorarsi; (die) perire. ~**able** adj deteriorabile

perjur|e /ˈpɜːdʒə(r)/ vt ~**e oneself** spergiurare. ~**y** n spergiuro m

perk /pɜːk/ n 🚻 vantaggio m

perm /pɜːm/ n permanente f • vt ~ **sb's hair** fare la permanente a qno

permanent /ˈpɜːmənənt/ adj permanente; (job, address) stabile. ~**ly** adv stabilmente

permissible /pəˈmɪsəbl/ adj ammissibile

permission /pəˈmɪʃn/ n permesso m

permit [1] /pəˈmɪt/ vt (pt/pp -mitted) permettere; ~ **sb to do sth** permet-

permit² /'pɜːmɪt/ n autorizzazione f

perpendicular /pɜːpən'dɪkjʊlə(r)/ adj perpendicolare ● n perpendicolare f

perpetual /pə'petjʊəl/ adj perenne. ~**ly** adv perennemente

perpetuate /pə'petjʊeɪt/ vt perpetuare

perplex /pə'pleks/ vt lasciare perplesso. ~**ed** adj perplesso. ~**ity** n perplessità f inv

persecut|e /'pɜːsɪkjuːt/ vt perseguitare. ~**ion** n persecuzione f

perseverance /pɜːsɪ'vɪərəns/ n perseveranza f

persever|e /pɜːsɪ'vɪə(r)/ vi perseverare. ~**ing** adj assiduo

Persian /'pɜːʃn/ adj persiano

persist /pə'sɪst/ vi persistere; ~ **in doing sth** persistere nel fare qcsa. ~**ence** n persistenza f. ~**ent** adj persistente. ~**ently** adv persistentemente

person /'pɜːsn/ n persona f; **in** ~ di persona

personal /'pɜːsənl/ adj personale. ~ '**hygiene** n igiene f personale. ~ **organizer** n (Comput) agenda f elettronica. ~**ly** adv personalmente.

personality /pɜːsə'nælətɪ/ n personalità f inv; (on (TV)) personaggio m

personnel /pɜːsə'nel/ n personale m

perspective /pə'spektɪv/ n prospettiva f

persp|iration /pɜːspɪ'reɪʃn/ n sudore m. ~**ire** vi sudare

persua|de /pə'sweɪd/ vt persuadere. ~**sion** n persuasione f; (belief) convinzione f

persuasive /pə'sweɪsɪv/ adj persuasivo. ~**ly** adv in modo persuasivo

pertinent /'pɜːtɪnənt/ adj pertinente (to a)

perturb /pə'tɜːb/ vt perturbare

peruse /pə'ruːz/ vt leggere

pervers|e /pə'vɜːs/ adj irragionevole. ~**ion** n perversione f

pervert /'pɜːvɜːt/ n pervertito, -a mf

pessimis|m /'pesɪmɪzm/ n pessimismo m. ~**t** n pessimista mf. ~**tic** adj pessimistico. ~**tically** adv in modo pessimistico

pest /pest/ n piaga f; (🄸: person) peste f

pester /'pestə(r)/ vt molestare

pesticide /'pestɪsaɪd/ n pesticida m

pet /pet/ n animale m domestico; (favourite) cocco, -a mf ● adj prediletto ● v (pt/pp **petted**) ● vt coccolare ● vi (couple:) praticare il petting

petal /'petl/ n petalo m

petition /pə'tɪʃn/ n petizione f

pet 'name n vezzeggiativo m

petrol /'petrəl/ n benzina f

petroleum /pɪ'trəʊlɪəm/ n petrolio m

petrol: ~-**pump** n pompa f di benzina. ~ **station** n stazione f di servizio. ~ **tank** n serbatoio m della benzina

petticoat /'petɪkəʊt/ n sottoveste f

petty /'petɪ/ adj (-**ier**, -**iest**) insignificante; (mean) meschino. ~ '**cash** n cassa f per piccole spese

petulant /'petjʊlənt/ adj petulante

pew /pjuː/ n banco m (di chiesa)

phantom /'fæntəm/ n fantasma m

pharmaceutical /fɑːmə'sjuːtɪkl/ adj farmaceutico

pharmac|ist /'fɑːməsɪst/ n farmacista mf. ~**y** n farmacia f

phase /feɪz/ n fase f ● vt **phase in/out** introdurre/eliminare gradualmente

pheasant /'feznt/ n fagiano m

phenomen|al /fɪ'nɒmɪnl/ adj fenomenale; (incredibile) incredibile. ~**ally** adv incredibilmente. ~**on** n (pl -**na**) fenomeno m

philistine /'fɪlɪstaɪn/ n filisteo, -a mf

philosoph|er /fɪˈlɒsəfə(r)/ n filosofo, -a mf. ~**ical** adj filosofico. ~**ically** adv con filosofia. ~**y** n filosofia f

phlegm /flem/ n (Med) flemma f

phlegmatic /fleɡˈmætɪk/ adj flemmatico

phobia /ˈfəʊbɪə/ n fobia f

phone /fəʊn/ n telefono m; **be on the** ~ avere il telefono; (be phoning) essere al telefono ● vt telefonare a ● vi telefonare. □~ **back** vt/i richiamare. ~ **book** n guida f del telefono. ~ **box** n cabina f telefonica. ~ **call** telefonata f. ~ **card** n scheda f telefonica. ~-**in** n trasmissione f con chiamate in diretta. ~ **number** n numero m telefonico

phonetic /fəˈnetɪk/ adj fonetico. ~**s** n fonetica f

phoney /ˈfəʊnɪ/ adj (-ier, -iest) fasullo

phosphorus /ˈfɒsfərəs/ n fosforo m

photo /ˈfəʊtəʊ/ n foto f; ~ **album** album m inv di fotografie. ~**copier** n fotocopiatrice f. ~**copy** n fotocopia f ● vt fotocopiare

photogenic /fəʊtəʊˈdʒenɪk/ adj fotogenico

photograph /ˈfəʊtəɡrɑːf/ n fotografia f ● vt fotografare

photograph|er /fəˈtɒɡrəfə(r)/ n fotografo, -a mf. ~**ic** adj fotografico. ~**y** n fotografia f

phrase /freɪz/ n espressione f ● vt esprimere. ~-**book** n libro m di fraseologia

physical /ˈfɪzɪkl/ adj fisico. ~ **edu'cation** n educazione f fisica. ~**ly** adv fisicamente

physician /fɪˈzɪʃn/ n medico m

physic|ist /ˈfɪzɪsɪst/ n fisico, -a mf. ~**s** n fisica f

physiology /fɪzɪˈɒlədʒɪ/ n fisiologia f

physio'therap|ist /fɪzɪəʊ-/ n fi-

sioterapista mf. ~**y** n fisioterapia f

physique /fɪˈziːk/ n fisico m

pianist /ˈpɪənɪst/ n pianista mf

piano /pɪˈænəʊ/ n piano m

pick[1] /pɪk/ n (tool) piccone m

pick[2] n scelta f; **take your** ~ prendi quello che vuoi ● vt (select) scegliere; cogliere (flowers); scassinare (lock); borseggiare (pockets); ~ **and choose** fare il difficile; ~ **one's nose** mettersi le dita nel naso; ~ **a quarrel** attaccar briga; ~ **holes in** Ⓣ criticare; ~ **at one's food** spilluzzicare. □~ **on** vt (Ⓣ: nag) assillare; **he always** ~**s on me** ce l'ha con me. □~ **out** vt (identify) individuare. □~ **up** vt sollevare; (off the ground, information) raccogliere; prendere in braccio (baby); (learn) imparare; prendersi (illness); (buy) comprare; captare (signal); (collect) andare/venire a prendere; prendere (passengers, habit); (police:) arrestare (criminal); Ⓣ rimorchiare (girl); ~ **oneself up** riprendersi ● vi (improve) recuperare; (weather:) rimettersi

'pickaxe n piccone m

picket /ˈpɪkɪt/ n picchettista mf ● vt picchettare. ~ **line** n picchetto m

pickle /ˈpɪkl/ n ~**s** pl sottaceti mpl; **in a** ~ fig nei pasticci ● vt mettere sottaceto

pick: ~**pocket** n borsaiolo m. ~-**up** n (truck) furgone m; (on record-player) pickup m inv

picnic /ˈpɪknɪk/ n picnic m ● vi (pt/pp -nicked) fare un picnic

picture /ˈpɪktʃə(r)/ n (painting) quadro m; (photo) fotografia f; (drawing) disegno m; (film) film m inv; **put sb in the** ~ fig mettere qcno al corrente; **the** ~**s** il cinema ● vt (imagine) immaginare. ~**sque** adj pittoresco

pie /paɪ/ n torta f

piece /piːs/ n pezzo m; (in game) pedina f; **a** ~ **of bread/paper** un pezzo di pane/carta; **a ~ of news/ advice** una notizia/un consiglio; **take to ~s** smontare. **~meal** *adv* un po' alla volta. **~work** *n* lavoro m a cottimo ● **piece together** *vt* montare; *fig* ricostruire

pier /pɪə(r)/ *n* molo m; (*pillar*) pilastro m

pierc|e /pɪəs/ *vt* perforare; **~e a hole in sth** fare un buco in qcsa. **~ing** *n* [body] *~* piercing m inv ● *adj* penetrante

pig /pɪg/ *n* maiale m

pigeon /pɪdʒɪn/ *n* piccione m. **~-hole** *n* casella f

piggy /pɪgɪ/ **~back** *n* **give sb a ~back** portare qcno sulle spalle. **~ bank** *n* salvadanaio m

pig'headed *adj* 🔲 cocciuto

pigtail *n* (*plait*) treccina f

pile *n* (*heap*) pila f ● *vt* **~ sth on to sth** appilare qcsa su qcsa. □ **~ up** *vt* accatastare ● *vi* ammucchiarsi

piles /paɪlz/ *npl* emorroidi *fpl*

'pile-up *n* tamponamento m a catena

pilgrim /pɪlgrɪm/ *n* pellegrino, -a *mf*. **~age** *n* pellegrinaggio m

pill /pɪl/ *n* pillola f

pillar /pɪlə(r)/ *n* pilastro m. **~-box** *n* buca f delle lettere

pillow /pɪləʊ/ *n* guanciale m. **~case** *n* federa f

pilot /paɪlət/ *n* pilota *mf* ● *vt* pilotare. **~-light** *n* fiamma f di sicurezza

pimple /pɪmpl/ *n* foruncolo m

pin /pɪn/ *n* spillo m; (*Electr*) spinotto m; (*Med*) chiodo m; **I have ~s and needles in my leg** 🔲 mi formicola una gamba ● *vt* (*pt/pp* **pinned**) appuntare (**to/on** su); (*sewing*) fissare con gli spilli; (*hold down*) immobilizzare; **~ sb down to a date** ottenere un appuntamento da qcno; **~ sth on sb** 🔲 addossare a qcno la colpa di qcsa. □ **~ up** *vt* appuntare; (*on wall*) affiggere

pinafore /pɪnəfɔː(r)/ *n* grembiule m. **~ dress** *n* scamiciato m

pincers /pɪnsəz/ *npl* tenaglie *fpl*

pinch /pɪntʃ/ *n* pizzicotto m, (*of salt*) presa f; **at a ~** 🔲 in caso di bisogno ● *vt* pizzicare; (🔲: *steal*) fregare ● *vi* (shoe:) stringere

pine[1] /paɪn/ *n* (tree) pino m

pine[2] *vi* **she is pining for you** le manchi molto. □ **~ away** *vi* deperire

pineapple /paɪn-/ *n* ananas m inv

'ping-pong *n* ping-pong m

pink /pɪŋk/ *adj* rosa m

pinnacle /pɪnəkl/ *n* guglia f

PIN number *n* codice m segreto

pin: **~point** *vt* definire con precisione. **~stripe** *adj* gessato

pint /paɪnt/ *n* pinta f (= 0,571, *Am:* 0,47 l); **a ~** 🔲 una birra media

pioneer /paɪəˈnɪə(r)/ *n* pioniere, -a *mf* ● *vt* essere un pioniere di

pious /paɪəs/ *adj* pio

pip /pɪp/ *n* (*seed*) seme m

pipe /paɪp/ *n* tubo m; (*for smoking*) pipa f; **the ~s** (*Mus*) la cornamusa ● *vt* far arrivare con tubature (water, gas etc). □ **~ down** *vi* 🔲 abbassare la voce

pipe: **~dream** *n* illusione f. **~line** *n* conduttura f; **in the ~line** 🔲 in cantiere

piping /paɪpɪŋ/ *adj* **~ hot** bollente

pirate /paɪrət/ *n* pirata m

Pisces /paɪsiːz/ *n* (*Astr*) Pesci *mpl*

piss /pɪs/ *vi* 🔀 pisciare

pistol /pɪstl/ *n* pistola f

piston /pɪstn/ *n* (*Techn*) pistone m

pit /pɪt/ *n* fossa f; (*mine*) miniera f; (*for orchestra*) orchestra f ● *vt* (*pt/pp* **pitted**) *fig* opporre (**against** a)

pitch[1] /pɪtʃ/ *n* (*tone*) tono m; (*level*) altezza f; (*in sport*) campo m; (*fig:* degree) grado m ● *vt* montare (tent). □ **~ in** *vi* 🔲 mettersi sotto

pitch[2] *n* **~-black** *adj* nero come la pece. **~-'dark** *adj* buio pesto

P

'pitfall /n fig trabocchetto m

pith /pɪθ/ n (of lemon, orange) interno m della buccia

piti|ful /'pɪtɪfl/ adj pietoso. **~less** adj spietato

pittance /'pɪtns/ n miseria f

pity /'pɪtɪ/ n pietà f; **what a ~l** che peccato!; **take ~ on** avere compassione di ● vt aver pietà di

pivot /'pɪvət/ n perno m; fig fulcro m ● vi imperniarsi (on su)

pizza /'piːtsə/ n pizza f

placard /'plækɑːd/ n cartellone m

placate /plə'keɪt/ vt placare

place /pleɪs/ n posto m; (☒: house) casa f; (in book) segno m; **feel out of ~** sentirsi fuori posto; **take ~** aver luogo; **all over the ~** dappertutto ● vt collocare; (remember) identificare; **~ an order** fare un'ordinazione; **be ~d** (in race) piazzarsi. **~-mat** n sottopiatto m

placid /'plæsɪd/ adj placido

plague /pleɪg/ n peste f

plaice /pleɪs/ n inv platessa f

plain /pleɪn/ adj chiaro; (simple) semplice; (not pretty) scialbo; (not patterned) normale; (chocolate) fondente; **in ~ clothes** in borghese ● adv (simply) semplicemente ● n pianura f. **~ly** adv francamente; (simply) semplicemente; (obviously) chiaramente

plaintiff /'pleɪntɪf/ n (Jur) parte f lesa

plait /plæt/ n treccia f ● vt intrecciare

plan /plæn/ n progetto m, piano m ● vt (pt/pp planned) progettare; (intend) prevedere

plane[1] /pleɪn/ n (tree) platano m

plane[2] n aeroplano m

plane[3] n (tool) pialla f ● vt piallare

planet /'plænɪt/ n pianeta m

plank /plæŋk/ n asse f

planning /'plænɪŋ/ n pianificazione f. **~ permission** n licenza f edilizia

plant /plɑːnt/ n pianta f; (machinery) impianto m; (factory) stabilimento m ● vt piantare. **~ation** n piantagione f

plaque /plɑːk/ n placca f

plasma /'plæzmə/ n plasma m

plaster /'plɑːstə(r)/ n intonaco m; (Med) gesso m; (sticking ~) cerotto m; **~ of Paris** gesso m ● vt intonacare (wall); (cover) ricoprire. **~ed** adj ☒ sbronzo. **~er** n intonacatore m

plastic /'plæstɪk/ n plastica f ● adj plastico

plastic surgery n chirurgia f plastica

plate /pleɪt/ n piatto m; (flat sheet) placca f; (gold and silverware) argenteria f; (in book) tavola f [fuori testo] ● vt (cover with metal) placcare

platform /'plætfɔːm/ n (stage) palco m; (Rail) marciapiede m; (Pol) piattaforma f; **~ 5** binario 5

platinum /'plætɪnəm/ n platino m ● attrib di platino

platitude /'plætɪtjuːd/ n luogo m comune

platonic /plə'tɒnɪk/ adj platonico

plausible /'plɔːzəbl/ adj plausibile

play /pleɪ/ n gioco m; (Theat), (TV) rappresentazione f; (Radio) sceneggiato m radiofonico; **~ on words** gioco m di parole ● vt giocare a; (act) recitare; suonare (instrument); giocare (card) ● vi giocare; (Mus) suonare; **~ safe** non prendere rischi. □ **~ down** vt minimizzare. □ **~ up** vi ☒ fare i capricci

play: **~er** n giocatore, -trice mf. **~ful** adj scherzoso. **~ground** n (Sch) cortile m (per la ricreazione). **~group** n asilo m

playing: **~-card** n carta f da gioco. **~-field** n campo m da gioco

play: **~-pen** n box m inv. **~wright** /-raɪt/ n drammaturgo, -a mf

plc n abbr (public limited company) s.r.l.

plea /pliː/ n richiesta f; **make a ~**

for fare un appello a

plead /pliːd/ vi fare appello (for a); ~ **guilty** dichiararsi colpevole; ~ **with sb** implorare qcno

pleasant /'plezənt/ adj piacevole; **~ly** adv piacevolmente; (say, smile) cordialmente

pleas|e /pliːz/ adv per favore; **~e do** prego ● vt far contento; **~e one-self** fare il proprio comodo; **~e yourself!** come vuoi; pej fai come ti pare!. **~ed** adj lieto; **~ed with/about** contento di. **~ing** adj gradevole

pleasure /'pleʒə(r)/ n piacere m; **with ~** con piacere, volentieri

pleat /pliːt/ n piega f ● vt pieghettare. **~ed 'skirt** n gonna f a pieghe

pledge /pledʒ/ n pegno m; (promise) promessa f ● vt impegnarsi a; (pawn) impegnare

plentiful /'plentɪfl/ adj abbondante

plenty /'plentɪ/ n abbondanza f; ~ **of money** molti soldi; ~ **of people** molta gente; **I've got ~** ne ho in abbondanza

pliable /'plaɪəbl/ adj flessibile

pliers /'plaɪəz/ npl pinze fpl

plight /plaɪt/ n condizione f

plimsolls /'plɪmsəlz/ npl scarpe fpl da ginnastica

plod /plɒd/ vi (pt/pp plodded) trascinarsi; (work hard) sgobbare

plot /plɒt/ n complotto m; (of novel) trama f; ~ **of land** appezzamento m [di terreno] ● vt/i complottare

plough /plaʊ/ n aratro m; **~man's lunch** piatto m di formaggi e sottaceti, servito con pane. ● vt/i arare. □ **~ back** vt (Comm) reinvestire

ploy /plɔɪ/ n [] manovra f

pluck /plʌk/ n fegato m ● vt strappare; depilare (eyebrows); spennare (bird); cogliere (flower). □ **~ up** vt ~ **up courage** farsi coraggio

plucky /'plʌkɪ/ adj (-ier, -iest) coraggioso

plug /plʌg/ n tappo m; (Electr) spina f; (Auto) candela f; ([] : advertisement) pubblicità f inv ● vt (pt/pp plugged) tappare; ([] : advertise) pubblicizzare con insistenza. □ **~ in** vt (Electr) inserire la spina di

plum /plʌm/ n prugna f; (tree) prugno m

plumage /'pluːmɪdʒ/ n piumaggio m

plumb|er /'plʌmə(r)/ n idraulico m. **~ing** n impianto m idraulico

plume /pluːm/ n piuma f

plump /plʌmp/ adj paffuto ● **plump for** vt scegliere

plunge /plʌndʒ/ n tuffo m; **take the ~** [] buttarsi ● vt tuffare; fig sprofondare ● vi tuffarsi

plural /'plʊərəl/ adj plurale ● n plurale m

plus /plʌs/ prep più ● adj in più; **500 ~ più di 500** n più m; (advantage) extra m inv

plush /plʌʃ/ adj lussuoso

plutonium /pluː'təʊnɪəm/ n plutonio m

ply /plaɪ/ vt (pt/pp plied) ~ **sb with drink** continuare a offrire da bere a qcno. **~wood** n compensato m

p.m. abbr (post meridiem) del pomeriggio

PM n abbr Prime Minister

pneumonia /njuː'məʊnɪə/ n polmonite f

P.O. abbr Post Office

poach /pəʊtʃ/ vt (Culin) bollire; cacciare di frodo (deer); pescare di frodo (salmon); **~ed egg** uovo m in camicia. **~er** n bracconiere m

pocket /'pɒkɪt/ n tasca f; **be out of ~** rimetterci ● vt intascare. **~-book** n taccuino m; (wallet) portafoglio m. **~-money** n denaro m per le piccole spese

pod /pɒd/ n baccello m

poem /'pəʊɪm/ n poesia f

poet /'pəʊɪt/ n poeta m. ∼**ic** adj
poetico

poetry /'pəʊɪtrɪ/ n poesia f

poignant /'pɔɪnjənt/ adj emo-
zionante

point /pɔɪnt/ n punto m; (sharp end)
punta f; (meaning, purpose) senso m;
(Electr) presa f [di corrente]; ∼s pl
(Rail) scambio m; ∼ of view punto m
di vista; good/bad ∼s aspetti mpl
positivi/negativi; what is the ∼? a
che scopo?; the ∼ is il fatto è; I
don't see the ∼ non vedo il senso;
up to a ∼ fino a un certo punto; be
on the ∼ of doing sth essere sul
punto di fare qcsa ● vt puntare (at
verso) ● vi (with finger) puntare il dito; ∼
at/to (person): mostrare col dito;
(indicator): indicare. □ ∼ **out** vt far
notare (fact). ∼ **sth out to sb** far
notare qcsa a qcno

point-'blank adj a bruciapelo

point|ed /'pɔɪntɪd/ adj appuntito;
(question) diretto. ∼**ers** npl (advice)
consigli mpl. ∼**less** adj inutile

poise /pɔɪz/ n padronanza f. ∼**d** adj
in equilibrio; ∼**d** to sul punto di

poison /'pɔɪzn/ n veleno m ● vt av-
velenare. ∼**ous** adj velenoso

poke /pəʊk/ n (piccola) spinta f ● vt
spingere; (fire) attizzare; (put) ficcare;
∼ **fun at** prendere in giro. □ ∼
about vi frugare

poker[1] /'pəʊkə(r)/ n attizzatoio m

poker[2] n (Cards) poker m

poky /'pəʊkɪ/ adj (-ier, -iest)
angusto

Poland /'pəʊlənd/ n Polonia f

polar /'pəʊlə(r)/ adj polare. ∼ '**bear**
n orso m bianco. ∼**ize** vt polarizzare

pole[1] n palo m

pole[2] n (Geog, Electr) polo m

Pole /pəʊl/ n polacco, -a mf

police /pə'li:s/ npl polizia f ● vt pattugliare (area)

police: ∼**man** n poliziotto m. ∼
station n commissariato m.

∼**woman** n donna f poliziotto

policy[1] /'pɒlɪsɪ/ n politica f

policy[2] n (insurance) polizza f

polio /'pəʊlɪəʊ/ n polio f

polish /'pɒlɪʃ/ n (shine) lucentezza f;
(substance) lucido m; (for nails) smalto
m; fig raffinatezza f ● vt lucidare; fig
smussare. □ ∼ **off** vt ▣ finire in
fretta; spazzolare (food)

Polish /'pəʊlɪʃ/ adj polacco ● n (language) polacco m

polished /'pɒlɪʃt/ adj (manner) raffinato; (performance) senza sba-
vature

polite /pə'laɪt/ adj cortese. ∼**ly** adv
cortesemente. ∼**ness** n cortesia f

politic|al /pə'lɪtɪkl/ adj politico.
∼**ally** adv dal punto di vista politico.
∼**ian** n politico m

politics /'pɒlɪtɪks/ n politica f

poll /pəʊl/ n votazione f; (election)
elezioni fpl; opinion ∼ sondaggio m
d'opinione; **go to the** ∼**s** andare
alle urne ● vt ottenere (votes)

pollen /'pɒlən/ n polline m

pollut|e /pə'lu:t/ vt inquinare. ∼**ion**
n inquinamento m

polo /'pəʊləʊ/ n polo m. ∼-**neck** n
collo m alto. ∼ **shirt** n dolcevita f

polythene /'pɒlɪθi:n/ n politene m.
∼ **bag** n sacchetto m di plastica

polyun'saturated adj polinsaturo

pomp /pɒmp/ n pompa f

pompous /'pɒmpəs/ adj pomposo

pond /pɒnd/ n stagno m

ponder /'pɒndə(r)/ vt/i ponderare

pony /'pəʊnɪ/ n pony m. ∼-**tail** n
coda f di cavallo. ∼-**trekking** n
escursioni fpl lente

poodle /'pu:dl/ n barboncino m

pool[1] /pu:l/ n (of water, blood) pozza
f; [swimming] ∼ piscina f

pool[2] n (common fund) cassa f comune; (in cards) piatto m; (game) biliardo m a buca. ∼**s** npl ≈ totocalcio
msg ● vt mettere insieme

poor /pʊə(r)/ adj povero; (not good) scadente; **in** ~ **health** in cattiva salute ● npl **the** ~ i poveri. ~**ly** adj **be** ~**ly** non stare bene ● adv male

pop¹ /pɒp/ n botto m, (drink) bibita f gasata ● v (pt/pp popped) ● vt ⚂: put) mettere; (burst) far scoppiare ● vi (burst) scoppiare. □ ~ **in/out** vi ⚂ fare un salto/un salto fuori

pop² n ⚂ musica f pop ● attrib pop

'popcorn n popcorn m inv

pope /pəʊp/ n papa m

poplar /'pɒplə(r)/ n pioppo m

poppy /'pɒpi/ n papavero m

popular /'pɒpjʊlə(r)/ adj popolare; (belief) diffuso. ~**ity** n popolarità f inv

populat|e /'pɒpjʊleɪt/ vt popolare. ~**ion** n popolazione f

'pop-up n popup m inv

porcelain /'pɔːsəlɪn/ n porcellana f

porch /pɔːtʃ/ n portico m; Am veranda f

porcupine /'pɔːkjʊpaɪn/ n porcospino m

pore¹ /pɔː(r)/ n poro m

pore² vi ~ **over** immergersi in

pork /pɔːk/ n carne f di maiale

porn /pɔːn/ n ⚂ porno m. ~**o** adj ⚂ porno inv

pornograph|ic /pɔːnə'græfɪk/ adj pornografico. ~**y** n pornografia f

porpoise /'pɔːpəs/ n focena f

porridge /'pɒrɪdʒ/ n farinata f di fiocchi d'avena

port¹ /pɔːt/ n porto m

port² n (Naut: side) babordo m

port³ n (wine) porto m

portable /'pɔːtəbl/ adj portatile

porter /'pɔːtə(r)/ n portiere m; (for luggage) facchino m

'porthole n oblò m inv

portion /'pɔːʃn/ n parte f; (of food) porzione f

portrait /'pɔːtrɪt/ n ritratto m

portray /pɔː'treɪ/ vt ritrarre; (represent) descrivere; (actor:) impersonare. ~**al** n ritratto m

Portug|al /'pɔːtjʊgl/ n Portogallo m. ~**uese** adj portoghese ● n portoghese mf

pose /pəʊz/ n posa f ● vt porre (problem, question) ● vi (for painter) posare; ~ **as** atteggiarsi a

posh /pɒʃ/ adj ⚂ lussuoso; (people) danaroso

position /pə'zɪʃn/ n posizione f; (job) posto m; (status) ceto m [sociale] ● vt posizionare

positive /'pɒzɪtɪv/ adj positivo; (certain) sicuro; (progress) concreto ● n positivo m. ~**ly** adv positivamente; (decidedly) decisamente

possess /pə'zes/ vt possedere. ~**ion** n possesso m; ~**ions** pl i beni mpl

possess|ive /pə'zesɪv/ adj possessivo. ~**iveness** n carattere m possessivo. ~**or** n possessore, -ditrice mf

possibility /pɒsə'bɪlətɪ/ n possibilità f inv

possib|le /'pɒsɪbl/ adj possibile; ~**ly** adv possibilmente; **I couldn't** ~**ly accept** non mi è possibile accettare; **he can't** ~**ly be right** non è possibile che abbia ragione; **could you** ~**ly...?** potrebbe per favore...?

post¹ /pəʊst/ n (pole) palo m ● vt affiggere (notice)

post² n (place of duty) posto m ● vt appostare; (transfer) assegnare

post³ n (mail) posta f; **by** ~ per posta ● vt spedire; (put in letter-box) imbucare; (as opposed to fax) mandare per posta; **keep sb** ~**ed** tenere qcno al corrente

post- pref dopo

postage /'pəʊstɪdʒ/ n affrancatura f. ~ **stamp** n francobollo m

postal /'pəʊstl/ adj postale. ~ **order** n vaglia m postale

post: ~**box** n cassetta f delle lettere. ~**card** n cartolina f. ~**code** n

p

codice m postale

poster /'pəʊstə(r)/ n poster m inv; (advertising, election) cartellone m

posterity /pɒ'sterəti/ n posterità f

posthumous /'pɒstjʊməs/ adj postumo. ~ly adv dopo la morte

post: ~man n postino m. ~mark n timbro m postale

post-mortem /-'mɔːtəm/ n autopsia f

'**post office** n ufficio m postale

postpone /pəʊst'pəʊn/ vt rimandare. ~ment n rinvio m

posture /'pɒstʃə(r)/ n posizione f

pot /pɒt/ n vaso m; (for tea) teiera f; (for coffee) caffettiera f; (for cooking) pentola f; ~s of money 🔲 un sacco di soldi; **go to** ~ 🔲 andare in malora

potato /pə'teɪtəʊ/ n (pl -es) patata f

poten|t /'pəʊtənt/ adj potente. ~tate n potentato m

potential /pə'tenʃl/ adj potenziale ● n potenziale m. ~ly adv potenzialmente

pot: ~hole n cavità f inv; (in road) buca f. ~shot n take a ~shot at sparare a casaccio a

potter¹ /'pɒtə(r)/ vi ~ about gingillarsi

potter² n vasaio, -a m. ~y n lavorazione f della ceramica; (articles) ceramiche fpl; (place) laboratorio m di ceramiche

potty /'pɒtɪ/ adj (-ier, -iest) 🔲 matto ● n vasino m

pouch /paʊtʃ/ n marsupio m

poultry /'pəʊltrɪ/ n pollame m

pounce /paʊns/ vi balzare; ~ **on** saltare su

pound¹ /paʊnd/ n libbra f (= 0,454 kg); (money) sterlina f

pound² vt battere ● vi (heart:) battere forte; (run heavily) correre pesantemente

pour /pɔː(r)/ vt versare ● vi riversarsi;

(with rain) piovere a dirotto. □ ~ **out** vi riversarsi fuori ● vt versare (drink); sfogare (troubles)

pout /paʊt/ vi fare il broncio ● n broncio m

poverty /'pɒvəti/ n povertà f

powder /'paʊdə(r)/ n polvere f; (cosmetic) cipria f ● vt polverizzare; (face) incipriare. ~y adj polveroso

power /'paʊə(r)/ n potere m; (Electr) corrente f [elettrica]; (Math) potenza f. ~ **cut** n interruzione f di corrente. ~ed adj ~ed by electricity dotato di corrente [elettrica]. ~ful adj potente. ~less adj impotente. ~-station n centrale f elettrica

PR n abbr public relations

practicable /'præktɪkəbl/ adj praticabile

practical /'præktɪkl/ adj pratico. ~ **joke** n burla f. ~ly adv praticamente

practice /'præktɪs/ n pratica f; (custom) usanza f; (habit) abitudine f; (exercise) esercizio m; (Sport) allenamento m; **in** ~ (in reality) in pratica; **out of** ~ fuori esercizio; **put into** ~ mettere in pratica

practise /'præktɪs/ vt fare pratica in; (carry out) mettere in pratica; esercitare (profession) ● vi esercitarsi; (doctor:) praticare. ~d adj esperto

praise /preɪz/ n lode f ● vt lodare. ~worthy adj lodevole

pram /præm/ n carrozzella f

prank /præŋk/ n tiro m

prawn /prɔːn/ n gambero m. ~ '**cocktail** n cocktail m inv di gamberetti

pray /preɪ/ vi pregare. ~er n preghiera f

preach /priːtʃ/ vt/i predicare. ~er n predicatore, -trice mf

pre-ar'range /priː-/ vt predisporre

precarious /prɪ'keərɪəs/ adj precario. ~ly adv in modo precario

precaution /prɪ'kɔːʃn/ n precauzione f; **as a** ~ per precauzione.

~ary adj preventivo

precede /prɪ'si:d/ vt precedere

preceden|ce /'presɪdəns/ n precedenza f. ~t n precedente m

preceding /prɪ'si:dɪŋ/ adj precedente

precinct /'pri:sɪŋkt/ n (traffic-free) zona f pedonale; (Am: district) circoscrizione f

precious /'preʃəs/ adj prezioso; (style) ricercato ● adv § ~ **little** ben poco

precipice /'presɪpɪs/ n precipizio m

precipitate /prɪ'sɪpɪtət/ vt precipitare

precis|e /prɪ'saɪs/ adj preciso. ~ely adv precisamente. ~ion n precisione f

precursor /pri'kɜ:sə(r)/ n precursore m

predator /'predətə(r)/ n predatore, -trice mf. ~y adj rapace

predecessor /'pri:dɪsesə(r)/ n predecessore m

predicament /prɪ'dɪkəmənt/ n situazione f difficile

predict /prɪ'dɪkt/ vt predire. ~able adj prevedibile. ~ion n previsione f

preen /pri:n/ vt lisciarsi; ~ **oneself** fig farsi bello

pre|fab /'pri:fæb/ n § casa f prefabbricata. ~'fabricated adj prefabbricato

preface /'prefɪs/ n prefazione f

prefect /'pri:fekt/ n (Sch) studente, -tessa mf della scuola superiore con responsabilità disciplinari, ecc

prefer /prɪ'fɜ:(r)/ vt (pt/pp preferred) preferire

prefera|ble /'prefərəbl/ adj preferibile (to a). ~bly adv preferibilmente

preferen|ce /'prefərəns/ n preferenza f. ~tial adj preferenziale

pregnan|cy /'pregnənsɪ/ n gravidanza f. ~t adj incinta

prehi'storic /pri:-/ adj preistorico

prejudice /'predʒʊdɪs/ n pregiudizio m ● vt influenzare (against contro); (harm) danneggiare. ~d adj prevenuto

preliminary /prɪ'lɪmɪnərɪ/ adj preliminare

prelude /'prelju:d/ n preludio m

premature /'premətjʊə(r)/ adj prematuro

pre'meditated /pri:-/ adj premeditato

premier /'premɪə(r)/ adj primario ● n (Pol) primo ministro m, premier m inv

première /'premɪeə(r)/ n prima f

premises /'premɪsɪz/ npl locali mpl; **on the ~** sul posto

premium /'pri:mɪəm/ n premio m; **be at a ~** essere una cosa rara

premonition /premə'nɪʃn/ n presentimento m

preoccupied /pri:'ɒkjʊpaɪd/ adj preoccupato

preparation /prepə'reɪʃn/ n preparazione f. ~s preparativi mpl

preparatory /prɪ'pærətrɪ/ adj preparatorio ● adv ~ **to** in preparazione a

prepare /prɪ'peə(r)/ vt preparare ● vi prepararsi (for per); ~d **to** disposto a

preposition /prepə'zɪʃn/ n preposizione f

preposterous /prɪ'pɒstərəs/ adj assurdo

prerequisite /pri:'rekwɪzɪt/ n condizione f sine qua non

prescribe /prɪ'skraɪb/ vt prescrivere

prescription /prɪ'skrɪpʃn/ n (Med) ricetta f

presence /'prezns/ n presenza f; ~ **of mind** presenza f di spirito

present[1] /'preznt/ adj presente ● n presente m; **at** ~ attualmente

present[2] n (gift) regalo m; **give sb sth as a ~** regalare qcsa a qcno

present³ /prɪˈzent/ vt presentare; ~ sb with an award consegnare un premio a qcno. **~able** adj be ~able essere presentabile

presentation /preznˈteɪʃn/ n presentazione f

presently /ˈprezntlɪ/ adv fra poco; (Am: now) attualmente

preservation /prezəˈveɪʃn/ n conservazione f

preservative /prɪˈzɜːvətɪv/ n conservante m

preserve /prɪˈzɜːv/ vt preservare; (maintain, Culin) conservare ● n (in hunting & fig) riserva f; (jam) marmellata f

preside /prɪˈzaɪd/ vi presiedere (over a)

presidency /ˈprezɪdənsɪ/ n presidenza f

president /ˈprezɪdənt/ n presidente m. **~ial** adj presidenziale

press /pres/ n (machine) pressa f; (newspapers) stampa f ● vt premere; pressare (flower); (iron) stirare; (squeeze) stringere ● vi (urge) incalzare. □ ~ **for** vi fare pressione per; be ~ed for essere a corto di. □ ~ **on** vi andare avanti

press: ~ **conference** n conferenza f stampa. ~ **cutting** n ritaglio m di giornale. **~ing** adj urgente. **~-up** n flessione f

pressure /ˈpreʃə(r)/ n pressione f ● vt = **pressurize**. **~-cooker** n pentola f a pressione. ~ **group** n gruppo m di pressione

pressurize /ˈpreʃəraɪz/ vt far pressione su. **~d** adj pressurizzato

prestige /preˈstiːʒ/ n prestigio m. **~ious** adj prestigioso

presumably /prɪˈzjuːməblɪ/ adv presumibilmente

presume /prɪˈzjuːm/ vt presumere; ~ **to do sth** permettersi di fare qcsa

presup'pose /priː-/ vt presupporre

pretence /prɪˈtens/ n finzione f; (pretext) pretesto m; **it's all** ~ è tutta una scena

pretend /prɪˈtend/ vt fingere; (claim) pretendere ● vi fare finta

pretentious /prɪˈtenʃəs/ adj pretenzioso

pretext /ˈpriːtekst/ n pretesto m

pretty /ˈprɪtɪ/ adj (-ier, -iest) carino ● adv (🔲: fairly) abbastanza

prevail /prɪˈveɪl/ vi prevalere; ~ **on sb to do sth** convincere qcno a fare qcsa. **~ing** adj prevalente

prevalen|ce /ˈprevələns/ n diffusione f. **~t** adj diffuso

prevent /prɪˈvent/ vt impedire; ~ **sb** [from] impedire a qcno di fare qcsa. **~ion** n prevenzione f. **~ive** adj preventivo

preview /ˈpriːvjuː/ n anteprima f

previous /ˈpriːvɪəs/ adj precedente. **~ly** adv precedentemente

prey /preɪ/ n preda f; **bird of** ~ uccello m rapace ● vi ~ **on** far preda di; ~ **on sb's mind** attanagliare qcno

price /praɪs/ n prezzo m ● vt (Comm) fissare il prezzo di. **~less** adj inestimabile; (🔲: amusing) spassosissimo. **~y** adj 🔲 caro

prick /prɪk/ n puntura f ● vt pungere. ~ **up one's ears** rizzare le orecchie

prickl|e /ˈprɪkl/ n spina f; (sensation) formicolio m. **~y** adj pungente; (person) irritabile

pride /praɪd/ n orgoglio m ● vt ~ **oneself on** vantarsi di

priest /priːst/ n prete m

prim /prɪm/ adj (primmer, primmest) perbenino

primarily /ˈpraɪmərɪlɪ/ adv in primo luogo

primary /ˈpraɪmərɪ/ adj primario; (chief) principale. ~ **school** n scuola f elementare

prime[1] /praɪm/ adj principale, primo; (first-rate) eccellente ● **n be in one's ~** essere nel fiore degli anni

prime[2] vt preparare (surface, person)

Prime Minister n Primo m Ministro

primeval /praɪˈmiːvl/ adj primitivo

primitive /ˈprɪmɪtɪv/ adj primitivo

primrose /ˈprɪmrəʊz/ n primula f

prince /prɪns/ n principe m

princess /prɪnˈses/ n principessa f

principal /ˈprɪnsəpl/ adj principale ● n (Sch) preside m

principally /ˈprɪnsəpli/ adv principalmente

principle /ˈprɪnsəpl/ n principio m; **in ~** in teoria; **on ~** per principio

print /prɪnt/ n (mark, trace) impronta f; (Phot) copia f; (picture) stampa f; **in ~** (printed out) stampato; (book) in commercio; **out of ~** esaurito ● vt stampare; (write in capitals) scrivere in stampatello. ~**ed matter** n stampe fpl

print|er /ˈprɪntə(r)/ n stampante f; (Typ) tipografo, -a mf. ~**er port** n (Comput) porta f per la stampante. ~**ing** n tipografia f

printout /ˈprɪntaʊt/ n (Comput) stampa f

prior /ˈpraɪə(r)/ adj precedente. ~ **to** prep prima di

priority /praɪˈɒrəti/ n precedenza f; (matter) priorità f pr

prise /praɪz/ vt ~ **open/up** forzare

prison /ˈprɪz(ə)n/ n prigione f. ~**er** n prigioniero, -a mf

privacy /ˈprɪvəsi/ n privacy f inv

private /ˈpraɪvət/ adj privato; (car, secretary, letter) personale ● n (Mil) soldato m semplice; **in ~** in privato. ~**ly** adv (funded, educated etc) privatamente; (in secret) in segreto; (confidentially) in privato; (inwardly) interiormente

privation /praɪˈveɪʃn/ n privazione

f; ~**s** npl stenti mpl

privilege /ˈprɪvɪlɪdʒ/ n privilegio m. ~**d** adj privilegiato

prize /praɪz/ n premio m ● adj (idiot etc) perfetto ● vt apprezzare. ~**-giving** n premiazione f. ~**-winner** n vincitore, -trice mf. ~**-winning** adj vincente

pro /prəʊ/ n (1: professional) professionista mf; **the ~s and cons** il pro e il contro

probability /prɒbəˈbɪləti/ n probabilità f inv

probabl|e /ˈprɒbəbl/ adj probabile. ~**y** adv probabilmente

probation /prəˈbeɪʃn/ n prova f; (Jur) libertà f vigilata. ~**ary** adj in prova; ~**ary period** periodo m di prova

probe /prəʊb/ n sonda f; (fig: investigation) indagine f ● vt sondare; (investigate) esaminare a fondo

problem /ˈprɒbləm/ n problema m ● adj difficile. ~**atic** adj problematico

procedure /prəˈsiːdʒə(r)/ n procedimento m

proceed /prəˈsiːd/ vi procedere ● vt ~ **to do sth** proseguire facendo qcsa

proceedings /prəˈsiːdɪŋz/ npl (report) atti mpl; (Jur) azione fsg legale

proceeds /ˈprəʊsiːdz/ npl ricavato msg

process /ˈprəʊses/ n processo m; (procedure) procedimento m; **in the** ~ nel far ciò ● vt trattare; (Admin) occuparsi di; (Phot) sviluppare

procession /prəˈseʃn/ n processione f

processor /ˈprəʊsesə(r)/ n (Comput) processore m; (for food) robot m inv da cucina

proclaim /prəˈkleɪm/ vt proclamare

procure /prəˈkjʊə(r)/ vt ottenere

prod /prɒd/ n colpetto m ● vt (pt/pp prodded) punzecchiare; fig incitare

produce[1] /'prɒdjuːs/ n prodotti mpl; ~ **of Italy** prodotto in Italia

produce[2] /prə'djuːs/ vt produrre; (bring out) tirar fuori; (cause) causare; (🔲: give birth to) fare. ~r n produttore m

product /'prɒdʌkt/ n prodotto m. ~ion n produzione f; (Theat) spettacolo m

productiv|e /prə'dʌktɪv/ adj produttivo. ~ity n produttività f

profession /prə'feʃn/ n professione f. ~al adj professionale; (not amateur) professionista; (piece of work) da professionista; (man) di professione ● n professionista mf. ~ally adv professionalmente

professor /prə'fesə(r)/ n professore m [universitario]

proficien|cy /prə'fɪʃnsɪ/ n competenza f. ~t adj be ~t in essere competente in

profile /'prəʊfaɪl/ n profilo m

profit /'prɒfɪt/ n profitto m ● vi ~ **from** trarre profitto da. ~able adj proficuo. ~ably adv in modo proficuo

profound /prə'faʊnd/ adj profondo. ~ly adv profondamente

profus|e /prə'fjuːs/ adj ~e apologies/flowers una profusione di scuse/fiori. ~ion n profusione f; in ~ion in abbondanza

prognosis /prɒg'nəʊsɪs/ n (pl -oses) prognosi f inv

program /'prəʊgræm/ n programma m ● vt (pt/pp programmed) programmare

programme /'prəʊgræm/ n Br programma m. ~r n (Comput) programmatore, -trice mf

progress[1] /'prəʊgres/ n progresso m; in ~ in corso; make ~ fig fare progressi

progress[2] /prə'gres/ vi progredire; fig fare progressi

progressive /prə'gresɪv/ adj pro-gressivo; (reforming) progressista. ~ly adv progressivamente

prohibit /prə'hɪbɪt/ vt proibire. ~ive adj proibitivo

project[1] /'prɒdʒekt/ n progetto m; (Sch) ricerca f

project[2] /prə'dʒekt/ vt proiettare (film, image) ● vi (jut out) sporgere

projector /prə'dʒektə(r)/ n proiettore m

prolific /prə'lɪfɪk/ adj prolifico

prologue /'prəʊlɒg/ n prologo m

prolong /prə'lɒŋ/ vt prolungare

promenade /prɒmə'nɑːd/ n lungomare m inv

prominent /'prɒmɪnənt/ adj prominente; (conspicuous) di rilievo

promiscu|ity /prɒmɪ'skjuːətɪ/ n promiscuità f. ~ous adj promiscuo

promis|e /'prɒmɪs/ n promessa f ● vt promettere; ~e sb that promettere a qcno che; I ~ed to l'ho promesso. ~ing adj promettente

promot|e /prə'məʊt/ vt promuovere; be ~ed (Sport) essere promosso. ~ion n promozione f

prompt /prɒmpt/ adj immediato; (punctual) puntuale ● adv in punto ● vt incitare (to a); (Theat) suggerire a ● vi suggerire. ~er n suggeritore, -trice mf. ~ly adv puntualmente

Proms /prɒmz/ npl rassegna f di concerti estivi di musica classica presso l'Albert Hall a Londra

---

i

Proms I Proms sono una serie di concerti di musica classica che ogni estate, per otto settimane, si tengono giornalmente all'Albert Hall di Londra. Istituiti nel 1895 per iniziativa di Sir Henry Wood, il loro nome è l'abbreviazione di promenade concerts, concerti durante i quali a parte del pubblico in sala sono riservati posti in piedi.

prone /prəʊn/ adj be ~ to do sth essere incline a fare qcsa

pronoun /'prəʊnaʊn/ n pronome m

pronounce /prə'naʊns/ vt pronunciare; (declare) dichiarare. ~d adj (noticeable) pronunciato

pronunciation /prənʌnsɪ'eɪʃn/ n pronuncia f

proof /pru:f/ n prova f; (Typ) bozza f, prova f ● adj ~ against a prova di

propaganda /propə'gændə/ n propaganda f

propel /prə'pel/ vt (pt/pp propelled) spingere. ~ler n elica f

proper /'prɒpə(r)/ adj corretto; (suitable) adatto; (ⓘ: real) vero [e proprio]. ~ly adv correttamente. ~ 'name, ~ 'noun n nome m proprio

property /'prɒpətɪ/ n proprietà f inv. ~ developer n agente m immobiliare. ~ market n mercato m immobiliare

prophecy /'prɒfəsɪ/ n profezia f

prophesy /'prɒfəsaɪ/ vt (pt/pp -ied) profetizzare

prophet /'prɒfɪt/ n profeta m. ~ic adj profetico

proportion /prə'pɔ:ʃn/ n proporzione f; (share) parte f; ~s pl (dimensions) proporzioni fpl. ~al adj proporzionale. ~ally adv in proporzione

proposal /prə'pəʊzl/ n proposta f; (of marriage) proposta f di matrimonio

propose /prə'pəʊz/ vt proporre; (intend) proporsi ● vi fare una proposta di matrimonio

proposition /prɒpə'zɪʃn/ n proposta f; (ⓘ: task) impresa f

proprietor /prə'praɪətə(r)/ n proprietario, -a f

prose /prəʊz/ n prosa f

prosecut|e /'prɒsɪkju:t/ vt intentare azione contro. ~ion n azione f giudiziaria; the ~ion l'accusa f. ~or n [Public] P~or il Pubblico Ministero m

prospect¹ /'prɒspekt/ n (expectation) prospettiva f

prospect² /prə'spekt/ vi ~ for cercare

prospect|ive /prə'spektɪv/ adj (future) futuro; (possible) potenziale. ~or n cercatore m

prospectus /prə'spektəs/ n prospetto m

prosper /'prɒspə(r)/ vi prosperare; (person:) stare bene finanziariamente. ~ity n prosperità f

prosperous /'prɒspərəs/ adj prospero

prostitut|e /'prɒstɪtju:t/ n prostituta f. ~ion n prostituzione f

prostrate /'prɒstreɪt/ adj prostrato; ~ with grief fig prostrato dal dolore

protagonist /prəʊ'tægənɪst/ n protagonista mf

protect /prə'tekt/ vt proteggere (from da). ~ion n protezione f. ~ive adj protettivo. ~or n protettore, -trice mf

protein /'prəʊti:n/ n proteina f

protest¹ /'prəʊtest/ n protesta f

protest² /prə'test/ vt/i protestare

Protestant /'prɒtɪstənt/ adj protestante ● n protestante mf

protester /prə'testə(r)/ n contestatore, -trice mf

protocol /'prəʊtəkɒl/ n protocollo m

protrude /prə'tru:d/ vi sporgere

proud /praʊd/ adj fiero (of di). ~ly adv fieramente

prove /pru:v/ vt provare ● vi ~ to be a lie rivelarsi una bugia. ~n adj dimostrato

proverb /'prɒvɜ:b/ n proverbio m. ~ial adj proverbiale

provide /prə'vaɪd/ vt fornire; ~ sb with sth fornire qcsa a qcno ● vi ~ for (law:) prevedere

provided /prə'vaɪdɪd/ conj ~ [that] purché

providen|ce /ˈprɒvɪdəns/ n provvidenza f. **~tial** adj provvidenziale

providing /prəˈvaɪdɪŋ/ conj = provided

provinc|e /ˈprɒvɪns/ n provincia f; fig campo m. **~ial** adj provinciale

provision /prəˈvɪʒn/ n (of food, water) approvvigionamento m (of di); (of law) disposizione f; **~s** pl provviste fpl. **~al** adj provvisorio

provocat|ion /prɒvəˈkeɪʃn/ n provocazione f. **~ive** adj provocatorio; (sexually) provocante. **~ively** adv in modo provocatorio

provoke /prəˈvəʊk/ vt provocare

prow /praʊ/ n prua f

prowess /ˈpraʊɪs/ n abilità f inv

prowl /praʊl/ vi aggirarsi ●n on the **~** in cerca di preda. **~er** n tipo m sospetto

proximity /prɒkˈsɪmətɪ/ n prossimità f

proxy /ˈprɒksɪ/ n procura f; (person) persona f che agisce per procura

prude /pruːd/ n be a **~** essere eccessivamente pudico

pruden|ce /ˈpruːdəns/ n prudenza f. **~t** adj prudente; (wise) oculatezza f

prudish /ˈpruːdɪʃ/ adj eccessivamente pudico

prune¹ /pruːn/ n prugna f secca

prune² vt potare

pry /praɪ/ vi (pt/pp pried) ficcare il naso

psalm /sɑːm/ n salmo m

psychiatric /saɪkɪˈætrɪk/ adj psichiatrico

psychiatr|ist /saɪˈkaɪətrɪst/ n psichiatra mf. **~y** n psichiatria f

psychic /ˈsaɪkɪk/ adj psichico; **I'm not ~** non sono un indovino

psychological /saɪkəˈlɒdʒɪkl/ adj psicologico

psycholog|ist /saɪˈkɒlədʒɪst/ n psicologo, -a mf. **~y** n psicologia f

pub /pʌb/ n ⓘ pub m inv

Pub In Gran Bretagna, molti pubs (abbreviazione di public house) fanno parte di catene e sono proprietà di grandi birrerie, mentre invece sono indipendenti (free houses). Oltre che per bere, si va al pub per socializzare e giocare a freccette, biliardo, ecc.; alcuni organizzano serate di quiz a gruppi. L'orario di apertura è diverso a seconda della licenza dell'esercizio, ma quello più comune va dalle 11 alle 23.

puberty /ˈpjuːbətɪ/ n pubertà f

public /ˈpʌblɪk/ adj pubblico ●n the **~** il pubblico; **in ~** in pubblico. **~ly** adv pubblicamente

publican /ˈpʌblɪkən/ n gestore, -trice mf/proprietario, -a mf di un pub

publication /pʌblɪˈkeɪʃn/ n pubblicazione f

public: ~ 'holiday n festa f nazionale. **~'house** n pub m

publicity /pʌbˈlɪsɪtɪ/ n pubblicità f

publicize /ˈpʌblɪsaɪz/ vt pubblicizzare

public: ~ relations pubbliche relazioni fpl. **~ 'school** n scuola f privata; Am scuola f pubblica

public schools In Inghilterra sono, al contrario di quanto si è soliti pensare, scuole secondarie private a pagamento, in cui spesso gli allievi risiedono in collegio.

publish /ˈpʌblɪʃ/ vt pubblicare. **~er** n editore m; (firm) editore m, casa f editrice. **~ing** n editoria f

pudding /ˈpʊdɪŋ/ n dolce m cotto al vapore; (course) dolce m

puddle /ˈpʌdl/ n pozzanghera f

puff /pʌf/ n (of wind) soffio m; (of

smoke) tirata *f*; (*for powder*) piumino *m*
● *vt* sbuffare. puff at *vt* tirare boc-
cate da (pipe). □ ∼ out *vt* lasciare
senza fiato (person); spegnere (candle). ∼ed *adj* (*out of breath*) senza
fiato. ∼ pastry *n* pasta *f* sfoglia

puffy /'pʌfɪ/ *adj* gonfio

pull /pʊl/ *n* trazione *f*; (*fig: attraction*)
attrazione *f*; (⽥: *influence*) influenza *f*
● *vt* tirare; estrarre (tooth); stirarsi
(muscle); ∼ faces far boccace; ∼
oneself together cercare di controllarsi; ∼ one's weight mettercela
tutta; ∼ sb's leg ⽥ prendere in
giro qcno. □ ∼ down *vt* (*demolish*)
demolire. □ ∼ in *vi* (Auto) accostare.
□ ∼ off *vt* togliere; ⽥ azzeccare.
□ ∼ out *vt* tirar fuori ● *vi* (Auto) spostarsi; (*of competition*) ritirarsi. □ ∼
through *vi* (*recover*) farcela. □ ∼ up
vt sradicare (plant); (*reprimand*) rimproverare ● *vi* (Auto) fermarsi

pullover /'pʊləʊvə(r)/ *n* pullover *m*

pulp /pʌlp/ *n* poltiglia *f*; (*of fruit*)
polpa *f*; (*for paper*) pasta *f*

pulpit /'pʊlpɪt/ *n* pulpito *m*

pulse /pʌls/ *n* polso *m*

pummel /'pʌml/ *vt* (*pt/pp* pum-
melled) prendere a pugni

pump /pʌmp/ *n* pompa *f* ● *vt* pompare; ⽥ cercare di estorcere da.
□ ∼ up *vt* (*inflate*) gonfiare

pumpkin /'pʌmpkɪn/ *n* zucca *f*

pun /pʌn/ *n* gioco *m* di parole

punch[1] /pʌntʃ/ *n* pugno *m*; (*device*)
pinza *f* per forare ● *vt* dare un pugno
a; forare (ticket); perforare (hole)

punch[2] *n* (*drink*) ponce *m inv*

punctual /'pʌŋktjʊəl/ *adj* puntuale.
∼ity *n* puntualità *f*. ∼ly *adv* puntualmente

punctuat|e /'pʌŋktjʊeɪt/ *vt* pun-
teggiare. ∼ion *n* punteggiatura *f*.
∼ion mark *n* segno *m* di inter-
punzione

puncture /'pʌŋktʃə(r)/ *n* foro *m*;

(*tyre*) foratura *f* ● *vt* forare

punish /'pʌnɪʃ/ *vt* punire. ∼able *adj*
punibile. ∼ment *n* punizione *f*

punk /pʌŋk/ *n* punk *m inv*

punt /pʌnt/ *n* (*boat*) barchino *m*

punter /'pʌntə(r)/ *n* (*gambler*) scom-
mettitore, -trice *mf*; (*client*) consumatore, -trice *mf*

puny /'pjuːnɪ/ *adj* (-ier, -iest) stri-
minzito

pup /pʌp/ *n* = puppy

pupil /'pjuːpl/ *n* alunno, -a *mf*; (*of
eye*) pupilla *f*

puppet /'pʌpɪt/ *n* marionetta *f*;
(*glove* ∼, *fig*) burattino *m*

puppy /'pʌpɪ/ *n* cucciolo *m*

purchase /'pɜːtʃəs/ *n* acquisto *m*;
(*leverage*) presa *f* ● *vt* acquistare. ∼r *n*
acquirente *mf*

pure /pjʊə(r)/ *adj* puro. ∼ly *adv* pu-
ramente

purgatory /'pɜːgətrɪ/ *n* purga-
torio *m*

purge /pɜːdʒ/ (*Pol*) *n* epurazione *f*
● *vt* epurare

puri|fication /pjʊərɪfɪ'keɪʃn/ *n*
purificazione *f*. ∼fy *vt* (*pt/pp* -ied)
purificare

puritan /'pjʊərɪtən/ *n* puritano, -a
mf. ∼ical *adj* puritano

purity /'pjʊərɪtɪ/ *n* purità *f*

purple /'pɜːpl/ *adj* viola

purpose /'pɜːpəs/ *n* scopo *m*; (*determination*) fermezza *f*; on ∼ apposta.
∼-built *adj* costruito ad hoc. ∼ful
adj deciso. ∼fully *adv* con decisione.
∼ly *adv* apposta

purr /pɜː(r)/ *vi* (*cat*:) fare le fusa

purse /pɜːs/ *n* borsellino *m*; (Am:
handbag) borsa *f* ● *vt* increspare (lips)

pursue /pə'sjuː/ *vt* inseguire; (*fig*) proseguire. ∼r *n* inseguitore, -trice *mf*

pursuit /pə'sjuːt/ *n* inseguimento *f*;
(*fig: of happiness*) ricerca *f*; (*pastime*)
attività *f inv*; in ∼ all'inseguimento

p

pus /pʌs/ n pus m

push /pʊʃ/ n spinta f; (fig: effort) sforzo m; (drive) iniziativa f; **at a ~** in caso di bisogno; **get the ~** 🔲 essere licenziato • vt spingere; premere (button); (pressurize) far pressione su; **be ~ed for time** 🔲 non avere tempo • vi spingere. **□ ~ aside** vt scostare. **□ ~ back** vt respingere. **□ ~ off** vt togliere vi (🔲: leave) levarsi dai piedi. **□ ~ on** vi (continue) continuare. **□ ~ up** vt alzare (price)

push: ~-chair n passeggino m. **~-up** n flessione f

pushy /ˈpʊʃɪ/ adj 🔲 troppo intraprendente

put /pʊt/ vt (pt/pp put, pres p putting) mettere; **~ the cost of sth at** valutare il costo di qcsa • vi **~ to sea** salpare. **□ ~ aside** vt mettere da parte. **□ ~ away** vt mettere via. **□ ~ back** vt rimettere; mettere indietro (clock). **□ ~ by** vt mettere da parte. **□ ~ down** vt mettere giù; (suppress) reprimere; (kill) sopprimere; (write) annotare; **~ one's foot down** 🔲 essere fermo; (Auto) dare un'accelerata; **~ down to** (attribute) attribuire. **□ ~ forward** vt avanzare; mettere avanti (clock). **□ ~ in** vt (insert) introdurre; (submit) presentare • vi **~ in for** far domanda di. **□ ~ off** vt spegnere (light); (postpone) rimandare; **~ sb off** tenere a bada qcno; (deter) smontare qcno; (disconcert) distrarre qcno; **~ sb off sth** (disgust) disgustare qcno di qcsa. **□ ~ on** vt mettersi (clothes); mettere (brake); (Culin) mettere su; accendere (light); mettere in scena (play); prendere (accent); **~ on weight** mettere su qualche chilo. **□ ~ out** vt spegnere (fire, light); tendere (hand); (inconvenience) creare degli inconvenienti a. **□ ~ through** vt far passare; (Teleph) I'll **~ you through to him** glielo passo. **□ ~ up** vt alzare; erigere (building); montare (tent); aprire

(umbrella); affiggere (notice); aumentare (price); ospitare (guest); **~ sb up to sth** mettere qcsa in testa a qcno • vi (at hotel) stare; **~ up with** sopportare • adj **stay ~!** rimani lì!

puzzl|e /ˈpʌzl/ n enigma m; (jigsaw) puzzle m inv • vt lasciare perplesso • vi **~e over** scervellarsi su. **~ing** adj inspiegabile

pygmy /ˈpɪgmɪ/ n pigmeo, -a mf

pyjamas /pəˈdʒɑːməz/ npl pigiama msg

pylon /ˈpaɪlən/ n pilone m

pyramid /ˈpɪrəmɪd/ n piramide f

python /ˈpaɪθn/ n pitone m

Qq

quack¹ /kwæk/ n qua qua m inv • vi fare qua qua

quack² n (doctor) ciarlatano m

quadrangle /ˈkwɒdræŋgl/ n quadrangolo m; (court) cortile m quadrangolare

quadruped /ˈkwɒdrʊped/ n quadrupede m

quadruple /ˈkwɒdrʊpl/ adj quadruplo • vt quadruplicare • vi quadruplicarsi. **~ts** npl quattro gemelli mpl

quagmire /ˈkwɒgmaɪə(r)/ n pantano m

quaint /kweɪnt/ adj pittoresco; (odd) bizzarro

quake /kweɪk/ n 🔲 terremoto m • vi tremare

qualif|ication /kwɒlɪfɪˈkeɪʃn/ n qualifica f. **~ied** adj qualificato; (limited) con riserva

qualify /ˈkwɒlɪfaɪ/ v (pt/pp -ied) • vt (course): dare la qualifica a (as di); (entitle) dare diritto a; (limit) precisare

quality | quote

●*vi* ottenere la qualifica; (*Sport*) qualificarsi

quality /'kwɒlətɪ/ *n* qualità *f inv*

qualm /kwɑːm/ *n* scrupolo *m*

quandary /'kwɒndərɪ/ *n* dilemma *m*

quantity /'kwɒntɪtɪ/ *n* quantità *f inv*; **in** ~ in grande quantità

quarantine /'kwɒrəntiːn/ *n* quarantena *f*

quarrel /'kwɒrəl/ *n* lite *f* ●*vi* (*pt/pp* **quarrelled**) litigare. ~**some** *adj* litigioso

quarry¹ /'kwɒrɪ/ *n* (*prey*) preda *f*

quarry² *n* cava *f*

quart /kwɔːt/ *n* 1.14 litro

quarter /'kwɔːtə(r)/ *n* quarto *m*; (*of year*) trimestre *m*; *Am* 25 centesimi *mpl*. ~**s** *pl* (*Mil*) quartiere *msg*; **at** [a] ~ **to six** alle sei meno un quarto ●*vt* dividere in quattro. ~'**final** *n* quarto *m* di finale

quarterly /'kwɔːtəlɪ/ *adj* trimestrale ● *adv* trimestralmente

quartz /kwɔːts/ *n* quarzo *m*. ~ **watch** *n* orologio *m* al quarzo

quay /kiː/ *n* banchina *f*

queasy /'kwiːzɪ/ *adj* **I feel** ~ ho la nausea

queen /kwiːn/ *n* regina *f*. ~ **mother** *n* regina *f* madre

queer /kwɪə(r)/ *adj* strano; (*dubious*) sospetto; (**I**: *homosexual*) finocchio ●*n* (**I**) finocchio *m*

quench /kwentʃ/ *vt* ~ **one's thirst** dissetarsi

query /'kwɪərɪ/ *n* domanda *f*; (*question mark*) punto *m* interrogativo ●*vt* (*pt/pp* -**ied**) interrogare; (*doubt*) mettere in dubbio

quest /kwest/ *n* ricerca *f* (**for** di)

question /'kwestʃn/ *n* domanda *f*; (*for discussion*) questione *f*; **out of the** ~ fuori discussione; **without** ~ senza dubbio; **in** ~ in questione ●*vt*

interrogare; (*doubt*) mettere in dubbio. ~**able** *adj* discutibile. ~ **mark** *n* punto *m* interrogativo

questionnaire /kwestʃə'neə(r)/ *n* questionario *m*

queue /kjuː/ *n* coda *f*, fila *f* ●*vi* ~ [**up**] mettersi in coda (**for** per)

quick /kwɪk/ *adj* veloce; **be** ~ sbrigati!; **have a** ~ **meal** fare uno spuntino ●*adv* in fretta ●*n* **be cut to the** ~ *fig* essere punto sul vivo. ~**ly** *adv* in fretta. ~**-tempered** *adj* collerico

quid /kwɪd/ *n inv* (**I**) sterlina *f*

quiet /'kwaɪət/ *adj* (*calm*) tranquillo; (*silent*) silenzioso; (*voice, music*) basso; **keep** ~ **about** (**I**) non raccontare a nessuno ●*n* quiete *f*; **on the** ~ di nascosto. ~**ly** *adv* (*peacefully*) tranquillamente; (*say*) a bassa voce

quiet|en /'kwaɪətn/ *vt* calmare. □ ~ **down** *vi* calmarsi. ~**ness** *n* quiete *f*

quilt /kwɪlt/ *n* piumino *m*, trapuntino *m*. ~**ed** *adj* trapuntato

quintet /kwɪn'tet/ *n* quintetto *m*

quirk /kwɜːk/ *n* stranezza *f*

quit /kwɪt/ *v* (*pt/pp* **quitted, quit**) ●*vt* lasciare; (*give up*) smettere (**doing** di fare) ●*vi* (**I**: *resign*) andarsene; (*Comput*) uscire; **give sb notice to** ~ (*landlord*:) dare a qcno il preavviso di sfratto

quite /kwaɪt/ *adv* (*fairly*) abbastanza; (*completely*) completamente; (*really*) veramente; ~ [**so**]! proprio così!; ~ **a few** parecchi

quits /kwɪts/ *adj* pari

quiver /'kwɪvə(r)/ *vi* tremare

quiz /kwɪz/ *n* (*game*) quiz *m inv* ●*vt* (*pt/pp* **quizzed**) interrogare

quota /'kwəʊtə/ *n* quota *f*

quotation /kwəʊ'teɪʃn/ *n* citazione *f*; (*price*) preventivo *m*; (*of shares*) quota *f*. ~ **marks** *npl* virgolette *fpl*

quote /kwəʊt/ *n* (**I**) = **quotation**; **in** ~**s** tra virgolette ●*vt* citare; quotare (*price*)

q

Rr

rabbi /'ræbaɪ/ n rabbino m; (title) rabbi

rabbit /'ræbɪt/ n coniglio m

rabies /'reɪbiːz/ n rabbia f

race¹ /reɪs/ n (people) razza f

race² n corsa f ● vi correre ● vt gareggiare con; fare correre (horse)

race: ~**course** n ippodromo m. ~**horse** n cavallo m da corsa. ~**track** n pista m

racial /'reɪʃl/ adj razziale. ~**ism** n razzismo m

racing /'reɪsɪŋ/ n corse fpl; (horse-) corse fpl dei cavalli. ~ **car** n macchina f da corsa. ~ **driver** n corridore m automobilistico

racis|m /'reɪsɪzm/ n razzismo m. ~**t** adj razzista m e f

rack¹ /ræk/ n (for bikes) rastrelliera f; (for luggage) portabagagli m inv; (for plates) scolapiatti m inv ● vt ~ one's brains scervellarsi

rack² n go to ~ and ruin andare in rovina

racket¹ /'rækɪt/ n (Sport) racchetta f

racket² n (din) chiasso m; (swindle) truffa f; (crime) racket m inv, giro m

radar /'reɪdɑː(r)/ n radar m inv

radian|ce /'reɪdɪəns/ n radiosità f inv. ~**t** adj raggiante

radiat|e /'reɪdɪeɪt/ vt irradiare ● vi (heat:) irradiarsi. ~**ion** n radiazione f

radiator /'reɪdɪeɪtə(r)/ n radiatore m; (Auto) radiatore m

radical /'rædɪkl/ adj radicale ● n radicale m f. ~**ly** adv radicalmente

radio /'reɪdɪəʊ/ n radio f inv

radio'active adj radioattivo. ~**ac'tivity** n radioattività f

radish /'rædɪʃ/ n ravanello m

radius /'reɪdɪəs/ n (pl -**dii** /-dɪaɪ/) raggio m

raffle /'ræfl/ n lotteria f

raft /rɑːft/ n zattera f

rafter /'rɑːftə(r)/ n trave f

rag /ræg/ n straccio m; (pej: newspaper) giornalaccio m; **in** ~**s** stracciato

rage /reɪdʒ/ n rabbia f; **all the** ~ 🆂 all'ultima moda ● vi infuriarsi; (storm:) infuriare; (epidemic:) imperversare

ragged /'rægɪd/ adj logoro; (edge) frastagliato

raid /reɪd/ n (by thieves) rapina f; (Mil) incursione f, raid m inv; (police) irruzione f ● vt (Mil) fare un'incursione in; (police, burglars:) fare irruzione in. ~**er** n (of bank) rapinatore, -trice mf

rail /reɪl/ n ringhiera f; (hand-) ringhiera f; (Naut) parapetto m; **by** ~ per ferrovia

'railroad n Am = railway

'railway n ferrovia f. ~**man** n ferroviere m. ~ **station** n stazione f ferroviaria

rain /reɪn/ n pioggia f ● vi piovere

rain: ~**bow** n arcobaleno m. ~**coat** n impermeabile m. ~**fall** n precipitazione f [atmosferica]

rainy /'reɪnɪ/ adj (-ier, -iest) piovoso

raise /reɪz/ n Am aumento m ● vt alzare; levarsi (hat); allevare (children, animals); sollevare (question); ottenere (money)

raisin /'reɪzn/ n uva f passa

rake /reɪk/ n rastrello m ● vt rastrellare. □ ~ **up** vt raccogliere col rastrello; 🆂 rivangare

rally /'rælɪ/ n raduno m; (Auto) rally m inv; (Tennis) scambio m ● vt (pt/pp -ied) radunare ● vi radunarsi; (recover strength) riprendersi

ram /ræm/ n montone m; (Astr) Ariete m ● vt (pt/pp rammed) cozzare contro

RAM /ræm/ n [memoria f] RAM f

rambl|e /ˈræmbl/ n escursione f • vi gironzolare; (in speech) divagare. ~er n escursionista mf; (rose) rosa f rampicante. ~ing adj (in speech) sconnesso; (club) escursionistico

ramp /ræmp/ n rampa f; (Aeron) scaletta f mobile (di aerei)

rampage /ˈræmpeɪdʒ/ n be/go on the ~ scatenarsi • vi ~ through the streets scatenarsi per le strade

ramshackle /ˈræmʃækl/ adj sgangherato

ran /ræn/ ▷RUN

ranch /rɑːntʃ/ n ranch m

random /ˈrændəm/ adj casuale; ~ sample campione m a caso • n at ~ a casaccio

rang /ræŋ/ ▷RING¹

range /reɪndʒ/ n serie f; (Comm, Mus) gamma f; (of mountains) catena f; (distance) raggio m; (for shooting) portata f; (stove) cucina f economica; at a ~ of a una distanza di • vi estendersi; ~ from... to... andare da... a..... ~r n guardia f forestale

rank /ræŋk/ n (row) riga f; (Mil) grado m; (social position) rango m; the ~ and file le fanze f; ~s (Mil) i soldati mpl semplici • vt (place) annoverare (among tra) • vi (be placed) collocarsi

ransack /ˈrænsæk/ vt rovistare; (pillage) saccheggiare

ransom /ˈrænsəm/ n riscatto m; hold sb to ~ tenere qcno in ostaggio (per il riscatto)

rant /rænt/ vi ~ [and rave] inveire; what's he ~ing on about? cosa sta blaterando?

rap /ræp/ n colpo m [secco]; (Mus) rap m • v (pt/pp rapped) • vt dare colpetti a • vi ~ at bussare a

rape /reɪp/ n (sexual) stupro m • vt violentare, stuprare

rapid /ˈræpɪd/ adj rapido. ~ity n rapidità f. ~ly adv rapidamente

rapids /ˈræpɪdz/ npl rapida fsg

rapist /ˈreɪpɪst/ n violentatore m

raptur|e /ˈræptʃə(r)/ n estasi f. ~ous adj entusiastico

rare¹ /reə(r)/ adj raro. ~ly adv raramente

rare² adj (Culin) al sangue

rarefied /ˈreərɪfaɪd/ adj rarefatto

rarity /ˈreərətɪ/ n rarità f inv

rascal /ˈrɑːskl/ n mascalzone m

rash¹ /ræʃ/ n (Med) eruzione f

rash² adj avventato. ~ly adv avventatamente

rasher /ˈræʃə(r)/ n fetta f di pancetta

rasp /rɑːsp/ n (noise) stridio m. ~ing adj stridente

raspberry /ˈrɑːzbərɪ/ n lampone m

rat /ræt/ n topo m; (fam: person) carogna f; smell a ~ fam sentire puzzo di bruciato

rate /reɪt/ n (speed) velocità f; (of payment) tariffa f; (of exchange) tasso m; ~s pl (taxes) imposte fpl comunali sui beni immobili; at any ~ in ogni caso; at this ~ di questo passo • vt stimare; ~ among annoverare tra • vi ~ as essere considerato

rather /ˈrɑːðə(r)/ adv piuttosto; ~! eccome!; ~ too... un po' troppo...

rating /ˈreɪtɪŋ/ n ~s pl (Radio, TV) indice m d'ascolto, audience f inv

ratio /ˈreɪʃɪəʊ/ n rapporto m

ration /ˈræʃn/ n razione f • vt razionare

rational /ˈræʃənl/ adj razionale. ~ize vt/i razionalizzare

rattle /ˈrætl/ n tintinnio m; (toy) sonaglio m • vi tintinnare • vt (shake) scuotere; fam innervosire. □ ~ off fam sciorinare

raucous /ˈrɔːkəs/ adj rauco

rave /reɪv/ vi vaneggiare; ~ about andare in estasi per

raven /ˈreɪvn/ n corvo m imperiale

ravenous /ˈrævənəs/ adj (person)

affamato

ravine /rə'viːn/ n gola f

raving /'reɪvɪŋ/ adj ~ **mad** T matto da legare

ravishing /'rævɪʃɪŋ/ adj incantevole

raw /rɔː/ adj crudo; (not processed) grezzo; (weather) gelido; (inexperienced) inesperto; **get a** ~ **deal** T farsi fregare. ~ **ma'terials** npl materie fpl prime

ray /reɪ/ n raggio m; ~ **of hope** barlume m di speranza

raze /reɪz/ vt ~ **to the ground** radere al suolo

razor /'reɪzə(r)/ n rasoio m. ~ **blade** n lametta f da barba

re /riː/ prep con riferimento a

reach /riːtʃ/ n portata f; **within** ~ a portata di mano; **out of** ~ fuori dalla portata di; **within easy** ~ facilmente raggiungibile • vt arrivare a (place, decision); (contact) contattare; (pass) passare; **I can't** ~ **it** non ci arrivo • vi arrivare (**to** a); ~ **for** allungare la mano per prendere

re'act /rɪ-/ vi reagire

re'action /rɪ-/ n reazione f. ~**ary** adj reazionario, -a mf

reactor /rɪ'æktə(r)/ n reattore m

read /riːd/ vt (pt/pp **read** /red/) leggere; (Univ) studiare • vi leggere; (instrument:) indicare. □ ~ **out** vt leggere ad alta voce

readable /'riːdəbl/ adj piacevole a leggersi; (legible) leggibile

reader /'riːdə(r)/ n lettore, -trice mf; (book) antologia f

readily /'redɪlɪ/ adv volentieri; (easily) facilmente. ~**ness** n disponibilità f inv; (quick) pronto

reading /'riːdɪŋ/ n lettura f

rea'djust /riː-/ vt regolare di nuovo • vi riabituarsi (**to** a)

ready /'redɪ/ adj (**-ier, -iest**) pronto; (quick) veloce; **get** ~ prepararsi

ready-'made adj confezionato

real /riːl/ adj vero; (increase) reale • adv Am T veramente. ~ **estate** n beni mpl immobili

realism /'rɪəlɪzm/ n realismo m. ~**t** n realista mf. ~**tic** adj realistico

reality /rɪ'ælətɪ/ n realtà f inv; ~ **TV** n reality TV f

realization /rɪəlaɪ'zeɪʃn/ n realizzazione f

realize /'rɪəlaɪz/ vt realizzare

really /'rɪəlɪ/ adv davvero

realm /relm/ n regno m

realtor /'rɪəltə(r)/ n Am agente mf immobiliare

reap /riːp/ vt mietere

reap'pear /riː-/ vi riapparire

rear[1] /rɪə(r)/ adj posteriore; (Auto) di dietro; ~ **end** T didietro m • n **the** ~ (of building) il retro m; (of bus, plane) la parte f posteriore; **from the** ~ da dietro

rear[2] vt allevare • vi ~ [**up**] (horse:) impennarsi

rear'range /riː-/ vt cambiare la disposizione di

reason /'riːzn/ n ragione f; **within** ~ nei limiti del ragionevole • vi ragionare; ~ **with** cercare di far ragionare. ~**able** adj ragionevole. ~**ably** adv (in reasonable way, fairly) ragionevolmente

reas'surance /riː-/ n rassicurazione f. ~ **e** vt rassicurare; ~ **sb of** sth rassicurare qcno su qcsa. ~**ing** adj rassicurante

rebate /'riːbeɪt/ n rimborso m; (discount) deduzione f

rebel[1] /'rebl/ n ribelle mf

rebel[2] /rɪ'bel/ vi (pt/pp **rebelled**) ribellarsi. ~**lion** n ribellione f. ~**lious** adj ribelle

re'bound[1] /rɪ-/ vi rimbalzare; fig ricadere

'rebound[2] /riː-/ n rimbalzo m

rebuff /rɪ'bʌf/ n rifiuto m

re'build /riː-/ vt (pt/pp -built) ricostruire

rebuke /rɪˈbjuːk/ vt rimproverare

re'call /rɪ-/ n richiamo m; **beyond ~** irrevocabile ● vt richiamare; riconvocare (diplomat, parliament); (remember) rievocare

recap /ˈriːkæp/ vt/i 🄸 = recapitulate ● n ricapitolazione f

recapitulate /riːkəˈpɪtjʊleɪt/ vt/i ricapitolare

re'capture /riː-/ vt riconquistare; ricatturare (person, animal)

recede /rɪˈsiːd/ vi allontanarsi. **~ing** adj (forehead, chin) sfuggente; **have ~ing hair** essere stempiato

receipt /rɪˈsiːt/ n ricevuta f; (receiving) ricezione f; **~s** pl (Comm) entrate fpl

receive /rɪˈsiːv/ vt ricevere. **~r** n (Teleph) ricevitore m; (Radio, TV) apparecchio m ricevente; (of stolen goods) ricettatore, -trice m

recent /ˈriːsnt/ adj recente. **~ly** adv recentemente

reception /rɪˈsepʃn/ n ricevimento m; (welcome) accoglienza f; (Radio) ricezione f; **~ [desk]** (in hotel) reception f inv. **~ist** n persona f alla reception

receptive /rɪˈseptɪv/ adj ricettivo

recess /rɪˈses/ n rientranza f; (holiday) vacanza f; Am (Sch) intervallo m

recession /rɪˈseʃn/ n recessione f

re'charge /riː-/ vt ricaricare

recipe /ˈresəpɪ/ n ricetta f

recipient /rɪˈsɪpɪənt/ n (of letter) destinatario, -a mf; (of money) beneficiario, -a mf

recital /rɪˈsaɪtl/ n recital m inv

recite /rɪˈsaɪt/ vt recitare; (list) elencare

reckless /ˈreklɪs/ adj (action, decision) sconsiderato; **be a ~** driver guidare in modo spericolato. **~ly** adv in modo sconsiderato. **~ness** n

sconsideratezza f

reckon /ˈrekən/ vt calcolare; (consider) pensare. □ **~ on/with** vt fare i conti con

re'claim /rɪ-/ vt reclamare; bonificare (land)

recline /rɪˈklaɪn/ vi sdraiarsi. **~ing** adj (seat) reclinabile

recluse /rɪˈkluːs/ n recluso, -a mf

recognition /rekəgˈnɪʃn/ n riconoscimento m; **beyond ~** irriconoscibile

recognize /ˈrekəgnaɪz/ vt riconoscere

re'coil /rɪ-/ vi (in fear) indietreggiare

recollect /rekəˈlekt/ vt ricordare. **~ion** n ricordo m

recommend /rekəˈmend/ vt raccomandare. **~ation** n raccomandazione f

recon|cile /ˈrekənsaɪl/ vt riconciliare; conciliare (facts); **~cile oneself to** rassegnarsi a. **~ciliation** n riconciliazione f

reconnaissance /rɪˈkɒnɪsns/ n (Mil) ricognizione f

reconnoitre /rekəˈnɔɪtə(r)/ vt (pres p -tring) fare una ricognizione

recon'sider /riː-/ vt riconsiderare

recon'struct /riː-/ vt ricostruire. **~ion** n ricostruzione f

record¹ /rɪˈkɔːd/ vt registrare; (make a note of) annotare

record² /ˈrekɔːd/ n (file) documentazione f; (Mus) disco m; (Sport) record m inv; **~s** pl (files) schedario msg; **keep a ~ of** tener nota di; **off the ~** in via ufficiosa; **have a [criminal] ~** avere la fedina penale sporca

recorder /rɪˈkɔːdə(r)/ n (Mus) flauto m dolce

recording /rɪˈkɔːdɪŋ/ n registrazione f

'record-player n giradischi m inv

recount /rɪˈkaʊnt/ vt raccontare

re-'count¹ /riː-/ vt ricontare

r

're-count² /'ri:-/ n (Pol) nuovo conteggio m

recover /rɪ'kʌvə(r)/ vt/i recuperare. **~y** n recupero m; (of health) guarigione m.

re·'cover /ri:-/ vt rifoderare

recreation /rekrɪ'eɪʃn/ n ricreazione f. **~al** adj ricreativo

recruit /rɪ'kru:t/ n (Mil) recluta f; **new ~** (member) nuovo, -a adepto, -a mf; (worker) neoassunto, -a mf ● vt assumere (staff). **~ment** n assunzione f

rectang|le /'rektæŋgl/ n rettangolo m. **~ular** adj rettangolare

rectify /'rektɪfaɪ/ vt (pt/pp -ied) rettificare

recuperate /rɪ'ku:pəreɪt/ vi ristabilirsi

recur /rɪ'kɜ:(r)/ vi (pt/pp recurred) ricorrere; (illness): ripresentarsi

recurren|ce /rɪ'kʌrəns/ n ricorrenza f; (of illness) ricomparsa f. **~t** adj ricorrente

recycle /ri:'saɪkl/ vt riciclare

red /red/ adj (redder, reddest) rosso ● n rosso m; **in the ~** (account) scoperto. **R~ Cross** n Croce f rossa

redd|en /'redn/ vt arrossare ● vi arrossire. **~ish** adj rossastro

re'decorate /ri:-/ vt (paint) ridipingere; (wallpaper) ritappezzare

redeem /rɪ'di:m/ vt **~ing quality** unico aspetto m positivo

redemption /rɪ'dempʃn/ n riscatto m

red: ~-haired adj con i capelli rossi. **~-handed** adj **catch sb ~-handed** cogliere qcno con le mani nel sacco. **~ herring** n diversione f. **~-hot** adj rovente

red: ~ light n (Auto) semaforo m rosso

re'double /ri:-/ vt raddoppiare

red 'tape n 1 burocrazia f

reduc|e /rɪ'dju:s/ vt ridurre; (Culin)

far consumare. **~tion** n riduzione f

redundan|cy /rɪ'dʌndənsɪ/ n licenziamento m; (payment) cassa f integrazione. **~t** adj superfluo; **make ~t** licenziare; **be made ~t** essere licenziato

reed /ri:d/ n (Bot) canna f

reef /ri:f/ n scogliera f

reek /ri:k/ vi puzzare (of di)

reel /ri:l/ n bobina f ● vi (stagger) vacillare. **□ ~ off** vt fig snocciolare

refectory /rɪ'fektərɪ/ n refettorio m; (Univ) mensa f universitaria

refer /rɪ'fɜ:(r)/ v (pt/pp referred) ● vt rinviare (matter) (to a); indirizzare (person) ● vi **~ to** fare allusione a; (consult) rivolgersi a (book)

referee /refə'ri:/ n arbitro m; (for job) garante mf ● vt/i (pt/pp refereed) arbitrare

reference /'refərəns/ n riferimento m; (in book) nota f bibliografica; (for job) referenza f; (Comm) **'your ~** 'con riferimento'; **with ~ to** con riferimento a; **make [a] ~ to** fare riferimento a. **~ book** n libro m di consultazione. **~ number** n numero m di riferimento

referendum /refə'rendəm/ n referendum m inv

re'fill¹ /ri:-/ vt riempire di nuovo; ricaricare (pen, lighter)

'refill² /ri:-/ n (for pen) ricambio m

refine /rɪ'faɪn/ vt raffinare. **~d** adj raffinato. **~ment** n raffinatezza f; (Techn) raffinazione f. **~ry** n raffineria f

reflect /rɪ'flekt/ vt riflettere; **be ~ed in** essere riflesso in ● vi (think) riflettere (on su); **~ badly on sb** fig mettere in cattiva luce qcno. **~ion** n riflessione f; (image) riflesso m; **on ~ion** dopo riflessione. **~ive** adj riflessivo. **~or** n riflettore m

reflex /'ri:fleks/ n riflesso m ● attrib di riflesso

reflexive /rɪ'fleksɪv/ adj riflessivo

reform /rɪˈfɔːm/ n riforma f ● vt riformare ● vi correggersi. **R~ation** n (Relig) riforma f. **~er** n riformatore, -trice mf

refrain[1] /rɪˈfreɪn/ n ritornello m

refrain[2] vi astenersi (**from** da)

refresh /rɪˈfreʃ/ vt rinfrescare. **~ing** adj rinfrescante. **~ments** npl rinfreschi mpl

refrigerat|e /rɪˈfrɪdʒəreɪt/ vt conservare in frigo. **~or** n frigorifero m

re'fuel /riː-/ v (pt/pp -fuelled) ● vt rifornire (di carburante) ● vi fare rifornimento

refuge /ˈrefjuːdʒ/ n rifugio m; **take ~** rifugiarsi

refugee /refjʊˈdʒiː/ n rifugiato, -a mf

'refund[1] /ˈriː-/ n rimborso m

re'fund[2] /rɪ-/ vt rimborsare

refusal /rɪˈfjuːzl/ n rifiuto m

refuse[1] /rɪˈfjuːz/ vt/i rifiutare; **~ to do sth** rifiutare di fare qcsa

refuse[2] /ˈrefjuːs/ n rifiuti mpl. **~ collection** n raccolta f dei rifiuti

refute /rɪˈfjuːt/ vt confutare

re'gain /rɪ-/ vt riconquistare

regal /ˈriːgl/ adj regale

regard /rɪˈgɑːd/ n (heed) riguardo m; (respect) considerazione f; **~s** pl saluti mpl; **send/give my ~s to your brother** salutami tuo fratello ● vt (consider) considerare (**as** come); **as ~s** riguardo a. **~ing** prep riguardo a. **~less** adv lo stesso; **~less of** senza badare a

regatta /rɪˈgætə/ n regata f

regime /reɪˈʒiːm/ n regime m

regiment /ˈredʒɪmənt/ n reggimento m. **~al** adj reggimentale. **~ation** n irreggimentazione f

region /ˈriːdʒən/ n regione f; **in the ~ of** fig approssimativamente. **~al** adj regionale

register /ˈredʒɪstə(r)/ n registro m ● vt registrare; mandare per raccomandata (letter); assicurare (luggage); immatricolare (vehicle); mostrare (feeling) ● vi (instrument:) funzionare; (student:) iscriversi (**for** a); **~ with** iscriversi nella lista di (doctor)

registrar /redʒɪˈstrɑː(r)/ n ufficiale m di stato civile

registration /redʒɪˈstreɪʃn/ n (of vehicle) immatricolazione f; (of letter) raccomandazione f; (of luggage) assicurazione f; (for course) iscrizione f. **~ number** n (Auto) targa f

registry office /ˈredʒɪstrɪ-/ n anagrafe f

regret /rɪˈgret/ n rammarico m ● vt (pt/pp regretted) rimpiangere; **I ~ that** mi rincresce che. **~fully** adv con rammarico

regrettab|le /rɪˈgretəbl/ adj spiacevole. **~ly** adv spiacevolmente; (before adjective) deplorevolmente

regular /ˈregjʊlə(r)/ adj regolare; (usual) abituale ● n cliente mf abituale. **~ity** n regolarità f. **~ly** adv regolarmente

regulat|e /ˈregjʊleɪt/ vt regolare. **~ion** n (rule) regolamento m

rehears|al /rɪˈhɜːsl/ n (Theat) prova f. **~e** vt/i provare

reign /reɪn/ n regno m ● vi regnare

reinforce /riːɪnˈfɔːs/ vt rinforzare. **~d 'concrete** n cemento m armato. **~ment** n rinforzo m

reiterate /riːˈɪtəreɪt/ vt reiterare

reject /rɪˈdʒekt/ vt rifiutare. **~ion** n rifiuto m; (Med) rigetto m

rejoic|e /rɪˈdʒɔɪs/ vi liter rallegrarsi. **~ing** n gioia f

rejuvenate /rɪˈdʒuːvəneɪt/ vt ringiovanire

relapse /rɪˈlæps/ n ricaduta f ● vi ricadere

relate /rɪˈleɪt/ vt (tell) riportare; (connect) collegare ● vi **~ to** riferirsi a; identificarsi con (person). **~d** adj imparentato (**to** a); (ideas etc) affine

    r

relation /rɪˈleɪʃn/ n rapporto m; (person) parente mf. ~ship n rapporto m (blood tie) parentela f; (affair) relazione f

relative /ˈrelətɪv/ n parente m ● adj relativo. ~ly adv relativamente

relax /rɪˈlæks/ vt rilassare; allentare (pace, grip) ● vi rilassarsi. ~ation n rilassamento m, relax m inv; (recreation) svago m. ~ing adj rilassante

relay[1] /ˈriːˈleɪ/ vt ritrasmettere; (Radio, TV) trasmettere

relay[2] /ˈriːˈleɪ/ n (Electr) relais m inv; work in ~s fare i turni. ~ [race] n [corsa f a] staffetta f

release /rɪˈliːs/ n rilascio m; (of film) distribuzione f ● vt liberare; lasciare (hand); togliere (brake); distribuire (film); rilasciare (information etc)

relegate /ˈrelɪgeɪt/ vt relegare; be ~d (Sport) essere retrocesso

relent /rɪˈlent/ vi cedere. ~less adj inflessibile; (unceasing) incessante. ~lessly adv incessantemente

relevan|ce /ˈreləvəns/ n pertinenza f. ~t adj pertinente (to a)

reli|ability /rɪlaɪəˈbɪlətɪ/ n affidabilità f. ~le adj affidabile a. ~bly adv in modo affidabile; be ~bly informed sapere da fonte certa

relian|ce /rɪˈlaɪəns/ n fiducia f (on in). ~t adj fiducioso (on in)

relic /ˈrelɪk/ n (Relig) reliquia f; ~s npl resti mpl

relief /rɪˈliːf/ n sollievo m; (assistance) soccorso m; (distraction) diversivo m; (replacement) cambio m; (in art) rilievo m; in ~ in rilievo. ~ map n carta f in rilievo. ~ train n treno m supplementare

relieve /rɪˈliːv/ vt alleviare; (take over from) dare il cambio a; ~ of liberare da (burden)

religion /rɪˈlɪdʒən/ n religione f

religious /rɪˈlɪdʒəs/ adj religioso. ~ly adv (conscientiously) scrupolosamente

relinquish /rɪˈlɪŋkwɪʃ/ vt abbandonare; ~ sth to sb rinunciare a qcsa in favore di qcno

relish /ˈrelɪʃ/ n gusto m; (Culin) salsa f ● vt fig apprezzare

reluctan|ce /rɪˈlʌktəns/ n riluttanza f. ~t adj riluttante. ~tly adv a malincuore

rely /rɪˈlaɪ/ vi (pt/pp -ied) ~ on dipendere da; (trust) contare su

remain /rɪˈmeɪn/ vi restare. ~der n resto m. ~ing adj restante. ~s mpl resti mpl; (dead body) spoglie fpl

remand /rɪˈmɑːnd/ n on ~ in custodia cautelare ● vt ~ in custody rinviare con detenzione provvisoria

remark /rɪˈmɑːk/ n osservazione f ● vt osservare. ~able adj notevole. ~ably adv notevolmente

remarry /riː-/ vi risposarsi

remedy /ˈremədɪ/ n rimedio m (for contro) ● vt (pt/pp -ied) rimediare a

remember /rɪˈmembə(r)/ vt ricordare, ricordarsi; ~ to do sth ricordarsi di fare qcsa; ~ me to him salutamelo ● vi ricordarsi

remind /rɪˈmaɪnd/ vt ~ sb of sth ricordare qcsa a qcno. ~er n ricordo m; (memo) promemoria m; (letter) lettera f di sollecito

reminisce /remɪˈnɪs/ vi rievocare il passato. ~nces npl reminiscenze fpl. ~nt adj be ~ of richiamare alla memoria

remnant /ˈremnənt/ n resto m; (of material) scampolo m; (trace) traccia f

remorse /rɪˈmɔːs/ n rimorso m. ~ful adj pieno di rimorso. ~less adj spietato. ~lessly adv senza pietà

remote /rɪˈməʊt/ adj remoto; (slight) minimo. ~ access n (Comput) accesso m remoto. ~ con'trol n telecomando m. ~-con'trolled adj telecomandato. ~ly adv lontanamente; be not ~ly... non essere lontanamente...

re'movable /rɪ-/ adj rimovibile

removal /rɪˈmuːvl/ n rimozione f;

(*from house*) trasloco *m.* ~ **van** *n* camion *m inv* da trasloco

remove /rɪ'muːv/ *vt* togliere; togliersi (clothes); eliminare (stain, doubts)

render /'rendə(r)/ *vt* rendere (service)

renegade /'renɪgeɪd/ *n* rinnegato, -a *mf*

renew /rɪ'njuː/ *vt* rinnovare (contract). ~**al** *n* rinnovo *m*

renounce /rɪ'naʊns/ *vt* rinunciare a

renovat|e /'renəveɪt/ *vt* rinnovare. ~**ion** *n* rinnovo *m*

renown /rɪ'naʊn/ *n* fama *f*. ~**ed** *adj* rinomato

rent /rent/ *n* affitto *m* • *vt* affittare; ~ **[out]** dare in affitto. ~**al** *n* affitto *m*

renunciation /rɪnʌnsɪ'eɪʃn/ *n* rinuncia *f*

re'open /riː-/ *vt/i* riaprire

re'organize /riː-/ *vt* riorganizzare

rep /rep/ *n* (Comm) □ rappresentante *mf*; (Theat) ≈ teatro *m* stabile

repair /rɪ'peə(r)/ *n* riparazione *f*; **in good/bad** ~ in cattive/buone condizioni • *vt* riparare

repatriat|e /riː'pætrɪeɪt/ *vt* rimpatriare. ~**ion** *n* rimpatrio *m*

re'pay /riː-/ *vt* (*pt/pp* -**paid**) ripagare. ~**ment** *n* rimborso *m*

repeal /rɪ'piːl/ *n* abrogazione *f* • *vt* abrogare

repeat /rɪ'piːt/ *n* (TV) replica *f* • *vt/i* ripetere; ~ **oneself** ripetersi. ~**ed** *adj* ripetuto. ~**edly** *adv* ripetutamente

repel /rɪ'pel/ *vt* (*pt/pp* **repelled**) respingere; *fig* ripugnare. ~**lent** *adj* ripulsivo

repent /rɪ'pent/ *vi* pentirsi. ~**ance** *n* pentimento *m*. ~**ant** *adj* pentito

repertoire /'repətwɑː(r)/ *n* repertorio *m*

repetit|ion /repɪ'tɪʃn/ *n* ripetizione

f. ~**ive** *adj* ripetitivo

re'place /rɪ-/ *vt* (*put back*) rimettere a posto; (*take the place of*) sostituire; ~ **sth with sth** sostituire qcsa con qcsa. ~**ment** *n* sostituzione *m*; (*person*) sostituto, -a *mf*. ~**ment** *part* *n* pezzo *m* di ricambio

'replay /'riː-/ *n* (Sport) partita *f* ripetuta; [**action**] ~ replay *m inv*

replenish /rɪ'plenɪʃ/ *vt* rifornire (stocks); (*refill*) riempire di nuovo

replica /'replɪkə/ *n* copia *f*

reply /rɪ'plaɪ/ *n* risposta *f* (**to** a) • *vt/i* (*pt/pp* **replied**) rispondere

report /rɪ'pɔːt/ *n* rapporto *m*; (TV, Radio) servizio *m*; (Journ) cronaca *f*; (Sch) pagella *f*; (*rumour*) diceria *f* • *vt* riportare; ~ **sb to the police** denunciare qcno alla polizia • *vi* riportare; (*present oneself*) presentarsi (**to** a). ~**edly** *adv* secondo quanto si dice. ~**er** *n* cronista *m*, reporter *mf inv*

reprehensible /reprɪ'hensəbl/ *adj* riprovevole

represent /reprɪ'zent/ *vt* rappresentare

representative /reprɪ'zentətɪv/ *adj* rappresentativo • *n* rappresentante *mf*

repress /rɪ'pres/ *vt* reprimere. ~**ion** *n* repressione *f*. ~**ive** *adj* repressivo

reprieve /rɪ'priːv/ *n* commutazione *f* della pena capitale; (*postponement*) sospensione *f* della pena capitale; *fig* tregua *f* • *vt* sospendere la sentenza a; *fig* risparmiare

reprimand /'reprɪmɑːnd/ *n* rimprovero *m* • *vt* rimproverare

reprisal /rɪ'praɪzl/ *n* rappresaglia *f*; **in** ~ **for** per rappresaglia contro

reproach /rɪ'prəʊtʃ/ *n* ammonimento *m* • *vt* ammonire. ~**ful** *adj* riprovevole. ~**fully** *adv* con aria di rimprovero

repro'duc|e /riː-/ *vt* riprodurre • *vi*

r

riprodursi. ~**tion** n riproduzione f. ~**tive** adj riproduttivo

reprove /rɪˈpruːv/ vt rimproverare

reptile /ˈreptaɪl/ n rettile m

republic /rɪˈpʌblɪk/ n repubblica f. ~**an** adj repubblicano • n repubblicano, -a mf

repugnan|ce /rɪˈpʌɡnəns/ n ripugnanza f. ~**t** adj ripugnante

repuls|ion /rɪˈpʌlʃn/ n repulsione f. ~**ive** adj ripugnante

reputable /ˈrepjʊtəbl/ adj affidabile

reputation /repjʊˈteɪʃn/ n reputazione f

request /rɪˈkwest/ n richiesta f • vt richiedere. ~ **stop** n fermata f a richiesta

require /rɪˈkwaɪə(r)/ vt (need) necessitare di; (demand) esigere. ~**d** adj richiesto; I am ~**d** to do si esige che io faccia. ~**ment** n esigenza f; (condition) requisito m

rescue /ˈreskjuː/ n salvataggio m • vt salvare. ~**r** n salvatore, -trice mf

research /rɪˈsɜːtʃ/ n ricerca f • vt fare ricerche su; (Journ) fare un'inchiesta su • vi ~ **into** fare ricerche su. ~**er** n ricercatore, -trice mf

resem|blance /rɪˈzembləns/ n somiglianza f. ~**ble** vt rassomigliare a

resent /rɪˈzent/ vt risentirsi per. ~**ful** adj pieno di risentimento. ~**fully** adv con risentimento. ~**ment** n risentimento m

reservation /rezəˈveɪʃn/ n (booking) prenotazione f; (doubt, enclosure) riserva f

reserve /rɪˈzɜːv/ n riserva f; (shyness) riserbo m • vt riservare; riservarsi (right). ~**d** adj riservato

reservoir /ˈrezəvwɑː(r)/ n bacino m idrico

re'shuffle /riː-/ n (Pol) rimpasto m • vt (Pol) rimpastare

residence /ˈrezɪdəns/ n residenza f; (stay) soggiorno m. ~ **permit** n permesso m di soggiorno

resident /ˈrezɪdənt/ adj residente • n residente mf. ~**ial** adj residenziale

residue /ˈrezɪdjuː/ n residuo m

resign /rɪˈzaɪn/ vt dimettersi da; ~ **oneself** to rassegnarsi a • vi dare le dimissioni. ~**ation** n rassegnazione f; (from job) dimissioni fpl. ~**ed** adj rassegnato

resilient /rɪˈzɪliənt/ adj elastico; fig con buone capacità di ripresa

resin /ˈrezɪn/ n resina f

resist /rɪˈzɪst/ vt resistere a • vi resistere. ~**ance** n resistenza f. ~**ant** adj resistente

resolute /ˈrezəluːt/ adj risoluto. ~**ely** adv con risolutezza. ~**ion** n risolutezza f

resolve /rɪˈzɒlv/ vt ~ **to do** decidere di fare

resort /rɪˈzɔːt/ n (place) luogo m di villeggiatura; **as a last** ~ come ultima risorsa • vi ~ **to** ricorrere a

resource /rɪˈsɔːs/ n ~**s** pl risorse fpl. ~**ful** adj pieno di risorse; (solution) ingegnoso. ~**fulness** n ingegnosità f inv

respect /rɪˈspekt/ n rispetto m; (aspect) aspetto m; **with** ~ **to** per quanto riguarda • vt rispettare

respect|able /rɪˈspektəbl/ adj spettabile. ~**ably** adv rispettabilmente. ~**ful** adj rispettoso

respective /rɪˈspektɪv/ adj rispettivo. ~**ly** adv rispettivamente

respiration /respɪˈreɪʃn/ n respirazione f

respite /ˈrespaɪt/ n respiro m

respond /rɪˈspɒnd/ vi rispondere; (react) reagire (**to** a); (patient:) rispondere (**to** a)

response /rɪˈspɒns/ n risposta f; (reaction) reazione f

responsibility /rɪspɒnsɪˈbɪlɪtɪ/ n responsabilità f inv

responsib|le /rɪˈspɒnsəbl/ adj responsabile; (job) impegnativo

responsive /rɪ'spɒnsɪv/ adj be ~ (audience etc:) reagire; (brakes:) essere sensibile

rest[1] /rest/ n riposo m; (Mus) pausa f; have a ~ riposarsi ● vi riposare; (lean) appoggiare (on su); (place) appoggiare ● vi riposarsi; (elbows:) appoggiarsi; (hopes:) riposare

rest[2] n the ~ il resto m; (people) gli altri mpl ● vi it ~s with you sta a te

restaurant /'restərɒnt/ n ristorante m. ~ car n vagone m ristorante

restful /'restfl/ adj riposante

restive /'restɪv/ adj irrequieto

restless /'restlɪs/ adj nervoso

restoration /restə'reɪʃn/ n (of building) restauro m

restore /rɪ'stɔː(r)/ vt ristabilire; restaurare (building); (give back) restituire

restrain /rɪ'streɪn/ vt trattenere; ~ oneself controllarsi. ~ed adj controllato. ~t n restrizione f; (moderation) ritegno m

restrict /rɪ'strɪkt/ vt limitare; ~ to limitarsi a. ~ion n limite m; (restraint) restrizione f. ~ive adj limitativo

'rest room n Am toilette f inv

result /rɪ'zʌlt/ n risultato m; as a ~ a causa di ● vi ~ from risultare da; ~ in portare a

resume /rɪ'zjuːm/ vt/i riprendere

résumé /'rezjʊmeɪ/ n riassunto m; Am curriculum vitae m inv

resurrect /rezə'rekt/ vt fig risuscitare. ~ion n the R~ion (Relig) la Risurrezione

resuscitat|e /rɪ'sʌsɪteɪt/ vt rianimare. ~ion n rianimazione f

retail /'riːteɪl/ n vendita f al minuto o al dettaglio ● adj & adv al minuto ● vt vendere al minuto ● vi ~ at essere venduto al pubblico al prezzo di. ~er n dettagliante mf

retain /rɪ'teɪn/ vt conservare; (hold back) trattenere

retaliat|e /rɪ'tælɪeɪt/ vi vendicarsi. ~ion n rappresaglia f; in ~ion for per rappresaglia contro

retarded /rɪ'tɑːdɪd/ adj ritardato

rethink /riː'θɪŋk/ vt (pt/pp rethought) ripensare

reticen|ce /'retɪsəns/ n reticenza f. ~t adj reticente

retina /'retɪnə/ n retina f

retinue /'retɪnjuː/ n seguito m

retire /rɪ'taɪə(r)/ vi andare in pensione; (withdraw) ritirarsi ● vt mandare in pensione (employee). ~d adj in pensione. ~ment n pensione f; since my ~ment da quando sono andato in pensione

retiring /rɪ'taɪərɪŋ/ adj riservato

retort /rɪ'tɔːt/ n replica f ● vt ribattere

re'trace /riː-/ vt ripercorrere; ~ one's steps ritornare sui propri passi

retract /rɪ'trækt/ vt ritirare; ritrattare (statement, evidence) ● vi ritrarsi

re'train /riː-/ vt riqualificare ● vi riqualificarsi

retreat /rɪ'triːt/ n ritirata f; (place) ritiro m ● vi ritirarsi; (Mil) battere in ritirata

re'trial /riː-/ n nuovo processo m

retrieval /rɪ'triːvəl/ n recupero m

retrieve /rɪ'triːv/ vt recuperare

retrograde /'retrəɡreɪd/ adj retrogrado

retrospect /'retrəspekt/ n in ~ guardando indietro. ~ive adj retrospettivo; (legislation) retroattivo ● n retrospettiva f

return /rɪ'tɜːn/ n ritorno m; (giving back) restituzione f; (Comm) profitto m; (ticket) biglietto m di andata e ritorno; by ~ [of post] a stretto giro di posta; in ~ in cambio (for di); many happy ~s! cento di questi

giorni! ● vi ritornare ● vt (give back)
restituire; ricambiare (affection, invitation); (put back) rimettere; (send
back) mandare indietro; (elect)
eleggere

return: ~ **match** n rivincita f. ~
ticket n biglietto m di andata e
ritorno

reunion /riːˈjuːnɪən/ n riunione f

reunite /riːjuːˈnaɪt/ vt riunire

rev /rev/ n (Auto), 🔧 giro m (di motore)
● v (pt/pp revved) ● vt ~ [up] far andare su di giri ● vi andare su di giri

reveal /rɪˈviːl/ vt rivelare; (dress:)
scoprire. ~**ing** adj rivelatore;
(dress) osé

revel /ˈrevl/ vi (pt/pp revelled) ~ **in**
sth godere di qcsa

revelation /revəˈleɪʃn/ n rivelazione f

revelry /ˈrevlrɪ/ n baldoria f

revenge /rɪˈvendʒ/ n vendetta f;
(Sport) rivincita f; **take** ~ vendicarsi
● vt vendicare

revenue /ˈrevənjuː/ n reddito m

revere /rɪˈvɪə(r)/ vt riverire. ~**nce** f
riverenza f

Reverend /ˈrevərənd/ adj re-
verendo

reverent /ˈrevərənt/ adj riverente

reverse /rɪˈvɜːs/ adj opposto; **in** ~
order in ordine inverso ● n contrario
m; (back) rovescio m; (Auto) marcia m
indietro ● vt invertire; ~ **the car
into the garage** entrare in garage a
marcia indietro; ~ **the charges**
(Teleph) fare una telefonata a carico
● vi (Auto) fare marcia indietro

revert /rɪˈvɜːt/ vi ~ **to** tornare a

review /rɪˈvjuː/ n (survey) rassegna
f; (re-examination) riconsiderazione f;
(Mil) rivista f; (of book, play) recensione f ● vt riesaminare (situation);
(Mil) passare in rivista; recensire
(book, play). ~**er** n critico, -a mf

revis|e /rɪˈvaɪz/ vt rivedere; (for
exam) ripassare. ~**ion** n revisione f;

(for exam) ripasso m

revive /rɪˈvaɪv/ vt resuscitare; riani-
mare (person) ● vi riprendersi; (person:) rianimarsi

revolt /rɪˈvəʊlt/ n rivolta f ● vi ribellarsi ● vt rivoltare. ~**ing** adj rivoltante

revolution /revəˈluːʃn/ n rivolu-
zione f; (Auto) ~**s per minute** giri
mpl al minuto. ~**ary** adj & n rivoluzio-
nario, -a mf. ~**ize** vt rivoluzionare

revolve /rɪˈvɒlv/ vi ruotare; ~
around girare intorno

revolver /rɪˈvɒlvə(r)/ n rivoltella f,
revolver m inv. ~**ing** adj ruotante

revue /rɪˈvjuː/ n rivista f

revulsion /rɪˈvʌlʃn/ n ripulsione f

reward /rɪˈwɔːd/ n ricompensa f ● vt
ricompensare. ~**ing** adj gratificante

re'write /riː-/ vt (pt rewrote, pp re-
written) riscrivere

rhetoric /ˈretərɪk/ n retorica f. ~**al**
adj retorico

rhinoceros /raɪˈnɒsərəs/ n rinoce-
ronte m

rhubarb /ˈruːbɑːb/ n rabarbaro m

rhyme /raɪm/ n rima f; (poem) filastrocca f ● vi rimare

rhythm /ˈrɪðm/ n ritmo m. ~**ic[al]**
adj ritmico. ~**ically** adv con ritmo

rib /rɪb/ n costola f

ribbon /ˈrɪbən/ n nastro m; **in** ~**s** a
brandelli

rice /raɪs/ n riso m

rich /rɪtʃ/ adj ricco; (food) pesante
● n **the** ~ i ricchi mpl; ~**es** pl ric-
chezze fpl. ~**ly** adv riccamente; (deserve) largamente

ricochet /ˈrɪkəʃeɪ/ vi rimbalzare ● n
rimbalzo m

rid /rɪd/ vt (pt/pp rid, pres p ridding)
sbarazzare (**of** di); **get** ~ **of** sbarazzarsi di

riddance /ˈrɪdns/ **good** ~! che
liberazione!

ridden /ˈrɪdn/ ▷RIDE

riddle /ˈrɪdl/ n enigma m

ride /raɪd/ n (on horse) cavalcata f; (in vehicle) giro m; (journey) viaggio m; **take sb for a ~** ▯ prendere qcno in giro ● v (pt **rode**, pp **ridden**) ● vt montare (horse); andare su (bicycle) ● vi andare a cavallo; (jockey:) cavalcare; (cyclist:) andare in bicicletta; (in vehicle) viaggiare. **~r** n cavallerizzo, -a mf; (in race) fantino m; (on bicycle) ciclista mf; (in document) postilla f

ridge /rɪdʒ/ n spigolo m; (on roof) punta f; (of mountain) cresta f

ridicule /ˈrɪdɪkjuːl/ n ridicolo m ● vt mettere in ridicolo

ridiculous /rɪˈdɪkjʊləs/ adj ridicolo

rife /raɪf/ adj be ~ essere diffuso; ~ **with** pieno di

rifle /ˈraɪfl/ n fucile m; **~-range** tiro m al bersaglio ● vt ~ **[through]** mettere a soqquadro

rift /rɪft/ n fessura f; fig frattura f

rig[1] /rɪɡ/ n equipaggiamento m; (at sea) piattaforma f per trivellazioni subacquee ● **rig out** vt (pt/pp **rigged**) equipaggiare. ▫ ~ **up** vt allestire

rig[2] vt (pt/pp **rigged**) manovrare (election)

right /raɪt/ adj giusto; (not left) destro; **be ~** (person:) aver ragione; (clock:) essere giusto; **put ~** mettere all'ora (clock); correggere (person); rimediare a (situation); **that's ~!** proprio così ● adv (correctly) bene; (not left) a destra; (directly) proprio; (completely) completamente; ~ **away** immediatamente ● n giusto m; (not left) destra f; (what is due) diritto m; **on/to the ~** a destra; **be in the ~** essere nel giusto; **know ~ from wrong** distinguere il bene dal male; **by ~s** secondo giustizia; **the R~** (Pol) la destra f ● vt raddrizzare; ~ **a wrong** fig riparare a un torto. ~ **angle** n angolo m retto

rightful /ˈraɪtfl/ adj legittimo

right: ~**-handed** adj che usa la mano destra. ~**-hand 'man** n fig braccio m destro

rightly /ˈraɪtlɪ/ adv giustamente

right: ~ **of way** n diritto m di transito; (path) passaggio m; (Auto) precedenza f. ~**-'wing** adj (Pol) di destra ● n (Sport) ala f destra

rigid /ˈrɪdʒɪd/ adj rigido. ~**ity** n rigidità f inv

rigorous /ˈrɪɡərəs/ adj rigoroso

rim /rɪm/ n bordo m; (of wheel) cerchione m

rind /raɪnd/ n (on fruit) scorza f; (on cheese) crosta f; (on bacon) cotenna f

ring[1] /rɪŋ/ n (circle) cerchio m; (on finger) anello m; (boxing) ring m inv; (for circus) pista f; **stand in a ~** essere in cerchio

ring[2] n suono m; **give sb a ~** (Teleph) dare un colpo di telefono a qcno ● v (pt **rang**, pp **rung**) ● vt suonare; ~ **[up]** (Teleph) telefonare a ● vi suonare; (Teleph) ~ **[up]** telefonare. ▫ ~ **back** vt/i (Teleph) richiamare. ▫ ~ **off** vi (Teleph) riattaccare

ring: ~**leader** n capobanda m. ~**road** n circonvallazione f. ~**tone** n suoneria f

rink /rɪŋk/ n pista f di pattinaggio

rinse /rɪns/ n risciacquo m; (hair colour) cachet m inv ● vt sciacquare

riot /ˈraɪət/ n rissa f; (of colour) accozzaglia f; ~**s** pl disordini mpl; **run ~** impazzare ● vi creare disordini. ~**er** n dimostrante mf. ~**ous** adj sfrenato

rip /rɪp/ n strappo m ● vt (pt/pp **ripped**) strappare; ~ **open** aprire con uno strappo. ▫ ~ **off** vt ▯ fregare

ripe /raɪp/ adj maturo; (cheese) stagionato

ripen /ˈraɪpn/ vi maturare; (cheese:) stagionarsi ● vt far maturare; stagionare (cheese)

'rip-off n ▯ frode f

ripple /ˈrɪpl/ n increspatura f; (sound) mormorio m

rise /raɪz/ n (of sun) levata f; (fig: to fame, power) ascesa f; (increase) aumento *m*; **give ~ to** dare adito a ● *vi* (*pt* **rose**, *pp* **risen**) alzarsi; (sun:) sorgere; (dough:) lievitare; (prices, water level:) aumentare; (*to power, position*) arrivare (**to** a). **~r** *n* early **~r** persona *f* mattiniera

rising /'raɪzɪŋ/ *adj* (sun) levante; **~ generation** nuova generazione *f* ● *n* (*revolt*) sollevazione *f*

risk /rɪsk/ *n* rischio *m*; **at one's own ~** a proprio rischio e pericolo ● *vt* rischiare

risky /'rɪskɪ/ *adj* (-ier, -iest) rischioso

rite /raɪt/ *n* rito *m*; **last ~s** estrema unzione *f*

ritual /'rɪtjʊəl/ *adj* rituale ● *n* rituale *m*

rival /'raɪvl/ *adj* rivale ● *n* rivale *mf*; **~s** *pl* (*Comm*) concorrenti *mpl* ● *vt* (*pt/pp* **rivalled**) rivaleggiare con. **~ry** *n* rivalità *f inv*; (*Comm*) concorrenza *f*

river /'rɪvə(r)/ *n* fiume *m*. **~-bed** *n* letto *m* del fiume

rivet /'rɪvɪt/ *n* rivetto *m* ● *vt* rivettare; **~ed by** *fig* inchiodato da

road /rəʊd/ *n* strada *f*, via *f*; **be on the ~** viaggiare

road: **~-map** *n* carta *f* stradale. **~side** *n* bordo *m* della strada. **~-works** *npl* lavori *mpl* stradali. **~worthy** *adj* sicuro

roam /rəʊm/ *vi* girovagare

roar /rɔː(r)/ *n* ruggito *m*; **~s of laughter** scroscio *msg* di risa ● *vi* ruggire; (lorry, thunder:) rombare; **~ with laughter** ridere fragorosamente. **~ing** *adj* **do a ~ing trade** 🔢 fare affari d'oro

roast /rəʊst/ *adj* arrosto; **~ pork** arrosto *m* di maiale ● *n* arrosto *m* ● *vt* arrostire (meat) ● *vi* arrostirsi

rob /rɒb/ *vt* (*pt/pp* **robbed**) derubare (**of** di); svaligiare (bank). **~ber** *n* rapinatore *m*. **~bery** *n* rapina *f*

robe /rəʊb/ *n* tunica *f*; (*Am: bathrobe*) accappatoio *m*

robin /'rɒbɪn/ *n* pettirosso *m*

robot /'rəʊbɒt/ *n* robot *m inv*

robust /rəʊ'bʌst/ *adj* robusto

rock[1] /rɒk/ *n* roccia *f*, (in sea) scoglio *m*; (*sweet*) zucchero *m* candito. **on the ~s** (ship) incagliato; (marriage) finito; (drink) con ghiaccio

rock[2] *vt* cullare (baby); (shake) far traballare; (shock) scuotere ● *vi* dondolarsi

rock[3] *n* (*Mus*) rock *m inv*

rock-'bottom *adj* bassissimo ● *n* livello *m* più basso

rocket /'rɒkɪt/ *n* razzo *m* ● *vi* salire alle stelle

rocky /'rɒkɪ/ *adj* (-ier, -iest) roccioso; *fig* traballante

rod /rɒd/ *n* bacchetta *f*; (*for fishing*) canna *f*

rode /rəʊd/ ▷**RIDE**

rodent /'rəʊdnt/ *n* roditore *m*

rogue /rəʊg/ *n* farabutto *m*

role /rəʊl/ *n* ruolo *m*

roll /rəʊl/ *n* rotolo *m*; (bread) panino *m*; (list) lista *f*; (of ship, drum) rullio *m* ● *vi* rotolare; **be ~ing in money** 🔢 nuotare nell'oro ● *vt* spianare (lawn, pastry). **~ over** *vi* rigirarsi. **~ up** *vt* arrotolare; rimboccarsi (sleeves) ● *vi* 🔢 arrivare

'roll-call *n* appello *m*

roller /'rəʊlə(r)/ *n* rullo *m*; (*for hair*) bigodino *m*; (list) lista *f*. **~ blades** *npl* pattini *npl* in linea. **~ blind** *n* tapparella *f*. **~-coaster** *n* montagne *fpl* russe. **~-skate** *n* pattino *m* a rotelle

'rolling-pin *n* mattarello *m*

Roman /'rəʊmən/ *adj* romano ● *n* romano, -a *mf*. **~ Catholic** *adj* cattolico ● *n* cattolico, -a *mf*

romance /rəʊ'mæns/ *n* (love affair) storia *f* d'amore; (book) romanzo *m* rosa

Romania /rəʊ'meɪnɪə/ *n* Romania *f*. **~n** *adj* rumeno ● *n* rumeno, -a *mf*

romantic /rəʊ'mæntɪk/ *adj* romantico. **~ally** adv romanticamente. **~ism** n romanticismo m

Rome /rəʊm/ n Roma f

romp /rɒmp/ n gioco m rumoroso ● vi giocare rumorosamente. **~ers** npl pagliaccetto msg

roof /ruːf/ n tetto m; (of mouth) palato m ● vt mettere un tetto su. **~-rack** n portabagagli m inv. **~-top** n tetto m

rook /rʊk/ n corvo m; (in chess) torre f

room /ruːm/ n stanza f; (bedroom) camera f; (for functions) sala f; (space) spazio m. **~y** adj spazioso; (clothes) ampio

roost /ruːst/ vi appollaiarsi

root[1] /ruːt/ n radice f; take ~ metter radici ● **root out** vt fig scovare

root[2] vi ~ about vi grufolare; ~ for sb Am 🄴 fare il tifo per qcno

rope /rəʊp/ n corda f; know the ~s 🄴 conoscere i trucchi del mestiere ● **rope in** vt 🄴 coinvolgere

rose[1] /rəʊz/ n rosa f; (of watering-can) bocchetta f

rose[2] ▷ RISE

rosé /ˈrəʊzeɪ/ n [vino m] rosé m inv

rot /rɒt/ n marciume m; (🄴: nonsense) sciocchezze fpl ● vi (pt/pp rotted) marcire

rota /ˈrəʊtə/ n tabella f dei turni

rotary /ˈrəʊtərɪ/ adj rotante

rotat|e /rəʊˈteɪt/ vt far ruotare; avvicendare (crops) ● vi ruotare. **~ion** n rotazione f; in ~ a turno

rote /rəʊt/ n by ~ meccanicamente

rotten /ˈrɒtn/ adj marcio; 🄴 schifoso; (person) penoso

rough /rʌf/ adj (not smooth) ruvido; (ground) accidentato; (behaviour) rozzo; (sport) violento; (area) malfamato; (crossing, time) brutto; (estimate) approssimativo ● adv (play) grossolanamente; sleep ~ dormire sotto i

ponti ● vt ~ **it** vivere senza comfort. □ ~ **out** vt abbozzare

roughage /ˈrʌfɪdʒ/ n fibre fpl

rough|**ly** /ˈrʌflɪ/ adv rozzamente; (more or less) pressappoco. **~ness** f ruvidità f; (of behaviour) rozzezza f

roulette /ruːˈlet/ n roulette f inv

round /raʊnd/ adj rotondo ● n tondo m; (slice) fetta f; (of visits, drinks) giro m; (of competition) partita f; (boxing) ripresa f, round m inv; do one's ~s (doctor:) fare il giro delle visite ● prep intorno a; **open ~ the clock** aperto ventiquattr'ore ● adv **all ~** tutt'intorno; **ask sb ~** invitare qcno; **go/come ~ to** (a friend etc) andare da; **turn/look ~** girarsi. □ ~ **about** (approximately) intorno a ● vt arrotondare; girare (corner). □ ~ **down** vt arrotondare (per difetto). □ ~ **off** vt (end) terminare. □ ~ **on** vt aggredire. □ ~ **up** vt radunare; arrotondare (prices)

roundabout /ˈraʊndəbaʊt/ adj indiretto ● n giostra f; (for traffic) rotonda f

round: ~ **'trip** n viaggio m di andata e ritorno

rous|**e** /raʊz/ vt svegliare; risvegliare (suspicion, interest). **~ing** adj di incoraggiamento

route /ruːt/ n itinerario m; (Aeron, Naut) rotta f; (of bus) percorso m

routine /ruːˈtiːn/ adj di routine ● n routine f inv; (Theat) numero m

row[1] /rəʊ/ n (line) fila f; **three years in a** ~ tre anni di fila

row[2] /rəʊ/ vi (in boat) remare

row[3] /raʊ/ n 🄴 (quarrel) litigata f; (noise) baccano m ● vi 🄴 litigare

rowdy /ˈraʊdɪ/ adj (-ier, -iest) chiassoso

rowing boat /ˈrəʊɪŋ-/ n barca f a remi

royal /ˈrɔɪəl/ adj reale

royal|**ty** /ˈrɔɪəltɪ/ n appartenenza f

r

alla famiglia reale; (persons) i membri mpl della famiglia reale. ~ies npl (payments) diritti mpl d'autore

rub /rʌb/ n give sth a ~ dare una sfregata a qcsa ●vt (pt/pp rubbed) sfregare. □~ **in** vt don't ~ it **in** non rigirare il coltello nella piaga. □~ **off** vt mandar via sfregando (stain); (from blackboard) cancellare ●vi andar via; ~ **off on** essere trasmesso a. □~ **out** vt cancellare

rubber /'rʌbə(r)/ n gomma f; (eraser) gomma f [da cancellare]. ~**band** n elastico m. ~**y** adj gommoso

rubbish /'rʌbɪʃ/ n immondizie fpl; (🔲: nonsense) idiozie fpl; (🔲: junk) robaccia f ●vt 🔲 fare a pezzi. ~**bin** n pattumiera f. ~**dump** n discarica f; (official) discarica f comunale

rubble /'rʌbl/ n macerie fpl

ruby /'ru:bɪ/ n rubino m ●attrib di rubini; (lips) scarlatta

rucksack /'rʌksæk/ n zaino m

rudder /'rʌdə(r)/ n timone m

rude /ru:d/ adj scortese; (improper) spinto. ~**ly** adv scortesemente. ~**ness** n scortesia f

ruffian /'rʌfɪən/ n farabutto m

ruffle /'rʌfl/ n gala f ●vt scompigliare (hair)

rug /rʌɡ/ n tappeto m; (blanket) coperta f

rugby /'rʌɡbɪ/ n ~ [football] rugby m

rugged /'rʌɡɪd/ adj (coastline) roccioso

ruin /'ru:ɪn/ n rovina f; **in** ~s in rovina ●vt rovinare. ~**ous** adj estremamente costoso

rule /ru:l/ n regola f; (control) ordinamento m; (for measuring) metro m; ~s regolamento m; **as a** ~ generalmente ●vt governare; dominare (colony, behaviour); ~ **that** stabilire che ●vi governare. □~ **out** vt escludere

ruler /'ru:lə(r)/ n capo m di Stato;

(sovereign) sovrano, -a mf; (measure) righello m, regolo m

ruling /'ru:lɪŋ/ adj (class) dirigente; (party) di governo ●n decisione f

rum /rʌm/ n rum m inv

rumble /'rʌmbl/ n rombo m; (of stomach) brontolio m ●vi rombare; (stomach) brontolare

rummage /'rʌmɪdʒ/ vi rovistare (in/through in)

rumour /'ru:mə(r)/ n diceria f ●vt it **is** ~ed that si dice che

run /rʌn/ n (on foot) corsa f; (distance to be covered) tragitto m; (outing) giro m; (Theat) rappresentazioni fpl; (in skiing) pista f; (Am: ladder) smagliatura f (in calze); at a ~ di corsa; ~ **of bad luck** periodo m sfortunato; **on the** ~ in fuga; **have the** ~ **of** avere a disposizione; **in the long** ~ a lungo termine ●v (pt ran, pp run, pres p running) ●vi correre; (river:) scorrere; (nose, make-up:) colare; (bus:) fare servizio; (play:) essere in cartellone; (colours:) sbiadire; (in election) presentarsi [come candidato] ●vt (manage) dirigere; tenere (house); (drive) dare un passaggio a; correre (risk); (Comput) lanciare; (Journ) pubblicare (article); (pass) far scorrere (eyes, hand); ~ **a bath** far scorrere l'acqua per il bagno. □~ **across** vi (meet, find) imbattersi in. □~ **away** vi scappare [via]. □~ **down** vi scaricarsi; (clock:) scaricarsi (stocks:) esaurirsi ●vt (Auto) investire; (reduce) esaurire; (🔲: criticize) denigrare. □~ **in** vi entrare di corsa. □~ **into** vi (meet) imbattersi in; (knock against) urtare. □~ **off** vi andare via di corsa ●vt stampare (copies). □~ **out** vi uscire di corsa; (supplies, money:) esaurirsi; ~ **out of** rimanere senza. □~ **over** vi correre; (overflow) traboccare ●vt (Auto) investire. □~ **through** vi scorrere. □~ **up** vi salire di corsa; (towards) arrivare di corsa ●vt accumulare (debts, bill);

(*sew*) cucire

'runaway n fuggitivo, -a mf

run-'down adj (area) in abbandono; (person) esaurito ●n analisi f

rung[1] /rʌŋ/ n (of ladder) piolo m

rung[2] ▷RING[2]

runner /'rʌnə(r)/ n podista mf; (in race) corridore, -trice mf; (on sledge) pattino m. ~ **bean** n fagiolino m. ~**-up** n secondo, -a mf classificato, -a

running /'rʌnɪŋ/ adj in corsa; (water) corrente; **four times ~** quattro volte di seguito ●n corsa f; (management) direzione f; **be in the ~** essere in lizza. ~ **'commentary** n cronaca f

runny /'rʌnɪ/ adj semiliquido; ~ **nose** naso che cola

runway n pista f

rupture /'rʌptʃə(r)/ n rottura f; (Med) ernia f ●vt rompere; ~ **one-self** farsi venire l'ernia ●vi rompersi

rural /'rʊərəl/ adj rurale

ruse /ruːz/ n astuzia f

rush[1] /rʌʃ/ n (Bot) giunco m

rush[2] n fretta f; **in a ~** di fretta ●vi precipitarsi ●vt far premura a; ~ **sb to hospital** trasportare qcno in corsa all'ospedale. ~**-hour** n ora f di punta

Russia /'rʌʃə/ n Russia f. ~**n** adj & n russo, -a mf; (language) russo m

rust /rʌst/ n ruggine f ●vi arrugginirsi

rustle /'rʌsl/ vi frusciare ●vt far frusciare; Am rubare (cattle). □ ~ **up** vt 🇬🇧 rimediare

'rustproof adj a prova di ruggine

rusty /'rʌstɪ/ adj (-ier, -iest) arrugginito

rut /rʌt/ n solco m; **in a ~** 🇬🇧 nella routine

ruthless /'ruːθlɪs/ adj spietato. ~**ness** n spietatezza f

rye /raɪ/ n segale f

Ss

sabot|age /'sæbətɑːʒ/ n sabotaggio m ●vt sabotare. ~**eur** n sabotatore, -trice mf

saccharin /'sækərɪn/ n saccarina f

sachet /'sæʃeɪ/ n bustina f; (scented) sacchetto m profumato

sack[1] /sæk/ vt (plunder) saccheggiare

sack[2] n sacco m; **get the ~** 🇬🇧 essere licenziato ●vt 🇬🇧 licenziare. ~**ing** n tela f per sacchi; (🇬🇧: dismissal) licenziamento m

sacrament /'sækrəmənt/ n sacramento m

sacred /'seɪkrɪd/ adj sacro

sacrifice /'sækrɪfaɪs/ n sacrificio m ●vt sacrificare

sacrilege /'sækrɪlɪdʒ/ n sacrilegio m

sad /sæd/ adj (sadder, saddest) triste. ~**den** vt rattristare

saddle /'sædl/ n sella f ●vt sellare; **I've been ~d with...** fig mi hanno affibbiato...

sad|ly /'sædlɪ/ adv tristemente; (unfortunately) sfortunatamente. ~**ness** n tristezza f

safe /seɪf/ adj sicuro; (out of danger) salvo; (object) al sicuro; ~ **and sound** sano e salvo ●n cassaforte f. ~**guard** n protezione f ●vt proteggere. ~**ly** adv in modo sicuro; (arrive) senza incidenti; (assume) con certezza

safety /'seɪftɪ/ n sicurezza f. ~**-belt** n cintura f di sicurezza. ~**-deposit box** n cassetta f di sicurezza. ~**-pin** n spilla f di sicurezza o da balia. ~**-valve** n valvola f di sicurezza

sag /sæg/ vi (pt/pp **sagged**) abbassarsi

saga /'sɑːgə/ n saga f

sage /seɪdʒ/ n (herb) salvia f

Sagittarius /sædʒɪ'teərɪəs/ n Sagittario m

said /sed/ ▷ SAY

sail /seɪl/ n vela f; (trip) giro m in barca a vela ● vi navigare; (Sport) praticare la vela; (leave) salpare ● vt pilotare

sailing /'seɪlɪŋ/ n vela f. **~-boat** n barca f a vela. **~-ship** n veliero m

sailor /'seɪlə(r)/ n marinaio m

saint /seɪnt/ n santo, -a mf. **~ly** adj da santo

sake /seɪk/ n for the ~ of (person) per il bene di; (peace) per amor di; for the ~ of it per il gusto di farlo

salad /'sæləd/ n insalata f. ~ **bowl** n insalatiera f. ~ **cream** n salsa f per condire l'insalata; **~-dressing** n condimento m per insalata

salary /'sælərɪ/ n stipendio m

sale /seɪl/ n vendita f (at reduced prices) svendita f; **for/on** ~ in vendita

sales|man /'seɪlzmən/ n venditore m; (traveller) rappresentante m. **~woman** n venditrice f

saliva /sə'laɪvə/ n saliva f

salmon /'sæmən/ n salmone m

saloon /sə'luːn/ n (Auto) berlina f; (Am: bar) bar m

salt /sɔːlt/ n sale m ● adj salato; (fish, meat) sotto sale ● vt salare; (cure) mettere sotto sale. **~-cellar** n saliera f. ~ '**water** n acqua f di mare. **~y** adj salato

salute /sə'luːt/ n (Mil) saluto m ● vt salutare ● vi fare il saluto

salvage /'sælvɪdʒ/ n (Naut) recupero m ● vt recuperare

salvation /sæl'veɪʃn/ n salvezza f. **S~ 'Army** n Esercito m della Salvezza

same /seɪm/ adj stesso (as di) ● pron the ~ lo stesso; **be all the** ~ essere tutti uguali ● adv the ~ nello stesso

modo; **all the** ~ (however) lo stesso; **the** ~ **to you** altrettanto

sample /'sɑːmpl/ n campione m ● vt testare

sanction /'sæŋkʃn/ n (approval) autorizzazione f; (penalty) sanzione f ● vt autorizzare

sanctuary /'sæŋktjʊərɪ/ n (Relig) santuario m; (refuge) asilo m; (for wildlife) riserva f

sand /sænd/ n sabbia f ● vt ~ [**down**] carteggiare

sandal /'sændl/ n sandalo m

sandpaper /'sænpeɪpə(r)/ n carta f vetrata ● vt cartavetrare

sandwich /'sænwɪdʒ/ n tramezzino m ● vt **~ed between** schiacciato tra

sandy /'sændɪ/ adj (**-ier, -iest**) (beach, soil) sabbioso; (hair) biondiccio

sane /seɪn/ adj (not mad) sano di mente; (sensible) sensato

sang /sæŋ/ ▷ SING

sanitary /'sænɪtərɪ/ adj igienico; (system) sanitario. ~ **napkin** n Am, ~ **towel** n assorbente m igienico

sanitation /sænɪ'teɪʃn/ n impianti mpl igienici

sanity /'sænɪtɪ/ n sanità f inv di mente; (common sense) buon senso m

sank /sæŋk/ ▷ SINK

sapphire /'sæfaɪə(r)/ n zaffiro m ● adj blu zaffiro

sarcasm /'sɑːkæzm/ n sarcasmo m. **~tic** adj sarcastico

sardine /sɑː'diːn/ n sardina f

sash /sæʃ/ n fascia f; (for dress) fusciacca f

sat /sæt/ ▷ SIT

satchel /'sætʃl/ n cartella f

satellite /'sætəlaɪt/ n satellite m. ~ **dish** n antenna f parabolica. ~ **television** n televisione f via satellite

satin /'sætɪn/ n raso m ● attrib di raso

satire /'sætaɪə(r)/ n satira f

satirical /sə'tɪrɪkl/ adj satirico

satisfaction /sætɪsˈfækʃn/ n soddisfazione f; **be to sb's ~** soddisfare qcno

satisfactor|y /sætɪsˈfæktərɪ/ adj soddisfacente. **~ily** adv in modo soddisfacente

satisf|y /ˈsætɪsfaɪ/ vt (pp/pp -fied) soddisfare; (convince) convincere; **be ~ied** essere soddisfatto. **~ying** adj soddisfacente

satphone /ˈsætfəʊn/ n telefono m satellitare

saturat|e /ˈsætʃəreɪt/ vt inzuppare (with di); (Chem), fig saturare (with di). **~ed** adj saturo

Saturday /ˈsætədeɪ/ n sabato m

sauce /sɔːs/ n salsa f; (cheek) impertinenza f. **~pan** n pentola f

saucer /ˈsɔːsə(r)/ n piattino m

saucy /ˈsɔːsɪ/ adj (-ier, -iest) impertinente

Saudi Arabia /saʊdɪəˈreɪbɪə/ n Arabia f Saudita

sauna /ˈsɔːnə/ n sauna f

saunter /ˈsɔːntə(r)/ vi andare a spasso

sausage /ˈsɒsɪdʒ/ n salsiccia f; (dried) salame m

savage /ˈsævɪdʒ/ adj feroce; (tribe, custom) selvaggio ● n selvaggio, -a mf ● vt fare a pezzi. **~ry** n ferocia f

save /seɪv/ n (Sport) parata f ● vt salvare (from da); (keep, collect) tenere; risparmiare (time, money); (avoid) evitare; (Sport) parare (goal); (Comput) salvare, memorizzare ● vi ~ [up] risparmiare ● prep salvo

saver /ˈseɪvə(r)/ n risparmiatore, -trice mf

savings /ˈseɪvɪŋz/ npl (money) risparmi mpl. **~ account** n libretto m di risparmio. **~ bank** n cassa f di risparmio

saviour /ˈseɪvjə(r)/ n salvatore m

savour /ˈseɪvə(r)/ n sapore m ● vt assaporare. **~y** adj salato; fig rispettabile

saw[1] /sɔː/ see **see**1

saw[2] n sega f ● vt/i (pt sawed, pp sawn or sawed) segare. **~dust** n segatura f

saxophone /ˈsæksəfəʊn/ n sassofono m

say /seɪ/ n **have one's ~** dire la propria; **have a ~** avere voce in capitolo ● vt/i (pt/pp said) dire; **that is to ~** cioè; **that goes without ~ing** questo è ovvio; **when all is said and done** alla fine dei conti. **~ing** n proverbio m

scab /skæb/ n crosta f; pej crumiro m

scald /skɔːld/ vt scottare; (milk) scaldare ● n scottatura f

scale[1] /skeɪl/ n (of fish) scaglia f

scale[2] n scala f; **on a grand ~** su vasta scala ● vt (climb) scalare. □ **~ down** vt diminuire

scales /skeɪlz/ npl (for weighing) bilancia fsg

scalp /skælp/ n cuoio m capelluto

scamper /ˈskæmpə(r)/ vi **~ away** sgattaiolare via

scan /skæn/ n (Med) scanning m inv, scansioscintigrafia f ● vt (pt/pp scanned) scrutare; (quickly) dare una scorsa a; (Med) fare uno scanning di

scandal /ˈskændl/ n scandalo m; (gossip) pettegolezzi mpl. **~ize** vt scandalizzare. **~ous** adj scandaloso

Scandinavia /skændɪˈneɪvɪə/ n Scandinavia f. **~n** adj e n scandinavo, -a mf

scanner /ˈskænə(r)/ n (Comput) scanner m inv

scant /skænt/ adj scarso

scant|y /ˈskæntɪ/ adj (-ier, -iest) scarso; (clothing) succinto. **~ily** adv scarsamente; (clothed) succintamente

scapegoat /ˈskeɪp-/ n capro m

s

espiatorio

scar /skɑː(r)/ n cicatrice f • vt (pt/pp **scarred**) lasciare una cicatrice a

scarc|e /skeəs/ adj scarso; fig raro; **make oneself ~e** 🗓 svignarsela; **~ely** adv appena; **~ely anything** quasi niente. **~ity** n scarsezza f

scare /skeə(r)/ n spavento m; (panic) panico m • vt spaventare; **be ~d** aver paura (of di)

'scarecrow n spaventapasseri m inv

scarf /skɑːf/ n (pl **scarves**) sciarpa f; (square) foulard m inv

scarlet /ˈskɑːlət/ adj scarlatto. **~ 'fever** n scarlattina f

scary /ˈskeərɪ/ adj **be ~** far paura

scathing /ˈskeɪðɪŋ/ adj mordace

scatter /ˈskætə(r)/ vt spargere; (disperse) disperdere • vi disperdersi. **~-brained** adj 🗓 scervellato. **~ed** adj sparso

scavenge /ˈskævɪndʒ/ vi frugare nella spazzatura. **~r** n persona f che fruga nella spazzatura

scenario /sɪˈnɑːrɪəʊ/ n scenario m

scene /siːn/ n scena f; (quarrel) scenata f; **behind the ~s** dietro le quinte

scenery /ˈsiːnərɪ/ n scenario m

scenic /ˈsiːnɪk/ adj panoramico

scent /sent/ n odore m; (trail) scia f; (perfume) profumo m. **~ed** adj profumato (with di)

sceptic|al /ˈskeptɪkl/ adj scettico. **~ism** n scetticismo m

schedule /ˈʃedjuːl/ n piano m, programma m; (of work) programma m; (timetable) orario m; **behind ~** in ritardo; **on ~** nei tempi previsti; **according to ~** secondo i tempi previsti • vt prevedere. **~d flight** n volo m di linea

scheme /skiːm/ n (plan) piano m, (plot) macchinazione f • vi pej macchinare

scholar /ˈskɒlə(r)/ n studioso, -a mf. **~ly** adj erudito. **~ship** n erudizione f; (grant) borsa f di studio

school /skuːl/ n scuola f; (in university) facoltà f; (of fish) branco m

school: **~boy** n scolaro m. **~girl** n scolara f. **~ing** n istruzione f. **~-teacher** n insegnante mf

sciatica /saɪˈætɪkə/ n sciatica f

scien|ce /ˈsaɪəns/ n scienza f; **~ce fiction** fantascienza f. **~tific** adj scientifico. **~tist** n scienziato, -a mf

scissors /ˈsɪzəz/ npl forbici fpl

scoff[1] /skɒf/ vi **~ at** schernire

scoff[2] vt 🗓 divorare

scold /skəʊld/ vt sgridare. **~ing** n sgridata f

scoop /skuːp/ n paletta f; (Journ) scoop m inv • **scoop out** vt svuotare. **□ ~ up** vt tirar su

scope /skəʊp/ n portata f; (opportunity) opportunità f inv

scorch /skɔːtʃ/ vt bruciare. **~er** n 🗓 giornata f torrida. **~ing** adj caldissimo

score /skɔː(r)/ n punteggio m; (individual) punteggio m; (Mus) partitura f; (for film, play) musica f; **a ~** [of] (twenty) una ventina [di]; **keep [the] ~** tenere il punteggio; **on that ~** a questo proposito • vt segnare (goal); (cut) incidere • vi far punti; (in football etc) segnare; (keep score) tenere il punteggio. **~r** n segnapunti m inv; (of goals) giocatore, -trice mf che segna

scorn /skɔːn/ n disprezzo m • vt disprezzare. **~ful** adj sprezzante

Scorpio /ˈskɔːpɪəʊ/ n Scorpione m

scorpion /ˈskɔːpɪən/ n scorpione m

Scot /skɒt/ n scozzese mf

scotch vt far cessare

Scotch /skɒtʃ/ adj scozzese • n (whisky) whisky m [scozzese]

Scot|land /ˈskɒtlənd/ n Scozia f. **~s**, **~tish** adj scozzese

Scottish Parliament Istituto nel 1999 con sede a Edimburgo, il Parlamento scozzese ha funzione legislativa e esecutiva riguardo agli affari interni della Scozia. Dei 129 parlamentari o *MSPs* (*Members of the Scottish Parliament*), 73 sono eletti direttamente dai cittadini scozzesi secondo un sistema di maggioranza relativa; i restanti 56 (*Additional Members*) vengono eletti col sistema proporzionale.

scoundrel /ˈskaʊndrəl/ *n* mascalzone *m*

scour[1] /ˈskaʊə(r)/ *vt* (*search*) perlustrare

scour[2] *vt* (*clean*) strofinare

scourge /skɜːdʒ/ *n* flagello *m*

scout /skaʊt/ *n* (*Mil*) esploratore *m* ● *vi* ~ **for** andare in cerca di

Scout *n* [Boy] ~ [boy]scout *m inv*

scowl /skaʊl/ *n* sguardo *m* torvo ● *vi* guardare [di] storto

scram /skræm/ *vi* ⚅ levarsi dai piedi

scramble /ˈskræmbl/ *n* (*climb*) arrampicata *f* ● *vi* (*clamber*) arrampicarsi; ~ **for** azzuffarsi per ● *vt* (*Teleph*) creare delle interferenze in; (*eggs*) strapazzare

scrap[1] /skræp/ *n* (⚅: *fight*) litigio *m*

scrap[2] *n* pezzetto *m*; (*metal*) ferraglia *f*; ~**s** *pl* (*of food*) avanzi *mpl* ● *vt* (*pt/pp* **scrapped**) buttare via

'scrap-book *n* album *m inv*

scrape /skreɪp/ *vt* raschiare; (*damage*) graffiare. □ ~ **through** *vi* passare per un pelo. □ ~ **together** *vt* racimolare

scraper /ˈskreɪpə(r)/ *n* raschietto *m*

'scrap-yard *n* deposito *m* di ferraglia; (*for cars*) cimitero *m* delle macchine

scratch /skrætʃ/ *n* graffio *m*; (*to relieve itch*) grattata *f*; **start from** ~

partire da zero; **up to** ~ (*work*) all'altezza ● *vt* graffiare; (*to relieve itch*) grattare ● *vi* grattarsi. □ ~ **card** *n* gratta e vinci *m inv*

scrawl /skrɔːl/ *n* scarabocchio *m* ● *vt/i* scarabocchiare

scream /skriːm/ *n* strillo *m* ● *vt/i* strillare

screech /skriːtʃ/ *n* stridore *m* ● *vi* stridere ● *vt* strillare

screen /skriːn/ *n* paravento *m*; (*Cinema, TV*) schermo *m* ● *vt* proteggere; (*conceal*) riparare; proiettare (*film*); (*candidates*) passare al setaccio; (*Med*) sottoporre a visita medica. ~**ing** *n* (*Med*) visita *f* medica; (*of film*) proiezione *f*. ~**play** *n* sceneggiatura *f*

screw /skruː/ *n* vite *f* ● *vt* avvitare. □ ~ **up** *vt* (*crumple*) accartocciare; strizzare (*eyes*); storcere (*face*); (⚅: *bungle*) mandare all'aria. ~**driver** *n* cacciavite *m*

scribble /ˈskrɪbl/ *n* scarabocchio *m* ● *vt/i* scarabocchiare

script /skrɪpt/ *n* scrittura *f* (*a mano*); (*of film*) sceneggiatura *f*

scroll /skrəʊl/ *n* rotulo *m* (*di pergamena*); (*decoration*) voluta *f*. □ ~ **down** *vi* scorrere in giù

scrounge /skraʊndʒ/ *vt/i* scroccare. ~**r** *n* scroccone, -a *mf*

scrub[1] /skrʌb/ *n* (*land*) boscaglia *f*

scrub[2] *vt/i* (*pt/pp* **scrubbed**) strofinare; (⚅: *cancel*) cancellare (*plan*)

scruff /skrʌf/ *n* **by the** ~ **of the neck** per la collottola

scruffy /ˈskrʌfɪ/ *adj* (-**ier**, -**iest**) trasandato

scruple /ˈskruːpl/ *n* scrupolo *m*

scrupulous /ˈskruːpjʊləs/ *adj* scrupoloso

scrutin|ize /ˈskruːtɪnaɪz/ *vt* scrutinare. ~**y** *n* (*look*) esame *m* minuzioso

scuffle /ˈskʌfl/ *n* tafferuglio *m*

sculpt /skʌlpt/ *vt/i* scolpire. ~**or** *n* scultore *m*. ~**ure** *n* scultura *f*

s

scum /skʌm/ n schiuma f; (people) feccia f

scurry /'skʌrɪ/ vi (pt/pp -ied) affrettare il passo

scuttle /'skʌtl/ vi (hurry) ~ away correre via

sea /si:/ n mare m; at ~ in mare; fig confuso; by ~ via mare. ~board n costiera f. ~food n frutti mpl di mare. ~gull n gabbiano m

seal¹ /si:l/ n (Zool) foca f

seal² n sigillo m; (Techn) chiusura f ermetica ● vt sigillare; (Techn) chiudere ermeticamente. □ ~ off vt bloccare (area)

'sea-level n livello m del mare

seam /si:m/ n cucitura f; (of coal) strato m

'seaman n marinaio m

seamy /'si:mɪ/ adj sordido; (area) malfamato

seance /'seɪɑ:ns/ n seduta f spiritica

search /sɜ:tʃ/ n ricerca f; (official) perquisizione f; in ~ of alla ricerca di ● vt frugare (for alla ricerca di); perlustrare (area); (officially) perquisire ● vi ~ for cercare. ~ing adj penetrante

search: ~light n riflettore m. ~-party n squadra f di ricerca

sea: ~sick adj be/get ~ avere il mal di mare. ~side n at/to the ~side al mare

season /'si:zn/ n stagione f ● vt (flavour) condire. ~able adj, ~al adj stagionale. ~ing n condimento m

'season ticket n abbonamento m

seat /si:t/ n (chair) sedia f; (in car) sedile m; (place to sit) posto m [a sedere]; (bottom) didietro m; (of government) sede f; take a ~ sedersi ● vt mettere a sedere; (have seats for) aver posti [a sedere] per. ~belt n cintura f di sicurezza

sea: ~weed n alga f marina. ~worthy adj in stato di navigare

seclu|ded /sɪ'klu:dɪd/ adj appartato. ~sion n isolamento m

second¹ /sɪ'kɒnd/ vt (transfer) distaccare

second² /'sekənd/ adj secondo; on ~ thoughts ripensandoci meglio ● n secondo m; ~s pl (goods) merce fsg di seconda scelta; have ~s (at meal) fare il bis; John the S~ Giovanni Secondo ● adv (in race) al secondo posto ● vt assistere; appoggiare (proposal)

secondary /'sekəndrɪ/ adj secondario. ~ school n ≈ scuola f media (inferiore e superiore)

second: ~ 'class adv (travel, send) in seconda classe. ~-class adj di seconda classe

'second hand n (on clock) lancetta f dei secondi

second-'hand adj & adv di seconda mano

secondly /'sekəndlɪ/ adv in secondo luogo

second-'rate adj di second'ordine

secrecy /'si:krəsɪ/ n segretezza f; in ~ in segreto

secret /'si:krɪt/ adj segreto ● n segreto m

secretarial /sekrə'teərɪəl/ adj (work, staff) di segreteria

secretary /'sekrətərɪ/ n segretario, -a mf

secretive /'si:krətɪv/ adj riservato. ~ness n riserbo m

sect /sekt/ n setta f. ~arian adj settario

section /'sekʃn/ n sezione f

sector /'sektə(r)/ n settore m

secular /'sekjʊlə(r)/ adj secolare; (education) laico

secure /sɪ'kjʊə(r)/ adj sicuro ● vt proteggere; chiudere bene (door); rendere stabile (ladder); (obtain) assicurarsi. ~ly adv saldamente

securit|y /sɪ'kjʊərətɪ/ n sicurezza f;

(for loan) garanzia f. ~ies npl titoli mpl

sedate¹ /sɪˈdeɪt/ adj posato

sedate² vt somministrare sedativi a

sedation /sɪˈdeɪʃn/ n somministrazione f di sedativi; be under ~ essere sotto l'effetto di sedativi

sedative /ˈsedətɪv/ adj sedativo • n sedativo m

sediment /ˈsedɪmənt/ n sedimento m

seduce /sɪˈdjuːs/ vt sedurre

seduct|ion /sɪˈdʌkʃn/ n seduzione f. ~ive adj seducente

see /siː/ v (pt saw, pp seen) • vt vedere; (understand) capire; (escort) accompagnare; go and ~ andare a vedere; (visit) andare a trovare; ~ you! ci vediamo!; ~ you later! a più tardi!; ~ing that visto che • vi vedere; (understand) capire; ~ that (make sure) assicurarsi che; ~ about occuparsi di. ~ off vt veder partire; (chase away) mandar via. □ ~ through vi vedere attraverso; fig non farsi ingannare da • vt portare a buon fine. □ ~ to vi occuparsi di

seed /siːd/ n seme m; (Tennis) testa f di serie; go to ~ fare seme; fig lasciarsi andare. ~ed player n (Tennis) testa f di serie. ~ling n pianticella f

seedy /ˈsiːdɪ/ adj (-ier, -iest) squallido

seek /siːk/ vt (pt/pp sought) cercare

seem /siːm/ vi sembrare. ~ingly adv apparentemente

seen /siːn/ ▷ SEE¹

seep /siːp/ vi filtrare

see-saw /ˈsiːsɔː/ n altalena f

seethe /siːð/ vi ~ with anger ribollire di rabbia

'see-through adj trasparente

segment /ˈsegmənt/ n segmento m; (of orange) spicchio m

segregat|e /ˈsegrɪgeɪt/ vt segregare. ~ion n segregazione f

seize /siːz/ vt afferrare; (Jur) confi-

scare. □ ~ up vi (Techn) bloccarsi

seizure /ˈsiːʒə(r)/ n (Jur) confisca f; (Med) colpo m [apoplettico]

seldom /ˈseldəm/ adv raramente

select /sɪˈlekt/ adj scelto; (exclusive) esclusivo • vt scegliere; selezionare (team). ~ion n selezione f. ~ive adj selettivo. ~or n (Sport) selezionatore, -trice mf

self /self/ n io m

self: ~-ad'dressed adj con il proprio indirizzo. ~-'catering adj in appartamento attrezzato di cucina. ~-'centred adj egocentrico. ~-'confidence n fiducia f in se stesso. ~-'confident adj sicuro di sé. ~-'conscious adj impacciato. ~-con'tained adj (flat) con ingresso indipendente. ~-con'trol n autocontrollo m. ~-de'fence n autodifesa f; (Jur) legittima difesa f. ~-em'ployed adj che lavora in proprio. ~-'evident adj ovvio. ~-in'dulgent adj indulgente con se stesso. ~-'interest n interesse m personale

self|ish /ˈselfɪʃ/ adj egoista. ~ishness n egoismo m. ~less adj disinteressato

self: ~-pity n autocommiserazione f. ~-'portrait n autoritratto m. ~-re'spect n amor m proprio. ~-'righteous adj presuntuoso. ~-'sacrifice n abnegazione f. ~-'satisfied adj compiaciuto di sé. ~-'service n self-service m inv • attrib self-service. ~-suf'ficient adj autosufficiente

sell /sel/ v (pt/pp sold) • vt vendere; be sold out essere esaurito • vi vendersi. □ ~ off vt liquidare

seller /ˈselə(r)/ n venditore, -trice mf

Sellotape® /ˈseləʊ-/ n nastro m adesivo, scotch® m

'sell-out n (囗: betrayal) tradimento m; be a ~ (concert:) fare il tutto esaurito

semblance /'sembləns/ n parvenza f

semester /sɪ'mestə(r)/ n Am semestre m

semi /'semɪ/: ~**breve** /'semɪbriːv/ n semibreve f. ~**circle** n semicerchio m. ~**circular** adj semicircolare. ~**colon** n punto e virgola m. ~**detached** adj gemella ● n casa f gemella. ~**final** n semifinale f

seminar /'semɪnɑː(r)/ n seminario m. ~**y** n seminario m

senate /'senət/ n senato m. ~**or** n senatore m

send /send/ vt/i (pt/pp sent) mandare; ~ **for** mandare a chiamare (person); far venire (thing). ~**er** n mittente mf. ~**off** n commiato m

senile /'siːnaɪl/ adj arteriosclerotico; (Med) senile. ~**ity** n senilismo m

senior /'siːnɪə(r)/ adj più vecchio; (in rank) superiore ● n (in rank) superiore mf; (in sport) senior mf; **she's two years my** ~ è più vecchia di me di due anni. ~**citizen** n anziano, -a mf

seniority /siːnɪ'ɒrətɪ/ n anzianità f inv di servizio

sensation /sen'seɪʃn/ n sensazione f. ~**al** adj sensazionale. ~**ally** adv in modo sensazionale

sense /sens/ n senso m; (common ~) buon senso m; **in a** ~ in un certo senso; **make** ~ aver senso ● vt sentire. ~**less** adj insensato; (unconscious) privo di sensi

sensibl|e /'sensəbl/ adj sensato; (suitable) appropriato. ~**y** adv in modo appropriato

sensitiv|e /'sensətɪv/ adj sensibile; (touchy) suscettibile. ~**ely** adv con sensibilità. ~**ity** n sensibilità f

sensual /'sensjʊəl/ adj sensuale. ~**ity** n sensualità f inv

sensuous /'sensjʊəs/ adj voluttuoso

sent /sent/ ▷**SEND**

sentence /'sentəns/ n frase f; (Jur) sentenza f; (punishment) condanna f

● vt ~ **to** condannare a

sentiment /'sentɪmənt/ n sentimento m; (opinion) opinione f; (sentimentality) sentimentalismo m. ~**al** adj sentimentale; pej sentimentalista. ~**ality** n sentimentalità f inv

sentry /'sentrɪ/ n sentinella f

separable /'sepərəbl/ adj separabile

separate[1] /'sepərət/ adj separato. ~**ly** adv separatamente

separate[2] /'sepəreɪt/ vt separare ● vi separarsi. ~**ion** n separazione f

September /sep'tembə(r)/ n settembre m

septic /'septɪk/ adj settico; **go** ~ infettarsi. ~ **tank** n fossa f biologica

sequel /'siːkwəl/ n seguito m

sequence /'siːkwəns/ n sequenza f

Serbia /'sɜːbɪə/ n Serbia f

serenade /serə'neɪd/ n serenata f ● vt fare una serenata a

seren|e /sɪ'riːn/ adj sereno. ~**ity** n serenità f inv

sergeant /'sɑːdʒənt/ n sergente m

serial /'sɪərɪəl/ n racconto m a puntate; (TV) sceneggiato m a puntate; (Radio) commedia f radiofonica. ~**ize** vt pubblicare a puntate; (Radio, TV) trasmettere a puntate. ~ **killer** n serial killer mf inv. ~ **number** n numero m di serie. ~ **port** n (Comput) porta f seriale

series /'sɪəriːz/ n serie f inv

serious /'sɪərɪəs/ adj serio; (illness, error) grave. ~**ly** adv seriamente; (ill) gravemente; **take** ~**ly** prendere sul serio. ~**ness** n serietà f inv; (of situation) gravità f inv

sermon /'sɜːmən/ n predica f

serum /'sɪərəm/ n siero m

servant /'sɜːvənt/ n domestico, -a mf

serve /sɜːv/ n (Tennis) servizio m ● vt servire; scontare (sentence); ~ **its purpose** servire al proprio scopo; **it** ~**s you right!** ben ti sta!; ~**s two**

per due persone ● *vi* prestare servizio; (*Tennis*) servire; **~ as** servire da. **~r** n (*Comput*) server *m inv*

service /'sɜːvɪs/ n servizio *m*; (*Relig*) funzione *f*; (*maintenance*) revisione *f*; **~s** *pl* forze *fpl* armate; (*on motorway*) area *f* di servizio; in the **~s** sotto le armi; **of ~ to** utile a; **out of ~** (*machine*) guasto ● *vt* (*Techn*) revisionare. **~able** *adj* utilizzabile; (*hard-wearing*) resistente; (*practical*) pratico

service: ~ charge n servizio *m*. **~ station** n stazione *f* di servizio

serviette /sɜːvɪ'et/ n tovagliolo *m*

servile /'sɜːvaɪl/ adj servile

session /'seʃn/ n seduta *f*; (*Jur*) sessione *f*; (*Univ*) anno *m* accademico

set /set/ n serie *f*, set *m inv*; (*of crockery, cutlery*) servizio *m*; (*Radio, TV*) apparecchio *m*; (*Math*) insieme *m*; (*Theat*) scenario *m*; (*Cinema, Tennis*) set *m inv*; (*of people*) circolo *m*; (*of hair*) messa *f* in piega ● *adj* (*ready*) pronto; (*rigid*) fisso; (*book*) in programma; **be ~ on doing sth** essere risoluto a fare qcsa; **be ~ in one's ways** essere abitudinario ● *v* (*pt/pp* **set**, *pres p* **setting**) ● *vt* mettere, porre, mettere (*alarm clock*); assegnare (*task, homework*); fissare (*date, limit*); chiedere (*questions*); montare (*gem*); assestare (*bone*); apparecchiare (*table*); **~ fire to** dare fuoco a; **~ free** liberare ● *vi* (*sun:*) tramontare; (*jelly, concrete:*) solidificare; **~ about doing sth** mettersi a fare qcsa. **□ ~ back** *vt* mettere indietro; (*hold up*) ritardare; (ⅠⅠ: *cost*) costare a. **□ ~ off** *vi* partire ● *vt* avviare; mettere (*alarm*); fare esplodere (*bomb*). **□ ~ out** *vi* partire; **~ out to do sth** proporsi di fare qcsa ● *vt* disporre; (*state*) esporre. **□ ~ to** *vi* mettersi all'opera. **□ ~ up** *vt* fondare (*company*); istituire (*committee*)

'set-back n passo *m* indietro

settee /se'tiː/ n divano *m*

setting /'setɪŋ/ n scenario *m*; (*pos-*

ition) posizione *f*; (*of sun*) tramonto *m*; (*of jewel*) montatura *f*

settle /'setl/ *vt* (*decide*) definire; risolvere (*argument*); fissare (*date*); calmare (*nerves*); saldare (*bill*) ● *vi* (*to live*) stabilirsi; (*snow, dust, bird:*) posarsi; (*subside*) assestarsi; (*sediment:*) depositarsi. **□ ~ down** *vi* sistemarsi; (*stop making noise*) calmarsi. **□ ~ for** *vt* accontentarsi di. **□ ~ up** *vi* regolare i conti

settlement /'setlmənt/ n (*agreement*) accordo *m*; (*of bill*) saldo *m*; (*colony*) insediamento *m*

settler /'setlə(r)/ n colonizzatore, -trice *mf*

'set-to n ⅠⅠ zuffa *f*; (*verbal*) battibecco *m*

'set-up n situazione *f*

seven /'sevn/ adj sette. **~teen** adj diciassette. **~teenth** adj diciassettesimo

seventh /'sevnθ/ adj settimo

seventieth /'sevntɪɪθ/ adj settantesimo

seventy /'sevntɪ/ adj settanta

sever /'sevə(r)/ *vt* troncare (*relations*)

several /'sevrəl/ adj & pron parecchi

sever|e /sɪ'vɪə(r)/ adj severo; (*pain*) violento; (*illness*) grave; (*winter*) rigido. **~ely** adv severamente; (*ill*) gravemente. **~ity** n severità *f inv*; (*of pain*) violenza *f*; (*of illness*) gravità *f*; (*of winter*) rigore *m*

sew /səʊ/ *vt/i* (*pt* **sewed**, *pp* **sewn** or **sewed**) cucire. **□ ~ up** *vt* ricucire

sewage /'suːɪdʒ/ n acque *fpl* di scolo

sewer /'suːə(r)/ n fogna *f*

sewing /'səʊɪŋ/ n cucito *m*; (*work*) lavoro *m* di cucito. **~ machine** n macchina *f* da cucire

sewn /səʊn/ ▷ **SEW**

sex /seks/ n sesso *m*; **have ~** avere rapporti sessuali. **~ist** adj sessista. **~ offender** n colpevole *mf* di delitti a sfondo sessuale

sexual /ˈseksjʊəl/ adj sessuale. ~ 'intercourse n rapporti mpl sessuali. ~ity n sessualità f inv. ~ly adv sessualmente

sexy /ˈseksɪ/ adj (-ier, -iest) sexy

shabb|y /ˈʃæbɪ/ adj (-ier, -iest) scialbo; (treatment) meschino. ~iness n trasandatezza f; (of treatment) meschinità f inv

shack /ʃæk/ n catapecchia f ● **shack up with** vt 🔢 vivere con

shade /ʃeɪd/ n ombra f; (of colour) sfumatura f; (for lamp) paralume m; (Am: for window) tapparella f; a ~ better un tantino meglio ● vt riparare dalla luce; (draw lines on) ombreggiare. ~s npl 🔢 occhiali mpl da sole

shadow /ˈʃædəʊ/ n ombra f; S~ Cabinet governo m ombra ● vt (follow) pedinare. ~y adj ombroso

shady /ˈʃeɪdɪ/ adj (-ier, -iest) ombroso; (🔢: disreputable) losco

shaft /ʃɑːft/ n (Techn) albero m; (of light) raggio m; (of lift, mine) pozzo m; ~s pl (of cart) stanghe fpl

shaggy /ˈʃægɪ/ adj (-ier, -iest) irsuto; (animal) dal pelo arruffato

shake /ʃeɪk/ n scrollata f ● v (pt shook, pp shaken) ● vt scuotere; agitare (bottle); far tremare (building); ~ hands with stringere la mano a ● vi tremare. □ ~ **off** vt scrollarsi di dosso. ~-**up** n (Pol) rimpasto m; (Comm) ristrutturazione f

shaky /ˈʃeɪkɪ/ adj (-ier, -iest) tremante; (table etc) traballante; (unreliable) vacillante

shall /ʃæl/ v aux I ~ go andrò; we ~ see vedremo; what ~ I do? cosa faccio?; I'll come too, ~ I? vengo anch'io, no?; thou shalt not kill liter non uccidere

shallow /ˈʃæləʊ/ adj basso, poco profondo; (dish) poco profondo; fig superficiale

sham /ʃæm/ adj falso ● n finzione f;

(person) spaccone, -a mf ● vt (pt/pp shammed) simulare

shambles /ˈʃæmblz/ n baraonda fsg

shame /ʃeɪm/ n vergogna f; it's a ~ that è un peccato che; what a ~! che peccato! ~-faced adj vergognoso

shame|ful /ˈʃeɪmfl/ adj vergognoso. ~less adj spudorato

shampoo /ʃæmˈpuː/ n shampoo m inv ● vt fare uno shampoo a

shape /ʃeɪp/ n forma f; (figure) ombra f; take ~ prendere forma; get back in ~ ritornare in forma ● vt dare forma a (into di) ● vi ~ [up] mettere la testa a posto; ~ up nicely mettersi bene. ~less adj informe

share /ʃeə(r)/ n porzione f; (Comm) azione f ● vt dividere; condividere (views) ● vi dividere. ~holder n azionista mf

shark /ʃɑːk/ n squalo m, pescecane m; fig truffatore, -trice mf

sharp /ʃɑːp/ adj (knife etc) tagliente; (pencil) appuntito; (drop) a picco; (reprimand) severo; (outline) marcato; (alert) acuto; (unscrupulous) senza scrupoli ● **pain** fitta f ● adv in punto; (Mus) fuori tono; **look** ~! sbrigati! ● n (Mus) diesis m inv. ~en vt affilare (knife); appuntire (pencil)

shatter /ˈʃætə(r)/ vt frantumare; fig mandare in frantumi; ~ed (🔢: exhausted) a pezzi ● vi frantumarsi

shav|e /ʃeɪv/ n rasatura f; have a ~e farsi la barba ● vt radere ● vi radersi. ~er n rasoio m elettrico. ~ing-brush n pennello m da barba; ~ing foam n schiuma f da barba; ~ing soap n sapone m da barba

shawl /ʃɔːl/ n scialle m

she /ʃiː/ pron lei

sheaf /ʃiːf/ n (pl sheaves) fascio m

shear /ʃɪə(r)/ vt (pt sheared, pp shorn or sheared) tosare

shears /ʃɪəz/ npl (for hedge) cesoie fpl

shed¹ /ʃed/ n baracca f; (for cattle) stalla f

shed² vt (pt/pp shed, pres p shedding) perdere; versare (blood, tears); ~ light on far luce su

sheep /ʃiːp/ n inv pecora f. ~**-dog** n cane m da pastore

sheepish /ʃiːpɪʃ/ adj imbarazzato. ~**ly** adv con aria imbarazzata

sheer /ʃɪə(r)/ adj puro; (steep) a picco; (transparent) trasparente ● adv a picco

sheet /ʃiːt/ n lenzuolo m; (of paper) foglio m; (of glass, metal) lastra f

shelf /ʃelf/ n (pl shelves) rIplano m; (set of shelves) scaffale m

shell /ʃel/ n conchiglia f; (of egg, snail, tortoise) guscio m; (of crab) corazza f; (of unfinished building) ossatura f; (Mil) granata f ● vt sgusciare (peas); (Mil) bombardare. □ ~ **out** vi ⊞ sborsare

'**shellfish** n inv mollusco m; (Culin) frutti mpl di mare

shelter /ʃeltə(r)/ n rifugio m; (air raid ~) rifugio m antiaereo ● vt riparare (from da); fig mettere al riparo; (give lodging to) dare asilo a ● vi rifugiarsi. ~**ed** adj (spot) riparato; (life) ritirato

shelve /ʃelv/ vt accantonare (project)

shelving /ʃelvɪŋ/ n (shelves) ripiani mpl

shepherd /ʃepəd/ n pastore m ● vt guidare. ~'**s pie** n pasticcio m di carne tritata e patate

sherry /ʃerɪ/ n sherry m

shield /ʃiːld/ n scudo m; (for eyes) maschera f; (Techn) schermo m ● vt proteggere (from da)

shift /ʃɪft/ n cambiamento m; (in position) spostamento m; (at work) turno m ● vt spostare; (take away) togliere; riversare (blame) ● vi spostarsi; (wind) cambiare; (⊞: move quickly) darsi una mossa

shifty /ʃɪftɪ/ adj (-ier, -iest) pej losco; (eyes) sfuggente

shimmer /ʃɪmə(r)/ n luccichio m ● vi luccicare

shin /ʃɪn/ n stinco m

shine /ʃaɪn/ n lucentezza f; give sth a ~ dare una lucidata a qcsa ● v (pt/pp shone) ● vi splendere; (reflect light) brillare; (hair, shoes): essere lucido ● vt ~ a light on puntare una luce su

shingle /ʃɪŋɡl/ n (pebbles) ghiaia f

shiny /ʃaɪnɪ/ adj (-ier, -iest) lucido

ship /ʃɪp/ n nave f ● vt (pt/pp shipped) spedire; (by sea) spedire via mare

ship: ~**ment** n spedizione f; (consignment) carico m. ~**ping** n trasporto m; (traffic) imbarcazioni fpl. ~**shape** adj & adv in perfetto ordine. ~**wreck** n naufragio m. ~**wrecked** adj naufragato. ~**yard** n cantiere m navale

shirk /ʃɜːk/ vt scansare. ~**er** n scansafatiche mf inv

shirt /ʃɜːt/ n camicia f; in ~-**sleeves** in maniche di camicia

shit /ʃɪt/ ⊞ n & int merda f ● vi (pt/pp shit) cagare

shiver /ʃɪvə(r)/ n brivido m ● vi rabbrividire

shoal /ʃəʊl/ n (of fish) banco m

shock /ʃɒk/ n (impact) urto m; (Electr) scossa f [elettrica]; fig colpo m, shock m inv; (Med) shock m inv; get a ~ (Electr) prendere la scossa ● vt scioccare. ~**ing** adj scioccante; (⊞: weather, handwriting etc) tremendo

shod /ʃɒd/ ▷ **SHOE**

shoddy /ʃɒdɪ/ adj (-ier, -iest) scadente

shoe /ʃuː/ n scarpa f; (of horse) ferro m ● vt (pt/pp shod, pres p shoeing) ferrare (horse)

shoe: ~**horn** n calzante m. ~**lace** n laccio m da scarpa

shone /ʃɒn/ ▷ **SHINE**

shoo /ʃuː/ vt ~ away cacciar via ● int sciò

shook /ʃʊk/ ▷SHAKE

shoot /ʃuːt/ n (Bot) germoglio m; (hunt) battuta f di caccia ● v ~ (pt/pp shot) ● vt sparare; girare (film) ● vi (hunt) andare a caccia. □ ~ **down** vt abbattere. □ ~ **out** vi (rush) precipitarsi fuori. □ ~ **up** vi (grow) crescere in fretta; (prices:) salire di colpo

shop /ʃɒp/ n negozio m; (workshop) officina f; **talk** ~ 🄸 parlare di lavoro ● vi (pt/pp **shopped**) far compere; **go** ~**ping** andare a fare compere. □ ~ **around** vi confrontare i prezzi

shop: ~ **assistant** n commesso, -a mf. ~**keeper** n negoziante mf. ~**lifter** n taccheggiatore, -trice mf. ~**lifting** n taccheggio m; ~**per** n compratore, -trice mf

shopping /ˈʃɒpɪŋ/ n compere fpl; (articles) acquisti mpl; **do the** ~ fare la spesa. ~ **bag** n borsa f per la spesa. ~ **centre** n centro m commerciale. ~ **trolley** n carrello m

shop: ~-**steward** n rappresentante mf sindacale. ~-'**window** n vetrina f

shore /ʃɔː(r)/ n riva f

shorn /ʃɔːn/ ▷SHEAR

short /ʃɔːt/ adj corto; (not lasting) breve; (person) basso; (curt) brusco; **a** ~ **time ago** poco tempo fa; **be** ~ **of** essere a corto di; **be in** ~ **supply** essere scarso; fig essere raro; **Mick is** ~ **for Michael** Mick è il diminutivo di Michael ● adv bruscamente; **in** ~ in breve; ~ **of doing** a meno di fare; **go** ~ essere privato (**of** di); **stop** ~ **of doing sth** non arrivare fino a fare qcsa; **cut** ~ interrompere (meeting, holiday); **to cut a long story** ~ per farla breve

shortage /ˈʃɔːtɪdʒ/ n scarsità f inv

short: ~**bread** n biscotto m di pasta frolla. ~ '**circuit** n corto m circuito. ~**coming** n difetto m. ~ '**cut** n scorciatoia f

shorten /ˈʃɔːtn/ vt abbreviare; accorciare (garment)

shorthand n stenografia f

short|ly /ˈʃɔːtlɪ/ adv presto; ~**ly before/after** poco prima/dopo. ~**ness** n brevità f inv; (of person) bassa statura f

shorts /ʃɔːts/ npl calzoncini mpl corti

short-'sighted adj miope

shot /ʃɒt/ ▷SHOOT ● n colpo m; (person) tiratore m; (Phot) foto f; (injection) puntura f; (🄸: attempt) prova f; **like a** ~ 🄸 come un razzo. ~**gun** n fucile m da caccia

should /ʃʊd/ v aux I ~ **go** dovrei andare; I ~ **have seen him** avrei dovuto vederlo; I ~ **like** mi piacerebbe; **this** ~ **be enough** questo dovrebbe bastare; **if he** ~ **come** se dovesse venire

shoulder /ˈʃəʊldə(r)/ n spalla f ● vt mettersi in spalla; fig accollarsi. ~-**bag** n borsa f a tracolla. ~-**blade** n scapola f. ~-**strap** n spallina f; (of bag) tracolla f

shout /ʃaʊt/ n grido m ● vt/i gridare. □ ~ **at** vi alzar la voce con. □ ~ **down** vt azzittire gridando

shove /ʃʌv/ n spintone m ● vt spingere; (🄸: put) ficcare ● vi spingere. □ ~ **off** vi 🄸 togliersi di torno

shovel /ˈʃʌvl/ n pala f ● vt (pt/pp **shovelled**) spalare

show /ʃəʊ/ n (display) manifestazione f; (exhibition) mostra f; (ostentation) ostentazione f; (Theat), (TV) spettacolo m; (programme) programma m; **on** ~ esposto ● v (pt **showed**, pp **shown**) ● vt mostrare; (put on display) esporre; proiettare (film) ● vi (film:) essere proiettato; **your slip is** ~**ing** ti si vede la sottoveste. □ ~ **in** vt fare accomodare. □ ~ **off** vi 🄸 mettersi in mostra ● vt mettere in mostra. □ ~ **up** vi risaltare; (🄸: arrive) farsi vedere ● vt (🄸: embarrass) far fare una brutta figura a

'show-down n regolamento m dei conti

shower /'ʃaʊə(r)/ n doccia f; (of rain) acquazzone m; **have a ~** fare la doccia ●vt ~ **with** coprire di ●vi fare la doccia. **~proof** adj impermeabile. **~y** adj da acquazzoni

'show-jumping n concorso m ippico

shown /ʃəʊn/ ▷**SHOW**

'show-off n esibizionista mf

showy /'ʃəʊɪ/ adj appariscente

shrank /ʃræŋk/ ▷**SHRINK**

shred /ʃred/ n brandello m; fig briciolo m ●vt (pt/pp **shredded**) fare a brandelli; (Culin) tagliuzzare. **~der** n distruttore m di documenti

shrewd /ʃruːd/ adj accorto. **~ness** n accortezza f

shriek /ʃriːk/ n strillo m ●vt/i strillare

shrift /ʃrɪft/ n **give sb short ~** liquidare qcno rapidamente

shrill /ʃrɪl/ adj penetrante

shrimp /ʃrɪmp/ n gamberetto m

shrine /ʃraɪn/ n (place) santuario m

shrink /ʃrɪŋk/ vi (pt **shrank**, pp **shrunk**) restringersi; (draw back) ritrarsi (**from** da)

shrivel /'ʃrɪvl/ vi (pt/pp **shrivelled**) raggrinzare

shroud /ʃraʊd/ n sudario m; fig manto m

Shrove /ʃrəʊv/ n **~ Tuesday** martedì m grasso

shrub /ʃrʌb/ n arbusto m

shrug /ʃrʌg/ n scrollata f di spalle ●vt/i (pt/pp **shrugged**) ~ **[one's shoulders]** scrollare le spalle

shrunk /ʃrʌŋk/ ▷**SHRINK.** **~en** adj rimpicciolito

shudder /'ʃʌdə(r)/ n fremito m ●vi fremere

shuffle /'ʃʌfl/ vi strascicare i piedi ●vt mescolare (cards)

shun /ʃʌn/ vt (pt/pp **shunned**)

rifuggire

shunt /ʃʌnt/ vt smistare

shush /ʃʊʃ/ int zitto!

shut /ʃʌt/ v (pt/pp **shut**, pres p **shutting**) ●vt chiudere ●vi chiudersi; (shop): chiudere. □ ~ **down** vt/i chiudere. □ ~ **up** vt chiudere; 🔲 far tacere ●vi 🔲 stare zitto; ~ **up!** stai zitto!

shutter /'ʃʌtə(r)/ n serranda f; (Phot) otturatore m

shuttle /'ʃʌtl/ n navetta f ●vi far la spola

shuttle: **~cock** n volano m. **~ service** n servizio m pendolare

shy /ʃaɪ/ adj (timid) timido. **~ness** n timidezza f

Sicil|y /'sɪsɪlɪ/ n Sicilia f. **~ian** adj & n siciliano, -a mf

sick /sɪk/ adj ammalato; (humour) macabro; **be ~** (vomit) vomitare; **be ~ of sth** 🔲 essere stufo di qcsa; **feel ~** aver la nausea

sick|ly /'sɪklɪ/ adj (-ier, -iest) malaticcio. **~ness** n malattia f; (vomiting) nausea f. **~ness benefit** n indennità f di malattia

side /saɪd/ n lato m; (of person, mountain) fianco m; (of road) bordo m; (on the ~ (as sideline) come attività secondaria; ~ **by** ~ fianco a fianco; **take** ~ immischiarsi; **take sb's** ~ prendere le parti di qcno; **be on the safe** ~ andare sul sicuro ●attrib laterale ●vi ~ **with** parteggiare per

side: **~board** n credenza f. **~effect** n effetto m collaterale. **~lights** npl luci fpl di posizione. **~line** n attività f inv complementare. **~show** n attrazione f. **~step** n schivare. ~ **vt** schivare. **~track** vt sviare. ~ **walk** n Am marciapiede m. **~ways** adv obliquamente

siding /'saɪdɪŋ/ n binario m di raccordo

sidle /'saɪdl/ vi camminare furtivamente (**up to** verso)

siege /siːdʒ/ n assedio m

sieve /sɪv/ n setaccio m • vt setacciare

sift /sɪft/ vt setacciare; ~ [through] fig passare al setaccio

sigh /saɪ/ n sospiro m • vi sospirare

sight /saɪt/ n vista f; (on gun) mirino m; the ~s pl le cose da vedere; at first ~ a prima vista; be within/out of ~ essere/non essere in vista; lose ~ of perdere di vista; know by ~ conoscere di vista; have bad ~ vederci male • vt avvistare

'sightseeing n go ~ andare a visitare posti

sign /saɪn/ n segno m; (notice) insegna f • vt/i firmare. □~ on vi (as unemployed) presentarsi all'ufficio di collocamento; (Mil) arruolarsi

signal /'sɪgnl/ n segnale m • v (pt/pp signalled) • vt segnalare • vi fare segnali; ~ to sb far segno a qcno (to do). ~-box n cabina f di segnalazione

signature /'sɪgnətʃə(r)/ n firma f. ~ tune sigla f [musicale]

significan|ce /sɪg'nɪfɪkəns/ n significato m. ~t adj significativo

signify /'sɪgnɪfaɪ/ vt (pt/pp -ied) indicare

signpost /'saɪn-/ n segnalazione f stradale

silence /'saɪləns/ n silenzio m • vt far tacere. ~r n (on gun) silenziatore m; (Auto) marmitta f

silent /'saɪlənt/ adj silenzioso; (film) muto; remain ~ rimanere in silenzio. ~ly adv silenziosamente

silhouette /sɪlʊ'et/ n sagoma f, silhouette f inv • vt be ~d profilarsi

silicon /'sɪlɪkən/ n silicio m. ~ chip piastrina f di silicio

silk /sɪlk/ n seta f • attrib di seta. ~worm n baco m da seta

silky /'sɪlkɪ/ adj (-ier, -iest) come la seta

silly /'sɪlɪ/ adj (-ier, -iest) sciocco

silt /sɪlt/ n melma f

silver /'sɪlvə(r)/ adj d'argento; (paper) argentato • n argento m; (silverware) argenteria f

silver: ~-**plated** adj placcato d'argento. ~**ware** n argenteria f

SIM card /'sɪmkɑːd/ n carta f SIM

similar /'sɪmɪlə(r)/ adj simile. ~ity n somiglianza f. ~ly adv in modo simile

simile /'sɪmɪlɪ/ n similitudine f

simmer /'sɪmə(r)/ vi bollire lentamente • vt far bollire lentamente. □~ down vi calmarsi

simple /'sɪmpl/ adj semplice; (person) sempliciotto. ~-**minded** adj sempliciotto

simplicity /sɪm'plɪsətɪ/ n semplicità f inv

simply /'sɪmplɪ/ adv semplicemente

simulat|e /'sɪmjʊleɪt/ vt simulare. ~**ion** n simulazione f

simultaneous /sɪml'teɪnɪəs/ adj simultaneo

sin /sɪn/ n peccato m • vi (pt/pp sinned) peccare

---

since /sɪns/

● prep as I've been waiting ~ Monday aspetto da lunedì

● adv da allora

● conj da quando; (because) siccome

---

sincere /sɪn'sɪə(r)/ adj sincero. ~**ly** adv sinceramente; Yours ~ly distinti saluti

sincerity /sɪn'serətɪ/ n sincerità f inv

sinful /'sɪnfl/ adj peccaminoso

sing /sɪŋ/ vt/i (pt sang, pp sung) cantare

singe /sɪndʒ/ vt (pres p singeing) bruciacchiare

singer /'sɪŋə(r)/ n cantante mf

single /'sɪŋgl/ adj solo; (not double) semplice; (unmarried) celibe; (woman) nubile; (room) singolo; (bed) a una piazza ●n (ticket) biglietto m di sola andata; (record) singolo m; ~s pl (Tennis) singolo ●n single out vt scegliere; (distinguish) distinguere

single-handed adj & adv da solo

singular /'sɪŋgjʊlə(r)/ adj (Gram) singolare ●n singolare m. ~ly adv singolarmente

sinister /'sɪnɪstə(r)/ adj sinistro

sink /sɪŋk/ n lavandino m ●v (pt sank, pp sunk) ●vi affondare ●vt affondare (ship); scavare (shaft); investire (money). □ ~ in vi penetrare; it took a while to ~ in ① be understood) c'è voluto un po' a capirlo

sinner /'sɪnə(r)/ n peccatore, -trice mf

sip /sɪp/ n sorso m ●vt (pt/pp sipped) sorseggiare

siphon /'saɪfn/ n (bottle) sifone m ●siphon off vt travasare (con sifone)

sir /sɜː(r)/ n signore m; S~ (title) Sir m; Dear S~s Spettabile ditta

siren /'saɪrən/ n sirena f

sister /'sɪstə(r)/ n sorella f; (nurse) [infermiera f] caposala f. ~ in law n (pl ~s-in-law) cognata f. ~ly adj da sorella

sit /sɪt/ v (pt/pp sat, pres p sitting) ●vi essere seduto; (sit down) sedersi; (committee) riunirsi ●vt sostenere (exam). □ ~ back vi fig starsene con le mani in mano. □ ~ down vi mettersi a sedere. □ ~ up vi mettersi seduto; (not slouch) star seduto diritto; (stay up) stare alzato

site /saɪt/ n posto m; (Archaeol) sito m; (building ~) cantiere m ●vt collocare

sit-in /'sɪtɪn/ n occupazione f (di fabbrica, ecc.)

sitting /'sɪtɪŋ/ n seduta f; (for meals) turno m. ~-room n salotto m

situate /'sɪtjʊeɪt/ vt situare. ~ed adj situato. ~ion /-'eɪʃn/ n situazione f; (location) posizione f; (job) posto m

six /sɪks/ adj sei. ~teen adj sedici.

~teenth adj sedicesimo

sixth /sɪksθ/ adj sesto

sixtieth /'sɪkstɪɪθ/ adj sessantesimo

sixty /'sɪkstɪ/ adj sessanta

size /saɪz/ n dimensioni fpl; (of clothes) taglia f, misura f; (of shoes) numero m; what ~ is the room? che dimensioni ha la stanza? ● size up vt ① valutare

sizzle /'sɪzl/ vi sfrigolare

skate¹ /skeɪt/ n inv (fish) razza f

skate² n pattino m ●vi pattinare

skateboard /'skeɪtbɔːd/ n skateboard m inv

skater /'skeɪtə(r)/ n pattinatore, -trice mf

skating /'skeɪtɪŋ/ n pattinaggio m. ~-rink n pista f di pattinaggio

skeleton /'skelɪtn/ n scheletro m. ~ 'key n passe-partout m inv. ~ 'staff n personale m ridotto

sketch /sketʃ/ n schizzo m; (Theat) sketch m inv ●vt fare uno schizzo di

sketch|y /'sketʃɪ/ adj (-ier, -iest) abbozzato. ~ily adv in modo abbozzato

ski /skiː/ n sci m inv ●vi (pt/pp skied, pres p skiing) sciare; go ~ing andare a sciare

skid /skɪd/ n slittata f ●vi (pt/pp skidded) slittare

skier /'skiːə(r)/ n sciatore, -trice mf

skiing /'skiːɪŋ/ n sci m

skilful /'skɪlfl/ adj abile

'ski-lift n impianto m di risalita

skill /skɪl/ n abilità f inv. ~ed adj dotato; (worker) specializzato

skim /skɪm/ vt (pt/pp skimmed) schiumare; scremare (milk). □ ~ off vt togliere. □ ~ through vt scorrere

skimp /skɪmp/ vi ~ on lesinare su

skimpy /'skɪmpɪ/ adj (-ier, -iest) succinto

skin /skɪn/ n pelle f; (on fruit) buccia f ●vt (pt/pp skinned) spellare

skin: ~-deep adj superficiale.

s

~-diving n nuoto m subacqueo

skinny /'skɪnɪ/ adj (-ier, -iest) molto magro

skip[1] /skɪp/ n (container) benna f

skip[2] n salto m ● v (pt/pp skipped) ● vi saltellare; (with rope) saltare la corda ● vt omettere.

skipper /'skɪpə(r)/ n skipper m inv

skipping-rope /'skɪpɪŋrəʊp/n corda f per saltare

skirmish /'skɜːmɪʃ/ n scaramuccia f

skirt /skɜːt/ n gonna f ● vt costeggiare

skittle /'skɪtl/ n birillo m

skulk /skʌlk/ vi aggirarsi furtivamente

skull /skʌl/ n cranio m

sky /skaɪ/ n cielo m. **~light** n lucernario m. **~ marshal** n guardia f armata a bordo di un aereo. **~scraper** n grattacielo m

slab /slæb/ n lastra f; (slice) fetta f; (of chocolate) tavoletta f

slack /slæk/ adj lento; (person) fiacco ● vi fare lo scansafatiche. □ **~ off** vi rilassarsi

slacken /'slækn/ vi allentare; **~** [off] (trade:) rallentare; (speed, rain:) diminuire ● vt allentare; diminuire (speed)

slain /sleɪn/ ▷SLAY

slam /slæm/ n ● v (pt/pp slammed) ● vt sbattere; ([T]: criticize) stroncare ● vi sbattere

slander /'slɑːndə(r)/ n diffamazione f ● vt diffamare. **~ous** adj diffamatorio

slang /slæŋ/ n gergo m. **~y** adj gergale

slant /slɑːnt/ n pendenza f; (point of view) angolazione f; **on the ~** in pendenza ● vt pendere; fig distorcere (report) ● vi pendere

slap /slæp/ n schiaffo m ● vt (pt/pp slapped) schiaffeggiare; (put) schiaffare ● adv in pieno

slap: **~dash** adj [T] frettoloso

slash /slæʃ/ n taglio m ● vt tagliare; ridurre drasticamente (prices)

slat /slæt/ n stecca f

slate /sleɪt/ n ardesia f ● vt [T] fare a pezzi

slaughter /'slɔːtə(r)/ n macello m; (of people) massacro m ● vt macellare; massacrare (people). **~house** n macello m

slave /sleɪv/ n schiavo, -a mf ● vi **~** [away] lavorare come un negro. **~-driver** n schiavista mf

slav|ery /'sleɪvərɪ/ n schiavitù f inv. **~ish** adj servile

slay /sleɪ/ vt (pt slew, pp slain) ammazzare

sleazy /'sliːzɪ/ adj (-ier, -iest) sordido

sledge /sledʒ/ n slitta f. **~-hammer** n martello m

sleek /sliːk/ adj liscio, lucente; (well-fed) pasciuto

sleep /sliːp/ n sonno m; **go to ~** addormentarsi; **put to ~** far addormentare ● v (pt/pp slept) ● vi dormire ● vt **~** six ha sei posti letto. **~er** n (Rail) treno m con vagoni letto; (compartment) vagone m letto; **be a light/heavy ~er** avere il sonno leggero/pesante

sleeping: **~-bag** n sacco m a pelo. **~-car** n vagone m letto. **~-pill** n sonnifero m

sleepless adj insonne

sleepy /'sliːpɪ/ adj (-ier, -iest) assonnato; **be ~** aver sonno

sleet /sliːt/ n nevischio m ● vi **it is ~ing** nevischia

sleeve /sliːv/ n manica f; (for record) copertina f. **~less** adj senza maniche

sleigh /sleɪ/ n slitta f

slender /'slendə(r)/ adj snello; (fingers, stem) affusolato; fig scarso; (chance) magro

slept /slept/ ▷SLEEP

slew[1] /sluː/ vi girare

slew[2] ▷SLAY

slice /slaɪs/ n fetta f ● vt affettare; ~d bread pane m a cassetta

slick /slɪk/ adj liscio; (cunning) astuto ● n (of oil) chiazza f di petrolio

slid|e /slaɪd/ n scivolata f; (in playground) scivolo m; (for hair) fermaglio m (per capelli); (Phot) diapositiva f ● v (pt/pp slid) ● vi scivolare ● vt far scivolare. ~-rule n regolo m calcolatore. ~ing adj scorrevole; (door, seat) scorrevole; ~ing scale scala f mobile

slight /slaɪt/ adj leggero; (importance) poco; (slender) esile. ~est adj minimo; not in the ~est niente affatto ● vt offendere ● n offesa f. ~ly adv leggermente

slim /slɪm/ adj (slimmer, slimmest) snello; fig scarso; (chance) magro ● vi dimagrire

slim|e /slaɪm/ n melma f. ~y adj melmoso; fig viscido

sling /slɪŋ/ n (Med) benda f al collo ● vt (pt/pp slung) lanciare

slip /slɪp/ n scivolata f; (mistake) lieve errore m; (petticoat) sottoveste f; (for pillow) federa f; (paper) scontrino m; give sb the ~ 🔲 sbarazzarsi di qcno; ~ of the tongue lapsus m inv ● v (pt/pp slipped) ● vi scivolare; (go quickly) sgattaiolare; (decline) retrocedere ● vt he ~ped it into his pocket se l'è infilato in tasca; ~ sb's mind sfuggire di mente a qcno. □ ~ away vi sgusciar via; (time) sfuggire. □ ~ into vi infilarsi (clothes). □ ~ up vi 🔲 sbagliare

slipper /ˈslɪpə(r)/ n pantofola f

slippery /ˈslɪpərɪ/ adj scivoloso

slip-road n bretella f

slipshod /ˈslɪpʃɒd/ adj trascurato

'slip-up n 🔲 sbaglio m

slit /slɪt/ n spacco m; (tear) strappo m; (hole) fessura f ● vt (pt/pp slit) tagliare

slither /ˈslɪðə(r)/ vi scivolare

slobber /ˈslɒbə(r)/ vi sbavare

slog /slɒg/ n [hard] ~ sgobbata f ● vi (pt/pp slogged) (work) sgobbare

slogan /ˈsləʊgən/ n slogan m inv

slop /slɒp/ v (pt/pp slopped) ● vt versare. □ ~ over vi versarsi

slop|e /sləʊp/ n pendenza f; (ski ~) pista f ● vi essere inclinato, inclinarsi. ~ing adj in pendenza

sloppy /ˈslɒpɪ/ adj (-ier, -iest) (work) trascurato; (worker) negligente; (in dress) sciatto; (sentimental) sdolcinato

slosh /slɒʃ/ vi 🔲 (person, feet:) squazzare; (water:) scrosciare ● vt (🔲: hit) colpire

slot /slɒt/ n fessura f; (time-~) spazio m ● vt (pt/pp slotted) ● vt infilare. □ ~ in vi incastrarsi

'slot-machine n distributore m automatico; (for gambling) slot-machine f inv

slouch /slaʊtʃ/ vi (in chair) stare scomposto

Slovakia /sləˈvækɪə/ n Slovacchia f

Slovenia /sləˈviːnɪə/ n Slovenia f

sloven|ly /ˈslʌvnlɪ/ adj sciatto. ~iness n sciatteria f

slow /sləʊ/ adj lento; be ~ (clock:) essere indietro; in ~ motion al rallentatore ● adv lentamente ● ~ down/up vt/i rallentare

slowly adv lentamente

sludge /slʌdʒ/ n fanghiglia f

slug /slʌg/ n lumacone m; (bullet) pallottoia f. ~gish adj lento

slum /slʌm/ n (house) tugurio m; ~s pl bassifondi mpl

slumber /ˈslʌmbə(r)/ vi dormire

slump /slʌmp/ n crollo m; (economic) depressione f ● vi crollare

slung /slʌŋ/ ▷SLING

slur /slɜː(r)/ n (discredit) calunnia f ● vt (pt/pp slurred) biascicare

slush /slʌʃ/ n pantano m nevoso; fig sdolcinatezza f. ~ fund n fondi mpl

s

neri. ~**y** *adj* fangoso; (*sentimental*) sdolcinato

sly /slaɪ/ *adj* (-er, -est) scaltro ● **on the** ~ di nascosto

smack[1] /smæk/ *n* (*on face*) schiaffo *m*; (*on bottom*) sculaccione *m* ● *vt* (*on face*) schiaffeggiare; (*on bottom*) sculacciare; ~ **one's lips** far schioccare le labbra ● *adv* ⓘ in pieno

smack[2] *vi* ~ **of** *fig* sapere di

small /smɔːl/ *adj* piccolo; **be out/ work etc until the** ~ **hours** fare le ore piccole ● *adv* **chop up** ~ fare a pezzettini ● **n the** ~ **of the back** le reni *fpl*

small: ~ **ads** *npl* annunci *mpl* [commerciali]. ~ **'change** *n* spiccioli *mpl*. ~**pox** *n* vaiolo *m*. ~ **talk** *n* chiacchiere *fpl*

smart /smɑːt/ *adj* elegante; (*clever*) intelligente; (*brisk*) svelto; be ~ ⓘ cheeky) fare il furbo ● *vi* (*hurt*) bruciare

smash /smæʃ/ *n* fragore *m*; (*collision*) scontro *m*; (*Tennis*) schiacciata *f* ● *vt* spaccare; (*Tennis*) schiacciare ● *vi* spaccarsi; (*crash*) schiantarsi (**into** contro). ~ **[hit]** *n* successo *m*. ~**ing** *adj* ⓘ fantastico

smattering /'smætərɪŋ/ *n* infarinatura *f*

smear /smɪə(r)/ *n* macchia *f*; (*Med*) striscio *m* ● *vt* imbrattare; (*coat*) spalmare (**with** di); *fig* calunniare

smell /smel/ *n* odore *m*; (*sense*) odorato *m* ● *v* (*pt/pp* smelt *or* smelled) ● *vt* odorare; (*sniff*) annusare ● *vi* odorare (**of** di)

smelly /'smelɪ/ *adj* (-ier, -iest) puzzolente

smelt[1] /smelt/ ▷**SMELL**

smelt[2] *vt* fondere

smile /smaɪl/ *n* sorriso *m* ● *vi* sorridere; ~ **at** sorridere a (**sb**); sorridere di (**sth**)

smirk /smɜːk/ *n* sorriso *m* compiaciuto

smithereens /smɪðə'riːnz/ *npl*

smock /smɒk/ *n* grembiule *m*

smog /smɒg/ *n* smog *m inv*

smoke /sməʊk/ *n* fumo *m* ● *vt/i* fumare. ~**less** *adj* senza fumo; (*fuel*) che non fa fumo

smoker /'sməʊkə(r)/ *n* fumatore, -trice *mf*; (*Rail*) vagone *m* fumatori

smoky /'sməʊkɪ/ *adj* (-ier, -iest) fumoso; (*taste*) di fumo

smooth /smuːð/ *adj* liscio; (*movement*) scorrevole; (*sea*) calmo; (*manners*) mellifluo ● *vt* lisciare. □ ~ **out** *vt* lisciare. ~**ly** *adv* in modo scorrevole

smother /'smʌðə(r)/ *vt* soffocare

smoulder /'sməʊldə(r)/ *vi* fumare; (*with rage*) consumarsi

smudge /smʌdʒ/ *n* macchia *f* ● *vt/i* imbrattare

smug /smʌg/ *adj* (smugger, smuggest) compiaciuto. ~**ly** *adv* con aria compiaciuta

smuggl|e /'smʌgl/ *vt* contrabbandare. ~**er** *n* contrabbandiere, a *mf*. ~**ing** *n* contrabbando *m*

snack /snæk/ *n* spuntino *m*. ~**-bar** *n* snack bar *m inv*

snag /snæg/ *n* (*problem*) intoppo *m*

snail /sneɪl/ *n* lumaca *f*; **at a** ~**'s pace** a passo di lumaca

snake /sneɪk/ *n* serpente *m*

snap /snæp/ *n* colpo *m* secco; (*photo*) istantanea *f* ● *attrib* (*decision*) istantaneo ● *v* (*pt/pp* snapped) ● *vt* (*break*) spezzarsi; ~ **at** (*dog:*) cercare di azzannare; (*person:*) parlare seccamente a ● *vt* (*break*) spezzare; (*say*) dire seccamente; (*Phot*) fare un'istantanea di. □ ~ **up** *vt* afferrare

snappy /'snæpɪ/ *adj* (-ier, -iest) scorbutico; (*smart*) elegante; **make it** ~! sbrigati!

'snapshot *n* istantanea *f*

snare /sneə(r)/ *n* trappola *f*

snarl /snɑːl/ *n* ringhio *m* ● *vi*

ringhiare

snatch /snætʃ/ n strappo m; (*fragment*) brano m; (*theft*) scippo m; **make a ~ at** cercare di afferrare qcsa • vt strappare [di mano] (**from** a); (*steal*) scippare; rapire (child)

sneak /sniːk/ n 🔢 spia mf • vi (🔢: *tell tales*) fare la spia • vt (*take*) rubare; **~ a look at** dare una sbirciata a. □ **~ in/out** vi sgattaiolare dentro/fuori

sneakers /ˈsniːkəz/ npl Am scarpe fpl da ginnastica

sneaky /ˈsniːkɪ/ adj sornione

sneer /snɪə(r)/ n ghigno m • vi sogghignare; (*mock*) ridere di

sneeze /sniːz/ n starnuto m • vi starnutire

snide /snaɪd/ adj 🔢 insinuante

sniff /snɪf/ n (*of dog*) annusata f • vi tirare su col naso • vt odorare (flower); sniffare (glue, cocaine); (dog:) annusare

snigger /ˈsnɪɡə(r)/ n risatina f soffocata • vi ridacchiare

snip /snɪp/ n taglio m; (🔢: *bargain*) affare m • vt/i (*pt/pp* snipped) **~** [at] tagliare

snippet /ˈsnɪpɪt/ n **a ~ of** information/news una breve notizia/informazione

snivel /ˈsnɪvl/ vi (*pt/pp* snivelled) piagnucolare. **~ling** adj piagnucoloso

snob /snɒb/ n snob mf. **~bery** n snobismo m. **~bish** adj da snob

snooker /ˈsnuːkə(r)/ n snooker m

snoop /snuːp/ n spia f • vi 🔢 curiosare

snooze /snuːz/ n sonnellino m • vi fare un sonnellino

snore /snɔː(r)/ vi russare

snorkel /ˈsnɔːkl/ n respiratore m

snort /snɔːt/ n sbuffo m • vi sbuffare

snout /snaʊt/ n grugno m

snow /snəʊ/ n neve f • vi nevicare; **~ed under with** fig sommerso di

snow: **~ball** n palla f di neve • vi fare a palle di neve. **~board** n snowboard m. **~-drift** n cumulo m di neve. **~fall** n nevicata f. **~flake** n fiocco m di neve. **~man** n pupazzo m di neve. **~-plough** n spazzaneve m. **~storm** n tormenta f. **~y** adj nevoso

snub /snʌb/ n sgarbo m • vt (*pt/pp* snubbed) snobbare

'snub-nosed adj dal naso all'insù

snug /snʌɡ/ adj (snugger, snuggest) comodo; (*tight*) aderente

so /səʊ/

• adv così; **so far** finora; **so am I** anch'io; **so I see** così pare; **that is so** è così; **so much** così tanto; **so much the better** tanto meglio; **so it is** è proprio così; **if so** se è così; **so as to** in modo da; **so long!** 🔢 a presto!

• pron **I hope/think/am afraid so** spero/penso/temo di sì; **I told you so** te l'ho detto; **because I say so** perché lo dico io; **I did so!** è vero!; **so saying/doing,...** così dicendo/facendo,...; **or so** circa; **very much so** sì, molto; **and so forth** o **on** e così via

• conj (*therefore*) perciò; (*in order that*) così; **so that** affinché; **so there** ecco!; **so what!** e allora?; **so where have you been?** allora, dove sei stato?

soak /səʊk/ vt mettere a bagno • vi stare a bagno; **~ into** (liquid:) penetrare. □ **~ up** vt assorbire

soaking /ˈsəʊkɪŋ/ n ammollo m • adj & adv (**wet**) 🔢 fradicio

so-and-so /ˈsəʊənsəʊ/ n Tal dei Tali mf; (*euphemism*) specie f di imbecille

soap /səʊp/ n sapone m. **~ opera** n telenovela f, soap opera f inv. **~ powder** n detersivo m in polvere

soapy /ˈsəʊpɪ/ adj (-ier, -iest) insaponato

soar /sɔː(r)/ vi elevarsi; (prices:) salire alle stelle

sob /sɒb/ n singhiozzo m ● vi (pt/pp **sobbed**) singhiozzare

sober /ˈsəʊbə(r)/ adj sobrio; (serious) serio ● **sober up** vi ritornare sobrio

'so-called adj cosiddetto

soccer /ˈsɒkə(r)/ n calcio m

sociable /ˈsəʊʃəbl/ adj socievole

social /ˈsəʊʃl/ adj sociale; (sociable) socievole

socialis|m /ˈsəʊʃəlɪzm/ n socialismo m. ~**t** adj socialista ● n socialista mf

socialize /ˈsəʊʃəlaɪz/ vi socializzare

social: ~ **se'curity** n previdenza f sociale. ~ **worker** n assistente mf sociale

society /səˈsaɪətɪ/ n società f inv

sociolog|ist /səʊsɪˈɒlədʒɪst/ n sociologo, -a mf. ~**y** n sociologia f

sock¹ /sɒk/ n calzino m; (kneelength) calza f

sock² n 🔲 pugno m ● vt 🔲 dare un pugno a

socket /ˈsɒkɪt/ n (wall plug) presa f [di corrente]; (for bulb) portalampada m inv

soda /ˈsəʊdə/ n soda f; Am gazzosa f. ~ **water** n seltz m inv

sodium /ˈsəʊdɪəm/ n sodio m

sofa /ˈsəʊfə/ n divano m. ~ **bed** n divano m letto

soft /sɒft/ adj morbido, soffice; (voice) sommesso; (light, colour) tenue; (not strict) indulgente; (🔲: silly) stupido; **have a ~ spot for sb** avere un debole per qcno. ~ **drink** n bibita f analcolica

soften /ˈsɒfn/ vt ammorbidire; fig attenuare ● vi ammorbidirsi

softly /ˈsɒftlɪ/ adv (say) sottovoce; (treat) con indulgenza; (play music) in sottofondo

software n software m

soggy /ˈsɒgɪ/ adj (-ier, -iest) zuppo

soil¹ /sɔɪl/ n suolo m

soil² vt sporcare

solar /ˈsəʊlə(r)/ adj solare

sold /səʊld/ ▷ SELL

solder /ˈsəʊldə(r)/ n lega f da saldatura ● vt saldare

soldier /ˈsəʊldʒə(r)/ n soldato m ● **soldier on** vi perseverare

sole¹ /səʊl/ n (of foot) pianta f; (of shoe) suola f

sole² n (fish) sogliola f

sole³ adj unico, solo. ~**ly** adv unicamente

solemn /ˈsɒləm/ adj solenne. ~**ity** n solennità f inv

solicitor /səˈlɪsɪtə(r)/ n avvocato m

solid /ˈsɒlɪd/ adj solido; (oak, gold) massiccio ● n (figure) solido m; ~**s** pl (food) cibi mpl solidi

solidarity /sɒlɪˈdærətɪ/ n solidarietà f inv

solidify /səˈlɪdɪfaɪ/ vi (pt/pp -ied) solidificarsi

solitary /ˈsɒlɪtərɪ/ adj solitario; (sole) solo. ~ **con'finement** n cella f di isolamento

solitude /ˈsɒlɪtjuːd/ n solitudine f

solo /ˈsəʊləʊ/ n (Mus) assolo m ● adj (flight) in solitario ● adv in solitario. ~**ist** n solista mf

solstice /ˈsɒlstɪs/ n solstizio m

soluble /ˈsɒljʊbl/ adj solubile

solution /səˈluːʃn/ n soluzione f

solve /sɒlv/ vt risolvere

solvent /ˈsɒlvənt/ adj solvente ● n solvente m

sombre /ˈsɒmbə(r)/ adj tetro; (clothes) scuro

some /sʌm/ adj (a certain amount of) del; (a certain number of) qualche, alcuni; ~ **day** un giorno o l'altro; **I need ~ money/books** ho bisogno di soldi/libri; **do ~ shopping** fare qualche acquisto ● pron (a certain amount) un po'; (a certain number) alcuni; **I want ~** ne voglio

some: ∼**body** /-bədɪ/ *pron & n* qualcuno *m.* ∼**how** *adv* in qualche modo; ∼**how or other** in un modo o nell'altro. ∼**one** *pron & n =* **somebody**

somersault /'sʌməsɔːlt/ *n* capriola *f*; **turn a** ∼ fare una capriola

'**something** *pron* qualche cosa, qualcosa, ∼ **different** qualcosa di diverso; ∼ **like un po'** come; (*approximately*) qualcosa come; **see** ∼ **of sb** vedere qcno un po'

some: ∼**time** *adv* un giorno o l'altro; ∼**times** *adv* qualche volta. ∼**what** *adv* piuttosto. ∼**where** *adv* da qualche parte ●*pron* ∼**where to eat** un posto in cui mangiare

son /sʌn/ *n* figlio *m*

sonata /sə'nɑːtə/ *n* sonata *f*

song /sɒŋ/ *n* canzone *f*

sonic /'sɒnɪk/ *adj* sonico. ∼ '**boom** *n* bang *m inv* sonico

'**son-in-law** *n* (*pl* ∼**s-in-law**) genero *m*

sonnet /'sɒnɪt/ *n* sonetto *m*

soon /suːn/ *adv* presto; (*in a short time*) tra poco; **as** ∼ **as** [non] appena; **as** ∼ **as possible** il più presto possibile; ∼**er or later** prima o poi; **the** ∼**er the better** prima è, meglio è; **no** ∼**er had I arrived than...** ero appena arrivato quando...; **I would** ∼**er go** preferirei andare; ∼ **after** subito dopo

soot /sʊt/ *n* fuliggine *f*

soothe /suːð/ *vt* calmare

sooty /'sʊtɪ/ *adj* fuligginoso

sophisticated /sə'fɪstɪkeɪtɪd/ *adj* sofisticato

sopping /'sɒpɪŋ/ *adj & adv* **be** ∼ [**wet**] essere bagnato fradicio

soppy /'sɒpɪ/ *adj* (**-ier, -iest**) 🔲 svenevole

soprano /sə'prɑːnəʊ/ *n* soprano *m*

sordid /'sɔːdɪd/ *adj* sordido

sore /sɔː(r)/ *adj* dolorante; (*Am:*

vexed) arrabbiato; **it's** ∼ fa male; **have a** ∼ **throat** avere mal di gola ●*n* piaga *f.* ∼**ly** *adv* (*tempted*) seriamente

sorrow /'sɒrəʊ/ *n* tristezza *f.* ∼**ful** *adj* triste

sorry /'sɒrɪ/ *adj* (**-ier, -iest**) (*sad*) spiacente; (*wretched*) pietoso; **you'll be** ∼! te ne pentirai!; **I am** ∼ mi dispiace; **be** *or* **feel** ∼ **for** provare compassione per; ∼! scusa!; (*more polite*) scusi!

sort /sɔːt/ *n* specie *f*; (🔲: *person*) tipo *m*; **it's a** ∼ **of fish** è un tipo di pesce; **be out of** ∼**s** (🔲: *unwell*) stare poco bene ●*vt* classificare. ▢ ∼ **out** *vt* selezionare (papers); *fig* risolvere (problem); occuparsi di (person)

'**so-so** *adj & adv* così così

sought /sɔːt/ ▷**SEEK**

soul /səʊl/ *n* anima *f*

'**sound**[1] /saʊnd/ *adj* sano; (*sensible*) saggio; (*secure*) solido; (*thrashing*) clamoroso ●*adv* ∼ **asleep** profondamente addormentato

sound[2] *n* suono *m*; (*noise*) rumore *m*; **I don't like the** ∼ **of it** 🔲 non mi suona bene ●*vi* suonare; (*seem*) avere l'aria ●*vt* (*pronounce*) pronunciare; (*Med*) auscoltare (chest). ∼ **barrier** *n* muro *m* del suono. ∼ **card** *n* (*Comput*) scheda *f* sonora. ∼**less** *adj* silenzioso. ▢ ∼ **out** *vt fig* sondare

soundly /'saʊndlɪ/ *adv* (*sleep*) profondamente; (*defeat*) completamente

'**sound:** ∼**proof** *adj* impenetrabile al suono. ∼**-track** *n* colonna *f* sonora

soup /suːp/ *n* minestra *f.* ∼**ed-up** *adj* 🔲 (*engine*) truccato

sour /saʊə(r)/ *adj* agro; (*not fresh & fig*) acido

source /sɔːs/ *n* fonte *f*

south /saʊθ/ *n* sud *m*; **to the** ∼ **of** a sud di ●*adj* del sud, meridionale

● adv verso il sud
south: S~ 'Africa n Sudafrica m. S~ A'merica n America f del Sud. S~ American adj & n sudamericano, -a mf. ~'east n sudest m

southerly /'sʌðəlɪ/ adj del sud

southern /'sʌðən/ adj del sud, meridionale; ~ Italy il Mezzogiorno m. ~er n meridionale mf

'southward[**s**] /-wəd[z]/ adv verso sud

souvenir /suːvə'nɪə(r)/ n ricordo m, souvenir m inv

sovereign /'sɒvrɪn/ adj sovrano ● n sovrano, -a mf. ~ty n sovranità f inv

Soviet /'səʊvɪət/ adj sovietico; ~ Union Unione f Sovietica

sow[1] /saʊ/ n scrofa f

sow[2] /səʊ/ vt (pt sowed, pp sown or sowed) seminare

soya /'sɔɪə/ n ~ bean soia f

spa /spɑː/ n stazione f termale

space /speɪs/ n spazio m ● adj (research etc) spaziale ● vt ~ [out] distanziare

space: ~ship n astronave f. ~ shuttle n navetta f spaziale

spade /speɪd/ n vanga f; (for child) paletta f; ~s pl (in cards) picche fpl. ~work n lavoro m preparatorio

Spain /speɪn/ n Spagna f

spam /spæm/ n spam m

span[1] /spæn/ n spanna f; (of arch) luce f; (of time) arco m; (of wings) apertura f ● vt (pt/pp spanned) estendersi su

span[2] ▷ SPICK

Span|**iard** /'spænjəd/ n spagnolo, -a mf. ~ish adj spagnolo ● n (language) spagnolo m; the ~ish pl gli spagnoli

spank /spæŋk/ vt sculacciare. ~ing n sculacciata f

spanner /'spænə(r)/ n chiave f inglese

spare /speə(r)/ adj (surplus) in più;

(additional) di riserva ● n (part) ricambio m ● vt risparmiare; (do without) fare a meno di; **can you** ~ **five minutes?** avresti cinque minuti?; **to** ~ (surplus) in eccedenza. ~ **part** n pezzo m di ricambio. ~ **time** n tempo m libero. ~ 'wheel n ruota f di scorta

spark /spɑːk/ n scintilla f. ~ing-plug n (Auto) candela f

sparkl|**e** /'spɑːkl/ n scintillio m ● vi scintillare. ~ing adj frizzante; (wine) spumante

sparrow /'spærəʊ/ n passero m

sparse /spɑːs/ adj rado. ~ly adv scarsamente; ~ly populated a bassa densità di popolazione

spasm /'spæzm/ n spasmo m. ~odic adj spasmodico

spat /spæt/ ▷ SPIT[1]

spate /speɪt/ n (series) successione f; **be in full** ~ essere in piena

spatial /'speɪʃl/ adj spaziale

spatter /'spætə(r)/ vt schizzare

spawn /spɔːn/ n uova fpl (di pesci, rane, ecc.) ● vi deporre le uova ● vt fig generare

speak /spiːk/ v (pt spoke, pp spoken) ● vi parlare (to a); ~ing! (Teleph) sono io! ● vt dire; ~ one's mind dire quello che si pensa. □ ~ for vi parlare a nome di. □ ~ up vi parlare più forte; ~ up for oneself parlare a favore di

speaker /'spiːkə(r)/ n parlante mf; (in public) oratore, -trice mf; (of stereo) cassa f

spear /spɪə(r)/ n lancia f

special /'speʃl/ adj speciale. ~ist n specialista mf. ~ity n specialità f inv

special|**ize** /'speʃəlaɪz/ vi specializzarsi. ~ly adv specialmente; (particularly) particolarmente

species /'spiːʃiːz/ n specie f inv

specific /spə'sɪfɪk/ adj specifico. ~ally adv in modo specifico

specify /'spesɪfaɪ/ vt (pt/pp -ied)

specificare

specimen /'spesɪmən/ n campione m

speck /spek/ n macchiolina f; (particle) granello m

specs /speks/ npl 🔢 occhiali mpl

spectacle /'spektəkl/ n (show) spettacolo m. ~s npl occhiali mpl

spectacular /spek'tækjʊlə(r)/ adj spettacolare

spectator /spek'teɪtə(r)/ n spettatore, -trice mf

spectre /'spektə(r)/ n spettro m

spectrum /'spektrəm/ n (pl -tra) spettro m; fig gamma f

speculat|e /'spekjʊleɪt/ vi speculare. ~ion n speculazione f. ~ive adj speculativo. ~or n speculatore, -trice mf

sped /sped/ ▷SPEED

speech /spi:tʃ/ n linguaggio m; (address) discorso m. ~less adj senza parole

speed /spi:d/ n velocità f inv; (gear) marcia f; at ~ a tutta velocità ● vi (pt/pp sped) andare veloce; (pt/pp speeded) (go too fast) andare a velocità eccessiva. □ ~ **up** (pt/pp speeded up) vt/i accelerare

speed: ~boat n motoscafo m. ~ **camera** n Autovelox® m inv. ~ **ing** n speed dating m. ~ **limit** n limite m di velocità

speedometer /spi:'dɒmɪtə(r)/ n tachimetro m

speed|y /'spi:dɪ/ adj (-ier, -iest) rapido. ~**ily** adv rapidamente

spell[1] /spel/ n (turn) turno m; (of weather) periodo m

spell[2] /spel/ vt (pt/pp spelled, spelt) ● vt how do you ~...? come si scrive...?; **could you** ~ that **for me?** me lo può compitare?; ~ **disaster** essere disastroso ● vi he can't ~ fa molti errori d'ortografia

spell[3] n (magic) incantesimo m. ~**bound** adj affascinato

spelling /'spelɪŋ/ n ortografia f

spelt /spelt/ ▷SPELL[2]

spend /spend/ vt/i (pt/pp spent) spendere; passare (time)

sperm /spɜ:m/ n spermatozoo m; (semen) sperma m

spew /spju:/ vt/i vomitare

spher|e /sfɪə(r)/ n sfera f. ~**ical** adj sferico

spice /spaɪs/ n spezia f; fig pepe m

spick /spɪk/ adj ~ **and span** lindo

spicy /'spaɪsɪ/ adj piccante

spider /'spaɪdə(r)/ n ragno m

spike /spaɪk/ n punta f; (Bot, Zool) spina f; (on shoe) chiodo m. ~**y** adj (plant) pungente

spill /spɪl/ v (pt/pp spilt or spilled) ● vt versare (blood) ● vi rovesciarsi

spin /spɪn/ v (pt/pp spun, pres p spinning) ● vt far girare; filare (wool); centrifugare (washing) ● vi girare; (washing machine:) centrifugare in rotazione f; (short drive) giretto m. □ ~ **out** vt far durare

spinach /'spɪnɪdʒ/ n spinaci mpl

spin-'drier n centrifuga f

spine /spaɪn/ n spina f dorsale; (of book) dorso m; (Bot, Zool) spina f. ~**less** adj fig smidollato

'**spin-off** n ricaduta f

spiral /'spaɪrəl/ adj a spirale ● n spirale f ● vi (pt/pp spiralled) formare una spirale. ~ '**staircase** n scala f a chiocciola

spire /'spaɪə(r)/ n guglia f

spirit /'spɪrɪt/ n spirito m; (courage) ardore m ● vi (pl) (alcohol) liquori mpl; **in good ~s** di buon umore; **in low ~s** abbattuto

spirited /'spɪrɪtɪd/ adj vivace; (courageous) pieno d'ardore

spiritual /'spɪrɪtjʊəl/ adj spirituale ● n spiritual m. ~**ism** n spiritismo m. ~**ist** n spiritista mf

spit[1] /spɪt/ n (for roasting) spiedo m

spit[2] /spɪt/ n sputo m ● vt/i (pt/pp spat, pres

p spitting) sputare; (cat:) soffiare; (fat:) sfrigolare; **it's ~ting [with rain]** piovviggina; **the ~ting image** of il ritratto spiccicato di

spite /spaɪt/ *n* dispetto *m*; **in ~ of** malgrado. ● *vt* far dispetto a. **~ful** *adj* indispettito

spittle /'spɪtl/ *n* saliva *f*

splash /splæʃ/ *n* schizzo *m*; (*of colour*) macchia *f*; (fig: *drop*) goccio *m* ● *vt* schizzare; **~ sb with** sth schizzare qcno di qcsa ● *vi* schizzare. □ **~ about** *vi* schizzarsi. □ **~ down** *vi* (spacecraft:) ammarare

splendid /'splendɪd/ *adj* splendido

splendour /'splendə(r)/ *n* splendore *m*

splint /splɪnt/ *n* (Med) stecca *f*

splinter /'splɪntə(r)/ *n* scheggia *f* ● *vi* scheggiarsi

split /splɪt/ *n* fessura *f*; (*quarrel*) rottura *f*; (*division*) scissione *f*; (*tear*) strappo *m* ● *v* (*pt/pp* split, *pres p* splitting) ● *vt* dividere; (*share, divide*) dividere; (*tear*) strappare ● *vi* spaccarsi; (*tear*) strapparsi; (*divide*) dividersi. □ **~ on sb** fig denunciare qcno ● *adj* a **~ second** una frazione *f* di secondo. □ **~ up** *vi* dividersi ● *vi* (*couple*) separarsi

splutter /'splʌtə(r)/ *vi* farfugliare

spoil /spɔɪl/ *n* **~s** *pl* bottino *msg* ● *v* (*pt/pp* spoilt *or* spoiled) ● *vt* rovinare; viziare (person) ● *vi* andare a male. **~sport** *n* guastafeste *mf inv*

spoke[1] /spəʊk/ *n* raggio *m*

spoke[2], **spoken** /'spəʊkn/ ▷SPEAK

'spokesman *n* portavoce *m inv*

sponge /spʌndʒ/ *n* spugna *f* ● *vt* pulire (con la spugna) ● *vi* **~ on** scroccare da. **~-cake** *n* pan *m* di Spagna

sponsor /'spɒnsə(r)/ *n* garante *m*; (Radio, TV) sponsor *m inv*; (*god-parent*) padrino *m*, madrina *f*; (*for membership*) socio, -a *mf* garante ● *vt* sponsorizzare. **~ship** *n* sponsorizzazione *f*

spontaneous /spɒn'teɪnɪəs/ *adj* spontaneo

spoof /spu:f/ *n* 𝟙 parodia *f*

spooky /'spu:kɪ/ *adj* (-ier, -iest) 𝟙 sinistro

spool /spu:l/ *n* bobina *f*

spoon /spu:n/ *n* cucchiaio *m* ● *vt* mettere col cucchiaio. **~-feed** *vt* (*pt/ pp* -fed) *fig* imboccare. **~ful** *n* cucchiaiata *f*

sporadic /spə'rædɪk/ *adj* sporadico

sport /spɔ:t/ *n* sport *m inv* ● *vt* sfoggiare. **~ing** *adj* sportivo; **~ing chance** possibilità *f* inv

sports: **~car** *n* automobile *f* sportiva. **~man** *n* sportivo *m*. **~woman** *n* sportiva *f*

spot /spɒt/ *n* macchia *f*; (*pimple*) brufolo *m*; (*place*) posto *m*; (*in pattern*) pois *m inv*; (*of rain*) goccia *f*; (*of water*) goccio *m*; **~s** *pl* (rash) sfogo *msg*; **a ~ of** 𝟙 un po' di; **a ~ of bother** qualche problema; **on the ~** sul luogo; (*immediately*) immediatamente; **in a [tight] ~** 𝟙 in difficoltà ● *vt* (*pt/pp* spotted) macchiare; (𝟙: *notice*) individuare

spot: **~check** *n* (*without warning*) controllo *m* a sorpresa; **do a ~ check on** sth dare una controllata a qcsa. **~less** *adj* immacolato. **~light** *n* riflettore *m*

spotted /'spɒtɪd/ *adj* (material) a pois

spotty /'spɒtɪ/ *adj* (-ier, -iest) (*pimply*) brufoloso

spouse /spaʊz/ *n* consorte *mf*

spout /spaʊt/ *n* becco *m* ● *vi* zampillare (from da)

sprain /spreɪn/ *n* slogatura *f* ● *vt* slogare

sprang /spræŋ/ ▷SPRING[2]

spray /spreɪ/ *n* spruzzo *m*; (*preparation*) spray *m inv*; (*container*) spruzzatore *m inv* ● *vt* spruzzare. **~-gun** *n* pistola *f* a spruzzo

spread /spred/ *n* estensione *f*; (of

disease) diffusione *f*; (*paste*) crema *f*; (🍴 *feast*) banchetto *m* ● *v* (*pt/pp*
spread) ● *vt* spargere; spalmare (butter, jam); stendere (cloth, arms); diffondere (news, disease); dilazionare (payments); ~ **sth with** spalmare qcsa di ● *vi* spargersi; (butter:) spalmarsi; (disease:) diffondersi. ~**sheet** *n* (*Comput*) foglio *m* elettronico. □ ~ **out** *vt* sparpagliare ● *vi* sparpagliarsi

spree /spriː/ *n* 🍴 **go on a** ~ far baldoria; **go on a shopping** ~ fare spese folli

sprightly /ˈspraɪtlɪ/ *adj* (-**ier**, -**iest**) vivace

spring[1] /sprɪŋ/ *n* primavera *f* ● *attrib* primaverile

spring[2] *n* (*jump*) balzo *m*; (*water*) sorgente *f*; (*device*) molla *f*; (*elasticity*) elasticità *f inv* ● *v* (*pt* **sprang**, *pp* **sprung**) ● *vi* balzare; (*arise*) provenire (from da) ● *vt* **he just sprang it on me** me l'ha detto a cose fatte compiuto. □ ~ **up** balzare; *fig* spuntare

spring: ~**board** *n* trampolino *m*. ~**time** *n* primavera *f*

sprinkl|e /ˈsprɪŋkl/ *vt* (*scatter*) spruzzare (liquid); spargere (flour, cocoa); ~ **sth with** spruzzare qcsa di (liquid); cospargere qcsa di (flour, cocoa). ~**er** *n* sprinkler *m inv*; (*for lawn*) irrigatore *m*. ~**ing** *n* (*of liquid*) spruzzatina *f*; (*of pepper, salt*) pizzico *m*; (*of flour, sugar*) spolveratina *f* (*of knowledge*) infarinatura *f*; (*of people*) pugno *m*

sprint /sprɪnt/ *n* sprint *m inv* ● *vi* fare uno sprint; (*Sport*) sprintare. ~**er** *n* sprinter *mf inv*

sprout /spraʊt/ *n* germoglio *m*; [**Brussels**] ~**s** *pl* cavolini *mpl* di Bruxelles ● *vi* germogliare

sprung /sprʌŋ/ ▷**SPRING**[2] ● *adj* molleggiato

spud /spʌd/ *n* 🍴 patata *f*

spun /spʌn/ ▷**SPIN**

spur /spɜː(r)/ *n* sperone *m*; (*stimulus*)

stimolo *m*; (*road*) svincolo *m*; **on the** ~ **of the moment** su due piedi ● *vt* (*pt/pp* **spurred**) ~ [**on**] *fig* spronare [a]

spurn /spɜːn/ *vt* sdegnare

spurt /spɜːt/ *n* getto *m*; (*Sport*) scatto *m*; **put on a** ~ fare uno scatto ● *vi* sprizzare; (*increase speed*) scattare

spy /spaɪ/ *n* spia *f* ● *v* (*pt/pp* **spied**) ● *vi* spiare ● *vt* (🍴 *see*) spiare. □ ~ **on** *vi* spiare

squabble /ˈskwɒbl/ *n* bisticcio *m* ● *vi* bisticciare

squad /skwɒd/ *n* squadra *f*; (*Sport*) squadra

squadron /ˈskwɒdrən/ *n* (*Mil*) squadrone *m*, (*Aeron*), (*Naut*) squadriglia *f*

squalid /ˈskwɒlɪd/ *adj* squallido

squalor /ˈskwɒlə(r)/ *n* squallore *m*

squander /ˈskwɒndə(r)/ *vt* sprecare

square /skweə(r)/ *adj* quadrato; (*meal*) sostanzioso; (🍴 *old-fashioned*) vecchio stampo; **all** ~ 🍴 pari ● *n* quadrato *m*; (*in city*) piazza *f*; (*on chessboard*) riquadro *m* ● *vt* (*settle*) far quadrare; (*Math*) elevare al quadrato ● *vi* (*agree*) armonizzare

squash /skwɒʃ/ *n* (*drink*) spremuta *f*; (*sport*) squash *m*; (*vegetable*) zucca *f* ● *vt* schiacciare; soffocare (rebellion)

squat /skwɒt/ *adj* tarchiato ● *n* 🍴 edificio *m* occupato abusivamente ● *vi* (*pt/pp* **squatted**) accovacciarsi; ~ **in** occupare abusivamente. ~**ter** *n* occupante *mf* abusivo, -a

squawk /skwɔːk/ *n* gracchio *m* ● *vi* gracchiare

squeak /skwiːk/ *n* squittio *m*; (*of hinge, brakes*) scricchiolio *m* ● *vi* squittire; (hinge, brakes:) scricchiolare

squeal /skwiːl/ *n* strillo *m*; (*of brakes*) cigolio *m* ● *vi* strillare; 🗷 spifferare

squeamish /ˈskwiːmɪʃ/ *adj* dallo stomaco delicato

squeeze /skwiːz/ *n* stretta *f*; (*crush*)

pigia pigia *m inv* ● *vt* premere; (*to get juice*) spremere; stringere (hand); (*force*) spingere a forza; (🔲: *extort*) estorcere (out of da). □ ~ **in/out** *vi* sguscire dentro/fuori. □ ~ **up** *vi* stringersi

squid /skwɪd/ *n* calamaro *m*

squiggle /'skwɪgl/ *n* scarabocchio *m*

squint /skwɪnt/ *n* strabismo *m* ● *vi* essere strabico

squirm /skwɜːm/ *vi* contorcersi; (*feel embarrassed*) sentirsi imbarazzato

squirrel /'skwɪrəl/ *n* scoiattolo *m*

squirt /skwɜːt/ *n* spruzzo *m*; (🔲: *person*) presuntuoso *m* ● *vt/i* spruzzare

St *abbr* (Saint) S; *abbr* Street

stab /stæb/ *n* pugnalata *f*, coltellata *f*; (*sensation*) fitta *f*; (🔲: *attempt*) tentativo *m* ● *vt* (*pt/pp* stabbed) pugnalare, accoltellare

stability /stə'bɪlɪtɪ/ *n* stabilità *f inv*

stabilize /'steɪbɪlaɪz/ *vt* stabilizzare ● *vi* stabilizzarsi

stable[1] /'steɪbl/ *adj* stabile

stable[2] *n* stalla *f*; (*establishment*) scuderia *f*

stack /stæk/ *n* catasta *f*; (*of chimney*) comignolo *m*; (*chimney*) ciminiera *f*; (🔲: *large quantity*) montagna *f* ● *vt* accatastare

stadium /'steɪdɪəm/ *n* stadio *m*

staff /stɑːf/ *n* (*stick*) bastone *m*; (*employees*) personale *m*; (*teachers*) corpo *m* insegnante; (*Mil*) Stato *m* Maggiore ● *vt* fornire di personale. ~**-room** *n* (*Sch*) sala *f* insegnanti

stag /stæg/ *n* cervo *m*

stage /steɪdʒ/ *n* palcoscenico *m*; (*profession*) teatro *m*; (*in journey*) tappa *f*; (*in process*) stadio *m*; go on the ~ darsi al teatro; by or in ~s a tappe ● *vt* mettere in scena; (*arrange*) organizzare

stagger /'stægə(r)/ *vi* barcollare ● *vt* sbalordire; scaglionare (holidays etc); I was ~ed sono rimasto sbalordito

● *n* vacillamento *m*. ~**ing** *adj* sbalorditivo

stagnant /'stægnənt/ *adj* stagnante

stagnat|e /stæg'neɪt/ *vi fig* [ri]stagnare. ~**ion** *n fig* inattività *f*

'stag party *n* addio *m* al celibato

staid /steɪd/ *adj* posato

stain /steɪn/ *n* macchia *f*; (*for wood*) mordente *m* ● *vt* macchiare; (wood) dare il mordente a; ~**ed glass** vetro *m* colorato; ~**ed-glass window** vetrata *f* colorata. ~**less** *adj* senza macchia; (steel) inossidabile. ~ **remover** *n* smacchiatore *m*

stair /steə(r)/ *n* gradino *m*; ~**s** *pl* scale *fpl*. ~**case** *n* scale *fpl*

stake /steɪk/ *n* palo *m*; (*wager*) posta *f*; (*Comm*) partecipazione *f*; at ~ in gioco ● *vt* puntellare; (*wager*) scommettere

stale /steɪl/ *adj* stantio; (air) viziato; (*uninteresting*) trito [e ritrito]. ~**mate** *n* (*in chess*) stallo *m*; (*deadlock*) situazione *f* di stallo

stalk[1] /stɔːk/ *n* gambo *m*

stalk[2] *vt* inseguire ● *vi* camminare impettito

stall /stɔːl/ *n* box *m inv*; (*in market*) bancarella *f*; ~**s** *pl* (*Theat*) platea *f* ● *vi* (engine) spegnersi; *fig* temporeggiare ● *vt* far spegnere (engine); tenere a bada (person)

stallion /'stæljən/ *n* stallone *m*

stalwart /'stɔːlwət/ *adj* fedele

stamina /'stæmɪnə/ *n* [capacità *f inv* di] resistenza *f*

stammer /'stæmə(r)/ *n* balbettio *m* ● *vt/i* balbettare

stamp /stæmp/ *n* (*postage* ~) francobollo *m*; (*instrument*) timbro *m*; *fig* impronta *f* ● *vt* affrancare (letter); timbrare (bill); battere (feet). □ ~ **out** *vt* spegnere; *fig* soffocare

stampede /stæm'piːd/ *n* fuga *f* precipitosa; (🔲) fuggi-fuggi *m* ● *vi* fuggire precipitosamente

stance /stɑːns/ *n* posizione *f*

stand /stænd/ n (for bikes) rastrelliera f; (at exhibition) stand m inv; (in market) bancarella f; (in stadium) gradinata f inv; fig posizione f ● v (pt/pp stood) ● vi stare in piedi; (rise) alzarsi [in piedi]; (be) trovarsi; (be candidate) essere candidato (for a); (stay valid) rimanere valido; ~ still non muoversi; **I don't know where I** ~ non so qual'è la mia posizione; ~ **firm** fig tener duro; ~ **together** essere solidali; ~ **to lose/gain** rischiare di perdere/vincere; ~ **to reason** essere logico ● vt (withstand) resistere a; (endure) sopportare; (place) mettere; ~ **a chance** avere una possibilità; ~ **one's ground** tener duro; ~ **the test of time** superare la prova del tempo; ~ **sb a beer** offrire una birra a qcno. □ ~ **by** vi stare a guardare; (be ready) essere pronto ● vt (support) appoggiare. □ ~ **down** vi (retire) ritirarsi. □ ~ **for** vt (mean) significare; (tolerate) tollerare. □ ~ **in for** vt sostituire. □ ~ **out** vi spiccare. □ ~ **up** vi alzarsi [in piedi]. □ ~ **up for** vt prendere le difese di; ~ **up for oneself** farsi valere. □ ~ **up to** vt affrontare

standard /'stændəd/ adj standard; **be** ~ **practice** essere pratica corrente ● n standard m inv; (Techn) norma f; (level) livello m; (quality) qualità f inv; (flag) stendardo m; ~**s** pl (morals) valori mpl; ~ **of living** tenore m di vita. ~**ize** vt standardizzare

'**standard lamp** n lampada f a stelo

'**stand-by** n riserva f; **on** ~ (at airport) in lista d'attesa

'**stand-in** n controfigura f

standing /'stændɪŋ/ adj (erect) in piedi; (permanent) permanente ● n posizione f; (duration) durata f. ~ '**order** n addebitamento m diretto. ~**room** n posti mpl in piedi

stand: ~**point** n punto m di vista. ~**still** n come to a ~**still** fermarsi; **at a** ~**still** in un periodo di stasi

stank /stæŋk/ ▷**STINK**

staple¹ /'steɪpl/ n (product) prodotto m principale

staple² n graffa f ● vt pinzare. ~**r** n pinzatrice f, cucitrice f

star /stɑː(r)/ n stella f; (asterisk) asterisco m; (Cinema, Sport, Theat) divo, -a mf, stella f ● vi (pt/pp starred) essere l'interprete principale

starboard /'stɑːbəd/ n tribordo m

starch /stɑːtʃ/ n amido m ● vt inamidare. ~**y** adj ricco di amido; fig compito

stare /steə(r)/ n sguardo m fisso ● vi it's rude to ~ è da maleducati fissare la gente; ~ **at** fissare; ~ **into space** guardare nel vuoto

'**starfish** n stella f di mare

stark /stɑːk/ adj austero; (contrast) forte ● adv completamente; ~ **naked** completamente nudo

starling /'stɑːlɪŋ/ n storno m

starry /'stɑːrɪ/ adj stellato

start /stɑːt/ n inizio m; (departure) partenza f; (jump) sobbalzo m; from the ~ [fin] dall'inizio; for a ~ tanto per cominciare; **give sb a** ~ dare un vantaggio a qcno ● vi [in]cominciare; (set out) avviarsi; (engine, car:) partire; (jump) trasalire; to ~ **with,...** tanto per cominciare,... ● vt [in]cominciare; (cause) dare inizio a; (found) mettere su; mettere in moto (car); mettere in giro (rumour). ~**er** n (Culin) primo m [piatto m]; (in race: giving signal) starter m inv; (participant) concorrente mf; (Auto) motorino m d'avviamento. ~**ing-point** n punto m di partenza

startle /'stɑːtl/ vt far trasalire; (news:) sconvolgere

starvation /stɑː'veɪʃn/ n fame f

starve /stɑːv/ vi morire di fame ● vt far morire di fame

state /steɪt/ n stato m; (grand style) pompa f; ~ **of play** punteggio m; **be in a** ~ (person:) essere agitato;

lie in ~ essere esposto ● *attrib* di Stato; (*Sch*) pubblico; (*with ceremony*) di gala ● *vt* dichiarare; (*specify*) precisare. ~**less** *adj* apolide

stately /ˈsteɪtlɪ/ *adj* (**-ier, -iest**) maestoso. ~ '**home** *n* dimora *f* signorile

statement /ˈsteɪtmənt/ *n* dichiarazione *f*; (*Jur*) deposizione *f*; (*in banking*) estratto *m* conto; (*account*) rapporto *m*

---

state schools In Gran Bretagna sono le scuole elementari, medie e superiori pubbliche, contrapposte alle **public schools** (scuole private).

'**statesman** *n* statista *mf*

static /ˈstætɪk/ *adj* statico

station /ˈsteɪʃn/ *n* stazione *f*; (*police*) commissariato *m* ● *vt* appostare (*guard*); **be** ~**ed in Germany** essere di stanza in Germania. ~**ary** *adj* immobile

'**station-wagon** *n Am* familiare *f*

statistic|al /stəˈtɪstɪkl/ *adj* statistico. ~**s** *n & pl* statistica *f*

statue /ˈstætjuː/ *n* statua *f*

stature /ˈstætʃə(r)/ *n* statura *f*

status /ˈsteɪtəs/ *n* condizione *f*; (*high rank*) alto rango *m*. ~ **symbol** *n* status symbol *m inv*

statut|e /ˈstætjuːt/ *n* statuto *m*. ~**ory** *adj* statutario

staunch /stɔːntʃ/ *adj* fedele. ~**ly** *adv* fedelmente

stave /steɪv/ *vt* ~ **off** tenere lontano

stay /steɪ/ *n* soggiorno *m* ● *vi* restare, rimanere; (*reside*) alloggiare; ~ **the night** passare la notte; ~ **put** non muoversi ● *vt* ~ **the course** resistere fino alla fine. □ ~ **away** *vi* stare lontano. □ ~ **behind** *vi* non andare con gli altri. □ ~ **in** *vi* (*at home*) stare in casa; (*Sch*) restare a scuola dopo le

lezioni. □ ~ **up** *vi* stare su; (*person:*) stare alzato

stead /sted/ *n* **in his** ~ in sua vece; **stand sb in good** ~ tornare utile a qcno. ~**fast** *adj* fedele; (*refusal*) fermo

steadily /ˈstedɪlɪ/ *adv* (*continually*) continuamente

steady /ˈstedɪ/ *adj* (**-ier, -iest**) saldo, fermo; (*breathing*) regolare; (*job, boyfriend*) fisso; (*dependable*) serio

steak /steɪk/ *n* (*for stew*) spezzatino *m*; (*for grilling, frying*) bistecca *f*

steal /stiːl/ *v* (*pt* **stole**, *pp* **stolen**) ● *vt* rubare (**from** da). □ ~ **in/out** *vi* entrare/uscire furtivamente

stealth /stelθ/ *n* **by** ~ di nascosto. ~**y** *adj* furtivo

steam /stiːm/ *n* vapore *m*; **under one's own** ~ Ⅱ da solo ● *vt* (*Culin*) cucinare a vapore ● *vi* fumare. □ ~ **up** *vi* appannarsi

'**steam-engine** *n* locomotiva *f*

steamer /ˈstiːmə(r)/ *n* piroscafo *m*; (*saucepan*) pentola *f* a vapore

'**steamroller** *n* rullo *m* compressore

steamy /ˈstiːmɪ/ *adj* appannato

steel /stiːl/ *n* acciaio *m* ● *vt* ~ **oneself** temprarsi

steep[1] /stiːp/ *vt* (*soak*) lasciare a bagno

steep[2] /stiːp/ *adj* ripido; (Ⅱ: *price*) esorbitante. ~**ly** *adv* ripidamente

steeple /ˈstiːpl/ *n* campanile *m*. ~**chase** *n* corsa *f* ippica a ostacoli

steer /stɪə(r)/ *vt/i* guidare; ~ **clear of** stare alla larga da. ~**ing** *n* (*Auto*) sterzo *m*. ~**ing-wheel** *n* volante *m*

stem[1] /stem/ *n* stelo *m*; (*of glass*) gambo *m*; (*of word*) radice *f* ● *vi* (*pt/pp* **stemmed**) ~ **from** derivare da

stem[2] *vt* (*pt/pp* **stemmed**) contenere

stench /stentʃ/ *n* fetore *m*

step /step/ *n* passo *m*; (*stair*) gradino *m*; ~**s** *pl* (*ladder*) scala *f* portatile; **in**

stepping-stone | stink

~ **al passo; be out of** ~ non stare al passo; ~ **by** ~ un passo alla volta ●*vi* (*pt/pp* **stepped**) ~ **into** entrare in; ~ **out of** uscire da; ~ **out of line** sgarrare. □ ~ **down** *vi fig* dimettersi. □ ~ **forward** *vi* farsi avanti. □ ~ **in** *vi fig* intervenire. □ ~ **up** *vt* (*increase*) aumentare

step: ~**brother** *n* fratellastro *m*. ~**daughter** *n* figliastra *f*. ~**father** *n* patrigno *m*. ~**ladder** *n* scala *f* portatile. ~**mother** *n* matrigna *f*

'**stepping-stone** *n* pietra *f* per guadare; *fig* trampolino *m*

step: ~**sister** *n* sorellastra *f*. ~**son** *n* figliastro *m*

stereo /'steriəʊ/ *n* stereo *m*; **in** ~ **in** stereofonia. ~**phonic** *adj* stereofonico

stereotype /'steriətaip/ *n* stereotipo *m*. ~**d** *adj* stereotipato

steril|e /'sterail/ *adj* sterile. ~**ity** *n* sterilità *f inv*

sterling /'stɜ:lɪŋ/ *adj fig* apprezzabile; ~ **silver** argento *m* pregiato ●*n* sterlina *f*

stern¹ /stɜ:n/ *adj* severo

stern² *n* (*of boat*) poppa *f*

stethoscope /'steθəskəʊp/ *n* stetoscopio *m*

stew /stju:/ *n* stufato *m*; **in a** ~ *fig* agitato ●*vt/i* cuocere in umido; ~**ed fruit** frutta *f* cotta

steward /'stjʊəd/ *n* (*at meeting*) organizzatore, -trice *mf*; (*on ship, aircraft*) steward *m inv*. ~**ess** *n* hostess *f inv*

stick¹ /stɪk/ *n* bastone *m*; (*of celery, rhubarb*) gambo *m*; (*Sport*) mazza *f*

stick² *v* (*pt/pp* **stuck**) ●*vt* (*stab*) [con]ficcare; (*glue*) attaccare; (฿: *put*) mettere; (฿: *endure*) sopportare ●*vi* (*adhere*) attaccarsi (**to** a); (*jam*) bloccarsi; ~ **to** attenersi a (*facts*); mantenere (*story*); perseverare in (*task*); ~ **at it** ฿ tener duro; ~ **at nothing** ฿ non fermarsi di fronte a niente; **be stuck** (*vehicle, person*:)

essere bloccato; (*drawer*:) essere incastrato; **be stuck with sth** ฿ farsi incastrare con qcsa. □ ~ **out** *vi* (*project*) sporgere; (฿: *catch the eye*) risaltare ●*vt* ฿ fare (*tongue*). □ ~ **up for** *vt* ฿ difendere

sticker /'stɪkə(r)/ *n* autoadesivo *m*

'**sticking plaster** *n* cerotto *m*

stickler /'stɪklə(r)/ *n* **be a** ~ **for** tenere molto a

sticky /'stɪkɪ/ *adj* (**-ier, -iest**) appiccicoso; (*adhesive*) adesivo; (*fig: difficult*) difficile

stiff /stɪf/ *adj* rigido; (*brush, task*) duro; (*person*) controllato; (*drink*) forte; (*penalty*) severo; (*price*) alto; **bored** ~ ฿ annoiato a morte; ~ **neck** torcicollo *m*. ~**en** *vt* irrigidire ●*vi* irrigidirsi. ~**ness** *n* rigidità *f inv*

stifl|e /'staifl/ *vt* soffocare. ~**ing** *adj* soffocante

still¹ /stɪl/ *n* distilleria *f*

still² *adj* fermo; (*drink*) non gasato; **keep/stand** ~ stare fermo ●*n* quiete *f*; (*photo*) posa *f* ●*adv* ancora; (*nevertheless*) nondimeno, comunque; **I'm** ~ **not sure** non sono ancora sicuro

'**stillborn** *adj* nato morto

still 'life *n* natura *f* morta

stilted /'stɪltɪd/ *adj* artificioso

stilts /stɪlts/ *npl* trampoli *mpl*

stimulant /'stɪmjʊlənt/ *n* eccitante *m*

stimulat|e /'stɪmjʊleɪt/ *vt* stimolare. ~**ion** *n* stimolo *m*

stimulus /'stɪmjʊləs/ *n* (*pl* **-li** /-laɪ/) stimolo *m*

sting /stɪŋ/ *n* puntura *f*; (*from nettle, jellyfish*) sostanza *f* irritante; (*organ*) pungiglione *m* ●*v* (*pt/pp* **stung**) ●*vt* pungere; (*jellyfish*:) pizzicare ●*vi* (*insect*:) pungere. ~**ing nettle** *n* ortica *f*

stingy /'stɪndʒɪ/ *adj* (**-ier, -iest**) tirchio

stink /stɪŋk/ *n* puzza *f* ●*vi* (*pt* **stank,**

s

pp **stunk**) puzzare

stipulat|e /'stɪpjʊleɪt/ *vt* porre come condizione. **~ion** *n* condizione *f*

stir /stɜː(r)/ *n* mescolata *f*; (*commotion*) trambusto *m* ● *v* (*pt/pp* **stirred**) ● *vt* muovere; (*mix*) mescolare ● *vi* muoversi

stirrup /'stɪrəp/ *n* staffa *f*

stitch /stɪtʃ/ *n* punto *m*; (*in knitting*) maglia *f*; (*pain*) fitta *f*; **have sb in ~es** 🆎 far ridere qcno a crepapelle ● *vt* cucire

stock /stɒk/ *n* (*for use or selling*) scorta *f*, stock *m inv*; (*livestock*) bestiame *m*; (*lineage*) stirpe *f*; (*Fin*) titoli *mpl*; (*Culin*) brodo *m*; **in ~** disponibile; **out of ~** esaurito; **take ~** *fig* fare il punto ● *adj* solito ● *vt* (*shop*:) vendere; approvvigionare (*shelves*). □ **~ up** *vi* far scorta (**with** di)

stock: **~broker** *n* agente *m* di cambio. **S~ Exchange** *n* Borsa *f* Valori

stocking /'stɒkɪŋ/ *n* calza *f*

stock: **~pile** *vt* fare scorta di ● *n* riserva *f*. **~-still** *adj* immobile. **~-taking** *n* (*Comm*) inventario *m*

stocky /'stɒkɪ/ *adj* (**-ier, -iest**) tarchiato

stodgy /'stɒdʒɪ/ *adj* indigesto

stoke /stəʊk/ *vt* alimentare

stole¹ /stəʊl/ *n* stola *f*

stole², **stolen** /stəʊln/ ▷**STEAL**

stomach /'stʌmək/ *n* pancia *f*; (*Anat*) stomaco *m* ● *vt* 🆎 reggere. **~-ache** *n* mal *m* di pancia

stone /stəʊn/ *n* pietra *f*; (*in fruit*) nocciolo *m*; (*Med*) calcolo *m*; (*weight*) *6,348 kg* ● *adj* di pietra; (*wall, Age*) della pietra ● *vt* snocciolare (*fruit*). **~-cold** *adj* gelido. **~-'deaf** *adj* 🆎 sordo come una campana

stony /'stəʊnɪ/ *adj* pietroso; (*glare*) glaciale

stood /stʊd/ ▷**STAND**

stool /stuːl/ *n* sgabello *m*

stoop /stuːp/ *n* curvatura *f* ● *vi* stare curvo; (*bend down*) chinarsi; *fig* abbassarsi

stop /stɒp/ *n* (*break*) sosta *f*; (*for bus, train*) fermata *f*; (*Gram*) punto *m*; **come to a ~** fermarsi; **put a ~ to sth** mettere fine a qcsa ● *v* (*pt/pp* **stopped**) ● *vt* fermare; arrestare (*machine*); (*prevent*) impedire; **~ sb doing sth** impedire a qcno di fare qcsa; **~ doing sth** smettere di fare qcsa; **~ that!** smettila! ● *vi* fermarsi; (*rain*:) smettere ● *int* fermo!. □ **~ off** *vi* fare una sosta. □ **~ up** *vt* otturare (*sink*); tappare (*hole*). □ **~ with** *vi* fermarsi da

stop: **~gap** *n* palliativo *m*; (*person*) tappabuchi *m inv*. **~-over** *n* sosta *f*; (*Aeron*) scalo *m*

stoppage /'stɒpɪdʒ/ *n* ostruzione *f*; (*strike*) interruzione *f*; (*deduction*) trattenute *fpl*

stopper /'stɒpə(r)/ *n* tappo *m*

stop-watch *n* cronometro *m*

storage /'stɔːrɪdʒ/ *n* deposito *m*; (*in warehouse*) immagazzinaggio *m*; (*Comput*) memoria *f*

store /stɔː(r)/ *n* (*stock*) riserva *f*; (*shop*) grande magazzino *m*; (*depot*) deposito *m*; **in ~** in deposito; **what the future has in ~ for me** cosa mi riserva il futuro; **set great ~ by** tenere in gran conto ● *vt* tenere; (*in warehouse, Comput*) immagazzinare. **~-room** *n* magazzino *m*

storey /'stɔːrɪ/ *n* piano *m*

stork /stɔːk/ *n* cicogna *f*

storm /stɔːm/ *n* temporale *m*; (*with thunder*) tempesta *f* ● *vt* prendere d'assalto. **~y** *adj* tempestoso

story /'stɔːrɪ/ *n* storia *f*; (*in newspaper*) articolo *m*

stout /staʊt/ *adj* (*shoes*) resistente; (*fat*) robusto; (*defence*) strenuo

stove /stəʊv/ *n* stufa *f*; (*for cooking*) cucina *f* [*economica*]

stow /stəʊ/ *vt* metter via. **~away** *n*

passeggero, -a *mf* clandestino, -a

straggl|e /'stræg,l/ *vi* crescere disordinatamente; (*dawdle*) rimanere indietro. ~**er** *n* persona *f* che rimane indietro. ~**y** *adj* in disordine

straight /streɪt/ *adj* diritto, dritto; (*answer, question, person*) diretto; (*tidy*) in ordine; (*drink, hair*) liscio ● *adv* diritto, dritto; (*directly*) direttamente; ~ **away** immediatamente; ~ **on** *or* **ahead** diritto; ~ **out** *fig* apertamente; **go** ~ 🄸 rigare diritto; **put sth** ~ mettere qcsa in ordine; **sit/stand up** ~ stare diritto

straighten /'streɪtn/ *vt* raddrizzare ● *vi* raddrizzarsi; ~ **[up]** (*person:*) mettersi diritto. □ ~ **out** *vt fig* chiarire (*situation*)

straight'forward *adj* franco; (*simple*) semplice

strain[1] /streɪn/ *n* (*streak*) vena *f*; (*Bot*) varietà *f inv*; (*of virus*) forma *f*

strain[2] *n* tensione *f*; (*injury*) stiramento *m*. ~**s** *pl* (*of music*) note *fpl* ● *vt* tirare; sforzare (*eyes, voice*); stirarsi (*muscle*); (*Culin*) scolare ● *vi* sforzarsi. ~**ed** *adj* (*relations*) teso. ~**er** *n* colino *m*

strait /streɪt/ *n* stretto *m*; **in dire** ~**s** in serie difficoltà. ~**jacket** *n* camicia *f* di forza. ~**-laced** *adj* puritano

strand[1] /strænd/ *n* (*of thread*) gugliata *f*; (*of beads*) filo *m*; (*of hair*) capello *m*

strand[2] *vt* **be** ~**ed** rimanere bloccato

strange /streɪndʒ/ *adj* strano; (*not known*) sconosciuto; (*unaccustomed*) estraneo. ~**ly** *adv* stranamente; ~ **ly enough** curiosamente. ~**r** *n* estraneo, -a *mf*

strangle /'stræŋgl/ *vt* strangolare, *fig* reprimere

strap /stræp/ *n* cinghia *f* (*to grasp in vehicle*) maniglia *f*; (*of watch*) cinturino *m*; (*shoulder* ~) bretella *f*, spallina *f* ● *vt*

(*pt/pp* **strapped**) legare; ~ **in** *or* **down** assicurare

strategic /strəˈtiːdʒɪk/ *adj* strategico

strategy /'strætədʒɪ/ *n* strategia *f*

straw /strɔː/ *n* paglia *f*; (*single piece*) fuscello *m*; (*for drinking*) cannuccia *f*; **the last** ~ l'ultima goccia

strawberry /'strɔːbərɪ/ *n* fragola *f*

stray /streɪ/ *adj* (*animal*) randagio ● *n* randagio *m* ● *vi* andarsene per conto proprio; (*deviate*) deviare (*from* da)

streak /striːk/ *n* striatura *f*; (*fig: trait*) vena *f* ● *vi* sfrecciare. ~**y** *adj* striato; (*bacon*) grasso

stream /striːm/ *n* ruscello *m*; (*current*) corrente *f*; (*of blood, people*) flusso *m*; (*Sch*) classe *f* ● *vi* scorrere. □ ~ **in/out** *vi* entrare/uscire a fiotti

streamer /'striːmə(r)/ *n* (*paper*) stella *f* filante; (*flag*) pennone *m*

'streamline *vt* rendere aerodinamico; (*simplify*) snellire. ~**d** *adj* aerodinamico

street /striːt/ *n* strada *f*. ~**car** *n Am* tram *m inv*. ~**lamp** *n* lampione *m*

strength /streŋθ/ *n* forza *f*; (*of wall, bridge etc*) solidità *f inv*; ~**s** punti *mpl* forti; **on the** ~ **of** grazie a. ~**en** *vt* rinforzare

strenuous /'strenjʊəs/ *adj* faticoso; (*attempt, denial*) energico

stress /stres/ *n* (*emphasis*) insistenza *f*; (*Gram*) accento *m* tonico; (*mental*) stress *m inv*; (*Mech*) spinta *f* ● *vt* (*emphasize*) insistere su; (*Gram*) mettere l'accento [tonico] su. ~**ed** *adj* (*mentally*) stressato. ~**ful** *adj* stressante

stretch /stretʃ/ *n* stiramento *m*; (*period*) periodo *m* di tempo; (*of road*) estensione *f*; (*elasticity*) elasticità *f inv*; **at a** ~ di fila; **have a** ~ stirarsi ● *vt* tirare; allargare (*shoes, arms etc*); (*person:*) allungare ● *vi* (*become wider*) allargarsi; (*extend*) estendersi; (*person:*) stirarsi. ~**er** *n* barella *f*

strict /strɪkt/ *adj* severo; (*precise*)

preciso. ~ly *adv* severamente; ~ly speaking in senso stretto

stride /straɪd/ n [lungo] passo m; take sth in one's ~ accettare qcsa con facilità ● vi (pt strode, pp stridden) andare a gran passi

strident /'straɪdənt/ adj stridente; (colour) vistoso

strife /straɪf/ n conflitto m

strike /straɪk/ n sciopero m; (Mil) attacco m; on ~ in sciopero ● v (pt/pp struck) ● vt colpire; accendere (match); trovare (oil, gold); (delete) depennare; (occur to) venire in mente a; (Mil) attaccare ● vi (lightning:) cadere; (clock:) suonare; (Mil) attaccare; (workers:) scioperare; ~ lucky azzeccarla. □ ~ off, strike out ● vt eliminare. □ ~ up vt fare (friendship); attaccare (conversation). ~-breaker n persona f che non aderisce a uno sciopero

striker /'straɪkə(r)/ n scioperante mf

striking /'straɪkɪŋ/ adj impressionante; (attractive) affascinante

string /strɪŋ/ n spago m; (of musical instrument, racket) corda f; (of pearls) filo m; (of lies) serie f; the ~s (Mus) gli archi; pull ~s 🔢 usare le proprie conoscenze ● vt (pt/pp strung) (thread) infilare (beads). ~ed adj (instrument) a corda

stringent /'strɪndʒənt/ adj rigido che

strip /strɪp/ n striscia f ● v (pt/pp stripped) ● vt spogliare; togliere le lenzuola da (bed); scrostare (paint, furniture); smontare (machine); (deprive) privare (of di) ● vi (undress) spogliarsi. ~ cartoon n striscia f. ~ club n locale m di strip-tease

stripe /straɪp/ n striscia f; (Mil) gallone m. ~d adj a strisce

strip-'tease n spogliarello m, striptease m inv

strive /straɪv/ vi (pt strove, pp striven) sforzarsi (to di); ~ for sforzarsi di ottenere

strode /strəʊd/ ▷STRIDE

stroke¹ /strəʊk/ n colpo m; (of pen) tratto m; (in swimming) bracciata f; (Med) ictus m inv; ~ of luck colpo m di fortuna; put sb off his ~ far perdere il filo a qcno

stroke² vt accarezzare

stroll /strəʊl/ n passeggiata f ● vi passeggiare. ~er n (Am: push-chair) passeggino m

strong /strɒŋ/ adj (-er /-gə(r)/, -est /-gɪst/) forte; (argument) valido

strong-~hold n roccaforte f. ~ly adv fortemente. ~-room n camera f blindata

stroppy /'strɒpɪ/ adj scorbutico

strove /strəʊv/ ▷STRIVE

struck /strʌk/ ▷STRIKE

structural /'strʌktʃərəl/ adj strutturale. ~ly adv strutturalmente

structure /'strʌktʃə(r)/ n struttura f

struggle /'strʌgl/ n lotta f; with a ~ lottare con ● vi lottare; ~ for breath respirare con fatica; ~ to do sth fare fatica a fare qcsa; ~ to one's feet alzarsi con fatica

strum /strʌm/ vt (pt/pp strummed) strimpellare

strung /strʌŋ/ ▷STRING

strut¹ /strʌt/ n (component) puntello m

strut² vi (pt/pp strutted) camminare impettito

stub /stʌb/ n mozzicone m; (counterfoil) matrice f ● vt (pt/pp stubbed) ~ one's toe sbattere il dito del piede (on contro). □ ~ out vt spegnere (cigarette)

stubble /'stʌbl/ n barba f ispida. ~ly adj ispido

stubborn /'stʌbən/ adj testardo; (refusal) ostinato

stuck /stʌk/ ▷STICK². ~-'up adj 🔢 snob

stud¹ /stʌd/ n (on boot) tacchetto m;

(on jacket) borchia f; (for ear) orecchino m [a bottone]

stud² n (of horses) scuderia f

student /ˈstjuːdənt/ n studente m, studentessa f; (school child) scolaro, -a mf. ~ **nurse** n studente, studentessa infermiere, -a

studio /ˈstjuːdɪəʊ/ n studio m

studious /ˈstjuːdɪəs/ adj studioso; (attention) studiato

study /ˈstʌdɪ/ n studio m ● vt/i (pt/pp studied) studiare

stuff /stʌf/ n materiale m; (🔲: things) roba f ● vt riempire; (with padding) imbottire; (Culin) farcire; ~ **sth into a drawer/one's pocket** ficcare qcsa alla rinfusa in un cassetto/in tasca. ~**ing** n (padding) imbottitura f; (Culin) ripieno m

stuffy /ˈstʌfɪ/ adj (-ier, -iest) che sa di chiuso; (old-fashioned) antiquato

stumble /ˈstʌmbl/ vi inciampare; ~**e across** or **on** imbattersi in. ~**ing-block** n ostacolo m

stump /stʌmp/ n ceppo m; (of limb) moncone m. ~**ed** adj 🔲 perplesso ● **stump up** vt/i 🔲 sganciare

stun /stʌn/ vt (pt/pp **stunned**) stordire; (astonish) sbalordire

stung /stʌŋ/ ▷ **STING**

stunk /stʌŋk/ ▷ **STINK**

stunning /ˈstʌnɪŋ/ adj 🔲 favoloso; (blow, victory) sbalorditivo

stunt¹ /stʌnt/ n 🔲 trovata f pubblicitaria

stunt² vt arrestare lo sviluppo di. ~**ed** adj stentato

stupendous /stjuːˈpendəs/ adj stupendo. ~**ly** adv stupendamente

stupid /ˈstjuːpɪd/ adj stupido. ~**ity** n stupidità f. ~**ly** adv stupidamente

stupor /ˈstjuːpə(r)/ n torpore m

sturdy /ˈstɜːdɪ/ adj (-ier, -iest) robusto; (furniture) solido

stutter /ˈstʌtə(r)/ n balbuzie f ● vt/i balbettare

sty, stye /staɪ/ n (pl **styes**) (Med) orzaiolo m

style /staɪl/ n stile m; (fashion) moda f; (sort) tipo m; (hair~) pettinatura f; **in** ~ in grande stile

stylish /ˈstaɪlɪʃ/ adj elegante. ~**ly** adv con eleganza

stylist /ˈstaɪlɪst/ n stilista mf; (hair~) parrucchiere, -a mf. ~**ic** adj stilistico

stylus /ˈstaɪləs/ n (on record player) puntina f

suave /swɑːv/ adj dai modi garbati

subconscious /sʌb-/ adj subcosciente ● n subcosciente m. ~**ly** adv in modo inconscio

subdivide vt suddividere. ~**sion** n suddivisione f

subject¹ /ˈsʌbdʒɪkt/ adj ~ **to** soggetto a; (depending on) subordinato a; ~ **to availability** nei limiti della disponibilità ● n soggetto m; (of ruler) suddito, -a mf; (Sch) materia f

subject² /səbˈdʒekt/ vt (to attack, abuse) sottoporre; assoggettare (country)

subjective /səbˈdʒektɪv/ adj soggettivo. ~**ly** adv soggettivamente

subjunctive /səbˈdʒʌŋktɪv/ adj & n congiuntivo m

sublime /səˈblaɪm/ adj sublime. ~**ly** adv sublimemente

submarine /ˈsʌbməriːn/ n sommergibile m

submerge /səbˈmɜːdʒ/ vt immergere; **be** ~**d** essere sommerso ● vi immergersi

submission /səbˈmɪʃn/ n sottomissione f. ~**ive** adj sottomesso

submit /səbˈmɪt/ v (pt/pp -mitted, pres p -mitting) ● vt sottoporre ● vi sottomettersi

subordinate /səˈbɔːdɪnət/ vt subordinare (to a)

subscribe /səbˈskraɪb/ vi contribuire; ~ **to** abbonarsi a (newspaper); sottoscrivere (fund); fig aderire a. ~**r** n abbonato, -a mf

subscription /səb'skrɪpʃn/ n (to club) sottoscrizione f; (to newspaper) abbonamento m

subsequent /'sʌbsɪkwənt/ adj susseguente. ~ly adv in seguito

subside /səb'saɪd/ vi sprofondare; (ground:) avvallarsi; (storm:) placarsi

subsidiary /səb'sɪdɪərɪ/ adj secondario ● n ~ [company] filiale f

subsid|ize /'sʌbsɪdaɪz/ vt sovvenzionare. ~y n sovvenzione f

substance /'sʌbstəns/ n sostanza f

sub'standard adj di qualità inferiore

substantial /səb'stænʃl/ adj solido; (meal) sostanzioso; (considerable) notevole. ~ly adv notevolmente; (essentially) sostanzialmente

substitut|e /'sʌbstɪtjuːt/ n sostituto m ● vt ~e A for B sostituire B con A ● vi ~e for sb sostituire qcno. ~ion n sostituzione f

subterranean /sʌbtə'reɪnɪən/ adj sotterraneo

'subtitle n sottotitolo m

sub|tle /'sʌtl/ adj sottile; (taste, perfume) delicato. ~tlety n sottigliezza f. ~tly adv sottilmente

subtract /səb'trækt/ vt sottrarre. ~ion n sottrazione f

suburb /'sʌbɜːb/ n sobborgo m; in the ~s in periferia. ~an adj suburbano. ~ia n sobborghi mpl

subversive /səb'vɜːsɪv/ adj sovversivo

'subway n sottopassaggio m; (Am: railway) metropolitana f

succeed /sək'siːd/ vi riuscire; (follow) succedere a; ~ in doing riuscire a fare ● vt succedere a (king). ~ing adj successivo

success /sək'ses/ n successo m; be a ~ (in life) aver successo. ~ful adj riuscito; (businessman, artist etc) di successo. ~fully adv con successo

succession /sək'seʃn/ n successione f; in ~ di seguito

successive /sək'sesɪv/ adj successivo. ~ly adv successivamente

successor /sək'sesə(r)/ n successore m

succulent /'sʌkjʊlənt/ adj succulento

succumb /sə'kʌm/ vi soccombere (to a)

such /sʌtʃ/ adj tale; ~ a book un libro di questo genere; ~ a thing una cosa di questo genere; ~ a long time ago tanto tempo fa; there is no ~ thing non esiste una cosa così; there is no ~ person non esiste una persona così ● pron as ~ come tale; ~ as chi; and ~ e simili; ~ as it is così com'è. ~like adj 🔲 di tal genere

suck /sʌk/ vt succhiare. □ ~ up vt assorbire. □ ~ up to vt 🔲 fare il lecchino con

sucker /'sʌkə(r)/ n (Bot) pollone m; (🔲: person) credulone, -a mf

suction /'sʌkʃn/ n aspirazione f

sudden /'sʌdn/ adj improvviso ● n all of a ~ all'improvviso. ~ly adv improvvisamente

sue /suː/ vt (pres p suing) fare causa a (for per) ● vi fare causa

suede /sweɪd/ n pelle f scamosciata

suet /'suːɪt/ n grasso m di rognone

suffer /'sʌfə(r)/ vi soffrire (from per) ● vt soffrire; subire (loss etc); (tolerate) subire. ~ing n sofferenza f

suffice /sə'faɪs/ vi bastare

sufficient /sə'fɪʃənt/ adj sufficiente. ~ly adv sufficientemente

suffix /'sʌfɪks/ n suffisso m

suffocat|e /'sʌfəkeɪt/ vt/i soffocare. ~ion n soffocamento m

sugar /'ʃʊgə(r)/ n zucchero m ● vt zuccherare. ~ basin, ~-bowl n zuccheriera f. ~y adj zuccheroso; fig sdolcinato

suggest /sə'dʒest/ vt suggerire; (indicate, insinuate) fare pensare a. ~ion n suggerimento m; (trace) traccia f.

~**ive** *adj* allusivo. ~**ively** *adv* in modo allusivo

suicidal /suːɪˈsaɪdl/ *adj* suicida

suicide /ˈsuːɪsaɪd/ *n* suicidio *m*; (person) suicida *mf*; **commit** ~ suicidarsi

suit /suːt/ *n* vestito *m*; (woman's) tailleur *m inv*; (in cards) seme *m*; (Jur) causa *f*; **follow** ~ *fig* fare lo stesso ● *vt* andare bene a; (adapt) adattare (to a); (be convenient for) andare bene per; **be** ~**ed to** *or* **for** essere adatto a; ~ **yourself!** fa' come vuoi!

suitabl|e /ˈsuːtəbl/ *adj* adatto. ~**y** *adv* convenientemente

'**suitcase** *n* valigia *f*

suite /swiːt/ *n* suite *f inv*; (of furniture) divano *m* e poltrone *fpl* assortiti

sulk /sʌlk/ *vi* fare il broncio. ~**y** *adj* imbronciato

sullen /ˈsʌlən/ *adj* svogliato

sulphur /ˈsʌlfə(r)/ *n* zolfo *m*. ~**ic acid** *n* acido *m* solforico

sultana /sʌlˈtɑːnə/ *n* uva *f* sultanina

sultry /ˈsʌltrɪ/ *adj* (-ier, -iest) (weather) afoso; *fig* sensuale

sum /sʌm/ *n* somma *f*; (Sch) addizione *f* ● ~ **up** (pt/pp summed) *vi* riassumere ● *vt* valutare

summar|ize /ˈsʌməraɪz/ *vt* riassumere. ~**y** *n* sommario *m* ● *adj* sommario; (dismissal) sbrigativo

summer /ˈsʌmə(r)/ *n* estate *f*. ~**house** *n* padiglione *m*. ~**time** *n* (season) estate *f*

summery /ˈsʌmərɪ/ *adj* estivo

summit /ˈsʌmɪt/ *n* cima *f*. ~**conference** *n* vertice *m*

summon /ˈsʌmən/ *vt* convocare; (Jur) citare. □ ~ **up** *vt* raccogliere (strength); rievocare (memory)

summons /ˈsʌmənz/ *n* (Jur) citazione *f* ● *vt* citare in giudizio

sumptuous /ˈsʌmptjʊəs/ *adj* sontuoso. ~**ly** *adv* sontuosamente

sun /sʌn/ *n* sole *m* ● *vt* (pt/pp sunned) ~ **oneself** prendere il sole

sun: ~**bathe** *vi* prendere il sole. ~**burn** *n* scottatura *f* (solare). ~**burnt** *adj* scottato (dal sole)

Sunday /ˈsʌndeɪ/ *n* domenica *f*

'**sunflower** *n* girasole *m*

sung /sʌŋ/ ▷SING

'**sun-glasses** *npl* occhiali *mpl* da sole

sunk /sʌŋk/ ▷SINK

sunken /ˈsʌŋkn/ *adj* incavato

'**sunlight** *n* luce *f* del sole

sunny /ˈsʌnɪ/ *adj* (-ier, -iest) assolato

sun: ~**rise** *n* alba *f*. ~**roof** *n* (Auto) tettuccio *m* apribile. ~**set** *n* tramonto *m*. ~**shine** *n* luce *f* del sole *m*. ~**stroke** *n* insolazione *f*. ~**tan** *n* abbronzatura *f*. ~**tan oil** *n* olio *m* solare

super /ˈsuːpə(r)/ *adj* fam fantastico

superb /sʊˈpɜːb/ *adj* splendido

supercilious /suːpəˈsɪlɪəs/ *adj* altezzoso

superficial /suːpəˈfɪʃl/ *adj* superficiale. ~**ly** *adv* superficialmente

superfluous /sʊˈpɜːflʊəs/ *adj* superfluo

super'human *adj* sovrumano

superintendent /suːpərɪnˈtendənt/ *n* (of police) commissario *m* di polizia

superior /sʊˈpɪərɪə(r)/ *adj* superiore ● *n* superiore, -a *mf*. ~**ity** *n* superiorità *f*

superlative /suːˈpɜːlətɪv/ *adj* eccellente ● *n* superlativo *m*

'**supermarket** *n* supermercato *m*

super'natural adj soprannaturale

'superpower n superpotenza f

supersede /suːpəˈsiːd/ vt rimpiazzare

super'sonic adj supersonico

superstiti|on /suːpəˈstɪʃn/ n superstizione f. **~ous** adj superstizioso

supervis|e /ˈsuːpəvaɪz/ vt supervisionare. **~ion** n supervisione f. **~or** n supervisore m

supper /ˈsʌpə(r)/ n cena f

supple /ˈsʌpl/ adj slogato

supplement /ˈsʌplɪmənt/ n supplemento m ● vt integrare. **~ary** adj supplementare

supplier /səˈplaɪə(r)/ n fornitore, -trice mf

supply /səˈplaɪ/ n fornitura f; (in economics) offerta f; **supplies** pl (Mil) approvvigionamenti m ● vt (pt/pp -ied) fornire; **~ sb with sth** fornire qcsa a qcno

support /səˈpɔːt/ n sostegno m; (base) supporto m; (keep) sostentamento m ● vt sostenere; mantenere (family); (give money to) mantenere finanziariamente; (Sport) fare il tifo per. **~er** n sostenitore, -trice mf; (Sport) tifoso, -a mf. **~ive** adj incoraggiante

suppose /səˈpəʊz/ vt (presume) supporre; (imagine) pensare; **be ~d to do** dover fare; **not be ~d to** 🔲 non avere il permesso di; **I ~ so** suppongo di sì. **~dly** adv presumibilmente

suppress /səˈpres/ vt sopprimere. **~ion** n soppressione f

supremacy /suːˈpreməsɪ/ n supremazia f

supreme /suːˈpriːm/ adj supremo

sure /ʃʊə(r)/ adj sicuro, certo; **make ~** accertarsi; **be ~ to do it** mi raccomando di farlo ● adv Am 🔲 certamente; **~ enough** infatti. **~ly** adv certamente, (Am: gladly) volentieri

surety /ˈʃʊərətɪ/ n garanzia f; **stand**

~ for garantire

surf /sɜːf/ n schiuma f ● vt (Comput) **~ the Net** surfare in Internet

surface /ˈsɜːfɪs/ n superficie f; **on the ~** fig in apparenza ● vi (emerge) emergere. **~ mail** n **by ~ mail** per posta ordinaria

'surfboard n tavola f da surf

surfing /ˈsɜːfɪŋ/ n surf m inv

surge /sɜːdʒ/ n (of sea) ondata f; (of interest) aumento m; (in demand) impennata f; (of anger, pity) impeto m ● vi riversarsi; **~ forward** buttarsi in avanti

surgeon /ˈsɜːdʒən/ n chirurgo m

surgery /ˈsɜːdʒərɪ/ n chirurgia f; (place, consulting room) ambulatorio m; (hours) ore fpl di visita; **have ~** subire un'intervento [chirurgico]

surgical /ˈsɜːdʒɪkl/ adj chirurgico

surly /ˈsɜːlɪ/ adj (-ier, -iest) scontroso

surmise /səˈmaɪz/ vt supporre

surmount /səˈmaʊnt/ vt sormontare

surname /ˈsɜːneɪm/ n cognome m

surpass /səˈpɑːs/ vt superare

surplus /ˈsɜːpləs/ adj d'avanzo ● n sovrappiù m

surprise /səˈpraɪz/ n sorpresa f ● vt sorprendere; **be ~ed** essere sorpreso (**at** da). **~ing** adj sorprendente. **~ingly** adv sorprendentemente

surrender /səˈrendə(r)/ n resa f ● vi arrendersi ● vt cedere

surreptitious /sʌrəpˈtɪʃəs/ adj & adv di nascosto

surround /səˈraʊnd/ vt circondare. **~ing** adj circostante. **~ings** npl dintorni mpl

surveillance /səˈveɪləns/ n sorveglianza f

survey¹ /ˈsɜːveɪ/ n sguardo m; (poll) sondaggio m; (investigation) indagine f; (of land) rilevamento m; (of house) perizia f

survey² /sə'veɪ/ vt esaminare; fare un rilevamento di (land); fare una perizia di (building); fare una perizia di (building). **~or** n perito m; (of land) topografo, -a mf

survival /sə'vaɪvl/ n sopravvivenza f; (relic) resto m

surviv|e /sə'vaɪv/ vt sopravvivere a ● vi sopravvivere. **~or** n superstite mf; **be a ~or** fig riuscire sempre a cavarsela

susceptible /sə'septəbl/ adj influenzabile; **~ to** sensibile a

suspect¹ /sə'spekt/ vt sospettare; (assume) supporre

suspect² /'sʌspekt/ adj & n sospetto, -a mf

suspend /sə'spend/ vt appendere; (stop, from duty) sospendere. **~er belt** n reggicalze m inv. **~ers** npl giarrettiere fpl; (Am: braces) bretelle mpl

suspense /sə'spens/ n tensione f; (in book etc) suspense f

suspension /sə'spenʃn/ n (Auto) sospensione f. **~ bridge** n ponte m sospeso

suspici|on /sə'spɪʃn/ n sospetto m; (trace) pizzico m; **under ~on** sospettato. **~ous** adj sospettoso; (arousing suspicion) sospetto. **~ously** adv sospettosamente; (arousing suspicion) in modo sospetto

sustain /sə'steɪn/ vt sostenere; mantenere (life); subire (injury)

swab /swɒb/ n (Med) tampone m

swagger /'swægə(r)/ vi pavoneggiarsi

swallow¹ /'swɒləʊ/ vt/i inghiottire. **□ ~ up** vt divorare; (earth, crowd:) inghiottire

swallow² n (bird) rondine f

swam /swæm/ ▷**SWIM**

swamp /swɒmp/ n palude f ● vt fig sommergere. **~y** adj paludoso

swan /swɒn/ n cigno m

swap /swɒp/ n scambio m ● vt (pt/pp swapped) ① scambiare (for con) ● vi fare cambio

swarm /swɔːm/ n sciame m ● vi sciamare; **be ~ing with** brulicare di

swarthy /'swɔːðɪ/ adj (-ier, -iest) di carnagione scura

swat /swɒt/ vt (pt/pp swatted) schiacciare

sway /sweɪ/ n fig influenza f ● vi oscillare; (person:) ondeggiare ● vt (influence) influenzare

swear /sweə(r)/ v (pt swore, pp sworn) vt giurare ● vi giurare; (curse) dire parolacce; **~ at sb** imprecare contro qcno; **~ by** ① credere ciecamente in. **~-word** n parolaccia f

sweat /swet/ n sudore m ● vi sudare

sweater /'swetə(r)/ n golf m inv

swede /swiːd/ n rapa f svedese

Swed|e n svedese mf. **~en** n Svezia f. **~ish** adj svedese

sweep /swiːp/ n scopata f, spazzata f; (curve) curva f; (movement) movimento m ampio; **make a clean ~** fig fare piazza pulita ● v (pt/pp swept) ● vt scopare, spazzare; (wind:) spazzare ● vi (go swiftly) andare rapidamente; (wind:) soffiare. **□ ~ away** vt fig spazzare via. **□ ~ up** vt spazzare

sweeping /'swiːpɪŋ/ adj (gesture) ampio; (statement) generico; (changes) radicale

sweet /swiːt/ adj dolce; **have a ~ tooth** essere goloso ● n caramella f; (dessert) dolce m. **~ corn** n mais m

sweeten /'swiːtn/ vt addolcire. **~er** n dolcificante m

sweetheart n innamorato, -a mf; **hi, ~** ciao, tesoro

swell /swel/ v (pt swelled, pp swollen or swelled) ● vi gonfiarsi; (increase) aumentare ● vt gonfiare; (increase) far salire. **~ing** n gonfiore m

swept /swept/ ▷**SWEEP**

swerve /swɜːv/ vi deviare bruscamente

swift /swɪft/ adj rapido. ~**ly** adv rapidamente

swig /swɪg/ n 🔊 sorso m ● vt (pt/pp swigged) 🔊 scolarsi

swim /swɪm/ n have a ~ fare una nuotata ● v (pt swam, pp swum) ● vi nuotare; (room:) girare; **my head is** ~**ming** mi gira la testa ● vt percorrere a nuoto. ~**mer** n nuotatore, -trice mf

swimming /ˈswɪmɪŋ/ n nuoto m. ~-**baths** npl piscina fsg. ~ **costume** n costume m da bagno. ~-**pool** n piscina f. ~ **trunks** npl calzoncini mpl da bagno

'swim-suit n costume m da bagno

swindle /ˈswɪndl/ n truffa f ● vt truffare. ~**r** n truffatore, -trice mf

swine /swaɪn/ n 🔊 porco m

swing /swɪŋ/ n oscillazione f; (shift) cambiamento m; (seat) altalena f; (Mus) swing m; **in full** ~ in piena attività ● v (pt/pp swung) ● vi oscillare; (on swing, sway) dondolare; (dangle) penzolare; (turn) girare ● vt oscillare; far deviare (vote). ~-**'door** n porta f a vento

swipe /swaɪp/ n 🔊 botta f ● vt colpire; (steal) rubare; far passare nella macchinetta (credit card); ~ **card** n pass m inv magnetico

Swiss /swɪs/ adj & n svizzero, -a mf; **the** ~ pl gli svizzeri. ~ **'roll** n rotolo m di pan di Spagna ripieno di marmellata

switch /swɪtʃ/ n interruttore m; (change) mutamento m ● vt cambiare; (exchange) scambiare ● vi cambiare; ~ **to** passare a. □ ~ **off** vt spegnere. □ ~ **on** vt accendere

switchboard n centralino m

Switzerland /ˈswɪtsələnd/ n Svizzera f

swivel /ˈswɪvl/ v (pt/pp swivelled) ● vt girare ● vi girarsi

swollen /ˈswəʊlən/ ▷ SWELL ● adj gonfio. ~-**headed** adj presuntuoso

swoop /swuːp/ n (by police) incur-

sione f ● vi ~ [**down**] (bird:) piombare; fig fare un'incursione

sword /sɔːd/ n spada f

swore /swɔː(r)/ ▷ SWEAR

sworn /swɔːn/ ▷ SWEAR

swot /swɒt/ n 🔊 sgobbone, -a mf ● vt (pt/pp swotted) 🔊 sgobbare

swum /swʌm/ ▷ SWIM

swung /swʌŋ/ ▷ SWING

syllable /ˈsɪləbl/ n sillaba f

syllabus /ˈsɪləbəs/ n programma m [dei corsi]

symbol /ˈsɪmbl/ n simbolo m (of di). ~**ic** adj simbolico. ~**ism** n simbolismo m. ~**ize** vt simboleggiare

symmetr|ical /sɪˈmetrɪkl/ adj simmetrico. ~**y** n simmetria f

sympathetic /sɪmpəˈθetɪk/ adj (understanding) comprensivo; (showing pity) compassionevole. ~**ally** adv con comprensione/compassione

sympathize /ˈsɪmpəθaɪz/ vi capire; (in grief) solidarizzare; ~ **with sb** capire qcno/solidarizzare con qcno. ~**r** n (Pol) simpatizzante mf

sympathy /ˈsɪmpəθi/ n comprensione f; (pity) compassione f; (condolences) condoglianze fpl; **in** ~ **with** (strike) per solidarietà con

symphony /ˈsɪmfəni/ n sinfonia f

symptom /ˈsɪmptəm/ n sintomo m. ~**atic** adj sintomatico (of di)

synagogue /ˈsɪnəgɒg/ n sinagoga f

synchronize /ˈsɪŋkrənaɪz/ vt sincronizzare

syndicate /ˈsɪndɪkət/ n gruppo m

synonym /ˈsɪnənɪm/ n sinonimo m. ~**ous** adj sinonimo

syntax /ˈsɪntæks/ n sintassi f inv

synthesize /ˈsɪnθəsaɪz/ vt sintetizzare. ~**r** n (Mus) sintetizzatore m

synthetic /sɪnˈθetɪk/ adj sintetico ● n fibra f sintetica

syringe /sɪˈrɪndʒ/ n siringa f

syrup /ˈsɪrəp/ n sciroppo m; treacle tipo m di melassa

system /'sɪstəm/ n sistema m.
~**atic** adj sistematico

Tt

tab /tæb/ n linguetta f; (with name) etichetta f; keep ~s on [T] sorvegliare; pick up the ~ [T] pagare il conto

table /'teɪbl/ n tavolo m; (list) tavola f; at [the] ~ a tavola; ~ of contents tavola f delle materie ● vt proporre. ~**cloth** n tovaglia f. ~**spoon** n cucchiaio m da tavola. ~**spoon**[**ful**] n cucchiaiata f

tablet /'tæblɪt/ n pastiglia f; (slab) lastra f; ~ of soap saponetta f

table tennis n tennis m da tavolo; (everyday level) ping pong m

tabloid /'tæblɔɪd/ n [giornale m formato] tabloid m inv; pej giornale m scandalistico

taboo /tə'buː/ adj tabù inv ● n tabù m inv

tacit /'tæsɪt/ adj tacito

taciturn /'tæsɪtɜːn/ adj taciturno

tack /tæk/ n (nail) chiodino m; (stitch) imbastitura f; (Naut) virata f; fig linea f di condotta ● vt inchiodare; (sew) imbastire ● vi (Naut) virare

tackle /'tækl/ n (equipment) attrezzatura f; (football etc) contrasto m, tackle m inv ● vt affrontare

tacky /'tækɪ/ adj (paint) non ancora asciutto; (glue) appiccicoso; fig pacchiano

tact /tækt/ n tatto m. ~**ful** adj pieno di tatto; (remark) delicato. ~**fully** adv con tatto

tactic|al /'tæktɪkl/ adj tattico. ~**s** npl tattica fsg

tactless /'tæktlɪs/ adj privo di tatto.

~**ly** adv senza tatto. ~**ness** n mancanza f di tatto; (of remark) indelicatezza f

tadpole /'tædpəʊl/ n girino m

tag[1] /tæg/ n (label) etichetta f ● vt (pt/pp tagged) attaccare l'etichetta a. □ ~ **along** vi seguire passo passo

tag[2] n (game) acchiapparello m

tail /teɪl/ n coda f; ~s pl (tailcoat) frac m inv ● vt ([T]: follow) pedinare. □ ~ **off** vi diminuire

tail light n fanalino m di coda

tailor /'teɪlə(r)/ n sarto m. ~-**made** adj fatto su misura

taint /teɪnt/ vt contaminare

take /teɪk/ n (Cinema) ripresa f ● v (pt took, pp taken) ● vt prendere; (to a place) portare (person, object); (contain) contenere (passengers etc); (endure) sopportare; (require) occorrere; (teach) insegnare; (study) studiare (subject); fare (exam, holiday, photograph, walk, bath); sentire (pulse); misurare (sb's temperature); ~ sb prisoner fare prigioniero qcno; be ~ ill ammalarsi; ~ sth calmly prendere con calma qcsa ● vi (plant): attecchire. □ ~ **after** vt assomigliare a. □ ~ **away** vt (with one) portare via; (remove) togliere; (Math) sottrarre; 'to ~ away' 'da asporto'. □ ~ **back** vt riprendere; ritirare (statement); (return) riportare [indietro]. □ ~ **down** vt portare giù; (remove) tirare giù; (write down) prendere nota di. □ ~ **in** vt (bring indoors) portare dentro; (to one's home) ospitare; (understand) capire; (deceive) ingannare; riprendere (garment); (include) includere. □ ~ **off** vt togliersi (clothes); (deduct) togliere; (mimic) imitare; ~ **time off** prendere delle vacanze; ~ **oneself off** andarsene ● vi (Aeron) decollare. □ ~ **on** vt farsi carico di; assumere (employee); (as opponent) prendersela con. □ ~ **out** vt portare fuori; togliere (word, stain); (withdraw) ritirare (money, books); ~

s

t

out a subscription to sth abbonarsi a qcsa; ~ **it out on sb** ① prendersela con qcno. □ ~ **over** vt assumere il controllo di (firm) ● vi ~ **over from sb** sostituire qcno; (permanently) succedere a qcno. □ ~ **to** vt (as a habit) darsi a; **I took to her** (liked) mi è piaciuta. □ ~ **up** vt turare (hole); cominciare (hobby); prendere (time); occupare (space); tirare su (floor-boards); accorciare (dress); ~ **sth up with sb** discutere qcsa con qcno ● vi ~ **up with sb** legarsi a qcno

take: ~**-off** n (Aeron) decollo m. ~**-over** n rilevamento m

takings /'teɪkɪŋz/ npl incassi mpl

tale /teɪl/ n storia f; pej fandonia f

talent /'tælənt/ n talento m. ~**ed** adj [ricco] di talento

talk /tɔːk/ n conversazione f; (lecture) conferenza f; (gossip) chiacchere fpl; **make small ~** parlare del più e del meno ● vi parlare ● vt parlare di (politics etc); ~ **sb into sth** convincere qcno di qcsa. □ ~ **over** vt discutere

talkative /'tɔːkətɪv/ adj loquace

tall /tɔːl/ adj alto. ~**boy** n cassettone m. ~ **order** n impresa f difficile. ~ **'story** n frottola f

tally /'tælɪ/ n conteggio m; **keep a ~ of** tenere il conto di ● vi coincidere

tambourine /tæmbə'riːn/ n tamburello m

tame /teɪm/ adj (animal) domestico; (dull) insulso ● vt domare. ~**ly** adv docilmente. ~**r** n domatore, -trice mf

tamper /'tæmpə(r)/ vi ~ **with** manomettere

tampon /'tæmpɒn/ n tampone m

tan /tæn/ adj marrone rossiccio ● n marrone m rossiccio; (from sun) abbronzatura f ● v (pt/pp **tanned**) ● vt conciare (hide) ● vi abbronzarsi

tang /tæŋ/ n sapore m forte; (smell)

odore m penetrante

tangent /'tændʒənt/ n tangente f

tangible /'tændʒɪbl/ adj tangibile

tangle /'tæŋgl/ n groviglio m; (in hair) nodo m ● vt ~ [**up**] aggrovigliare ● vi aggrovigliarsi

tango /'tæŋgəʊ/ n tango m inv

tank /tæŋk/ n contenitore m; (for petrol) serbatoio m; (fish ~) acquario m; (Mil) carro m armato

tanker /'tæŋkə(r)/ n nave f cisterna; (lorry) autobotte f

tantrum /'tæntrəm/ n scoppio m d'ira

tap /tæp/ n rubinetto m; (knock) colpo m; **on ~** a disposizione ● (pt/pp **tapped**) ● vt dare un colpetto a; sfruttare (resources); mettere sotto controllo (telephone) ● vi picchiettare. ~**-dance** n tip tap m ● vi ballare il tip tap

tape /teɪp/ n nastro m; (recording) cassetta f ● vt legare con nastro; (record) registrare

tape-measure n metro m [a nastro]

taper /'teɪpə(r)/ n candela f sottile ● **taper off** vi assottigliarsi

tape recorder n registratore m

tapestry /'tæpɪstrɪ/ n arazzo m

tar /tɑː(r)/ n catrame m ● vt (pt/pp **tarred**) incatramare

target /'tɑːgɪt/ n bersaglio m; fig obiettivo m

tarnish /'tɑːnɪʃ/ vi ossidarsi ● vt ossidare; fig macchiare

tart¹ /tɑːt/ adj aspro; fig acido

tart² n crostata f; (individual) crostatina f; (🗙 : prostitute) donnaccia f ● **tart up** vt ① ~ **oneself up** agghindarsi

tartan /'tɑːtn/ n tessuto m scozzese, tartan m inv ● attrib di tessuto scozzese

task /tɑːsk/ n compito m; **take sb to ~** riprendere qcno. ~ **force** n (Pol) commissione f; (Mil) task-force f inv

tassel /'tæsl/ n nappa f

taste /teɪst/ n gusto m; (sample) assaggio m; get a ~ of sth fig assaporare il gusto di qcsa ● vt sentire il sapore di; (sample) assaggiare ● vi sapere (of di); it ~s lovely è ottimo. ~**ful** adj di [buon] gusto. ~**fully** adv con gusto. ~**less** adj senza gusto. ~**lessly** adv con cattivo gusto

tasty /'teɪstɪ/ adj (-ier, -iest) saporito

tat /tæt/ ▷ **TIT²**

tatter|ed /'tætəd/ adj cencioso; (pages) stracciato. ~s npl in ~s a brandelli

tattoo¹ /tæ'tuː/ n tatuaggio m ● vt tatuare

tattoo² n (Mil) parata f militare

tatty /'tætɪ/ adj (-ier, -iest) (clothes, person) trasandato; (book) malandato

taught /tɔːt/ ▷ **TEACH**

taunt /tɔːnt/ n scherno m ● vt schernire

Taurus /'tɔːrəs/ n Toro m

taut /tɔːt/ adj teso

tax /tæks/ n tassa f; (on income) imposte fpl; before ~ (price) tasse escluse; (salary) lordo ● vt tassare; fig mettere alla prova; ~ with accusare di. ~**able** adj tassabile. ~**ation** n tasse fpl. ~ **evasion** n evasione f fiscale. ~**-free** adj esentasse. ~ **haven** n paradiso m fiscale

taxi /'tæksɪ/ n taxi m inv ● vi (pt/pp taxied, pres p taxiing) (aircraft:) rullare. ~ **driver** n tassista m f. ~ **rank** n posteggio m per taxi

'taxpayer n contribuente m f

tea /tiː/ n tè m inv. ~**-bag** n bustina f di tè. ~**-break** n intervallo m per il tè

teach /tiːtʃ/ vt/i (pt/pp taught) insegnare; ~ sb sth insegnare qcsa a qcno. ~**er** n insegnante m f; (primary)

maestro, -a m f. ~**ing** n insegnamento m

teacup n tazza f da tè

team /tiːm/ n squadra f; fig équipe f inv ● **team up** vi unirsi

'team-work n lavoro m di squadra; fig lavoro m d'équipe

'teapot n teiera f

tear¹ /teə(r)/ n strappo m ● v (pt tore, pp torn) ● vt strappare ● vi strappare; (material:) strapparsi; (run:) precipitarsi. □ ~ **apart** vt (fig: criticize) fare a pezzi; (separate) dividere. ~ **away** vt ~ **oneself away** riuscire a staccarsi; ~ **oneself away from** staccarsi da (television). □ ~ **open** vt aprire strappando. □ ~ **up** vt strappare; rompere (agreement)

tear² /tɪə(r)/ n lacrima f. ~**ful** adj (person) in lacrime; (farewell) lacrimevole. ~**fully** adv in lacrime. ~**gas** n gas m lacrimogeno

tease /tiːz/ vt prendere in giro (person); tormentare (animal)

tea: ~**-set** n servizio m da tè. ~**spoon** n cucchiaino m [da tè]

teat /tiːt/ n capezzolo m; (on bottle) tettarella f

'tea-towel n strofinaccio m [per i piatti]

technical /'teknɪkl/ adj tecnico. ~**ity** n tecnicismo m; (Jur) cavillo m giuridico. ~**ly** adv tecnicamente; (strictly) strettamente

technician /tek'nɪʃn/ n tecnico, -a m f

technique /tek'niːk/ n tecnica f

technological /teknə'lɒdʒɪkl/ adj tecnologico

technology /tek'nɒlədʒɪ/ n tecnologia f

tedious /'tiːdɪəs/ adj noioso

tedium /'tiːdɪəm/ n tedio m

teem /tiːm/ vi (rain) piovere a dirotto; be ~**ing with** (full of) pullulare di

t

teenage /ˈtiːneɪdʒ/ adj per ragazzi; ~ **boy/girl** adolescente mf. ~ r n adolescente mf

teens /tiːnz/ npl the ~ l'adolescenza fsg; be in one's ~ essere adolescente

teeny /ˈtiːnɪ/ adj (-ier, -iest) piccolissimo

teeter /ˈtiːtə(r)/ vi barcollare

teeth /tiːθ/ ▷ TOOTH

teeth|e /tiːð/ vi mettere i [primi] denti. ~ing troubles npl fig difficoltà fpl iniziali

telecommunications /telɪkəmjuːnɪˈkeɪʃnz/ npl telecomunicazioni fpl

telegram /ˈtelɪɡræm/ n telegramma m

telepathy /tɪˈlepəθɪ/ n telepatia f

telephone /ˈtelɪfəʊn/ n telefono m; be on the ~ avere il telefono; (be telephoning) essere al telefono ● vt telefonare a ● vi telefonare

telephone: ~ **booth** n, ~ **box** n cabina f telefonica. ~ **directory** n elenco m telefonico

telephonist /tɪˈlefənɪst/ n telefonista mf

telescop|e /ˈtelɪskəʊp/ n telescopio m. ~ic adj telescopico

televise /ˈtelɪvaɪz/ vt trasmettere per televisione

television /ˈtelɪvɪʒn/ n televisione f; watch ~ guardare la televisione. ~ **set** n televisore m

teleworking /ˈtelɪwɜːkɪŋ/ n telelavoro m

telex /ˈteleks/ n telex m inv

tell /tel/ vt (pt/pp told) dire; raccontare (story); (distinguish) distinguere (from da); ~ **sb** dire qcsa a qcno; ~ **the time** dire l'ora; I couldn't ~ why... non sapevo perché... ● vi (produce an effect) avere effetto; time will ~ il tempo te lo dirà; his age is beginning to ~ l'età comincia a farsi sentire [per lui]; you mustn't ~ non devi dire niente. □ ~ **off** vt sgridare

teller /ˈtelə(r)/ n (in bank) cassiere, -a mf

telling /ˈtelɪŋ/ adj significativo; (argument) efficace

telly /ˈtelɪ/ n ① tv f inv

temp /temp/ n ① impiegato, -a mf temporaneo, -a

temper /ˈtempə(r)/ n (disposition) carattere m; (mood) umore m; (anger) collera f; lose one's ~ arrabbiarsi; be in a ~ essere arrabbiato; keep one's ~ mantenere la calma

temperament /ˈtemprəmənt/ n temperamento m. ~al adj (moody) capriccioso

temperate /ˈtempərət/ adj (climate) temperato

temperature /ˈtemprətʃə(r)/ n temperatura f; have a ~ avere la febbre

temple[1] /ˈtempl/ n tempio m

temple[2] (Anat) tempia f

tempo /ˈtempəʊ/ n ritmo m; (Mus) tempo m

temporar|y /ˈtempərərɪ/ adj temporaneo; (measure, building) provvisorio. ~ily adv temporaneamente; (introduced, erected) provvisoriamente

tempt /tempt/ vt tentare; sfidare (fate); ~ **sb** to indurre qcno a; be ~ed essere tentato (to di); I am ~ed by the offer l'offerta mi tenta. ~ation n tentazione f. ~ing adj allettante; (food, drink) invitante

ten /ten/ adj dieci

tenaci|ous /tɪˈneɪʃəs/ adj tenace. ~ty n tenacia f

tenant /ˈtenənt/ n inquilino, -a mf; (Comm) locatario, -a mf

tend vi ~ **to do sth** tendere a far qcsa

tendency /ˈtendənsɪ/ n tendenza f

tender[1] /ˈtendə(r)/ n (Comm) offerta

f; **be legal ~** avere corso legale ● *vt* offrire; presentare (resignation)

tender² *adj* tenero; (*painful*) dolorante. **~ly** *adv* teneramente. **~ness** *n* tenerezza *f*; (*painfulness*) dolore *m*

tendon /'tendən/ *n* tendine *m*

tennis /'tenɪs/ *n* tennis *m*. **~-court** *n* campo *m* da tennis. **~ player** *n* tennista *mf*

tenor /'tenə(r)/ *n* tenore *m*

tense¹ /tens/ *n* (*Gram*) tempo *m*

tense² *adj* teso ● *vt* tendere (muscle). □ **~ up** *vt* tendersi

tension /'tenʃn/ *n* tensione *f*

tent /tent/ *n* tenda *f*

tentacle /'tentəkl/ *n* tentacolo *m*

tentative /'tentətɪv/ *adj* provvisorio; (smile, gesture) esitante. **~ly** *adv* timidamente; (accept) provvisoriamente

tenterhooks /'tentəhʊks/ *npl* **be on ~** essere sulle spine

tenth /tenθ/ *adj* decimo ● *n* decimo, -a *mf*

tenuous /'tenjʊəs/ *adj fig* debole

tepid /'tepɪd/ *adj* tiepido

term /tɜːm/ *n* periodo *m*; (Sch) (Univ) trimestre *m*; (expression) termine *m*; **~s** *pl* (conditions) condizioni *fpl*; **~ of office** carica *f*; **in the short/long ~** a breve/lungo termine; **be on good/bad ~s** essere in buoni/cattivi rapporti; **come to ~s with** accettare (past, fact); **easy ~s** facilità *f* di pagamento

terminal /'tɜːmɪn(ə)l/ *adj* finale; (Med) terminale ● *n* (Aeron) terminal *m inv*; (Rail) stazione *f* di testa; (of bus) capolinea *m*; (on battery) morsetto *m*; (Comput) terminale *m*. **~ly** *adv* **be ~ly ill** essere in fase terminale

terminat|e /'tɜːmɪneɪt/ *vt* terminare; rescindere (contract); interrompere (pregnancy) ● *vi* terminare; **~e** **in** finire in. **~ion** *n* termine *m*; (Med) interruzione *f* di gravidanza

terminology /tɜːmɪ'nɒlədʒɪ/ *n*

terminologia *f*

terrace /'terəs/ *n* terrazza *f*; (houses) fila *f* di case a schiera; **the ~s** (Sport) le gradinate. **~d house** *n* casa *f* a schiera

terrain /te'reɪn/ *n* terreno *m*

terrible /'terəbl/ *adj* terribile

terrific /tə'rɪfɪk/ *adj* 🆏 (excellent) fantastico; (huge) enorme. **~ally** *adv* 🆏 terribilmente

terri|fy /'terɪfaɪ/ *vt* (pt/pp -ied) atterrire; **be ~fied** essere terrorizzato. **~fying** *adj* terrificante

territorial /terɪ'tɔːrɪəl/ *adj* territoriale

territory /'terɪtərɪ/ *n* territorio *m*

terror /'terə(r)/ *n* terrore *m*. **~ism** *n* terrorismo *m*. **~ist** *n* terrorista *mf*. **~ize** *vt* terrorizzare

terse /tɜːs/ *adj* conciso

test /test/ *n* esame *m*; (in laboratory) esperimento *m*, (of friendship, machine) prova *f*; (of intelligence, aptitude) test *m inv*; **put to the ~** mettere alla prova ● *vt* esaminare; provare (machine)

testament /'testəmənt/ *n* testamento *m*; **Old/New T~** Antico/Nuovo Testamento *m*

testicle /'testɪkl/ *n* testicolo *m*

testify /'testɪfaɪ/ *vt/i* (pt/pp -ied) testimoniare

testimonial /testɪ'məʊnɪəl/ *n* lettera *f* di referenze

testimony /'testɪmənɪ/ *n* testimonianza *f*

'test: ~ match *n* partita *f* internazionale. **~-tube** *n* provetta *f*

tether /'teðə(r)/ *n* **be at the end of one's ~** non poterne più

text /tekst/ *n* testo *m*. **~book** *n* manuale *m*

textile /'tekstaɪl/ *adj* tessile ● *n* stoffa *f*

text message *n* sms *m inv*, breve messaggio *m* di testo

texture /'tekstʃə(r)/ *n* (of skin)

t

grana *f*; (*of food*) consistenza *f*; **of a smooth ~** (*to the touch*) soffice al tatto

Thames /temz/ *n* Tamigi *m*

than /ðæn/, *accentato* /ðæn/ *conj* che; (*with numbers, names*) di; **older ~ me** più vecchio di me

thank /θæŋk/ *vt* ringraziare; **~ you [very much]** grazie [mille]. **~ful** *adj* grato. **~fully** *adv* con gratitudine; (*happily*) fortunatamente. **~less** *adj* ingrato

thanks /θæŋks/ *npl* ringraziamenti *mpl*; **~!** ① grazie!; **~ to** grazie a

that /ðæt/
● *adj & pron* (*pl* **those**) quel, quei *pl*; (*before s + consonant, gn, ps and z*) quello, quegli *pl*; (*before vowel*) quell' *mf*, quegli *mpl*, quelle *fpl*; **~ one** quello; **I don't like those** quelli non mi piacciono; **~ is** cioè; **is ~ you?** sei tu?; **who is ~?** chi è?; **what did you do after ~?** cosa hai fatto dopo?; **like ~** in questo modo, così; **a man like ~** un uomo così; **~ is why** ecco perché; **~'s it!** (*you've understood*) ecco!; (*I've finished*) ecco fatto!; (*I've had enough*) basta così!; (*there's nothing more*) tutto qui!; **~'s ~!** (*with job*) ecco fatto!; (*with relationship*) è tutto finito!; **and ~'s ~!** punto e basta! **all ~ I know** tutto quello che so
● *adv* così; **it wasn't ~ good** non era poi così buono
● *rel pron* che; **the man ~ I spoke to** l'uomo con cui ho parlato; **the day ~ I saw him** il giorno in cui l'ho visto; **all ~ I know** tutto quello che so
● *conj* che; **I think ~...** penso che...

thaw /θɔː/ *n* disgelo *m* ● *vt* fare scongelare (*food*) ● *vi* (*food*): scon-

gelarsi; **it's ~ing** sta sgelando

the /ðə/, *di fronte a una vocale* /ðiː/
● *def art* il, la *f*; i *mpl*, le *fpl*; (*before s + consonant, gn, ps and z*) lo, gli *mpl*; (*before vowel*) l' *mf*, gli *mpl*, le *fpl*; **at ~ cinema/station** al cinema/alla stazione; **from ~ cinema/station** dal cinema/dalla stazione
● *adv* **~ more ~ better** più ce n'è meglio è; (*with reference to pl*) più ce ne sono, meglio è; **all ~ better** tanto meglio

theatre /ˈθɪətə(r)/ *n* teatro *m*; (*Med*) sala *f* operatoria

theatrical /θɪˈætrɪkl/ *adj* teatrale; (*showy*) melodrammatico

theft /θeft/ *n* furto *m*

their /ðeə(r)/ *adj* il loro *m*, la loro *f*; i loro *mpl*, le loro *fpl*; **~ mother/father** la loro madre/il loro padre

theirs /ðeəz/ *poss pron* il loro *m*, la loro *f*, i loro *mpl*, le loro *fpl*; **a friend of ~** un loro amico; **friends of ~** dei loro amici; **those are ~** quelli sono loro; (*as opposed to ours*) quelli sono i loro

them /ðem/ *pron* (*direct object*) li *m*, le *f*; (*indirect object*) gli, loro *fml*; (*after prep: with people*) loro; (*after preposition: with things*) essi; **we haven't seen ~** non li/le abbiamo visti/viste; **give ~ the money** dai loro or dagli i soldi; **give it to ~** daglielo; **I've spoken to ~** ho parlato con loro; **it's ~** sono loro

theme /θiːm/ *n* tema *m*. **~ park** *n* parco *m* a tema. **~ song** *n* motivo *m* conduttore

them'selves *pron* (*reflexive*) si; (*emphatic*) se stessi; **they poured ~ a drink** si sono versati da bere; **they said so ~** lo hanno detto loro stessi; **they kept it to ~** se lo sono tenuti per sé; **by ~** da soli

then /ðen/ *adv* allora; (*next*) poi; **by**

~ (in the past) ormai; (in the future) per allora; **since** ~ sin da allora; **before** ~ prima di allora; **from** ~ on da allora in poi; **now and** ~ ogni tanto; **there and** ~ all'istante ● adj di allora

theoretical /θɪə'retɪkl/ adj teorico

theory /'θɪərɪ/ n teoria f; **in** ~ in teoria

therapeutic /θerə'pju:tɪk/ adj terapeutico

therap|ist /'θerəpɪst/ n terapista mf. ~y n terapia f

there /ðeə(r)/ adv là, lì; (down/up) ~ laggiù/lassù; ~ **is/are** c'è/ci sono; **he/she is** eccolo/eccola ● int ~, ~! dai, su!

there: ~**abouts** adv [or] ~**abouts** (roughly) all'incirca. ~**fore** /-fɔ:(r)/ adv perciò

thermometer /θə'mɒmɪtə(r)/ n termometro m

thermostat /'θɜ:məstæt/ n termostato m

thesaurus /θɪ'sɔ:rəs/ n dizionario m dei sinonimi

these /ði:z/ ▷**THIS**

thesis /'θi:sɪs/ n (pl **-ses** /-si:z/) tesi f inv

they /ðeɪ/ pron loro; ~ **are** tired sono stanchi; **we're going, but** ~ **are not** noi andiamo, ma loro no; ~ **say** (generalizing) si dice; ~ **are building a new road** stanno costruendo una nuova strada

thick /θɪk/ adj spesso; (forest) fitto; (liquid) denso; (hair) folto; (fig: stupid) ottuso; (fig: close) molto unito; **be 5 mm** ~ essere 5 mm di spessore ● adv densamente ● n **in the** ~ **of** nel mezzo di. ~**en** vi ispessire (sauce) ● vi ispessirsi; (fog:) infittirsi. ~**ly** adv densamente; (cut) a fette spesse. ~**ness** n spessore m

thief /θi:f/ n (pl **thieves**) ladro, -a mf

thigh /θaɪ/ n coscia f

thimble /'θɪmbl/ n ditale m

thin /θɪn/ adj (**thinner, thinnest**) sottile; (shoes, sweater) leggero; (liquid) liquido; (person) magro; (fig: excuse, plot) inconsistente ● adv = **thinly** ● v (pt/pp **thinned**) ● vt diluire (liquid) ● vi diradarsi. □ ~ **out** vi diradarsi. ~**ly** adv (populated) scarsamente; (disguised) leggermente; (cut) a fette sottili

thing /θɪŋ/ n cosa f; ~**s** pl (belongings) roba fsg; **for one** ~ in primo luogo; **the right** ~ la cosa giusta; **just the** ~! proprio quel che ci vuole!; **how are** ~**s**? come vanno le cose?; **the latest** ~ l'ultima cosa; **the best** ~ **would be** la cosa migliore sarebbe; **poor** ~! poveretto!

think /θɪŋk/ vt/i (pt/pp **thought**) pensare; (believe) credere; **I** ~ **so** credo di sì; **what do you** ~? (what is your opinion?) cosa ne pensi?; ~ **of/about** pensare a; **what do you** ~ **of it?** cosa ne pensi di questo?. □ ~ **over** vt riflettere su. □ ~ **up** vt escogitare

third /θɜ:d/ adj & n terzo, -a mf. ~**ly** adv terzo. ~**-rate** adj scadente

thirst /θɜ:st/ n sete f. ~**ily** adv con sete. ~**y** adj assetato; **be** ~**y** aver sete

thirteen /θɜ:'ti:n/ adj tredici. ~**th** adj tredicesimo

thirtieth /'θɜ:tɪɪθ/ adj trentesimo

thirty /'θɜ:tɪ/ adj trenta

this /ðɪs/ adj (pl **these**) questo; ~ **man/woman** quest'uomo/questa donna; **these men/women** questi uomini/queste donne; ~ **one** questo; ~ **morning/evening** stamattina/stasera ● pron (pl **these**) questo; **we talked about** ~ **and that** abbiamo parlato del più e del meno; **like** ~ così; ~ **is Peter** questo è Peter; (Teleph) sono Peter; **who is** ~ chi è?; (Teleph) chi parla? ● adv così; ~ **big** così grande

thistle /'θɪsl/ n cardo m

thorn /θɔ:n/ n spina f. ~**y** adj

spinoso

thorough /'θʌrə/ adj completo; (knowledge) profondo; (clean, search, training) a fondo; (person) scrupoloso

thorough: ~bred n purosangue m inv. ~fare n via f principale; 'no ~fare' 'strada non transitabile'

thorough|ly /'θʌrəlɪ/ adv (clean, search, know sth) a fondo; (extremely) estremamente. ~ness n completezza f

those /ðəʊz/ ▷THAT

though /ðəʊ/ conj sebbene; as ~ come se ● adv 🎧 tuttavia

thought /θɔːt/ ▷THINK ● n pensiero m; (idea) idea f. ~ful adj pensieroso; (considerate) premuroso. ~fully adv pensierosamente; (considerately) premurosamente. ~less adj (inconsiderate) sconsiderato. ~lessly adv con noncuranza

thousand /'θaʊznd/ adj one/a ~ mille m inv ● n mille m inv; ~s of migliaia fpl di. ~th adj millesimo ● n millesimo, -a mf

thrash /θræʃ/ vt picchiare; (defeat) sconfiggere. □ ~ out vt mettere a punto

thread /θred/ n filo m; (of screw) filetto m ● vt infilare (beads); ~ one's way through farsi strada fra. ~bare adj logoro

threat /θret/ n minaccia f

threaten /'θretn/ vt minacciare (to do sth/fare) ● vi fig incalzare. ~ing adj minaccioso; (sky, atmosphere) sinistro

three /θriː/ adj tre. ~fold adj & adv triplo. ~some n trio m

threshold /'θreʃəʊld/ n soglia f

threw /θruː/ ▷THROW

thrift /θrɪft/ n economia f. ~y adj parsimonioso

thrill /θrɪl/ n emozione f; (of fear) brivido m ● vt entusiasmare; be ~ed with essere entusiasta di. ~er n

(book) [romanzo m] giallo m; (film) [film m] giallo m. ~ing adj eccitante

thrive /θraɪv/ vi (pt thrived or throve, pp thrived or thriven /'θrɪvn/) (business): prosperare; (child, plant): crescere bene; I ~ on pressure mi piace essere sotto tensione

throat /θrəʊt/ n gola f; sore ~ mal di gola

throb /θrɒb/ n pulsazione f; (of heart) battito m ● vi (pt/pp throbbed) (vibrate) pulsare; (heart): battere

throes /θrəʊz/ npl in the ~ of fig alle prese con

throne /θrəʊn/ n trono m

throng /θrɒŋ/ n calca f

throttle /'θrɒtl/ n (on motorbike) manopola f di accelerazione ● vt strozzare

through /θruː/ prep attraverso; (during) durante; (by means of) tramite; (thanks to) grazie a; Saturday ~ Tuesday Am da sabato a martedì incluso ● adv attraverso; ~ and ~ fino in fondo; wet ~ completamente bagnato; read sth ~ dare una lettura a qcsa; let ~ lasciar passare (sb) ● adj (train) diretto; be ~ (finished) aver finito; (Teleph) avere la comunicazione

throughout /θruː'aʊt/ prep per tutto ● adv completamente; (time) per tutto il tempo

throw /θrəʊ/ n tiro m ● vt (pt threw, pp thrown) lanciare; (throw away) gettare; azionare (switch); disarcionare (rider); (🎧: disconcert) disorientare; 🎧 dare (party). □ ~ away vt gettare via. □ ~ out vt gettare via; rigettare (plan); buttare fuori (person). □ ~ up vt alzare ● vi (vomit) vomitare

thrush /θrʌʃ/ n tordo m

thrust /θrʌst/ n spinta f ● vt (pt/pp thrust) (push) spingere; (insert) conficcare; ~ [up]on imporre a

thud /θʌd/ n tonfo m

thug /θʌg/ n delinquente m

thumb /θʌm/ n pollice m; **as a rule of ~** come regola generale; **under sb's ~** succube di qcno ● vt ~ **a lift** fare l'autostop. **~-index** n indice m a rubrica. **~-tack** n Am puntina f da disegno

thump /θʌmp/ n colpo m; (noise) tonfo m ● vt battere su (table, door); battere (fist); colpire (person) ● vi battere (on su); (heart:) battere forte. □ ~ **about** vi camminare pesantemente

thunder /'θʌndə(r)/ n tuono m; (loud noise) rimbombo m ● vi tuonare; (make loud noise) rimbombare. **~clap** n rombo m di tuono. **~storm** n temporale m. **~y** adj temporalesco

Thursday /'θɜ:zdeɪ/ n giovedì m inv

thus /ðʌs/ adv così

thwart /θwɔ:t/ vt ostacolare

Tiber /'taɪbə(r)/ n Tevere m

tick /tɪk/ n (sound) ticchettio m; (mark) segno m; (🔲: instant) attimo m ● vi ticchettare. □ ~ **off** vt spuntare; (🔲: scold) sgridare. □ ~ **over** vi (engine:) andare al minimo

ticket /'tɪkɪt/ n biglietto m; (for item deposited, library) tagliando m; (label) cartellino m; (fine) multa f. **~-collector** n controllore m. **~-office** n biglietteria f

tick|le /'tɪkl/ n solletico m ● vt fare il solletico a; (amuse) divertire ● vi fare prurito. **~lish** adj che soffre il solletico

tide /taɪd/ n marea f; (of events) corso m; **the ~ is in/out** c'è alta/ bassa marea ● vt ~ **sb over** aiutare qcno a andare avanti

tidily /'taɪdɪlɪ/ adv in modo ordinato

tidiness /'taɪdɪnɪs/ n ordine m

tidy /'taɪdɪ/ adj (-ier, -iest) ordinato; (🔲: amount) bello ● vt (pt/pp -ied) ~ [up] ordinare; **~ oneself up** mettersi in ordine

tie /taɪ/ n cravatta f; (cord) legaccio m; (fig: bond) legame m; (restriction) im-

pedimento m; (Sport) pareggio m ● v (pres p **tying**) ● vt legare; fare (knot); be ~d (in competition) essere in parità ● vi pareggiare. □ ~ **in with** vi corrispondere a. □ ~ **up** vt legare; vincolare (capital); **be ~d up** (busy) essere occupato

tier /tɪə(r)/ n fila f; (of cake) piano m; (in stadium) gradinata f

tiger /'taɪgə(r)/ n tigre f

tight /taɪt/ adj stretto; (taut) teso; (🔲: drunk) sbronzo; (🔲: mean) spilorcio; ~ **corner** 🔲 brutta situazione f ● adv strettamente; (hold) forte; (closed) bene

tighten /'taɪtn/ vt stringere; (screw); intensificare (control) ● vi stringersi

tight: ~-fisted adj tirchio. **~ly** adv strettamente; (hold) forte; (closed) bene. **~rope** n fune f (da funamboli)

tights /taɪts/ npl collant m inv

tile /taɪl/ n mattonella f; (on roof) tegola f ● vt rivestire di mattonelle (wall)

till¹ /tɪl/ prep & conj = **until**

till² n cassa f

tilt /tɪlt/ n inclinazione f; **at full ~ a** tutta velocità ● vt inclinare ● vi inclinarsi

timber /'tɪmbə(r)/ n legname m

time /taɪm/ n tempo m; (occasion) volta f; (by clock) ora f; **two ~s four** due volte quattro; **at any ~** in qualsiasi momento; **this ~** questa volta; **at ~s, from ~ to ~** ogni tanto; **~ and again** cento volte; **two at a ~** due alla volta; **on ~** in orario; **in ~** in tempo; (eventually) col tempo; **in no ~ at all** velocemente; **in a year's ~** fra un anno; **behind ~** in ritardo; **behind the ~s** antiquato; **for the ~ being** per il momento; **what is the ~?** che ora è?; **by the ~ we arrive** quando arriviamo; **did you have a nice ~?** ti sei divertito?; **have a good ~!** divertiti! ● vt

scegliere il momento per; cronome-
trare (race); **be well ~d** essere ben
calcolato

time: ~ bomb n bomba f a orolo-
geria. **~ly** adj opportuno. **~table** n
orario m

timid /'tɪmɪd/ adj (shy) timido; (fearful) timoroso

tin /tɪn/ n stagno m; (container) barattolo m ● vt (pt/pp tinned) inscatolare.
~ foil n [carta f] stagnola f

tinge /tɪndʒ/ n sfumatura f ● vt **~d
with** fig misto a

tingle /'tɪŋgl/ vi pizzicare

tinker /'tɪŋkə(r)/ vi armeggiare

tinkle /'tɪŋkl/ n tintinnio m; (🔝:
phone call) colpo m di telefono ● vi tintinnare

tinned /tɪnd/ adj in scatole

'tin opener n apriscatole m inv

tint /tɪnt/ n tinta f ● vt tingersi (hair)

tiny /'taɪnɪ/ adj (-ier, -iest) mi-
nuscolo

tip¹ /tɪp/ n punta f

tip² n (money) mancia f; (advice) consiglio m; (for rubbish) discarica f ● v (pt/
pp tipped) ● vt (tilt) inclinare; (pour)
versare; (reward) dare una mancia a ● vi inclinarsi;
(overturn) capovolgersi. **□ ~ off** vt **~
sb off** (inform) fare una soffiata a
qcno. **□ ~ out** vt rovesciare. **□ ~
over** vt capovolgere ● vi capovolgersi

tipped /tɪpt/ adj (cigarette) col filtro

tipsy /'tɪpsɪ/ adj 🔝 brillo

tiptoe /'tɪptəʊ/ n **on ~** in punta
di piedi

tiptop /tɪp'tɒp/ adj 🔝 in condizioni
perfette

tire /'taɪə(r)/ vt stancare ● vi stancarsi. **~d** adj stanco; **~d of** stanco
di; **~d out** stanco morto. **~less** adj
instancabile. **~some** adj fastidioso

tiring /'taɪərɪŋ/ adj stancante

tissue /'tɪʃuː/ n tessuto m; (handkerchief) fazzolettino m di carta.

~-paper n carta f velina

tit¹ /tɪt/ n (bird) cincia f

tit² n **~ for tat** pan per focaccia

title /'taɪtl/ n titolo m. **~-deed** n
atto m di proprietà. **~-role** n ruolo
m principale

---

to /tuː/, atono /tə/

● prep a; (to countries) in; (towards)
verso; (up to, until) fino a; **I'm
going to John's/the butcher's**
vado da John/dal macellaio;
come/go to sb venire/andare
da qcno; **to Italy/Switzerland**
in Italia/Svizzera; **I've never
been to Rome** non sono mai
stato a Roma; **go to the market** andare al mercato; **to the
toilet/my room** in bagno/
camera mia; **to an exhibition** a
una mostra; **to university** all'u-
niversità; **twenty/quarter to
eight** le otto meno venti/un
quarto; **5 to 6 kilos** da 5 a 6
chili; **to the end** alla fine; **to
this day** fino a oggi; **to the
best of my recollection** per
quanto mi possa ricordare;
give/say sth to sb dare/dire
qcsa a qcno; **give it to me**
dammelo; **there's nothing to it**
è una cosa da niente

● verbal constructions **to go** andare;
learn to swim imparare a nuotare; **I want to/have to go**
voglio/devo andare; **it's easy to
forget** è facile da dimenticare;
too ill/tired to go troppo
malato/stanco per andare; **you
have to do it** devi; **I don't want to**
non voglio; **live to be 90** vivere
fino a 90 anni; **he was the last
to arrive** è stato l'ultimo ad arrivare; **to be honest,...** per essere sincero,...

● adv **pull to** chiudere; **to and fro**
avanti e indietro

toad /təʊd/ n rospo m. ~**stool** n fungo m velenoso

toast /təʊst/ n pane m tostato; (drink) brindisi m ● vt tostare (bread); (drink a ~ to) brindare a. ~**er** n tostapane m inv

tobacco /təˈbækəʊ/ n tabacco m. ~**nist's** [shop] n tabaccheria f

toboggan /təˈbɒɡən/ n toboga m ● vi andare in toboga

today /təˈdeɪ/ adj & adv oggi m; a week ~ una settimana a oggi; ~'s paper il giornale di oggi

toddler /ˈtɒdlə(r)/ n bambino, -a m f ai primi passi

toe /təʊ/ n dito m del piede; (of footwear) punta f; **big** ~ alluce m ● vt **the line** rigar diritto. ~**nail** n unghia f del piede

toffee /ˈtɒfɪ/ n caramella f al mou

together /təˈɡeðə(r)/ adv insieme; (at the same time) allo stesso tempo; ~ **with** insieme a

toilet /ˈtɔɪlɪt/ n (lavatory) gabinetto m. ~ **paper** n carta f igienica

toiletries /ˈtɔɪlɪtrɪz/ npl articoli mpl da toilette

toilet roll n rotolo m di carta igienica

token /ˈtəʊkən/ n segno m; (counter) gettone m; (voucher) buono m ● attrib simbolico

told /təʊld/ ▷TELL ● adj **all** ~ in tutto

tolerabl|e /ˈtɒl(ə)rəbl/ adj tollerabile; (not bad) discreto. ~**y** adv discretamente

toleran|ce /ˈtɒl(ə)r(ə)ns/ n tolleranza f. ~**t** adj tollerante. ~**tly** adv con tolleranza

tolerate /ˈtɒləreɪt/ vt tollerare

toll[1] /təʊl/ n pedaggio m; **death** ~ numero m di morti

toll[2] vi suonare a morto

tomato /təˈmɑːtəʊ/ n (pl -es) pomodoro m. ~ **ketchup** n ketchup m.

~ **purée** n concentrato m di pomodoro

tomb /tuːm/ n tomba f

'tombstone n pietra f tombale

tomorrow /təˈmɒrəʊ/ adj & adv domani m; ~ **morning** domani mattina; **the day after** ~ dopodomani; **see you** ~! a domani!

ton /tʌn/ n tonnellata f (= 1,016 kg.); ~**s of** 🅱 un sacco di

tone /təʊn/ n tono m; (colour) tonalità f inv ● vt **tone down** attenuare. □ ~ **up** vt tonificare (muscles)

tongs /tɒŋz/ npl pinze fpl

tongue /tʌŋ/ n lingua f; ~ **in cheek** (say) ironicamente. ~**-twister** n scioglilingua m inv

tonic /ˈtɒnɪk/ n tonico m; (for hair) lozione f per i capelli; fig toccasana m inv; ~ [**water**] acqua f tonica

tonight /təˈnaɪt/ adj & adv stanotte; (evening) stasera ● n questa notte f; (evening) questa sera f

tonne /tʌn/ n tonnellata f metrica

tonsil /ˈtɒnsl/ n (Anat) tonsilla f. ~**litis** n tonsillite f

too /tuː/ adv troppo; (also) anche; ~ **many** troppi; ~ **much** troppo; ~ **little** troppo poco

took /tʊk/ ▷TAKE

tool /tuːl/ n attrezzo m

tooth /tuːθ/ n (pl teeth) dente m

tooth: ~**ache** n mal m di denti. ~**brush** n spazzolino m da denti. ~**paste** n dentifricio m. ~**pick** n stuzzicadenti m inv

top[1] /tɒp/ n (toy) trottola f

top[2] n in cima f; (Sch) primo, -a m f; (upper part or half) parte f superiore; (of page, list, road) inizio m; (upper surface) superficie f; (lid) coperchio m; (of bottle) tappo m; (garment) maglia f; (blouse) camicia f; (Auto) marcia f più alta; **at the** ~ fig al vertice; **at the** ~ **of one's voice** a squarciagola; **on** ~/**on** ~ **of** sopra; **on** ~ **of that** (besides) per di più; **from** ~ **to bottom**

da cima a fondo • *adj* in alto; (official, floor) superiore; (pupil, musician etc) migliore; (speed) massimo • *vt* (*pt/pp* topped) essere in testa a (list); (exceed) sorpassare; ~ped with ice-cream ricoperto di gelato. □ ~ up *vt* riempire

top: ~ 'floor *n* ultimo piano *m*. ~hat *n* cilindro *m*. ~-heavy *adj* con la parte superiore sovraccarica

topic /'tɒpɪk/ *n* soggetto *m*; (*of conversation*) argomento *m*. ~al *adj* d'attualità

topless *adj* & *adv* topless

topple /'tɒpl/ *vt* rovesciare • *vi* rovesciarsi. □ ~ **off** *vi* cadere

top-'secret *adj* segretissimo, top secret *inv*

torch /tɔːtʃ/ *n* torcia *f* [elettrica]; (*flaming*) fiaccola *f*

tore /tɔː(r)/ ▷**TEAR**¹

torment¹ /'tɔːment/ *n* tormento *m*

torment² /tɔː'ment/ *vt* tormentare

torn /tɔːn/ ▷**TEAR**¹

tornado /tɔː'neɪdəʊ/ *n* (*pl* -es) tornado *m inv*

torpedo /tɔː'piːdəʊ/ *n* (*pl* -es) siluro *m* • *vt* silurare

torrent /'tɒrənt/ *n* torrente *m*. ~ial *adj* (rain) torrenziale

tortoise /'tɔːtəs/ *n* tartaruga *f*

torture /'tɔːtʃə(r)/ *n* tortura *f* • *vt* torturare

Tory /'tɔːrɪ/ *adj* & *n* 🇬🇧 conservatore, -trice *mf*

toss /tɒs/ *vt* gettare; (*into the air*) lanciare in aria; (*shake*) scrollare; (*horse:*) disarcionare; mescolare (salad); rivoltare facendo saltare in aria (pancake); ~ **a coin** fare testa o croce • *vi* ~ **and turn** (*in bed*) rigirarsi; let's ~ **for it** facciamo testa o croce

tot¹ /tɒt/ *n* bimbetto, -a *mf*; (🇬🇧: *of liquor*) goccio *m*

tot² *vt* (*pt/pp* totted) ~ **up** 🇬🇧 fare la somma di

total /'təʊtl/ *adj* totale • *n* totale *m* • *vt* (*pt/pp* totalled) ammontare a; (*add up*) sommare

totalitarian /təʊtælɪ'teərɪən/ *adj* totalitario

totally /'təʊtəlɪ/ *adv* totalmente

totter /'tɒtə(r)/ *vi* barcollare; (*government:*) vacillare

touch /tʌtʃ/ *n* tocco *m*; (*sense*) tatto *m*; (*contact*) contatto *m*; (*trace*) traccia *f*; (*of irony, humour*) tocco *m*; **get/be in** ~ mettersi/essere in contatto • *vt* toccare; (*lightly*) sfiorare; (*equal*) eguagliare; (*fig: move*) commuovere • *vi* toccarsi. □ ~ **down** *vi* (Aeron) atterrare. □ ~ **on** *vt fig* accennare a. **touch up** *vt* ritoccare (painting). ~**ing** *adj* commovente. ~**screen** *n* touch screen *m inv*. ~**tone** *adj* a tastiera. ~**y** *adj* permaloso; (*subject*) delicato

tough /tʌf/ *adj* duro; (*severe, harsh*) severo; (*durable*) resistente; (*resilient*) forte

toughen /'tʌfn/ *vt* rinforzare. □ ~ **up** *vt* rendere più forte (person)

tour /tʊə(r)/ *n* giro *m*; (*of building, town*) visita *f*; (Theat), (Sport) tournée *f inv*; (*of duty*) servizio *m* • *vt* visitare • *vi* fare un giro turistico; (Theat) essere in tournée

touris|m /'tʊərɪzm/ *n* turismo *m*. ~**t** *n* turista *mf* • *attrib* turistico. ~**t office** *n* ufficio *m* turistico

tournament /'tʊənəmənt/ *n* torneo *m*

tousle /'taʊzl/ *vt* spettinare

tout /taʊt/ *n* (ticket ~) bagarino *m*; (*horse-racing*) informatore *m* • *vi* ~ **for** sollecitare

tow /təʊ/ *n* rimorchio *m*; **'on** ~' 'a rimorchio'; **in** ~ 🇬🇧 *adj* nel rimorchiare. □ ~ **away** *vt* portare via col carro attrezzi

toward[s] /tə'wɔːd(z)/ *prep* verso (*with respect to*) nei riguardi di.

towel /'taʊəl/ *n* asciugamano *m*.

~ling *n* spugna *f*

tower /'taʊə(r)/ *n* torre *f* ● *vi* ~ **above** dominare. ~ **block** *n* palazzone *m*. ~ing *adj* torreggiante; (*rage*) violento

town /taʊn/ *n* città *f inv*. ~ 'hall *n* municipio *m*

toxic /'tɒksɪk/ *adj* tossico

toy /tɔɪ/ *n* giocattolo *m*. ~shop *n* negozio *m* di giocattoli. ~ with *v* giocherellare con

trace /treɪs/ *n* traccia *f* ● *vt* seguire le tracce di; (*find*) rintracciare; (*draw*) tracciare; (*with tracing-paper*) ricalcare

track /træk/ *n* traccia *f*; (*path*, (*Sport*)) pista *f*; (*Rail*) binario *m*; **keep ~ of** tenere d'occhio. ~ *vt* seguire le tracce di. □ ~ **down** *vt* scovare

tracksuit *n* tuta *f* da ginnastica

tractor /'træktə(r)/ *n* trattore *m*

trade /treɪd/ *n* commercio *m*; (*line of business*) settore *m*; (*craft*) mestiere *m*; **by ~** di mestiere ● *vt* commerciare; ~ **sth for sth** scambiare qcsa per qcsa ● *vi* commerciare. □ ~ **in** *vt* (*give in part exchange*) dare in pagamento parziale

'**trade mark** *n* marchio *m* di fabbrica

trader /'treɪdə(r)/ *n* commerciante *mf*

trades 'union *n* sindacato *m*

tradition /trə'dɪʃn/ *n* tradizione *f*. ~al *adj* tradizionale. ~ally *adv* tradizionalmente

traffic /'træfɪk/ *n* traffico *m* ● *vi* (*pt/pp* **trafficked**) trafficare

traffic: ~ **circle** *n Am* isola *f* rotatoria. ~ **jam** *n* ingorgo *m*. ~ **lights** *npl* semaforo *msg*. ~ **warden** *n* vigile *m* [urbano]; (*woman*) vigilessa *f*

tragedy /'trædʒədɪ/ *n* tragedia *f*

tragic /'trædʒɪk/ *adj* tragico. ~ally *adv* tragicamente

trail /treɪl/ *n* traccia *f*; (*path*) sentiero *m* ● *vi* strisciare; (*plant*) arrampicarsi; ~ **[behind]** rimanere indietro; (*in

competition*) essere in svantaggio ● *vt* trascinare

trailer /'treɪlə(r)/ *n* (*Auto*) rimorchio *m*; (*Am: caravan*) roulotte *f inv*; (*film*) presentazione *f* (*di un film*)

train /treɪn/ *n* treno *m*; ~ **of thought** filo *m* dei pensieri ● *vt* formare professionalmente; (*Sport*) allenare; (*aim*) puntare; educare (*child*); addestrare (*animal, soldier*) ● *vi* fare il tirocinio; (*Sport*) allenarsi. ~ed *adj* (*animal*) addestrato (**to do** a fare)

trainee /treɪ'ni:/ *n* apprendista *mf*

train|er /'treɪnə(r)/ *n* (*Sport*) allenatore, -trice *mf*; (*in circus*) domatore, -trice *mf*; (*of dog, race-horse*) addestratore, -trice *mf*; ~ers *pl* scarpe *fpl* da ginnastica. ~ing *n* tirocinio *m*; (*Sport*) allenamento *m*; (*of animal, soldier*) addestramento *m*

trait /treɪt/ *n* caratteristica *f*

traitor /'treɪtə(r)/ *n* traditore, -trice *mf*

tram /træm/ *n* tram *m inv*. ~-lines *npl* rotaie *fpl* del tram

tramp /træmp/ *n* (*hike*) camminata *f*; (*vagrant*) barbone, -a *mf*; (*of feet*) calpestio *m* ● *vi* camminare con passo pesante; (*hike*) percorrere a piedi

trample /'træmpl/ *vt/i* ~ **[on]** calpestare

trampoline /'træmpəli:n/ *n* trampolino *m*

trance /trɑ:ns/ *n* trance *f inv*

tranquil /'træŋkwɪl/ *adj* tranquillo. ~lity *n* tranquillità *f*

tranquillizer /'træŋkwɪlaɪzə(r)/ *n* tranquillante *m*

transatlantic /trænzət'læntɪk/ *adj* transatlantico

transcend /træn'send/ *vt* trascendere

transfer¹ /'trænsfɜ:(r)/ *n* trasferimento *m*; (*Sport*) cessione *f*; (*design*) decalcomania *f*

transfer² /træns'fɜ:(r)/ *v* (*pt/pp

transferred) ● vt trasferire; (Sport) cedere ● vi trasferirsi; (when travelling) cambiare. **~able** adj trasferibile

transform /træns'fɔːm/ vt trasformare. **~ation** n trasformazione f. **~er** n trasformatore m

transfusion /træns'fjuːʒn/ n trasfusione f

transient /'trænzɪənt/ adj passeggero

transistor /træn'zɪstə(r)/ n transistor m inv; (radio) radiolina f a transistor

transit /'trænzɪt/ n transito m; in **~** (goods) in transito

transition /træn'zɪʃn/ n transizione f. **~al** adj di transizione

transitive /'trænzɪtɪv/ adj transitivo

translat|e /trænz'leɪt/ vt tradurre. **~ion** n traduzione f. **~or** n traduttore, -trice mf

transmission /trænz'mɪʃn/ n trasmissione f

transmit /trænz'mɪt/ vt (pt/pp transmitted) trasmettere. **~ter** n trasmettitore m

transparen|cy /træn'spærənsɪ/ n (Phot) diapositiva f. **~t** adj trasparente

transplant¹ /'trænsplɑːnt/ n trapianto m

transplant² /træns'plɑːnt/ vt trapiantare

transport¹ /'trænspɔːt/ n trasporto m

transport² /træn'spɔːt/ vt trasportare. **~ation** n trasporto m

trap /træp/ n trappola f; (🔲: mouth) boccaccia f ● vt (pt/pp trapped) intrappolare; schiacciare (finger in door). **~door** n botola f

trapeze /trə'piːz/ n trapezio m

trash /træʃ/ n robaccia f; (rubbish) spazzatura f; (nonsense) sciocchezze fpl. **~can** n Am secchio m della spazzatura. **~y** adj scadente

travel /'trævl/ n viaggi mpl ● v (pt/pp travelled) ● vi viaggiare; (to work) andare ● vt percorrere (distance). **~ agency** n agenzia f di viaggi. **~ agent** n agente mf di viaggio

traveller /'trævələ(r)/ n viaggiatore, -trice mf; (Comm) commesso m viaggiatore; **~s** pl (gypsies) zingari mpl. **~'s cheque** n traveller's cheque m inv

trawler /'trɔːlə(r)/ n peschereccio m

tray /treɪ/ n vassoio m; (for baking) teglia f; (for documents) vaschetta f per ticarta; (of printer, photocopier) vassoio m

treacher|ous /'tretʃərəs/ adj traditore; (weather, currents) pericoloso. **~y** n tradimento m

treacle /'triːkl/ n melassa f

tread /tred/ n andatura f; (step) gradino m; (of tyre) battistrada m inv ● v (pt trod, pp trodden) ● vi camminare. □ **~ on** vt calpestare (grass); pestare (foot)

treason /'triːzn/ n tradimento m

treasure /'treʒə(r)/ n tesoro m ● vt tenere in gran conto. **~r** n tesoriere, -a mf

treasury /'treʒərɪ/ n the T**~** il Ministero del Tesoro

treat /triːt/ n piacere m; (present) regalo m; **give sb a ~** fare una sorpresa a qcno ● vt trattare; (Med) curare; **~ sb to sth** offrire qcsa a qcno

treatise /'triːtɪz/ n trattato m

treatment /'triːtmənt/ n trattamento m; (Med) cura f

treaty /'triːtɪ/ n trattato m

treble /'trebl/ adj triplo ● n (Mus: voice) voce f bianca ● vt triplicare ● vi triplicarsi. **~ clef** n chiave f di violino

tree /triː/ n albero m

trek /trek/ n scarpinata f; (as holiday) trekking m inv ● vi (pt/pp trekked) farsi una scarpinata; (on holiday) fare trekking

tremble /'trembl/ vi tremare

tremendous /trɪ'mendəs/ adj (huge) enorme; (⊡: excellent) formidabile. ~ly adv (very) straordinariamente; (adj lot) enormemente

tremor /'tremə(r)/ n tremito m; [earth] ~ scossa f [sismica]

trench /trentʃ/ n fosso m; (Mil) trincea f. ~ coat n trench m inv

trend /trend/ n tendenza f; (fashion) moda f. ~y adj (-ier, -iest) ⊡ di o alla moda

trepidation /trepɪ'deɪʃn/ n trepidazione f

trespass /'trespəs/ vi ~ on introdursi abusivamente in; fig abusare di. ~er n intruso, -a mf

trial /'traɪəl/ n (Jur) processo m; (test, ordeal) prova f; on ~ in prova; (Jur) in giudizio; by ~ and error per tentativi

triang|le /'traɪæŋgl/ n triangolo m. ~ular adj triangolare

tribe /traɪb/ n tribù f inv

tribulation /trɪbjʊ'leɪʃn/ n tribolazione f

tribunal /traɪ'bju:nl/ n tribunale m

tributary /'trɪbjʊtərɪ/ n affluente m

tribute /'trɪbju:t/ n tributo m; pay ~ rendere omaggio

trick /trɪk/ n trucco m; (joke) scherzo m; (in cards) presa f; do the ~ ⊡ funzionare; play a ~ on fare uno scherzo a ● vt imbrogliare

trickle /'trɪkl/ vi colare

trick|ster /'trɪkstə(r)/ n imbroglione, -a mf. ~y adj (-ier, -iest) adj (operation) complesso; (situation) delicato

tricycle /'traɪsɪkl/ n triciclo m

tried /traɪd/ ▷ TRY

trifl|e /'traɪfl/ n inezia f; (Culin) zuppa f inglese. ~ing adj insignificante

trigger /'trɪgə(r)/ n grilletto m ● vt ~ [off] scatenare

trim /trɪm/ adj (trimmer, trimmest) curato; (figure) snello ● n (of hair, hedge) spuntata f; (decoration) rifinitura f; in good ~ in buono stato; (person) in forma ● vt (pt/pp trimmed) spuntare (hair etc); (decorate) ornare; (Naut) orientare. ~ming n bordo m; ~mings pl (decorations) guarnizioni fpl; with all the ~mings (Culin) guarnito

trinket /'trɪŋkɪt/ n ninnolo m

trio /'tri:əʊ/ n trio m

trip /trɪp/ n (excursion) gita f; (journey) viaggio m; (stumble) passo m falso ● v (pt/pp tripped) ● vt far inciampare ● vi inciampare (on/over in). □ ~ up vt far inciampare

tripe /traɪp/ n trippa f; (⊡: nonsense) fesserie fpl

triple /'trɪpl/ adj triplo ● vt triplicare ● vi triplicarsi

triplets /'trɪplɪts/ npl tre gemelli mpl

triplicate /'trɪplɪkət/ n in ~ in triplice copia

tripod /'traɪpɒd/ n treppiede m

trite /traɪt/ adj banale

triumph /'traɪʌmf/ n trionfo m ● vi trionfare (over su). ~ant adj trionfante. ~antly adv (exclaim) con tono trionfante

trivial /'trɪvɪəl/ adj insignificante. ~ity n banalità f inv

trolley /'trɒlɪ/ n carrello m; (Am: tram) tram m inv. ~ bus n filobus m inv

trombone /trɒm'bəʊn/ n trombone m

troop /tru:p/ n gruppo m; ~s pl truppe fpl ● vi ~ in/out entrare/uscire in gruppo

trophy /'trəʊfɪ/ n trofeo m

tropic /'trɒpɪk/ n tropico m; ~s pl tropici mpl. ~al adj tropicale

trot /trɒt/ n trotto m ● vi (pt/pp trotted) trottare

trouble /'trʌbl/ n guaio m; (difficulties) problemi mpl; (inconvenience, (Med) disturbo m; (conflict) conflitto m; **be in ~** essere nei guai; (swimmer, climber:) essere in difficoltà; **get into ~** finire nei guai; **get sb into ~** mettere qcno nei guai; **take the ~ to do sth** darsi la pena di far qcsa ● vt (worry) preoccupare; (inconvenience) disturbare; (conscience, old wound:) tormentare ● vi don't ~! non ti disturbare! **~maker** n be a **~maker** seminare zizzania. **~some** adj fastidioso

trough /trɒf/ n trogolo m; (atmospheric) depressione f

troupe /truːp/ n troupe f inv

trousers /ˈtraʊzəz/ npl pantaloni mpl

trout /traʊt/ n inv trota f

trowel /ˈtraʊəl/ n (for gardening) paletta f; (for builder) cazzuola f

truant /ˈtruːənt/ n **play ~** marinare la scuola

truce /truːs/ n tregua f

truck /trʌk/ n (lorry) camion m inv

trudge /trʌdʒ/ n camminata f faticosa ● vi arrancare

true /truː/ adj vero; **come ~** avverarsi

truffle /ˈtrʌfl/ n tartufo m

truly /ˈtruːlɪ/ adv veramente; **Yours ~** distinti saluti

trump /trʌmp/ n (in cards) atout m inv

trumpet /ˈtrʌmpɪt/ n tromba f. **~er** n trombettista m f

truncheon /ˈtrʌntʃn/ n manganello m

trunk /trʌŋk/ n (of tree, body) tronco m; (of elephant) proboscide f; (for travelling, storage) baule m; (Am: of car) bagagliaio m; **~s** pl calzoncini mpl da bagno

truss /trʌs/ n (Med) cinto m erniario

trust /trʌst/ n fiducia f; (group of companies) trust m inv; (organization) associazione f; **on ~** sulla parola ● vt fidarsi di; (hope) augurarsi ● vi **~ in** credere in; **~ to** affidarsi a. **~ed** adj fidato

trustee /trʌsˈtiː/ n amministratore, -trice mf fiduciario, -a

'trust|ful /ˈtrʌstfl/ adj fiducioso. **~ing** adj fiducioso. **~worthy** adj fidato

truth /truːθ/ n (pl -s /truːðz/) verità f inv. **~ful** adj veritiero. **~fully** adv sinceramente

try /traɪ/ n tentativo m, prova f; (in rugby) meta f ● v (pt/pp **tried**) ● vt provare; (be a strain on) mettere a dura prova; (Jur) processare (person); discutere (case); **~ to do sth** provare a fare qcsa ● vi provare. □ **~ on** vt provarsi (garment). □ **~ out** vt provare

trying /ˈtraɪɪŋ/ adj duro; (person) irritante

T-shirt /ˈtiː-/ n maglietta f

tub /tʌb/ n tinozza f; (carton) vaschetta f; (bath) vasca f da bagno

tuba /ˈtjuːbə/ n (Mus) tuba f

tubby /ˈtʌbɪ/ adj (**-ier, -iest**) tozzo

tube /tjuːb/ n tubo m; (of toothpaste) tubetto m; (Rail) metro f

tuberculosis /tjuːbɜːkjuˈləʊsɪs/ n tubercolosi f

tubular /ˈtjuːbjʊlə(r)/ adj tubolare

tuck /tʌk/ n piega f ● vt (put) infilare. □ **~ in** vt rimboccare; **~ sb in** rimboccare le coperte a qcno ● vi (**!**: eat) mangiare con appetito. □ **~ up** vt rimboccarsi (sleeves); (in bed) rimboccare le coperte a

Tuesday /ˈtjuːzdeɪ/ n martedì m inv

tuft /tʌft/ n ciuffo m

tug /tʌɡ/ n strattone m; (Naut) rimorchiatore m ● v (pt/pp **tugged**) ● vt tirare ● vi dare uno strattone. **~ of war** n tiro m alla fune

tuition /tjuˈɪʃn/ n lezioni fpl

tulip /ˈtjuːlɪp/ n tulipano m

tumble /ˈtʌmbl/ n ruzzolone m ● vi ruzzolare. **~down** adj cadente. **~-drier** n asciugabiancheria f

tumbler /ˈtʌmblə(r)/ n bicchiere m

(senza stelo)

tummy /'tʌmɪ/ n 🔲 pancia f

tumour /'tjuːmə(r)/ n tumore m

tumult /'tjuːmʌlt/ n tumulto m. **~uous** adj tumultuoso

tuna /'tjuːnə/ n tonno m

tune /tjuːn/ n motivo m; out of/in ~ (instrument) scordato/accordato; (person) stonato/intonato; to the ~ of 🔲 per la modesta somma di ● vt accordare (instrument); sintonizzare (radio, TV); mettere a punto (engine). □ ~ **in** vt sintonizzare ● vi sintonizzarsi (to su). □ ~ **up** vi (orchestra:) accordare gli strumenti

tuneful /'tjuːnfl/ adj melodioso

tuner /'tjuːnə(r)/ n accordatore, -trice mf; (Radio, TV) sintonizzatore m

tunic /'tjuːnɪk/ n tunica f; (Mil) giacca f; (Sch) ≈ grembiule m

tunnel /'tʌnl/ n tunnel m inv ● vi (pt/pp tunnelled) scavare un tunnel

turban /'tɜːbən/ n turbante m

turbine /'tɜːbaɪn/ n turbina f

turbulen|ce /'tɜːbjʊləns/ n turbolenza f. **~t** adj turbolento

turf /tɜːf/ n erba f; (segment) zolla f erbosa ● **turf out** vt 🔲 buttar fuori

Turin /tjuˈrɪn/ n Torino f

Turk /tɜːk/ n turco, -a mf

turkey /'tɜːkɪ/ n tacchino m

Turk|ey n Turchia f. **~ish** adj turco

turmoil /'tɜːmɔɪl/ n tumulto m

turn /tɜːn/ n (rotation, short walk) giro m; (in road) svolta f, curva f; (development) svolta f; (Theat) numero m; (🔲: attack) crisi f inv; a ~ for the better/ worse un miglioramento/ peggioramento; do sb a good ~ rendere un servizio a qcno; take ~s fare a turno; in ~ a turno; out of ~ (speak) a sproposito; it's your ~ tocca a te ● vt girare; voltare (back, eyes); dirigere (gun, attention) ● vi girare; (person:) girarsi; (leaves:) ingiallire; (become) diventare; ~ right/

left girare a destra/sinistra; ~ sour inacidirsi; ~ to sb girarsi verso qcno; fig rivolgersi a qcno. □ ~ **against** vi diventare ostile a ● vt mettere contro. □ ~ **away** vt mandare via (people); girare dall'altra parte (head) ● vi girare dall'altra parte. □ ~ **down** vt piegare (collar); abbassare (heat, gas, sound); respingere (person, proposal). □ ~ **in** vt ripiegare in dentro (edges); consegnare (lost object) ● vi (🔲: go to bed) andare a letto; ~ **into the drive** entrare nel viale. □ ~ **off** vt spegnere; chiudere (tap, water) ● vi (car:) girare. □ ~ **on** vt accendere; aprire (tap, water); (🔲: attract) eccitare ● vi (attack) attaccare. □ ~ **out** vt (expel) mandar via; spegnere (light, gas); (produce) produrre; (empty) svuotare (room, cupboard) ● vi (transpire) risultare; ~ **out well/badly** (cake, dress:) riuscire bene/male; (situation:) andare bene/male. □ ~ **over** vt girare ● vi girarsi; **please ~ over** vedi retro. □ ~ **round** vi girarsi; (car:) girare. □ ~ **up** vt tirare su (collar); alzare (heat, gas, sound, radio) ● vi farsi vedere

turning /'tɜːnɪŋ/ n svolta f. **~-point** n svolta f decisiva

turnip /'tɜːnɪp/ n rapa f

turn: ~over n (Comm) giro m d'affari; (of staff) ricambio m. **~pike** n Am autostrada f. **~stile** n cancelletto m girevole. **~table** n piattaforma f girevole; (on record-player) piatto m (di giradischi). **~up** n (of trousers) risvolto m

turquoise /'tɜːkwɔɪz/ adj (colour) turchese ● n turchese m

turret /'tʌrɪt/ n torretta f

turtle /'tɜːtl/ n tartaruga f acquatica

tusk /tʌsk/ n zanna f

tussle /'tʌsl/ n zuffa f ● vi azzuffarsi

tutor /'tjuːtə(r)/ n insegnante mf privato, -a; (Univ) insegnante mf universitario, -a che segue individualmente un ristretto

numero di studenti. ~**ial** n discussione f
col tutor

tuxedo /tʌk'si:dəʊ/ n *Am* smoking
m inv

TV n abbr (television) tv f inv, tivù f inv

twang /twæŋ/ n (in voice) suono m
nasale ● vt far vibrare

tweezers /'twi:zəz/ npl pinzette fpl

twelfth /twelfθ/ adj dodicesimo

twelve /twelv/ adj dodici

twentieth /'twentiiθ/ adj ven-
tesimo

twenty /'twenti/ adj venti

twice /twais/ adv due volte

twiddle /'twidl/ vt giocherellare
con; ~ **one's thumbs** fig girarsi i
pollici

twig[1] /twig/ n ramoscello m

twig[2] vt/i (pt/pp twigged) 🟥 intuire

twilight /'twar–/ n crepuscolo m

twin /twin/ n gemello, -a mf ● attrib
gemello. ~ **beds** npl letti mpl gemelli

twine /twain/ n spago m ● vi intrec-
ciarsi; (plant:) attorcigliarsi ● vt intrecciare

twinge /twindʒ/ n fitta f; ~ **of**
conscience rimorso m di coscienza

twinkle /'twiŋkl/ n scintillio m ● vi
scintillare

twirl /tws:l/ vt far roteare ● vi volteggiare ● n piroetta f

twist /twist/ n torsione f; (curve)
curva f; (in rope) attorcigliata f; (in
book, plot) colpo m di scena ● vt attor-
cigliare (rope); torcere (metal); girare (knob, cap); (distort) distorcere;
~ **one's ankle** storcersi la caviglia
● vi attorcigliarsi; (road:) essere
pieno di curve

twit /twit/ n 🟥 cretino, -a mf

twitch /twitʃ/ n tic m inv; (jerk)
strattone m ● vi contrarsi

twitter /'twitə(r)/ n cinguettio m
● vi cinguettare; (person:) cianciare

two /tu:/ adj due

two: ~**-faced** adj falso. ~**-piece** adj

(swimsuit) due pezzi m inv; (suit) completo m. ~**-way** adj (traffic) a doppio
senso di marcia

tycoon /tar'ku:n/ n magnate m

tying /'taiŋ/ ▷**TIE**

type /taip/ n tipo m; (printing) carattere m [tipografico] ● vt scrivere a
macchina ● vi scrivere a macchina.
~**writer** n macchina f da scrivere.
~**written** adj dattiloscritto

typical /'tipikl/ adj tipico. ~**ly** adv
tipicamente; (as usual) come al solito

typify /'tipifai/ vt (pt/pp -ied) essere
tipico di

typing /'taipiŋ/ n dattilografia f

typist /'taipist/ n dattilografo, -a mf

tyrannical /ti'rænikl/ adj tirannico

tyranny /'tirəni/ n tirannia f

tyrant /'tairənt/ n tiranno, -a mf

tyre /'taiə(r)/ n gomma f, pneumatico m

* * *

Uu

* * *

udder /'ʌdə(r)/ n mammella f (di
vacca, capra etc)

ugly /'ʌgli/ adj (-ier, -iest) brutto

UK n abbr United Kingdom

ultimate /'ʌltimət/ adj definitivo;
(final) finale; (fundamental) fondamentale. ~**ly** adv alla fine

ultimatum /ʌltɪ'meɪtəm/ n ultimatum m inv

ultra'violet /ʌm'brelə/ adj ultravioletto

umbrella /ʌm'brelə/ n ombrello m

umpire /'ʌmpaiə(r)/ n arbitro m
● vt/i arbitrare

umpteen /ʌmp'ti:n/ adj 🟥 innumerevole. ~**th** adj 🟥 ennesimo; **for the**
~**th time** per l'ennesima volta

UN n abbr (United Nations) ONU f

un'able /ʌn-/ *adj* be ~ to do sth non potere fare qcsa; (*not know how*) non sapere fare qcsa

unac'companied *adj* non accompagnato; (*luggage*) incustodito

unac'customed *adj* insolito; be ~ to non essere abituato a

un'aided *adj* senza aiuto

unanimous /juː'nænɪməs/ *adj* unanime. **~ly** *adv* all'unanimità

un'armed *adj* disarmato; ~ **combat** *n* lotta *f* senza armi

unat'tended *adj* incustodito

una'voidable *adj* inevitabile

una'ware *adj* be ~ of sth non rendersi conto di qcsa. **~s** *adv* catch sb **~s** prendere qcno alla sprovvista

un'bearabl|e *adj* insopportabile. **~y** *adv* insopportabilmente

unbeat|able /ʌn'biːtəbl/ *adj* imbattibile. **~en** *adj* imbattuto

unbe'lievable *adj* incredibile

un'biased *adj* obiettivo

un'block *vt* sbloccare

un'bolt *vt* togliere il chiavistello di

un'breakable *adj* infrangibile

un'button *vt* sbottonare

uncalled-for /ʌn'kɔːldfɔː(r)/ *adj* fuori luogo

un'canny *adj* sorprendente; (*silence, feeling*) inquietante

un'certain *adj* incerto; (*weather*) instabile; **in no ~ terms** senza mezzi termini. **~ty** *n* incertezza *f*

un'charitable *adj* duro

uncle /'ʌŋkl/ *n* zio *m*

Uncle Sam *i* Personaggio immaginario che rappresenta gli Stati Uniti, il suo governo e i suoi cittadini. Nell'iconografia è tradizionalmente rappresentato con la barba bianca, vestito dei colori nazionali bianco, rosso e azzurro, con un gran cappello a cilindro con le stelle della bandiera americana. Spesso utilizzato quando si fa appello al patriottismo americano.

---

un'comfortabl|e *adj* scomodo; imbarazzante (*silence, situation*); **feel ~e** *fig* sentirsi a disagio. **~y** *adv* (*sit*) scomodamente; (*causing alarm etc*) spaventosamente

un'common *adj* insolito

un'compromising *adj* intransigente

uncon'ditional *adj* incondizionato. **~ly** *adv* incondizionatamente

un'conscious *adj* privo di sensi; (*unaware*) inconsapevole; be ~ **of sth** non rendersi conto di qcsa. **~ly** *adv* inconsapevolmente

uncon'ventional *adj* poco convenzionale

un'cork *vt* sturare

uncouth /ʌn'kuːθ/ *adj* zotico

un'cover *vt* scoprire; portare alla luce (*buried object*)

unde'cided *adj* indeciso; (*not settled*) incerto

undeniabl|e /ʌndɪ'naɪəbl/ *adj* innegabile. **~y** *adv* innegabilmente

under /'ʌndə(r)/ *prep* sotto; (*less than*) al di sotto di; ~ **there** lì sotto; ~ **repair/construction** in riparazione/costruzione; ~ **way** *fig* in corso ● *adv* (~ *water*) sott'acqua; (*unconscious*) sotto anestesia

'undercarriage *n* (*Aeron*) carrello *m*

'underclothes *npl* biancheria *fsg* intima

under'cover *adj* clandestino

'undercurrent *n* corrente *f* sottomarina; *fig* sottofondo *m*

'underdog *n* perdente *m*

under'done *adj* (*meat*) al sangue

under'estimate *vt* sottovalutare

under'fed *adj* denutrito

under'foot adv sotto i piedi; **trample ~** calpestare

under'go vt (pt -went, pp -gone) subire (operation, treatment); **~ repair** essere in riparazione

under'graduate n studente, -tessa mf universitario, -a

under'ground[1] adv sottoterra

'underground[2] adj sotterraneo; (secret) clandestino ● n (railway) metropolitana f. **~ car park** n parcheggio m sotterraneo

'undergrowth n sottobosco m

under'hand adj subdolo

under'lie vt (pt -lay, pp -lain, pres p -lying) fig essere alla base di

under'line vt sottolineare

under'lying adj fig fondamentale

under'mine vt fig minare

underneath /ʌndə'niːθ/ prep sotto; **~ it** sotto ● adv sotto

under'paid adj mal pagato

'underpants npl mutande fpl

'underpass n sottopassaggio m

under'privileged adj non ab-biente

under'rate vt sottovalutare

'undershirt n Am maglia f della pelle

under'stand vt (pt/pp -stood) capire; **I ~ that...** (have heard) mi risulta che... ● vi capire. **~able** adj comprensibile. **~ably** adv comprensibilmente

under'standing adj comprensivo ● n comprensione f; (agreement) accordo m; **on the ~ that** a condizione che

'understatement n understatement m inv

under'take vt (pt -took, pp -taken) intraprendere; **~ to do sth** impegnarsi a fare qcsa

'undertaker n impresario m di pompe funebri; **[firm of] ~s** n impresa f di pompe funebri

under'taking n impresa f; (promise) promessa f

'undertone n fig sottofondo m; **in an ~** sottovoce

under'value vt sottovalutare

'underwater[1] adj subacqueo

under'water[2] adv sott'acqua

'underwear n biancheria f intima

under'weight adj sotto peso

'underworld n (criminals) malavita f

unde'sirable adj indesiderato; (person) poco raccomandabile

un'dignified adj non dignitoso

un'do vt (pt -did, pp -done) disfare; slacciare (dress, shoes); sbottonare (shirt); fig, (Comput) annullare

un'doubted adj indubbio. **~ly** adv senza dubbio

un'dress vt spogliare; **get ~ed** spogliarsi ● vi spogliarsi

un'due adj eccessivo

un'duly adv eccessivamente

un'earth vt dissotterrare; fig scovare; scoprire (secret). **~ly** adj soprannaturale; **at an ~ly hour** 🅣 a un'ora impossibile

uneco'nomic adj poco remunerativo

unem'ployed adj disoccupato ● npl **the ~** i disoccupati

unem'ployment n disoccupazione f. **~ benefit** n sussidio m di disoccupazione

un'ending adj senza fine

un'equal adj disuguale; (struggle) impari; **be ~ to a task** non essere all'altezza di un compito

unequivocal /ʌnɪ'kwɪvəkl/ adj inequivocabile; (person) esplicito

un'ethical adj immorale

un'even adj irregolare; (distribution) ineguale; (number) dispari

unex'pected adj inaspettato. **~ly** adv inaspettatamente

un'fair adj ingiusto. **~ly** adv ingiustamente. **~ness** n ingiustizia f

un'faithful adj infedele

unfa'miliar adj sconosciuto; be ∼ with non conoscere

un'fasten vt slacciare; (detach) staccare

un'favourable adj sfavorevole; (impression) negativo

un'feeling adj insensibile

un'fit adj inadatto; (morally) indegno; (Sport) fuori forma; ∼ for work non in grado di lavorare

un'fold vt spiegare; (spread out) aprire; fig rivelare ● vi (view:) spiegarsi

unfore'seen adj imprevisto

unfor'gettable /ʌnfə'getəbl/ adj indimenticabile

unfor'givable /ʌnfə'gɪvəbl/ adj imperdonabile

un'fortunate adj sfortunato; (regrettable) spiacevole; (remark, choice) infelice. ∼ly adv purtroppo

un'founded adj infondato

unfurl /ʌn'fɜːl/ vt spiegare

un'gainly /ʌn'geɪnlɪ/ adj sgraziato

un'grateful adj ingrato. ∼ly adv senza riconoscenza

un'happy adj infelice; (not content) insoddisfatto (with di)

un'harmed adj incolume

un'healthy adj poco sano; (insanitary) malsano

un'hurt adj illeso

unification /juːnɪfɪ'keɪʃn/ n unificazione f

uniform /'juːnɪfɔːm/ adj uniforme ● n uniforme f. ∼ly adv uniformemente

unify /'juːnɪfaɪ/ vt (pt/pp -ied) unificare

uni'lateral /juːnɪ-/ adj unilaterale

uni'maginable adj inimmaginabile

unim'portant adj irrilevante

unin'habited adj disabitato

unin'tentional adj involontario. ∼ly adv involontariamente

union /'juːnɪən/ n unione f; (trade ∼) sindacato m. U∼ Jack n bandiera f del Regno Unito

unique /juː'niːk/ adj unico. ∼ly adv unicamente

unison /'juːnɪsn/ n in ∼ all'unisono

unit /'juːnɪt/ n unità f inv; (department) reparto m; (of furniture) elemento m

unite /juː'naɪt/ vt unire ● vi unirsi

unity /'juːnətɪ/ n unità f; (agreement) accordo m

universal /juːnɪ'vɜːsl/ adj universale. ∼ly adv universalmente

universe /'juːnɪvɜːs/ n universo m

university /juːnɪ'vɜːsətɪ/ n università f ● attrib universitario

un'just adj ingiusto

un'kind adj scortese. ∼ly adv in modo scortese. ∼ness n mancanza f di gentilezza

un'known adj sconosciuto

un'lawful adj illecito, illegale

unleaded /ʌn'ledɪd/ adj senza piombo

un'leash vt fig scatenare

unless /ən'les/ conj a meno che; ∼ I am mistaken se non mi sbaglio

un'like adj (not the same) diversi ● prep diverso da; that's ∼ him non è da lui; ∼ me, he... diversamente da me, lui...

un'likely adj improbabile

un'limited adj illimitato

un'load vt scaricare

un'lock vt aprire (con chiave)

un'lucky adj sfortunato; it's ∼ to... porta sfortuna...

un'married adj non sposato. ∼ 'mother n ragazza f madre

un'mask vt fig smascherare

unmistakabl|e /ʌnmɪ'steɪkəbl/ adj inconfondibile. ∼y adv chiaramente

un'natural *adj* innaturale; *pej* anormale. ~**ly** *adv* in modo innaturale; *pej* in modo anormale

un'necessar|y *adj* inutile. ~**ily** *adv* inutilmente

un'noticed *adj* inosservato

unob'tainable *adj* (product) introvabile; (phone number) non ottenibile

unob'trusive *adj* discreto. ~**ly** *adv* in modo discreto

unof'ficial *adj* non ufficiale. ~**ly** *adv* ufficiosamente

un'pack *vi* disfare le valigie ● *vt* svuotare (parcel); spacchettare (books); ~ **one's case** disfare la valigia

un'paid *adj* da pagare; (work) non retribuito

un'pleasant *adj* sgradevole; (person) maleducato. ~**ly** *adv* sgradevolmente; (behave) maleducatamente. ~**ness** *n* (bad feeling) tensioni *fpl*

un'plug *vt* (pt/pp -plugged) staccare

un'popular *adj* impopolare

un'precedented *adj* senza precedenti

unpre'dictable *adj* imprevedibile

unpre'pared *adj* impreparato

unpro'fessional *adj* non professionale; **it's** ~ è una mancanza di professionalità

un'profitable *adj* non redditizio

un'qualified *adj* non qualificato; (fig: absolute) assoluto

un'questionable *adj* incontestabile

unravel /ʌnˈrævl/ *vt* (pt/pp -ravelled) districare; (in knitting) disfare

un'real *adj* irreale; 🆃 inverosimile

un'reasonable *adj* irragionevole

unre'lated *adj* (fact) senza rapporto (to con); (person) non imparentato (to con)

unre'liable *adj* inattendibile; (person) inaffidabile, che non dà affidamento

un'rest *n* fermenti *mpl*

un'rivalled *adj* ineguagliato

un'roll *vt* srotolare ● *vi* srotolarsi

un'ruly /ʌnˈruːlɪ/ *adj* indisciplinato

un'safe *adj* pericoloso

unsatis'factory *adj* poco soddisfacente

un'savoury *adj* equivoco

unscathed /ʌnˈskeɪðd/ *adj* illeso

un'screw *vt* svitare

un'scrupulous *adj* senza scrupoli

un'seemly *adj* indecoroso

un'selfish *adj* disinteressato

un'settled *adj* in agitazione; (weather) variabile; (bill) non saldato

unshakeable /ʌnˈʃeɪkəbl/ *adj* categorico

unshaven /ʌnˈʃeɪvn/ *adj* non rasato

un'sightly /ʌnˈsaɪtlɪ/ *adj* brutto

un'skilled *adj* non specializzato. ~ **worker** *n* manovale *m*

un'sociable *adj* scontroso

unso'phisticated *adj* semplice

un'sound *adj* (building, reasoning) poco solido; (advice) poco sensato; **of** ~ **mind** malato di mente

un'stable *adj* instabile; (mentally) squilibrato

un'steady *adj* malsicuro

un'stuck *adj* **come** ~ staccarsi; (🆃: project) andare a monte

unsuc'cessful *adj* fallimentare; **be** ~ (in attempt) non aver successo. ~**ly** *adv* senza successo

un'suitable *adj* (inappropriate) inadatto; (inconvenient) inopportuno

unthinkable /ʌnˈθɪŋkəbl/ *adj* impensabile

un'tidiness *n* disordine *m*

un'tidy *adj* disordinato

un'tie *vt* slegare

until /ən'tɪl/ *prep* fino a; **not ~** non prima di; **~ the evening** fino alla sera; **~ his arrival** fino al suo arrivo ● *conj* finché, fino a quando; **~ you've seen it** non prima che tu l'abbia visto

un'told *adj* (wealth) incalcolabile; (suffering) indescrivibile; (story) inedito

un'true *adj* falso; **that's ~** non è vero

unused¹ /ʌn'juːzd/ *adj* non [ancora] usato

unused² /ʌn'juːst/ *adj* **be ~ to** non essere abituato a

un'usual *adj* insolito. **~ly** *adv* insolitamente

un'veil *vt* scoprire

un'wanted *adj* indesiderato

un'welcome *adj* sgradito

un'well *adj* indisposto

un'wieldy /ʌn'wiːldɪ/ *adj* ingombrante

un'willing *adj* riluttante. **~ly** *adv* malvolentieri

un'wind *v* (*pt/pp* unwound) ● *vt* svolgere, srotolare ● *vi* svolgersi, srotolarsi; (🄵: relax) rilassarsi

un'wise *adj* imprudente

un'worthy *adj* non degno

un'wrap *vt* (*pt/pp* -wrapped) scartare (present, parcel)

un'written *adj* tacito

up /ʌp/ *adv* su; (not in bed) alzato; (road) smantellato; (theatre curtain, blinds) alzato; (shelves, tent) montato; (notice) affisso; (building) costruito; **prices are up** i prezzi sono aumentati; **be up for sale** essere in vendita; **up here/there** quassù/lassù; **time's up** tempo scaduto; **what's up?** 🄵 cosa è successo?; **up to** (as far as) fino a; **be up to** essere all'altezza di (task); **what's he up to?** 🄵 cosa sta facendo?; (plotting) cosa sta combinando?; **I'm up to page 100** sono arrivato a pagina 100; **feel up to it** sentirsela; **be one up on sb** 🄵 essere in vantaggio su qcno; **go up** salire; **lift up** alzare; **up against** *fig* alle prese con ● *prep* su; **the cat ran is up the tree** il gatto è salito di corsa/è sull'albero; **further up this road** più avanti su questa strada; **row up the river** risalire il fiume; **go up the stairs** salire su per le scale; **be up the pub** 🄵 essere al pub; **be up on** *or* **in sth** essere bene informato su qcsa ● *n* **ups and downs** *npl* alti e bassi

'upbringing *n* educazione *f*

up'date¹ *vt* aggiornare

'update² *n* aggiornamento *m*

up'grade *vt* promuovere (person); modernizzare (equipment)

upheaval /ʌp'hiːvl/ *n* scompiglio *m*

up'hill *adj* in salita; *fig* arduo ● *adv* in salita

up'hold *vt* (*pt/pp* upheld) sostenere (principle); confermare (verdict)

upholster /ʌp'həʊlstə(r)/ *vt* tappezzare. **~er** *n* tappezziere, -a *mf*. **~y** *n* tappezzeria *f*

'upkeep *n* mantenimento *m*

up-'market *adj* di qualità

upon /ə'pɒn/ *prep* su; **~ arriving home** una volta arrivato a casa

upper /'ʌpə(r)/ *adj* superiore ● *n* (of shoe) tomaia *f*

upper class *n* alta borghesia *f*

'upright *adj* dritto; (piano) verticale; (honest) retto ● *n* montante *m*

'uprising *n* rivolta *f*

'uproar *n* tumulto *m*; **be in an ~** essere in trambusto

up'set¹ *vt* (*pt/pp* upset, *pres p* upsetting) rovesciare; sconvolgere (plan); (distress) turbare; **get sth** prendersela per qcsa; **be very ~** essere sconvolto; **have an ~ stomach** avere l'intestino disturbato

'upset² *n* scombussolamento *m*

'upshot *n* risultato *m*

upside 'down adv sottosopra; turn ~ capovolgere

up'stairs[1] adv [al piano] di sopra

up'stairs[2] adj del piano superiore

'upstart n arrivato, -a mf

up'stream adv controcorrente

'uptake n be slow on the ~ essere lento nel capire; be quick on the ~ capire le cose al volo

up-to-'date adj moderno; (news) ultimo; (records) aggiornato

'upturn n ripresa f

upward /'ʌpwəd/ adj verso l'alto, in su; ~ slope salita f ● adv ~[s] verso l'alto; ~s of oltre

uranium /jʊ'reɪnɪəm/ n uranio m

urban /'ɜːbən/ adj urbano

urge /ɜːdʒ/ n forte desiderio m ● vt esortare (to a). □ ~ **on** vt sponare

urgen|cy /'ɜːdʒənsɪ/ n urgenza f. ~**t** adj urgente

urinate /'jʊərɪneɪt/ vi urinare

urine /'jʊərɪn/ n urina f

us /ʌs/ pron ci; (after prep) noi; they know us ci conoscono; give us the money dateci i soldi; give it to us datecelo; they showed it to us ce l'hanno fatto vedere; they meant us, not you intendevano noi, non voi; it's us siamo noi; she hates us ci odia

US[A] n[pl] abbr (United States [of America]) U.S.A. mpl

usage /'juːsɪdʒ/ n uso m

use[1] /juːs/ n uso m; be of ~ essere utile; be of no ~ essere inutile; make ~ of usare; (exploit) sfruttare; it is no ~ è inutile; what's the ~? a che scopo?

use[2] /juːz/ vt usare. □ ~ **up** vt consumare

used[1] /juːzd/ adj usato

used[2] /juːst/ pt be ~ to sth essere abituato a qcsa; get ~ to abituarsi a; he ~ to live here viveva qui

useful /'juːsfl/ adj utile. ~**ness** n

utilità f

useless /'juːslɪs/ adj inutile; (🔢: person) incapace

user /'juːzə(r)/ n utente mf. ~-'friendly adj facile da usare

usher /'ʌʃə(r)/ n (Theat) maschera f; (Jur) usciere m; (at wedding) persona f che accompagna gli invitati a un matrimonio ai loro posti in chiesa ● usher in vt fare entrare

usherette /ʌʃə'ret/ n maschera f

usual /'juːʒʊəl/ adj usuale; as ~ come al solito. ~**ly** adv di solito

utensil /juː'tensl/ n utensile m

utilize /'juːtɪlaɪz/ vt utilizzare

utmost /'ʌtməʊst/ adj estremo ●n one's ~ tutto il possibile

utter[1] /'ʌtə(r)/ adj totale. ~**ly** adv completamente

utter[2] vt emettere (sigh, sound); proferire (word). ~**ance** n dichiarazione f

U-turn /'juː-/ n (Auto) inversione f a U; fig marcia f in dietro

. . . .

. . . .

vacan|cy /'veɪk(ə)nsɪ/ n (job) posto m vacante; (room) stanza f disponibile. ~**t** adj libero; (position) vacante; (look) assente

vacate /və'keɪt/ vt lasciare libero

vacation /və'keɪʃn/ n vacanza f

vaccinat|e /'væksɪneɪt/ vt vaccinare. ~**ion** n vaccinazione f

vaccine /'væksiːn/ n vaccino m

vacuum /'vækjʊəm/ n vuoto m ● vt passare l'aspirapolvere in/su. ~ **cleaner** n aspirapolvere m inv. ~ **flask** n thermos® m inv. ~**-packed** adj confezionato sottovuoto

vagina /vəˈdʒaɪnə/ n (Anat) vagina f

vague /veɪg/ adj vago; (outline) impreciso; (absent-minded) distratto; **I'm still ~ about it** non ho ancora le idee chiare in proposito. **~ly** adv vagamente

vain /veɪn/ adj vanitoso; (hope, attempt) vano; **in ~** invano. **~ly** adv vanamente

valentine /ˈvæləntaɪn/ n (card) biglietto m di San Valentino

valiant /ˈvæliənt/ adj valoroso

valid /ˈvælɪd/ adj valido. **~ate** vt (confirm) convalidare. **~ity** n validità f

valley /ˈvælɪ/ n valle f

valour /ˈvælə(r)/ n valore m

valuable /ˈvæljuəbl/ adj di valore; fig prezioso. **~s** npl oggetti mpl di valore

valuation /væljuˈeɪʃn/ n valutazione f

value /ˈvæljuː/ n valore m; (usefulness) utilità f ● vt valutare; (cherish) apprezzare. **~ added tax** n imposta f sul valore aggiunto

valve /vælv/ n valvola f

vampire /ˈvæmpaɪə(r)/ n vampiro m

van /væn/ n furgone m

vandal /ˈvændl/ n vandalo, -a mf. **~ism** n vandalismo m. **~ize** vt vandalizzare

vanilla /vəˈnɪlə/ n vaniglia f

vanish /ˈvænɪʃ/ vi svanire

vanity /ˈvænətɪ/ n vanità f. **~ bag or case** n beauty-case m inv

vapour /ˈveɪpə(r)/ n vapore m

variable /ˈveərɪəbl/ adj variabile; (adjustable) regolabile

variance /ˈveərɪəns/ n **be at ~** essere in disaccordo

variant /ˈveərɪənt/ n variante f

variation /veərɪˈeɪʃn/ n variazione f

varied /ˈveərɪd/ adj vario; (diet) diversificato; (life) movimentato

variety /vəˈraɪətɪ/ n varietà f inv

various /ˈveərɪəs/ adj vario

varnish /ˈvɑːnɪʃ/ n vernice f; (for nails) smalto m ● vt verniciare; **~ one's nails** mettersi lo smalto

vary /ˈveərɪ/ vt/i (pt/pp -ied) variare. **~ing** adj variabile; (different) diverso

vase /vɑːz/ n vaso m

vast /vɑːst/ adj vasto; (difference, amusement) enorme. **~ly** adv (superior) di gran lunga; (different, amused) enormemente

vat /væt/ n tino m

VAT /viːeɪˈtiː, /væt/ n abbr (value added tax) I.V.A. f

vault[1] /vɔːlt/ n (roof) volta f; (in bank) caveau m inv; (tomb) cripta f

vault[2] n salto m ● vt/i [over] saltare

VDU n abbr (visual display unit) VDU m

veal /viːl/ n carne f di vitello ● attrib di vitello

veer /vɪə(r)/ vi cambiare direzione; (Auto, Naut) virare

vegetable /ˈvedʒtəbl/ n (food) verdura f; (when growing) ortaggio m ● attrib (oil, fat) vegetale

vegetarian /vedʒɪˈteərɪən/ adj & n vegetariano, -a mf

vehicle /ˈviːɪkl/ n veicolo m; (fig: medium) mezzo m

veil /veɪl/ n velo m ● vt velare

vein /veɪn/ n vena f; (mood) umore m; (manner) tenore m. **~ed** adj venato

velocity /vɪˈlɒsɪtɪ/ n velocità f

velvet /ˈvelvɪt/ n velluto m. **~y** adj vellutato

vendetta /venˈdetə/ n vendetta f

vending-machine /ˈvendɪŋ-/ n distributore m automatico

veneer /vəˈnɪə(r)/ n impiallacciatura f; fig vernice f. **~ed** adj impiallacciato

venereal /vɪˈnɪərɪəl/ adj **~ disease** malattia f venerea

Venetian /vɪˈniːʃn/ adj & n veneziano, -a mf. **v~ blind** n persiana f alla veneziana

vengeance /'vendʒəns/ n vendetta f; **with a ~** 🔢 a più non posso

venison /'venɪsn/ n (Culin) carne f di cervo

venom /'venəm/ n veleno m. **~ous** adj velenoso

vent¹ /vent/ n presa f d'aria; **give ~ to** fig dar libero sfogo a ● vt fig sfogare (anger)

vent² n (in jacket) spacco m

ventilat|e /'ventɪleɪt/ vt ventilare. **~ion** n ventilazione f; (installation) sistema m di ventilazione. **~or** n ventilatore m

ventriloquist /ven'trɪləkwɪst/ n ventriloquo, -a mf

venture /'ventʃə(r)/ n impresa f ● vt azzardare ● vi avventurarsi

venue /'venju:/ n luogo m (di convegno, concerto, ecc.)

veranda /və'rændə/ n veranda f

verb /vɜːb/ n verbo m. **~al** adj verbale

verdict /'vɜːdɪkt/ n verdetto m; (opinion) parere m

verge /vɜːdʒ/ n orlo m; **be on the ~ of doing sth** essere sul punto di fare qcsa ● **verge on** vt fig rasentare

verify /'verɪfaɪ/ vt (pt/pp -ied) verificare; (confirm) confermare

vermin /'vɜːmɪn/ n animali mpl nocivi

versatil|e /'vɜːsətaɪl/ adj versatile. **~ity** n versatilità f

verse /vɜːs/ n verso m; (of Bible) versetto m; (poetry) versi mpl

versed /vɜːst/ adj **~ in** versato in

versus /'vɜːsəs/ prep contro

vertebra /'vɜːtɪbrə/ n (pl -brae /-briː/) (Anat) vertebra f

vertical /'vɜːtɪkl/ adj & n verticale m

vertigo /'vɜːtɪɡəʊ/ n (Med) vertigine f

verve /vɜːv/ n verve f

very /'verɪ/ adv molto; **~ much**

molto; **~ little** pochissimo; **~ many** moltissimi; **~ few** pochissimi; **~ probably** molto probabilmente; **~ well** benissimo; **at the ~ most** tutt'al più; **at the ~ latest** al più tardi ● adj **the ~ first** il primissimo; **the ~ thing** proprio ciò che ci vuole; **at the ~ end/beginning** proprio alla fine/all'inizio; **that ~ day** proprio quel giorno; **the ~ thought** la sola idea; **only a ~ little** solo un pochino

vessel /'vesl/ n nave f

vest /vest/ n maglia f della pelle; (Am: waistcoat) gilè m inv. **~ed interest** n interesse m personale

vestige /'vestɪdʒ/ n (of past) vestigio m

vet /vet/ n veterinario, -a mf ● vt (pt/pp vetted) controllare minuziosamente

veteran /'vetərən/ n veterano, -a mf

veterinary /'vetərɪnərɪ/ adj veterinario. **~ surgeon** n medico m veterinario

veto /'viːtəʊ/ n (pl -es) veto m ● vt proibire

vex /veks/ vt irritare. **~ation** n irritazione f. **~ed** adj irritato; **~ed question** questione f controversa

via /'vaɪə/ prep via; (by means of) attraverso

viable /'vaɪəbl/ adj (life form, relationship, company) in grado di sopravvivere; (proposition) attuabile

viaduct /'vaɪədʌkt/ n viadotto m

vibrat|e /vaɪ'breɪt/ vi vibrare. **~ion** n vibrazione f

vicar /'vɪkə(r)/ n parroco m (protestante). **~age** n casa f parrocchiale

vice¹ /vaɪs/ n vizio m

vice² n (Techn) morsa f

vice versa /vaɪsɪ'vɜːsə/ adv viceversa

vicinity /vɪ'sɪnətɪ/ n vicinanza f; **in the ~ of** nelle vicinanze di

vicious /ˈvɪʃəs/ adj cattivo; (attack) brutale; (animal) pericoloso. ~ **'circle** n circolo m vizioso. ~**ly** adv (attack) brutalmente

victim /ˈvɪktɪm/ n vittima f. ~**ize** vt fare delle rappresaglie contro

victor /ˈvɪktə(r)/ n vincitore m

victor|ious /vɪkˈtɔːrɪəs/ adj vittorioso. ~**y** n vittoria f

video /ˈvɪdɪəʊ/ n video m; (cassette) videocassetta f; (recorder) videoregistratore m ● attrib video ● vt registrare

video: ~ **recorder** n videoregistratore m. ~**-tape** n videocassetta f

vie /vaɪ/ vi (pres p vying) rivaleggiare

view /vjuː/ n vista f; (photographed, painted) veduta f; (opinion) visione f; **look at the** ~ guardare il panorama; **in my** ~ secondo me; **in** ~ **of** in considerazione di; **on** ~ esposto; **with a** ~ **to** con l'intenzione di ● vt visitare (house); (consider) considerare ● vi (TV) guardare. ~**er** n (TV) telespettatore, -trice mf; (Phot) visore m

view: ~**finder** n (Phot) mirino m. ~**point** n punto m di vista

vigilan|ce /ˈvɪdʒɪləns/ n vigilanza f. ~**t** adj vigile

vigorous /ˈvɪɡərəs/ adj vigoroso

vigour /ˈvɪɡə(r)/ n vigore m

vile /vaɪl/ adj disgustoso; (weather) orribile; (temper, mood) pessimo

village /ˈvɪlɪdʒ/ n paese m. ~**r** n paesano, -a mf

villain /ˈvɪlən/ n furfante m; (in story) cattivo m

vindicate /ˈvɪndɪkeɪt/ vt (from guilt) discolpare; **you are** ~**d** ti sei dimostrato nel giusto

vindictive /vɪnˈdɪktɪv/ adj vendicativo

vine /vaɪn/ n vite f

vinegar /ˈvɪnɪɡə(r)/ n aceto m

vineyard /ˈvɪnjɑːd/ n vigneto m

vintage /ˈvɪntɪdʒ/ adj (wine) d'annata ● n (year) annata f

viola /vɪˈəʊlə/ n (Mus) viola f

violat|e /ˈvaɪəleɪt/ vt violare. ~**ion** n violazione f

violen|ce /ˈvaɪələns/ n violenza f. ~**t** adj violento

violet /ˈvaɪələt/ adj violetto ● n (flower) violetta f; (colour) violetto m

violin /vaɪəˈlɪn/ n violino m. ~**ist** n violinista mf

VIP n abbr (very important person) vip mf

virgin /ˈvɜːdʒɪn/ adj vergine ● n vergine f. ~**ity** n verginità f

Virgo /ˈvɜːɡəʊ/ n Vergine f

viril|e /ˈvɪraɪl/ adj virile. ~**ity** n virilità f

virtual /ˈvɜːtjʊəl/ adj effettivo. ~ **reality** n realtà f virtuale. ~**ly** adv praticamente

virtue /ˈvɜːtjuː/ n virtù f inv; (advantage) vantaggio m; **by** or **in** ~ **of** a causa di

virtuous /ˈvɜːtjʊəs/ adj virtuoso

virulent /ˈvɪrʊlənt/ adj virulento

virus /ˈvaɪərəs/ n virus m inv

visa /ˈviːzə/ n visto m

visibility /vɪzəˈbɪlɪtɪ/ n visibilità f

visibl|e /ˈvɪzəbl/ adj visibile. ~**y** adv visibilmente

vision /ˈvɪʒn/ n visione f; (sight) vista f

visit /ˈvɪzɪt/ n visita f ● vt andare a trovare (person); andare da (doctor etc); visitare (town, building). ~**ing hours** npl orario m delle visite. ~**or** n ospite mf; (of town, museum) visitatore, -trice mf; (in hotel) cliente mf

visor /ˈvaɪzə(r)/ n visiera f; (Auto) parasole m

visual /ˈvɪzjʊəl/ adj visivo. ~ **aids** npl supporto m visivo. ~ **dis'play unit** n visualizzatore m. ~**ly** adv visualmente; ~**ly handicapped** non vedente

visualize /ˈvɪzjʊəlaɪz/ vt visualizzare

v

vital /'vaɪtl/ adj vitale. **~ity** n vitalità f. **~ly** adv estremamente

vitamin /'vɪtəmɪn/ n vitamina f

vivaci|ous /vɪ'veɪʃəs/ adj vivace. **~ty** n vivacità f

vivid /'vɪvɪd/ adj vivido. **~ly** adv in modo vivido

vocabulary /və'kæbjʊlərɪ/ n vocabolario m; (list) glossario m

vocal /'vəʊkl/ adj vocale; (vociferous) eloquente. **~ cords** npl corde fpl vocali

vocalist /'vəʊkəlɪst/ n vocalista mf

vocation /və'keɪʃn/ n vocazione f. **~al** adj di orientamento professionale

vociferous /və'sɪfərəs/ adj vociante

vogue /vəʊg/ n moda f; in ~ in voga

voice /vɔɪs/ n voce f ● vt esprimere. **~mail** n posta f elettronica vocale

void /vɔɪd/ adj (not valid) nullo; ~ of privo di ● n vuoto m

volatile /'vɒlətaɪl/ adj volatile; (person) volubile

volcanic /vɒl'kænɪk/ adj vulcanico

volcano /vɒl'keɪnəʊ/ n vulcano m

volley /'vɒlɪ/ n (of gunfire) raffica f; (Tennis) volée f inv

volt /vəʊlt/ n volt m inv. **~age** n (Electr) voltaggio m

volume /'vɒljuːm/ n volume m; (of work, traffic) quantità f inv. ~ **control** n volume m

voluntar|y /'vɒləntərɪ/ adj volontario. **~y work** n volontariato m. **~ily** adv volontariamente

volunteer /vɒlən'tɪə(r)/ n volontario, -a mf ● vt offrire volontariamente (information) ● vi offrirsi volontario; (Mil) arruolarsi come volontario

vomit /'vɒmɪt/ n vomito m ● vt/i vomitare

voracious /və'reɪʃəs/ adj vorace

vot|e /vəʊt/ n voto m; (ballot) votazione f; (right) diritto m di voto; take

a **~e on** votare su ● vi votare ● vt **~e sb president** eleggere qcno presidente. **~er** n elettore, -trice mf. **~ing** n votazione f

vouch /vaʊtʃ/ vi **~ for** garantire per. **~er** n buono m

vow /vaʊ/ n voto m ● vt giurare

vowel /'vaʊəl/ n vocale f

voyage /'vɔɪdʒ/ n viaggio m [marittimo]; (in space) viaggio m [nello spazio]

vulgar /'vʌlgə(r)/ adj volgare. **~ity** n volgarità f inv

vulnerable /'vʌlnərəbl/ adj vulnerabile

vulture /'vʌltʃə(r)/ n avvoltoio m

vying /'vaɪɪŋ/ ▷VIE

Ww

wad /wɒd/ n batuffolo m; (bundle) rotolo m. **~ding** n ovatta f

waddle /'wɒdl/ vi camminare ondeggiando

wade /weɪd/ vi guadare; ~ **through** 🔢 procedere faticosamente in (book)

wafer /'weɪfə(r)/ n cialda f, wafer m inv; (Relig) ostia f

waffle[1] /'wɒfl/ vi 🔢 blaterare

waffle[2] n (Culin) cialda f

waft /wɒft/ vt trasportare ● vi diffondersi

wag /wæg/ v (pt/pp wagged) ● vt agitare ● vi agitarsi

wage[1] /weɪdʒ/ vt dichiarare (war); lanciare (campaign)

wage[2] n, & **~s** pl salario msg. **~ packet** n busta f paga

waggle /'wægl/ vt dimenare ● vi dimenarsi

wagon /'wægən/ n carro m; (Rail) vagone m merci

wail /weɪl/ n piagnucolio m; (of wind) lamento m; (of baby) vagito m ● vi piagnucolare; (wind:) lamentarsi; (baby:) vagire

waist /weɪst/ n vita f. ~coat n gilè m inv, (of man's suit) panciotto m. ~line n vita f

wait /weɪt/ n attesa f; lie in ~ for appostarsi per sorprendere ● vi aspettare; ~ for aspettare ● vt one's turn aspettare il proprio turno. □ ~ on vt servire

waiter /'weɪtə(r)/ n cameriere m

waiting: ~-list n lista f d'attesa. ~-room n sala f d'aspetto

waitress /'weɪtrɪs/ n cameriera f

waive /weɪv/ vt rinunciare a (claim); non tener conto di (rule)

wake[1] /weɪk/ n veglia f funebre ● v (pt woke, pp woken) ~ [up] ● vt svegliare ● vi svegliarsi

wake[2] n (Naut) scia f; in the ~ of fig nella scia di

Wales /weɪlz/ n Galles m

walk /wɔːk/ n passeggiata f; (gail) andatura f; (path) sentiero m; go for a ~ andare a fare una passeggiata ● vi camminare; (as opposed to drive etc) andare a piedi; (ramble) passeggiare ● vt portare a spasso (dog); percorrere (streets). □ ~ out vi (husband, employee:) andarsene; (workers:) scioperare. □ ~ out on vt lasciare

walker /'wɔːkə(r)/ n camminatore, -trice mf; (rambler) escursionista mf

walk-out n sciopero m

wall /wɔːl/ n muro m; go to the ▯ andare a rotoli; drive sb up the ~ ▯ far diventare matto qcno ● wall up vt murare

wallet /'wɒlɪt/ n portafoglio m

wallop /'wɒləp/ n ▯ colpo m ● vt (pt/pp walloped) ▯ colpire

wallow /'wɒləʊ/ vi sguazzare; (in self-pity, grief) crogiolarsi

'wallpaper n tappezzeria f ● vt tappezzare

walnut /'wɔːlnʌt/ n noce f

waltz /wɔːlts/ n valzer m inv ● vi ballare il valzer

wand /wɒnd/ n (magic ~) bacchetta f [magica]

wander /'wɒndə(r)/ vi girovagare; (fig: digress) divagare. □ ~ about vi andare a spasso

wane /weɪn/ n be on the ~ essere in fase calante ● vi calare

wangle /'wæŋgl/ vt ▯ rimediare (invitation, holiday)

want /wɒnt/ n (hardship) bisogno m; (lack) mancanza f ● vt volere; (need) aver bisogno di; ~ [to have] sth volere qcsa; ~ to do sth volere fare qcsa; we ~ to stay vogliamo rimanere; I ~ you to go voglio che tu vada; it ~s painting ha bisogno d'essere dipinto; you ~ to learn to swim bisogna che impari a nuotare ● vi ~ for mancare di. ~ed adj ricercato. ~ing adj be ~ing mancare; be ~ing in mancare di

WAP /wæp/ n abbr (wireless application protocol) WAP m inv

war /wɔː(r)/ n guerra f; fig lotta f (on contro); at ~ in guerra

ward /wɔːd/ n (in hospital) reparto m; (child) minore m sotto tutela. ~ off vt evitare; parare (blow)

warden /'wɔːdn/ n guardiano, -a m

warder /'wɔːdə(r)/ n guardia f carceraria

wardrobe /'wɔːdrəʊb/ n guardaroba m

warehouse /'weəhaʊs/ n

w

magazzino m

war: ~**fare** n guerra f. ~**head** n testata f

warm /wɔːm/ adj caldo; (welcome) caloroso; **be** ~ (person:) aver caldo; **it is** ~ (weather) fa caldo ● vt scaldare. □ ~ **up** vt scaldare ● vi scaldarsi; fig animarsi. ~**-hearted** adj espansivo. ~**ly** adv (greet) calorosamente; (dress) in modo pesante. ~**th** n calore m

warn /wɔːn/ vt avvertire. ~**ing** n avvertimento m; (advance notice) preavviso m

warp /wɔːp/ vt deformare; fig distorcere ● vi deformarsi

warped /wɔːpt/ adj fig contorto; (sexuality) deviato; (view) distorto

warrant /'wɒrənt/ n (for arrest, search) mandato m; (justify) giustificare; (guarantee) garantire. ~**y** n garanzia f

warrior /'wɒrɪə(r)/ n guerriero, -a mf

'**warship** n nave f da guerra

wart /wɔːt/ n porro m

'**wartime** n tempo m di guerra

war|y /'weərɪ/ adj (-ier, -iest) (careful) cauto; (suspicious) diffidente

was /wɒz/ ▷**BE**

wash /wɒʃ/ n lavata f; (clothes) bucato m; (in washing machine) lavaggio m; **have a** ~ darsi una lavata ● vt lavare; (sea:) bagnare. □ ~ **one's hands** lavarsi le mani ● vi lavarsi. □ ~ **out** vt sciacquare (soap); sciacquarsi (mouth). □ ~ **up** vt lavare ● vi lavare i piatti; Am lavarsi

washable /'wɒʃəbl/ adj lavabile

wash-basin n lavandino m

washer /'wɒʃə(r)/ n (Techn) guarnizione f; (machine) lavatrice f

washing /'wɒʃɪŋ/ n bucato m. ~**-machine** n lavatrice f. ~**-powder** n detersivo m. ~**-'up** n do the ~**-up** lavare i piatti. ~**-'up liquid** n detersivo m per i piatti

wash: ~**-out** n disastro m. ~**-room** n bagno m

wasp /wɒsp/ n vespa f

waste /weɪst/ n spreco m; (rubbish) rifiuto m; ~ **of time** perdita f di tempo ● adj (product) di scarto; (land) desolato; **lay** ~ devastare ● vt sprecare. □ ~ **away** vi deperire

waste: ~**-di'sposal unit** n eliminatore m di rifiuti. ~**ful** adj dispendioso. ~**-'paper basket** n cestino m per la carta [straccia]

watch /wɒtʃ/ n guardia f; (period of duty) turno m di guardia; (timepiece) orologio m; **be on the** ~ stare all'erta ● vt guardare (film, match, television); (be careful of, look after) stare attento ● vi guardare. □ ~ **out** vi (be careful) stare attento (for a). □ ~ **out for** vt (look for) fare attenzione all'arrivo di (person)

watch: ~**-dog** n cane m da guardia. ~**man** n guardiano m

water /'wɔːtə(r)/ n acqua f ● vt annaffiare (garden, plant); (dilute) annacquare ● vi (eyes:) lacrimare; **my mouth was** ~**ing** avevo l'acquolina in bocca. □ ~ **down** vt diluire; fig attenuare

water: ~**-colour** n acquerello m. ~**-cress** n crescione m. ~**-fall** n cascata f

'**watering-can** n annaffiatoio m

water: ~**-lily** n ninfea f. ~ **logged** adj inzuppato. ~**-proof** adj impermeabile. ~**-skiing** n sci m nautico. ~**tight** adj stagno; fig irrefutabile. ~**way** n canale m navigabile

watery /'wɔːtərɪ/ adj acquoso; (eyes) lacrimoso

watt /wɒt/ n watt m inv

wave /weɪv/ n onda f; (gesture) cenno m; fig ondata f ● vt agitare; ~ **one's hand** agitare la mano ● vi far segno; (flag:) sventolare. ~**length** n lunghezza f d'onda

waver /'weɪvə(r)/ vi vacillare;

wavy | weed

(hesitate) esitare

wavy /'weɪvɪ/ *adj* ondulato

wax[1] /wæks/ *vi (moon:)* crescere; *(fig: become)* diventare

wax[2] *n* cera *f; (in ear)* cerume *m* ● *vt* dare la cera a. **~works** *n* museo *m* delle cere

way /weɪ/ *n* percorso *m; (direction)* direzione *f; (manner, method)* modo *m;* **~s** *pl (customs)* abitudini *fpl*; **be in the ~** essere in mezzo; **on the ~ to Rome** andando a Roma; **I'll do it on the ~** lo faccio mentre vado; **it's on my ~** è sul mio percorso; *(like this)* così; **by the ~** a proposito; **by ~ of** come; *(via)* via; **either ~** *(whatever we do)* in un modo o nell'altro; **in some ~s** sotto certi aspetti; **in a ~** in un certo senso; **in a bad ~** *(person)* molto grave; **out of the ~** fuori mano; **under ~** in corso; **lead the ~** far strada; *fig* aprire la strada; **make ~** far posto *(for* a); **give ~** *(Auto)* dare la precedenza; **go out of one's ~** *fig* scomodarsi *(to* per); **get one's [own] ~** averla vinta ● *adv* **~ behind** molto indietro. **~ in** *n* entrata *f*

way·lay *vt (pt/pp* **-laid**) aspettare al varco *(person)*

way 'out *n* uscita *f; fig* via *f* d'uscita

way-'out *adj* 🔲 eccentrico

we /wiː/ *pron* noi; **we're the last** siamo gli ultimi; **they're going, but we're not** loro vanno, ma noi no

weak /wiːk/ *adj* debole; *(liquid)* leggero. **~en** *vt* indebolire ● *vi* indebolirsi. **~ling** *n* smidollato, -a *mf*. **~ness** *n* debolezza *f; (liking)* debole *m*

wealth /welθ/ *n* ricchezza *f; fig* gran quantità *f*. **~y** *adj* (**-ier, -iest**) ricco

weapon /'wepən/ *n* arma *f;* **~s of mass destruction** *npl* armi *mpl* di distruzione di massa

wear /weə(r)/ *n (clothing)* abbiglia-

mento *m;* **for everyday ~** da portare tutti i giorni; **in ~** [and tear] usura *f* ● *v (pt* **wore**, *pp* **worn**) ● *vt* portare; *(damage)* consumare; **~ a hole in sth** logorare qcsa fino a fare un buco; **what shall I ~?** cosa mi metto? ● *vi* consumarsi; *(last)* durare. **□ ~ off** *vi* consumarsi; *(effect:)* finire. **□ ~ out** *vt* consumare [fino in fondo]; *(exhaust)* estenuare ● *vi* estenuarsi

wear·y /'wɪərɪ/ *adj* (**-ier, -iest**) sfinito ● *v (pt/pp* **wearied**) ● *vt* sfinire ● *vi* **~y of** stancarsi di. **~ily** *adv* stancamente

weather /'weðə(r)/ *n* tempo *m;* **in this ~** con questo tempo; **under the ~** 🔲 giù di corda ● *vt* sopravvivere a *(storm)*

weather: ~-beaten *adj (face)* segnato dalle intemperie. **~ forecast** *n* previsioni *fpl* del tempo

weave[1] /wiːv/ *vi (pt/pp* **weaved**) *(move)* zigzagare

weave[2] *n* tessuto *m* ● *vt (pt* **wove**, *pp* **woven**) tessere; intrecciare *(flowers* etc); intrecciare le fila di *(story* etc). **~r** *n* tessitore, -trice *mf*

web /web/ *n* rete *f; (spider's)* ragnatela *f.* **W~** *(Comput)* Web *m* inv, Rete *f.* **~bed feet** *npl* piedi *mpl* palmati. **~cam** *n* webcam *f* inv. **~ master** *n* webmaster *m* inv. **~ page** *n* pagina *f* web. **~ site** *n* sito web.

wed /wed/ *vt (pt/pp* **wedded**) sposare ● *vi* sposarsi. **~ding** *n* matrimonio *m*

wedding: ~ cake *n* torta *f* nuziale. **~-ring** *n* fede *f*

wedge /wedʒ/ *n* zeppa *f; (for splitting wood)* cuneo *m; (of cheese)* fetta *f* ● *vt (fix)* fissare

Wednesday /'wenzdeɪ/ *n* mercoledì *m* inv

wee[1] /wiː/ *adj* 🔲 piccolo

wee[2] *vi* 🔲 fare la pipì

weed /wiːd/ *n* erbaccia *f;* (🔲: *person)*

w

mollusco *m* ●*vt* estirpare le erbacce da. □ ~ **out** *vt* fig eliminare

'**weed-killer** *n* erbicida *m*

weedy /'wi:dɪ/ *adj* 🄸 mingherlino

week /wi:k/ *n* settimana *f*. ~**day** *n* giorno *m* feriale. ~**end** *n* fine settimana *m*

weekly /'wi:klɪ/ *adj* settimanale ●*n* settimanale *m* ●*adv* settimanalmente

weep /wi:p/ *vi* (*pt/pp* wept) piangere

weigh /weɪ/ *vt/i* pesare; ~ **anchor** levare l'ancora. □ ~ **down** *vt* fig piegare. □ ~ **up** *vt* fig soppesare; valutare (person)

weight /weɪt/ *n* peso *m*; put on/lose ~ ingrassare/dimagrire. ~**ing** *n* (allowance) indennità *f inv*

weight-lifting *n* sollevamento *m* pesi

weir /wɪə(r)/ *n* chiusa *f*

weird /wɪəd/ *adj* misterioso; (bizarre) bizzarro

welcome /'welkəm/ *adj* benvenuto; you're ~! prego!; you're ~ to have it/to come prendilo/vieni pure ●*n* accoglienza *f* ●*vt* accogliere; (appreciate) gradire

weld /weld/ *vt* saldare. ~**er** *n* saldatore *m*

welfare /'welfeə(r)/ *n* benessere *m*; (aid) assistenza *f*. **W**~ **State** *n* Stato *m* assistenziale

well[1] /wel/ *n* pozzo *m*; (of staircase) tromba *f*

well[2] *adv* (better, best) bene; as ~ anche; as ~ as (in addition) oltre a; ~ done! bravo!; very ~ benissimo ●*adj* he is not ~ non sta bene; get ~ soon! guarisci presto! ●*int* beh!; ~ I never! ma va!

well-behaved *adj* educato

well: ~**-known** *adj* famoso. ~**-off** *adj* benestante. ~**-to-do** *adj* ricco

Welsh /welʃ/ *adj* & *n* gallese; the ~ *pl* i gallesi. ~**man** *n* gallese *m*. ~ **rabbit** *n* toast *m inv* al formaggio

went /went/ ▷**GO**

wept /wept/ ▷**WEEP**

were /wɜ:(r)/ ▷**BE**

west /west/ *n* ovest *m*; to the ~ of a ovest di; the **W**~ l'Occidente *m* ●*adj* occidentale ●*adv* verso occidente; go ~ 🄸 andare in malora. ~**erly** *adj* verso ovest; occidentale (wind). ~**ern** *adj* occidentale ●*n* western *m*

West: ~ '**Indian** *adj* & *n* antillese *mf.* ~ '**Indies** /'ɪndɪz/ *npl* Antille *fpl*

'**westward[s]** /-wəd[z]/ *adv* verso ovest

wet /wet/ *adj* (wetter, wettest) bagnato; fresco (paint); (rainy) piovoso; (🄸: person) smidollato; get ~ bagnarsi ●*vt* (*pt/pp* wet, wetted) bagnare. ~ '**blanket** *n* guastafeste *mf inv*

whack /wæk/ *n* 🄸 colpo *m* ●*vt* 🄸 dare un colpo a. ~**ed** *adj* 🄸 stanco morto. ~**ing** *adj* (🄸: huge) enorme

whale /weɪl/ *n* balena *f*; have a ~ of a time 🄸 divertirsi un sacco

wham /wæm/ *int* bum

wharf /wɔ:f/ *n* banchina *f*

what /wɒt/ *pron* che, [che] cosa; ~ for? perché?; ~ is that for? a che cosa serve?; ~ is it? (what do you want) cosa c'è?; ~ is it like? com'è?; ~ is your name? come ti chiami?; ~ is the weather like? com'è il tempo?; ~ is the film about? di

599 | **whatever | whisker**

cosa parla il film?; ~ is he talking about? di cosa sta parlando?; he asked me ~ she had said mi ha chiesto cosa ha detto; ~ about going to the cinema? e se andassimo al cinema?; ~ about the children? (what will they do) e i bambini?; ~ if it rains? e se piove? ● adj quale, che; take ~ books you want prendi tutti i libri che vuoi; ~ kind of a che tipo di; at ~ time? a che ora? ● adv che; ~ a lovely day! che bella giornata! ● int ~! [che] cosa!; ~? [che] cosa?

what'ever adj qualunque ● pron qualsiasi cosa; ~ is it? cos'è?; ~ he does qualsiasi cosa faccia; ~ happens qualunque cosa succeda; nothing ~ proprio niente

whatso'ever adj & pron = whatever

wheat /wiːt/ n grano m, frumento m

wheel /wiːl/ n ruota f; (steering ~) volante m; at the ~ al volante ● vt (push) spingere ● vi (circle) ruotare; ~ [round] ruotare

wheel: ~**barrow** n carriola f. ~**chair** n sedia f a rotelle. ~**clamp** n ceppo m bloccaruote

wheeze /wiːz/ vi ansimare

when /wen/ adv & conj quando; the day ~ il giorno in cui; ~ swimming/reading nuotando/leggendo

when'ever adv & conj in qualsiasi momento; (every time that) ogni volta che; ~ did it happen? quando è successo?

where /weə(r)/ adv & conj dove; the street ~ I live la via in cui abito; ~ do you come from? da dove vieni?

whereabouts¹ /weərə'baʊts/ adv dove

'whereabouts² n nobody knows his ~ nessuno sa dove si trova

where'as conj dal momento che; (in contrast) mentre

wher'ever adv & conj dovunque; ~

is he? dov'è mai?; ~ possible dovunque sia possibile

whet /wet/ vt (pt/pp whetted) aguzzare (appetite)

whether /'weðə(r)/ conj se; ~ you like it or not che ti piaccia o no

which /wɪtʃ/ adj & pron quale; ~ one? quale?; ~ one of you? chi di voi?; ~ way? (direction) in che direzione? ● rel pron (object) che; ~ he does frequently cosa che fa spesso; after ~ dopo di che; on/in ~ su/in cui

which'ever adj & pron qualunque; ~ it is qualunque sia; ~ one of you chiunque tra voi

while /waɪl/ n a long ~ un bel po'; a little ~ un po' ● conj mentre; (as long as) finché; (although) sebbene ● while away vt passare (time)

whilst /waɪlst/ conj see while

whim /wɪm/ n capriccio m

whimper /'wɪmpə(r)/ vi piagnucolare; (dog:) mugolare

whine /waɪn/ n lamento m; (of dog) guaito m ● vi lamentarsi; (dog:) guaire

whip /wɪp/ n frusta f; (Pol: person) parlamentare m incaricato, -a di assicurarsi della presenza dei membri del suo partito alle votazioni ● vt (pt/pp whipped) frustare; (Culin) sbattere; (snatch) afferrare; (🔲: steal) fregare. □ ~ up vt (incite) stimolare; (🔲) improvvisare (meal). ~**ped 'cream** n panna f montata

whirl /wɜːl/ n (movement) rotazione f; my mind's in a ~ ho le idee confuse ● vi girare rapidamente; vt far girare rapidamente. ~**pool** n vortice m. ~ **wind** n turbine m

whirr /wɜː(r)/ vi ronzare

whisk /wɪsk/ n (Culin) frullino m ● vt (Culin) frullare. □ ~ **away** vt portare via

whisker /'wɪskə(r)/ n ~s (of cat) baffi mpl; (on man's cheek) basette fpl;

w

by a ~ per un pelo

whisky /'wɪskɪ/ n whisky m inv

whisper /'wɪspə(r)/ n sussurro m; (rumour) diceria f •vt/i sussurrare

whistle /'wɪsl/ n fischio m; (instrument) fischietto m •vt fischiare •vi fischiettare; (referee) fischiare

white /waɪt/ adj bianco; go ~ (pale) sbiancare •n bianco m; (of egg) albume m; (person) bianco, -a mf

white: ~ **'coffee** n caffè m inv macchiato. ~-**'collar worker** n colletto m bianco

white 'lie n bugia f pietosa

whiten /'waɪtn/ vt imbiancare •vi sbiancare

'whitewash n intonaco m; fig copertura f •vt dare una mano d'intonaco a; fig coprire

Whitsun /'wɪtsn/ n Pentecoste f

who /huː/ inter pron chi •rel pron che; **the children,** ~ **were all tired,...** i bambini, che erano tutti stanchi,...

who'ever pron chiunque; ~ **can that be?** chi può mai essere?

whole /həʊl/ adj tutto; (not broken) intatto; **the** ~ **truth** tutta la verità; **the** ~ **world** il mondo intero; **the** ~ **lot** (everything) tutto; (pl) tutti; **the** ~ **lot of you** tutti voi •n tutto m; **as a** ~ nell'insieme; **on the** ~ tutto considerato; **the** ~ **of Italy** tutta l'Italia

whole: ~-**'hearted** adj di tutto cuore. ~**meal** adj integrale

'wholesale adj & adv all'ingrosso; fig in massa. ~ **r** n grossista mf

wholesome /'həʊlsəm/ adj sano

wholly /'həʊlɪ/ adv completamente

whom /huːm/ rel pron che; **the man I saw** l'uomo che ho visto; **to/with** ~ a/con cui •inter pron chi; **to** ~ **did you speak?** con chi hai parlato?

whooping cough /'huːpɪŋ/ n pertosse f

whore /hɔː(r)/ n ▣ puttana f

whose /huːz/ rel pron il cui; **people** ~ **name begins with D** le persone i cui nomi cominciano con la D •inter pron di chi; ~ **is that?** di chi è quello? •adj ~ **car did you use?** di chi è la macchina che hai usato?

why /waɪ/ adv (inter) perché; **the reason** ~ la ragione per cui; **that's** ~ per questo •int diamine

wick /wɪk/ n stoppino m

wicked /'wɪkɪd/ adj cattivo; (mischievous) malizioso

wicker /'wɪkə(r)/ n vimini mpl •attrib di vimini

wide /waɪd/ adj largo; (experience, knowledge) vasto; (difference) profondo; (far from target) lontano; **10 cm** ~ largo 10 cm; **how** ~ **is it?** quanto è largo? •adv (off target) lontano dal bersaglio; ~ **awake** del tutto sveglio; ~ **open** spalancato; **far and** ~ in lungo e in largo. ~**ly** adv largamente; (known, accepted) generalmente; (different) profondamente

widen /'waɪdn/ vt allargare •vi allargarsi

'widespread adj diffuso

widow /'wɪdəʊ/ n vedova f. ~**ed** adj vedovo. ~**er** n vedovo m

width /wɪdθ/ n larghezza f; (of material) altezza f

wield /wiːld/ vt maneggiare; esercitare (power)

wife /waɪf/ n (pl **wives**) moglie f

wig /wɪg/ n parrucca f

wiggle /'wɪgl/ vi dimenarsi •vt dimenare

wild /waɪld/ adj selvaggio; (animal, flower) selvatico; (furious) furibondo; (applause) fragoroso; (idea) folle; (with joy) pazzo; (guess) azzardato; **be** ~ **about** (keen on) andare pazzo per •adv **run** ~ crescere senza controllo •n **in the** ~ allo stato naturale; **the** ~**s** pl le zone fpl sperdute

w

wilderness /'wɪldənɪs/ n deserto m; (fig: garden) giungla f

'**wildfire** n spread like ~ allargarsi a macchia d'olio

wild: ~'**goose chase** n ricerca f inutile. ~**life** n animali mpl selvatici

---

will¹ /wɪl/ v aux he ~ arrive tomorrow arriverà domani; I won't tell him non glielo dirò; you ~ be back soon, won't you? tornerai presto, no?; he ~ be there, won't he? sarà là, no?; she ~ be there by now sarà là ormai; ~ you go? (do you intend to go) pensi di andare?; ~ you go to the baker's and buy...? puoi andare dal panettiere a comprare...?; ~ you be quiet! vuoi stare calmo!; ~ you have some wine? vuoi del vino?; the engine won't start la macchina non parte

---

will² n volontà f inv; (document) testamento m

willing /'wɪlɪŋ/ adj disposto; (eager) volonteroso. ~**ly** adv volentieri. ~**ness** n buona volontà f

willow /'wɪləʊ/ n salice m

'**will-power** n forza f di volontà

wilt /wɪlt/ vi appassire

win /wɪn/ n vittoria f; have a ~ riportare una vittoria ●v (pt/pp won; pres p winning) ●vt vincere; conquistare (fame) ●vi vincere. □ ~ **over** vt convincere

wince /wɪns/ vi contrarre il viso

winch /wɪntʃ/ n argano m

wind¹ /wɪnd/ n vento m; (breath) fiato m; (🔲: flatulence) aria f; get/ have the ~ **up** 🔲 aver fifa; get ~ of aver sentore di; in the ~ nell'aria ●vt ~ sb lasciare qcno senza fiato

wind² /waɪnd/ v (pt/pp wound) ●vt (wrap) avvolgere; (move by turning) far girare; (clock) caricare ●vi (road:) serpeggiare. □ ~ **up** vt caricare (clock); concludere (proceedings); 🔲 prendere in giro (sb)

windfall /'wɪndfɔːl/ n fig fortuna f inaspettata

'**wind farm** n centrale f eolica

winding /'waɪndɪŋ/ adj tortuoso

wind: ~ **instrument** n strumento m a fiato. ~**mill** n mulino m a vento

window /'wɪndəʊ/ n finestra f; (of car) finestrino m; (of shop) vetrina f

window: ~-**box** n cassetta f per i fiori. ~-**sill** n davanzale m

'**windscreen** n, Am '**windshield** n parabrezza m inv. ~ **washer** n getto m d'acqua. ~-**wiper** n tergicristallo m

wine /waɪn/ n vino m

wine: ~**glass** n bicchiere m da vino. ~-**list** n carta f dei vini

'**wine-tasting** n degustazione f di vini

wing /wɪŋ/ n ala f; (Auto) parafango m; ~**s** pl (Theat) quinte fpl. ~**er** n (Sport) ala f

wink /wɪŋk/ n strizzata f d'occhio; not sleep a ~ non chiudere occhio ●vi strizzare l'occhio; (light:) lampeggiare

winner /'wɪnə(r)/ n vincitore, -trice mf

wint|er /'wɪntə(r)/ n inverno m. ~**ry** adj invernale

wipe /waɪp/ n passata f; (to dry) asciugata f ●vt strofinare; (dry) asciugare. □ ~ **off** vt asciugare; (erase) cancellare. □ ~ **out** vt annientare; eliminare (village); estinguere (debt). □ ~ **up** vt asciugare (dishes)

wire /waɪə(r)/ n fil m di ferro; (electrical) filo m elettrico

wiring /'waɪərɪŋ/ n impianto m elettrico

wisdom /'wɪzdəm/ n saggezza f; (of action) sensatezza f. ~ **tooth** n dente

w

m del giudizio

wise /waɪz/ *adj* saggio; (*prudent*) sensato. **~ly** *adv* saggiamente; (*act*) sensatamente

wish /wɪʃ/ *n* desiderio *m*; make a **~** esprimere un desiderio; with best **~**es con i migliori auguri • *vt* desiderare; **~** sb well fare tanti auguri a qcno; I **~** you every success ti auguro buona fortuna; I **~** you could stay vorrei che tu potessi rimanere • *vi* **~** for sth desiderare qcsa. **~ful** *adj* **~ful** thinking illusione *f*

wistful /ˈwɪstfl/ *adj* malinconico

wit /wɪt/ *n* spirito *m*; (*person*) persona *f* di spirito; be at one's **~**s' end non saper che pesci pigliare

witch /wɪtʃ/ *n* strega *f*. **~craft** *n* magia *f*. **~-hunt** *n* caccia *f* alle streghe

with /wɪð/ *prep* con; (*fear, cold, jealousy etc*) di; I'm not **~** you 🔲 non ti seguo; can I leave it **~** you? (*task*) puoi occupartene tu?; **~** no regrets/money senza rimpianti/soldi; be **~** it 🔲 essere al passo coi tempi; (*alert*) essere concentrato

with'draw *v* (*pt* -drew, *pp* -drawn) • *vt* ritirare; prelevare (*money*) • *vi* ritirarsi. **~al** *n* ritiro *m*; (*of money*) prelevamento *m*; (*from drugs*) crisi *f inv* di astinenza; (*Psych*) chiusura *f* in se stessi. **~al symptoms** *npl* sintomi *mpl* da crisi di astinenza

with'drawn ▷**WITHDRAW** • *adj* (*person*) chiuso in se stesso

wither /ˈwɪðə(r)/ *vi* (*flower:*) appassire

with'hold *vt* (*pt/pp* -held) rifiutare (*consent*) (from a); nascondere (*information*) (from a); trattenere (*smile*)

with'in *prep* in; (*before the end of*) entro; **~** the law legale • *adv* all'interno

with'out *prep* senza; **~** stopping senza fermarsi

with'stand *vt* (*pt/pp* -stood) resistere a

witness /ˈwɪtnɪs/ *n* testimone *mf* • *vt* autenticare (signature); essere testimone di (accident). **~-box** *n*, Am **~-stand** *n* banco *m* dei testimoni

witticism /ˈwɪtɪsɪzm/ *n* spiritosaggine *f*

witty /ˈwɪtɪ/ *adj* (-ier, -iest) spiritoso

wives /waɪvz/ ▷**WIFE**

wizard /ˈwɪzəd/ *n* mago *m*. **~ry** *n* stregoneria *f*

wobb|le /ˈwɒbl/ *vi* traballare. **~ly** *adj* traballante

woe /wəʊ/ *n* afflizione *f*

woke, woken /wəʊk/, /ˈwəʊkn/ ▷**WAKE**¹

▷**wolf** /wʊlf/ *n* (*pl* wolves /wʊlvz/) lupo *m*; (🔲: *womanizer*) donnaiolo *m* • *vt* **~** [down] divorare. **~-whistle** *n* fischio *m* • *vi* **~-whistle** at sb fischiare dietro a qcno

woman /ˈwʊmən/ *n* (*pl* women) donna *f*. **~izer** *n* donnaiolo *m*. **~ly** *adj* femmineo

womb /wuːm/ *n* utero *m*

women /ˈwɪmɪn/ ▷**WOMAN**. W**~**'s Libber *n* femminista *f*. W**~**'s Liberation *n* movimento *m* femminista

won /wʌn/ ▷**WIN**

wonder /ˈwʌndə(r)/ *n* meraviglia *f*; (*surprise*) stupore *m*; no **~**! non c'è da stupirsi!; it's a **~** that... è incredibile *m*... • *vi* restare in ammirazione; (*be surprised*) essere sorpreso; I **~** è quello che mi chiedo; I **~** whether she is ill mi chiedo se è malata?. **~ful** *adj* meraviglioso. **~fully** *adv* meravigliosamente

wood /wʊd/ *n* legno *m*; (*for burning*) legna *f*; (*forest*) bosco *m*; out of the **~** *fig* fuori pericolo; touch **~**! tocca ferro!

wood: **~ed** /-ɪd/ *adj* boscoso. **~en** *adj* di legno; *fig* legnoso. **~wind** *n* strumenti *mpl* a fiato. **~work** *n* (*wooden parts*) parti *fpl* in legno; (*craft*) falegnameria f. **~worm** n tarlo m. **~y** adj legnoso; (hill) boscoso

wool /wʊl/ n lana f ● attrib di lana. **~len** adj di lana. **~lens** npl capi mpl di lana

woolly /'wʊlɪ/ adj (-ier, -iest) (sweater) di lana; fig confuso

word /wɜːd/ n parola f; (news) notizia f; by **~** of mouth a viva voce; **have a ~ with** dire due parole a; **have ~s** bisticciare; **in other ~s** in altre parole. **~ing** n parole fpl. **~ processor** n programma m di videoscrittura, word processor m inv

wore /wɔː(r)/ ▷ WEAR

work /wɜːk/ n lavoro m; (of art) opera f; **~s** pl (factory) fabbrica fsg; (mechanism) meccanismo msg; **at ~** al lavoro; **out of ~** disoccupato ● vi lavorare; (machine, ruse:) funzionare; (study) studiare ● vt far funzionare (machine); far lavorare (employee); far studiare (student). □ **~ off** vt sfogare (anger); lavorare per estinguere (debt); fare sport per smaltire (weight). □ **~ out** vt elaborare (plan); risolvere (problem); calcolare (bill); **I ~ed out how he did it** ho capito come l'ha fatto ● vi evolvere. □ **~ up** vt **I've ~ed up an appetite** mi è venuto appetito; **don't get ~ed up** (anxious) non farti prendere dal panico; (angry) non arrabbiarti

workable /'wɜːkəbl/ adj (feasible) fattibile

worker /'wɜːkə(r)/ n lavoratore, -trice mf; (manual) operaio, -a mf

working /'wɜːkɪŋ/ adj (clothes etc) da lavoro; (day) feriale; in **~ order** funzionante. **~ class** n classe f operaia. **~-class** adj operaio

work: **~man** n operaio m. **~manship** n lavorazione f. **~shop** n officina f; (discussion) dibattito m

world /wɜːld/ n mondo m; a **~ of difference** una differenza abissale; **out of this ~** favoloso; **think the ~ of sb** andare matto per qcno. **~ly**

adj materiale; (person) materialista. **~'wide** adj mondiale ● adv mondialmente

worm /wɜːm/ n verme m ● vt **~ one's way into sb's confidence** conquistarsi la fiducia di qcno in modo subdolo. **~-eaten** adj tarlato

worn /wɔːn/ ▷ WEAR ● adj sciupato. **~-out** adj consumato; (person) sfinito

worried /'wʌrɪd/ adj preoccupato

worry /'wʌrɪ/ n preoccupazione f ● v (pt/pp worried) ● vt preoccupare; (bother) disturbare ● vi preoccuparsi. **~ing** adj preoccupante

worse /wɜːs/ adj peggiore ● adv peggio ● n peggio m

worsen /'wɜːsn/ vt/i peggiorare

worship /'wɜːʃɪp/ n culto m; (service) funzione f; **Your/His W~** (to judge) signor giudice/il giudice ● v (pt/pp -shipped) ● vt venerare ● vi andare a messa

worst /wɜːst/ adj peggiore ● adv peggio [di tutti] ● n the **~** il peggio; **get the ~ of it** avere la peggio; **if the ~ comes to the ~** nella peggiore delle ipotesi

worth /wɜːθ/ n valore m; £10 **~ of petrol** 10 sterline di benzina ● adj **be ~** valere; **be it** fig valerne la pena; **it's ~ trying** vale la pena di provare; **it's ~ my while** mi conviene. **~less** adj senza valore. **~while** adj che vale la pena; (cause) lodevole

worthy /'wɜːðɪ/ adj degno; (cause, motive) lodevole

would /wʊd/ v aux **I ~ do it** lo farei; **~ you go?** andresti?; **~ you mind if I opened the window?** ti dispiace se apro la finestra?; **he ~ come if he could** verrebbe se potesse; **he said he ~n't** ha detto di no; **~ you like a drink?** vuoi

w

qualcosa da bere?; **what** ~ you
like to drink? cosa prendi da
bere?; **you** ~**n't,** ~ **you?** non
lo faresti, vero?

wound¹ /wuːnd/ n ferita f ● vt ferire

wound² /waʊnd/ ▷**WIND**²

wrangle /ˈræŋɡl/ n litigio m ● vi litigare

wrap /ræp/ n (shawl) scialle m ● vt (pt/pp wrapped) ~ (up) avvolgere; (present) incartare; **be** ~**ped up in** fig essere completamente preso da ● vi ~ **up warmly** coprirsi bene. ~**per** n (for sweet) carta f [di caramella]. ~**ping** n materiale m da imballaggio. ~**ping paper** n carta f da pacchi; (for gift) carta f da regalo

wrath /rɒθ/ n ira f

wreak /riːk/ vt ~ **havoc with sth** scombussolare qcsa

wreath /riːθ/ n (pl ~s /-ðz/) corona f

wreck /rek/ n (of ship) relitto m; (of car) carcassa f; (person) rottame m ● vt far naufragare; demolire (car). ~**age** n rottami mpl; fig brandelli mpl

wrench /rentʃ/ n (injury) slogatura f; (tool) chiave f inglese; (pull) strattone m ● vt (pull) strappare; slogarsi (wrist, ankle etc)

wrestl|e /ˈresl/ vi lottare corpo a corpo; fig lottare. ~**er** n lottatore, -trice mf. ~**ing** n lotta f libera; (all-in) catch m

wretch /retʃ/ n disgraziato, -a mf. ~**ed** adj odioso; (weather) orribile; **feel** ~**ed** (unhappy) essere triste; (ill) sentirsi malissimo

wriggle /ˈrɪɡl/ n contorsione f ● vi contorcersi; (move forward) strisciare; ~ **out of sth** 🔢 sottrarsi a qcsa

wring /rɪŋ/ vt (pt/pp wrung) torcere (sb's neck); strizzare (clothes); ~ **one's hands** torcersi le mani; ~**ing wet** inzuppato

wrinkle /ˈrɪŋkl/ n grinza f; (on skin) ruga f ● vt/i raggrinzire. ~**d** adj (skin,

face) rugoso; (clothes) raggrinzito

wrist /rɪst/ n polso m. ~**-watch** n orologio m da polso

writ /rɪt/ n (Jur) mandato m

write /raɪt/ vt/i (pt wrote, pp written, pres p writing) scrivere. □ ~ **down** vt annotare. □ ~ **off** vt cancellare (debt); distruggere (car)

'write-off n (car) rottame m

writer /ˈraɪtə(r)/ n autore, -trice mf; **she's a** ~ è una scrittrice

writhe /raɪð/ vi contorcersi

writing /ˈraɪtɪŋ/ n (occupation) scrivere m; (words) scritte fpl; (handwriting) scrittura f; **in** ~ per iscritto. ~**-paper** n carta f da lettera

written /ˈrɪtn/ ▷**WRITE**

wrong /rɒŋ/ adj sbagliato; **be** ~ (person:) sbagliare; **what's** ~? cosa c'è che non va? ● adv (spelt) in modo sbagliato; **go** ~ (person:) sbagliare; (machine:) funzionare male; (plan:) andar male ● n ingiustizia f; **in the** ~ dalla parte del torto; **know right from** ~ distinguere il bene dal male ● vt fare torto a. ~**ful** adj ingiusto. ~**ly** adv in modo sbagliato; (accuse, imagine) a torto; (informed) male

wrote /rəʊt/ ▷**WRITE**

wrought iron /rɔːt-/ n ferro m battuto ● attrib di ferro battuto

wrung /rʌŋ/ ▷**WRING**

wry /raɪ/ adj (-er, -est) (humour, smile) beffardo

• •

X x

• •

Xmas /ˈkrɪsməs/ n 🔢 Natale m

'X-ray n (picture) radiografia f; **have an** ~ farsi fare una radiografia ● vt passare ai raggi X

Yy

yacht /jɒt/ n yacht m inv; (for racing) barca f a vela. **~ing** n vela f

yank /jæŋk/ vt 🔟 tirare

Yank n 🔟 americano, -a mf

yap /jæp/ vi (pt/pp **yapped**) (dog:) guaire

yard¹ /jɑːd/ n cortile m; (for storage) deposito m

yard² n iarda f (= 91,44 cm). **~stick** n fig pietra f di paragone

yarn /jɑːn/ n filo m; (🔟: tale) storia f

yawn /jɔːn/ n sbadiglio m ● vi sbadigliare. **~ing** adj **~ing gap** sbadiglio m

yeah /jeə/ adv sì

year /jɪə(r)/ n anno m; (of wine) annata f; for **~s** 🔟 da secoli. **~book** n annuario m. **~ly** adj annuale ● adv annualmente

yearn /jɜːn/ vi struggersi. **~ing** n desiderio m struggente

yeast /jiːst/ n lievito m

yell /jel/ n urlo m ● vi urlare

yellow /'jeləʊ/ adj & n giallo m

yelp /jelp/ n (of dog) guaito m ● vi (dog:) guaire

yes /jes/ adv sì ● n sì m inv

yesterday /'jestədeɪ/ adj & adv ieri m inv; **~'s paper** il giornale di ieri; **the day before ~** l'altroieri

yet /jet/ adv ancora; **as ~** fino ad ora; **not ~** non ancora; **the best ~** il migliore finora ● conj eppure

yield /jiːld/ n produzione f; (profit) reddito m ● vt produrre; fruttare (profit) ● vi cedere; Am (Auto) dare la precedenza

yoga /'jəʊgə/ n yoga m

yoghurt /'jɒgət/ n yogurt m inv

yoke /jəʊk/ n giogo m; (of garment) carré m inv

yokel /'jəʊkl/ n zotico, -a mf

yolk /jəʊk/ n tuorlo m

you /juː/ pron (subject) tu, voi pl; (formal) lei, voi pl; (direct/indirect object) ti, vi pl; (formal: direct object) la; (formal: indirect object) le; (after prep) te, voi pl; (formal: after prep) lei;

tu is used when speaking to friends, children and animals. **lei** is used to speak to someone you do not know. **voi** is used to speak to more than one person. Note that you is often not translated when it is the subject of the sentence

~ are very kind (sg) sei molto gentile; (formal) è molto gentile; (pl & formal pl) siete molto gentili; **~ can stay, but he has to go** (sg) tu puoi rimanere, ma lui deve andarsene; (pl) voi potete rimanere, ma lui deve andarsene; **all of ~** tutti voi; **I'll give ~ the money** (sg) ti darò i soldi; (pl) vi darò i soldi; **I'll give it to ~** (sg) te/(pl) ve lo darò; **it was ~!** (sg) eri tu!; (pl) eravate voi!; **~ have to be careful** (one) si deve fare attenzione

young /jʌŋ/ adj giovane ● npl (animals) piccoli mpl; **the ~** (people) i giovani mpl. **~ lady** n signorina f. **~ man** n giovanotto. **~ster** n ragazzo, -a mf; (child) bambino, -a mf

your /jɔː(r)/ adj il tuo m, la tua f, i tuoi mpl, le tue fpl, (formal) il suo m, la sua f, i suoi mpl, le sue fpl; (pl & formal pl) il vostro m, la vostra f, i vostri mpl, le vostre fpl; **~ mother/father** tua madre/tuo padre; (formal) sua madre/suo padre; (pl & formal pl) vostra madre/vostro padre

y

yours /jɔːz/ poss pron il tuo m, la tua f, i tuoi mpl, le tue fpl; (formal) il suo m, la sua f, i suoi mpl, le sue fpl; (pl & formal pl) il vostro m, la vostra f, i vostri mpl, le vostre fpl; a friend of ∼ un tuo/suo/vostro amico; friends of ∼ dei tuoi/vostri/suoi amici; that is ∼ quello è il tuo/vostro/suo; (as opposed to mine) quello è il tuo/il vostro/il suo

your'self pron (reflexive) ti; (formal) si; (emphatic) te stesso; (formal) sé, se stesso; do pour ∼ a drink versati da bere; (formal) si versi da bere; you said so ∼ lo hai detto tu stesso; (formal) lo ha detto lei stesso; you can be proud of ∼ puoi essere fiero di te/di sé; by ∼ da solo

your'selves pron (reflexive) vi; (emphatic) voi stessi; do pour ∼ a drink versatevi da bere; you said so ∼ lo avete detto voi stessi; you can be proud of ∼ potete essere fieri di voi; by ∼ da soli

youth /juːθ/ n (pl youths /-ðz/) gioventù f inv; (boy) giovanetto m; the ∼ (young people) i giovani mpl. ∼ful adj giovanile. ∼ hostel n ostello m [della gioventù]

Yugoslav /'juːgəslɑːv/ adj & n jugoslavo, -a mf

Yugoslavia /-'slɑːvɪə/ n Jugoslavia f

Zz

zeal /ziːl/ n zelo m

zealous /'zeləs/ adj zelante. ∼ly adv con zelo

zebra /'zebrə/ n zebra f. ∼-'crossing n passaggio m pedonale, zebre fpl

zero /'zɪərəʊ/ n zero m

zest /zest/ n gusto m

zigzag /'zɪgzæg/ n zigzag m inv ● vi (pt/pp -zagged) zigzagare

zilch /zɪltʃ/ n 🔲 zero m assoluto

zinc /zɪŋk/ n zinco m

zip /zɪp/ n [fastener] cerniera f [lampo] ● vt (pt/pp zipped) ∼ [up] chiudere con la cerniera [lampo]

'Zip code n Am codice m postale

zipper /'zɪpə(r)/ n Am cerniera f [lampo]

zodiac /'zəʊdɪæk/ n zodiaco m

zombie /'zɒmbɪ/ n 🔲 zombi mf inv

zone /zəʊn/ n zona f

zoo /zuː/ n zoo m inv

zoolog|ist /zəʊ'ɒlədʒɪst/ n zoologo, -a mf. ∼y zoologia f

zoom /zuːm/ vi sfrecciare. ∼ lens n zoom m inv

Verbi inglese irregolari

Infinito	Passato	Participio passato	Infinito	Passato	Participio passato
be	was	been	**drive**	drove	driven
bear	bore	borne	**eat**	ate	eaten
beat	beat	beaten	**fall**	fell	fallen
become	became	become	**feed**	fed	fed
begin	began	begun	**feel**	felt	felt
bend	bent	bent	**fight**	fought	fought
bet	bet,	bet,	**find**	found	found
	betted	betted	**flee**	fled	fled
bid	bade, bid	bidden, bid	**fly**	flew	flown
bind	bound	bound	**forecast**	forecast,	forecast,
bite	bit	bitten		forecasted	forecasted
bleed	bled	bled	**forget**	forgot	forgotten,
blow	blew	blown			forgot US
break	broke	broken	**freeze**	froze	frozen
breed	bred	bred	**get**	got	got, gotten US
bring	brought	brought	**give**	gave	given
build	built	built	**go**	went	gone
burn	burnt,	burnt,	**grow**	grew	grown
	burned	burned	**hang**	hung,	hung,
burst	burst	burst		hanged	hanged
buy	bought	bought	**have**	had	had
catch	caught	caught	**hear**	heard	heard
choose	chose	chosen	**hide**	hid	hidden
cling	clung	clung	**hit**	hit	hit
come	came	come	**hold**	held	held
cost	cost,	cost,	**hurt**	hurt	hurt
	costed (vt)	costed	**keep**	kept	kept
cut	cut	cut	**kneel**	knelt	knelt
deal	dealt	dealt	**know**	knew	known
dig	dug	dug	**lay**	laid	laid
do	did	done	**lead**	led	led
draw	drew	drawn	**lean**	leaned,	leaned,
dream	dreamt,	dreamt,		leant	leant
	dreamed	dreamed	**leap**	leaped,	leaped,
drink	drank	drunk		leapt	leapt

Infinito	Passato	Participio passato	Infinito	Passato	Participio passato
learn	learnt, learned	learnt, learned	**smell**	smelt, smelled	smelt, smelled
leave	left	left	**speak**	spoke	spoken
lend	lent	lent	**spell**	spelled, spelt	spelled, spelt
let	let	let			
lie	lay	lain	**spend**	spent	spent
lose	lost	lost	**spit**	spat	spat
make	made	made	**spoil**	spoilt, spoiled	spoilt, spoiled
mean	meant	meant			
meet	met	met	**spread**	spread	spread
pay	paid	paid	**spring**	sprang	sprung
put	put	put	**stand**	stood	stood
quit	quitted, quit	quitted, quit	**steal**	stole	stolen
			stick	stuck	stuck
read	read	read	**sting**	stung	stung
ride	rode	ridden	**stride**	strode	stridden
ring	rang	rung	**strike**	struck	struck
rise	rose	risen	**swear**	swore	sworn
run	ran	run	**sweep**	swept	swept
say	said	said	**swell**	swelled	swollen, swelled
see	saw	seen			
seek	sought	sought	**swim**	swam	swum
sell	sold	sold	**swing**	swung	swung
send	sent	sent	**take**	took	taken
set	set	set	**teach**	taught	taught
sew	sewed	sewn, sewed	**tear**	tore	torn
shake	shook	shaken	**tell**	told	told
shine	shone	shone	**think**	thought	thought
shoe	shod	shod	**throw**	threw	thrown
shoot	shot	shot	**thrust**	thrust	thrust
show	showed	shown	**tread**	trod	trodden
shut	shut	shut	**understand**	understood	understood
sing	sang	sung			
sink	sank	sunk	**wake**	woke	woken
sit	sat	sat	**wear**	wore	worn
sleep	slept	slept	**win**	won	won
sling	slung	slung	**write**	wrote	written

Italian verb tables

1. in **-are** (eg compr|are)

Present ~o, ~i, ~a, ~iamo, ~ate, ~ano
Imperfect ~avo, ~avi, ~ava, ~avamo, ~avate, ~avano
Past historic ~ai, ~asti, ~ò, ~ammo, ~aste, ~arono
Future ~erò, ~erai, ~erà, ~eremo, ~erete, ~eranno
Present subjunctive ~i, ~i, ~i, ~iamo, ~iate, ~ino
Past subjunctive ~assi, ~assi, ~asse, ~assimo, ~aste, ~assero
Present participle ~ando
Past participle ~ato
Imperative ~a (fml ~i), ~iamo, ~ate
Conditional ~erei, ~eresti, ~erebbe, ~eremmo, ~ereste, ~erebbero

2. in **-ere** (eg vend|ere)

Pres ~o, ~i, ~e, ~iamo, ~ete, ~ono
Impf ~evo, ~evi, ~eva, ~evamo, ~evate, ~evano
Past hist ~ei or ~etti, ~esti, ~è or ~ette, ~emmo, ~este, ~erono or ~ettero
Fut ~erò, ~erai, ~erà, ~eremo, ~erete, ~eranno
Pres sub ~a, ~a, ~a, ~iamo, ~iate, ~ano
Past sub ~essi, ~essi, ~esse, ~essimo, ~este, ~essero
Pres part ~endo
Past part ~uto
Imp ~i (fml ~a), ~iamo, ~ete
Cond ~erei, ~eresti, ~erebbe, ~eremmo, ~ereste, ~erebbero

3. in **-ire** (eg dorm|ire)

Pres ~o, ~i, ~e, ~iamo, ~ite, ~ono
Impf ~ivo, ~ivi, ~iva, ~ivamo, ~ivate, ~ivano
Past hist ~ii, ~isti, ~ì, ~immo, ~iste, ~irono
Fut ~irò, ~irai, ~irà, ~iremo, ~irete, ~iranno
Pres sub ~a, ~a, ~a, ~iamo, ~iate, ~ano
Past sub ~issi, ~issi, ~isse, ~issimo, ~iste, ~issero
Pres part ~endo
Past part ~ito
Imp ~i (fml ~a), ~iamo, ~ite
Cond ~irei, ~iresti, ~irebbe, ~iremmo, ~ireste, ~irebbero

Notes

• Many verbs in the third conjugation take *isc* between the stem and the ending in the first, second, and third person singular and in the third person plural of the present, the present subjunctive, and the imperative: fin|ire *Pres* ~isco, ~isci, ~isce, ~iscono. *Pres sub* ~isca, ~iscano *Imp* ~isci.

• The three forms of the imperative are the same as the corresponding forms of the present for the second and third conjugation. In the first conjugation the forms are also the same except for the second person singular: present *compri*, imperative *compra*. The negative form of the second person singular is formed by putting *non* before the infinitive for all conjugations: *non comprare*. In polite forms the third person of the present subjunctive is used instead for all conjugations: *compri*.

Irregular verbs:

Certain forms of all irregular verbs are regular (except for *essere*). These are: the second person plural of the present, the past subjunctive, and the present participle. All forms not listed below are regular and can be derived from the parts given. Only those irregular verbs considered to be the most useful are shown in the tables.

accadere *as* **cadere**

accendere
Past hist accesi, accendesti
Past part acceso

affliggere
Past hist afflissi, affliggesti
Past part afflitto

ammettere *as* **mettere**

andare
Pres vado, vai, va, andiamo, andate, vanno
Fut andrò *etc*
Pres sub vada, vadano
Imp va', vada, vadano

apparire
Pres appaio *or* apparisco, appari *or* apparisci, appare *or* apparisce, appaiono *or* appariscono
Past hist apparvi *or* apparsi, apparisti, apparve *or* appari *or* apparse,

apparvero *or* apparirono *or* apparsero
Pres sub appaia *or* apparisca

aprire
Pres apro
Past hist aprii, apristi
Pres sub apra
Past part aperto

avere
Pres ho, hai, ha, abbiamo, hanno
Past hist ebbi, avesti, ebbe, avemmo, aveste, ebbero
Fut avrò *etc*
Pres sub abbia *etc*
Imp abbi, abbia, abbiate, abbiano

bere
Pres bevo *etc*
Impf bevevo *etc*
Past hist bevvi *or* bevetti, bevesti
Fut berrò *etc*
Pres sub beva *etc*
Past sub bevessi *etc*
Pres part bevendo
Cond berrei *etc*

cadere
Past hist caddi, cadesti
Fut cadrò *etc*

chiedere
Past hist chiesi, chiedesti
Pres sub chieda *etc*
Past part chiesto *etc*

chiudere
Past hist chiusi, chiudesti
Past part chiuso

cogliere
Pres colgo, colgono
Past hist colsi, cogliesti

Pres sub colga
Past part colto

correre

Past hist corsi, corresti
Past part corso

crascere

Past hist crebbi
Past part cresciuto

cuocere

Pres cuocio, cuociamo, cuociono
Past hist cossi, cocesti
Past part cotto

dare

Pres do, dai, dà, diamo, danno
Past hist diedi or detti, desti
Fut darò *etc*
Pres sub dia *etc*
Past sub dessi *etc*
Imp da' (*fml* dia)

dire

Pres dico, dici, dice, diciamo, dicono
Impf dicevo *etc*
Past hist dissi, dicesti
Fut dirò *etc*
Pres sub dica, diciamo, diciate, dicano
Past sub dicessi *etc*
Pres part dicendo
Past part detto
Imp di' (*fml* dica)

dovere

Pres devo or debbo, devi, deve, dobbiamo, devono or debbono
Fut dovrò *etc*
Pres sub deva or debba, dobbiamo, dobbiate, devano or debbano
Cond dovrei *etc*

essere

Pres sono, sei, è, siamo, siete, sono
Impf ero, eri, era, eravamo, eravate, erano
Past hist fui, fosti, fu, fummo, foste, furono
Fut sarò *etc*
Pres sub sia *etc*
Past sub fossi, fossi, fosse, fossimo, foste, fossero
Past part stato
Imp sii (*fml* sia), siate
Cond sarei *etc*

fare

Pres faccio, fai, fa, facciamo, fanno
Impf facevo *etc*
Past hist feci, facesti
Fut farò *etc*
Pres sub faccia *etc*
Past sub facessi *etc*
Pres part facendo
Past part fatto
Imp fa' (*fml* faccia)
Cond farei *etc*

fingere

Past hist finsi, fingesti, finsero
Past part finto

giungere

Past hist giunsi, giungesti, giunsero
Past part giunto

leggere

Past hist lessi, leggesti
Past part letto

mettere

Past hist misi, mettesti
Past part messo

morire

Pres muoio, muori, muore, muoiono
Fut morirò or morrò *etc*

Pres sub muoia
Past part morto

muovere

Past hist mossi, movesti
Past part mosso

nascere

Past hist nacqui, nascesti
Past part nato

offrire

Past hist offersi or offrii, offristi
Pres sub offra
Past part offerto

parere

Pres paio, pari, pare, pariamo, paiono
Past hist parvi or parsi, paresti
Fut parrò *etc*
Pres sub paia, paiamo or pariamo, pariate, paiano
Past part parso

placere

Pres piaccio, piaci, piace, piacciamo, piacciono
Past hist piacqui, piacesti, piacque, piacemmo, piaceste, piacquero
Pres sub piaccia *etc*
Past part piaciuto

porre

Pres pongo, poni, pone, poniamo, ponete, pongono
Impf ponevo *etc*
Past hist posi, ponesti
Fut porrò *etc*
Pres sub ponga, poniamo, poniate, pongano
Past sub ponessi *etc*

potere

Pres posso, puoi, può, possiamo, possono
Fut potrò *etc*
Pres sub possa, possiamo, possiate, possano
Cond potrei *etc*

prendere

Past hist presi, prendesti
Past part preso

ridere

Past hist risi, ridesti
Past part riso

rimanere

Pres rimango, rimani, rimane, rimaniamo, rimangono
Past hist rimasi, rimanesti
Fut rimarrò *etc*
Pres sub rimanga
Past part rimasto
Cond rimarrei

salire

Pres salgo, sali, sale, saliamo, salgono
Pres sub salga, saliate, salgano

sapere

Pres so, sai, sa, sappiamo, sanno
Past hist seppi, sapesti
Fut saprò *etc*
Pres sub sappia *etc*
Imp sappi (*fml* sappia), sappiate
Cond saprei *etc*

scegliere

Pres scelgo, scegli, sceglie, scegliamo, scelgono
Past hist scelsi, scegliesti *etc*
Past part scelto

scrivere

Past hist scrissi, scrivesti *etc*
Past part scritto

sedere

Pres siedo *or* seggo, siedi, siede, siedono

Pres sub sieda *or* segga

spegnere

Pres spengo, spengono

Past hist spensi, spegnesti

Past part spento

stare

Pres sto, stai, sta, stiamo, stanno

Past hist stetti, stesti

Fut starò *etc*

Pres sub stia *etc*

Past sub stessi *etc*

Past part stato

Imp sta' (*fml* stia)

tacere

Pres taccio, tacciono

Past hist tacqui, tacque, tacquero

Pres sub taccia

tendere

Past hist tesi

Past part teso

tenere

Pres tengo, tieni, tiene, tengono

Past hist tenni, tenesti

Fut terrò *etc*

Pres sub tenga

togliere

Pres tolgo, tolgono

Past hist tolsi, tolse, tolsero

Pres sub tolga, tolgano

Past part tolto

Imp fml tolga

trarre

Pres traggo, trai, trae, traiamo, traete, traggono

Past hist trassi, traesti

Fut trarrò *etc*

Pres sub tragga

Past sub traessi *etc*

Past part tratto

uscire

Pres esco, esci, esce, escono

Pres sub esca

Imp esci (*fml* esca)

valere

Pres valgo, valgono

Past hist valsi, valesti

Fut varrò *etc*

Pres sub valga, valgano

Past part valso

Cond varrei etc

vedere

Past hist vidi, vedesti

Fut vedrò *etc*

Past part visto *or* veduto

Cond vedrei *etc*

venire

Pres vengo, vieni, viene, vengono

Past hist venni, venisti

Fut verrò *etc*

vivere

Past hist vissi, vivesti

Fut vivrò *etc*

Past part vissuto

Cond vivrei *etc*

volere

Pres voglio, vuoi, vuole, vogliamo, volete, vogliono

Past hist volli, volesti

Fut verrò etc

Pres sub voglia etc

Imp vogliate

Cond vorrei *etc*

Numbers/Numeri

Cardinal numbers/ Numeri cardinali

0	zero **zero**
1	one **uno**
2	two **due**
3	three **tre**
4	four **quattro**
5	five **cinque**
6	six **sei**
7	seven **sette**
8	eight **otto**
9	nine **nove**
10	ten **dieci**
11	eleven **undici**
12	twelve **dodici**
13	thirteen **tredici**
14	fourteen **quattordici**
15	fifteen **quindici**
16	sixteen **sedici**
17	seventeen **diciassette**
18	eighteen **diciotto**
19	nineteen **diciannove**
20	twenty **venti**
21	twenty-one **ventuno**
22	twenty-two **ventidue**
30	thirty **trenta**
40	forty **quaranta**
50	fifty **cinquanta**
60	sixty **sessanta**
70	seventy **settanta**
80	eighty **ottanta**
90	ninety **novanta**
100	a hundred **cento**
101	a hundred and one **centouno**
110	a hundred and ten **centodieci**
200	two hundred **duecento**
1,000	one thousand **mille**
10,000	ten thousand **diecimila**
100,000	a hundred thousand **centomila**
1,000,000	a million **un million**

Ordinal numbers/ Numeri ordinali

1st	first **primo**
2nd	second **secondo**
3rd	third **terzo**
4th	fourth **quarto**
5th	fifth **quinto**
6th	sixth **sesto**
7th	seventh **settimo**
8th	eighth **ottavo**
9th	ninth **nono**
10th	tenth **decimo**
11th	eleventh **undicesimo**
20th	twentieth **ventesimo**
30th	thirtieth **trentesimo**
40th	fortieth **quarantesimo**
50th	fiftieth **cinquantesimo**
100th	hundredth **centesimo**
1,000th	thousandth **millesimo**

Abbreviations/Abbreviazioni

adjective	*adj*	aggettivo
abbreviation	*abbr*	abbreviazione
administration	*Admin*	amministrazione
adverb	*adv*	avverbio
aeronautics	*Aeron*	aeronautica
American	*Am*	americano
anatomy	*Anat*	anatomia
archaeology	*Archeol*	archeologia
architecture	*Archit*	architettura
astrology	*Astr*	astrologia
attributive	*attrib*	attributo
automobiles	*Auto*	automobile
auxiliary	*aux*	ausiliario
biology	*Biol*	biologia
botany	*Bot*	botanica
British English	*Br*	inglese britannico
chemistry	*Chem*	chimica
commerce	*Comm*	commercio
computers	*Comput*	informatica
conjunction	*conj*	congiunzione
cooking	*Culin*	cucina
definite article	*def art*	articolo determinativo
et cetera	*ecc*	eccetera
electricity	*Electr*	elettricità
et cetera	*etc*	eccetera
feminine	*f*	femminile
figurative	*fig*	figurato
formal	*fml*	formale
geography	*Geog*	geografia
geology	*Geol*	geologia
grammar	*Gram*	grammatica
humorous	*hum*	umoristico
indefinite article	*indef art*	articolo indeterminativo
interjection	*int*	interiezione
interrogative	*inter*	interrogativo
invariable	*inv*	invariabile
law	*Jur*	legge/giuridico
literary	*liter*	letterario
masculine	*m*	maschile
mathematics	*Math*	matematica
mechanics	*Mech*	meccanica
medicine	*Med*	medicina